EVIDENCE-BASED PRACTICES
FOR SOCIAL WORKERS

Related books of interest

**Essential Skills of Social Work Practice:
Assessment, Intervention, Evaluation, Second Edition**
Thomas O'Hare

Modern Social Work Theory, Fourth Edition
Malcolm Payne

**Clinical Assessment for Social Workers:
Qualitative and Quantitative Methods, Third Edition**
Catheleen Jordan and Cynthia Franklin

Best Practices in Community Mental Health: A Pocket Guide
Vikki L. Vandiver

An Experiential Approach to Group Work, Second Edition
Rich Furman, Kimberly Bender, and Diana Rowan

Advocacy Practice for Social Justice, Second Edition
Richard Hoefer

**Case Management: An Introduction to Concepts and Skills,
Third Edition**
Arthur J. Frankel and Sheldon R. Gelman

**Doing Research: The Hows and Whys of Applied Research,
Third Edition**
Nel Verhoeven

**Spirituality, Religion, and Faith in Psychotherapy:
Evidence-Based Expressive Methods for Mind, Brain, and Body**
Helen Land

**From Task-Centered Social Work to Evidence-Based and
Integrative Practice: Reflection on History and Implementation**
Tina Rzepnicki, Stanley G. McCracken, and Harold E. Briggs

EVIDENCE-BASED PRACTICES FOR SOCIAL WORKERS

AN INTERDISCIPLINARY APPROACH

Second edition

Thomas O'Hare
Boston College

LYCEUM
BOOKS, INC.

Chicago, Illinois

© 2015 by Lyceum Books, Inc.

Published by

LYCEUM BOOKS, INC.
5758 S. Blackstone Avenue
Chicago, Illinois 60637
773-643-1903 fax
773-643-1902 phone
lyceum@lyceumbooks.com
www.lyceumbooks.com

6 5 4 3 2 1   14 15 16 17 18

ISBN 978-1-935871-70-5

Printed in the United States of America.

Library of Congress Cataloging-in-Publication Data

O'Hare, Thomas.
    Evidence based practices for social workers : an interdisciplinary approach /
Thomas O'Hare, Boston College. — Second edition.
        pages cm
    Includes bibliographical references and index.
    ISBN 978-1-935871-70-5
    1. Psychiatric social work. 2. Evidence-based social work. I. Title.
HV689.O43   2015
361.3′2—dc23
                                                                    2014016940

CONTENTS

PREFACE TO THE SECOND EDITION

Approaching the 10-year mark since the initial publication of *EBPSW* in 2005, I have found the task of updating this text simultaneously daunting and exhilarating. Research in human behavior theory, assessment, and intervention continues to expand rapidly in most areas of mental health practice. Evidence continues to support the need for interdisciplinary research as well as the use of multidimensional, functional, and systemic approaches to assessment accompanied by a coherent yet flexible intervention model that includes supportive engagement, cognitive-behavioral, family, and contingency management approaches within a systems framework. There has also been a steady increase in research on Internet-based services, including early intervention and treatment for a range of client needs. These include a combination of online help resources and individual practitioner feedback for a range of problems, including depression, anxiety, substance abuse, and eating disorders, among others. In the coming years, social workers are likely to divide their professional time between online and face-to-face contact with clients in order to optimize their assessment, intervention, monitoring, and evaluation efforts for more cost-effective services.

The rapidly expanding literature on evidence-based practices with people from different races, cultures, and countries is also reflected in this second edition and will help clarify the aspirations of culturally competent practice. As one reviews the empirical literature, it becomes increasingly clear that, with some commonsense modifications (e.g., language, an understanding of local cultural beliefs and customs), evidence-based practices (EBPs) appear to work comparably well across races, cultures, and international borders. Future research will continue to elucidate the extent to which major modifications are necessary in order to enhance treatment effectiveness from one group to another. However, it is more likely that modifications in treatment approaches will continue to be heavily based on individual differences (e.g., age, gender, temperament, problem severity) rather than broad population characteristics.

Every effort has been made in this text to represent practice outcome research in a balanced and unbiased manner. As in the first edition, for practical reasons, I strove for representative, not exhaustive, reviews of the literature. Despite the continued advances in EBPs, however, they continue to be underused in community practice, as many practitioners cling to familiar but less empirically supported approaches. Transfer of effective practices from clinical research to the field continues to lag and remains a serious challenge for educators, administrators, and policy makers.

In addition, I recognize that there are somewhat varying definitions of evidence-based practice. Although controlled trials are the best tool we have for testing interventions, I do not rely on them exclusively when other evidence is compelling. It is also important to consider using approaches that have garnered modest evidence of efficacy when there is a lack of effective alternatives. For example, substance abuse interventions with people with severe mental illnesses have not shown impressive results. However, given the risks of ignoring substance use in that population, not providing such services would be clinically negligent, given that some benefits can accrue. I have also made it clear in both the previous edition and this one that evidence-based practices include the reciprocal efforts of both practitioners in the field and practitioner-researchers. I have also noted interventions in current use that have *not* been shown to be effective (an equally edifying point) or that do not offer any methods that are uniquely effective when compared with current practices.

I have also deliberately avoided making a fetish of terminology (*depressed* vs. *depressive disorder*) and overstating hypothetical "rigor" with respect to research methods or how uniformly practitioners should adhere to evidence-based guidelines. A purely academic perspective on research methods and practice suggests a naive view of both, leaving little room for the real-world indeterminacies of both research and practice. EBP guidelines are just that: *guidelines* based on statistical estimates that have been gleaned from repeated testing. As such, they can reduce needless variation in practice and eliminate the use of ineffective practices. The effective implementation of evidence-based practices, however, must also rely on the skill and judgment of experienced practitioners in tailoring interventions to the needs of individual clients, given the prevalence of comorbid disorders, complex problems, and a range of other individual client differences often not reflected in the research. However, practitioners should not overinterpret this need for craft and spontaneity in practice as a repudiation of the need for practice to be supported by methodologically sound evidence.

I have also sidestepped some academic debates over semantics and straw-man issues regarding the definition and meaning of *evidence-based practice* and other matters regarding education, dissemination, training, administration, and policy. The emphasis here is squarely on *evidence-based practices*, that is, the use of those assessment and intervention methods that have been shown to be most effective with people who share similar psychiatric disorders and problems-in-living. As an experienced practitioner, I gave these matters the utmost priority in this text. Hopefully, the many case studies and sample treatment plans will help bring some of the more abstract principles of evidence-based practices to life for student-practitioners so they can better envision how they would proceed with similar cases.

I have made some relatively minor changes in terminology and in the organization of this second edition. Changes from the DSM-IV-TR to the DSM-5 are noted. Some changes are minor, but others are more significant. Changes in the DSM-5 followed considerable controversy about moving toward a dimensional system rather than the familiar categorical one; however, the DSM-5 committees fell short of this goal. Nevertheless, diagnostic criteria are a useful starting point for treatment planning, but they must be augmented with multidimensional, functional, and systems-oriented assessment in order to highlight the unique aspects of individual, couple, and family functioning in a social context. This second edition continues to emphasize this approach in order to more fully understand clients' needs and challenges. To this end, I also made some minor changes in terminology. I have changed the label for a multidimensional/functional assessment (MDF) to multidimensional-functional-systems (MFS) assessment, to place more emphasis on what was previously implied (i.e., a systems perspective). Also, I have replaced the ambiguous term *therapeutic coping skills* with *cognitive-behavioral skills*, recognizing that intervention skills that collectively constitute cognitive-behavioral interventions are ubiquitously and eclectically applied in evidence-based practices.

I also expanded the previous edition's chapter 9 ("Depression") to include bipolar disorder in a new chapter 6 ("Depressive and Bipolar Disorders"), and placed it adjacent to chapter 5 ("Schizophrenia Spectrum Disorders") for pragmatic reasons. Although many people with major mood disorders are treated on an outpatient basis, these disorders are generally considered severe mental illnesses, and as such, they are often treated in community-based programs with approaches very similar to those used with people who have schizophrenia spectrum disorders. Also, in the first edition, chapter 13 ("Conduct Disorders and ADHD") included content on co-occurring substance use disorders in adolescents. Although this is acknowledged in the new chapter 13, the material on substance use in young people is now consolidated in chapter 16 ("Substance Abuse and Co-occurring Problems in Adolescents and Young Adults") to more efficiently apply a common literature.

This second edition continues to emphasize the need to have a solid grasp of relevant human behavior research specific to one's field of practice to support both qualitative and quantitative assessment. The use of contemporary behavioral science as a basis for understanding human problems and how to assess them is often sorely lacking in available social work texts, some of which continue to cling to relatively untested, untestable, or even soundly repudiated theories of human behavior. I also continue to emphasize the need to move toward dimensional approaches to assessment and to teach a common core of evidence-based methods that, with some variation, can be applied across many disorders in mental health, as the approaches share the common skill set described in these chapters. Expecting students to learn and master a dozen or more different yet overlapping evidence-based practices is neither efficient nor necessary. As for evaluation methods, this second edition continues to emphasize the use of practical qualitative and quantitative methods that can be used in everyday practice with individual clients as well as on the program level. Some of the evaluation designs promoted in social work academia (e.g., controlled single-subject experiments) are not suitable for everyday use in practice settings.

Last, the ten years that have passed since publishing the first edition lend perspective and provide the opportunity not just to update the literature but also to repair mistakes and smooth out some of the more turgid passages, which resulted from my efforts to translate and integrate a wide variety of literature across disciplines replete with often unnecessary and overwritten jargon. However, with the benefit of hindsight, I've made every effort to make this single-authored text more readable, informative, coherent, and practical, and perhaps even enjoyable.

Tom O'Hare
Charlestown, RI, United States

PART I

DEFINING EVIDENCE-BASED PRACTICE
FOR SOCIAL WORKERS

CHAPTER 1

DEFINITION, PROCESSES, AND PRINCIPLES

This first chapter covers a general definition of core concepts, processes, and principles that characterize evidence-based practices for social workers (EBPSW). In addition, the chapter addresses the manner in which the term *practice theory* has been traditionally used in social work, along with the important role of critical thinking and ethics in evidence-based practice. Last, this chapter summarizes basic principles relevant to implementing EBPSW.

THE TRADITIONAL "PRACTICE THEORY" APPROACH TO SOCIAL WORK

Proponents of social work practice theories have been challenged by three main questions. First, what is the nature of human problems and adaptation in the social environment? Second, what are the key mechanisms of change that practitioners can address to achieve good outcomes? Third, which interventions are most likely to be effective for a particular problem or disorder? Variants of practice theories (e.g., schools of thought, orientations, perspectives) range from the conceptually specific to the general and abstract. These include psychodynamic approaches; social cognitive theory and cognitive-behavioral interventions; various family systems theories and practices; general systems and ecosystems models; and—more recently—empowerment, solution-focused, and other phenomenological or constructivist (i.e., experiential) approaches. Students and practitioners typically use one or two preferred practice theories to guide assessment and intervention methods.

However, practice theories vary considerably to the extent that they address salient questions regarding human behavior theory and provide sufficient detail to guide assessment and intervention methods, and to the degree that they are supported by a body of critically reviewed scientific evidence. For example, humanist, constructivist, empowerment, solution-focused, and strengths-based models are guided by value-based assertions and are relatively atheoretical, but they offer some practical techniques for enhancing clients' coping abilities. There is, however, limited evidence to support the effectiveness of most of these methods. In an apparent effort to avoid any critical review, proponents of some of these approaches even deny that research methods are suitable for enhancing our understanding of treatment effectiveness. As for psychodynamic approaches, relevant theories of psychopathology have long lacked empirical support, and there is little evidence to support uniquely effective aspects of psychodynamic techniques beyond those methods that are common to other approaches (e.g., engagement, problem solving). Although family systems theories have highlighted the importance of interactions among family members, evidence for the effectiveness of some specific family treatment models remains thin, except for behaviorally oriented family therapies. Last, while cognitive-behavioral interventions have garnered the lion's share of research on efficacy, and researchers have identified some mechanisms of change (e.g., self-efficacy, desensitization), some argue that a disproportionate emphasis has been placed on the role of cognition at the expense of other social-environmental determinants. In brief, *no single practice theory provides a sufficiently comprehensive and valid foundation for understanding and treating the full range of serious human problems that social workers confront.*

In contrast to endorsing any one practice theory as the basis for intervention, the current approach to EBPSW requires an interdisciplinary understanding of human problems and of adaptation, mechanisms of change, and effective intervention. Current understanding of human behavior is increasingly interdisciplinary and requires a greater integration of efforts in neuroscience and the behavioral and social sciences. However, the current lack of a full understanding of human problems and their solutions should not impede our efforts to determine which interventions are currently most effective with certain disorders and problems-in-living. That can be largely achieved through controlled comparisons of different approaches and with follow-up, naturalistic evaluation in the field.

EFFICACIOUS OR EFFECTIVE PRACTICE? THE PRESSURES OF ACCOUNTABILITY

Although many social workers and practitioner-researchers in the allied professions have long endorsed the development and use of effective practices, there is a growing mandate from funding bodies, regulatory agencies, and other professional organizations to ensure accountability in service delivery. As a result of these influences, the endorsement of certain psychosocial interventions is increasingly guided by outcome research instead of theoretical or ideological preferences (e.g., Bond, Drake, & Becker, 2010; Gambrill, 2004; Howard, McMillen, & Pollio, 2003; O'Hare, 1991, 2009; Rosen, 2003; Thyer, 2004). However, there are several interpretations among practitioners, policy makers, administrators, and academics as to what becoming more "accountable" means. One might suggest that there have been two prevailing strategies in social work. The first emphasizes *efficacy*, that is, selecting and implementing interventions that have been shown to be efficacious in controlled practice research. In this approach, practitioners use the existing outcome research to help guide their selection of an intervention once they have conducted a thorough assessment. The second approach emphasizes the routine use of practice evaluation methods to demonstrate practice *effectiveness*. In this approach, practitioners incorporate evaluation methods into practice and, on the basis of feedback from the client, make incremental changes to the intervention in the hopes of achieving optimal client outcomes.

As for the *efficacy* model, the body of research used to guide treatment selection is typically based on a series of randomized controlled trials (RCTs). In this approach to practice research, practitioners are usually trained specifically in the interventions that are being tested; clients are sampled using specific selection criteria; and multiple standardized measures are employed at assessment, at planned intervals during intervention, and at one or more follow-up periods to measure client change. Controlled trials may be the best tool researchers have to test whether an intervention model is more efficacious than no intervention or some alternative intervention (often defined as *treatment as usual* in the community). After several controlled trials have shown an intervention to be efficacious across different samples, the approach may be deemed an evidence-based practice by a committee of experts who are qualified to critically review outcome research. Practitioners can then learn these new approaches and implement them in their own practice. Over the past few decades, many social work practitioners, researchers, and educators have endorsed the use of outcome research to guide the selection of social work interventions (e.g., Fischer, 1973; Gambrill, 2001; Gray, Joy, Plath, & Webb, 2013; O'Hare, 1991, 2009; Reid, 1997a, 1997b; Thyer, 2004; Wood, 1978).

In contrast, the *effectiveness* approach to evidence-based practice emphasizes the process of evaluating social work interventions in everyday practice. However, there are two variations of this "process-oriented" approach. First, earlier proponents of "empirical practice" in social work focused almost exclusively on evaluating one's own practice (Bloom, Fischer, & Orme, 2009; Corcoran & Gingerich, 1994), whereby practitioners employ qualitative case analysis or single-subject designs to monitor and evaluate an intervention. However, early proponents of practice monitoring and evaluation paid little attention to a key question: Which knowledge base and decision-making criteria guided the initial choice of intervention? More recently, the social work literature has offered a second "process-oriented" strategy. Although access to and use of existing outcome research is acknowledged by many practitioners as an important first step, it is also stressed that applying the findings of outcome research to unique cases requires a considerable degree of flexibility and "practice wisdom." Practitioners need to make incremental adjustments to an intervention on the basis of ongoing evaluation (Klein & Bloom, 1995; Rosen, 2003). In other words, iterative and reciprocal feedback between client and practitioner are needed to demonstrate whether treatment is going well, and any new information can then be used to make adjustments that will hopefully lead to an optimal outcome for the client. Although few might argue with this model in principle, clinical decision making is not well researched and not well understood (Lambert & Ogles, 2004; McCracken & Marsh, 2008; O'Hare & Geertsma, 2013; Schottenauer, Glass, & Arnkoff, 2007). At this point, practitioners should use evidence-based practice guidelines to help select their approach, and they should be prepared to monitor and evaluate the progress of their interventions and adjust their approach as needed.

In reality, the concepts of both *efficacy* and *effectiveness* are essential to implementing EBPSW. In this text, EBPSW emphasizes the use of outcome research to help guide the initial choice of intervention, followed by monitoring and evaluation methods to facilitate optimal implementation. The use of knowledge gleaned from reviews of the research literature (i.e., controlled trials) is essential and increasingly required for the provision of clinical services. However, because of considerable variability in client characteristics, needs, and preferences, flexibility and incremental adjustments to the initial intervention plan are usually necessary to optimize the intervention. Although current guidelines for decision making during the implementation process are far from clear, practitioners should consider themselves on very firm empirical grounds when they employ the core ingredients of effective helping: good listening skills, empathic attunement, positive regard, and motivational enhancement, along with clients' active participation in monitoring and evaluating their own progress. Having clients test out the results of an intervention in their everyday environment is not only a useful form of self-evaluation but also an empowering therapeutic tool that can enhance self-efficacy by putting clients in the driver's seat, so to speak. With a sound practitioner-client working relationship in place, both qualitative and quantitative evaluation methods can be seamlessly integrated into routine practice to help practitioners and clients collaborate in the optimal implementation of evidence-based practices.

DEFINING EBPSW: A COMPREHENSIVE STRATEGY FOR CONDUCTING ASSESSMENT, INTERVENTION, AND EVALUATION

Although practitioner-researchers and others have advocated for the use of outcome research to guide practice, the term *evidence-based practice* (EBP) did not become formalized in the mental health field until the 1990s, as an offshoot of the evidence-based medicine movement (Sackett, Straus, Richardson, Rosenberg, & Haynes, 2000). The American Psychological Association set EBP standards (Chambless & Ollendick, 2001) that have since become a reference point for debate regarding what constitutes EBP. Other professional bodies have weighed in as well, but most emphasize controlled trials as the core criteria for determining intervention efficacy.

Evidence-based practices for social workers involve the use of research-based knowledge to inform assessment, the selection of an intervention strategy, and ongoing monitoring and evaluation of a client's progress. It is also understood that clinical judgment will guide these decisions. Some social work scholars have emphasized the use of the term *evidence-based practice* as a metaconcept or broader movement within the field that includes critical reviews of relevant literature, teaching and supervising students in evidence-based practices, the administration of evidence-based programming, knowledge dissemination, education, training, and transfer of technologies, among other important professional functions (Beidas & Kendall, 2010; Bellamy, Bledsoe, Mullen, Fang, & Manuel, 2008; Bellamy et al., 2013; Gambrill, 2006; Thyer & Myers, 2010). This text, however, focuses squarely on matters of primary importance to social work practitioners: the application of *evidence-based practices*, that is, specific interventions supported by substantial controlled research, to be implemented in collaboration with clients to ameliorate the symptoms of psychiatric disorders, to reduce problems-in-living, to enhance adaptive capabilities, and to improve clients' overall psychosocial well-being.

Writing in the context of mental health practice with people who have severe mental illnesses, Bond et al. (2010) outlined nine characteristics of evidence-based practices that can be widely generalized to practice with other populations: interventions should (1) be well-defined, (2) be commensurate with the client's goals, (3) be congruent with society's goals, (4) be supported by methodologically rigorous controlled research and evaluation in real-world settings, (5) have minimal side effects, (6) have good long-term outcomes, (7) have reasonable implementation costs, (8) involve straightforward training and implementation, and (9) be adaptable to diverse communities. Clearly, these criteria can be generalized to other treatment populations and are works in progress, that is, guidelines to follow given the current state of the research and knowledge of best practices. However, despite general support for the adoption of general principles of EBP, implementation in everyday practice lags far behind. Reasons include the training capacities of graduate schools and agencies to promote and supervise evidence-based practices, and practitioner resistance to using formal research-based evidence to guide practice (Adams, Matto, & LeCroy, 2009; Glasgow, 2009; Lehman, 2010).

A WORKING MODEL FOR IMPLEMENTING EBPSW

Social workers need an operable framework for guiding assessment, intervention, and evaluation to accommodate a wide range of practice situations. In this text, *EBPSW* is defined as the planned use of empirically supported assessment and intervention methods, combined with the judicious use of monitoring and evaluation strategies for the purpose of improving the

psychosocial well-being of clients. Evidence-based social work is characterized primarily by the following:

- Conducting qualitative assessment informed by current human behavior
  research and accompanied by the use of reliable and valid quantitative
  assessment tools (e.g., scales, indexes). These instruments also provide a
  baseline for monitoring and evaluation.

- Selecting and implementing interventions that have been shown to be
  efficacious in controlled outcome research. Flexibility in implementing
  evidence-based practices is encouraged to accommodate client needs,
  preferences, and circumstances.

- Implementing evaluation methods as part of practice at the individual and
  program levels.

Evidence-based practice is not a new practice theory. It is a procedural
framework that emphasizes the use of current scientific knowledge to support assessment and intervention, and it employs qualitative and quantitative
evaluation methods to determine effectiveness. When conducting *evidence-
based assessment*, the practitioner does the following:

- Goes beyond general theoretical perspectives to use *problem-specific
  knowledge* (e.g., research on schizophrenia, child abuse, drug addiction,
  eating disorders, depression in the elderly) to identify important biopsychosocial risk and protective factors that cause and maintain the client's
  problems

- Assesses clients' well-being on multiple levels (e.g., psychological, social)

- Employs functional analysis to describe how more proximate cognitive,
  behavioral, physiological, interpersonal, and social factors interact over
  time and across situations

- Uses a systemic perspective to examine interactions among family members, and families and communities (e.g., schools, workplaces)

- Incorporates the client's understanding of the problem into the assessment

- Uses multiple methods of data collection from multiple sources

- Pragmatically emphasizes problems that are amenable to change

- Employs scales and indexes to enhance the reliability and validity of the
  assessment and to provide a baseline for monitoring and evaluation

Intervention is guided by the following:

- The use of practice outcome research to guide the initial selection of an
  approach

- Flexibility in implementation, to accommodate the client's understanding
  of the problem, individual-specific differences, circumstances, and preferences, as well as the unpredictability of day-to-day events and client
  responses to the intervention

- Gives priority to those interventions shown to be effective in controlled trials, but incorporates other evidence-based techniques as needed even though interventions, especially with complex cases, are often eclectic

Monitoring and evaluation methodologies are used to do the following:

- Incrementally adjust the interventions to optimally meet client needs
- Conduct qualitative evaluation
- Continue to use scales (for baseline assessment) to monitor progress
- Aggregate data across cases for the purposes of quality assurance and program evaluation when scales can be used to measure the same outcomes (e.g., overall well-being, depression, alcohol abuse—as is suitable to the program's mission). Routine data aggregation is increasingly required by funding bodies as a condition of contracting for services in both the public and the private sector.

Figure 1.1 illustrates the relationships among assessment, intervention, and evaluation that define EBPSW.

FIGURE 1.1   Micromodel of evidence-based practice

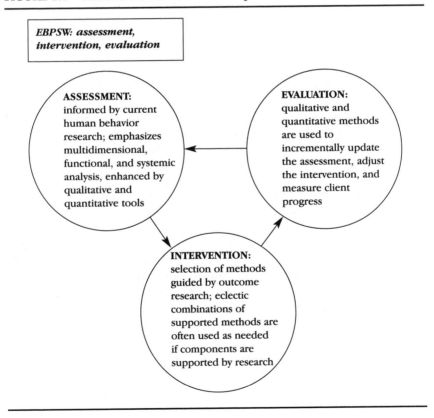

ASSUMPTIONS ABOUT KNOWLEDGE BUILDING

Much of the debate among social work scholars in recent decades has contrasted traditional scientific methods (e.g., measurement, controlled research) (Fischer, 1981; Hudson, 1982b; O'Hare, 1991; Reid, 2001) with qualitative (heuristic) methods (e.g., naturalistic observation, practice wisdom), a view associated with postmodernism and social constructionism (Heineman-Pieper, 1985; Hudson, 2009; Tyson, 1992; Witkin, 1998). This debate over "how we know what we know" (i.e., epistemology) has often been erroneously portrayed as antagonism between practitioners and researchers or as conflict regarding whether qualitative or quantitative research and evaluation methods are superior.

The social constructionist perspective emphasizes the uniqueness, contextual variability, and complexity of each client's experience and each practice situation. Proponents of practice wisdom (e.g., Gould, 2010; Hudson, 2009) champion the importance of intuition, judgment, creativity, and spontaneity in both choice of intervention and the evaluation of an intervention's effectiveness. Heuristic and constructivist practitioners view themselves as part of the process of inquiry rather than independent of it, and they maintain that informed qualitative, "subjective" judgment is no less valid than "objective" scientific inquiry (indeed, "radical" constructivist reject the very idea of objectivity). They maintain that the emphasis on evaluating theories and practice methods should focus on their usefulness (heuristic value) and that explanations can be valid without measuring key concepts or testing the relationships among them (i.e., research). Heuristic and constructivist practitioners object to the notions that a client's problem can be measured, that interventions can be cataloged and applied to specific clients in any meaningful way, and that important unseen (subjective) aspects of the client's treatment experience can be evaluated. Social constructionist practitioners tend to resent generalizations about human behavior and treatment effectiveness. From their perspective, the scientific method is understood not to be context-free or value-free, objective or unbiased, but it is as much a social and political construction as anything else, perhaps merely a manifestation of the practitioner-researcher's personal narrative.

Evidence-based practitioners believe that research methods, both qualitative and quantitative, can help inform us about human problems and adaptive capacities, and can contribute to the development of more effective interventions. Human problems are considered complex (i.e., multidimensional, interactional, context dependent), and although they understand the uniqueness of each individual, evidence-based practitioners believe that limited generalizations based on data derived from research with representative samples can inform assessment and intervention. Rather than indulging in philosophical debate regarding what is "objective" versus what is "subjective," social and behavioral scientists recognize that human thoughts, feelings, and behaviors are often ambiguous with respect to their definition and understanding, but defining and measuring human behavior (e.g., depression, suicide risk, child abuse, domestic violence) is critical to testing theories, developing valid assessment tools, improving intervention methods, and evaluating the results of our efforts. Replication and generalization of important findings and treatments are key to building a professional knowledge base, and employing such evidence is understood to be necessary for the conduct of competent and ethical professional practice.

Evidence-based practitioners reject the notion that knowledge is merely the product of personal interpretation. Evidence-based practitioners endorse the view that the conduct of informed assessment and treatment selection is a more responsible, professional way of operating than treatment planning by inspiration. Evidence-based practitioners see claims of intuition, deep and rich insights as arbitrary (and self-indulgent) and in need of some agreed-on definitions and external testing (Dawes, 1989). Individual judgment is necessary but fallible. Judgment needs to be exercised with caution given the variety of cognitive vulnerabilities that result from one's own personal experiences, preconceptions, biases, and motives. Evidence-based practitioners tend to see constructivists' claims of "neutrality" in the inquiry process as naive and self-serving, and to see their rejection of external reality as imprudent. Evidence-based practitioners also see the tendency to make claims without evidence as argument by authority (Gambrill, 2001), a weak foundation for ethical and effective practice.

The failure of the social constructionist or postmodern view lies primarily in the untestability of its assertions regarding theories and practices. Social constructionists apparently want to make claims about human behavior problems, interventions, and policies without empirical challenge. This perspective hinders social work's efforts to make substantive contributions to improving mental health interventions, an endeavor that cannot exclusively rely on philosophical speculation or artistic inspiration. Social constructionists offer case study as proof without apparently realizing that, although case studies make for useful illustrations, they are highly prone to biased interpretation and cannot rule out competing explanations for outcomes. Their portrayal of qualitative research methods as unique to their approach or superior to quantitative reveals either a lack of knowledge in this regard or disingenuousness. Qualitative research methods have long been an important tool of the behavioral and social sciences, albeit a preliminary (exploratory) first step in a broader process of rigorous scientific inquiry. Given their heavy reliance on case study and self-reflection, social constructionists turn serious inquiry into little more than an exercise in confirmation bias, that is, selective attendance to evidence that supports one's point of view while simultaneously ignoring evidence that disconfirms it. By obviating the need for more objective testing of their theories and practices, social constructionists seem to expect their positions to be accepted out of hand or confirmed by a show of hands.

EBPSW is clearly commensurate with the scientist-practitioner tradition. However, notwithstanding the caricature of the cold, uncaring technician, the implementation of evidence-based practices requires the capacity for empathic engagement with clients, keen judgment (grounded in knowledge), good critical-thinking skills, the use of both qualitative and quantitative data-collection methods, and the ability to collaborate flexibly with clients to optimize treatment outcomes (Gambrill, 1990; Klein & Bloom, 1995; O'Hare, 1991, 2009; Reid, 1997b; Rosen, 2003; Thyer, 2004). Implementing assessment and intervention procedures that are not supported by research is no longer acceptable practice in social work or the other helping professions. Ultimately, professional decision making is a complex process that is fraught, at times, with ambiguity, but social work practitioners can reduce assessment and treatment errors by learning and using evidence-based practices.

THE ROLE OF CRITICAL THINKING IN EBPSW

Practitioners must rely on good critical-thinking skills to effectively apply the existing practice knowledge base for at least two reasons: First, scientific evidence does not speak for itself. Some degree of interpretation is involved. Second, applying knowledge gleaned from research to individual cases and circumstances does require some judgment calls. Although findings from research offer helpful guidelines, they provide probability estimates, not predictive guarantees. Even the most informed and experienced practitioners make mistakes, partly because there is much we still do not know about human problems or how to ameliorate them.

All people make thinking errors, and social workers (including myself) are no exception. We are, after all, human, and therefore subject to the often arbitrary influences of our own life experiences, cultural background, preferred ideologies, political opinions, gaps in professional training, psychological and emotional problems, seduction by practice fads, collegial peer pressure, the need for money, ambition, and professional status seeking. Others succumb to more self-serving influences, including serious ethics violations (e.g., sexual impropriety and other boundary violations, financial exploitation) (Houston-Vega, Nuehring, & Daguio, 1997; Reamer, 1992, 1995, 2000, 2012). However, even assuming the best of intentions on the part of an informed and ethical social work practitioner, there exists a host of systematic thinking errors with which practitioners should be familiar (Gambrill, 1990, 2004; Nurius & Gibson, 1990; Tversky & Kahneman, 1974). These are as follows:

- Confusing description with inference by substituting handy labels (e.g., "She's a 'borderline,'" "He's an 'Axis II'") as a substitute for a thoughtful analysis of the person and situation (e.g., the client has suffered from many chronic and stressful experiences, and has not learned effective ways to cope)
- Focusing on dramatic stereotypes (e.g., "She's just a lying, drug abuser") rather than seeing client behavior in context (e.g., a mother is trying not to lose custody of children and to avoid imprisonment)
- Relying on easily accessible information (e.g., an emotionally compelling case study, recommendations from a charismatic "celebrity therapist") to make practice judgments rather than acquiring a more accurate view of the problem through relevant research
- Ascribing too much or too little importance to some data when formulating an assessment (e.g., an adverse childhood event) at the expense of other important influences (e.g., multiple chronic environmental stressors, such as poverty or long-term psychological abuse)
- Failing to employ accurate base rates of a problem by becoming infatuated with rare phenomena (e.g., multiple-personality disorder) rather than first considering more common explanations (e.g., feigning mental illness, drug abuse, medical disorder)
- Engaging in dichotomous thinking (e.g., treatment success or failure) rather than measuring behavior on a continuum (e.g., client is now less anxious, demonstrates better communication skills, has decreased alcohol or drug consumption)
- Overgeneralizing (e.g., "All traumatized women develop post-traumatic stress disorder, or PTSD") rather than considering individual variability and accurate base rates (e.g., "Some traumatized women develop PTSD")
- Engaging in hindsight bias to create the illusion of predictive expertise (e.g., "You should have known the client would attempt suicide!"), when, in fact, predicting relatively rare events on a case-by-case basis has proved very difficult under the best of circumstances
- Confusing correlation with causation (e.g., co-occurring heavy drinking and depression) rather than considering a range of causal relationships that may involve multiple factors (e.g., client drinks heavily because he is depressed; client is depressed because he drinks heavily; depression and alcohol abuse share common risk factors)
- Engaging in circular reasoning (e.g., client can't remember incidents of child abuse because of repressed memories; repressed memories are an indication of childhood trauma, and so the client must have been sexually abused because she cannot recall the incident) rather than examining multiple factors (including the possibility of trauma) and multiple sources of evidence as part of a thorough objective assessment

- Selectively attending to evidence that confirms one's theoretical or practice opinions (i.e., confirmation bias) rather than considering alternative explanations (e.g., citing only studies that appear to support one's point of view rather than conducting a representative review of the existing research using rigorous methodological criteria)
- Engaging in basic logical fallacies, such as non sequiturs (e.g., some traditional mental health services have failed our clients, and so unconventional or alternative therapies will be more effective), as the ineffectiveness of one approach does not lend support (by default) to an alternative strategy

The implementation of evidence-based methods requires informed judgment and careful reasoning. Although all practitioners are susceptible to personal biases and logical lapses, employing sound assessments based on well-founded human behavior research, implementing evidence-based practices, and carefully monitoring and evaluating each case can reduce errors. Evidence-based treatment planning keeps practitioners' focus on our highest priority: implementing valid assessments, effective interventions, and thoughtful evaluations for the benefit of our clients.

THE ETHICAL ARGUMENT FOR EVIDENCE-BASED SOCIAL WORK PRACTICE

All social work practitioners, researchers, academics, and administrators should be familiar with and adhere to the National Association of Social Workers' (NASW) Code of Ethics. The code outlines the ethical duty of social workers to use and promote scientifically sound theories and practices, and to engage in ethical research and evaluation activities. Evidence-based practices not only conform to the Code of Ethics but also enhance and facilitate its implementation. Ethical guidelines for conducting both social work practice and research are actually quite similar (Houston-Vega et al., 1997; O'Hare, 2009; Reamer, 1994, 1995, 2012).

Three basic guidelines must be adhered to with respect to both research and practice: (1) client confidentiality, (2) informed consent, and (3) a mandate to first "do no harm." Confidentiality has always been one of the foremost ethical principles for social workers, and it has been robustly supported in past court decisions (e.g., see *Jaffee v. Redmond*, in Appelbaum, 1996) and by federal legislation, specifically the Health Insurance Portability and Accountability Act of 1996. Practitioners and researchers also share the responsibility to provide adequate informed consent to clients by explaining the nature of the intervention or the research or evaluation project, and by indicating whether there is any potential for it to cause psychological distress. Practitioners and researchers are also required to be responsive should clients become distressed in the course of an intervention or research and evaluation procedure. With increasing frequency, practice and evaluation activities are occurring simultaneously (e.g., using clinical scales as part of assessment and evaluation), thus blurring the distinction between the two activities. A sensible policy would be for social workers to concentrate on applying good ethical principles whether the professional activity is defined as practice, evaluation, research, or a combination of those.

Because few social workers engage in controlled experimental research with innovative or potentially controversial treatments (e.g., drug trials, other medical research), most of the concerns about breaches of ethics, practically speaking, are relevant to social work practice, not research. There have been numerous malpractice claims related to incorrect treatment, sexual impropriety, breaches of confidentiality, failure to diagnose correctly, client abandonment (i.e., terminating prematurely), and suicide attempts (Appelbaum, 1993; Beutler, Clarkin, & Bongar, 2000; Houston-Vega et al., 1997; Reamer, 1995, 2012). Although anyone can inadvertently breach ethical principles or be sued for malpractice, evidence-based practice guidelines can help mitigate those threats by providing an accountable basis for assessment, intervention, and evaluation. Practitioners are well advised to document their efforts by citing authoritative evidence-based sources when writing intervention plans.

PRINCIPLES OF EBPSW

The working principles of EBPSW are listed here; we will examine them further in subsequent chapters.

1.   Social work is a profession based on values, ethics, knowledge, and skills. Value-based professional decision making requires the use of scientifically derived knowledge and skills as applied to assessment and intervention, guided by critical thinking and good judgment honed by practice experience.

2.   The knowledge base of social work is rooted in the behavioral and social sciences. People's problems and adaptive capabilities are understood to be caused by or associated with biological, psychological, and social-environmental factors that interact in complex ways over time and vary by situation. These influences have both remote and proximate effects on the cause and maintenance of psychosocial problems and adaptive capacities. The behavioral and social sciences inform our ability to conduct valid assessments and help us understand biopsychosocial mechanisms that might be amenable to change.

3.   Although the client's view of the problem, coping capacities, and suggestions for potential solutions should be given the utmost consideration in professional assessment and treatment planning, practitioners are primarily responsible for that consideration. Funding

sources, regulatory agencies, and the courts recognize licensed social workers, not their clients, as the experts, and they hold the social workers, not the clients, accountable for assessment and treatment planning.

4.   Personal identity factors such as age, gender, sexual orientation, race, ethnicity, and cultural and religious affiliation interact in complex and sometimes indeterminate ways. Consideration of these client characteristics is essential for advancing our understanding of human behavior theories, improving assessment protocol, and providing effective interventions to specific client groups.

5.   Outcome research provides substantial guidance for practitioners when developing effective intervention strategies. Nevertheless, interventions shown to be effective in controlled studies often require flexible, eclectic adaptation as a result of client preferences, circumstances, and the unpredictable events that occur during intervention.

6.   Evidence-based practitioners have many evaluation research methods at their disposal. All have strengths and weaknesses. Evidence-based practitioners use the design that is most suitable and practical given their practice context.

7.   Above all, the development, teaching, and dissemination of evidence-based practices are guided by the time-honored tradition of rational, scholarly discourse. Critical thinking and peer-reviewed, methodologically sound research are the currency of ethical, professional knowledge building and debate.

8.   In contrast to depictions of EBPSW as a simplistic, rigid application of "manualized interventions," the implementation of EBPSW requires flexibility to adapt practices to complex cases in fluid service environments.

9.   At the levels of both practitioner and agency, the assessment, intervention, and evaluation processes are integrated to provide effective care. Qualitative and quantitative methodologies are often combined to evaluate and improve the quality of service.

10.   For social work to remain a vital profession well into the future, social workers must play an active role in the development, implementation, and evaluation of EBPSW.

CHAPTER 2

QUALITATIVE AND
QUANTITATIVE ASSESSMENT

Assessment in social work practice is a form of problem analysis. It is an attempt on the part of the practitioner, client, and often other collaborators to identify which factors appear to have caused and currently maintain the client's problems, to assess client capacities for adaptation and change (i.e., assess strengths), and to specify those aspects of the client's problems that are amenable to change. Setting goals and objectives, selecting effective intervention methods, and designing the evaluation plan are inextricably linked to assessment as part of the intervention-planning process. These processes are discussed further in this and subsequent chapters.

Currently, there is little consensus in the practice literature regarding the composition of an adequate assessment for psychosocial disorders and problems-in-living. Practitioners tend to stress the form of assessment that is commensurate with their preferred theoretical model: proponents of the medical model offer diagnosis, traditional behaviorists emphasize functional assessment, family therapists use a systems perspective, cognitivists emphasize dysfunctional thinking, constructivists focus on the client's personal narrative, and so on. All of these methods have advantages, but relying exclusively on any one approach is not sufficient for adequate treatment planning. Although psychosocial, family systems, and ecosystems assessment models provide useful organizing frameworks for examining an individual's behavior, they must be supplemented with problem-specific research findings to meaningfully inform the assessment.

HOW BEHAVIORAL SCIENCE INFORMS ASSESSMENT

Although it is understood that every person's life experience is unique, problem-specific knowledge derived from the behavioral and social sciences provides the foundation for conducting a competent assessment. The significance of individuals' thoughts, feelings, and behaviors, and how they function in their social environment have little salience unless informed by knowledge relevant to schizophrenia, substance abuse, depression, domestic violence, childhood disorders, and so forth. The behavioral sciences inform assessment in the following ways:

- Providing base rate estimates (incidence and prevalence) of specific problems in the community
- Estimating the rates of co-occurring problems
- Identifying key risk and resiliency factors (both developmental and current) that are likely to contribute to a client's problems or predict recovery (these factors may be cognitive, physiological, familial, social, environmental, or cultural)
- Providing estimates of the relative strength of risk and resiliency factors
- Accounting for the multidimensional nature of client problems
- Providing support for some theories and invalidating others
- Providing an empirical and theoretical foundation for instrument development

Contemporary behavioral science explains human behavior as a complex interaction of intraindividual (i.e., cognitive, behavioral, and physiological) and systemically related social-environmental factors (e.g., familial, social, cultural). These risks, stressors, deficits, protective factors, and strengths interact reciprocally over time and across situations as people develop and adapt within their social environment. Behavioral science also emphasizes the importance of "personal identity factors," such as age, gender, race/ethnicity, cultural background, and sexual orientation, to more fully inform us about the similarities and differences across various groups of people (Basic Behavioral Science Task Force, 1996; Pinderhughes, 1989; Sue & Zane, 2006; Sue, Zane, & Young, 1994). Although findings from research on white males have historically been overextended to assessment and intervention guidelines for women and persons of color (Beckman, 1994; Carter, 1995; Schliebner, 1994), research emphasizing personal identity factors has expanded rapidly in recent decades. Still, much more needs to be done.

Although it is critical that personal identity factors be taken into account in both research and practice, one must exercise caution to avoid making overly broad generalizations about various groups of people, and in effect, stereotyping them (Gopaul-McNicol & Brice-Baker, 1998; Manoleas, 1996; Uba, 1994; Vasquez, 1994). For example, women of color may share a common bond of oppression, but they also manifest considerable differences (i.e., heterogeneity) between and within racial groups. Indeed, some theoreticians have suggested an alternative strategy to assessing group differences. Rather than emphasizing broad ethnic categories to describe culturally disparate peoples, for example, finer-grained approaches may provide greater sensitivity (Cheung, 1990; Heath, 1991; O'Hare & Tran, 1998; Sue & Zane, 2006; Trimble, 1990). Such guidelines include identifying the birthplace of the client and other family members over two or three generations;

analyzing ethnicity-specific behavior patterns, such as language use, ethnic identity of friends and acquaintances, use of various media, participation in ethnic activities such as cultural and religious events, and music and food preferences; and exploring subjective assessments of ethnic identity, acculturation and assimilation status, value preferences, role models and preferred reference groups, and attitudes toward out-groups.

These ethnic and cultural differences must also be seen in a temporal or developmental context. Rather than seeing acculturation as a linear transition from immigrant culture to host culture, it is better to understand it as bidirectional. Accordingly, multiple psychological and behavioral aspects of acculturation vary between the immigrant and host culture. Individuals may acquire, retain, or discard various aspects of cultural identification to one extent or another (Anderson et al., 1993; Marino, Stuart, & Minas, 2000). Berry (1986) conceptualizes four possible outcomes of the acculturation process: assimilation toward the dominant culture, integration of both cultures, reaffirmation of the traditional culture, and marginalization from both cultures. Overall, characterizing large groups of persons by, for example, gender, race, or sexual orientation as though "they" share a common characteristic is fraught with peril and can blind practitioners to the uniqueness of each client's experience.

A growing number of assessment instruments have been designed to address matters related to race and culture, for example, race-related stress (Utsey & Ponterotto, 1996) and language proficiency among recent immigrants (Anderson et al., 1993). Other scales address common problems that can vary by cultural background, such as mental health (Mollica, Wyshak, de Marneffe, Khuon, & Lavelle, 1987) and substance abuse (Saunders, Aasland, Amundsen, & Grant, 1993), among others. In addition, more attention has been given to refining methodological processes for valid scale construction with persons from different cultural groups (Tran, 1997, 2009). Practitioners who include scales in their assessment procedures should check to see that the selected scale has been validated with the client's reference group.

THE MULTIDIMENSIONAL-FUNCTIONAL-SYSTEMIC (MFS) APPROACH TO ASSESSMENT

Given the assumption that valid assessment must consider both problem-specific knowledge about the client's condition and a detailed accounting of the client's unique experience, a comprehensive assessment should incorporate three core organizing concepts: *multidimensionality*, *functionality*, and the *systemic nature of human behavior* (table 2.1). All three concepts are at the heart of what this text defines as evidence-based assessment, and they are drawn from a range of sources on assessment in mental health and human services (Antony & Swinson, 2000; Franklin & Jordan, 2011; Hartmann, Roper, & Bradford, 1979; Haynes, 1998; Karls & Wandrei, 1994; O'Hare, 2009; Persons & Fresco, 1998).

TABLE 2.1   Conceptual Domains of Evidence-Based Assessment

Multidimensionality	Functionality	A systems perspective
Assess developmental and current causes of client difficulties and the trajectory of problems over time. Analysis is informed by problem-specific human behavior research.	Examine temporal sequencing and patterning of problem behaviors over time and across situations; focus on current functioning and key problems.	Analyze interactional and systemic influences and behaviors over time in family, organizational, and community settings.
Conduct a thorough examination of current biopsychosocial difficulties across multiple domains (e.g., mental status, relationships, work, health).	Measure important problems on a continuum (e.g., frequency, severity, or duration) with either self-anchored indexes or dimensional scales.	Examine both positive and dysfunctional interactions, and how they play out over time.
Carefully consider the role of individual factors (e.g., gender, race, ethnicity, sexual orientation, spirituality) on problems and potential solutions.	Identify important contingencies, that is, rewards and sanctions that appear to maintain current conditions.	Identify reinforcers that cause positive or negative interactions to continue.
	Set problem priorities and develop hierarchies for achieving objectives toward resolving problems.	Examine the relationships among various systems: family, school, work, community.
	Explore client's unique problem constructions and expectations of resolving problems.	Estimate the strength of various bonds, boundaries, alliances, and subsystems within families and communities.
	Emphasize problems that are amenable to change, or changes that can be measured incrementally over time for monitoring and evaluation purposes.	

Multidimensionality requires knowledge about the nature and severity of the client's specific difficulties and adaptive capabilities across a variety of life domains: psychological functioning (e.g., cognition, emotion), behavioral problems (e.g., impulsivity, substance abuse), social well-being (e.g., family, community), and overall health status. The problems and strengths associated with these domains are usually interrelated, and the factors that cause and maintain them tend to interact over time and across situations. *Functionality* is assessed primarily through an understanding of the patterns unique to the client's experience based on reports from multiple sources, including the client, the family, collaborating professionals, and others when needed. Emphasis is placed on understanding those antecedents and consequences that seem to cause or maintain the problem, or to result in better coping and adaptation. Although *systemic interaction* is implicit in both concepts of multidimensionality and functionality, it is important to be explicit about the fact that people's problems are best understood within the interactive context of family, friends and acquaintances, organizations, community, and society as a whole. Although these assessment concepts may seem somewhat abstract, all chapters in parts II and III of this text offer many examples of how MFS assessment is applied in practice.

Multidimensionality

Assessment is multidimensional to the extent that it has the following characteristics: First, the practitioner's understanding of the client's overall well-being and problem-specific history is informed by contemporary human behavior research. Human development, problems, and adaptive capacities are understood to be caused by *reciprocally and systemically interacting biopsychosocial processes*. Second, a multidimensional assessment describes client distress across multiple domains of psychosocial functioning or well-being. These domains minimally include mental status (e.g., psychiatric symptoms, dysfunctional thinking, mood disturbance), substance abuse, social functioning in immediate social relationships (e.g., partners, family) and extended relationships (e.g., work, school, community), access to and use of environmental resources (e.g., housing, health care, transportation, housing and safety concerns), gainful vocational activity (e.g., job, education), general health status, leisure activities, criminal involvement, and spiritual well-being. Third, the expression of a client's problems and life circumstances are recognized as moderated by gender, age, cultural identity, and other defining characteristics as already noted here.

Functionality

Although human behavior research informs assessment in a general way, assessment must also address the client's experiences, patterns, and behavioral responses to the contingencies of everyday life. This examination of daily behavior and the factors that maintain the problem and support adaptation is known as functional analysis. Knowledge of schizophrenia, for example, is helpful for understanding the condition of clients who share this disorder. However, persons with schizophrenia are unique in many ways. An MFS assessment reflects functionality to the extent that it provides an in-depth analysis of the patterning and sequencing of client-specific experiences (i.e., thoughts, feelings, behaviors, coping skills and deficits) that interact with day-to-day events (i.e., antecedents and consequences) in their social environment. A functional assessment is unique to each individual. Thus, the practitioner and client must work collaboratively to describe, explain, understand, and together build a detailed working model of the client's problems in order to identify factors (e.g., symptoms, dysfunctional thinking, other people, situations) that will be either problematic or helpful in resolving the target problem.

The functional assessment emphasizes the following: (1) *temporal sequencing and patterning* of thoughts, feelings, behaviors, and events related to the problem; (2) measuring the *frequency, severity (intensity), or duration* of specific problems to detect changes over time; (3) identifying salient *contingencies* (i.e., antecedent events, responses to those events, and resulting consequences) that influence the client's behavior and overall well-being; (4) *setting priorities among different problems*; (5) establishing *progressive hierarchies* to gradually address intervention objectives; (6) paying close attention to the *client's construction of the problem and expectations for change*; and (7) focusing on problems that are *amenable to change.*

A Systems Perspective

Although most assessment models emphasize work with individuals, assessment is best done when we examine individual behavior in a social context, including immediate social relationships (e.g., close relationships, family) and extended relationships (e.g., school, work, community). For example, family systems assessment complements both multidimensional and functional aspects of the assessment. The practitioner must examine problem behaviors and strengths in individual members but at the same time examine the interactional and temporal patterning among family members to understand *how the system functions* (e.g., who does what, when, to whom, what is the response). This approach can help identify both positive and dysfunctional patterns of communications among individuals and between individuals and larger social systems. Those patterns can then become a focus for intervention.

THE ROLE OF MEASUREMENT IN MFS ASSESSMENT

Practitioners are called on at assessment to make frequent judgments regarding the severity of problems, for purposes of treatment planning, referral, or evaluation (e.g., changes in severity of hallucinations, anxiety level, level of hope for recovery, number of drinks per day, suicidal risk). Suffice it to say that practitioners are constantly gauging the well-being of their clients to determine whether they are improving. The only remaining question is how consistent (i.e., reliable) and how accurate (i.e., valid) those judgments are.

Assessment can be greatly enhanced when practitioners incorporate a combination of simple indexes and user-friendly standardized instruments into assessment and evaluation procedures. Simple indexes (e.g., days sober, days absent from school, number of panic attacks per week) can be quite accurate (depending on the reliability of the source) and are useful for determining progress. Standardized scales can be practical to use and can contribute much to the validity of an overall assessment. The use of reliable, valid, and practical instruments enhances assessment by (1) engendering increased reliability and validity of the overall assessment; (2) identifying high-risk behaviors (e.g., drug use, suicidal ideation, self-harm); (3) helping clients identify specific complaints, clarify their definition of their problems, and become more knowledgeable about the presenting problem (e.g., panic attacks don't mean that one is "going crazy"; sleep problems can be associated with depression); (4) prompting more in-depth discussion about the problem with the practitioner and thus providing an opportunity for more targeted assessment; and (5) providing a mechanism for monitoring and evaluation of client progress.

Client problems are measured in several different ways: by *classification* (e.g., diagnosis), *frequency* with which the problem occurs (e.g., number of obsessional thoughts in a day), *intensity* or *severity* (e.g., degree of suicidal intent), and *duration* (e.g., time procrastinating before commencing homework). Types of instruments also vary by degree of complexity, from simple classification and single-item indexes to one-dimensional and multidimensional scales.

DIAGNOSTIC CLASSIFICATION

For many social workers, conducting an assessment also includes, by necessity, the use of the *Diagnostic and Statistical Manual of Mental Disorders* (American Psychiatric Association, APA, 2000, 2013). The utility and limitations of the DSM must be addressed first. Indeed, the DSM has become an essential tool for many social workers, and it has contributed greatly to the recognition of serious mental disorders. It also provides a common nomenclature for practitioners and has stimulated and guided much clinical research. Social work practitioners should be familiar with it and know how to use it competently. However, there are limitations to the DSM as a tool for assessment, and long-standing criticisms about the validity of some of the diagnostic categories and the DSM's overall approach have become more acute with the introduction of the fifth edition of the DSM (DSM-5).

First, DSM diagnosis is premised on the notion that the locus of dysfunction (i.e., mental disorder) is within the individual: "Whatever its original cause [the disorder] must currently be considered a manifestation of a behavioral, psychological, or biological dysfunction in the individual" (APA,

2000, p. xxxi). This assumption, however, is somewhat constrained by growing research on the influences of psychosocial stressors and other socio-environmental factors.

Second, DSM categories lack differentiation. Classification systems work best when the categories are relatively homogenous, have clear boundaries between them, and are mutually exclusive. Generally, homogeneity is more the exception than the rule in DSM diagnoses, since many symptoms and behaviors are common to more than one disorder (e.g., anxiety disorders, externalizing disorders of children). The authors of the DSM-5 seem to have become more circumspect on this issue, noting in the preface that "mental disorders do not always fit completely within the boundaries of a single disorder" (APA, 2013, p. xii).

Third, aside from determining the presence of serious mental illness presumably caused, in part, by some physiological dysfunction (e.g., schizophrenia, bipolar disorder, major depression, some anxiety disorders), many believe that the DSM is misapplied to conditions in which psychosocial factors play a prominent, if not dominant, role (e.g., a woman who meets the criteria for depression associated with severe domestic violence). Some DSM categories also appear to be merely descriptions of behaviors that are sometimes troubling to the client or, especially, to others (Kutchins & Kirk, 1997; Peele, 1989; Sroufe, 1997; Wakefield, 1997). Criticisms regarding diagnosis of personality disorders, for example, are long-standing, particularly with respect to matters of reliability (Zimmerman, 2012). The lack of empirical evidence for the biological etiology of many disorders includes diagnoses applied to children with psychosocial or behavioral difficulties (e.g., oppositional-defiant disorder) (Achenbach, 1995). However, even with disorders such as severe mental illness in which biological factors have been shown to play a dominant etiological role, social and environmental factors weigh heavily in the exacerbation of symptoms, access to treatment, and long-term outcomes.

Fourth, according to critics within and without psychiatry, reviews of the field trials and data related to the development of the DSM have consistently concluded that the methods employed in reliability and validity testing were seriously flawed and remain so (Frances & Nardo, 2013; Kutchins & Kirk, 1988, 1997). Last, aside from setting general treatment expectations for practitioners (e.g., persons with schizophrenia are likely to benefit from antipsychotic drugs), diagnosis provides relatively little practical guidance for treatment planning and evaluation, given that clients' problems are typically multidimensional and specific to the individual, and diagnosis, being categorical, lacks sensitivity to change. However, in acknowledgment of some professionals' preference for a dimensional approach to assessment, the DSM-5 now includes a section on instruments to measure crosscutting symptoms.

SCREENING DEVICES

Screening devices in social work practice also play an important role as prelude to a more thorough assessment. Screening tools are scales that use a cut score determined by research to detect the likelihood of a client having a particular problem. Instruments such as the Michigan Alcoholism Screening Test (Seltzer, 1971) or the Drug Abuse Screening Test (Skinner, 1982) use specific cut scores to identify people who may be at risk of a serious substance abuse problem. Although some screening devices (because of the wording of items or scoring method) cannot be used as outcome measures because they cannot show change over short periods of time (e.g., 3 months), others are more sensitive to change and can be employed as both a screening and an evaluation tool. For example, the Geriatric Depression Scale (Yesavage et al., 1983) can be used with an empirically determined cut score (see chapter 6) to serve as a screening device with elderly clients, but it is also sensitive to change, and thus can be used as an assessment or evaluation tool. Before using screening devices, however, practitioners should be sure that the recommended cut score is based on research similar to the client's reference group. As with all instruments, screening devices should be validated with samples that reflect the population with whom they are intended to be used. In addition, the results of a screening instrument should not be considered a confirmation of the problem but simply a "warning light" signaling that a more detailed assessment is warranted.

SINGLE-ITEM INDEXES

Sometimes clients' most pressing concerns can be summed up in a simple index: number of drinks, frequency of panic attacks, level of postoperative pain, number of suicidal thoughts, level of depression, and so on. One-item indexes were originally associated with early behavioral interventions in which "target" problems were the focus of treatment (Bloom, Fischer, & Orme, 2009; Hersen, 1985). For example, for a child with severe autism, reduced head banging or hair pulling may be used to judge the success of behavior modification. For another client, the intensity of trauma-related flashbacks using a self-anchored scale from 0 to 100 can assess progress in response to stress management and guided imagery. The number of successfully completed homework assignments for a child struggling with attention-deficit hyperactivity disorder (ADHD) can be measured with a brightly colored chart indicating small rewards as incentives. When applied to more complex problems, the adjunctive use of simple indexes can help focus an intervention on key problems and provide a straightforward basis for evaluation.

Table 2.2 provides a template for considering how to define target problems (i.e., thoughts, feelings, behaviors) and how to measure them (e.g., frequency, intensity, duration). For treatment planning, these indexes can also represent specific treatment objectives. How the problem or objective is defined and measured should be the result of client-practitioner discussion to maximize the salience for clients, to encourage their willingness to participate, and to reflect whatever seems most congruent with their situation. For example, for serious suicidal thoughts (cognition), frequency may be the main concern for one client but severity or intensity of the thoughts for another. For an assaultive adolescent, intensity of anger may be the main focus of change rather than frequency. For the person with agoraphobia, the frequency of panic attacks may be most critical, or the amount of time (duration) he or she can remain in the supermarket without "freaking out" and running outside. For a couple struggling to improve communications and intimacy, reducing the frequency of interruptions during conversations (i.e., behavior) may be their initial objective, and later, increasing the amount of recreational or romantic time spent together may become the new objective. As treatment objectives are accomplished, they can be modified to reflect greater improvement or changed to focus on a different problem. When defining these indexes, careful attention should be given to the context within which the target symptom or problem occurs. The chart below can be used with clients to help define specific problems and objectives.

TABLE 2.2   Template for defining and measuring target problems

	Frequency	Intensity or severity	Duration
Cognitive (thoughts)			
Emotional (feelings)			
Physiological (symptoms)			
Behavioral (actions)			

Unidimensional Scales

Unidimensional scales measure only one dimension of client well-being, such as depression, anxiety, self-esteem, and so forth, but they do so with multiple items. Although less flexible in use than simple one-item indexes, unidimensional scales have usually been tested for reliability and validity. Notable examples include the Beck Depression Inventory (Beck, Ward, Mendelson, Mock, & Erbaugh, 1961), the HAM-D for depression (Hamilton, 1960), the Obsessive Compulsive Inventory (Foa, Kozak, Salkovskis, Coles, & Amir, 1998), and the Index of Marital Relations (Hudson, 1982a), among many others. Although unidimensional scales can be a valuable adjunct to a comprehensive assessment, they are limited in focus and need to be employed on a case-by-case basis. However, they can be used routinely in specialized intervention settings (e.g., depression or anxiety clinic) or as a supplement to multidimensional instruments that do not include a particular domain of interest.

Multidimensional Scales

One remedy for dealing with the potential "jumbled array" (Hudson & McMurty, 1997) of unidimensional scales is to employ multidimensional instruments, which measure several important areas of psychosocial well-being with one instrument. Multidimensional measures provide a quantitative counterpart to a comprehensive qualitative assessment. There has been considerable growth in the development of reliable and valid instruments to measure clients' functioning across an array of psychiatric, psychosocial, and health-related domains for adults and children (e.g., Dickerson, 1997; Hurley, Huscroft-D'Angelo, Trout, Griffith, & Epstein, 2014; Srebnik et al., 1997) and many have been translated into other languages to advance culturally informed research. Many scales designed to balance reliability, validity, and utility are highlighted throughout this text.

Although some practitioners might question the measurement of problems other than those "target problems" for which the client requested treatment, mental health and other human services settings often require multidimensional measures to gauge clients' overall functioning. Some can be used for both assessment and outcome evaluation purposes. The Psycho-Social Well-Being Scale (PSWS) (O'Hare & Geertsma, 2013; O'Hare et al., 2002; O'Hare et al., 2003) is an example of a broad-spectrum instrument. There are others cited in this text, and practitioners should employ those that best fit their assessment and evaluation needs. The PSWS was developed as a comprehensive yet easy-to-use "debriefing" tool or final "scorecard" to quantitatively summarize clinical judgments regarding problem severity on a range of important psychosocial domains. Clinicians are encouraged to use a broad array of sources (e.g., client self-report, clinical records, input from significant others and collaborating professionals) before making a final judgment about problem severity. Because the PSWS was developed for use with adults in a comprehensive community mental health center, it may have wide applicability.

Practitioners rate the 12 items that constitute the PSWS on a 5-point scale (excellent = 4, good = 3, marginal = 2, impaired = 1, poor = 0), and the items cover the following problem domains: First, there are two four-item subscales, psychological well-being (cognition, mood, impulse control, and coping skills) and social well-being (immediate social network, extended social network, recreational activities, living environment). (The four items of each of these two subscales can be added into a subscale score and divided by 4 to obtain a relative measure of severity.) In addition, there are four one-item indexes, including global measures of substance abuse, health, activities of daily living, and work satisfaction. These four items can be used as "stand-alone" indexes. The PSWS has been shown to have good reliability and concurrent validity, in that its subscales have correlated well with other valid scales, and the PSWS appears to be sensitive to change over time (O'Hare et al., 2002; O'Hare et al., 2003; O'Hare & Geertsma, 2013). The PSWS is best used as part of a comprehensive strategy of assessment, monitoring, and evaluation that incorporates the observations and judgments of client, practitioner, and other corroborating sources. After scoring each item on the scale, practitioners should qualitatively describe the client's specific problem in the lines provided for each item. In this way, the PSWS serves as both a quantitative and a qualitative assessment and outcome instrument. The PSWS is available in appendix A and can be used without obtaining special permission from the author.

Broad-based scales for assessment of childhood disorders are also available. The Child Behavior Check List (CBCL) (Achenbach, 1995; Lowe, 1998; Wild, Furtado, & Angalakuditi, 2012), a widely used and well-regarded multidimensional scale of child functioning, measures both social competence and behavior problems in children. Different versions have been developed for use by parents, teachers, and children themselves, and it has been validated by gender and race. The CBCL is proprietary and requires special permission from its author in order to use it.

The Shortform Assessment for Children (SAC) (Glisson, Hemmelgarn, & Post, 2002; Hemmelgarn, Glisson, & Sharp, 2003) is a viable alternative to the CBCL. The SAC is a brief and reliable broad scale that measures both emotional and behavioral problems in children. The SAC is a recent addition to a series of scales developed with the support of the National Institute of Mental Health (NIMH) from behavioral items created in the 1940s and 1950s (Tyson & Glisson, 2005). Validated with a sample of 3,790 children (age 5–18) served by the child welfare and juvenile justice systems, the SAC works comparably well with children of different ages, by gender and by respondent groups (e.g., parents and teachers) (Glisson et al., 2002). Internal consistency reliability coefficients ranged between .86 and .96 with either parents or teachers as respondents, and subscales showed significant correlations with child placement decisions and other validity criteria. Furthermore, an additional independent sample of 1,252 children indicated the SAC to be equally valid with African American and white children (Tyson & Glisson, 2005). The SAC can be completed by parents or teachers, or preferably both. The SAC is available at no cost from its authors, and it is accompanied by software-based scoring guidelines normed for child's age and gender, and respondent. (To obtain the scale and access to the scoring software, contact Children's Mental Health Services Research Center, Henson Hall, University of Tennessee, Knoxville, TN 37996-3332.) A copy of the Shortform Assessment for Children appears in appendix B.

Other broad scales are available to accommodate a range of assessment needs. The Family Adaptability and Cohesion Evaluation Scales (FACES IV) measures levels of cohesiveness (i.e., enmeshed to disengaged) and flexibility (i.e., chaotic to rigid) in family functioning (Franklin, Streeter, & Springer, 2001; Groenenberg, Sushma, Green, & Fleming, 2013; Olsen, Russell, & Sprenkle, 1989). It was developed from a systems perspective, and the scale is intended to be self-administered. The Addiction Severity Index (Denis, Cacciola, & Alterman, 2013; McLellan, Luborsky, O'Brien, & Woody, 1980) measures degree of distress from alcohol and drug use across several problem domains, including legal, medical, family, social, and occupational functioning (see chapter 7). The Social Functioning Scale is a widely used, brief instrument that accurately measures physical and mental health (see Ware, Kosinski, & Keller, 1996). Lehman's (1988) Quality of Life Scale measures seven areas, including living situation, family and social relations, leisure, work and religious activity, finances, safety, and health. All of these instruments have been shown to be reliable and valid with specific populations to one degree or another, provide continuous measures to gauge treatment progress, and can generally be completed in less than an hour.

BASIC GUIDELINES FOR DEVELOPING A MEASUREMENT STRATEGY

There are several basic criteria that should be considered before selecting and using scales and developing a measurement strategy. An overall measurement package should do the following:

- Measure multiple dimensions of client well-being on continuous scales
- Support and enhance the overall qualitative psychosocial assessment
- Be relevant to the treatment agenda of all members of an interdisciplinary team

- Facilitate the treatment-planning process by providing a template for measuring treatment goals and outcomes (evaluation)
- Have a published record of reliability and validity, and be relatively easy to use with little training
- Produce scores (for individual items and aggregate scores) that have straightforward face validity and resonance with clients, practitioners, administrators, and policy makers

MATTERS OF RELIABILITY AND VALIDITY

Reliability and validity must be considered when developing or choosing scales for assessment, research, or evaluation (Devellis, 2000; Kazdin, 1994a). First, a scale should have *face validity* and be considered by both practitioner and client to be relevant to the client's overall problems. Second, it should have a track record of research supporting its *internal consistency reliability* (i.e., items of the scale show good interitem correlation), *test-retest reliability* (i.e., scale is consistent when filled out at two different points in time), and *interrater reliability* (i.e., two observers who use the same scale with the same client show a high degree of agreement). Third, instruments should ideally meet criteria for three forms of validity: *construct validity* (i.e., the scale measures what it purports to measure), *criterion validity* (i.e., it correlates with similar measures concurrently and predicts relevant outcomes), and *content validity* (i.e., it includes a reasonably representative array of relevant items). Although ideally a scale should meet all of these standards, most published scales are considered acceptable if they meet at least one or two forms of reliability and show both construct validity and some form of criterion validity with relevant target populations.

Various statistical methods are used to demonstrate the degree of reliability and validity. A statistic called Cronbach's alpha is used to measure internal consistency reliability. Ranging from 0 to 1, a Cronbach's alpha of .70 is considered "adequate," .80 or greater is "good," and .90 is "excellent." Interrater reliability is measured using a range of different statistics, and depending on how it is measured, agreement between two raters should be at least considered "good" to be acceptable. Concurrent validity of scales is indicated by moderate to high correlations (>.50), and predictive validity is shown when a scale score predicts an intended outcome significantly better than chance alone. Testing for construct validity involves a more detailed analysis of the underlying factor structure and requires advanced statistical techniques known as exploratory and confirmatory factor analysis to demonstrate that the scale items individually and collectively measure the theoretical construct of interest (e.g., anxiety, psychopathy, alcohol dependence). In addition, a scale's reliability and validity should be replicated across different samples. Last, instruments intended to be used for monitoring and evaluation purposes should be sensitive to change with respect to the client's target problems. Although practitioners should be familiar with the basic concepts of reliability and validity, persons who have expertise in instrument development and validation can provide helpful consultation as to the selection of scales.

METHODS FOR GATHERING ASSESSMENT INFORMATION

After practitioners compile a package of scales and simple indexes suitable for assessment and evaluation, there are a number of different approaches to take to collecting data. For the most part, social workers depend on client self-report in *face-to-face interviews*, which may range from relatively unstructured to highly structured (i.e., standardized) formats. To obtain a more complete picture of the client's situation (e.g., child having problems in school) and to ensure accurate self-report (e.g., for a court-ordered client), practitioners may also need to obtain *collateral* or *corroborating information* (e.g., legal records, medical records, employer's report of job performance). Other methods include observing clients in their natural environment (e.g., hospital ward, school, summer camp); asking clients to *demonstrate* (role-play or "act out") a problem situation (e.g., a troubled couple discusses finances for the practitioner to observe their communication skills; a person with a mental illness "interviews" with you for a job); asking clients to participate in an extended assessment by requesting that they self-monitor their thoughts, feelings, and behaviors in different circumstances for a week or two (e.g., client keeps a diary of negative self-statements; parent keeps a chart noting their child's compulsive hand washing) to develop a better working model of the problem. All of these assessment activities may include the collection of qualitative data, quantitative data, or (preferably) both. Scales and other quantitative indexes should complement the qualitative assessment.

Practitioner judgment is required to conduct the optimal MFS assessment. In some instances, client self-report may be sufficiently valid if there appears to be no compelling motive for the clients to misrepresent the truth and the client does not appear to have a problem with long-term memory. In other instances, because of cognitive impairment, minimizing a problem, or lying, practitioners should obtain corroborating information. Given that effective intervention is, in part, contingent on an accurate assessment, practitioners should be assertive in obtaining an overall accurate, thorough, and balanced view of the client's problems. In the final analysis, assessment is both art and science, inductive and deductive, focused on unique individual behavior but informed by problem-specific research findings.

SUMMARY

In summary, assessment in EBPSW is informed by problem-specific research findings, describes and measures problems across multiple psychosocial domains, includes a functional analysis of behavioral patterns and related factors, examines problems in a systems context, and uses both qualitative and quantitative methods to support intervention planning.

CHAPTER 3

SELECTING AND
IMPLEMENTING INTERVENTIONS

This chapter addresses general considerations regarding the selection and implementation of evidence-based practices: (1) defining the intervention; (2) identifying essential practice components common to many evidence-based interventions; (3) clarifying the debate on "flexibility" versus "manualization"; (4) providing a brief overview of current findings in controlled outcome research; and (5) offering a summary of basic guidelines for the critical review of outcome studies, a key step in understanding and selecting evidence-based practices.

DEFINING INTERVENTIONS

Intervention in evidence-based practice for social workers (EBPSW) is defined as those professional activities engaged in by practitioners, clients, and perhaps other collaborators for the purpose of solving specific problems, enhancing clients' adaptive capabilities (i.e., strengths), and modifying social-environmental contingencies to improve a client's psychosocial well-being. If *intervention* is the overarching term, then *skills* are the most elemental components, and *strategies or techniques* are combinations of skills that summatively constitute the intervention. It has been long understood that social work interventions often comprise various combinations of both basic and advanced skills, techniques, and strategies (Hepworth, Rooney, Rooney, & Strom-Gottfried, 2012; O'Hare, 2009; Shulman, 1992). Novice social workers may initially focus on learning a few discrete basic skills (e.g., listening, empathic response to help a client cope with a loss), specific behavioral techniques (e.g., parental use of positive reinforcement to improve a child's homework completion), or case management methods (e.g., coordinating services to enhance instrumental and social supports for socially isolated older people.

Evidence-based interventions, however, are *combinations of skills and techniques that have been shown to be efficacious in controlled outcome studies with serious and complex psychosocial problems and psychiatric disorders*. These interventions may include, for example, psychoeducation and behavioral family therapy for people with severe mental illness, community reinforcement or contingency management interventions with paroled inmates addicted to drugs, cognitive and interpersonal psychotherapies for depressed clients, exposure with response prevention for persons with obsessive-compulsive disorder; cognitive-behavioral intervention for clients with bulimia nervosa, dialectical behavior therapy for borderline personality disorder, and behavioral family therapy for conduct-disordered and delinquent adolescents, to name a few. In addition, more difficult and complex problems often require collaboration with other professionals. Case management skills are often required to coordinate these interdisciplinary efforts.

CULTURALLY COMPETENT PRACTICE: CURRENT REALITY OR ASPIRATION?

Sue and Zane (2006) have defined *cultural competency* as "having the cultural knowledge or skills to deliver effective interventions to members of particular culture" (p. 335). They have also rightly noted that research on evidence-based practices has not sufficiently represented racial and cultural minorities. Although such research has greatly increased over the past few decades, more needs to be done. In addition, methodological complications such as finding representative samples of clients (e.g., Native Americans who meet a particular diagnostic criteria) or having ready access to culturally valid measurement tools have hampered efforts to conduct rigorous clinical studies with different minority groups.

Aside from commonsense issues such as speaking the client's language, being familiar with culturally defined customs, and understanding and respecting the general cultural worldview of clients, the phrase "culturally competent practice" suggests that there are known culturally specific modifications to intervention strategies that improve outcomes for people in certain cultural groups. Research findings on these matters, though somewhat limited, have shown rather ambiguous, if not negative, results. According to Sue and Zane (2006), some interventions appear to work comparably well across various groups, and wholesale modification of such interventions do not appear to be necessary. One review of outcome studies revealed that practices shown to be effective in controlled research (e.g., many cognitive-behavioral treatments) appear to work comparably well across racial, ethnic, and cultural lines (Whaley & Davis, 2007). Another review of 23 studies in which specific efforts were made to tailor interventions culturally for Hispanic clients showed no statistical association between such modifications and treatment outcomes (Jani, Ortiz, & Aranda, 2009). Another study comparing highly experienced clinicians with psychology-student interns revealed that, although the experienced practitioners endorsed the basic principles of culturally competent practice, they showed little difference from their student counterparts with respect to what they would actually do in a particular practice situation (Seghal et al., 2011). One qualitative focus group study with Latina mothers found that some aspects of parent training programs were found to be acceptable but others less so, as a result of different cultural expectations regarding parenting (e.g., spanking) (Calzada, Basil, & Fernandez, 2012). The authors of that study recommended aligning parent and practitioner goals at the outset with respect to what competent parenting meant to each. This admonition could just as easily apply to regional differences or individual differences. Given that caveat, it is understood that agreeing on goals is standard procedure when working with any and all clients. Whether specific modifications to interventions can be deemed culturally competent remains to be seen.

The failure to demonstrate that culturally congruent techniques improve outcomes does not necessarily mean that being knowledgeable about a client's cultural background is not important. Being familiar with customs, behaviors, and rituals, and perhaps speaking the language, is likely to be critical to successfully engaging a client in the treatment process and could facilitate the overall helping relationship and whether the client believes the treatment is acceptable. Mental health disorders, stigma, and even specific symptoms can also be associated with culturally specific beliefs (Corin, Thara, & Padmavati, 2005; Green, 2009; Prasadarao, 2009). However, making broad generalizations about people's cultures can backfire and come across as presumptuous, stereotyping, and offensive, given that cultural identity is a complex and personal matter. Cultural identity varies considerably by an individual's degree of assimilation and acculturation to the host country, political views about one's native and host country, subjective ethnic identity within a broader culture, religious beliefs, historical allegiances, and other idiosyncratic reasons. In addition, there are other personal identity factors that weigh into the culture mix: age, generational differences, gender, sexual orientation, socioeconomic status, and so on. Social work practitioners can best serve their clients by treating them as unique individuals and by keeping an open mind regarding how clients think and feel about their own cultural identity. At this point, we can tentatively conclude that "cultural competence" remains a theoretical aspiration based on certain values, assumptions, and principles, but core intervention techniques need not be substantially modified for EBPs to be effective with different cultural groups. If evidence from practice research suggests otherwise, then modifications should be made on the basis of that evidence.

Some critics of evidence-based practices have questioned whether the scientific method is appropriate for addressing matters related to culture. Reasons cited include the assertions that the scientific method is too narrow, that EBPs are not universally applicable to all groups of people, that EBPs have not resolved disparities in service delivery among various ethnic groups, and that EBPs were designed to accommodate managed-care systems (e.g., Aisenberg,

2008; Roysircar, 2009). Critics, though, proffer these arguments, rooted in postmodern and social constructionist thinking, without evidence. First, claiming that culture (as all other personal identity factors) is not a suitable topic for research makes about as much sense as suggesting that gender, sexual orientation, or age be considered off-limits in the behavioral, social, or health sciences. Practitioners have opined for years, and rightly so, that racial/ethnic and cultural minorities and women, among others, have been underrepresented in behavioral science research. Now that these disparities are being addressed, some assert that research is somehow not an appropriate tool to examine the role of culture in the development, persistence, and treatment of serious psychosocial disorders. Second, acceptability is a key criteria in practice research, and there is evidence aplenty that EBPs are well accepted by people from all walks of life and in other countries around the world (O'Hare & Tran, 1998; Sue & Zane, 2006; Whaley & Davis, 2007; Wong, 2013). Third, the fact that there are disparities in health care and social service delivery is a long-standing and complex problem rooted in socio-economic differences; inequities in health-care policy and insurance coverage; cultural stigma; and the begrudging pace with which evidence-based practices have been disseminated, implemented, and evaluated in everyday practice. Last, practice outcome research predates "managed care" by decades, and during this time practitioner-researchers have been busy developing many effective interventions to address many serious disorders and problems-in-living while some social work scholars have been fiddling with semantics about the relationship between practice and research. In addition, research-based recommendations for optimal treatment duration for various disorders typically exceed those authorized by managed-care case managers. Social work has an ethical obligation to promote the use of interventions that have been shown to be effective. Whether or not people from different cultures respond well to evidence-based practices will be judged in the light of empirical testing. Results to date are very promising.

THE ESSENTIAL SKILLS OF EVIDENCE-BASED SOCIAL WORK PRACTICE

It is difficult to define the actual skills and interventions that practitioners employ without implying some intended outcome or change process in the client. *Skills*, *techniques*, and *strategies* (i.e., collectively, the intervention) are terms that emphasize what the practitioners do. Change processes, however, are primarily psychological, emotional, physiological, behavioral, and social processes that can be modified to facilitate the attainment of the client's intervention goals, and they have been subjected to considerable research (Dobson, 2009; Elliot, 2010; Goldfried, 2010; Lambert & Ogles, 2004). To distinguish the intervention from change processes, consider this example: A practitioner uses good listening and empathy skills with a mentally ill client, and as a result, the client responds with feelings of trust toward the practitioner. The practitioner then uses cognitive techniques to help the client identify a dysfunctional pattern of always "expecting the worst" in social encounters, and with further discussion, the client comes to recall that social encounters in the past have sometimes gone well. The practitioner then conducts a role-play with the client to practice him asking someone out on a date. The client responds by gaining a feeling of confidence that he just might be able to attempt it. The client then asks a woman for a date, and she accepts, disconfirming his exaggerated belief that he is generally unlikable. This example highlights using basic relationship-building skills, challenging dysfunctional beliefs, and rehearsing a change in behavior. The client then tries out the new skills in real life (i.e., in vivo) to solidify the changes, a critical step for long-term success and genuine insight. Hundreds of studies on practice research have demonstrated that many different practice methods, despite their theoretical differences, share common skills and common change processes (Elliot, 2010; Goldfried, 1980, 1995, 2010; Grencavage & Norcross, 1990; Lambert & Bergin, 1994; O'Hare, 2009; O'Hare & Geertsma, 2013; Orlinsky, Grawe, & Parks, 1994; Orlinsky & Howard, 1986; Walborn, 1996).

Identifying common change processes across various approaches to intervention is the focus of practice theory *integrationists*. Those practitioners who emphasize the use of a variety of skills and techniques borrowed from different approaches are referred to as *eclecticists*. Although integration and eclecticism are somewhat overlapping concepts, and are sometimes used interchangeably, they emphasize different aspects of theory and practice. Integrationists (e.g., Elliot, 2010; Goldfried, 1980, 1995, 2010; Wachtel, 1977, 1987) are primarily concerned with reconciling theoretical explanations about how psychosocial interventions engender client change (change-process theory). Eclecticists emphasize the optimal configuration of observable skills, techniques, and intervention strategies that are most likely to help clients solve problems, improve coping skills, and enhance psychosocial well-being. To clarify the difference between *change processes* and *interventions*, consider the following examples: if insight is the change process, interpretation could be the intervention (i.e., the technique the practitioner employs); if altering dysfunctional thinking is the change process, then Socratic questioning and behavioral disconfirmation (i.e., testing out one's beliefs) could be the interventions; if shifting power (authority) dynamics in a family is the change process, directed role-play and practicing better communication skills among family members may help to achieve that.

Although the "common elements" approach implies that client change processes and intervention skills are overlapping constructs, the emphasis in EBPSW is clearly on the *eclectic* application of intervention skills, techniques, and interventions. Psychosocial change processes have to be inferred, which makes it a greater challenge to identify them and link them to outcomes.

Interventions, however, are more readily observed and more amenable to research efforts to determine efficacy and effectiveness. Practice skills can be grouped into three major categories:

1. Supportive and facilitative skills, such as engagement; therapeutic alliance; communication of warmth, empathy, and genuineness; motivation

2. Cognitive behavioral skills, including cognitive change techniques (e.g., challenging dysfunctional beliefs, explanation and interpretation, reframing, rehearsal), physiological and emotion self-regulation techniques (e.g., relaxation, mediation, and physical exercise), and behavior change techniques (e.g., behavioral self-regulation, problem-solving and communication skills, role-play, rehearsal, modeling, in vivo practice)

3. Case management skills, such as providing instrumental and social supports, coordinating complex intervention plans, and advocacy

Effective interventions typically comprise some combination of these intervention skills. The case for an eclectic, empirically based social work model drawn from interdisciplinary sources is now stronger than ever. More than 40 years of controlled practice research has produced an eclectic, multidisciplinary amalgam of supportive and facilitative skills, cognitive-behavioral skills, and case management strategies that collectively have come to represent evidence-based social work practice (Fischer, 1973, 1981, 1993; MacDonald, Sheldon, & Gillespie, 1992; Reid, 1997a, 1997b; O'Hare, 1991, 2009; Wood, 1978).

Supportive and Facilitative Skills

Supportive and facilitative skills include putting the client at ease, basic listening and communication, engendering trust, communicating empathy, expressing genuineness and positive regard, enhancing client confidence and morale, and motivating the client to change. Dimensions of the therapeutic relationship have been researched extensively in the counseling, psychotherapy, and social work literature for many years (e.g., Duan & Hill, 1996; Elliot, 2010; Hill, Nutt, & Jackson, 1994; Horvath & Greenberg, 1989; Miller & Rollnick, 2013; O'Hare, Tran, & Collins, 2002; Rice & Greenberg, 1984; Rogers, 1951; Truax & Carkhuff, 1967; Walborn, 1996).

Research on "readiness to change" has also helped practitioners estimate clients' level of motivation. Prochaska, DiClemente, and Norcross (1992) have developed a useful model whereby clients can be assessed to be at one of five stages of change: *precontemplation*, when clients do not agree that they have a problem, may see others as the cause of their difficulties, or may feel coerced into treatment by the courts or significant others; *contemplation*, when clients are aware of a problem and may want to find out whether therapy can help; *preparation*, when clients are taking initial steps toward change; *action*, when clients may take more significant steps toward working on the problem and seek help in the change process; and last, *maintenance*, when clients have already made changes with regard to a problem and have sought treatment to consolidate previous improvements (McConnaughy, DiClemente, Prochaska, & Velicer, 1989). Clients may cycle through these stages of change. A person with an addiction, for example, may consider change many times before taking action or may even relapse numerous times before stabilizing (DiClemente & Hughes, 1990). Judging a client's readiness to change is particularly relevant in work with clients who are pressured or coerced into receiving social work services and are often labeled by practitioners as "resistant," "hard to reach," "hostile," and "unmotivated" (Goldstein, 1986; Miller & Rollnick, 2013; O'Hare, 1996b; Rooney, 1992).

Although supportive and facilitative skills are an essential dimension of effective intervention, they are also insufficient for establishing lasting change with more challenging psychosocial conditions (Lambert & Bergin, 1994). More robust interventions require expert use of cognitive and behavioral coping skills.

Cognitive-Behavioral Skills

Empirically supported interventions that emphasize the use of cognitive-behavioral coping skills and strategies are overwhelmingly represented in evidence-based practices given the growing body of evidence that such methods are effective. Cognitive-behavioral skills have been combined into a wide array of interventions that help clients reduce cognitive distortions; improve their ability to identify and express feelings; better self-regulate troubling emotions (i.e., mood) and disabling physiological responses (e.g., anxiety, panic attacks); improve behavioral coping capacities; enhance problem solving, communication, and interpersonal skills; and generally develop more effective ways of dealing with psychosocial and environmental challenges. They are now used extensively in individual, couples, and family work, and they have been widely adapted to group interventions as well. Practitioners may initially promote and teach clients these skills, but clients are expected to practice and incorporate them into their daily life in order to maintain gains over time (Craighead, Craighead, Kazdin, & Mahoney, 1994; Dobson, 2009; Dobson & Craig, 1996).

Self-monitoring techniques are combinations of self-assessment skills that clients use to increase understanding of their problems and track progress in coping with them. This approach is highly flexible, can use both qualitative (e.g., diaries) and quantitative (e.g., weekly charts, scales) data collection methods, and should be crafted to reflect the client's unique problems and treatment goals. As part of the functional assessment, self-monitoring can be used to identify psychological, physical, behavioral, interpersonal, or situational factors that seem to cause or maintain the client's problem. Emphasis is placed on honing the client's skills in self-assessment by tracking the frequency, intensity, or duration of the problem, and by noting patterns, sequences, and psychosocial cues associated with the reoccurrence of the problem. These skills may include identifying triggers for substance abuse relapse, anticipating events that provoke trauma-related flashbacks, learning to recognize angry feelings in order to practice prosocial and constructive responses, and identifying cues that trigger a child's obsessive-compulsive behaviors, to name but a few examples. Self-monitoring skills are key to bridging functional assessment with the monitoring and evaluation of the intervention, and thus they become an assessment, intervention, and evaluative tool all in one.

Psychoeducation provides factual information to help inform clients about the nature of their problem and ways to cope. Often a preliminary and important component of intervention, psychoeducation can take many beneficial forms (e.g., reducing self-blame in families of persons with severe mental illness; as a brief intervention for problem drinkers to emphasize feedback on medical and behavioral consequences; as a basis for educating and reassuring a client with anxiety disorder that he is not "going to die" or "go crazy" as a result of the disorder; teaching basic parenting skills to an overwhelmed young, single mother). Psychoeducation can be part of either a multifaceted or a stand-alone intervention.

Changing dysfunctional thinking has also become a first-line strategy for implementing cognitive-behavioral therapies. Clients' difficulties are sometimes grounded in erroneous, distorted, exaggerated, or otherwise dysfunctional beliefs about themselves, others, and the future. Negative schema can promote negative automatic thoughts and subsequently lead to systematic errors in thinking as well as poor coping abilities (Beck, 1976, 1996; Beck, Rush, Shaw, & Emery, 1979; Ellis, 1962; Young, Rygh, Weinberger, & Beck, 2008). Cognitive-behavioral coping skills rely heavily on changing thinking patterns through a combination of Socratic questioning and "behavioral disconfirmation" (i.e., testing out dysfunctional thinking to refute it) rather than simply rational discussion. Cognitive change techniques typically combine cognitive and behavior change methods and are often referred to as *cognitive restructuring* (Young et al., 2008).

Examining beliefs and attitudes that appear to be causing clients' trouble has long been considered an important part of basic counseling and psychosocial interventions generally. Although theoretical considerations regarding the cause of troubled thinking and techniques for intervening differ depending on one's approach, *explanation* and *interpretation* (traditionally associated with psychodynamic therapy), have come to be seen as relatively generic aspects of other effective therapies as well, and one need not assume a role for the "unconscious" (Jones & Pulos, 1993; Lambert & Bergin, 1994; Safran, 1998). Dysfunctional thinking is often focused on interpersonal relationships. In addition to providing support and facilitating change, the therapeutic relationship can serve as a proxy for clarifying cognitive distortions regarding interpersonal conflict (past or present). Psychodynamic practitioners have usually considered these distortions the product of unconscious conflict. However, there is little reason to assume that cognitive distortions related to interpersonal relations are rooted in early relationships with parents; nor is there much evidence to support the assertion that the interpretation of unconscious motives is a uniquely effective approach for dealing with interpersonal problems or emotional disorders (Clarkin, Levy, Lenzenweger, & Kernberg, 2007; Henry, Strupp, Schacht, & Gaston, 1994; Kantrowitz, 1995). A more parsimonious explanation for the causes of interpersonal distortion (between client and practitioner or client and others) is that people often overgeneralize (knowingly or unwittingly) from prior experiences in life (e.g., childhood abuse, sexual assault during adolescence, traumatic loss, having been the victim of a hate crime, having been betrayed in love). These overgeneralizations and false attributions can distort one's view of the self, others, and the world, and can cause emotional distress or interpersonal conflict that is generally unrelated to the original perceived psychological insult.

Practitioners can help clients clarify and disconfirm these misattributions by examining the meaning of the distortion or conflict and then testing out the client's inferences and negative expectations experientially. For example, if a young woman was emotionally abused by an important person in her childhood and continues to find herself in emotionally abusive relationships as an adult, it might be helpful for her to identify what characteristics she looks for in an intimate relationship and then reexamine those assumptions. If these interpersonal distortions lead to repeated conflict though her misinterpretation of others' behaviors, testing out her expectations may lead to behavioral disconfirmation of some of her more negative and distorted beliefs (e.g., "He can't help that he is controlling and abusive. He acts like this because he really loves me," "If I respond to his abuse with love, I know I can really change him!"). Challenging these assumptions and behaviorally disconfirming them can lead to lasting change.

Facilitating the expression and regulation of emotions has also long been a mainstay of basic counseling and has been widely incorporated into cognitive-behavioral strategies as well. Dialectical behavior therapy, for example, emphasizes these skills to facilitate better regulation of emotions in people diagnosed with borderline personality disorder (Linehan & Dexter-Mazza, 2008). These skills have long been incorporated into effective treatments with children and adolescents with emotional disorders as well (e.g., Kendall, 1993, 1994; Tandon, Cardeli, & Luby, 2009). People often experience a range of troubling emotions and feelings (e.g., anger, fear, sadness, guilt), but for whatever reason, they are not always able to clearly identify what their feelings are, what causes them, or how to cope with them in adaptive ways. Thoughtful and empathic listening can help identify emotions, link them to dysfunctional thinking, and provide an opportunity for catharsis and relief. Mindfulness, relaxation training, and learning to cope through a range of other strategies can then help clients gain some ability to regulate their feelings rather than being hampered by them. In addition, when working with couples or families, facilitating the identification and expression of emotions can be very helpful in improving communications and reducing interpersonal conflict. Emotion-focused therapy with couples has successfully placed strong emphasis on the use of these skills for resolving couples' conflicts (Johnson & Greenberg, 1988).

Physiological self-regulation skills can also be an important preliminary step toward real and sustained change. Debilitating anxiety in children and adults often accompanies a range of problems, including relationship conflict, substance abuse, phobias, depression, and school- or work-related stress, and is the core symptom of other serious disorders, including agoraphobia, panic attacks, obsessive-compulsive disorder, and post-traumatic stress disorder, among others. Anxiety reduction and stress management techniques include progressive muscle relaxation (Jacobsen, 1938; Schroder, Heider, Zaby, & Gollner, 2013), breathing and meditation techniques (Benson, 1975), combined meditation and mindfulness techniques (Edenfield & Saeed, 2012), and systematic desensitization (Pagoto, Kozak, Spates, & Spring, 2006; Wolpe, 1958, 1973), often accompanied by the creative use of imagery to help clients confront their fears. Cognitive-behavioral approaches have also incorporated mindfulness training, yoga, meditation, and a physical exercise plan (with a physician's approval in some cases) into an overall intervention strategy. These skills have all been shown to be effective adjunctive methods for reducing anxiety and depression, and for facilitating interventions with a range of psychological, interpersonal, and some physical disorders (Blanchard, 1994; Blechman & Brownell, 1998; Edenfield & Saeed, 2012; Linehan, 1993a).

Once a good therapeutic alliance has been established, dysfunctional thinking has been explored, feelings identified and expressed, and anxiety brought under control, an array of *behavioral coping skills* can be employed to help clients "test out" dysfunctional beliefs, improve emotion regulation, and establish more effective coping skills that can lead to lasting change (Craighead et al., 1994; Dobson, 2009; Dobson & Craig, 1996; Thorpe & Olson, 1997). For many conditions, such as major mental illness, addictions, marital and family problems, child abuse and neglect, and health-related disorders, among others, behavioral coping skills and strategies have come to be considered essential for competent social work mental health practice. These skills and techniques include *modeling, role-playing, rehearsal, graduated exposure*, and *in vivo practice* of new behaviors in the real world. Graduated exposure and ongoing practice in clients' own environment is key to intervention success, because unless clients can put what they've learned into everyday practice, there is little chance of them generalizing new skills across situations or maintaining their therapeutic gains over time.

Communication skills are often an essential component of an overall treatment strategy and can be applied across a wide array of settings for many different disorders and problems-in-living (Bedell & Lennox, 1997; Hadas-Lidor, Weiss, & Redlich, 2011). Although individual clients can often benefit from communication skills, communications training can be especially useful when dealing directly with couples and families. Communications approaches often appear deceptively simple but require skills and subtlety to apply. When done well, communications training can be very effective at improving interpersonal understanding and overall functioning in couples and families. The basic paradigm involves the following steps: (1) one person expresses thoughts and feelings calmly as the other party listens in silence; (2) the first person asks whether the second party understood what was communicated; (3) the second party demonstrates an empathic response to show that he or she did understand; (4) the second party expresses his or her grievance in the same manner as the first party listens carefully and empathically responds. The steps are repeated until the communication "loop" is completed several times successfully. Quiet conversation, mutual understanding, and respect then allow for a more productive tone for addressing target problems. Although the practitioner often begins this process by acting as referee if communications are especially dysfunctional, with some practice, improved communications can lay the groundwork for progress in other areas.

Problem-solving skills are often embedded in evidence-based intervention packages for use with both adults and children. As with communications training, this approach is highly flexible and is meant to be adapted to the target problem. Although there are slight variations in the models (e.g., Bedell & Lennox, 1997; D'Zurilla & Goldfried, 1971; Meichenbaum, 1974; Vidrine et al., 2013), problem-solving generally includes (1) recognizing, exploring, and defining the problem; (2) generating alternative solutions and developing a plan; (3) anticipating consequences and obstacles to problem resolution; and (4) performing, monitoring, and evaluating the problem-solving plan.

Contingency management techniques (Alessi, Rash, & Petry, 2011; Higgins et al., 1993) are also an essential component of many effective interventions. A contingency is a quid pro quo; that is, "You do this, and I'll do that." Reinforcement is contingent on successful completion of the task or achievement of the goals. Implementing reinforcement procedures to reduce problem behaviors and increase adaptive and prosocial behaviors is an essential skill for use with many serious childhood and adult conditions, including self-regulation of risky health behaviors, parenting skills to help children with emotional and behavioral disorders, couples counseling, behavioral family interventions with adolescents, and social skills training for people with serious developmental disabilities. In addition, contingency management skills are sometimes incorporated into *community reinforcement approaches* for court-ordered and other involuntary clients, many of whom struggle with substance abuse or addiction. Social supports, incentives, and negative contingencies are combined to help these clients reduce problem behaviors and improve their overall psychosocial well-being.

Although cognitive-behavioral skills can be used as individual techniques, they are typically used in some combination as part of an overall approach to dealing with more challenging psychosocial problems. The overall goal is to combine an optimal range of skills to help clients reduce dysfunctional thinking, facilitate emotional expression, improve emotional regulation, enhance coping skills, and apply these skills in everyday life. For example, a young man with schizophrenia may learn to self-monitor delusional symptoms, engage in behaviors to disconfirm frightening thoughts, participate in behavioral family therapy, and practice social skills in the community. A woman suffering from agoraphobia will first learn about the disorder to reduce fearful thoughts based on erroneous notions about the disorder, establish control over anxiety symptoms through relaxation methods and imaginal exposure (i.e., gradually approaching the feared situation in her mind's eye), and then gradually spend increasing amounts of time outdoors or in a specific situation (e.g., supermarket) until the anxiety dissipates and her range of activities increases. Couples experiencing serious conflict may work on basic communication skills and emotional expression, and then focus on clarifying interpersonal distortions that they may have generalized in a harmful way from previous relationships (e.g., distrust). A single mom with a rebellious teenage son might benefit from learning better communication and negotiating skills, and setting better limits through the use of contingency management (i.e., rewards and sanctions). Persons with chronic addictions may learn to self-monitor triggers (i.e., risky thoughts, feelings, and situations associated with substance use), use imagery to focus on negative consequences of use, and learn alternatives for dealing with negative or painful feelings that could precipitate relapse. How these cognitive-behavioral skills and effective skills derived from other approaches are combined in treatment planning will become increasingly evident in subsequent chapters.

Case Management Skills

Although many psychosocial difficulties can be effectively addressed through supportive, cognitive, and behavioral coping skills, these methods are often not robust enough to overcome the environmental pressures and barriers that weigh on many clients (Bouton, 2000; Hopps, Pinderhughes, & Shankar, 1995; Sherrer & O'Hare, 2008). Practitioners are remiss when they place disproportionate emphasis on psychological causes of the client's problems or focus solely on the client's need to change. Evidence for the impact of social-environmental pressures (e.g., homelessness, poverty, discrimination) on the psychological well-being of individuals is compelling (Avison & Gotlib, 1994;

Dohrenwend, 1998; Moos & Moos, 1992). Although large-scale political and socioeconomic change may not be the primary target of the clinical or direct-practice social worker, evidence-based interventions demand a thorough assessment of social-environmental factors that affect clients directly. Some of these barriers and problems may be amenable to direct influence, or clients may learn to cope with them more effectively. If nothing else, an accurate and thorough assessment of socio-environmental factors, even those beyond clients' direct influence, can provide an opportunity for psychoeducation, reduced self-blame, and a more realistic intervention plan by emphasizing those problems that are amenable to change.

Case management skills include an array of social work strategies that enhance client functioning through the coordination of complex interventions and improved access to other social, material, and environmental resources. This role often requires a broad scope of knowledge concerning comprehensive assessment and treatment needs, as well as a good degree of professional initiative, leadership, and communication skills to make interdisciplinary services and bureaucratic systems work in concert for clients. Beyond the mere "brokering" of services, case management skills have come to be seen as essential for coordinating multiple services and enhancing instrumental and social supports with a range of problems, including mental illness (Kondrat & Teater, 2012; Mueser, Bond, Drake, & Resnick, 1998), child abuse and neglect (Dauber, Neighbors, Dasaro et al., 2012; Lewis, Walton, & Fraser, 1995), conduct-disordered adolescents (Henggeler, Schoenwald, Borduin, Rowland, & Cunningham, 2009), and other groups as well.

Enhancing social supports is a critical goal of case management. The quality of social supports is associated with several factors, including a sense of self-efficacy and personal empowerment (Gutierrez, 1990; Sarason, Pierce, & Sarason, 1994). Social supports can also be either naturally occurring or orchestrated as part of formal social work interventions (Dawe & Harnett, 2007; Streeter & Franklin, 1992). Social supports may be both social (i.e., increased contact and emotional support from others) and instrumental (i.e., concrete and tangible goods and services) (Richey, 1994; Sarason et al., 1994). Social supports should also be understood both structurally (e.g., connections; networks; relations with different groups such as family, coworkers, other social organizations) and functionally (e.g., availability, accessibility, satisfaction with support received). Enhancing social supports may take many forms, ranging from encouraging clients to try out mutual-help groups such as Alcoholics Anonymous (Humphreys, 1999) to facilitating the development of a consumer group for people with mental illness (Heinssen, Levendusky, & Hunter, 1995; Kondrat & Teater, 2012), and providing social supports to buffer the stressful effects of grief on the elderly (Fitzpatrick, 1998). Practitioners may have to help clients optimize the potential benefits from social supports by helping them improve their social skills (Richey, 1994).

Case management methods have often been treated as the "poor cousin" to psychotherapeutic skills, perhaps because using these skills is often associated with less prestigious practice settings. For evidence-based practitioners, it is understood that failing to provide effective coordination of services or ignoring social and environmental needs may preclude solid long-term outcomes with even the most skillfully delivered intervention. Case management skills, when used judiciously and assertively, can often be the most powerful agent of stable change.

THE MANUALIZATION VERSUS FLEXIBILITY DEBATE

Much of the debate regarding the adoption of evidence-based practices has centered on the "manualization" of treatments that are derived largely from controlled practice research. Opinions vary regarding the use of treatment manuals to guide interventions (Hudson, 2009; Kirk, 1999; Mitchell, 2001). First, some practitioners resist any perceived pressure to use interventions that are not congruent with their own preferred approaches, feel that evidence-based practices are a challenge to their professional autonomy, consider manualization little more than a cost-control strategy of managed-care organizations, or just do not believe that evidence-based guidelines are relevant (Amodeo et al., 2011; Gould, 2010; Nelson & Steele, 2007). Second, some practitioners see that, for some mild conditions, clients have been shown to respond positively to different approaches, and they erroneously conclude that choice of intervention really does not matter. Third, practitioners note that DSM classifications drive outcome research, and as a result, manualized interventions are designed for artificially narrow clinical disorders. In general, then, practitioners' styles as well as complex problems and situational factors often preclude strict adherence to manualized approaches (Borntrager, Chorpita, Higa-McMillan, & Weisz, 2009; Garfield, 1996).

Proponents of manualization respond to these criticisms by pointing out that clinician preferences can be somewhat arbitrary and should not be the primary driver of treatment selection; that there is no evidence that "experience" or "practice wisdom" or treating professional practice as an "art" is a sound or even testable basis for professional decision making; and that mental health professionals are, in fact, accountable to funding bodies and to ethical and legal guidelines. Society generally expects licensed professionals in the health-related and human service fields to be trained in assessment and intervention methods that are grounded in scientific research. Manuals are meant to be used as guidelines drawn from practice research, not to be followed in cookie-cutter fashion, as critics of evidence-based practices sometimes caricature it.

The charge that the endorsement of evidence-based practices is somehow serving the interests of managed care (Gould, 2010) can be readily dismissed because clinical researchers have been conducting controlled trials for decades, long before managed care arrived on the health-care scene. It is more reasonable to assume that practitioner-researchers have been motivated to discover which interventions work best with which problems, for which clients, and under what circumstances. If there is evidence that these practitioner-researchers are in cahoots with managed care, then critics of EBP should be more forthcoming with such evidence. In addition, many manualized guidelines are at odds with managed-care recommendations and call for two to four times the number of treatment sessions typically authorized by managed-care utilization review boards (Weisz & Hawley, 1998).

With respect to the question of relevance, investigations suggest that manualized evidence-based approaches have been well received by clients (Mitchell, 2001), including many from non-Western cultures (e.g., Wong, 2013). Measuring acceptability in the development and testing of evidence-based practices is a routine aspect of controlled practice research. In addition, contrary to some claims that controlled research is artificial, evidence suggests that interventions conducted in the context of controlled investigations are often quite comparable to "real" treatment conditions (Franklin, Abramowitz, Kozak, Levitt, & Foa, 2000). "Treatment as usual" in community care agencies is often the control group in randomized trials. The use of treatment manuals in the research and teaching of clinical practice can go a long way toward providing social work practitioners with the necessary guidelines for working with serious psychosocial problems and can improve fidelity to evidence-based models (Hogue & Dauber, 2013; Wilson, 1996).

Although different intervention approaches might share common factors, research demonstrates that there are differential outcomes among intervention methods for more serious psychosocial disorders. All treatments are not equally effective with certain disorders and problems, and some professional bodies have explicitly advised against using certain interventions when little evidence of effectiveness has been forthcoming, as is the case for psychodynamic interventions with severe mental illnesses, for example (Dixon et al., 2010; Kreyenbuhl, Buchanan, Dickerson, & Dixon, 2010).

Diagnosis-driven practice guidelines are, indeed, sometimes, artificially narrow. However, there is an increasing consensus that there is a need for a pragmatic approach to the training, research, and evaluation of evidence-based mental health practice that capitalizes on common etiological and maintenance factors associated with a range of psychiatric disorders (Glasgow, 2009; O'Hare, 2009; Westen, Novotny, & Thompson-Brenner, 2004) and common change processes and practice skills effective with a range of psychiatric disorders and problems-in-living (Goldfried, 2010; Goodheart, Kazdin, & Sternberg, 2006; Lambert & Bergin, 1994; Nathan & Gorman, 2007; O'Hare, 2009; Orlinsky et al., 1994; Taylor & Clark, 2009). Rather than teaching a variety of overlapping intervention methods as discrete practice approaches, some practitioner-researchers are calling for the teaching of *readily accessible skill sets* that are applicable across different intervention approaches and treatment modalities (e.g., couples, family, groups). These common skill sets can then be applied flexibly to accommodate a wide range of psychiatric disorders and common psychosocial problems (Glasner-Edwards & Rawson, 2010; O'Hare, 2009; O'Hare & Geertsma, 2013). At this time, however, those learning evidence-based practices should first learn effective interventions "by the book," and only then adapt them to complex psychosocial problems—with judgment, flexibility, and keen attention to the client's unique treatment expectations and goals—and monitor and evaluate clients' response to the intervention.

A BRIEF OVERVIEW OF THE CURRENT FINDINGS OF OUTCOME RESEARCH

Up to this point, the discussion of EBPSW has focused mostly on specific skills, the essential components of effective interventions, and a rationale for flexibly combining them. Although articulating these skills is necessary in order to provide the practitioner with the "ingredients" to be eclectic, evidence-based practices are primarily delineated through the use of randomized controlled studies demonstrating how combinations of these skills and techniques are efficaciously applied to serious psychosocial disorders.

Mullen and Shuluk (2010) have noted that some practitioners have been slow to adopt EBPs because they have come to erroneously believe in the so-called dodo verdict ("Everyone has won, and all must have prizes," a reference to Lewis Carroll's *Alice's Adventures in Wonderland*, 1865; Sloan, Staples, Cristol, Yorkston, & Whipple, 1975). The implication suggests that all forms of psychotherapeutic interventions are equally effective. Although there is considerable evidence that different mental health practices are effective for mild psychosocial conditions and common problems-in-living (e.g., relationship troubles, mild depression), there is growing evidence that some interventions are more effective than others for many moderate to severe mental health problems and psychiatric disorders. Results of early meta-analyses (i.e., summary quantitative analyses of multiple outcome studies) in the 1970s and 1980s suggested some equivalence, but further reviews identified methodological flaws in those studies, including failure to measure the effects of mediators, or therapeutic activities that target specific problems (e.g., Shadish & Sweeney, 1991). In more recent years, evidence-based recommendations devised from rigorous reviews of the research have shown substantial differences in efficacy. Outcome research has come a long way since the early meta-analyses of the 1970s and 1980s upon which the dodo verdict was based.

Eysenck (1952) in psychology and Fischer (1973) in social work initially challenged the helping professions to demonstrate the effectiveness of psychosocial interventions. By the early 1980s a substantial body of clinical outcome research had emerged (Lambert, Shapiro, & Bergin, 1986). Traditional scholarly (e.g., Luborsky, Singer, & Luborsky, 1975) and later meta-analytic (e.g., Smith, Glass, & Miller, 1980) reviews of the clinical research demonstrated the overall effectiveness of psychotherapy interventions. Early reviews of the literature in social work (Fischer, 1973, 1981; Reid & Hanrahan, 1982; Rubin, 1985; Wood, 1978) reported mixed results. Initial reviews of outpatient treatment problems revealed comparable results for psychodynamic and behavioral therapies (Lambert et al., 1986; Sloan et al., 1975), but behavior therapies demonstrated superior outcomes with more serious disorders in both adults (Kazdin & Wilson, 1980) and children (Weisz, Weiss, Alicke, & Klotz, 1987). Positive findings for cognitive-behavioral approaches continued to grow throughout the 1990s (Lambert & Bergin, 1994; Nathan & Gorman, 1998; Reid, 1997a; Weiss, Catron, Harris, & Phung, 1999; Weisz, Donenberg, Han, & Weiss, 1995) and were often combined with case management skills for treating the most challenging client groups, such as those with severe mental illness.

Over the past 40 years, a modest body of research has emerged that provides moderate support for short-term psychodynamic therapies for depression, some anxiety disorders, some eating disorders, and borderline personality disorder (Leichsenring, 2009; Shedler, 2010). Overall the number of outcome studies is relatively small, especially when parsed by specific mental health problems. However, with the exception of very few studies, psychodynamic therapies have not been shown to yield superior outcomes than cognitive-behavioral treatments for similar disorders. Evidence for the effectiveness of long-term psychodynamic therapies is even less promising. In addition, what appears to be effective about psychodynamic interventions is likely attributable to "common factors" (i.e., empathy, listening skills, engagement, working alliance). Little is known about any uniquely effective psychodynamic "ingredients" that result in substantial clinical benefit.

In contrast, more than 16 meta-analyses covering more than 10,000 client-participants, and well over 300 studies with more than 500 treatment comparisons, have been shown to provide solid support for cognitive-behavioral therapies for major depression, certain applications for people with schizophrenia, borderline personality disorder, agoraphobia-related panic, obsessive-compulsive disorder, post-traumatic stress disorder, marital dysfunction, and childhood emotional and behavioral disorders, among others (Butler, Chapman, Forman, & Beck, 2006). Cognitive-behavioral treatments remain the most rigorously and frequently studied to date, and overall they have been shown to be the most effective approaches overall for a wide range of psychiatric disorders and problems-in-living. With increasing frequency they are being implemented within a family systems modality, particularly when couples, children, and the family are the focus of the intervention.

Practice outcome research has continued to expand rapidly. What follows are highlights of current outcome research that supports interventions for common and serious psychosocial interventions. The list here is not exhaustive, but coming chapters explore EBPs in greater detail. Although cognitive-behavioral interventions have come to dominate the EBP field, other approaches have garnered significant evidence of effectiveness as well and will also be described in later chapters. In addition, many of these evidence-based practices have been tested and applied across individual, couples, families, and group modalities covering the elderly, other adults, adolescents, and children. Cognitive-behavioral and similar variants have been shown to be effective with the following disorders and problems-in-living:

- Severe and persistent mental illness (e.g., Dixon et al., 2010; Huxley, Rendall, & Sederer, 2000; Kreyenbuhl et al., 2010; Lehman, Steinwachs, & Co-Investigators of the PORT Project, 1998)

- Depression (e.g., Hollon & Beck, 1994; Mazzucchelli, Kane, & Rees, 2009; Young et al., 2008)

- Binge eating (e.g., Shekter-Wolfson, Woodside, & Lackstrom, 1997; Stein et al., 2001; Wilson, 2011; Wilson & Fairburn, 1993)

- Anxiety, including obsessive-compulsive disorder (e.g., Abramowitz, Brigidi, & Roche, 2001; Rosa-Alcázar, Sánchez-Meca, Gómez-Conesa, & Marín-Martínez, 2008; Steketee, 1993), agoraphobia and panic attacks (e.g., Antony & Swinson, 2000; Arch & Craske, 2009; Emmelkamp, 1994; Hollon & Beck, 1994; Sánchez-Meca, Rosa-Alcázar, Marín-Martínez, & Gómez-Conesa, 2010), and post-traumatic stress disorder (e.g., Powers, Halpern, Ferenschak, Gillihan, & Foa, 2010; Rothbaum, Meadows, Resick, & Foy, 2000)

- Substance abuse and dependence (e.g., Abbott, Weller, Delaney, & Moore, 1998; Acierno, Donohue, & Kogan, 1994; Barber, 1995; Higgins et al. 1993; Higgins, Sigmon, & Heil, 2008; Magill & Ray, 2009; McCrady, 2008; Miller, 1992; Miller, Meyers, & Hiller-Sturmhöfel, 1999; Monti & Rohsenow, 1999; Schilling, El-Bassel, Hadden, & Gilbert, 1995)

- Borderline personality disorder (e.g., Linehan, 1993a; Simpson et al., 1998; Zanarini, 2009) and some court-ordered offenders (e.g., Gendreau, 1996a; McGuire & Hatcher, 2001; Rooney, 1992).

- Couples' conflict (e.g., Alexander, Holtzworth-Munroe, & Jameson, 1994; Fals-Stewart, Lam, & Kelly, 2009; Hahlweg & Markman, 1988; Jacobson & Addis, 1993; Lebow, 2000; Lebow & Gurman, 1995; O'Farrell & Fals-Stewart, 1999; Thomas & Corcoran, 2001), including when substance abuse is involved (O'Farrell & Schein, 2011)

- Emotional and behavioral disorders of children and adolescents (e.g., Alexander, Waldron, Newberry, & Liddle, 1988; Brown et al., 2008; Farmer, Compton, Burns, & Robertson, 2002; Foster, 1994; Henggeler et al., 2009; Kazdin, 1994b; Kazdin & Weisz, 1998; Kendall, 1993; McMahon & Forehand, 1984; Northey, Wells, Silverman, & Bailey, 2003; Ollendick & King, 1994a, 1998; Saavedra, Silverman, Morgan-Lopez, & Kurtines, 2010; Sexton, 2011; Silverman & Berman; 2001; Tandon et al., 2009; Thyer, 1995; Webster-Stratton & Herbert, 1994)

- Child abuse and neglect (e.g., Barth, 2009; Howing, Wodarski, Gaudin, & Kurtz, 1989; Kazdin & Weisz, 1998; Lutzker, Bigelow, Doctor, Gershater, & Greene, 1998; Smokowski & Wodarski, 1996; Wolfe & Wekerle, 1993)

Other approaches have also been consistently shown to be effective in controlled trials for certain conditions. Interpersonal psychotherapy has been shown to be effective for depression (e.g., Elkin, 1994; Grote et al., 2009; Markowitz, 1999; Seligman, 1998; Weissman, Markowitz, & Klerman, 2000) and binge eating disorder (e.g., Klerman, Weissman, Rounsaville, & Chevron, 1984; Wilson, 2011). Emotion-focused therapy (Johnson, 2007; Johnson & Greenberg, 1995) has been well researched and shown to be effective for couples' conflict. A psychodynamic approach that is focused in the present on emotion regulation has also been shown to have good results for people with borderline personality disorder, and in some cases with results comparable to those of dialectical behavior therapy (e.g., McMain et al., 2009).

A QUICK GUIDE TO REVIEWING OUTCOME RESEARCH

Although reviews of the outcome research in journal articles and an increasing array of texts on evidence-based practices are available to students and practitioners, social workers should understand the methodologies that support outcome research in order to better understand the nature of practice research, to be able to read and understand outcome studies, and to stay abreast of state-of-the-art practices. Terms such as *evidence-based* and *best practices* are likely to become marketing tools in the human services industry, and perhaps to be used without regard to core criteria that primarily define what evidence-based practices are: *those interventions that are consistently shown to be efficacious in controlled trials.* Social work students should learn basic research methodology in their first-year graduate courses so they can develop basic proficiency in accessing the proper databases and digital library resources, and, if they do not critically review research in their own practice areas of interest, they should at least become literate in the language of outcome research to be able to appreciate the findings in critical reviews and other secondary sources. Although authors differ somewhat as to the level of methodological rigor that should be employed in determining efficacy and effectiveness, (e.g., Chambless & Hollon, 1998; Kazdin, 2002; Kazdin & Kendall, 1998; Thyer, 2001), the following are minimal considerations for judging the quality of outcome studies (some of the design terminology referred to in this list is examined in chapter 4):

- For an original research article, the literature review should be representative of the current available research and cover a range of refereed journals from social work, clinical psychology, psychiatry, marriage and family publications, and other relevant specialty journals (e.g., child welfare, substance abuse, gerontology).

- Review articles (those in which relevant research has already been critically reviewed and summarized) should reflect representative coverage of the available evidence.

- The purpose of the study should be made clear. Does it examine the predictive validity of client, clinician, or practice processes, or does it primarily test the effectiveness of a specific treatment approach?

- The author should clearly define client descriptors (e.g., age, sex, ethnicity), sources of referral, and diagnostic and other formal selection criteria. Client problems should be clearly defined, with valid baseline measures taken before the intervention.

- If the article is a controlled outcome study, clients should be randomly assigned to treatment conditions or specifically matched to different interventions on several variables (e.g., age, gender, problem severity). The intervention should be compared with some alternative treatment (or no treatment). Replication of controlled studies by independent research groups substantially strengthens an argument of efficacy.

- Single-subject designs, particularly ABAB and multiple-baseline designs, can provide strong support for treatment efficacy if they are replicated with at least three study participants. Again, replication by other researchers further strengthens the argument of efficacy.

- If the evaluation study is uncontrolled (i.e., has no control or comparison group), statistical controls can help identify client and treatment factors that predict outcomes. Although these designs are not as strong as randomized studies, such investigations are valuable because they sometimes reflect everyday practice conditions (effectiveness) more realistically than do some controlled investigations.

- If the investigation tested the cause-effect relationship between specific intervention components and client outcomes, a clear link must be established between the intervention component and changes in client functioning in one or more areas.

- If the study is an investigation of theoretical change processes hypothesized to be activated by a specific intervention, a clear theoretical rationale must be defined before causal inferences can be made regarding the effect of a specific intervention component on client outcomes. Demonstrating change process (i.e., *how* the treatment works) is much more difficult than demonstrating that the intervention *does* work.

- Investigators should employ at least one standardized scale (preferably more) with a history of adequate validity and reliability for the particular population. Simple indexes with clear face validity (e.g., number of panic attacks, drinks, or days in the hospital) are also useful. Measures should ideally focus on target problems as well as broader measures of psychosocial well-being.

- The treatment procedure (i.e., what practitioners and clients actually do) should be clearly defined rather than referring vaguely to perspectives, orientations, or practice theories. Treatment manuals, evidence of close supervision, adequacy of therapists' training in the specific interventions employed, and use of fidelity measures (i.e., scales that demonstrate the faithful implementation of the model; see chapter 4) are a plus.

- Outcome data should include baseline measures, additional measures taken at regular intervals (e.g., 3 or 6 months, or whatever makes sense given the duration of the program), and termination and follow-up (e.g., 1 year after service ends).

- Methodological flaws and alternative explanations for outcomes should be examined in the discussion of the results.

- Evidence that the intervention methods can be transferred and implemented in typical community service settings after some staff training is essential to argue for generalizable effectiveness.

- Generalizability to populations other than that of the study participants should be considered.

SUMMARY

Effective social work interventions are likely to be defined by some optimal amalgam of supportive and/or facilitative skills, cognitive-behavioral coping skills, and case management strategies. Practitioners should initially consult the published outcome research and available clinical manuals and texts describing these interventions, and ideally should obtain adequate training, supervision, and ongoing mentorship in their use. Practitioners should also be prepared to apply the interventions with cautious flexibility within an eclectic practice framework and to adjust the approach to clients' needs and expectations via monitoring and evaluation of their response.

CHAPTER 4

TESTING INTERVENTIONS AND
EVALUATING PROGRAMS

Assuming that evidence-based practices are taught in professional schools and written into an agency's policies and procedures, there is still no guarantee that they will be implemented effectively. Interventions shown to be efficacious in controlled trials may not be implemented effectively because of a number of factors, including lack of training in specific practices, practitioner resistance, poor transfer of training, lack of funds for professional development among staff, organizational structures and processes that militate against the implementation of evidence-based practices, and inadequate supervision, among other reasons. This chapter examines a number of different evaluation designs to determine their relative strengths, weaknesses, and suitability for ensuring the effective implementation of evidence-based practices. Although randomized controlled designs are not used very often in program evaluations, we examine this basic methodology here since it is the primary method for testing the *efficacy* of evidence-based practices. The emphasis in this chapter, however, is on the use of naturalistic monitoring and evaluation methods to test the *effectiveness* of programs when integrated into routine care at both the individual and program levels.

DESIGNS OF EVIDENCE-BASED PRACTICE RESEARCH AND EVALUATION

Social workers and other allied professionals have been trying to "bridge the gap" between practice and research for some time with modest success. Many practice scholars have engaged in spirited debate regarding what the "best" evaluation design is and whether qualitative or quantitative methods are superior. Before proceeding with an examination of the roles of different research and evaluation designs relevant to social work practice, some basic clarification is required.

As noted in chapter 1, practice research and evaluation of practice have two somewhat overlapping purposes. Practice research tests whether interventions work under controlled conditions (to demonstrate efficacy), and

54

practice evaluation tests whether interventions work under everyday practice conditions (to demonstrate effectiveness) (Hargreaves, Shumway, Hu, & Cuffel, 1998; Kazdin, 2002; Mechanic, Schlesinger, & McAlpine, 1995; O'Hare, 2009; Rossi & Freeman, 1993; Royse, Thyer, & Padgett, 2009). This distinction, however, is not always very neat. Some well-designed outcome studies can often closely replicate real-world treatment conditions, and evaluation designs can range from *naturalistic evaluation*, in which few efforts are made to control treatment conditions, to controlled *evaluation research*. Thus, the differences between controlled outcome research and naturalistic evaluation may be best understood on a continuum of methodological rigor. As this chapter examines in more detail, this continuum of control roughly corresponds to the classic distinctions among pre-experimental, quasi-experimental, and experimental designs. Table 4.1 illustrates this continuum.

Distinguishing controlled outcome research, evaluative research, and naturalistic monitoring and evaluation is a matter of degree, and any distinction should become increasingly blurred as agency-based evaluation improves in methodological quality. However, in addition to pragmatic considerations (e.g., cost, design feasibility, purpose of the research or evaluation project), the differences in research and evaluation designs can be explained as differences in balancing internal and external threats to validity.

TABLE 4.1   Testing and evaluation practice: A continuum of design control

High control (efficacy)	*Moderate control*	*Low control* (effectiveness)
Experimental design	*Quasi-experimental design*	*Pre-experimental design*
Controlled outcome studies: Client(s) (groups of clients or single-subject experiment) are carefully selected, practitioners are trained to the treatment manual, clients are matched or randomly assigned to the experimental and comparison (control) groups, and multiple outcome measures are employed (in single-subject studies, clients serve as their own control).	Evaluation research: Clients may be selected or matched across two different approaches; or two programs are compared and statistical controls used to determine treatment effectiveness; outcome measures are used.	Naturalistic program evaluation or monitoring of a single case using qualitative or quantitative methods to measure outcomes; no efforts are made to control treatment conditions, but statistical controls might be used to isolate associations among client factors, intervention factors, and outcomes.

As was discussed in chapter 1, there are many potential sources of error that should prevent practitioners and evaluators from being supremely confident in assuming that their positive treatment outcomes are the direct result of the intervention. These "threats" to drawing valid conclusions are referred to as problems of *internal validity*. One must consider whether the intervention was implemented faithfully (i.e., treatment fidelity); whether the client would have improved with no treatment or with some alternative intervention; whether other factors, such as the client's history, maturation, or other external factors played a role; whether the practitioner-evaluator is selecting "good" clients; whether there were problems in using the instruments to collect data; and whether statistical analysis (when data are aggregated) was done correctly and with sufficiently large samples.

Practitioners should also be concerned with how well the intervention will generalize to other similar practice environments and with other client groups. These ambiguities are caused by threats to *external validity*. For many reasons, one cannot assume that a successful intervention with one person or even a whole program can be successfully exported and applied to other situations. As noted earlier, practitioners often feel that interventions shown to be effective in well-controlled outcome studies do not seem to fit their own practice situation. This transition from *efficacy* studies (results of controlled outcome research) to *effectiveness* (results of real-world programming) gets at the heart of generalization, that is, external validity. What is certain is that all approaches to evaluation research have their share of strengths and weaknesses, as well as their place in the seamless continuum of reasoned inquiry into matters of practice efficacy and effectiveness.

The commonalties and shared purposes of clinical social work practice and evaluation methods have long been recognized (Corcoran & Gingerich, 1994; Corcoran, Gingerich, & Briggs, 2001; O'Hare, 1991, 2009; Siegel, 1984). Both activities require that clients and practitioners define, analyze, and assess the severity of a problem; determine which kind of intervention should be used; measure whether the client's problems improve over time; and infer whether the intervention had anything to do with the outcome. Although it may seem to some practitioners that drawing conclusions about the effectiveness of their practice with a specific case should be a relatively straightforward matter, such conclusions can often be misleading. In addition, when one has to answer the same question regarding 10, 100, or 1,000 clients in a program, evaluation becomes even more challenging. Nevertheless, practitioners and evaluators must begin in the same place: define the problem, define the intervention, and establish some criteria and method for judging success. What follows is a review of the more common designs used in evaluation and outcome research, and their relative strengths and weaknesses in providing sound answers to matters of efficacy and effectiveness.

QUALITATIVE APPROACHES TO RESEARCH AND EVALUATION

Qualitative evaluation employs an array of observational data collection techniques and methods of analysis to obtain a detailed and highly textured description of the client's experience and to judge the effectiveness of an intervention. Despite some attempts to pose qualitative research as an antidote to "positivist" research, qualitative methods have long been a key method of social science. As with quantitative research, the conduct of qualitative research requires reviews of the existing literature, sampling strategies, data collection procedures, and data analysis, and it often is combined with quantitative data methods (i.e., mixed-methods design). Qualitative researchers investigating social work practice might employ focus groups, in-depth interviews, case studies, and structured or semistructured questionnaires. Qualitative methods provide nuance, detail, and exploratory flexibility, which are not usually obtainable with experimental or most large-sample survey methods. Although there is often a greater emphasis on thick description in qualitative case study, the approach also requires making cause-effect links between interventions and outcomes based on observations. Case studies are a unique complement to experimental research, often spawning innovative assessment or intervention hypotheses. Qualitative methods are good for studying rare phenomena, can provide some degree of disconfirmation of a prevailing theory or claims of practice effectiveness (by demonstrating exceptions to the rule), and have persuasive and motivational value (Kazdin, 1998; Marshall & Rossman, 1995).

In response to the romanticizing of qualitative methods in social work literature (Heineman-Pieper, 1985; Tyson, 1992), others have highlighted its limitations (Gambrill, 1995; Mullen, 1995; Stake, 1995). Qualitative inquiry is highly susceptible to personal bias and the tendency to force observations to fit to one's preferred theories (i.e., Procrustean reasoning), provides a generally weak basis for inferring causation, often raises more questions than it answers, is extremely labor intensive, and yields few generalizable results because of small sample sizes. Although an important first, and usually exploratory, step in a broader research endeavor, qualitative studies generally contribute relatively little overall knowledge to the social sciences.

Although qualitative *research* can be highly controlled, qualitative *evaluation* is typically used in uncontrolled (i.e., naturalistic) designs to assist practitioners in evaluating their own practice (i.e., the standard case study). However, conclusions about treatment effectiveness from single case analyses should be taken with a grain of salt. Observing that clients have improved, stayed about the same, or gotten worse since an initial assessment simply tells us how clients are doing. Drawing conclusions that client changes were the *direct result* of the intervention is more ambiguous.

SINGLE-SYSTEM DESIGNS

Single-system design (a.k.a. single-subject design, "$n = 1$") in social work practice generally refers to the evaluation of an intervention with a client or a family. In single-system design, the baseline measure is typically represented graphically as A (which provides a measure of current performance and a criterion against which one predicts change in the client's problem), and the intervention is represented as B (and C, D, and the like, if more than one intervention is employed). Although single-subject designs are typically used for uncontrolled (naturalistic) monitoring of cases, some single-system designs are referred to as "experimental," because the underlying logic of control is similar to that of classic group experimental designs: the design compares intervention effects under different treatment conditions (e.g., treatment is withdrawn or a new intervention introduced), and clients serve as their own "control." Variations on experimental single-subject designs include the withdrawal and reintroduction of an intervention (i.e., ABAB design, called the "reversal design"), the introduction of an alternative intervention (e.g., ABAC), or the use of combinations of interventions (e.g., ABCA). Obviously, many other design variations are possible (Bloom, Fischer, & Orme, 2009; Hersen, 1985; Kazdin, 1978).

Given that the baseline constitutes the criteria against which the success of treatment is judged, a stable baseline (with several observations) is generally preferred, as an improving baseline would make it more difficult to argue that a successful outcome resulted from the intervention and not just from spontaneous improvement or other nontreatment factors. The new level of performance provides a new baseline to predict future changes in the treatment condition. Treatment can be withdrawn to determine whether performance deviates from the predicted level under treatment or whether the original baseline would have continued. "Baselining" is often done retrospectively, since collecting assessment data and withholding the intervention can be impractical or even unethical in some cases. In actual practice, intervention withdrawal also happens spontaneously, as clients sometimes drop out of treatment unannounced and return at a later date.

There are a number of benefits to employing single-subject, or $n = 1$, methodology. First, simple designs (e.g., ABA) are relatively easy to implement as a monitoring and evaluation tool. Second, the methodology is quite flexible and can be designed to fit unique practice situations. Third, single-subject designs provide some degree of structure for treatment planning by necessitating clear definitions of problems, interventions, and goals. Fourth, clients often see the utility of evaluation and are willing to participate by using self-monitoring devices (e.g., charts) to baseline their problems and track their own progress. Defining a particular problem (e.g., urges to drink, number of positive interactions between a couple, number of panic attacks) becomes a self-monitoring tool in addition to providing baseline data for tracking progress and outcomes. Although conclusions about the effectiveness of the intervention with a single case should be made cautiously (as with qualitative evaluation), replication with similar cases using controlled experimental single-subject designs can provide some basis for further generalization regarding the efficacy of an innovative intervention method.

However, methodological problems with single-subject designs can be formidable as well (Bloom et al., 2009; Kazdin, 1978; Royse et al., 2009). These include several threats to internal validity: (1) obtaining stable baselines is often impractical; (2) altering phases or conditions during intervention can cause ambiguity in the interpretation of outcomes; (3) clients often do not improve in linear, incremental fashion but take "two steps forward, one step back"; (4) it is difficult to attribute changes in the client to specific interventions when multiple interventions are employed (e.g., ABCA); and (5) cause-effect reasoning can be confounded by "history" or "carry-over effects" when clients' recollections of previous events effect their future behavior (Wakefield & Kirk, 1995).

Originally employed to evaluate behavior modification methods in populations with the most severe disorders, single-subject design has become less useful with more complex interventions, since it is more difficult to link client improvements to specific treatment methods (e.g., coping skills, motivational skills) or different phases of treatment (e.g., early or middle phase). In addition, aside from naturalistic monitoring and evaluation in which no treatment conditions are altered, it is unrealistic to expect busy practitioners to employ well-planned single-subject designs in everyday practice, and it is unethical to manipulate treatment conditions without clients' informed consent. However, perhaps the most serious problem with single-system designs is that, since they can be applied to only a handful of cases at one time, generalizing results to other clients and treatment situations is impractical. Beyond simple monitoring and evaluation, the question becomes, what can be inferred about the effectiveness of the intervention? Some social work commentators have suggested that social work go beyond the limitations of single case designs and naturalistic monitoring to emphasize program evaluation instead (Benbenishty, 1996; O'Hare, 2009; O'Hare & Geertsma, 2013).

Others have argued that single-subject evaluation has advantages over group designs because, first, problems and interventions can be more specifically defined for the individual client, and second, making causal linkages between interventions and outcomes appears to be more straightforward (Bloom et al., 2009; Mattaini, 1996). However, ambiguity in defining the intervention is not an inherent weakness of group designs, and making causal connections between treatment and outcomes is certainly no easier in single-subject design than in group designs. The use of treatment manuals and intervention process measures can capture much of the salient dimensions of the intervention in group designs, and group designs can provide a stronger basis for inferring causality between intervention and outcome, along with helping make a stronger case for generalization because of random case assignment and larger samples. In addition, the use of single-subject designs without reference to treatment selection presents a more fundamental dilemma for social work practitioners: what criteria do we use to guide our choice of intervention in the first place? In summary, single-subject designs provide a sound basis for routine monitoring and evaluation, and when used as a controlled experimental design with several cases, they serve as a valuable tool for investigating the efficacy of innovative treatments, which is an important first step toward controlled (i.e., group designs) outcome research.

GROUP DESIGNS FOR EVALUATION RESEARCH AND CONTROLLED OUTCOME RESEARCH

Controlled group designs are not typically employed in the routine evaluation of social work interventions but constitute a methodological gold standard for conducting outcome research (i.e., efficacy studies). More advanced group designs (randomized experimental designs) do a good job of controlling for internal threats to validity, although generalizing to everyday practice environments should be done with caution. In group designs, relationships among intervention and outcome variables are examined in several configurations (Campbell & Stanley, 1963; Kazdin, 1994a, 1998; Royse et al., 2009). These strategies include larger numbers of clients (at least 20 under each condition, although more is preferable), and they might compare the experimental treatment to no intervention (i.e., control group) or an alternative intervention (i.e., a comparison treatment group, often "treatment as usual"). Although there are many group designs, the basic models are considered here.

The elements of experimental design include the initial observation (measurement) (O1) of the client's difficulties (e.g., degree of anxiety, drinking problem, couples' arguments), the intervention (X) (e.g., stress management, motivational enhancement therapy, emotion-focused therapy), and a subsequent measure of the client's problem (O2) to determine some degree of change. If only these basic elements are employed with no comparison or control group, the design is referred to as a pre-experimental or pre-post design. As noted in table 4.1, this design reflects a low level of control. The model conceptually can be portrayed as follows:

$$O1 \qquad X \qquad O2$$

This design illustrates the basic components of controlled research but is itself a weak argument for drawing conclusions regarding the efficacy of the intervention, since there is no basis for comparison (i.e., clients could improve for reasons other than the intervention).

A typical quasi-experimental design compares the original intervention to some alternative treatment:

O1	X1	O2
O3	X2	O4

This design provides a stronger basis for inferring treatment efficacy or effectiveness than the first design because of the presence of a comparison group. But there are still some difficulties in drawing firm conclusions. How clients are assigned to the different groups also matters considerably. If in this design clients chose their own treatment condition (e.g., sought help in two different mental health agencies, X1 and X2), then the design would be considered quasi-experimental. The weakness of this design, of course, is that little consideration is given to the impact of differences in the agencies themselves or the effect of clients' treatment expectations or other factors that may have influenced their decision to select one agency over another (e.g., socioeconomic status, location). The two groups of clients are considered "nonequivalent." This model reflects a moderate degree of control, although alterations in the design could strengthen the level of control (e.g., matching clients in both groups on selected demographic variables).

However, if clients are randomly assigned to these different treatment conditions, then the design becomes experimental, which can be depicted as follows:

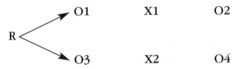

R represents random assignment to the two groups. Purists, however, might contend that this design is still quasi-experimental due to the lack of a true control group. The classic experimental design does, in fact, compare the effects of one intervention with a "placebo" or no intervention at all (usually a waiting-list control group) and would be illustrated as follows:

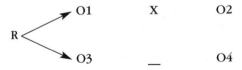

In this design, "___" represents the control group.

One way to strengthen this design would be to collect follow-up data to see how stable the changes are over 3–6 months or more. With that addition, the previous model would look as follows:

Although not foolproof, random assignment tends to reduce the likelihood of outcomes being affected by client differences, such as client selection factors or treatment expectations, rather than the effects of the intervention.

Experimental designs can be more complex. For example, researchers may decide to measure two variations of an experimental treatment with a comparison or control group. To maintain experimental quality, cases would have to be randomly assigned to three treatment groups. In addition, if researchers wanted to compare the effects of treatment on equal numbers of men and women across all three groups, the participants would also have to be randomly assigned to both treatment groups and the "treatment as usual" comparison or control group. When specific client or practitioner factors (e.g., level of experience) are controlled for, these are referred to as factorial designs.

Controlled comparisons have the potential to provide robust evidence to support whether an intervention is efficacious. Depending on the complexity of the design, they can also account for the role of client and practitioner factors, the effects of individual treatment components themselves, and interactions among factors. They have other advantages as well: (1) pretesting allows for better client matching and accounts for different pretest performance levels among clients; (2) data allow for measures of change both within and between treatment groups; (3) they can also control for the effects of attrition (i.e., client dropouts). Controlled experimental designs can make a strong case for treatment efficacy when clients are well chosen, practitioners are well trained, and the employed instruments are reliable and valid. Results can also be sufficiently robust to justify a claim of superiority of one treatment over an alternative treatment or control group, particularly if several similar studies replicate the findings. Last, intervention effects should continue to be evident at follow-up over the course of at least a few months.

These approaches are not without limitations, however. Drawing conclusions about the relationship between the interventions and changes in clients' problems can still be difficult because of a number of threats to validity (Kazdin, 1994a). There may be (1) variations in the way the interventions were provided; (2) disproportionate or excessive attrition (dropouts); (3) aspects of the intervention that were unaccounted for in the design; (4) unintentional cues that participants in the experimental group were getting the "better" intervention, which can distort findings; (5) low statistical power (e.g., insufficient number of clients relative to number of variables), which can yield ambiguous results; (6) use of instruments with poor reliability, validity, or sensitivity to change, which can distort outcomes. Perhaps one of the most difficult problems is in generalizing the results of controlled trials to real practice situations (i.e., external validity). However, despite their limitations, replicated controlled trials provide the strongest basis for establishing intervention efficacy and provide the foundation for intervention planning in EBPSW.

NATURALISTIC PROGRAM EVALUATION

Although controlled designs provide valuable guidelines for the initial choice of intervention, they are rarely used as a method of routine evaluation in human services agencies because of the exacting demands required to implement them. One strategy for evaluating whether evidence-based practices are implemented effectively is to use an evaluative design that accommodates the demands of day-to-day agency practice. This approach is referred to as *naturalistic evaluation* (also known as passive-observational design) (Hargreaves et al., 1998; Kazdin, 1998; O'Hare, 2009; Rossi & Freeman, 1993).

Naturalistic evaluation strategies can accommodate the classic organizational model, which integrates agency structure, service processes, and client outcomes (Donabedian, 1980; Salzer, Nixon, Schut, Karver, & Bickman, 1997). Structurally, programs should be well designed, with a clear organizational mission and goals that support the administration, training, implementation, supervision, and evaluation of evidence-based interventions. Naturalistic designs employ assessment and evaluation methods that can be readily integrated into the normal clinical and administrative functions of human services agencies (e.g., routine assessment). As the term *naturalistic* implies, no extraordinary means (e.g., random assignment, control groups) are used to manipulate the treatment conditions. Agencies function as usual in terms of general service delivery, but great emphasis is placed on developing quality programming based on careful reviews of the relevant practice outcome literature; training staff in best practices; and integrating the use of brief, reliable, and valid measures into assessment and evaluation procedures to capture pretest, posttest, and (in sampled cases) follow-up data over time. These data collectively link client characteristics, elements of the intervention, outcomes, and (with increasing emphasis) service costs in one coherent model (Lyons, Howard, O'Mahoney, & Lish, 1997; Newman, Howard, Windle, & Hohmann, 1994; Royse et al., 2009; Salzer et al., 1997; Smith, Fischer, Nordquist, Mosley, & Ledbetter, 1997). Meaningful and useful reports can then be designed to enhance administrative decision making and respond to accountability expectations of insurers, funding agencies, and accrediting organizations.

Although the ideal scenario for developing such systems is to start from scratch, the implementation of evidence-based practices and evaluation procedures can be initiated at any time, and often in fluid service environments. Achieving a reasonable measure of both practicality and scientific validity is a constant balancing act when conducting program evaluation. Establishing regular intervals for data collection during the intervention and at some follow-up period will vary on the basis of the treatment environment. For example, for outpatient mental health programs that provide brief interventions of generally fewer than eight visits, data may be collected at baseline, termination, and (with sampled clients) at 3-month follow-up, as indicated in the following paradigm: O1 X O2 . . . O3. For a program that serves persons with severe mental illness, the design would likely require repeated measures over longer periods of time during which different components of intervention were offered (e.g., psychiatric services, case management): O1 X1 X2 O2 O3 X3 O4 . . ., and so on. In addition to basic univariate data reports (i.e., baseline and outcome data periodically reported for groups of clients), more sophisticated statistical techniques are needed to examine the relationships among several types of variables, including client characteristics (e.g., age, race, diagnosis, problem type), intervention type (e.g., interpersonal psychotherapy, stress management, behavioral family therapy, case management), frequency of visits, service costs, and client outcomes (e.g., psychosocial well-being).

Because naturalistic evaluation is generally based on the pre-experimental paradigm (i.e., O1 X O2 O3), there are inherent threats to validity. Nevertheless, selection and development of key measures can strengthen the design. A data collection package should minimally include the following: key client characteristics (e.g., gender, age, race, income, insurance coverage, education, source of referral); brief, reliable, and valid assessment or outcome measures that are sensitive to detecting changes in client functioning and well-being over the course of the intervention; client satisfaction measures; fidelity measures (to be discussed later) that can capture key aspects of the interventions employed (e.g., type, frequency of methods used); and a range of other indexes that may be useful for other external reporting requirements. At the individual case level, the combination of both qualitative and quantitative data provides the basis for monitoring and evaluating intervention with an individual case. When quantitative data from scales and indexes are aggregated, they provide the basis for program evaluation. This combination of client, intervention process, and assessment or outcome measures provides a comprehensive system for naturalistic program evaluation that can be seamlessly integrated into the routine delivery of evidence-based practices (Joint Commission on the Accreditation of Healthcare Organizations, 2004; Lyons et al., 1997; Newman et al., 1994; O'Hare, 2009; Royse & Thyer, 1996; Salzer et al., 1997; Yates, 1996).

Although naturalistic designs reflect considerable external validity in their real-world application, this approach incurs some degree of threats to internal validity even when they are well designed and carefully implemented. Potential problems include the inability to consider other explanations for client improvement (e.g., alternative programming), substandard implementation of intervention methods, poor data collection procedures (e.g., poor choice of instruments, problems with unreliable or missing data), regression to the mean (e.g., moderating effects of repeated data collecting), history and maturational effects of the clients themselves (i.e., people often improve without treatment), and client selection factors (e.g., more motivated clients are likely to show up, but a program is intended to target the "hard to reach"), among other problems (Corcoran & Vandiver, 1996; Hargreaves et al., 1998; Lyons et al. 1997; Rossi & Freeman, 1993). The strength of naturalistic evaluation is in its external validity. The quality of practice and service delivery is judged in the context of the typically complex and unpredictable environment of the human service agency.

FIDELITY ASSESSMENT: MEASURING WHETHER EVIDENCE-BASED PRACTICES ARE IMPLEMENTED "FAITHFULLY"

Simply because an agency or an individual practitioner claims to use evidence-based practices does not mean that those practice are in fact implemented with a high degree of skill. Although evaluation usually brings to mind client outcomes, measuring various aspects of the intervention is becoming increasingly important and, in some instances, mandated by funding sources. The main purpose of measuring the intervention process itself is to ensure that evidence-based interventions are implemented with *fidelity*; that is, that actual service delivery is faithful to the intervention as described in "the manual." In an agency setting there are basically three methods available to achieve this end: (1) the use of qualitative case analysis in supervision or supervised focus groups; (2) direct observation (e.g., the one-way window); (3) the use of fidelity and other process measures completed by staff and/or clients as part of routine clinical documentation (e.g., a brief checklist completed immediately after an office session or home visit). These data can also be entered into a database, then aggregated and linked to client characteristics and client outcomes to enhance program evaluation (e.g., "What was the problem?" "What did we do?" "How did the client respond?").

Qualitative process evaluation (case-study analysis) is an invaluable tool for examining implementation at the individual client level. Through supervision or focus groups, practitioners can examine the intervention process through case discussions and scenario building ("What if?") as a brainstorming method to discuss how to deal with more challenging and less predictable cases. This constructive sharing of practice experience can help staff learn to anticipate problems that may arise and address them in a way that maintains the essential integrity of an evidence-based approach. Under selected circumstances, practitioners can be observed in vivo with clients (with client consent), in order to compare practitioners' intervention approach with the model and help practitioners deal with unanticipated occurrences. As with program monitoring and evaluation in general, these activities should be undertaken in a context of mutual support to help refine methods and learn to adapt evidence-based practices creatively to complex client problems. However, case studies must be balanced against larger databases compiled through the use of fidelity scales and other intervention process indicators (e.g., type, frequency, duration of service). One way to ensure reasonable congruency between a model and actual implementation is to allow for some degree of flexibility in the application of evidence-based approaches so that practitioners can adjust manualized approaches to the needs of more complex cases. The thoughtfully planned application of both qualitative and quantitative methods for measuring intervention fidelity can help ensure delivery of high-quality services.

There are several "process" instruments that measure different dimensions of psychosocial interventions (Hill, Nutt, & Jackson, 1994; O'Hare & Collins, 1997; O'Hare & Geertsma, 2013). Most of these, however, focus on the interpersonal aspects of psychotherapy, an important but incomplete view of psychosocial interventions. Many promising initiatives have demonstrated that the implementation of practice skills for social work practice can be measured reliably. These scales include the Inpatient Measure of Adolescent and Child Services and Treatment (I-MACST) (Pottick, Hansell, & Barber, 1998), the Hospital Social Work Self-Efficacy Scale (Holden, Cuzzi, Rutter, Rosenberg, & Chernack, 1996), the Practice Skills Inventory (O'Hare & Geertsma, 2013; O'Hare, Tran, & Collins, 2002), the Substance Abuse Treatment Self-Efficacy Scale (SATSES) (Kranz, 2003; Kranz & O'Hare, 2006), and a fidelity measure of service delivery with persons who have severe mental illness and substance abuse problems (Teague, Bond, & Drake, 1998). Fidelity instruments vary in the level of service delivery being measured. Variations include measurement of service program processes (e.g., indicators that assessments were conducted, clients referred for treatment), the use of certain "packaged" intervention models (e.g., motivational interviewing, behavioral family therapy), the use of practice skills (e.g., empathic attunement, self-monitoring, modeling, brokering, advocacy), and basic administrative aspects of service delivery (e.g., type, frequency, duration, cost of services).

The Practice Skills Inventory (PSI) developed by O'Hare and colleagues is presented here as one illustration of a process measure that can be adapted for use as a fidelity scale (O'Hare & Collins, 1997; O'Hare, Tran, & Collins, 2002). Based on reviews of the practice literature, the PSI measures three major categories of intervention skills: supportive skills that focus on facilitating a sound working relationship; coping skills interventions that include a range of cognitive-behavioral methods shown to be essential for moderate to severe psychosocial disorders; and case management skills, which are essential for coordinating complex cases. One study with experienced practitioners also supported the use of an insight facilitation skill (O'Hare, Collins, & Walsh, 1998), a subscale that represents more interpersonal approaches to psychosocial treatment. The PSI has been shown to have good to excellent internal consistency reliability for all its subscales, and it has demonstrated a good factor structure with both student and experienced social work practitioners (O'Hare & Collins, 1997; O'Hare, Tran, & Collins, 2002). It also was shown to be sensitive to client change over time when used in an outpatient mental health center (O'Hare & Geertsma, 2013).

There are many potential uses for the PSI that social work students, practitioners, researchers, and evaluators can explore: (1) to examine patterns of skill application in practice, (2) as a fidelity measure to examine the implementation of evidence-based guidelines, (3) to examine whether skill application varies with different types of problems or severity of problems presented by clients, (4) to examine variations in skill application over time within the same case, and (5) as an evaluation tool for linking processes with outcomes. A slightly modified version of the PSI is included in appendix C to be used as an exploratory device by students and practitioners in individual cases. The instructions direct the practitioner first to indicate the number of client contacts on which completion of the scale is based. The number of contacts can range from one to several, depending on patterns of service delivery. Second, respondents then report the "frequency" with which they used certain skills with a particular client during that period of time. Third, respondents then describe in more detail the particular skill used (discussed further later). Students and practitioners can use the scale for self-review or in supervision to compare the configuration of practice skills they relied on with those recommended in the literature. At the program level, evaluators can aggregate data with the PSI to determine whether the proper category of skills generally conforms to best practices, and then use the results of such a report as a basis for providing feedback to staff. These data can then be used to prompt further supervision, consultation, or staff development.

The individual items of the PSI were designed to be somewhat general so the scale could have broad application to social work service settings. Practitioners should estimate the frequency with which they used the general skills, but then describe more specifically which skill they actually used with the client. In this way, the PSI can serve as a tool for both quantitative and qualitative analyses. For example, for an item on the coping skills subscale (e.g., "manage their own problem behaviors"), practitioners could more specifically define which intervention skill they actually employed with the client (in parentheses under the specific item). For an adolescent with conduct disorder, it might read: "taught and role played anger management skills." Although more research regarding the validity of the PSI is needed, students and practitioners are encouraged to use the scale in an exploratory way to examine practice patterns relative to guidelines provided in evidence-based practice texts and treatment manuals. The scale can be reproduced without the permission of the author.

The Substance Abuse Treatment Self-Efficacy Scale (SATSES) (Kranz, 2003; Kranz & O'Hare, 2006), noted earlier, was designed to measure practitioners' confidence in carrying out substance abuse intervention skills. This scale has 32 items and measures five domains of substance abuse skills employed by social workers: assessment and/or treatment planning, individual counseling, group counseling, case management, and ethics. The instructions direct practitioners to rate their own level of confidence in using specific skills for working with substance-abusing clients (from very low to very high). The scale can be used to evaluate practitioners' training needs or, with minor modification, as a fidelity tool in environments where it is important to measure how consistently practitioners use core substance abuse intervention processes and skills. To be used as a fidelity scale, the instructions could be modified to have respondents measure how confidently they applied each skill with a particular client. The instrument was validated through exploratory and confirmatory factor analysis, and it showed excellent internal consistency reliabilities for all subscales (.89–.96). Further field testing across an array of service environments is needed to strengthen its external validity. Practitioners can use the scale without permission of the author (see appendix D).

SUMMARY OF RECOMMENDATIONS FOR IMPLEMENTING AND EVALUATING EVIDENCE-BASED PRACTICES

The inherent challenges of implementing evidence-based practices can be facilitated through the development of a sound evaluation plan. Many experts in the field have outlined guidelines for evaluation (e.g., Hargreaves et al., 1998; Lyons et al. 1997; Smith et al., 1997). To ensure the effective implementation of EBPSW, agencies need to do the following:

- Get their organization's top management on board, and educate staff and clients about the need to learn and use evidence-based practices and sound evaluation methods.

- Construct a sound mission and program plan that incorporates the use of evidence-based practices. The use of interventions shown to be efficacious in controlled trials strengthens the argument for their effectiveness but does not guarantee effective implementation.

- Hire well-trained staff, and invest in staff development to upgrade knowledge and skills in evidence-based practices and evaluation methods.

- Provide skilled management and assertive supervision to ensure effective implementation of the plan.

- Hire trainers in evidence-based practices as needed.

- Develop a data collection plan that includes measures of client characteristics, intervention processes, client outcomes, consumer satisfaction, and service costs.

- Develop a battery of assessment and outcome instruments that can be integrated with routine clinical documentation at assessment, during continuing care reviews, at termination, and at follow-up. These instruments should be well chosen on the basis of psychometric value (i.e., reliability and validity), utility, and salience to the clients' problems and services provided.

- Use a total instrument package that incorporates important indexes not captured by standardized scales. These data include items such as duration of hospital stay, relapses, days worked, and days homeless. Some of these data may be required for reporting purposes to outside funding or accreditation agencies.

- Include checklists or indexes that capture high-risk indicators (e.g., suicide attempts, arrests, reported incidents of abuse). These indexes include low-frequency events that have a potentially high impact on client well-being (e.g., suicide, homicide, criminal activity, victimization) and are often associated with greater liability exposure for the agency and practitioner. Designing a report on "high-risk" clients can support decision making for both practitioners and managers.

- Use fidelity instruments to assess the consistency with which practitioners are using evidence-based practices.

- Protect client confidentiality in all databases, as mandated by the Health Insurance Portability and Accountability Act of 1996.

- Hire and train the right mix of staff and consultants to provide expertise in quality assurance, evaluation design, and statistics to analyze and report data clearly and accurately. Statistical reporting errors can have a negative impact on an organization by implying unjustifiably positive or negative reports. Statistical accuracy is essential if process and outcome data are to be used to support management decision making.

- Conduct careful statistical analysis of the data to integrate the effects of client characteristics, intervention processes, outcomes, and costs.

- Use data for troubleshooting, self-evaluation, in-house staff development, training, strategic planning, and (most of all) to improve the quality of client care. Avoid using the data for punitive administrative purposes.

- Provide administrative safeguards so that quality assurance and evaluation personnel are not easily leveraged for expedient political reasons but can operate relatively unencumbered to produce relatively unbiased evaluation reports.

As human services funding policies continue to evolve, it is likely that the demands for evidence-based, cost-effective practices and sound evaluative expertise will increase (Mechanic et al., 1995; O'Hare, 2002; Wells, Astrachan, Tischler, & Unutzer, 1995).

THE EBPSW SERVICE PLAN: ASSESSMENT, INTERVENTION, AND EVALUATION

The service delivery plan links client treatment with individual and program evaluation. Most practitioners and agencies are required to document their services to clients. This documentation takes many forms and is far from standardized. The format of such documentation varies by funding source, accreditation organizations, and state and federal regulatory agencies. Although documentation varies considerably, some basic assumptions are suggested here. First, documentation is required, necessary, and important for a variety of contractual, legal, risk management, and ethical reasons. Second, although service documentation is often (and sometimes justifiably) considered a time-consuming and expensive nuisance, documentation can be an essential part of delivering and evaluating evidence-based practices for a number of important reasons. For example, when conceptually well designed, service plan documentation can improve the validity (e.g., accuracy, thoroughness) and reliability (e.g., consistency) of assessment; clarify the goals, objectives, and methods used in the intervention; and detail the methods used for monitoring and evaluation. Third, a well-conducted assessment, intervention, and evaluation plan is essential for guiding individual service for clients, and when data from individual service plans are aggregated, they can provide a sound basis for program-level evaluation.

Assessment

As outlined in chapter 2, the assessment should include a number of basic considerations: a thorough psychosocial history and problem formulation that is informed by contemporary human behavior theory, an assessment of the severity of client problems across multiple problem domains (e.g., psychological, family, social, health, substance abuse), a detailed functional assessment of psychosocial factors that affect the client's main difficulties, and a systems perspective. This detailed multidimensional-functional-systems (MFS) assessment should be accompanied by the use of thoughtfully chosen instruments that also serve as outcome measures. These instruments are likely to be a combination of both individual indexes specific to client problems and standardized instruments that provide a foundation for naturalistic evaluation.

Intervention Plan

Once the assessment data have been collected, practitioners and clients need to collaboratively define problems and goals. This process includes, first, developing a definition of the client's problem(s) based on the MFS assessment. Although the assessment may provide a somewhat complex understanding of the factors involved in the client's problems, the final problem definition should be relatively straightforward.

Second, practitioner and client should decide on reasonable intervention goals (e.g., achievable resolution of problems, acquisition of certain coping abilities). Goals can be stated somewhat generally, although they should represent a reasonable and clinically significant improvement in the client's condition and ability to cope.

Third, practitioners should reference evidence-based practices, discuss them with the client, and discuss how to collaboratively and flexibly implement the intervention to accommodate the client's individual needs and circumstances. Interventions should be defined by both the formal "title" of the approach (e.g., interpersonal psychotherapy, exposure with response prevention, social skills training, behavioral marital therapy), but the actual implementation should be spelled out in more detail.

Fourth, practitioner and client must define intervention objectives, that is, short-term and hierarchically ranked stepping-stones that lead to the ultimate treatment goal. Objectives are a linchpin between the practitioners' intervention skills and clients' efforts to problem solve and strengthen their own coping skills. Objectives are likely to unfold and change as the client improves, as new problems arise, or if a new approach is taken. Treatment plans should be updated as objectives are achieved. Objectives may be defined as incremental steps toward a treatment goal, but they may also overlap with interventions for one simple reason: an intervention is not simply something that is *done to* the client. The objectives are often the main vehicle by which the client participates in the implementation of the intervention. So, for example, the practitioner might provide psychoeducation and a brief intervention to encourage a client to try out his first Alcoholics Anonymous meeting (the objective) in the coming week. A traumatized young woman who has become agoraphobic may benefit from an intervention that includes support, psychoeducation, anxiety management skills, and exposure treatment (i.e., in vivo practice to gradually confront the anxiety). The objective may be for her to walk down the street a quarter of a mile to mail a letter or pick up a few groceries every day for the following 2 weeks. For a child struggling with shyness and depression, the intervention may emphasize couples therapy to reduce marital conflicts that affect the child's emotional well-being. The objective may be for the couple to encourage the child to attend a birthday party unaccompanied by the parents. The interventions are the skills and techniques the practitioner brings to the table. The objectives are intermediate goals for the client to achieve, and they should be thoughtfully chosen in collaboration with the client in a way that helps drive progress toward the treatment goals. Intermittent and meaningful successes increase a client's self-efficacy and chances of coping successfully with difficulties. Achieving meaningful objectives is empowering for clients and helps them enhance their own coping skills.

Evaluation

Last, a brief description of the evaluation plan should be provided in the overall service plan. This includes the standardized measures and unique indexes that were discussed in the assessment (see chapter 2). The plan should also include a brief description of the data collection process (i.e., who will collect the data, at which intervals, under which circumstances). The evaluation plan serves two purposes: it provides a foundation for qualitative and quantitative evaluation with the individual case, and (if standardized measures are used) the data can be aggregated with data from other clients for program evaluation.

Linking well-chosen, clear problem definitions and intervention goals, selecting evidence-based approaches, constructing key objectives, and implementing clinically useful evaluation tools is a highly skilled craft. When done well, the service plan can reduce complex information regarding the client's problems and recommended interventions to a relatively simple model focused on problem solving and improving a client's ability to cope. The client service plan serves many useful purposes: it is a necessary bureaucratic tool used to meet contractual and regulatory obligations, it is a blueprint for clinical intervention that reflects expertise in clinical assessment and intervention, and it stipulates the assessment or evaluation tools to be employed. The complete service plan should thoughtfully reflect all three components of EBPSW: assessment, intervention, and evaluation (see figure 4.1).

FIGURE 4.1   Model client service plan to integrate assessment, intervention planning, and evaluation

Problems	Goals	Objectives (samples)	Interventions	Assessment and evaluation tools

SUMMARY

Evaluation should be seamlessly integrated into the assessment and intervention plan. Although evaluation designs are derived from various research methods, evaluation in routine care, whether done with one client or with an entire program, is typically uncontrolled for both practical and ethical purposes. Well-chosen scales and indexes can be incorporated into routine assessment to provide a baseline for further monitoring and evaluation. When data regarding client characteristics, intervention methods, and outcomes are aggregated across an entire program, those data can also serve as a foundation for program evaluation.

PART II

ADULT DISORDERS

CHAPTER 5

SCHIZOPHRENIA SPECTRUM DISORDERS

Schizophrenia spectrum disorders include schizophrenia, schizoaffective disorder, and other residual diagnoses when the person does not fit the full criteria. Persons with schizophrenia struggle with one of the most challenging of psychiatric disorders. Those with schizoaffective disorder share many of the same symptoms of schizophrenia, but depression or mania is also required to be concurrently present most of the time. (For convenience, the term *schizophrenia* is used here to refer to schizophrenia spectrum disorders.) Much of what is discussed in this chapter regarding assessment and intervention with schizophrenia spectrum disorders is also relevant to other serious mental illnesses, such as major mood disorders (e.g., bipolar disorder, severe chronic depression; see chapter 6), given the amount of overlapping or shared symptoms with diagnoses of severe mental illnesses (Abrams, Rojas, & Arciniegas, 2008; Baynes et al., 2000) in addition to a range of common social, functional, and occupational deficits. In addition to biological causes of schizophrenia spectrum disorders, many psychosocial risk factors, resiliencies, and personal identity factors, such as gender, race, and socioeconomic level affect the course of schizophrenia and its response to treatment. Cultural interpretation of symptoms is also relevant for accurate assessment and diagnosis, and social stigma, which is culturally determined, also strongly affects how severe mental illness is perceived. This chapter also highlights two common problems that often co-occur with people diagnosed with schizophrenia: substance abuse and post-traumatic stress disorder. Several assessment instruments are available to reliably measure key psychosocial symptoms of schizophrenia. This chapter highlights the Brief Psychiatric Rating Scale, a well-established and widely used measure of psychiatric symptoms. In addition to a range of medications that have been shown to be effective in reducing the severity of major symptoms, research on effective psychosocial interventions has grown considerably and offers much hope for improved functioning and better quality of life for clients living with these disorders. These interventions include cognitive-behavioral coping skills, social skills training, psychoeducation, and behavior therapy with the families of persons with mental illness, and assertive case management.

ASSESSMENT

Background Data

Schizophrenia covers a spectrum of related diseases marked by thought disorders (e.g., hallucinations, delusions), disorganized speech and behavior, flattened emotional response, and a deterioration in social functioning. Lifetime prevalence for the disorder ranges from .5% to 1% of the general population, it is more or less evenly divided between genders (rates for women may be slightly lower), and it is fairly equally distributed globally (Messias, Chen, & Eaton, 2007; Tandon, Keshavan, & Nesrallah, 2008a, 2008b; World Health Organization, 2010). Clients with schizophrenia often have little awareness of being ill or needing treatment. The course of schizophrenia is quite variable and defies easy summation. Although many face considerable psychosocial deterioration over time, some clients experience early remission, manage the disorder quite well, and may even see their symptoms level off rather than face inexorable deterioration and decline (American Psychiatric Association, APA, 2000, 2013; Kaplan & Sadock, 1998; Johnson, 1997). Those who have later and acute onset, have good predisease functioning, are female, and have good social supports appear to have a better chance of recovery. When young persons who have experienced their first psychotic episode are treated in a timely manner with both medication and psychosocial interventions, prognosis for good recovery improves (Falloon, Roncone, Malm, & Coverdale, 1998). In addition, larger social networks and more social supports have been shown to be associated with requiring less inpatient treatment and having better outcomes (Albert, Becker, McCrone, & Thornicroft, 1998).

Gender Differences.   Persons with schizophrenia are far from all alike. In addition to individual differences, person factors such as gender and race are related to variation in the onset, course, and outcomes of schizophrenia. Women have a slightly lower prevalence of schizophrenia and later onset than men (late 20s to early 30s vs. late teens to early 20s, respectively); more related mood disturbance; better premorbid history; fewer negative symptoms (e.g., social withdrawal); and better outcomes, social adjustment, and response to medication overall (APA, 2013). It has been suggested that differential response to family interventions between men and women may be due to different gender-role expectations (i.e., men are expected to demonstrate more "independent" behavior) (Angermeyer, Kuhn, & Goldstein, 1990; Goldstein & Tsuang, 1990). Men also tend to show more recidivism than women (Test, Burke, & Wallach, 1990). Although there are few differences overall between men and women in hospitalization, treatment utilization, and aftercare (Klinkenberg & Calsyn, 1998), women who are seriously mentally ill incur additional risks, including a greater chance of contracting HIV as a result of having been sexually victimized, a risk that is also compounded by associated substance abuse and poverty (Carey, Carey, & Kalichman, 1997; Cournos & McKinnon, 1997; Otto-Salaj, Heckman, Stevenson, & Kelly, 1998). Many women with mental illness also struggle to retain custody of their children, a monumental challenge given the adversities they face (Mowbray, Oyserman, Bybee, McFarland, & Rueda-Riedle, 2001). Research regarding co-occurring schizophrenia and substance abuse has revealed similar rates of abuse between men and women but differences in associated risk factors such as better social supports among women, more criminal involvement for men, and more abuse victimization of women (Burnette & Drake, 1997; Goodman et al., 2001). With regard to treatment, preliminary evidence suggests that women may do at least as well as men in programs that address both substance abuse and severe mental illness (Jerrell & Ridgely, 1995).

Race Differences.   Although schizophrenia has been shown to occur at similar rates across different ethnic and racial groups, cultural biases and racism have been noted as mediating factors in diagnosis (APA, 2000) and in service-delivery patterns. For example, Whaley (1998) noted a tendency of practitioners to see the guarded behavior of African American clients as "paranoid." Other evidence suggests more difficulty in procuring aftercare housing for black men with mental illness (Uehara, 1994). There is also a higher risk of contracting HIV among African American men with mental illness (Carey et al., 1997; Cournos & McKinnon, 1997). Clearly, risk factors associated with racism, poverty, and mental illness may reciprocally interact. However, some research has reported comparable service utilization patterns and outcomes for mentally ill black and white men in a Veterans Administration residential program (Leda & Rosenheck, 1995), perhaps underscoring the positive association between outcomes and having comparable health benefits. Persons with schizophrenia also experience a disproportionate degree of psychosocial stressors that increase the risk of developing post-traumatic stress disorder (Drake, Green, Mueser, & Goldman, 2003; Harris, 1996; Osborn, 2001). For persons with mental illness in general, there is also negative stigma, particularly in regard to the exaggerated perception of a propensity toward violent behavior (Monahan, 1996; Ryan, 1998).

Schizophrenia and Substance Abuse Problems.   Although a more thorough examination of general substance abuse assessment appears in chapter 7, a brief overview of the problem of "dual diagnosis," or co-occurring substance abuse and mental illness, is warranted here. There is considerable evidence from both epidemiological studies and surveys of clinical populations that roughly half of all clients with serious mental illness (including schizophrenia, bipolar disorder, and major depression) are likely to have been identified at some time in their lives as abusers of alcohol or other drugs (Drake & Mueser, 2000; Helzer & Pryzbeck, 1988; Kessler, Birnbaum et al., 2005; Kessler et al., 1996; Regier et al., 1990). Six-month incidence rates are somewhat lower and range from 25% to 35% (Graham et al., 2001; Rosenberg et al., 1998). Numerous studies support the view that when mentally ill persons abuse alcohol and other drugs, they increase their risk of exacerbated psychiatric symptoms, increased hospitalizations, poorer treatment compliance and outcomes, polysubstance use, high-risk sexual behavior, and other health difficulties. Additional risks include homelessness, financial problems, and involvement with the criminal justice system (Clark, Ricketts, & McHugo, 1999; Drake, Alterman, & Rosenberg, 1993; Drake, McHugo et al., 1998; Drake, Mueser, Clark, & Wallach, 1996; Drake, Osher, & Wallach, 1989; Drake & Wallach, 2000; O'Hare, 1992; O'Hare, Bennett, & Leduc, 1991). The findings on long-term outcomes for substance-abusing people with mental illness are ambiguous, but evidence suggests that they are at considerable risk of remission and recidivism (Drake & Mueser, 1996; Drake et al., 1989; Turner & Tsuang, 1990).

It is understood that the relationship among substance abuse, mental illness, and a host of other psychosocial factors is complex, and simple cause-effect explanations (e.g., self-medication) of any relationship lack explanatory power (Kassel, Wardel, Heinz, & Greenstein, 2010; Turner & Tsuang, 1990). At the pharmacological level, the interaction among alcohol and other drugs, schizophrenic disease processes, and medications is not well understood. Current theories of co-occurring substance use disorders and serious mental illness posit a range of explanations, including the existence of common biopsychosocial factors and the potential of one condition to increase risk for the other. At the practical level, the use of alcohol or other drugs may precipitate or exacerbate symptoms and behavior problems, as well as interfere with assessment and the effects of psychotropic medication.

Trauma in People with Schizophrenia.   Rates of trauma and posttraumatic stress disorder (PTSD) in people with schizophrenia are higher than for the general public (O'Hare & Sherrer, 2009). Most of the research on trauma and PTSD includes samples of people with either a schizophrenia spectrum or major mood disorder (see also chapter 6). Rates of lifetime trauma in people with a severe mental illness in general have been reported to be about 90% (for a review, see, e.g., Grubaugh, Zinsow, Paul, Egede, & Freuh, 2011; Mueser, Goodman et al., 1998; O'Hare, Shen, & Sherrer, 2013a; O'Hare & Sherrer, 2009; Resnick, Bond, & Mueser, 2003), compared to about two-thirds of the general population (Kessler, Sonnega, Bromet, Hughes, & Nelson, 1995), and rates of PTSD have been shown to be from four to five times higher (ranging from 29% to 43%) (Mueser et al., 1998; O'Hare, Sherrer, & Shen, 2006; Resnick et al., 2003) than the roughly 8% estimated for the general public (Kessler et al., 1995). Hypothesized explanations for higher rates of trauma and PTSD in persons with severe mental illness include shared genetic and environmental vulnerabilities, correlated or shared symptoms (e.g., depression) (Brady & Sinha, 2005), and the possible mediating effects of PTSD (Mueser, Rosenberg, Goodman, & Trumbetta, 2002).

The most common trauma in this population appears to be having experienced physical and sexual abuse (especially in women), having witnessed violence (more so in men), and having experienced life-threatening illnesses. However, other severe stressors that might not meet diagnostic "Criterion A" status are also notable, including homelessness and having experienced sudden loss (e.g., death) of those close to the person (O'Hare & Sherrer, 2011). Trauma and PTSD in the severely mentally ill population have been correlated with more severe psychiatric symptoms, greater risk of additional trauma, more high-risk behaviors (e.g., suicide attempts, self-mutilation, unprotected sex), more substance use, and poorer treatment outcomes in general (Gearon, Kaltman, Brown, & Bellack, 2003; Lu, Mueser, Rosenberg, & Jankowski, 2008; O'Hare et al., 2006; O'Hare, Shen, & Sherrer, 2010; Rosenberg, Lu, Mueser, Jankowski, & Cournos, 2007). Physical abuse has been associated with suicide attempts as well (O'Hare, Shen, & Sherrer, 2013c). A thorough examination of lifetime trauma is clearly warranted when conducting assessments with people diagnosed with schizophrenia and other severe mental illnesses.

Suicide among People with Schizophrenia.   The number of people diagnosed with schizophrenia who commit suicide has been estimated to range from 5% to 13% (APA, 2013; Hawton, Sutton, Haw, Sinclair, & Deeks, 2005; Hor & Taylor; 2010; Palmer, Pankratz, & Bostwick, 2005; Pompili et al., 2006; Saha, Chant, & McGrath, 2007). Risk factors include being younger, male, white, unemployed, relatively well educated, unmarried, good premorbid functioning, a family history of suicide, having suffered from severe depression and hopelessness, experienced family stressors, a history of substance abuse, and made previous suicide attempts. Self-harming behaviors and previous suicide attempts are key predictors of completed suicide and should be examined carefully during routine assessment.

Theories

Before conducting a formal assessment with a person who suffers from schizophrenia, it is critical to have a basic understanding of both the biological nature of the disease and the relevance of environmental stressors in the exacerbation of symptoms and behavior problems. Decades of research have produced an abundance of evidence establishing biological explanations as the primary cause of schizophrenia (Bogerts, 1993; Downar & Kupar, 2008; Kaplan & Sadock, 1998; Johnson, 1997; Messias et al., 2007; Tandon et al., 2008a, 2008b; Taylor, 1987), although the exact nature of these processes is still not known. Genetic factors appear to contribute about 80% of the risk, although genetic studies have yet to identify the specific genes or nature of the link among suspected genes. Prenatal disease or trauma, birth trauma (e.g., asphyxia), and severe social stressors are also suspected as risk factors (Messias et al., 2007). Other risk factors include various abnormalities in brain structure and abnormal neurological processes (Tandon et al., 2008a, 2008b). In addition to genetic predisposition and other biological factors, a range of childhood developmental abnormalities may also be implicated as predictive of schizophrenia, including age of achieving developmental milestones, cognitive functioning, educational achievement, and social competence. The course of schizophrenia can be unpredictable, with periods of improvement and remission, but a small minority of people achieve good outcomes after steady improvement.

Much of the research has focused on the limbic system of the brain as the primary site of dysfunction. A review of more than 50 brain-imaging and postmortem brain studies (Bogerts, 1993) strongly suggests abnormal brain development, physiological dysfunction, and neuroanatomical anomalies that cannot be accounted for by psychosocial influences. These physiological changes occur at the higher integrative and associative (cortical) brain functions, as well as in brain structures controlling basic drives and emotions (i.e., the limbic system) (Bogerts, 1993). Because the exact organic etiology is not known, schizophrenia is considered a functional psychosis. Research suggesting that schizophrenia is related to temporal-lobe dysfunction extends back over a century. Technological advances in the form of computer tomography research in the 1970s and, more recently, magnetic resonance imaging (MRI) have provided more clearly delineated structural differences in the brains of persons with schizophrenia. These differences are primarily located in the temporal lobe, which is closely related to other brain functions. Psychotic symptoms caused by temporal-lobe abnormalities are presumably the result of genetic mechanisms or physical trauma (Shenton, 1996).

Other theories, most notably the dopamine hypothesis, have focused on dysfunction in neurotransmitter production and/or the reuptake of dopamine and serotonin as causing schizophrenic symptoms. It appears more likely that multiple interacting neurotransmitter systems are implicated (Downar & Kupar, 2008; Kaplan & Sadock, 1998). There is also growing evidence to support the hypothesis that schizophrenia is the consequence of anomalous synaptic reorganization caused by brain abnormalities (again, primarily in the limbic system) stimulated by hormone surges during late adolescence (Stevens, 1992). Hemsley (1996) suggested that since perception depends on the interaction between context-related stimuli and stored memories, behavioral abnormalities in schizophrenia are the result of a breakdown in the normal relationship between memory and sensory input. Brain-imaging research, particularly more recent MRI developments, have revealed abnormalities in the size of cerebral ventricles in many patients with schizophrenia. The higher concordance rates between identical twins raised apart and the higher rate of schizophrenia (by a factor of 10) in first-degree relatives with the disease has perhaps provided the strongest evidence to date for biogenetic influences as the primary cause of the disease (APA, 2013; Kaplan

& Sadock, 1998; Kety, 1996). Although environmental stress is seriously considered a precipitating factor in the etiology of schizophrenia, no specific environmental factor has ever been shown to play a significant causal role (Erlenmeyer-Kimling, 1996). Some environmental stressors may, however, increase risk for organic causes such as viruses, prenatal trauma, and autoimmune disorders.

Although schizophrenia is presumed to have a strong biological basis, there are an array of psychosocial factors that exacerbate the condition, and reciprocally, there are psychosocial consequences that result from symptoms and behaviors associated with the disease. Models emphasizing the interactions of biological vulnerability and environmental stressors have also provided important insights into the course and outcomes of schizophrenia, although the interactions of biological processes and environmental stressors are not yet thoroughly understood. However, once the disease process begins, understanding and mitigating the impact of environmental stressors becomes critical to the psychosocial assessment and intervention with persons who suffer from schizophrenia. It has been long recognized that people in the lowest socioeconomic stratum are much more likely to suffer from serious psychopathology, schizophrenia included (Dohrenwend & Dohrenwend, 1974; Kohn, Dohrenwend, & Mirotznik, 1998). Two prevailing theories have been proffered to account for this situation: the social causation hypothesis suggests that "rates of psychiatric disorders are higher in the lower socioeconomic strata because of greater environmental adversity. The selection theory argues that rates are higher in the lower strata because predisposed individuals drift down to or fail to rise out of the lower social strata" (Kohn et al., 1998, p. 275). In the case of schizophrenia (more so than with other disorders, such as depression, for which the cause of the disorder appears to be more reactive to social stressors), the selection theory ("downward drift") seems to account for the reasons people with schizophrenia are incapacitated in ways that prevent them from advancing socioeconomically (Dohrenwend et al., 1998). Although one cannot argue that schizophrenia is caused primarily by social factors, the social work practitioner must be acutely aware of how living in poverty and high-crime areas, living in substandard housing, experiencing trauma and stigma, and having an inconsistent work history can adversely affect clients. Schizophrenia, therefore, for all practical purposes, becomes more than a mental disease; it is a complex disorder-in-living on every level.

Key Elements of Multidimensional-Functional-Systemic Assessment

The diagnostic criteria for schizophrenia (APA, 2000, 2013) are widely considered to be reliable and valid. Minor changes were made to the diagnosis of schizophrenia for the DSM-5. The main criteria now include two or more symptoms (for duration of at least 1 month) that must include the presence of delusions, hallucinations, or disorganized speech (e.g., incoherence), and may also include grossly disorganized or catatonic behavior, or negative symptoms (e.g., diminished emotional expression). In addition to active symptoms, there must be some evidence of serious social or occupational dysfunction and continuous signs of the disorder for a duration of at least 6 months (including 1 month of active symptoms). Other disorders, including mood disorders, substance abuse, and medical conditions, must be ruled out as the primary cause of the client's symptoms.

Providing a diagnosis for schizophrenia is an important part of an overall assessment. However, given that the primary impact of medication is on "positive" symptoms (e.g., hallucinations, delusions) of schizophrenia with only limited benefits for "negative" symptoms (e.g., emotional withdrawal, interpersonal functioning), a multidimensional-functional-systemic (MFS) assessment is essential (Bedell, Hunter, & Corrigan, 1997; O'Hare et al., 2003) and should cover the following domains:

- Mental status (e.g., psychiatric symptoms including hallucinations, delusions, disorganized thinking, depression, anxiety, social withdrawal, motor retardation, blunted affect, among others)
- Highly stressful or traumatic events (e.g., rape and other assault, sudden loss)
- Use of medications (e.g., compliance with prescribed dose)
- Thorough examination of use of alcohol and other drugs (e.g., quantity and frequency of use, consequences of use, use of nonprescribed medications)
- Social functioning in proximate relationships (e.g., family, friends) and extended relationships (e.g., number and types of social supports, quality of connectedness with others in the community, signs of isolation and withdrawal)
- Ability to negotiate daily living activities (e.g., shopping, laundry, personal hygiene)
- Access to and use of environmental resources (e.g., housing, transportation, safety concerns)
- Money management and gainful vocational activity (e.g., job or education)
- General health status
- Leisure activities
- Civic responsibilities (e.g., criminal activity)

In conducting the MFS assessment, it is important to collate data from multiple sources, including other mental health professionals, primary physicians, case managers, counselors, community members, law enforcement, and family members—all with appropriate consent.

In addition to assessing the client's well-being across multiple domains, it is essential to conduct a careful functional assessment as well. Examining the day-to-day experiences of the client during a "typical" week is likely to reveal circumstances under which the client is likely to do particularly well or to experience stressors that may be associated with crises or deteriorated functioning. Antecedents to potential problems may include conflict with family members, acquaintances, coworkers, or others in the community; depression or anxiety associated with trauma-related symptoms (e.g., flash-backs, reexperiencing); abuse of alcohol or other drugs; and exacerbation of symptoms as a result of noncompliance. These difficulties can easily escalate into serious crises that may require emergency intervention, police involve-ment, or hospitalization. By learning self-monitoring skills as part of the ongoing assessment, clients can begin to link these experiences with the potential for decompensation, and perhaps identify emotional upset, dis-couragement, suicidal thoughts, anger, conflict, or other troubling experi-ences as "warning signals" to seek social supports or to contact someone on their mental health team to reduce the likelihood of further problems. The functional analysis can also identify areas of opportunity in which clients can practice their social and other coping skills to reduce the likelihood of crises and enhance their sense of self-efficacy, confidence, and overall well-being.

Assessment of Cognitive Impairments

In addition to lack of insight (awareness and understanding of their illness), people with schizophrenia often suffer from serious cognitive impairments. Cognitive impairments refer to problems in attention, memory, and informa-tion processing in general, and they predict functional impairments, includ-ing difficulties finding and retaining employment and housing, as well as establishing stable social relationships in the community (Harvey, 2011; McGurk, Twamley, Sitzer, McHugo, & Mueser, 2007). Noting the lack of a clin-ically practical and valid tool for evaluating cognitive impairments in the field, Hurford, Marder, Keefe, Reise, and Bilder (2011) combined elements of preexisting measures to develop the Brief Cognitive Assessment Tool for Schizophrenia (B-CATS). They found three tests to provide a reliable and valid test of cognitive ability: (1) the digit-symbol substitution test, in which clients pair numbers with a unique symbol by copying the pairings from an accompanying sheet; (2) the trail-making test, whereby clients link numbers and letter sequences in order with a pencil in a continuous effort (i.e., not lifting the pencil); (3) and the category-fluency test, in which clients list as many items per category (e.g., animals, plants) as they can in one minute. These tests have been shown to correlate strongly with a battery of more comprehensive neurological tests. These data enable clinicians with a mini-mum of training to administer the test and obtain readily interpretable results. Recommendations can then be made for cognitive remediation treat-ment, which is reviewed later in this chapter.

Instruments

Part of the MFS assessment should also include the use of instruments to enhance the qualitative assessment and provide a baseline for evaluation. There are several brief scales for measuring psychiatric symptoms and social functioning in persons with serious mental illnesses. Some focus on one specific domain (e.g., mental status, social functioning), whereas others cover various domains, including mental status, social well-being, community functioning, health, and other important areas. Some of these instruments can be used repeatedly (e.g., every 6 months) to track changes and monitor progress over time.

A number of instruments are suitable for use with people who have been diagnosed with serious mental illness. These include the Brief Psychiatric Rating Scale (BPRS) (Lachar et al., 2001), and the Positive and Negative Syndrome Scale (PANSS) (Kay, Fiszbein, & Opler, 1987), both of which are considered among the best measures of primary symptoms of schizophrenia. The Brief Symptom Inventory (BSI) (Derogatis & Melisaratos, 1983) is also well regarded but focuses on a wider range of psychiatric and psychological symptoms, beyond those experienced in people with schizophrenia. The Behavior and Symptom Identification Scale (BASIS-24) (Eisen, Dill, & Grob, 1994; Eisen, Normand, Belanger, Spiro, & Esch, 2004) is a practical tool that focuses on key areas of clinical concern: psychosis, depression, mood dysregulation, interpersonal relations, thoughts of self-harm, and substance abuse. All these scales have been extensively tested for reliability and validity. The Role Functioning Scale (RFS) (Goodman, Sewell, Cooley, & Leavitt, 1993) targets four distinct areas often overlooked in assessment: work productivity, independent living and self-care, immediate social network relationships, and extended social network relationships. Results of preliminary psychometric testing with 79 low-income African American women revealed excellent internal consistency and adequate test-retest reliability for this brief four-item scale. The RFS also predicted clients' diagnostic status and correlated as expected with other psychiatric- and role-functioning scales.

Other important measures include quality-of-life questionnaires (for a review, see Nieuwenhuizen, Schene, Boevink, & Wolf, 1997). Quality of life is understood to be a multidimensional concept that includes access to resources, as well as fulfillment and satisfaction in various social roles. One well-regarded example is Lehman's (1988) Quality of Life Interview (QLI), which has 143 items covering the following domains: living situation, family and social relations, leisure, work and religious activity, finances, safety, and health. The QLI takes about 45 minutes to complete, and it can be used with relatively little training. Subsequent confirmatory factor analysis strongly supported both the reliability and the validity of the scale (Lehman, McNary, & O'Grady, 1997).

Although conducting formal assessment and diagnosis of a client with serious mental illness requires advanced expertise (particularly if neurological impairments are suspected), a social worker with training and experience in conducting mental status exams can become proficient as well. Since recommendations for medications are often the purpose of a mental status exam, close collaboration with the client's psychiatrist is essential.

The Brief Psychiatric Rating Scale (BPRS; instrument 5.1) has been a mainstay in psychiatric assessment for more than 50 years and has undergone some revision over time (Lachar et al., 2001; Overall & Gorham, 1962; Roy-Byrne et al., 1995). The BPRS-A (anchored version) has acquired a solid record of reliability, validity, and utility in assessing clients for severity of psychiatric symptoms. One study with 3,000 hospitalized psychiatric clients (Lachar et al., 2001) demonstrated that the BPRS has good factorial validity, internal consistency, and interrater reliabilities for each of its subscales. Moreover, subscales of the BPRS add significantly to predictions of hospital length of stay (Hopko, Lachar, Bailley, & Varner, 2001), and scores are sensitive to clinical change (Bailley et al., 2004).

Instrument 5.1   BRIEF PSYCHIATRIC RATING SCALE-ANCHORED (BPRS-A)

Date of 24–48 Hours Rating: ___/___/___

Directions: The BPRS-A will be completed within 48 hours of admission (rate from initial interviews). Place one check mark to indicate the most descriptive BPRS-A level (1 through 7) for each dimension.

1. Somatic Concern: Degree of concern over present bodily health. Rate the degree to which physical health is perceived as a problem by the patient, whether the complaints have a realistic basis or not. Do not rate mere reporting of somatic symptoms. Rate only concern for (or worrying about) physical problems (real or imagined). [Rating based primarily on verbal report.]

1____**Not Reported**
2____**Very Mild:** Occasionally is somewhat concerned about body, symptoms, or physical illness
3____**Mild:** Occasionally is moderately concerned about body, or often is somewhat concerned
4____**Moderate:** Occasionally is very concerned, or often is moderately concerned
5____**Moderately Severe:** Often is very concerned
6____**Severe:** Is very concerned most of the time.
7____**Very Severe:** Is very concerned nearly all of the time

2. Anxiety: Worry, fear, or over concern for present or future. Rate solely on the basis of verbal report of patient's own subjective experiences. Do not infer anxiety from physical signs or from neurotic defense mechanisms. Do not rate if restricted to somatic concern. [Rating based primarily on verbal report.]

1____**Not Reported**
2____**Very Mild:** Occasionally feels somewhat anxious
3____**Mild:** Occasionally feels moderately anxious, or often feels somewhat anxious

4_____**Moderate:** Occasionally feels very anxious, or often feels moderately anxious

5_____**Moderately Severe:** Often feels very anxious

6_____**Severe:** Feels very anxious most of the time

7_____**Very Severe:** Feels very anxious nearly all of the time

3. Emotional Withdrawal: Deficiency in relating to the interviewer and to the interview situation. Overt manifestations of this deficiency include poor/absence of eye contact, failure to orient oneself physically toward the interviewer, a general lack of involvement or engagement in the interview. Distinguish from BLUNTED AFFECT, in which deficits in facial expression, body gesture, and voice pattern are scored. [Rating based primarily on observation.]

1_____**Not Observed**

2_____**Very Mild:** E.g., occasionally exhibits poor eye contact

3_____**Mild:** E.g., as above, but more frequent

4_____**Moderate:** E.g., exhibits little eye contact, but still seems engaged in the interview and is appropriately responsive to all questions

5_____**Moderately Severe:** E.g., stares at floor or orients self away from interviewer, but still seems moderately engaged

6_____**Severe:** E.g., as above, but more persistent or pervasive

7_____**Very Severe:** E.g., appears "spacey" or "out of it" (total absence of emotional elatedness), and is disproportionately uninvolved or unengaged in the interview. (Do not score if explained by disorientation.)

4. Conceptual Disorganization: Degree of speech incomprehensibility. Include any type of formal thought disorder (e.g., loose associations, incoherence, flight of ideas, neologisms). DO NOT include mere circumstantiality or pressured speech, even if marked. DO NOT rate on the patient's subjective impressions (e.g., "My thoughts are racing. I can't hold a thought." "My thinking gets all mixed up"). Rate ONLY on the basis of observations made during the interview.

1_____**Not Observed**

2_____**Very Mild:** E.g., Somewhat vague, but of doubtful clinical significance

3_____**Mild:** Frequently vague, but the interview is able to progress smoothly; occasional loosening of associations

4_____**Moderate:** E.g., Occasional irrelevant statements, infrequent use of neologisms, or moderate loosening of associations

5_____**Moderately Severe:** As above, but more frequent

6_____**Severe:** Formal thought disorder is present for most of the interview, and the interview is severely strained

7_____**Very Severe:** Very little coherent information can be obtained

5. Guilt Feelings: Overconcern or remorse for past behavior. Rate on the basis of the patient's subjective experiences of guilt as evidenced by verbal report. Do not infer guilt feelings from depression, anxiety, or neurotic defenses. [Rating based primarily on verbal report.]

1_____**Not Reported**

2_____**Very Mild:** Occasionally feels somewhat guilty

3_____**Mild:** Occasionally feels moderately guilty, or often feels somewhat guilty

4____**Moderate:** Occasionally feels very guilty, or often feels moderately guilty

5____**Moderately Severe:** Often feels very guilty.

6____**Severe:** Feels very guilty most of the time, or encapsulated delusion of guilt

7____**Very Severe:** Agonizing constant feelings of guilt, or pervasive delusions(s) of guilt

6. Tension: Rate motor restlessness (agitation) *observed* during the interview. DO NOT rate on the basis of subjective experiences reported by the patient. Disregard suspected pathogenesis (e.g., tardive dyskinesia).

1____**Not Observed**

2____**Very Mild:** Occasionally fidgets

3____**Mild:** E.g., frequently fidgets

4____**Moderate:** E.g., frequently fidgets, wrings hands and pulls clothing

5____**Moderately Severe:** E.g., constantly fidgets, wrings hands and pulls clothing

6____**Severe:** E.g., cannot remain seated (i.e., must pace)

7____**Very Severe:** E.g., paces in a frantic manner

7. Mannerisms and Posturing: Unusual and unnatural motor behavior. Rate only abnormality of movements. Do not rate simple heightened motor activity here. Consider frequency, duration, and degree of bizarreness. Disregard suspected pathogenesis. [Rating based on observation.]

1____**Not Observed.**

2____**Very Mild:** Odd behavior but of doubtful clinical significance, e.g., occasional unprompted smiling, infrequent lip movements.

3____**Mild:** Strange behavior but not obviously bizarre, e.g., infrequent head-tilting (from side to side) in a rhythmic fashion, intermittent abnormal finger movements

4____**Moderate:** E.g., assumes unnatural position for a brief period of time, infrequent tongue protrusions, rocking, facial grimacing

5____**Moderately Severe:** E.g., assumes and maintains unnatural position throughout interview, unusual movements in several body areas

6____**Severe:** As above, but more frequent, intense, or pervasive

7____**Very Severe:** E.g., bizarre posturing throughout most of the interview, continuous abnormal movements in several body areas

8. Grandiosity: Inflated self-esteem (self-confidence), or inflated appraisal of one's talents, powers, abilities, accomplishments, knowledge, importance, or identity. Do not score mere grandiose quality of claims (e.g., "I'm the worst sinner in the world," "The entire country is trying to kill me") unless the guilt and/or persecution is related to some special exaggerated attributes of the individual. Also, *the patient* must claim exaggerated attributes: e.g., if patient denies talents, powers, etc., even if he/she states that others indicate that he/she has these attributes, this should not be reported. [Rating based primarily on verbal report.]

1____**Not Reported**

2____**Very Mild:** E.g., is more confident than most people, but of only possible clinical significance

3____**Mild:** E.g., definitely inflated self-esteem or exaggerates talents somewhat out of proportion to the circumstances

4____**Moderate:** E.g., inflated self-esteem clearly out of proportion to the circumstances, or suspected grandiose delusion(s)

5____**Moderately Severe:** E.g., a single (definite) encapsulated grandiose delusion, or multiple (definite) fragmentary grandiose delusions

6____**Severe:** E.g., a single (definite) grandiose delusion/delusional system, or multiple (definite) grandiose delusions that the patient seems preoccupied with

7____**Very Severe:** E.g., as above, but nearly all conversation directed towards the patient's grandiose delusion(s)

9. Depressive Mood: Subjective report of feeling depressed, blue, "down in the dumps," etc. Rate only degree of reported depression. Do not rate on the basis of inferences concerning depression based upon general retardation and somatic complaints. [Rating based primarily on verbal report.]

1____**Not Reported**

2____**Very Mild:** Occasionally feels somewhat depressed

3____**Mild:** Occasionally feels moderately depressed, or often feels somewhat depressed

4____**Moderate:** Occasionally feels very depressed, or often feels moderately depressed

5____**Moderately Severe:** Often feels very depressed

6____**Severe:** Feels very depressed most of the time

7____**Very Severe:** Feels very depressed nearly all of the time

10. Hostility: Animosity, contempt, belligerence, disdain for other people outside the interview situation. Rate solely on the basis of the verbal report of feelings and actions of the patient toward others. Do not infer hostility from neurotic defenses, anxiety or somatic complaints.

1____**Not Reported**

2____**Very Mild:** Occasionally feels somewhat angry

3____**Mild:** Often feels somewhat angry, or occasionally feels moderately angry

4____**Moderate:** Occasionally feels very angry, or often feels moderately angry

5____**Moderately Severe:** Often feels very angry

6____**Severe:** Has acted on his anger by becoming verbally or physically abusive on one or two occasions.

7____**Very Severe:** Has acted on his/her anger on several occasions

11. Suspiciousness: Belief (delusional or otherwise) that others have now, or have had in the past, malicious or discriminatory intent toward the patient. On the basis of verbal report, rate only those suspicions which are currently held whether they concern past or present circumstance.

1____**Not Reported**

2____**Very Mild:** Rare instance of distrustfulness which may or may not be warranted by the situation

3____**Mild:** Occasional instances of suspiciousness that are definitely not warranted by the situation

4_____**Moderate:** More frequent suspiciousness, or transient ideas of reference

5_____**Moderately Severe:** Pervasive suspiciousness, frequent ideas of reference, or an encapsulated delusion

6_____**Severe:** Definite delusion(s) of reference or persecution that is (are) not wholly pervasive (e.g., an encapsulated delusion)

7_____**Very Severe:** As above, but more widespread, frequent, or intense

12. Hallucinatory Behavior: Perceptions (in any sense modality) in the absence of an identifiable external stimulus. Rate only those experiences that have occurred during this rating period. DO NOT rate "Voices in my head" or "Visions in my mind" unless the patient can differentiate between these experiences and his or her thoughts. [Rating based primarily on verbal report.]

1_____**Not Reported**

2_____**Very Mild:** Suspected hallucinations only

3_____**Mild:** Definite hallucinations, but insignificant, infrequent, or transient (e.g., occasional formless visual hallucinations, a voice calling the patient's name)

4_____**Moderate:** As above, but more frequent or extensive (e.g., frequently sees the devil's face, two voices carry on lengthy conversations)

5_____**Moderately Severe:** Hallucinations are experienced nearly every day, or are a source of extreme distress

6_____**Severe:** As above and has had a moderate impact on the patient's behavior (e.g., concentration difficulties leading to impaired work functioning)

7_____**Very Severe:** As above, and has had a severe impact (e.g., attempts suicide in response to command hallucinations)

13. Motor Retardation: Reduction in energy level evidenced in slowed movements. Rate on the basis of observed behavior of the patient only. Do not rate on the basis of the patient's subjective impression of his or her own energy level.

1_____**Not Observed**

2_____**Very Mild** and of doubtful clinical significance.

3_____**Mild:** E.g., conversation is somewhat retarded, movements somewhat slowed

4_____**Moderate:** E.g., conversation is notably retarded but not strained

5_____**Moderately Severe:** E.g., conversation is strained, moves very slowly

6_____**Severe:** E.g., conversation is difficult to maintain, hardly moves at all

7_____**Very Severe:** E.g., conversation is almost impossible, does not move at all throughout the interview

14. Uncooperativeness: Evidence of resistance, unfriendliness, resentment, and lack of readiness to cooperate with the interviewer. Rate only on the basis of the patient's attitude and responses to the interviewer and the interview situation. Do not rate on the basis of reported resentment or uncooperativeness outside the interview situation.

1_____**Not Observed**

2_____**Very Mild:** E.g., does not seem motivated

3_____**Mild:** E.g., seems evasive in certain areas

4____**Moderate:** E.g., monosyllabic, fails to elaborate spontaneously, somewhat unfriendly

5____**Moderately Severe:** E.g., expresses resentment and is unfriendly throughout the interview

6____**Severe:** E.g., refuses to answer a number of questions

7____**Very Severe:** E.g., refuses to answer most questions

15. Unusual Thought Content: Severity of delusions of any type—consider conviction, and effect on actions. Assume full conviction if patient has acted on his or her beliefs. [Rating based primarily on verbal report.]

1____**Not Reported**

2____**Very Mild:** Delusion(s) suspected or likely

3____**Mild:** At times, patient questions his or her belief(s) (partial delusion)

4____**Moderate:** Full delusional conviction, but delusion(s) has little or no influence on behavior

5____**Moderately Severe:** Full delusional conviction, but delusion(s) has only occasional impact on behavior

6____**Severe:** Delusion(s) has significant effect, e.g., neglects responsibilities because of preoccupation with belief that he/she is God

7____**Very Severe:** E.g., delusion(s) has major impact, e.g. stops eating because believes food is poisoned

16. Blunted Affect: Diminished affective responsivity, as characterized by deficits in facial expression, body gesture, and voice pattern. Distinguish from EMOTIONAL WITHDRAWAL, in which the focus is on interpersonal impairment rather than affect. Consider degree and consistency of impairment. [Rating based on observations made during interview.]

1____**Not Observed**

2____**Very Mild:** E.g., occasionally seems indifferent to material that is usually accompanied by some show of emotion

3____**Mild:** E.g., somewhat diminished facial expression, or somewhat monotonous voice or somewhat restricted gestures

4____**Moderate:** E.g., as above, but more intense, prolonged, or frequent

5____**Moderately Severe:** E.g., flattening of affect, including at least two of the three features: severe lack of facial expression, monotonous voice, or restricted body gestures

6____**Severe:** E.g., profound flattening of affect

7____**Very Severe:** E.g., totally monotonous voice, and total lack of expressive gestures throughout the evaluation

17. Excitement: Heightened emotional tone, including irritability and expansiveness (hypomanic affect). Do not infer affect from statements of grandiose delusions. [Rating based on observations made during interview.]

1____**Not Observed**

2____**Very Mild** and of doubtful clinical significance

3____**Mild:** E.g., irritable or expansive at times

4____**Moderate:** E.g., frequently irritable or expansive

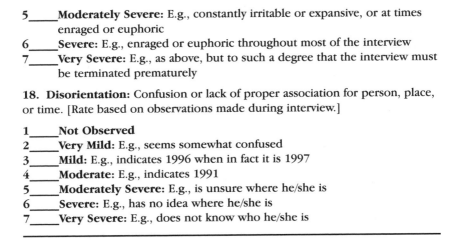

5_____**Moderately Severe:** E.g., constantly irritable or expansive, or at times enraged or euphoric

6_____**Severe:** E.g., enraged or euphoric throughout most of the interview

7_____**Very Severe:** E.g., as above, but to such a degree that the interview must be terminated prematurely

18. Disorientation: Confusion or lack of proper association for person, place, or time. [Rate based on observations made during interview.]

1_____**Not Observed**

2_____**Very Mild:** E.g., seems somewhat confused

3_____**Mild:** E.g., indicates 1996 when in fact it is 1997

4_____**Moderate:** E.g., indicates 1991

5_____**Moderately Severe:** E.g., is unsure where he/she is

6_____**Severe:** E.g., has no idea where he/she is

7_____**Very Severe:** E.g., does not know who he/she is

Individual subscale scores (rather than a global score) should be used for assessment and evaluation purposes. Based on an examination of factor structure (Lachar et al., 2001), the four subscales included resistance (i.e., grandiosity, hostility, uncooperativeness, excitement), positive symptoms (i.e., conceptual disorganization, suspiciousness, hallucinations, unusual thought content, disorientation), negative symptoms (i.e., blunted affect, emotional withdrawal, motor retardation), and psychological discomfort (i.e., somatic concern, anxiety, guilt feelings, tension, depressed mood). "Mannerisms and posturing" is not currently factored into any subscale. (Each item of this 18-item scale is scored from 1, "not reported/not observed," to "7, very severe.")

Assessment with Mentally Ill Clients Who Abuse Alcohol and Other Drugs

Reviews of the assessment literature on persons who experience both mental illness and substance abuse reveal a pattern of underdetection in daily practice (Drake et al., 1993; Drake & Mueser, 1996; Drake & Wallach, 2000). Since most assessment strategies and techniques have both strengths and limitations, a multidimensional approach that includes both qualitative interviewing and quantitative instruments is recommended. The clinical interview involves the following areas of thorough investigation:

- Determining the type, quantity, and frequency of specific substances used

- Examining the temporal history related to the course of substance use and the onset of schizophrenia

- Taking a detailed family history of mental health and substance abuse problems

- Tentatively sorting out any cause-effect relationships between substance abuse and mental health problems up to the present time (although this can be a time-consuming and difficult task, one can look for psychosocial and physiological correlates of substance use and important psychosocial problems or crises)

- Noting that other important factors associated with abuse may include demographics (e.g., gender, cultural background), alcohol expectancies (i.e., strong beliefs that alcohol or drugs are helpful in alleviating tensions or other problems), physiological and health indicators, social and environmental difficulties, abuse of prescription medication, trouble with the law, and other impulse-related problems.

In general, accurate retrospective information can be difficult to come by, and a period of client abstinence may be illuminating in sorting out the complex interplay of drugs and other psychiatric symptoms (Brems & Johnson, 1997; Buckstein, Brent, & Kaminer, 1989).

Given the critical importance of assessing and monitoring substance abuse problems, it is important for practitioners to incorporate the use of brief measures to gauge clients' involvement with alcohol and other drugs. Although lab tests, self-report, observation of physical signs and symptoms, and use of collateral information are all valuable sources of assessment data, practitioners should not overlook one of the most effective methods for detecting substance abuse problems in persons with mental illness: the use of simple paper-and-pencil screening tools (Wolford et al., 1999). The Alcohol Use Scale (AUS) and the Drug Use Scale (DUS) are single-item, clinician-rated indexes of alcohol and drug abuse (Carey, Cocco, & Simons, 1996; Drake, McHugo et al. 1998; Mueser, Noordsy, Drake, & Fox, 2003). Responses to the one-item AUS and DUS (done separately for alcohol and drugs, respectively) are as follows

- Abstinent
- Use without impairment
- Abuse
- Dependence
- Dependence with institutionalization

Although the DSM-5 downplays the distinction between abuse and dependence, the AUS and/or DUS can still be used as a practical measure to suggest severity of the problem. Also recent evidence has suggested that simple substance abuse indexes correlate well with more extensive batteries (Carey et al., 1996; Drake, McHugo et al., 1998) and should be included as part of a brief, multidimensional assessment.

Assessing readiness to change in clients who abuse alcohol or other drugs (O'Hare, 2002) has become an expected part of a substance use assessment. This assessment model has been accompanied by more gradual and flexible approaches to setting treatment goals through motivational interviews and harm reduction approaches (Drake, Rosenberg, & Mueser, 1996; Osher & Kofoed, 1989). This staged assessment approach to intervention is reflected in the Substance Abuse Treatment Scale (SATS) (see McHugo, Drake, Burton, & Ackerson, 1995), which can also be used to monitor clients' treatment progress. These stages are as follows:

- Preengagement
- Engagement
- Early persuasion
- Late persuasion
- Early active treatment
- Late active treatment
- Relapse prevention
- Remission or recovery

Psychometric evaluation of the SATS reveals good to excellent test-retest and interrater reliabilities, as well as good concurrent validity between researchers and case managers. Revised versions of the AUS, DUS, and SATS are available to clinicians in *Integrated Treatment for Dual Disorders: A Guide to Effective Practice* (Mueser et al., 2003).

In addition to these brief indexes, other "mainstream" substance abuse instruments have been shown to be reliable when used with people who have a severe mental illness. The Alcohol Use Disorders Identification Test (AUDIT) (Saunders, Aasland, Babor, de la Fuente, & Grant, 1993) (which is discussed in more detail in chapter 7) has been shown to be valid when used with persons who have serious mental illnesses, although cut points lower than the standard cut score of 8 have been suggested for this population (e.g., O'Hare, Sherrer, LaButti, & Emrick, 2004).

In summary, conducting a thorough and valid assessment with persons who have severe mental illness presents a considerable challenge. Many types and sources of data are required, including through the use of both qualitative and quantitative methods, and a thoughtful summary of the information also requires considered judgment regarding which problems are to be addressed first, and which intervention methods are to be employed.

SELECTING EFFECTIVE INTERVENTIONS

Despite advances in medications for the mentally ill, pharmacotherapy alone is often not sufficient to help increase clients' overall psychosocial well-being or improve their overall adjustment in the community (Dixon et al., 2010; Johnson, 1997; Kaplan & Sadock, 1998; Kreyenbuhl, Buchanan, Dickerson, &

Dixon, 2010; Mueser, Drake, & Bond, 1997). The preponderance of outcome research on psychosocial interventions with persons suffering from schizophrenia can be roughly classified into three major categories that reviewers have collectively deemed efficacious practices: assertive case management, a range of cognitive-behavioral coping skills approaches (alone and in combination), and psychoeducation and behavior therapy with families (Dixon et al., 2010; Falloon et al., 1998; Huxley, Rendall, & Sederer, 2000; Kreyenbuhl et al., 2010; Lehman, Steinwachs, & Co-Investigators of the PORT Project, 1998; Mueser, Deavers, Penn, & Cassisi, 2013). Other approaches have shown increasing evidence of effectiveness as well: supported housing and supported employment, cognitive remediation, and integrated mental health and substance misuse intervention, among others (Dixon et al., 2010; Mueser, Deavers et al., 2013). Because there is a robust body of research in some of these areas, summaries of findings from controlled investigations are presented here along with exemplar studies and descriptions of the interventions. General comprehensive critical reviews of the literature have been used as sources for this summary, with an emphasis on controlled studies, though findings are supplemented with uncontrolled studies when randomized designs are sparse.

Assertive Community Treatment

The case management movement has developed in response to initiatives in the 1960s of the National Institute of Mental Health (Drake, 1998; Stein & Test, 1980) and has evolved into variations on the Programs for Assertive Community Treatment (PACT) model, such as mobile treatment teams and intensive community treatment programs. Such programs are typically marked by the coordination of comprehensive services provided by a multidisciplinary team, with 24-hour coverage for open-ended treatment, and (ideally) a low (e.g., 10:1) client-to-staff ratio. Assertive community treatment programs focus on efforts to prevent relapse and rehospitalization, and enhance psychosocial functioning in seriously mentally ill clients. Case management is a key coordinating element in the system and is meant to orchestrate seamless integration of service components. Over the course of the history of the case management movement, however, the system has been marked by various degrees of fragmentation (Drake, 1998; Mechanic, 1996; Mueser, Bond, Drake, & Resnick, 1998; Solomon, 1992) and has often not lived up to its potential.

Reviews of case management literature in the 1980s concluded that research efforts were in their infancy and characterized relevant data as "sparse and contradictory" (Anthony & Blanch, 1989). However, there is now a substantial body of controlled evaluation research on assertive case management with the mentally ill. Although there are considerable methodological weaknesses, there are some relatively consistent findings based on numerous reviews of controlled studies. In general, assertive case management programs (mostly derivatives of the PACT model) have been shown to reduce hospitalization. There is some additional evidence that case management also has resulted in better treatment adherence, increased employment, increased social contact, increased life satisfaction, some reduction in symptoms (perhaps through medication compliance), increased family and patient satisfaction, improved social functioning, and improved residential stability and independent living. Some limited evidence suggests that time in jail may also be reduced (Burns & Santos, 1995; Dixon et al., 2010; Draine, 1997; Kreyenbuhl et al., 2010; Mueser et al., 1997; Mueser et al. 1998; Rubin, 1992; Scott & Dixon, 1995; Solomon, 1992).

Exemplar Study: An Experimental Comparison of PACT versus Broker-Style Case Management

In one experimental study (Morse, Calsyn, Klinkenberg, Trusty et al., 1997), two conditions of assertive case management (i.e., one with the addition of paraprofessional community workers) were compared with brokered case management. The study included 135 of 165 originally selected participants, who were randomly assigned to the three treatment groups. All had serious mental illnesses and were eligible for social service benefits. The experimental treatment was a form of assertive case management in which workers were responsible for treatment coordination with assertive follow-up, treatment was conducted in the community with a client-to-staff ratio of 10 to 1, and no time limits were placed on services. Practitioners cultivated a positive working relationship with clients, emphasized practical problem solving, enhanced community-living skills, provided supportive services, assisted with money management, and facilitated transportation. One assertive case management condition included having paraprofessional community workers spend additional time with clients. In contrast, brokered case management (the comparison group) focused on developing treatment plans and purchasing services from various agencies. Client-to-staff ratio was 85 to 1. Treatment process measures accounted for service activities in housing; employment; job training; financial assistance; and legal, mental health, substance abuse, health, and supportive services. Outcome measures included client satisfaction, income, stability of housing, psychiatric symptoms, and substance abuse. A 3 × 3 factorial design was employed (i.e., three treatment conditions with outcome measures taken over three time periods: 6, 12, and 18 months). Overall, assertive case management groups provided considerably more assistance (i.e., housing, finances, health, and support), and both assertive community treatment conditions resulted in greater satisfaction and better psychiatric ratings. There were no differences among the groups in substance abuse outcomes. It is worth noting that 33% of clients in the brokered group received no services at all, the addition of paraprofessionals in one assertive case management group made little difference overall, and cost differentials among groups were not calculated. The authors pointed out that this study was one of only a few that showed improvement in psychiatric symptoms in the experimental group.

Results of controlled studies of case management in general must be viewed with caution given some methodological weaknesses (see McHugo et al., 1998). These problems include the following:

- Inconsistent model conceptualization
- Inadequate sample size
- Lack of pretreatment data on clients
- Problems with random assignment of cases
- High rates of attrition from some studies
- Poor sensitivity to measuring changes over time
- Poor utilization of existing standardized instruments
- Violations of statistical assumptions and a lack of multivariate analysis
- Vague definitions of the interventions resulting in a lack of distinction among treatment conditions
- Lack of attention to intervention fidelity (i.e., faithfulness to the practice model)

Despite some evidence that intensive or assertive case management reduces hospitalization and, in some cases, improves levels of functioning, evidence suggests that cost-effectiveness advantages may be realized only if assertive case management is targeted at those clients *most at risk* or those most likely to benefit from the service (Essock, Frisman, & Kontos, 1998). In addition, despite some general positive effects of case management programs, it has been difficult to sort out the specific contributory effects of case management activities from overall treatment effects. However, some correlation data strongly suggest that case managers themselves have a positive effect on client outcomes in that their relationship with clients may make a discernible difference, even when types of service and client characteristics are statistically controlled (Ryan, Sherman, & Judd, 1994).

Although the community mental health model is primarily associated with Western approaches to mental health, particularly the United States, this model is gaining adherents in non-Western countries as well. For example, the psychosocial and physical needs of people with schizophrenia in India are great and exceed the unmet needs of their counterparts in the West (Kulhara et al., 2010). Chatterjee, Pillai, Jain, Cohen, and Patel (2009) conducted a longitudinal evaluation of a community mental health program (i.e., medication, medication adherence, psychoeducation, psychosocial rehabilitation, mutual help groups, vocational support) with 256 patients with mixed severe mental illnesses in rural India. At a median of 46 months follow-up, more than 90% showed substantial participation in treatment and considerable gains in community adjustment measures. Medication adherence and participation in support groups were associated with better gains. One outreach study near Bangalore recruited 100 people with untreated schizophrenia and demonstrated substantial reductions in symptoms and family burden after the implementation of pharmacological and psychosocial interventions (Murthy et al., 2005).

Although assertive community treatment can be considered a standalone program in its own right, it is increasingly viewed as a broad intervention framework for offering a growing range of services for people with schizophrenia and other severe mental illnesses.

Coping Skills Approaches

There is an eclectic array of evidence-based coping skills interventions and programs available for people with severe mental illnesses. In general, coping skills approaches include a somewhat overlapping group of interventions such as social skills training, and cognitive-behavioral interventions, and they are often incorporated into broader rehabilitation packages, such as illness, management, and recovery and assertive community treatment programs. Coping skills approaches have evolved from a number of therapeutic traditions, including counseling, psychoeducation, cognitive and behavioral therapies, problem-solving and communications training, and psychosocial rehabilitation models. Coping skills approaches can also be applied to a range of different problems associated with severe mental illness (e.g., PTSD, substance abuse). When focused on specific interpersonal or situational problems, coping skills treatments have shown substantial benefits, and often long-lasting results, and they have been effectively adapted for people from different cultural backgrounds (Dixon et al., 2010; Kreyenbuhl et al., 2010).

In general, coping skills approaches share several key ingredients to some degree:

- Nurturing of a sound therapeutic relationship
- Motivational enhancement
- Problem identification and teaching self-monitoring skills
- Appraisal of cognitive dysfunction
- Teaching of new skills via role-play, modeling, and practice with corrective feedback
- Graduated exposure and practice to disconfirm irrational or unfounded beliefs and expectancies

- Stress management (e.g., physically focused tension reduction exercises, anxiety management)
- Skill development in dealing with interpersonal and community relationships (e.g., communication skills training)
- Community-based support, reinforcement, guidance, and consistent follow-up—coordinated by skillful case management

Exemplar Study: Evaluation of an Eclectic Coping Skills Program

A controlled study of a structured group intervention with persons with schizophrenia provides a good example of one coping skills approach (Bradshaw, 1996). This eclectic intervention consists of four modules: anxiety management, time management, cognitive restructuring, and social skills training. The rationale of the intervention was to improve overall psychosocial functioning and prevent relapse (including rehospitalization). Sixteen clients (two later dropped out) were randomly assigned to two interventions: the experimental group (coping skills) and a comparison or control group (problem solving). The experimental intervention included the following:

- Development of treatment goals specific to each client
- Relaxation training (physically oriented relaxation methods to reduce anxiety)
- Time management (self-monitoring to identify stressful situations and pleasurable activities)
- Planned activities intended to be constructive and enjoyable, and geared toward increasing social supports that would mitigate stress
- Cognitive restructuring (thought stopping, developing constructive self-statements in response to troubling thoughts)
- Learning additional coping skills to deal with anticipated stressful situations through modeling, role-play, practice, and self-reinforcement techniques
- Learning social skills (e.g., identification of a specific deficiency in a social skill, goal setting, modeling, role-play, practice, evaluation of performance)

The intervention was conducted in the context of a structured group approach, in part, to take advantage of socialization aspects of group interaction. The problem-solving group (i.e., the comparison or control group), in contrast, required more initiative on the part of the clients to develop problem-solving methods, and group-process methods were not emphasized. Both groups met for 90-minute sessions for 24 weeks. Global attainment scaling, The Global Assessment of Functioning, rehospitalization, and time in the hospital were used as outcome measures. The coping skills group showed better goal attainment and fewer hospitalizations than the problem-solving group. Results, however, were only suggestive. The small sample size and the inability to infer which intervention components were effective (i.e., which specific skills in the overall treatment package had the most impact) preclude firm conclusions about the effectiveness of the treatment. Nevertheless, the study illustrates a thoughtful and innovative multimodal approach to a coping skills intervention for persons who have schizophrenia.

Cognitive-Behavior Therapy

There has been growing interest in the use of cognitive-behavior therapy (CBT) with persons who have schizophrenia (Alford & Correia, 1994; Kingdon & Turkington, 1991; Morrison, 2008). These approaches help clients directly analyze the dysfunctional cognitions (e.g., delusions, other anxieties) and test out the validity of those beliefs in the context of a supportive and collaborative relationship with practitioners. CBT can be an effective part of an overall coping skills strategy as well. Alford and Correia (1994) summarize the basic steps of CBT:

- The problematic belief is identified.
- Clients are encouraged to keep a log and further examine the belief, and rate their level of conviction for the belief.
- Beliefs are then examined for content, and discussions ensue regarding the reasons for and plausibility of the beliefs.
- The practitioner encourages "distancing" (i.e., help clients see the disturbing thought more objectively) to help them gain perspective on the belief.
- Clients are encouraged to consider another perspective or alternative reaction to the specific belief.
- Alternative explanations for the belief are generally explored.
- Clients may be encouraged, as part of the intervention, to test out these beliefs and examine evidence that confirms or disconfirms the belief.
- Monitoring and evaluation of the client's progress is essential.

Kingdon and Turkington (1991) conducted an exploratory (qualitative) investigation of the effectiveness of cognitive therapy with 64 patients with schizophrenia. The intervention focused on psychoeducation to help clients rationally examine some of their psychosocial experiences; normalize some of those perceptions, thoughts, and experiences; help correct faulty cognitions (e.g., "I am being controlled by alien beings"); and use homework assignments to test out the validity of some of their troubling beliefs. Stress management techniques were taught to deal with anxiety and help de-catastrophize specific fears. Clients were helped to cope with family emotional responses, and use support groups, and were encouraged to accept medication. Although the study was not a controlled comparison, results were quite promising. Clients achieved good results and showed genuine acceptance of the treatment, and the intervention was used safely with relatively low doses of medication. Hospitalization occurred less often, and clients reported acceptable levels of psychological symptoms and social well-being.

Recently, some randomized trials have been conducted with cognitive-behavior therapy. A controlled trial of 144 persons with schizophrenia (or related disorder) was carried out for a 12-month period (Gumley et al., 2003). During that time, a five-session engagement phase was introduced, followed by two to three sessions per week when a client showed evidence of possible relapse. The CBT intervention (combined with treatment as usual and compared to a separate treatment-as-usual control condition) focused on an examination of cognitive and emotional "triggers" associated with possible relapse and helped clients increase self-efficacy through enhancing their coping skills to maintain medication compliance and avoid relapse. After 12 months it was evident that those in the CBT condition were about half as likely to relapse or be hospitalized, and general psychosocial well-being improved significantly. Rector, Seeman, and Segal (2003) carried out a randomized control trial (RCT) with a smaller sample ($n = 42$) by similarly adding CBT to treatment as usual, yet their study failed to demonstrate significant effects post-treatment for CBT. Last, meta-analyses underscore the early stage of research with cognitive therapies for seriously mentally ill persons, but suggest that results to date should be considered promising. However, more recent reviews, including two meta-analyses, suggest that the effects of cognitive-behavior therapy on severe mental illness are quite positive and enduring, with low dropout rates (Pilling, Bebbington, Kuipers, Garety, Geddes, Orbach et al., 2002; Zimmermann, Favrod, Trieu, & Pomini, 2005). Results appear fairly consistent, showing reductions in positive and negative symptoms, and improvements in social functioning, although some studies have not found these results. In addition, there is less evidence for the effectiveness of CBT on suicide risk and relapse, rehospitalization, or for relief of onset or acute exacerbation of schizophrenia (Dixon et al., 2010; Kreyenbuhl et al., 2010).

There also is some evidence that cognitive-behavioral interventions with people who have schizophrenia can be effectively delivered in group format with good long-term (12-month) effects (Penn et al., 2009); however, some studies suffer from poor methodological quality (Lawrence, Bradshaw, & Mairs, 2006). Recent findings that cognitive restructuring can help reduce PTSD symptoms in clients with severe mental illnesses (Mueser et al., 2008) underscore the need to better understand the links among dysfunctional cognitions, emotional distress, comorbid symptoms, and maladaptive coping behaviors. Positive coping strategies aimed at dealing with negative cognitions could be readily incorporated into multifaceted interventions for clients diagnosed with severe mental illness and PTSD (Frueh et al., 2009).

After noting that nonwhite people with psychiatric disorders often avoid or drop out of mental health services, Lu et al. (2009) conducted an uncontrolled test of cognitive-behavior therapy (psychoeducation, breathing retraining, cognitive restructuring) with 19 participants who had severe mental illnesses and met criteria for PTSD, half of whom were of minority background (African American and Hispanic). They found comparable reductions for minority clients in PTSD symptoms and comparable treatment retention rates as for white clients. These results add to the growing body of evidence that EBPs generalize very well to nonwhites.

Social Skills Training

A considerable amount of research has been conducted on social skills training. This is primarily the adaptation of traditional behavioral interventions that focus on the clients' ability to appraise and respond to social situations in a way that enhances their ability to relate to others, communicate effectively, and adapt better in the community. The need for improved social skills is based on the premise that one of the more debilitating problems for a mentally ill person is the ability to relate to others effectively. Well-documented reviews of the literature (Liberman, Kopelowicz, & Young, 1994; Mueser et al., 1997; Penn & Mueser, 1996; Pilling, Bebbington, Kuipers, Garety, Geddes, Martindale et al., 2002; Smith, Bellack, & Liberman, 1996) reveal that social skills training yields significant improvements in assertiveness and reductions in anxiety and other problems. A meta-analysis of 40 years of research on social skills training for people with schizophrenia supports the view that the approach substantially improves functional outcomes, including social adjustment and independent living (Kurtz & Mueser, 2008).

Exemplar Study: A Controlled Trial of Social Skills Training

Hayes, Halford, and Varghese (1995) compared social skills training for 63 persons who had schizophrenia with a supportive discussion group (control). Patients were assessed for level of social skills and anxiety in standardized role-plays in different interpersonal situations, and community functioning was assessed through the coding of client diary entries. Assessment also included the BPRS, the Global Assessment of Functioning, and a quality-of-life scale. Both treatments were conducted for 36 sessions of 75 minutes each over the course of 18 weeks. The skills group focused on standard behavioral approaches, including instructions in social skills, modeling, rehearsal, feedback, and structured homework tasks to generalize the results outside of the sessions. Therapists received 10 hours of specific instruction on the intervention methods. Thirty-seven participants completed the intervention, and 34 were assessed at follow-up. Although both groups showed improvements in psychiatric symptoms and quality of life, the social skills group showed greater improvement on some social skills measures. However, generalizations of gains were somewhat limited.

It is important to note the lack of research and evaluation on social skills training with clients from other cultures. The assumption that treatment goals are intended to result in independent living may be presumptuous in a culture where better integration with the family, extended family, and immediate community may be considered preferable. Behaviorally oriented social skills interventions might be modified for use with Latino families, for example, by incorporating culturally congruent staff and other helpers to facilitate better family and social adjustment (Kopelowicz, 1997). The goals may emphasize interdependence among family and other social supports rather than the independent functioning that may be more highly valued in "Anglo" families. Patterson et al. (2005) compared a culturally informed psychoeducational approach to a (randomized) control support group and found only modest improvements in daily functioning outcomes over 12-month follow-up, and no difference in psychopathology between the two groups. Although the authors considered the infusion of Latino cultural elements such as the importance of family, respect, and close relationships, they did not test whether these elements made any specific difference in outcomes.

Social skills training has been exported to countries outside the West. Conducting the first RCT of the Community Re-entry Module in China, Xiang et al. (2007) compared this social skills training program (psychoeducation regarding medication, stress and coping in the community, role-play, rehearsal, in vivo exercises, feedback) in an RCT with a more conventional psychoeducation approach over 24 months with a fairly large sample of clients with schizophrenia. Results revealed less severe symptoms, better social functioning, higher employment, and lower recidivism for the skills-based approach.

Assuming that practitioners have conducted a thorough multidimensional assessment, a more focused functional assessment is in order to specifically ascertain clients' strengths and deficits in being able to interact comfortably and competently with others in their social sphere. Bellack, Mueser, Gingerich, and Agresta (1997) posited four questions for guiding functional assessment before social skills training: (1) Does the client manifest some dysfunctional interpersonal behavior? This can be determined through observation of the client in various social circumstances and can be guided by some common sense regarding normal social behavior and discourse. (2) What are the specific circumstances in which the dysfunction occurs? Ideally, assessment should cover a range of circumstances, for example, with familiar acquaintances in a social club environment to more stressful circumstances (e.g., waiting in a long line at the supermarket, inquiring about a job opportunity, being challenged by a proprietor in the local coffee shop for acting "strangely"). (3) What is the probable source of the dysfunction? This can include severe shyness, depression, a lack of effective conversational skills, or distraction from obsessional thoughts or hallucinations. (4) What specific skill deficits does the client have? Difficulty in listening attentively or responding in a congruent way to "keep the conversation going"? Assessment interviewing techniques should include a good detailed history; observation of role-playing situations; and observation of the client in vivo, if possible.

Mueser et al. (1997) enumerated core intervention steps typically applied in social skills training. The practitioner should

- Provide a clear rationale for learning the skill
- Demonstrate the skill in a role-play with the client
- Collaborate with the client in a role-play of the skill
- Provide positive and corrective feedback about how well the client performed the skill
- Engage the client in additional role-plays followed by positive and corrective feedback
- Assign homework assignments for the client to practice the skill in real-life situations

These processes should be repeated and advanced gradually as the client gains confidence and demonstrates mastery of the technique. There are many variations on effective social skills training. Some social skills interventions may also include live modeling of the skill, videotape modeling, assertiveness training, communication and problem-solving skills, and increased social supports (Bedell et al., 1997; Liberman et al., 1994). Providing homework assignments for clients to practice on their own is also essential.

Illness, Management, and Recovery

Illness, management, and recovery (IMR) is a more recent development in the treatment of people with schizophrenia and other severe mental illnesses that emphasizes empowering clients to take more initiative in their own lifelong recovery. This approach is a good example of how multiple coping skills, some reviewed already, are often "packaged" into more comprehensive strategies. IMR is rooted to some degree in psychiatric rehabilitation methods. Similar to IMR, personal therapy, developed by Gerald Hogarty and colleagues (Hogarty, 2002; Hogarty et al., 1995), is a multifaceted coping skills approach that addresses mentally ill clients' problems in thinking, difficulties in expressing emotions, and behavioral deficits. Commensurate with the long-term goals of psychiatric rehabilitation, personal therapy requires a long-term commitment to a client; emphasizes the development of a strong therapeutic alliance; and incorporates a range of coping skills, including psychoeducation, self-monitoring, problem solving, communication skills, rehearsal, feedback, and homework (in vivo practice). Although few controlled studies have been done on personal therapy as a model, the components are well represented in other evidence-based approaches.

However, IMR has been more thoroughly researched (Mueser et al., 2002; Silverstein & Bellack, 2008). IMR emphasizes (in addition to medication and formal treatment) educating clients to take more personal initiative in managing their illness, with more emphasis on a collaborative relationship with treatment providers (e.g., shared decision making) and increased peer-assisted treatment management, and less emphasis on the hierarchical "doctor-patient" relationship. The concept of recovery (as a process) emphasizes the client's aspiration to set and pursue personal goals that make life more meaningful and de-emphasizes the "sick role." As such, the intent of IMR is to encourage clients to take on more personal responsibility for their treatment and to collaborate with them in using evidence-based methods as part of a comprehensive approach (Frese, Stanley, Kress, & Vogel-Scibilia, 2001; Liberman & Kopelowicz, 2005).

The research-supported components of IMR include psychoeducation and cognitive-behavioral techniques. These appear to improve medication adherence, reduce relapse (i.e., avoid hospitalization), and reduce symptoms (Mueser et al., 2002). Several controlled trials and quasi-experimental studies support IMR (McGuire et al., 2013). Furthermore, IMR programs can also include social skills training and supported employment (discussed later in this chapter). Yet generalizations about the effectiveness of IMR should be made with caution, given the heterogeneity of how these programs are implemented. Some have suggested that IMR and assertive community treatment can be integrated with an emphasis on client-peer assistants as part of the treatment teams (Salyers et al., 2010). More research is needed not only to define which recovery processes are most essential but also to determine the optimal mix of treatment components (Liberman & Kopelowicz, 2005; Mueser et al., 2002; Silverstein & Bellack, 2008). A few controlled trials in various countries have also shown IMR programs to be effective (Mueser & Gingerich, 2013a).

Interventions for Co-occurring Severe Mental Illness and Substance Abuse

Given that a large proportion of clients in treatment have a co-occurring substance abuse problem, it is essential to address that problem as a priority in the overall treatment plan. Fortunately, many of the coping skills approaches outlined here can be readily adapted to clients who also abuse alcohol and other drugs, with the understanding that a thorough assessment of substance abuse has been conducted. In addition, interventions with mentally ill persons who have substance abuse problems are better implemented if both conditions are addressed simultaneously in well-integrated treatment programs rather than treated sequentially (i.e., one after the other) or in parallel programs (Minkoff, 2000; Mueser & Gingerich, 2013b; Mueser et al., 2003).

Helping clients reduce their abuse or dependence on substances is a goal that can be directly and effectively addressed in the context of coping skills, family treatment, and case management interventions. The results of studies that have focused on the integration of these effective methods into an assertive case management framework appear promising. Although controlled investigations are few, they provide initial support for behaviorally oriented, long-term, integrated programs for reducing substance abuse and recidivism among the mentally ill (Blankertz & Cnaan, 1994; Herman et al., 2000; Jerrell & Ridgely, 1995; RachBeisel, Scott, & Dixon, 1999). Integrated substance abuse programs have resulted in better treatment engagement, better housing, and better overall adjustment than standard case management approaches (Drake, Mercer-McFadden, Mueser, Hugo, & Bond, 1998; Drake, McHugo et al., 1998; Drake, Yovetich, Bebout, Harris, & McHugo, 1997; Mueser et al., 1997). One meta-analysis of 15 controlled studies of interventions for persons with co-occurring disorders (Dumaine, 2003) provided good support for combined intensive case management and psychopharmacology.

Integrated treatment for co-occurring mental illness and substance use might include a combination of substance use screening, psychoeducation, motivational interviewing, harm-reduction treatment goals, relapse-prevention skills, coping-skills training, and contingency management (Tenhula, Bennett, & Kinnaman, 2009). Although the PORT committee unambiguously recommends providing substance use treatment in an integrated framework, methodological diversity among studies (e.g., diagnostically mixed samples; different mental health and/or substance use program configurations) makes specific evidence-based recommendations less than certain. Evidence provides moderate support for improved treatment attendance, reduced substance use and relapse, symptom improvement, and overall functioning. Recent studies suggest modest but clinically important improvements for clients overall. Baker et al. (2006) compared a combination of motivational interviewing and cognitive behavior therapy (10 sessions total) with treatment as usual in a relatively large sample of participants with severe mental illnesses ("psychotic disorders") and combinations of alcohol, cannabis, and other drug use. After 6- and 12-month follow-ups, the experimental group showed modest success, compared with no change in the treatment-as-usual group. Noting the lack of head-to-head comparisons between trained case managers and more experienced clinicians, Craig et al.'s (2008) study showed little differences in treatment outcomes with regard to substance use. Substance use outcomes have not been shown to be significant in some studies of integrated treatment. For example, in a randomized trial of integrated assertive community treatment versus a control group, Morse et al. (2006) showed no difference in substance use outcomes, although there were some cost savings in the integrated approach.

Attempts have also been made to incorporate substance abuse treatment into family approaches for dual disorders. Mueser, Glynn et al. (2013) tested a family intervention for dual disorders that emphasizes recovery from substance abuse within a psychoeducational and behavioral family therapy model. Although no significant differences were found in levels of substance use between the enhanced family approach and a brief family education control group, families did benefit from reduced stress and family burden. However, both groups did show improvements in psychiatric symptoms, substance abuse, and family functioning, thereby underscoring the feasibility and moderate effectiveness of family approaches to substance abuse reduction.

On the basis of the evidence to date, the following skills should minimally be included in an integrated program to address co-occurring substance abuse and serious mental disorders (Bellack & DiClemente, 1999; Carey, 1996a, 1996b; Mercer, Mueser, & Drake, 1998; Mueser et al., 2003; Osher & Kofoed, 1989):

- Development of a good working alliance that is marked by a nonjudgmental attitude about the use of substances
- Identification and monitoring of problematic thoughts, feelings, and situations that are associated with increased risk of drug use
- Helping clients make consistent connections between their psychosocial complaints and their substance use; gauging of the client's level of engagement and self-confidence (self-efficacy) in dealing with risky situations
- Use of motivational interviewing to engage clients in constructive change
- Application of interventions in a staged format (see SATS scale noted earlier)
- Provision of psychoeducation to teach clients about the negative consequences of use and to challenge their beliefs and expectancies regarding the use of substances
- Role-play of new skills with clients and in vivo practice (e.g., communication skills, stress management, substance use refusal skills)
- Provision of constructive feedback
- Enhancement of available social supports
- Generalization of their improved skills in the community to reduce and prevent relapse
- Teaching clients to monitor and evaluate their own progress by keeping a chart, log, or diary, and review of actual problem situations, their responses to them, and outcomes of their efforts

It is understood that there may be a considerable degree of "two steps forward, one step back" on the road to stable moderation or abstinence. As opposed to dichotomous goal setting (e.g., abstinence vs. failure), partial successes are encouraged and rewarded (Drake, Rosenberg, & Mueser, 1996; Osher & Kofoed, 1989). Clinical guidelines are readily available to help guide practitioners in implementing evidence-based strategies for their mentally ill clients who abuse substances (Bellack et al., 1997; Mueser et al., 2003; Roberts, Shaner, & Eckman, 1999).

Family Psychoeducational and Behavioral Interventions

Family psychoeducation and behavioral family therapy approaches overlap considerably. Although psychoeducation can be applied separately, psychoeducation and behavioral techniques are usually combined in some fashion. Treatments should last at least 6–9 months and include illness education, crisis intervention, emotional support, coping skills, communication skills, and problem solving. Practitioners work with the families of a person with severe mental illness to help them better understand the nature of mental illness; reduce self-blame; and learn coping skills to create a calmer atmosphere in the home, emphasize problem solving and improving communications, cope more effectively with crises, and generally try to create a better life for themselves and their mentally ill family member.

Family psychoeducation and behavioral family therapy share several assumptions (Dixon & Lehman, 1995; Dixon et al., 2001):

- Schizophrenia is regarded as an illness.
- Family members' behaviors do not cause schizophrenia.
- Family members are potentially effective therapeutic agents.
- Interventions are not intended to stand alone but are part of an overall approach to treatment that includes medication.

Basic family approaches include the following strategies in some configuration:

- Psychoeducation about mental illness and its effects
- Family support
- Communications training
- Behavioral problem solving
- Crisis intervention

These approaches may differ in

- Modality (single family or family groups)
- Whether the patient is included in each session
- Whether treatment is conducted in the home, a professional setting, or other setting
- Phase of the illness during which the intervention is provided

Evidence for the effectiveness of family approaches is substantial (Dixon, Adams, & Lucksted, 2000; Dixon et al., 2010; Dixon & Lehman, 1995; Dixon et al., 2001; Falloon & Coverdale, 1994; Kreyenbuhl et al., 2010; McFarlane et al., 1995; Penn & Mueser, 1996; Pilling, Bebbington, Kuipers, Garety, Geddes, Orbach et al., 2002; Tarrier & Barrowclough, 1995). Family approaches have shown robust outcomes in the following problem areas:

- Reducing family stress
- Reducing caregiver burden
- Reducing symptoms
- Improving coping skills and social functioning
- Reducing relapse and recidivism

On the basis of these reviews, general common effective ingredients among family therapies for the mentally ill have been identified:

- Employing both multidimensional and functional assessment to better tailor treatment to the family's needs and goals and foster the development of all family members
- Obtaining detailed assessment information on each family member's thoughts, feelings, and behaviors related to the situation
- Instilling optimism but anchoring expectations realistically
- Offering emotional support, reframing the problem, and giving advice when it seems needed
- Developing good working relationships with families and respecting them as "experts" for their experience and point of view
- Providing psychoeducation about the illness, including avoiding blaming families for causing it or characterizing their attempts to cope as pathological
- Encouraging medication compliance
- Identifying interactional patterns among family members and weighing the strengths and weaknesses of the family as a unit
- Monitoring indicators of possible relapse
- Conducting treatment for long periods of time rather than attempting short-term therapy
- Working with multiple families when practical
- Improving communication and problem-solving skills in all family members
- Using homework activities to practice skills learned in sessions
- Using stress management techniques
- Coping with special problems as they arise
- Focusing on current problems of clients and their families
- Employing crisis intervention when needed

Family therapy should be implemented as part of a comprehensive approach that includes psychiatric consultation for medication; crisis management; and case management of other services, such as facilitating employment, maintaining residential stability, and cultivating additional social supports.

Although there are variations in the way effective family interventions are conducted, a brief descriptive overview of behavioral family therapy (Mueser & Glynn, 1999) is presented here as a representative example that includes the most effective common ingredients found across several reviews of controlled studies. Ideally, both adolescent and adult family members and the client should be included, although practitioners should be prepared, at times, to work with only family members. Initially, practitioners should conduct more frequent (e.g., weekly) visits, gradually tapering off to monthly visits over the course of 1–2 years. There are several major components of family interventions that are loosely sequenced. These include engagement, assessment, education, communications training, problem solving, and dealing with special problems.

During engagement, practitioners should apply their general knowledge and skills concerning basic counseling (e.g., listening, positive regard, empathy, allowing clients to vent) and make an effort to engender hope and motivate clients. After a brief period of joining, practitioners should augment their multidimensional assessment and history taking by conducting a functional analysis of their clients' specific complaints (i.e., analyzing problem events and patterns of family members' reactions in sequence to determine factors that reinforce problem behaviors). Practitioners may also introduce and use standardized scales or client-specific indexes at this point to enhance the assessment and provide a baseline for evaluation. After a case assessment is summarized and goals are agreed on with client and family, practitioners educate family members about the nature of the disease to help them better understand positive and negative symptoms, and the potential positive effects all members can have toward improving the family situation.

Communications training then commences, to reduce negative emotional states in the family, help them communicate more effectively with their mentally ill family member (who may have serious problems processing information, especially under stress or when emotions are high), and improve interpersonal skills. Demonstrating basic listening skills and social skills can help family members relate more effectively and reduce negative emotional states. Standard problem-solving methods can be effective in helping families cope with a variety of specific problems as they arise. These well-known steps include (1) defining the problem; (2) brainstorming potential solutions; (3) evaluating alternative solutions; (4) choosing an agreed-on "best" solution; (5) planning an implementation; and (6) reviewing and revising, as needed, on the basis of the family's evaluation of their "homework" efforts.

When working with families coping with a member who has a severe mental illness (Finley, 1998), practitioners should recognize that family support should take place in the context of the family's culture. Important points to note in assessment include kinship relationships, communication and problem-solving styles, various role expectations, attitudes around help seeking, attributions about illness and its meaning, the role of spirituality and indigenous healers, and level of acculturation, among other matters. Preliminary empirical evidence suggests that these differences may be more than theoretical. One exploratory survey (Guarnaccia & Parra, 1996) of 90 families with a mentally ill family member (45 Latino, 29 African American, and 16 European Americans) demonstrated differences by culture: Latinos and African Americans were much more likely to have the mentally ill family member living with them, and they were more involved in kinship networks. There was also a greater likelihood that the European American mentally ill family member was in a residential treatment facility. Families expressed a variety of views regarding the causes of the problem, and African American families expressed more distrust of mental health professionals.

Family approaches to the treatment of mental illness have been well received outside of Western culture as well. In one recent randomized controlled trial in six rural Chinese communities, where many people see the symptoms of mental illness as the work of witchcraft, family psychoeducation and medication were shown to be superior to medication alone in increasing knowledge about mental illness, and somewhat more effective in engendering more understanding and caring and less negligent attitudes on the part of family members toward the mentally ill person (Ran et al., 2003). Another controlled study (Chien & Wong, 2007) in Hong Kong with Chinese families demonstrated that a US-based psychoeducational model (engagement, support, educational workshops, family role, independence, and strength building) with 18 sessions over 12 months showed significant reduction in family burden, fewer hospitalizations, and better functioning in family members and in the patient with schizophrenia. A pilot study with a smaller sample (14 patients) in Canada used multifamily psychoeducation group intervention within an assertive community treatment program for Chinese and Tamil families (Chow et al., 2010). Members met for 2 hours per month for 12 months. Using qualitative evaluation methods, they showed reduced family burden and stress levels, improved understanding of mental illness, and less frustration toward the individual with schizophrenia. The first randomized trial of family psychoeducation in Pakistan (Nasr & Kausar, 2009) showed that nine sessions significantly reduced family burden in families who received the combination of medication and family psychoeducation, compared to families who received medication alone. Psychoeducation was compared with behavioral family therapy and standard care (medication and advice) with families in Tehran, Iran in which one member had schizophrenia (Koolaee & Etemadi, 2010) and found that, after 6 months, behavioral family intervention that did not include the patient and emphasized communication and social skills showed somewhat better results in lowering expressed emotion among mothers, although both approaches were superior than standard care with regard to lowering expressed emotion and family burden. Although generalization of evidence-based family approaches appears very promising in non-Western cultures, more research is needed to delineate cultural differences in assessment and intervention as well as optimal effective components of these approaches with families who have a member with a serious mental illness.

Cognitive Rehabilitation Therapy

Cognitive rehabilitation therapy focuses on helping clients with schizophrenia reduce the impact of cognitive deficits that interfere with their maintaining employment and cause other problems in daily functioning. A series of RCTs has shown very positive results for cognitive remediation therapy. One randomized trial comparing cognitive enhancement therapy (CET) with enriched supportive therapy (EST) (Eack, Hogarty, Greenwald, Hogarty, & Keshavan, 2011) in 46 individuals with schizophrenia revealed significantly improved employment outcomes (i.e., time employed, money earned, and satisfaction) over 2 years. The CET comprised 60 hours of computer-based rehabilitation that focused on improving attention, memory, and problem solving, along with 45 hours of in vivo social skills training. EST (based on Hogarty's Personal Therapy) also emphasized relaxation training to reduce stress in social situations. McGurk, Mueser, DeRosa, and Wolfe (2009) compared cognitive remediation training in combination with a vocational rehabilitation program with vocational rehabilitation alone in 34 individuals with schizophrenia and found that cognitive remediation resulted in greater improvements in cognitive abilities, weeks worked, and wages earned at 2-year follow-up. Hodge et al. (2010) showed similar results for improved cognitive performance in 69 people with schizophrenia at 4-month follow-up after 15 weeks of treatment. A meta-analysis of 26 studies of interventions for cognitive impairments showed moderate improvements in cognitive performance (e.g., problem solving, reasoning, memory) for clients with schizophrenia, slightly less benefit for social functioning, and only modest improvement in symptoms of schizophrenia (McGurk et al., 2007). Clearly, cognitive remediation interventions show considerable promise for improved functioning in people with schizophrenia, and the approaches should be disseminated more broadly in the future to enhance individuals' functioning and well-being.

Increasing Environmental Supports for Seriously Mentally Ill Clients

Supported Housing.   Even with the most skillfully applied psychosocial interventions, clients' long-term outcome will be threatened if their living conditions and financial supports are not adequate or stable. Researchers have long understood that persons with schizophrenia experience difficulties maintaining steady residences and employment (Anthony & Blanch, 1989; Herman, Susser, & Struening, 1998). One review of the literature estimated that lifetime prevalence of serious mental illness and substance abuse is more than twice as high for the homeless as for the general population. In addition, when homelessness is associated with the loss of familial and social support, there appears to be greater risk of depression. Therefore, homelessness must be understood as a pronounced stressor associated with the loss of critical social and emotional supports (Herman et al., 1998).

In response to deinstitutionalization and subsequent homelessness in the 1980s, residential programs grew rapidly. By the end of that decade, most state-affiliated community residential programs across the United States included group homes (23%), supervised apartments (21%), board and care homes (10%), and supportive housing (9%) (Randolph, Ridgway, & Carling, 1991). A survey of 158 (mostly) African American adults in the Washington, DC, area (Bebout, Drake, Xie, McHugo, & Harris, 1997) provided suggestive evidence that housing stability was associated with reduced substance abuse. Other data have shown that, among the mentally ill, African Americans, the poor, and those with substance abuse problems are most at risk of being homeless (Kuno, Rothbard, Averyt, & Culhane, 2000).

Supported Employment.   Recent reviews of controlled and uncontrolled studies of supported employment provide evidence that direct placement into real, paying jobs (without pretraining), ongoing support, attention to client preferences, and integration of vocational services into the service model appear to result in superior rates of job placement, time worked, and wages earned in contrast to traditional train-and-place approaches or sheltered workshops (Bond et al., 2001; Bond, Drake, Mueser, & Becker, 1997; Lehman, 1995). Bond et al. (1997) found that, across six experimental studies, almost three times as many clients achieved competitive employment in comparison to those who received traditional vocational services. Mueser et al. (1997) concluded from a review of seven controlled studies that supportive approaches are more effective when clients are given direct assistance in finding and maintaining employment (as opposed to general job counseling). However, more research is needed to determine whether benefits of employment generalize to other areas of psychosocial functioning.

Individual placement and support (IPS) is the current evidence-based model for supported employment; it is guided by seven basic principles: (1) a focus on competitive employment, (2) consumer choice, (3) rapid job search, (4) integrated mental health and employment services, (5) consumer preference in job search, (6) individualized job supports, and (7) personalized benefits counseling (Bond, 2004). Noting that there have been up to 20 experimental tests of IPS (i.e., supported employment) showing twice the rate of successful job placement than usual vocational services, Burns et al.

(2007) tested IPS in six centers across Europe using a randomized controlled design to account for local employment conditions. They found that those in IPS showed twice as much successful placement and substantially fewer hospitalizations than those in traditional vocational programs. Noting that severely mentally ill clients in IPS programs in urban areas have been shown to be twice as likely to secure employment as those in other vocational programs, Gold, Meisler, Santos et al. (2006) used an RCT design to compare integrated ACT and IPS with a parallel vocational program in rural environments. They found that those in the experimental program were more than twice as likely to secure employment over the course of an 18-month trial. In a randomized controlled study in Hong Kong, Wong et al. (2008) compared IPS with conventional vocational programs over 18 months and showed that, although there were no between- or within-group differences over time in symptom levels, the IPS group (as in previous studies) was more than twice as successful in helping participants obtain and maintain work and earn more income. More recent meta-analysis (Bond, Drake, & Becker, 2008) of 11 RCTs with 6–24 months of follow-up of supported employment programs showed that IPS resulted in almost three times as much employment than controls and had more robust effects than approaches that are not as congruent with current evidence-based guidelines.

Working with the Criminal Justice System

There has also been an increase in awareness of the rates of mental illness and substance abuse problems among those in prison and otherwise involved in the criminal justice system. People with mental illness are arrested more often than those without mental illness, and they are often held without formal charges being filed and are not adequately treated for their mental illnesses during incarceration. Indeed, there have been calls to integrate services across the mental health, substance abuse, and criminal justice systems (Fisher, Packer, Grisso, McDermeit, & Brown, 2000; Godley et al., 2000; Lamb & Weinberger, 1998; Rock, 2001). Some have argued convincingly for more research and consistent implementation of civil commitment procedures to help clients comply with treatment on an outpatient basis (as opposed to forced incarceration in mental hospitals or prison) (Geller, 1995; Swartz et al., 1995). Considerable debate is likely to accompany these developments with respect to balancing the civil rights of clients who refuse treatment and implementing more humane alternatives to mental health care for those who commit crimes.

Although a high number of incarcerated people have some form of mental illness, only about 3.6% of people with severe mental illness in the general population have committed a violent act in the previous 6 months (Lamb & Weinberger, 2008). In addition, there is currently a lack of measures for acts of violence in this population that have good predictive validity (Singh, Serper, Reinharth, & Faxel, 2011). Although media depictions of mentally ill persons as violence-prone have created an unfair stigma, a number of factors have independently and additively increased the relatively low risk that a mentally ill person will commit a serious violent act. These include a history of conduct disorder and antisocial personality disorder, a co-occurring substance abuse disorder, having been a victim of violence in childhood or adulthood, and noncompliance with psychiatric medication (Eronen, Angermeyer, & Schulze, 1998; Fulwiler & Ruthazer, 1999; Swartz et al., 1998; Tehrani, Brennan, Hodgins, & Mednick, 1998). However, most violence by mentally ill persons is not directed at the general public; instead victims are likely to be the mentally ill person's family members (Eronen et al., 1998).

Over the years, mental health courts have made a more concerted effort to divert people with mental illness from incarceration to community treatment. The courts coordinate all relevant expertise to determine an individual's suitability for effective treatment while keeping public safety a priority. Courts can also mandate treatment. This general approach of using the leverage of the courts to effect positive psychosocial change in individuals is referred to as therapeutic jurisprudence, that is, the use of legal contingencies (i.e., using rewards and sanctions as leverage) to enhance a person's psychosocial well-being and to protect the community (Elbogen & Tomkins, 2000; Wexler, 1991). Positive outcomes require close monitoring and evaluation of client progress (e.g., keeping of appointments, medication compliance, reduced substance use, lack of criminal activities) (Lamb & Weinberger, 2008).

Although there have been only few controlled trials involving court-involved treatment, the results are promising for mandatory outpatient treatment (Appelbaum, 2001; Gerbasi, Bonnie, & Binder, 2000) and will, hopefully, lead to more humane alternatives to treating persons with major mental illness who commit crimes. Moore and Hiday (2006), for example, showed in a study of 82 individuals in mental health court (various diagnoses) that those who received the "full dose" of mental health court intervention were significantly less likely to be rearrested. One randomized controlled trial utilized a forensic approach to comprehensive assertive community treatment and compared it with treatment as usual (mental health services available in the community) for 134 individuals with a "major mental disorder" who were on probation (Cusack, Morrissey, Cuddeback, Prins, & Williams, 2010). Results showed significantly less criminal involvement, less likelihood of returning to prison, fewer days of hospitalization, and lower overall costs than for treatment-as-usual clients. For a variety of methodological reasons (e.g., inadequate design, heterogeneous samples), it is unclear at this time what constitutes "best practices" in mental health courts. More research, particularly using RCTs with more homogeneous samples of people with specific disorders, is needed before mental health courts can be deemed an evidence-based practice. This point is critical given the priority that should be placed on public safety as well as humane treatment of people with mental illness who have committed crimes.

Antipsychotic Medications

Social workers who treat serious mental illnesses should be familiar with antipsychotic medications so they can conduct accurate assessments, identify signs of noncompliance and side effects, and work collaboratively with psychiatric physicians and nurses. Reviews of the research on these drugs have summarized the most salient data regarding the effective use of antipsychotic medication (Bentley, 1998; Buchanan et al., 2010; Dixon, Lehman, & Levine, 1995; Kreyenbuhl et al., 2010).

Experts in psychiatric pharmacology classify antipsychotics in terms of first-, second-, and third-generation medications (Kutscher, 2008). Although they generally all provide comparable effects in reducing positive symptoms of schizophrenia spectrum disorders, second- and third-generation drugs appear to do so with fewer side effects. First-generation (also referred to as typical) antipsychotics (e.g., haloperidol, fluphenazine) act primarily by suppressing dopamine activity in the limbic system of the brain. Second-generation (i.e., atypical) antipsychotics antagonize both dopamine and serotonin receptors in the brain and have more potential for alleviating negative symptoms. Clozapine is, perhaps, the most widely used second-generation antipsychotic, and is useful for refractory illness (i.e., frequent relapsing), but because of side effects (i.e., reduces white-blood-cell counts) calls for a conservative approach to dosing with close monitoring (Buchanan, 1995). Third-generation medications (e.g., aripiprazole) are beginning to emerge and appear to have a more complex effect on brain functioning, and to show benefits for negative symptoms. Side effects of long-term use of antipsychotic drugs can be serious, including tardive dyskinesia marked by involuntary muscle movements, particularly in the face (e.g., unusual tongue, jaw, and mouth movements). These medications can also cause uncomfortable anticholinergic effects, such as blurred vision, dry mouth, constipation, and urinary retention. Some of the newer drugs appear to have fewer long-term side effects (Umbricht & Kane, 1995).

Aggregate findings from more than 600 studies have demonstrated that, on the whole, antipsychotic medications are effective with the majority of patients when they adhere to a treatment regimen, although noncompliance remains a persistent problem. More than 70% of clients show improvements in positive symptoms, and the drugs also substantially reduce risk of relapse for at least the first 12 months after the initial psychotic episode. Results, however, are not as good for negative symptoms or other social adjustment outcomes. Depot medication (i.e., by injection) reduces risk of relapse better than oral medication does, but many other factors that influence effectiveness in clinical application include accurate dosing, medication compliance, long-term outcomes, and the interrelationships of pharmacotherapy and other psychosocial interventions. First-generation antipsychotics are still considered a first-line treatment for people with acute onset and those who respond favorably to continued maintenance use. Second-generation antipsychotic drugs (e.g., clozapine) are then considered for patients who continue to experience significant symptoms and high levels of hostility or suicidal intent. Although antianxiety agents and antidepressants are widely prescribed for people with schizophrenia, evidence regarding their effectiveness is unconvincing. Most of the therapeutic gains for antipsychotics are realized within the first few weeks and months after the initial prescription. Regarding various prescribing practices, rapid neuroleptization (i.e., aggressive use of large doses), for example, has not been shown to yield superior results, and the use of clinical judgment in dosing has not been shown to be more effective than standard dosing. After clients' symptoms stabilize, many can be maintained on lower standard doses (not intermittently targeted doses) without increased risk of relapse (Buchanan et al., 2010; Dixon et al., 1995; Kreyenbuhl et al., 2010).

Kutscher (2008) notes key considerations for physicians prescribing antipsychotic medications: (1) use well-established treatment guidelines for each drug; (2) use family history (which can give clues to likelihood of good response); (3) involve the patient in the decision; and (4) use the STEPS decision model for prescribing medication, or safety (how safe is the medication for the individual patient?) tolerability (how well can the patient tolerate the side effects?), efficacy (might some medications work better than others for certain patients), price and affordability, and simplicity with regard to dosing (which might affect adherence).

IMPLEMENTING AND EVALUATING THE EVIDENCE-BASED INTERVENTION PLAN

CASE STUDY: MARTIN

Martin, a 26-year-old African American man, was referred to a social worker Jim, because he had not shown up at his maintenance job at a fast-food restaurant for 4 days and had not returned home during that time. This was the third time Martin's supervisor had referred him for help. The assessment revealed that Martin had been diagnosed with schizophrenia in his late teens, and had been hospitalized several times since then, but had not become consistently engaged in a community support program. It also became clear that Martin did not take his medication regularly and periodically abused street drugs, most recently, crack and amphetamines, during his hiatus from work. He often did this when he became paranoid and experienced command hallucinations to hurt people around him, particularly when he was at work. These voices frightened him, and he felt that drugs temporarily quieted the voices and took his mind off them. His live-in girlfriend, Maria, worried about him and came with him to the consultation with the social worker. Martin revealed that after his parents divorced when he was in his teens, he ran away from home. He did not finish high school but had been living on his own much of the time for the previous 10 years. He presented as friendly and cooperative but appeared suspicious, depressed, and remorseful about his recent absences from work. He was appreciative of his girlfriend's and his employer's continuing faith in him. Martin was willing to take his medication and go back to work, but he was afraid that he would slip again and that people would lose patience with him.

MFS Assessment: Defining Problems and Goals

Martin presented as soft spoken and willing to engage with the social worker, Jim, although he seemed, at times, suspicious and a little guarded. Nevertheless, he was reasonably forthcoming and remorseful at times about having run away from his girlfriend and abandoned his boss again. Face-to-face interviewing provided a good deal of information, and it seemed likely that Martin's girlfriend and boss would also be good sources of corroborating data. They would provide further insight into his behavior at home and at work.

Historically, his family life was relatively uneventful. Neither parent had a major mental illness, although Martin's father had a drinking problem. His paternal uncle and grandfather had psychiatric histories (i.e., hospitalizations), but it was not clear what the specific diagnoses were. His parents divorced when he was about 16 years old. He has a brother and a sister with whom he has had little contact. He did not report having been abused, although he remembered having been afraid of his father when his dad was drinking heavily. His father also disappeared for days at a time when he went on a drinking binge.

Martin often went for relatively long periods of time without displaying overtly psychotic symptoms. Although he was usually "standoffish," behaved suspiciously, and muttered to himself at work, his auditory hallucinations were generally tolerable as long as he stayed on his antipsychotic medication. He often seemed depressed, edgy and anxious, and he spent most of his time alone. He took his coffee breaks and lunches alone, and went outside to smoke behind the restaurant when he had a chance. When he stopped taking his medication (sometimes because he felt he was being poisoned by the government as "part of a conspiracy to make blacks insane"), he became hostile, lashed out at his coworkers verbally, responded loudly to command hallucinations to "kill the white devils," and generally was uncooperative at work. Once he yelled at and pushed a young white man (an "enemy agent") who, Martin claimed, put "poison" in his lunch. He told his African American boss about the incident. His boss often mediated arguments among his young staff and was aware that there had been racial tensions among them and occasions when racial epithets had been exchanged. His boss was having difficulty sorting out how much of the racial content was real and how much was in Martin's imagination.

After consulting with Maria, Martin's Latina girlfriend, it seemed to Jim that Martin was generally able to trust her. She described Martin as "sweet" and said "He does stuff for me," but she added that he sometimes went for days without speaking to her and would become preoccupied with watching the news. He seemed very interested in computer technology, talked about Internet security features a lot, and worried about whether the government was monitoring his Internet browsing. She said that she was afraid for him when he disappeared for days, did not know where he went, was afraid that he might get HIV if he was having sex in crack houses, and was afraid that he might infect her. She said she loved him and felt that she could help him. She worried about him a lot but felt that she needed help in dealing with his problems.

To date, Martin seemed to have avoided any serious encounters with the police, although they were aware of him because he had appeared from time to time in the local hospital emergency room. He had never been caught in possession of drugs and usually didn't carry any with him or even use them, except for occasional binges, when he would disappear for 3–4 days. In general, his health was reported to be good; he worked for 3–4 months at a time with good attendance and performance; and generally took care of his hygiene and appearance, although his hygiene deteriorated during his more paranoid phases. He stopped showering during those times, and his coworkers and customers would complain. His boss seemed to be the only person from whom he would take constructive criticism of his appearance and hygiene when the matters were brought to Martin's attention.

Although Martin was (based on previous diagnoses) apparently suffering from schizophrenia, he had been doing reasonably well over the previous few years. Aside from periodic hospitalizations when his symptoms become acute, he had been able to maintain a job and a relationship for more than 2 years. However, as he became more suspicious and hostile to those around him, they in turn responded more negatively to him, thus increasing his feelings that others didn't like him or were out to harm him. The flash point in this sequence of events could have been a relatively innocuous event: a nasty look; the innocent laugh of a colleague; a news report on the television regarding war, a terrorist attack, or the arrest of a black media personality.

Jim worked with Martin to keep the problems well defined, goals reasonable, and the treatment plan manageable. He also arranged for psychiatric consultation to manage Martin's medication. Working together, Jim and Martin agreed that there were some people at work who probably were racist but that Martin's reactions may have worsened his paranoid delusions. He spent a lot of time withdrawing from those around him, and the estrangement from his coworkers left room for his imagination and delusions to "fill in the gaps." It appeared that, as he became more wary of others, including his white therapist and white female psychiatrist, he sometimes stopped taking his medication because he felt that they were tying to "control his mind." As his delusions increased in intensity, and as his command hallucinations grew louder, Martin became increasingly frightened and belligerent, which led eventually to a crisis at home or at work, and the possibility of a crack binge.

In brief, Martin appeared to suffer from paranoid delusions and occasional hallucinations that had a persecutory quality but seemed to worsen when racial tensions added to their plausibility. At some point, he would stop taking his medication regularly, and his paranoid delusions and hallucinations would subsequently increase. His behavior would become more belligerent, and those around him would respond and reinforce his behavior accordingly. Things would escalate and a crisis ensue. This sequential pattern had played out several times within the previous year, and it provided a good, workable functional assessment to guide at least part of the intervention plan.

Martin had other difficulties as well. He was chronically depressed and anxious, did not sleep well, and felt that the medications he took interfered with his lovemaking when he and his girlfriend, on occasion, were intimate. He also had real strengths in that he was diligent in his work, related well to Maria from time to time, and received considerable social support from both her and his boss. Preliminary intervention goals included improved medication compliance to reduce symptoms, improved social supports and coping skills at work, and abstinence from alcohol and other drugs.

Selecting and Designing the Intervention: Defining Strategies and Objectives

Jim and Martin worked out an intervention plan that initially included the following approaches: First, cognitive-behavior therapy was initiated to test out and gain some control over the paranoid delusions, particularly at work. Second, social skills training was employed to help Martin cope better with interpersonal exchanges at work (e.g., communicate better with his boss when he was feeling angry or frightened, engage in friendly conversation with some of his coworkers). Third, psychoeducation and behavioral couples therapy was implemented with Martin and Maria together. This approach was intended to engage Maria as a therapeutic ally, to help her better understand Martin's condition, to help her learn to deal with him more effectively, and to provide support for her as well. Fourth, Martin focused on self-monitoring and coping skills to identify triggers and seek help before taking off on a binge. Last, assertive case management was initiated to coordinate psychiatric care and enhance social supports in the community.

A number of specific objectives were designed to help engage Martin in treatment and move him toward his goals in a step-by-step approach (table 5.1). Jim helped Martin examine some of his delusions carefully and

TABLE 5.1   The Client Service Plan for Martin

Problems	Goals	Objectives (samples)	Interventions	Assessment and evaluation tools
Frightening paranoid delusions; feels the government and coworkers are out to harm him	Reduce frequency and intensity of fearful delusions; help gain better cognitive understanding of link between symptoms and exaggerated fears	Monitor, identify, and record level of intensity of delusions daily; think about alternative interpretations and record them	Cognitive therapy to examine and challenge delusional thinking; test out alternative interpretations	*Scales:* BPRS to monitor changes in mental status; BASIS-32 to measure psychological and social functioning Role Functioning Scale to measure social and occupational functioning
Withdraws from others; fails to communicate his fears to others; lashes out angrily when he feels threatened	Improve ability to reach out to social supports when he feels the need	Initiate at least one conversation daily at home and work; when confused by someone's comment, ask other person to clarify meaning	Social skills training: role-playing and in vivo practice of basic communication skills: focus on clarifying meaning of others' communications and responding in a friendly manner	AUS and DUS to monitor involvement with drugs; SATS to gauge his level of involvement in dealing with episodic but risky drug problem
Does not take his medication consistently	Improve medication compliance close to 100%	Take meds daily in front of girlfriend (after she is given instructions by nurse, case manager)	Psychoeducation for client and partner to help girlfriend cope Assertive case management to consult with doctor to	*Other indexes* (linked specifically to objectives): • Create a credibility index (5-point, low to high) regarding paranoid delusions
Occasional drug binges and engages in risky sexual behaviors	Eliminate the binges; develop an alternative to running away when he is in a crisis; join "persuasion" group at mental health center	Identify thoughts of bingeing and other related thoughts daily, and note feelings or situations that provoke it for discussion with social worker	ensure medicine compliance, coach client's boss to monitor and assist Martin; provide support for Maria and reinforce her "co-therapist" role Self-monitoring and related coping skills: because client occasionally binges, focus on identifying triggers associated with thinking about drug use and devise and discuss a written "crisis plan" to put into effect; direct-deposit of paycheck; refer to "persuasion" group for co-occurring mental illness and substance abuse clients	• Weekly count of the frequency of positive interactions at work with others (have boss keep a log); qualitatively review meaning and salience • Weekly count of conversations initiated at home (have girlfriend keep score); keep record of successful medication administrations

distinguish those aspects of them that might have some validity (e.g., blacks and whites are often hostile to one another in our society; the government does monitor Internet communications), but he helped him understand that not *every* white person was out to hurt him because he is black, and that the government was not necessarily out get him in particular. The practitioner then tried to help Martin see that, when he kept to himself and acted unfriendly or was angry toward others at work, his coworkers might have thought he did not like them or might have felt threatened by him. Considering these alternative explanations seemed to be helpful in encouraging Martin to actually test out his more troubling beliefs. Martin and Jim role-played a typical situation at work. Martin was gradually able to consider that perhaps some of his suspicions were blown out of proportion. With some practice, Martin was later able to better identify his reactions to some of the relative minor incidents at work, and by talking with his coworkers and his boss, he was able to clarify some matters before he responded angrily or in a threatening manner. His communication skills seemed to improve a bit on the job, at least enough to forestall further serious conflict.

A similar application of self-monitoring and coping skills were also used to identify precipitating factors (i.e., antecedents, "triggers") for drug use. These triggers were often associated with anxiety or emotional distress at work. A crisis plan was developed and written down with important phone numbers (and kept in his wallet) so that Martin would pause and consider more constructive alternatives before taking off from work impulsively. Jim taught Martin how to stop and review a list of potentially negative consequences he might bring upon himself and others if he gave in to the impulse to run away and use drugs (e.g., becoming a victim of violence, contracting HIV, losing his girlfriend, losing his job, getting arrested, going to prison). In addition, through couples therapy, Martin agree to have his paycheck deposited directly to his account to reduce the chances that he would impulsively go off on a binge, since he knew from past experience that he needed cash to buy drugs. Martin also agreed to attend a treatment group for co-occurring disorders.

Couples' psychoeducation was also helpful in that it helped Maria better understand Martin's problems and helped her recognize when he was becoming "symptomatic" and then intervene before his condition deteriorated. Maria also monitored his medication regimen more carefully. She practiced role-playing and communication skills that Martin had learned with Jim. Those skills were reinforced during couples' visits. Maria also appeared to benefit from the support provided during the sessions. In addition, both agreed to undergo physical exams to test for sexually transmitted diseases.

Selecting Scales and Creating Indexes to Monitor and Evaluate Client Progress

Several scales are suitable for assessment and evaluation in this case. The BPRS subscales (i.e., positive and negative symptoms, resistance and psychological distress) were used to target Martin's specific mental status symptoms; the AUS, DUS, and SATS to track his substance use and engagement in treatment; and the RFS to monitor his social and work functioning. However, these measures could have also been supplemented with specific indexes to measure and track individual problems related to Martin's immediate concerns, such as employing a 5-point severity scale to have him judge the intensity of his suspiciousness that others (e.g., coworkers, the government) were specifically out to harm him, how strongly he felt about taking his medication according to prescription, how strong his urges were to run away and go on a crack binge, and how frequently he constructively used social supports (e.g., talked to his girlfriend and his boss to let them know that he was troubled by some frightening thoughts).

SUMMARY

Given the multidimensional nature of problems experienced by persons with serious mental illnesses such as schizophrenia, an eclectic evidence-based strategy can help clients improve their cognitive, emotional, behavioral, and interpersonal skills; make better adjustments to family life; and function more effectively in the community. Comprehensive reviews of the research have concluded that psychosocial interventions should emphasize the use of cognitive-behavioral coping skills, family psychoeducation and behavioral family therapy, and supported employment—all delivered in the context of integrated assertive case management. The skills for working with mentally ill persons who also abuse alcohol and other drugs can be readily integrated into the psychosocial interventions reviewed in this chapter. Together these evidence-based strategies can empower the person with mental illness to make a more satisfactory adjustment to life in the community (Corrigan, 1997). Advanced and highly skilled clinical social workers are needed to address the needs of the seriously mentally ill.

CHAPTER 6

DEPRESSIVE AND BIPOLAR DISORDERS

For some time, depressive and bipolar disorders were classified together as "major mood disorders," a phrase commonly used in the extant research. Suggesting that bipolar disorders represent a metaphorical bridge between schizophrenia spectrum and depressive disorders "in terms of symptomatology, family history and genetics" (American Psychiatric Association, APA, 2013, p. 123), the authors of the DSM-5 have separated depressive and bipolar disorders into two distinct diagnostic categories. Nevertheless, there are clear overlaps in depressive symptoms between depressive and bipolar disorders, and to some extent, they share common elements with respect to psychosocial treatment approaches. Other related but less severe diagnoses include dysthymia (a chronic depressive disorder), cyclothymia (varying hypomanic and moderate depressive symptoms), and bipolar II disorder (a variant of bipolar I, with less intensive manic symptoms). Although there is extensive research on psychosocial treatment of depressive disorders, research on psychosocial interventions for bipolar disorders is only emerging. For that and other pragmatic reasons, including the overlap in symptoms and treatment approaches, this chapter addresses the two classes of disorders.

Despite the categorical distinctions, severe depression and bipolar disorders also lie on the spectrum of disorders generally referred to as severe mental illnesses, a group that includes schizophrenia spectrum disorders. It has been long recognized that these disorders share a range of common symptoms, including depression, mood disturbances, and psychosis (Abrams, Rojas, & Arciniegas, 2008; Baynes et al., 2000). Although many people with depressive and bipolar disorders are treated successfully on an outpatient basis and are eventually able to manage quite well in their daily lives, many others suffer more severe symptoms, lack family and other social supports, cannot maintain employment, lack daily self-care skills, and experience much more disability overall. These clients might require more intensive and comprehensive community support services, similar to those provided to people with schizophrenia spectrum disorders (see chapter 5). Thus, despite categorical and diagnostic distinctions, clinical pragmatism requires that clients with major depressive disorders and bipolar disorder be assessed on a continuum of symptom severity and psychosocial disability, and that interventions be crafted accordingly.

The current chapter addresses background data, assessment, and current psychosocial interventions for major depressive and bipolar disorders. In addition, although dysthymia, cyclothymia, bipolar II, and other variants of these two disorders are not assumed to be simply diluted versions of major depression and bipolar I, it is understood that practitioners will make the necessary adjustments in assessment and treatment planning on the basis of symptom severity and overall psychosocial dysfunction. This chapter also highlights research on treatment of depression in the elderly, not because depressive disorders are more common among elderly people, but because the consequences of depression, including heightened risk of suicide, can be more challenging to treat. Last, current medications used to treat the primary symptoms of these disorders are briefly reviewed at the end of this chapter.

ASSESSMENT

Background Data

Major mood disorders are among the most common and debilitating of health problems in the world (World Health Organization, 2012). Hasin, Goodwin, Stinson, and Grant (2005) reported that about 13% of the US population has a major mood disorder (including either major depression or bipolar disorder), and also estimated that women are about twice as likely to meet diagnostic criteria (17% vs. 9%). General population estimates from the National Comorbidity Study (Kessler et al., 1994) revealed that about 17% of US citizens were estimated to have met diagnosis of major depressive *episode* at some point in their lives, with women almost twice as likely to be diagnosed as men. Lifetime prevalence of major depressive disorder was estimated to be 12.7%, with 7.7% of the population diagnosed within a 12-month time period. Women are more likely than men to have met the criteria for major depression in both their lifetime (21.3% vs. 17.1%) and within the previous 12 months (8% vs. 6.4%). Other estimates of rates of depression (APA, 2000; Kaplan & Sadock, 1998) in community samples vary from 10% to 25% for women and from 5% to 12% for men, suggesting that rates of depression among women may be 2.5 times those of men (Blumenthal, 1994; Chen, Eaton, Gallo, Nestadt, & Crum, 2000; Hankin et al., 1998; Sprock & Yoder, 1997; Sullivan, Neale, & Kendler, 2000). In the United States, rates of depression may be increasing more rapidly among women than among men (Weissman, Markowitz, & Klerman, 2000).

Rates of mania and bipolar disorder in the general population have been reported to be about .4%. (Helzer & Pryzbeck, 1988; Kessler, Rubinow, Holmes, Abelson, & Zhao, 1997). However, using adjusted diagnostic criteria and more representative samples in the National Epidemiologic Survey on

Alcohol and Related Conditions study, Grant et al. (2005) estimated lifetime bipolar disorder to considerably higher, at 3.84%, with comparable rates for both men and women. The APA (2013) reports 12-month prevalence of .6%.

Suicide Risk.   Suicide is of major concern for people with major mood disorders, as they have a much higher rate of suicide attempts than do people with other psychiatric disorders (Bolton & Robinson, 2010; Kessler, Borges, & Walters, 1999). Several major reviews (Dutta et al., 2007; Hawton, Sutton, Haw et al., 2005; Simon, Hunkeler, Fireman, Lee, & Savarino, 2007) have revealed that individuals with bipolar disorder exhibit risk factors similar to those of people with schizophrenia. Risk factors for completed suicides include being younger, male, white, unemployed, relatively well educated, unmarried, having had good premorbid functioning, having a family history of suicide, having suffered from severe depression and hopelessness, having experienced family stressors, having a history of substance abuse, and having made previous suicide attempts and/or self-harming behaviors. Although it appears that previous suicide attempts are the most robust risk factor for eventually completed suicide, self-harming behaviors, particularly multiple events, have also been shown to be a strong predictor of suicide in people with major mood disorders, especially women (Harris & Barraclough, 1997; Hawton, Sutton, Haw, Sinclair, & Harriss, 2005b).

Comorbidity of Depressive and Bipolar Disorders and Substance Abuse.   Major mood disorders show high comorbidity with substance use disorders. The National Longitudinal Alcohol Epidemiologic Survey (NLEAS) (Grant & Harford, 1995) demonstrated that the co-occurrence of depression and substance abuse disorders not only is prevalent in society; it is even higher among women, African Americans, and middle-age to older Americans. An Australian survey of persons ranging in age from 18 to 80 (Rodgers et al., 2000) revealed that, although there is a strong association between persons who drink heavily and symptoms of anxiety and depression, the relationship may be curvilinear, specifically U shaped (abstainers and heavy drinkers are at greater risk), and is similar for both men and women. The NESARC study (Hasin et al., 2005) revealed that 4.5% of people diagnosed with major depression in the previous 12 months and 17.2% diagnosed with depression in their lifetime met criteria for a drug use disorder. Of those diagnosed with a lifetime major mood disorder, about 40% also were diagnosed with an alcohol use disorder and 41% with an anxiety disorder (Hasin et al., 2005).

Helzer and Pryzbeck (1988) reported that persons with mania were more than six times as likely to be diagnosed with alcohol abuse or dependence than the general population. Kessler, Crum, Warner et al. (1997) reported that 6.2% of men and 6.8% of women with alcohol dependence also met criteria for mania (i.e., two to six times the rate of mania in the general population, depending on the particular estimate). Almost 10% of persons diagnosed with lifetime alcohol dependence were also diagnosed with co-occurring mania (i.e., about 3 to 10 times previous estimates of mania in the general population) (Kessler et al., 1996). More recently, 40% of clients who met lifetime criteria for a bipolar I disorder also met criteria for alcohol dependence, and 58% met criteria for any alcohol use disorder (Grant et al., 2005). Clearly, as with most clients, those with major mood disorders should be screened and assessed carefully for any substance use given the correlations among mood disturbances, substance abuse, and suicide risk.

Culture.   Lifetime major depression has been estimated as roughly twice as high in US-born versus foreign-born groups in the United States, with some exceptions, and major depression was higher among Puerto Ricans, Mexican Americans, and African Americans than among whites (Gonzalez, Tarraf, Whitfield, & Vega, 2010). Rates of bipolar disorder are about equal across various racial groups (with the possible exception of Native Americans, who are diagnosed at a higher rate) and are highly comorbid with substance use and anxiety disorders (Merikangas & Pato, 2009). Other than prevalence rates, little research has been conducted on cultural differences in bipolar disorders.

Koss-Chioino (1999) has noted that, although rates of depression among Puerto Rican women are comparable to women in the United States, the causes of depression may be somewhat culturally determined. For example, she cites evidence that "traditional sex-role socialization encourages inhibition of assertiveness, which in turn leads to psychological problems, such as depression and psychosomatic symptoms" (Koss-Chiono, 1999, p. 335). Depressive episodes may also be triggered by negative life events or role strains in family relations that may be somewhat distinct from other cultural contexts. Women's depression in primary health-care settings is likely to go undetected, and minority women appear less likely than white women to seek help from mental health or social service workers (Van Hook, 1999).

Older persons of color, in addition to being subjected to other challenges of old age, are also more likely than younger people of color to have suffered from discrimination and other forms of oppression, especially if they grew up even before the civil rights movement brought many of these issues to a head (Beckett & Dungee-Anderson, 2000). Even more so than their white counterparts, African American, Native American, Latino, and Asian Americans are likely to have experienced poverty, fewer benefits from either public or private insurance as a result of employment discrimination, poorer housing, and more health problems because of a lack of access to health care. Racial minorities disproportionately experience socioeconomic problems, and factors related to poverty appear to increase depression.

In decades past, many immigrants from Southeast Asia came to the United States having been traumatized by decades of war, and many experienced imprisonment or torture. Many arrived as political refugees, and as a result of the stressors they experienced, they showed disproportionate signs of psychological strain, including symptoms of depression. Much of the continued symptoms of stress are associated with poverty, poor English-language proficiency, lack of social supports, low self-esteem, and depression (Kinzie et al., 1982; Nicassio, 1983; Tran, 1993). For many immigrants, there appeared to be a direct dose-response relationship between the extent of traumatic stress and psychological and health-related consequences (Mollica, Poole, & Tor, 1998). However, level of acculturation may moderate premigration stressors. Those immigrants who become more acculturated in their new host country are also likely to suffer less stress and depression from their premigration trauma experiences (Ngo, Tran, Gibbons, & Oliver, 2001). There are also signs that the symptoms of stress and strain may co-occur with an increase in substance abuse problems (O'Hare & Tran, 1998). Samples of persons from Southeast Asia, including those who have experienced war-related trauma, seem to experience depression and stress symptoms, in part as somatic distress, an important factor that should be included in conceptualizations and measurement of depression (Kinzie et al., 1982; Uehara, Morelli, & Abe-Kim, 2001). Last, some evidence suggests that Asian Americans (who have lower rates of depression than the general population overall) might rely on culturally determined forms of disengaging coping strategies if they see their depressive symptoms as caused by internal factors. Thus, they are more readily accepting of the cause of depression, less likely to disclose depression (to save face), and less likely to see depression as a problem to solve with more engagement oriented coping strategies (Wong, Kim, & Tran, 2010). Although the focus here was on Asian immigrants to illustrate links between mental health concerns and immigration, the basic principles are likely to apply to other groups as well, especially those who have left war and political oppression.

Depression in the Elderly. As the population of elderly persons in the United States continues to grow, so will the demand and costs for interdisciplinary health and social work services. Increasing political, technological, ethical, and service-delivery challenges are increasingly the focus of social work with the elderly (Feit & Cuevas-Feit, 1996). Epidemiological studies generally use diagnostic criteria to determine the presence of psychiatric disorders, but one 30-year review of the literature revealed that older adults suffer from high rates of *subthreshold* depression, many of whom go on to develop major depression. Most of these cases are women with the following risk factors: medical burden, disability, and low social support (Meeks, Vahia, Lavretsky, Kulkarni, & Jeste, 2011). However, other nationally representative data have shown that mood and anxiety disorders tend to decline with age, although rates remain significant, with considerable comorbidity in both disorders, and with women suffering from higher rates of both disorders than men (Byers, Yaffe, Covinsky, Friedman, & Bruce, 2010). An extensive review of the literature revealed that risk factors for depression in the elderly included "chronic diseases, poor self-perceived health, functional disability, personality traits, inadequate coping strategies, previous psychopathology, smaller network size, being unmarried, qualitative aspects of social network, stressful life events and female gender" (Vink, Aartsen, & Schoevers, 2008, p. 40). Some of these risk factors were associated with anxiety problems as well, in addition to a sense of loss of control, neuroticism, and poor coping strategies.

Although the rates of depression in older adults appear to be generally comparable to those of the general population, high-risk groups include older women and those with moderate to severe illnesses. In addition, older adults tend to be underdiagnosed for depression, partly because they tend to minimize depression, and because professionals do not detect it and/or confound psychiatric and medical symptoms (Dick & Gallagher-Thompson, 1996). Underdetection of depression can increase risk of suicide, so practitioners should always screen for such risks. Caution should be taken with differential diagnosis as well. Sorting out depression from cognitive impairments and other medical complaints, bereavement, substance abuse, and side effects of medication can be challenging. Focusing on the course of the disorder, duration, and progression of symptoms, and relying on multiple sources of data can help practitioners sort out the right diagnoses and causes of psychosocial distress. Expertise in mental status examinations for serious cognitive impairments is required to conduct a thorough assessment and diagnosis.

Depression is also a common ailment in older persons with Alzheimer's disease (AD) (Teri, 1996), as well as a possible predictor of AD (Bartolini, Coccia, Luzzi, Leandro, & Ceravolo, 2004). Given that the likelihood of developing AD increases with age, clinicians must be vigilant for its possible onset. Memory problems can be related to several disorders, including depression and dementia. In turn, dementia can be related to various medical conditions (e.g., substance abuse, cerebrovascular disease). However, most often dementia is associated with AD, which accounts for half or more of all cases of dementia, is the fourth leading cause of death in the United States, and may last 3-20 years from onset to end of life. Estimates of the prevalence of dementia in the community are about 3%, with rates climbing from about 1.5% for individuals in their late 60s to 30% for persons age 85 years and older (APA, 2013; Callaway, 1998; Kaplan & Sadock, 1998).

The primary cognitive deficits associated with AD include aphasia (deterioration in the use of meaningful language), apraxia (inability to perform ordinary motor activities, such as brushing one's teeth), and agnosia (inability to recognize and name common objects, such as a chair). For an AD diagnosis these disturbances must be severe enough to indicate impairment and decline in social or occupational functioning. Deterioration in cortical functioning can manifest as difficulty with or inability to plan and carry out task-oriented behaviors that involve several sequential steps (e.g., preparing a meal) or difficulty coping with novel situations (e.g., being in an unfamiliar setting with strangers). In general, AD has a progressive and irreversible course. Early-stage AD is marked by short-term memory loss, disorientation, and personality changes, along with impaired judgment and information processing, as well as compromised problem-solving skills. Middle-stage AD is characterized by difficulties in both short- and long-term memory, language, social skills, abstract reasoning, and problems with activities of daily living. Late-stage AD, which lasts less than 2 years, includes problems with mobility, speech deficits, greater disorientation, self-care difficulties, incontinence, and disinterest in eating. Because memory deterioration may be an early sign of AD, it is important that clinicians make note of it and pursue further clinical diagnostic investigation rather than assuming that it is related to depression. As a result of memory deterioration, orientation to time, place, and person may also be affected with AD. Over time, personality changes may become apparent, changes that may be particularly disturbing to the client's family members (APA, 2013; Callaway, 1998; Kaplan & Sadock, 1998). Thus, given the complex diagnostic concerns regarding depression and related psychiatric and other medical conditions, clinical social workers who serve the elderly should collaborate closely with medical specialists for assessment and intervention planning.

Anxiety disorders also commonly co-occur with depression and bipolar disorders (APA, 2013; Smith, Sherrill, & Colenda, 1995; Vink et al., 2008). One study conducted in the Netherlands (Beekman et al., 2000) examined the co-occurrence and risk factor patterns for both anxiety and depression in a random sample of older persons (age 55–85) as part of a 10-year longitudinal study. Using well-validated standardized measures, the authors found that almost 48% of those who met the criteria for depressive disorder also met criteria for anxiety disorder. Conversely, about 26% of those with anxiety disorder were also depressed. Anxiety disorders were particularly associated with a range of vulnerability and stress-related factors. Again, social workers should be acutely aware that psychopathology is highly variable and highly interactive with current stressors in clients' lives, including the lives of their elderly clients. There are multiple possible sources of anxiety for the elderly person: stressors associated with retirement and the loss of friends and loved ones, accompanied by subsequent feelings of loneliness, uselessness, and hopelessness. Medical problems, including the loss of eyesight and hearing, may add to fears of dying or becoming incapacitated. Other financial and situational stressors can exacerbate anxiety as well (Smith et al., 1995).

Alcohol abuse is also a serious problem among older Americans (Blazer & Wu, 2011) and often co-occurs with major mood disorders. Liberto, Oslin, and Ruskin (1996) reported that estimates of daily drinking among older persons range from 10% to 22% and estimates of heavier drinking from 3% to

9%. They also report that about half of these persons would likely meet DSM criteria for an alcohol use disorder. Drinking rates among the elderly are higher for men, and consumption levels appear to be comparable among older African American, Hispanic, and white men. Older persons who drink are also more likely to experience co-occurring anxiety disorders; drug abuse (especially prescription drugs); and other psychosocial stressors, such as caretaker burden (e.g., caring for an incapacitated spouse), poverty, and loneliness associated with grief and loss (Sanjuan & Langenbucher, 1999). The elderly are also more vulnerable to negative health effects from alcohol even when they consume less than their younger counterparts. Such problems include alcoholic liver disease, organic brain syndrome, obstructive pulmonary disease, strokes, gastritis, pancreatitis, and sleep disorders, among other things. Detoxification also carries greater risks for the elderly and is associated with a higher rate of mortality. Alcohol abuse can also cloud the diagnostic picture and distort the clinical presentation of other disorders, such as dementia, and other organic illnesses associated with old age.

Theories

A range of biological, psychological, interpersonal, and stress-diathesis theories have been posited to explain the causes and maintenance of major mood disorders, but it has become increasingly clear that they are best understood as the result of interacting biopsychosocial processes that predispose some people to mood disturbances and dysregulation more than others. One 20-year review of the literature covering more than 5,000 patients revealed the following risk factors for chronic depression: earlier age of onset, family history, and longer duration of depressive episodes in addition to comorbidity (e.g., anxiety, substance abuse, personality disorder) (Holzel, Harter, Reese, & Kriston, 2011). However, evidence is growing with respect to the role of genetic risk factors. Evidence from studies comparing monozygotic and dizygotic twins, studies of twins (separated at birth) raised by adoptive parents, and studies of first-degree relatives strongly suggests that biological factors have a substantial role in causing major mood disorders (APA, 2000, 2013; Kaplan & Sadock, 1998; Schwartz & Schwartz, 1993; Sullivan et al., 2000). Meta-analysis (based mostly on twin studies) revealed that familial genetic influence almost triples the risk of developing depression (Sullivan et al., 2000), and estimates of the inheritability of depression range from 31% to 42% (as compared to schizophrenia and bipolar disorder, which may be as high as 70%). Risk of bipolar disorders might be as much as 10 times greater if bipolar disorder is present in blood relatives, with increased risk with degree of kinship, and it appears that bipolar disorders and schizophrenia share common genetic links (APA, 2013). Some researchers have suggested that cognitive dysfunctions (e.g., emotion comprehension, empathy) and personality factors (e.g., neurotic temperament) might be predictive of the emotional instability that is characteristic of bipolar disorders (McKinnon,

Cusi, & MacQueen, 2013). Environmental stressors can also play a major role in the onset, trajectory, treatment, and outcome of major mood disorders.

Adolescence may be an especially critical time for the development of depression. In a longitudinal study of university students, several measures taken over 10 years revealed a surge in rates of depression between the ages of 15 and 18, but the rate among female adolescents rose to twice that of their male counterparts (Hankin et al., 1998). Reviews of the research concerning women and depression (Blumenthal, 1994; Sprock & Yoder, 1997) have revealed evidence strongly suggesting that the differences are likely due to interacting causes, including biological factors (e.g., hormonal differences emerging during puberty), psychosocial stressors (e.g., multiple competing roles at home and work, sexual and physical abuse, sensitivity to loss, insufficient social supports, discrimination), and differences in socialization factors (e.g., gender-role expectations). How these factors interact and change over time requires further investigation. Although multiple factors appear to be at work in the increased risk of depression among women, a recent investigation of a clinical population demonstrated that women were more likely to have experienced a severe negative stressful event before the onset of their depressive episode (Spangler, Simons, Monroe, & Thase, 1996). Adult women's increased risk factors for depression include longer episodes of depression that are more likely to develop into chronic and recurrent depression and a greater likelihood of depression being triggered by negative life events; seasonal sensitivity; hormonal differences related to menstrual cycle, pregnancy, birth (postpartum depression), and menopause; and increased comorbidity with other disorders, such as anxiety disorders and bulimia.

As with several mental disorders, depression appears to be related to the dysregulation of neurotransmitters (Kaplan & Sadock, 1998; Schwartz & Schwartz, 1993). Depletion of serotonin may precipitate depression, and dopamine activity may also be reduced. Research on animals (including primates) and preliminary findings in studies of humans have demonstrated that depression appears to be associated with hypersecretion of corticotropin-releasing hormone and subsequent overactivation of the hypothalamic-adrenal-pituitary axis, glands directly involved in hormone regulation and mood. There is suggestive evidence that these hormonal oversecretions may be influenced by genetic factors and by environmental stressors (O'Keane, 2000). Nevertheless, to date no laboratory findings have confirmed a diagnosis of major depression. These various biophysiological processes may be related, and further research is needed to delineate their relationship to the various symptoms of depression and their degree of severity.

Cognitive Theory of Depression.   Although there is relatively little cognitive theory devoted to understanding bipolar disorders, an understanding of the cognitive theory of depression can contribute to a better understanding of bipolar disorders, as most people with that disorder suffer from periods of severe depression. A number of theories have contributed to our understanding of depression over the years (Dobson & Jackman-Cram, 1996), including learned helplessness theory (Abramson, Seligman, & Teasdale, 1978; Seligman, 1975) and behavioral theory (Lewinsohn, 1974). Learned helplessness theory posits that individuals with depression are more likely to have stable, global, and internal attributions in response to negative life events (vs. external attributions: seeing problems caused by situational factors beyond their immediate control). These negative internal attributions can lead to hopelessness, helplessness, and depression. Lewisohn's (1974) behavioral theory focuses on the role of reinforcement contingencies inherent in interpersonal skills and the interpretation of social reinforcers. According to Persons and Fresco (1998), Lewisohn's model posits that a person's depression or happiness is, in part, contingent on the amount of positive reinforcement in one's life, the number and range of stimuli that a person finds reinforcing, the availability of reinforcers, and an individual's skill in obtaining reinforcers.

Although behavioral theories have increased our awareness of the role of reinforcement with respect to depression and its treatment, cognitive and social-cognitive theories of depression have clearly come to dominate the psychological literature over the past few decades (Beck, 1976; Beck, Rush, Shaw, & Emery, 1979; Clark & Beck, 1999, 2010). Cognitive theory of depression is an important development because it has shed light on psychological processes relevant to problems other than depression, including anxiety disorders. Beck's cognitive theory has evolved since the 1960s. The earlier formulation (Beck, 1976; Beck et al., 1979) laid down the fundamental components that remain relevant to the current, albeit more complex, model. Although no assertions are made in cognitive theory regarding the ultimate cause of depression, it gives priority to cognitive events within the reciprocal interactions of physiological, behavioral, and environmental factors. Evidence from neuropsychiatric research is growing and suggests that cognitive changes do mediate depression and anxiety, and that those effects may result from active cognitive control of negative emotions (Clark & Beck, 2010).

Three concepts constitute the major building blocks of the cognitive theory: the cognitive triad, schemas, and cognitive errors. The *cognitive triad* consists of three major cognitive patterns: first, a negative view of the self, or seeing oneself as defective in some way, worthless, the cause of bad things happening, and so forth; second, a negative view of the world, that is, seeing the world as placing major obstacles in one's path to happiness; and third, a negative view of the future, that is, being pessimistic and expecting poor outcomes for one's efforts. These negative expectations of the self, the world, and the future are likely to negatively affect motivation, resulting in a sense of helplessness, hopelessness, and dependency, and they may promote physiological symptoms of depression (e.g., low energy).

Negative schemas, the second major component of the cognitive theory of depression, are relatively stable cognitive patterns by which a person interprets life's experiences. Schemas may not always be active, but when activated by some external event, they are likely to determine how the person will respond. If these schemas result in a distortion of life's events, they may lead to faulty information processing and misinterpretations, which result in less-than-optimal or even maladaptive responses. The more distorted the interpretations, the more likely the negative schema could affect behavior in a negative way. The more severe the distortions, the less likely the person is to be willing to consider that negative interpretations are erroneous. Negative schemas appear to have their origins in one's social learning experience, including early life experiences.

The third major component of the cognitive theory of depression is *cognitive errors,* which result from faulty information processing, whereby illogical or distorted thinking serves to reinforce the negative view of self, the world, and the future. These faulty thinking processes may include arbitrary inference (i.e., drawing conclusions with little or no evidence to support the belief), selective abstraction (i.e., giving disproportionate weight to a small sample of evidence, perhaps, viewed out of context), overgeneralization (i.e., erroneously applying conclusions based on small amounts of observational data), magnification or minimization (i.e., grossly over- or underestimating the significance of a particular event), personalization (i.e., erroneously relating external events to oneself), and absolutist or dichotomous thinking (i.e., seeing events as polar extremes rather than on a continuum).

More recent developments in cognitive theory have provided a modified and more detailed construction of key concepts (Clark & Beck, 1999). A superordinate framework subsumes most of the prior theoretical developments within three categories: *cognitive structure, information processing,* and the *products of cognitive structures.* Cognitive structures subsume the earlier concept of cognitive schema but delineate various types, including cognitive-conceptual, affective, physiological, behavioral, and motivational schema. The content of schema (when activated in a depressed person) is constituted with elements of the cognitive triad as defined above.

Information processing may vary by different *levels of activation* (i.e., matching of environmental input to relevant schema and modes), *accessibility* (i.e., ease with which information can be transferred from long- to short-term memory), levels of *attention* (i.e., level of priority for processing), and *consciousness* (i.e., awareness of conscious information processing). Products of cognitive structures constitute those thoughts, feelings, and behaviors that interact in adaptive or maladaptive ways. Key cognitive products relevant to pathological conditions such as depression are those negative automatic thoughts presumably related to an individual's problems. Faulty information processes also produce cognitive errors, which become even more pronounced when individuals are affected by high-emotion states (e.g., depression, anxiety). Cognitive constructions are ultimately the conceptual constructions (e.g., persons, experiences, events) that provide meaning. The interacting cognitive structures, processes, and products are subject to self-referent activity that results in self-schema (i.e., cognitive constructions of the self). The interaction of depression-causing schema and the continuation of cognitive errors can become self-perpetuating. In the depressed person, this process may be expressed as "pervasive negativity toward the self" (Clark & Beck, 1999, p. 109).

In a somewhat parallel evolution, social-cognitive theory evolved empirically from early behavioral models (Bandura, 1977, 1986), and although the theory emphasizes cognitive processes it more explicitly emphasizes the reciprocal interaction of psychological, physiological, and environmental factors. Social learning theory (Bandura, 1977) engendered a revolution (Mahoney, 1977) in behaviorism by demonstrating the necessity of cognitive mediating factors to account for some of the limitations in stimulus-response reinforcement theories (i.e., classic and operant conditioning). Immediate, observable reinforcement in human behavior may be *facilitative* for behavior change, but social learning theorists demonstrated that observable reinforcement was not *necessary* for behavior change. Social-cognitive theory emphasizes the role of cognitive processes that mediate external stimuli and behavioral responses, including attention, retention, motor reproduction, and motivational processes. People essentially learn through information gathering, observational learning (i.e., vicarious learning through observation of others' modeling behavior), and experience (i.e., enactive engagement). Social-cognitive theorists see the development of psychosocial disorders as primarily the result of learning dysfunctional and maladaptive ways of thinking, interpreting emotional and physiological cues, and behaving in response to social and environmental contingencies. As such, changing dysfunctional patterns of thinking, feeling, and behaving in the context of an individual's unique situation (i.e., change processes or mechanisms) becomes the focus of psychosocial interventions.

Cognitive-behavioral interventions are informed by cognitive theory, social-cognitive theory, and stimulus-response behavioral theories. Current emphasis in cognitive-behavioral treatment clearly emphasizes changing cognitions through direct cognitive means and behavioral change techniques to disconfirm dysfunctional beliefs. This disconfirmation experience is likely to be reinforcing to the individual and to result in increased self-efficacy (i.e., the belief in one's ability to cope with challenging situations) by improving coping skills across different situations (Bandura, 1986). Although much theoretical and empirical work in cognitive and social-cognitive theories has been done in the area of depression and anxiety disorders, the contributions have been readily applied to other problems as well (e.g., substance abuse, eating disorders, major mental illness, childhood and adolescent disorders).

Cognitive factors related to depression are best understood when viewed in the context of social and environmental influences, which may provide a degree of competing risk and protective factors to precipitate or buffer an individual against the development of serious depression. Beck and colleagues (e.g., Clark & Beck, 2010; Clark & Beck, 1999) have begun to pay more attention, for example, to the appraisal of environmental factors in the causes of depression and have incorporated stress-environment theoretical concepts into a more interactive model of cognitive theory (e.g., Lazarus & Folkman, 1984). Negative appraisal of traumatic events, for example, has become a major focus in understanding post-traumatic stress disorder, a disorder that is often comorbid with depression (e.g., Ehlers & Clark, 2000; Sherrer, 2011). Evidence for the relationship between depression and socioenvironmental conditions and stressful life events such as loss (Brown, 1998; O'Hare & Sherrer, 2011; Stueve, Dohrenwend, & Skodol, 1998) has been known for some time. Other socio-environmental stressors, such as racism and discrimination, have been linked to stress and symptoms of depression (Utsey & Ponterotto, 1996). However, in a large national study (Chen et al., 2000), stressful life events were shown to be associated only with mild and episodic forms of depression rather than major depression. Nevertheless, the addition of environmental stressors may increase overall vulnerability, and those environmental influences are likely to be unique to individuals, as is the way individuals cognitively appraise those stressors. Although cognitive processes play a critical role, pathways to changing depressogenic cognitions might be attained via other routes, such as biological interventions or environmental changes. Despite the lack of consensus among theoreticians regarding the specific causal pathways of factors related to depression, evidence suggests that facilitating social and other environmental supports can have some preventive value (e.g., Shoevers et al., 2000).

Key Elements of Multidimensional-Functional-Systems Assessment

Depressive Disorders.   A considerable amount of research has informed the diagnostic criteria for depressive disorders (APA 2000, 2013), and the data currently reflect a multidimensional view that includes physiological and psychosocial indicators of distress. Criteria for major depressive disorder include the presence of a major depressive episode, defined by experiencing five relevant symptoms during the same 2-week period. The symptoms represent a change from previous functioning (at least one of the symptoms must be either depressed mood or loss of interest or pleasure). The relevant symptoms include a consistently depressed mood; markedly diminished interest or pleasure in almost all activities; significant (unintended) weight loss or consistent decrease or increase in appetite; near-daily insomnia or hypersomnia; near-daily psychomotor agitation or retardation; near-daily fatigue or loss of energy; feelings of worthlessness or excessive or inappropriate guilt (which may be delusional); difficulty concentrating; and recurrent thoughts of death (not just fear of dying), which may include recurrent suicidal ideation (without a specific plan) or a suicide attempt or a specific plan for committing suicide. There should not be any evidence of manic episode (other than substance induced). Persistent depressive disorder (dysthymia) shares some of the same symptoms as major depressive disorder but to a lesser degree and is more chronic (must be present for at least 2 years). As with other psychosocial conditions, the assessment is strengthened if data are collected from both the client and collateral observers.

Bipolar Disorders.   A diagnosis of bipolar I disorder requires the presence of a manic episode, which might be preceded by or follow with a depressive or hypomanic (i.e., not full manic) episode. This episode of a persistently elevated, expansive, or irritable mood; high energy; or intensively goal-directed activity must last a full week and be characterized by at least three or more of the following: inflated self-esteem or grandiosity, decreased need for sleep, extreme talkativeness and/or pressured speech, racing thoughts, easy distraction by irrelevant details, increased goal-directed activity and/or psychomotor agitation, and engagement in risky behaviors (e.g., unaffordable spending sprees, heightened sexual activity). Although an experience of a major depressive episode is not required to diagnose bipolar I disorder, the overwhelming majority of people with bipolar disorder have experienced major depression and often cycle in and out of manic and depressive episodes. Bipolar II is diagnosed if a person does not meet the 7-day criteria for manic episode, has had at least one major depressive episode (lasting 2 weeks), and has had a hypomanic episode (i.e., similar symptoms as manic episode) that lasts at least 4 days.

Multidimensional-functional-systems assessment requires going beyond the mere enumeration of the symptoms of mood disorders and demands an examination of the reciprocal nature of symptoms in the client's social context. Depression, particularly, is not just a matter of disordered mood; it is also often experienced as an interpersonal problem. Depression and mood disturbances, including the cycling of bipolar disorders, can be brought on or exacerbated by interpersonal strains and conflict, victimization (e.g., psychological abuse, neglect), and substance abuse. Conversely, living with a person suffering with a depressive or bipolar disorder can put considerable strain on those who live with him or her, reciprocally adding to stress and strain on the client. A depressed person may be relatively inactive (e.g., lie around the house brooding in silence for hours, be glued inattentively to the television), relatively uncommunicative with others in the household (e.g., leaving partners to wonder what is wrong or, for children, what they have done wrong). The depressed person may be irritable, argumentative, and uncooperative at work; actively avoid social gatherings; show little enthusiasm regarding leisure time on the weekends, or planning vacations; and or may be generally apathetic about making future plans. A seriously depressed person can cast a gloom over a household for months or years, and conflict may often erupt as, over time, empathy from loved ones erodes as they come to increasingly resent the person's relative inactivity and apparent apathy. Over time, the lack of cooperation, aloofness, and sparse communication or argumentativeness can lead to disaffection from family, friends, and coworkers.

A person with a bipolar disorder who is experiencing a manic phase can also be disruptive. Imagine a family member suddenly awake most of the night, talking very excitedly about some new but apparently completely unrealistic venture, pacing nonstop around the house, gesticulating wildly at each key point he is making, and becoming abusive and argumentative should his "grand plan" be challenged. Without foreknowledge of the signs and symptoms of bipolar disorder, such an experience is likely to be strange, puzzling, and possible very frightening for family members, especially young children. Understanding depressive and bipolar disorders in a broader psychosocial context can also help in planning an intervention that goes beyond symptom reduction to provide the family with an opportunity to better understand what is happening to their loved one; to take the client's strange or aggressive behavior less personally; to provide a calmer and less emotionally reactive environment; and to give the client the needed support to stabilize, adjust, and perhaps recover from illness.

With the stress-vulnerability model in mind, practitioners should conduct a detailed functional assessment that focuses on how the mood-disordered client's symptoms vary day to day in their social context (Miklowitz, 2008; Persons & Fresco, 1998). Clients might experience their depression or mania more acutely at different times or in different situations. Practitioners should examine the type, frequency, and severity of a client's signs and symptoms over time and across different social contexts, including work, friends, family, and so on. Practitioners should also help clients track the occurrence of other emotional disturbances (e.g., anxiety), behavioral problems (e.g., drinking), and interpersonal difficulties (e.g., conflicts, role strain, loss), all of which may be affected by or linked to mood disturbances.

Screening for Suicide.   Client suicide can be one of the more worrisome concerns for practitioners, and clients with mood disorders are at a much higher risk of attempting and completing suicides than is the general population. Although no social worker can offer 100% certainty of predicting and preventing client suicide, there are well-researched guidelines that can heighten awareness of potential suicide and help practitioners know when to take preventative action. Based on a range of demographic and clinical data, guidelines for assessing suicide risk include both general indicators and specific risk factors for suicide (Peruzzi & Bongar, 1999). General indicators of suicide risk include being male, having a serious mental disorder (e.g., schizophrenia, alcoholism, depression), having a history of suicide attempts or a history of suicide attempt in the family, being unemployed or experiencing other job-related problems, being unmarried or socially isolated, communicating suicidal intent, having made previous suicide attempts, possessing the lethal means to complete a suicide, communicating a sense of hopelessness (possibly a more reliable predictor than depression itself), having experienced chronic and stressful life events (including traumatic events), having aggressive and/or angry feelings, and suffering from serious physical illness. In addition, Song et al. (2012) found early age of onset, a history of auditory hallucinations, and antidepressant use to be strong predictors of suicide attempts in bipolar patients.

In addition to general indicators, Peruzzi and Bongar (1999) suggest the following as predictors for clients specifically diagnosed with major depression: attraction to death (fantasies about it), experience of anhedonia (i.e., loss of pleasure in life), suffering from anxiety, having acute suicidal ideation, engaging in acute alcohol abuse, and experiencing interpersonal stress (especially losses and separations). These items should be assessed in all clients, with an increasingly detailed focus on any item that a client positively indicates. As a rule of thumb, all these risk factors should be gauged individually on a continuum from mild to moderate to severe, and they should be seen as additive, that is, suicide risk increases as the number of risk factors increases. When practitioners identify risk factors, they should follow them up over the course of treatment until it becomes clear that clients have improved, that some of the acute problems are resolved, and that clients appear to be no longer at significant risk. Inpatient hospitalization should be seriously considered for clients who appear to be suicidal. If a client is to be treated on an outpatient basis, the practitioners should increase supervision of the client by increasing his or her availability to the client (e.g., more frequent visits, phone contact) and should inform and recruit significant others to monitor the client.

There are some pitfalls to avoid in conducting suicide assessments. Bongar, Maris, Berman, and Litman (1992) examined malpractice data and clinical literature to identify common practice failures that can be avoided. They point out that predicting suicide, which is a relatively rare event, is difficult. It also constitutes a troubling legal burden for practitioners because they are asked, essentially, to assume partial responsibility for another person's behavior. Nevertheless, social workers are expected to provide a reasonable degree of protection for clients against their suicidal actions. Bongar et al. (1992) itemized procedural failures that practitioners can avoid in outpatient care, including failure to

- Provide a diagnosis
- Conduct a thorough mental status exam
- Complete a formal treatment plan
- Provide a safe outpatient treatment environment
- Document clinical rationale, judgment, and significant observations
- Refer a client for a medication evaluation
- Specify criteria for hospitalization and/or implement hospitalization
- Provide adequate supervision (if the social worker is a supervisor)

- Evaluate for suicide at intake and periodically at points in treatment
- Secure prior records for medical and/or mental health history data

Although there are no guarantees that even the most thorough and skilled practitioner can prevent every potential suicide over years of practice, social workers can exercise prudence by providing thorough and well-documented assessments, keeping the client's interests paramount, and documenting their efforts to provide competent care. Conducting evidence-based assessment improves risk management practices for social workers and their employers, and it helps assure clients that they will receive the best care possible.

Special Considerations When Evaluating Depression in the Elderly. When conducting an assessment for depression with an elderly person, practitioners often have to consider other related problems: cognitive impairment, functional capacity, decision-making ability, whether to bring in outside caretakers (e.g., home health, visiting nurses), or whether the client needs to be placed outside the home (e.g., nursing home) (Edelstein, Staats, Kalish, & Northrop, 1996). As with MFS assessment in general, gerontology researchers stress the need for a biopsychosocial framework and emphasize that practitioners should avail themselves of multiple sources of data, first-hand observation of the environment, use of reliable and valid measurement instruments, observations of the individual's interactions with significant others in the environment, notes on the consequences of the elderly client's behaviors for others, and testing out of assessment hypotheses. Practitioners should also be mindful of their own biases about the elderly (e.g., being elderly means an end to productivity and disengagement from society, old folks are inflexible and get "set in their ways," senility is inevitable). Performance decrements (related to depression and other forms of psychopathology) may manifest themselves differently in the elderly than in younger adults (e.g., more concerns with performance fears, lower expectations, memory problems, poor concentration, fatigue), and other physical problems may also affect the elderly client's presentation and symptoms. For example, visual and auditory senses may be compromised, individuals lose physical flexibility and strength, and they may experience problems (e.g., pain) related to chronic illnesses and the effects of medications.

Depression and symptoms of physical illnesses can be intertwined in complex ways. The physical illness and depression can be reciprocally exacerbating; symptoms of both illnesses may be similar; medications can cause or exacerbate depression; and alcohol abuse may negatively affect medications, physical symptoms, and depression. The institutionalized elderly person and those undergoing medical treatment are more likely to be depressed. Practitioners should be alert to stressful negative events, health problems, loss, changes in social roles, lower income, a late-life caregiving role, and other acute and chronic stressors as possible risk factors for depression (Meeks et al., 2011; Wolfe, Morrow, & Fredrickson, 1996).

One of the most important assessment tasks may be to distinguish depressive symptoms from dementia (Bartolini et al., 2004; Safford, 1997; Wolfe et al., 1996). Cognitive, affective, and behavioral symptoms of dementia and depression overlap, but depression is generally more treatable than are symptoms of dementia. In terms of distinguishing depression from dementia (Alzheimer's type), the depressed patient is more likely not to be confused or have significant problems with everyday tasks, more likely to be anxious, and more likely to manifest the other classic symptoms of depression (e.g., waking up very early). Depressed patients also appear to show more rapid onset and progression, to have more problems with social skills, to complain more about forgetfulness, to underestimate their cognitive performance more, and to experience more negative memories. Those clients with dementia have slower onset and progression, minimize or overlook performance deficits, show fewer classic symptoms of depression, show a decline in short-term memory, do worse on formal tests of cognitive performance, show more confusion and confabulation, and demonstrate cognitive performance that is more consistently and pervasively impaired.

Most, if not all, of what was discussed here earlier regarding assessment of suicide risk in adult populations generally applies to the elderly as well. However, there may be some special considerations. Suicide appears to be more common among the elderly than younger adult populations (Kennedy, Metz, & Lowinger, 1996; Wolfe et al., 1996). Up to 70% of late-life suicides are related to serious illness, and suicide attempts are often made after having consulted a physician. Although illness may play a central role, the degree of hopelessness regarding whether the illness can be treated may be an even stronger predictor. Other stressful life events such as loss of a loved one can precipitate suicide (Lapierre et al., 2011). Research on prevention and intervention with elderly suicide appears to be growing internationally.

Instruments

The Beck Depression Inventory (BDI) (Beck, Ward, Mendelson, Mock, & Erbaugh, 1961) is one of the best-known scales for assessment of depression, and its psychometric properties have been thoroughly documented. The BDI's item pool was derived from observations of clinically depressed and other psychiatric patients, then compiled as a 21-item self-report scale that measures mood, pessimism, sense of failure, lack of satisfaction, guilt, sense of punishment, self-dislike, self-accusation, suicidal wishes, crying, irritability, social withdrawal, indecisiveness, distortion of body image, work inhibition, sleep disturbance, fatigability, loss of appetite, weight loss, somatic preoccupation, and loss of libido. These items are scored on a 0–3 scale, with cutoff scores as follows: 0–9 (none or minimal depression), 10–18 (mild to moderate), 19–29 (moderate to severe), and 30–63 (severe depression). Reviews of the psychometric properties have revealed that the BDI has very good internal consistency (mid-.80s, on average) for both clinical and nonclinical populations, good test-retest reliability, and good factorial validity (measuring negative attitudes toward self, as well as behavioral and somatic disturbances related to depression), although factor structures in various studies varied somewhat by study sample (Beck, Steer, & Garbin, 1988). The BDI-II was developed later, with some modifications in item content and formatting to cover a 2-week (vs. 1-week) reporting period (Dozois, Dobson, & Ahnberg, 1998). Overall, however, the new version is quite similar to the original BDI. The BDI is a proprietary instrument, and agencies must pay to use it.

Although scale developers often claim that their instrument measures unique features of a construct, the nuanced differences often have little clinical significance. Depression scales, including the BDI and the Hamilton Depression Rating Scale (HAM-D) (Hamilton, 1960), tend to correlate highly (e.g., Hotopf, Sharp, & Lewis, 1998). The HAM-D has also been shown to be valid for detecting depression in patients with dementia, for whom a cut-score of 10 is recommended (other than the usual 17 for all others) (Kertzman, Treves, Treves, Vainder, & Korczyn, 2002). The HAM-D is one of the most extensively used and well-validated scales in clinical research and has been a mainstay in clinical practice for more than half a century. It requires that the practitioner have a competent grasp of assessment for depression. There are no specific prompts, as such, and the interviewer must probe and examine each symptom category in a face-to-face, semistructured interview format. The HAM-D is in the public domain and can be used without cost (instrument 6.1).

Brief depression screens can improve the detection and assessment of depression in the elderly (Dorfman et al., 1995). The Geriatric Depression Scale (GDS) (Yesavage et al., 1983) was designed specifically to detect depression in elderly clients. It is a screening tool, and as such, a positive score (11–14) should prompt a more in-depth assessment and diagnosis for depression. The GDS was developed from a pool of 100 items suggested by practitioners and researchers. It was administered to a sample of nondepressed elderly persons (older than age 55 years) and hospitalized elderly. The 30 items that correlated best with a diagnosis of depression were retained for the scale. Items that emphasized somatic symptoms were not included because they also correlated with physical symptoms experienced by nondepressed older adults. The yes-no format of the GDS allows for easy administration. The GDS was shown to have both high internal consistency and split-half reliability. Edelstein et al. (1996) reviewed the literature regarding the GDS and cited evidence that supports good sensitivity and specificity, but as might be expected, they suggested that the GDS may not be as accurate for adults with serious cognitive impairment. The GDS appears to be more sensitive to detecting depression in the elderly than the HAM-D, the BDI, or the Zung Depression Scale are (Dick & Gallagher-Thompson, 1996).

A comprehensive review of the GDS (Stiles & McGarrahan, 1998) summarized the psychometric data and administrative recommendations. Although there are briefer versions of the GDS, the original 30-item version of the scale is recommended, given that it is the most researched version and

INSTRUMENT 6.1   Hamilton Depression Rating Scale

The total Hamilton Depression (HAM-D) Rating Scale provides an indication of depression and, over time, provides a valuable guide to progress.

- Classification of symptoms which may be difficult to obtain can be scored as:
  0 = absent, 1 = doubtful or trivial, 2 = present
- Classification of symptoms where more detail can be obtained can be expanded to:
  0 = absent, 1 = mild, 2 = moderate, 3 = severe, 4 = incapacitating

In general, the higher the total score the more severe the depression.

HAM-D score level of depression:
10–13 mild; 14–17 mild to moderate; >17 moderate to severe.
Assessment is recommended at 2-week intervals.

HAM-D Symptoms	Date
1 Depressed mood	0 1 2 3 4
2 Guilt feelings	0 1 2 3 4
3 Suicide	0 1 2 3 4
4 Insomnia, early	0 1 2
5 Insomnia, middle	0 1 2
6 Insomnia, late	0 1 2
7 Work and activities	0 1 2 3 4
8 Retardation, psychomotor	0 1 2 3 4
9 Agitation	0 1 2 3 4
10 Anxiety, psychological	0 1 2 3 4
11 Anxiety, somatic	0 1 2 3 4
12 Somatic symptoms, GI	0 1 2
13 Somatic symptoms, general	0 1 2
14 Sexual dysfunction, menstrual disturbance	0 1 2
15 Hypochondrias	0 1 2 3 4
16 Weight loss, by history	0 1 2
Weight loss, by scales	0 1 2
17 Insight	0 1 2

Total Score _____

can be administered in a few minutes. It can be used as self-report instrument but is probably better administered by clinical staff. Recommended cut scores range from 11 to 14 as an indicator of depression (use of 11 might increase false positives; 14 will reduce false positives). In the original scoring (with individual items rated "yes" = 1 and "no" = 0), 0–10 is generally considered "normal"; 11–19, "mildly depressed"; and 20–30, "severely depressed." Research on the GDS shows relatively consistent support for its reliability and validity, including good internal consistency, test-retest reliability, and good sensitivity and specificity in discriminating between depressed and nondepressed individuals. Using the GDS with clients with serious dementia is probably of questionable validity, although it should be considered valid for those who show only mild to moderate symptoms of dementia. Most studies have shown moderate to high correlations between the GDS and other standardized depression scales, in support of its concurrent validity. The GDS has been translated into many languages, although data regarding reliability and validity data with other cultures and races are mixed. More cross-cultural research with the GDS is needed. The GDS is in the public domain, and so can be used free of charge (instrument 6.2).

INSTRUMENT 6.2   The Geriatric Depression Scale

Answer "yes" (1) or "no" (0) to the following questions for how you felt over the past week:

1. Are you basically satisfied with your life? ___
2. Have you dropped many of your activities and interests? ___
3. Do you feel that your life is empty? ___
4. Do you often get bored? ___
5. Are you hopeful about the future? ___
6. Are you bothered by thoughts that you can't get out of your head? ___
7. Are you in good spirits most of the time? ___
8. Are you afraid that something bad is going to happen to you? ___
9. Do you feel happy most of the time? ___
10. Do you often feel helpless? ___
11. Do you often get restless and fidgety? ___
12. Do you prefer to stay at home rather than going out and doing new things? ___
13. Do you frequently worry about the future? ___
14. Do you feel you have more problems with memory than most? ___
15. Do you think it is wonderful to be alive now? ___
16. Do you often feel downhearted and blue? ___
17. Do you feel pretty worthless the way you are now? ___
18. Do you worry a lot about the past? ___
19. Do you find life very exciting? ___
20. Is it hard for you to get started on new projects? ___
21. Do you feel full of energy? ___
22. Do you feel that your situation is hopeless? ___
23. Do you think that most people are better off than you are? ___
24. Do you frequently get upset over little things? ___
25. Do you frequently feel like crying? ___
26. Do you have trouble concentrating? ___
27. Do you enjoy getting up in the morning? ___
28. Do you prefer to avoid social gatherings? ___
29. Is it easy for you to make decisions? ___
30. Is your mind as clear as it used to be? ___

Total Score ___

One example of a scale specifically designed for a culturally specific group is the Vietnamese Depression Scale (VDS) (Dinh, Yamada, & Yee, 2009; Kinzie et al., 1982), a 15-item scale instrument developed with a clinical group of Vietnamese in the United States who met DSM-III criteria for depressive disorder. The initial 45 items were reduced to 15 by selecting those that best distinguished Vietnamese clinic patients with depression from a comparable community (without depression) group. With a cut score of 13 (out of a possible 34), the VDS was highly accurate in distinguishing clinical and community subjects employing DSM-III criteria. The 15 items measure the following: feelings of desperation, downheartedness and low-spiritedness, feelings of being sad and bothered, feelings of going crazy, physical pains, feeling shameful and dishonored, decreased appetite, hopelessness, anger, difficulty concentrating, low-spiritedness and boredom, diurnal variation, and exhaustion. The additional emphasis on somatic complaints is culturally congruent with an Asian experience of depression. The VDS was also shown to have good internal consistency and reliability, and it distinguished levels of depression among different Vietnamese subgroups (Amerasians, their non-Amerasian siblings, and other Vietnamese immigrants) (Webb, McKelvey, & Strobel, 1997).

Because depression scales do not target common co-occurring symptoms in the very elderly, scales that measure cognitive impairment may also need to be included in an assessment and implemented by practitioners trained specifically in conducting thorough mental status exams. One of the better validated and most commonly used scales for measuring cognitive impairments is the Mini Mental State Exam (MMSE) (Folstein, Folstein, & McHugh, 1975), considered perhaps the best all-around screen for cognitive impairment including dementia. It takes 5–10 minutes to administer, and a score of 23 or less is the general cutoff for cognitive impairment with high sensitivity. The 20-item screen for cognitive functioning measures orientation, attention and concentration, recall memory, ability to follow a three-step command, and other gross indicators of problems with cognitive functioning.

Should practitioners suspect symptoms of mania and bipolar disorder after an initial assessment, the use of the brief Young Mania Rating Scale (YMRS) is a valid tool for both supplementing and confirming a diagnosis of bipolar disorder and is useful for monitoring changes over time. The YMRS (Young, Biggs, Ziegler, & Meyer, 1978) is an 11-item scale that measures key signs and symptoms of mania, including elevated mood, motor activity, sexual interest, sleep, irritability, rate of speech, language related to thought disorders (e.g., tangential speech), disordered content (e.g., delusions), aggressiveness, appearance, and degree of insight. The scale is meant to be completed by the practitioner during or immediately following a clinical interview. Each item is rated by the practitioner on a 5-point severity scale that is tailored to each sign or symptom. In its initial development, the YMRS showed very good reliability and correlated highly with other valid measures of mania. Higher scores on the YMRS appear to be associated with greater psychosis in bipolar mania (Canuso, Bossie, Zhu, Youseff, & Dunner, 2008) (see instrument 6.3).

INSTRUMENT 6.3   Young Mania Rating Scale (YMRS)

Guide for Scoring Items: The purpose of each item is to rate the severity of that abnormality in the patient. When several keys are given for a particular grade of severity, the presence of only one is required to qualify for that rating. The keys provided are guides. One can ignore the keys if that is necessary to indicate severity, although this should be the exception rather than the rule. Scoring between the points given (whole or half points) is possible and encouraged after experience with the scale is acquired. This is particularly useful when severity of a particular item in a patient does not follow the progression indicated by the keys.

1. *Elevated Mood*

    0. Absent
    1. Mildly or possibly increased on questioning
    2. Definite subjective elevation; optimistic, self-confident; cheerful; appropriate to content
    3. Elevated, inappropriate to content; humorous
    4. Euphoric; inappropriate to content; singing

2. *Increased Motor Activity—Energy*

    0. Absent
    1. Subjectively increased
    2. Animated; gestures increased
    3. Excessive energy; hyperactive at times; restless (can be calmed)
    4. Motor excitement; continuous hyperactivity (cannot be calmed)

3. *Sexual Interest*

    0. Normal; not increased
    1. Mildly or possibly increased
    2. Definitive subjective increase on questioning
    3. Spontaneous sexual content; elaborates on sexual matters; hypersexual by self-report
    4. Overt sexual acts (towards patients, staff, or interviewer)

4. *Sleep*

    0. Reports no decrease in sleep
    1. Sleeping less than normal amount by up to one hour
    2. Sleeping less than normal by more than one hour
    3. Reports decreased need for sleep
    4. Denies need for sleep

5. *Irritability*

    0. Absent
    1. Subjectively increased
    2. Irritable at times during interview; recent episodes of anger or annoyance on ward
    3. Frequently irritable during interview; short, curt throughout
    4. Hostile, uncooperative; interview impossible

6. *Speech (Rate and Amount)*

0. No increase
1. Feels talkative
2. Increased rate or amount at times, verbose at times
3. Push; consistently increased rate and amount; difficult to interrupt
4. Pressured; uninterruptible, continuous speech

7. *Language—Thought Disorder*

0. Absent
1. Circumstantial; mild distractibility; quick thoughts
2. Distractible; loses goal of thought; changes topics frequently; racing thoughts
3. Flight of ideas; tangentiality; difficult to follow; rhyming; echolalia
4. Incoherent; communication impossible

8. *Content*

0. Normal
1. Questionable plans, new interests
2. Special project(s); hyperreligious
3. Grandiose or paranoid ideas; ideas of reference
4. Delusions; hallucinations

9. *Disruptive—Aggressive Behavior*

0. Absent; cooperative
1. Sarcastic; loud at times; guarded
2. Demanding; threats on ward
3. Threatens interviewer; shouting; interview difficult
4. Assaultive; destructive; interview impossible

10. *Appearance*

0. Appropriate dress and grooming
1. Minimally unkempt
2. Poorly groomed; moderately disheveled; overdressed
3. Disheveled; partly clothed; garish makeup
4. Completely unkempt; decorated; bizarre garb

11. *Insight*

0. Present; admits illness; agrees with need for treatment
1. Possibly ill
2. Admits behavior change but denies illness
3. Admits possible change in behavior but denies illness
4. Denies any behavior changes

SELECTING EFFECTIVE INTERVENTIONS

Over the past few decades, most research on psychosocial interventions for mood disorders has focused on depressive disorders, with little attention given to bipolar disorders. However, much of what has been learned about treating severe depression is quite applicable to bipolar disorder as well. In addition, in cases in which depression or bipolar disorders are severe, and clients have severe difficulties in day-to-day functioning and require community support services, treatments designed for people with severe mental illnesses might be more suitable, as described in chapter 5.

Cognitive-Behavioral Therapy and Interpersonal Therapy for Depression

Most of the controlled research on psychosocial interventions for depression over the past 30 years has focused on two approaches: cognitive therapy, which for the sake of consistency is referred to here as cognitive-behavioral therapy (CBT) (Beck, 1976; Beck et al., 1979; Clark & Beck 1999; Hollon, Shelton, & Davis, 1993) and interpersonal psychotherapy (IPT) (Elkin et al., 1989; Klerman & Weissman, 1993; Klerman, Weissman, Rounsaville, & Chevron, 1984; Weissman et al., 2000). Leading professional organizations have endorsed both approaches as evidence-based practices, although evidence specifying the effective mechanisms of change has not been clearly demonstrated (Hollon & Carter, 1994; Oei & Shuttlewood, 1996), as is the case for many disorders.

Although some of the outcome data have been mixed with regard to the effectiveness of CBT for severe depression or its relative effectiveness when compared to antidepressant medication, CBT has accumulated a solid record of effectiveness when compared to control and comparison groups treated with other psychotherapies (Clark et al., 1999; Hollon et al., 1993). However, findings from the National Institute of Mental Health's (NIMH) Treatment of Depression Collaborative Research Program (Elkin, 1994; Elkin, Parloff, Hadley, & Autry, 1985; Elkin et al., 1989) revealed a relatively poor early showing for CBT. The study compared the efficacy of CBT, IPT, and tricyclic antidepressant (TCA) pharmacotherapy with a placebo condition that included minimal supportive therapy. It is considered the most ambitious test to date comparing cognitive therapy to pharmacotherapy. Conducting the study simultaneously at three different sites, the investigators randomly assigned 250 nonpsychotic, unipolar depressed outpatient clients to 16 weeks of treatment in one of the four conditions. Results indicated little difference among the three treatment conditions, and relatively little difference in outcomes between the CBT and IPT in symptoms or levels of functioning. For more severely depressed clients, pharmacotherapy was superior to placebo controls, and IPT seemed to fare better than CBT. However, according to Hollon, Shelton, and Loosen (1991), CBT outperformed the placebo group on some measures, and long-term follow-up at 18 months showed the long-term effects of CBT to be somewhat better than those of the other treatments (Shea et al., 1992). These results echoed previous findings (Kovacs, Rush, Beck, & Hollon, 1981), although long-term outcomes for all the interventions were unimpressive overall. More recent evidence has also provided modest support for the relapse prevention potential of cognitive-behavioral treatment when applied after a trial of antidepressant medication (Fava, Rafanelli, Grandi, Canestrari, & Morphy, 1998).

In the first comprehensive meta-analytic review of cognitive therapy (CT) using a common outcome measure (the BDI), Dobson (1989) examined 28 controlled studies from which 39 contrasts could be made between cognitive therapy and non-cognitive therapies and pharmacotherapy. Ten studies demonstrated that those clients receiving CT improved significantly better than 98% of those who received no treatment (including waiting-list control clients). Nine studies showed that those receiving CT had better outcomes than 67% of those receiving behavior therapy. Eight studies demonstrated that CT clients fared better than 70% of clients receiving pharmacotherapy, and seven studies showed that clients receiving CT obtained significantly better results than 70% of those receiving other forms of psychotherapies. Although Dobson's (1989) findings were generally favorable toward CT versus medications, Hollon et al. (1991) noted methodological weaknesses in some of the core studies Dobson (1989) had reviewed.

Noting that previous data concerning comparisons of cognitive and pharmacological therapies had been flawed for several reasons, Hollon et al. (1992) conducted a controlled trial to offset some of those weaknesses. In their study, 107 depressed clients who met strict diagnostic criteria and cut scores on the HAM-D and the BDI were assigned randomly to four conditions: pharmacotherapy without continuation, pharmacotherapy with continuation, cognitive-behavioral therapy, and combined CBT and pharmacotherapy. Randomization continued until 16 clients had completed each protocol, yielding a final complete sample of 64. Data showed there to be no differences in attrition among the four groups. Clients were assessed at intake, 6 weeks, and 12 weeks (post-treatment) by evaluators blind to the treatment condition. Data showed there to be no difference in outcomes between cognitive-behavioral therapy and imipramine treatments, and no advantage to combining treatments over implementing them alone.

Noting the mixed findings resulting from comparisons of CBT and tricyclic antidepressant pharmacotherapy, Thase et al. (2000) conducted the first comparison of CBT with the newer generation of antidepressants: selective serotonin reuptake inhibitors, SSRIs. Their sequential comparison of two groups of male clients demonstrated that SSRI medications outperformed cognitive-behavioral therapy on four of six outcome measures, including the HAM-D (Hamilton, 1960), the Automatic Thoughts Questionnaire (Hollon & Kendall, 1980), the Dysfunctional Attitudes Scale (Beck, Brown, Steer, & Weissman, 1980) and the Affects Balance Scale (Bradburn, 1969). They attributed some of the apparent advantages of SSRIs to better treatment compliance, given what they surmised to be fewer and less severe side effects of these medications. Additional studies are needed to replicate comparisons of SSRIs, CBT, and other therapies.

Some researchers have cited the so-called heterogeneity hypothesis to account for the inconsistency in outcomes for CBT; that is, differential outcomes may be a function of various interactions of dysfunctional thinking and different degrees of life stress. Simons, Gordon, Monroe, and Thase (1995) conducted a study in which 53 clients who had completed the treatment protocol provided data on several valid measures of depression, electroencephalogram (EEG) readings, and two environmental stressor scales. Results demonstrated that severe negative life events lessened the expected impact of treatment on dysfunctional attitudes. In a follow-up study, Spangler, Simons, Monroe, and Thase (1997) tested whether the interaction of cognitive dysfunction and negative stress predicted the participant's response to CBT. As in the initial study, participants generally showed good improvement with treatment, but findings indicated that CBT was effective regardless of the individual's degree of cognitive dysfunction or occurrence of recent and severe stressful life events. The authors concluded that in general CBT is effective regardless of interactions between specific cognitive dysfunctions and stressful events.

Since the NIMH collaborative study, evidence that IPT is a viable intervention for depression has continued to accumulate (Klerman & Weissman, 1993; Weissman et al., 2000) and has been shown to be culturally adaptable (Grote et al., 2009). In a brief review of IPT, Markowitz (1999) concluded that the results of IPT were often comparable to those achieved with a trial of the TCA imipramine, that clients developed new social skills up to a year following the termination of treatment, and that IPT provided more benefits for some clients than CBT did. IPT also has shown substantial benefits across all age groups. Combining IPT and tricyclic antidepressants has been shown to yield good long-term outcomes for elderly patients with depression. In a randomized controlled study of older clients (Reynolds et al., 1999), elderly depressed clients were assigned to four treatment groups: medication (nortriptyline) and IPT, medication and medication clinic visits, placebo pill and IPT, and placebo pill and medication clinic. Those receiving IPT plus medication were least likely to relapse.

Although CBT has come to be seen as a first-line psychosocial approach for treating depression (Young, Rygh, Weinberger, & Beck, 2008), research demonstrating its versatility with diverse groups, including those with co-occurring problems, continues to grow. For example, with regard to treating co-occurring depression and substance use problems, CBT has been shown in one review of the literature to be efficacious, with durable outcomes for co-occurring depression and substance use disorders, although with results comparable to other therapies such as motivational interviewing and brief intervention (Hides, Samet, & Lubman, 2010). Results of one meta-analytic study suggested that for those with co-occurring alcohol use disorders and either anxiety or depressive disorder, the addition of psychiatric medication (antidepressants primarily) to CBT (primarily) could confer additional benefits on clients (Hobbs, Kushner, Lee, Reardon, & Maurer, 2011).

CBT and components of it have been shown to be reasonably well accepted by and effective with diverse client groups as well. Enumerating the profound effects of depression on low-income women and their children, Levy and O'Hara (2010) concluded from their review that evidence-based practices appear to be effective with this group, although a range of modifications might be in order to increase engagement in treatment. These include using psychoeducation regarding the nature of depression and its treatment, addressing practical barriers (e.g., transportation problems), and attempting to make treatment more culturally relevant. A randomized trial comparing CBT with a sample of depressed pregnant (mostly Mexican) young women (in the United States) with a control group showed short-term benefits but mixed results overall, possibly as a result of relatively low levels of depression in either group (Le, Perry, & Stuart, 2011). The authors noted that the results of previous studies of programs to reduce postpartum depression have also been mixed.

Another randomized controlled trial tested a culturally relevant intervention based on interpersonal psychotherapy versus usual care with a mixed sample of African Americans and whites. It showed both a higher rate of participation and better response both during and after pregnancy for up to 6 months than in the usual care group (i.e., psychoeducational materials and access to counseling) (Grote et al., 2009).

CBT furthermore has been shown to be efficacious in individuals with HIV. One randomized controlled trial (Safren et al., 2009) compared a version of CBT focused on retroviral medication adherence (psychoeducation and dealing with barriers to adherence) in a sample of men and women with either major depression or bipolar disorder. Over the course of 12 months, CBT led to superior outcomes in both depressive symptoms and adherence level.

Behavioral Activation Therapy

There has been a resurgence of interest in basic behavioral approaches, lately in the form of behavioral activation therapy (BAT), a behaviorally focused intervention that emphasizes motivating clients to become more engaged in daily reinforcing activities. BAT emphasizes enhancement of self-regulatory skills (e.g., self-monitoring of mood, activities), graduated goal setting, and self-reinforcement with a focus on incremental success. Problem solving, reducing avoidance behavior, and making lifestyle changes that increase overall life satisfaction are ultimate goals. Evidence for the efficacy of BAT is growing (Dimidjian, Martell, Addis, & Herman-Dunn, 2008). A recent meta-analysis revealed that BAT showed a large average effect size when compared with other interventions for those with major depression. BAT involves increasing clients' behavioral interactions with environmental reinforcement contingencies, particularly those activities that bring pleasure and satisfaction, and enhancing clients' self-regulation so they can continue activities on their own via self-monitoring and self-maintenance (Mazzucchelli, Kane, & Rees, 2009). Results showed that BAT is comparable in both effect size and durability (up to 24 months) to cognitive and cognitive-behavioral therapies.

Interventions Designed for Elderly Clients

Given that depression in the elderly is often linked to loss, loneliness, withdrawal, and social deficits, improving clients' instrumental and social supports may be essential for maintaining therapeutic improvements. Naleppa and Reid (1998) conducted preliminary research on integrating a short-term task-oriented intervention into a long-term case management model. Sowers-Hoag (1997) also emphasized the need for multiple "traditional" case management services for the elderly, including case finding, multidimensional assessment, comprehensive care planning, coordination, monitoring, and evaluation of services. Although there are several interventions (including medication and psychotherapy) that are effective for treating depression in elderly persons, they are of little use if clients, especially those who lack social and instrumental supports, do not have the means to obtain treatment or cannot be monitored effectively in the community. One innovative program (Morrow-Howell, Becker-Kemppainen, & Lee, 1998) uses frequent phone contact to increase socialization and maximize autonomy in the elderly. The intervention (called Link-Plus) combines supportive therapy with case management services to provide meals, transportation, opportunities for socialization, and psychiatric services. In addition to helping clients accessing these services, case managers help clients overcome environmental and psychological barriers to using the services, and ensure service quality and continuity through monitoring and evaluation. Initial evaluation of this model proved promising.

Supportive, psychoeducational, and problem-solving interventions can be readily incorporated into an eclectic model that includes both psychotherapeutic and case management components. For example, a brief 8-week psychoeducational program for helping grandparents who are raising their grandchildren was evaluated (Burnette, 1998). The eclectic intervention included enhancement of social supports, stress management skills, dealing with family and/or interpersonal problems, parenting skills for a "new" generation of children, examining the availability of legal and social services, addressing neighborhood and community problems, and accessing available services. The evaluation demonstrated significant improvement in client depression scores. Rife and Belcher (1994) developed an innovative job-finding service (Job Club) for elderly unemployed workers who instructed participants in such areas as job interviewing, writing résumés, and completing applications, and facilitated social support and the sharing of job leads among participants. Results demonstrated significantly better outcomes for finding employment compared to traditional job-finding services, and participants had significantly lower scores on the Geriatric Depression

Scale at post-test. Cummings (2003) demonstrated in an uncontrolled evaluation that brief motivational enhancement therapy for elders in an assisted living residence improved psychological well-being and social supports. The program emphasized participants' social interaction with hands-on participation in gardening-related activities. Such programs can be a cost-effective addition to comprehensive strategies to improve quality of life for the elderly.

A recent Austrian controlled trial demonstrated that home care for depressed elderly people that included phone calls, counseling in coping skills, and enhancing access to resources resulted in reduced depressive symptoms and improved quality of life compared with the control group receiving standard outpatient psychiatric services (Klug et al., 2010). In another study of 170 individuals (age 75 and older) receiving primary care in the Netherlands, the use of cognitive-behavioral therapy (including bibliotherapy) and problem solving reduced the rate of diagnosed major depressive disorder by half over the course of 12 months compared with a treatment-as-usual control group (Van't Veer-Tazelaar et al., 2009). However, given the limitations of the design, it was unclear which components of the intervention conferred the most benefit.

In the first randomized trial of its kind, a home-based six-session problem-solving intervention was also shown to be significantly more effective at reducing depression and improving problem solving for medically ill elderly patients (Gellis et al., 2007). Incorporation of mindfulness and related meditation practices has been shown to be effective with a sample of those who had at least one major depressive episode in a randomized controlled trial (64 experimental, 66 control). Geschwind, Peeters, Drukker, van Os, and Wichers (2011) showed that incorporation of mindfulness practice increased participants' focus on improved mood linked to more positive appraisal of everyday occurrences and resulted in an increase in partaking of pleasant activities.

Interventions Adapted for People with Bipolar Disorder

As noted earlier in this chapter, some aspects of treatment of people with severe mental illnesses in general are likely to be effective with people diagnosed with bipolar disorder as well. Psychoeducation, cognitive-behavioral therapy, and family interventions share what appear to be common effective ingredients: learning about the disease and its course, learning to self-monitor moods and related symptoms, coping with stress, and improving family communications and adherence to a medication regimen (Buila, 2009). Evidence seems to support this view. For example, Miklowitz et al. (2000) found that a family psychoeducational program for those with a bipolar member was significantly more effective at reducing symptoms and relapse than standard clinical management. A randomized trial of group-based psychosocial intervention with people diagnosed with bipolar disorder (all taking medication) focused on self-monitoring and coping strategies, and showed considerably fewer relapses for the treatment group (n = 32) then for the control group (n = 40) over the course of a 12-week program with 9-month follow-up (Castle et al., 2010).

As with interventions for people with other severe mental illnesses, CBT appears to be a key component to an overall intervention strategy. Although practitioners should be cautious about extrapolating the results of CBT treatments from unipolar to bipolar depression, one review of the literature suggests that research on cognitive models of unipolar depression have relevance for understanding bipolar disorder as well. In addition, the few studies conducted on cognitive-behavioral treatments for bipolar disorder have suggested that CBT reduces relapse (Nusslock, Abramson, Harmon-Jones, Alloy, & Coan, 2009). Scott, Garland, and Moorhead (2001) showed a 60% reduction in relapse in bipolar patients, global improvements, and better medication adherence in a randomized controlled trial of cognitive therapy. In a review of the nascent literature on psychotherapeutic approaches to treating bipolar disorders, Miklowitz (2008) noted that individual, couple, and family interventions, when used as an adjunctive intervention with medication, appear to improve functioning overall and reduce relapse.

Evidence for the effectiveness of community practice for bipolar disorder (in contrast to randomized controlled trials, or RCTs) has been mixed, however. In a large naturalistic study carried out across five sites in Great Britain with a large sample of about 250 cases of people diagnosed with bipolar disorder, cognitive-behavioral therapy (over 26 weeks) was added to pharmacotherapy (n = 127) and compared with medication alone (n = 126). Results showed a modest overall difference in outcomes between the two treatment conditions, with some evidence that CBT might be helpful for patients with fewer manic-depressive episodes (Scott et al., 2006). More research on the transfer of EBP from controlled research to naturalistic settings appears warranted, and the addition of fidelity measures might help determine which components of care are most effective in daily practice.

Internet-Based Treatments for Depression

CBT, typically accompanied by telephone or email contact with a licensed provider, has been shown to result in moderate improvements and hold considerable promise as a public mental health tool. Internet-based approaches to CBT for depression are on the rise. In one RCT, Christensen, Griffiths, Mackinnon, and Brittliffe (2006) recruited almost 2,800 online volunteers who agreed to be randomized to one of six treatment conditions: (1) brief CBT; (2) brief CBT and problem solving; (3) brief CBT, stress management, and problem solving; (4) extended CBT and problem solving; (5) extended CBT, behavioral strategies, and problem solving; and (6) a module that included all programs. The findings suggested that extended online CBT was likely responsible for the small to moderate improvements that many participants experienced.

One web-based approach (Ruwaard et al., 2009) used an interactive workbook in which client and therapist could post, but they could not interact in real time. The practitioner used a manual for guidance in the therapeutic process. The treatment took about 11 weeks to complete, with a commitment of about 22–44 hours of client time and 7–14 hours of therapist time. Steps included inducing awareness of negative thoughts and feelings, monitoring those over time, adding structure to daily activities, challenging negative thoughts, engaging in cognitive restructuring (i.e., testing out negative thinking in behavioral experiments), practicing self-reinforcement, practicing social skills, and preventing relapse (by anticipating slips). Results showed clinically significant results in a reduction of both depression and anxiety, with good stability up to 18 months, and clients were generally very satisfied with their experience.

Physical Activity and Exercise

Although there is growing evidence for the positive effects of physical activity on disorders associated with mood disturbance (e.g., depression, anxiety), clinical application as a primary or adjunct treatment lags far behind (Salmon, 2001; Strohl, 2009). A recent meta-analysis demonstrated the benefits of exercise in depressed elderly people (Bridle, Spanjers, Patel, Atherton, & Lamb, 2012). However, methodological issues in the current research need to be disentangled (e.g., age, medication, types of exercise) before firm recommendations can be made (Steffens, 2013).

Electroconvulsive Therapy

Electroconvulsive therapy (ECT) is sometimes a viable option for treating severe depression in adults, including the elderly. Research for use of ECT with bipolar disorder, however, is lacking. The safety and efficacy of ECT for depression has been well documented (Dick & Gallagher-Thompson, 1996; McClintock, Brandon, Husain & Jarrett, 2011; Petrides, Tobias, Kellner, & Rudorfer, 2011), but others note potential complications associated with ECT, including hypoxia, arrhythmias, delirium, transient hypertension, and memory disturbances (Wolfe et al., 1996). There is also a lack of research establishing the effectiveness of ECT for depressed clients with dementia (Oudman, 2012). Relapse is common, and clients often receive some combination of ECT, medication, and psychotherapy. Nevertheless, many elderly persons who do not respond well to medications or other therapies obtain substantial relief from their depression with ECT, and many suffer few, if any, adverse side effects.

Change-Process Theory: How and Why Psychosocial Interventions for Depression Work

Comparable outcomes among different interventions for depression (e.g., CBT, IPT) make it difficult to establish the efficacy of specific mechanisms of change. Common or different therapeutic processes might be at work within different approaches. Despite the relative effectiveness of CBT, no change processes have been shown to be specifically or uniquely related to positive outcomes with depressed clients. "The pattern of findings for cognitive therapy has paralleled other findings for other therapies; clear superiority over no treatment conditions, but little difference in comparison with other forms of therapy. . . . Taken as a whole . . . meta-analyses do not provide strong evidence for specific action in cognitive therapy for depression" (Oei & Shuttlewood, 1996, p. 95).

In cognitively oriented interventions, the task in therapy is to change schematic models from dysfunctional (e.g., negative, pessimistic) ones to more adaptive ones (Teasdale, 1995), but the pathways to accomplishing that goal might be multiple, not just cognitive. Proponents of behavioral approaches (e.g., BAT) emphasize that, although the process by which the problem is maintained may be cognitive, effective interventions often focus on behavior change, where corrective learning experiences may have multiple impacts on cognitive, emotional, and behavioral functioning (Wilson 1995). Behavioral homework activities in CBT (e.g., testing out dysfunctional thoughts) may largely account for the effectiveness of cognitive therapy (Robins & Hayes, 1993). Medication and other interventions (e.g., regular vigorous exercise) can also cause clinically significant changes in mood, cognition, physiological functioning, and behavior. Because clients' depressive concerns often manifest in the context of interpersonal problems, it is quite possible that CBT, IPT, and some experiential therapies—though ostensibly different in technique—operate effectively through a combination of either different or common change processes that focus on interpersonal distortions, associated negative moods, and behavior changes to actively alter those processes (Ablon & Jones, 2002; Jensen, 1994; Johnson & Greenberg, 1995; Watson, Gordon, Stermac, Kalogerokos, & Steckley, 2003). Perhaps variations in both intervention techniques and change processes among different approaches will have to be accounted for, at least in part, by client differences.

Exemplar Study of Treatment for Depression: Testing Change Processes in Cognitive Therapy

One controlled investigation (Jacobson et al., 1996) compared key intervention components of CBT to the complete CBT model to examine whether all components of CBT are necessary to achieve the desired therapeutic effect. According to Beck et al.'s (1979) theory, the key active ingredient in CBT is the targeting of core cognitive structures (schemas) for change. Jacobson et al. (1996) compared behavioral activation (BA) (i.e., engaging in semistructured activities) and identifying and modifying automatic thoughts (ATs) with the full CBT package (which also includes identifying and modifying core dysfunctional cognitive schemas). One hundred fifty-two participants (110 women, 42 men) who met diagnostic criteria and scored above the conventional cutoffs on the BDI and the HAM-D were randomly assigned to three treatment conditions, and measures were taken at intake; termination; and 6-, 12-, 18-, and 24-week follow-up. Data were analyzed on the basis of 137 clients (resulting in an only 8% attrition rate) who completed between 12 and the maximum 20 sessions. Experienced cognitive therapists provided all services. Fidelity checks were conducted randomly on 20% of sessions to ensure that each specific treatment protocol was adhered to.

Treatment conditions were as follows:

- *Behavioral activation (BA)*: This condition included monitoring daily activities, assessing pleasure and mastery associated with those activities, engaging in increasingly more challenging tasks that engendered pleasure and mastery, cognitive rehearsal of engaging in those activities and identifying obstacles in the process, identifying behavioral techniques to use to overcome obstacles, and enhancing of social skills to overcome obstacles.

- *Activation and modification of dysfunctional thoughts (AT)*: This condition involved identifying cognitive distortions and thoughts that preceded mood shifts during sessions, using a diary as a self-monitoring tool to identify negative thoughts and circumstances, challenging the rationality of those thoughts, developing more functional responses to them, examining cause-effect reasoning with regard to how participants made attributions regarding successes or failures in their lives, and homework to evaluate negative interpretations. In this treatment condition, all BA activities could be incorporated as well.

- *CBT (complete form)*: emphasized the identification and modification of more stable core beliefs (schemas) that underlie the negative automatic thoughts and distortions in reasoning through a careful deductive analysis of underlying assumptions and challenging of them through homework assignments. In addition to the full CBT condition, which incorporated both BA and AT, eight sessions were specifically targeted toward core assumptions.

Results showed that a complete regimen of CBT was no more effective than either BA or AT. In fact, BA was as effective as the full CBT protocol. A follow-up study (Gortner, Gollan, Dobson, & Jacobson, 1998) examined data at 6, 12, 18, and 24 months after active treatment. One hundred thirty-seven participants (more than 90% of whom completed treatment of 12–20 visits) were followed up with measures used in the original study. At 2-year follow-up, there were no significant differences among the three treatment groups with regard to relapse indicators. The authors summarized: "The three treatment conditions were virtually identical on every criterion measure, including recovery and relapse rates, number of well weeks, and survival time to relapse" (Gortner et al., 1998, pp. 380–381). This study is but one that challenges a major tenet of cognitive theory and practice: core negative schema must be addressed directly to cause stable improvement in depressed mood. Because behavioral activation is a relatively straightforward intervention method, it is possible that either core cognitive schema can be changed through behavior changes alone or that other change processes alone or in combination result in reduced depression.

Effective Interventions for Depression

Cognitive-Behavioral Therapy.   CBT for depression is a set of integrated cognitive and behavioral techniques used to identify, assess, and change negative and dysfunctional beliefs and associated problem behaviors (Beck, 1976; Beck et al., 1979; Clark & Beck, 1999; Hollon & Carter, 1994; Young et al., 2008). Clients are helped to modify dysfunctional thinking through rational discussion and behavioral disconfirmation in the form of "homework" assignments. These assignments may also include one or more standard behavioral interventions (e.g., coping skills, problem-solving and communication skills, stress management) in some combination. In actual practice, considerable latitude is employed in crafting a CBT treatment plan for individual clients.

Cognitive-behavioral therapists are expected to be actively engaged in the process of collaborative empiricism with the client (i.e., testing out dysfunctional beliefs). It is understood that practitioners will cultivate a sound therapeutic alliance based on a foundation of the "core ingredients" of the helping relationship (i.e., warmth, genuineness, positive regard, and basic trust) (Beck, 1976; Klosko & Sanderson, 1999; Orlinsky, Grawe, & Parks, 1994; Young et al., 2008). The process of CBT for depression is generally sequenced as follows:

1. A thorough biopsychosocial assessment is conducted.

2. Suicide assessment is carefully carried out.

3. A therapeutic structure is established and respective roles delineated.

4. Tasks are planned to jump-start the client's level of activity (e.g., spend an hour per day organizing work at home, begin long-neglected tasks); seemingly complex tasks are broken down into manageable steps.

5. The cognitive model of depression is explained (i.e., schemas, negative automatic thoughts, dysfunctional information processing); the CBT practitioner avoids judging or labeling, but accepts the client's initial construction of the problem.

6. The practitioner sets about actively engaging the client in a Socratic exploration of the problem and discovering where some of the sources of the problem may be.

7. Client is taught how to self-monitor and record automatic thoughts and associated moods; examination of the client's negative automatic thoughts may lead to an exploration of underlying assumptions, perhaps themes that permeate different areas of the client's life and recur over time.

8. Client is taught how to examine evidence of troubling thoughts, consider alternative explanations, and identify the real implications of a belief if it is true.

9. Client learns how to identify cognitive distortions and perform agreed on tasks to test out hypotheses regarding negative assumptions or negative automatic thoughts (i.e., collaboratively planned homework assignments).

10. Client is encouraged to participate in active self-monitoring of thoughts and record responses to them. (e.g., diaries, logs, charts). Significant others may participate as needed to assist in the assessment or play a part in carrying out homework assignments with the client. With repeated homework experiences and associated tasks, dysfunctional beliefs are likely to be disconfirmed.

11. Practitioner helps the client to identify underlying assumptions (schemas) that maintain the negative automatic thoughts.

12. Practitioner works with the client to develop a plan to cope with the possibility of relapse and to focus on how the client will implement new coping strategies in the face of future stressors and disappointments that may reactivate negative automatic thoughts.

Practitioners may be relatively active in the beginning stage of the intervention, becoming gradually less active as clients take more initiative in questioning and testing their own negative or depressing thinking, associated feelings, and behaviors. During each session, an agenda is set, homework reviewed, new homework assigned, and feedback obtained on each visit. In addition to the homework tasks designed to test out dysfunctional beliefs, other behavioral treatments employed may include assertiveness training, anger management, relaxation techniques, methods to improve productivity (e.g., time management, organization), managing of panic attacks, guided imagery for covert rehearsal, and lifestyle changes (e.g., regular exercise), among other activities.

CBT for Late-Life Depression.   A meta-analysis of interventions with the elderly demonstrated considerable promise for a number of interventions, particularly cognitive and reminiscence therapy (Scogin & McElreath, 1994). Case-study research has also provided some support for cognitive therapy for depression in the elderly (e.g., Gupta, 2000). Thompson (1996) outlined recommendations for adapting CBT for older clients, given that they may be experiencing some degree of cognitive impairment. He recommends the use of the Geriatric Depression Scale and a thorough mental status exam as part of a comprehensive assessment. Brief CBT should be used in combination with medication for maximum therapeutic benefit. Although CBT for depression is usually provided in 16–20 sessions, practitioners should be prepared to be flexible with treatment duration. In addition, presenting material more slowly and using memory aids (e.g., writing down homework assignments, using a notebook, presenting information on a whiteboard or projector screen) are all modifications that can be helpful for older clients.

Thompson (1996) suggests a three-phase approach. In the early phase (sessions 1–3) a good working alliance is established, and clients are instructed in the basic principles of cognitive theory and CBT. Clients are also instructed in how to self-monitor dysfunctional thoughts (e.g., negative automatic thoughts) that occur between sessions. In the middle phase (sessions 4–12), clients are taught core cognitive and behavioral skills for identifying dysfunctional thoughts, and practitioners then gently challenge those beliefs through rational examination and behavioral hypothesis testing. Clients are also encouraged to identify and increase pleasurable activities in their lives. In the final phase (sessions 13–16) clients focus on honing their skills for dealing with stressful situations to prevent relapse. Some clients may also be referred for follow-up interventions, such as continued medication or electroconvulsive therapy.

Thompson (1996) recommends that individual sessions be structured as follows:

1. The agenda is presented.

2. Assessment is conducted (including the use of measures).

3. Problem assumptions or dysfunctional beliefs are identified and discussed.

4. Homework assignments are reviewed.

5. Practitioner addresses areas of apparent resistance.

6. A new or continued topic is presented as needed.

7. Session is summarized and new homework assignment is given.

A similar application of CBT for anxiety in the elderly has also been found to be effective; results showed clinically substantive reductions in co-occurring depression (Stanley et al., 2003). Because many depressed elderly clients also suffer from anxiety disorders, it may be fruitful to incorporate anxiety management skills into CBT for older clients.

Interpersonal Psychotherapy for Depression.   Although Weissman et al. (2000) refer to a number of theoretical influences in the development of IPT, they explicitly endorse a firm commitment to the basic principles of evidence-based practice: "We are convinced . . . that all theories and schools require evidence from testing, and that the most powerful evidence comes from carefully designed, well-controlled investigative trials" (p. 4). IPT emphasizes three main component processes: symptom function (main physiological symptoms such as disturbances in sleep, appetite, and energy), social and interpersonal relations (based on learning experiences, current social supports, personal coping skills and competence), and personality and character problems (i.e., more enduring dysfunctional traits, including poor self-esteem, and chronic difficulties relating to others). The IPT practitioner intervenes in the first of these two processes: physiological symptoms of depression and problems of interpersonal relations. Although IPT does not focus on character change, improved coping skills may compensate for problems in those areas as well. Although IPT shares "generic" psychotherapeutic skills such as basic counseling techniques, and improving interpersonal problem solving and communication, the authors assert that it is more than merely "supportive" therapy:

> IPT . . . intervenes with symptom formation, social adjustment and interpersonal relations, working predominantly on current problems and at conscious and preconscious levels. Although the IPT therapist may recognize unconscious factors, they are not directly addressed. The emphasis is on current disputes, frustrations, anxieties, and wishes as defined in the interpersonal context. IPT aims to help clients *change* rather than to understand and simply accept their current life situation. The influence of early childhood experience is recognized as significant but not emphasized in the therapy. Rather, the work focuses on the "here and now." Overall treatment goals are to encourage mastery of current social roles and adaptation to interpersonal situations. (Weissman et al., 2000, p. 9)

IPT is to be understood within the broader framework of the medical model, and its adherents actively endorse the notion of clients adopting the patient role. IPT practitioners recognize that other interventions may be preferable for some clients, and its developers do not claim that IPT is universally effective for all depressed clients. IPT is a goal-focused intervention and is of relatively short duration. The main techniques are exploration, encouragement of affect, clarification, communication analysis, use of the therapeutic relationship, behavior change techniques, and other adjunctive techniques. Although past relationships are recognized as potentially important in understanding the genesis of the client's main problem, the therapeutic focus is on current relationships. Because IPT is rooted somewhat in a neo-Freudian tradition, practitioners of IPT may recognize the importance of defense mechanisms, but the focus is squarely on improving current interpersonal relations. IPT differs from CBT in at least one significant way: although distorted thinking may be acknowledged along the way in therapy, no systematic effort is made to analyze the content of these thoughts other than to better understand them in the context of the client's interpersonal functioning. The IPT practitioner is active, not neutral or passive, and emphasizes the core ingredients of basic helping. Transference (i.e., the displacement of client's unconscious thoughts, wishes, fantasies, and so on, onto the practitioner), though recognized as a legitimate construct by IPT practitioners, does not become a focus of treatment. Positive transference is left untouched, negative interpersonal interactions with the therapist are dealt with openly in an effort to resolve them. Above all, client autonomy (not dependency) is encouraged.

Based on the writings of the leading developers and proponents of IPT (Markowitz, 1999; Weissman et al., 2000), the basic IPT approach is outlined as follows:

- In the initial sessions, practitioners conduct a thorough review of depressive symptoms, characterize the depression as an illness, and evaluate the client for medication.

- Both past and present relationships are examined for quality and satisfaction, significant problems, met and unmet expectations, and changes the client would like to see in his or her relationships.

- The problem is defined as a relationship-based formulation, and the practitioner and client plan intervention goals together.

- The client is provided with a basic introduction to the philosophy and procedures of IPT.

- In intermediate sessions, the practitioner and client focus on one of three major problem areas: grief, interpersonal role disputes, or role transitions.

  - For grief, the practitioner facilitates the mourning process, examines the loss and attending symptoms, and helps the client to reconnect with other social supports to alleviate the depressive symptoms associated with loss.

  - For an interpersonal role dispute, the conflict should be identified and problem-solving strategies reviewed to help ameliorate the conflict.

  - For role transition, the practitioner might assist the client in mourning the old role by examining thoughts and facilitating the expression of feelings about the loss. The client can then address the new role in a more positive light, with an emphasis on mastering the new role and accessing support systems to facilitate the new role.

- If the client has interpersonal deficits, the practitioner should help the client to reduce isolation and encourage the formation of new relationships.

- If the client's interpersonal problems seem to recapitulate in the context of the therapeutic relationship, the practitioner should use that opportunity to help the client resolve the interpersonal dispute. In other words, the therapeutic context becomes a laboratory for helping the client better understand and manage interpersonal problems.

- Termination focuses on helping the client plan to maintain gains into the future.

IPT for Treating Depression in Elderly Persons. Weissman et al. (2000) note that mood disorders are common among the elderly population and are often accompanied by disproportionately high suicide rates. Effective psychosocial interventions for the elderly are important given the higher risks associated with taking medication (e.g., side effects, drug interactions). In addition, losses and role transitions experienced by the elderly lend themselves to goals of IPT (Klerman & Weissman, 1993). Controlled trials of IPT with elderly clients have demonstrated that IPT can be effective when administered in much the same way as it is for younger clients, although a variation on the original IPT model geared toward maintenance of late-life depression (IPT-LLM) has been developed. However, in addition to balancing dependency needs with the need to maintain independence, practitioners should expect to remain active in the treatment and should encourage small gains, be flexible in scheduling meetings, and help clients tolerate some of their interpersonal difficulties if making major changes is impractical or unwanted (Klerman & Weissman, 1993).

Medications for Depression and Bipolar Disorders

Overall, data support the effectiveness of SSRIs, serotonin and norepinephrine-reuptake inhibitors (SNRIs), and tricyclic antidepressants for the treatment of depressive disorders. However, the research regarding for whom antidepressants work best and whether medication, psychotherapy, or combined treatments is superior is somewhat indeterminate given the current state of research (Cuijpers et al., 2012). The most common side effects from antidepressants involve headache, sexual dysfunction, nervousness, insomnia, drowsiness, and anxiety. Fluoxetine, and other SSRIs may cause sleep interruption as well, prompting physicians to add a more sedative drug to the medication regimen. SSRIs have been considered generally safer than other antidepressants in the case of overdose (Kaplan & Sadock, 1998; National Institute of Mental Health [NIMH], 2013).

Although not prescribed as frequently for depression anymore, tricyclic antidepressants (TCAs) are still considered a viable option for some depressed clients (Kaplan & Sadock, 1998; NIMH, 2013). TCAs also have a reputation for more serious anti-cholinergic side effects and greater potential toxicity than SSRIs. These side effects, which are shared with SSRIs, include blurred vision, dry mouth, constipation, and urinary retention. TCAs also have a reputation of being more sedating than the SSRIs. Social work practitioners should be aware that the risks associated with overdose through error or by suicide attempt are not uncommon, and overdoses of TCAs can be fatal, particularly in a physically compromised elderly person.

Monoamine oxidase inhibitors (MAOIs) have come to be considered a third option for an antidepressant (Dzieglielewski & Leon, 1998; Kaplan & Sadock, 1998; NIMH, 2013). These drugs work by increasing amine neurotransmitter levels. MAOIs carry a risk of hypertensive crisis resulting from potential interactions with ingredients in common foods. MAOIs also tend to interrupt normal sleep and may cause insomnia and daytime drowsiness. Other side effects include edema, weight gain, and sexual dysfunction. Overdose of MAOIs may induce coma, and an overdose of these drugs with other antidepressants may be fatal.

Dzieglielewski and Leon (1998) offer prudent suggestions for social workers providing interventions for clients who are taking antidepressant medication. In general, clients need to take these medications for several months to achieve their full benefit. However, as a client prepares to discontinue their use, social workers can help plan for this transition by

- Increasing clients' awareness of possible recurrence of symptoms
- Ensuring that clients have good social supports
- Encouraging clients to consider the continuation of psychosocial intervention after discontinuing medications
- Preparing clients with an action plan in case depressive symptoms recur
- Involving significant others in a relapse prevention plan

First-line medications for bipolar disorder specifically include lithium carbonate and divalproex sodium, and their efficacy is well established. However, people with bipolar disorders might also benefit from anticonvulsants or antipsychotic medications depending on the presence of other symptoms (e.g., psychosis) (NIMH, 2013).

TREATMENT PLANNING AND EVALUATION

CASE STUDY: GRANDMA LONG

Grandma Long came into the social worker's office led by her daughter, An. She was obviously quite depressed, staring down at the floor, and refusing to look at the social worker, Jen, and, except for occasionally sighing and crying softly to herself, said very little throughout the interview. An recounted the story and the reasons she had reluctantly come to the clinic.

About a month earlier Grandma Long's 16-year-old grandson Thu (An's nephew) was shot and killed during a robbery outside the family's restaurant after closing hours. The funeral was a few days later, and the extended family was greatly distraught. Thu had been a hard worker in the restaurant and a good student at school. The family had worked hard to keep their sons and daughters out of the growing gang culture that had evolved over the past few years in nearby neighborhoods. It was not clear who committed the crime and no arrests had been made.

Before the killing, Grandma Long had been increasingly despondent. An's husband, and Grandma

Long's son-in-law, Hung, had recently purchased the restaurant that he had worked in for the previous few years with Grandma Long and his wife, An. Hung, now the boss (after many years of working more than 80 hours per week) wanted to make it clear that he was in charge. He asked that Grandma Long no longer be allowed in the kitchen. Grandma Long had for many years been manager and head chef in a number of restaurants in Vietnam and in the United States. She and Hung had often butted heads, but the former owner had a way of keeping them focused on different tasks. In the previous few months, she had been pushed out altogether and was feeling, in her words, "used up, worthless, no longer needed." After the killing, she became incapacitated by depression, refused to eat, was losing weight, and expressed a desire to die as soon as possible. Other family members were coming by often to offer her tea and conversation, and to keep an eye on her.

Grandma Long had left Vietnam just before the fall of Saigon. She was in her late 40s then, had witnessed many years of war, had lost several extended family members, and felt she had left such violence behind when she came to the United States.

She brought her daughter, An, who was 21 at the time, with her. They lived in Vietnamese neighborhoods in the Midwest for a number of years and worked in restaurants. After An met Hung and got married, they moved east so Hung could take a new job. An and Hung had a daughter, and since then have been living and working in the same neighborhood. They lived near the restaurant in a three-story house with Grandma Long and other family members. Everyone worked hard, and child care and other domestic duties were shared along traditional lines. Grandma Long (whose name means "the dragon") lived up to her name as the one in charge (the children called her "dragon lady" behind her back). Grandma Long often opined that the old ways were fading, that children did not respect their elders in the United States. She tried to exercise her authority over the children in the household but feared they were being pulled too easily into the fast and seductive American culture outside the extended family's enclave. When Thu, her favorite grandson (and An's nephew), was killed, it was the validation of the worst of her lifelong fears. War and more killing, she felt, had followed her to the United States.

MFS Assessment: Defining Problems and Goals

Just before the killing, Grandma Long had been somewhat despondent and more irritable than usual. She seemed less assertive around the house, and less inclined to orchestrate domestic duties, and she seemed to be giving up her position of authority, since she had been "demoted" at the restaurant by her son-in-law, Hung. She seemed distracted, staring out the window for long periods, and often was forgetful, once leaving the teakettle on and falling asleep in her easy chair. The smell of the burning kettle brought one of the other family members downstairs. When Hung found out, he was angry and said if it happened again, Grandma Long would have to move out and go to an "old folks' home."

At other times, Grandma Long seemed fidgety and nervous; she would sigh a lot and sometimes cry. She did not sleep well at night, often getting out of bed early in the morning and sitting in her chair in the main room. Often she would repeat the refrain, "I'm no use to anyone. I should just die soon. It would make things a lot easier for everyone." She seemed to feel a great sense of shame because of her lowered status in the family. She often complained of pains and feeling ill, and she had visited the neighborhood herbalist. She was drinking various teas, and felt that the admixtures ameliorated her physical symptoms. Still, her mood had not improved. She also visited the doctor at the local clinic, who suggested Grandma Long was depressed but ruled out any incipient dementia and offered medication (an SSRI), which Grandma Long declined. Grandma Long had little faith in standard American medical practices. Other than her somatic complaints, her health was deemed to be very good.

Although she was felt everyone had abandoned her and pushed her aside, Grandma Long actually had many social supports and was still respected in the family. Some members still felt that she was the go-to person on cooking and other domestic matters. Younger members of the community would often come by to see her and ask her about the "old days" in Vietnam or obtain recipes from her. It was at these times that she seemed to be a little more animated and (her daughter related) demonstrated some of her "old spark." But when her visitors left, she would relapse into a sense of despair. Nevertheless, she had considerable family and community support despite her depressed state, feelings of shame, and sense of worthlessness. After the news of Thu's death reached her, she became incapacitated. Her day-to-day functioning declined even further, and she no longer would accept visitors. She stopped eating. She lay in bed and said she just wanted to die.

Selecting and Designing Interventions: Defining Strategies and Objectives

During the week after the killing, neighbors and friends came and went in the household, helping with meals and cleaning, and keeping an eye on Grandma Long. There was not much else they could do at the time. A week after the funeral, household routines and restaurant duties resumed despite the cloud of sadness and anger that remained. Grandma Long seemed to be fading away, and the family knew they had to take action. After An conferred with Jen, the clinical social worker at the local mental health clinic, Grandma Long was admitted to a local general hospital that had a special geriatric psychiatric unit. Grandma Long remained there for a few days, as she was losing weight and somewhat dehydrated. After a number of examinations and multiple tests, the psychiatrist in charge said she needed to be discharged, as the insurance would not cover an extended stay. The recommendation for medication was again made. Jen would continue to follow the case on an outpatient basis. Jen met with the family and established a plan for individual grief counseling for Grandma Long, but she also encouraged An, Hung, and other family members to participate in family sessions for grief counseling and to work out some of the interpersonal conflicts that emerged in the initial assessment with Grandma Long. Eventually, Jen set up a case management plan to make occasional home visits with the family to see that improvements would be maintained.

In this case the social work practitioner was well versed in evidence-based approaches to working with depression in the elderly. She was also attuned to the local Vietnamese culture, and had considerable experience working with families and community helpers (e.g., the apothecary, the Vietnamese Catholic priest). Jen met with Grandma Long, An, and Hung, and decided that Grandma Long needed, at least initially, some individual attention to grieve the loss of Thu. She made it clear that she also wanted to include An and Hung at some point in family sessions but felt that it was premature to deal with family conflicts at this time. She also recognized the family's grief over the loss of their nephew, and invited An, Hung, and other family members to attend a group session that included other Vietnamese community members who had also lost loved ones.

Jen concluded that IPT would be helpful for Grandma Long. Initially, the emphasis on addressing her grief seemed to be in order. Grandma Long spoke for long time and glowingly of Thu and how he would stop by often to see her. She was obviously very proud of him, and she brought in pictures of him and documents that attested to his academic successes and other accomplishments. He had won second prize for a story he had written about his grandmother and her experiences in Vietnam before coming to the United States. Over the course of 2–3 months, Grandma Long had begun to brighten. She was sleeping better (which may have been attributed to the antidepressant medication that she finally agreed to try along with her herbal teas), and she had gained back a significant amount of weight. She was not talking about suicide, and some of her attention was refocused on domestic duties. Nevertheless, she continued to feel that her status in the family had been seriously diminished.

At some point into the third month, the social worker asked Grandma Long if, perhaps, she would like to have her daughter and husband return for a few visits to see if they could work out some of their differences. Grandma Long's belief that she was "useless" seemed intractable. The practitioner felt that Grandma Long's negative beliefs about herself could be resolved, but not without resolving some of the family-role conflicts. Grandma Long was still in good health and could certainly contribute more to the family at home and perhaps in the restaurant. It seemed that IPT could be used to resolve the role conflicts in a family intervention, and at the same time, elements of CBT could be applied to help Grandma Long examine and (through behavior changes) disconfirm her negative view of herself as "used up, and worthless."

Jen had developed a strong alliance with her client, and she felt that it was time for Grandma Long, An, and Hung to meet together. However, during the week, Jen began to think that perhaps she had miscalculated by scheduling both the grandmother and the couple together. She felt that perhaps she should see the couple first to report on Grandma Long's progress but also to test out the possibility that the son-in-law, Hung, would relent somewhat on having banished Grandma Long from the restaurant altogether. When they all met in the waiting room, the social worker asked Grandma Long if it would be OK to meet with her daughter and son-in-law alone for a few minutes. Grandma Long seemed pleased to be deferred to in this decision, and she agreed. During the couple's visit, Jen explained that Grandma Long had become a bit less depressed, although she would probably always grieve the loss of her grandson on some level. Jen then posed the problem of the long-standing conflict between Hung and Grandma Long. As Hung spoke it became clear that he had worked incredibly long and hard under an abusive boss. When he finally had his "own place," he felt he had to establish complete control over the business to ensure its success. Nothing, in his eyes, could be worse than if his business failed. He did not feel that he could expend energy or stress on fighting with his mother-in-law in the kitchen, run his business, and maintain his marriage. Jen acknowledged these as reasonable concerns. But she suggested that, as the business was going very well and Hung had a sense that things were under his command, perhaps they could discuss the possibility of delegating some important role to Grandma Long—not make-work, but a real contribution to the business.

The social worker met with Grandma Long, and suggested that all three of them could meet again the following week to discuss some things about the home and the business. Grandma Long agreed. In the discussion that ensued the following week, they all agreed that the business was going well and that there was considerably more help in the kitchen than before. Many of the employees were young people engaged in preparatory cooking work and other ancillary jobs (e.g., running the dishwasher). Hung agreed that, at times, things were getting out of hand in the restaurant. He had also discussed with other restaurant owners down at his social club that his employees lacked training, a task for which Hung had not the time or the patience.

It occurred to Hung in conversations with his wife that he had been disrespectful to Grandma Long and that she might be the ideal person to take over training of the younger employees and to keep them "in line." (She was, after all, the "dragon lady.") Hung had become frustrated at dealing with them, and felt the need to delegate more responsibility to his head chef, spend some time talking to his customers, get out of the restaurant once in a while, and deal more directly with his suppliers. It might also give him more time to look into opening up another restaurant on the other side of town. Hung realized he had been somewhat abrupt in the past with Grandma Long. Jen motioned to him to talk with Grandma Long directly. He picked up the cue and, after apologizing to her for showing disrespect, asked if she would be willing to take over the training and supervision of the kitchen help. Grandma Long agreed (after telling him in so many words "I told you so"). Jen made follow-up visits to the home and the restaurant (she was invited). Grandma Long appeared to be doing well; she was once again energetic in the kitchen and attending to her new charges. Although the psychiatrist recommended that Grandma Long continue taking her antidepressant medication for now, An reported that her serious symptoms of depression had not returned. Grandma Long seemed to have "adopted" some of the young people who worked for her, which seemed to please her very much. Still pinned up over the calendar at the far end of the kitchen was a photo of Grandma Long and her grandson, Thu, always in view.

Selecting Scales and Creating Indexes to Monitor and Evaluate Client Progress

Instruments useful in this case included the Mini-Mental Status Exam (MMSE) (Folstein et al., 1975), which was used during Grandma Long's hospital stay, and the GDS and VDS, which the social worker used for both assessment and periodic monitoring. Individual indexes included her level of activity around the house (e.g., how often she engaged in domestic duties), hours sleeping, and number of meals she took daily. Other important indexes included suicide risk factors, particularly indications of hopelessness or suicidal ideation.

SUMMARY

Major mood disorders are among the most common debilitating disorders globally, and they co-occur with the full range of psychosocial disorders. Contemporary theories emphasize the interaction of biological, cognitive, behavioral, and situational factors in the etiology and trajectory of depression. After a thorough assessment, social workers can avail themselves of at least two psychosocial interventions that have been shown to be effective with depression: cognitive-behavioral therapy and interpersonal psychotherapy. Behavioral activation therapy is also gaining adherents. Because social and instrumental supports are critical to the long-term maintenance of gains, particularly for elderly clients, case management provides a coherent framework for coordinating evidence-based practices for clients with major mood disorders.

TABLE 6.1   The Client Service Plan for Grandma Long

Problems	Goals	Objectives (samples)	Interventions	Assessment and evaluation tools
Symptoms of major depression that appear to be exacerbated by acute grief reaction (favorite grandson killed during a robbery)	Alleviate acute symptoms related to grief; sort out assessment of prior depression from grief reaction	Allow for expressions of grief during weekly visits; review and reminisce about her relationship with her grandson; review mementos and pictures; help her express grief over other past losses in her family	Eclectic use of both interpersonal psychotherapy and cognitive-behavioral therapy Short-term IPT to initiate resolution of acute grief symptoms IPT to address grief and role conflicts with family members that appear to be related to grandmother's sense of "worthlessness"	MMSE (Folstein et al., 1975) Geriatric Depression Scale Vietnamese Depression Scale Other functional indexes (hours of sleep, meals eaten, hours of activity at home and at the restaurant, suicidal indicators)
Suicidal thinking, feelings of shame, guilt, worthlessness; lowered activity level, sleep disturbance, loss of appetite and pleasure in life; other somatic complaints (e.g., references to aches and pains)	Ameliorate symptoms related to major depression; return to normal level of functioning	When she begins to show some increase in energy, activate daily routine gradually over time; plan domestic activities one at a time; increase as needed	CBT to examine cognitions regarding "sense of worthlessness," and disconfirm that by improving role performance (e.g., return her to a position of some authority, give her suitable responsibility at home or in family business)	
Problem in family relations: specifically, conflict with son-in-law over authority and respective roles	Resolve family dispute; ideally, adjust respective family roles to reasonable satisfaction of all members	As depression abates and energy increases, plan to reintroduce her to the business; incorporate her role as trainer initially for 2 hours, 1–2 days per week; increase as needed and required	Family session(s) to clarify communications and assist in resolving role conflicts that involve the grandmother Case management activities: coordinate monitoring and evaluation with psychiatrist regarding medication compliance; confer with local community helpers as needed	

CHAPTER 7

SUBSTANCE USE DISORDERS

Millions of Americans abuse alcohol and other drugs. "Other drugs" refers to the use of "recreational" or "street drugs" and the abuse of prescription medications. These problems result in billions of dollars of costs to the *health* and *psychosocial well-being* of the nation (Bouchery, Harwood, Sacks, Simon, & Brewer, 2011; Hasin, Stinson, Ogburn, & Grant, 2007; Johnston, O'Malley, Bachman, & Schulenberg, 2013; US Department of Health and Human Services, USDHHS, 2000), as well as enormous human costs. No single prevailing theory dominates the current scientific understanding of the causes, course, or consequences of substance abuse. Biological, psychological, cultural, and economic perspectives compete in a field that has become increasingly interdisciplinary. Research has demonstrated a range of moderately effective interventions, including brief psychoeducation, motivational enhancement therapy, cognitive-behavioral therapy, behavioral couples' and family interventions, 12-step facilitation strategies, and community reinforcement and contingency management approaches. These methods share overlapping intervention components that focus on self-monitoring and skill building to reduce relapse. Practitioners have become more flexible with regard to treatment goals, which now range from harm reduction and moderation to abstinence and long-term recovery. Efforts to predict choice of treatment on the basis of client characteristics (i.e., treatment matching) have not produced substantive results, but research in this area continues.

The purpose of this chapter is to provide an evidence-based overview of assessment and interventions that social workers can provide as primary treatments or integrate into mental health practice when substance abuse co-occurs with other problems. Adults struggling with substance abuse and dependence are the main focus of this chapter. Adolescents and young adults who abuse substances are often experiencing other behavioral difficulties as well (e.g., delinquency, conduct disorder, problems in school), and thus are addressed more fully in chapter 16.

ASSESSMENT

Background Data

Definitions of substance abuse and dependence cover a continuum from experiencing moderate distress in daily life (e.g., work, mood, relationships) to developing some degree of physiological dependence (e.g., tolerance, cravings, loss of control) on one or more substances. Although current diagnostic nomenclature is examined in more detail here later, the dividing line between abuse and dependence has always been unclear. This empirical reality has recently been recognized by changes in the DSM-5 (American Psychiatric Association, APA, 2013) for diagnosis of a substance use disorder; the DSM-5 no longer distinguishes abuse from dependence, as was the case in the DSM-IV. Disordered substance use is better reflected as a heterogeneous collection of cognitive, physiological, and behavioral signs and symptoms that are associated with an array of problems across a continuum of severity.

Multidimensional-functional-systems (MFS) assessment of substance abuse and dependence is critical, given that the problem manifests itself quite differently depending on personal factors (e.g., gender, age, type of employment, life circumstances) and on individual cognitive, physiological, behavioral, situational, and cultural differences. This approach to assessment requires an examination of the quantity and frequency of substances used and measurement of psychosocial, physiological, and clinical health consequences.

About two-thirds of Americans drink alcoholic beverages with, for the most part, few associated problems. Another large proportion of Americans also use illegal drugs, and many others abuse prescription medication. Although epidemiological data for alcohol and other drugs vary from year to year, overall Americans use more substances than they did in the past, and the traditional gap between men (who generally use more substances) and women has been closing over the past few decades. Although whites traditionally consumed more alcohol per capita than Hispanic Americans and African Americans, risks for these racial groups have increased in recent years.

Rates of Alcohol Use Disorders.   Data from the National Longitudinal Alcohol Epidemiologic Survey (NLAES) (Grant & Dawson, 1999; Grant et al., 1994) indicated that 66% of adults (age 18 and older) were lifetime drinkers who had consumed at least 12 alcoholic drinks during any 12-month period of their life. In addition, almost half (44.4%) had consumed 12 or more drinks in the preceding year. Almost 25% were classified as lifetime heavy drinkers, and about 9% were classified as heavy drinkers within the past year. Reports of alcohol abuse versus alcohol dependence vary somewhat as a result of shifting diagnostic criteria and other methodological differences in epidemiologic studies. Also, one should note the difference between *12-month* prevalence (i.e., diagnosed within the past year) and *lifetime* prevalence (i.e., diagnosed at least once in a person's lifetime). The estimate for 12-month alcohol use disorder (based on DSM-5 criteria) is about 8.5% (APA, 2013; Grant et al., 2004). Kessler et al. (1994) reported that about 14% of US citizens have met diagnostic criteria for alcohol dependence at some point in their lives, with men about 2.5 times as likely to meet those criteria as women. Hasin et al. (2007) estimated lifetime prevalence for alcohol abuse at 17.8% and lifetime dependence at 12.5%. They also pointed out that about 75% of people with alcohol dependence never received treatment.

The highest rates of abuse appear to be in younger individuals, mostly men, from age 18 to 29, whereas most dependence occurs in middle-age men (Hasin et al., 2007). Men showed more than double the rates of women for both abuse and dependence over the lifetime and in the previous year. Those in the 18–29 age group drank the most in the previous year. Men were almost three times as likely as women to drink heavily during their lifetime and within the previous year, a profile similar by gender among drinkers age 18–29. For both men and women, rates of heavy drinking in the previous year declined after age 30 (Grant & Dawson, 1999; Grant et al., 1994).

College-age youth and their noncollege cohorts continue to drink prodigious amounts of alcohol on average, and a sizable proportion also use illegal drugs during their young adult years. More than 20 years of research on college drinking show that more than 67% of college students drink alcohol, about 40% are considered binge drinkers (i.e., consumed five or more drinks in one sitting within the previous 2 weeks), and rates of alcohol use have not changed substantially for decades (Johnston et al., 2013; O'Malley & Johnston, 2002). Data on alcohol and drug use in young adults are more thoroughly reviewed in chapter 16.

Recently, more attention has been focused on military veterans returning from Iraq and Afghanistan. Heavy alcohol use is common among veterans (33% or more), yet relatively few seek out substance use services (Burnett-Zeigler et al., 2011). Substance abuse is highly comorbid with post-traumatic stress disorder (PTSD) in veterans (Goodson et al., 2011), and this matter is addressed more thoroughly in chapter 9.

There are variations in alcohol consumption patterns among racial groups in the United States. Between 1984 and 1995, rates of abstinence from alcohol increased somewhat among white, black, and Hispanic men and women. However, frequent heavy drinking declined among white men and women, stayed about the same among black men and women, and increased among Hispanic men and women. Rates of frequent heavy drinking among these three racial groups (by men and women, respectively) were estimated at 12% and 2% for whites, 15% and 5% for blacks, and 18% and 3% for Hispanics. Problems related to alcohol either declined or stayed about the same for whites and blacks, but problems increased notably for Hispanic males and females (Caetano & Clark, 1998; Galvan & Caetano, 2003). More recently, 12-month prevalence rates in the United States for alcohol use disorder have been estimated at 12.1% for Native Americans and Alaskan Natives, 8.9% for whites, 7.9% for Hispanics, 6.9% for African Americans, and 4.5% for Asian Americans and Pacific Islanders (APA, 2013; Huang et al., 2006).

Perhaps most of the research regarding the negative consequences of substance abuse and dependence is based on alcohol use, and the consequences for health and psychosocial well-being are considerable (Hasin et al., 2007). It is now well recognized that, although light to moderate drinking among otherwise healthy adults has significant cardiovascular health benefits, excessive bingeing and chronic abuse significantly increase the likelihood of serious illnesses such as heart disease and various cancers (Rehm, Gmel, Sempos, & Trevisan, 2003). About 88,000 deaths per year are attributable to alcohol abuse (Centers for Disease Control and Prevention, CDC, 2013a), other prominent consequences include 20,000 alcohol-related deaths in traffic accidents; 25,000 deaths due to cirrhosis; and increased risk of death by other traumatic events, including fires, falls, drowning, and interpersonal and domestic violence (Bouchery et al., 2011; Rehm et al., 2003; USDHHS, 1997, 2000). The overall costs of alcohol use in the United States were estimated at $223 billion in 2006, with more than $20 billion attributed to health-care costs alone (Bouchery et al., 2011). Young men between the ages of 22 and 45 are at the greatest risk of driving under the influence and being involved in fatal alcohol-related accidents. The risk of an alcohol-related fatal crash is dose dependent (i.e., the higher the blood alcohol level, the greater is the risk of an accident). In one study of all vehicular fatalities in the United States from 2005 to 2009, more than half (57%) had been using alcohol or other drugs at the time, and about 20% were using more than one drug (Brady & Li, 2013). Although fatalities related to substance use have generally dropped over the past 30 years (Dang, 2008; Hingson & Winter, 2003), this progress might be threatened by increases in the abuse of other drugs, including the sharp rise in prescription drug abuse (Brady & Li, 2013; Johnston et al., 2013; McCarthy, 2007).

Drugs Other Than Alcohol.   The National Household Survey on Drug Abuse (NHSDA) (USDHHS, 1998) estimated the percentages of persons who have *ever used* an illicit drug in the following age groups: 12–17 years (23.7%), 18–25 (45.4%), 26–34 (50.8%), and older than 35 (31.5%). Rates of drug use among men tend to be higher than for women, ranging from 1% to 10%, with differences increasing with age. The following proportions are for those persons who had used an illicit drug in the previous year: age 12–17 (18.8%), 18–25 (25.3%), 26–34 (14.3%), and older than 35 (6.1%), again with comparable differences between men and women.

The NLAES data (Grant & Dawson, 1999) also revealed that more than 15% (15.6%) of the US adult population reported having used illicit drugs at least 12 times in their lifetime, mostly marijuana (13.9%), amphetamines

(4.1%), and cocaine (3.7%), and about 2% each for tranquilizers, hallucinogens, opioids, and sedatives. Those in the age range of 18–29 years used almost twice as much as those older than age 30, men used more than women by a margin of 19.5% to 12.0%, and men used more drugs than women in all drug categories. The percentage of previous-year use was 4.9% for any drug, with marijuana topping the list at 3.9% and all other drugs estimated at less than 1%. Previous-year drug use for men was almost twice that for women, and those age 18–29 were more than three times as likely to use as those over 30.

The NLAES study (Grant & Dawson, 1999; Grant et al., 1994), also demonstrated high rates of co-occurring abuse of alcohol and other drugs. Sixty-nine percent of those with any drug use disorder also were classified with an alcohol use disorder. Those classified with an alcohol use disorder were about 10 times as likely to have a drug use disorder as those with no alcohol use disorder. Results were fairly consistent over the different major classes of licit and illicit drugs (Grant & Pickering, 1996).

The abuse of illicit drugs, particularly marijuana, cocaine, and amphetamine "designer" drugs are relatively common among adolescents and young adults. According to the Monitoring the Future Survey (USDHHS, 1999), although there were some variations in types of drugs used and in their rates of use, drug abuse rates continue to be relatively stable among those age 19–28. There has been an increasing trend among college students' use of marijuana, 3,4-Methylenedioxyamphetamine/3,4-Methylenedioxy-methamphetamine (i.e., MDA/MDMA or ecstasy), and cocaine. Between 1991 and 1998 the rates of marijuana use among eighth graders nearly tripled from 6% to 17%, nearly doubled among tenth graders (15% to 31%), and grew by 80% among twelfth graders (22% to 38%). Among high school seniors, the use of any illicit drug has risen from 15% to 21% since 1992. Although brief trends emerge in the data, no steady downward trends have been recorded in drug use overall since 2002 (National Center for Health Statistics, 2014). Drug use disorders were more prevalent among younger adults and those who never married (Compton, Thomas, Stinson, & Grant, 2007).

Examination of substance use with diagnostic criteria reveals a similar picture. The National Epidemiologic Survey on Alcohol and Related Conditions (NESARC) (based on responses from more than 43,000 respondents) (Compton et al., 2007) revealed that approximately 2% (2.8% male, 1.2% female) of the US population has been diagnosed with a drug use disorder within 12 months, and 10.3% (13.8% male, 7.1% female) met lifetime criteria for a drug use disorder. In general, drug abuse disorders were about three times more common than drug dependence. Rates of nonprescription use of sedatives, tranquilizers, opioids, and amphetamines range from 3.4% to 4.7% in the United States, and rates of abuse and/or dependence range from about 1% to 2%, according to NESARC data (Huang et al., 2006). The same data revealed that men were roughly twice as likely to abuse drugs as women across all categories, and that those who had a prescription drug use disorder were 11–16 times as likely to have an alcohol use disorder, up to 200 times as likely (particularly tranquilizers and sedatives) to have another category of nonmedical prescription drug use disorder, and from 28–70 times as likely to have any other illicit drug use disorder. Overuse of pain control medications has been openly acknowledged as a serious public health problem, and deaths from pain medication have risen precipitously over the past 25 years (CDC, 2013b; McCarthy, 2007).

Race in Relation to Drug Abuse.   Race comparison data from the National Household Survey on Drug Abuse (USDHHS, 1998) revealed that whites have a higher lifetime rate of marijuana use (35.6%) than Hispanics (22.3%) or African Americans (28.5%), and both whites and African Americans showed comparable rates of marijuana use in the previous year (9.1% vs. 9.9%), which exceeded that of Hispanics (7.5%). Whites also had higher rates of lifetime cocaine use (11.8%) than Hispanics (7.3%) and African Americans (6.5%), but whites were slightly less likely to have used in the previous year (1.9%) than Hispanics (2.0%) or African Americans (2.4%). Whites' rates of drug use in both lifetime and previous-year categories for inhalants, hallucinogens, stimulants, tranquilizers, and analgesics also exceeded the rates for both Hispanics and African Americans. Other researchers have compared data on whites, African Americans, Hispanics, Asian Americans, and Native Americans and have drawn similar conclusions (Caetano, Clark, & Tam, 1998; Kitano, 1989). Using diagnostic criteria with more recent data than the NHSDA, NESARC (Compton et al., 2007) revealed that Native Americans (4.9%), followed by African Americans (2.4%), whites (1.9%), Hispanics (1.7%) and Asians (1.4%), met 12-month criteria for a drug use disorder. Similarly, Native Americans (18.4%), followed by whites (11.3%), African Americans (8.7%), Hispanics (7.2%), and Asians (3.8%), met lifetime criteria for a drug use disorder.

Substance Use and Comorbid Conditions.   Substance abuse problems co-occur with the full range of psychosocial and health problems social workers encounter in their daily practice. These problems include mental health disorders (Drake & Mueser, 2002; Kessler et al., 1996; Petrakis, Gonzalez, Rosenheck, & Krystal, 2002), health problems (USDHHS, 2000), child and family disruptions (Azzi-Lessing & Olsen, 1996; Orford, 1990), domestic violence (Gmel & Rehm, 2003), and the full range of other psychosocial disorders commonly seen in social service environments (O'Hare, 1993; USDHHS, 2000; Weisner & Schmidt, 1993).

The Epidemiological Catchment Area (ECA) survey (Helzer & Pryzbeck, 1988), the National Comorbidity Survey (NCS) (Kessler et al., 1996), and the National Longitudinal Alcohol Epidemiologic Survey (NLAES) (Grant & Harford, 1995) have shown significant correlations among anxiety, depression, and antisocial behavior and borderline personality with substance abuse and addiction (Grant et al., 2009; Hasin et al., 2007). Across all drug categories, those with drug use disorders were about 2.5 times more likely than the general population to meet diagnostic criteria for major depression, between 5 and 6 times as likely to have bipolar I disorder, and 3–5 times as likely to meet criteria for bipolar II (Huang et al., 2006). When controlling for demographic characteristics, those with any drug use disorder were nine times more likely to meet criteria for an alcohol use disorder than people with no drug use disorder, and diagnoses for depression, bipolar I disorder, bipolar II disorder, and personality disorder were 2.2, 5.1, 2.4, and 4 times more likely, respectively. Slightly more than one-third of people with a drug use disorder had ever sought treatment for that disorder during their lifetime (Compton et al., 2007).

Women have consistently shown a disproportionate degree of co-occurrence of emotional distress (e.g., anxiety, depression) and substance abuse, whereas substance-abusing men are more likely to engage in antisocial behaviors. Persons with serious mental illnesses also show a disproportionate degree of substance abuse problems (as reviewed in chapter 5). The Methods for the Epidemiology of Child and Adolescent Mental Disorders (MECA) study (Kandel et al., 1997) also demonstrated that the use of alcohol, cigarettes, and other illicit substances, even at relatively low doses, were significantly associated with anxiety, mood, and disruptive behavior disorders in young people, with gender differences essentially mirroring data for adults.

Prominent Risk Factors Associated with Substance Abuse and Addiction

Although there are many potential risk factors for substance abuse (generally, factors that correlate or have been shown to predict substance abuse), only some of the more prominent empirically validated risk factors are noted here. In addition to other forms of psychopathology noted already, these risk factors include age, gender, cognitive mediators, family history, and cultural factors. It should be understood that these risk factors may be accounted for by interacting biological, psychosocial, and cultural processes.

Age.   As noted already, young adults are among the highest consumers of alcohol and drugs in the nation, and consequently, they run relatively high risks of psychosocial problems, such as depression, anxiety, and suicide, as well as health and physical problems, such as contracting HIV, and accidental injury and death, often associated with drinking and driving (Johnston, O'Malley, & Bachman, 1996; Johnston et al., 2013; O'Hare, 1997a, 1997b; Quigley & Marlatt, 1996; USDHHS, 2000). Although most substance use problems are transitory for youth, it has been long established that the earlier young people begin to abuse drugs, the more likely they are to have long-term problems (Chen & Kandel, 1995).

By comparison with their younger counterparts, the elderly drink considerably less (Liberto, Oslin, & Ruskin, 1992) but suffer greater psychological and health risks, in part because of the inherent vulnerabilities of aging as well as interactions with medications. Older adults also take increasing amounts of prescription drugs with age, and have diminished physical health and capacities (e.g., slower metabolism, cognitive decline, depression, fewer social supports) (Gossop & Moos, 2008). An elderly person may have been struggling since early adulthood (early onset) or may have begun to abuse alcohol more recently (e.g., after retirement, after loss of a spouse). Late-onset drinkers, however, are more likely to respond positively to an intervention (Brennan & Moos, 1996; Liberto et al., 1992).

Gender.   Although substance abuse research has been traditionally focused on men (Floyd, Monahan, Finney, & Morley, 1996; Wilk, 1994), research on women has steadily increased. Despite using less alcohol and fewer street drugs than men, women suffer higher risks because of associations between alcohol and health, depression, anxiety, and polysubstance use (including prescription medications), as well as the consequences of sexual abuse and other trauma, role disruption, and domestic violence (Bennett, 1995; Corrigan, 1985; Gomberg, 1994; Greenfield, Back, Lawson, & Brady, 2010; Greenfield et al., 2011; Hurley, 1991; Klee, Schmidt, & Ames, 1991; Lex, 1994; Norris, 1994; O'Hare, 1995; Project Worth, 1997; USDHHS, 2000; Wilsnack, Wilsnack, & Hiller-Sturmhöfel, 1994).

Children of Alcoholic Parents.   In addition to genetic influences from biological parents, children (and later those same children as adults) who grew up with substance-abusing parents incur some degree of increased risk for emotional, behavioral, and social problems. The level of risk, however, is likely to be predicted by a range of interacting factors, including genetic influences on both substance abuse and psychopathology, quality of parenting, level of marital conflict, degree of job-related problems, and role modeling with respect to drinking practices and risk-taking behaviors (Johnson, Sher, & Rolf, 1991; Pandina & Johnson, 1990; Sher, 1997; Windle, 1996; Zucker & Fitzgerald, 1991). Not all adult children of alcoholics (ACOAs) share the same experience or list of pathologies as a result of their experiences with parents who have a drinking problem.

Race and Culture.   Differences in substance use patterns exist among Americans from different cultural and racial-ethnic backgrounds. However, generalizations about the drinking patterns of broad racial/ethnic groups should be made cautiously because of the high degree of heterogeneity among interethnic subgroups (Caetano et al., 1998; Heath, 1991; Huang et al., 2006). Asian Americans, for example, generally consume the least alcohol overall, but as among other cultural groups, acculturation pressures have resulted in higher alcohol consumption than prevously (Kitano, 1989). Native Americans' use of alcohol varies widely; some groups are relatively abstemious, yet others show profound alcohol problems, with death rates in excess of five times the national norm (Beauvais, 1998; Huang et al., 2006). Although concerns related to methamphetamine abuse among Native Americans in the US Southwest have been on the rise, alcohol abuse continues to be the primary concern (Forcehimes et al., 2011). Culture is a risk factor, but a complex one in which ethnic identity and degree of assimilation and acculturation to American drinking norms must be considered. Despite increasing research on substance abuse in ethnic minorities, nonwhites continue to be underrepresented in research, including in clinical trials. Researchers examining these concerns in detail have recommended more assertive and community-based efforts to recruit people of color into research trials (Burlew et al., 2011).

Theories

Assessment models of substance abuse necessarily reflect theoretical assumptions. Although there are a range of competing theories that purport to account for the causes of alcohol abuse and dependence, the major dialectic in substance abuse research has been between predominantly disease-oriented explanations (biological causes) and learning-based theories (beliefs, behavior, and sociocultural factors). Modern biological explanations for the causes of alcoholism have focused on studies of heredity and vulnerabilities associated with alcohol abuse, including central nervous system (CNS) response to alcohol ingestion, temperament, and other related forms of psychopathology (Goodwin, 1985; Heath, 1995; Hesselbrock, Hesselbrock, & Epstein, 1999; Pickens & Svikis, 1991). Genetic researchers have most prominently employed studies of children of alcoholic parents who were adopted and raised by presumably nonalcoholic parents (to control for environmental factors) and studies of identical and fraternal twins (identical twins should have higher rates of alcoholism). Overall, these types of genetic studies have accounted for about 50% or more of variance in alcoholism. Various approaches in genetic research are attempting to identify specific genes and connections among genes that might account for addiction (Faroud, Edenberg, & Crabbe, 2010; Heath, 1995). Proponents of disease-oriented explanations acknowledge no clearly identified etiology as of yet but maintain:

> At the heart of the disease model is the fundamental tenet that alcohol and drug dependence is a physical illness. The disease is neither the end result nor the symptom of another disorder, but a primary, progressive, chronic illness. Rather than a singular personality disorder or maladaptive learned behavior, alcohol and drug dependence involves the biological fabric of the individual and eventually impacts every phase of the afflicted person's life. (Sheehan & Owen, 1999, p. 269)

Biological models incorporate learning processes as well but subordinate them to neurological functioning. These models understand drug addiction to be primarily a response of the brain to the reinforcing qualities of drugs, a key to the process of addiction (Gold, 1994).

Social-cognitive theorists recognize that biological vulnerabilities provide a partial explanation for addiction, but they emphasize learning processes in the development of abuse, addiction, and recovery. The social-cognitive theory of addiction (Abrams & Niaura, 1987; Bandura, 1986, 1999; Maisto, Carey, & Bradizza, 1999; Marlatt & Gordon, 1985; Moos, 2007; O'Hare & Shen 2013) emphasizes interacting physiological and psychosocial influences on the initiation and course of abuse and/or addiction, as well as personal agency (e.g., volition, choice, self-efficacy, decision making) and self-regulatory strategies (i.e., coping skills) as mechanisms of change. Although early stimulus-response theories continue to resonate through modern addictions theory and treatment models, research has shifted to cognitive mediating factors such as alcohol expectancies and self-efficacy. A contemporary social-cognitive view, however, incorporates physiological factors and their interactions with cognitive expectancies and behavior. Social and environmental influences including family, peers, culture, and the environmental context of use also play a significant role. Cultural factors have long been recognized as powerful predictors of problematic use (Amodeo & Kay, 1997; Moos, 2007; Vaillant, 1983), although definitions of problem use vary widely by culture (Bennett, Janca, Grant, & Sartorius, 1993).

The social-cognitive theory of substance use and abuse focuses on three related constructs: *expectancies* (Brown, Goldman, Inn, & Anderson, 1980; McKellar, Harris, & Moos, 2006) or enduring beliefs in the effects of alcohol or other drugs (e.g., alcohol or a specific drug can help relieve tension, make one more sociable, or promote pleasure); *motives* (Cooper, 1994; O'Hare & Shen, 2012), or more proximate "reasons" for using substances (e.g., "I use when I am depressed," or "I want to get high"); and abstinence *self-efficacy* (Annis & Davis, 1991; Hasking & Oei, 2007), or the belief that one can cope with specific situations and not resort to using alcohol or other drugs (e.g., "when other people are socializing," "when I feel depressed"). These three sets of constructs have been shown to correlate with and, to some degree, predict substance use and related problems. Although substance use expectancies are considered more behaviorally fundamental because people can learn them vicariously before initiating substance use, motives for using alcohol and other drugs are considered a more proximate cause of substance use (Cooper, 1994). In addition, coping motives appear to be more strongly associated with problem drinking and drug use than enhancement motives in the general population and in clinical samples (Cooper, 1994; Holahan, Moos, Holahan, Cronkite, & Randall, 2004; O'Hare & Shen, 2012). It is theorized that these cognitive mediators of substance use, particularly the boosting of abstinence self-efficacy, are potential change mechanisms that can be successfully targeted by cognitive-behavioral interventions to improve substance use treatment outcomes (Longabaugh et al., 2005; Moos, 2007).

In a similar vein, other researchers have conceptualized the development of substance abuse and addiction in a contemporary transactional model in which biological temperament associated with early behavioral problems (e.g., self-control) is hypothesized to interact with a host of social and environmental risk and resiliency factors (e.g., stressful events, family relations, academic and peer experiences) to predict future substance abuse (Tarter et al., 1999; Wills, Sandy, & Yaeger, 2000). Given the growth in biopsychosocial evidence concerning the causes, course, and consequences of addictions in recent years, a contemporary addictions model has become increasingly heterogeneous (Abrams & Niaura, 1987; Coccozelli & Hudson, 1989; Finney & Moos, 1991; Finney, Moos, & Timko, 1999; Nordstrom & Berglund, 1987; Pattison, Sobell, & Sobell, 1977; Peele, 1989; Schuckit, 1998; Sobell, Cunningham, & Sobell, 1996; Vaillant & Hiller-Sturmhöfel, 1996; Tarter et al., 1999; Wills et al., 2000; Zucker & Gomberg, 1986). It is also more commensurate with social work's person-in-environment paradigm (Freeman, 1991) than is the traditional disease model. In summary, a contemporary evidence-based model reflects the following findings:

- Rather than being a dichotomous (i.e., diagnostic) phenomenon, substance abuse problems span a continuum from mild to moderate to severe.

- The causes, course, and consequences of substance use and abuse vary widely according to a host of interacting physiological, psychological, interpersonal, and environmental risks and resiliencies.

- Substance abuse problems usually follow a variable course over time and do not necessarily follow a predictable trajectory of a progressive, irreversible disease. Substance abuse problems and addiction may improve or worsen with or without formal treatment through self-directed moderation, elective abstinence, self-regulated recovery (perhaps as a response to the assistance of normal social supports), or other negative social consequences.

- The type, severity, and interpretation of substance abuse problems varies by situational factors as well as by age, gender, race, and culture.

- Substance use disorders are typically intertwined with health, mental health, and psychosocial problems, and severity is only partly related to consumption level and symptoms of physiological dependence, such as craving or loss of control.

- Many consequences of drug abuse are often determined by the context of illegal use (e.g., HIV infection through sharing dirty needles, contaminants in street drugs, injury or death related to involvement in the illegal drug trade, overdose due to the unreliable contents of street drugs) rather than by the pharmacological characteristics of the drugs themselves.

Prelude to Assessment: A Basic Knowledge about Drugs and Their Effects

Because social workers treat many persons with primary or co-occurring substance abuse problems, a basic knowledge of the pharmacology of alcohol and other drugs, prescribed or otherwise, is essential for conducting a competent assessment. Such basic information includes the main chemical actions of drugs; the various routes of transmission and use patterns; their acute and long-term cognitive, physiological, and behavioral effects; risks for overdose and withdrawal; and the potential for physical addiction and psychological dependence. Knowledge of the actions and effects of drugs can not only help identify risks of overdose and withdrawal but also help differentially assess mental health and assorted behavioral problems from drug-related symptoms. The information for major drug groups—sedatives (e.g., alcohol, benzodiazepines, barbiturates), stimulants (e.g., cocaine, amphetamines, related "designer" drugs such as MDMA and caffeine), narcotics (e.g., heroin, methadone, codeine, oxycodone), and others (e.g., hallucinogens, marijuana, PCP, inhalants, over-the-counter drugs)—can be found in an array of sources (e.g., Frances & Miller, 1998; Hart & Ksir, 2013; McCrady & Epstein, 1999; Ray & Ksir, 1999).

Important pharmacological concepts include knowing the effective dose (i.e., the amount of the drug that will deliver the desired effect), being aware of dangerous drug interactions (e.g., such as when CNS depressants are mixed), recognizing behavioral tolerance (i.e., demonstrated when a person who uses substances is able to control behavioral manifestations of being intoxicated), and physiological tolerance (i.e., when the substance-abusing person requires a higher dose to obtain the same desired effect or alleviate withdrawal symptoms). Practitioners should also be aware of the various routes of transmission: drugs may be taken orally, insufflated (sniffed), injected, or smoked.

Tolerance and withdrawal are important considerations when determining whether a person is drug dependent and whether a person needs medical assistance to stop using the drug and avoid potentially dangerous effects of withdrawal. Interventions for serious withdrawal symptoms include initial medical detoxification either on an inpatient (for those with potentially dangerous withdrawal symptoms or other compromising health conditions) or outpatient (for those with mild to moderate withdrawal symptoms) basis. Detoxification may be followed up with aversive medications (e.g., disulfiram) or anticraving medications (e.g., naltrexone) (Anton et al., 2006; Hayashida, 1998; Litten & Allen, 1999; Myric & Anton, 1998). In addition to social and psychological supports, clients may also need medication (e.g., antianxiety drugs) to help reduce withdrawal symptoms, and they may receive intravenous fluids and vitamin supplements. Although drugs may be helpful for blocking cravings or as treatment for secondary psychiatric symptoms (e.g., depression, anxiety), medication is not yet considered a primary form of treatment for addictions. However, research efforts are currently being directed toward this goal. Beyond detoxification, substance abuse intervention remains a primarily psychosocial endeavor.

The risks of overdose and withdrawal are a critical concern for the practitioner, since both conditions can be fatal. Advising clients to decrease or abstain from use without medical supervision carries risks. Clients may suffer convulsions when detoxifying from alcohol, benzodiazepines, barbiturates, and other CNS depressants. Although the elimination of some drugs (e.g., marijuana, cocaine) poses little risk of serious physiological withdrawal, psychological consequences such as depression may require acute mental health intervention. For clients who are willing to openly discuss their history of alcohol and drug use, questions about prior treatment and incidents of overdose or withdrawal may be very telling. For those clients in the range of light to moderate abuse, specific questions about how much (i.e., quantity of the drug) and how often (i.e., frequency) are also critical. As noted already, many clients may be vulnerable to acute negative effects of substances even at low to moderate doses (e.g., elderly, seriously physically ill), particularly if multiple substances are involved.

Although all drugs are different in dosing, effects, interactions with other drugs, side effects, time needed to metabolize (half-life), and withdrawal symptoms, four classifications are employed here for heuristic purposes: central nervous system (CNS) depressants (e.g., alcohol, sedatives, and hypnotics), stimulants (e.g., amphetamines, cocaine), opioids (e.g., heroin, narcotics), and other commonly abused illicit drugs (e.g., marijuana, hallucinogens, PCP, inhalants). Again, it is emphasized here that social workers make liberal use of medical consultation in regard to matters relevant to detoxification, often a necessary step before psychosocial interventions can be employed.

CNS Depressants.   Alcohol is the most widely used psychoactive drug and causes the greatest amount of psychological, social, and long-term health problems in the nation. Although use patterns and responses to alcohol use vary according to gender, age, weight, cultural expectancies, drinking experience (e.g., behavioral and physical tolerance), and drinking context, in general low to moderate doses (i.e., a couple of drinks) are considered pleasantly relaxing and are associated with sociability in most societies. After a few drinks (e.g., 3–6), the drinker is likely to experience impaired motor functioning, and gradually worsening cognitive functioning, and after heavy drinking (e.g., 7–15 drinks, depending on level of tolerance), the drinker is probably quite drunk, unconscious, or possibly dead. Signs of alcohol intoxication include slurred speech, loss of coordination, unsteadiness on one's feet, difficulty focusing, impaired attention or memory, and stupor or coma. Persons sometimes die from rapid ingestion of high doses of alcohol (e.g., at fraternity initiations), and withdrawals after long-term heavy drinking can be dangerous or even fatal for those who have experienced long-term dependence.

In the alcohol-dependent person, withdrawals may begin a few hours after the last drink and last up to 5 days, usually peaking somewhere between 24 and 48 hours. Nervous system hyperactivity resulting from a rebound effect of alcohol's depressant effects can be marked by moderate to severe anxiety, increased heart rate, hand tremors, increased blood pressure, nausea, and insomnia, and may result in an alcohol withdrawal seizure. At the severe end of the spectrum, delirium tremens (the DTs) may occur within 2–3 days, and a person has a 10–15% chance of dying if withdrawals are left untreated. Long-term effects of heavy alcohol abuse include damage to virtually all major organ systems, including gastrointestinal disorders, liver damage (e.g., scarring, cirrhosis), cardiovascular disease, stroke, and circulatory problems, as well as severe cognitive impairments, including organic brain disorders associated with thiamin deficiencies (e.g., Wernicke's syndrome, which is marked by confusion and loss of mental activity, and can lead to coma and death, and Korsakoff's syndrome, which is marked by severe memory loss, the inability to form new memories, confabulation, and hallucinations).

Sedatives and hypnotics are also CNS depressants. At lower doses they are meant to have a calming effect (sedative), at higher doses, they are used to induce sleep (hypnotic). Barbiturates also have the capacity to induce general anesthesia, although benzodiazepines (e.g., Xanax, Valium) do not. In addition to anxiety reduction and sleep induction, these drugs are also used as anticonvulsive medications. Sedatives and hypnotics vary in both half-life and in their specific therapeutic effect. Benzodiazepines, alleged by some to be widely overprescribed (Ashton, 2005), have a more specific antianxiety effect, whereas barbiturates have a more general sedative effect on the nervous system. Signs of intoxication by these drugs are very similar to those related to alcohol. Dangers of lethal overdose are more prominent with barbiturates than with benzodiazepines. Sedative effects of both types of drugs are magnified when mixed with alcohol, and a mix of alcohol and barbiturates may be fatal. Withdrawal symptoms vary depending on the specific drug, but care should be taken to refer clients who have a history of sedative or hypnotic use to a physician if they are considering discontinuing use. Withdrawal symptoms can begin anywhere from 1–3 days (for drugs with a shorter half-life) to 4–7 days or longer. Most persons who withdraw from sedative or hypnotic drugs under medical supervision experience a range of mild to moderate anxiety. However, for more severely dependent persons, withdrawal can be very similar to that for alcohol and may include increased heart rate, insomnia, hand tremors, nausea and vomiting, transient hallucinations, anxiety, and grand mal seizures. For social workers, distinguishing between withdrawal symptoms and the reemergence of anxiety symptoms in some clients can be difficult.

Most persons who take these drugs under prescription do not abuse them; however, those who do also tend to abuse other drugs as well and often use them to regulate the withdrawal symptoms associated with other drugs. Long-term abuse can be associated with common mental health symptoms including depression and anxiety. Newer classes of benzodiazepines (e.g., buspirone) appear to have lower risks for abuse.

CNS Stimulants. Central nervous system stimulants are generally cocaine and amphetamine-related products. Cocaine has a shorter half-life than most amphetamines. The fact that a client does not use these drugs daily does not necessarily indicate the lack of a problem. Abusers often go on binges or "runs" for days at a time, marked by a cycle of craving, bingeing, withdrawal, depression, more craving, and a resumption of use. General effects of these drugs include CNS arousal, increased libido, energy, decreased appetite, hyperalertness, increased self-confidence, talkativeness, and repetitive behavior. Intoxication results in increased heart rate, dilation of pupils, elevated blood pressure, chills, nausea, vomiting, psychomotor agitation or retardation, cardiac arrhythmia, muscular weakness, confusion, and seizures, among other signs and symptoms. Chronic abuse can result in depression, fatigue, and poor concentration.

Despite the reinforcing qualities of amphetamines and cocaine, relatively few of the many people who try these drugs develop a serious problem or an addiction to them (less than 15%). Methamphetamines and related designer drugs such as ecstasy (i.e., MDA/MDMA) have effects that combine those produced by amphetamines and hallucinogens: general arousal, and feelings of well-being and intimacy with others. Although in higher doses they share some of the potentially toxic effects of other amphetamines, users also run the risk of dehydration and hyperthermia from prolonged frenetic activity (e.g., dancing at all-night raves). Although injection produces the quickest high, smoking results in full absorption as well. Snorting is the least efficient method to transmit these drugs.

A stimulant can result in a cardiac emergency, stroke or convulsions, and toxic "psychosis," which can last for hours with longer-acting amphetamines. Withdrawal symptoms commence soon after stimulant abuse ends. Users experience the "crash" (i.e., rapid reduction in mood and energy), and chronic abusers may experience anxiety, depression, and paranoia. Symptoms may last for a few days. Depression, boredom, memory problems, and malaise (perhaps accompanied by suicidal ideation) may continue for a few days or weeks. If substance-abusing individuals do not relapse during this period, they may experience cravings for months or years after they have stopped using stimulants. Other specific long-term effects of abuse include damage to the heart (e.g., cardiomyopathy), "crack lung" (i.e., chronic cough producing black sputum), and damage to nasal membranes for those who snorted powdered cocaine.

Opioids. Opium-based drugs such as morphine and its derivative heroin, originally designed for pain relief, can result in a dependence syndrome when abused. Intoxication from abuse can produce euphoria and relief from anxiety, followed by apathy, depression, psychomotor agitation or retardation, "nodding" or a dreamy twilight state, constriction of pupils, decreased respiration, slurred speech, and impaired judgment. Although many occasional users of opioids do not develop dependence, tolerance can develop with repeated use. Severe intoxication or overdose may present a medical emergency, indicated by pinpoint pupils, depressed respiration, and coma. Withdrawal from opioids is considered generally safe if users are not also addicted to CNS depressants. Withdrawal symptoms may begin within a few hours of the last dose but last up to a few days. Symptoms are similar to those of a 24-hour bout with influenza: depressed mood, nausea and vomiting, muscle aches, runny nose, watery eyes, gooseflesh, dilation of pupils, diarrhea, yawning, fever, and insomnia. Withdrawals are also likely to be accompanied by craving for the drug, which often leads to relapse and drug seeking. Treatment of withdrawals is often accompanied by the use of opioid agonists (e.g., methadone) or antagonists (e.g., naltrexone) or some combination of drugs.

Other Drugs.   The active ingredient in marijuana (*Cannabis sativa*) is delta-9-tetrahydrocannabinol (THC). The percentage of this active ingredient ranges from 5% to 15%. Hashish is more potent, and the THC content in hashish oil may be as high as 60%. Most people who use cannabis report the subjective experience of being high as mild euphoria and relaxation, but effects vary considerably depending on one's mood, state of mind, and social context, among other factors. Abuse of cannabis can result in panic reactions among inexperienced or anxious users, a problem addressed effectively with calming reassurance and the passage of time. In other respects, the immediate risk of overdose is minimal. Negative effects can include short-term memory loss and attention lapses, as well as disjointed thought patterns, symptoms that may be problematic depending on the context of use (e.g., driving a bus vs. listening to music at home). Some individuals who are heavy, regular users of marijuana can develop some degree of tolerance, but withdrawals are generally mild and may include some sleep disturbance, nervousness, moodiness, and appetite changes. Chronic heavy use poses a serious risk to the health of the lungs. Amotivational syndrome is not unique to the abuse of marijuana, and marijuana has not been empirically demonstrated to be a gateway drug for any pharmacological reasons. However, because of its current status in many jurisdictions as an illegal substance, it may increase the likelihood of other drug use by exposing users to a wide array of products available on the illicit drug market. Recently, some US states have relaxed the outright prohibition of marijuana. It remains to be seen if such changes to the law increase drug use overall.

Hallucinogens are another type of drug and come in many varieties. There are more than 100 different types, with varying molecular structures.

The better-known hallucinogens are LSD (lysergic acid diethylamide), mescaline, and psilocybin (e.g., magic mushrooms, peyote). These substances produce physiological effects (e.g., elevated blood pressure, temperature) soon after ingestion and hallucinogenic effects within a few hours. Effects may last for several hours after ingestion. Visual hallucinations are the most commonly cited effects, although all senses may be affected. Users report alterations in aesthetic experience, slowing of time, synesthesia (i.e., mixing of senses, such as hearing colors, or seeing musical tones), fluctuation in emotional state, increased vividness of memories, and a perception of deep insight regarding philosophical or spiritual matters. There are no risks of serious overdose from LSD, although a lethal dose of mescaline is estimated to be about 10–30 times higher than the effective dose. Some users have reported ingesting and surviving prodigious amounts of hallucinogens, and others have reported "bad trips" or panicky feelings that can make the experience seem endless. Tolerance to these drugs develops rapidly and dissipates just as rapidly. There is little danger of physiological withdrawals from hallucinogens and little risk of physiological dependence. For some, hallucinogen abuse has resulted in long-term psychological problems.

PCP, often misrepresented on the street as THC or LSD, is not a true hallucinogen, but at lower doses it can produce feelings of relaxation or numbness, confusion, disorientation, and distorted body image. Higher doses can result in depression, anxiety, confusion, and paniclike states. Persons who use PCP sometimes become belligerent or out of control. It is often sprinkled into a marijuana joint or a standard cigarette. PCP effects begin within about 5 minutes, plateau within 30 minutes, and may last for several hours with effects lingering for up to 2 days. An overdose can result in coma.

Inhalant abuse is associated with hundreds of chemicals often easily available in the home or workplace. These products include gasoline, cleaning solvents, glues, and aerosol products (e.g., toluene in spray paint). They are sniffed (i.e., huffed) through a rag soaked in the chemical or from some kind of container. Users anticipate the "rush," that is, feelings of euphoria, floating, hallucinations, and other perceptual distortions. Repeated use often leaves individuals with a characteristic smell and a rash around the mouth. Central nervous system damage and occasionally seizures can result. Long-term use of some of these chemicals can lead to damage to organ systems and increased risk of serious diseases. Death can result from sniffing certain products, and some children have died when the chemicals were inadvertently ignited (they tend to be highly flammable). Tolerance can develop, and withdrawal may include cramps, nausea, vomiting, diarrhea, tremors, and irritability.

Having a familiarity with the basic effects, patterns of use, routes of transmission, and risks of tolerance and withdrawal of these substances is key to conducting evidence-based assessment for the abuse of alcohol and other drugs. Although most social workers are not employed in primary addictions facilities, conducting routine screening and assessment for substance abuse and addiction is essential for all clients because of the high rates of co-occurrence with other psychosocial disorders and problems-in-living.

Key Elements of MFS Assessment

In the DSM-IV (APA, 2000), substance abuse was diagnosed when maladaptive use occurred over the previous 12 months in at least one of the following areas: failure to fulfill major role obligations (e.g., work, school, home), recurrent use in hazardous situations (e.g., driving under the influence), recurrent legal problems, and continued use despite persistent or recurrent social or interpersonal problems. Dependence was diagnosed when three or more of the following conditions were met: tolerance; withdrawal symptoms; use of more of the substance than intended; difficulty cutting down; frequent drug-seeking behavior; impairment of social, occupational, or recreational activities; and continued use despite persistent or recurrent psychological or physical problems.

Acknowledging that the distinction between abuse and dependence is somewhat ambiguous, the American Psychiatric Association (2013) modified the diagnostic criteria for a substance use disorder in the DSM-5 by dropping the abuse-dependence distinction. DSM-5 criteria are similar, with some minor differences across an array of substances including alcohol, marijuana, opiates, hallucinogens, stimulants, and sedatives. Practitioners are directed to identify a "problematic pattern of alcohol use leading to clinically significant impairment or distress, as manifested by at least two of the following, occurring within a 12-month period" (APA, 2013, p. 490). Signs and symptoms include using more than intended; having trouble cutting down; spending much time and effort devoted to obtaining the substance; experiencing cravings; not following through on social, occupational, or other responsibilities; high-risk use (e.g., driving while intoxicated); using despite negative psychological or health consequences; developing tolerance (using more to achieve desired effect); and, experiencing withdrawal (distressing physical reaction when substance use is discontinued).

The call for practitioners to conduct routine substance abuse assessment has been well articulated, given the high rates of comorbidity of substance use disorders with other health and mental health disorders, as well as with a wide array of psychosocial problems (Carey & Teitelbaum, 1996; Donovan, 1999; Griffin, 1991; Sobell, Toneatto, & Sobell, 1994). Although a brief screening tool may be helpful initially, a more thorough MFS assessment is required if there are positive indications that a client is experiencing significant problems with alcohol or other drugs. Although the diagnostic criteria for substance use disorders touch on the major points of an MFS assessment, the practitioner should examine each of these domains of living (e.g., psychological, family, interpersonal, work, health) in more detail, examine their systemic interaction, and employ multiple sources of data as needed (e.g., collateral family or friends, other professionals, court records, employment data).

Assessment should be considered an ongoing process that serves multiple purposes. Given the demonstrated effectiveness of self-monitoring in substance abuse assessment and treatment (Annis & Davis, 1991; Carey & Teitelbaum, 1996), client collaboration becomes an effective therapeutic tool in the following ways: (1) it helps clients to specify which substances they use, how much, and how often; (2) it assists them in making connections between substance abuse and variations in other health or psychosocial complaints; (3) it provides therapeutic structure and clarity concerning treatment goals and objectives; (4) it provides confirmation concerning their motivations for use (e.g., enhancement or coping style); (5) it signals inconsistencies in self-report; and (6) it provides clear evidence of improvement or the need to reassess and alter the treatment plan. Evidence suggests that Internet-based assessment and self-monitoring can be a reliable and useful tool for self-help for both men and women struggling with abuse or addictions, as well as an important adjunct to professional help (Sinadinovic, Berman, Hasson, & Wennberg, 2010).

There are five major questions that frame the substance-focused assessment: (1) Which substances (e.g., legal or illicit, prescribed or nonprescribed) are used? (2) How much of the substance(s) (e.g., estimated ounces, grams, milligrams, "joints," "hits," "lines") is used? (3) How often (e.g., daily, weekly, monthly) is it used? (4) Which precipitating factors (e.g., negative mood, cravings, situational factors) appear to be associated with problem use? (5) What are the consequences (acute and chronic) of substance use across physiological, psychosocial, and health domains?

Although some have overgeneralized the notion that alcohol and drug abusers are not to be trusted, evidence generally supports the validity of self-report of alcohol and drug use (Babor, Stephens, & Marlatt, 1987; Del Boca & Darkes, 2003; Hesselbrock, Babor, Hesselbrock, Meyer, & Workman, 1983; Sobell et al., 1994). Although there are some circumstances under which clients may be inclined to lie, deny, or minimize their use and related consequences, clinical research has consistently demonstrated that the self-report of substance use and abuse is relatively valid and reliable in the hands of a skilled interviewer. Response demands, personal characteristics (e.g., race, age), and other situational factors can affect the degree of validity. More research is needed on substance use self-report; however, people are usually relatively forthcoming when confidentiality is ensured and they are not threatened with negative consequences (e.g., discharge from a zero-tolerance treatment environment, threatening that children will be taken by child welfare services). An evaluation of the client's relative veracity should also consider the referral source and the client's level of motivation for seeing the practitioner. Techniques for improving the accuracy of self-report include the following:

- Desensitizing clients to a discussion of the use of psychoactive chemicals rather than approaching the topic in an accusatory, judgmental manner (e.g., "Are you a drinker? A drug abuser?")
- For clients who are guarded, approaching questions in the context of health concerns: (e.g., "Do you smoke? Use alcoholic beverages? Take medication? Nonprescription, recreational or street drugs?")
- Expressing concern about not being able to help clients unless they are honest about drug use and abuse
- Ensuring confidentiality to the extent possible
- Reducing or eliminating negative program contingencies for honest reporting at assessment, ongoing evaluation, or follow-up
- Anchoring the client's recent and long-term memory with important life events (e.g., trauma, loss, milestones, significant relationships, emotionally charged situations)
- Using clear and specific terminology regarding what constitutes, for example, a "drink," and the types of drugs, routes of transmission, and dosage, etc.
- If necessary, informing the clients that collateral sources of information can be obtained from significant others and/or other agencies (e.g., law enforcement, medical records)
- Discussing preliminary causal associations between clients' drug use and presenting complaints
- Tactfully confronting contradictory information
- Estimating acute physiological risks associated with potential overdose or withdrawal, and arranging for medical consultation if any risks seem apparent; sharing these concerns with the client

Once preliminary drug use data have been collected, clinicians can then conduct a more detailed functional assessment by helping the client make connections between drug use and other problematic psychological, social, health-related, and situational experiences that have occurred over time. *This cause-effect sequencing of antecedent events, drug use, and consequences is the heart of a good functional analysis.* Research findings have suggested that persons concerned with their substance use and abuse tend to make changes by weighing the pros and cons of using, and many decide to reduce or eliminate use on their own because (in their estimation) the cost of using has become too high (Cunningham, Sobell, Sobell, & Kapur, 1995). Focusing on a nonconfrontational approach that appeals to clients' self-interest and sense of autonomy is commensurate with what is referred to as motivational interviewing (DiClemente, Bellino, & Neavins, 1999; Miller & Rollnick, 2013). Emphasizing the client's self-interest rather than "extracting a confession" through confrontation seems to be a more constructive way to engage clients in the initial stage of intervention. It is important to be specific and concrete in one's questions: if you do not ask, clients might not volunteer the information.

Setting Intervention Goals

The assessment is not complete until tentative treatment goals have been negotiated with the client. Given the heterogeneity and range of seriousness of substance abuse problems, reducing both substance use and associated harms are often considered legitimate goals on a continuum along with abstinence (as a possible ultimate goal) (Ambrogne, 2002; Rosenberg & Davis, 1994). The range of goal possibilities includes harm reduction, moderation, and abstinence. A review of the empirical literature for alcohol treatment goals (Ambrogne, 2002) summarizes the findings of more than two decades of research: reduced-risk drinking as an intervention goal is a viable option for some problem drinkers and some dependent drinkers; abstinence and non-abstinence-based interventions are comparably effective; those individuals with moderate to severe dependence should be advised to eventually strive for abstinence; and providing clients with some choice in treatment goals seems to promote treatment effectiveness. Given that clinician-recommended treatment goals are often not good predictors of outcome (Finney & Moos, 1991; Nordstrom & Berglund, 1987), a collaborative approach to goal setting may enhance client engagement and commitment to treatment from the start. Recently, Adamson, Heather, Morton, Raistrick, and Slegg (2010) found somewhat better outcomes for those choosing abstinence over moderation, but there were differences in severity of abuse and motivation at baselines between the two groups. In addition, there were significant correlations between initial goal choice and type of successful outcome achieved (i.e., both groups equally satisfied with progress). The authors caution against an abstinence-only treatment philosophy, which can discourage clients from engaging in treatment and ultimately choosing abstinence as a goal should moderation fail. The relationship between initial goal choice and outcome is complex and deserves further study.

A few basic considerations are in order before goals are established:

- Clients enter treatment at different stages of readiness to change, and a clinician's ability to meet clients "where they are" can start treatment off on the right foot. Many practitioners have become familiar with the stages of change (DiClemente & Hughes, 1990; Prochaska & DiClemente, 1986) defined in chapter 3: precontemplation, contemplation, preparation, action, and maintenance.

- For many substance abusers, an insistence on abstinence might discourage them from engaging in treatment (Adamson et al., 2010). For others it may set up a series of failure contingencies, which is referred to as the abstinence-violation effect (Larimer, Palmer, & Marlatt, 1999; Marlatt & George, 1984; Marlatt & Gordon, 1985), in which a "slip" is equated with failure. Depending on clients' readiness to make some changes, social workers should help them first to experiment with cutting down or trying periodic abstinence, to make tentative changes in the context of use in order to minimize serious consequences (e.g., drinking on the job, while driving), or to eliminate one or two substances if the client is using multiple drugs (with consideration given to risks for withdrawals). Including clients in formulation of the treatment plan and selection of treatment goals has been shown to contribute to treatment retention and positive outcomes (Miller, 1992; Sanchez-Craig, 1980; Sanchez-Craig & Lei, 1986);

- Although practitioners do not want to unwittingly engage in "enabling" clients, caution must be used when imposing treatment goals that reduce the likelihood of even partial improvement. While a client's response to the initial assessment may be negative, resistance can be approached constructively by accepting initial reluctance, avoiding unnecessary confrontation, and working collaboratively with the client to provide choice in treatment methods and goals (Miller & Rollnick, 2013);

- Equivocal outcomes of controlled drinking studies suggest a conservative approach to setting treatment goals (Ambrogne, 2002; Nathan & McCrady, 1987). *Clients who appear to have trouble with loss of control or abstaining from use, who have serious psychiatric disorders, few social supports, a history of treatment failure, or health problems resulting from substance abuse, should be encouraged to make abstinence their goal.* Nevertheless, any reduction in harm on the way toward elective abstinence should be considered progress, and practitioners should give first priority to the client's treatment goal preference.

A graduated self-testing approach in the initial stages of treatment may help clients decide on optimal treatment goals. Although completely problem-free abstinence will always be an ideal goal for many clients, maximizing harm reduction for all clients may be a more flexible and realistic clinical strategy (Marlatt, 1996). Once treatment goals have been negotiated, practitioners need to consistently associate reduction of alcohol or other drug use with progress in the client's major complaints (e.g., depression, panic attacks, marital difficulties). Because substance abuse problems and other psychosocial difficulties exacerbate one another, client progress in one area is often associated with progress in the other (Brownell, Marlatt, Lichtenstein, & Wilson, 1986; Rounsaville, Dolinsky, Babor, & Meyer, 1987).

Instruments

There are many substance use assessment tools available to clinicians (Alcohol and Drug Abuse Institute, 2011; Allen & Mattson, 1993; Carey & Teitelbaum, 1996; Donovan, 1999; Hasin, 1991; National Institute of Alcohol Abuse and Alcoholism, 2006). These include brief screening devices; simple indexes for tracking changes and treatment progress; and multidimensional scales that measure problems, consequences, and other psychological aspects of substance abuse and dependence. Assessment tools are best used when they are incorporated into the comprehensive psychosocial assessment. Many of these instruments are now available in languages other than English. Paper-and-pencil brief screening devices have been shown to be reasonably sensitive to the detection of substance abuse (Babor, Kranzler, & Lauerman, 1989) and have good clinical utility in signaling the need for early intervention.

The Alcohol Use Disorders Identification Test (AUDIT) (Babor & Grant, 1989; Babor, Higgins-Biddle, Saunders, & Monteiro, 2001; Saunders, Aasland, Amundsen, & Grant, 1993), originally developed in 10 countries under the auspices of the World Health Organization, was designed to detect harmful or hazardous drinking in addition to alcohol dependence. The 10-question AUDIT includes questions on alcohol consumption (i.e., how much, how often, and a question for peak drinking or "six or more"), along with four questions on dependence (i.e., unable to stop, failed responsibilities, eye opener, guilt) and three on consequences (i.e., memory loss, injury to others, advised to cut down). The AUDIT is scored on a frequency continuum (rather than dichotomously), requests measures over the previous year (rather than lifetime), and appears to have broader applicability by discriminating hazardous and harmful drinkers (i.e., at-risk drinkers) rather than just those who are alcohol dependent (Bohn, Babor, & Kranzler, 1995). The AUDIT appears to have good potential as a brief screen in mental health and other social service environments where problem drinking frequently co-occurs with other complaints (instrument 7.1).

The Drug Abuse Screening Test (DAST) (Skinner, 1982; Yudko, Lozhinka, & Fouts, 2007) is a 28-item self-report screening instrument intended to measure the extent of involvement with drugs other than alcohol. It uses a cutoff score of 6 or more (≥ 6) to indicate a level of clinical concern. It provides a global measure of drug abuse, discriminates between drug abusers from those with mixed alcohol and other drug problems, and correlates well with a diagnosis of substance abuse. The DAST discriminated drug abusing psychiatric patients with a primary DSM-III diagnosis of substance abuse and showed excellent internal consistency (alpha = .94) (Staley & El Guebaly, 1990). Although it constitutes a useful valid screening tool for detecting drug abuse and dependence, the DAST is designed to diagnose lifetime dependence

INSTRUMENT 7.1   Alcohol Use Disorders Identification Test

Please circle the answer that is correct for you.

1. How often do you have a drink containing alcohol?

| Never | Monthly or less | Two to four times per month | Two to three times per week | Four or more times per week |

2. How many drinks containing alcohol do you have on a typical day when you are drinking?

| 1 or 2 | 3 or 4 | 5 or 6 | 7 to 9 | 10 or more |

3. How often do you have six or more drinks on one occasion?

| Never | Less than monthly | Monthly | Two to three times per week | Four or more times per week |

4. How often during the last year have you found that you were not able to stop drinking once you had started?

| Never | Less than monthly | Monthly | Two to three times per week | Four or more times per week |

5. How often during the last year have you failed to do what was normally expected from you because of drinking?

| Never | Less than monthly | Monthly | Two to three times per week | Four or more times per week |

6. How often during the last year have you needed a first drink in the morning to get yourself going after a heavy drinking session?

| Never | Less than monthly | Monthly | Two to three times per week | Four or more times per week |

7. How often during the last year have you had a feeling of guilt or remorse after drinking?

| Never | Less than monthly | Monthly | Two to three times per week | Four or more times per week |

8. How often during the last year have you been unable to remember what happened the night before because you had been drinking?

| Never | Less than monthly | Monthly | Two to three times per week | Four or more times per week |

9. Have you or someone else been injured as the result of your drinking?

| No | Yes, but not in the last year | Yes, during the last year |
| 0 | 2 | 4 |

10. Has a relative, friend or doctor or other health worker been concerned about your drinking or suggested you cut down?

| No | Yes, but not in the last year | Yes, during the last year |
| 0 | 2 | 4 |

Procedures for scoring the AUDIT: Questions 1–8 are scored 0, 1, 2, 3 or 4. Questions 9 and 10 are scored 0, 2, or 4 only. The minimum score (for non-drinkers) is 0 and the maximum possible score is 40. A score of 8 or more indicates a strong likelihood of hazardous or harmful alcohol consumption.

rather than actual consumption, and thus, it is not useful as an outcome measure. A 10-item version of the DAST (DAST-10) was developed and was shown to correlate very highly with the full DAST in a population of mentally ill persons with co-occurring substance abuse disorders (Cocco & Carey, 1998; Maisto, Carey, Carey, Gordon, & Gleason, 2000). The Spanish version of the DAST-10 has also been shown to have excellent psychometric qualities (Bedregal, Sobell, Sobell, & Simco, 2006). In the same study, the DAST-10 showed good interrater reliability, very good internal consistency, and good concurrent validity with other substance abuse measures. With "yes" = 1 and "no" = 0, the recommended cutoff for detecting a probable drug problem is 3 or greater. The DAST-10 is presented here (instrument 7.2).

INSTRUMENT 7.2   The DAST–10

The following questions concern information about your possible involvement with drugs *not including alcoholic beverages* during the past 12 months. Carefully read each statement and decide if your answer is yes or no. Then circle the appropriate response beside the question.

In the statements, "drug abuse" refers to (1) the use of prescribed or over-the-counter drugs in excess of the directions and (2) any nonmedical use of drugs. The various classes of drugs may include cannabis (e.g., marijuana, hash), solvents, tranquilizers (e.g., Valium), barbiturates, cocaine, stimulants (e.g., speed), hallucinogens (e.g., LSD), or narcotics, (e.g., heroin). Remember that the questions *do not* include alcoholic beverages.

Please answer every question. If you have difficulty with a statement, then choose the response that is mostly right.

These questions refer to the past 12 months	Circle your response	
1. Have you used drugs other than those required for medical reasons?	Yes	No
2. Do you abuse more than one drug at a time?	Yes	No
3. Are you always able to stop using drugs when you want to?	Yes	No
4. Have you had "blackouts" or "flashbacks" as a result of drug use?	Yes	No
5. Do you ever feel bad or guilty about your drug use?	Yes	No
6. Does your spouse (or parents) ever complain about your involvement with drugs?	Yes	No
7. Have you neglected your family because of your use of drugs?	Yes	No
8. Have you engaged in illegal activities in order to obtain drugs?	Yes	No
9. Have you ever experienced withdrawal symptoms (felt sick) when you stopped taking drugs?	Yes	No
10. Have you had medical problems as a result of your drug use (e.g., memory loss, hepatitis, convulsions, bleeding)?	Yes	No

Multidimensional measures are recommended so practitioners can evaluate assessment and treatment outcomes in a number of problem domains. One example is the Addiction Severity Index (ASI) (McLellan, Luborsky, O'Brien, & Woody, 1980; Stoffelmayer, Mavis, & Kasim, 1994), a well-regarded multidimensional substance abuse assessment instrument that is sensitive to change and can therefore be used to measure treatment outcomes. Because the ASI takes about an hour to complete, it should be used after a client has met initial screening criteria for a substance abuse problem. It provides both subjective (severity) ratings to determine need for treatment as well as composite scores for seven areas of functioning: psychiatric status, physical health, employment, legal status, alcohol and drug use, family functioning and social functioning. Evidence obtained from substance-abusing men and women supports the ASI's interrater and test-retest reliability, it has good concurrent and discriminant validity, and it has good stability when used in longitudinal evaluations (Denis et al., 2012; McLellan et al., 1980; Stoffelmayr et al., 1994). A copy of the ASI (version 5) appears in appendix E. The scale is in the public domain, and training materials to use the ASI can be obtained free of charge at www.tresearch.org.

An indirect approach to measuring problem drinking emphasizes the respondent's ability to resist drinking under "at-risk" circumstances. One such scale includes the Inventory of Drinking Situations (IDS) (Annis, 1982), which was designed to estimate the likelihood of relapse in persons struggling with alcohol (or other drugs). The eight dimensions include unpleasant emotions, physical discomfort, pleasant emotions, testing personal control, urges and temptations to drink, conflicts with others, social pressure, and pleasant times with others. In one treatment population (Isenhart, 1993), high scores on some of these subscales (i.e., negative emotions, social pressures, testing control, pleasant emotions, and physical distress) were associated with heavy drinking. Other similar instruments include the Situational Confidence Questionnaire (Kirisci, Moss, & Tarter, 1996; O'Hare & Shen, 2013) and the Alcohol Abstinence Self-Efficacy Scale (DiClemente, Carbonari, Montgomery, & Hughes, 1994).

SELECTING EFFECTIVE INTERVENTIONS

Overview

Treating substance abuse in the United States costs billions of dollars per year in a combination of private and public treatment facilities, and billions of dollars more in treating related illnesses (CDC, 2013a; USDHHS, 2000). On any given day, more than 700,000 persons are receiving alcoholism treatment (about 25% women, almost 67% white, and 86% on an outpatient basis) (USDHHS, 1997, 2000), although most people with substance use disorders never receive treatment. A considerable amount has been learned about the effectiveness of substance abuse treatment from uncontrolled naturalistic evaluation data and matched treatment and community samples. Early detection of substance abuse and access to a range of intervention options and treatment goals appears to be the best course for making a positive impact on a substance-abusing person's long-term well-being (Finney & Moos, 1991; Finney et al., 1999). Although treatment may shorten the trajectory of substance abuse and addiction, psychosocial pressures and health consequences also play a powerful role in long-term recovery. Treatment and policy initiatives should capitalize on these naturally occurring social factors to mitigate the effects of substance use disorders (Finney et al., 1999).

A few large, uncontrolled evaluation studies of drug treatment facilities in the United States have been conducted over the past decades (i.e., Drug Abuse Reporting Program or DARP; Treatment Outcome Prospective Study or TOPS; Drug Abuse Treatment Outcome Study or DATOS). Results suggest that treatment is moderately successful in helping clients overcome addiction when they remain in treatment for 3 months or longer. These positive outcomes included reduced heroin and cocaine abuse and decreased criminal activity. Nevertheless, effective treatment components are often poorly defined, so it is difficult to say exactly which components of the intervention were helpful or effective. In addition, high dropout rates make it difficult to determine whether positive outcomes were due to effective treatment or resulted from more highly motivated clients remaining in treatment (Fletcher, Tims, & Brown, 1997; Hubbard, Craddock, Flynn, Anderson, & Etheridge, 1997). Nevertheless, when representative samples of addicted persons in the community are matched with those in treatment, evidence suggests that treatment shows positive results at 12-month follow-up for both abstinence and nonproblematic use. Poorer outcomes are associated with co-occurring psychiatric disorders, drug abuse, and more negative social consequences (Weisner, Matzger, & Kaskutas, 2003).

Traditional psychotherapy has not been shown to be particularly effective in helping clients who have problems with substance abuse (Emrick, 1974, 1982; Miller, 1992). However, an array of more effective interventions are available, and social workers who do not work in primary substance abuse treatment facilities can integrate these methods into their practice repertoire. These interventions help clients reduce or eliminate consumption, reduce harm, recover, and prevent relapse. On the basis of an extensive analysis of controlled studies for alcoholism treatments, it is clear that expensive inpatient services are no longer assumed to be the gold standard of treatment and do not generally result in superior outcomes (Holder, Longabaugh, Miller, & Rubonis, 1991; Miller & Hester, 1986).

Overall, treating alcohol use and other drug use disorders remains a challenge for clinicians with long-term positive outcomes difficult to achieve. Nevertheless, the more effective interventions appear to use some combination of initial detoxification or cutting down, self-monitoring of "triggers" (e.g., thoughts, feelings, situational cues that provoke urges to use substances), use of cognitive-behavioral coping skills that increase more functional responses to urges in order to prevent relapse (e.g., spending time with sober friends, planned alternative activities to using, accessing mutual help groups), and improvement in lifestyle behaviors in general (e.g., lowering stress, getting exercise, cultivating healthful relationships, improving diet). External reinforcement such as the use of positive and negative contingencies (e.g., rewards and threats of sanctions) has also been shown to be effective for many individuals, particularly if coordinated with court-ordered treatments (Higgins, Sigmon & Heil, 2008; McCrady, 2008).

Critical reviews of *controlled* outcome studies demonstrate that there are a range of moderately effective interventions available for persons who abuse alcohol and other drugs. Degree of evidence varies, but the interventions include the following:

- Brief interventions in which practitioners provide a few psychoeducational and motivational sessions focused on negative health-related consequences of drinking (DiClemente et al., 1999; Gryczynski et al., 2011; Heather, 1995; USDHHS, 1997, 2000).
- Motivational interviewing (MI) or motivational enhancement therapy (MET) (Miller & Rollnick, 2013).
- Cognitive-behavioral coping skills strategies (Kadden, 1994; Longabaugh & Morgenstern, 1999; Magill & Ray, 2009; Miller, 1992) that emphasize learning to self-monitor, detect and avoid urges and situations that increase risk of drinking or drug use, and replace substance abuse with more adaptive coping skills and a healthier lifestyle.
- Behavioral marital and family therapies (McCrady, Epstein, Cook, Jensen, & Hildebrandt, 2009; O'Farrell & Fals-Stewart, 1999, 2003; Stanton & Shadish, 1997; Thomas & Santa, 1982) that include communications, problem solving, contingency management, and coping skills.
- Community reinforcement approach (CRA) and contingency management (CM) strategies (Acierno, Donohoe, & Kogan, 1994; Alessi, Rash, & Petry, 2011; Azrin, Sisson, Meyers, & Godley, 1982; Higgins et al., 1993; Higgins, Wong, Badger, Ogden, & Dantona, 2000) that combine coping skills interventions with positive payoffs for abstinence and negative sanctions for relapse, and can be linked with court-ordered treatments.
- Twelve-step facilitation (TSF) (Humphreys, 1999; Nowinski, 1999; Ries, Galantner, & Tonigan, 2008; Walitzer, Dermen, & Barrick, 2008) by substance abuse professionals to orient, encourage, and guide the addicted person through the first few steps of 12-step programs.

Brief Interventions

Brief interventions refer to a general collection of strategies used as a form of early intervention or to ameliorate a more serious degree of problem drinking or dependence (DiClemente et al., 1999; Gryczynski et al., 2011; Heather,

1995; USDHHS, 1997, 2000). The crux of the brief intervention is a thorough assessment accompanied by informed, structured feedback about the consequences of the client's drinking, including data from medical tests, advice on methods for avoiding drinking situations, and psychoeducation about the effects of alcohol. This approach can be provided over a few visits and may include two or three sessions of assessment, psychoeducation, and advice giving—often accompanied by reading materials. Given the wide range of problems that social workers treat, they are in an ideal circumstance to screen, diagnose, assess, and provide early intervention and/or referral. Goal setting is oriented toward moderation or initial moderation with the intent of pursuing more extensive intervention for long-term abstinence, if needed.

In recent years, a new brief intervention model, Screening, Brief Intervention, Referral, and Treatment (SBIRT), has been disseminated in healthcare settings to reach a larger pool of potential clients. In addition to highlighting the effectiveness of SBIRT in reducing alcohol and drug use in their brief review of the literature, Gryczynski et al. (2011) reported on a naturalistic study ($N = 1,208$) that SBIRT showed sharper reductions in alcohol use than brief intervention, but there were no differences between the two approaches with respect to drug use outcomes. Results add support for SBIRT but pose questions about the optimal service mix. Others have suggested that brief interventions in general might reduce emergency room visits (Bray, Cowell, & Hinde, 2011).

Motivational Enhancement Therapy

Motivational enhancement therapy (MET) is an elaboration on earlier work in motivational interviewing (MI) (DiClemente et al., 1999; Miller & Rollnick, 2013; USDHHS, 2000). Clients typically come to intervention at different levels (stages) of readiness to change (DiClemente & Hughes, 1990; O'Hare, 1996b; Prochaska, DiClemente, & Norcross, 1992). Many minimize or outright deny the existence of a substance abuse problem, have little intention of changing, and may view others as being the source of the problem. Given the levels of dropout in treatment, initial efforts to meet clients "where they are" have focused on initially motivating clients in a nonconfrontational manner. This approach can be incorporated into a brief intervention (as described earlier) or can be used as a prelude to a lengthier engagement process (DiClemente et al., 1999). In some respects, MI reflects the basics of good client-centered counseling techniques and reemphasizes the importance of being nonjudgmental, using good listening skills, engaging clients in a process of gradually weighing the benefits and costs of their substance use, and ultimately relying on clients' ability to make decisions in their own best interest. In addition to providing psychoeducation, the practitioner helps clients compare personal goals with their actual situation, especially the problems incurred as a result of their abuse of alcohol and other drugs. MET practitioners essentially combine MI methods with brief structured intervention and after extensive assessment, they offer client feedback, which may include results of other tests, including health measures (e.g., in collaboration with a physician), and use data to compare substance use and consequences with population norms. Practitioners then focus on engaging and motivating the client, developing a specific plan of change, and examining ambivalent feelings and other potential roadblocks to change (DiClemente et al., 1999; Miller & Rollnick, 2013).

Brief MI was tested with young army conscripts in Switzerland, and results showed a significant drop in alcohol consumption among binge drinkers compared to those who received assessment only in a randomized controlled trial (RCT) (Daeppen et al., 2011). However, there might be limitations to how well MI generalizes to other groups. In a relatively large-sample, multisite RCT with African American participants, Montgomery, Burlew, Kosinski, and Forcehimes (2011) demonstrated that MI resulted in worse outcomes for both men and women than did a more traditional approach to substance abuse counseling.

Cognitive-Behavioral Approaches

Cognitive-behavioral therapy (CBT) can be employed with those experiencing the full range of disordered substance use. A range of goals might be considered depending on a client's needs and preferences. These include harm reduction, moderation, abstinence, relapse prevention (Acierno et al., 1994; Kadden, 1994; Magill & Ray, 2009; Miller, 1992; Monti & Rohsenow, 1999; Nunes-Dinis & Barth, 1993). These skills have also been incorporated into efforts to assist substance abusers who also are at risk for other serious problems, such as HIV transmission (El-Bassel et al., 1995; Pomeroy, Kiam, & Abel, 1999; Schilling, El-Bassel, Hadden, & Gilbert, 1995). A solid body of outcome research provides moderate support for CBT with substance use disorders. CBT might be most effectively used as part of a comprehensive treatment strategy that includes motivational interviewing and 12-step approaches (Longabaugh & Morgenstern, 1999). Coping skills interventions were derived from a number of related approaches, including cognitive therapy (Beck, Rush, Shaw, & Emery, 1979; Moorey, 1989), self-monitoring and cue exposure (Monti & Rohsenow, 1999), social skills training and stress management techniques (Kadden, 1994), and relapse prevention (Larimer et al., 1999; Marlatt & Gordon, 1985). Although CBT is considered among the more effective approaches to treating substance abuse, a recent meta-analysis of 53 studies demonstrated generally moderate effectiveness overall (Magill & Ray, 2009).

CBT methods have also been incorporated into behavioral couples and family therapy and community reinforcement approaches, both of which are discussed here.

Core coping skills strategies include

- Developing rapport and enhancing motivation
- Reviewing dysfunctional thinking regarding denial, rationalization, or hopelessness regarding the client's situation
- Conducting a functional assessment with emphasis on high-risk situations (e.g., client's thoughts, moods, situations, triggers) in which clients are most vulnerable to using drugs
- Teaching self-monitoring of positive or negative thoughts, feelings, behaviors, and situations that could enhance or hinder, respectively, moderation or sobriety
- Identifying and learning to cope with cravings
- Coping with intense or troubling thoughts and feelings (e.g., guilt, anger, depression, stress)
- Practicing assertiveness and social skills when confronted with risky circumstances
- Practicing stress management skills to cope with daily general and specific stressors (e.g., use of imagery, self-desensitization skills, physical exercise, non-drug-centered recreation)
- Learning and sharpening problem-solving skills (e.g., brain-storming solutions, trying out new solutions, considering alternatives)
- Teaching and practicing drink-refusal skills through the use of modeling, role-play, rehearsal, and in vivo practice (e.g., assertively turning down offers to drink: "no thanks," "I'm all set," "I'm good," "I'm not drinking today," or whatever seems to work for the client)
- Teaching communications skills to help the client deal with a wider variety of social situations through use of the following: learning to give and take positive or negative criticism, improving conversational skills, using conflict resolution techniques, and developing sober social supports, as well as enlisting the help of friends, family members, romantic partners, coworkers, employers, and other social supports such as AA buddies or sponsors

Coping skills methods have also been packaged for clients who have made considerable progress in treatment but whose current goal is to prevent relapse (Annis & Davis, 1991; Daley, 1987; Larimer et al., 1999; Magill & Ray, 2009; Marlatt & Gordon, 1985). The purpose of relapse prevention is to increase the client's self-efficacy in the use of these specific skills and to reduce the chances of relapsing in at-risk situations. The overall strategy includes cognitive self-assessment (e.g., pausing to think, reviewing the negative consequences of using and the positive consequences of abstaining or moderating use, taking one's mind off the urge to use), behavior change (e.g., seeking out alternative activities, avoiding or leaving high-risk situations), planning stress-reducing activities, coping with distressing or negative emotions (e.g., letting go of things that can't be controlled or changed, emphasizing positive feelings), and seeking social supports (e.g., spending more time with family and friends who are supportive of the client's efforts to cut down or abstain).

Homework tasks are planned to practice self-monitoring skills and increase clients' confidence in their ability to cope (i.e., build self-efficacy) with at-risk situations. These tasks can include the use of self-rewards for dealing effectively with risky situations, rehearsal and role-play of coping skills with the clinician and significant others, and gaining practice experience (in vivo) in the community. The level of challenge should be gradually increased to promote self-efficacy in high-risk situations. If the person does relapse, coping skills can help mitigate the abstinence violation effect (i.e., catastrophic thinking that a slip is equal to total failure) by preparing the client to interrupt the slip as soon as possible with a minimum of negative consequences. Long-term gains are encouraged by developing healthier and preventative lifestyle changes to maintain gains over the long run.

Behavioral Couples' and Family Therapy

Family members often play an important role in the recovery of a person with a substance use disorder. A number of different approaches to dealing with couples and families have been developed. The family disease model (based on the "Minnesota model" developed at Hazelden) (e.g., Johnson, 1973) considers alcoholism a "family disease." The family systems model (Steinglass, Bennett, Wolin, & Reiss, 1987) is built on the premise that substance abuse develops or is maintained as part of an interactional family process, and both the drinker's behavior and the compensatory behaviors of the other family members help maintain a homeostatic equilibrium. In both the family disease and the family systems approaches, the practitioner attempts to help family members reduce their overinvolvement in the client's behavior and take a more adaptive stance for their own sake and for the health of the client. Little research, however, has been conducted to establish the effectiveness of either model.

Behavioral couples' and family therapy (McCrady et al., 1986; McCrady et al., 2009; Noel & McCrady, 1993; O'Farrell, Choquette, Cutter, Brown, & McCourt, 1993; O'Farrell & Fals-Stewart, 1999, 2003) is grounded in the premise that substance use disorders and associated maladaptive behaviors are learned, and that other family members (including spouses, generally referred to as "concerned significant others," or CSOs) sometimes unwittingly get caught up in attempts to cope with, ameliorate, cover up, or compensate for the behavior of the substance-abusing person. Often, CSOs inadvertently reinforce drinking by shielding (e.g., excuse making), caretaking (e.g., comforting), or punishing the family member (e.g., refraining from talking, intimacy, or sex). In behavioral couple and family approaches, the practitioner works with CSOs to lessen these behaviors and helps them capitalize on opportunities to engage the substance-using client in productive problem solving and improved communication. For example, rather than arguing with a husband who comes home intoxicated, the spouse is encouraged to refrain from addressing the situation at the time and to deal with it the next day when the husband is sober and perhaps in a better state of mind to discuss his drinking. If someone calls to inquire why the husband did not come into work that day, the spouse will refrain from "covering" for her husband. No doubt, there are risks to be run, including withdrawal of the substance-using spouse, retribution, suspension from work, loss of a job, and so forth. These matters need to be discussed thoroughly with family members so they are prepared for such eventualities. Although behavioral therapists share the view that family members' behaviors interact reciprocally, they do not contend that the person abusing substances has a disease, nor do they hold to the belief that other family members cause the client's problems or are codependent. In addition, because they assume that substance abuse and related behaviors are primarily learned (and thus can be changed), behaviorally oriented practitioners do assert that non-substance-abusing family members can help themselves to cope better and have a positive impact on the family member's drinking or drug use.

A meta-analysis of controlled trials covering 3,500 clients and significant others showed that marital and family interventions produced superior outcomes compared to individual, peer group, or family psychoeducation (Stanton & Shadish, 1997). Family interventions also appear to be a cost-effective adjunct to methadone maintenance. These strategies are mostly used with problem adolescents, although they appear to work equally well for both adolescent and adult substance abusers and demonstrate relatively higher levels of client retention. Because of the high rates of co-occurrence between teenage substance abuse and behavioral disorders, family interventions for substance-abusing adolescents will be addressed more thoroughly in chapter 13.

Behavioral Couples Therapy.   Behavioral couples therapy (BCT) has received strong empirical support (McCrady et al., 1986; McCrady et al., 2009; Noel & McCrady, 1993; O'Farrell, Choquette, & Cutter, 1998; O'Farrell & Fals-Stewart, 1999, 2000, 2003). Research repeatedly has shown more positive outcomes in reduced drinking days and reduced drug use, improved marital relationships, reduced domestic violence, and improved psychosocial functioning in children (O'Farrell & Fals-Stewart, 2003). These approaches have also been shown to be cost-effective (Fals-Stewart, O'Farrell, & Birchler, 1997; O'Farrell & Fals-Stewart, 2003). Behavioral contracting, particularly with the use of disulfiram (which causes severe nausea as a person drinks alcohol), has been shown to be an especially effective component of BCT. Key components of BCT include

- Seeing the couple, family, or individuals alone or together as needed
- Conducting a thorough MFS assessment of marital and family problems
- Engaging in crisis intervention as needed
- Using an (optional) disulfiram contract (e.g., the drinking spouse agrees to take daily disulfiram accompanied by the non-abusing spouse's observation and reinforcement)
- Implementing homework assignments and behavioral rehearsal
- Learning to deal with urges to drink, identifying at-risk interventions (incorporating CBT methods discussed earlier)
- Practicing daily caring behaviors between spouses and planning rewarding activities for them together
- Practicing better communications and problem-solving skills for both the actual substance abuse and other related problems
- Incorporating relapse prevention strategies into behavioral marital and family methods

Exemplar Study: Behavioral Couples Therapy

In a key study, O'Farrell et al. (1993) recruited 59 couples with husbands who had recently become abstinent. They agreed to participate in behavioral marital therapy weekly for 5 months and were then randomly assigned either to receive 15 sessions of conjoint relapse prevention treatment over the course of a year or to a control group. In addition to baseline and outcomes measured before and after behavioral marital therapy, couples also reported results at 3-, 6-, and 12-month follow-ups. The intervention included several pregroup sessions, with a thorough assessment, crisis intervention, disulfiram contract, feedback about the assessment of alcohol and marital problems, and efforts to enhance motivation. The couples group sessions consisted of 10 weekly meetings of four to five couples and emphasized the use of homework assignments and behavioral rehearsal. The intervention plan was designed to maintain abstinence, decrease arguments, maintain the disulfiram contract, provide crisis intervention for drinking episodes, monitor and initiate interpersonal caring behaviors, plan and share recreational activities, work on communication skills, and practice problem solving.

After the couples' groups were completed, the couples were then randomly assigned to relapse prevention (RP) or non-RP treatment conditions. Couples with RP received 15 sessions with decreasing frequency over the following year, and RP skills focused on maintaining drinking gains in part by continuing the disulfiram contract for several months along with AA or

Al-Anon. They also practiced behavioral skills to reduce marital problems, improve their relationship, and increase problem-solving skills. Each couple practiced and rehearsed the RP plan by identifying high-risk situations and deciding how to respond to them successfully when they occurred. Those who received the additional RP sessions demonstrated more days abstinent, fewer days drinking, and better marital adjustment than did those who received behavioral couples treatment alone, although drinking measures were comparable between groups at further follow-up. RP subjects were also more likely to use specific treatment-targeted behaviors (i.e., disulfiram contract and marital improvements) at follow-up.

A follow-up study (O'Farrell et al., 1998) reported the results of 12 additional months of RP with 18-month follow-up after termination of treatment. The RP sessions were conducted jointly and had three major goals: to maintain the behavioral gains targeted by BCT (i.e., reduction in drinking and improvement in marital relations), to deal with unresolved marital problems, and to rehearse standard RP methods. Well-established standardized questionnaires were employed to measure both drinking and relational outcomes. Results demonstrated that the combination of BCT and RP resulted in somewhat better marital adjustment overall for the full 30-month period, and alcoholic men (in both treatment groups) remained significantly improved after the full 30-month period.

Research on BCT continues. When 102 women with alcohol use disorders were randomized into behavioral couples' therapy and individual therapy, couples' therapy resulted in significantly better outcomes in days abstinent and reduction of heavy drinking days at 18 months, including for those women with more severe relationship problems (McCrady et al., 2009).

Unilateral Couples Therapy.   A number of interventions have been developed to either help the CSO persuade the substance-abusing spouse to engage in treatment or to help the CSO cope better on his or her own because the partner refuses treatment. Several somewhat similar approaches generally referred to as unilateral family interventions (Sisson & Azrin, 1986; Thomas & Ager, 1993; Thomas & Santa, 1982) have been designed and evaluated for this situation. Two examples of unilateral approaches that have produced promising results in engaging a reluctant spouse and/or improving the coping abilities for the non-substance-abusing spouse include the Pressures to Change model (Barber & Gilbertson, 1996, 1997) and the Community Reinforcement and Family Training Approach (CRAFT) (Miller, Meyers, & Tonigan, 1999; Sisson & Azrin, 1986). In these unilateral approaches, the practitioners generally work with the CSO over several months, provide psychoeducation about the nature of addiction, and try to help the CSO understand the futility of some of his or her own compensatory and reinforcing behaviors (i.e., "enabling"). They may also develop and rehearse a plan to move the substance-abusing spouse toward treatment. Specific supporting skills are also enhanced to help the CSO cope with emotional distress associated with trying to tolerate or influence the substance-abusing spouse. In general, the major intervention steps include variations on the following key elements:

- Education about the nature of the intervention itself, and its methods, purposes, and goals
- An extensive assessment of the behaviors of the person who drinks and the partner's response
- Coaching the CSO to understand the nature of the substance-abusing partner's behaviors, to learn ways of enhancing the relationship (when the spouse is sober), and to reduce behaviors that may be inadvertently reinforcing, such as shielding or nagging
- Developing specific contracts (e.g., contingency management skills) to reinforce moderation or sobriety
- Developing and rehearsing a plan to enlist the help of others to participate in the persuasion activities or, in some cases, prepare family members to participate in an "intervention," in which the CSO (and perhaps others) express concern for the client but demand certain changes (e.g., specific drinking reduction goals or abstinence, participation in treatment)
- Providing support for the CSO in dealing with the emotional distress of living with an addicted or substance-troubled person
- Including some psychoeducation to help the CSOs deal with potentially abusive situations (toward themselves or their children)
- Applying relapse prevention methods if the spouse who drinks makes improvements
- In the event that the client fails to change, focusing the intervention more exclusively on the spouse should he or she need further support in dealing with the current situation or decide to leave the relationship

Although these approaches are quite similar in methods and purpose, practitioners should consult specific models and accompanying treatment manuals before implementing unilateral approaches, since they vary in technique and specific treatment goals.

Community Reinforcement and Contingency Management Approaches

Despite the fact that community reinforcement approaches (CRAs) were originally developed and tested successfully with some of the most debilitated alcohol-dependent persons (Azrin, 1976; Azrin et al., 1982), they have been largely overlooked until recently. The CRA was originally designed to help the severely alcoholic person maintain sobriety through the use of community-based rewards (e.g., social connections, family relations, jobs, supported housing), and it was later adapted to include the use of disulfiram and coping skills. CRAs have come to be considered one of the more effective forms of substance abuse intervention (Alessi et al., 2011; Miller, Meyers, & Hiller-Sturmhöfel, 1999).

Assessment in a CRA emphasizes functional analysis of the client's substance use problem, that is, the identification of behaviors and situation-specific antecedents and consequences that appear to maintain substance abuse. Clients are taught to engage in sobriety sampling (i.e., experimental periods of abstinence or reduced use) to better understand the relationship between substance use and its consequences. Clients are then urged to gradually extend the duration of sobriety with each effort. The goals of the CRA are to reduce or eliminate substance use and to improve overall lifestyle and build social supports. Practitioners who use a CRA may incorporate some of the CBT methods discussed earlier, but they must link the client's performance directly to concrete rewards (Alessi et al., 2011; Higgins & Petry, 1999; Meyers & Smith, 1995).

As with many effective treatments, a CRA may begin more intensively (i.e., more frequent visits), with a gradual increase in time between sessions as the client gains confidence in self-management methods. Outcomes for CRAs have been very positive. Overall, results have shown that clients reduce their substance use substantially more than do counseling controls, need fewer days of institutionalization, work more days, and demonstrate greater social stability. A CRA provides a flexible framework, can be used on an outpatient basis, can be integrated into a family treatment model and 12-step approaches, and can incorporate the use of disulfiram or other similar medications. Although flexible in format, the core components are essential: a thorough MFS assessment, as well as provision of specific and valued concrete and social rewards for reducing or eliminating substance use.

Contingency management (CM) approaches are similar to CRAs, but are often used as interventions for court-ordered drug offenders. CM is structured around two basic principles: the withholding of incentives (i.e., negative reinforcement) or punishment if drug use is detected (e.g., legal sanctions) and positive reinforcers for substance reduction or abstinence and treatment participation (e.g., taking medication, attending sessions, participating in a 12-step program). Although CM may also incorporate the positive reward aspects of CRA, the threat of punishment (e.g., return to prison) because of failed drug tests might be part of court-ordered agreements (Higgins & Petry, 1999; Higgins et al., 2000). It has also been demonstrated that vouchers for goods alone are not as effective overall in reducing substance use or maintaining paid employment as when rewards are contingent on clean urinalysis (Higgins et al., 2003). Both CRA and CM approaches are commensurate with social work approaches, given that many clients are court ordered (Rooney, 1992) and because case management is a critical element in coordinating and optimizing complex and interdisciplinary substance abuse treatment efforts (Sullivan, Hartmann, Dillon, & Wolk, 1994).

Exemplar Study: Combining CRA and CM

One randomized controlled study of cocaine-addicted persons recruited through newspaper advertisements (Higgins et al., 1993) compared a combined CRA-CM approach with a 12-step counseling model based on the disease model. CRA-CM comprised stimulus avoidance plus community reinforcement for clean drug screens (i.e., vouchers for up to $1,000 of approved purchases); self-monitoring of cognitive, emotional, and situational antecedents; relationship counseling; skills training for drug refusal; problem solving; recreational counseling; HIV/AIDS prevention counseling; and job training for drug abstinence. Of participants in the CRA-CM condition, 53% remained in treatment, compared with 11% of the comparison group. In the CRA-CM group, 42% also received disulfiram, an important component of this approach. Sixty-eight percent maintained 8 weeks of cocaine abstinence, compared with 11% of the control group. Forty-two percent of the CRA-CM group achieved 16 weeks of cocaine abstinence versus 5% for the comparison group. In a subsequent controlled study (Higgins et al., 1994), cocaine-dependent individuals were randomly assigned to CRA-CM using vouchers or CRA alone. Clients in the combined treatment (CRA-CM) showed a higher retention rate by completing the 24-week treatment (75% vs. 40%) and achieved a greater proportion of sobriety at 5 weeks (70% vs. 50%), 10 weeks (55% vs. 15%), and 20 weeks (30% vs. 5%). The CRA-CM group also demonstrated almost twice the duration (11.7 vs. 6.0 weeks) of continuous cocaine abstinence as did the CRA without CM group.

Contingency management has been shown to be effective with cocaine abusers, including those with pretreatment marijuana use (Alessi et al., 2011), and it has been shown to be effective with cocaine-dependent pregnant women and women with young children (Schottenfeld, Moore, & Pantalon, 2011). However, in that study, contingency management was not differentially more effective when combined with community reinforcement approach or 12-step facilitation. CM has also been shown to have comparable success with alcohol abuse when added to standard treatment that includes relapse prevention and 12-step groups. Treatment completion at 8 weeks was almost four times greater for the CM group, and abstinence rates were significantly improved as well in a group of alcohol-dependent veterans (Petry, Martin, Cooney, & Kranzler, 2000). Similar CRA programs have also been shown to have robust effects for opiate-addicted persons (Abbott, Weller, Delaney, & Moore, 1998).

12-Step Facilitation (TSF)

The 12-step model is a nonprofessional voluntary form of self-help or, as some refer to it, mutual help. For some, it might also be seen as a form of spiritual help, since it is based on assumptions about the influence of a "higher power." As such, 12-step models (which have been adapted to a wide array of other behavioral problems) are not meant to be evaluated with the standards of evidence-based practice. However, 12-step approaches, primarily Alcoholics Anonymous (AA), is voluntary, free of charge, widely available in many countries, and has had a broad and deep impact on millions of alcohol-disordered people for many decades. Thus, many behavioral health professionals consider AA and similar groups (e.g., Narcotics Anonymous) to be a viable "adjunct" treatment. A growing body of evidence suggests that facilitating a client's introduction and orientation to AA is one more intervention tool available to mental health and substance abuse professionals. This approach is referred to as 12-step facilitation.

Although the 12-step model does not explicitly endorse any scientific theory, it has traditionally been associated with the disease model of alcoholism and recovery (Miller & Kurtz, 1994). The Minnesota (Hazelden) Model came to represent the traditional approach to treating alcoholism in the United States. The traditional recovery model typically employs a multi-level approach, including initial detoxification, education about alcohol addiction and the associated psychosocial and medical consequences, family and group therapy, nutrition and recreation counseling, and regular attendance at 12-step meetings. Outpatient follow-up and continued involvement with AA (or Alanon, or Alateen for other family members) is typically emphasized (Nowinski, 1999). AA rightfully boasts tens of thousands of registered groups and 2 million or more members worldwide. Non-spiritually-oriented mutual help recovery groups are also available and include Rational Recovery, SMART recovery, and Moderation Management, which focus on drinking reduction, not abstinence.

Pioneering efforts to assist alcohol-dependent persons and their families were developed by the Johnson Institute (Johnson, 1973). The primary strategy, known as "the intervention," involves the development of a team of professionals and concerned others in the client's life, and then a well-planned confrontation to persuade the alcohol-dependent person to enter treatment (Liepman, 1993). This approach is firmly embedded in the traditional disease or recovery model and incorporates concepts about resistance and denial, as well as some concepts commensurate with family systems theory, including the codependence of other family members. Not only can the family wield considerable leverage to help the alcohol-dependent person come to a better understanding about their drinking and its consequences; the family can also be an important source of social support during recovery. In addition, family members often need assistance themselves in overcoming many of their "enabling" behaviors. Preparation for the intervention includes a thorough assessment of the problem, analysis of family structure and function, and selection of "team" members. Training for the actual confrontation includes psychoeducation about alcoholism and the family disease concept, an examination of family members' feelings and experiences, negotiation of desired outcomes, an examination of members' willingness to follow through on their commitments to helping the alcohol-dependent person, and rehearsal of the confrontation. Assuming that the confrontation is successful, assessment and evaluation of the situation continues, further adjustments to the family system are examined, and additional plans for recovery are pursued. The popularity of the Minnesota Model is largely based on tradition and anecdotal reports, and there is limited evidence of effectiveness to be gleaned from controlled trials. Nevertheless, clinicians should be familiar with this popular model.

There is some (mostly) uncontrolled research that supports the efficacy of AA for many people (Emrick, 1993), but few studies have evaluated this approach adequately using controlled designs (Morgenstern, Labouvie, McCrady, Kahler, & Frey, 1997). However, a 10-year follow-up of data from the Matching Alcoholism Treatment to Client Heterogeneity study showed significant support for the effectiveness of AA attendance and 12-step work (Pagano, White, Kelly, Stout, & Tonigan, 2013). Although most persons who initiate contact with AA drop out within a few months, evidence suggests that those who "work the program" (i.e., progress through the steps) are more likely to do well than those who drop out prematurely. Perhaps those who do well (a self-selected group) are those motivated to "stick with it." In addition, those clients who combine AA with another professional treatment program have been shown to do better than those who do not attend AA (Emrick, 1993).

However, data are mixed regarding whether 12-step approaches are effective alone or as an add-on to formal substance use treatment. Some have suggested that treatment approaches infused with 12-step beliefs are no more effective than treatments that do not refer to 12-step beliefs (e.g., step work) (Miller, 2008). One randomized controlled trial compared a directive intervention with a motivational approach, both of which included 12-step facilitation, and both were compared with a treatment-as-usual condition in which no 12-step facilitation was employed with 169 cases (about 33% women). The directive approach, but not the motivational approach, resulted in more days abstinent, and the outcome was mediated by the frequency of AA attendance (Walitzer et al., 2008). Overall, evidence is generally positive regarding the moderate effectiveness of TSF (Ries et al., 2008).

Others have examined the "to AA or not to AA" dilemma from a process-change perspective. Some clinician-researchers have noted the compatibility of coping skills and self-help wisdom offered in 12-step programs. Morgenstern et al. (1997) demonstrated that 100 post-treatment AA participants showed increased self-efficacy, coping, and commitment to sobriety as a result of their affiliation in AA. These findings suggest the importance of encouraging clients to try mutual-help groups as well as the potential effectiveness of combining coping skills interventions with mutual-help approaches.

There may be similar change processes between coping skills approaches and mutual help. Clients in recovery often demonstrate self-monitoring skills when they talk about identifying factors associated with risk of relapse (e.g., "people, places, and things," "stinkin' thinkin'). Taking "one day at a time," putting "first things first," and complying with the exhortation of 12-step colleagues to "take it easy" seem comparable to CBT practitioners' efforts to help clients reduce stress, set priorities, and strive for a healthier lifestyle. Other comparisons can be made, including the enhancement of communications and interpersonal skills that come with consistent attendance at 12-step or similar mutual-help meetings. Going beyond rigid distinctions between "professional" and "self-help" jargon can help practitioners learn about mutual-help groups that might be beneficial for some clients. Practitioners can effectively promote the use of AA by encouraging and guiding clients through the first few steps, but practitioners should be cautious not to confuse incongruent treatment goals (Humphreys, 1999). For example, CBT methods should be employed only in conjunction with 12-step approaches when the common goal is abstinence, not moderation. At the very least, all practitioners should be familiar with the 12-steps of Alcoholics Anonymous (1981):

Step 1: We admitted we are powerless over alcohol—that our lives had become unmanageable.

Step 2: Came to believe that a power greater than ourselves could restore us to sanity.

Step 3: Made a decision to turn our will and our lives over to the care of God as we understood him.

Step 4: Made a searching and fearless moral inventory of ourselves.

Step 5: Admitted to God, to ourselves, and to another human being the exact nature of our wrongs.

Step 6: Were entirely ready to have God remove all these defects of character.

Step 7: Humbly asked Him to remove our shortcomings.

Step 8: Made a list of all persons we had harmed, and became willing to make amends to them all.

Step 9: Made direct amends to such people wherever possible, except when to do so would injure them or others.

Step 10: Continued to take personal inventory and when we were wrong promptly admitted it.

Step 11: Sought through prayer and meditation to improve our conscious contact with God as we understood him, praying only for knowledge of His will for us and the power to carry that out.

Step 12: Having had a spiritual awakening as the result of these steps, we tried to carry this message to alcoholics and to practice these principles in all our affairs.

Internet Interventions

Recent reviews of the literature suggest optimism regarding the impact of Internet-based interventions for a range of addictions (e.g., Gainsbury & Blaszczynski, 2008). Those based on CBT principles have shown sound evidence of effectiveness (Barak, Hen, Boniel-Nissim, & Shapira, 2008). One RCT compared CBT-based Internet therapy (i.e., self-monitoring, self-regulatory skills, motivational enhancement, and social support via chat forum) with Internet-based self-help for problem-drinking adults ($N = 205$; about 50% women) and found superior outcomes for the CBT approach at 6 months (Blankers, Koeter, & Schippers, 2011). More research on Internet-based substance use interventions is likely to be forthcoming.

Medication for Substance Use Disorders

For many years, medication intervention for substance abuse has been heralded as the next major treatment advance. One review of the literature suggests that naltrexone (intended to reduce craving for alcohol), perhaps the best-known medication of this type, is a promising treatment option for postrelease prisoners with alcohol use disorders and could reduce HIV-risk behaviors (Springer, Azar, & Altice, 2011). However, the bulk of the evidence does not support this optimistic view. The Combined Pharmacotherapies and Behavioral Interventions for Alcohol Dependence (COMBINE) study is the largest study to date examining the effects of both medication and behavioral treatment in more than 1,300 alcohol-dependent participants Naltrexone and behavioral interventions appeared to be most effective (alone or in combination) when provided in a medical management treatment context, and they were comparably effective for both men and women (Anton et al., 2006; Greenfield, Pettinati, O'Malley, Randall, & Randall, 2010). However, medication did not appear to be superior to behavioral intervention alone. As with Project MATCH (Project Match Research Group, 1997), it remains unclear which elements of the respective treatments (e.g., medication, motivational interviewing, 12 step) are directly related to outcomes (Bergmark, 2008).

Slow-release amphetamine (e.g., dextroamphetamine) showed some initial promise for people addicted to methamphetamine in a small randomized controlled trial (Longo et al., 2009). Other pharmacological studies have shown little or no benefit from medication therapies, and overall the evidence for the superiority of medication therapies over behavioral interventions is sparse.

Person and Treatment Factors That Affect Treatment Outcomes

Because of the heterogeneity and variation in treatment effectiveness, researchers have long wondered about the extent to which client factors and change processes make a difference in treatment outcomes. Perhaps the best-known study to examine the potential congruity between client and treatment factors is the heavily funded Project Match. This ambitious controlled study was conducted to compare both the relative effectiveness of 12-step facilitation (TSF), motivational enhancement therapy (MET), and cognitive-behavioral therapy (CBT), and to identify client factors that predicted positive outcomes for one approach or another. A year after treatment, results were shown to be comparable for the three treatment groups, with slightly higher rates of abstinence reported for the TSF group. TSF showed some slight advantage for severely dependent individuals whose social networks supported drinking (Fuller & Hiller-Sturmhöfel, 1999; Project Match Research Group, 1997). On the whole, Project Match revealed relatively little new information to help guide matching clients to treatment (USDHHS, 2000).

Other studies have shown significant positive correlations between client and treatment process factors with client outcomes. Some of these include degree of financial supports (e.g., health insurance) (Lordan, Kelley, Peters, & Siegfried, 1997), pretreatment motivation and abstinence self-efficacy (Adamson, Sellman, & Frampton, 2009), quality of the client-worker relationship (Raytek, McCrady, Epstein, & Hirsch, 1999; Simpson, Joe, Rowan-Szal, & Greener, 1997), level of social support (McLellan, Luborsky, Woody, & O'Brien, 1983), baseline severity of dependence and co-occurring psychopathology (Adamson et al., 2009; McLellan et al., 1983), impulsivity (Blonigen, Timko, Finney, Moos, & Moos, 2011), use of legal coercion and history of positive treatment experiences (Hser, Maglione, Polinsky, & Anglin, 1998), use of CBT processes (Ogborne, Wild, Braun, & Newton-Taylor, 1998), and use of a 12-step treatment philosophy (Moos & Moos, 1998), among others. Despite this smattering of findings, prescriptive guidelines for matching clients and treatment with any confidence remain elusive (Longabaugh et al., 2005; Mattson et al., 1994; Saxon, Wells, Fleming, Jackson, & Calsyn, 1996).

Women.   One area of the research that has recently generated positive results regarding client-treatment factors concerns the needs of women. It has been long recognized that substance abuse treatment designed primarily for men fell short in addressing women's specific needs. Barriers to women receiving adequate care include a lack of support for reproductive health, pregnancy, and child care; additional stigma for women who abuse substances; and lack of insurance coverage, among other things (Beckman, 1994; Carten, 1996; Greenfield et al., 2011; Haskett, Miller, Whitworth, & Huffman, 1992; Nelson-Zlupko, Dore, Kauffman, & Kaltenbach, 1996; Schliebner, 1994). A recent review of the literature, which included seven randomized controlled trials, demonstrated that when specific components of women-oriented programs were included (e.g., prenatal services, child care, mental health and psychoeducational services geared to women), more women successfully completed treatment with lower rates of substance abuse, fewer mental health problems, improved health, and reduced HIV risk (Ashley, Marsden, & Brady, 2003). However, some studies have shown little advantage in programs designed specifically for women (e.g., Bride, 2001). One rigorous meta-analysis of the literature on treatment of women who were pregnant or parenting showed that treatment was significantly better than no treatment, but there were no significant differences in outcomes between integrated and nonintegrated programs (Milligan et al., 2010). Nevertheless, high-risk sexual behaviors, child abuse trauma, post-traumatic stress disorder, and eating disorders are more common in women in treatment for substance use, and whether services for these issues are integrated or not, it is essential that they be addressed in an overall treatment strategy (Greenfield et al., 2011).

Prisoners.   Although estimates vary, prison inmates are diagnosed with substance use disorders at rates that are substantially higher than those of the larger community. Fazel, Bains, and Doll (2006) reviewed general prison population studies from 1966 through 2004 (mostly US studies but some included England, New Zealand, and Canada) and reported that the prevalence for alcohol abuse and dependence ranged from 18% to 30% in male prisoners and from 10% to 24% in female prisoners. Regarding drug abuse and dependence, estimates ranged from 10% to 48% in male prisoners and 30% to 60% in female prisoners. Substance use is associated with a host of other co-occurring problems including mental health disorders and HIV infection. Drug treatment courts (e.g., deferred sentencing, early release) have proliferated over the past 25 years, and although they are generally referred to as "voluntary," there is clearly an element of coercion (e.g., reduced sentencing upon successful program completion). Participants must consistently attend treatment (including urine screens), and a mix of sanctions and incentives are used to reinforce participant compliance (see the previous section on contingency management). However, results for drug courts are mixed and hard to interpret because of methodological differences in the research. Client characteristics, for example, are complex and need to be better accounted for in some studies. Brown (2010) examined data from 573 drug court participants and found poverty, low educational attainment, and cocaine use to be predictive of failure to comply with the drug court regimen. At this point, it seems that the jury is still out with respect to the effectiveness of drug courts.

Cultural Factors.   Although commonsense guidelines such as understanding cultural mores, mannerisms, language (when necessary), other concerns of the local community, and relevant cultural or ethnic characteristics could potentially facilitate the engagement process with clients, evidence for the superior effectiveness of cultural matching or infusing cultural components into treatment is elusive. Caetano (1993) points out, for example, that cultural minorities in the United States have shown substantial acceptance of 12-step programs. Another study demonstrated that, although Hispanic and non-Hispanic whites in alcohol treatment used somewhat different routes to recovery, outcomes were comparable, and differences may have been largely due to income level, not cultural difference (Arroyo, Westerberg, & Tonigan, 1998). In contrast, with some Hispanic families, one might be especially aware of the importance of family and kinship relationships (although these qualities are certainly not unique to Hispanic people alone), the possible reticence to address problems in the family (i.e., the need to keep things smooth), the recognition of culturally defined family roles, and the importance of spirituality in the family (Gloria & Peregoy, 1996). However, Suarez-Morales et al. (2010) examined secondary data ($N = 235$) extracted from a large controlled trial of motivational enhancement therapy and found no outcome effects associated with birthplace and acculturation matching of clients and practitioners. Other evidence suggests that many Asian Americans have found mainstream psychoeducational and coping-skills-oriented approaches to be acceptable given cultural expectations for a professional advice-giving (i.e., teaching) style accompanied by practical take-home recommendations (O'Hare & Tran, 1998). Given the current state of the research, it may be reasonable for practitioners to begin with the assumption that standard treatments, on the whole, are likely to be acceptable to most clients, but efforts should be made to adapt them to the client's or family's cultural and individual expectations on a case-by-case basis, given the heterogeneity of attitudes and cultural expectations within specific cultural and ethnic groups.

IMPLEMENTING AND EVALUATING THE EVIDENCE-BASED INTERVENTION PLAN

CASE STUDY: CARLA

Carla, a practicing nurse in her mid-30s, had been using cocaine and drinking excessively for 6–9 months. She said she did so as a way of "dealing with her stressful job." After her divorce from a man who had a serious substance abuse problem, she moved in with a new boyfriend, who also used drugs. One day, Carla was accused of making a minor procedural error on her unit at the hospital. She became very upset and was referred by her supervisor to a social worker who did employee assistance contract work for the hospital. The supervisor, a divorced mother of three, was sympathetic to Carla's situation, valued her work, and was willing to give her an opportunity "to get herself together." Carla told the social worker during the assessment that she "was depressed and having a relationship problem," and was now worried about losing her job. During a detailed evaluation over the following few weeks, Carla gradually revealed that she had been abusing alcohol and cocaine. She was snorting cocaine in the evening, having four to five "stiff" drinks per night to get to sleep, and using cocaine in the morning to energize herself for work. She was readily able to recognize and admit the "possible" role substance abuse played in her apparent depression, anxiety, problems in her relationship, and her compromised attention at work. The therapist offered to continue to work with her and help her maintain her employment if she were willing to further explore the possible links between her substance abuse and other problems in her life.

MFS Assessment: Defining Problems and Goals

Employing a multidimensional framework, the social worker, Anne, reviewed with Carla how things were going in the other areas of her life. Because Carla was primarily concerned about her job, she agreed that she had not been at "her best," but she felt that much of her upset was due to her difficult relationship with her boyfriend. Upon further investigation, it became clear that her boyfriend (Terry) was involved with a group of people who were dealing cocaine. When she went home at night to her apartment, there was usually a group of "six or eight people sitting around doing lines of coke." Carla was simply expected to join in. On one recent occasion when she felt that she needed to slow down her "partying" because it was affecting her mood and job performance, she said she didn't feel like using that night. Terry pulled her aside in the bedroom, pushed her down on the bed, and in a threatening tone queried whether she wanted to be "part of things" anymore. At that point, Carla felt that Terry could be potentially violent. She knew that he kept a firearm in the apartment, and sometimes he carried it with him when he went out on business. She was experiencing that "here I go again" feeling with another abusive man in her life. She felt that joining in with routine cocaine use, for the time being, was the only way she could cope with the situation.

This was not the first time Carla had felt trapped and somewhat hopeless about her relationship. Upon further exploration she reflected that she had always been attracted to men who were a "little dangerous," but this time, it appeared that she had gotten herself in more deeply than she wanted, and she was involved in illegal activities that could threaten her career. Her previous marriage was to a similar type of man, and although he was verbally abusive, he had never hit her, was not involved in illegal activities, and usually just got drunk and didn't bother her. She thought about her parents, with whom she was not currently close, who seemed to be locked in an unhappy marriage. Her dad continued to drink and hang out with his buddies at the local tavern. Her mom stayed home most of the time and was usually in treatment for some kind of health-related problem that Carla felt was mostly related to anxiety. Her mom took prescribed tranquilizers and had been taking them (without prescription) from friends as well. Although Carla said she missed her parents sometimes, she found it too depressing to go home and was afraid she would end up in a relationship like theirs. She said she wanted to have a family sometime but did not want to be trapped in a relationship with a "loser."

Anne examined the depth of Carla's mood disturbance and found it difficult to sort out the factors related to her depression and anxiety. Since she had been abusing alcohol off and on for years since college, had been abusing cocaine (up to a gram per day) more recently, and had been unhappy in her relationships for some time, it was hard to pinpoint when the anxiety and depression began and whether they were the cause or result of the substance abuse. As a working hypothesis, the social worker suggested that the only way to find out would be to attempt some period of cutting down, and eventually abstaining, at least for a while. Carla was concerned that she would not be able to do that.

Carla was particularly concerned about the status of her job. She had been going to work on the 7 a.m. shift after snorting cocaine in her car in the parking lot. She had become upset when she thought one of the doctors had seen her snorting lines of coke off her pocket mirror. Generally, she felt pretty good for the first couple of hours on her floor, but by late morning she would become exhausted and often go into the bathroom to snort some more cocaine. She had been feeling increasingly anxious about getting caught, and with this recent incident on her floor, she was becoming very anxious about losing her job.

Carla's health was good, and she did not have any pressing financial problems. Her boyfriend liked paying for things and "taking care of her," but she was beginning to feel that this arrangement was part of a deal, and not because he genuinely cared for her.

After three or four visits, Carla begrudgingly began to agree that her drug abuse was in some way connected with her other concerns: anxiety and depression, job performance, and relationship problems. As she felt more comfortable and was more forthcoming with Anne about her problems, Carla began to see that dealing with her drug problem might help her get a handle on her life in many ways. The social worker assured Carla that she was willing to do her best to help her maintain her job (after a 2-week "vacation," that is, a leave of absence), but Carla would have to be completely forthright in her reporting of drug use and related problems.

To help Carla get a handle on the tentative links between her alcohol and cocaine use and her other symptoms, they developed a 7-day diary with which Carla would note the thoughts, feelings, and situations that stimulated her desire to use, the intensity of her desire to use, the type and quantity of substances used, and any consequences of use (table 7.1).

TABLE 7.1   Diary for substance use

	Monday	*Tuesday*	*Wednesday*	*Thursday*	*Friday*	*Saturday*	*Sunday*
Thoughts, feelings, situations							
Amount of coke used							
Number of drinks							
Consequences of use							

The social worker and Carla began to work immediately on developing alternative ways of coping to cut down and eventually eliminate Carla's use of alcohol and other drugs. Given her history, it appeared that Carla was unlikely to experience dangerous withdrawal symptoms from her drinking. Five or six drinks (each drink probably larger than the "standard" 1.5 ounces of 86-proof liquor) was a considerable amount of alcohol, but she had not been drinking this much for a long period of time, had never consumed more than that for any regular period of time, and had never suffered from serious withdrawal symptoms. However, she would probably experience some anxiety and perhaps disrupted sleep for a while. The social worker suggested a medical consultation, but Carla knew that tranquilizers would probably be prescribed (she could get them for free if she wanted them), and she did not want to use prescription medications since it conjured up images of her becoming "like her mother": hopeless, helpless, and unable to extricate herself from a failed, and unhappy relationship. Withdrawals from cocaine did not pose any physical threat, but Anne noted that Carla would likely feel even more depressed for a period of time, and she let Carla know that she could call her once per day at an agreed-on time if she needed to talk. A psychiatric consultation was arranged for possible prescription of antidepressants.

After using the diary for a couple of weeks while she began to cut down her alcohol and drug use, Carla began to see for herself the day-to-day links among her depressed mood, negative outlook, edginess, poor quality of sleep, and drug abuse. Whereas she would normally fall asleep after two or three drinks, the use of cocaine would stimulate her and keep her awake in the evening, thus drinking more than she normally could handle. To get up in the morning, she would use or want to use more cocaine. She felt depressed and anxious beginning each day like this, and since she had not been working for a couple of weeks, she did not really know what to do with herself. She became more despondent thinking about feeling trapped in what was becoming apparent to her—a dead-end relationship with someone who really didn't care about her. She was feeling exploited. Her mood worsened during the day, but as she and her therapist agreed, she would leave the apartment for a while everyday and find other constructive things to do: errands she had neglected (e.g., taking care of her dry-cleaning, getting her hair done, scheduling car maintenance, going to the dentist).

Her boyfriend Terry became suspicious about her not working, and he began to query her about what she was telling the social worker. Because Terry was involved in dealing cocaine, he became angry when he realized Carla had been talking about him, felt betrayed that she did not want to live this lifestyle anymore, and became belligerent. He hit her hard across the face, causing her nose to bleed profusely. She became angry and, after he went out, packed her belongings and left the apartment. She was somewhat afraid that he would come after her, but afterward she mostly felt depressed about her circumstances and a little panicked. She decided to look up an old friend, Tara, whom she had been neglecting and decided to stay with her for a few days to get reacquainted. Her friend agreed and told Carla that she had noticed changes in her over the previous year or so and had been worried about her. She invited Carla to stay with her a while and meet some of her other friends.

During this time, Carla (more or less) kept up with her diary and noticed that, despite her decrease in drinking (and lack of cocaine use in the previous 3 days), she felt depressed and was crying a lot. Her girlfriend called the social worker and told her that Carla had expressed some desire to "end it all," but she did not feel there was any imminent danger. Tara accompanied Carla to her next session, where further assessment of her depression was conducted. Carla's drinking had been reduced to one or two drinks per day ("to take the edge off at night"), but her cocaine use had been eliminated. Anne and Tara agreed, however, that if Carla moved back in with her boyfriend Terry (who had located her by calling friends of Carla's at work), she would probably begin to use again. The substance abuse appeared to be somewhat contextually dependent, linked closely to her involvement with her drug-abusing boyfriend. Although Carla was depressed about her relationship (or unhappy about it ending,—she wasn't sure which), the depression was exacerbated significantly by her withdrawals from her daily gram of cocaine. She was sleeping more and feeling little energy during the day. Nevertheless, she forced herself to go out and do something, or at least to help out around her friend's apartment. Carla was convinced about the links among her drug use, negative mood, relationship problems, and dissatisfaction in the way her life was going. She and her social worker both agreed that, first, she needed to remain sober and drug-free, and then make some decisions about her relationship and how to extricate herself from it. She also needed to meet with her work supervisor and discuss her progress and a timetable for returning to work. Carla agreed that she should establish a goal of abstaining completely from illicit drug use, but she was less sure about abstinence regarding alcohol.

Selecting and Designing the Intervention: Defining Strategies and Objectives

As the assessment period blended into the beginning stages of intervention, it became apparent that a solid working alliance had been developed. Anne had employed good motivational enhancement methods to help Carla examine the role of drugs as a factor in her presenting problems and test out her own commitment to change. She had, in 4 weeks, moved from being rather ambivalent (i.e., in the contemplation stage) about whether substance abuse played a role in her difficulties to feeling that she had proved the links between her problems and drugs to herself, and being prepared to take action. As she gradually began to sleep better and feel more optimistic about getting her job back on track, Carla moved into a more self-motivated, action-oriented stage of change.

Her social worker began to introduce coping skills methods in a more formal way. After her psychiatric consultation and decision to begin a trial of antidepressants, Carla's energy gradually began to improve, and she returned to work. She was still staying with Tara, but she felt that she was becoming an imposition, and she did not want to go back to her boyfriend's apartment. Since she had taken most of her things when she packed and left, she did not want to go back and recover the few things she had left behind.

She and Anne focused on improving her day-to-day coping skills. First, they addressed her negative thinking about ever having a good relationship. A brief history taking revealed that she previously had a good relationship with a man, but she had decided to leave him for the person who became her husband. She recalled that she had wanted someone "stronger," but as they examined this further, it appeared that her boyfriend simply wanted to control the relationship. The more they examined her cognitive schema around "caring," the more it became apparent that Carla equated "caring" with "control." As a result, she engaged in relationships with men who were more likely to tell her what to do, and they become angry when she didn't comply. Anne noted that, early on, Carla also expected much direction from the social worker as well.

As a result of reviewing her daily diary from a few weeks, Anne and Carla agreed that there were a number of specific high-risk thoughts, feelings, and situational triggers that Carla would have to watch out for if she was going to maintain long-term sobriety, maintain good job performance, and develop healthier relationships. These included some exaggerated negative expectations of relationships ("I'll *never* find someone who will love me," "I'll *never* have a family," "I'll *never* feel good about myself"), lack of confidence in herself on the job, and doubts in her ability to feel OK about living by herself for a while without jumping into a relationship with someone or making a sudden commitment to live with someone. In response to these thoughts, Carla worked on labeling them "old thinking" and on countering them with other more optimistic and realistic alternatives, for example:

> I am attractive and I am a good person to be with, but I must use better judgment and get to know the person I want to be with. I will do well at work if I stay clean and sober, and if I take work one day at a time. When I am depressed about what is going on or scared of what lies ahead, these feelings will pass. In the meantime, I can talk to people, and find other ways to enjoy my life as I work on making things better. I know that all of this will not be easy, it will take hard work and patience, but I know that there are people who can help me.

Occasionally, when Carla felt cravings to buy cocaine or have a drink, she distracted herself with television, read, called a friend, took a walk, or engaged in some other constructive activity. She did drink wine now and then, but she had not consumed more than two drinks on any given occasion. She discussed this with both her social worker and her psychiatrist, who both advised against drinking alcohol, at least for now. She felt that knowing she might be able to have a glass of wine or two in the future made her feel better by not having to commit herself, at this point, to lifetime abstinence. The social worker agreed that she was making great progress but that she should be careful right now about tripping herself up. Carla agreed to put off social drinking for a while. In social situations she also had the opportunity to successfully turn down offers of drinks, and she felt that she could manage the challenge for now. Sometimes she would dwell on regrets and guilt about lost opportunities or the time she spent in bad relationships. Sometimes she felt that she would have liked to have been a better daughter and perhaps visited her parents more often. She discussed these feelings with her social worker, who pointed out that Carla seemed to take on a disproportionate amount of the responsibility in relationships and to blame herself when things didn't go well. She and Carla discussed various scenarios with her boyfriend and parents, and they role-played alternative ways that Carla might deal with others when they laid blame on her.

After a couple of months it became apparent that Carla was doing much better at work, was sleeping better, and was coping adequately living alone, although this was distressing for her at times, and she missed being in a romantic relationship. She was, however, coming home and feeling alone and stressed, and she began to think about drinking excessively again, or even getting back together with her old boyfriend to patch things up. She was feeling vulnerable. She and Anne discussed this and carefully reviewed what had led up to her crisis a few months earlier, and where she was now. Carla decided to stay the course but felt she needed to do more in her life to keep it from going "backward." She joined an exercise group and began to meet different people who had interests other than drinking and drug use. Although Carla had never smoked cigarettes, she did not have much experience with regular exercise such as biking, aerobics, or jogging. She fell in with a "beginner" group and felt that she was meeting people that she felt pretty comfortable with. In collaboration with her social worker, she developed her own daily coping strategies by continuing to reflect on her self-monitoring diary daily (it appealed to her familiarity with nursing protocol and her sense of "healing thyself"), used meditation to counter some of her fears and replace them with more constructive and goal-oriented thinking, and used relaxation (stretching) exercises that she learned in her workout group to relieve tension. The social worker encouraged Carla to continue with her exercise and new social group, since it could help her deal with the physiological stressors that she often interpreted as fear and depression, and it helped her get involved with people who had more constructive and healthful lifestyles. She began to increase the amount of time between visits to the social worker. Together they developed a plan by which Carla would develop personal goals in her personal and work life and report back periodically (every month, then every 3 months) to see how she was doing.

The social worker regularly conferred with the nursing supervisor, and without going into too much detail (to respect client privacy, although all informed consent procedures were in order), she informed her that Carla was making good progress. But given the possibility of relapse, they all agreed that the contingency management plan should remain in place. The terms were not written down but were discussed with Carla: as long as her performance remained acceptable and there was no further evidence of drug relapse, her job was secure. Carla expressed relief in knowing that she was valued by her supervisor, but she also felt a sense of comfort knowing that she had a very compelling incentive to continue to take care of herself and to watch out for situations where she might become vulnerable and slip.

Selecting Scales and Creating Indices to Monitor and Evaluate Client Progress

The AUDIT and the DAST-10 both served as excellent screening tools during the preliminary assessment. In addition, the AUDIT was used to provide a baseline assessment and was repeated periodically (every 3 months) to measure changes. The instructions were modified from "previous year" to "the past 3 months." In addition, individual indexes were employed to help Carla measure the frequency or intensity of key triggers. These included level of depression, anxiety, and simply the urge to use. The Addictions Severity Index was used to provide baseline and outcome measures across multiple domains of well-being (table 7.2).

TABLE 7.2   The Client Service Plan for Carla

Problems	Goals	Objectives (samples)	Interventions	Assessment and evaluation tools
Daily abuse of alcohol (8–10 oz. of liquor) and about 1 gram of cocaine of fairly high purity	Reduce use and abuse of alcohol and other drugs; eliminate cocaine use permanently; abstain from alcohol for the time she is in treatment; revisit this goal on termination	Engage in daily self-monitoring: record thoughts, feelings, situations related to substance use; record exact amounts of substances used; consequences of use	Motivational enhancement therapy to begin the engagement process and help client "own" her intervention goals and methods	AUDIT AND DAST-10 as initial screens

Daily self-monitoring chart to record triggers and level of substance use; rate intensity of triggers on self-anchored scale (1–10) |
| Depression symptoms: negative view of self as hopeless in relationships and failing at work, guilt, remorse, lack of self-confidence, sleep disturbance | Alleviate depressive symptoms: improve self-image and negative view of herself in relationships; build self-confidence through accomplishing her treatment goals; improve sleep through improved health habits | Identify and provide counterargument to daily negative thoughts about herself, her value in a relationship or as an employee; challenge negative outlook for the future | Coping skills interventions tailored to the client's specific needs:

• Teach self-monitoring skills (daily charting)

• Cognitive reappraisal of her dysfunctional thinking regarding her own worth and expectations in relationships, and her negative view of the future | Recommended: weekly use of Inventory of Drinking Situations (modify for alcohol and drugs) or Situational Confidence Questionnaire

AUDIT to track alcohol use every 3 months |
| Anxiety symptoms: worried about losing job, concerned about getting caught with drugs, muscle tension, nervousness, sleeplessness | Similar to above: alleviate anxiety symptoms through abstinence and improved health habits | Engage in daily reflection on her chart combined with 10 minutes of meditation on positive planning and stretching and relaxation exercises to reduce tension | • Develop daily alternative ways of coping to deal with depression, anxiety, and urges to drink or use drugs | ASI as a multidimensional measure for assessment and evaluation |
| Poor relationship with abusive boyfriend; relationship lacks intimacy, based on common interest in drug use | Improve judgment in partner selection and social supports | Reach out to healthful social supports: friends and acquaintances in social support and health activities group; initiate a conversation with one of them daily | • Engage in tension-reducing healthful exercises alone and with others

• Later, focus these self-monitoring and healthful lifestyle changes on relapse prevention when she feels discouraged again | |
| Work performance suffering: client "on probation" informally, will be closely evaluated on return | Achieve and maintain satisfactory work performance | Keep in touch with supervisor; after returning to work, meet with her weekly to review performance on the job | Case management and related interventions:

• Contingency management: continue to link her progress with job performance through liaison and consultation with supervisor

• Enhance social supports through continued contact with health activities group

• Medication consultation with psychiatrist to monitor use of antidepressant medication | |

SUMMARY

Substance abuse and addiction present complex challenges across all social work fields of practice. These problems vary by types of substances used, range of co-occurring problems and consequences, and a host of personal factors that affect the client's response to intervention. Effective substance abuse interventions represent an eclectic array of supportive, cognitive-behavioral skills, and case management skills that are key components of brief treatment, motivational interviewing, and CBT among others, that can be applied with individuals, couples, and families. Despite the availability of evidence-based practices for substance use disorders, however, they continue to be underutilized in practice.

CHAPTER 8

PANIC DISORDER, AGORAPHOBIA, AND OBSESSIVE-COMPULSIVE DISORDER

Anxiety disorders cover a wide array of disabling conditions that may be accompanied by dreadful and terrifying thoughts (e.g., fears of "going crazy," dying of a heart attack), uncontrollable physiological symptoms (e.g., racing heart rate, shortness of breath, trembling), and avoidance behavior (e.g., not leaving home, keeping away from social situations). Although diagnoses depict anxiety disorders as discrete syndromes, different anxiety disorders share many symptoms. In addition, over time individuals may experience signs and symptoms related to more than one anxiety disorder. For example, a person who experienced specific phobias as a child, and has suffered from long-standing generalized anxiety may at other points also experience problems with obsessive thinking or panic attacks, with avoidance of important activities such as driving, flying, and going out in public. To fully appreciate the suffering of a person with a serious anxiety disorder, it is necessary to go beyond discrete categorization (diagnosis) and understand how the anxiety-related thoughts, feelings, and behaviors vary over time and across situations, and how these debilitating conditions can affect other areas of the individual's life. Decades of extensive clinical research have confirmed that cognitive-behavioral therapy is a first-line treatment for anxiety disorders in general and for panic disorder, agoraphobia, and obsessive-compulsive disorder, specifically. These CBT interventions include the development of a sound working alliance between practitioner and client; challenging dysfunctional thinking regarding the perceived threat; learning physiological coping mechanisms (e.g., imagery and relaxation exercises) to mitigate anxiety and counter feelings of losing control; and engaging in graduated, frequent, and prolonged exposure to feared thoughts or situations. Over time, this process has a high likelihood of helping clients gain a sense of self-efficacy (e.g., empowerment, mastery) over their anxiety and improve their overall psychosocial well-being. Case management skills are also needed to coordinate care (e.g., medication) and engender social supports to aid clients.

ASSESSMENT: PANIC DISORDER AND AGORAPHOBIA

Background Data

A considerable amount of research has provided an improved understanding of debilitating anxiety, including both panic disorder and agoraphobia (American Psychiatric Association, APA, 2013; Antony & Swinson, 2000; Barlow, 1997; Craske, 1999). The two disorders were previously linked in the DSM-IV, but the DSM-5 treats them as separate disorders (APA, 2013). Although they are now uncoupled, agoraphobia avoidance behaviors often accompany panic disorder, and panic attacks often accompany agoraphobia. For practical reasons including the fact that most extant research has addressed the two disorders together, this chapter combines them in discussion.

Panic attacks are marked by feelings of overwhelming fear and are accompanied by very distressing physiological symptoms, including a racing heartbeat, shortness of breath, dizziness, and nausea. Panic disorder often causes individuals to begin avoiding situations in which they believe panic attacks are more likely to occur, such as going to the supermarket, driving, being in other public places, or simply going outside the home. The disorder may begin with one panic attack in a stressful or relatively arbitrary situation but with anticipatory fear of another attack, cause the individuals to gradually avoid more and more situations in which they feel vulnerable to another attack. In the extreme, clients may become virtually immobilized and homebound (i.e., agoraphobic).

Experts have described three types of panic attacks: (1) unexpected or "out of the blue" panic attacks; (2) panic that results in response to specific situations; and (3) situationally predisposed panic, in which a person may experience panic associated with a particular situation, but the connection is less predictable. Cues relevant to the panic attack can be either internal (e.g., physical symptoms, frightening thoughts) or external (e.g., being on a bus, in an elevator, in a grocery store). The frequency and severity of panic attacks vary widely, but the associated fears can be quite persistent, despite much reassurance to the contrary. Fears about the next attack (i.e., anticipatory dread) often lead to avoidance behaviors, as in agoraphobia. Persons with panic disorder may also be generally anxious about other matters, including health, work, finances, and other life changes (e.g., separations, sudden losses). Panic disorder may also be associated with depression or substance abuse and co-occur with other anxiety disorders. Agoraphobia can exist without panic disorder, but the two generally co-occur. "The essential feature of agoraphobia is marked, or intense, fear or anxiety triggered by the real or anticipated exposure to a wide range of situations" (APA, 2013, p. 218). Such situations might include riding public transportation, being in open spaces, or being in a crowd. The person then begins to avoid such places for fear of being unable to escape or for fear of experiencing a panic attack.

Lifetime prevalence of panic disorder is estimated to be between 1% and 2%, although some estimates are as high as 3.5% (Antony & Swinson, 2000; Craske, 1999; Kessler et al., 1994), and lifetime prevalence of agoraphobia is estimated at 6.7% (Magee, Eaton, Wittchen, McGonagle, & Kessler, 1996). More recently, the National Comorbidity Study Replication (Kessler et al., 2006) revealed that 28.3% of the US population reported having experienced at least one panic attack in their lifetime, 3.7% met criteria for panic disorder without agoraphobia, 1.1% panic disorder with agoraphobia, and .8% had experienced at least one panic attack with agoraphobia (but did not meet criteria for panic disorder). Onset for panic disorder can occur from the late teens to the early 30s. The course of panic disorder seems to be somewhat chronic, but it waxes and wanes (APA, 2013). The relationship of agoraphobic symptoms to panic attacks is also variable, with some predictable development of symptoms following panic attacks. In other cases, agoraphobia may persist despite a lessening of attacks (possibly because the individual avoids specific situations). Although most people with panic disorder eventually seek treatment, the treatments provided, both psychotherapeutic and pharmacological, have not met evidence-based treatment guidelines (Kessler et al., 2006).

Rates of panic disorder and agoraphobia appear to be slightly higher in women (Kessler et al., 2006). The National Epidemiologic Survey on Alcohol & Related Conditions study (Chou, 2009) revealed very similar lifetime prevalence rates in people age 55 and older for panic disorder without agoraphobia (3.7%), and they found high rates of the disorder with major mood disorders, higher rates in those from a lower socioeconomic status, and higher rates among those who had experienced recent stressful life events. Others have noted that stressful life events such as unemployment, divorce, and death (and positive events such as weddings, births, and graduations) may increase the likelihood of an onset of panic (Antony & Swinson, 2000; Barlow, 1988).

Fokias and Tyler (1995) addressed an often overlooked factor that appears to play a compelling role in the development and maintenance of agoraphobia: quality of social support as a buffer against environmental stressors. They argued that a conceptualization of social support should include the perception of support, a range of different types of support covering a range of situations and activities, degree of satisfaction with the supports, and identification of a confidante within the social support network. They suggested that reviews of research showed a consistent correlation between the absence of social support and the level of psychological distress. The marital relationship may also be an important factor in the etiology, maintenance, and/or successful intervention with agoraphobia, although the review showed conflicting evidence in this regard. Situational stressors may not be the primary cause of debilitating anxiety, but they can exacerbate an existing anxiety disorder and can be mediated (for better or for worse) by the quality of available social supports.

A large epidemiological sample (based on a composite of national surveys) found that whites reported more panic symptoms overall than did
African Americans, Hispanics, and Asian Americans, who reported the lowest
rates (Asnaani, Gutner, Hinton, & Hofmann, 2009). There also appear to be
cultural differences in the meaning of anxiety (Guarnaccia, 1997). For example, *ataques de nervios* in some Latino communities include such behaviors
as screaming uncontrollably or having crying attacks. Although this concept
is similar to panic attack as defined in the DSM-5, it also seems to be associated with a specific upsetting event, and the signature dread of future panic
attacks might not be present. *Ataques de nervios* may also be associated with
affective disorders, anger, loss of impulse control, and possible dissociative
features. Other symptoms may include verbal or physical aggression and suicidal gestures—a general symptom of being out of control. Caution and a
familiarity with cultural norms are important when interpreting or judging
the clinical relevance of some culturally based behaviors.

Hispanic Americans, however, are less likely to access mental health services because of cultural and language barriers (Friedman, 1997). Some feel
great stigma associated with being perceived as needing help or as being
"crazy" (*loco*). Those with a higher level of acculturation are more likely to
use mental health services. Some Hispanic Americans seek help through normal medical and social service channels; others may seek assistance through
indigenous healers in their community (i.e., *curanderas*). Overall, Hispanic
Americans tend to be less informed about white mainstream views of mental
health problems and available services in the United States. Ultimately, however, outcomes for treatment of panic disorder with agoraphobia show little
variation by gender or culture (Steketee & Shapiro, 1995).

In the National Comorbidity Study, people who reported at least one
panic attack revealed some degree of comorbidity with other disorders, and
those who reported panic disorder with agoraphobia had the highest rates of
comorbidity that included another anxiety disorder (93.6%), post-traumatic
stress disorder (PTSD) (39.6%), any mood disorder (73.3%), an impulse disorder (59.5%), and/or a substance use disorder (37.3%) (Bibb & Chambless,
1986; Kessler et al., 1996; Kessler et al., 2006). Persons with serious alcohol
abuse problems are likely to experience more anxiety-related symptoms from
withdrawal, as well as psychosocial stressors caused by drinking (e.g., legal
and occupational problems, marital difficulties, medical concerns). Conversely, persons with anxiety disorders may be more likely to use alcohol as
a coping mechanism to dampen the effects of anxiety (Sher, 1987). Understanding the link between panic with agoraphobia and alcohol abuse suggests that improvement in one problem can improve treatment outcomes in
the other (Lehman, Brown, & Barlow, 1998). Panic attacks also co-occur with
other disorders, including obsessive-compulsive disorder and major depressive disorders (Fava et al., 2000; Steketee, Chambless, & Tran, 2001). Assessment of other problems is important, as evidence suggests that co-occurring

problems such as major depression can have a direct, negative effect on outcomes with otherwise effective interventions (Steketee et al., 2001).

Theories

Historically, the two most prominent theories proffered to explain panic and agoraphobia evolved from early psychoanalytic explanations (e.g., abandonment fears) and early classical and operant conditioning theories (e.g., generalization of a frightening experience). Contemporary scientific models generally eschew early attachment explanations as a cause of panic and instead emphasize biologically inherited anxiety sensitivity and conditioning experiences that lead to subsequent fear reactions in response to bodily sensations associated with anxiety and panic (Pilecki, Arentoft, & Mckay, 2011). Thus, current theories tend to look at the complex and reciprocal interplay of biological predisposition (i.e., inherited temperament, anxiety sensitivity); developmental learning experiences (e.g., innate inhibitions having been reinforced or challenged); the persistence of anxiety-driven cognitive schema; misinterpretation of physiological cues; and behavioral avoidance, in part related to the specific social context or other situational factors (Barlow, 1988; Craske, 1999; Kagan, 1997; McHugh, Smits, & Otto, 2009; Schmidt & Keough, 2009; Zinbarg, Barlow, Brown, & Hertz, 1992). Occurring in the context of life stressors, the initial panic attack can be seen as a possible "false alarm," since it would have happened at an inappropriate, coincidental, or unnecessary time rather than at a time of actual mortal danger (Barlow, 1997; Craske & Barlow, 2008). However, this false alarm may become associated with internal bodily (i.e., interoceptive) cues (e.g., rapid heart rate, dizziness) that lead to additional learned panic responses. The possible reexperiencing of the initial panic may become a source of genuine dread. Some persons begin to avoid situations that they feel will trigger another false alarm, and by reinforcing their anticipatory anxiety, they become increasingly agoraphobic.

Cognitive appraisal and interpretation (e.g., perceptions, attributions, expectancies) give *meaning* to events and interact with anxious feelings. Cognitive theories (Beck, 1976, 1996) emphasize the role of dysfunctional attributions or appraisals by means of automatic thoughts rooted in negative schema and information-processing errors. Beck and Emery (1985) see cognitive, emotional, behavioral, and physiological dimensions of behavior as interactive, and they understand biological processes as essentially innate. However, cognition is the primary activating agent in that the appraisal of threat gives it meaning and subsequently determines, to some extent, the type and severity of physiological response. In the anxious person, the cognitive schema is defined by an overvigilant expectation of risk or danger, and these distortions extend through the person's view of him- or herself, the world, and the future. Thus, anxiety-tinged automatic thoughts precipitate anxious responses through physiological arousal and avoidant behavior.

Cognitive models (see Bandura, 1986; Beck, 1976, 1996) emphasize beliefs centered on danger (i.e., danger schemata), which "serve as pre-dispositional cognitions, leading to processing of information about the world, self and future in a framework of automatic thoughts and images of danger. Danger-related schemata contrast with negative self-evaluation and schemata related to loss, a cognitive style typical of depressed mood. Schemata are posited to cause preferential encoding of threatening, or schema-congruent, information that produces cognitive biases, which in turn are responsible for initiating an anxious state" (Beck & Emery, 1985, p. 64).

Other researchers stress the interaction of cognitive, physiological, behavioral, and situational factors. Parental behavior can contribute to the development and shaping of specific anxiety problems by sending out excessive "danger signals" to a child, but it is not clear whether parents primarily cause the anxiety or are merely responding to an already-anxious child. Genetic predisposition (i.e., a general tendency toward anxiety) is probably nonspecific and is likely to be mediated by environmental experiences (Barlow, 1988; Craske, 1999; Craske & Barlow, 2008), including the appraisal of those stressors as determined by cognitive schemata and the ability of the person to cope with those stressors (Bandura, 1986; Beck & Emery, 1985; Holahan & Moos, 1994; Lazarus & Folkman, 1984). Stressful life events can shape the development of anxiety disorders and precipitate relapse. These effects may vary by type, frequency, and severity of the event; other circumstantial and interpersonal factors; and degree of controllability. Although what constitutes "stress" is certainly subject to one's unique appraisal, stressful conditions associated with lower socioeconomic status have been shown to predict higher rates of panic disorder (Chou, 2009; Kessler et al., 1994; Kohn, Dohrenwend, & Mirotznik, 1998).

Given the combined risk factors of temperament, stressful environmental factors, compromised coping skills, and limited social supports, acute stressors are likely to be appraised as uncontrollable and unpredictable, which results in subsequent dread and avoidance of seemingly related events. The focus of fear may then narrow to a certain thought, feeling, or circumstance, and the resultant anxiety may increase in intensity and generalize to other areas of the person's life (Barlow, 1988, 1997; Craske, 1999; Craske & Barlow, 2008). One can easily imagine how the confluence of these risk factors could increasingly immobilize an anxious person. For example, an innately "nervous" girl grows up in an uncertain, unsupportive, unpredictable environment; struggles with shyness and low self-confidence throughout adolescence; and is thrust suddenly into the challenges of adulthood as a single parent. She experiences an initial panic attack while waiting in line at a grocery store trying to finish the shopping with not enough money in her checking account and knowing that she will be late picking up her daughter from day care for the third time this week. She is afraid she will again be asked to remove her daughter from day care after she has once again adjusted to a new set of friends and caretakers. With racing heartbeat, feeling as though she is about to faint, she rushes to the day-care center, almost has a car accident along the way, and is told at the center that she can no longer bring her daughter there. She places her daughter in the car and has her first full-blown panic attack. This episode of feeling as though one has almost "lost one's mind" can then launch a period of incapacitating daily dread as the person faces each new day uncertain about when the feelings will return and whether he or she will be able to cope sufficiently to survive the day. It appears that the etiology and development of panic disorder is a complex interplay of biological predisposition, developmental learning experiences, life circumstances, and environmental stressors, with the development of panic disorder hinging on the psychological interpretation of these interacting internal and external stimuli.

Key Elements of MFS Assessment

The DSM-5 diagnosis of panic disorder and agoraphobia (APA, 2013) is well researched and is considered reasonably reliable and valid. To meet the diagnostic criteria, the individual must experience recurrent, unexpected panic attacks. Symptoms of panic attack may be one or more of the following: some combination of pounding heartbeat and accelerated heart rate, sweating, trembling or shaking, shortness of breath, feelings of smothering, a choking sensation, chest pain, nausea, feeling faint, and experiencing de-realization (i.e., feelings of unreality) or depersonalization (being detached from oneself). The individual may also experience an intense fear of losing control, losing "one's mind" or "going crazy," a fear of dying, paresthesia (i.e., numbness or tingling sensations), and chills or hot flashes. Attacks must also be followed by persistent concerns about having another panic attack or the consequences of having another attack (i.e., anticipatory dread), and the individual must demonstrate a significant change in behavior related to the attacks. An individual might also meet diagnostic criteria for agoraphobia, indicated by anxiety about being in places or situations from which escape might be difficult (or embarrassing) or situations in which help may not be available in the event of having a panic attack. Individuals avoid situations that they fear may trigger an attack, or they do not limit their movements but endure the experience with marked distress about having a panic attack, or they require the presence of a companion. Agoraphobic fears are usually related to being alone in situations outside the home, such as being in a crowd; standing in a line (e.g., at the supermarket); being stuck in traffic on a bridge; or traveling in a bus, train, airplane, or automobile.

As outlined already, the DSM-5 provides a well-researched list of symptoms associated with panic disorder and agoraphobia. The MFS assessment should include a close review of these problems, with careful analysis of the frequency, severity, and duration of symptoms. However, the signs and symptoms need to be understood in the broader context of a client's psychosocial well-being. Many persons struggle on their own with anxiety disorders; may not be aware of what is happening to them; and/or do not bring their concerns to the attention of professionals until a crisis such as a suicide attempt, "nervous breakdown," or false "heart attack" has occurred.

The MFS assessment should also include other aspects of the client's mental status and co-occurring problems, including depression and any suicidal thoughts, impulsive behaviors, and substance abuse. A routine health screening by a physician is also important, given the significant rates of co-occurrence for anxiety disorders and other health problems. A thoughtful examination of important relationships is crucial, since important people in the client's life may be either exerting stress on the client, thereby exacerbating anxiety, or preventing the person from getting and benefiting from treatment. For example, a young woman with a history of trouble with anxiety may be trapped in an abusive relationship, perhaps living each day with the realistic fear of being physically assaulted. She may be exerting much of her energy just getting through the day and protecting her children, and she may be too frightened to go for help. Substance abuse might be a readily available coping mechanism for her to deal with her fears. The existence of other co-occurring problems, such as depression, serious interpersonal conflicts, traumatic events, changes, losses, and other stressful changes (e.g., marriage, relocation, job loss), should be examined carefully as precipitants or factors that exacerbate the existing condition. A thorough history taking can also provide clues regarding when the problems with severe anxiety began, including panic attacks or agoraphobic behavior, and which circumstances may have precipitated the attack.

A careful analysis of the client's living circumstances, safety in environment, working conditions, and financial well-being is essential, since any or all of these common life stressors can increase the client's day-to-day anxiety (e.g., being evicted from an apartment or house, losing one's job, a child's health crisis, safety concerns given the prevalence of violence and other crimes in a neighborhood). *In brief, practitioners should not overlook any potential sources of acute or chronic stressors.* Although the causes of panic and agoraphobia are mixed and not always clearly linked to situational factors, daily stressors in a client's life can make the struggle much more difficult and become a barrier to successful coping with panic and related avoidance behaviors. Last, practitioners should carefully consider the cultural significance of the client's beliefs or fears.

An accurate functional assessment is essential to helping clients implement coping skills as part of the intervention. Practitioners should focus on the specifics of clients' thoughts, feelings, behaviors, and circumstances and work with them to describe a detailed patterning and sequencing of factors related to anxiety and related problems. Practitioners should also examine the day-to-day impact of other situational stressors and co-occurring problems, such as marital and family problems, substance abuse, poverty, safety concerns, and other social factors that might be exacerbating the problem. Panic attacks can be measured in general ways. Most clients are terrified of an attack happening at all, but practitioners should teach clients to measure the frequency of occurrence, the intensity of the attacks on a self-anchored scale (0–10), and the duration of the attacks (in minutes). It would also be important for clients to note the circumstances at the time, what they were thinking and feeling, what they did in response, and any other relevant factors that may have made the situation more stressful (or less stressful, should clients initiate their own coping responses). Asking clients to collect these data on a calendar grid (7- or 14-day diary) gets them quickly involved in their own treatment and can provide some sense of clinical perspective and control over the problem. The functional analysis also provides rich clues and useful benchmarks to help develop the intervention plan. Practitioners could enhance the face-to-face assessment by acquiring the observations and insights of significant others, who can accompany the client if possible. Antony and Swinson (2000) suggest capturing data on the following key points:

- Development and course of the problem
- Impact on functioning
- Pattern of physical symptoms
- Cognitive factors (e.g., general beliefs, expectancies, dysfunctional thinking, cognitive biases)
- Focus of apprehension (e.g., internal vs. external)
- Patterns of overt avoidance and subtle avoidance strategies (e.g., distraction, overprotective behaviors, safety signals)
- Parameters of fear (i.e., variables affecting fear)
- Family factors and social supports (e.g., family history of the problem, family accommodation, potential for family and friends to help with treatment)
- Treatment history
- Skills deficits (e.g., communication skills, driving skills)
- Medical history and physical limitations

In addition to identifying the characteristics of panic symptoms and avoidance, practitioners and clients should collaborate to develop a fear and avoidance hierarchy that includes a list (from least fear inducing to most fear inducing) and a graduated hierarchy for approaching (i.e., gradually confronting) each individual fear. For example, a client may be afraid of a number of situations (in ascending order): going outside the house, driving, being in a crowd of people, and standing in line at a grocery store. Although the first two problems may be more manageable and may be dealt with directly through graduated daily practice, a more challenging problem, such as going into a grocery store and patiently standing in line, may have to be broken down into smaller steps as part of a thorough assessment (e.g., driving to the store; going inside; spending 2, 5, 10, then 20 minutes shopping; standing in line; checking out). Because it is unlikely that a seriously agoraphobic person who has not shopped in years is likely to accomplish this in one session, breaking the process down into increasingly challenging smaller steps (i.e., an ascending hierarchy of objectives) provides a clear plan by which the client can gain control gradually instead of feeling pressured to accomplish the final goal at one time. The details of developing such a hierarchy are key to developing a good functional assessment, since during the discussion of each step, clients will provide important clues as to the nature of their fears (i.e., symptoms, specific frightening thoughts, likely behavioral responses) which can be discussed early on. This information can help practitioners and clients anticipate problems and tailor the intervention to obtain maximum effect. The Subjective Units of Distress Scale (SUDS), a self-anchored 0–10 anxiety scale developed as an assessment tool as part of systematic desensitization (Wolpe, 1973) (described later) can be used to help clients gauge their anxiety level during the development of the hierarchy, and it provides a baseline by which clients can judge their progress when they implement in vivo exposure. SUDS is a useful tool that can be employed with other anxiety disorders as well, or with any problem for which overcoming anxiety is key to achieving therapeutic goals. The details of developing a graduated hierarchy are examined more thoroughly later, in the discussion on effective interventions for panic disorder with agoraphobia.

Instruments

Although a detailed functional assessment of the frequency, severity, and duration of panic symptoms and the circumstances of avoidance behavior provide important measurable benchmarks for assessment and evaluation, standardized scales are an important adjunct to the overall assessment process. There are general scales available for measuring panic symptoms and agoraphobic avoidance. The Panic Attack Symptoms Questionnaire (PASQ) measures the duration of autonomic symptoms associated with panic. The Panic Attack Cognitions Questionnaire (PACQ), a companion scale (Clum, Broyles, Borden, & Watkins, 1990), measures how thoroughly catastrophic cognitions dominate an individual's thinking.

Clum et al. (1990) examined 93 individuals (age 18–57; 30 men) with various anxiety diagnoses. In addition to the PASQ and the PACQ, clients completed well-established measures of general anxiety and depression.

Items from the PACQ were generated from DSM-III criteria as well as items from client self-report and other scales. Each item is rated on a four-point scale (1 = not at all, 4 = totally dominated) that indicates the degree of preoccupation with each cognition during a panic attack. The subject rates the severity of the thought before, during, and after an anxiety episode. Scores are summed across individual items. Those who experienced panic attacks scored higher on 8 of the scale's 25 items. Internal consistency for the PACQ was .88. PASQ items were generated from DSM-III descriptors of panic symptoms and from interviews with clients and another standardized scale. Each item is rated on a six-point scale that indicates duration of symptoms ranging from 1 (do not experience this) to 6 (protracted period from 24–48 hours or more). Results of the analysis indicated that all 18 items of the PASQ significantly differentiated persons with a diagnosis of panic disorder. Internal consistency for the PASQ was .88. The PASQ appears to be a more accurate measure of panic attacks than the PACQ.

Although both the PASQ and the PACQ are both well-regarded scales, the Agoraphobia Scale (AS) (Ost, 1990) is recommended here for practical reasons. With only 20 items, it measures two primary symptoms of agoraphobia: fear and avoidance. The respondent rates a variety of situations for anxiety and avoidance after reading brief descriptions of potential fear- and avoidance-inducing situations, and then rates each item according to the following scale: 0 = no anxiety whatsoever, 1 = a little, 2 = moderate, 3 = much, 4 = very much anxiety. The same situations are then rated for avoidance: 0 = do not avoid at all, 1 = avoid if possible, 2 = always avoid. Two samples of agoraphobic and community clients were obtained to validate the instrument along with DSM diagnosis, other validated agoraphobic questionnaires, results from behavioral tests (i.e., the percentage of hierarchically ordered anxiety-provoking tasks completed), and other standardized measures of anxiety and depression. Results of the analysis showed the AS to have high internal consistency (.87 for the anxiety subscale, .89 for the avoidance subscale), it significantly correlated with other agoraphobia scales, but discriminated from other general psychopathology scales including the Beck Depression Inventory (Beck et al., 1961) and the Hamilton Anxiety Rating Scale (Hamilton, 1959). In addition, the anxiety and avoidance subscales both predicted the individual's degree of avoidance based on the behavioral avoidance test. Both subscales also showed good sensitivity to individual change during treatment. Each of the 20 items below of the Agoraphobia Scale (Ost, 1990) should be scored twice using the two scales shown in instrument 8.1.

An evidence-based assessment of a client with panic disorder with agoraphobia combines the best of an MFS analysis with simple indexes and standardized scales. These complementary approaches will provide practitioners and clients with a unique portrait of client strengths and vulnerabilities in dealing with a potentially incapacitating disorder.

INSTRUMENT 8.1   The Agoraphobia Scale

Anxiety level: 0 = no anxiety whatsoever, 1 = a little, 2 = moderate, 3 = much, 4 = very much anxiety

Avoidance: 0 = do not avoid at all, 1 = avoid if possible, 2 = always avoid

---

1. Being alone in your home
2. Shopping unaccompanied in small shops, (e.g., grocery, tobacco shop, or pharmacy)
3. Crossing a street in the city alone
4. Being in a crowd without the company of a friend
5. Unaccompanied, riding the bus at rush hour
6. Walking straight across large open spaces in the city (e.g., a square)
7. Driving a car alone through a long tunnel
8. Walking away from your home alone
9. Going by train or subway unaccompanied, when it is crowded
10. Standing in long lines in the post office, bank, or department store, unaccompanied
11. Sitting in a chair for a long time, in the company of other people
12. Eating at a restaurant or lunch bar
13. Going to a cinema or theater and sitting in the middle of a row
14. Shopping unaccompanied in a department store full of people
15. Crossing a bridge where there is a lot of traffic, unaccompanied
16. Driving a car alone over a viaduct or bridge
17. Having a haircut at the hairdresser, unaccompanied
18. Shopping unaccompanied in a large supermarket, crowded with people
19. Unaccompanied walking in crowded streets
20. Riding in an elevator alone.

SELECTING EFFECTIVE INTERVENTIONS

Although earlier literature reviews (e.g., Jansson & Ost, 1982; Marks, 1987) almost exclusively emphasized the importance of in vivo exposure as the intervention of choice for panic disorder with agoraphobia, more recent evidence provides some tentative support for adding cognitive techniques to the overall intervention package (Craske, 1999; Craske & Barlow, 2008). Cognitive-behavioral therapy (CBT) appears to enhance treatment for persons with panic disorder by helping them change their cognitions about bodily sensations that they have misinterpreted as potentially catastrophic (e.g., impending heart attack) and that often provoke panic and subsequent avoidance. Treatments may include some combination of breathing retraining to reduce hyperventilation, cognitive restructuring to correct catastrophic misinterpretations of harmless bodily sensations, and exposure to somatic cues (e.g., hyperventilation) (Chambless & Gillis, 1996; Craske, 1996a, 1996b; Emmelkamp, 1994; Zinbarg et al., 1992). Effective interventions often require an eclectic blend of treatments tailored to client's needs. Antony and Swinson (2000) categorize CBT methods for panic disorder with agoraphobia into four types of strategies: in vivo exposure to feared situations (e.g., driving on busy highways), interceptive exposure (IE) exercises (e.g., repeatedly spinning in a chair to overcome a fear of becoming dizzy), cognitive strategies (e.g., examining evidence that supports or contradicts anxious beliefs), and relaxation-based strategies (e.g., learning to breathe more slowly and for relaxation). They also suggest that adjunctive interventions, such as the use of mobile phones to communicate during graduated exposure tasks and self-guided instructional manuals might be helpful.

Critical reviews of the outcome literature have established that CBT treatments are most effective for treating panic disorder and agoraphobia, and result in lasting positive outcomes for many people (Antony & Swinson, 2000; Arch & Craske, 2009; Barlow, 1988, 1997; Craske, 1999; Emmelkamp, 1994; Hollon & Beck, 1994; Zinbarg et al., 1992). A recent meta-analysis of more than 25 years of studies on treatment of panic disorder with or without agoraphobia controlled for different components of variations of CBT and found that exposure (both covert and in vivo), relaxation, and breath control in response to a client's physiological symptoms were the most effective methods. Treatments worked best when they included homework and follow-up (Sanchez-Meca, Rosa-Alcazar, Marin-Martinez, & Gomez-Conesa, 2010). These findings showed moderate to large effect sizes, and larger effect sizes were associated with studies of higher methodological quality. CBT yields moderate to large effect sizes for anxiety disorders in general and for panic disorder specifically, with good long-term stability in clinical gains. About 75% of participants can expect to be virtually free of panic at completion and at 6-month follow-up (for up to 2 years and more). Long-term outcomes appear to include improvements in overall quality of life, with relatively low attrition rates. Clients with more serious debilitation may benefit from booster interventions to maintain gains over time. Nevertheless, about half of clients with more severe agoraphobia achieve substantial improvement. No other psychosocial interventions for panic with agoraphobia have been shown to be nearly as effective in the short or long term as cognitive-behavioral methods. However, long-term maintenance of gains with co-occurring disorders remains a challenge (Arch & Craske, 2009). Although medication may be of assistance, CBT alone may be as effective as when it is combined with medication.

Medications Used with Panic Disorder

Four types of medications have been found to be potentially helpful in the treatment of panic disorder (McHugh et al., 2009; Kaplan & Sadock, 1998; Schmidt & Keough, 2009; Sundel & Sundel, 1998): selective serotonin reuptake inhibitors (SSRIs), tricyclic antidepressants (TCAs), benzodiazepines (BZDs), and monoamine oxidase inhibitors (MAOIs).

CBT versus Medication

Although medication may be of assistance with panic disorder, CBT alone may be as effective as a combination of CBT and medication (Barlow, 1997; Craske, 1999; Craske & Barlow, 2008). Some atudies have suggested that medication may actually interfere with the long-term effectiveness of CBT because clients attribute progress to medication rather than to their efforts to make psychosocial and behavior changes (Antony & Swinson, 2000; Craske & Barlow, 2008). A meta-analysis of 124 studies (Mitte, 2005) revealed CBT to be substantially effective for panic and agoraphobia, and medications (both antianxiety and antidepressant) were also shown to be effective. However, one class of medication did not appear to be superior in efficacy to the other, and adding pharmacological treatment to CBT did not appear to enhance treatment outcomes. CBT also resulted in lower attrition than behavior therapy alone, which supports the view that cognitive components improved outcomes.

Exemplar Study: Comparing Medication Alone versus Medication and CBT in a Managed-Care Setting

Mitchell (1999) examined the following question: "Do cognitive-behavioral interventions for panic disorder have an effect that goes beyond the effect of medication alone?" (p. 192). To answer this question, a quasi-experimental design was employed. Fifty-six adults diagnosed with panic disorder were free to select either group CBT and medication or medication alone. Medication regimens followed standardized dosing protocol for either BZDs or SSRIs, and those who also received CBT participated in one of four separate therapy groups (all run by the same therapist, who followed the same 8-week protocol of weekly sessions of 1.5 hours). The intervention is summarized as follows: week 1, psychoeducation about panic disorder and breathing retraining; week 2, development of a personal anxiety management program; week 3, progressive muscle relaxation and physical exercise; week 4, imaginal relaxation techniques; week 5, desensitizing interoceptive cues (i.e., internal physiological symptoms); week 6, phobic desensitization (covert and in vivo); week 7, countering cognitive distortions related to anxiety; and week 8, examining core beliefs regarding anxiety, plus a final review and discussion of post-treatment follow-up.

A multidimensional scale that measured cognitive, behavioral, and physiological symptoms of anxiety was used at baseline and at post-treatment. As noted earlier, clients self-selected their choice of medication or medication plus CBT. Findings significantly demonstrated that those clients who received the medication plus CBT intervention fared better on all three outcome measures than those who only received medication. Although this particular investigation demonstrates the superior effectiveness of providing both CBT plus medication over medication alone, there are some limitations to the study. The fact that clients chose their intervention protocol suggests that client treatment expectancies may have affected the outcome. In addition, the study does not provide evidence for maintenance of gains at follow-up.

Including Spouses in Evidence-Based Interventions with Panic Disorder and Agoraphobia

Although there is little evidence for the effectiveness of family or couples therapy when panic disorder or agoraphobia is treated as a "symptom" of family dysfunction, there is growing consensus in the evidence-based literature that spousal participation in behavioral couples therapy can help effect positive outcomes. In their review of the literature on behavioral couples therapy and implications for treatment of agoraphobia, Daiuto, Baucom, Epstein, and Dutton (1998) suggested that partner-assisted exposure treatment enhances maintenance of gains in relatively healthy couples who demonstrate adequate communication and problem-solving skills. However, partner-assisted exposure may be countertherapeutic for more seriously troubled couples. In otherwise well-functioning couples, the assisting partner can help the client by providing support, acting as coach, otherwise assisting his or her partner in following through on homework exercises (e.g., working on daily graduated exposure), actively discouraging avoidance behaviors, praising and supporting intervention efforts and client progress, countering the client's dysfunctional anxiety-producing cognitions, problem solving with the client, and facilitating better communications (Antony & Swinson, 2000; Baucom, Mueser, Shoham, Daiuto, & Stickle, 1998). By working with the couple, the practitioner can also identify otherwise unhelpful partner behaviors that interfere with therapeutic progress. Although some evidence supports couples work with agoraphobic clients (e.g., Jacobson, Holzworth-Munroe, & Schmaling, 1989), others contend that the evidence is mixed (Fokias & Tyler, 1995).

Evidence for Other Treatments

Psychodynamic Therapy.   The efficacy of psychodynamic treatments for panic with and without agoraphobia is relatively undetermined: there are few available studies, and it is unclear which aspects of the intervention (e.g., common factors vs. transference interpretation) account for the positive effects (McHugh et al., 2009; Schmidt & Keough, 2009). For example, in the first randomized controlled trial (RCT) of psychodynamic treatment for panic disorder, Milrod et al. (2007) compared a manualized form of psychoanalytically informed treatment (e.g., explore meaning of symptoms, transference interpretation) with relaxation therapy in 49 people with panic disorder. The psychodynamic treatment resulted in almost twice as many participants substantially reducing their symptoms (73% vs. 39%). However, the authors note that such findings do not illuminate the specific techniques that might account for the results, nor can they rule out the effects of "common factors" (e.g., working relationship) accounting for the successful outcomes. In addition, relaxation therapy does not provide a robust comparison treatment.

Physical Exercise.   McHugh et al. (2009) cite several studies in which aerobic exercise (e.g., brisk walking, running) shows substantial benefits in terms of reducing anxiety and panic symptoms. However, practitioners should encourage vigorous exercise only after having documentation of a physician's approval.

Internet Therapies.   Internet therapy and treatments administered and/or facilitated by computer (in coordination with live providers) have shown considerable promise but await more controlled research (Reger & Gahm, 2009).

Description of Effective Psychosocial Intervention for Panic Disorder with Agoraphobia

Cognitive-behavioral interventions for panic disorder accompanied by agoraphobia include several main components (Antony & Swinson, 2000; Barlow, 1997; Craske, 1999; Craske & Barlow, 2008): (1) psychoeducation regarding the nature of the disorder and basic components of the intervention; (2) the development of self-monitoring skills to assess the patterns of anxiety and specific situational factors related to implementing the new techniques; (3) cognitive reappraisal skills to challenge dysfunctional thinking that reinforces panic and avoidance; (4) anxiety reduction skills, including breathing retraining and perhaps imaginal exposure (i.e., desensitization) to frightening thoughts and images; (5) in vivo graduated exposure to the feared situation; (6) lifestyle changes (e.g., exercise, reduced substance use, solving personal and interpersonal problems, reducing other sources of stress)—all of which should be addressed to help clients maintain their gains and prevent relapse. Although published protocols vary somewhat, core effective elements in the CBT literature are similar, and practitioners flexibly tailor a treatment plan to client needs, preferences, and circumstances. A more detailed breakdown is presented in the lists that follow.

Psychoeducation

- Provide didactic information regarding the nature of fear and anxiety (e.g., "fear of the fear" model, anticipatory dread) and other false beliefs about the harmful nature of the physical symptoms themselves (assuming client has received a clean bill of health in a medical exam).

- Examine other erroneous cognitions and thinking errors that often accompany panic attacks; help clients understand that physical symptoms can be brought under control through CBT methods and that fears often lead to avoidance behaviors; explain how biopsychosocial aspects of the symptoms work; help clients understand the sequencing and patterning of thoughts, feelings, behaviors, and situations and how these can be modified to reduce distress associated with the disorder.

- Provide an overview of the specific treatment strategies to be employed.

Cognitive Restructuring

- Identify and challenge core cognitions and common thinking errors associated with dysfunctional misinterpretations of bodily sensations (e.g., heart palpitations) or frightening thoughts ("I'm going to faint in front of everyone."); help clients identify and challenge overestimations of danger, catastrophic thinking (e.g., "This problem will never end!"), identify and avoid overgeneralizing (e.g., "I'm afraid of *everything.*"), dichotomous thinking (e.g., "I'm either going to get better or die."), and generally help clients consider more realistic and plausible interpretations. Practitioners should gently challenge clients' overall appraisal of the threat of their symptoms to their health and future well-being.

- Cognitive restructuring should focus on teaching clients to identify the anxiety-producing belief; generating alternative explanations, predictions, or beliefs; examining the respective evidence for the original belief and the alternative belief; choosing a more realistic interpretation or prediction.

- Other cognitive tasks can facilitate the intervention, such as using self-monitoring strategies (practicing between visits) and developing exposure hierarchies (i.e., a scenario of approaching the feared situation that is broken down into gradual steps). These are used later for either in-session (imaginal) exposure or in vivo exposure.

Managing Physiological Symptoms of Anxiety

- Teach breathing retraining (e.g., diaphragm breathing to reduce the hyperventilation often associated with panic attacks).

- Demonstrate hyperventilation (to help correct misconceptions about anxiety symptoms as being very dangerous) and educate the clients about physiology of respiration; demonstrate that overbreathing leads to feelings of dizziness and lightheadedness that often trigger panic but can be controlled through deep, slowed breathing. Teach clients to hold deep breaths and let them out slowly.

- Teach imaginal exposure methods to help clients focus on interoceptive stimuli (i.e., internal body, somatic sensations) that they have come to associate with panic attacks. Using the hierarchy of a feared situation developed earlier, clients should gradually confront the feared thought and situation in their mind's eye (i.e., covertly) and learn to maintain exposure until the anxiety is reduced substantially. Have clients tailor the imaginal scenario to be as salient and as emotionally compelling for them as possible.

- Perhaps the most common form of imaginal exposure is systematic desensitization, noted earlier. After assisting clients in developing a fear-inducing hierarchy—from low anxiety (e.g., leaving the house) to high anxiety (e.g., standing in line at the grocery store)—clients use basic relaxation techniques (e.g., breathing techniques, progressive muscle relaxation) and learn to use the Subjective Units of Distress Scale (SUDS), a self-anchored 0–10 anxiety scale, which clients score verbally when prompted. After a client is in a relaxed state, the practitioner introduces images from the hierarchy that increase incrementally from low anxiety to higher levels of anxiety. Periodically, clients are asked how anxious they are on a scale from 0 to 10. As clients begin to report some degree of discomfort (e.g., images of "getting into the car" generate an anxiety level of 4), clients are asked to hold onto the image and use their relaxation exercises (e.g., deep, slow breathing) at the same time. This may be repeated several times, until clients indicate that their fear has been greatly reduced and they can move further up the hierarchy. This approach gradually helps clients move to a point at which they can imagine, for example, being in line at the grocery store (e.g., originally rated as 8 on the SUDS) and can maintain imaginal exposure until the score drops to a 4 or less. Imaginal exposure is not typically the core intervention for agoraphobia, but it might be helpful as a warm-up before beginning in vivo, graduated exposure sessions.

In Vivo Exposure

- During in vivo, graduated exposure, clients incrementally confront the frightening situation and remain in that situation for a prolonged period while practicing their anxiety-reducing coping skills (e.g., breathing, self-soothing talk, reassuring images).

- In vivo sessions should be carefully planned (step by step) and structured (i.e., what the client will do, how long it will take).

- In vivo exposure sessions are behavioral experiments designed to challenge clients' dysfunctional beliefs about their fears and the potential effects of anxiety. They, in effect, create a cognitive "contest" whereby clients' catastrophic anxieties are pitted against the reality that, if they remain long enough in the situation, they will be able to maintain control and the anxiety will dissipate, thus "disproving" (i.e., provide disconfirming evidence) their terrifying expectations.

- With practice, self-efficacy (i.e., the belief of being able to cope with these situations) increases and provides clients with a more assured sense of empowerment and self-control.

- Graduated exposure is generally recommended over rapid exposure (flooding), but progress should be made expeditiously. The pace of exposure should be gradual, but tasks should be at least moderately fear-inducing. The practitioner should challenge clients to do a little more than they think they are capable of doing at each threshold, so that they can make steady progress.

- Counsel the client not to use subtle avoidance strategies (e.g., drinking beforehand, arriving late, leaving early).

- Encourage clients to give in to the fear, and not fight it. Reassure clients that, at worst, they will feel uncomfortable, but their catastrophic fears will not be realized.

- Exposure sessions should be fairly frequent and spaced close together, and the duration of exposure should be long enough to significantly decrease anxiety. Clients should expect to feel uncomfortable and not to obtain quick and easy results.

- Clients should be directed to use their cognitive coping strategies to challenge negative automatic thoughts during the exercise.

- Depending on the situation, clients should attempt to generalize the exposure to other relevant situations. Although therapist-directed exposure is important in the beginning, clients should be encouraged to practice on their own and to continue practicing as treatment contacts are reduced or terminated. Booster (i.e., follow-up) sessions are encouraged to help maintain gains.

- Clients can engage in self-directed exposure, be accompanied by a practitioner, or have a trained significant other coach them. Agoraphobic self-help groups have become increasingly sophisticated in using behavioral techniques, and they often provide "buddy systems" to help newer members overcome their fears. Use of technologies may be helpful where in vivo practice is not practical. Mobile phones may be useful for assisting an agoraphobic person who is engaged in exposure therapy.

- Socially phobic clients may also benefit from social skills training.

- In addition to booster sessions after termination, clients should leave treatment with a plan to maintain other positive changes, such as consistently exposing themselves to an anxiety-inducing situation if it is practical (so they don't backslide), and maintaining other positive habits, such as anxiety management techniques and abstinence or moderation in substance use, as warranted. If the client has been given medical clearance, physical exercise can help substantially in reducing the anxiety and depression that often accompany panic and agoraphobia.

TREATMENT PLANNING AND EVALUATION

CASE STUDY: MILAGRA

Milagra, a 17-year-old Latina woman, was brought to an outpatient mental health clinic by her mother and local parish priest Padre Reyes. Although she had experienced "nervios" in the past, she recently began experiencing panic attacks several times a week. As a result, she was terrified of driving and did not even want to think about leaving her immediate neighborhood for any reason whatsoever. Since her mother (who never learned how to drive) had come to rely on her to run errands, this turn of events was disruptive for the entire household. In addition, Milagra shared some of the parenting responsibilities for her two younger siblings: Raul, age 10, and Pablo, 8. The family emigrated from Mexico twelve years earlier, and moved into a community that strongly maintained its heritage, language, and customs. Because of her early school experiences, Milagra grew up speaking excellent English, and thus acquired much of the responsibility of household translator. Her father, an intermittently heavy drinker, worked two or three jobs to survive financially. Her mom, "a worrier," coped with her anxieties by maintaining close ties to her church, often volunteering hours of her time. She had also sought help for own anxieties in the past, but she later avoided the physician, who was not a Latino, and relied instead on her rosary beads and occasional visits to the neighborhood curandera. After Gloria, the social worker, took a thorough history, it appeared that a happy event precipitated the onset of panic attack symptoms. Milagra was accepted to the state university with a full tuition scholarship. The family was at first ecstatic, very proud, and the envy of all their neighbors. However, as the late spring and early summer wore on, Milagra grew increasingly anxious: "How will I get to school? My car is too old. It will need many repairs. What about all my responsibilities at home? When will I have time to study? There are no buses or trains that travel reliably or conveniently to the campus." After she accepted that she would have to visit the university, she planned a day to check out the campus and interview with university officials. On her way there, she experienced a full-blown panic attack, an experience that went well beyond the usual "nervios." Terrified, she pulled off the road and remained there, with her heart racing, and she was gasping for breath until a state police car pulled up to investigate. When she explained her situation, the police officer told her to move the vehicle off the bridge or it would be towed. Feeling as if she were going to pass out, she calmed herself enough to travel down the highway; got off at the next exit at a gas station and convenience mart; and called home tearful, terrified, and feeling defeated. Once home, her mother thought her daughter was going insane (because Milagra said as much), and her mother brought her to the parish priest. Padre Reyes recognized the symptoms of panic attack immediately (having ministered for years at the local psychiatric hospital) and referred her to a social worker. Milagra's mother called and set up the appointment, which was outside the immediate neighborhood, and Padre Reyes brought them there. When she showed up for the first visit, Milagra expressed embarrassment at having to be brought by her mother and the parish priest.

MFS Assessment: Defining Problems and Goals

A brief screening of Milagra's symptoms and concerns met many of the criteria for panic disorder with agoraphobia, including recurrent, unexpected panic attacks characterized by heart palpitations and an accelerated heart rate, sweating, shaking, shortness of breath, nausea, and lightheadedness. Milagra thought at times that she was losing her mind, and she began to dread the possibility of having another attack, which made her avoid going out even more, especially to public places, where she might make a "fool" of herself by "fainting or running out" of the grocery store. She curtailed doing any of her chores alone, and she usually took her mother or one of her brothers "along for the ride." In addition to her anxiety, Milagra was becoming increasingly depressed about her college prospects. Although she had successfully put college out of her mind, she could no longer avoid it. Fortunately, she did not abuse alcohol or other drugs, but she coped by burying herself in her books. She had no impulse control problems of note, had a couple of good close friends, but no romantic interest, and was highly respected and depended on by her own family members. Her dad was a little distant from her, but she had good relations with him. Although he had always been a strict disciplinarian and had high standards for his children, he was never abusive in any way. She was in excellent health.

Her anxiety about leaving home was compounded by her sense of obligation to her family and her feelings that she was betraying her community. Her family was ostensibly proud of her and bragged to the neighbors and extended family but quietly voiced their own anxieties about what they would do when Milagra "left" there. In addition, many of her peers at school were not planning to go to college, and when word got around that she was accepted into school with a scholarship, she found it hard to endure accusations that she was going to abandon her roots. These conflicted feelings added to her distress.

A functional analysis revealed a fairly straightforward correlation between symptoms and impending emancipation from home. After the initial excitement of having been accepted to the university, she became increasingly tense the more she thought about leaving home. Although she would avoid thinking about it much of the time, correspondence from the school began to arrive, and Milagra realized that she would soon have to confer with university personnel and register for courses, as well as arrange to move and live on campus. She only had 4 months before classes were to begin, and she knew she could not put off her trip any longer. When she thought about leaving, she became increasingly panicked and began to find reasons to stay at home, or at least not leave her neighborhood. The symptoms would worsen, and she would find herself in her room crying and trembling. Milagra's panic attacks increased, as did her avoidance of thinking about school until she received her letter to come to the university for a meeting. It was at that point that she had a panic attack, when she tried to force herself to drive out of town.

After this initial assessment and rapport building with Milagra, she and the practitioner decided that the goal of treatment was to get her to drive to the university and begin her new adventure. After a couple of visits, the social worker Gloria expressed her appreciation for the help her mother and the priest provided but suggested that Milagra come alone. The clinic was only a few blocks past Milagra's usual "boundary." Although the thought of driving to the university, which was about an hour away (and included crossing a half-mile-long bridge) frightened her, she felt a sense of confidence that Gloria was knowledgeable and communicated an optimism that she would be able to succeed.

Selecting and Designing the Intervention: Defining Strategies and Objectives

Although there would be time for a more in-depth history taking, the social worker prioritized understanding the recent events that led to the incident and engendering a collaborative working alliance. Although the client, Milagra, was encouraged to see a physician for a checkup and consultation, she did not fill the prescription because of her own skepticism of traditional medicine and her anxiety about taking medication. Because the abuse of alcohol or other drugs had been carefully ruled out, in-depth assessment focused on the psychosocial factors potentially exacerbating her anxiety and panic symptoms.

The second step of the first session was to provide psychoeducation concerning the prevalence, patterns, and contributing causes of panic. Although Milagra's mother tended to imbue her daughter's experience with religious overtones, Gloria did not challenge those interpretations. Milagra, however, having read about panic disorder in a magazine, was more inclined to consider physiological predisposition and psychosocial stressors. The social worker then met with Milagra alone to develop a treatment plan and initiate coping skills strategies that she could begin immediately on her own. Gloria showed her basic breathing and muscle relaxation techniques and she offered her psychoeducation to help Milagra reinterpret her physiological symptoms. She also recommended a book to her. These preliminary efforts at psychoeducation and relaxation training provided the client with some immediate symptom relief.

For the second visit, Milagra got a ride from a friend and her mother came along. Milagra reported that she was still experiencing panic attacks, albeit a little less frequently, and was unable to go outside for more than a few minutes because she dreaded another attack. However, thoughts about being trapped at home and not being able to go to college upset her even more. Although the social worker empathized with her concerns, she did not give her any false reassurance that Milagra would make it to college. In addition to educating Milagra about the physical aspects of anxiety and how the mind misinterprets these events, Gloria wanted to discuss her fears about leaving home. Milagra expressed a number of concerns: "What about my dad? He's not always there for my mom. What about my little brothers? I'm not sure Mom can keep up with them, and she spends a lot of time at the church. What about my friends? They are already telling me I'm too good for them now, that I just want to be like the rich white girls." The social worker responded that it appeared that Milagra felt extraordinarily responsible for the welfare of many people and might be afraid of losing their affection. However, rather than challenge these beliefs directly, Milagra was encouraged to listen to herself "talk out loud" about her worst fears and what she really thought would happen to her and to her relationships with others if she successfully pursued her dreams—and to consider alternative interpretations and scenarios.

During the following four weekly sessions, Milagra continued to practice meditation, breathing, and reinterpretation of her cognitive cues, and with journal writing she appeared to come to an accommodation about how she could still be responsive to her family (by living at home for now) and her community (by eventually becoming a doctor and volunteering some time in the barrio). However, she had six weeks before classes began. The social worker explained that although Milagra had a better understanding of the role of anxiety, some skills to control it, and a better understanding of other contributing causes, these insights would not be enough to relieve Milagra's terror of driving to the university on her own. The only way to overcome this irrational fear of driving out of town would be to confront it. "There's no way I'm going to do that. That scares the heck out of me! And what if I can't get home this time, or what if I get arrested?!"

Gloria agreed that, yes, this must be quite frightening. So to make it a little easier, their discussion focused on how Milagra would learn to use her imagination along with relaxation exercises to create a step-by-step hierarchy that she could use repeatedly to approach her fears in her mind's eye and practice remaining calm while covertly "driving" out of town before attempting it in vivo. Since Milagra had already felt some relief from relaxation exercises, she was positively disposed to try this approach. Gloria asked Milagra to close her eyes, and practice her breathing exercise for a minute or two while concentrating on a neutral image in her mind's eye. The social worker then asked Milagra to imagine herself at home, comfortable, at ease, and relatively free from anxiety. She then said: "I want you to tell me by raising your finger when it becomes a little frightening for you (raised a little), moderately frightening (a little higher), or extremely frightening (straight up). When you start feeling anxious, use your breathing and muscle relaxation exercise to calm yourself as much as you can." Then the social worker began to walk Milagra through a "typical" day of getting up, getting ready for classes, preparing her lunch, going out to the car, driving down the street to the edge of town by way of the main avenue, then onto the exit ramp of the highway, to the exit for the university a half hour away, into the parking lot, and into her first class. After several trials, she was able to complete the exercise with, at worst, a moderate degree of anxiety. She agreed to practice daily at home using a tape of the session.

For the next week, Milagra practiced this "mental walk-through" (i.e., covert rehearsal) daily. Although it was quite frightening at first, she was determined not to allow the panicky feelings to keep her from something she really wanted. After a week of daily practice, she felt that she was ready to try driving, but she did not think she would make it all the way. During her meditations, however, she spontaneously conjured an internal image of a strong, older, courageous woman whom she felt she could rely on to help her through this trial. Gloria asked, "Is there anyone you know like that?" Milagra said there was an old woman in her neighborhood, a *curandera,* whom she often thought of as someone who was both loving and strong and, like her, a bit on the mystical side. The social worker agreed that the *curandera* seemed to be a person whom others relied on in times of trouble. Gloria offered that perhaps Milagra could obtain a figurine in one of the local tiendas, and bring it along with her for the ride as a representation of this woman. Milagra agreed this might help. The social worker also assisted Milagra in sketching out a map of the area, to plan some "bail-out points," in case she felt that she could not complete her journey.

Over several days, Milagra gradually increased her driving distance, first down the street (completing errands), then down the main thoroughfare until she approached the highway entrance ramp. It became clear that she actually had desensitized herself to much of the anxiety associated with getting back into the car and driving locally; she also was not overwhelmed in her fears of panic anymore, feeling that the experience was transitory and probably would not be as bad as before. However, it also became clear to her that her terror rose precipitously when she approached the highway ramp; once on it, she felt there would be no turning back, no escape route for at least a few miles. For 2 more weeks she drove locally but could not approach the ramp. Comments such as "Maybe college just isn't for me" and "Maybe I could just put things off for a year" were expected by Gloria and understandable. Gloria reflected that, yes, maybe she was right: "Perhaps a year off would do you good, and what would staying at home for the next year or so be like for you?" As they both played out this scenario, it became clear that Milagra considered this an unacceptable alternative. She felt she was approaching an inevitable and critical moment in her life: "I'm terrified, but I won't be left behind and stuck at home for the rest of my life. I have to do it now."

Realizing that time was closing in, it appeared that Milagra needed an additional incentive to make the final leap. The social worker suggested that she borrow a friend's "hands-free" cell phone and keep the line open during the in vivo driving session. Milagra agreed to the plan. When Milagra called Gloria, she was in town and just about to begin her approach to the highway ramp. The social worker coached her through her breathing exercises and provided gentle encouragement. Milagra became noticeably more afraid as the ramp approached but was well in control. It was also apparent that she found considerable comfort in the fact that she had a connection on the line to someone who could confront this threshold with her and talk her through it. The practitioner reminded her of the strength and confidence of the *curandera* whom she wanted to emulate. However, as Milagra drove out onto the highway, the cellular phone connection broke up, and they lost communication. Ten minutes later (it seemed much longer), Gloria received a call from the other side: "I've done it! And you know what? It wasn't half as bad as I thought it would be! I can't believe it! I've done it!" For the next 3 weeks, Milagra drove back and forth to school, wandered the campus, imagined herself going to class. She purchased her books and a parking sticker, and she met a staff person at the student center who was also Latina. She thought to herself, "Maybe this won't be so terrifying after all."

Selecting Scales and Creating Indexes to Monitor and Evaluate Client Progress

A combination of the Agoraphobia Scale (measuring anxiety level and avoidance) coupled with the Hamilton Depression Rating Scale (HAM-D) provided a sound accompaniment to the qualitative assessment. In addition, a series of indexes including frequency of panic attacks, time or distance driving, and SUDS (to gauge anxiety level) were indispensable to evaluating change over the course of the intervention.

TABLE 8.1   The Client Service Plan

Problems	Goals	Objectives (samples)	Interventions	Assessment and evaluation tools
Long-term anxiety with recent onset of panic disorder	Leave home, enroll in school, develop coping skills to eliminate panic disorder and avoidance behaviors (timetable: 4 months)	Become knowledgeable about panic disorder and agoraphobia through discussions, watching videos, reading a book provided by social worker (2 weeks)	Establish solid working alliance with client; examine relationship of treatment expectations and impact of prospective outcomes on cultural beliefs	Agoraphobia Scale to gauge overall anxiety and avoidance levels
Exacerbation of avoidance behavior brought on by the prospect of leaving home and community for college				HAM-D for co-occurring symptoms
Depression: sense of guilt, betrayal, and loss at the thought of leaving home	Reduce and eliminate depression; redefine separation as normal "moving on"; find other ways to compensate family and community	Examine and keep diary of anxiety-provoking thoughts; challenge them in discussion with social worker about "thinking errors" (daily)	Cognitive-behavioral coping skills including psychoeducation on panic disorder and CBT; use of standard CBT techniques to	Individual indexes: • Frequency of panic attacks • Distance driven from home • Amount of time away from home

Problems	Goals	Objectives (samples)	Interventions	Assessment and evaluation tools
		Practice anxiety reduction: meditation and breathing exercises (10 minutes twice a day); gradually (as introduced by social worker) incorporate covert exposure to "car-trip" hierarchy	examine dysfunctional thinking around leaving home, unrealistic fears of panic symptoms, normative feelings of depression and betrayal of family and culture	• SUDS to measure subjective level of anxiety
		Begin daily in vivo graduated exposure (unaccompanied) by driving and parking as prescribed by "trip map" designed with social worker according to hierarchy of objectives; couple relaxation exercises and challenge cognitive errors until anxiety subsides to less than 5 on SUDS scale	Imaginal desensitization in combination with in vivo exposure to reduce fear of driving out of town and going to public places alone	
		2 months before school begins, drive over the bridge and to university; biweekly trips after that to "hang around" campus and get comfortable	Case management: recommend a physical and psychiatric evaluation; work with community (e.g., church) to assist family as needed; later contact and confer with university counseling to facilitate follow-up treatment as needed (e.g., adjustments at school; dealing with social anxiety, depression, sense of loss)	
		Make contacts with Latino club members during summer; plan to meet a representative if possible		
		Examine cognitive errors regarding betrayal and guilt; focus on alternative ways to "give back" to family and culture as a college grad and professional; delegate household jobs to brothers; work with church to organize help for mom		

ASSESSMENT: OBSESSIVE-COMPULSIVE DISORDER

Background Data

Obsessive-compulsive disorder (OCD) shares some commonalities with other anxiety disorders in both assessment and intervention methods. OCD can be severe and debilitating to an individual and can have negative impacts on family life. Some consider OCD among the most debilitating of psychiatric disorders (Stein et al., 2009). OCD is marked by intrusive dysfunctional thinking (obsessions), physiological symptoms of anxiety (and depression), and futile attempts to ward off anxiety through repetitive behaviors (compulsions). OCD can be mitigated by challenging obsessive thinking, learning new coping skills, and engaging in interventions whereby the client is confronted with obsession-related stimuli (e.g., touching a used towel) while simultaneously withholding compulsive responses (e.g., hand washing). Medication can also be helpful as an adjunctive treatment.

Obsessive-compulsive disorder (OCD) is estimated to afflict about 2.5% of the population (Craske, 1999; Karno, Goldman, Sorenson, & Burnam, 1988; Ruscio, Stein, Chiu, & Kessler, 2010). Onset typically occurs in childhood or adolescence for males and in young adulthood for women. Obsessions and compulsions are very common in the general population (Craske, 1999), but the degree of impairment varies widely. Clients who meet the diagnostic criteria are at the severe end of the spectrum. OCD co-occurs with other disorders, especially other anxiety disorders, depression, and substance use disorders (APA, 2013; Barlow, 1988; Craske, 1999; Ruscio et al., 2010; Steketee, 1993). Stress is a common precipitant to obsessive thinking and compulsions, and biological and psychological vulnerabilities are important predictors. OCD is twice as common in women as in men, and it is most prevalent in younger people age 18–29 (Ruscio et al., 2010). Although cultural themes often color the nature of obsessions and compulsions, there appears to be little variation by gender or culture in treatment outcomes (Steketee & Shapiro, 1995).

Steketee (1997) has summarized important dimensions regarding functional impairment and family burden concerning the person with OCD. On the basis of a review of the literature, she reports that persons with OCD are disproportionately unemployed, less likely to be married (as a result of impaired social and sexual functioning), and often experience other problems in family functioning. Although most of the data on the burden incurred by a family with a member suffering from OCD are anecdotal, many family members seem to complain about the client's "manipulative behavior," which may include attempts to involve family members in the client's rituals. Clients may also demonstrate poor grooming and personal hygiene habits, among other behavioral problems. It appears that most families suffer some degree of burden from caring for a family member with OCD, and most of that burden is carried by the principal caregiver. Family members suffer from feelings of frustration, anger, guilt, financial burden, and interrupted family activities. Although outcome data are largely limited to primary symptoms, Steketee (1997) recommends that practitioners pay more specific attention to understanding clients' social and occupational adjustments, and include family members in treatment to provide them with support and psychoeducation regarding the disorder and ways to manage it.

Theories

Psychodynamic explanations for the causes of obsessive-compulsive neuroses have generally focused on an individual's difficulties in resolving love-hate feelings (ambivalence) toward the "love object," accompanied by defensive responses (e.g., isolation, undoing, reaction formation) to the perceived loss of mother's love. However, aside from using case-study analyses to justify these theories, no developmentally sound research has ever provided substantive scientific support for them. Early conditioning theorists (e.g., Mowrer, 1960) conceptualized obsessive-compulsive behaviors as a two-stage process in which some thought or image (obsession) was initially associated with a fear-inducing stimulus, and in response, an avoidance behavior (compulsive ritual) became reinforcing because it briefly reduced the anxiety. Conditioning theories, however, came to be seen as insufficient to explain the *continuation* of obsessive-compulsive behaviors (i.e., when the original stimulus is no longer active, the compulsive behavior should be extinguished).

Contemporary theories regarding the cause and course of the disorder tend to focus on the interaction of genetic, developmental, cognitive, and behavioral factors (Barlow, 1988; Craske, 1999; Franklin & Foa, 2011; Grados, 2010; Iervolino, Rijsdijk, Cherkas, Fullana, & Mataix-Cols, 2011; Riggs & Foa, 1993; Steketee, 1993). Although the initial anxiety-producing thought may be triggered by some environmental event, perhaps under a period of stress, the obsession is deemed very unacceptable, and may be tied to an overwrought sense of responsibility, and the person responds by engaging in behavioral rituals in a vain attempt to neutralize the negative thought. Recent contributions of social-cognitive theory have illuminated the dynamics of obsessive thinking and the role of compulsive rituals. Building on the foundation of Beck's (1976) cognitive model, Salkovskis (1985) points out that negative automatic thoughts are usually distressing because of their plausible nature, whereas obsessions are not plausible (e.g., a client's fear that touching a doorknob will give him HIV), and the person experiencing them also finds them irrational and unacceptable. Salkovskis (1985) goes on to argue that although many people have intrusive thoughts, those thoughts become a source of considerable distress "only when they result in negative automatic thoughts through interaction between the unacceptable intrusions and the individual's belief system" (p. 573). These individuals must evaluate the thoughts as "bad" in some way. Often they appear to be related to the idea that the individual is responsible for causing harm to himself or to another person. The person becomes distressed about the negative automatic thoughts that result from the intrusion and may feel like a bad person merely for having had bad thoughts. Depression often accompanies these negative self-evaluations. The compulsive thoughts or behaviors (rituals) then become futile efforts at neutralize the distressing obsession. Attempts to neutralize the thoughts through cognitive efforts alone are not likely to be successful. Salkovskis (1989) further hypothesized that treatment must focus on helping clients realize that obsessive thoughts are irrelevant to further action (i.e., to prevent harm to oneself or others). That is, the intervention must focus on disengaging the cognitive link between obsessive thoughts and ritualistic "protecting" behaviors. Personal values embedded in cultural or religious influences may account for some of these fixed beliefs (Craske, 1999).

Key Elements of MFS Assessment

Essential features of OCD (APA, 2013; Barlow, 1988) include recurrent obsessions or compulsions that a person typically has come to recognize as excessive or unreasonable, are debilitating in that they take up more than one hour per day, and cause marked stress or impairment. Common obsessions include implausible thoughts about contamination (e.g., germs), persistent doubts (e.g., left the coffee pot on, therefore, the house will burn down), excessive orderliness (e.g., spends hours repeatedly arranging objects on the top of one's desk until they are "perfectly ordered"), or unacceptable thoughts of engaging in sexual or aggressive acts. Compulsions include repetitive behaviors (e.g., checking, ordering, counting, hand washing) as well as mental rituals intended to ward off anxiety or undo troubling thoughts. The client typically recognizes that engaging in the ritualized behavior cannot prevent the imagined negative consequences that they feel will result (e.g., "My mother will become mortally ill if I don't fold my laundry in perfect piles").

The following lists show essential criteria for a DSM-5 (APA, 2013) diagnosis of OCD.

Obsessions

- Having recurrent and persistent thoughts, impulses, or images that are experienced as intrusive and inappropriate and cause marked anxiety or distress, and that are not simply excessive worries about real-life problems

- Attempting to ignore or suppress such thoughts, impulses, or images or to neutralize them with some other thought or action

- Recognizing that the obsessive thoughts, impulses, or images are a product of a person's own mind (not imposed from without as in thought insertion)

Compulsions

- Repetitive behaviors or mental acts that an individual feels driven to perform in response to an obsession or according to rules that must be applied rigidly
- Behaviors or mental acts aimed at preventing or reducing distress or preventing some dreaded event or situation—these are not connected in a realistic way with what they are designed to neutralize or prevent, or they are clearly excessive

At some point, adults recognize that the thoughts or behaviors are excessive (although children may not recognize them as such), and the obsessions or compulsions cause marked distress and interfere with interpersonal, occupational, or academic functioning. Practitioners should be aware that obsessions are fairly common and that it is important to distinguish OCD from obsessive rumination and excessive worrying associated with depression and anxiety. Obsessions associated with OCD tend to be unrealistic (and the client does not see them as realistic), whereas obsessions associated with other problems (e.g., ruminating over having actually caused an accident) may be congruent with a client's depressed mood. As noted earlier, OCD can co-occur with other disorders, including other anxiety disorders, depression, substance abuse, and eating disorders, and many persons with OCD also have a history of tic disorders. A careful analysis of the effects of the person's OCD on social well-being is also important. Clients may go to considerable lengths to hide their ritualistic behavior or obsessions. The practitioner should also closely assess the behaviors of family members to see if they engage in behaviors that inadvertently reinforce clients' obsessions and compulsions.

Functional assessment of OCD involves a more detailed accounting of the type, frequency, severity, and duration of both the obsessive thinking and the ritualistic behaviors. Determining the nature of these obsessions and compulsions, when they occur, and under which circumstances is critical to helping clients monitor and track their occurrence. The social worker and client can then develop a hierarchy of obsessions as prelude to implementing graduated imaginal or in vivo exposure with response prevention (discussed later). Assessment of obsessions should include information about external sources of fear (i.e., tangible objects), internal triggers for fear (i.e., thoughts, images or impulses), and worries about the consequences of not engaging in compulsive behaviors (e.g., disease, harm coming to others) (Franklin & Foa, 2008; Steketee, 1993).

A variety of information-gathering methods should be employed, including self-report, behavioral tests, observation, reports of significant others, and standardized assessment. Sequentially, the assessment should proceed according to a general plan. In the first two sessions, psychoeducation about the nature of OCD and cognitive-behavioral therapy (i.e., exposure with response prevention) should be explained. A functional assessment should be completed to identify internal and external cues for obsessions, note obsession-cueing situations, list avoidance behaviors and mental rituals, and describe the involvement of significant others in rituals. The client should report the information gathered in their self-monitoring diary or chart in the second session, and the practitioner should carefully confirm the diagnosis of OCD. In the third and fourth sessions, further review of self-monitoring is essential, and the practitioner should describe treatment in detail, help the client develop a hierarchy of obsessive situations, plan adjunctive activities such as involvement of significant others and homework, and schedule future sessions (Franklin & Foa, 2008; Steketee, 1993).

Taylor (1995) has summarized different approaches to the assessment of OCD. These methods include the use of behavioral avoidance tests in which the client is presented with the feared situation (e.g., for a client who has an extreme fear of germs, testing to see how long the client can avoid hand-washing after touching a doorknob). Clients can report their level of subjec-tive units of distress (SUDS) as described earlier in the assessment of panic disorder. An in vivo assessment can be compelling but may be somewhat lim-ited with respect to understanding other obsessive patterns or associated problems. Other less obvious obsessions (e.g., privately counting, ritualistic thought patterns) may be more difficult to assess. Direct observation or use of diaries can also be helpful for more covert compulsions.

Instruments

A literature review suggests that the Yale-Brown Obsessive-Compulsive Scale (YBOCS) (Goodman et al., 1989) is a valid tool for the assessment and eval-uation of treatment outcomes. Most investigators use the 10 "core" items, which measure five parameters of obsessions and compulsions: duration and frequency, interference in social and occupational functioning, associated distress, degree of resistance, and perceived control over obsessions or com-pulsions. Each core item is rated by average severity over the previous week by the interviewer on a five-point scale (0 = none, 4 = extreme). Separate subscales for obsessions and compulsions are summed, although the 10 items are usually summed as a global score. In a review of the psychometric literature on the YBOCS, Taylor (1995) states that the scale has excellent interrater reliability, acceptable to good internal consistency, good test-retest reliability, distinguishes persons with OCD from persons with other anxiety disorders, and correlates well with other OCD-related scales. It does, how-ever, tend to correlate significantly with measures of anxiety and depression, which suggests some weakness in discriminant validity.

The Obsessive-Compulsive Inventory (OCI) (Foa, Kozak, Salkovskis, Coles, & Amir, 1998) is an excellent alternative to the YBOCS and was devel-oped with three goals in mind: to be more comprehensive than existing instruments, to allow for a wider range of severity scores than used with other scales, and to be easily administered to clinical and nonclinical populations.

However, an 18-item version of the OCI has been developed that improves the utility of the original instrument, but retains excellent psychometric properties (Foa, Huppert, Leiberg, Langner, Dichic, Hajcak, & Salkovskis, 2002). The short version of the OCI comprises six subscales with three items each: washing (5,11,17), obsessing (6,12,18), hoarding (1,7,13), ordering (3,9,15), checking (2,8,14), and neutralizing (4,10,16). Internal consistency for the total OCI is good, test-retest reliability is very good overall for subscales and total score, and the subscales of the short OCI correlate very well in general with those of the longer version. Factor analysis supports the internal structure of the scale, and correlational analysis supports both convergent and discriminant validity. The 18-item OCI is scored by simply summing all items, and a cut score of 21 is recommended for identifying persons who are likely to meet DSM-IV-TR criteria for obsessive-compulsive disorder. Individual items and subscale scores should also be examined to gauge the client's unique symptom configuration as well as subclinical distress. (see instrument 8.2).

INSTRUMENT 8.2   Obsessive-Compulsive Inventory, Revised

The following statements refer to experiences that many people have in their everyday lives. Circle the number that best describes **How much** that experience has **distressed or bothered you during the past month**. The numbers refer to the following verbal labels:

	0 Not at all	1 A little	2 Moderately	3 A lot	4 Extremely
1. I have saved up so many things that they get in the way.	0	1	2	3	4
2. I check things more often than necessary.	0	1	2	3	4
3. I get upset if objects are not arranged properly.	0	1	2	3	4
4. I feel compelled to count while I am doing things.	0	1	2	3	4
5. I find it difficult to touch an object when I know it has been touched by strangers or certain people.	0	1	2	3	4
6. I find it difficult to control my own thoughts.	0	1	2	3	4
7. I collect things I don't need.	0	1	2	3	4
8. I repeatedly check doors, windows, drawers, etc.	0	1	2	3	4
9. I get upset if others change the way I have arranged things.	0	1	2	3	4
10. I feel I have to repeat certain numbers.	0	1	2	3	4
11. I sometimes have to wash or clean myself simply because I feel contaminated.	0	1	2	3	4
12. I am upset by unpleasant thoughts that come into my mind against my will.	0	1	2	3	4
13. I avoid throwing things away because I am afraid I might need them later.	0	1	2	3	4
14. I repeatedly check gas and water taps and light switches after turning them off.	0	1	2	3	4
15. I need things to be arranged in a particular order.	0	1	2	3	4
16. I feel that there are good and bad numbers.	0	1	2	3	4
17. I wash my hands more often and longer than necessary.	0	1	2	3	4
18. I frequently get nasty thoughts and have difficulty getting rid of them.	0	1	2	3	4

Copyright 2002 by Edna B. Foa.

SELECTING EFFECTIVE INTERVENTIONS

Research has not supported the use of psychodynamic interventions for persons with OCD. In addition, early behavioral treatments such as thought stopping and mild aversive procedures were not shown to have any long-term positive effects (Foa & Kozak, 1996; Riggs & Foa, 1993). A strong consensus, however, has emerged among leading clinician-researchers that a specific application of CBT, exposure with response prevention (EXRP), implemented over long periods, is the most effective psychosocial intervention for OCD. From 50% to 75% of individuals appear to obtain substantial relief from their obsessive-compulsive symptoms and show good long-term maintenance of gains. Those who relapse can be successfully treated with follow-up booster sessions and relapse prevention methods (Emmelkamp, 1994; Foa & Kozak, 1996; Franklin & Foa, 2011; Riggs & Foa, 1993; Steketee, 1993; Zinbarg et al., 1992). Studies have even revealed measurable changes in brain functioning, which demonstrates the deep and lasting effects of cognitive-behavioral therapy for OCD (e.g., Schwartz, 1998).

One meta-analysis of 19 RCTs (24 comparisons to control groups) of cognitive therapy alone, cognitive therapy combined with EXRP, and EXRP alone revealed comparably robust outcomes (Rosa-Alcazar, Sanchez-Meca, Gomez-Conesa, & Marin-Martinez, 2008). The analysis also demonstrated positive outcomes for co-occurring depression, anxiety, and social adjustment. Combining both covert and in vivo exposure appeared to result in greater improvements, overall. EXRP in 70 outpatient adults was also shown to result in clinically significant improvements including substantive improvements in overall quality of life (Diefenbach, Abramowitz, Norberg, & Tolin, 2007). Both cognitive and behavioral change processes in the client appear to be bidirectionally related and necessary for change, although the heterogeneity of dysfunctional beliefs in people with OCD defies simple generalization (Polman, Bouman, van Hout, de Jong, & den Boer, 2010). Adults with more severe symptoms of OCD are likely to require more treatment sessions, as was shown in one study of 39 adults that employed cognitive therapy (Steketee, Siev, Fama et al., 2011). Despite superior outcomes of EXRP and its transportability to more complex cases in everyday treatment settings, EXRP (as with other evidence-based practices, or EBPs) remains underused by practicing clinicians (Franklin & Foa, 2011).

Many clients with OCD report obsessions without any overt compulsive behavior. To address this problem, an intervention has been developed for these clients to engage in prolonged exposure sessions by listening to a self-recorded audiotape of their own obsessive rumination (thought, impulse, or image), and then focus on avoiding the psychological compulsion to neutralize it or engage in avoidance responses. An RCT with 15 clients and 14 controls demonstrated that audiotape exposure resulted in clinically significant gains, with good maintenance of progress at 6 month follow-up for about 67% of participants (Freeston et al., 1997). Brief self-directed treatments that include combinations of bibliotherapy, self-directed in vivo exposure, and imaginal exposure to a planned hierarchy have also shown promising results (Fritzler, Hecker, & Losee, 1997). This brief intervention may be a cost-effective intervention for less debilitated OCD clients.

Clients from racial minorities have been markedly underrepresented in studies of OCD. One case analysis of two African American women diagnosed with OCD demonstrated that current behavior therapies for this disorder were well received and showed positive results (Williams, Chambless, & Steketee, 1998). EXRP has also been successfully implemented in partial hospitalization programs when combined with medication and other psychosocial interventions. Long-term outcomes at 18 months were very positive (Bystritsky et al., 1996).

Evidence for the effectiveness of interventions that include family members show results similar to findings reported here for panic disorder and agoraphobia. Without addressing relationship problems directly, it appears that the significant other can enhance treatment and improve outcomes in some cases by assisting the client in carrying out EXRP (Baucom et al., 1998; Franklin & Foa, 2008).

Exposure with Response Prevention versus Medication

SSRIs have been demonstrated to be reasonably effective in the treatment of obsessive-compulsive disorders (Foa & Kozak, 1996; Franklin & Foa, 2008; Kaplan & Sadock, 1998; Riggs & Foa, 1993), although about half of clients with OCD do not respond adequately to SSRIs alone (McDonough & Kennedy, 2002). There may be an initial increase in anxiety during the first 2–3 weeks of taking medication, but many clients obtain long-term relief after that initial period (Kaplan & Sadock, 1998).

Comparisons of CBT with and without medication have been examined in recent years. Results of a meta-analytic study demonstrated that EXRP had outcomes comparable to antidepressants, but some evidence suggested that combined treatments may be preferable (Kobak, Greist, Jefferson, Katzelnick, & Henk, 1998). Other controlled trials have not shown that a combination of drugs and CBT (e.g., EXRP) is superior to CBT alone (Van Balkom et al., 1998). Other reviewers have concluded that although both interventions are effective, neither results in complete remission of symptoms. CBT results in better overall outcomes, particularly when relapse rates, dropouts, and treatment refusals are considered. Relapse rates for those treated with medication alone, however, are considerably high (Stanley & Turner, 1995). Much remains to be learned about what constitutes "best practices" for OCD, including the need for more exploration of optimal treatment matching to client characteristics. It is likely that social work practitioners who employ

CBT approaches will collaborate with psychiatrists to find the right combination on a case-by-case basis. Exposure with response prevention in combination with medication is currently considered the standard of care for OCD (Barletta, Beamish, Patrick, Andersen, & Pappas, 1996).

In summary, SSRIs and EXRP are both considered first-line treatments. Medications yield earlier response, but EXRP yields longer maintenance of gains. Although studies of combined treatments yield mixed results for superior outcomes versus either treatment alone, expert committees are pragmatic in recommending a combined treatment strategy (Stein et al., 2009).

Exemplar Study: The Efficacy and Effectiveness of EXRP

Qualitative researchers often contend that the controlled conditions under which outcome research is conducted do not reflect real-world practice. In partial response to these critics, Franklin, Abramowitz, Kozak, Levitt, and Foa (2000) conducted a study to compare the effectiveness of EXRP in a "service as usual" environment to results from four previously conducted controlled experiments. Participants were 58 men and 52 women treated on a fee-for-service basis in a university-affiliated outpatient clinic. They ranged from age 18 to 74 years, and almost all of them were white. Forty percent were not taking medication at the time of the study. Outcome measures included the YBOCS, the Hamilton Scale for Depression, and the Beck Depression Inventory. All clients received EXRP, including 3 treatment-planning sessions (i.e., information gathering, developing an exposure hierarchy, psychoeducation on OCD, and rationale for EXRP), and 15 sessions of exposure with response prevention (including the exposure and response prevention exercises, review of homework, and involvement of family and support persons as determined by clinical judgment). Each session lasted 2 hours, and treatment was conducted over the course of 4 weeks. Exposure exercises were "designed to trigger the patient's specific obsessive concerns. Patients were encouraged to persist with each exposure until the distress decreased noticeably. Exposure exercises were arranged hierarchically, beginning with moderately distressing ones. Exposure exercises gradually progressed toward the most distressing situation or object, which was typically confronted during exposure session 6" (Franklin et al., 2000, p. 596). Clients were also assigned exposure homework for 2 hours between each daily session. Patients were instructed to refrain from engaging in their rituals throughout the entire treatment period. Clients were taught self-monitoring to become more aware of situations that triggered the urge to ritualize. If clients "slipped," therapists reviewed coping strategies with them. Clients were encouraged to seek help from supports or family members to resist ritualizing, or to call their practitioner for support and assistance.

All practitioners received training in EXRP, but level of experience among practitioners ranged considerably. To offset this disparity, inexperienced practitioners received more supervision. Cases were assigned nonrandomly to practitioners. Of those who completed treatment, 86% (100 of 110) improved significantly on three main outcome measures. The mean progress was comparable to results obtained in previous controlled trials. The study illustrates that the treatment context of clinical research may indeed be comparable to that of "natural" treatment environments.

Descriptions of Effective Interventions

A number of clinician-researchers have provided clear evidence-based guidelines for conducing EXRP (Franklin & Foa, 2008; Foa & Kozak, 1996; Riggs & Foa, 1993; Steketee, 1993). Although there are minor variations among authors, a synthesis of key treatment elements is compiled in the lists that follow.

General Considerations

- The practitioner clearly explains the basic rationale for EXRP to the client. After conducting a detailed functional assessment of the client's obsessions and ritualized thoughts or behaviors, the client is then exposed progressively from the least anxiety-provoking item on the hierarchy to the most as he or she successfully reduces anxiety at each predetermined stage. As clients are exposed to each level, they are prevented from responding with their compulsive rituals until the anxiety subsides to a planned minimal level, measured on the SUDS. Although the exposure and response prevention components are discussed separately later, they are implemented simultaneously. After the client has "conquered" the most anxiety-provoking obsession in the hierarchy, maximum exposure and response prevention to the most troubling item is maintained over the remaining sessions. If this process is conducted frequently and long enough for the anxiety to subside during each exposure, clients stand a very good chance of overcoming this debilitating disorder.

- EXRP can be conducted in the office, in the natural environment, with or without the help of others, and with or without medication, depending on circumstances and client needs. The exposure and response prevention plan is developed collaboratively during a detailed assessment, is tailored to the individual client, and often requires considerable creativity and ingenuity in its implementation.

- Practitioners explain all details of the procedure to clients. Others (e.g., family members, physicians) may collaborate in treatment. These persons should be in regular contact with the practitioner.

- The general format for the intervention proceeds as follows: The first two or three sessions (which can last 4–6 hours, as needed) are devoted to a detailed examination of client obsessions and compulsions. About 15 sessions are required for active exposure and response prevention to be completed. By the eighth or tenth visit, clients should be receiving maximum exposure to the most anxiety-provoking step on the hierarchy. The sessions may last 2 hours or longer, often with 2 hours or more for homework to carry out the intervention alone or with the assistance of a supportive partner or other family member. Although this format may vary somewhat, case analysis suggests that more intensive and frequent visits are more effective than ones carried out less frequently. A typical session is divided into 10–15 minutes for discussing homework and progress, but the bulk of the session is devoted to engaging in EXRP. The remaining few minutes are devoted to discussing the next homework assignment.

Assessment

- Assuming that the practitioner has conducted a thorough MFS assessment and has identified or ruled out other co-occurring problems, one or two visits may be devoted to a detailed functional assessment of the type, frequency, intensity, and duration of obsessions and compulsions, and the circumstances in which they occur. Obsessions are listed hierarchically from the least troubling to the most troubling. In each subsequent intervention, practitioner and client work "up the list" toward more anxiety-provoking stimuli. Confronting each anxiety-provoking stimulus (covertly or in vivo) is done in turn until the anxiety level for each is substantially diminished, then clients can move on to the next objective on the list.

- The practitioner helps clients develop and keep a chart or diary of thoughts or situations (i.e., triggers) that provoke obsessive thinking and the subsequent compulsive ritual, gauge the degree of discomfort provoked by the obsessive thought, and measure the amount of time spent engaging in the compulsive ritual. The nature of these obsessive thoughts may be internal (e.g., "bad" thoughts about sex, harming someone, having done something that unrealistically might have caused harm to someone), external (e.g., concerns about germs from touching doorknobs, toilet seats, or other people's hands), or about safety (e.g., leaving on a lightbulb or the coffee maker after having left the house). Common themes may characterize these internal and external cues for persons with OCD, but themes are often highly idiosyncratic in their detail and meaning.

- Keeping a chart or diary of obsessive concerns during the initial assessment continues to serve an important self-monitoring and evaluative function as clients track their own progress. By taking on this collaborative role in treatment, clients also begin to develop some autonomy and sense of control over their distress. They use the self-monitoring tool to guide their homework assignments and measure progress.

- During the assessment, the practitioner teaches clients how to use the Subjective Distress Scale (i.e., SUDS), with scores ranging from 0 to 100. The level of distress associated with the feared thought or situation is measured at frequent intervals during the time they initially develop the fear hierarchy, and subsequently when they are practicing actual exposure with response prevention. In this way, clients can judge and indicate their subjective level of distress for themselves, the practitioner, and supportive assistant, and they can gauge how much progress they are making during the procedure.

Exposure

• Clients engage in and focus on the feared situation (e.g., touching doorknobs) and exaggerate other "dirty" behaviors (e.g., touch, rub, wipe hands all over the doorknob). Clients must then refrain from exercising the compulsion to undo, avoid the anxiety, or neutralize the obsessive thought until their distress subsides substantially (using the self-reported SUDS, based on a predetermined objective, e.g., a drop from 80 to 30). Clients should continue to move along the hierarchy only after each objective has been successfully achieved. Every 5–10 minutes, the practitioner (or assistant) should ask clients what their anxiety level is (0–100). Although the amount of time clients can hold the exposure may vary, it is critical that the exposure be prolonged and that it be maintained long enough for the anxiety to decrease significantly.

• In vivo exposure begins with the least anxiety-provoking situation and progresses gradually to the most anxiety-provoking situation, usually within six to eight treatment sessions. The most anxiety-provoking items continue to be practiced for the remainder of treatment. Flexibility is key, as clients may need more or less time. As with exposure treatment for agoraphobia, the practitioner should gently but firmly push clients to expose to moderately or highly anxiety-provoking thoughts or situations. If the thought or situation is not sufficiently anxiety provoking, they should move up the hierarchy to the next objective.

• During exposure, practitioners can periodically gauge clients' anxiety every 5–10 minutes by querying the client and then applying anxiety coping skills, which may include a cognitive challenge to the realistic degree of danger associated with the obsession, breathing or relaxation exercises, or some form of paradoxical intervention (e.g., humor, absurd exaggeration of the danger).

• Although in vivo exposure is generally considered the most effective method, some clients may also benefit from imaginal exposure with or without the additional use of EXRP in vivo or as a warm-up to in vivo exposure. Although some clients find it hard to hold images in their mind's eye, the practitioner can assist them by painting a mental picture with them to re-create the anxiety-inducing situation. This part of the procedure can be done during the assessment phase, when the practitioner carefully examines the nature of the obsessions and compulsive rituals. As with in vivo exposure, more anxiety-provoking scenes are generated gradually for imaginal exposure. The intervention process is similar to in vivo: develop a hierarchy, construct the scenes, expose clients to the mental pictures, and monitor clients' efforts to use behavioral or mental neutralizing techniques as compulsions to reduce anxiety. This procedure should last most of the 2-hour session, and SUDS should be used every 5–10 minutes.

Response Prevention

- Response prevention requires that the practitioner and clients devise a way to block the response, which may include either compulsive thoughts or behaviors. Covert or subtle compulsions, such as subvocalizations, ritualistic blinking, or unusual hand gestures, must be identified and neutralized so as to not undermine the effectiveness of the exposure. Of course, the compulsive behavior may also be quite overt, such as repeated hand washing or tapping loudly in specific numerical patterns. However, regardless of the type of compulsion, it is critical that maximum response prevention be employed. Although some graduated approach to response prevention may be necessary initially (i.e., progressively allowing less of the response), maximum response prevention is the ultimate goal. Partial response prevention may actually make the problem worse by reinforcing the compulsion. Response prevention is planned at the same time that the fear hierarchy is planned, and the practitioner should anticipate sabotage (e.g., subtle or covert mini rituals); teach the supportive assistant to watch out for these; and as clients progress through their hierarchy, eventually fade the intervention out.

- Practitioner and clients should estimate how far they are likely to progress in the hierarchy for each session, although this can be adjusted as needed. New situations can be added as things progress. Clients should be encouraged gently but firmly to expose themselves to situations that are challenging for them, but practitioners should avoid being overly ambitious or impatient. In general, the more autonomy a client has during the progression of treatment, the better. The point of intervention is for clients to take as much control of resolving this problem as they can and maintain gains over time. In a phrase, expose the client, check anxiety, wait, and then urge the client to go further.

- The typical session involves a review of the homework assignment and a detailed report of the success of the response prevention (e.g., time spent on homework, exposures accomplished, anxiety responses to exposures). Were there any violations? If so, have clients describe them. What obstacles got in the way of successfully completing the EXRP homework? Did the client take any shortcuts or sabotage the response prevention? Did the client use any subtle neutralizing thoughts or behaviors to reduce their anxiety? In general, in addition to the time spent conducting the procedure with the practitioner, it is recommended that clients continue practicing EXRP for an additional 2 hours on their own (or with an agreed on support person), for a total of at least 4 hours of exposure treatment per day. It is agreed to from the start that clients are restricted from engaging in all compulsive rituals from the start of treatment. For example, "washers" are not permitted to wash beyond a timed shower (e.g., every 2–3 days), and only one check of lights and appliances is permitted for compulsive checkers when they leave the house.

- Toward the end of the intervention, a home visit can be used to reinforce gains and assess for subtle attempts to avoid the full exposure. The practitioner should also note the behavior of other family members to see if they are helping or unwittingly hindering the client's progress. Active intervention (EXRP) should be carried out in the home to solidify gains in the client's home environment, often the site of compulsive ritualizing.

- After the client has succeeded in reducing anxiety and eliminating ritual responses, the practitioner should gradually disengage from involvement with the client. Clients gradually take control of the treatment by doing more on their own, and practitioner and clients should develop a follow-up maintenance plan. Supportive sessions or occasional "booster" visits may help solidify gains for the long run. At that point, clients may turn their attention to other problems in their life. Since EXRP was never offered as an intervention that would solve all their problems or forever inoculate clients against other difficulties, other interventions such as interpersonal psychotherapy, couples therapy, or cognitive therapy may be required.

TREATMENT PLANNING AND EVALUATION

CASE STUDY: GEORGE

George, a 34-year-old married white man, arrived at the local mental health clinic with his wife, Jan, age 32. He decided to come in for a long-standing problem that had recently gotten worse. In the waiting room, George decided after a brief discussion to come in alone, and Jan suggested that she might join him later in some sessions if it would be helpful. In the first visit, George was quite forthcoming about his troubles. Although he discussed things in a somewhat roundabout manner, he finally got to the point: "I've been having a lot of trouble with an old problem. It has been taking me a long time to get home from work. Although my job is only 20 minutes away from home, I've been taking almost an hour and a half, almost two hours sometimes. Whenever I hear a bump in the road in my pickup truck, I am fearful that I have hit someone, a pedestrian, and even though I know rationally I have not hit anyone, I have to stop the truck and get out of it and look around to make sure I did not. Sometimes, I have to make myself leave even though I cannot be 100 percent certain that I did not hit someone. I lie awake at night worried that in the newspapers the next morning they will report that a body was found off the side of the road in that area. This would make me think that I had actually hit and killed someone, but the body went flying and I could not find them during dusk." When the social worker, Ted, inquired how long this had been going on, George indicated that he had been ok for a few years, since his two little girls came along (they are age 4 and 6). But he said, "Since I am responsible for them and working hard to keep up I have not had much time to think about this old problem."

The "old problem" apparently was a repeated obsession that he had been responsible for the death of a young boy who was hit and killed by the car George's father was driving when George was a young boy himself. The boy had come down a hill through a stop sign onto the main road near their home in the early evening. The child appeared without warning, and George's father could not avoid hitting him. He never even hit the brakes. George, 8 years old at the time, always remembered that he and his father were talking and laughing when the accident occurred, and he felt that he must have distracted his dad and was therefore at fault. He had overheard his father say when the police arrived, "I was just talking with my son, and I turned my head, and there was this kid on a bicycle right in front of us." George always thought his father secretly blamed

him for this. His dad was depressed for some time after that, and he drank more heavily than usual. George recalls that he would come downstairs and his dad would be talking to himself, angrily sometimes, as though arguing with someone. George said his dad was never the same after that, and he died of a heart attack a few years later.

At his dad's funeral, someone said to George, who was then 12, "You're the man now. You've got to be responsible. Be good and help out your mother and sisters." The neighbors and parish priests tried to be helpful, but George always felt that he needed to "take care of things" in a way most of his friends didn't understand. His mother, was "a religious fanatic. She made sure I went to church every Sunday, and she made me go to confession every week. I never felt like I could confess everything adequately, and felt guilty for overlooking things. I was afraid of having thoughts about sex, and I couldn't talk to anyone about it. As I got older, I worked hard in school, but knew I had to get a job to help myself if I wanted to have a car or get money for college. My friends thought I was too serious, and I usually felt like I didn't fit in with them. I kind of forgot the incident as I got older, I guess, because I kept myself pretty busy. I drank a lot in college, but a couple of years after I got out, I stopped for a while. In the past few years I've started having few again on the weekends. If I get drunk once in a while, it seems to quiet the noise in my head. I didn't think it would be any harm. I am captain of my bowling team, and we like to knock back a few during the games. I get on their case when they don't show up for practices on time or don't do their part with the equipment and so forth. They tell me to lighten up and not take it so seriously. I got the job in the post office when I was 25. It seemed like a steady thing, a secure job. It's boring sometimes, and the people in my location don't work too hard, but there's not much I can do about it."

"A few months ago, I heard that a guy in another post office got drunk and hit a kid and sent him to the hospital. For some reason I've started thinking about the old incident again, and my concern that I've hit something or someone when I'm driving just started up, like some kind of trigger was switched on. The problem I'm having is that I can't stop the thoughts, and I can't stop myself from stopping the truck and getting out to look and see if someone is lying in the road. I know the thoughts are crazy, but I can't make myself believe it. Sometimes I just go home and go down in the basement to hide from my wife and kids and cry. I can't stand the stress it's causing me. I worry about every report in the morning paper, every accident or body they've found, and I have to find out exactly where it was, and whether it could possibly have been me. I can't take this anymore. It's making me think about killing myself. It takes the fun out of everything I'm doing. I have a great wife and two beautiful little girls and I'm miserable most of the time. I can't stop thinking about this. I can't sleep. You gotta help me."

MFS Assessment: Defining Problems and Goals

Although the content of George's obsessive thinking seemed triggered by a past event, a thorough assessment was done of the functional patterns of the obsession and compulsive checking. George appeared to meet the criteria for an OCD diagnosis, but his depressive symptoms and episodic binge drinking were significant as well. He seemed very tense much of the time. He reported trouble sleeping and was irritable with his coworkers. He also discussed responsibility as a recurrent theme in several areas of his life, and his friends often characterized him as the "serious one."

Important relationships in his life appeared to be satisfying and going well. He and Jan loved each other, and their two children were doing well. However, at times he was overbearing at home, making sure "rules" about cleaning up and so forth were adhered to. When he was feeling particularly edgy and obsessing a lot, he was hard to approach and critical of those around him, sometimes alienating his wife for the day and being a little harsh with his daughters for them to "behave" themselves. His job was steady, and he had no immediate financial concerns. He was in good health.

George described his upbringing as "strict," although he felt that his parents had loved him. He had always a hard time letting himself "off the hook" from relatively minor mistakes. His recent experience with obsessive-compulsive symptoms was not altogether new. Upon further examination, it became evident that he had, off and on, experienced an array of compulsive behaviors since he was young: compulsive blinking or ritualistic praying under his breath to ward off guilty feelings about "bad thoughts" as a young teenager. This new twist on an already-overwrought sense of responsibility was enough to cause additional compulsions to ward off guilt. These symptoms were exacerbated during times of stress in his life, and they further marginalized him from ordinary social experiences such as dating, dances, prom, and other normative social activities.

A careful functional analysis of his presenting symptoms and reemergence of his compulsions seems connected to several things: an increase in stress at work as a result of "efficiency" changes, an increase in drinking on weekends, and the report that one of his coworkers in another location (who was apparently driving under the influence of alcohol) had hit a child in a car accident. The child later died. Upon hearing this report, George felt flush with anxiety and as though he were going to pass out. He took a break and went to sit in his truck for a few minutes, going over and over in his mind the last time he drove home on Saturday evening after having had four or five beers in 2 hours after a bowling league tournament. He felt flush and panicky trying to remember if he had heard any "bumps" on the way home. Since the tournament had been over for 2 weeks with no adverse reports of accidents since then, he was able to calm himself to the point that he could go back inside to work. But the feeling lingered. His reaction to the news of his coworker's accident had been so acute that Ted began to think George may also be suffering from post-traumatic stress.

On his way home from work, George began to think about it again and started to observe every sound emanating from the suspension system in his old truck. It was dusk, and if he ever wanted to avoid feeling that sense of guilt again, he thought that he had better be exceptionally careful on the way home. Over the next few weeks, the sounds he heard, whether driving through the busy downtown area on the approach to work or when on more rural, out-of-town roads, were enough to make him think something awful had happened. He began to stop the truck and look around "just to make sure" nothing had happened. This type of experience began to happen more often, until it began to take up considerable time on his way home (he didn't do this in the morning—he seemed to be able to shake off the thoughts to get to work on time). But at the end of the day, he found himself more keyed up. Jan began to wonder what the problem was, but George made excuses and was not comfortable talking about it. After a few weeks, Jan became anxious about his evasiveness, began to think there was a problem, and confronted him about it. George responded angrily, "Everybody needs to get off my back," and he attacked her verbally, saying he was doing everything he could as a father and husband and she should just trust him. This outburst and the unresolved nature of the lateness created a "cold war" atmosphere for about a week. George's struggles, however, worsened. It seemed that the more he stopped his truck and looked around, the more obsessional he became, the more the thoughts bothered him, and the more anxious and desperate he felt. He was drinking more on the weekends, and his relations with Jan were not getting better. One night he couldn't contain his feelings anymore and told her so. He sobbed uncontrollably, saying that he couldn't live like this anymore. Jan began to understand what the problem had been all along. She thought he had left these problems behind long ago.

With the MFS assessment as backdrop, the practitioner, Ted, and George developed a hypothetical summation of the problem: when under stress, George began to ruminate about being responsible for events beyond his control. He automatically began to think, "What have I done? What could I have done differently?" His belief that he could undo or neutralize his troubling, anxiety-provoking thoughts by thoroughly checking every move he made was a futile endeavor and a long-standing problem. The argument for his guilt was unassailable: he could never completely disprove that he had harmed someone. However, the more he tried to prove that nothing happened while he was driving home, the harder it was for him to keep himself from stopping to look and double-check that he hadn't hit anyone. He became increasingly anxious and despondent, began to drink more (which further exacerbated his depression, anxiety, and obsessive thinking), and he became further alienated from those who could comfort and support him, especially his wife. This made him feel more isolated and guilty.

Ted and George decided that they had to address this problem directly. After a long discussion and examination of the developmental contributions to George's current difficulties, George knew he had to let go of this old way of dealing with his troubles and develop better ways of coping with his troubled feelings and daily stressors. He knew intellectually that the guilt was completely irrational, and he knew that the compulsive checking was futile. He could never resolve his anxieties by checking. He even laughed when he recounted the stories he made up to cover for himself when one of his friends stopped to help him on the side of the road: "If they knew what I was really up to, they would think I was crazy."

After a few visits, George seemed a bit more at ease with himself and with the practitioner. Ted described to George how EXRP works. He also suggested that George stop drinking for a while, at least until the obsessive symptoms and compulsive checking subsided. George agreed to try and felt that he probably would not have a problem with abstaining, since he only drank on weekends. He also agreed to discuss his symptoms with a psychiatrist and at least consider taking medication if the psychiatrist recommended it. George said he understood the gist of the intervention and that he wanted to "get to work" as soon as possible. They together developed a hierarchy that gradually detailed the types of sounds that would trigger George's anxiety-ridden obsessive thoughts and his need to check what happened. This seemed to occur only when he was driving alone, and he only drove his old pickup truck. The strength of the compulsion to check would depend on the type and force of the sound he heard. In general, they ranged from minor sounds he could sometimes overlook (e.g., a stone banging under the wheel well) to a louder "clunk" (e.g., a branch hitting the bottom of the truck), and a loud bang (e.g., the sound of the old suspension hitting a pot hole). His anxious responses to these various sounds were rated on a SUDS scale. To hit a maximum of 100, there would have to be a loud bang and several people in the vicinity, say, on a busy downtown street. It also became apparent that the sound did not have to emanate directly from the truck; it could be a loud noise produced from some occurrence nearby. In George's thinking, he could not *guarantee* that a sound did not come from his truck; therefore, he had to confirm it. His goal was to reduce his SUDS score to less than 20; at that point, he felt he could "shake the sound off" and not have to check out each noise.

Selecting and Designing the Intervention: Defining Strategies and Objectives

The implementation of the EXRP plan began right away. For George to implement it, however, he agreed to have his wife accompany him a few times, at least in the beginning. After a couples session, during which the procedure was described and Jan's role explained, they were ready to start.

However, since George could not systematically and progressively control the loudness of the sounds that would occur, he would have to be prepared to pull off the road and maintain his exposure (tolerating the fact that he had heard the noise) without responding to it by getting out of the truck and checking what had happened (response prevention). For two prolonged 2-hour sessions, George agreed to "warm up" with imaginal exposure sessions to prepare for in vivo exposure. The social worker prepared George by teaching him relaxation exercises accompanied by deep breathing. He also learned to use a mantra, "Nothing happened, everyone is fine," to challenge the obsessive thought that he had struck someone with his truck. Gradually, Ted presented the obsession-inducing stimuli in ascending order of intensity, and when George indicated that he had the image in mind, the practitioner directed him to imagine sitting in his truck, suspended as if traffic had come to a stop. In his mind's eye he would have to remain sitting in his truck looking forward (not checking in his mirrors) and practice his deep breathing and his mantra. As they traveled up the hierarchy, George became increasingly anxious (after a large "bang" was inserted into the image). George shifted in his chair uncomfortably and was not breathing in a slow, relaxed way. The practitioner asked him his SUDS level, which was 80. At that point, the social worker directed George to breathe deeply, focus on his mantra, and maintain the image in his mind. They sat for at least 30 minutes, and the practitioner occasionally requested a reading of George's SUDS. Gradually, the rating began to decline until it came down to 30. The social worker directed George to practice this imaginal exercise daily at home for an hour each night, with extra practice on the weekends (at least 2 hours). After a week of covert desensitization, they decided to begin in vivo exposure with response prevention.

Everyday for the next week, Jan agreed to meet George at work and drive home with him in the truck to get the process rolling. After that, George would be on his own, but they would go out together after he got home and on weekends for "extra" practice. The social worker explained that EXRP would have to be done intensely and in a prolonged way for it to work. They met after work daily, and Jan (whom Ted trained to be the coach) was prepared to assist George by sitting with him as he pulled to the side of the road after he heard a "40 or better" sound, and she would guide him in practicing his relaxation without getting out of the truck to check what happened. He found this very difficult at first, and, sobbing, he begged Jan to tell him if anything had happened. Of course, the social worker had instructed Jan not to reassure him, since she would be reinforcing the compulsive need to check. Jan, upset, called the practitioner one night and told him she didn't know if she could continue doing this. It was hard for her to see George suffer. Ted encouraged her not to give up, and he told her that if she stuck with it for a few more days, George would begin to get some relief from his suffering and she would see some positive results.

The exposure sessions continued, and after a few days, George was breathing better during exposure and response prevention, even after some of the loudest bangs. He felt that he was ready to try it alone. The following week he was able to maintain exposure without checking, although he did find himself peeking in the mirror now and then, but eventually he curtailed that too. (Later, when he had full control after even the loudest noises, he resumed checking "one time," as would be considered "normal" for responsible driving.) After 1 week of covert exposure and 3 weeks of daily in vivo exposure for about 2 hours a day (plus weekends), George felt like he was over the worst of it. In addition to the in vivo exposure, George had eliminated his drinking during this time; was sleeping better; and was taking an antidepressant, the therapeutic effects of which he felt might have begun to work. The practitioner agreed that this was an excellent beginning, but some follow-up was in order to prevent any backsliding. In addition to continuing his self-guided EXRP on the way home from work for an hour each day, George wanted to work on becoming a more relaxed and fun person with his wife and kids, "not so serious all the time." They agreed to meet weekly in a couples session, since George agreed that his marriage would be a good vehicle for addressing some of his interpersonal concerns. Other lifestyle changes included having one or two beers on the weekends only after he discontinued his medication, and only if his OCD symptoms were well under control. He would avoid the use of alcohol to "quiet the noise" again. In addition, he decided to start running again, three times a week (because he agreed that bowling could not be considered serious exercise) to reduce generalized anxiety symptoms. Overall, his long-term prospects looked good, and he knew that he could always come by for a booster session if he felt that his obsessions were coming back to haunt him.

Selecting Scales and Creating Indexes to Monitor and Evaluate Client Progress

To gauge his progress, George, his wife, and Ted relied primarily on George's own self-anchored subjective level of distress to gauge progress. Later, he relied on the number of days that had gone by when he felt relatively trouble-free. Scores on the OCI were also checked periodically with the practitioner. As George improved, however, qualitative indicators began to tell the broader benefits of the relief he began to feel: his ability to laugh and have fun again with his kids and his friends; his general feeling of ease and lightness in his life; his lack of preoccupation with depressing thoughts, and best of all, a renewed sense of intimacy with his wife who didn't give up on him during treatment.

SUMMARY

Helping clients with serious anxiety disorders is both very challenging and very gratifying. These disorders cause enormous suffering for millions of people. Social workers who learn cognitive-behavioral and exposure-based interventions for these and other anxiety disorders will find that they are using their clinical skills to the maximum. Clients often suffer from other co-occurring problems as well. However, clients with anxiety disorders will not take the necessary risks to get better unless they feel that the practitioner is competent, is confident in his or her skills, and can imbue the client with hope when dealing with what are often long-standing problems. Case management skills are often required to coordinate interventions that sometimes include collaborations with physicians, paraprofessionals, and social supports in the family and community.

TABLE 8.2   The Client Service Plan

Problems	Goals	Objectives (samples)	Interventions	Assessment and evaluation tools
Anxiety, guilty obsessive thinking about striking pedestrians with his truck	Reduce, eliminate anxiety regarding dysfunctional thinking	Read short manual and watch brief film on what OCD is and how EX/RP works	Relationship building: develop atmosphere of openness and trust so he can commit to working the treatment plan	SUDS to gauge progress with level of fear
Compulsive checking to confirm whether he actually struck anyone; moderately debilitating, spending up to 2 hours daily struggling with compulsion	Eliminate obsessive thoughts and checking behaviors	Practice imaginal exposure daily at home for at least half an hour	Psychoeducation on the nature of OCD and how EXRP works; include his wife in the discussions and implementation as supportive assistant	Periodic OCI assessment — Other qualitative indicators of quality of life
Depression: trouble sleeping, thoughts of hopelessness, suicidal thoughts	Reduce depressive symptoms; further assessment needed	Practice in vivo EXRP daily for two-four hours. First week: accompanied by wife; second week: alone — Keep diary of progress daily for both imaginal and in vivo exposure — Talk to wife daily about progress he is making with his difficulties	EXRP: — • Incorporate SUDS into the functional assessment during development of the hierarchy of fears (e.g., loudness of sounds while driving)	
Interpersonal trouble: irritability with wife and coworkers; possibly related to his struggles with guilt-ridden obsessive thinking	Improve ability to express feelings to his wife and children; ask wife for support when he is troubled		• Teach imaginal exposure and relaxation exercises as preparation for in vivo exposure	
Episodic excessive alcohol use, mostly on weekends; reports drinking to cope with anxious obsessive thinking	Abstinence for now; pending further assessment after OCD symptoms abate		• Daily (2–4 hours) in vivo exposure while driving — • Referral for psychiatric evaluation for possible antidepressants — Lifestyle changes: increase aerobic exercise to reduce generalized anxiety and depression	

CHAPTER 9

POST-TRAUMATIC STRESS DISORDER

Having participated in combat, endured torture, witnessed a killing, been victimized by crime, escaped an attack on one's life, experienced a terrorist bombing, survived a natural disaster, suffered domestic violence, or been victimized by sexual assault—these are all horrific events. Any one of them can have serious, long-term negative effects on the psychological and social well-being of an adult or a child. These events are generally understood to be extreme psychological experiences, and many persons have experienced at least one such traumatic event in their lives. Although many resilient persons rebound from such experiences by virtue of innate temperament, ongoing social supports, or other protective factors, many persons continue to suffer from the residual effects of these stressful events for years. The cluster of anxiety-related symptoms and behaviors that include hyperarousal, reexperiencing of the traumatic event, and avoidance and numbing of stimuli that remind a person of a traumatic event is referred to as post-traumatic stress disorder (PTSD).

Much of the previous chapter on the assessment and treatment of anxiety disorders is directly applicable to evidence-based practice with traumatized persons. However, because of the nature of traumatic events and their effects, there are some unique aspects to assessment and intervention with PTSD. Assessment of PTSD demands the standard multidimensional overview of a client's well-being, as well as a thorough functional multidimensional-systemic analysis (i.e., MFS assessment) that links key antecedents in everyday life to a client's worsening or improving symptoms. Although working with people who suffer from PTSD is challenging, there is a good chance the condition responds favorably to cognitive-behavioral therapies (CBTs) that include some form of prolonged exposure to the thoughts and/or situations that provoke disabling anxiety.

ASSESSMENT

Background Data

Several major studies conducted in recent decades have provided estimates for the prevalence, consequences, and costs of PTSD in the general population. These include the National Comorbidity Study (NCS) (Kessler, Sonnega, Bromet, Hughes, & Nelson, 1995); Norris's (1990) survey of 1,000 persons in the southeastern United States; Resnick, Kilpatrick, Dansky, Saunders, and Best's (1993) telephone survey with a national sample of 4,008 women; and Breslau, Davis, Andreski, and Peterson's (1991) survey of 1,007 adults. Although data collection methods, measures, and diagnostic criteria have varied somewhat, results demonstrated that between 60% and 70% of persons surveyed reported experiencing at least one traumatic event in their lifetime. More recently, the National Epidemiologic Survey on Alcohol and Related Conditions (NESARC) revealed that the most commonly reported traumas for those with PTSD were unexpected death of a significant other, serious injury or illness of someone close, and sexual assault (Pietrzak, Goldstein, Southwick, & Grant, 2011).

However, the fact that someone has experienced a traumatic event does not mean that he or she will develop PTSD. Factors that mediate whether someone develops the disorder include the nature and severity of the stressful event, its cognitive appraisal and interpretation, the inherent resiliency or vulnerability of the person, and the responsiveness and quality of social supports post-trauma. Lifetime prevalence of PTSD has been estimated at 7.8% in the general population (10.4% for women, 5.0% for men; Kessler et al., 1995). More recently, NESARC data revealed lifetime prevalence rates of PTSD to be 6.4% overall (8.6% for women, 4.1% for men). Rates for lifetime "partial" PTSD were slightly higher (Pietrzak et al., 2011). PTSD also is more common among younger, previously married, and lower-income individuals (Pietrzak et al., 2011). African Americans report higher rates of PTSD than do Asian Americans, whites, and Hispanics (Asnaani, Richey, Dimaite, Hinton, & Hofmann, 2010). Thus, large proportions of the population are exposed to traumatic events, often to multiple types of events and on multiple occasions, and many demonstrate signs and symptoms associated with PTSD as a result (Kilpatrick, Resnick, Saunders, & Best, 1998; Kilpatrick, Saunders, Veronen, Best, & Von, 1987). Costs associated with the effects of traumatic events have been estimated in the hundreds of billions of dollars (Solomon & Davidson, 1997).

Military Service Trauma and PTSD.   In the twentieth century, war-related trauma (known as shell shock) during World War I focused attention on the psychological effects of exposure to intense bombardment and associated death and dismemberment, and the condition fell into the realm of medical interest. This work continued after World War II and set the stage for a more formal recognition of PTSD as a psychiatric disorder (Keane, 1998). The National Vietnam Veterans Readjustment Study (NVVRS) was initiated in the mid-1980s to compensate for the methodological limitations of previous efforts to determine the effects of combat-related service in Vietnam. The study aimed to measure pre-military service, military service, and post-military service factors and their relationship to the psychosocial well-being of veterans years after service. The goals of the study (Kulka et al., 1988)—funded by the Department of Veterans Affairs—were to determine the prevalence of PTSD and other psychological disorders that might have occurred as a result of participating in the Vietnam War, to examine the current life adjustment of individuals who participated in the war, and to study factors related to the development of PTSD (Keane, 1998).

The study revealed that veterans who served in the Vietnam War were estimated to have rates of PTSD about six times higher (15.2% for men, 8.5% for women) than other veterans who served during the Vietnam era (2.5% for men, 1.1% for women) and than the civilian population (1.2% for men, and .3% for women). Lifetime prevalence rates for Vietnam-theater veterans were 30.9% for men and 26.9% for women. PTSD rates for those who experienced low to moderate stress were 8.5% for men and 2.5% women, and for high war-zone stress, 35.8% for men and 17.5% for women. These differences were significant even after controlling for a wide range of demographic and other psychiatric and psychosocial measures. Various other psychosocial disorders also accompanied a diagnosis of PTSD. These included substance abuse, marital and family adjustment problems, unemployment, and homelessness. The data revealed that symptoms were directly related to the severity of the stressor.

With more recent military engagements, data reveal high rates of anger among male veterans and high rates of PTSD among active-duty soldiers and veterans of Iraq and Afghanistan, ranging from 11% to 12% (for a brief review, see Kulkarni, Porter, & Rauch, 2012). The effects of PTSD in veterans are highly comorbid (e.g., depression, substance abuse), and these conditions can last for many years, as one 20-year longitudinal analysis of Israeli soldiers demonstrated (Ginzburg, Ein-Dor, & Solomon, 2010).

It is important to remember that combat veterans were not the only victims of war. Civilians also suffer extensively from warfare. For example, there is extensive literature on the effects of war-related trauma and atrocities on civilians in Southeast Asia. The effects of war, imprisonment, loss of homeland, torture, traumatic emigration experiences, and dislocation result in a higher-than-expected range of psychiatric disorders, including PTSD, depression, and substance abuse (e.g., Carlson & Russer-Hogan, 1991; O'Hare & Tran, 1998).

Gender Differences in Trauma and PTSD.   There is some evidence that women are more prone to post-trauma negative appraisal, with a greater tendency than men to engage in self-blame, to view themselves as incompetent or damaged, and to be inclined to hold strong beliefs that the world is dangerous (Sherrer, 2011; Tolin & Foa, 2006). These differences might partially account for the higher rates of PTSD and more severe symptoms in women overall (Olff, Langeland, Draijer, & Gersons, 2007; Tolin & Foa,

2006). Norris (1992) examined traumatic exposure in a large sample (*n* = 1,000) of men and women, and revealed that women were more likely to have suffered sexual assault, but men were more likely to have suffered automobile accidents, physical assault, and combat exposure. Although men experienced higher rates of exposure to traumatic events in general, women suffered more severe symptoms overall, much of it associated with having been sexually assaulted. Among those who were victims of crime, women suffered more symptoms than men did. Resnick et al. (1993) interviewed a random sample of more than 4,000 Americans by phone and found that 69% of women reported exposure to traumatic events, and 36% reported exposure to sexual or aggravated assault or the homicide of a close friend or family member. The overall sample showed a lifetime prevalence of PTSD of 12.3%, and rates were much higher for those who had been victimized by crime (26%) than for those who reported noncrime events (9%). Although rates of PTSD appear to be very high following a completed rape (greater than 90%), almost half of women who have been raped show considerable remission of symptoms 3 months after the event (Rothbaum, Foa, Riggs, Murdock, & Walsh, 1992). Women with preexisting psychiatric difficulties also are more likely to develop PTSD symptoms after the traumatic event.

Trauma and PTSD Associated with Rape and Other Interpersonal Violence.   Rape is generally underreported because respondents do not respond in the affirmative when asked if they have been raped, even though the event may meet the legal definition of rape. In addition, victims often know the perpetrators and are reluctant to identify them and press charges. Rates of rape across studies also vary because of inconsistencies in definitions of rape, as well as the varying sensitivity of screening questions for identifying rape (Koss, 1993). Rape is one of the more frequent risk factors for PTSD in women because it often involves additional physical injury or even threat to life, and some women have been raped multiple times. However, as traumatic as rape is for a woman, long-term emotional disability is not inevitable. Rothbaum et al. (1992) studied the course of PTSD symptoms in 95 women assessed several days after sexual assault. Although most met PTSD criteria soon after the event, about half gradually showed a reduction in symptoms to subdiagnostic levels. Those who did not improve by the first month (post-rape) showed little improvement afterward. Symptoms of rape-related distress included intrusive thoughts and images, anxiety, and depression. The authors demonstrated that those less likely to improve were identified soon after the sexual assault from scores on the Rape Aftermath Symptom Test (RAST) and the Impact of Events Scale (IES). As noted earlier, a host of factors mediates the likelihood of developing PTSD, including early childhood neglect and abuse (including sexual abuse), substance abuse, history of other psychopathology, history of multiple violent events, and history of inordinate physical and social risk taking (i.e., sensation seeking). However, rates of

PTSD are higher for those who have been raped than for those who have been the victim of other crimes. Substantial proportions of Americans are subjected to crimes against their persons, including rape and other physical assaults (Bisson & Shepherd, 1995).

In addition to rape, other crimes also precipitate the development of PTSD (Kilpatrick & Resnick, 1993). Criminal victimization is a relatively common occurrence, and rates of victimization are generally higher than those reflected in government statistics. Psychological reactions to being a crime victim are often similar to those of persons who experience PTSD symptoms, and victims of crime are more likely than accident victims to manifest symptoms 3 months after the event. Kilpatrick et al. (1987) interviewed 391 adult females from South Carolina about lifetime criminal victimization experiences, crime reporting behavior, and psychological impact. More than 75% of the women reported having been the victim of a crime. Of all 547 crimes reported, almost half (49%) were sexual assaults, and 38.6% were burglaries. More than half of the crimes were not reported to the police. A subsequent analysis of the same sample (Kilpatrick et al., 1989) demonstrated that the development of crime-related PTSD (in about 20% of crime victims) was predicted by age (those younger were more likely to develop symptoms), number of years since the crime occurred, having sustained a physical injury, having perceived threat of serious harm or death when the crime was being committed, and having been a victim of a completed rape. As with other traumatic events, the effects of having been the victim of a crime were dependent on a host of factors, particularly the degree to which one feared for one's life.

PTSD and Co-occurring Disorders. Most persons with PTSD also have at least one other psychiatric disorder, and the prevalence of co-occurring disorders is somewhat similar for men and women (Kessler et al., 1995; Pietrzak et al., 2011). Many problems co-occur with PTSD, including depression, anxiety, substance abuse, somatization disorders, and other functional psychosocial impairments that affect life at home and work. PTSD symptoms are also related to medical problems, particularly for women who have been sexually assaulted. Determining the sequencing of the development of these symptoms is more difficult, although it appears that a history of anxiety and depressive disorders may signal an increased risk of PTSD. Persons who have a prior history of depression and substance abuse have an increased risk for direct personal exposure to traumatic events (Breslau, Davis, Andreski, Federman, & Anthony, 1998).

Recently, the relatively common co-occurrence of PTSD and substance abuse has received more attention. Although it appears intuitively appealing that substance abuse develops as a way of coping with the physiological arousal that accompanies PTSD (e.g., the self-medication hypothesis), the relationship is actually more complex (Hoffman & Sasaki, 1997; Stewart,

1996). Despite methodological limitations in the research, evidence is emerging on the following:

- Traumatic events and PTSD symptoms correlate directly with substance abuse.
- PTSD symptoms tend to precede a substance abuse problem.
- Those who drink following a traumatic event are more likely to do so episodically.
- Symptom severity may be directly related to substance abuse.
- Substance abuse may not only enhance a person's readiness to experience a traumatic event (e.g., a car accident in which the drinker's passenger dies) but also physiologically prime the person to develop PTSD as a result of the event.
- PTSD symptoms may exacerbate an existing substance abuse problem or precipitate the development of a substance abuse problem.
- Both disorders may share common causal factors (e.g., genetic or environmental).
- An individual's response to trauma may be more related to alcohol abuse than to exposure to the trauma itself.
- Although PTSD symptoms appear to precede the onset of problem drinking, the interrelationship is complex and reciprocal in that withdrawal symptoms from abuse tend to exacerbate anxiety, depression, and other related symptoms serving to maintain the cycle of alcohol abuse and PTSD symptoms.

To quote Stewart (1996): "It appears that a single unidirectional pathway to explain the overlap between PTSD and alcohol abuse is unlikely to be found. Instead, it seems possible that both self-medication and alcohol intoxication or withdrawal-induced intensification of PTSD symptoms contribute to the high degree of comorbidity between alcohol abuse and PTSD diagnoses" (p. 102).

Theories

Early Trauma Theories.   At the turn of the nineteenth century, psychoanalytic theories paved the way for the exploration of psychological trauma and its effects. The causes of "hysterical neuroses" (Freud, 1920/1966; Herman, 1992) were generally attributed to the failure of the individual to successfully repress infantile sexual impulses. However, psychoanalytic theorists have argued over the years whether hysterical neurosis was the result of actual childhood sexual seduction or unconscious fantasy on the part of the individual (Herman, 1992; Horowitz, 1997). These debates were accompanied by a lack of empirical evidence, which contributed to decades of confusion about the validity of a causal link between childhood sexual abuse and the development of future psychopathology. Nevertheless, some continue to believe that the causes of psychopathology of various kinds lie predominantly in the lack of "secure attachment" or other failures of parental nurturance during early childhood, which would otherwise have provided a buffer, presumably, against future mental illnesses, including PTSD (Finkelhor & Browne, 1985; Herman, 1992; Van der Kolk, Weisaeth, & Van der Hart, 1996). Theoretically, it has been asserted that traumatic events appear to interfere with children's ability to regulate their arousal level (through adequate functioning of the ego and its defenses), which, in turn, may lead to problems in learning, mood regulation, aggression, and other interpersonal difficulties. Most of these theories, however, have been based on post hoc analysis of case studies and correlational data between childhood experiences and adult psychopathology. More recently, longitudinal studies have been brought to bear on the causal connection between early childhood trauma as a predictor of adult psychopathology, but these studies either do not consider the relative predictive power of childhood experiences in the context of other psychosocial influences over time or make unsubstantiated inferences regarding factors and causal links that could be explained more parsimoniously.

Although childhood victimization (e.g., physical and sexual abuse, other related forms of neglect) appears to increase risk for adult psychopathology (including PTSD), retrospective diagnosis is fraught with complexity, ambiguity, and reliability problems. Widom (1998) is articulate about the complexities inherent in drawing cause-effect inferences about adult psychopathology from childhood data:

> Childhood experiences such as physical and sexual abuse and neglect are adverse events with immediate and long-term consequences. However, in considering child abuse and neglect as examples of adverse life events that have the potential to affect development and subsequent psychopathology, the assumptions of "well-being" in the child's life before the victimization experience may not be a reasonable one. Although certain forms of childhood victimization may indeed be acute stressors, child abuse and neglect often occur against a background of more chronic adversity in multiproblem homes. Child abuse and neglect may be only one of the family's problems. Thus, the general effects of other family characteristics, such as poverty, unemployment, parental alcoholism or drug problems, or other inadequate social and family functioning, must be recognized and disentangled from the specific effects of childhood abuse and neglect. (p. 81)

Sorting out the effects of child abuse from other past and current contributing factors is difficult for clinicians and researchers alike. Clinicians should be cautious about attributing all complaints from adolescent or adult clients to a child abuse history, lest they overlook other important contributing factors and co-occurring problems that may be more amenable to effective intervention. Long-term outcomes of child abuse may also depend largely on other contextual factors, that is, how others responded at the time, including the criminal justice and social service systems. Those surrounding the child can buffer or exacerbate the effects of the traumatic event itself. Much more needs to be established regarding the long-term effects of childhood victimization. It is likely, as with most of the problems addressed in this text, that the long-term consequences are the result of multiple interacting biological, psychosocial, and environmental factors that take a variety of developmental pathways.

Current Cognitive Theories.   In recent decades, learning theories embedded in a biopsychosocial framework have come to dominate the literature regarding the cause and maintenance of pathological reactions to trauma and highly stressful events. Theories regarding the etiology of PTSD are, as one might expect, subject to genetic, learning, and social-environmental (including cultural) influences. In addition to evidence that some people might be physiologically predisposed to more negative responses to trauma, learning processes appear to play a prominent role. Relevant learning theories include basic conditioning (i.e., severe emotional response paired with a severe stressor) to social-cognitive theory and information-processing theories that emphasize (1) an interplay of memory structures, emotional responses, and activation of neural fear networks combined with other emotional responses (e.g., guilt, shame, anger); (2) negative cognitive appraisals of the event; and (3) maladaptive behavioral responses that reinforce fear (e.g., avoidance) (Brewin & Holmes, 2003; Dalgleish, 2004; Ehlers & Clark, 2000; Foa, Huppert, & Cahill, 2006; Foa & Kozak, 1986; Foa & Rothbaum, 1998; Resick, Monson, & Rizvi, 2008; Sherrer, 2011). Although there is significant overlap and variation in these cognitively based theories, the key mechanism of change appears to be prolonged covert (imaginal) and/or in vivo exposure to the feared stimuli (i.e., the trauma and similar or related events) until the fear associated with it is gradually lessened and, possibly, extinguished. This point is addressed more in a subsequent discussion regarding change processes in the section "Selecting Effective Interventions."

Stress-Coping Theories.   Stress-coping theories are much needed to provide a "horizontal" complement to the "vertical" view of developmental psychopathology as a predictive model of PTSD. Multivariate theories now provide a more complete framework for understanding the complex links between traumatic events and PTSD symptoms. It is well established that various life stressors predispose people to greater health risks and mental health risks (for relevant reviews, see Dohrenwend, 1998). Although one should not underestimate the potential consequences of childhood abuse or other past traumas, chronic daily stressors can also be major contributors to mental health disorders and overall well-being (Wheaton, 1994).

Problems abound with the developmental-diagnostic view as applied to PTSD. First, what constitutes traumatic versus not traumatic is highly variable (Shalev, 1996). Second, the vast majority of persons exposed to extreme stressors do not develop PTSD (McFarlane & Yehuda, 1996; Resnick et al., 1993; Shalev, 1996). Most acute trauma symptoms remit soon after the event, thus making acute symptoms poor predictors of who will manifest PTSD symptoms later. Conversely, PTSD symptoms can result from distressing but relatively common occurrences, such as nonfatal automobile accidents. Third, symptoms associated with PTSD are generally not unique to the disorder (King, Leskin, King, & Weathers, 1998; McFarlane & Girolamo, 1996). The symptoms overlap considerably with depression, anxiety, somatization, and personality disorders, and they co-occur with medical illnesses as well (Friedman, 1997). Fourth, factors that predict the development of the disorder may have less to do with traumatic events themselves and more to do with individual differences in the appraisal of traumatic events (Ehlers & Clark, 2000), as well as differences in personality traits (e.g., negative worrying style) and gender (i.e., women are more likely to be diagnosed with PTSD despite less frequent exposure to traumatic events) (Bowman, 1999). Traumatic events can trigger other psychological vulnerabilities related to various other causes. This variability in the link between traumatic events and the development of PTSD may account, in part, for some of the inconsistent findings in the effectiveness of some treatments.

It has been suggested that research on PTSD has been too narrow or truncated. Shalev (1996) notes a disconnection between psychiatric research on PTSD and stress-coping theory (Holahan & Moos, 1994; Lazarus & Folkman, 1984). She outlines several factors that should be considered in a more complete multivariate model: pre-trauma vulnerability (e.g., biological temperament, family history, and social stressors), severity of the stressor, preparedness for the event, acute responses, and coping resources that may provide a sense of control. She emphasizes that a distinction should be made between post-traumatic pathological symptoms and normative responses to a stressful event. The overlap in symptoms between PTSD and other anxiety disorders suggests that more attention needs to be paid to the interaction of developmental and stress-coping theories to provide a broader and more valid context for understanding PTSD symptoms on a continuum of severity.

Stressful events occur throughout the life span. Although the emphasis for assessment is on current functioning and adaptation (Holahan & Moos, 1994), how the events are appraised and whether a person's coping capacities are overtaxed depends on general individual cognitive mediating factors that vary considerably from one individual to the next (Bandura, 1986; Lazarus & Folkman, 1984). Thus, stress-coping theories can be readily linked to the cognitive theories reviewed already (e.g., Ehlers & Clark, 2000; Foa et al., 2006). Current psychological theories emphasize traumatic events as an assault on an individual's formerly stable cognitive model of the world (i.e., schemata), followed by either a relatively rapid psychological accommodation to the new related stimuli without further undue distress, or a long-term struggle, vacillating between confrontation and avoidance. The person must then gradually reconcile these events by incrementally confronting them with gradually lessening psychophysiological distress (Horowitz, 1997; Rachman, 1980). Other psychological theories, such as conditioning and learned helplessness theories, may also provide partial and somewhat overlapping explanations for this psychological reconciliation process. Joseph, Williams, and Yule (1997) point out that dealing with traumatic events requires a balancing act of gradual exposure to frightening stimuli with time out for intermittent respite from the emotional stress caused by thinking about the traumatic event. Over time, this cognitive processing allows the individual to psychologically confront the event with a tolerable degree of discomfort. Although these theories vary somewhat in content and emphasis, they share a common theoretical core that points to the need for some level of covert exposure to the event and psychological reconciliation of the traumatic event and one's schema (i.e., sense of self and the world).

Psychological resolution, however, should not be understood as a process that takes place in a social vacuum. Social supports, both the emotional support of others and instrumental supports (meeting basic needs), can significantly moderate the effects of stress (Sarason, Pierce, & Sarason, 1994). The quality of social supports before and after the trauma may be an important determinant for both the manner in which a person responds to the traumatic event and how speedily the person recovers from it. For example, research supports the buffering effects of family relationships for individuals exposed to community violence (Gorman-Smith & Tolan, 1998). The presence or absence of social supports may be the determining factor in long-term outcomes for someone who has suffered a severe traumatic event.

Although it should be understood that cultural factors influence the appraisal of and response to traumatic events, there is relatively little research on the effects of culture on the development, course, and treatment of PTSD (Marsella, Friedman, & Spain, 1996). A major problem in determining the role of race, ethnicity, and culture in relation to PTSD is the lack of good measures for these constructs. A review of racial differences among veterans with combat-related PTSD suggests strongly that veterans of different races are probably more alike than different with respect to symptoms and treatment response (Frueh, Brady, & de Arellano, 1998). However, in the NVVRS study, Hispanics were shown to have higher rates of PTSD, even after controlling for combat exposure and other background variables (Ruef, Litz, & Schlenger, 2000). Differences in treatment outcomes, however, may have less to do with inherent differences in response to traumatic events and more to do with access to the treatment system (Rosenheck & Fontana, 1996).

Key Elements of MFS Assessment

The diagnostic criteria for PTSD have been modified somewhat in the DSM-5 (American Psychiatric Association, APA, 2013). In the DSM-IV (APA, 2000), individuals met the criteria for PTSD if they had been exposed to a traumatic event that involved actual or threatened death or serious injury, or a threat to the physical integrity of self or others, and their response involved intense fear, helplessness, or horror (or, in the case of children, if they demonstrated disorganized or agitated behavior). The individual must also have manifested three categories of symptoms for a period of at least 1 month. First, the individual persistently *reexperiences* the traumatic event through distressing recollections, dreams, "reliving" the experience, illusions, hallucinations, and/or dissociative flashbacks. The individual may also experience intense psychological distress when exposed to internal or external cues that symbolize or resemble an aspect of the traumatic event. Second, to meet the criteria, individuals must also demonstrate persistent *avoidance* of stimuli associated with the trauma and numbing of general responsiveness through efforts to avoid thoughts, feelings, conversations, or activities (including people and/or places) associated with the trauma, and have trouble recalling important aspects of the traumatic event.

The individual may show significantly diminished interest or participation in familiar activities, as well as a feeling of detachment from others and a restricted range of expressing emotions and feelings toward others. The individual may also experience a sense of a foreshortened future. Third, the client must experience persistent symptoms of increased *arousal* that were not present before the traumatic event as indicated by two of the following symptoms: difficulty falling or staying asleep, irritability or outbursts of anger, difficulty concentrating, hypervigilance, or an exaggerated startle response. The practitioner should examine the extent to which the symptoms cause significant distress or impairment in social, occupational, or other important areas of functioning.

In the DSM-5, criterion A1, which defines a trauma, is now more explicit about the nature of the event, and the DSM-IV's Criterion A2 (which previously focused on the subjective reaction to the trauma) has been eliminated. In addition to the symptom and behavioral criteria in the DSM-IV (i.e., reexperiencing, avoidance and/or numbing, hyperarousal), the DSM-5 has added a fourth symptom cluster that includes persistent negative alterations in cognitions and mood, effectively supplanting "numbing" as a separate symptom category that also includes signs of irritability and anger.

Given the heterogeneity of the causes and problems associated with PTSD, practitioners should go beyond diagnostic labeling of clients, to see the client's response to a traumatic event in a broader psychosocial context that takes into account both distal and more proximate contributing factors (Follette, Ruzek, & Abueg, 1998; Naugle & Follette, 1998). A recent traumatic event (e.g., rape) can directly affect all domains of a client's psychosocial well-being, including mental status (e.g., depression, anxiety, dissociation), substance abuse, quality of family and other interpersonal relationships, and community functioning (e.g., as student, on the job), among other problems. Nevertheless, clinicians should also be attuned to problems that existed before the traumatic event and recognize that the recent trauma may have compounded problems. For clients with a preexisting depression, substance abuse problem, or poor interpersonal relationships (e.g., subjected to domestic violence), a rape may exacerbate these, with additional psychosocial effects, including shame, humiliation, anger, interpersonal conflict, decreased functioning at work, and anxiety over health risks incurred (e.g., HIV testing). It is reasonable to expect that a client with preexisting psychological difficulties and lack of social supports will have a more difficult time recovering and dealing with a traumatic event than someone who has a better pre-trauma history. Although several preexisting problems may worsen the response to trauma, individuals may need to address those problems before they can make progress in reducing symptoms of PTSD.

Once major areas of well-being are reviewed (e.g., mental status, relationships, daily productivity, health, substance abuse), a detailed functional analysis of day-to-day coping is necessary to identify psychological distress and situational triggers that affect the client's symptoms and associated problems. The functional analysis provides a more focused assessment to tentatively identify causal relationships among factors relevant to the target problem (i.e., anxiety, panic, avoidance, dissociative experiences, and flashbacks). Specifically, these may include automatic negative thoughts and images associated with the traumatic event; physiological arousal in the form of startle or chronic anxiety; and avoidance of specific persons, places, or things that may remind one of the traumatic event. Linking these troubling thoughts, feelings, and behaviors with social and situational antecedents that trigger them can provide a useful and accurate working model for explaining which psychosocial factors affect the client's symptoms and overall sense of well-being. Problems that negatively affect the client's difficulties may include living with an addicted person or being in a violent relationship, dealing with immediate financial stressors (e.g., losing one's home, being evicted), or dealing with serious health problems and having no health insurance. A complete MFS assessment should accomplish the following: define the traumatic event or events that appear to be the primary precipitant of the client's distress along with other contributing problems; identify sequential patterning of everyday psychosocial stressors that potentially exacerbate the client's symptoms; define links among the client's distressing thoughts, feelings, behaviors, and situations that appear to alleviate or worsen distress; and describe systemic interactions between the client and significant others that might have precipitated the problem or might provide a social buffer from the negative effects. Clients can collaborate in this ongoing assessment by engaging in a self-monitoring regimen (e.g., chart or diary) and by identifying those thoughts, feelings, and circumstances in which they feel most vulnerable or most resilient.

Instruments

There are two classes of instruments related to trauma in general: those that measure the *types, frequency, or severity of traumatic events*, and those that measure the *respondent's reaction to traumatic events* (i.e., PTSD symptoms). A well-reviewed example of the former type of instrument is the Traumatic Stress Schedule (TSS) (Norris, 1990; Norris & Riad, 1997). Traumatic events measured by this scale include being a victim of a crime, such as robbery, assault, or rape; loss through homicide, suicide, or accident; personal injury; natural disaster; serving in combat; and experiencing a serious automobile accident. The scale is available in both English and Spanish, and it has shown very good test-retest reliability. Rates of trauma measured with the TSS have been shown to be relatively stable across several samples, and with 10 items, the scale can be easily incorporated into routine screening and assessment protocol.

However, the emphasis in this section is on the second type of scale—scales that measure symptoms associated with post-traumatic stress. Several scales have been developed to measure PTSD symptoms. The Mississippi Scale for Combat-Related PTSD (Keane, Caddell, & Taylor, 1988) contains 35 items that collectively measure reexperiencing, avoidance and numbing, arousal, and guilt and/or suicidality. The Civilian Mississippi Scale for PTSD uses an alternate instruction (i.e., "in the past" rather than "since I was in the military"). Different response categories are used depending on the question, but all are scored on a five-point scale. With a sample of 451 male and 217 female nonveterans, Vreven, Gudanowski, King, and King (1995) demonstrated very good internal consistency (.86), and a multidimensional factor structure but relatively weak relationships with other indicators of PTSD, which suggests that the Civilian Mississippi Scale may be a more general indicator of psychological distress. Authors concluded that evidence for the Civilian Mississippi Scale is somewhat mixed.

The Clinician-Administered PTSD Scale (CAPS-1) was developed at the National Center for PTSD (Blake et al., 1990; Blake et al. 1995). It covers the 17 PTSD symptoms included as DSM-IV diagnostic criteria, as well as others such as the impact of symptoms on social and occupational functioning, improvement in symptoms since previous CAPS-1 assessment, overall response validity, and global PTSD severity. Frequency and severity for each item are measured separately, and responses to each question are behaviorally anchored. The rating scheme allows for both dichotomous scoring (for diagnostic purposes) and continuous measures for evaluation. CAPS-1 shows good evidence of test-retest reliability (.77 to .98), good internal consistency (.85 to .87 for major symptom clusters and .94 for all 17 PTSD items), good sensitivity (.84) and specificity (.95), and good convergent validity in that it correlates well with other known measures of PTSD. A confirmatory factor analysis revealed a four-factor solution of moderately to highly intercorrelated subscales, which suggests that PTSD is more a collection of related symptoms and behaviors than a unified construct and that most of the symptoms are not unique to PTSD (King et al., 1998). An alternative version (CAPS-2) is designed to assess current symptoms over 1 week rather than 1 month (as in CAPS-1). CAPS-2 may be more sensitive to change and may better lend itself to treatment evaluation. The CAPS instrument does require interviewers to be experienced in diagnostic interviewing, especially with PTSD diagnosis, and requires some degree of training in its use. CAPS-1 and CAPS-2 also take about 45 minutes to complete.

The PTSD Symptom Scale (PSS), developed with female rape victims (Foa, Riggs, Dancu, & Rothbaum, 1993), comprises 17 items that correspond to DSM criteria for PTSD. It comes in both a client self-report form (PSS-SR) and practitioner structured-interview form (PSS-I). Coffey, Dansky, Falsetti, Saladin, and Brady (1998) tested the PSS-SR against measures of stressful life events and psychiatric symptoms with a sample of 118 persons admitted for chemical dependency who reported at least one traumatic event in their lives (e.g., rape, other violent assault). Internal consistency of the PSS-SR was excellent, at .95 and .94 for the severity and frequency subscales, respectively. Total score was significantly correlated with the SCL-90 PTSD scale and moderately correlated with the impact-of-events subscales that measure avoidance and intrusion. It also showed good sensitivity (89%) and specificity (65%), using a structured PTSD symptom interview as criteria. The PSS-SR shows good utility as well, in that it takes about 10–15 minutes to complete.

The PSS-I (interview version) provides a total score and subscale scores for reexperiencing, avoidance, and arousal. Items are measured on a four-point (0–3) frequency scale. The PSS-I shows good evidence of concurrent validity given significant correlations with measures of PTSD symptoms and measures of anxiety and depression, and it has demonstrated excellent sensitivity and specificity with the DSM structured-interview schedule (SCID) (Norris & Riad, 1997). The PSS-I was shown to compare favorably to CAPS-1 when administered with 39 persons (combined clinical and community sample), all of whom met PTSD criteria and had experienced traumatic events including sexual assault, other violent assault, or another traumatic event. Results showed good reliability and validity for the PSS-I, demonstrated by good internal consistency (.86 for all 17 items, .70 for reexperiencing, .74 for avoidance, and .65 for arousal), excellent interviewer rater reliability (all subscales well above 90%), and moderate to high subscale correlations with the CAPS-1 (Foa & Tolin, 2000). A copy of the PSS-I is provided here as instrument 9.1. The practitioner should, first, identify the client's "target trauma," and then use all available information to make judgments about the severity of each item.

INSTRUMENT 9.1   The PTSD Symptom Scale Interview (PSS-I)

Ask "In the past two weeks" (if < 2 weeks since trauma, ask "Since the trauma . . ."). Probe all positive responses (e.g., "How often has this been happening?")

0	1	2	3
Not at all	Once per week or less/a little	2 to 4 times per week/somewhat	5 or more times per week/very much

Re-experiencing (need one for DSM criteria): [probe, then quantify]

____   1. Have you had recurrent or intrusive distressing thoughts or recollections about the trauma?

____   2. Have you been having recurrent bad dreams or nightmares about the trauma?

____   3. Have you had the experience of suddenly reliving the trauma, flashbacks of it, acting or feeling as if it were re-occurring?

____   4. Have you been intensely EMOTIONALLY upset when reminded of the trauma (includes anniversary reactions)?

____   5. Have you been having intense PHYSICAL reactions (e.g., sweaty, heart palpitations) when reminded of the trauma?

Avoidance (need three for DSM criteria): [probe, then qualify]

____   6. Have you persistently been making efforts to avoid thoughts or feelings associated with the trauma?

____   7. Have you persistently been making efforts to avoid activities, situations, or places that remind you of the trauma?

____   8. Are there any important aspects about the trauma that you still cannot recall?

____   9. Have you markedly lost interest in free time activities since the trauma?

____   10. Have you felt detached or cut off from others around you since the trauma?

____   11. Have you felt that your ability to experience the whole range of emotions is impaired (e.g., unable to have loving feelings)?

____   12. Have you felt that any future plans or hopes have changed because of the trauma (e.g., no career, marriage, children, or long life)?

Increased Arousal (need two for DSM criteria): [probe then quantify]

____   13. Have you had persistent difficulty falling or staying asleep?

____   14. Have you been continuously irritable or have outbursts of anger?

____   15. Have you had persistent difficulty concentrating?

____   16. Are you overly alert (e.g., check to see who is around you, etc.) since the trauma?

____   17. Have you been jumpier, more easily startled, since the trauma?

PTSD severity is determined by totaling the 17 PSS-I item ratings. Scores range from **0 to 51.**

PTSD diagnosis is determined by counting the number of symptoms endorsed (a rating of 1 or greater) per symptom cluster: one re-experiencing, three avoidance, and two arousal symptoms are needed to meet diagnostic criteria.

SELECTING EFFECTIVE INTERVENTIONS

Because of a lack of controlled studies, little evidence exists regarding the effectiveness of psychodynamic therapies for PTSD (Foa & Meadows, 1997; Foa & Rothbaum, 1998; Kudler, Blank, & Krupnick, 2000; Shalev, Bonne, & Eth, 1996). Part of the difficulty in assessing the efficacy of psychodynamic treatments is that hypotheses about the relationship between the intervention and the outcomes are stated in ways that are difficult to test. Although descriptions of psychodynamic interventions for PTSD include common aspects of effective interventions (e.g., a working alliance, establishing a sense of safety, recounting events and mourning associated losses, regaining coping skills and a sense of connectedness to others), there does not appear to be any demonstrated elements of these interventions that are unique or specific to psychoanalytic practice. Other commonly employed interventions such as family or group methods have produced insufficient data from which to draw even marginally affirmative conclusions about their efficacy.

Overall, the most effective treatments for PTSD (tested mostly with combat and rape-related trauma) appear to be prolonged exposure (PE); eye-movement desensitization and reprocessing (EMDR); and other cognitive-behavioral coping skills, such as stress inoculation training (Emmelkamp, 1994; Foa & Meadows, 1997; Rothbaum, Meadows, Resick, & Foy, 2000; Van Etten & Taylor, 1998; Goodson et al., 2011). Although some form of imaginal (i.e., covert) exposure appears indicated for PTSD, no intervention has demonstrated great success in reducing all the associated symptoms, and particularly the associated physiological arousal. In addition, sensitivity to clients' ability to tolerate intense reimagining of traumatic events must be exercised through careful measuring of their subjective distress as memories are broached. Some clients, such as persons with serious co-occurring mental illnesses, may find the arousal induced through exposure overwhelming, and intervention can focus instead on developing better coping skills. However, many clients do obtain some degree of relief from physiological arousal, intrusive traumatic thoughts, sleep disturbance, anxiety, and fear. Positive effects may be enhanced with supplementary hospitalization, medication, and additional psychosocial interventions (Blake & Sonnenberg, 1998).

Rothbaum et al. (2000) reviewed 12 studies that employed exposure therapy, "all of which found positive results for this treatment with PTSD" (p. 67). Most of the studies met the methodological "gold standard" outlined in Foa and Meadows (1997). These standards include clearly defined target symptoms, sound measures, evaluators blind to treatment conditions, trained assessors, well-defined intervention programs, random assignment to treatment and control groups, and good fidelity to the intervention model. Four studies investigated exposure therapies with veterans of the Vietnam War, two with sexual assault survivors and four with a variety of other trauma-related conditions. The authors concluded that "compelling evidence from many well-controlled trials with a mixed variety of trauma survivors indicates that exposure therapy is quite effective. In fact, no other treatment modality has evidence this strong indicating its efficacy" (Rothbaum et al., 2000, p. 75). In general, exposure therapies have gained the most evidence of effectiveness and ease of use (by practitioners and clients), and they appear to be the most cost-effective methods. However, practitioners should be flexible and ready to use combinations of in vivo (real world) exposure, imaginal exposure, and other stress management techniques (similar to those examined in chapter 8) to help clients reduce symptoms, especially in the early stages of the intervention (Foa & Rothbaum, 1998).

Stress inoculation training (SIT) (Meichenbaum, 1974) has been employed as a component of a successful intervention for PTSD (as well as for other anxiety disorders for both adults and children). The intervention includes an array of well-established behavioral techniques, including psychoeducation, relaxation training (e.g., muscle relaxation, breathing retraining, meditation), covert modeling, and role-playing, among others. With regard to studies employing SIT with PTSD, only two met the methodological "gold standard" (Foa, Rothbaum, Riggs, & Murdock, 1991; Foa et al., 1999), and although both showed good results for SIT, it has been demonstrated to be effective only with rape trauma survivors. Overall, exposure treatments have garnered the most evidence of effectiveness in controlled trials, have been shown to be effective with a wide array of trauma populations, and are typically as effective alone as when combined with other treatments such as SIT (Rothbaum et al., 2000).

Eye-Movement Desensitization and Reprocessing.   Few treatments have spawned as much controversy in recent decades as eye-movement desensitization and reprocessing (EMDR). However, the efficacy of EMDR is supported by a growing number of controlled studies for use with non-war-related PTSD along with exposure therapy and stress inoculation therapy. It has earned a sound degree of credibility and should be considered a viable option for effective intervention with clients suffering from PTSD (Davidson & Parker, 2001; Edmond, Rubin, & Wambach, 1999; Shapiro, 1996, 2002; Van Etten & Taylor, 1998). Evidence supports the conclusion that EMDR is at least as effective as cognitive-behavioral interventions, and some studies have suggested that it is more efficient (i.e., require fewer sessions and related activities). However, more direct comparisons of EMDR and CBT are required before definitive conclusions can be drawn about the relative efficacy of the two interventions.

Although it has been debated whether EMDR is simply another variant on exposure therapy, the science to date has not supported the necessity of the dual attention (e.g., eye movement) component of the intervention. A meta-analysis of 34 controlled studies of EMDR (Davidson & Parker, 2001) revealed that (1) EMDR is an effective intervention (i.e., better than nonspecific therapies) for noncombatants with PTSD but is not superior to other exposure-based therapies; (2) the eye movements, or other alternating techniques, do not account for the effectiveness of the intervention; (3) when training was conducted by EMDR Institute–trained practitioners, the interventions were no more effective than when other practitioners conducted the interventions; and (4) EMDR is no more or less effective with one treatment population or another. Nevertheless, in another meta-analysis of 12 controlled studies, methodologically more rigorous studies of EMDR demonstrated robust effects (Maxfield & Hyer, 2002). However, serious criticisms have been brought to bear on methodologies employed in testing EMDR (Foa & Meadows, 1997) (e.g., lack of standardized measures, blind evaluations, measures of treatment adherence), and little evidence, as noted already, has provided compelling support for the specific efficacy of the signature "eye movement" component of EMDR (Blake & Sonnenberg, 1998; Chemtob, Tolin, van der Kolk, & Pittman, 2000; Davidson & Parker, 2001; Foa & Rothbaum, 1998; Lohr, Lilienfeld, Tolin, & Herbert, 1999; Shapiro, 1996).

An increasing number of comparisons of PE and EMDR have been conducted, with mixed results. Ironson, Freund, Strauss, and Williams (2002), treating rape and crime victims ($n = 22$), and Rogers et al. (1999), treating veterans ($n = 12$), both demonstrated superior results overall for EMDR in very brief, randomly controlled trials after three-session and one-session interventions, respectively. Ironson et al. (2002) also showed a significantly lower dropout rate from treatment for EMDR. However, both studies used relatively small samples and no follow-up measures. Lee, Gavriel, Drummond, Richards, and Greenwald (2002) compared a combination of SIT and PE to EMDR. At 3-month follow-up, the 24 completers all showed clinically significant gains, but those who received EMDR had made significantly greater gains. Contrary to these findings, Devilly and Spence (1999) showed that a combination of PE and CBT coping skills yielded superior outcomes to EMDR in a randomized controlled trial (RCT) with 23 participants who had experienced a traumatic event within 4 weeks of the study and met PTSD criteria. After both groups received 8 weeks of treatment, improvements for the CBT protocol were substantially greater for PTSD symptoms at post-treatment and 3-month follow-up. Taylor et al. (2003) compared PE, EMDR, and relaxation therapy in an RCT with 60 participants (45 treatment completers; dropouts did not differ across treatments) who met PTSD criteria; had suffered for a mean duration of almost 9 years; and had experienced a variety of trauma, including sexual assault, motor vehicle accidents, and witnessing a homicide, among others. Co-occurring disorders included depression (42%), panic disorder (31%), and social anxiety disorder (12%). Although all three interventions showed positive results in reducing PTSD symptoms, PE showed significantly greater reduction in both reexperiencing and avoidance symptoms, demonstrated a more rapid reduction of avoidance symptoms, and showed a greater reduction in clients who no longer met the criteria for PTSD. The authors added that their study met Foa and Meadow's (1997) gold standard, and to the best of their knowledge, it was the first study using EMDR to do so.

Overall, these studies met reasonable criteria for sound experimental design and used standardized measures of good reliability and utility. Although lively debate and further research is likely to continue in comparing matters of theory, change process, and the cost-effectiveness of PE and EMDR, evidence-based practitioners can take heart that there are at least two effective interventions available that are likely to provide clinically significant relief for clients suffering from PTSD. As research continues, some optimal integration or client-treatment matching protocol may emerge.

Recent Findings for Treating Combat PTSD.   The first randomized controlled trial of cognitive-processing therapy (CPT) compared this new variation of CBT with treatment as usual (i.e., an eclectic array of services including some CBT) with 59 combat veterans (Forbes et al., 2012). Cognitive-processing therapy is a 12-session cognitive-behavioral approach that combines psychoeducation, cognitive therapy (linking thoughts and feelings, Socratic questioning, and challenging dysfunctional thoughts), coping skills (e.g., enhancing safety measures, trust, intimacy), journaling the traumatic narrative (and reviewing and rewriting the narrative), and relapse prevention efforts. Results were superior to treatment as usual even at 3-month follow-up, and results generalized to other comorbid conditions, including depression, anxiety, and relationship functioning.

Behavioral activation therapy (BAT) (described in chapter 6) has also shown some promise for traumatized (including severely injured) veterans. BAT involves getting one's "life back on track" by mobilizing individuals through reconnecting with their peer group, getting physically active, focusing on vocational and education goals, and engaging in other reinforcing and pleasurable activities (for case study, see Turner & Jacupcak, 2010).

In their review of 24 controlled trials including more than 1,700 combat veterans, Goodson et al. (2011) found medium effect sizes for a range of exposure treatments (including prolonged exposure, systematic desensitization, and EMDR). Those veterans who received exposure treatment did better than two-thirds of those who do not. However, their analysis included a mix of both controlled trials and open trials. In their 20-year review of female veterans' trauma exposure Middleton and Craig (2012) reported that about 15% of female veterans had been exposed to unwanted or coerced sexual contact, 11% had experienced combat exposure, and almost 50% had experienced the death or disfigurement of others in service. In their review of treatments for women veterans, they found variations of CBT to be moderately effective, including prolonged exposure (Rauch et al., 2009; Schnurr et al., 2007) and safety seeking, which involves psychoeducation and coping skills (Desai, Harpaz-Rotem, Najavits, & Rosenheck, 2008). Given the harmful impact that combat-related trauma can have on the veteran's intimate relationships, more emphasis on research related to couples problems have been called for (Monson, Taft, & Fredman, 2009).

Recent Findings for Treating Sexual Assault.   Given the high rates of sexual assault in women and associated comorbid symptoms, a sexual assault history should be routinely screened in mental health settings. Prolonged exposure, stress inoculation training, cognitive-processing therapy, and EMDR have all been shown, alone or in combination, to be helpful with the effects associated with sexual assault (Butterfield & Becker, 2002; Vickerman & Margolin, 2009). Nevertheless, about one-third of women remain relatively unimproved after cognitive-behavioral treatments. And there is some evidence based on results from a controlled trial with 98 women (Resick, Nishith, Weaver, Astin, & Feuer, 2002) that cognitive-processing therapy might be more effective than prolonged exposure at resolving guilt feelings related to having been raped (Nishith, Nixon, & Resick, 2005). Ten-year follow-ups to the original study (Resick et al., 2002) showed very good stability of clinical gains for both prolonged exposure and cognitive processing therapy.

Change Processes in Exposure Interventions.   Social-cognitive theorists account for the effectiveness of exposure therapies by suggesting that covert or in vivo exposure promotes symptom reduction by allowing patients to realize that, contrary to their mistaken beliefs, (1) being in objectively safe situations that reminds them of the trauma is not dangerous; (2) remembering the trauma is not equivalent to experiencing it again; (3) anxiety does not remain indefinitely in the presence of feared situations or memories but rather decreases even without avoidance or escape; and (4) experiencing anxiety or PTSD symptoms does not lead to loss of control (Foa et al., 2006; Foa & Meadows, 1997; Foa & Rothbaum, 1998; Rothbaum et al., 2000). Cognitive change occurs not by direct cognitive intervention alone but also through behavior change.

Beck and associates (Beck, 1976; Beck, Rush, Shaw, & Emery, 1979; Oei & Shuttlewood, 1996) have provided much of the foundation for modern theories of PTSD and change process. They have theorized that individuals' interpretation of events is linked causally to the emotional response (cognition is primary), and in turn, individuals' negative thoughts (e.g., negative schema, negative automatic thoughts, information-processing errors) contribute to the persistence of negative emotional states, including both depression and anxiety. Subsequent dysfunctional behaviors are also likely to become part of this problematic interplay of thoughts, feelings, and emotions. The theoretical change process of cognitive restructuring involves targeting the dysfunctional thoughts and changing them through disconfirmation experiences (i.e., behavioral experiences that will successfully challenge negative or dysfunctional beliefs). These disconfirmation experiences theoretically work through exposure, habituation and extinction, increased self-efficacy, reduction in automatic negative thoughts, or some combination of these processes.

Emotional-processing models also reflect the increasingly cognitive emphasis in contemporary behavioral theories. Fear responses are conceptualized in emotional-processing theories as neural structures that contain memories and other cognitive components related to the anxiety, and they engender emotional, physiological, and behavioral responses (Foa & Kozak, 1998; Rachman, 1980; Rogers & Silver, 2002). The goal of treatment in the context of emotional-processing theory is to activate the fear structure, provide alternative corrective information, and attempt to disconnect stimuli from responses—in a sense, to dismantle the fear structure and change-related cognitions, physiological responses, and behaviors. In the long run, the client needs to learn and practice coping skills to maintain the more adaptive cognitive structures to prevent the reemergence of the original fear structure. The core intervention theoretically posited to cause changes in these fear structures is exposure to the feared mental images, and preferably prolonged exposure until the habituation, extinction, and dismantling of the fear structure occur.

Key findings in research on exposure therapies continue to support the view that the exposure must be directly focused on an unwavering elicitation of the feared image in the mind (or, as with other problems, in vivo) without letting the client use mental or behavioral avoidance mechanisms. However, in EMDR, exposure to the feared stimulus is not constant and prolonged; it is intermittent, with periods of attention to other matters. Despite this key difference, results appear to be comparable to more classic exposure-based therapies. However, Rogers and Silver (2002) support the view that, despite some incongruities with current emotional-processing theories, EMDR is more akin to an emotional reprocessing intervention (recalling traumatic memories and correcting distorted cognitions associated with them) than to simple exposure. Critical review of specific and nonspecific effects of EMDR strongly suggests that EMDR may be effective for the reasons that other cognitive-behavioral treatments are effective: exposure to the feared mental images. Although the change processes for EMDR may be different from those purported for PE, some maintain that there is no evidence to substantiate any unique or specific effect to the eye movement (or similar) alternating techniques (Lohr et al., 1999). Obviously, there are unanswered theoretical questions and competing explanations concerning why exposure therapies work, but it is also unclear why EMDR is effective (Cahill, Carrigan, & Frueh, 1999). Thus, conclusions on the identification and nature of specific change processes for these effective interventions remain tentative at this time (Tarrier, Sommerfield, Pilgrim, & Faragher, 2000).

Exemplar Study: Comparing Interventions Specifically Applied to Rape-Related PTSD

Two key studies (Foa et al., 1999; Foa et al., 1991) illustrate the supporting controlled research on exposure treatments and other cognitive-behavioral methods for PTSD, focusing specifically on the treatment of rape-related trauma. Foa et al. (1991) compared the effectiveness of three interventions— prolonged imaginal exposure (PE), stress inoculation training (SIT), and supportive counseling (SC)—for PTSD with a waiting-list control group (WL). The researchers designed the interventions so there would be a minimum of overlap, and they expected that both PE and SIT would result in better outcomes than SC and WL. Forty-five women who had been raped 3 months before the study were randomly assigned to the four groups, and measures were taken at assessment, post-treatment and follow-up (approximately 3 months). Treatment was provided by female therapists in nine 90-minute sessions for about 5 weeks. In addition to a thorough assessment and evaluation of PTSD symptoms, additional valid self-report measures were included to measure symptoms associated with the aftermath of rape, depression, and anxiety. Interventions were performed by a combination of psychologists and clinical social workers hired and trained for the project. Interventions were monitored through supervision to enhance fidelity to the respective intervention models. In all three active treatments, the first two sessions included assessment and explanation of the rationale for the treatment. For the PE group, the additional seven sessions included the following:

- Participants would repeat this scene several times over the course of 60 minutes in imaginal exposure. (i.e., reliving the rape scene in the mind's eye, as vividly as possible and describing it aloud in the present tense).

- Participants took a recording of the session home to listen to it once daily.

- Additional in vivo exposure to feared situations (judged to be safe) were added on the basis of participant-therapist discussions.

- The SIT group employed an array of standard cognitive-behavioral coping skills, including breathing exercises, muscle relaxation, thought stopping to counter obsessional thinking, self-talk, imaginal modeling, and role-playing.

- Practitioners in the SC group would provide standard unconditional support and facilitate general problem-solving techniques.

- WL participants were contacted periodically for 5 weeks and then randomly assigned to the PE or SIT group.

Of the 66 individuals offered services, 11 refused treatment and 10 dropped out, but attrition was comparable across treatment groups. Results demonstrated that both PE and SIT were effective interventions in the short run, and PE showed superior results at 3-month follow-up. Both the SC and the WL groups showed some reduction in arousal symptoms only. The investigators suggested that coping skills approaches in SIT provided more immediate relief from symptoms, but PE (which produces high levels of arousal initially as clients imaginally reenacted the rape experience) showed more durable gains at follow-up. The authors suggested that the data supported an eclectic blend of both approaches.

In a later study, Foa et al. (1999) examined whether combining PE and SIT would be more effective than each treatment alone. Sixty-nine women who had been sexually assaulted and 27 who were victims of nonsexual assault all met PTSD criteria. Extensive assessment included diagnostic interview and ratings of PTSD symptoms and social adjustment. Self-report measures included standardized anxiety and depression scales. Participants were randomly assigned to the following groups: combined PE and SIT, PE alone, SIT alone, and WL group (10 participants). Measures were taken at assessment and at 3, 6, and 12 months. Interventions were conducted by seven doctoral-level female psychologists supervised by Foa and Dancu. The intervention consisted of nine, twice-weekly sessions over 5 weeks, and the first two sessions were 120 minutes in duration. Interventions provided were very similar to those described in Foa et al. (1991). Although all active treatments showed good results, PE was clearly the superior treatment. The investigators suggested that because of lower demand on the participant to engage in a simpler intervention (PE), fewer participants who received PE dropped out of treatment.

Descriptions of Effective Interventions.   What follows is a brief overview of the essential components of both EMDR and cognitive-behavioral therapy for victims of rape trauma. Notwithstanding debates about the essential nature of the eye movement (and similar) techniques, EMDR is considered a viable treatment for PTSD. The intervention requires that the client identify a number of details related to the traumatic memory, identify affective and physiological response elements, define the negative self-representation triggered by the traumatic experience, and identify an alternate positive self-representation (Chemtob et al., 2000; Shapiro, 2002). To implement the basic elements of EMDR, one should do the following:

- Develop a sound working relationship with the client.
- Provide psychoeducation about trauma, the rationale for the treatment.
- Focus on trauma-specific memories and associated reminders.
- Teach coping skills to deal with trauma-related material as it emerges.
- Conduct a focused assessment of the trauma-related memory, including all associated negative and positive cognitions, associated emotions, and physical sensations, along with self-anchored scales (1) to rate the validity of the positive cognition (Validity of Cognition scale) and (2) to measure distress at regular intervals with the Subjective Unit of Distress Scale (SUDS).

- Instruct the client to hold the upsetting image in mind along with associated negative thoughts and bodily images connected with the traumatic memory, and instruct the client to visually track the therapist's finger, which moves side to side about a foot in front of the client's face. After 20 or so repetitions, the client is asked to release the memory; take a deep breath; and report any cognitive, physical, or emotional changes. The practitioner may adjust verbal instructions depending on the client's response.

- After subjective distress has been reduced to an acceptable level, the exercise begins again; however, this time the client works with the practitioner to install the positive image (using the VOC scale), and additional coping skills may be rehearsed to deal with future situations.

- After each session, care is taken to help the client recover from experiencing the traumatic images. The intervention is repeated and continuous reevaluation is conducted until the client meets his or her respective goals.

Shapiro (2002) points out that dual stimulation (of which the eye-movement component of treatment is but one form) is only one of several techniques that make up EMDR. She claims that the intervention is not merely a desensitization method but also "includes the elicitation of positive affects, evoked insights, belief alterations, and behavioral shifts" (Shapiro, 2002, p. 1). The core of the technique, however, does not focus on behavior indexes but rather is the "reprocessing of maladaptive information upon which experientially forged psychopathology is assumed to be based" (Shapiro, 2002, p. 2).

PE protocol for sexual assault victims has been clearly delineated as well. A more thorough, detailed examination is available in Foa and Rothbaum (1998). Although it is understood that a fair amount of judgment is required in the choice of respective technique, Foa and Rothbaum (1998) recommend three basic treatment configurations based on their work and on exhaustive reviews of the available controlled research: (1) use of prolonged exposure (PE) alone, given its relative ease of use and lower demand on both client and practitioner; (2) PE and cognitive restructuring (CR) in combination for clients who have persistent ruminative or obsessive thoughts associated with disabling anger, shame, or guilt; and (3) PE and SIT for clients who need more work to deal with disabling anxiety symptoms before they can benefit more fully from PE. It is understood, regardless of the specific treatment regimen, that a thorough diagnostic and MFS assessment is required before the intervention can commence. Practitioners should spend a good amount of time connecting with the client, gaining trust, providing some initial psychoeducation about the nature of the problem and the intervention, and (as with all evidence-based practices) projecting expertise and confidence that they can help the client. Practitioners should be empathic and as active as necessary, and intervention should be relatively brief, with adjustments to length as needed. In general, these treatments share some common elements: a thorough assessment, psychoeducation, and use of taped treatment sessions at home by the client. Specifically, an intervention that emphasizes PE includes both in vivo and imaginal exposure along with breathing exercises. PE may also be used with cognitive restructuring. The combination of PE and SIT incorporates PE skills and a variety of coping skills, including thought stopping, guided self-dialogue, deep muscle relaxation, covert modeling (imaginal rehearsal), and role-playing with the practitioner.

Specific components of interventions are described in the following lists (see also Foa & Rothbaum, 1998). Modifications to the intervention plan depend on a number of things, including what the client is willing to try, how debilitated the client is (does the client need covert exposure as a warm-up before engaging in vivo?), and the detection of other co-occurring problems.

Cognitive Restructuring

- Identify the source of the emotional distress and the specific emotional reaction (e.g., guilt, shame).
- Identify the troubling thought that preceded the distress and underlying beliefs (through Socratic questioning).
- Help the client challenge the belief by examining evidence to support or refute it; help the client understand the dysfunctional or irrational nature of the belief and then change it.
- Thought-stopping techniques may be helpful; clients say "stop" aloud when the thought intrudes, say "stop" and simultaneously use some image to distract their thoughts, or say "stop" silently to themselves.
- Assign homework to practice techniques.

Progressive Muscle Relaxation

- Proceed through all muscle groups.
- Select and associate a cue word or phrase to instill relaxation as needed during the day (e.g., "calm," "easy does it," "I'm doing fine");
- Teach cue-controlled relaxation by identifying a source of physical tension (e.g., neck) and using it as a stimulus to relax (e.g., breathe deeply, exhale slowly).

Imaginal Exposure

- Have the client close his or her eyes and narrate the traumatic event vividly in the present tense.
- Gradually increase the intensity of the imaginal event (with practitioner's direct questioning and encouragement after one or two visits).
- Take SUDS ratings every 10 minutes or so, and leave time for the client to "come down" and talk about the experience of reliving the traumatic event.
- The practitioner should be available by phone between visits.

Role-Play

- Give the client the opportunity to practice a new skill or improve on one (e.g., being more assertive at work).
- Collaboratively develop a troubling scenario for the client that he or she wants to work on, then act it out, changing roles.
- Give encouragement, feedback, and make constructive suggestions for improvement as needed.
- Through covert modeling, clients can rehearse similar activities by "practicing" in their mind's eye at home; by doing so, they can prepare to engage in live exposure experiences by seeing themselves coping with troubling situations successfully.

In Vivo Exposure

- Explain the procedure thoroughly.
- Describe the use of SUDS.
- Construct a hierarchy of feared situations with SUDS ratings for each situation.
- Develop homework assignments based on the hierarchy.
- Have client place him- or herself in a moderately anxiety-producing situation (e.g., shopping center parking lot) until anxiety reduces by at least half.
- Have client record SUDS ratings before and after each exposure.

The design of exposure-based therapies can be as creative as the situation warrants. Clients typically provide their own narrative accounts in the development of hierarchical scenarios, and the therapist may embellish them to increase therapeutic effect. Treatments may vary in duration of exposure per treatment event, and length may vary. Clients can practice these techniques at home, and they can be facilitated by significant others who have been trained to collaborate in the intervention.

Interventions for Clients with PTSD and Co-occurring Substance Abuse.   Given that CBT methods have been shown to be effective for both PTSD and substance abuse, combinations of skills can be used to address both problems (Najavits, Weiss, & Liese, 1996). An evidence-based eclectic approach could include, for example, (1) establishing a working relationship; (2) psychoeducation on the reciprocal links between substance abuse and PTSD symptoms; (3) the need for brief medical intervention, perhaps including detoxification; (4) self-monitoring of substance using "triggers" (which may be related to trauma symptoms); (5) teaching coping skills to avoid relapse related to reexperiencing trauma symptoms or substance use; (6) using graduated covert exposure treatments to reduce trauma-related

distress; and (7) facilitating increased social supports for long-term maintenance of gains. These methods can be readily incorporated into a comprehensive intervention plan for co-occurring PTSD and substance abuse.

Emerging Approaches.   Mindfulness, a Zen Buddhist approach to
meditation that focuses on the connections between thoughts and emotions
in a nonjudgmental manner in the present moment, has shown some promising results (Owens, Walter, Chard, & Davis, 2011). As with other areas of
mental health, there is a growing interest in using "telehealth" (e.g., telephone, Internet video conferencing) to provide treatments to veterans who
live in outlying areas or who have physical limitations. On the basis of preliminary data, various approaches have been used in this manner with
promising results, including behavioral activation (Strachan, Gros, Ruggiero,
Lejuez, & Acierno, 2012), prolonged exposure (Strachan, Gros, Yuen et al.,
2012), and mindfulness therapy (Niles et al., 2012).

Medications for PTSD.   Evidence has accumulated that although antidepressants and benzodiazepines can provide some temporary relief from
symptoms of PTSD, they do not provide long-term relief and are not considered first-line treatment (Bastien, 2010; Foa & Rothbaum, 1998; Shalev, 2009;
Shalev et al., 1996).

TREATMENT PLANNING AND EVALUATION
CASE STUDY: JULIA

Julia is an 18-year-old college freshman who left home to attend a
medium-size, out-of-state university.
She had always been an excellent
student but was somewhat anxious
socially and was looking forward, she
said, to "meeting people right
away—I want to get out of my shell a
bit." She met other young women in
her dormitory and seemed to hit it
off with them right away. She was
feeling right at home in no time. She
called her parents, with whom she
had always been close (she was the
only child), and told them how
happy she was that she had decided
to attend the university.

Julia's first semester passed
uneventfully, and she continued to
do well in school and enjoyed the
company of her female companions.
She was enthusiastic about picking
up where she left off after returning
to school for the spring semester.
About halfway through the semester,
just before spring break began, she
attended a party at a local fraternity
house. There was considerable
drinking and rumored use of illicit
drugs going on, but aside from a
drink or two, Julia had little experience abusing alcohol or other drugs.
Her best friend had wanted to
attend the party because her boy-

friend was one of the fraternity members. At one point, they became separated, and Julia couldn't find her friend. "Oh well," she mused, "I need to work on getting over my shyness anyway. Here's my chance." She found herself in one room with three young men who seemed like they were having a good time. They invited her over, and as they talked, they seemed to have a lot in common. One of them was from her home state. They talked for some time, and Julia agreed to have some of the fruit punch they were serving.

With the loud music, talking, and the unexpectedly strong punch going to her head, she did not notice the time pass or that almost everyone had left the party. One of the guys got up and put a video on the television and closed the door. They invited Julia over to sit on a big couch in front of the TV. At that point, Julia assumed they were going to watch a movie, and since she was having such a good time, she figured, "Why not?" It became apparent in a hurry that the movie was a pornographic film. The guys laughed and cheered, and Julia, though surprised at first, was intoxicated and intrigued herself at that point. It did not become apparent to her that the young men in the room were going to try to encourage her to participate in sexual activity herself until one of them reached over and kissed her full on the mouth and cupped his hands around her breast. After that, things spun out of her control.

In recounting the following events, Julia was somewhat vague, only recalling images and feelings as she recollected what had happened that night several months past. She recalled being pushed down on the couch and her clothes being pulled off by one of the young men. Before she could even react, one of the men was on top of her with his fingers inside her vagina. Another had his mouth on her breasts. She was then quickly pulled up by her legs, and the first young man penetrated her forcefully. She recalled the penetration being somewhat painful, but then simply remembered being terrified and feeling completely out of control. She was raped again by the other male. In hindsight she remembered the two young men who raped her, and she vaguely recalled the name of the young man who had been in the room earlier. She remembered crying, and the two men sitting her up at one point and giving her another drink of punch. She was completely confused at that moment, since they seemed to be acting very nicely to her.

The next thing Julia remembered was waking up on a couch in the front of her own dormitory in the rain. Her clothes were disheveled and felt like they didn't fit right. She went into her dorm and found her girlfriend. She started crying, and when she was able to communicate some of what had happened, her girlfriend took her to the infirmary. She received a medical exam and was referred to the university counseling department for an appointment later that day. She reported the incident to the campus police and later gave a statement to state police. The third young man at the scene was also contacted during the investigation. Although he later reported that he thought things might get out of hand, he was not actually there when the rape occurred. The two others were later suspended from the university on the basis of Julia's complaint and the police investigation, but the criminal trial would not take place for some time. The two men and their parents retained an attorney who maintained that Julia had been a willing participant in the sexual activity. She became additionally distressed because of that assertion.

With rape crisis counseling and the support of her family and friends, Julia was able to finish the semester, but she felt like she was on "automatic pilot." She felt some vindication that two of the men had been suspended, but she continued to feel somewhat humiliated, depressed, and guilty about what had occurred. She left for home that summer with the hope that she would be able to put it behind her. During the summer, however, she became increasingly depressed and withdrawn, and thought about the event in frightening images in her waking hours, and sometimes in her dreams. At her job as a server at a local restaurant, she was having trouble keeping her mind on her work, sometimes mixing up customers' orders. The manager of the restaurant had to talk to her on a

number of occasions. She was asked out on dates by some of the male patrons but automatically refused. She often felt angry, bordering on hostile, in response to these inquiries. Although she kept busy reading during the day and working in the evenings, her social life was minimal, and her parents queried her about spending so much time alone, but they didn't push—they were happy that she seemed to be content to spend much of her time at home. Occasionally, her parents would hear her sobbing in her room, sometimes late at night, but when they asked, she said she was all right. When her dad asked if the assault was still bothering her, she responded that she thought about it sometimes, but that she would be all right. Her parents did not press her further to discuss it, and she did not bring it up.

As September approached, she seemed to her parents to be very anxious and irritable. They asked some more, but Julia began to say that she wasn't sure this was the right school for her anymore. As her annual medical exam for school was overdue anyway, she saw her physician, who noticed that she seemed depressed and anxious. She told Julia that she might still not be over the effects of the rape, and for the first time, Julia heard the words *traumatic stress* used in the context of her own experience. Her doctor told her that she would call the university and talk to Amy, a social worker on the staff of the university counseling center. The physician encouraged her not to avoid school but to go back (it would start in a few weeks), and she said that she should see someone to help her deal with her fears, anger, and depression. She prescribed an antidepressant to help "take the edge off some symptoms" but insisted that Julia follow through, and perhaps talk to the social worker on the phone, as soon as possible. After the initial phone call with that social worker, Julia felt somewhat better. She was not harboring these feelings alone, and she had a name to put to what she was experiencing: post-traumatic stress disorder.

MFS Assessment: Defining Problems and Goals

Although Julia had spoken to the social worker, Amy, at length over the phone, she conducted a full assessment with her during the first visit. Although some of the sleep disturbance had abated, her mental status exam revealed a young woman who was considerably depressed, had some suicidal ideation during the summer, avoided social situations and found herself very frightened (e.g., lightheaded, heart pounding) at times, for example, if she found herself in a corner in the library when a group of male students approached. She often jumped if someone quietly walked up behind her or if she suddenly encountered someone coming around the corner in the laundry room. She ruminated about how she must have done something herself: "Did I set myself up? I mean, how could I have been so stupid?" Although her parents were very supportive, she thought she sensed her dad's disapproval at her having put herself in that situation. She wondered if he blamed her too. As she wondered about these things, Julia found it hard to concentrate on her work. Her mind wandered, and she found herself reliving the experience (or what she recalled of it) in her mind's eye, as if watching the same movie over and over again. She also found herself getting impatient with her new roommate, and she became testy over things that normally didn't bother her. She felt more possessive about her things and "her space" in her room, and she felt the need to have more control over her surroundings. She was afraid she would alienate her new roommate, and end up feeling even more isolated.

Her relationship with her best friend (who had brought her to the fraternity party) became somewhat strained. Although they discussed it, Julia could not shake the feeling that her friend also blamed her. Although Julia was struggling through the day preoccupied and with low energy, she pushed herself to keep up with her work but had little time for socializing. She was in good health and avoided any use of alcohol since she was taking medication. As she discussed with her social worker, the medication was not going to make her problems go away. She was going to have to cope with the feelings better, deal with what happened to her once and for all. She felt angry that those young men had taken away her joy of living and were "keeping me from enjoying my time at college."

The social worker suggested they take a more focused or functional view to capture how the troubling thoughts, feelings, and behaviors were affecting her in different situations. Julia seemed to be mostly concerned about her feelings of depression, feeling detached from people but also wanting to feel comfortable and not afraid of talking with men again. The social worker agreed that these three specific areas not only were all related but also were a good place to begin. On a daily basis, it appeared that one problem affected another: Julia awakened everyday feeling somewhat pessimistic and even had feelings of dread about accomplishing her work and dealing with people. She thought about how stupid others must think she was to have been taken advantage of. Perhaps some people who knew about the incident even blamed her for what happened, since those two guys still had friends around campus. These thoughts added to her negative mood and then seemed to precipitate a need to avoid others and "just stick to my work," since that, at least, was something she felt she had some control over and could feel good about. However, her avoidance of other people seemed to continue to cause further rumination, and she had become increasingly withdrawn even from her good friend (who was also feeling guilty and somewhat responsible for leaving her alone the night of the party).

The social worker and Julia decided that these three problems—feelings of guilt and harsh criticism of herself, depression, and anxious avoidance of other people—seemed to be interrelated and stuck in a self-defeating cycle, making her feel helpless and more isolated. The seemingly automatic negative thoughts she had about herself added to her depression and exacerbated her anxiety in social situations. The more she avoided them, the more anxious she became and the more demoralized she felt, saying, "I feel more afraid of people now than before I came to college. I thought I'd be over this by now!" Her frustration at continuing to feel out of control enhanced her motivation to work on her problems. She wanted to feel better and not be afraid of people, particularly men, any longer. Her social worker, whom she now felt she could trust and who she felt understood her, agreed that these were good treatment goals.

Selecting and Designing the Intervention: Defining Strategies and Objectives

After an extensive assessment, Amy outlined a tentative intervention plan to discuss with Julia, which is laid out here.

Psychoeducation.   The social worker explained to Julia that much of the distress she was experiencing looked very much like the problems and symptoms associated with post-traumatic stress disorder. Although the social worker didn't like using these labels, her depression, anxiety, guilt, startle reaction, and avoidance, among other problems, often occurred in people after they had experienced a horrible event, such as rape. Julia even had trouble admitting that she had been raped or even saying, "I was raped."

Amy explained that the feelings could linger for months or even years in people, interrupting their lives in many ways. She explained that her feelings were quite common and normal in someone who was raped, but that because she had a supportive family and some real psychological strengths, she had a very good chance of learning to deal with them and gain some control over her life again. When she said "control," Julia began to cry, saying, "That's what they did to me. They took my life away from me, my fun, my hopes in college to meet people, and I want it back."

Cognitive Restructuring.   Together they examined Julia's negative thinking about the event and about everyday events as well. She did feel somewhat to blame, and she asked herself repeatedly: "Why did I go to that party? What was I doing alone in a frat house with those boys? Why was I drinking? Why did they pick me?" As they both examined her own thoughts, feelings, and behaviors, the social worker Julia asked in response: "Well, why shouldn't you have gone? What's wrong with going to a party? What was wrong with staying and talking with two or three male students? They seemed to be nice, didn't they? How could you have known that two of them were going to rape you? How were you supposed to have known? Should you never be alone with men again? Did you know how much alcohol they had snuck into your drink? Were there any other drugs in your drink? How do you know?" The more they collaboratively explored the situation, it became clear to Julia that she had been focusing mostly on blaming herself these past few months rather than examining the culpability of the two men. She and Amy began to catalog challenges to these intrusive and troubling thoughts. The more Julia discussed them out loud, the more clearly she saw how hard she had been on herself since the incident and how many factors related to the event had been out of her control.

As this line of inquiry proceeded, the social worker and Julia began to develop a daily diary (in chart form) so that she could note some of these more troubling thoughts and her challenges to them. She was also to note the time of day and any important situational details. She said she found this easy to do, because she was able to create one on her portable computer, which she had with her most of the time anyway. She discovered that the rape had hurt her deeply because she really thought that those guys had been interested in her, not just in using her. She discussed these thoughts and feelings with her social worker, who encouraged her to continue to explore this on her own as she kept her diary. She continued to note her challenges to negative automatic thoughts for the next few weeks, although she sometimes felt like giving up, since the thoughts were often very distressing. Specific treatment objectives began to emerge: daily identification of self-critical thoughts, feelings, and situations, and then identification of a counterargument to them.

Imaginal Exposure (with Anxiety Management Skills and SUDS). It became evident that, although they were discussing the events of the night Julia was raped, Julia had not really confronted the rape and examined the details. Although there was some ambiguity about the event, she was remembering more as time passed. The social worker explained to Julia the rationale for imaginal exposure, a graduated process by which she could learn to recount the rape experience in detail and, at the same time, learn to control and diminish her anxiety. She would have to reexperience some of the intense thoughts and feelings that had occurred to develop some sense of mastery over her feelings and to diminish the negative influence they were having on her life. Additional intervention objectives would be to learn controlled breathing, practice SUDS, and engage in daily imaginal exposure until she reduced her anxiety to a score of 3 or less.

After Julia agreed, Amy explained to her how to develop and use SUDS and to signal when she was becoming too anxious (if she reached a score of 7). Together they discussed a detailed hierarchy of events that transpired before, during, and after the rape. As they discussed the hierarchy, it became clear that Julia was becoming increasingly anxious, and the social worker was careful to gauge her anxiety to help her client get a feel for how the process worked. The social worker also taught Julia some deep breathing methods and encouraged her to breathe deeply and steadily, hold the image of what was occurring during the particular scene in her mind, and not mentally turn away from it. If she wanted to, Julia could stop the exposure intervention any time she wanted. She was in control of the pacing of events, and Amy was there to guide her through it.

Over the next few visits they worked their way up the hierarchy, and Julia become increasingly composed and less emotionally distressed and anxious as she slowly recounted each detail of the rape. She also conducted the exposure in private every day for at least half an hour, as agreed with the therapist. Over the next 3 weeks, she was beginning to feel "stronger," that the rape no longer "had a hold over me," she said.

Role-Play and In Vivo Practice for Social Anxiety.   As they talked, it became clearer to Julia that what she really wanted to work on directly was talking to other people, including guys, and eventually being comfortable alone with other males. As she had already learned anxiety management techniques (e.g., breath control, gauging her anxiety) when using imaginal exposure for the sexual assault, she was able to readily apply them in vivo when meeting people and engaging them in conversation. The social worker reviewed with her the deep breathing exercises and also encouraged Julia to couple deep breathing with her cognitive challenges to her "old tapes" that people would not like her or would reject her outright. She also took it upon herself to begin charting (i.e., self-monitoring) thoughts about initiating conversations with others, particularly men, to examine what she had been thinking and what was making her afraid. She discovered that she had always been shy because she was afraid that they would not want to talk to her or would give her the brush-off.

Together Julia and Amy discussed social situations in which Julia would want to approach another person, and they arranged these situations hierarchically. First a young woman about her age in the college quad, the cafeteria, then at a party (increasingly personal settings). Then she would use the same hierarchy with young male students. A series of opening questions or topics of conversations were added to the proposed in vivo scenarios. Her objective was to make at least one social overture every day. She continued to keep her chart-diary and reported good successes in initiating conversations over the following 2 weeks. She was beginning to feel relaxed and reported that much of the depression that had been burdening her for months was beginning to lift. She was beginning to feel like she was starting to have fun again, and she was finally beginning to feel like she was engaged in college life.

Although one might want to attribute the good results to the intervention itself, other events can also contribute to clinical improvement. One evening when Julia was working in the library, she went downstairs into a lounge to get a soda and a snack from the vending machines. When she turned the corner, she encountered the third young man who had been at the scene just before the rape. They had not spoken together since the incident. He became very flustered. But Julia took a deep breath as she saw he became very anxious and said, "Hello, Todd, how are you?" Todd immediately began to apologize for not contacting Julia since the incident. He said he felt horrible and could not think about what to say to her, that he was very sorry. As she spoke with him, she felt a mixture of anger and compassion for him. He had not hurt her, but he had walked away when he felt things were becoming uncomfortable. At one point during the conversation she suggested to him that perhaps he should talk to someone about what happened, but that he should not blame himself. At that point, his eyes welled up, and he wiped his face with his shirtsleeve. He said that he did blame himself and that he had felt like a coward since the rape. He had cut off relations with his fraternity buddies, who wouldn't have anything to do with him anymore. She later recounted in her diary how confident she felt speaking with him and how she wished she could have done more to comfort him.

Selecting Scales and Creating Indexes to Monitor and Evaluate Client Progress

Fortunately, Julia was quite comfortable keeping a chart-diary, and her willingness to engage in self-monitoring provided an ideal opportunity for personal evaluation. Self-anchored indexes were used to measure depression, the number of times she initiated conversations, and her level of anxiety when thinking about the rape incident, among other things. The 17-item PTSD scale provided an ideal overall composite measure of PTSD related distress symptoms.

TABLE 9.1 The Client Service Plan

Problems	Goals	Objectives (samples)	Interventions	Assessment and evaluation tools
Problems and symptoms associated with PTSD as a result of sexual assault:	Reduce symptoms to a minimum	Use of chart-diary to self-monitor situational-specific negative thoughts, and response to them	Combined prolonged exposure and cognitive-behavioral coping skills	PTSD 17-item scale for overall symptoms (consider use of standardized depression scale)
Depression: guilt, self-blame, tearful, harsh self-criticism, trouble concentrating, some suicidal ideation	Reduce depression and related symptoms to pre-trauma level		Psychoeducation, cognitive restructuring, anxiety management, imaginal and in vivo exposure	Self-anchored indexes to examine degree of suicidal ideation
Anxiety, edginess, startles easily; troubled by mental images of rape	Reduce excessive anxiety, sense of control over images, develop anxiety management skills	Learn breath control, use of SUDS, and practice daily; develop hierarchy of rape incident details; practice imaginal exposure daily for 30 minutes	Cognitive therapy and restructuring to examine negative critical thoughts and develop refutations	Develop chart to monitor and examine patterns of thoughts, feelings, behaviors, and situations related to daily episodes of distress
Social anxiety, avoidance of social situations, especially encountering men alone	Improve social assertiveness and confidence in social situations	Develop hierarchy of social encounters; practice in vivo exposure daily	Use of anxiety management skills with imaginal exposure to gain control over arousal associated with mental images of rape	Use SUDS to measure anxiety during imaginal or in vivo exposure exercises when coping with symptoms related to recollecting rape or dealing with social anxiety
			Use of anxiety management skills in conjunction with in vivo exposure to practice social skills and reduce social anxiety in social encounters	
			Case management:	
			• Consultation with MD regarding antidepressants	
			• Referral to student organization dealing with rape on campus; peer consultation	

SUMMARY OF CHAPTER

Persons suffering from the effects of traumatic events present serious clinical challenges to even the most experienced clinical social workers. There are a number of valid assessment instruments to accompany a thorough qualitative assessment. Cognitive-behavioral skills and exposure-based therapies are the most thoroughly researched approaches, and they have been shown to be effective with PTSD. EMDR is also considered a viable option for treating PTSD. Although medication can be helpful in ameliorating some of the more troubling symptoms of PTSD, it is not considered optimal care without effective psychosocial methods as well. Further research and practice innovation, however, is needed, since a sizable proportion of people diagnosed with PTSD do not respond well to current treatments or relapse over time.

CHAPTER 10

ANTISOCIAL AND BORDERLINE
PERSONALITY DISORDERS

Among the most challenging, intriguing, and often frustrating clients whom social work practitioners encounter are those referred to as "personality disordered." Often enduring from childhood or adolescence, the problems of these clients can confound even the most attentive and skilled practitioners. The causes of these chronic disorders of thinking, affect, behavior, and relating to others include inherited temperament, childhood abuse, role modeling of significant adults, maladaptive coping in pathogenic environments (e.g., growing up in a violent home or crime-ridden neighborhood), and any combination of these. Psychoanalytic theories, based primarily on correlational studies and case analyses, have not provided explanations that have stood up to longitudinal research. Aside from research on psychopathy, personality trait theories (e.g., Cattell, 1965; Eysenck, 1960; Goldberg, 1993; Millon & Davis, 1995) have found relatively little utility in mainstream mental health services. Practitioners, by necessity, usually refer to diagnostic descriptions that define *personality disorder* as "an enduring pattern of inner experience and behavior that deviates markedly from the expectations of the individual's culture" in ways that include cognition, expression of emotion, interpersonal relationships, and impulse control (APA, 2013, p. 647). The DSM-5 criteria do not differ significantly from those of the DSM-IV. Nevertheless, there remains considerable controversy regarding the reliability and essential validity of personality disorder diagnostic categories, with growing consensus that diagnostic criteria for personality disorders particularly need to be overhauled from a categorical approach to a dimensional one (Crits-Christoph, 1998; Hare & Hart, 1995; Johnston & Alozie, 2001; Skodol, Bender, Morey, & Oldham, 2013; Tryer, 1995; Widiger & Corbitt, 1995). Still, this chapter focuses on antisocial personality disorder and borderline personality disorder, which are more commonly diagnosed among the personality disorders, are clinically challenging conditions to address in treatment, and have solid records of accompanying research that support their diagnostic reliability and relatively well-developed bodies of treatment literature.

310

Although not all individuals who run afoul of the law have a personality disorder, many individuals with personality disorders do so, and they are sometimes treated in the informal framework referred to as forensic social work (Odiah & Wright, 2000; Roberts & Brownell, 1999), an outgrowth of forensic psychiatry (Jager, 1999). In this professional context, social workers might be involved in writing reports or providing expert testimony on the determination of, for example, a self-mutilating and drug-addicted young woman's fitness to stand trial, a violent husband's likelihood of repeating further domestic violence, or an adolescent sex offender's chances of relapsing in the community. Social workers are also required to be knowledgeable about informed consent, confidentiality, and what constitutes professional malpractice, and they may be called on to advocate for clients involved in the criminal justice system. They often provide primary interventions for clients as well.

Personality disorders also tend to co-occur with other psychosocial problems, including anxiety, depression, severe mental illnesses, interpersonal and community problems, and substance use disorders, among others. Some have argued that two of the more common personality disorders, antisocial personality disorder (APD) and borderline personality disorder (BPD), share a common etiology and behavioral characteristics (e.g., manipulativeness, suicidality, substance abuse) and may be variations of the same disorder, with men and women disproportionately diagnosed with APD and BPD, respectively (Paris, 1997a). Despite the challenge in caring for these clients, a body of outcome research for treating APD and BPD has begun to emerge. Given that APD and BPD are two of the more commonly treated personality disorders in human service environments, they are the focus of this chapter.

ASSESSMENT: ANTISOCIAL PERSONALITY DISORDER

Background Data

In general, there are two somewhat-overlapping approaches to defining persons referred to generally as antisocial: the DSM diagnostic description of antisocial personality disorder (APD) and a personality type described as psychopathic. First, the DSM-5 (APA, 2013) criteria for a diagnosis of antisocial personality disorder emphasize a pervasive pattern of disregard and violation of the rights and safety of others (e.g., unlawful acts, chronic deceitfulness, impulsiveness, violence), chronic irresponsibility with regard to work or financial commitments, and lack of remorse when having hurt or otherwise infringed on others' rights. Although not synonymous with criminality, there is considerable overlap among persons, mostly male, who run afoul of the law and meet criteria for APD. Second, the concept of psychopathy, originating with Cleckley's (1941) classic book *The Mask of Sanity*, has been operationalized as the Psychopathy Check List (PCL-r) (Hare et al., 1990). Psychopathy emphasizes two major factors: first, selfishness, callousness, and remorseless use of others; second, a chronically unstable and antisocial lifestyle, which are elements that overlap with a diagnosis of APD (Coid & Ullrich, 2010; Hare & Neumann, 2010; Skeem & Cooke, 2010). Thus, psychopathy constitutes a narrower construct in the framework of antisocial personalities, and it should be screened for separately and in addition to diagnosing APD.

Prevalence rates for APD are estimated at 1–3% in the general population—3% in males and 1% in females—and rates in clinical samples have ranged from 3% to 30%. Kessler et al. (1994) estimated lifetime DSM-III-R diagnoses of APD at 5.8% for men, 1.2% for women, and 3.5% for the general adult population. Although persons diagnosed with APD are not always involved in criminal activity, about 75% of persons in prison are considered to have antisocial personalities. Over time, from the teen years until around age 40, the criminal activities of persons later diagnosed with APD are relatively constant, but these begin to decline after age 40 and virtually cease beyond age 50 (Hare, McPherson, & Forth, 1988; Kessler et al., 1994; Robins, 1966). Those diagnosed with APD are also less likely to have completed high school and show much lower incomes overall than the general population (Kessler et al., 1994). During the time when such persons are criminally active, they tend to be criminal generalists, not specialists, engaging in various criminal activities, such as drug use, domestic violence, robbery, and rape (Simon, 1997).

There is also a high rate of co-occurrence of APD and substance abuse. About 70% of persons diagnosed as APD abuse alcohol, and 33% or more abuse other drugs (Regier et al., 1990). Sexual excesses, substance abuse, child abuse and neglect, and domestic violence are often part of their behavioral repertoire. In addition, APD might also co-occur with a range of other disorders, including those related to anxiety, depression, somatization, and gambling, as well as borderline, narcissistic, and other personality disorders.

Persons who fit the criteria for APD should also be carefully screened for having perpetrated domestic violence. A sizable proportion of domestic batterers are also sociopathic and/or antisocial (Gleason, 1997). As chapter 11 covers more thoroughly, Bograd and Mederos (1999) have noted several risk factors for domestic violence that mirror characteristic behaviors of persons with APD, including unresolved substance abuse; a history of two or more acts of domestic violence or sexual assault; and a history of violent criminal acts, including violation of restraining order, previous use of weapons, ongoing threats of violence, and obsessive behaviors toward a partner (e.g., intense jealousy, stalking, harassing, bizarre forms of violence marked by sadism, an attempt to depersonalize the victim).

Given the high rates of disorders that co-occur with APD, practitioners are likely to confront these problems in a variety of combinations (Hotaling & Sugarman, 1986). For example, Brown, Werk, Caplan, and Seraganian (1999) found that almost 67% of 53 adult males (age 23–61) from three domestic violence treatment facilities had a current substance abuse disorder, and almost all of them met criteria for a lifetime diagnosis of a substance use disorder. More than 50% had a polysubstance use problem as well. Severity of substance abuse was directly related to severity of psychiatric symptoms, including acts of verbal and physical violence. Although this was a small clinical sample, the group was screened for willingness to participate in treatment and to take responsibility for their actions. One might infer that this group represents a less psychopathic and antisocial sample than other groups. Dutton, Bodnarchuck, Kropp, Hart, and Ogloff (1997) demonstrated in a combined group of both mandated and voluntary men in domestic violence treatment (about 75% of whom had a substance abuse disorder) that those with personality disorders (including both BPD and APD) were more likely to perpetrate violent acts after treatment. Male batterers have also been found to show greater levels of personality disorder traits commensurate with APD and BPD (Dutton, Starzomski, & Ryan, 1996; Gleason, 1997), and excessive drinking seems to exacerbate their level of abusiveness (Hamberger & Hastings, 1991; Hastings & Hamberger, 1988). Although not all batterers meet criteria for psychopathy, APD, or other personality disorders, there is likely to be a subgroup of batterers who do, and these individuals are more likely to be less responsive to treatment and more likely to repeat their offenses (Huss & Langhinrichsen-Rohling, 2000).

The co-occurrence of conduct disorder, APD, and substance abuse has also been shown to be present among persons diagnosed with severe mental illnesses (e.g., schizophrenia, major affective disorders) (Mueser et al., 1999) and among depressed outpatients (Carter, Joyce, Mulder, Sullivan, & Luty, 1999). Those with co-occurring substance abuse disorders and APD are more likely to engage in at-risk HIV behaviors, including unprotected sex and IV drug use (Kelly & Petry, 2000). In a study by Compton et al. (2000), 44% of substance-abusing clients admitted to a drug treatment facility in the Midwest were diagnosed with APD, with no significant differences found between white and African American clients. However, rates of APD among men significantly exceeded the rate for women, as would be expected in the general population as well. Surveys of incarcerated individuals (a group with a disproportionately high rate of persons with APD) also show higher rates of persons with drinking disorders (Wright, 1993). Among alcoholic incarcerated offenders, men also show greater degrees of psychopathy than women do (Walsh, 1997).

Theories on the Cause of APD and Psychopathy

Both genetic and environmental factors appear to increase the risks of developing APD and substance abuse among offspring of persons with APD. Antisocial personality and psychopathy appear to have a substantial genetic component, a conclusion supported by various research designs (Daghestani,

Dinwiddie, & Hardy, 2001; Ferguson, 2010). Low arousal levels in such persons seem to lead to sensation seeking and possibly increased tendencies toward criminal behavior. There also appear to be differences in brain structures, significant social learning influences (e.g., criminality in parents), and neurodevelopmental deficiencies (Vien & Beech, 2006). Having a first-degree relative with APD may increase the likelihood of manifesting these signs and symptoms by a factor of five (Kaplan & Sadock, 1998).

Children with a history of abuse and neglect, conduct disorder, and attention-deficit/hyperactivity disorder (ADHD) appear to have an increased likelihood of later being diagnosed with APD. On the basis of data from the nationally representative National Epidemiologic Survey on Alcohol and Related Conditions (NESARC), adult antisocial personality disorder is more strongly predicted by childhood onset of conduct disorder than by adolescent onset (Goldstein, Grant, Ruan, Smith, & Saha, 2006). Childhood abuse and neglect also appear to contribute to adult antisocial behavior and psychopathology traits associated with male sexual offenders (Graham, Kimonis, Wasserman, & Kline, 2011). In addition, many of the traits of psychopathy are evident not just in the mainstream antisocial and criminal population but also in so-called white-collar criminals: lack of empathy for others; lack of remorse for taking advantage of others; and premeditated exploitation of others in business, political activities, or other professional roles. Risk of recidivism and repeat violent behavior is very high in psychopaths, including sexual offenders (Hare & Neumann, 2009; Vien & Beech, 2006).

Men are more frequently diagnosed with APD than are women. Studies of adoptees have demonstrated that for both men and women, genetic predisposition for petty criminality is well established, but the risks are moderated by gender relative to social status, institutionalization during childhood, and being raised in an urban setting, among other social influences (Sigvardsson, Cloninger, Bohman, & von Knorring, 1982). Biological research on the causes of aggressiveness and impulsivity often associated with antisocial and criminal behavior has demonstrated a negative correlation between serotonin levels and aggressive behavior. Although the influences may be genetic in origin, environmental influences can exacerbate or mitigate them (Lane & Cherek, 2000).

APD and substance abuse and dependence are both partly genetically transmitted, and there appears to be some interaction between these two sources of genetic influence in some persons (Van den Bree, Svikis, & Pickens, 2000). A child born to at least one mentally ill parent and placed in an adoptive home soon after birth is more likely to show an increased risk of antisocial behavior if that child has a biological parent who was alcoholic or antisocial, or if the child has experienced adverse environmental stressors (Cadoret & Cain, 1980). Electroencephalogram (EEG) and neuropsychological testing with young males have shown greater frontal lobe activity in persons with childhood conduct problems and antisocial personality indicators (Deckel, Hesselbrock, & Bauer, 1996). Such findings suggest a common biological substrate among antisocial personality, substance abuse, and biological reinforcement processes.

Biological processes, however, probably interact with environmental liabilities and risks to reveal a portrait of a disorder that is determined by multiple factors interacting over time (Martens, 2000). The preponderance of evidence suggests that those diagnosed with APD are of low socioeconomic status (Kessler et al., 1994; Kohn, Dohrenwend, & Mirotznik, 1998), which suggests at least some environmental factors contributing to the development of antisocial behavior. The interactive and reciprocally reinforcing effects of biological and environmental factors may result in cognitive structures (i.e., negative schema, dysfunctional beliefs, expectancies, thought processes) related to problems with self-regulation, impulsivity, emotional dysregulation, and aggression. However, although childhood risk factors in general have been known for some time to be good predictors of APD in later adulthood, genetic and environmental influences are difficult to disentangle (Rutter, 1997).

One longitudinal study begun in South London in the early 1960s (Farrington, 2000) examined a sample of white boys age 8–10 and in primary school. Survey response rates in (roughly) 10-year intervals over 30 years remained high at each measurement point (>90%). Results revealed that males identified to have a diagnosis of APD at age 18 were more than three times as likely to be arrested between age 21 and 40. The most important predictive factors for future diagnosis of APD and criminal convictions included having a parent who was convicted of a crime, having a large family, having low intelligence, having a disrupted family life, and having been raised by a young single mother. Another longitudinal study of a representative population in New Zealand (Moffitt, Caspi, Dickson, Silva, & Stanton, 1996) followed boys from age 3 to 18. A battery of measures was taken every 2 years for more than 1,000 subjects. Although it was the rare boy who did not engage in some kind of antisocial behavior at some point (< 6%), the children manifesting behavioral disorders by age 3 were much more likely to develop long-term patterns of conduct disordered and, later, antisocial behavior. Late-onset problems, usually precipitated around puberty, were more transitory and less likely to persist. The problems associated with early onset were primarily associated with a range of early learning and neurological problems, including "cognitive, language and motor deficits, comorbid attention deficit and hyperactivity, extreme aggressiveness, reading difficulties, impulsivity, adverse family social contexts, and poor parenting" (Moffit et al., 1996, p. 419). Similar conclusions have been drawn for populations of adult offenders (e.g., Vitelli, 1997). In follow-up with adults with APD, long-term outcomes appear to be best predicted by the initial severity of APD symptoms (Black, Monahan, Baumgard, & Bell, 1997). Given the proclivity for early-onset conduct-disordered children to engage in violence, as one would expect, adults with APD are also more likely to engage in a range of violent acts, especially those with higher indicated levels of psychopathy, a personality trait marked by "callousness, impulsivity, egocentricity, grandiosity, irresponsibility, lack of empathy, guilt, or remorse" (Hare, 1999, p. 185). These traits are especially dangerous and troubling when identified in violent sex offenders, persons who are virtually nonresponsive to treatment (Hare, 1999).

Fishbein (2000) notes that there has been a lack of interdisciplinary research on antisocial personality, and this lack of communication among various disciplines has been to the detriment of understanding the interactions among biological, psychological, social, and criminal justice processes.

> Studies indicate that vulnerability to antisocial behavior is partially a function of genetic and biological makeup that manifests during childhood as particular behavioral, cognitive, and psychological traits (e.g., impulsivity, attention deficits, or conduct disorder) and are measurable in physiological and biochemical responses. . . . Instead of viewing evidence from these various disciplines as independent sources of biological and social dysfunction, sources of evidence should be seen as a continuous, developmental sequence of interacting factors. That is, basic genetic or acquired biological traits contribute to measurable biochemical and physiological conditions that predispose individuals to a constellation of particular behavioral and temperamental outcomes. . . . Biological vulnerabilities are, in turn, influenced by socioenvironmental factors that act as triggers, offering one explanation for the disproportionate number of residents prone to antisocial behavior in lower income neighborhoods where triggers are more prevalent. Put simply, abnormalities in certain neurobiological mechanisms heighten sensitivity to adverse environmental circumstances, increasing the risk for an antisocial outcome (Fishbein, 2000, pp. 1–3).

Widom and Toch (2000) describe a transactional view that incorporates the contributions of temperament, early attachment and loss, parental guidance and modeling (e.g., influence of parenting skills, proper disciplining, adequate nurturance, parent's own modeling of self-control and pro-social behaviors), and environmental contingencies (e.g., intermittent rewards and punishments for committing crimes). All these influences can theoretically be examined within a transactional and ecological framework where cognitive, behavioral, physiological, interpersonal, and environmental factors interact over time and across situations to increase or decrease the likelihood of antisocial behavior (Martens, 2000; Rutter, 1997). An interdisciplinary view of the causes, course, and consequences of APD would likely lead to more integrated understanding and more effective interventions and policies rather than approaches that are largely driven by political ideology.

Key Elements of MFS Assessment

The DSM-5 (APA, 2013) diagnosis of antisocial personality disorder includes four basic criteria. First, evidence of a pervasive pattern of disregard and violation of the rights of others occurring since age 15, as indicated by at least three of the following: repeated unlawful acts, chronic deceitfulness, impulsiveness, hyperaggression (e.g., fights, assaults), reckless disregard for the safety of self or others, consistent irresponsibility with regard to work or financial commitments, and lack of remorse when having hurt others or otherwise infringed on others' rights. Second, the individual should be at least age 18 (although the diagnosis can be applied to minors). Third, there is evidence of the onset of conduct disorder before age 15. Last, antisocial behavior did not occur exclusively during a period of major mental illness. Again, practitioners should be aware of problems with reliability in applying this diagnosis as well as of a high rate of co-occurrence with other problems and diagnoses (Cunningham & Reidy, 1998). A more complete diagnostic picture should include elements that emphasize psychopathy in addition to criminal behavior. The Psychopathy Check List (Hare et al., 1990) is reviewed in more detail later in this chapter.

Social workers are likely to encounter many clients who demonstrate some of the behaviors described in the current diagnostic criteria. Key considerations include the chronicity and pervasiveness of antisocial behaviors, psychopathic attitudes regarding the rights of others, and the context in which the behaviors occur. A multidimensional assessment should draw heavily on a historical timeline to substantiate these facts across various domains of living (e.g., work, relationships) and to avoid diagnosing in response to a client's recent presentation in one particular situation. Regardless of whether a client clearly meets the criteria for APD, it is important to examine potential co-occurring problems and disorders (e.g., other mental illnesses, substance abuse). Given the predictive value of childhood and adolescent risk factors, a thorough history is in order, particularly evidence of behavioral problems (e.g., school disruption, truancy, fighting, stealing, run-ins with the law, substance abuse) from childhood through adolescence (Daghestani et al., 2001). Consistency should be sought and congruence with current problems in interpersonal relations, job disruption, and evidence of dangerousness to others (e.g., domestic and community violence).

Assessing risk for violent behavior is one of the more challenging and critical goals of an MFS assessment of persons diagnosed with APD. Research findings support a range of risk factors that contribute to an assessment of violent behaviors and the reasons for it. These factors include temperament, childhood history of abuse and neglect, history of conduct disorder, hyperactivity, family conflict, witnessing or being a victim of domestic violence, growing up in a violent community, previous involvement with alcohol and other drugs, and criminal involvement. Given the heterogeneity of risk factors and the unique combination of factors that contribute to the proclivity toward violence, Howells and Day (2002) emphasized the critical importance of conducting a functional analysis of factors that may precipitate aggressive or violent behavior. This detailed sequential analysis of proximate factors that maintain the cycle of violence in the individual's life is essential for focusing intervention planning. Gendreau (1996b) argues for the benefits of combining both population risk data (i.e., actuarial and risk assessment data) with a client-specific functional analysis of day-to-day behavior. A systemic perspective on influences and consequences of the client's behavior with respect to others is critical. This assessment needs to be linked to intervention planning that targets specific problems and needs of the client (e.g., criminal and antisocial attitudes, impulse control, substance abuse, use of leisure time, social relationships, work).

Risk assessment research strongly suggests that *predicting* violent behavior in an individual client is a difficult task for even the most seasoned and scrupulous practitioner. Prediction is not an activity that lends itself to "clinical intuition." There is a difference between prediction based on cross-sectional risk assessment research and predicting *if, when, and under which circumstances an individual is likely to become violent*. Nevertheless, practitioners are called on in clinical and legal settings to make their best estimates of risk. In recent years, some progress has been made in this regard. A study conducted with 799 violent offenders discharged from a maximum security therapeutic community (Rice & Harris, 1995) demonstrated that the following factors (measured with the Violence Risk Appraisal Guide, VRAG) were predictive of further violence: a positive score on the PCL-r, separation from parents before age 16, having never been married, having had behavior problems in elementary school, having failed on prior conditional release, having had a property offense history, having a history of alcohol abuse, and having a diagnosis of APD. Those less likely to be violent included those with a diagnosis of schizophrenia and older clients. On the basis of these factors, the investigators accurately predicted 75% of the cases that failed (which were 43% of those released). Cunningham and Reidy (1999) suggest that practitioners improve their estimates by using a number of evidence-based strategies, including referencing population base rates and clinical sample base rates, clearly defining the severity of the behavior in question, and considering contextual factors (e.g., drug use at the time of the violent event). They also recommend that practitioners avoid the following practices: relying on illusory correlations (i.e., things often appear to be related when they are not), putting too much confidence in one's own clinical impressions (which tend to selectively and disproportionately focus on previous "correct" guesses while forgetting "wrong" ones), using projective testing for diagnostic purposes, and avoiding an overemphasis on a DSM-5 APD diagnosis. Monahan (1996), a well-known authority on the challenges of predicting violence, suggests that future research should (1) disaggregate dangerousness into risk factors, including type and degree of harm, and likelihood of its occurrence; (2) employ a multidimensional approach to assessment and risk evaluation; (3) measure harm on a severity continuum and employ multiple measures; (4) estimate risk over time and across different contexts; (5) use known statistical data to predict harm from known risk factors; and (6) use representative samples in research and include research goals that both assess and manage risk. There may be serious consequences to the use of well-intended treatments not supported by evidence-based assessment of violence risk. For example, Rice (1997) notes that early enthusiastic efforts to treat psychopathic violent offenders demonstrated not only failure but also an actual increase in the chances of future violence. She concludes that there are currently no psychological treatments that significantly reduce risk of reoffending.

Practitioners must also be aware of the pernicious influences of racial stereotypes in making evidence-based assessments. In addition to the tendency to give harsher sentences to racial minorities for drug offenses, African Americans are also likely to be sentenced more harshly because of the perception that they are less likely than whites to reduce criminal behavior with age. Given the evidence that antisocial behavior tends to remit during middle age, it is reasonable to hypothesize that criminal sentencing for older citizens should show a tendency to be less severe for many drug-related crimes. Johnston and Alozie (2001) conducted a multivariate analysis of about 5,700 arrested persons in Arizona and found that although white defendants began to receive more lenient sentences at around age 52, those shorter sentences were not extended as often to blacks and Hispanics. Not only are many persons of color more likely to be sentenced and more harshly; this bias continues even when offenders have reached the declining years of their criminal careers.

Instruments

Given the risk of violence by clients diagnosed with APD, the predictive validity of assessment for the purpose of making decisions regarding court-ordered interventions or conditional release to the community are of critical importance. Thus, an instrument that can accurately reduce the likelihood of making the wrong decision about releasing criminals back into the community would be particularly valuable. Evidence consistently supports the use of the Psychopathy Check List (revised) (PCL-r) (Hare, 1991; Hare et al., 1990) as a valuable aid in making these decisions. Bodholdt, Richards, and Gacono (2000) discuss the historical and conceptual roots of the PCL-r and note that its items are similar to the profile of the psychopathic personality conceptualized by Cleckley (1941) in *The Mask of Sanity*. These traits include superficial charm, absence of thought disorders, lack of anxiety, untruthfulness, lack of remorse, failure to learn by experience, lack of insight, and lack of any life plan, among others. In contrast, the current criteria of the DSM-5 focus almost exclusively on criminal behavior and are understood to be based more on a model of social deviance (Bodholdt et al., 2000). Other items on the PCL-r overlap with some of these indicators as well.

A series of studies with several forensic samples has supported the reliability and validity of the PCL-r. Hart, Kropp, and Hare (1988) used the PCL-r with a cutoff of 34 (to identify the high-risk group) with more than 200 inmates who were released back to the community. The data clearly demonstrated that the PCL-r improved predictive ability of practitioners beyond the statistical contributions of age, criminal history, and release type. Those who scored high performed very poorly following conditional release from prison by participating in more frequent and more serious criminal activities and by failing to develop a stable, noncriminal lifestyle.

Although earlier factor analyses of the PCL showed several factors measuring psychopathy, many of the samples were of inadequate size, and there were other problems in interpretation of the analyses. Harpur, Hakstian, and Hare (1988) examined the factor structure of the PCL using exploratory factor analysis (EFA) from five samples of male prison inmates (mostly white) and found good congruence of factor structure across different samples, with good to excellent interrater reliabilities and internal consistencies. The best solution appeared to contain two factors: selfishness, callousness, and remorseless exploitation of others (factor 1) and a chronically unstable and antisocial lifestyle (factor 2). In multiple samples of prison and forensic inmates, Harpur et al. (1989) demonstrated very good internal consistencies (mid-.80s) for factors 1 and 2. The PCL-r also demonstrated good concurrent and discriminant validity in that factor 1, as expected, correlated significantly and more highly than factor 2 with standardized measures of anxiety (−.20 and −.26) and narcissism (.45), whereas factor 2 correlated with a diagnosis of APD (.55, .61, .66) in three separate samples. In a similar study with 80 forensic patients, Hart and Hare (1989) showed good concurrent validity between the PCL and APD, but good discrimination between the PCL and Axis I diagnoses. Studies with similar populations provided equally strong support (Forth, Hart, & Hare, 1990). A study of a Swedish forensic population (violent offenders with schizophrenia) demonstrated that the PCL-r was the strongest predictor of recidivism (using a cut score of 26) than several other factors over the course of a follow-up of more than 4 years (Tengstrom, Grann, Langstrom, & Kulgren, 2000). The PCL-r has also been shown to be reliable and valid for adolescents, including African American youths (Brandt, Kennedy, Patrick, & Curtin, 1997), and for both African American and white adult inmates (Cooke & Michie, 1997). One rigorous validation of the PCL-r using item-response theory (IRT) showed strong support for the factor structure, reliability, and validity of the subscales (Cooke & Michie, 1997). Item-response theory focuses on the performance of each individual item as it relates to the overall factor it is theoretically expected to measure.

The PCL-r (Hare et al., 1990) is a 20-item instrument, with each item scaled to indicate the degree to which the trait or behavior applies to the respondent (as reported in Hart & Hare, 1989) (0 = definitely does not apply, 1 = may or may not apply, and 2 = definitely applies). The PCL-r is a proprietary instrument. It cannot be used without purchasing the instrument and the training materials, and it requires expertise in forensic evaluations. Nevertheless, the PCL-r items may be a helpful guide for detecting psychopathy in nonforensic settings as well. The 20 items (reported in Hare et al., 1990) are as follows:

1. Glibness/superficial charm
2. Grandiose sense of self-worth
3. Need for stimulation
4. Pathological lying
5. Conning/manipulative
6. Lack of remorse or guilt
7. Shallow affect
8. Callous/lack of empathy
9. Parasitic lifestyle
10. Poor behavioral controls
11. Promiscuous sexual behavior
12. Early behavior problems
13. Lack of realistic goals
14. Impulsivity
15. Irresponsibility
16. Failure to accept responsibility
17. Many short-term relationships
18. Juvenile delinquency
19. Revocation of conditional release
20. Criminal versatility

Factor 1 (selfishness, callousness and remorseless use of others) is scored by summing items 1, 2, 4, 5, 6, 7, 8, 16. Factor 2 (chronically unstable and antisocial lifestyle) is scored by summing items 3, 9, 10, 12, 13, 14, 15, 18, and 19.

In summary, reviews of the PCL-r (Bodholdt et al., 2000; Cunningham & Reidy, 1998) have demonstrated that it has very good internal consistency, interrater and test-retest reliability, and good construct and criterion validity, and it has been normed with prison inmates and forensic psychiatric patients. The PCL-r is also highly intercorrelated with the brief PCL screening version, but the screening version is not intended as a substitute for the full PCL-r when used as part of a comprehensive assessment. Again, these items can be a basis for raising concern about the presence of psychopathy in a client, but the PCL-r should be administered by persons with special training and experience in working with correctional or forensic populations. Despite the strengths of the PCL-r, it has limitations and should be used in the context of a broad MFS assessment that includes known base rates for recidivism (Freedman, 2001; Serin & Brown, 2000).

SELECTING EFFECTIVE INTERVENTIONS

Persons who meet the criteria for APD may be encountered in any number of treatment environments, including outpatient or inpatient mental health and substance abuse treatment settings, court-ordered treatment, specialized forensic settings, and prison-connected therapeutic communities among others (Daghestani et al., 2001). Simon (1998) points out that 70% of inmates meet criteria for APD, but most individuals under correctional supervision are not in prison. Many of these persons are on probation or parole, and many are not adequately supervised in the community. Reviewers of the current research literature generally agree on the importance of employing well-controlled studies to justify the use of interventions with offenders, given the risks to the community.

Overall, traditional treatment approaches, including psychodynamic psychotherapies and therapeutic community approaches for antisocial clients, have not yielded substantially positive results (Daghestani et al., 2001; Gendreau, 1996a, 1996b; Lipsey & Wilson, 1993; Simon, 1998), and some cognitive-behavioral programs have yielded moderately positive outcomes (Hare & Neumann, 2009; Vien & Beech, 2006). However, these outcomes should be tempered by overall reviews that have shown not very promising results for adults with clinically significant psychopathy scores (Salekin, Worley, & Grimes, 2010).

Despite the lukewarm results of behaviorally oriented programs, prison-based therapeutic communities (TCs) have become increasingly accepted by the criminal justice system and the public, particularly for nonviolent drug offenders. Some results have shown some reduction in drug use, crime, and recidivism, as well as an increase in pro-social behaviors (Wexler, 1995). The TC movement began with Synanon in the late 1950s, as an alternative to Alcoholics Anonymous and conventional therapeutic treatments geared more toward middle-class patients. The Synanon movement has evolved, but the basic concept lives on in well-known programs such as Daytop Village and Phoenix House, residential programs modeled on the TC concept. According to Wexler (1995), TCs have several core components: the overarching principles of self-help, a hierarchical structure and strict rules of conduct in the residence, emotionally charged group encounters, and educational seminars. Lengths of stay of at least a year are strongly recommended. Implementing TCs in prison has become an increasingly popular approach, and Wexler (1995) recommends that they be developed with the following "central features": a clear and consistent treatment philosophy; an empathic and safe environment; recruitment of committed staff; clear rules of conduct; employment of ex-offenders and ex-addicts; use of peer role models and peer pressure; use of relapse prevention strategies; continuity of care from residential to aftercare in the community; and "maintenance of treatment program integrity, autonomy, flexibility, and openness" (p. 63). Attention to TC programming has increasingly focused on problems that co-occur with substance abuse.

Although drug-court treatment diversionary programs have shown some positive outcomes, most evaluation studies have suffered from methodological weaknesses, including high attrition rates from the original sample (and possibly oversampling less dysfunctional and more motivated inmates), lack of random assignment, and lack of long-term follow-up. In one nonrandomized, quasi-experimental evaluation, Vito and Tewksbury (1998) compared drug-court graduates of a diversionary program in Kentucky to those who chose not to participate in the program. Both African American and white participants who successfully completed the yearlong treatment program showed substantively lower reconviction rates than did those who did not participate. The others speculated that reasons for the apparent success were good mutual support between the criminal justice and treatment communities, adequate screening of potential candidates for the program, implementation of evaluation technologies, and reliable systems for monitoring drug abuse (e.g., urine testing).

In evaluating three similar prison-based drug rehabilitation programs in Delaware, New York, and Texas, Knight, Hiller, and Simpson (1999) noted that all three demonstrated that prisoners who received the standard prison drug program plus an aftercare follow-up program showed less relapse than those who received just the standard prison program, who in turn showed less recidivism that those who received no treatment. Nevertheless, even the best-performing groups showed considerable rates of recidivism overall. However, the authors point out that a key problem in making comparisons across studies is the lack of consistency in measuring relapse (i.e., how to detect and measure drug use), recidivism (i.e., rearrest or reincarceration), and a lack of broad-based psychosocial measures to account for other outcomes.

Exemplar Study: Staged Approaches to Prison Aftercare Programs

The trend in the offender literature has begun to support the emphasis of staged long-term approaches to intervention with inmates in drug therapeutic communities (TCs) while in prison and then after release. A noted program in Delaware (Inciardi, Martin, Butzin, Hooper, & Harrison, 1997; Martin, Butzin, & Inciardi, 1995) evaluated combinations of a three-stage model against a comparison group (who received no TC in-prison treatment but managed to obtain some treatment after release). Stage 1 included an in-prison TC intervention (focused on reducing criminal attitudes, engendering pro-social attitudes, and planning a drug-free life). In stage 2, inmates worked at jobs in the community during the day but returned to prison or an associated facility at night. In stage 3, work release was completed, and the offender was placed on parole. The offender attended counseling sessions, periodically returned to the prison TC for "booster" sessions, and kept in touch with a counselor. Of the 448 mostly male African American study participants (of

1,002 originally interviewed), 77% of those who completed the three-stage program were not arrested at 18-month follow-up, compared to 57% who received the two-stage program, 43% who received prison TC only, and 46% of the comparison group. Similar results were found for clean urine analysis (47% for three-stage intervention, 31% for two-stage intervention, 22% for TC only, and 16% for the comparison group). In general, the more treatment received, the better the results. However, findings must be tempered by the lack of clear analysis of the effects of nonrandom assignment and the sample's high rate of attrition. Nevertheless, the project shows that a stepped approach is feasible and may have considerable promise if participants are closely supervised.

Although in-prison TCs with aftercare are a positive development in the field of correctional rehabilitation, confidence in the outcome research must be tempered given the methodological weaknesses in the evaluation designs. In addition to sample attrition and a lack of random assignment to treatment conditions, there is also the overarching problem of how and why many of these persons come to be imprisoned in the first place. The "war on drugs" has resulted in disproportionate imprisonment of African Americans and Hispanics, and these groups also receive longer sentences than whites do. Even the best psychosocial interventions will not mitigate the essential injustice of this disproportionate imprisonment of persons who are poor and racial minorities.

Sex Offender Outcome Studies

Sex offenders are considered a subset of persons who may otherwise fit criteria for APD and, some more specifically, psychopathy. Their calculated exploitation of children and lack of remorse qualify them as criminally antisocial and possibly psychopathic. Methodologically sound outcome studies on sexual offenders including those with psychopathic traits are still scarce. Nevertheless, some believe that cognitive-behavioral approaches that focus on self-regulation show some promise in adults (Abracen, Looman, & Langton, 2008; Losel & Schmucker, 2005). Maletzky and Steinhouser (2002) reported on the treatments of more than 7,000 clients over 25 years. Various cognitive-behavioral therapy (CBT) methods were employed, but the elements of treatment packages were not consistent. Nevertheless, *less severe clients* (i.e., exhibitionists and child molesters vs. aggressive pedophiles) demonstrated modest gains. Although 62% of clients were followed for up to 5 years, those who dropped out are considered treatment failures. Overall, it is reasonable to cautiously conclude that CBT methods may have a modest positive effect with less severe sex offenders. Emmelkamp and Vedel (2010), however, have called into question the National Institute for Health and Clinical Excellence guidelines for treating juvenile and adult offenders in group and therapeutic communities, citing the modest evidence for success of these programs and noting that such environments can encourage networking among inmates who are sex offenders.

In his review, Marshall (1996) concludes that, although results from cognitive-behavioral programs have been encouraging particularly for young offenders, these approaches have not yet been subjected to a sufficient amount of controlled research to justify placing a high degree of confidence in them. These types of CBT programs are generally conducted in a group format and include empathy training, respectful confrontation to reduce denial and minimization of the offense, masturbatory reconditioning to reduce deviant sexual fantasies and to increase "normal" fantasies, and relapse prevention strategies. Hall (1995) reviewed 92 studies and found 12 in which treatment groups were compared to alternative treatment or control conditions. Although participants across studies had been convicted of heterogeneous offenses, 10 of the 12 studies included adult male sex offenders who committed their crimes against children. Results showed some modest success for cognitive-behavioral and hormonal treatments. Quinsey, Harris, Rice, and Lalumiere (1993) carefully examined the methodological shortcomings of many of the studies that had been reviewed by others. The major limitations of sex offender research include lack of random assignment and control groups (i.e., treatment as usual), inadequacy in dealing with attrition and dropouts when calculating results, and the use of comparison data from other populations to estimate the significance of recidivism in treatment groups. The authors argue that with more rigorous methodological criteria, there is little evidence to conclude that interventions for sex offenders are effective. Although some cognitive-behavioral programs with close external (law enforcement) supervision appear promising for some offenders, outcomes do not reach levels that are sufficient to justify putting children in the community at risk. Furby, Weinrott, and Blackshaw (1989) concluded in their review that those clients deemed to be sexually aggressive should be considered intractable and nonresponsive to treatment.

Some who work with sex offenders have suggested that interventions should focus less on risk management of potential harm in the community and instead make "sexual offender treatment more positive and self-enhancing for our clients [to] increase their responsivity to treatment" (Marshall et al., 2005, p. 1098). Although it should be pointed out that enhancing a client's strengths and promoting risk management are not mutually exclusive, the authors offer no evidence that their strengths-based approach actually reduces risk of harm to children and adults in the community (Marshall et al., 2005). Risk reduction should remain the primary goal of any intervention with antisocial clients in general. Considering all the current evidence to date for more serious sexual offending, the priority for dealing with sex offenders must be protection of potential child victims by confinement and strict supervision of offenders upon release into the community. Some flexibility in this position may be justified for less severe adolescent offenders.

Descriptions of Effective Intervention Methods for Antisocial Clients

After thoroughly reviewing the extant empirical literature, several reviewers have concluded that behavioral programs conducted in the context of community reinforcement and/or contingency management approaches are the most effective psychosocial interventions (Gendreau, 1996a, 1996b; McGuire & Hatcher, 2001; Prendergast, Anglin, & Wellisch, 1995). Recommendations based on their reviews include the following:

- Place a strong emphasis on developing a sound working and sensitive relationship with each client

- Implement an individual multidimensional-functional-systems (MFS) assessment of each client's deficits, needs, strengths, and readiness to change

- Use standardized measures such as the PCL-r, as well as scales for common co-occurring problems, such as the Addictions Severity Index (see chapter 6)

- Use cognitive-behavioral coping skills to help clients challenge negative criminogenic attitudes, learn self-monitoring to detect at-risk situations, avoid triggers for crime-related activities (e.g., drug use), and learn self-regulation skills (e.g., emphasize impulse and anger control, stress management, improve poor motivation, cope more effectively with negative moods)—such skills are commensurate with the goals of relapse prevention (see chapter 7) for those offenders who abuse drugs

- Have clients observe the modeling behavior of others to learn alternative ways of dealing with situations that can provoke criminal acts

- Help clients develop better social problem-solving methods (i.e., deal better with social isolation, develop improved interpersonal skills)

- Implement community reinforcement strategies (e.g., social and occupational supports)

- Use contingency management methods (e.g., rewarding pro-social activities, sanctioning antisocial behaviors), including the possible reinstatement of punishment if necessary (e.g., return to prison for reoffending)

- Monitor interventions for treatment fidelity

- Implement long-term interventions, with long-term follow-up and good coordination with adjunctive services as needed

With these basic intervention principles, practitioners and program managers must also make an effort to match the intervention plan to the interests and needs of each individual client. Reinforcers and contingencies must be provided and enforced consistently. Positive reinforcers should be used in much greater proportion than the use of punishment. Traditional case management is also necessary to coordinate the community resources necessary to help clients avoid relapse and achieve their prosocial rehabilitative goals.

These community contacts may include drug testing and related service agencies (e.g., methadone maintenance), psychiatric services, job-site supervisors, probation or parole officers, and spouses or other family members.

Collaboration between Social Work and the Criminal Justice System: Therapeutic Justice and Therapeutic Jurisprudence

Individuals are ultimately responsible for their own decisions and actions. If social workers believe in "empowering" people, then they must simultaneously advocate for their clients' rights and communicate an expectation that clients respect the rights of others. When clients do something positive for themselves or for another person, social workers consider the act an expression of client free will. When a client performs a criminal act, social workers must hold the client accountable and responsible for his or her behavior. Although there are mitigating psychological and environmental factors to consider (e.g., florid psychosis at the time of the act, being in a life-threatening situation), a balanced approach to assessing client responsibility is needed to effectively apply therapeutic and criminal justice strategies for the common goals of improving the psychosocial well-being of clients and protecting innocent community members.

Nygaard (2000) has noted a disconnection between the criminal justice system and the behavioral sciences that tends to result in a reactionary and polarized approach to criminal behavior (i.e., punishment vs. treatment). An alternative to these extremes is a growing appreciation and understanding of two related concepts: therapeutic justice and therapeutic jurisprudence. Nygaard (2000) explains that therapeutic justice employs the criminal justice system not just as a means to confine and punish but also as an opportunity to engender change in a person by both leveraging the penal system and using a range of existing social forces, including professional therapeutic means. These efforts go beyond the prison walls to a continuum of efforts in the community to enhance change and prevent recidivism. Such an effort must be interdisciplinary in both research and practice. According to Nygaard (2000), therapeutic justice

> is all about change, about creating a clinical and penal climate in which transgressors are encouraged to change and, for the offenders who sincerely want to change, about assisting them in their endeavors. Nonetheless, people who are correctable or have treatable conditions bear the ultimate moral responsibility both for the change resulting from treatment and their condition afterwards; this applies whether one has a physical ailment, an addiction disease, a more complex emotional problem, or has committed a crime. The system can help one do what one cannot do for, or by, himself. It can restore hope where despair exists. It can coordinate individual and component efforts. It can intervene. But it cannot rehabilitate. We have learned that lesson. Change is tough. Therapeutic justice is not a soft, easy remedy. (p. 23-14)

Therapeutic jurisprudence is a focused effort to use the courts to advance therapeutic outcomes (Wexler, 1991). An example of therapeutic jurisprudence in the broader context of therapeutic justice is the civil commitment of a substance-abusing mentally ill man who has committed assault. Sentencing might include close monitoring and continued compliance with medical and psychosocial intervention. Individuals with mental illness are not exonerated from criminal behavior, but rather than being institutionalized indefinitely, they are simultaneously treated and held accountable for their actions. *Holding clients accountable for their behavior must be understood as a therapeutic process,* in order for clients' progress to be tied inextricably to community safety. Social workers have an ethical duty to enhance clients' psychosocial well-being, as well as an ethical duty to protect the larger community from dangerous clients when they can.

Social workers have long been ambivalent (somewhat justifiably perhaps) about their relationship with law enforcement and the criminal justice system, given some of the inherent biases and discriminatory policies found there. However, such excesses do not obviate the potential for collaboration when therapeutic and criminal justice goals are commensurate. Unfortunately, the practice of remanding a client for counseling from the bench is often a dubious practice at best. As O'Hare (1996a) has noted, social workers risk "participating in a muddled enterprise where clinicians pretend to treat and clients pretend to comply at the behest of the criminal justice system" (p. 421). A clarification of the goals and responsibilities of both the therapeutic community and the criminal justice system, however, can help reduce ambiguous goals and responsibilities and result in clearer accountability standards for clients. Current examples of potentially effective collaborations between social workers and the criminal justice system include outpatient civil commitment for treatment of the mentally ill who have committed crimes, diversionary treatment programs for nonviolent drug offenders, and advocacy for substance-abusing mothers (contingent on treatment compliance and sobriety) to regain custody of children in the child welfare system, among others. Rather than loose or informal arrangements, such collaboration of various social services and criminal justice requires more clearly defined integrative programs, including clearer mandates for the use of evidence-based practices, clearly defined intervention goals, adequate supervision and evaluation of client outcomes, and more rigorously designed program evaluation and research.

Rooney and Bibus (2001) provide the following guidelines for practitioners working in an ethical and legal framework with involuntary clients:

- Ensuring informed consent and protection of clients' legal rights (due process)

- Exercising beneficence and paternalism with judgment; intervening when necessary and within legal limits for the good of the client and/or to protect others in society

- Empowering the client to the extent possible to affirm his or her worth and dignity, enhance strengths, and take initiative in problem solving
- Keeping clients informed of their legal requirements as well as choices and options; communicating openly and honestly with clients and avoiding deceptive methods
- Advocating for the protection of clients' rights and fair treatment under the law

TREATMENT PLANNING AND EVALUATION

CASE ILLUSTRATION: TIM

Tim, a 26-year-old white male, was recently arrested for being drunk and disorderly and for possession of a small amount of methamphetamine. He was seen by a social worker, George, in a combined mental health and substance abuse treatment agency as part of a contracted diversionary program for first-time drug offenders. This was not, however, the first time Tim had broken the law.

Tim had been in trouble off and on since adolescence. Raised in an economically disadvantaged, mixed-race, working-class neighborhood, Tim vaguely recalls his father coming in and out of the picture during his childhood and adolescence. He clearly recalls his father violently beating his mother in their narrow galley kitchen, as well as the beatings he received himself. His father was often drunk, intermittently provided financial support, and at times would be present for months at a time while he was "on the wagon." Tim recalls these periods of sobriety as almost worse than when his father was drinking, since his father would become unbearably strict in an effort to "rehabilitate himself and everyone around him." As his father relapsed

and spent more time out of the picture, Tim began to skip school, started hanging out on the streets, began to shoplift, and began to engage in other forms of criminal activity. Later, he "graduated" to stealing objects out of cars and snatching purses. During this time, he began to drink; to sniff glue and other inhalants; and to occasionally smoke pot, when he could afford it or steal it. Occasionally, he was paid in drugs to act as courier for local drug dealers. Tim was remarkably adept at not being caught, and he maintained a reputation among adults in the community as a "nice boy." Eventually, he was sent to foster homes because of chronic truancy during early adolescence. His mom could not control his behavior, and his age virtually precluded adoption. At that point, his father was absent from his life.

After a few stays in foster homes, Tim eventually moved back home with his mother. Tim decided that moving from one place to another was not preferable to staying home. He remained there until he was 18 and worked sporadically. At age 18 (having failed to finish high school) he moved out and began working in phone sales (i.e., calling people at home) for a variety of companies selling a range of speculative products (e.g., vacation time shares, stocks and bonds, investment schemes). He was quite adept at these endeavors and was able to make a decent living, maintain an apartment, and drive a late-model car. He successfully lied about his age and qualifications on numerous occasions to obtain better-paying work, and his employers did not delve too deeply into his grandiose claims given his sales record. As he moved into more sophisticated sales jobs, he was able to afford better clothes and the desirable accoutrements of the high-powered salesperson. He was charming and engaging, he could converse well on any number of subjects, and he had a first-rate reputation in his product area. Tim also had to keep moving around because of his questionable sales methods. He showed little compunction for misrepresenting the truth to older persons and those with physical and mental vulnerabilities or disabilities when selling insurance policies. He came across as quite sincere and very credible, and he was very persuasive in person. He was also accused on more than one occasion of sexual assault. In one case, the young woman was 15 years old, but charges were dropped because of a lack of evidence. In another case, the woman was an adult, but she dropped charges for unknown reasons.

None of Tim's brushes with the law ever amounted to a conviction. He was arrested just before his intake at the clinic. He had been drinking heavily and snorting methamphetamine all day, celebrating yet another "big score" in his current sales job, and had gotten involved in a bar fight with someone who was also intoxicated. The bartender (with the help of other patrons) pushed them into the street, where the fight ensued, and called police. Upon emptying his pockets in the local police station, the methamphetamines were discovered, and Tim was arrested. He presented himself before the judge as suitably contrite and was mandated to outpatient substance abuse treatment at the local mental health center, an agency with a contract with the state drug-court diversionary program.

MFS Assessment: Defining Problems and Goals

George, the social worker, obtained Tim's previous criminal and social service records. It appeared from these data that he would easily have met the diagnostic criteria for conduct disorder and, now, antisocial personality disorder. Risk factors were congruent with Tim's increasing antisocial behavior: his father's alcoholism, Tim's impulsivity, having witnessed domestic violence and having been abused himself, feeling that there were few people in the world he could trust. His history and current presentation were of someone who clearly had developed the ability to be deceitful, lie, and otherwise take advantage of people while showing little remorse. His brushes with the law, which involved stealing, allegations of rape, chronic drug abuse, and other problem behaviors represented a long history of criminal activity from youth into adulthood. George was inclined to think that Tim played down these details and took little responsibility for the accusations. At times George observed that Tim would disproportionately focus on one relatively innocuous event in great detail with considerable affect while avoiding or glossing over other more egregious facts concerning his alleged illegal activities. He would admit as little as possible about crimes for which he had been charged or arrested and volunteer information for little else. His arrest for drug possession was his first time being charged as an adult for a serious crime. His day-to-day coping skills were generally good; he complained about being bored often; he had few friends outside of work acquaintances; and aside from moving from one job to another (not all that unusual in sales), he worked consistently. He had no steady romantic relationship but prided himself on "having an easy time getting any woman I want." He reported his health as excellent (despite the neglect of his health and poor health habits). Although he owned up to the possibility that he possibly drank a bit too much at times, he generally denied drug abuse ("aside from an occasional joint") and suggested that the drugs found on him at his arrest were not really his, that he was holding them for someone else that night.

Overall, it appeared to George that Tim was generally downplaying his drug use and otherwise illegal activities, and his sincerity about "getting better and improving myself" was somewhat affected. The tip seemed to come when he began to use psychotherapeutic clichés: "I want to get myself together and really, I mean, really deal with my issues." Nevertheless, George realized that there was little point in calling him on his apparent deceitfulness, but he would continue to gather more data and move forward with a detailed functional assessment.

In examining the details of Tim's everyday life, it appeared that he was not uniformly conning people, abusing drugs, or attempting to otherwise exploit people. Although these themes appeared somewhat consistent overall, he was not unlikable or without the ability to develop acquaintances, even a friendly relationship with another man or romantic relationship with a woman. These relationships, however, appeared to be somewhat short-lived, and Tim usually terminated them. Although he did not present his work or relationships as exploitive, there appeared to be a pattern of increasing his "con" behaviors when he was feeling threatened either at work or in his relationships. A sense of "I'll get them before they get me" clearly came through as the social worker discussed with him his "survival strategies" at work or in his dealings with women. He tended to see perceived slights or not getting his way as a very serious matter and a provocation he would not stand for. Compromise equaled capitulation, and "giving in is for losers," he said. His drinking and drug use appeared to increase during times of stress, and it seemed that his other problematic behaviors tended to increase simultaneously. These included quick sexual liaisons with women and increased conflict at work, often leading to a change of employment. At other times, he suggested that he actually felt quite good, but "it never lasts." When queried about what those times were like, Tim suggested that once, when he was 20, he had a relationship with someone and, during that time, felt better than he had ever felt in his life. But he said, "She left me for someone else. . . . I'll never let that happen again." Whether it was work, his relationships or something else, the pattern seemed to be this: (1) Tim experienced a sense of being threatened; (2) he drank more or used drugs; (3) he become more impulsive and somewhat exploitive to those around him with the consequences being creating more conflict and stress; and (4) at some point, a more serious problem would erupt, a problem he would have to escape or retreat from.

Over the course of a few visits (he was mandated for weekly counseling for a year, with monthly reports to his probation officer), Tim and George came to a tentative understanding on what the goals of their work together would be. They agreed on the following: to abstain from drug use for the time being (although Tim might continue to downplay it, he agreed in principle); to examine his relationships with other people, including his customers, coworkers, and any romantic associations; and to reduce incidents of explosive anger and conflict that caused him more problems. The social worker, after a few visits, put it succinctly: "You tend to treat people in a way that suggests that you just want to get something from them, like a sale, a favor, or sex, but you don't want to give them anything of yourself in return. Is that about right?" Despite appearing very angry at this suggestion that he was "just a user," Tim acknowledged, "There might be a little something to that."

However, for Tim, the most important consideration for being in treatment seemed to be to "comply with the courts and get this behind me." George made it clear that full reports regarding any illegal behavior would go to the probation officer, and that George, as social worker, and the probation officer were on the same side, working as a team. George was also realistic in his outcome expectations for Tim: there would be no personality reconstruction, but it was possible that a reduction, even an elimination, of illegal activities was possible. Tim might not cultivate deeper and genuine feelings, even empathy, for others, but he could reduce the threat he posed to others in the community with his drug use and exploitation of others. These latter goals would, however, be much more difficult to monitor and hard to hold him accountable for. Regarding Tim's taking advantage of people on the job, there appeared to be a fine line between his exploitive quasi-criminal behavior and what is often condoned in many work environments.

Selecting Interventions:
Defining Strategies and Objectives

Appealing to Tim's self-interest, George endeavored to find some motivation to work on his problems, other than simply "staying out of trouble." In using a motivational interviewing style, he was able to help Tim arrive at somewhat of a cost-benefit analysis (using the pros and cons approach one might use in sales) of what kind of trouble his conning others and use of illegal drugs (to the extent that he admitted it) had caused him. He was, after a time, willing to admit that his drug use didn't really "fill the void" all that well, and that, at times, he got sick of it and wondered why he was often "bored with reading or exercise or other activities that people seem to enjoy." Although many of his acquaintances in his line of work enjoyed golfing, he thought, "Golfing is stupid. Using sticks to hit little balls into holes. I don't get it." He didn't see that the companionship might be a big draw for some people aside from the nature of the activity itself. He clearly understood the drawbacks to being arrested. That was an easy evaluation for him to make. He also felt bad when he had to leave a job that he liked because his sales tactics raised one too many eyebrows. As for his relationships with women, he seemed to be unaware that they might be interested in anything other than just being with him. When George asked him what he "brought to the table" for the woman who had his interest, he seemed to be stumped by the question, suggesting (as though it were obvious), "Well, me, of course." When asked, "Well, what is it about you that makes a relationship such a good deal for the woman?" he became angry and sullen and wanted to end the session early.

The first goal was to help Tim avoid or cope with the triggers associated with his "occasional" drug use. Since he was not willing to own up to much, they decided to discuss his drug use as a "hypothetical" based on his past experiences. Triggers included, he said "when I'm bored, angry, frustrated, and lonely." Further exploration was conducted around these thoughts, feelings, behaviors, and situations, and they both came up with a useful list of realistic alternatives to drug use, ways to assuage his negative feelings and avoid using substances. (He had not agreed to abstinence with alcohol since it is legal, but George helped him identify alcohol use as a trigger for drug use.) Cognitive exercises focused on his real fear of being arrested and going to prison (he had never been incarcerated, except for a few hours once) and, conversely, a cognitive review of all the legal things he enjoyed about his freedom.

To cope with physiological tension, the social worker showed him some basic relaxation exercises and discovered that he had always had trouble sitting still, "ever since I was a kid," he said. Anger control exercises were also planned and carried out using a combination of imagery to recreate specific circumstances that elicited his anger, role-plays, rehearsal, and practice for situations that arose at work or in the community. He had underperformed in school all his life and had never graduated high school or received an equivalency (although he had fake high school and college diplomas available and regularly lied on his résumé). They also discussed the possibility of his getting a graduate equivalency degree from high school and perhaps taking a business class at the local community college, but the suggestions just seemed to anger him.

George also helped Tim develop a behavioral map to identify those times and circumstances in which he was most likely to feel the desire to drink heavily or use drugs and reviewed the list of alternative methods. To implement the contingency management part of the program, they also decided to meet bimonthly with the probation officer to reinforce the team approach, but the social worker agreed only to discuss those matters directly salient to the charges, and not reveal anything that was unnecessary, although absolute confidentiality on these matters could not be guaranteed. Over time, Tim began to show more interest in examining his transitory relationships and the lack of intimacy he felt with others, but it was difficult for the social worker to judge his level of sincerity on these matters. Nevertheless, Tim continued to show genuine interest in "staying out of trouble," the primary goal of the intervention.

Selecting Scales and Creating Indexes to Monitor and Evaluate Client Progress

The social worker used the PCL-r primarily to screen Tim for his level of psychopathy, although he was not expecting to detect substantive changes in scores at outcome. He also decided to use the Addiction Severity Index (ASI), although the extent to which he thought Tim would be honest about his use was questionable. Nevertheless, it served as a useful assessment and clinical tool over the course of the intervention. George and Tim also developed a series of one-item (0–10) self-anchored indexes to track his main objectives and goals. These included an "urge" scale to monitor thoughts, feelings, and situations in which he felt particularly at risk to "hypothetically" drink or use drugs, or lose his temper at work or other social circumstances, and he would use these situations to work on the communication skills that he practiced in sessions with George.

ASSESSMENT: BORDERLINE PERSONALITY DISORDER

Background Data

Persons diagnosed with borderline personality disorder (BPD) demonstrate a combination of characteristic behaviors that may include some combination of the following: severe mood swings, short-lived psychotic episodes, unpre-

TABLE 10.1   The Client Service Plan

Problems	Goals	Objectives (samples)	Interventions	Assessment and evaluation tools
Illegal activities, specifically drug use	Reduce and eventually abstain from substance use	Monitor triggers (cognitive, emotions, behaviors, situations) that increase likelihood of drug use	Cognitive-behavioral skills employed with contingency management; service implementation conducted in a case management framework to integrate mental health and substance abuse intervention with probationary requirements	PCL-r; possibly ASI, and/or other drug use indexes or index of "urge to use" to assess and evaluate ability to resist desire to use
Angry outbursts, desire to strike out, to hurt others when he feels provoked	Reduce intensity of anger and increase time between provocation and response; improve ability to respond verbally rather than physically	Practice identifying provocation and practice nonaggressive responses twice weekly; come to visits prepared to discuss examples		
Exploitive relationships; difficulty genuinely connecting with others; difficulty experiencing empathy	Define potential problems, explore them, provide education on how they may be problematic; have him at least consider further discussion	No specific objectives: client does not genuinely acknowledge a problem at this time	Cognitive appraisal of risks of use (imprisonment); relaxation exercises to reduce physiological tension	
			Contingency management plan: meet with social worker and probation officer to discuss progress and reinforce consequences if drug use resumes	
			Cognitive appraisal of provoking situations, role-play and rehearsal during sessions, homework practice	
			No intervention at this time	

dictable and often impulsive behaviors frequently associated with highly conflicted relationships, suicidal or parasuicidal gestures (e.g., nonlethal wrist lacerations), and other risky or dangerous behaviors. The mood, ideals, and aspirations of persons characterized as having BPD are often ephemeral, as they fly from one commitment or set of plans to another, depending on how they are feeling at any given moment, particularly in regard to their own self-worth, self-confidence, and self-image. These vacillations are often accompanied by wide mood swings (e.g., crying, screaming, raging outbursts, threats of harm to oneself or others) and are often followed by a brief return to tranquility or euphoria. Persons with BPD often describe themselves as feeling empty, bored, or confused about who they are, and they are often characterized as having an unstable self-image (i.e., identity diffusion). Persons diagnosed with BPD are often described as intolerant of being alone, although their relationships are often fraught with upset, drama, conflict, and sometimes violence. Moods and perceptions regarding those with whom they become involved tend to oscillate between two extremes on a continuum from "all bad" to "all good." These emotional extremes often accompany the heightened drama of their tumultuous relationships. Persons categorized as "borderline" appear to be particularly sensitive to any apparent change in a relationship that may trigger fears of "abandonment," even when the separation is time limited. Their relationships tend to be marked by initial euphoric attachment and overidealization of the other person, but disappointment and conflict seem inevitable and often arrive swiftly as clients with BPD becomes disillusioned in the focus of their previous affections. The borderline client often complains about the seeming inability of another person to supply them with adequate attention.

Perhaps the most troublesome behavior for clinicians is the tendency for individuals with BPD to threaten suicide and sometimes engage in frequent self-mutilation and other self-destructive acts (e.g., repeatedly exposing a vein in the wrist, throwing oneself out of a moving car, slamming one's head against a wall to emphasize distress). These acts of self-mutilation do not usually indicate an actual suicide attempt, although persons with this diagnosis are often severely depressed, which does put them at increased risk for suicide. Persons diagnosed with BPD might engage in other risky activities that indirectly put themselves or others at risk of harm (e.g., promiscuous and unprotected sex, reckless driving, spending money impulsively, abusing drugs and alcohol, engaging in outright aggression) (APA, 2013; Linehan, 1993a; Linehan, Kanter, & Comtois, 1999). Needless to say, the distorted cognitions, erratic emotions, and impulsive and at times dangerous behaviors of clients with BPD are challenging treatment management issues for even experienced practitioners.

Estimates of BPD range from 1.6% to 5.9% in the general population (Leichsenring, Leibing, Kruse, New, & Leweke, 2011; Pagura et al., 2010). Results of the National Epidemiologic Survey of Alcohol and Related Disorders study also showed that 30.2% of those diagnosed with BPD also met criteria for PTSD. Those with comorbid PTSD and BPD showed significantly poorer quality of life and more adverse childhood events, and they made more suicide attempts than people with either condition alone (Pagura et al., 2010). As many as 10% of clients in outpatient mental health facilities and 20% of inpatients reportedly fit the diagnostic criteria for BPD. From 33% to more than 50% of clients diagnosed with any personality disorder are also likely to fit the criteria for BPD. The symptoms of BPD are more prevalent in adolescents and young adults, and they tend to attenuate over time. Many clients diagnosed with BPD no longer meet the BPD criteria as they move into their 30s and 40s. BPD is likely to co-occur with other disorders, including mood and substance use disorder, and they may demonstrate symptoms of other personality disorders, such as narcissistic personality disorder and APD, among others (APA, 2013; Leichsenring et al., 2011; Sadock & Kaplan, 1998).

Evidence suggests that persons with BPD are more likely to have experienced violence and sexual abuse as children and/or adults. In one study (Zanarini et al., 1999), 290 hospitalized patients with BPD (average age 27, 85% white) were compared with 72 controls diagnosed with another Axis II disorder. Both groups were similar in age, marital status, and race. More of those in the BPD category were female. Results showed that violence was a fairly common experience among BPD patients: about 33% experienced abuse at the hands of their partner, almost 33% had been raped as an adult, 21% reported having been raped by a known perpetrator, and 11% reported multiple episodes of rape. About 50% of female patients with BPD reported an adult history of physical assault and/or rape. Male patients with BPD were about half as likely as female patients to have been physically assaulted and/or raped. Violence among the BPD patients was significantly more common than among controls. The patients were also more likely than other Axis II clients to have had a substance abuse problem before age 18 and to have experienced abuse and neglect as a child, including physical neglect, any form of sexual abuse, sexual abuse by a non-caretaker, emotional withdrawal by a caretaker, and failure by the caretaker to provide physical protection.

Although correlations between BPD and substance abuse have been shown to be significant, the cause-effect linkages are complex and potentially mediated by several important factors. After an extensive 10-year review of the research, Trull, Sher, Minks-Brown, Durbin, and Burr (2000) considered possible explanations for the correlation between BPD and substance abuse. First, the overlap between BPD symptoms and substance abuse may be an artifact, in that both problem areas are marked by impulsive behavior; second, they may share a common (but noncausal) factor, such as age of onset for the disorder (i.e., late teens, early 20s); third, both disorders may share a common risk factor (e.g., childhood trauma); fourth, they may be reciprocally causal (i.e., one causes and/or exacerbates the other). Although these are reasonable hypotheses for further testing, the authors concluded that "it is not possible at this point . . . to declare simply that BPD causes or leads to SUD (i.e., substance use disorder) or vice versa" (Trull et al., 2000, p. 244).

Although practitioners have observed that impulsivity is a common behavior among persons diagnosed with BPD, Hochhausen, Lorenz, and Newman (2002) noted that little laboratory research has provided support for this contention. They compared white and African American female inmates who met criteria for BPD with a similar group of inmates who did not meet the criteria on computer-based tests of impulse control, finding that both African American and white inmates with BPD showed significantly greater impulsivity than those without the diagnosis. Underscoring the heterogeneity of a diagnosis with BPD, they also found that BPD was correlated with APD, psychopathy as measured by the PCL-r, and established measures of depression and anxiety.

Theories

Perhaps because of a lack of competing alternatives, psychoanalytic conceptions of BPD and its treatment have dominated the mental health field until recently. Current psychodynamic conceptualizations derive from a combination of classical psychoanalytic theory (Freud, 1920/1966, 1923, 1938; A. Freud, 1946; Strean, 1986) and later from its derivatives, including developmental ego psychology, attachment theory, and Kohut's self-psychology (e.g., Baker & Baker, 1987; Bowlby, 1980; Mahler, 1968). Classic psychoanalytic theories involved several interacting systems, including the "structural view" (i.e. id, ego, and superego), the dynamic point of view (i.e., regulation of sexual and aggressive drives), the topographic perspective (i.e., unconscious, preconscious, and conscious mind), the functions of the ego and defense mechanisms (e.g., repression, projection, denial, rationalization, intellectualization), and the genetic or developmental perspective (i.e., oral, anal, phallic—including the Oedipal phase—and latency), continuing on to puberty and adolescence, when psychosocial elements from earlier phases might be recapitulated.

Developmental ego psychology, based on Sigmund Freud's later emphasis on the ego (see also A. Freud, 1946), was developed further by Mahler, Bowlby, and others into a more explicitly interpersonal developmental model. Healthful relationships were purported to derive from successful negotiation of psychosocial phases. Conversely, psychopathology resulted from serious failures to negotiate these important psychosocial developmental thresholds. The individual's internal mental representations of these relationships (i.e., object relations) developed sequentially as follows: the autistic phase (i.e., basic physiological needs are met), the symbiotic phase (i.e., a blending of self with the mother, who satisfies or frustrates needs), and the subphases of the separation-individuation stage (i.e., toddler gradually moves toward a degree of separate identity while maintaining a constant internalized and integrated image of the maternal object). In a healthful resolution, the toddler resolves the "splitting defense" and integrates the internalized representation, that is, does not vacillate between extremes of all good and all bad. Serious developmental failures in these stages may result in the vacillating moods, tumultuous relationships, and impulsive behaviors of a future "borderline" client.

The concept of the borderline personality was coined by Stern (1938) for patients who appeared to be on the "borderline" of psychoses and neuroses. This geographical metaphor reflects a theoretical developmental continuum of psychopathology (i.e., psychotic to borderline to neurotic) that mirrors the stages of developmental ego psychology: autism, symbiosis, separation-individuation. Failure in one stage theoretically results in a corresponding degree of psychopathology. Clients with more serious pathology but one that is less severe than psychosis may be characterized as demonstrating "primitive" defensive functioning (e.g., denial, projection, splitting, failures in normal repression), which reflects a disruption in ego development during the separation-individuation phase (Gunderson, 1984; Kernberg, 1975; Masterson, 1981). As Kernberg (1976) concisely puts it: "These patients' capacity for encompassing contradictory ("good" and "bad") self- and object-images is impaired" (p. 146). And, "Individualization includes the gradual replacement of primitive introjections and identifications with partial, sublimatory identifications fitting into the overall concept of the self. Emotional maturity is reflected in the capacity for discriminating subtle aspects of one's own self and of other people and in an increasing selectivity in accepting and internalizing the qualities of other people. Mature friendships are based on such selectivity and the capacity to combine love with independence and emotional objectivity" (Kernberg, 1976, p. 74). Although Kernberg's concepts of borderline personality organization are somewhat divergent from the more descriptive criteria for BPD in the DSM-5, the differences are more theoretical than practical for the average practitioner. The narcissistic personality also suffers from some of the same presumed ego deficits but is better organized and is behaviorally and emotionally more stable. The individual with narcissism is also markedly more grandiose, arrogant, and defensively more difficult to influence or confront. In this case, practitioners use interpretation to help clarify, explain, or gently confront clients on distortions related to communications in therapy or problems external to therapy (Baker & Baker, 1987; Kernberg, 1975).

These theoretical assertions, based primarily on correlational studies and uncontrolled case analyses, lead to the following treatment recommendations in psychoanalytic and/or psychodynamic practice: (1) identifying and interpreting emerging primitive part-objects (partial internalized representations of others, usually one's mother) in the context of the transference (e.g., unconscious projections that the therapist is mean, hurtful, or untrustworthy); (2) helping clients understand how self and object representations can oscillate or reverse (e.g., a client may start to act mean and see the therapist as a vulnerable, frightened victim); (3) helping clients understand that their positive and negative conceptualizations of the relationship with the therapist need to be reconciled into one whole, albeit more complex, relationship. "The successful integration of mutually dissociated or split-off, all-good and all-bad primitive object relations in the transference includes the integration not only of the corresponding self and object representations, but also of primitive affects, leading to affect modulation, to an increase in the capacity for affect control, to a heightened capacity for empathy with both self and others, and a corresponding deepening and maturing of all object relations" (Kernberg, 1999, p. 169). Stated concisely, the goal of treatment of the person with borderline personality disorder is to resolve identity diffusion and primitive defensive operations (e.g., denial, projection, splitting), and help him or her move toward a more integrated view of internalized self-object (Kernberg, 1999).

Psychodynamic psychotherapy with borderline clients has been modified somewhat from long-term interpretive analytic work into a briefer, more supportive approach that emphasizes current functioning and gentle confrontation. Interpretations of unconscious material, typically employed with healthier "neurotic" clients in psychoanalytic treatment circles, are saved for a later stage of treatment when clients are more stable and are on their way to better integration of "good-bad" self and other object representation. Premature interpretations of unconscious conflict with its genesis in early childhood could confuse the client's already unsteady grip on reality and possibly provoke "transference psychosis" (Kernberg, 1976). Interpretations are more focused on the present to help clients better cope with more immediate problems. Limit setting regarding session rules and reality clarification is dealt with more directly. Priorities in treatment include behaviors that are dangerous to self or others, behaviors that are potentially disruptive to treatment continuity, and communications that indicate a lack of honesty in treatment.

There have been efforts in recent years to empirically validate psychodynamic explanations of BPD. Stern, Herron, Primavera, and Kakuma (1997) conducted a correlational study comparing 55 hospitalized persons with BPD and 22 with major depression. Using a series of measures including psychiatric functioning scales and scales designed specifically to measure perceptions of self and others, they found some expected differences. Patients with BPD were found to be generally more hostile, emotionally labile, and unstable than persons with major depression. However, a good proportion of the findings was mixed or did not support study hypotheses. For example, there were no differences in perceptions of control or nurturance from early caregivers, and other differences washed out when age and gender were controlled for.

De Bonis, De Boeck, Lida-Pulik, Hourtane, and Feline (1998) used a qualitative and quantitative grid method to capture clients' unique positive and negative affect valences for self and others (a key object relations construct), and they compared small samples of depressed patients with BPD, depressed patients without BPD, and persons with no known psychiatric diagnosis. Results showed that self-descriptions of both depressed groups were more negative than the psychiatric controls. In addition, depressed patients with BPD had greater affect valence discrepancy for others, but the depressed-only group showed no differences on negative view of the self. As with the prior study, these data provided mixed support for object relations theory.

Fonagy et al. (1996) compared 82 psychiatric inpatients with matched outpatient controls on psychiatric measures, attachment style, and capacity for self-reflection (ability to reflect on their own and another's mental state, a theoretically important factor in object relations theory). As one would expect, inpatients showed significantly greater psychiatric problems and unresolved attachments than outpatients. With regard to patients with BPD, they were found to be more likely to have experienced childhood abuse, unresolved trauma, or loss; were less likely to have experienced their parents as loving but more neglectful; and had a lower ability to reflect on their own or another's state of mind. This impaired ability to conceptualize the mind of the abusive caregiver may be related to unresolved attachment conflicts and a factor in the development of borderline pathology (Fonagy, Target, & Gergely, 2000).

Goldman, D'Angelo, and DeMaso (1993) compared 44 children (about 10 years of age) with BPD and 100 without BPD and found greater rates of pathology in the parents in the families of the BPD group. Types of pathology in descending order of frequency included substance abuse problems, depression, and antisocial personality. There was no evidence that the interviewers were blind to the diagnostic status of the child during the interview. The authors suggested that interacting environmental and biological risk factors of one or two parents with significant psychopathology contribute to the development of BPD, although they also suggested that causality could not be inferred from the study.

Given that longitudinal designs would strengthen the cause-effect argument for the genesis of borderline personality disorder resulting from poor parenting, Bezirganian, Cohen, and Brook (1993) examined data collected over 3 years in an attempt to causally connect maternal inconsistency and high maternal overinvolvement with the development of BPD in a random sample of 776 adolescents. Given that DSM criteria for BPD were not available at the time of the baseline interviews, diagnoses were made after the fact according to other personality disordered-related items. Logistic regression was employed to examine whether theoretically relevant factors predicted BPD status. Results showed that an interaction of maternal overinvolvement and maternal inconsistency predicted BPD diagnostic status better than chance alone. However, most of the measures employed in the study, including those that measured maternal overinvolvement and maternal inconsistency, were below acceptable standards for internal consistency, and there was no indication how much of the variance of BPD was explained by maternal overinvolvement and/or inconsistency.

Although the investigators who made these long-overdue attempts to test the validity of psychodynamic theories of BPD should be applauded for their efforts, the studies suffer from fatal methodological flaws: (1) they are based primarily on clinical populations and thus vulnerable to Berkson's bias (i.e., clinical populations tend to have more correlating problems); (2) they are correlational in nature, in which case they merely suggest that certain current self-reported thoughts, feelings, or behaviors are associated with other presumably pathogenic processes or events (i.e., one cannot infer cause and effect); (3) they are based on retrospective data and thus subject to the distortions of recall memory; or (4) there are serious limitations in the measures employed. Thus, to date, the only substantive claim to be made is that chronic problems during childhood and adolescence are risk factors for increased psychological and interpersonal problems in adolescence and adulthood. The theoretical processes that may account for *how* past events cause BPD are not adequately addressed by these studies. Developmental cause-effect processes remain widely open to interpretation. From longitudinal data predictive of other disorders, it appears more likely that a combination of factors, including biological temperament, substantive child abuse and/or neglect (e.g., direct physical, sexual abuse, lack of nurturance, exposure to family violence, substance abuse), and a host of environmental stressors, is needed to account for increased risk for serious psychopathology.

Many persons subjected to abuse and other forms of trauma do not develop BPD, and many persons who manifest borderline symptoms have never been abused (Paris, 1997b; Sabo, 1997). Indeed, there is little evidence that early childhood abuse as an individual factor is more important that other environmental assaults that occur later in life (see Rutter & Rutter, 1993). Evidence, again, suggests that practitioners employ evidence-based multidimensional theories to support their assessment protocol. Childhood trauma, though not to be overlooked as a risk factor, is often not a sufficient explanation for adult psychopathology (Paris, 1997b; Sabo, 1997; Trull et al., 2000).

Cognitive-analytical theory (CAT) (Ryle, 1997) emphasizes influences from both cognitive and phenomenological psychology and psychoanalytic theory. This model conceptualizes BPD as a dysfunction marked by alternating multiple self-states. Self-states are cognitive-affective-behavioral psychic structures that represent internalized models of interpersonal functioning (i.e., repertoire of reciprocal roles) that develop over time. In a reasonably well-functioning person, these roles are adequate for giving and receiving what is necessary for healthy interpersonal relations. Persons with BPD seem to be "prone to abrupt and discomforting shifts between markedly contrasting states . . . accompanied by depersonalization-derealization experiences[,] . . . understood in the proposed model to be the effect of switches between partially dissociated self states" (Ryle, 1997, p. 83). Commonly encountered self-states reflect some of the key symptoms of BPD in character: idealization, emotional blankness, loss of control, rage. Ryle (1997) differentiates his model from psychoanalytic theory by emphasizing dissociation of these self-states rather than emphasizing the failure of repression and the reliance on splitting and projection as main defenses. The application of this theory to treatment emphasizes assisting the client in recognizing, understanding, modifying, and integrating these self-states with commensurate improvement in cognitive and interpersonal functioning. Although the research is in its early stages, the author recommends the use of controlled trials to compare the efficacy of treatment with other extant models. Uncontrolled evaluation suggests that about half of the participants benefited from CAT, but those with more severe symptoms tended to respond poorly to the intervention (Ryle & Golynkina, 2000).

The theoretical foundation for dialectical behavior therapy (Linehan, 1993a; Linehan et al., 1999) is a range of theories and conceptual frameworks. It is suggested that BPD is partly caused by a deficiency in the ability to regulate emotions, a deficiency that has its roots in genetic predisposition, prenatal trauma, or other early trauma. This temperamental vulnerability may include a high sensitivity to emotional stimuli, a tendency toward intense emotional reactions, difficulty returning to baseline emotional functioning (i.e., calming down), and poor modulation of emotional responses. This dysregulation in a child may then be exacerbated by what Linehan calls an "invalidating" environment, that is, circumstances in which emotional dysregulation and poor coping skills are reinforced through confusing and disconfirmatory communications in the home or by punishment of otherwise normal emotional expression. As a result, a child may begin to consistently doubt the veracity or genuineness of what he or she thinks and feels. In such an environment, painful emotions may be ignored or disregarded, and emotional expression discouraged in general. Persons in the environment (e.g., parents) may simply refuse to accept the accuracy of the child's labeling of his or her own emotions, or they may be generally unresponsive to the child's emotional needs. Theoretically, the consequences of such interactions may impair a child's ability to accurately identify and regulate his or her own feelings, a problem that may negatively affect identity development and future ability to cope with emotional distress, regulate behavior, and maintain stable interpersonal relations. As with similar theories that place the causes of psychopathology in family relations (e.g., dysfunctional family communications, the schizophrenogenic mother), more developmental research is needed to account for these specific processes.

As with other psychiatric disorders, consensus is emerging for a multivariate explanation of BPD. Various forms of evidence suggest that early childhood adversity (e.g., abuse, neglect, abandonment) has significant effects on emotion regulation and other neurocognitive abnormalities. Thus, current consensus considers a mix of genetic, neurocognitive, familial disruption, and other environmental stressors to contribute to the development of borderline personality disorder (Cole, Llera, & Pemberton, 2009; Crowell, Beauchaine, & Linehan, 2009; Leichsenring et al., 2011; Widom, Czaja, & Paris, 2009). In one prospective study, early separation from the mother before age 5 was also shown to increase symptoms of BPD while controlling for other factors, including temperament, child abuse, maternal problems, and other risks (Crawford, Cohen, Chen, Anglin, & Ehrensaft, 2009). The authors added that because they had no direct measure of parent-child interactions before age 5, and because the attachment measures used in the study could indicate only adolescent and adult interactions, they could not infer from the data that attachment insecurity mediated early separation and BPD symptoms. Thus, more longitudinal data are needed to understand better the biopsychosocial factors that contribute to this troubling condition.

Key Elements of MFS Assessment

Borderline personality disorder (BPD) (APA, 2013, p. 663) is marked by a "pervasive pattern of instability of interpersonal relationships, self-image, and affects, and marked impulsivity beginning by early adulthood and present in a variety of contexts," as indicated by five (or more) of the following: (1) frantic efforts to avoid real or imagined abandonment; (2) a pattern of unstable and intense interpersonal relationships characterized by alternating between extremes of idealization and devaluation; (3) identity disturbance, or a markedly and persistently unstable self-image or sense of self; (4) impulsivity in at least two areas that are potentially self-damaging (e.g., spending, sex, substance abuse, reckless driving, binge eating); (5) recurrent suicidal behaviors, gestures, or self-mutilating behavior; (6) affective instability due to a marked reactivity of mood (e.g., intense episodic dysphoria, irritability or anxiety usually lasting a few hours and only rarely more than a few days); (7) chronic feelings of emptiness; (8) inappropriate, intense anger or difficulty controlling anger (e.g., frequent displays of temper, constant anger, recurrent physical fights); (9) transient, stress-related paranoid ideation or severe dissociative symptoms.

In a thorough review of the literature regarding the reliability and validity of the DSM-IV criteria for BPD, Gunderson, Zanarini, and Kisiel (1995) concluded that BPD was rarely diagnosed alone, that there continues to be considerable overlap with other personality disorders (e.g., histrionic, avoidant), and that much of these criteria continue to be based on theoretical inferences versus observable behaviors. BPD also overlaps with Axis I diagnoses (e.g., mood disorders, PTSD), and although there is adequate reliability in identifying many of these signs and symptoms, there continues to be a lack of construct and predictive validity (Dahl, 1995). Narcissistic personality disorder appears to be even less reliable, and little evidence supports the validity of its presumed cause, course, or relevance to treatment (Gunderson, Ronningstam, & Smith, 1995; Paris, 1995).

Initially, a thorough examination of the client's presenting problems, signs, and symptoms are commensurate with the DSM-5 diagnosis for BPD particularly with regard to impulsive behaviors, highly conflicted relationships, self-harm and suicide risks, and mood disturbance. Fears regarding "abandonment" or problems with a stable self-image are more subject to inference and so less reliable. It is also important to carefully examine the historical consistency and duration of these behaviors and to examine factors in the current environment that may partly account for the client's emotional and behavioral instability.

Ongoing threats by an abusive partner, a history of domestic violence, sexual assault, involvement in criminal activity, and other situational factors may account for what appear to be "borderline" symptoms and behaviors. Practitioners should also carefully consider co-occurring disorders such as substance abuse, depression, major mental illness (e.g., bipolar disease), anxiety disorders (e.g., panic with agoraphobia, PTSD), and eating disorders, among others. These problems may be primary problems, not merely other manifestations of borderline personality. Given the variety of symptoms associated with a diagnosis of BPD, a thorough history taking is in order, and it should carefully consider cause-effect links between significant past events (e.g., traumatic events including sudden losses, physical or sexual abuse, victimization as result of a crime) and current co-occurring problems. A family history should note the presence of parental mental illnesses, substance abuse, domestic violence, criminal behavior and other significant pathology, and disruption in the client's childhood and adolescence. The fact that BPD symptoms overlap with a range of other disorders means that practitioners should be conservative in applying this label and should rule out other explanations.

A careful functional analysis of the client's daily encounters with stressful situations and his or her pattern of coping emotionally and behaviorally are essential. Those circumstances that clearly appear to precipitate the client's more egregious and potentially harmful behaviors should be highlighted (e.g., the client burning their own forearm with a cigarette after a domestic dispute). One might also expect periods of inactivity and low energy due to depression associated with disappointments or precipitated by what would otherwise be seen as normative stressors (e.g., an argument with someone at work). Given the likelihood of distortion, lying, or malingering, one should also make the attempt to engage significant others in the assessment and possibly include them in the intervention at some point. Obtaining collateral assessment data can go a long way toward clarifying incongruities in the client's self-report and obtaining the perspective of others who see the client within a broader systems context. The client's presentation in the consulting room or hospital can be quite different from at home or at work. A thorough MFS assessment that collates multiple points of view can provide a solid base for intervention planning.

Instruments

There are several scales that have been developed to identify BPD. The revised Personality Diagnostic Questionnaire (PDQ-R) (Hyler, Skodol, Kellman, Oldham, & Rosnick, 1990; Patrick, Links, Reekum, & Mitton, 1995) is a 152-item, self-administered, true-false instrument that includes subscales for 11 personality disorders, including BPD. It takes 20 minutes to complete. Patrick et al. (1995) examined three cutoff scores with inpatient and outpatient populations to determine the ideal scores for the BPD subscale that would provide the best sensitivity and specificity for psychiatrist-determined diagnosis of BPD. Overall, sensitivity and specificity ratings were inadequate and relatively inconsistent across three clinical samples. The PDQ-R was shown to have fairly high false-positive ratings with an inpatient sample ($n = 87$) (Hyler et al., 1990).

The Borderline Syndrome Index (Conte, Plutchik, Karasu, & Jerrett, 1980) comprises 52 dichotomous items to detect the presence of BPD. Until recently, little psychometric evaluation was conducted on this instrument. Marlowe, O'Neill-Byrne, Lowe-Ponsford, and Watson (1996) found modest correlations between the Borderline Syndrome Index, the Beck Depression Inventory, and a general index of psychopathology. However, the instrument performed poorly overall as a screening device for detecting BPD.

One BPD screening instrument has been developed to reflect Kernberg's (1975) theories on borderline personality organization. The Borderline Personality Inventory (BPI) is a short (53 items, yes or no) self-report instrument (Leichsenring, 1999). A four-part study was devised to test the factor structure, reliability, discriminant validity, and receiver operating characteristics of the scale (i.e., sensitivity and specificity cut scores). An initial 100-item version of the scale was administered to a small sample of clients diagnosed with BPD to establish interrater reliability (.90). In addition, 53 items correlated significantly with diagnostic criteria for BPD, and those 20 items with the highest correlations were scaled to determine a diagnosis of BPD. On the basis of additional samples of clients with and without BPD ($n = 484$), factor analysis was conducted and four subscales identified: identity diffusion, primitive defense mechanisms, impaired reality testing, and fear of fusion. Using the 20-item subscale, the BPI demonstrated very good sensitivity (85–89%) for accurately identifying persons diagnosed with BPD and very good specificity (82–90%) for identifying those who did not meet BPD criteria (i.e., "neurotic" and those diagnosed with schizophrenia). Internal consistency reliability for the four subscales ranged from acceptable to good, and test-retest reliabilities were good overall. Intercorrelations among the four subscales were moderate, as would be expected, and the subscales were invariant across sex and age. Thus, overall psychometric characteristics suggest the BPI could be used as a self-administered screening tool for BPD in mental health treatment environments.

The Borderline Personality Disorder Severity Index (BPDSI) (Arntz et al., 2003), a semistructured instrument based on DSM-IV criteria for BPD (with minor changes in the DSM-5), was developed and refined in a two-part study with a relatively small but mixed mental health clinic population (see instrument 10.1). The original interview format (Weaver & Clum, 1993) showed very good psychometric characteristics overall. The BPDSI is currently undergoing further psychometric evaluation, and factor structure, reliability, and validity appear strong. In addition, a score of 19 or higher appears at this time to be an indication of borderline psychopathology (personal communication, Dr. Giesen-Bloo, 2005; Giesen-Bloo, Wachters, Shouten, & Arntz, 2010).

Instrument 10.1   The Borderline Personality Disorder Severity Index,
Fourth Version

[ADMINISTRATOR:] This interview is about a number of things people can experience. You decide whether you feel you have experienced the particular item within the last three months and how often it has happened. All questions are asked in the same way, but if you don't understand them completely you can easily ask for some explanation. Do you have any questions about this so far?

Because we will only talk about the past three months, it's important to determine which period that was. Today is [date], three months ago it was [date]. That was around [important event/day in general and/or specific for the patient].

Notes preceding each question are meant for the interviewer and are not meant to be read out loud to the patient.

The following scale is used to provide a frequency score for all items except "Identity," which has an alternate scale. Record the scores for each item on the SCORING FORM [see appendix F].

0. Never
1. 1x in 3 months
2. 2x in 3 months
3. 3x in 3 months/1 x a month
4. 4 to 5x in 3 months/1x in 3 weeks
5. 6 to 7x in 3 months/1x in 2 weeks

6. 8 to 10x in 3 months/2x in 3 weeks
7. 1x week/11 to 15x in 3 months
8. Several times a week but less than half of the week
9. More than half of the week/almost daily
10. Daily

1. Abandonment: These items refer to frantic efforts attempted by the interviewee with the goal to prevent someone with whom interviewee has a relationship, is bonded with or is dependent on from abandoning him/her. Examples are, among other things, begging someone not to leave or physically trying to prevent someone from leaving.

1.1 Did you, in the last three months, ever become desperate when you thought that someone you care about was going to abandon you?
(when scoring positive, clear examples are required)

1.2 Did you, in the last three months, try to keep someone who's important to you and who wanted to avoid you (or whom you thought he/she wanted to avoid you) with you in a fanatic way? (e.g., continuous ringing up, checking, seducing—only exaggerated, forced, frenetic ways are scored)

(This item is about real and imagined abandonment; when scoring positive, clear examples of attempts are required) (Also scoring of examples and incidents that return at items 1.3, 1.4, and 1.5)

1.3 Did you, in the last three months, ever beg or cry for someone not to leave you?

1.4 Did you, in the last three months, ever threaten to do something to make sure that someone wouldn't leave you? (e.g., blackmail, lies, murder, suicide)

1.5 Did you, in the last three months, ever try to keep someone from leaving you in a physical way? (e.g., by standing in front of a door, hold on to someone)

1.6 How often did you, in the last three months, have a strong desire to hear someone tell you he/she loves you, cares about you, is not abandoning you, finds you attractive, et cetera.
(This can happen with both partners, family and friends)

1.7 How often did you, in the last three months, ask other people for affirmation, whereas the aim of the affirmation is reassurance that someone will not abandon you?

2. Interpersonal relationships: There are three characteristics for this criterion. First of all, there must be a pattern of instable relationships, which can be characterized by regular conflicts and imminent or actual break-up. Second, these relationships must be intense, meaning that strong emotions are involved (e.g., euphoria, aversion, anger, resentment, despair). Third, the interviewee must at some moments devaluate the other person (e.g., "he's really very mean"). At other moments the interviewee could idealize the other person (e.g., "my boyfriend is the most wonderful, attentive, and strongest person I ever met"). These persons use, in psychoanalytic terms, splitting as a defense mechanism.

Partner relationship

2.1 Were there moments, in the last three months, when you thought that your partner was everything you wanted and other moments at which you thought he/she was awful? (the conviction is essential, i.e., intrapsychological, so it's not necessarily about the actual relationship)

2.2 How often, in the last three months, did you have ups and downs in your partner relationship? (the focus is on the actual relationship)

2.3 How often, in the last three months, did you break up your partner relationship and/or get together again? (score both on and off, so two times of breaking up and getting together again receives a score of 4 not 2)

2.4 How often, in the last three months, did you start one or more *new* partner relationship(s) and/or did you end these? (score both 'on' and 'off' separately)

Other relationships

2.5 Were there moments, in the last three months, when you thought that your friends/family members/colleagues and/or other important persons were everything you wanted and other moments at which you thought that he/she were awful? (the conviction is essential, i.e., intrapsychological, so it's not necessarily about the actual relationship)

2.6 How often, in the last three months, did you have ups and downs in your relationships with friends/family members/colleagues and/or other important persons? (the focus is on the actual relationships)

2.7 How often, in the last three months, did you break up your relationships with friends/family members/colleagues and/or other important persons and/or got together again? (score both breaking up and getting together)

2.8 How often, in the last three months, did you start one or more *new* relationships with friends/family members/colleagues and/or important persons and/or did you end relationships? (score both breaking up and getting together)

3. Identity: Self-identity is a stable sense of self which provides unity of personality over time. The type of identity disturbance characteristic for borderline personality disorder exists as extreme shifts in the self-image of the person in question ("who am I?"). These shifts manifest themselves in sudden changes with respect to jobs, career goals, sexual orientation, personal values, friends, and the fundamental feeling one has about oneself (e.g., good or bad). These items must be scored only if the identity disturbance doesn't fit the developmental age of the person in question (i.e., normal adult identity shifts are not taken into account).

3.1 Were you, in the last three months, in diverse situations or with various people so different that you didn't always behave as the same person and that you didn't know anymore who you truly were?
0. absent
1. questionable/some support
2. probable not knowing who he/she is, but not very clearly defined
3. (quite) clear not knowing who he/she is, but not very dominant
4. dominant, clear and well-defined not knowing who he/she is

3.2 Did it happen, in the last three months, that the idea of who you are. changed strongly?
0. absent
1. questionable/some support
2. probable instability of self-image
3. (quite) clear instability of self-image
4. clear and dominant instability of self-image

3.3 Did it happen, in the last three months, that the feeling of you being a good or bad person changed strongly?
0. absent
1. questionable/some support
2. probable instability of sense of self
3. (quite) clear instability of sense of self
4. clear and dominant instability of sense of self

3.4 What have been your long-term goals for life in the last three months? For example, which education, job, and/or career would you want or wish for? Have these goals changed in the last three months? (clients in treatment often tell their only goal is to get better and/or finish treatment well; this is scored as avoidance)
0. absent
1. questionable/some support

2. probable instability of long term goals/probable avoidance of dealing with long term goals

3. (quite) clear instability of long term goals, but not very dominant/(quite) clear avoidance of dealing with long term goals, but not very dominant

4. clear and dominant instability of long term goals/clear and dominant avoidance of dealing with long term goals

3.5 Have you changed, in the last three months, in your view of what is morally right or wrong? (in your view about your standards and values/what you can and what you can't do/what's good and bad) (question intensity/direction/frequency of changes)

0. absent
1. questionable/some support
2. probable instability of moral values
3. (quite) clear instability of moral values, but not very dominant
4. clear and dominant instability of moral values

3.6 Have you had trouble, in the last three months, to determine what is important in your life? Has this changed in the last three months?

0. absent
1. questionable/some support
2. probable instability of personal values/probable avoidance
3. (quite) clear instability of personal values, but not very dominant/probable avoidance but not very dominant
4. clear and dominant instability of moral values/clear and dominant avoidance

3.7 Have you had trouble, in the last three months, to determine what sort of friends you would like to have? Does the sort of friends you have change often? (some people say they don't have friends; this is scored as avoidance)

0. absent
1. questionable/some support
2. probable instability with regard to friends/probable avoidance with regard to friends
3. (quite) clear instability with regard to friends, but not very dominant/probable avoidance with regard to friends but not very dominant
4. clear and dominant instability with regard to friends/clear and dominant avoidance with regard to friends

3.8 Did you, in the last three months, ever doubt if you wanted a sexual relationship with men *or* women? After the interviewee's reply: How often has this changed in the last three months? (stable heterosexual/bisexual/homosexual orientation is scored 0)

0. absent
1. rarely
2. has probably doubts with regard to sexual orientation
3. has (quite) clearly doubts with regard to sexual orientation
4. has serious doubts with regard to sexual orientation

4. Impulsivity: Next are a few examples of things people can act on impulsively. Things of which you later thought that you should not have done or things that caused or could have caused problems for you or your environment.

(behavior with the primary goal of eliminating negative feelings and/or inducing positive feelings is essential; *not* the behavior with the primary goal to damage oneself or others). The core characteristic of this criterion is the inability of the person to control his/her impulses, through which he/she gets involved in behavior that is satisfactory in the short term but can be damaging in the long term. The behaviors mentioned below are examples, they don't cover the full spectrum of impulsive behaviors.

4.1 How often, in the last three months, did you irresponsibly spend money and/or spend more money than you actually can spend? (e.g., gambling, impulsive buying, making many and long phone calls)

4.2 How often, in the last three months, did you have sex with people you didn't or hardly know?

4.3 How often, in the last three months, did you have unsafe sex? (sex without considering the possible self-damaging consequences and/or pregnancy)

4.4 How often, in the last three months, did you have too much alcohol and/or did you use alcohol at the wrong moments? (with alcoholic people: note the standard use of alcohol at 4.4.A on the score form; everything on top of that is scored at 4.4)

4.5 How often, in the last three months, did you use too much soft drugs and/or did you use soft drugs at the wrong moments? (with drug addicts: note the standard use of soft drugs at 4.5.A on the score form; everything on top of that is scored at 4.5)

4.6 How often, in the last three months, did you take pills? (not with the goal of suicide but with the goal of getting high)

4.7 How often, in the last three months, did you use hard drugs? (with drug addicts: note the standard use of hard drugs at 4.7.A on the score form; everything on top of that is scored at 4.7)

4.8 How often, in the last three months, did you have episodes of binge eating? (all binge eating is scored, so with or without loss of control, with or without planning, etc.)

4.9 How often, in the last three months, were you reckless in traffic? (e.g., driving too fast or under the influence of alcohol) (not caused by dissociation)

4.10 How often, in the last three months, have you committed theft? (with what intention? It's essential that it's done to get a good feeling or to push aside a bad feeling; it's not about enriching oneself)

4.11 How often, in the last three months, did you do things impulsively that could have gotten you in trouble or actually did get you in trouble? (e.g., cancel appointments, not keeping up to agreements, subscribe to a course/education, book a vacation) (not self-mutilation or suicidal behavior; note answers on score-form)

5. Parasuicidal behavior: The next questions inquire if you tried to hurt or wound yourself in the last three months.

Self-mutilation with self-injury as immediate consequence, (i.e., tissue damage or physical pain), <u>without any suicidal intention</u>

5.1 How often, in the last three months, did you deliberately hit yourself or did you hit your head, fist, knuckles, or other body part into something? Or smash a window with your fist and/or other body part?

5.2 How often, in the last three months, did you scratch or pinch yourself?

5.3 How often, in the last three months, did you bite yourself? (what generally speaking hurts, so not nail biting)

5.4 How often, in the last three months, did you tear your hair? (can also be eyebrows or eyelashes)

5.5 How often, in the last three months, did you cut yourself? (also cutting relatively shallow, more or less resulting in scratches)

5.6 How often, in the last three months, did you burn yourself? (cigarette, clothes iron)

5.7 How often, in the last three months, did you stick needles and such in your body?

5.8 How often, in the last three months, did you harm yourself on purpose? (e.g., swallow sharp objects, take dangerous substances, enter sharp/dangerous objects into body openings like the vagina, penis, ears, etc.; note well on the score form)

Suicide (plans/attempts)

5.9 How often, in the last three months, did you want to kill yourself?

5.10 How often, in the last three months, did you tell other people that you wanted to kill yourself? (not scored when it's about passive suicidal ideation (e.g., telling others "I wish I was dead")

5.11 How often, in the last three months, did you make plans to kill yourself? (when these plans lead to particular steps, score at 5.12)

5.12 How often, in the last three months, did you take steps towards killing yourself? (when these steps lead to an attempt, score at 5.13)

5.13 How often, in the last three months, did you attempt to take your own life?

6. Affective instability: I now want to ask you about mood changes. It is about striking changes with regard to a dejected/depressed, irritable, anxious, desperate and/or angry mood. Affective instability refers to the alternating, instable quality of mood of the interviewee. Even though the mood alteration is often abrupt, a sudden onset of the change in mood is not required. Instead, this criterion specifies frequent affective shifts that are indeed strong but of relative short endurance (rather hours than days or weeks).

6.1 Are you aware of such mood shifts towards a dejected (depressed) mood? How often, in the last three months, did this happen?
(Not due to Axis I diagnoses)

6.2 And how often, in the last three months, towards an irritable and/or edgy mood?
(Not because of Axis I)

6.3 And how often, in the last three months, towards an anxious mood?
(Not because of Axis I)

6.4 And how often, in the last three months, towards a desperate mood? (Not because of Axis I)

6.5 And how often, in the last three months, towards an angry mood? (Not because of Axis I)

(When in doubt of the influence of Axis I diagnoses score the items)

7. **Emptiness:** Chronic feelings of emptiness are often linked with feelings of boredom, loneliness, worthlessness or feelings "you can't define."

7.1 How often, in the last three months, did you feel bored or empty inside? (This is about feelings of emptiness or boredom resulting in stress or inadequate behavior. Inadequate behavior also includes the negative influence of these feelings on normal or adequate behavior. For example, not being able to do anything while it was desired or necessary to do something.)

7.2 How often, in the last three months, didn't you do anything as a consequence of these feelings of emptiness or boredom, while you actually did want to do something? (e.g., stay in bed instead of doing shopping)

7.3 How often, in the last three months, did you do things as a consequence of these feelings of emptiness or boredom, while you actually did want to do something else? (e.g., going out instead of working, alcohol and drug abuse can also belong to this criterion)

7.4 How often, in the last three months, did it happen that you couldn't take a moment to rest? (e.g., cleaning or pacing up and down, this is interpreted as avoidance of rest to keep feelings of emptiness away)

8. **Outbursts of anger:** The next questions are about outbursts of anger or rage. Inappropriate anger refers to the intensity of anger of the person, which is not in proportion to the cause of the anger. Manifestations of extreme physical (violent) behavior, like hitting people or throwing things, can indicate a lack of anger control with regard to anger/rage. The rage is often expressed in the context of an actual or experienced lack of care/attention, loss or neglect.

8.1 Does it happen that you experience a bad temper and/or have a fit of rage? How often, in the last three months, did this happen?

8.2 How often, in the last three months, did you act cynical and/or sarcastic to other people?
(stinging, sneering, mocking)

8.3 How often, in the last three months, did you swear, scream, and/or slam doors?
(make noise)

8.4 How often, in the last three months, were you so mad that you weren't approachable anymore, that you couldn't be brought to reason anymore?
(outbursts of anger)

8.5 How often, in the last three months, did you throw things, break things, et cetera?

8.6 How often, in the last three months, did you attack others?
(physically)

9. Dissociation and paranoid ideation: Some people strongly react to stressful events. Some people with borderline personality disorder develop transitory paranoid or dissociative symptoms during periods of stress. These symptoms are rarely of such severity that an additional diagnosis can be made (i.e. psychotic disorders). The stressor often is an actual, supposed or anticipated absence of the care/attention of a care-taker (e.g., partner, parent, or therapist). In such situations can the actual or supposed return of care/attention result in remission of the symptoms? The dissociative symptoms consist of periods of dissociative amnesia (sometimes expressed through the person's feeling of "losing time"), depersonalization (i.e. the feeling of becoming estranged from yourself or moving away from yourself) or derealization (i.e. the feeling that the external world is unreal or unusual). These periods usually last a few minutes or hours.

Dissociation: depersonalization (9.1), derealization (9.2), consciousness (9.3), memory (9.4 and 9.5)

9.1 To what extent, in the last three months, did you feel not like yourself anymore, as if you stood outside yourself, or did you experience yourself as in a movie or dream?
(Self is both body and mind) (Not because of drugs)

9.2 To what extent, in the last three months, did you perceive the world around you entirely different, or experience it entirely different, so that this appears very strange or unreal to you?
(e.g., other people look unfamiliar or like robots) (Not because of drugs)

9.3 To what extent, in the last three months, didn't you know anymore what you were doing or where you were?
(Not because of drugs)

9.4 To what extent, in the last three months, did you, all of a sudden, not recognize people and/or objects familiar to you anymore ?
(Not because of drugs)

9.5 To what extent, in the last three months, couldn't you quite remember important things anymore?
(Not because of drugs; clinical judgment of the importance of something, so not always out of the interviewee's perception)

Paranoid ideation

9.6 To what extent, in the last three months, did you have trouble with being very suspicious or distrusting other people?
(Not because of drugs) (The idea is essential)

9.7 To what extent, in the last three months, were you convinced that other people were out to get you, that you were being pursued?
(Not because of drugs) (This item is about a temporary delusion)

9.8 To what extent, in the last three months, were you convinced that other people were unfairly treating you?
(Not because of drugs) (This item is about a temporary delusion)

SELECTING EFFECTIVE INTERVENTIONS

There is little controlled intervention research with persons suffering from personality disorders in general (Crits-Christoph, 1998; Turkat, 1992), but research on interventions for BPD has increased in recent years. Overall, outcomes for treating BPD can be viewed with some optimism. In their narrative review, Leichsenring et al. (2011) summarized the findings of 24 controlled studies of treatment for borderline personality disorder including: ten studies of dialectical behavior therapy, six of cognitive and cognitive-behavioral therapies, and six on various psychodynamic treatments (e.g., mentalization, transference). They concluded that the various therapies show a reduction in some symptoms (outcomes vary in this regard), including suicidal ideation, self-injury, and affect regulation, with good maintenance of gains over time, yet most clients continue to meet the diagnostic criteria for BPD. Although the authors suggest that there are no substantial differences in outcomes among the various treatments, to date, treatments based on cognitive behavioral principles (including DBT for a total of 16 studies) have provided the largest body of replicated evidence to date for effectiveness. Evidence for various psychodynamic treatments remains slim, and it is unclear what the effective components of psychodynamic treatments are. Zanarini (2009) also concluded that cognitive-behavioral approaches for BPD have accrued the greatest amount of evidence to date for obtaining reasonably good outcomes (particularly in reduction of self-mutilation and/or suicide attempts), but it is not clear that other approaches are not comparably effective. Paris (2009) makes the point that both cognitive-behavioral and psychodynamic approaches appear to be effective with people diagnosed with BPD and might share some common elements, in that both focus on teaching clients to better recognize their thoughts and feelings, and to regulate emotional responses and behaviors (e.g., self-mutilation). He notes that the effectiveness of psychodynamic approaches does not appear to depend on exploration of the past as in traditional psychodynamic approaches but emphasizes examination of current interpersonal experiences and how they affect the client's thoughts, feelings, and behaviors in the present. In that broad sense, both psychodynamic and cognitive-behavioral interventions might share some key elements. Future studies should focus on key process elements (e.g., therapeutic relationship, efforts to change cognitions directly, emotion regulation, problem-solving skills, transference interpretations) to isolate those intervention and client behavioral mechanisms that are most strongly linked to sustained positive outcomes in these challenging-to-treat clients.

Psychodynamic Treatments for BPD.   There is modest evidence to support the effectiveness of psychodynamic therapies with clients diagnosed with BPD. Bateman and Fonagy (1999) compared psychoanalytically oriented partial hospitalization care with standard outpatient care for 38 borderline patients (19 completed treatment). The psychoanalytically oriented group consisted of combined individual and group therapy, weekly expressive therapy, weekly community meetings, and medication review. Therapy was provided by psychiatric nurses who "had no formal psychotherapy qualifications" (p. 1565). Control patients received outpatient services that included medication review, problem-solving therapy, community follow-up visits, and no formal psychotherapy of any kind. Results were measured over 18 months and showed generally superior outcomes for the experimental group on several measures, including depression, suicidal acts, self-harm, improved social functioning, and inpatient days. Interpretation of the results, however, is problematic. The experimental group received substantially more treatment overall. Thus, the study appears to be more a comparison of the structure, intensity, and amount of treatment rather than a test of psychoanalytic intervention.

Gregory et al. (2008) randomized two groups of clients who met diagnostic criteria for both BPD and a co-occurring substance use disorder and tested dynamic deconstructive psychotherapy (DDP) ($n = 15$) versus treatment as usual in the community ($n = 15$). According to the authors, the purpose of DDP, similar to other psychodynamically informed therapies, is to "foster verbalization of affects and elaboration of recent interpersonal experiences into simple narratives so that patients can begin to link their affective experiences to their verbal/symbolic attribution capacities. The therapist also tries to help the patient integrate polarized attributions toward self and other" (p. 33). After about 12 months of treatment, DDP showed better results for parasuicidal behaviors, alcohol misuse, and a need for institutional care. DDP also showed more improvement in core symptoms of BPD, depression, dissociation, and perceived social support.

Transference-focused psychodynamic psychotherapy (TFP) uses interpretation, clarification, and confrontation to help clients alter internalized views of themselves and others that were presumably distorted in early childhood as a result of inadequate or adverse parenting. These events might then become manifest as transference within the context of the practitioner-client relationship. One comparison study randomized 90 clients to three types of therapy: transference focused (twice weekly), dialectical behavior therapy (weekly individual and group sessions), and psychodynamic supportive therapy (once weekly plus more as needed). Of the 62 clients who completed three waves of measurement over 12 months of treatment, both TFP and DBT were associated with reduced suicidality, the two psychodynamic therapies showed improvements in anger and impulsivity, and TFP was shown to significantly improve secure attachment and reflective capacity (Clarkin, Levy, Lenzenweger, & Kernberg, 2007). Comparative analysis showed that TFP and DBT were only marginally more effective than general supportive treatment.

Doering et al. (2010) compared TFP with community treatment over a year in 104 women outpatients who met criteria for BPD. They found TFP to be more efficacious in reducing borderline symptoms, reducing suicide attempts (but not self-injury), improving psychosocial functioning, and personality organization, but they did not show differences in levels of depression, anxiety, and general psychopathology. Attrition rates were very high (38.5% in the TFP group, 67.3% in the community group), which calls into question any solid conclusions about the effectiveness of TFP in this study.

Mentalization Therapy.   Mentalization-based treatment (MBT) has been characterized by Paris (2009) as a combination of cognitive and psychodynamic approaches. The purpose of MBT is to help clients focus on and better understand how thoughts and feelings affect their behavior toward others. On the basis of earlier investigations, Bateman and Fonagy (1999, 2001, 2008) found that 8 years after initial partial hospitalization treatment, mentalization therapy resulted in substantially better outcomes than the treatment-as-usual group (general clinical management) in reduced suicide (23% vs. 74%), diagnostic status (13% vs. 87%), use of medication, and overall functioning. In a separate study, Bateman and Fonagy (2009) randomized 134 patients to structured clinical management programs in which one group received mentalization therapy and the other received support and problem solving. After 18 months, both groups had improved, but the MBT group had substantially fewer hospitalizations, suicide attempts, and acts of self-harm; lower depression and other symptoms; and better psychosocial functioning. The authors would not aver that mentalization was the core effective ingredient, but they emphasized practical aspects of the treatment: the use of a practical view of the mind and the lack of need for intensive specialized training.

Dialectical Behavior Therapy.   Linehan and associates have formulated a successful cognitive-behavioral approach—dialectical behavior therapy—to help clients diagnosed with BPD cope with negative affect while reducing self-destructive and other maladaptive behaviors. Results have also demonstrated better treatment compliance and fewer days in the hospital than those receiving alternative psychotherapy. Components of the approach were employed in a problem-solving framework and included cognitive modification, behavioral skills training, contingency management, and exposure to behavioral cues. On the basis of a number of controlled studies, cognitive-behavioral methods are considered the first-line approach (Leichsenring et al., 2011; Linehan, 1993a; Linehan et al., 1999). Dialectical behavior therapy is a cognitive-behavioral intervention intended to help persons with BPD learn to better self-regulate their dysfunctional thinking, problem behaviors, and emotions more effectively. The term *dialectic* implies one's struggle to better tolerate extremes of emotion and change from rigid dichotomous thinking about him- or herself and others to seeing oneself and others in a more balanced and less extreme way. For the practitioner's part, the dialectic

involves balancing the need to accept some of the client's distress and troubling behaviors while at the same time helping the client develop the skills to
better regulate emotions and control problem behaviors.

An early randomized controlled trial conducted by Linehan, Armstrong,
Suarez, Allmon, and Heard (1991) matched 44 women (22 in each group) on
diagnosis, number of parasuicidal behaviors, age, hospitalizations, and prognosis. The women were randomly assigned to either DBT or treatment-as-
usual (TAU) in the community. Individual therapists in the study used behavioral management skills, contingency management, cognitive modification,
and exposure to emotional cues. These techniques were balanced with standard supportive therapeutic methods, including empathy, reflection, and
acceptance. Group sessions employed a psychoeducational format that
included behavioral skills training in three areas: interpersonal functioning,
distress tolerance, and emotion regulation skills. Clients attended weekly
1-hour individual and 2.5-hour group sessions for a year. Assessment and
evaluation measures were taken at baseline, 4, 8, and 12 months. A combination of standardized and unstandardized scales were used in the study to
measure frequency of parasuicidal episodes, suicide attempts, amount of psychiatric and medical treatments received, and measures of depression and
hopelessness, among others. There were significant pre-treatment differences between the two groups on important clinical indicators. Results
showed fewer (i.e., median of 1.5 vs. 9) and less severe episodes of parasuicidal behavior and fewer days in the hospital compared to TAU clients, but no
differences in depression, hopelessness, suicidal ideation, or reasons for living. Attrition rate for the DBT group was less than one third than that for the
TAU group (16.7% vs. 58.3%). DBT patients also spent less time in psychiatric
hospitals (average 8.46 vs. 38.86 days) and had fewer admissions. In the last
4 months of treatment, the TAU group engaged in suicidal behavior almost
twice as often as did the DBT group. The authors suggested that the low attrition rate in the DBT group might be attributable to directly addressing ther-
apy-interfering behaviors and the development of a solid working relationship as an important component of the intervention.

Subsequent studies of the same clients also revealed less parasuicidal
behavior; less anger; and better adjustment with regard to social functioning,
work; and global adjustment for DBT clients (Linehan, Heard, & Armstrong,
1993; Linehan, Tutek, Heard, & Armstrong, 1994). Gains, which were generally maintained over the course of 1-year follow-up, did not appear to be an
artifact of experimental treatment factors, such as lower fee for DBT clients,
more therapy or phone contacts, or the novelty of being involved in an experimental treatment. With other psychiatric indicators (e.g., depression, hopelessness, suicidal ideation), there were no significant differences. Limitations
of the study include the fact that more than 25% of TAU clients never made it
into treatment, and DBT therapists had more experience in treating clients
diagnosed with BPD. Although generalizations from this one study of 22
women with BPD should be made cautiously, the differences with regard to

reduction in parasuicidal behaviors were substantial. Other reports have offered positive narrative accounts of implementing DBT (Corwin, 1996; Miller, 1995), including in partial hospital settings (Simpson et al., 1998) and inpatient programs (Swenson, Sanderson, Dulit, & Linehan, 2001).

In the Netherlands, Verheul et al. (2003) randomly assigned 58 women who met BPD criteria to DBT versus TAU (i.e., mental health or substance abuse treatment). The intervention began 4 weeks after random assignment, and clients were treated by psychologists and social workers for 12 months. The DBT group showed superior outcomes overall: almost three times as many patients were retained in the DBT group for the entire year, four times as many clients (8 vs. 2) attempted suicide in the TAU group (although the difference was not statistically significant), and DBT clients demonstrated significantly fewer self-mutilating behaviors (35% vs. 57%) than those in the TAU group.

Bohus et al. (2004) compared 4 months of inpatient DBT for women (after randomization) with TAU, finding significant reductions in 10 or 11 measures of psychopathology (e.g., depression, anxiety, dissociation) and reduced self-harming behaviors, compared with virtually no improvement for the TAU group. In another RCT, DBT was compared with TAU in the community with 101 women who met criteria for BPD and engaged in at least two suicide attempts or self-injuries over the previous 5 years (Linehan et al., 2006). After a year of treatment and a year of follow-up, clients receiving DBT were half as likely to attempt suicide, engage in self-harm, be hospitalized, or drop out of treatment. The authors noted that their findings were remarkably consistent with previous studies (e.g., Linehan et al., 1991). A follow-up study showed that co-occurring substance dependence was also more successfully treated in the DBT group (Harned et al., 2008).

Using the Linehan et al. (1991) intervention approach, Verheul et al. (2003) recruited a sample of women (ages 18–70) from both psychiatric service and addiction treatment referrals and offered 1 year of treatment to 62 eligible patients who were then randomized to either DBT or TAU. Attrition in the DBT group was half that of TAU, and DBT resulted in much lower rates of self-harming behaviors, a result that was not explained by medication use.

Other data from a large sample ($N = 180$) study comparing DBT to a psychodynamically informed treatment combined with general psychiatric management showed positive and comparable outcomes for both approaches with respect to suicidal and self-harming episodes, psychiatric symptoms, general social functioning, emergency visits, and days in the hospital (McMain et al., 2009). The authors took pains to point out differences between the two approaches (e.g., skills training vs. attention to negative transference), but they also had much in common, including psychoeducation, therapeutic relationship, here-and-now focus, and focus on emotion regulation. DBT also has been shown to translate well to "real world" clinical settings, with comparable results that extend to clients with co-occurring problems as well (Davidson et al., 2006; Kroger et al., 2006; Soler et al., 2009).

Although results of DBT with reduction in self-harming behaviors have been consistently good and support its use as an evidence-based practice, positive outcomes are not universal. In a randomized controlled trial in Australia, clients receiving DBT failed to show significantly greater reductions in self-harm or hospitalizations compared with wait-list controls. However, DBT did result in significantly better psychosocial functioning overall (Carter, Willcox, Lewin, Conrad, & Bendit, 2010).

Change-Process Considerations.   DBT has provided a promising alternative to previous treatments for BPD. However, in addition to the lack of replication, other substantive questions regarding the change-process theory behind the techniques as well as the relative effectiveness of individual components of the overall approach remain to be addressed. From an evidence-based perspective, it is far from clear that many of the theoretical assumptions are either valid or necessary to account for the effectiveness of DBT. In addition, although one can extrapolate from the efficacy studies of CBT with other serious problems (e.g., PTSD, substance abuse, anxiety disorders, depression, antisocial behaviors), it seems quite reasonable that the core components of DBT—including a sound working alliance, core CBT coping skills (e.g., self-monitoring, challenging dysfunctional cognitions, practicing emotional regulation and stress management skills, practicing interpersonal skills), facilitating social support, and contingency management strategies— are likely to hold up well in future research. Although the theoretical concepts and practices of DBT may appear daunting to the uninitiated, one study demonstrated that a diverse group of clinicians could, with adequate training, grasp the concepts of DBT (Hawkins & Sinha, 1998). However, as the authors pointed out: "Conceptual mastery does not guarantee adherence to a model, or even the ability to practice it adequately, and whether the knowledge acquired in this training initiative translates into practice approximate to Dr. Linehan's model remains to be determined" (Hawkins & Sinha, 1998, p. 384).

Descriptions of Effective Intervention Methods

Although she describes DBT as employing a wide range of standard CBT methods, Linehan (1993a, 1993b) stresses that DBT is different from CBT in the following ways: first, there is an emphasis on acceptance and validation of the client's behavior as the client experiences it in the moment; second, there is an emphasis on intervening with client behaviors that interfere with the process of therapy; third, there is an emphasis on therapeutic relationship and on dialectical processes. Although one could argue about whether these factors truly diverge from standard CBT practice, they are given priority in the practice of DBT.

Linehan's (1993a, 1993b) now-classic text and workbook describe DBT theory and intervention methods in great detail. At its core, DBT is an assertive combination of intensive social support for clients in the context of the practitioner-client relationship; a careful functional behavioral analysis; and the teaching of coping skills to decrease dysfunctional thoughts and behaviors, increase functional behaviors, and improve overall quality of life. Although there is some flexibility in how the treatment may be applied, formal DBT employs the use of several modalities, including individual therapy, supportive therapy group, structured skill training, phone consultation, and other ancillary treatments (e.g., hospitalization) as needed. An important dimension of DBT is an early emphasis on contracting with the client regarding attendance at sessions, commitment to staying in treatment for a substantial duration (e.g., at least 1 year), agreements to reduce suicidal and parasuicidal acts, and not engaging in behaviors that disrupt or interfere with treatment, among others. The practitioner is also explicit about adhering to other fairly standard guidelines for ethical practice. The tone of DBT, while commensurate with CBT methods in general, is a model for most forms of psychosocial intervention: the client contracts to participate constructively for specific reasons and the practitioner practices true informed consent by telling the client in clear terms what their work together is about and how it will be carried out.

The core goals of DBT are to help the client reduce dysfunctional (e.g., absolutistic, extreme, or nondialectical thinking); develop a "dialectical" way of thinking (i.e., moderation; balancing, integrating, or reconciling apparent contradictions); and reduce harmful behaviors by learning a range of coping skills to better regulate emotional expression, solve problems-in-living, and improve quality of life. In addition to experiencing depression, emotional turmoil, and suicidal feelings, persons diagnosed with BPD often struggle with tumultuous and often abusive relationships, other mental health disorders, substance abuse, problems with changing jobs, unstable housing, untreated health problems, criminal activity (e.g., shoplifting, prostitution, dealing drugs), risky sexual behaviors, and gambling, among others. Cognitive-behavioral methods employed successfully with these other problems are congruent with the methods employed in DBT. The emphasis on reducing dysfunctional thinking is quite similar to the methods employed in standard cognitive therapy. Dysfunctional thinking, for example, includes absolutist or dichotomous thinking (either-or, good or bad, "love him or hate him"), drawing conclusions from too little data, overgeneralizing from one occurrence, and catastrophizing problems. Reducing suicidal ideation as well as parasuicidal and potentially genuine suicidal acts are priorities as well. In addition to cognitive therapy methods, there is a strong emphasis on employing behavioral analysis and standard behavioral problem-solving methods. Linehan (1993a) summarizes: "In most cases, the behavioral analysis will show that there are skill deficits, problematic reinforcement contingencies, inhibitions resulting from fear and guilt, and faulty beliefs and assumptions. Thus, a treatment program integrating skill training, contingency management, exposure strategies, and cognitive modification is likely to be required. The behavioral target of each strategy, however, is dependent on the behavioral analysis" (p. 100). Clients are also helped to use problem-solving skills to move toward a more moderate approach to life that improves lifestyle functioning and overall psychosocial well-being.

The process of DBT occurs in four stages (Linehan et al., 1999). In stage 1, the practitioner addresses some of the most immediate and troubling behavioral disturbances typically associated with BPD: suicidal threats, treatment compliance, co-occurring problems (e.g., substance abuse, homelessness, hospitalizations, health problems), problems with interpersonal functioning, emotional dysregulation, and difficulties tolerating stress. In stage 2, although the more dramatic behavioral problems have hopefully been brought under some control, the client continues to suffer emotional pain in "quiet desperation," pain that may be related to PTSD. The goal of stage 2 is to help clients reduce some of their emotional distress through exposure methods (similar to those reviewed in chapters 8 and 9). In stages 3 and 4, the focus is geared toward moderating distress or unhappiness and moving toward more fulfilling engagement in life.

Linehan et al. (1999) discuss several general modes of service delivery. These include motivational enhancement of the client by (1) reinforcing client progress; (2) skill building (i.e., capability enhancement) to help clients learn to cope better with emotional distress through standard behavioral techniques (i.e., teaching, modeling, rehearsal, feedback, and practicing through homework assignments); (3) generalization through homework assignments, in vivo interventions, and phone consultations; (4) increasing environmental supports (e.g., a positive therapeutic environment, family sessions if warranted, seeking out therapeutically positive social supports); and (5) enhancing the practitioner's capabilities and motivation through support, consultation, and supervision.

Specific behavioral coping skills methods are geared toward the particular problems experienced by clients diagnosed with BPD and are further specified for the individual client. The major behavioral skill categories include the following:

- *Core mindfulness skills* (influenced by Zen teaching) help clients experience the moment through observation, reflecting on an event less emotionally and fully participating in events with less self-consciousness. Clients also learn to be less judgmental about events, focus on "one thing at a time," and emphasize being effective and achieving goals over getting caught up in emotion-driven contests to prove "I'm right."

- *Distress tolerance skills* help clients with the amount of emotional pain they continue to deal with. Learning how to accept distress as a part of life is an important goal for clients who may typically avoid it through numbing, cutting, drug abuse, promiscuity, or other unhealthful behaviors.

- *Emotion regulation skills* help clients be less controlled by their emotions. These skills include identification of the feeling, identification of what the function of the emotion is (e.g., often a form of communication), emphasis on reducing their vulnerability to the "emotion mind" through increased self-efficacy and problem-solving (e.g., mastery activities), engaging in activities that increase positive emotional events, acting in ways that are in apposition to the emotion evoked in a situation (e.g., respond pleasantly in an uncomfortable social situation), and increasing mindfulness (i.e., awareness and acceptance) of emotions.

- *Interpersonal effectiveness skills* emphasize clear and effective expression in routine or novel interpersonal and social situations in order to cope effectively. Many of the skills are similar to those in standard assertiveness and interpersonal skill training programs (e.g., expressing thoughts and feelings clearly, being assertive, saying no, asking for assistance).

- *Self-management skills* include (in addition to those skills listed immediately above) generic behavioral skills for solving problems and successfully getting things done. These skills include setting realistic goals, behavioral self-analysis and optimizing of the environment, self-reward techniques, and dealing realistically with relapses and partial successes.

- *Exposure and cognitive modification strategies* help change a client's cognitive and emotional responses to trauma-related stimuli (graduated covert exposure is a core component of dealing with the effects of trauma). CBT methods for PTSD were covered in chapter 9, but refer to Linehan (1993a) for the recommended application of these methods in work with clients with BPD. Once clients have achieved some level of emotional and behavioral stability, methods used to help them recognize the continuing effects of trauma can be employed to deal with them more effectively.

A more detailed accounting of all these cognitive-behavioral skills for addressing primary and secondary behavioral targets is found in Linehan's (1993a, 1993b) text and companion workbook.

TREATMENT PLANNING AND EVALUATION

CASE STUDY: FRANCINE

Francine is a 34-year-old white female who came to see a social worker, Gail, at the local mental health clinic at the urging of her husband. He was becoming increasingly concerned about her strange behavior. Francine and her husband, Geoff, live in a relatively isolated rural area with their 12-year-old daughter, Tabatha. Francine came to the social worker very depressed, talking of "ending it all," although she had no specific plan. She said she had been depressed all her life; she had not held a job for some time; and she was having a terrible time with

Tabatha, who virtually ignored Francine's attempts to set limits or get her to help around the house. She described her relationship with her husband as "OK, not great"; they had no specific problems, but she'd lost interest in having sex with him over the past few years. Geoff was a maintenance person for the local township, worked hard, and was typically dirty and very tired when he came home in the evening. Francine said she did not find him appealing anymore. Francine had worked as a receptionist in the past but had quit her job a few months earlier and had not worked since. She said she could not get along with the people at work, that they did not accept her. Upon further inspection, it seemed that in her first week on the job she found out that she had not been invited to a party. When she heard others discussing it around the lunch table she became upset and started screaming at them, "Don't fuck with me. If you don't like me just say so!"

Someone took her aside, apologized about the oversight, and tried to explain that the get-together was for a longtime employee who was leaving and that the party had been planned and people invited long before Francine started working there. No slight was intended. Francine then felt humiliated because of her behavior, left work, and did not return. She said she took off in her car to go home, sped out of the parking lot, and almost had an accident with a passing car. She pulled the car over to the side of the road and started gasping and crying; she was reaching for her tranquilizers when a police cruiser came by. He noticed the pills and the scratches and cuts on her arms, and transported her to the local hospital's emergency room. It was revealed later that she may have experienced a panic attack, which Francine described as "freaking out . . . something that happens now and then."

MFS Assessment: Defining Problems and Goals

Francine had recently found herself reminiscing about her mother, who died a few years earlier. Her dad was still alive. She described him as always having treated her very specially because her mother was sick often (depressed, she thinks, and had used a lot of medication), and Francine had to "take over the house" now and then. She described her father as being somewhat flirtatious with her when she was a teenager but does not recall it ever going beyond that. Her parents were never abusive, but she describes herself as often feeling alone. She had few friends because her parents discouraged it, and she characterized her home and family as "too weird to bring home any friends." Francine did attend a community college for a few years, during which time she struggled with a moderate drug problem (alcohol, marijuana, and cocaine). She described what sounded like a series of somewhat tumultuous and abusive relationships, and she had obtained counseling for a brief bout with bulimia during that time as well.

She sometimes described intense feelings of anger at herself, and she often felt guilty for not being a better person, wife, daughter, and mother. She described how she would like to hurt the "little demon-girl inside her" for not being better. During these times, she would often hide in the attic (when no one else was home) and cut up her arms with a hobby knife or broken pieces of glass. Although she usually hid her arms with long sleeves, she had recently exposed veins in her wrist that resulted in excessive bleeding and required emergency intervention at the hospital. Although her husband often worried about her depression, he became alarmed when he saw the scratches and scarring on her arms. Further examination over the course of a few weeks revealed that Francine did have a relationship with a friend who had been sharing some benzodiazepine medication with her, she said, to "help me with my nerves." Francine was taking them off and on when she wanted to "calm down." Her husband described Francine's intense emotional outbursts. He said he tried to help her, to calm her down, but she would not listen to him and just seemed to become more enraged at him the more he tried.

A detailed functional assessment revealed that Francine often awoke in the morning quite depressed, and had a hard time getting out of bed, but after some struggle, helped get her husband and daughter ready for the day. She would then sit over her coffee for an hour feeling "tired and empty." She would often brood for most of the morning, many of her thoughts focused on intense self-loathing, and "wanting to kill that little girl inside of me." Sometimes she drew pictures of herself or what she sees as the bad girl inside of her and marked up the picture with depictions of stab wounds. Over the past few months, she had become increasingly incapacitated and often would not leave the house for days. Sometimes she would go for 3–4 days without showering, and she increasingly did little in the way of housework, shopping, or meal preparation. In family meetings, her husband and daughter helped the social worker, Gail, obtain a more complete accounting of what their daily life was like. Apparently, Geoff and Tabatha would offer to assist with household responsibilities, but Francine would frustrate their attempts with emotional outbursts and accusations that they didn't like the way she did things and were trying to take over and push her out of the home altogether. Geoff tried patiently to assuage her anger, but Tabatha and Francine would end up in screaming matches. She would, however, expect her daughter to pick up the slack with the housework, although Francine would take little initiative to teach her daughter how to do anything. Francine was not actively looking for a job either, which caused considerable tension with her husband. The couple was barely making it financially; they were living just above the rural poverty line.

After these outbursts, Francine would become withdrawn and sulk, and Tabatha would make attempts to reconcile with her, apologizing for upsetting her. Francine would be inconsolable, and alternate between blaming Tabatha for being a bad daughter and blaming herself for being a bad mother, wife, and so on. The family felt they could no longer cope with her. Geoff described himself as one to "muddle through. . . . My mom had problems, so I'm kind of used to it." Tabatha appeared depressed during these sessions but said she had friends and was doing pretty well in school: "I just feel guilty when I leave the house because I don't know what it's going to be like when I get home."

Francine presented sufficient signs and symptoms of BPD (i.e., self-loathing, distorted self-image, self-mutilating and parasuicidal behavior, chronic feelings of emptiness, difficulty connecting with others, intense anger, vacillating feelings that caused considerable conflict in relationships) but also presented co-occurring problems: serious depression, possible panic disorder, drug abuse, and parenting skills deficits. On a daily basis, she appeared to be immobilized with depression from the first thing in the morning, had little structure to plan her day, became more avoidant of daily responsibilities, and spent more time ruminating about past regrets and problems; she also used tranquilizers to manage her moods. This pattern had become more stable over the previous 2 months or so, and her depression, anxiety, conflicts, and emotional outbursts with her family and self-harming behaviors appeared to have increased in intensity. Her own construction of the problem was put succinctly: "I need to die and come back as a new person. I hate myself. I need to be made new." Gail acknowledged Francine's self-loathing and recognized the pain she had been in for some time. With Francine's husband present, she provided the couple with some psychoeducation regarding these co-occurring problems and talked about how they might work together to help Francine learn how to better cope with her distress and enjoy her family and her life more than she was. She tried not to focus immediately on Francine's problems exclusively, so as not to further convince her that she was the "bad" one. But they did agree on tentative goals for the intervention: to eliminate the self-hatred and self-mutilation, to alleviate and help her cope better with some of the depression and anxiety, to help her sleep better, and to improve relations at home with her husband and daughter.

Selecting and Designing Interventions: Defining Strategies and Objectives

In response to Francine's query "So where do we start?" Gail suggested a psychiatric evaluation for the depression and panic attacks with a medically supervised withdrawal from the benzodiazepine to obtain a better assessment of the problems. In consultation with the psychiatrist, Gail agreed that Francine's self-mutilation did not appear to be suicidal in any way, but they would continue to monitor her for any intent to really harm herself. Geoff was provided with psychoeducation on suicidal risk factors, and he was encouraged to observe and discuss his concerns with Francine on a regular basis. Francine agreed and seemed to respond positively to the attention. Antidepressant medication was prescribed a few weeks later, and Geoff again was asked to monitor the dispensing of the medication to see that Francine took the prescribed amount on a regular basis. Little was said at this point about her self-harming behaviors.

After a few weeks of preliminary meetings, referral, and follow-up assessment, the social worker then recommended and described to Francine the use of DBT. Francine agreed that it was time to get some help. Gail focused immediately on Francine's main concerns: her depression and panicky feelings, maintaining a drug-free lifestyle, improving her relations with her husband and daughter, and reducing or eliminating her self-mutilating behavior. Gail taught Francine core mindfulness skills and cognitive therapy to help her to avoid "freaking out" every time something moderately upsetting happened around the house. Rather than react, the social worker taught Francine to be more focused on observing what was going on without making any immediate judgment about the event (e.g., her daughter would come home from school in a bad mood because one of her girlfriends or a boy she liked rebuffed her). Gail incorporated some basic cognitive therapy techniques to help Francine stop and consider what she herself was thinking and feeling, and to gauge whether her response was reasonable and measured given the situation. They role-played Francine listening, not reacting on the basis of her own feelings, but instead reaching out to her daughter with a query such as "Why don't you sit down with me and tell me what happened today." The phrase "it's not about me" seemed to come up spontaneously, and Francine (laughing for the first time) showed some awareness that others around her might have been experiencing distress as well and that not everything that happened was directed at Francine or was intended to upset her. Francine tersely, if inelegantly, characterized her self-absorption: "Perhaps it's time I pulled my head out of my ass and paid attention to others."

After the next few visits, Francine began to direct some of her anger and suspicion toward the therapist: "I don't think you really like me. You think I'm a head case, don't you? Why don't you just tell me I'm a fucking asshole and get it over with." In each case, Gail expressed concern about Francine's anger, asked her to talk more about how she was feeling and what was going on at home (and, later, on her job), and provided some honest feedback to Francine about how it felt to be attacked in that manner. She used the exchanges as opportunities to educate Francine about her inclination to assume that other people thought very poorly of her, despite there being no evidence that they intended to be negative toward her. After several encounters like this, Francine began to consider more realistically that perhaps these were distortions on her part. To the extent that people actually did respond to her negatively, it might have something to do with the way Francine was communicating to them, since she was often sarcastic or critical or ignored others altogether when she was "in a mood." Over time, Francine began to see that, rather than reacting negatively, "like everybody else," Gail made every attempt to use the exchanges as an opportunity to teach Francine something that could be helpful to her. This modeling behavior seemed to have a positive effect, as Francine commented on one occasion: "I wish I could not take things so personally like you. I have to get a grip when I think someone doesn't like me or doesn't like something I've said. I mean, so what if they don't? I can't freak out every time I think someone is angry at me or doesn't approve of me."

Having eliminated the use of benzodiazepines and having started taking her prescribed SSRI antidepressant medication, Francine began to have a little more energy in the morning. Self-management skills were discussed and used to focus on structuring her mornings, and she gradually took on more productive activities. They agreed that after completing her chores, she would reward herself with either a bath or a walk (e.g., depending on needs, the weather) at about midday. Over the next few weeks, these activities (e.g., basic house cleaning, shopping for groceries, preparing meals) were increased, and Francine became increasingly confident and less anxious about going into town and accomplishing basic errands. She did have a tendency at times to "space out" and discovered during her sessions that she would become immobilized and begin ruminating at certain times. She struggled with the desire to go upstairs and cut herself, as the ruminating often led to negative and critical thoughts about herself. Through negotiation, she and the social worker agreed that she could schedule a time to sit and "brood" for exactly 20 minutes late in the morning after she completed her chores, and then reward herself with a walk or a bath. Gail also showed her some simple relaxation and meditation exercises she could do for a few minutes when she felt some of her frustration and anger rising. Francine also told her friend next door that they could walk together only if she did not talk about using drugs anymore. When Francine asked about cutting herself (which often followed her intense brooding periods), Gail told her that not cutting herself would be preferred but that the decision was up to her. The social worker chose to focus on helping Francine self-monitor her own mood and use positive alternatives when she was feeling angry or depressed or desperate.

Over the a few weeks (with periodic brief visits that included her husband and daughter), Francine made considerable gains in being active during the morning, was more productive, was less depressed, and became more available to her daughter when she came home after school. She began to feel "like a real mom" as her daughter seemed happier to come home and looked forward to telling her mother all that was going on in school during the day. "Maybe I'm not as screwed up as my mother was," Francine quipped at one point. "I don't have to be a chronic nut job like her if I don't want to. I can be there for Tabatha. It doesn't even take much. I just have to put her needs ahead of mine for a few minutes a day. That's not really much to ask of someone."

Early afternoons seemed to be the toughest time of the day for Francine. By that time, her schedule was done, and she found herself becoming bored and preoccupied. She would begin to feel like going upstairs and cutting herself, and it was still a struggle not to give into it. She needed to find a way to "fill in the gap" before her daughter came home a couple hours later. Gail and Francine decided that this window of vulnerability had to be closed and dealt with directly. Enough of the depression had subsided, and Francine had developed enough confidence in her self-management skills so that the social worker felt she could challenge Francine a bit more. For the next few weeks, Gail helped Francine improve her self-management skills (i.e., distress tolerance and emotion regulation) by developing an imaginal hierarchy of things that caused her emotional pain (e.g., images of her mom being ill when Francine was a child; feelings of embarrassment that she could not invite friends over; other stressors such as being in a group of people and having a conversation without becoming upset, jealous, anxious, or angry). With a combination of guided imagery and relaxation exercises, the social worker helped Francine hierarchically list these covert stressors from most to least distressful. Starting with the least distressful image, the social worker helped Francine develop these images in her mind's eye, tolerate them while maintaining her composure, and accept them (if they were past events that could not be changed). Francine imagined herself coping with current stressors more effectively. As they worked their way down the list, Francine began to feel more confident that her emotional reactions to events past or present could be controlled or at least tolerated. This possibility came as a relief to her, and she began to feel, over time, that perhaps she could begin venturing out into the world again. Going out would provide more opportunities to fill up that troublesome part of the day.

Francine spontaneously asked the social worker for some advice on how to polish her résumé. Gail offered some pretty standard advice on how Francine could present her work experience and how to present herself at her best in a job interview. Francine's desire to get a part-time job outside the home presented an excellent opportunity to work on helping her gain confidence and overcome her anxiety about dealing with people again. She could further work on integrating her distress tolerance, and improving her emotional regulation skills and interpersonal effectiveness skills in a stressful situation (e.g., a job interview in which she felt she was being judged). A few different scenarios were drawn up, and the social worker provided the role-playing environment for Francine to field tough questions and challenging situations by learning to relax, breathe, not take it personally, and respond calmly knowing that her worth as a person was not "on the line" in every job interview. After a few sessions of role-play and rehearsal, she felt she was ready to try again.

Over the following weeks, Francine found a part-time job as a receptionist in a physician's office, and although she felt she would be somewhat overwhelmed by the task of dealing with people on a daily basis, she decided to take the position. She talked with her husband and daughter (who insisted they had to reschedule their private time for after dinner), and they agreed it was a good move. Her husband was relieved, as they needed the extra income. Francine decided to attend sessions every other week instead of weekly. She continued to struggle with anxieties regarding work and feeling comfortable dealing with other people. Her progress was reviewed, and she and Gail developed a relapse prevention plan together. They focused on identifying those potential "potholes" that Francine had to look out for and wrote down a menu of constructive positive coping responses. There were also daily routine skills she needed to continue to work on: identifying negative and self-destructive thoughts; practicing calm communication skills with her husband; spending undivided time with her daughter every day, if only for 5–10 minutes; and taking time out for herself daily to do something she found enjoyable. Since her job was about three-quarters of a mile from her home, she was able to walk and practice her relaxation skills to and from the job. During follow-up several months later, she appeared to be less preoccupied with her past ruminations. Her daily anxieties seemed to be much more focused on realistic concerns. Her confidence in being able to cope with them had grown. She continued her medication, although she talked with her physician about cutting down. She no longer used benzodiazepines. Her daughter seemed more at ease, and her husband more relaxed (although, as Francine agreed, "we need to work on us"). The scars on her wrists and forearms were still visible but with time would gradually fade. Rather than provocatively displaying her wounds, she wanted increasingly to hide them, particularly at work. Her daughter, who had taken up making costume jewelry with a friend, gave her mom a collection of bracelets, which Francine would wear in multiples and proudly show off to her new companions at work.

Selecting Scales and Creating Indexes to Monitor and Evaluate Client Progress

Any number of standardized and simple indexes would be helpful for both the initial assessment as well as for monitoring and evaluating client progress. The Borderline Personality Disorder Severity Index (BPDSI) would be useful for gauging the change in severity of symptoms over time, and the Hamilton Depression Rating Scale (HDRS) (see chapter 6) would be useful for assessing changes in depression level. Individual indexes could be employed to measure: severity of urge to cut, use of tranquilizers, severity of anxiety, frequency of cutting, time spent with daughter, and time problem solving with husband.

TABLE 10.2   The client service plan for Francine

Problems	Goals	Objectives (samples)	Interventions	Assessment and evaluation tools
Depression: mood disturbance, cognitive distortions regarding self-image, self-loathing, sleep disturbance (early a.m. waking), lack of self-care, withdrawal, low energy (poor personal hygiene, low activity level); feelings of emptiness	Alleviate most major depression symptoms; improve sleep; increase structured activities; improve hygiene; overall appearance, self-image	Identify specific cognitive distortions about self and others; test out at home and elsewhere as opportunities increase	DBT (with family visits) Psychoeducation on anxiety, depressive symptoms, and problems with regulating emotions and behavior; discuss core aspects of DBT Cognitive therapy: mindful consideration of distortions about self and others; test distortions in role-play and in vivo practice Core mindfulness to help cope with others' behaviors Structured daily activities with daily goals and rewards to increase activity Cognitive therapy to interpret provocative stimuli Stress management skills: breathing and relaxation exercises to cope with symptoms Role-playing to cope with interpersonal situations that cause anxiety and miscommunication Exposure therapy to approach anxiety-provoking situations socially or at work	Use any one depression or anxiety scale to help track symptoms Use BPDSI to track core BPD symptoms Select key indexes as self-anchored scales to help client self-monitor progress (e.g., on a 1–10 scale, degree of self-loathing, desire to cut and/or use drugs, level of depression, anxiety about a specific event) and frequency scales (e.g., number of times scratched or cut, minutes spent in productive conversation with daughter or husband)
Anxiety: generalized anxiety, anxiety attacks (rule out substance abuse withdrawal), interpersonal anxiety (anxious in social and work settings, self-conscious, easily upset, defensive)	Rule out panic attacks and substance withdrawals; improve anxiety management skills in social and work situations	Increase daily household objectives with target behaviors (e.g., washing dishes, vacuuming) as client improves		
Substance abuse: taking nonprescription benzodiazepines; history of drug abuse when younger	Eliminate use of alcohol and other drugs other than prescription use	Practice and increase breathing, meditation skills daily (initially 5 minutes, 10, 20)		
Self-mutilation: scratches wrists and forearms with blade or glass; no clear suicidal intent	Eliminate self-mutilation	Use relaxation skills when thinking of drug seeking; take "stress breaks" to do something enjoyable; later implement in vivo practice of interpersonal skills; initiate a conversation a week up to daily as she returns to work and has more social contacts		

Problems	Goals	Objectives (samples)	Interventions	Assessment and evaluation tools
Parenting problems with adolescent daughter; difficulty dealing with daughter's needs	Improve relations and parenting skills with daughter; improve attention to daughter's age-specific needs	Sit and talk (mostly listen) with daughter 5 minutes daily after school, longer as she becomes comfortable	Case management: coordinate medical, psychiatric review of medications and symptoms	
Minimal intimacy with husband; little affection; poor communication	Improve relationship with husband in taking care of daughter and household responsibilities; improve communication and empathy	Later in evening, initiate conversation with husband; first focus on daily home responsibilities, then each other; plan an activity together each weekend for 1 hour (e.g., a walk), longer if enjoyment increases	Plan brief structured time for daughter daily Communication and problem solving with husband to improve relationship, intimacy once symptoms abate	

SUMMARY

Social workers are likely to encounter clients who "fit the profile" of a personality disorder in both specialized and general practice environments. Acquiring multiple collateral reports is essential to conducting a thorough MFS assessment. Individuals with antisocial personality disorder continue to present serious challenges to the therapeutic and judicial professional communities. Treatment outcomes for BPD clients are more optimistic. Despite the difficulties and frequent frustrations associated with working with these troubled clients, emerging evidence-based practices offer optimism for substantively helping clients with a personality disorder reduce emotional distress, improve their self-management skills, enjoy better quality of life, and become less of a problem for their families and communities.

PART III

PROBLEMS AND DISORDERS OF COUPLES, CHILDREN, AND FAMILIES

CHAPTER 11

DISTRESSED COUPLES

Using evidence-based interventions with couples is important not only for improving intimate adult relationships but also for enhancing work with children and families. Thus, the current chapter serves as both a critical overview of assessment and intervention with distressed couples and a prelude to the following chapters on treating childhood and adolescent disorders. Although systems frameworks have helped practitioners expand their perspective from individual psychopathology to one that includes the family and community, many popular couple and family approaches remain relatively untested. However, this chapter emphasizes two major evidence-based couples approaches for which substantive bodies of outcome research exist: behavioral couples therapy (BCT) and emotion-focused therapy (EFT).

ASSESSMENT

Background Data

A range of psychosocial factors contribute to the problems and distress experienced by couples, and resulting distress can have serious consequences for the individual mental health of the respective partners and their children (Gottman, 1993a, 1998; Weiss & Heyman, 1997). Although divorce rates in North America have declined somewhat in recent years, divorce rates for first-time marriages still range from 40% to 50%, and divorce rates for previously divorced people are higher than for those in first marriages (Burditt, Brown, Orbuch, & McIlvane, 2010; Johnson, 2003). The consequences of couples conflict, separation, and divorce include increased automobile accidents and fatalities, physical illness, suicide, homicide, depression, anxiety, social withdrawal, and other behavioral problems. Dysfunctional couples are more likely to suffer stress-related health problems (e.g., compromised immune system response, higher blood pressure) as a result of their conflicts (Gottman, 1993a, 1998; Johnson, 2003; Weiss & Heyman, 1997).

Psychiatric Disorders in One or Both Partners. Psychiatric disorders in a partner can have a serious impact on a couple's relationship. These problems can include depression (Beach & O'Leary, 1992; O'Leary & Beach,

1990), alcoholism (O'Farrell, Choquette, Cutter, Brown, & McCourt, 1993; O'Farrell & Fals-Stewart, 2003), and anxiety disorders (Craske & Zoeller, 1995), among other problems. In their review of the literature, Joutsenniemi, Moustgaard, Koskinen, Ripatti, and Maritikainen (2011) found that the highest risk for a diagnosis of major depressive disorder was to be married to a spouse with both major depressive disorder and substance use disorder. In a study with a convenience sample (e.g., from counseling services) of 228 separated males and 142 separated females, men showed significantly higher rates of suicidal ideation than women (after controlling for demographics), but in both groups, those with a history of anxiety, mood disturbance, and/or substance abuse in the prior year were also at increased risk of suicide (Kolves, Ide, & de Leo, 2010). Marital distress has also been shown to result in increased use of mental health services, even when controlling for other factors, such as gender, age, race, or psychiatric disorders (Schonbrun & Whisman, 2010).

The relationship between individual psychopathology and couples problems, however, is complex. One must consider, at a minimum, the age of onset of the partner's disorder, whether it is recurrent, the impact of marital stress on the individual's disorder, the effects of the disorder as a stressor on the partner's psychological well-being, and quality of the couple's relationship. Theories that suggest that one partner is unconsciously gratifying dark, unresolved needs via a partner's disorder or that the disorder of the "identified patient" serves some form of regulatory function in the family system have given way to multivariate explanations for couple distress. A more accurate picture of the relationship between individual psychological disorders and marital distress is that the two problems are likely to interact reciprocally (Gottman, 1998; Halford & Bouma, 1997; Weiss & Heyman, 1997).

Intimate Partner Violence.   Findings regarding the cause and correlates of domestic violence have begun to accumulate (Field & Caetano, 2005; Gelles & Cornell, 1990; Holtzworth-Munroe, Bates, Smutzler, & Sandin, 1997; Holtzworth-Munroe, Smutzler, & Bates, 1997). Violence against women is far too common, and much of it goes unreported. About 25% of women have reported being physically abused by a partner in their lifetime, about 8% of women have been raped by their husbands, and many of these women die at the hands of their batterers (Pagelow, 1992; US Department of Justice, 2000). Almost 5 million women annually are raped or physically assaulted by partners (US Department of Justice, 2000). Field and Caetano (2005) reviewed 20 years of survey data on intimate partner violence (IPV) and found that more than 20% of couples engaged in some violent behavior with each other in a 12-month period. In addition, although men and women are about equally likely to engage in IPV, women are at higher risk of being victims of more serious violence and of receiving more severe injuries.

Women experiencing IPV were barely recognized in the research litera-ture until the 1980s (Holtzworth-Munroe, Bates et al., 1997), partly because it is a low priority in terms of national civil rights or the law, and it tends to be dismissed by therapists and emergency room attendants as the result of a woman's psychological problems (Pagelow, 1992). On the basis of a review and analysis of National Comorbidity Study–Replication data, Afifi et al. (2009) found that IPV is associated with a history of child abuse as well as more negative mental health outcomes, yet women are more likely to report depression, post-traumatic stress disorder (PTSD), other anxiety disorders, substance abuse, and chronic physical ailments. Age is negatively correlated with IPV, and both African Americans and Hispanics are more likely to engage in IPV than whites (Caetano, Vaeth, & Ramisetty-Mikler, 2008). Also, interra-cial couples appear to be more likely to engage in IPV than same-race cou-ples, findings borne out in one study of police reports in the US Northeast (Fusco, 2010). In response to the age-old query "Why do these women stay?" researchers have concluded, "Battered women have many understandable reasons for remaining with an abusive partner, including fear of further abuse, economic dependence, commitment to one's spouse, and the belief that the partner will change" (Holtzworth-Munroe, Smutzler, & Sandin, 1997, p. 197). However, they point out that many battered women do eventually leave their abusive husbands.

Violence has been reported by up to 25% of couples during courtship, and marital violence is more likely in newlyweds and those younger than age 30. Aggressive behavior among newlyweds has been shown to correlate with marital dissatisfaction even when controlling for negative communication styles and stressful life events (Lawrence & Bradbury, 2001). In a longitudinal study of couples, O'Leary et al. (1989) revealed that 31% of men and 44% of women had engaged in aggression against their partner in the year before they were married. At 18 months, the rates dropped to 27% and 36%, respec-tively, and at 30 months, to 25% and 32%. Women's violence, but not men's, declined significantly from one time interval to the next. The most common forms of aggression were pushing, grabbing, and shoving. Age appeared to be the most important determinant of rates of aggressive acts. In a follow-up investigation with the same research sample, O'Leary, Malone, and Tyree (1994) examined predictive factors of aggression and concluded that men's violence appeared to be more strongly related to a history of domestic vio-lence in their own family of origin, but women's violence in marriage appeared to be a continuation of previous violent behavior. Other factors such as personality characteristics and the influence of marital discord also contributed to what is a multivariate model of violent behavior. The authors stressed, however, that pathways to violence and the consequences for the object of that violence are quite different for both men and women. In addition, most of these violent acts are not severe or do not result in serious bodily harm. In their study, about 2% of aggressive acts resulted in the victim being "beaten up."

Men who abuse their spouses are more likely to score higher on various measures of psychopathology, including poor self-esteem, depression, aggressiveness, hostility and anger, personality disorders, dependency needs, and disturbed relationship patterns. Men who feel powerless (e.g., unemployed, underemployed, dissatisfied with their jobs) are also more likely to use violence. Other correlates of men's battering behavior include having more children in the family, financial problems, living in poor housing conditions, having had a violent childhood, experiencing disparity in the partner's educational and/or occupational status, having sexual difficulties, having poorly balanced power sharing in the relationship, and experiencing social stressors and social isolation. Minority rates of couples' violence also appear to be related to socioeconomic factors. Although substance abuse is a significant correlate of violence in couples, its causal relationship to the abuse is complex—either the result of disinhibiting effects or a ready excuse to be abusive. Regardless of its specific role, substance abuse appears to be a catalyst for couple violence (Gelles & Cornell, 1990; Holtzworth-Munroe, Bates et al., 1997; Pagelow, 1992).

Couple violence also appears to be related to negative communication patterns between partners. For example, a husband's controlling behavior tends to drive a communication pattern that is marked by anger, contempt, and belligerence, a cycle that is difficult to terminate once initiated. One reason it is important to study violent couples is that there appears to be a strong, direct relationship between marital distress and a husband's violence (Holtzworth-Munroe, Smutzler, & Bates, 1997). In a comprehensive review of studies from 1970 to 1984, Hotaling and Sugarman (1986) found four key factors associated with male violence toward a spouse: violence toward children, sexual aggression toward the wife, alcohol abuse, and having witnessed violence between his own parents as a child or adolescent. In two controlled case studies comparing both clinical and community samples (Hamberger & Hastings, 1991; Hastings & Hamberger, 1988), male batterers were found to show greater levels of personality-disordered traits commensurate with BPD and APD, and their abusiveness seemed to be mediated by alcohol abuse. Although drinking per se might not be a key precipitant of most IPV, data from one national survey have shown alcohol abuse to be a risk factor, and it is associated with IPV severity (McKinney, Caetano, Rodriguez, & Okoro, 2010). Marcus and Swett (2002), however, call for an emphasis on the violent couple's relationship to better understand couples violence rather than overemphasizing individual psychopathology, since evidence has consistently shown that both partners are likely to be violent. These violent relationships tend to be associated with high-risk emotions: anger, rage related to rejection sensitivity, insecurity, jealousy, negative affect.

Likewise, as one would expect, empathy, intimacy, trust, love, and a sense of security marked nonviolent relationships.

In the legal arena, domestic violence has increasingly become better recognized as a crime rather than a private family matter or personal problem. Nevertheless, law enforcement protection of women from their violent partners often fails with consequences that include further serious physical injury and often death at the hands of their abusers. Pagelow (1992) makes a key point on the importance of using social science evidence as a tool in the pursuit of social justice: "None of the legislative changes benefiting women could have occurred without empirical research findings" (p. 103). Evidence-based practice is more than employing psychosocial interventions that work; it is using social science evidence to inform policy analysis and support social action.

Gay and Lesbian Couples.   Gay and lesbian couples share many of the same concerns and challenges as heterosexual couples. They also face some particular psychosocial and political challenges (e.g., legal recognition of gay marriages). Like heterosexual couples, gay and lesbian couples seek constancy and intimacy in relationship, experience similar problems (e.g., money disputes, sharing of household duties, sexual relations, infidelity, parenting differences) and are as likely to be satisfied in their relationships as heterosexual couples are (Ossana, 2000). Kurdek (1998) surveyed more than 200 gay, lesbian, and heterosexual couples, finding many similarities in the overall affective appraisal of their relationships, problem solving, and relationship satisfaction over 5 years. In their in-depth study of 40 gay and lesbian couples using multiple behavioral, affective, and physiological measures, Gottman et al. (2003) came to similar conclusions.

Research on rates of IPV in same-sex couples versus straight couples has shown mixed results. Some data suggest that rates of IPV are comparable and that gay and heterosexual couples share similar problems related to control, power, dominance, sexual dissatisfaction, and struggles for autonomy (Blosnich & Bossarte, 2009; MacDonald, 1998). However, one review of the literature suggested that IPV might be higher in gay couples than in heterosexual couples, and although alcohol abuse is generally higher in gay couples, it is unclear if it is associated with greater IPV (Klostermann, Kelley, Milletich, & Mignone, 2011).

Researchers have also found that for gay and lesbian couples, balance and equality in relationships tends to be a sign of relationship health (as also seems to be the case in heterosexual couples). A recent qualitative analysis of a small sample of gay and lesbian persons in relationships found that gay couples were similar to straight couples in their use of maintenance behaviors such as task sharing, communication, and spending time together (Haas & Stafford, 1998). Even with regard to concerns such as HIV/AIDS, which at one time were perceived as a uniquely "gay issue," there may be more similarity than otherwise. In one survey of gay and straight couples with mixed HIV status, Beckerman, Letteneny, and Lorber (2000) found that couples were equally concerned about HIV transmission, effects of uncertainty on the relationship, and fluctuations in emotional closeness and distancing.

However, the different challenges gay and lesbian couples face should not be minimized. Kurdek (1998) found that lesbian couples reported more intimacy than heterosexual couples, and both gay and lesbian couples reported more autonomy in their relationships than heterosexual couples. MacDonald (1998) highlighted challenges for gay and lesbian couples in a thoughtful review of the literature: discrimination, stigma and homophobia, lack of comparable economic and political parity, the increased threat of HIV/AIDS, and alienation from their own families. As a result, gay and lesbian couples may be more inclined to keep their sexual orientation to themselves, a dilemma that places the resolution of a couple's conflict in a somewhat different social context from that of straight couples. Gay and lesbian couples may engage in relational maintenance behaviors that focus on solidifying their bond as a way of coping with sociopolitical pressures in society, that is, as a buffer against social stigma (Haas & Stafford, 1998). Practitioners should also not overlook within-group differences: one should not expect that all gay, lesbian, or heterosexual couples operate on the same principles.

Ossana (2000) points out some unique considerations for working with gay and lesbian couples: different developmental challenges for each member of the couple, the lack of available role models for gay couples' relationships, and the differences in gender-role identity formation that each partner brings to the relationship. One partner may be "out," and the other quietly "in the closet." Barriers to living openly as a couple continue in our society, and gay and lesbian couples continue to face public policy barriers, family rejection, and difficulties fitting into other typical social rituals (Ossana, 2000). Any and all of these stressors, past or present, can put psychological strain on the relationship.

Effects of Couple Distress on Children.   Couples who navigate the sometimes difficult waters of marital and family stress and conflict may provide positive role modeling and engender psychosocial resilience in their children. Lindahl, Clements, and Markman (1998) convincingly demonstrated that parents' ability to manage conflict in their marriage enhances their children's psychological well-being. However, raising children can introduce stress to a couple's relationship. These stressors may be due to differences in parenting philosophies; the accumulated role strain of balancing careers with children's activities; rigid gender roles regarding parenting responsibilities; and/or dealing with a behaviorally disturbed, disabled, or seriously ill child (Sanders, Nicholson, & Floyd, 1997). Reciprocally, marital distress and conflict associated with divorce increase the likelihood of greater psychological, emotional, behavioral, and interpersonal adjustment problems for children (Grych & Fincham, 1990; Sanders, Nicholson, & Floyd, 1997). Children who witness marital violence, particularly conflict that is open, frequent, intense, physically aggressive, and unresolved, are at much greater risk of suffering negative psychosocial effects (Holtzworth-Munroe, Smutzler, & Sandin, 1997). Children of divorce also suffer mental health problems both as children and later as adults. They are more likely to obtain less satisfaction from family life, are more anxious, and have more difficulty coping with life's stressors (Gottman, 1998; Sanders, Nicholson, & Floyd, 1997). These problems may vary somewhat by age and gender, and long-term outcomes may be mitigated to some degree if consistent parenting resumes post-divorce. The mechanisms by which these effects are processed may include modeling (e.g., overt hostility, violence), the direct stress caused by marital conflict, and the negative effects of marital conflict on parent-child relationships.

More recently, cross-sectional data have shown associations among marital conflict, divorce, and emotional and behavioral problems in children and adolescents. For example, Stutzman et al. (2011) showed in a sample of roughly 400 boys and girls that covert and overt marital conflict were related to both internal and externalizing problems in children; however, overt conflict seemed to be more strongly associated with internalizing problems, with similar findings in both Latino and European American youth. In a more rigorous test of the hypothesized link between marital distress and mental health risk in children, a longitudinal study (21 years from birth) revealed that divorce can contribute to long-term depression in children, even as mothers who repartner recover from prior post-divorce depression (Clavarino et al., 2011).

The implications of these findings are important for planning interventions with children and their families. As Sanders, Nicholson, and Floyd (1997) aptly point out, there has been very little overlap or integration in the literature on interventions with couples and interventions with children: "When a couple presents with parenting difficulties, therapists are encouraged to, first, diagnose the problem as primarily a marital problem or a parenting issue, and then, second, implement the appropriate course of marital or parenting intervention. It is rarely acknowledged that these two components may be inextricably linked, or that therapists should be experienced in treating both types of problems simultaneously" (p. 234). There is little research addressing how to modify marital interventions to address emotional and behavioral disorders in children. Although intervening with a couple during divorce to aid their children's adjustment has become popular, there is little research evaluating these programs. For some childhood and adolescent disorders, incorporating cognitive-behavioral interventions into a family therapy model has begun to receive more empirical attention, as we will see in subsequent chapters.

The Importance of Cultural, Racial, and Ethnic Differences in Couples Relationships.   Cultural, racial, and ethnic identity can be powerful forces in making or breaking a relationship. Cultivating a long-term relationship with someone can be greatly enhanced by mutual identification with common cultural ancestry, including a desire to share it with one's children. Conversely, the joining of different racial, ethnic, or cultural heritages through marriage can also be exciting. Appreciating and blending customs, beliefs, mythologies, rituals, music, food, and other traditions into a new family can result in a unique cultural pastiche. Although little research has been conducted on racially or culturally mixed couples, a number of clinical scholars have made thoughtful observations. Jones and Chao (1997) point out that couples should attempt to be consciously aware of cultural issues; see cultural differences as a potential enhancement to their relationship; and use their cultural mix to develop each person's own cultural, ethnic, or racial identity further in a positive and affirming way. However, they also warn of potential pitfalls: (1) having mismatched ethnic identity and acculturation conflict (e.g., a couple, both of Cantonese ancestry, may have differences in negotiating US norms given different levels of acculturation and assimilation); (2) minimizing the potential impact of cultural, ethnic, or racial differences (e.g., an Irish-Catholic and Reform Jewish woman of Orthodox parents may face friction as she plans for marriage and children); (3) having different strategies for coping with racial, ethnic, or cultural bias, as well as discrimination and oppression (e.g., one person avoids it, one confronts it openly). One nationally representative study of African Americans, Hispanics, and non-Hispanic whites revealed significant correlation between homogeneous religious beliefs and values and marital satisfaction in couples (Ellison, Burdette, & Wilcox, 2010).

Evidence suggests that there are both similarities and differences among couples by race and culture. For example, German couples were shown to be more likely to engage in negative and coercive interactions than Australian couples (Halford, Hahlweg, & Dunne, 1990). Hispanic and non-Hispanic white couples in the US Southwest appeared to be more similar than different in levels of marital distress after controlling for other demographic factors (e.g., education, employment), and they showed only a modest difference in the relationship between level of acculturation and marital distress among wives (Negy & Snyder, 1997). Oggins, Leber, and Veroff (1993) examined the sexual and marital satisfaction of both African American and white couples, finding that for both groups, men reported less of a contingency between sexual satisfaction and marital intimacy than women. However, lower-income black women (compared with white women) appeared to pay greater attention to sexual satisfaction in its own right. In a retrospective qualitative study of white, African American, and Mexican American couples who had been married for 20 years or more, conflict generally declined after the rearing of children, but African American men reported a more confrontational style over the years, an opinion with which their wives generally concurred (Mackey & O'Brien, 1998). However, the relationships among race, religion, spirituality, and other relationship factors are complex, and practitioners should use caution in making any generalizations (Ellison et al., 2010).

Theories

There is a striking split in the literature on couples' problems between theories based largely on speculation and those supported by empirical evidence. Pathological behavior in the context of psychodynamic couple assessment, for example, is seen largely as the result of poor ego development related to disturbances in early attachment or as object relations leading to interpersonal (i.e., relational) problems that affect choice of mate and later cause relationship dysfunction (Bowlby, 1969; Johnson, 2007; Johnson & Greenberg, 1995; Meissner, 1978; Scharff, 1995). The goal of treatment is to help the couple clarify interpersonal distortions (i.e., displacements, projections), see each other more realistically, interact less defensively, and obtain a more mature level of intimacy. Although these theories continue to have some intuitive appeal, there is relatively little evidence that specifically links early mother-infant and mother-toddler interactions with adult relationship problems. Indeed, any model linking childhood experiences and subsequent adult relationships is likely to involve a combination of factors that interact over time, such as innate temperament, early childhood experiences (nurturance vs. abuse and neglect), peer influences, intimate experiences in adolescence and young adulthood, social and cultural context of early romantic relationships, and a host of other psychosocial risks and resiliencies. Theories that overemphasize the influence of early childhood also fail to account for sources of change and variability during the course of the marital relationship itself (Karney & Bradbury, 1995).

Although multidimensional theories of relationship development await further investigation, current theories that attempt to explain couples' well-being and distress generally focus on the quality of interactional attributions and behaviors. Much of contemporary couple theory has its roots in social exchange theory (Thibaut & Kelly, 1959). Levinger (1976) applied these concepts to marriage and suggested that the success or failure of marriage depended on three main factors: each spouse weighing the attractions of the relationship, barriers to leaving, and the availability of attractive alternatives. Behavioral exchange theory is the bedrock of contemporary marital theory, and it emphasizes the importance of interacting rewards and punishments between partners and their correlation with overall marital satisfaction (Jacobson & Margolin, 1979; Stuart, 1969, 1980). Interventions developed in this tradition tend to focus on changing interactional behaviors to increase mutual satisfaction through improved communication and problem solving.

Recently, Johnson and O'Leary (1996) tested this hypothesized relationship between behavior exchange and marital satisfaction and demonstrated that they do, indeed, correlate significantly. In addition, the authors demonstrated that an individualized approach to assessment whereby couples identified 10 positive and 10 negative behaviors in their relationship was as reliable and valid as using validated psychometric instruments that included more than 100 items. Such findings illustrate the importance of using thoughtful individualized assessment.

The increased emphasis on cognitive theory has also had its impact on behavioral approaches to couples theory and practice. Several practitioner-researchers have incorporated traditional cognitive concepts (Baucom, Epstein, & Rankin, 1995; Kayser, 1997) to account for the interpersonal distortions and misattributions that occur between couples as a result of social learning history or current situational stressors. For example, couples may use selective attention (e.g., only focusing on a partner's mistakes), arbitrary inference (e.g., "You're late. Are you seeing someone else?"), overgeneralization (e.g., "You never do anything nice for me!"), dichotomous thinking (e.g., "I take all the responsibility around here and you take none!"), or mind reading (e.g., "You've been quiet all night. You're angry at me aren't you!"). Cognitive-behavioral intervention includes an examination of dysfunctional cognitive thinking about the relationship (without inferring unconscious motives), clarification through improved communications, and behavioral tasks to disconfirm distorted beliefs or erroneous expectations. The partners' respective cognitive schema—that is, their more enduring beliefs or expectancies about relationship and intimacy—may require more careful and probing examination. Beliefs and associated feelings and behaviors may need to be repeatedly challenged and disconfirmed over time in the relationship before they can change. For example, despite much reassurance, being generally suspicious or vigilant because of a former lover's infidelities can have long-term negative effects on mutual trust. Such problems with "basic trust" need not be rooted in early childhood but can be instilled as a result of a prior betrayal in adulthood. Other deeply hurtful experiences may require more "cognitive reconstruction" than just challenging distorted thinking. Only behavioral disconfirmation over time (e.g., constancy in a loving relationship) is likely to heal these psychological wounds.

Operating in the same general social exchange framework, Gottman (1993b) developed an empirical model that examines interpersonal processes over the course of the relationship. He contends that his structural model supports a "*process cascade* in which criticism leads to contempt, which leads to defensiveness, which leads to stonewalling. The findings of his research suggest that these four processes are particularly corrosive to marital stability" (p. 62). Divorce may not be far off when these behaviors far outweigh positive interchanges. Gottman's (1993b) research led him to suggest five typologies of marriage (three stable: validators, volatiles, and avoiders; and two unstable: hostile and hostile-detached) based on the couple's ability to balance positive and negative interactions. The stable marriages, in different ways, demonstrated a 5:1 ratio of positive to negative interactions. Gottman (1993a) suggested that marital therapy should focus on interrupting the negative reciprocal cycle between the couple by employing three main strategies: nondefensive and nonprovocative speaking, nondefensive listening and validation, and tactful editing (clarification of what was communicated). The process should be accompanied by physiological soothing (i.e., efforts to calm heightened arousal during marital discussions). As the negative interactions ease, the couple can use repair mechanisms to ease tensions and improve communications overall.

Karney and Bradbury (1995) also emphasized the central place of behavioral theory and its focus on mutual attributions and interactional rewards. However, they suggested that the focus on behavioral theory has been overly narrow, and lacks a sense of context in which the behavioral changes are occurring (e.g., environmental stressors). They also address another aspect of healthy relationships not addressed in contemporary couples' theory, the role of social support. Pasch and Bradbury (1998) demonstrated the importance of both positive interactions during problem solving and the need to provide social support to the other spouse when dealing with nonmarital problems. The provision of social support to the other partner predicted positive marital outcomes over 2 years during early marriage, the critical time during which most divorce proceedings are initiated.

Despite the limitations in the research, a multidimensional social-cognitive framework for marital theory is emerging (Karney & Bradbury, 1995; Lindahl, Malik, & Bradbury 1997). The vulnerability-stress-adaptation model suggests that marital outcomes emerge from the interaction of three domains: enduring vulnerabilities, adaptive processes, and stressful events. Enduring vulnerabilities include those intraindividual qualities partners individually bring to the relationship. Adaptive processes refer to communication between partners, attributions partners make about each other, and partners' ability to provide support and understanding to each other (Karney & Bradbury, 1995). Adaptive processes are shaped by the personal strengths and weaknesses (or enduring vulnerabilities) spouses bring to marriage, such as stable demographic, historical, personality, and experiential factors, and by the stressful events, developmental transitions, and chronic or acute circumstances that spouses and couples encounter. One implication of this theory is that even couples who are good problem solvers can succumb to marital failure if environmental stressors overwhelm them and they lack the resources to deal with them (Lindahl et al., 1997). Further research on the impact of social, environmental, and economic stressors on marriage is needed to enhance social-cognitive couples' theory.

Current theories of marital well-being and dysfunction clearly owe a debt to social exchange in the behavioral tradition. Much of the data has focused on negative reciprocal interactional processes that tend to spiral out of control once they become negative. Couples who are adept at "short-circuiting" those negative patterns by self-editing, lowering their own level of criticism, reducing arousal during exchanges, and sticking to the issue at hand tend to have better communications (e.g., good listening without interrupting), which results in a more constructive and supportive marital climate (Gottman, 1993a, 1998; Weiss & Heyman, 1997). Couples who practice good rules of engagement during arguments (i.e., fight well) may also store up a bank of goodwill or positive sentiment over-ride (Weiss & Heyman, 1997) that can be tapped during more stressful periods. However, there are limitations to theory built primarily on interactional processes. In addition to a host of methodological shortcomings, these theories tend to be *correlational* rather than *developmentally explanatory* (i.e., explain how relationships succeed or fail over time). Couples theory in the social-cognitive and social exchange arena would be enhanced by examining influences that develop in both individuals and couples over time within a broader social-environmental framework that includes a greater emphasis on cross-cultural factors as well (Gottman, 1993a; Halford, 1998; Karney & Bradbury, 1995).

Key Elements of Multidimensional-Functional-Systems Assessment

Multidimensional-functional-systems (MFS) assessment of distressed couples may be more challenging than assessing an individual. Couples assessment involves both individual assessments of each partner and the need to understand the development of interactional patterns between partners over time. Children may also be part of the assessment picture, but more attention will be paid to the broader family assessment and that of children in subsequent chapters. A thorough assessment of each partner is important for several reasons. First, each partner may have different reasons for seeking help, different motivation level, different goals, and different understanding of the problems at hand. Second, one or both of the partners may be suffering from individual problems or a psychiatric disorder that may require special attention beyond understanding the couple's behavior. Frequently, one partner is seriously depressed, won't travel outdoors because of panic attacks, suffers from obsessive-compulsive disorder, has a substance abuse problem, or is suffering from PTSD. It is a reasonable working assumption, however, that although individual problems may have their own developmental causes and trajectory, they are likely to strain the relationship, and in turn the couple's conflict may further exacerbate a partner's disorder. Third, one partner may not feel ready to disclose certain information in the presence of the other partner, and it may be critical for the practitioner to be informed of this matter (e.g., suspected physical or sexual abuse in the household, other criminal behavior, infidelity, other problems).

A thorough examination of each partner's own relationship history (beyond family of origin) may also reveal information salient to the current relationship. What does each partner bring to the relationship? Has either been married before? What were previous relationships like? Were they positive with pleasant memories, or were they fraught with conflict? Was there any history of abuse? What expectations did they bring and do they still have about the current relationship, and what do they want from their partner? Are these expectations reasonable? Are their impressions, attributions, and cognitions congruent with regard to the other partner's actual behavior? This relationship history can then provide a foundation for a developmental timeline. How long have they been together? At what point (in terms of major developmental milestones) are they in their relationship? Are they newlyweds, struggling with young children, or a more experienced couple trying to keep up with more adventurous adolescent sons or daughters? Are they struggling to finance their young adult's college education? Practitioners should avoid superimposing the expectations of standard "stage theories" on couples. However, they should take note of common milestones (e.g., having children, children leaving home, approaching retirement) and examine the unique aspects of the relationship at these points.

A functional assessment is necessary to capture the pattern and sequencing of a couple's positive and negative interactions over time (Floyd, Haynes, & Kelly, 1997; Fraenkel, 1997; Sayers & Sarwer, 1998). The functional analysis should include their unique developmental trajectory (i.e., courtship and marital lifecycle) and their day-to-day interactions concerning key problems (e.g., parenting differences, money, sharing household responsibilities, fidelity, sexual problems, and difficulties with in-laws). Processes to be described should include distorted cognitions (misattributions) about the relationship and each other, emotional expression, negative and positive communication patterns and deficits, and other situational problems. Relationships with families of origin, social supports, work relationships, and other community relations (e.g., friends and acquaintances) should be examined as well. Work-related stress or financial problems can seriously strain a couple's relationship. More severe environmental barriers due to poverty, discrimination, poor living conditions, and other social stressors must also be considered.

It is important that the couple have an opportunity to discuss a moderately distressing problem within the session during the assessment phase so that the practitioner can observe a representative example of how they interact and which problem-solving methods and communication styles they employ. After a period of observation, the practitioner can use a stop-action method to interrupt the couple and help them examine important aspects of their own communication process, including cognitions (beliefs, expectations, attributions) regarding the relationship and their partner, emotional content associated with those cognitions, and specific behavioral interactions. Both partners are likely to have different views regarding their partner's respective behaviors, the quality of the relationship as a whole, and different versions of "what happened and when" regarding day-to-day interactions. Nevertheless, practitioners should strive, at least initially, to keep the discussion purely descriptive, to keep the emotional timbre low and matter-of-fact, and to try to avoid making confirmatory judgments. This "neutral" position can help establish an overall sense of fairness (i.e., both partners feel that the practitioner is not taking sides). The practitioner can then begin to tentatively formulate a hypothetical model of a key problem: "Let me see if I understand this. First, you do X, then you say Y, and then Z happens. Do I have that right?"

Once the practitioner and couple generally agree on the problem content (e.g., sex, money, parenting) and a description of the problematic interactional process, it is important to establish a problem hierarchy and decide on intervention goals. Goals of treatment (i.e., changes each partner wants in the other and in the relationship as a whole) should be mutually agreed on. Which problem should be addressed first? Taking on the most challenging one may not be the best place to start. Beginning with a more manageable and less contentious but important issue (e.g., balancing the budget) may be a good starting point. Approaching problems gradually and achieving small successes along the way can help clients increase their self-efficacy in problem-solving, improve their emotional response to each other, and increase optimism that "we can work it out." Individual problems should also be broken down into steps (again, hierarchically) so that the couple can begin with a more manageable part of the problem (e.g., making a list of household expenses, attending a free budgeting seminar at the local high school, reviewing résumé writing tips), and lead gradually up to more contentious challenges (e.g., moving or changing jobs). Indeed, not every problem needs to be solved. Couples can live quite happily together by "agreeing to disagree" about some problems for which the resolution is not critical at the moment. Sometimes, as other problems are resolved, the improvements in mutual goodwill, problem solving, and communication skills generalize to these other problems as well.

As discussed in chapter 2, the practitioner should be prepared to use a few different methods of reporting to compare the consistency of responses: the face-to-face interview; self-monitoring techniques that the couple can work on at home (e.g., keeping individual diaries or a joint chart to record times they worked constructively on the problem together); and brief, reliable, and valid couple assessment scales, a few of which are discussed later.

Assessment of Couple Violence. Because violence between couples is not rare, and given the potential harm to both the partner and children, practitioners should always screen for domestic violence when working with couples or when working with individuals who report problems in their relationships (Bradford, 2010). An assessment of domestic violence should be considered necessary to determine whether couples work is even feasible. Although some practitioners maintain that domestic violence should always preclude couples work, there is growing consensus that this policy may be overly broad and may preclude effective work in cases where the violence is at a low to moderate level. Although there is an acute need for further research on the matter, assessment of couples' battering and determining which couples may be amenable to successful intervention can be informed by what is currently known about risk factors.

Bograd and Mederos (1999) suggest three preconditions for assessment with male-on-female violence (which can be modified for gay couples): (1) the man must be a voluntary participant in the therapy; (2) modification in disclosing confidential information during individual assessment interviews must be an option (e.g., the woman may disclose that she has been victimized to the practitioner but does not want the practitioner to disclose yet); (3) the practitioner must "be frank and clear about the allocation of responsibility and the inappropriateness of abusive behavior regardless of circumstances" (p. 296). In addition to a couple assessment session that focuses primarily on interactional concerns in the marriage, the practitioner should conduct individual meetings that explore domestic violence. Bograd and Mederos (1999) make clear that the practitioner cannot mislead victims into believing that the practitioner can guarantee their security, and clients must be well informed of the potential risks.

The goals of the individual assessment interview are the following:

- To learn about the nature of any violence between the couple and functional details (e.g., context; sequence of events leading up to it; the type, frequency, severity, consequences of the violence)
- To understand the intended function of the violence and its effects
- To evaluate the degree of intimidation used and fear elicited in the victim
- To examine whether there is a broader pattern of violence and intimidation
- To consider the real possibility of serious injury or death
- To arrive at an informed decision about the feasibility and wisdom of proceeding with couples' work

Bograd and Mederos (1999) further suggest that if any one of the following risk factors exists, practitioners should seriously consider forgoing couples' therapy:

- Unresolved substance abuse
- A history of two or more acts of domestic violence (to wife or children), including rape
- A history of violent criminal acts, including violation of restraining order
- Previous use of weapons
- Ongoing threats of violence
- Obsessional behaviors toward the partner, such as intense jealousy, stalking, or harassing
- Bizarre forms of violence marked by sadism or an attempt to depersonalize the victim.

Conversely, couples intervention *may* be considered if

- Both individuals freely agree to therapy
- Incidents of violence have been few and/or have been confined to less harmful forms of aggression, such as pushing, shoving, or open-handed slaps that do not result in physical injury (e.g., bruises)
- There is minimal psychological abuse
- There are no threats of lethality, and the woman does not fear violent reprisals
- The abusive partner takes responsibility for his behavior and for controlling his anger without making excuses or blaming others

This is a brief overview, so a thorough review of Bograd and Mederos (1999) is recommended. Assessment instruments such as the Conflict Tactics Scale and the Danger Assessment Scale also are recommended as useful adjuncts to a thorough clinical interview (Anderson, 2001).

Social workers may not always be the first in line to assess domestic violence cases. Often medical professionals are in a position to determine whether violence has taken place. Such data can be instrumental in the successful prosecution of domestic violence cases. Two key areas in which medical professionals can improve assessment and provide solid evidence for court proceedings are in documenting medical injuries accurately (e.g., clear descriptions, photographs) and accurately recording the verbal reports of their clients (in quotes) rather than making interpretations or inferences about what they thought their patients meant. Recording the time of the interview and the time the injuries were said to have occurred also strengthens the evidence (US Department of Justice, 2001). Social workers can also improve their recording of verbal reports from clients about the specific nature (who, what, where, and when) of the violence and can work closely with health-care professionals on a routine basis to gather solid evidence of physical abuse. Case management coordination of data gathering and, later, interventions may be invaluable to successful intervention with victims of domestic violence.

Instruments

There are several well-tested instruments that have been widely used in practice and research with couples and can serve as useful adjuncts to an MFS assessment. The Marital Adjustment Test (MAT) (Fredman & Sherman, 1987; Locke & Wallace, 1959) is one of the most widely used measures of marital satisfaction. The MAT is a 15-item scale that takes only a few minutes to complete and has weighted scores that sum to a potential total of 60. It has one global measure of marital satisfaction; eight questions regarding specific areas of possible disagreement (e.g., finances, recreation, affection, friends, sex); and six questions measuring conflict resolution, communication, and cohesion (e.g., how disagreements are resolved, leisure preferences, willingness to confide in the other). It has excellent internal consistency reliability and discriminates well between adjusted and maladjusted couples.

The Dyadic Adjustment Scale (DAS) (Spanier, 1976) is considered one of the more valid and useful scales for assessing marital adjustment. The original DAS is relatively brief (32 items) and has been shown to discriminate between distressed and nondistressed couples. Although there is some controversy regarding whether the DAS is a unidimensional or multidimensional scale, it was originally designed to measure four areas of marital adjustment: consensus on important areas of marital functioning, dyadic satisfaction, marital cohesion, and expression of affection. Busby, Christensen, Crane, and Larson (1995) undertook a reanalysis of the factor structure of the DAS with 242 couples. They demonstrated that, according to their data, the DAS is best conceptualized as a multidimensional instrument that measures three subscales in the following areas: consensus (in decision making, leisure activities, values, and affection), marital satisfaction (instability of the marriage and level of conflict), and cohesion (activities engaged in together and exchanging ideas of interest with one another). Their three-factor model resulted in a 14-item brief scale that demonstrated a high degree of construct and criterion validity, as well as good to excellent internal consistency and split-half reliability for brief subscales. The 14-item revised DAS is found in Busby et al. (1995). The revised DAS has also been shown to correlate highly ($r = .78$) with the Kansas Marital Satisfaction scale, which has yielded comparable results in distinguishing distressed from nondistressed couples (Crane, Middleton, & Bean, 2000). A limitation of these two scales, however, is that the samples overrepresent white couples. Validating the scales with minority couples is a potentially rich avenue for future social work research.

Should practitioners be primarily interested in measuring relationship satisfaction, then a practical and brief alternative may be the Relationship Assessment Scale (RAS) (Hendrick, 1981, 1988; Hendrick, Dicke, & Hendrick, 1998). The original RAS was based on research showing a correlation between self-disclosure and marital satisfaction with 51 couples (Hendrick, 1981). A more recent version of the RAS is a seven-item Likert-scale global measure of relationship satisfaction, with total scores ranging from 7 to 35. The scale's reliability has been shown to be high, and it correlates highly with the long version of the DAS (Hendrick, 1988; Vaughn & Matyastik Baier, 1999). The RAS also discriminates couples who stay together and couples who break up. It has also been shown to have relatively consistent measurement properties by gender and ethnic background, and it can be used with nonmarried persons involved in a relationship (Hendrick et al., 1998). This option is important, since practitioners can use this brief scale with "nontraditional" couples (e.g., gay, lesbian, or bisexual couples).

A more recent addition to the set of available instruments for assessing couple's relationships is the Marital Disaffection Scale (Kayser, 1996; Kersten, 1990). This 21-item self-report scale measures the degree to which individuals have lost their feelings of love and affection for their partner on a four-point scale (4 = very true, 1 = not at all true). Although the scale uses the term *marital*, the items do not preclude its use with any couple that has been in a relationship for a significant amount of time (i.e., the scale's term *spouse* can be replaced with *partner*). Two studies support the scale's reliability and criterion validity. Kayser (1996) administered the scale to 76 spouses recruited through community sources for the study. Mean age was about 32, and couples had been married for a mean of 8 years. In another study, 354 spouses were surveyed (mean age of 46 and mean length of marriage was 21 years). Internal consistency ratings were high (>.95), and the scale correlated with other related measures moderately to highly in the expected direction (e.g., disaffection vs. increased intimacy) (Kayser, 1996; Tuliatos, Perlmutter, & Holden, 2001). The scale also includes several reverse score items to measure intimacy (see instrument 11.1).

SELECTING EFFECTIVE INTERVENTIONS

Although there has been a tremendous amount of descriptive and theoretical literature written about couple therapy, surprisingly few formal interventions for couples have been thoroughly tested in controlled trials. The better-researched approaches include emotion-focused couples therapy (EFT) and behavioral couples therapy (BCT). Since the early 1990s, the pace of research on couples therapy has slowed, but theoretical developments with an eye toward integration and eclecticism have continued. What follows is a brief overview of interventions shown to be effective with distressed couples, followed by suggestions for incorporating the best of the approaches into flexible evidence-based guidelines.

Behavioral couples (marital) therapy (BCT) is clearly the most extensively researched of the couple interventions and has accumulated a solid record of demonstrated effectiveness in reducing couple's distress in dozens of controlled trials (e.g., Alexander, Holtzworth-Munroe, & Jameson, 1994; Baucom & Epstein, 1990; Gurman, Kniskern, & Pinsof, 1986; Hahlweg &

INSTRUMENT 11.1   The Marital Disaffection Scale

Instructions: Please answer all questions using the following scale:

Very true	Somewhat true	Not very true	Not at all true
4	3	2	1

1. If I could never be with my spouse, I would feel miserable.   4 3 2 1
2. I find it difficult to confide in my spouse about a number of things.   4 3 2 1
3. I enjoy spending time alone with my spouse.   4 3 2 1
4. I often feel lonely even though I am with my spouse.   4 3 2 1
5. I miss my spouse when we're not together for a couple days.   4 3 2 1
6. Most of the time I feel very close to my spouse.   4 3 2 1
7. I seem to enjoy just being with my spouse.   4 3 2 1
8. I look forward to seeing my spouse at the end of the day.   4 3 2 1
9. My love for my spouse has increased more and more over time.   4 3 2 1
10. I find myself withdrawing more and more from my spouse.   4 3 2 1
11. When I have a personal problem, my spouse is the first person I turn to.   4 3 2 1
12. Apathy and indifference best describe my feelings toward my spouse.   4 3 2 1
13. I feel little, if any, desire to have sex with my spouse.   4 3 2 1
14. My spouse has always been there when I needed him or her.   4 3 2 1
15. I would prefer to spend less time with my spouse.   4 3 2 1
16. I have more positive than negative thoughts about my partner.   4 3 2 1
17. I have a lot of angry feelings toward my spouse.   4 3 2 1
18. I am not as concerned about fulfilling my obligations and responsibilities in my marriage as I was in the past.   4 3 2 1
19. I try to avoid spending time with my spouse.   4 3 2 1
20. There are times when I do not feel a great deal of love and affection for my mate.   4 3 2 1
21. I enjoy sharing my feelings with my spouse.   4 3 2 1

After reversing the scores on items 1, 3, 5, 6, 7, 8, 9, 11, 14, 16, 21, sum all items. The higher the score, the greater the level of disaffection. Kersten, K. K. (1990) The process of marital disaffection: Interventions at various stages. *Family Relations*, 39, 257–265. (Copyright 1990 by the National Council on Family Relations, 3989 Central Ave., NE, Suite 550, Minneapolis, MN 55421. Reprinted by permission.)

Markman, 1988; Jacobson & Addis, 1993; Lebow, 2000; Lebow & Gurman, 1995; O'Farrell & Fals-Stewart, 2003). Usually, a BCT intervention includes three main components: behavioral exchange (quid pro quo contracting: "you do this for me, and I'll do that for you"); communication training, and problem-solving skills. In almost all controlled trials, BCT has been shown to be more effective than no treatment controls in reducing harmful conflict, improving communications and interpersonal behaviors, and increasing relationship satisfaction (Hahlweg & Markman, 1988; Halford, 1998; Lebow

& Gurman, 1995). However, only about 70–75% of clients show improvement from BCT, and many clients relapse over time. Although BCT has accumulated the most evidence as an established treatment for marital distress, it has not been shown to be markedly superior to other nonbehavioral approaches, such as insight-oriented couples' therapy (IOCT) or EFT in direct comparisons (e.g., Johnson, 2003; Snyder, Wills, & Grady-Fletcher, 1991), or through meta-analysis (Shadish et al., 1993). The addition of explicit cognitive elements has not markedly improved the outcomes of BCT (Baucom & Epstein, 1990; Halford, 1998; Jacobson & Addis, 1993), and (as with other approaches) the effective processes of BCT have not been clearly determined.

In the course of its evolution, BCT has incorporated modifications that go beyond behavior change as the only indication of success. Integrative behavioral couple therapy (IBCT) (Christensen, Jacobson, & Babcock, 1995) was developed to enhance "acceptance" between partners when some problems seem intractable. IBCT is based on the assumption that to be happy as a couple, not all problems need to be resolved. In fact, some couples can become more intimate by learning to accept some of their differences. To this end, the methods include empathic joining (i.e., trying to understand the partner's needs and feelings to reduce some of the pain felt mutually), detachment (i.e., developing some mutual intellectual understanding and distance from the problem), development of some degree of tolerance for the problem (i.e., diminishing the ongoing struggle to change it), and cultivation of self-care skills to reduce overreliance on the other person to satisfy all of one's particular needs). A preliminary randomized trial with 21 couples (treated for a mean of 21 sessions) demonstrated that IBCT resulted in greater satisfaction and more clinically significant gains than traditional BCT (Jacobson, Christensen, Prince, Cordova, & Eldridge, 2000). However, Baucom, Sevier, Eldridge, Doss, and Christensen (2011) found that couple communication patterns marked by negativity and withdrawal were significantly reduced 2 years after IBCT, but problem solving did not improve, and positivity toward each partner actually decreased.

Halford (1998) has also embellished BCT by changing the focus from changing the partner to each partner improving his or her own self-regulatory behaviors: "In the context of relationship problems, self-regulation involves focusing on each partner's attempts to change their own behavior, cognitions and affect to enhance their personal satisfaction with the relationship" (p. 621). Initial exploratory investigations appear to be promising. Investigators are hopeful that emphasizing self-regulatory mechanisms of change rather than changing the other person may lead to more lasting benefits of couple therapy.

The major alternatives to BCT include EFT (Goldman & Greenberg, 1992; James, 1991; Johnson, 2007; Johnson & Greenberg, 1985a, 1985b, 1988), and IOCT (Snyder & Wills, 1989; Snyder et al., 1991). Based somewhat on variants of psychodynamic theory and practice, both EFT and IOCT emphasize changing partners' behaviors by increasing understanding (i.e., insight) into their relationship through either direct interpretation (IOCT) or improved emotional expression (EFT). Both EFT and IOCT have been shown to be reasonably effective at improving relationship satisfaction (Halford, 1998), although these conclusions are based on a very limited number of trials and few direct comparisons to other approaches. In a study comparing BCT and EFT (Johnson & Greenberg, 1985a), EFT was shown to be superior when compared with one skill component of BCT (i.e., problem solving) in a sample of mildly distressed couples. In a comparison with BCT (Snyder & Wills, 1989; Snyder et al., 1991), IOCT was shown to have better long-term outcomes, although it was alleged that the BCT method employed did not include relational aspects that are part of BCT (Jacobson, 1991). Given the limited evidence from direct comparisons and meta-analytic studies, it is difficult to argue that one approach is markedly superior to another.

A few key outcome studies of EFT have been conducted since the mid-1980s. In the initial study, Johnson and Greenberg (1985a) assigned 45 couples (15 each) to eight 1-hour EFT sessions, to problem-solving training (PS, a component of BCT), or to a control group (waiting list). Several measures were taken at pre-treatment, post-treatment, and follow-up. Husbands in the EFT group reported significant improvement over the other two conditions, and wives in both the EFT and the PS reported improvements over the controls. Couples in both treatment groups had improved over controls on the following measures: intellectual intimacy, consensus, reduction in target problems, and overall goal attainment. EFT couples, however, reported greater cohesion, intellectual intimacy, reductions in target complaints, and conventionality than those couples receiving PS. Wives in the EFT condition also improved more in emotional expression and expression of affection. Follow-up measures at 2 months showed gains for the EFT couples consistent with those at post-test. The authors emphasized that EFT resulted in behavioral improvements (e.g., negotiations and other behavior changes) even though there was no explicit focus on these skills. They suggested that "it may be that the increase in trust and responsiveness, which is the goal of the EFT treatment, has an effect in these areas" (Johnson & Greenberg, 1985a, p. 181). In a follow-up study, Johnson and Greenberg (1985b) treated and evaluated those who had been on the wait list (i.e., the control group) in the previous study, and showed that, although no substantive improvements had occurred during the wait period, they improved after eight sessions of EFT in all outcomes and maintained gains after 2 months.

James (1991) conducted a controlled trial in which EFT was compared to EFT (12 sessions) augmented by the addition of communication training (CT), that is, eight sessions of EFT and four sessions of CT. Forty-two couples (average length of partnership about 10 years) were randomly assigned to three treatment conditions (including a wait-list control), and interventions were measured for fidelity to their respective models. Both treatment groups had generally superior outcomes at post-test and follow-up. But aside from improved communications in the group receiving EFT and CT, there were few differences between them, which suggests that the addition of CT to EFT resulted in only marginal improvement. In general, the results suggested that the goals of improving marital satisfaction and target complaints were more responsive to treatment than improving emotional bonds, a goal that may require more lengthy intervention.

Goldman and Greenberg (1992) compared EFT with integrated systemic marital therapy (IST) in which therapist consultants assisted the primary therapist in using systemic techniques such as reframing and prescribing the symptom. Forty-two couples were randomly assigned (14 each) to one of two treatment conditions (10 sessions) or to a wait-list control group. Couples were all white and had been together for 11 years on average. Fourteen therapists (with a master's degree in psychology, counseling, or social work) received 12 hours of instruction and additional supervision in their respective approach. Couples in the two treatment groups demonstrated more marital satisfaction, conflict resolution, reductions in target complaints, and goal attainment. Two-thirds of the treatment couples were rated in the nondistressed range after treatment, with no differences between the two treatment groups. The other 33 couples showed some clinical improvement, although they could not be considered treatment successes. Results for EFT couples deteriorated over time at follow-up, perhaps as the result of the persuasiveness of the team approach, or because the couples were more severely distressed than couples previously treated in studies of EFT. The IST approach was more explicit about changing couples' behaviors, whereas the EFT was more focused on changing emotional perceptions and interactive experience within the couples.

In recent years, there has been growing interest in "forgiveness" as a focus of therapy, particularly with respect to interpersonal emotional injury. Using EFT in an uncontrolled trial, Greenberg, Warwar, and Malcomb (2010) demonstrated that relationships damaged by betrayal, abandonment, or identity insult, overall, showed improvements over time with regard to forgiveness, although a few couples continued to deteriorate, and many could not improve with respect to trust. A forgiveness focus incorporates core aspects of EFT but includes an explicit focus on expressions of empathy from the "offender" to the "offendee," as well as a sincere apology for the hurtful act.

Exemplar Outcome Studies: IOCT versus BCT

Given the key theoretical and practical debate generated by comparing IOCT and BMT, the investigation by Snyder and associates (Snyder & Wills, 1989; Snyder et al., 1991) serve as this chapter's exemplar study.

As noted earlier, BCT was generally considered the only empirically demonstrated effective couple intervention until the mid-1980s. Snyder and Wills (1989) pointed out that although EFT (Johnson and Greenberg, 1985a) is based on psychodynamic principles, its implementation does not explicitly require identifying early, perhaps unconscious, causes of intrapsychic and interspousal difficulties. IOCT, however, was designed specifically to uncover and interpret unconscious conflict that is presumed to cause intrapsychic and interspousal conflict, to improve the couple's relationship. The investigators (Snyder & Wills, 1989) recruited 79 predominantly white Midwestern couples, who were randomly assigned to BCT (29) and IOCT (30). Therapists were four master's-level social workers and one psychiatric nurse. Pains were taken to examine treatment biases, but examination found that all practitioners were comfortable with eclectic practice. Considerable efforts were also taken to ensure treatment fidelity. As Snyder and Wills (1989) describe, IOCT:

> emphasized the resolution of conflictual emotional processes that exist either within one or both spouses separately, between spouses interactively, or within the broader family system. This approach attempted to integrate individual, couple, and family functioning by addressing developmental issues, collusive interactions, incongruent contractual expectations, irrational role assignments, and maladaptive relationship rules. Therapists used probes, clarification and interpretation in uncovering and explicating those feelings, beliefs, and expectations that spouses had toward themselves, their partners and their marriage, which were either totally or partially beyond awareness, so that these could be restructured or renegotiated at a conscious level. The emphasis was on the interpretation of underlying dynamics that contributed to the current, observable marital difficulties. (p. 41)

Both approaches were applied over an average of 19 sessions each, and attrition rates were negligible. Results showed that both interventions performed comparably well at termination and at 6-month follow-up on measures of both psychological distress, but more so on couples' satisfaction. The authors suggested that, despite the procedural differences in the two approaches, the comparable outcomes might be attributed to common core therapeutic processes.

Four years later, however, 55 couples were followed up and interviewed by phone. Results showed a striking difference in outcomes between the two groups. Those who had undergone BCT showed a divorce rate of 38%, whereas those who had received IOCT had a divorce rate of 3%. In addition, those in the IOCT group who were still married showed greater marital satisfaction. Results suggest that psychodynamically oriented methods may help modify underlying cognitive attributions about the interactional problems between partners. Perhaps understanding the "underlying rules" of the relationship is necessary for couples to generalize the benefits of marital therapy across situations and maintain their behavior changes.

These studies provoked lively debate regarding the relative efficacy of BCT and IOCT. Jacobson (1991) argued that the type of IOCT used appeared to have much in common as clinically sensitive BCT, thus demonstrating that enhanced BCT was better than the older, more behaviorally focused BCT. Respective camps also argued over which approach was more likely to benefit from investigational bias. However, it was clear in the original study (Snyder & Wills, 1989) that the investigators went to considerable pains to examine the biases of the investigators (who generally expected BCT to be superior) and noted that they used BCT as explicated in Jacobson and Margolin (1979) (described in more detail later here) without attention to later cognitive embellishments. Nevertheless, without further replication or additional efficacy and change-process studies, it is hard to determine which approach is superior or even which components of each intervention are essential. Results from a single study can easily be anomalous. Further research might reveal reliable differences.

Descriptions of EFT and BCT.   The following sections present basic steps for implementing emotion-focused therapy (EFT) and behavioral couples therapy (BCT). Practitioners should become familiar with both interventions and examine possibilities for eclectic implementation.

EFT.   There are two major tasks in EFT (Johnson & Greenberg, 1988): to access the couple's emotional experience and to change the couple's interactional positions. Johnson and Greenberg (1988) divide the descriptive intervention procedures into nine steps usually lasting up to 15 visits or so:

- "Focus on the partners' experience of the relationship, particularly on their emotional responses to each other and how these responses mediate the closeness or separateness of the bond between them and the process of self-definition" (p. 83)

- Identify the recurrent negative interactional cycle—the authors suggest that the "therapist must *see* the cycle" (p. 85)

- Access unacknowledged feelings underlying interactional positions (i.e., the therapist must help clients reenact the core emotional conflicts in the here and now)

- Redefine the problem(s) in terms of underlying feelings (i.e., the explanation or interpretation of the couples' enacted experience should integrate affective, cognitive, and behavioral experiences)

- Promote identification with disowned needs and aspects of self by helping clients reconnect with thoughts, needs, and feelings that they have not been relating to their dysfunctional reactions and subsequent conflicted cycles (e.g., a husband raised by hypercritical parents tends to be thin skinned when, for instance, his wife innocently asks about when a home project will be finished—the practitioner can help him identify his hurt feelings behind his angry and defensive responses)

- Encourage acceptance by each partner of the other's experience (i.e., help the couple to listen, acknowledge, empathize, and accept the other's feelings and experience without needing to discount or criticize those feelings or experience)
- Facilitate the expression of needs and wants to restructure the interaction (i.e., to help partners move from defensive postures to openly expressing their desires in ways that may engender more caring responses)
- Establish the emergence of new solutions (i.e., the couple attempts to solidify gains by practicing more emotionally open communication of thoughts, feelings, and needs, and replace old negative and dysfunctional interactions)
- Consolidate new positions; continue with new engendered practices but emphasize before-and-after differences of their interactive cycles; this review should include an examination of future scenarios that may threaten successes; couples should continue practicing clearer emotional expression to prevent returning to the old, negative interactive cycles

BCT.   Although there have been modifications to the basic BCT approach over the years (e.g., inclusion of explicit methods targeting changes in cognitions about the relationship), the basic behavioral methods of BCT are described in detail in Jacobson and Margolin (1979). In addition to a thorough assessment and relationship building with the client, the following lists illustrate what practitioners should incorporate into their intervention.

Cognitive Analysis

- Practitioners should closely examine cognitive distortions and faulty attributions made by each partner about the other and about the relationship.
- Over the course of treatment, practitioners should use the interactions in the sessions and homework to challenge distortions, attempt to "disconfirm" them, and allow for alternative and more constructive cognitions to replace them.

Behavioral Exchange

- A key behavioral component to BCT is rooted in behavioral exchange, that is, the increase in engaging in behaviors that are pleasing (i.e., positively reinforcing) for the other partner. This behavioral exchange not only can reduce tensions and conflict but also can increase a sense of goodwill and caring, and lead to greater relationship intimacy. The rationale is simply to reduce costs in the relationship and to increase rewards (benefits).

- Practitioners must focus on identifying those positive behaviors that please the other partner. The couple must test out hypotheses about what is pleasing or not.

- "Love days" are an effective way to highlight or concentrate on those behaviors that are mutually pleasing. Couples must practice being clear and explicitly letting the other know what is pleasing and what is not.

- Behavioral exchange contracts (also called contingency contracting) can accompany this method and can either be an explicit exchange of favors (known as the quid pro quo: "I'll do this, if you do that") or be built on a "good-faith contract," with no specific contingency or timetable, but a general agreement that each partner will follow through on his or her end of the bargain (e.g., "I'll pick up the house during the week, if you take care of the laundry on the weekends"). Ideally, contingency contracting should be a positive exchange rather than a form of coercion or threat (e.g., "If you don't come home on time, I'm leaving!").

Communication Skills

- Communication skills (e.g., empathy, listening, reflecting and validating, accepting what the partner feels, responding clearly, expressing thoughts and feelings assertively) are key for each partner to examine the other's thoughts and feelings and to create accurate expectations regarding what each partner likes and dislikes. Poor communication can easily lead to further misunderstanding and distress.

- Practitioners focus on sensitively providing good feedback regarding the couple's communication strengths and deficits and give instructions on how to improve it. The couple must then rehearse the skills during sessions and practice more effective communication skills at home.

- A hierarchy of topics should be addressed gradually, moving from moderately stressful areas of conflict to those that are more challenging as the couple increases the skills and capacity for tolerating talking about "touchy" subjects. Although maintaining effective communication skills appears to be an elementary aspect of intervention, they are challenging to maintain under stress and are among the more oft-cited problems that couples report in relationships.

Problem-Solving Skills

- Jacobson and Margolin (1979) define problem solving as "the process by which change agreements are reached" (p. 213). Effective problem-solving skills are also necessary to weather the normal stresses that can strain a long-term relationship. Although others have defined the problem-solving steps of behavior approaches somewhat differently (see, e.g., D'Zurilla & Goldfried, 1971), the steps are similar to those recommended in BCT: define the problem(s) specifically, express feelings assertively, each partner takes responsibility for his or her own contribution to the problem and its solution, each takes a turn briefly defining the problem, then emphasize solutions (avoid attributing blame), work toward compromise and maintain a sense of mutuality ("we're in this thing together"), and record the agreements.

Combining the Best Couples' Therapies: Theoretical Integration or Pragmatic Eclecticism?.   Having noted the lack of clear superiority for any of the evidence-based interventions for couples work, several practitioner-researchers have recommended integrated or eclectic approaches drawn from psychodynamic, emotionally focused, and behavioral approaches (Epstein, Baucom & Daiuto, 1997; Halford, 1998; Lawrence, Eldridge, & Christensen, 1998). However, the distinction made in chapter 3 between *integration* (i.e., common change-processes) and *eclecticism* (i.e., combined techniques) should be kept in mind.

In explaining their rationale for EFT, Johnson and Greenberg (1988) cite attachment theory and object relations theory (Bowlby, 1969; Guntrip, 1969), thus placing the theoretical foundation for EFT squarely in the psychoanalytic tradition. Snyder and Wills (1989) subscribe to a similar view regarding IOCT. Simply put, proponents of psychoanalytic couples theory aver that adult couples' problems are the consequence of disordered relational templates or prototypes laid down in early childhood that resulted from the failure of mothers (primarily) to adequately nurture their children. These disturbed early psychological templates are then recapitulated in future relationships. This assumption is the cornerstone of psychoanalytic theory. Nevertheless, Johnson and Greenberg (1988) later assert "The etiology of each couple's dance is a matter for speculation" (p. 77).

Other proponents of EFT (e.g., Lawrence et al., 1998) have elaborated on this theoretical premise. The emphasis on both the individual partner's relationship history and the dyadic development as a couple can provide a basis for identifying disordered attachment patterns (i.e., securely, avoidant, anxious, or ambivalent) based on the apparent similarity between the way adults behave in interpersonal relationships and how infants behave. References by these authors to attachment theory, then, appear to be more analogous than explanatory since causation cannot be inferred from "similarity" (i.e., correlation).

However, Johnson and Greenberg (1988) also claim to have identified the theoretical change processes that are engaged in the implementation of EFT:

> Emotionally focused couples therapy is an affective systemic approach in which the emphasis is on changing interactional cycles and changing each person's intrapsychic experience, which maintains, and is maintained by,

the cycle. In this treatment, the emphasis is first on identifying the negative interactional cycle early in treatment and then on accessing each partner's unexpressed underlying emotions, which serve to organize his or her views of self and partner. The problem cycle, the individuals, interactional positions, and their behaviors are then redefined in terms of the newly experienced underlying emotions. Thus, for example, the blaming of one partner may come to be seen as an expression of an underlying fear of abandonment, vulnerability, or loneliness, while the withdrawal or rejection of the other partner may come to be seen as an attempt at self-protection or fear of engulfment. This approach is based on an integration of experiential and systemic approaches. (p. 29)

Although EFT techniques may, in fact, activate processes by which the couple better recognizes their respective interpersonal "templates," there is no evidence that the templates were necessarily (or even primarily) created by disruptions in early childhood. In short, practitioners of different theoretical allegiances can agree that interpersonal change processes are related to "relational templates" without inferring that these templates (interpersonal schemata?) were created primarily by mother-toddler experiences.

Given the absence of developmental research supporting attachment theory as a necessary or sufficient explanation for couple conflict, a more reasonable theoretical model would include multiple independent, additive, and interactive influences on the emergence of interpersonal schemata over time: temperament, lifelong relationship experiences (including childhood family experiences, nonromantic friendships, adolescent and adult intimate relationships), and cultural disposition toward relationship roles (e.g., equality vs. subservience), among other factors. In addition, practitioner-researchers should be open to the possibility that several change processes may be at work (alone or in combination) during the intervention itself:

- The emotionally corrective experience of the therapeutic relationship
- Better insight and increased empathy regarding each partner's respective concerns, fears, complaints, and relationship patterns
- Increased hope and morale in dealing with marital distress
- Improved problem-solving skills
- Increased self-efficacy as communications and problem-solving efforts improve

These explanations are not mutually exclusive, nor are they necessarily incommensurate with early attachment explanations. However, given that relatively little research specifically targets change processes in couple therapy, it is currently not known how or why couple interventions are effective even when they do work successfully. It may be more fruitful for researchers and practitioners to focus on identifying and combining the most effective techniques of both EFT and BCT:

- Helping partners understand and clarify each other's cognitive appraisal and expectations of the other
- Identifying and understanding emotionally charged interactional patterns
- Changing behaviors through improved communication and problem solving to optimize interpersonal rewards
- Ameliorating the impact of individual disorders (e.g., substance abuse, depression) on the relationship

Given the available evidence for effective couples work, flexible eclecticism seems to be a reasonable option. Further research on couples work should emphasize the identification of optimal combinations of intervention skills and matching them to client needs and preferred change modalities (e.g., emotionally focused analysis, behavioral contracting, some combination).

Other Specific Applications for Couple Therapies

Couples therapies are used not only for general relationship distress, which includes emotional harm, communication problems, and disagreements about child rearing or household finances. Evidence-based couples approaches can also be adapted for use with more specific problems, although the amount of available research varies from problem to problem.

Couples Therapy for Specific Mental Health Problems.   A comprehensive review of the literature on empirically supported couples and family interventions for marital distress and adult mental health problems supports the view that couples and family interventions can often augment results for an individual with a specific disorder (Baucom, Mueser, Shoham, Daiuto, & Stickle, 1998). Using relatively strict methodological criteria for reviewing the literature, the authors noted that there are different purposes in applying couples and family interventions when one person is a primary target of the intervention. First, some interventions are seen as partner- or family-assisted treatments to help in the implementation of a treatment regimen (e.g., the partner or family helps a mother overcome agoraphobia). Second, a couple's or family's interactional behaviors may be the focus of treatment insofar as the behaviors have a negative impact on a family member with an individual disorder (e.g., helping family members not to reinforce a heavy drinking father's excuse making). Third, a couple or family may have difficulties that need to be addressed, and their collective behaviors may exacerbate the symptoms of a family member who may also be the focus of individual treatment (e.g., helping a family with a son with mental illness by reducing conflict and improving communications and problem solving to improve overall family climate and reduce stress). With respect to severe mental illness, evidence does not support early family therapy theories, which asserted that individual "identified patient's" symptoms or problems were caused by the family's behavior.

With regard to findings, Baucom et al. (1998) concluded that couples and family work may be as effective as individual interventions for obsessive-compulsive disorder, agoraphobia, and alcohol abuse disorders, and the use of couples and family work may enhance the individual client's therapeutic success. Involving a partner or other family member in assisting in exposure treatments for persons with obsessive-compulsive disorder or agoraphobia, for example, can help the individual succeed. Engaging a partner or family member in helping a drinking spouse or other family member can boost therapeutic outcomes as well. Family psychoeducation with mentally ill persons has now accumulated a wealth of evidence of effectiveness. Last, although it is not clear that couples interventions are superior to individual treatment when a partner is depressed, it appears that couples therapy "might be preferable to individual psychotherapy among maritally discordant couples with a depressed wife because it leads to improvement in both depression and marital discord" (Baucom et al., 1998, p. 68). However, if the partners are not distressed, individual treatment may be more effective in many cases.

Behavioral couples therapy is prominently represented in research on applying couples work to individual disorders. Behavioral couples therapy (e.g., McCrady et al., 1986; O'Farrell et al., 1993; O'Farrell & Fals-Stewart, 2003) was shown to be effective for couples in which an alcoholic spouse voluntarily participated in treatment (for a review and description of BCT for couples with alcohol-related problems, see chapter 7). This approach treats spouses together by focusing directly on reducing drinking and improving the relationship. BCT was also shown to be effective in reducing depressive symptoms in one spouse and improving marital functioning overall (Beach & O'Leary, 1992). In a controlled trial comparing couples therapy with medication, EFT was found to have superior results for the female spouse at 6 month follow-up (Dessaulles, Johnson, & Denton, 2003). Few controlled trials have been conducted with other couple approaches when applied to an individual partner's disorder.

Interventions for Sexual Dysfunction in Couples.   It is not uncommon for couples to experience some problems with sexual expression or one or both partners to experience a diagnosable sexual dysfunction. The DSM-IV (APA, 2000) categorized these as disorders of *sexual desire* (i.e., hypoactive or sexual aversion disorder), *sexual arousal* (i.e., female arousal disorder or male erectile disorder), *orgasmic disorders* (i.e., difficulty achieving orgasm in females or males, and premature ejaculation in males), and *sexual pain disorders*—dyspareunia (i.e., pain associated with intercourse) and vaginismus (i.e., involuntary contraction of outer muscles of the vagina causing marked distress). In the DSM-5, disorders of desire and arousal in women have been combined into "female sexual interest/arousal disorder," and dyspareunia and vaginismus have been combined as "genito-pelvic pain/penetration disorder." Sexual disorders are now considered in two subtypes: lifelong versus acquired, and generalized versus situational (APA, 2013).

In addition to the fact that the validity of the sexual disorder taxonomy has been questioned over the years (Rosen & Leiblum, 1995), it is also understood that the notion of sexual dysfunction is highly relative to cultural context. Reliable data on the prevalence of sexual dysfunctions are hard to come by because of the highly variable methods used in relevant surveys. However, estimates based on reviews of epidemiological data suggest that 25–50% of all women and about 15% of men experience disorders of low sexual desire; up to about 20% of men older than age 40 complain about not achieving an erection, a rate than increases with age. Although about 75% of men report always ejaculating during sex, 5–15% of men and women experience inhibited orgasm, and estimates of women having problems with orgasm vary widely, with about 10% reporting never having achieved orgasm. About 30–40% of men report experiencing premature ejaculation, and sexual pain disorders are much more common in women than men (15% vs. 3%) (APA, 2000, 2013; Dziegielewski, Resnick, Nelson-Gardell, & Harrison, 1998).

Sexual dysfunctions can be roughly divided into two categories: problems with desire and/or arousal (e.g., achieving an erection for men, becoming adequately lubricated for women) and problems with satisfactorily completing the act of sex (e.g., premature orgasm in men, lack of orgasm or experiencing pain related to sex in women). Each of these problems needs to be assessed carefully for a range of medical, psychological, and behavioral causes and addressed with a treatment plan tailored for each partner and for the couple together. Multidimensional assessment for sexual dysfunction is widely recommended for couples (Dziegielewski et al., 1998; Rosen & Leiblum, 1995). There is now a greater emphasis on understanding sexual dysfunction in the context of the individual's interpersonal history and the quality of the current relationship, in addition to a medical examination to identify physiological causes. In addition, special consideration should be given to a thorough history of sexual behavior, especially to history of sexual abuse. Rape, incest, and sexual molestation—depending on type, severity, and relationship to the abuser—may have a profound effect on a person's ability to enjoy sexual intimacy as an adult (Barnes, 1995).

In addition to a thorough history taking, assessment of current sexual functioning should focus on both the individual and the dyad. Individual factors that may impede sexual expression include depression, anxiety, distorted cognitions that inhibit sexual enjoyment, substance abuse, and overall fitness and other specific medical concerns. A medical examination should be given high priority when sexual dysfunction is present.

As for the couple, the sexual assessment should also be done in the context of the couple's overall relationship (Rosen & Leiblum, 1995). Relationship problems can either contribute to the cause of sexual difficulties or become a barrier to their amelioration. Couples' conflicts regarding parenting differences, money, conflict over sharing household or employment obligations, differences over spending recreational time together, and other mundane matters may lead to chronic anger, resentment, and control struggles, and further erode communications, mutual empathy, and emotional intimacy. Other problems such as chronic jealousy, lack of trust, and resentment due to previous infidelities can become barriers to sexual enjoyment. A detailed functional assessment of the nature of a couple's sexual problems and formal diagnosis is also required.

Masters and Johnson (1970) are credited with emphasizing anxiety reduction and gradually increasing and maintaining sensual and sexual pleasure through their pioneering "sensate focus" technique to address problems of arousal and sexual performance. However, current approaches have become more comprehensive. Despite readily available and well-advertised pharmaceuticals that have been shown to enhance sexual desire and performance, inhibited sexual desire can be a multifaceted problem. Effective intervention is possible and involves a few key methods: (1) the couple is encouraged to avoid blame and see inhibited sexual desire as a shared problem; (2) open communication and revelations about sexual secrets and fantasies are encouraged (e.g., past sexual abuse, fetishes); (3) each partner is coached to help the other develop a new sexual repertoire, with planned opportunities to engage in sexual encounters that combine both romantic and erotic elements (McCarthy, Ginsberg, & Fucito, 2006).

With regard to sexual performance, behavioral treatments have been shown to be effective for premature ejaculation. Practitioners should focus on improved communication (in general and with respect to sexual activity) and help the male partner (in collaboration with his partner) learn to self-regulate the speed and intensity of stimulation to develop better control (Betchen, 2007). Overall, clinical reports and uncontrolled studies (e.g., Sarwer & Durlak, 1997) have shown that a combination of cognitive-behavioral and medical interventions are the most promising strategies for reducing sexual dysfunction and increasing sexual desire and expression between partners (Dziegielewski et al., 1998; LoPiccolo, 1994; Rosen & Leiblum, 1995). These strategies focus on the following:

- Identifying and treating cognitive or interpersonal emotional barriers to intimacy
- Decreasing anxiety that may inhibit sexual arousal
- Gradually increasing sensual interactions through a combination of sexual stimulation aids including practicing sexual fantasy, watching adult videos, using sexual stimulation devices (i.e., sex toys)
- Increasing sensual interaction between the couples leading to mutual masturbation
- Engaging in other highly stimulating noncoital activities (e.g., oral sex, if acceptable to both partners) and ultimately sexual intercourse

Social workers can enhance their work with couples by mastering basic assessment skills regarding sexual problems in the context of their relationship and by incorporating some of these methods into their practice repertoire. Other interventions may require collaboration with specialists (licensed sex therapists) and physicians.

Interventions for Domestic Violence.   Despite years of research and public promotion of "model" programs that treat men who have been referred for perpetrating domestic violence, data have shown only marginal effectiveness overall. It has been argued that these programs lack a coherent theoretical and empirical base, and there is often a lack of a clear contingency management system that integrates treatment providers, the courts, and law enforcement (Day, Chung, O'Leary & Carson, 2009). Such a system may hold promise for reducing domestic battering, but reinforcement for treatment compliance and success as well as swift sanctions against perpetrators when they relapse has to be consistent and predictable in order to be effective.

Years ago, Rubin (1991) and Abel (2000) both noted the lack of evaluation research for interventions with battered women and other victims of domestic violence. Methodological limitations of the research included deficiencies in defining interventions and outcomes, lack of controlled trials, small samples, and little follow-up data. Nevertheless, some writers have made helpful recommendations based on their clinical experience. Jordan and Walker (1994) recommend the following: (1) more thorough individual assessments for abuse history; (2) multiple services, including consultation, education and prevention, crisis care, psychiatric services and inpatient facilities, counseling, and clinical and residential services; (3) support services for victims and close linkage with the police and criminal justice system to ensure compliance with services and reduce relapse in the perpetrators; (4) availability of residential services for victims, such as shelters, foster care as needed, and other transitional living arrangements; (5) endorsement of the assumption that domestic violence is a crime and that safety of the victims is the first priority. In addition to the immediate need to protect women and children from domestic violence, follow-up services are needed to maintain psychosocial improvements over time. Although there is a lack of research in this area, one promising uncontrolled evaluation of an intervention with 28 battered women demonstrated significant improvements in both appraised social support and self-esteem (Tutty, 1996). Given the enormity of the problem, much more research is needed.

The literature comparing conjoint versus separate treatment for domestic violence is also sparse. Brannen and Rubin (1996) found no outcome literature to support the superiority of one modality over another, in general. Although using conjoint interventions for domestic violence is generally discouraged, there is some evidence to suggest that for those couples for whom the violence is less severe (i.e., pushing, slapping, often by both partners), there is no evidence of serious injuries, or of enduring psychopathy on the part of the (usually) male partner, couples therapy may be as effective as individual therapy and does not seem to result in any more risk to the spouse (Stith, Rosen, & McCollum, 2003). In their controlled study comparing two cognitive-behavioral approaches (conjoint group therapy vs. gender-specific group therapy) as part of court-mandated services, Brannen and Rubin (1996) found that both groups made comparable gains, although there may have been some advantage for the conjoint group when the husband had an alcohol problem. For couples with co-occurring IPV and substance abuse, behavioral couples therapy has been shown to be effective in an RCT (N=207) at 12 months (32 sessions) in reducing both violence and substance use when compared to treating the male offender separately in individual behavior therapy (Fals-Stewart & Clinton-Sherrod, 2009). Similar results for BCT have been found with alcoholic female perpetrators of IPV as well (Schumm, O'Farrell, Murphy, & Fals-Stewart, 2009). Overall, a consensus seems to be building that conjoint approaches to mild to moderate domestic violence can be effective when provided in the context of an ongoing community and criminal justice framework whereby court orders and sanctions for poor compliance are used to enhance treatment outcomes and protect the (overwhelmingly) women victims (McCollum & Stith, 2008; Stith & McCollum, 2011).

Integrating Couples Therapy with Interventions for Child Behavior Problems.   Couples' dysfunction and problems in the couples' children often coincide. Although not all children's problems are the result of parental conflict, children's emotional and behavioral difficulties can, in fact, be the direct result of parental conflict or be exacerbated by a conflicted couple. Child and adolescent behavior problems and disorders can also place considerable strain on a couple as both intimate partners and parents. Couples who are having trouble communicating and resolving other problems are also likely to show some signs of difficulty cooperating as parents. Sanders, Markie-Dadds, and Nicholson (1997) point out the lack of controlled studies regarding childhood behavioral outcomes resulting from marital interventions. Nevertheless, some sensible guidelines are in order to address the challenging assessment issues when dealing with a family that is experiencing marital difficulties, parenting problems, and behavioral difficulties in their children.

Although sequencing the intervention is not easy to plan, addressing the conflicts in the couple is essential to help them "work from the same page" as parents. Some of the marital concerns may have to be put temporarily on the back burner. Sometimes getting together "for the sake of the children" can be a positive experience for the couple. Achieving some success in improving communication and problem solving regarding parenting may set the stage for improvements in their partner relationship as well. However, as Sanders et al. (1997) point out, "The key is to demonstrate rather than assume a functional relationship between child and marital problems. This requires close attention to the day-to-day co-variation between marital stress and child problems, as well as parents' own view of the relationship between parenting problems and their marriage" (p. 531). The next few chapters address the emotional and behavioral difficulties of children and adolescents. It is assumed that couple well-being and functioning as intimate partners and as parents (assuming a two-parent household) is a decided advantage, if not a critical one, for effective interventions with their children. As we will see in coming chapters, addressing childhood and adolescent disorders is often accomplished most effectively in a family therapy modality which lends itself to addressing couples problems as well to enhance family functioning as a whole.

TREATMENT PLANNING AND EVALUATION

CASE STUDY: CONNOR AND LUIS

Connor and Luis arrived for their first visit with the social worker, Brad, with telltale signs of a serious problem: Connor was sporting a fat lip, and Luis wore a neck brace, the kind people wear after a car collision. First, they needed to explain: "This type of thing has never happened before. We frightened ourselves because of it. We don't want it to ever happen again." According to Luis, they had been arguing about "Connor's avoiding commitment. It's time we move in together." Luis apparently "got in Connor's face"; Connor went to push him back, blows were exchanged, and Luis hit his target. Connor lost his temper after he saw his own blood on his shirt, got one of his arms around Luis's neck, and threw him over a chair. Sitting in the hospital emergency waiting room gave them time to calm down and talk. They decided to get some help. The social worker agreed that it was a good move for them to seek some help.

Connor, age 36, came from a white, working-class family. He has two younger sisters and two brothers. His father worked a variety of blue-collar jobs, often two at a time, to support the family. His mom worked at home, but as the kids got older, she also supplemented the family income by taking in sewing work from the neighbors or helping out in a local catering service on weekends. Connor and his family all knew he was a little different. When he came home from school crying because other kids called him "faggot" or "homo," his father and brothers would compensate by showing him, he said, "how to fight, to toughen me up." He has never discussed being gay with his family except for coming out to one of his sisters years later when she gently confronted him. His dad dismissed his lack of marrying as his being "just the bachelor type," and his mom is still waiting for him to "meet the right girl." Connor loves both his parents and his family, although it had been difficult socially over the years to deal with their questions about when he was "going to settle down." He never begrudged his family's lack of sensitivity to "gay issues": "I know they love me. That's just the way it is in their social circles." Connor himself still seemed to harbor some shame about being gay.

Luis, age 30, was born in a very poor section of San Juan, Puerto Rico. He was the son of a Puerto Rican father and Mexican mother. They both emigrated to the United States after they married. Luis was 8 years old at the time. He grew up in poverty in a city in the US Northeast and left home at age 16 after being threatened by members of a rival gang. After 2 years of wandering, lying about his age, and working menial jobs, he joined the army, obtained his GED, and served over-

seas in the first Gulf War, during which he was awarded a Purple Heart (the army didn't "ask" and Luis didn't "tell" about his homosexuality). Luis met Connor in a gay bar outside of the town they lived in. They hit it off immediately and have seen each other steadily over the past 2 years. Luis worked his way up to become regional manager of a chain of men's clothing stores. Luis is openly gay, active in gay politics, and since his stint in the army has become much less tolerant of people (like Connor) who are not "in-your-face gay," he says. Luis also reported no notable grievances with his parents; he says he "came out" a long time ago with his mom (whom he e-mails weekly), and has been on a conversational basis with his dad, but has kept his distance from his brothers, who "have major machismo," he says.

MFS Assessment: Defining Problems and Goals

Before the army, he says, "straightened him out," Luis had been a bit more reckless over the years with drug use (injecting) and had been more active sexually, but in recent years he has maintained abstinence from drugs (although he occasionally overindulges in dry martinis). He says he has been faithful to Connor for at least a year. Both partners have had HIV testing within the past year, and both tested negative. Luis reports no specific mental health problems (e.g., depression, anxiety); enjoys his work; and is otherwise on good terms with his coworkers, family, and friends. He reports no specific health problems, although he has unsuccessfully been trying to quit smoking, another bone of contention between him and Connor.

Aside from an early bout with heavy drinking and some depression in his early 20s before he "came out to myself, at least," Connor presented no mental health problems other than his distress over his conflicts with Luis. He always took good care of himself physically and continues in a well-paying career as loan manager at a bank. He expressed the wish that he could be more open with his family about being gay, but he was afraid that it would create distance.

The couple expressed to Brad many positives about their relationship, but they seemed to feel that it was seriously threatened if Connor remained unwilling to publicly acknowledge the relationship. As the issue of commitment and living together continued to come up, the matter of "coming out" became a potentially more explosive catalyst for conflict. Any number of situations triggered this recurring patterning and sequencing of escalating tension and subsequent conflict. For example, Luis was invited to a management dinner at which he was to receive an award for exceeding the company's production targets. He was quite proud of the honor and felt it would provide some stability in his career. Connor was also pleased for him. But when Luis asked him to come to the event, Connor began to make excuses. Given that they both worked in the same community, it became apparent that Connor was concerned about running into people with whom he conducted business. Luis, in detecting this hesitation, became angry; began to object and quarrel vehemently; and provoked Connor, who admitted that he was concerned about being seen with Luis in public. "I also felt shame, guilt and anger at being cornered," he said. After these types of arguments, Connor tended to withdraw from Luis for a few days and would wait for the anger to dissipate—until the next inevitable crisis. Although they had more easily avoided confrontations in the past, when "we gave each other more space," they have become more frequent after the subject of living together had been put on the table. Over the previous 2 months, the couple has had intense arguments at least once per week, with residual anger lasting days at a time. The proportionate increase of angry and hurt feelings had begun to erode an otherwise loving and considerate relationship. The recent physical fight brought matters to a head.

From their respective points of view, Luis saw Connor as not "serious about the relationship," and Connor saw Luis as "wanting too much too soon from me." They both said they loved each other but saw the relationship at a crossroads: either they would find some compromise or the relationship was over. Given the recent fight, they were not strongly optimistic that they could find a resolution. They felt that this difference about "coming out" may have "poisoned the well" and left only angry words and hurtful feelings. Although one of the goals of the intervention was to improve their ability to discuss this explosive issue without hurting each other it was not clear whether the goal was for Connor to become more openly gay.

Selecting and Designing Interventions: Defining Strategies and Objectives

The social worker, Brad, discussed with the couple his thoughts about using an eclectic approach to their dilemma. He briefly described the emotion-focused analysis of EFT and the problem-solving and communications aspects of BCT. The couple agreed that they thought they could benefit from both. Luis preferred the emphasis on understanding feelings, whereas

Connor was a bit more analytical and liked the problem-solving emphasis of BCT. Brad helped Luis express his frustration more calmly and explain to Connor how hurt he felt when Connor wouldn't show his commitment publicly. Conversely, the practitioner helped Connor identify his own fears that were provoked when Luis pressed him too hard to come out and say, "to hell with what everybody else thinks." Connor needed to express to Luis that he felt his career and relationship with his family and other friends were at stake. The practitioner helped them identify and express these feelings but also listen to the other partner without editing or contradicting him. He told them that they did not need to "buy in" to what the other partner was saying but simply accept it at face value though the problem remained unresolved for the time being.

BCT also provided a valuable complement to the initial progress with EFT. First, examining interpersonal misattributions (i.e., cognitive distortions about the other partner's motives or feelings) seemed to help clarify what the emotional conflicts were about. For example, in examining Luis's anger and hurt about Connor's reluctance to join him at his award ceremony, a cognitive analysis of what was "behind the feelings" revealed that Luis also thought Connor may have been seeing someone else. "If I'm at the award ceremony, where is he going to be? Does he have something more important to do or someone he'd rather be with?" Until that point, it had never occurred to Connor that his reluctance to "come out" was being interpreted (e.g., jumping to conclusions, misattributing) as showing a lack of interest or faithfulness to Luis. Conversely, Luis's intense expressions of anger evoked many difficult feelings in Connor, including anger, fear, and shame. When the practitioner examined the cognitions behind the feelings, Connor said it was quite similar to a lifetime of subtle rejection and the difference he had felt from other males (i.e., his dad, brothers, schoolmates). As in the past, these feelings caused him to withdraw and "clam up." Improved communications and improved behavioral exchange may have helped to disconfirm these distorted attributions.

Second, the use of communication skills seemed to complement the goals of EFT, that is, to improve a consistent, honest, and open expression of emotions. Maintaining eye contact, actively listening, not interrupting, and giving accurate feedback appeared to reduce the heat of an emotionally charged argument. Brad's coaching during sessions served as rehearsal for practice at home (e.g., three nights per week after dinner, for no more than 30 minutes and before their favorite television shows).

Third, behavioral exchange activities were used to help them gradually solidify their commitment and express caring to each other as they temporarily accepted that "coming out" might not happen right away. In this way, the decision about if, when, and how to "go public" did not represent the only indicator of their feelings for each other, but rather provided some breathing room as they learned how to discuss it in a more constructive light. They also agreed to a good-faith commitment: Connor agreed to have Luis over for a dinner of his choice once a week, and Luis (at Connor's request) agreed to attend a smoking cessation clinic, because, as Luis put it, "I plan on being with Connor for a while." In addition, on "love days" (i.e., Saturdays), they planned to do something together and agreed not to discuss any timetable for Connor during that time.

As the couple became more comfortable accepting each other's present position for the time being, and as they were able to calmly and (more empathically) discuss each other's thoughts and feelings about their dilemma, it became clear that their desire to commit to one another grew. "If we can work through this, we can probably work through anything," said Connor. "This is the big test," Luis agreed. In a more analytical way, they began to address this challenge as a problem to be solved rather than an unmovable barrier in their relationship. Brad encouraged them to address two questions in the session and during their planned discussions at home: using an accounting metaphor (since they are both in the business world), what were the costs and benefits of Connor's "coming out" versus the costs and benefits of "staying in"? The couple was asked to "submit a report" in 2 weeks' time. As they made improvements in communicating and problem solving, the social worker felt that there was less of a need for weekly visits. Clearly, they needed to work on the problem together. The practitioner provided a list of gay support groups in outlying areas for Connor to consider, since others might be able to provide some advice and support on how to navigate the coming-out process. Connor agreed to consider it.

The couple returned 2 weeks later with a rather thoughtful analysis. Coming out would probably cause Connor some temporary discomfort, but in the long run, there would be more problems if he didn't: "It's like a colleague of mine who goes to AA says: people change when they get 'sick and tired of being sick and tired.' Well, I'm sick and tired of hiding who I am. I don't know when I'm going to do this, or how I'm going to go about it, but I know I'm going to have to deal with it sooner or later. It might as well be sooner. Besides, I'm not the only gay guy working for my bank, and they seem to handle it OK. And when I come out, I want Luis to be there for me when I do."

Selecting Scales and Creating Indexes to Monitor and Evaluate Client Progress

Perhaps, with minor modifications, any of the standardized scales for couples (e.g., MAS, MDS) could have been useful for examining overall relationship satisfaction or couple distress. But given the specific nature of the problem, other individual indexes were included to target problems and monitor

TABLE 11.1   The Client Service Plan

Problems	Goals	Objectives (samples)	Interventions	Assessment and evaluation tools
Intense conflict over one partner's reluctance to live an openly gay life Repeated pattern of explosive arguments about "coming out," subsequent sullen retreats for days at a time	Improve ability to communicate on emotional matters Improve intimacy Reduce anger Work toward couple resolving the problem on their own	Identify core emotional conflicts at the center of the couple's differences Define the couple's repeated interactional cycle Examine cognitive distortions associated with intense feelings related to core conflict Improve communications to enhance emotionally charged discussions (coach in sessions; practice at home three times weekly) Plan and agree to carry out good-faith contract Problem-solving plan: engage in a cost-benefit analysis of coming out and submit a report to social worker	An eclectic combination of EFT (to identify emotionally charged patterns) BCT (with a cognitive component): emphasis on communication skills and problem solving Practitioner provides information on gay support group to get "other points of view on perils of coming out" (i.e., increased social support)	Modify Marital Disaffection Scale (substitute *couple* for *marital*); use monthly as a global measure of couple satisfaction and distress Use two self-anchored indexes (scored 1–10) to measure and track weekly progress: • Comfort in discussing mutual feelings about being more public with the relationship • Commitment They develop a chart to assess the pros and cons of coming out for Connor

progress: a self-anchored scale (1 = no discomfort at all, 10 = extremely uncomfortable) to gauge the level of comfort of each partner in discussing the "coming out" problem and a scale (1 = no commitment at all, and 10 = extremely committed) to assess level of commitment to the relationship.

SUMMARY

Working with couples often reveals a range of both individual and interacting problems including mental health disorders, substance abuse, domestic violence, child abuse and neglect, and the typical problems of partners themselves: distrust, frequent arguments, parenting differences, money problems, conflict over extended families, and sexual problems and dysfunctions, among others. Working with couples is also often the linchpin for working effectively with children and families. There are a number of validated instruments that can aid in the assessment of couples problems, and the body of research on effective couples practice has continued to grow. BCT and EFT provide sound approaches to helping couples enhance intimacy, improve communications, and become more adept at solving problems. Although less is known about how these interventions work, learning about these methods is essential for social workers who work with adults, children, and their families. The next few chapters, which address the problems of children and adolescents, further underscore how essential it is that social workers have a grasp of evidence-based work with couples.

CHAPTER 12

ANXIETY AND DEPRESSION IN CHILDREN AND ADOLESCENTS

Anxiety disorders and depression in children are often referred to as *internalizing disorders*. Although that term is descriptively not quite accurate (some symptoms of depression and anxiety are externalized, that is, observable), in children many of the symptoms of anxiety and depression are covert. Thus, finding out what is troubling children (especially very young children) can be a challenge for social workers. In addition to depression, a child may be experiencing a combination of generalized anxiety, social anxiety disorder, school phobia, obsessive concerns and/or compulsions, and post-traumatic stress symptoms. Variations in the course of both depression and anxiety disorders are common. Several brief, valid, and reliable scales for measuring internalizing disorders are available to enhance multidimensional-functional-systems (MFS) assessment. Given much similarity among the anxiety disorders in symptoms and both assessment and intervention strategies, we address a representative range of anxiety disorders here, including social anxiety disorder, simple phobias, obsessive-compulsive disorder, post-traumatic stress disorder, and separation anxiety disorder.

There are various effective cognitive-behavioral interventions for anxiety disorders and depression in children and adolescents. In addition to the practitioner developing empathic rapport with the child or adolescent, interventions can include self-monitoring (e.g., learning to recognize feelings in context), anxiety management, and other coping skills, and these are often combined with contingency management techniques implemented by parents, teachers, and other significant adults in a child's life. It has become increasingly recognized that implementing these approaches in behavioral family therapy may be ideal for many children with internalizing disorders. Helping children learn to cope better with depression and anxiety is challenging if the adults in children's lives are verbally or physically abusive, neglectful, apathetic, incompetent, or otherwise detrimental to children's coping efforts. Medications appear to have limited benefits for children and adolescents who experience depression and anxiety-related problems, except for those suffering from obsessive-compulsive disorder (OCD). Evidence-based interventions with children suffering from serious levels of anxiety and depression involve a multifaceted strategy of relationship building with the child, the family, school personnel, and other influential persons in a child's life.

ASSESSMENT OF ANXIETY DISORDERS IN CHILDREN AND ADOLESCENTS

Background Data

It is common for children to be afraid or anxious. Fortunately, these episodes usually pass quickly, and most children learn to cope with life's stressors and frightening situations. Fears and anxieties are also linked to development. Fears in early childhood tend to be more discrete (e.g., animals, strangers, a dark basement), whereas fears among older children and adolescents are more likely to manifest in response to social inhibitions, school performance, and health concerns. Fear reactions and anxiety may be linked to a combination of factors, including temperament, past experiences, and social and environmental context. Fears (or the appraisal of fear) may also be linked to culture-bound beliefs and gender roles. Anxiety in children may manifest in extreme behavior such as temper tantrums, clinging, and problems with peers. However, because childhood fears are ubiquitous, they should be considered a disorder only if they cause significant dysfunction in the child or adolescent (American Psychiatric Association, APA, 2013; Fonseca & Perrin, 2001; Last, 1989; Ronan & Deane, 1998). Such disorders include simple phobias, separation anxiety disorder, social anxiety disorder, OCD, post-traumatic stress disorder (PTSD), and generalized anxiety disorder. Childhood anxiety disorders also are a significant risk factor for experiencing mental health problems in adulthood (Ost & Treffers, 2001).

In children and adolescents anxiety disorders are likely to co-occur along with other problems, including depressive disorders. This co-occurrence may be considered a lack of evidence for the discriminative validity of internalizing disorders in children (Schniering, Hudson, & Rapee, 2000; Spence, 1997). From 25% to 50% of depressed youth also manifest an anxiety disorder, and about 10%–15% of youth with anxiety disorders also suffer from a depressive disorder. There are many suggested reasons for this co-occurrence: the two share common genetic risk factors, they are causally related, and/or they have independent but correlated risk factors. Spurious reasons for co-occurrence may include treatment-seeking factors (i.e., people who seek services for mental health problems are more likely to have other problems as well) (Verhulst, 2001).

A thorough review of epidemiological research reveals prevalence rates for all childhood anxiety disorders to be between 1% and 3% (Verhulst, 2001), but estimates of prevalence and incidence (including cross-cultural differences) vary across studies because of methodological differences. Prevalence estimates (Schniering et al., 2000) have been reported for separation anxiety (children, 3.5%–4.1%; adolescents, .6%–2.4%), generalized anxiety (children, 2.9%–4.6%; adolescents, 2.4%–4.2%), social anxiety disorder (children, less than 1%; adolescents, up to 6.3%), simple phobia (children, 2.4%; adolescents, 5.1%), OCD (children, .2%–1.2%; adolescents, 3%), and panic disorder ("rare" in children and young adolescents; older adolescents, .3%). Rates of anxiety disorders for children exposed to severe stressors such as fires or sexual abuse can be considerably higher. Perhaps half of adolescents, especially females, have experienced panic attacks at one time (although few ever meet the criteria for panic disorder), and the attacks appear to be related to life stressors such as family problems or school pressures (Ollendick, Mattis, & King, 1993). In an Australian study of 648 adolescents, female adolescents appeared to have more fears than male adolescents, and younger adolescents reported having more fears than older ones (Ollendick & King, 1994a). Most of the fears concerned physical danger and negative social evaluation.

Social anxiety disorder was not considered a clinically significant problem until the 1990s. Although many young persons are shy, most mature out of serious social inhibitions. More recently, though, social anxiety disorder has come to be seen as potentially debilitating, it can manifest as school phobia, and it may be a precursor for the later development of social inhibitions and related problems. Children who suffer from social anxiety disorder show considerable distress in a range of social situations, and that distress is likely to occur frequently as life demands more social interaction of them. Social anxiety disorder co-occurs with other childhood and adolescent phobias (e.g., avoidant disorder, separation anxiety disorder) and depression (Beidel & Morris, 1995).

Separation anxiety disorder manifests itself as extreme anxiety when a child is separated from his or her primary caretaker, and symptoms include the full range of anxiety symptoms. School refusal appears to be a common manifestation of separation anxiety disorder and may be related to social anxiety disorder. The onset may be sudden or gradual, and separation anxiety disorder appears to be linked to the onset of agoraphobia and panic attacks in adults (Black, 1995). In separation anxiety disorder, the child's behavior is marked by verbal and behavioral expressions of anxiety and fear (e.g., crying, clinging, screaming, tantrums, phobic reactions to specific situations), and problems are often accompanied by somatic complaints (e.g., stomachaches).

In children and adolescents OCD is similar to the diagnostic description of OCD for adults: unwanted obsessions, intrusive images, thoughts, impulses that cause distress, and compulsions (e.g., repetitive thoughts or behaviors) performed repeatedly or ritualistically in an effort to reduce distress caused by the obsessions. Children, however, may not recognize the obsessive thoughts as irrational, excessive, or unreasonable. The preoccupation with ritualizing in a fruitless attempt to escape the anxiety associated with obsessions can be incapacitating for children. Depression and social anxiety disorder often accompany childhood OCD. Children with OCD are likely to be anxious about germs and contamination, fear that harm might come to themselves or others, and display excessive religiosity and guilt. The most common compulsions (in descending order) include washing and cleaning, counting, repeating words or actions, touching, and ordering and/or straightening up. These symptoms can be very disruptive and interfere with functioning at home, in school, and with friends. Mean age of onset for OCD is 10, more boys than girls manifest OCD symptoms, and the parents of a child with OCD are more likely to have OCD than are other adults in the general population. There is considerable co-occurrence of OCD with other childhood disorders, including other anxiety disorders, depression, and specific developmental disorders. Many children with OCD also suffer from Tourette's syndrome and other tic-related disorders. Childhood OCD has a poor prognosis if left untreated, and at least half of children with OCD will continue to struggle with it into adolescence and adulthood. Before the introduction of the antidepressant selective serotonin reuptake inhibitors (SSRIs), the long-term outlook for children with OCD was quite negative (March, Leonard, & Swedo, 1995; Piacentini & Bergman, 2000; Shafran, 1998).

Children may also experience as an anxiety disorder the full range of symptoms associated with post-traumatic stress disorder (PTSD) (Amaya-Jackson & March, 1995; Yule, Perrin, & Smith, 2001). Children's symptoms are similar to those experienced by adults (i.e., reexperiencing, avoidance, arousal), but they manifest somewhat differently. Children may reexperience the trauma through repetitive acting out, ritualistic play, or nightmares. Avoidance and numbing may manifest as regressive behaviors such as thumb sucking, detaching, and shutting down feelings and expressiveness. Arousal is likely to be observed as nightmares, sleep problems, irritability, angry outbursts, depression, and poor concentration. Children suffering from PTSD are also likely to experience other anxiety disorders, depression, disordered behaviors including sexual and aggressive play, interpersonal difficulties, and conduct disorders. In children PTSD can be precipitated by a wide range of events, including kidnapping and assault, physical and sexual abuse, natural disasters, life-threatening illness, and medical procedures (e.g., bone-marrow transplants). There appears to be a proportional relationship between the severity of the traumatic event and its effect on the child: the more severe the trauma, the more severe the effects. Life-threatening events appear to be the most traumatic. However, as with adults, there is considerable variability in how children respond to traumatic events. These mediating factors include differences in temperament, appraisal of the threat, and attribution of blame. Although there is little reliable data from large epidemiological studies on the prevalence and incidence of PTSD in children, Yule et al. (2001) have estimated that about 33% of children who experience life-threatening accidents and more severe forms of trauma are likely to develop PTSD. However, not all children who are exposed to a traumatic event develop PTSD symptoms, so clinicians should avoid overdiagnosing the problem by attributing all of a child's anxieties and related symptoms to trauma (Amaya-Jackson & March, 1995; Yule et al., 2001). Although diagnosing children with PTSD remains controversial, it has come to be considered useful for theory development, assessment, and intervention planning (Smith, Perrin, & Yule, 1998).

Symptoms of anxiety and depression also vary by environmental stressors, including poverty and community violence. For example, given the disproportionate socioeconomic stressors and discrimination experienced by many racial minority youth, it is reasonable to investigate whether children of color experience more severe and qualitatively different types of anxiety and related symptoms. In a thoughtful review of the literature, Safren et al. (2000) found mixed results but emphasized the need for more racially, ethnically, and culturally informed research. Treadwell, Flannery-Schroeder, and Kendall (1995), however, showed that black and white youth shared very similar fears (e.g., death or dead people, getting lost, getting poor grades, getting burned in a fire, failing a test, being hit by a car, falling from high places, not being able to breathe). Research on racial and cultural differences in depression and anxiety in youth is likely to reveal considerable overlap as well as differences.

Theories on the Causes of Anxiety Disorders in Children and Adolescents

Anxiety has been defined as a broad collection of distressing cognitive, behavioral, and physiological responses, and fear refers to a situation-specific event. However, research suggests that there is little theoretical or practical value in distinguishing the terms *fear* and *anxiety* (Barrios & Hartmann, 1997). Thus, they are generally used interchangeably in the literature.

Psychoanalytic theorists have noted that anxiety disorders often emerge during childhood and adolescence, emphasizing inadequate nurturance in childhood as the primary cause (e.g., Erikson, 1950; Loevinger, 1976). Last (1989) suggested that the etiology of childhood separation anxiety, for example, is related to an overdependent relationship with the child's mother, although the theoretical mechanisms for this overdependency are open to explanation (e.g., common temperament, learning experiences, hostile-dependent relationship). Other theorists have contended that anxiety disorders in children are symbolic expressions of early fears, but they offer little evidence to explain how anxiety disorders develop over time.

Attachment theorists have argued that the roots of future anxiety disorders are related to anxious attachment style in early childhood (Ainsworth, Blehar, Waters, & Wall, 1978; Bowlby, 1980), an extension of earlier psychoanalytic theories. Cognitive maps of interpersonal relations between infants and their mothers (i.e., internal working models) are presumed to manifest in different attachment styles (e.g., secure vs. avoidant, ambivalent, disorganized). Proponents of attachment theory assert that anxiety originates in an infant's uncertainty about a caregiver's availability, and varied responses to that uncertainty account for different types of childhood anxieties. The early task of children is to gradually develop self-regulatory cognitive, behavioral, and physiological processes to cope with anxiety and stressful stimuli: "it is clear that caregiver-child social interactions are pivotal events that both exacerbate underlying constitutional problems and also function independently to produce difficulties in self-regulation" (Costanzo, Miller-Johnson, & Wencel, 1995, p. 87). However, although childhood anxiety problems often continue into adulthood, the causal mechanism for this link between early caregiving and adult anxiety problems is not well understood (Westenberg, Siebelink, & Treffers, 2001). Although attachment style can be considered one risk factor (Manassis, 2001), longitudinal data have never clearly demonstrated a substantive causal link between early childhood attachment and adult anxiety disorders. To establish such a link, one would have to account for a range of other independent and mediating factors (Costanzo et al., 1995). In general, developmental research reveals a decrease in the influences of childhood factors as children grow older and as other factors begin to affect their development. Attachment "styles" in adulthood could be better understood as behaviors that correlate with other factors and are not inferred to be the consequence of parenting experiences during childhood. A meta-analysis of 46 studies covering 25 years of research (Colonnesi et al., 2011) showed a moderate association overall between attachment styles and childhood anxiety, with ambivalent attachment mostly correlated with childhood anxiety. They also found little relationship between attachment style and specific type of anxiety disorder. Given the lack of longitudinal studies, such associations actually tell us little about any causal links between parenting and children's later anxiety problems, as both might be explained largely by genetic factors such as anxiety sensitivity.

Biological temperament (e.g., proneness to anxiety, arousal) appears to significantly contribute to the development of anxiety disorders (Kagan, 1989; Oosterlaan, 2001). Anxious temperament (e.g., shyness, social inhibition) appears to be largely inherited, and inhibition appears to be stable over time and across situations. Children at higher risk of developing anxiety disorders show greater temperament-related inhibition than children at less risk for anxiety disorders. In addition, it appears that parents of anxious children are also more likely to have anxiety disorders themselves. The longer children remain temperamentally inhibited, the more likely they are to develop anxiety disorders in later childhood. However, not all anxious children develop anxiety disorders as they age. Temperament is mediated by several psychosocial influences that can exacerbate or diminish a predisposition to anxiety. Although there is now a general assumption regarding the neurobiological links in anxiety between childhood and adulthood, much less is known about the specific pathways of the development of individual anxiety disorders (Biederman, Rosenbaum, Chaloff, & Kagan, 1995). In addition to psychosocial influences, these physiological processes apparently involve the neurotransmitter systems and the hypothalamic-pituitary-adrenal system (Sallee & Greenawald, 1995). Research on the links between neuropsychological patterns in children and adolescents and specific anxiety disorders is in its early stages (Caouette & Guyer, 2014; Hooper & March, 1995).

As discussed in chapter 8, a multivariate model of anxiety disorders is slowly emerging (Craske, 1997; Craske & Barlow, 2008; Rapoport, Swedo, & Leonard, 1992). Clearly, a combination of interacting genetic, temperament, parental and/or familial, psychological, and situational factors contribute to the development and maintenance of anxiety disorders in children. Behavioral inhibition appears to be a product of temperament and is characterized by "withdrawal, seeking comfort from a familiar person, and suppression of ongoing behavior, when confronted with unfamiliar people or novelty, as opposed to vocalizing, smiling, and interacting with the unfamiliar object or setting" (Craske, 1997, p. 14). Children with anxious temperaments are more likely to develop one or more anxiety disorders. Inhibited children also appear to be more prone to have fears related to social situations and social evaluation, and these children's parents are more likely to have anxiety disorders as well. Nevertheless, the emergence of an anxiety disorder appears to depend on environmental factors, including childhood stressors and parental reinforcement of fears. A mother's ability to promote healthy attachment with her children is directly affected by her level of social supports (including a helpful partner) and other social and environmental stressors (Manassis, 2001). Extreme environmental stressors related to poverty, poor access to health care, fear of crime, and domestic and community violence are likely to have a significant impact on parents' ability to nurture children in a constant and secure environment. Extreme stressors (e.g., early separation anxiety, trauma) can cause changes in neurological circuitry that may predispose a child to the development of a specific anxiety disorder. Whether physiological or environmental factors predominate may determine the type of anxiety disorder that develops (e.g., separation anxiety disorder vs. posttraumatic stress) (Sallee & March, 2001). More research is needed on the impact of social and environmental stressors on the development of specific anxiety disorders.

In the context of this biopsychosocial framework, there is a good deal of theoretical work on cognitive processes and anxiety disorders. Current theoretical formulations are the same as those for adults (see chapters 6, 8, and 9), and these theories tend to favor social-cognitive and information-processing models. The development of anxiety disorders in children seems to result from the interaction of cognitive, physiological, and behavioral components that reciprocally interact with stressful stimuli in the social environment (Craske & Barlow, 2008; Ronan & Deane, 1998). Cognitive models focus on both negative schema and maladaptive (dysfunctional) thinking, and information-processing models focus on how affective information is cognitively processed (Prins, 2001). In this perspective, the original traumatic event (e.g., as in the case of PTSD) is considered a conditioned stimulus, which sets a process in motion whereby cognitive, physiological, and behavioral components of the response to the traumatic event become somewhat repetitive and reinforcing. The child seems incapable of resolving the meaning of the event as a result of continued avoidance, emotional numbing, repetitive play, and other manifestations of the disorder. Cognitive, affective, physiological, and environmental cues accompanying the traumatic event then become conditioned stimuli, often called *traumatic reminders.* Through stimulus generalization, these reminders, in turn, become capable of eliciting a conditioned response in the form of PTSD symptoms. By trial and error, children attempt to reduce PTSD symptoms through avoidance and other anxiety-dampening rituals (Amaya-Jackson & March, 1995). Rather than extinguishing the anxiety, though, these behaviors tend to reinforce and sustain it. In general, anxious children tend to judge threats as more serious, underestimate their own coping abilities, report more catastrophizing thoughts than children without anxiety, and have more negative cognitions than nonanxious children (Prins, 2001). How these factors interact over time varies among children according to their strengths and vulnerabilities.

The theoretical explanations for cognitive processes associated with OCD (discussed at more length in chapter 8) are also similar in adults and children, and they are closely tied to the rationale for effective therapy: graded exposure with response prevention until the obsessions and compulsions associated with anxiety are extinguished (Shafran, 1998). The behavioral model emphasizes anxiety reduction by the process of habituation, that is, exposing the child or adolescent to the feared situation and preventing the compulsive response (i.e., exposure with response prevention, or EXRP). With repeated administration, individuals' fear that the anxiety will overwhelm them decreases along with the compulsive behavior. The core obsession appears to be related to children's exaggerated belief that they may be responsible for harm befalling someone and that engaging in certain repeated rituals will reduce the likelihood of harm (Barrett, Farrell, Pina, Peris, & Piacenti, 2008; Salkovskis, 1985). Although their obsessive concerns may be broader than just harm occurring to others, the emphasis on cognitive constructions in OCD focuses on the exaggerated and distorted belief in the oversignificance of one's thoughts, that is, the belief that the thoughts have some influence on external outcomes. Such preoccupations cause considerable psychological distress in young persons with OCD. Effective treatment, however, tends to focus on the behavioral components (e.g., EXRP), although some literature addresses the use of overt cognitive challenges to the intrusive and irrational thoughts as well.

Ollendick and Hirshfeld-Becker (2002) reviewed the theoretical literature on social anxiety disorder within the framework of developmental psychopathology. Noting that all children do not "grow out of" early social inhibitions, children and adolescents who suffer from social anxiety disorder show unreasonable responses to a number of often-unavoidable social situations in which they feel they will be harshly evaluated. These sometimes-incapacitating reactions include wariness, crying, and panic attacks. The average age of onset appears to be during mid-adolescence. As with other disorders, developmental pathways can be diverse, but they appear to involve an interacting combination of temperament, parental and peer influences, and other social learning experiences.

Regarding anxiety disorders in general, Kendall (1993) distinguishes cognitive deficits (i.e., lack of cognitive skill) and cognitive distortions (i.e., maladaptive cognitive processes and thought content). Maladaptive cognitive processes and content are presumed to begin developing in childhood. Although innate temperament also plays a role, distorted cognition can develop as a result of adults communicating exaggerated threats of perceived danger to a child. Overcontrol (or overprotection) may also influence children to believe that they are not capable of coping with perceived dangers, which thus leads to deficits in self-confidence and/or self-efficacy. Anxious cognitions and negative affect appear to be common among children who experience anxiety or depression, and it is believed that anxiety and depression in children are closely related psychological processes.

MFS Assessment of Childhood Anxiety Disorders

Assessment of anxiety disorders must go well beyond DSM-5 criteria, given the considerable overlap in symptoms, high comorbidity among anxiety disorders (and depression), and the various manifestations of anxiety disorders in children and adolescents. The qualitative aspects of conducting an MFS assessment with children experiencing anxiety disorders and depression are quite similar. Thus, much of what is discussed here with respect to the assessment of anxiety disorders also applies to the assessment of depression. More specific considerations for the assessment of depression are addressed in the second part of this chapter.

Assessment with children requires a basic developmental knowledge of children's cognitive and emotion-processing capacities. Assessment of childhood internalizing disorders must take into account the child's "acquisition of specific cognitive and social cognitive skills . . . language skills, understanding of emotions, concept of self and self-awareness, and perception of others" (Schniering et al., 2000, p. 470). To the greatest extent possible, the assessment of a child should use multiple informants: parents, family, the school, and other significant persons in the child's life. In addition, it should be understood that not all symptoms of anxiety or depression (which are common in children) need to be resolved. A key benchmark should include some determination that depression or anxiety is having a significant impact on the child's psychological and social well-being (Barrios & Hartmann, 1997).

Diagnostic criteria for anxiety and depressive disorders in children are similar to criteria for adults, as reviewed in previous chapters (APA, 2013). However, there may be some differences in symptom presentation. Generalized anxiety disorder shows symptoms similar to those in adults, including restlessness, trouble falling asleep, and chronic worrying, but it may also include fears about unlikely or unrealistic occurrences. Although panic disorder with agoraphobia is not typically diagnosed in children, similar symptoms may express themselves as separation anxiety disorder and/or school phobia. Symptoms of OCD in children mirror those in adults, but children may be less likely to consider their own behavior to be strange, whereas adults may know "rationally" that a behavior makes no sense. In a similar manner, a child with a simple (specific) phobia may not find the fear of a monster hiding in the closet to be an unreasonable one. Children also experience many of the same symptoms as adults when suffering from PTSD or acute stress responses (e.g., hypervigilance, dissociation, fear, avoidance, numbing), but they manifest others differently (e.g., repetition of the experience through play). As with adults, differential diagnosis among depression and specific anxiety disorders can be difficult, yet fine-grained distinctions in diagnostic categories probably serve little heuristic purpose given often-heterogeneous symptom profiles and the fact that effective intervention methods for these disorders use similar methods.

Given the high co-occurrence rates of anxiety and depression, children and adolescents suffering from symptoms of either problem should receive a thorough MFS assessment. In addition to a detailed and thorough history (i.e., trauma, recent stresses, abuse and neglect, family history of depression or other mental illnesses), children's distress should be examined across all areas of functioning, including mental status (e.g., specific fears, cognitive distortions, mood disturbances, somatic complaints), family and social functioning (e.g., parental nurturance and discipline, abuse or neglect, relations with peers, school performance), health, and general environmental stressors (e.g., poverty; violence; adequacy of food, clothing, and shelter). An MFS assessment results in a unique portrait of each child's distress. For example, shy children suffering from depression and obsessive worries may not outwardly manifest or verbalize serious concerns; they may be more severely isolated from their peers and be suffering in quiet distress. Younger children experiencing separation anxiety are likely to show those symptoms only in circumstances when they confront the threat of being "left alone" or "taken" from a parent (e.g., first day of kindergarten). A child who has been sexually abused may manifest any number of PTSD symptoms, such as numbing or dissociation, but may not meet all PTSD criteria. An older child or young adolescent who has suffered similar abuse may be more outwardly aggressive toward peers. Children suffering from internalizing disorders are likely to manifest complex and heterogeneous combinations of cognitive, physiological, and behavioral signs and symptoms that do not fit neatly into diagnostic categories, and assessment should consider all potential symptoms of internalizing disorders as they manifest across different social contexts.

A detailed functional analysis is essential for carefully mapping out how a child's anxiety and depression interact with everyday events in the systemic context of family functioning, school, community, and social activities

(Fonseca & Perrin, 2001; McGlynn & Rose, 1998). Multiple sources of information based on observation are essential because of many children's limitations regarding self-report, and attempts should be made to reconcile inconsistencies in collateral reports. Assessment of a child should increasingly focus on the cause-effect details that appear to determine the child's daily distress across three key response modes: cognitions (e.g., thoughts of death, fear of contamination by germs, fear of going to school), physiological responses (e.g., panicky feelings, general nervousness, somatic complaints, interrupted sleep), and behavior (e.g., withdrawal from others, avoidance of other children in play groups, fear of leaving home). For a child suffering from an anxiety disorder, for example, these three response modes are likely to emphasize fear-related cognitive appraisal of events, physiological arousal indicated by overt signs of fear, and behavioral avoidance of persons or situations that elicit the fear response (Ronan & Deane, 1998). This analysis should include a detailed cause-effect mapping of the relationship among antecedent events that the child appraises as frightening, physiological symptoms of anxiety, the resulting behaviors, and the ensuing social consequences that either mitigate or exacerbate the anxiety (e.g., parents may reinforce the avoidance and worsen the anxiety over time). For example, socially phobic children may dread going to a birthday party where they expect that nobody will like them. At the first sign of disinterest on the part of a fellow partygoer (antecedent), a child may become anxious, flushed, and panicked, and then run into a bedroom to hide (behavior), a response that temporarily reduces some anxiety but reinforces avoidance behavior. Either an attending adult can try to coax the child gradually back to the group (e.g., have the child sit and fold party napkins with another child at a distance from the group), or the child can be sent home with a parent, a move that would reinforce the child's expectations that "parties are not fun" and thus should be avoided. Sequential linking of cause and effect must be tied to specific events that have high salience for the child. In addition, the specifics must also be examined within and across a variety of different contexts: home, school, the playground, after-school activities, other relevant circumstances. As noted earlier, multiple sources of data from many points of view will help provide a comprehensive picture of the severity and contextual specificity of a child's distress.

Additional assessment tools and procedures can enhance the MFS assessment. Silverman and Serafini (1998) recommend the inclusion of problem behavior checklists (e.g., Child Behavior Check-List, depression and anxiety scales; Achenbach, 1991), observation in the natural environment, or analogue assessment (e.g., have child role-play a problem on the school playground or at home with parents). Self-monitoring techniques may also be illuminating and could be a constructive way to engage parents and/or the child in treatment. Depending on the child's age, he or she may be willing and able to keep a diary, complete a chart, use self-anchored mood-rating scales, or engage in other self-monitoring activities developed collaboratively with the practitioner. Another useful approach to the functional assessment of anxiety disorders is the use of the Behavioral Avoidance Test, by which specific anxiety problems can be observed in vivo as they unfold (Fonseca & Perrin, 2001). The child who may be fearful of going outside (agoraphobia), of approaching others in a social situation (socially phobic), or of touching a "dirty" doorknob (obsessive-compulsive) can be placed in these situations and encouraged to go as far as he or she can before the anxiety becomes too uncomfortable. This test can be performed across different situations to determine whether the fear is contextually specific or more generalized. Close attention must be paid to the antecedent events that appear to provoke the fearful or avoidant behavior and the ensuing consequences in specific circumstances.

MFS assessment is incomplete without conducting a thorough behavioral family systems assessment, either at home or in the consulting office. For children suffering from serious depression and anxiety disorders, a behavioral family systems assessment should include at a minimum the following considerations: quality of parental nurturance, disciplining and communication patterns and style with children, parental cooperation with each other regarding parenting matters, the quality of the marital (couple) relationship, ongoing problems between parents and children or between siblings, other co-occurring difficulties experienced by parents (e.g., mental illness, substance abuse, criminality), relations between the family and the immediate community (i.e., neighbors, school), and general health of family members. The key assessment hypothesis regarding the identified child's well-being is straightforward: how do parental and family behaviors affect the day-to-day psychosocial functioning of the child, and conversely, how does the child's behavior affect other family members? Which factors in this family system, the school, and community directly and negatively affect the child, and which specific psychological and social supports are available to the child? A detailed functional assessment of the influences on the child often readily reveals those factors that have the greatest impact on the child's mood and behavior. Some of those problems may be readily amenable to change; others may be more challenging. However, even if factors in the family and immediate social environment appear to cause or exacerbate a child's difficulties, it should not be assumed that those factors are the only causes. Temperamental influences and stressors external to the family should also be considered.

Instruments for Assessing Anxiety Disorders in Children and Adolescents

Broad scales such as the CBCL (Achenbach, 1991) and the Shortform Assessment for Children (SAC) (Glisson, Hemmelgarn, & Post, 2002) (both noted in chapter 2) measure both internalizing and externalizing disorders. There are also several well-established narrow scales for measuring anxiety disorders and depression (Costello & Angold, 1988; Greenhill, Pine, March, Birmaher, & Riddle, 1998; Myers & Winters, 2002; Reynolds, 1994; Smith et

al., 1998). Scales for measuring anxiety in children and adolescents are discussed in this section, but scales for measuring trauma and PTSD (Sauter &
Franklin, 1998) are examined in chapter 14 in the context of child abuse.

One of the most widely used scales for measuring anxiety in children is
the Fear Survey Schedule for Children (FSSC) (Scherer & Nakamura, 1968).
The FSSC was originally developed for children aged 9–12, but it was later
revised by Ollendick (1983) to make it more applicable to a wider age range
(aged 7–18). The current version uses a three-point scale ("none," "some,"
"much") and has been shown to have good internal consistency, good test-
retest reliability, and adequate convergent and discriminant validity. Some
studies have showed good cross-cultural validity for the FSSC. The Spence
Anxiety Scale for Children (SCAS) (Spence, 1997) has 45 items and is scored
from "never" to "always" on a four-point (0–3) scale. Five subscales derived
from factor analysis with a large community sample measure panic, agoraphobia, social anxiety, separation anxiety, obsessive-compulsive problems, generalized anxiety, and physical fears. The SCAS has good internal consistency and
test-retest reliability, as well as solid evidence for construct validity. The Children's Yale-Brown Obsessive-Compulsive Scale (CYBOCS) (Goodman, et al.,
1989) is the children's version of the YBOCS described in chapter 8 and is
scored in a similar manner to the YBOCS.

One scale that combines both good psychometric characteristics and
practicality for use in clinic settings is the Screen for Child Anxiety-Related
Emotional Disorders (SCARED), developed by Birmaher et al. (1997). The
initial scale was developed with an item pool of 85 randomly ordered questions representing the different types of anxiety disorders in the DSM-IV.
Three-hundred forty-one children (aged 9–18, 59% female, 82% white, 18%
African American) and 300 parents completed the initial questionnaire. Factor analysis was employed to identify the major factors. This process resulted
in almost-identical five-factor solutions for the children's sample and the parent's sample: somatic and/or panic, generalized anxiety, separation anxiety,
social anxiety disorder, and school phobia. The five subscales were formed
out of 38 remaining items, scored 0 ("not true or hardly ever true"), 1
("sometimes true"), and 2 ("true or often true"). Internal consistency for the
final 38-item scale was .93, and subscale alphas ranged from .74 to .89. Test-
retest reliability was .86 for the total scale, and subscale interrater reliabilities
ranged from .70 to .90. The SCARED showed good discriminant validity
among different anxiety disorders (using structured interview DSM criteria
scales) and other diagnoses (e.g., depression). Very few differences were
found in psychometric characteristics among gender, age, and race. In a replication study (Birmaher et al., 1999) with 190 outpatient children and adolescents and 166 parents (evenly split between boys and girls aged 9–18, with
25% of the sample African American and 25% Hispanic), a 41-item version of
the SCARED demonstrated the same factor structure as the original with comparable evidence for reliability and validity. A brief (five-item) version of the
scale was also developed by selecting the items that best predicted each

respective anxiety disorder. The brief scale demonstrated psychometric characteristics comparable to the original scale and performed well as a screening device. A score of 3 or more on the five-item scale indicates a serious problem with anxiety. The SCARED also showed good convergent and divergent validity with a sample of 295 children and adolescents in a mood disorders clinic when correlated with the CBCL and the State-Trait Anxiety Inventory for Children (STAIC) (Monga et al., 2000). Last, in a rigorous test using confirmatory factor analysis with 881 seventh graders, the SCARED was shown to work comparably well (i.e., be factor invariant) with African American, white, Hispanic, and Asian American youth (Skriner & Chu, 2014).

The 41-item SCARED appears here (instrument 12.1) as an exemplar instrument given its brevity, sound psychometric characteristics, and potential utility as a scale to monitor treatment outcomes (Birmaher et al., 1997; Birmaher et al., 1999). The five-item child-report version is highlighted in bold type in instrument 12.1. (The parent version is identical, but each item is prefaced with "My child . . .".). Practitioners can use the scale face-to-face, with the child reading along if necessary.

INSTRUMENT 12.1   Screen for Child Anxiety-Related Emotional Disorders
(SCARED)

Directions: Below is a list of sentences that describe how people feel. Read each phrase and decide if it is "Not true or hardly ever true," or "Somewhat true or sometimes true," or "very true or often true" for you. Then for each sentence, fill in one circle that corresponds to the response that seems to describe you for the *last 3 months*.

Client/parent scores the following items according to this scale:

   0 = not true or hardly ever true
   1 = somewhat true or sometimes true
   2 = very true or often true.

 1. When I feel frightened, it is hard to breathe
 2. I get headaches when I am at school
 3. I don't like to be with people I don't know well
 4. I get scared if I sleep away from home
 5. **I worry about other people liking me**
 6. When I get frightened, I feel like passing out
 7. I am nervous
 8. I follow my mother or father wherever they go
 9. People tell me I look nervous
10. I feel nervous with people I don't know well
11. I get stomachaches at school
12. When I get frightened, I feel like I am going crazy
13. I worry about sleeping alone
14. I worry about being as good as other kids
15. When I get frightened, I feel like things are not real
16. I have nightmares about something bad happening to my parents

17. I worry about going to school
18. When I get frightened, my heart beats fast
19. I get shaky
20. I have nightmares about something bad happening to me
21. I worry about things working out for me
22. When I get frightened, I sweat a lot
23. I am a worrier
24. **I get really frightened for no reason at all**
25. **I am afraid to be alone in the house**
26. It is hard for me to talk with people I don't know well
27. When I get frightened, I feel like I am choking
28. **People tell me I worry too much**
29. I don't like to be away from my family
30. I am afraid of having anxiety (or panic) attacks
31. I worry that something bad might happen to my parents
32. I feel shy with people I don't know well
33. I worry about what is going to happen in the future
34. When I get frightened, I feel like throwing up
35. I worry about how well I do things
36. **I am scared to go to school**
37. I worry about things that have already happened
38. When I get frightened, I feel dizzy
39. I feel nervous when I am with other children or adults and I have to do something while they watch me (for example: read aloud, speak, play a game, play a sport)
40. I feel nervous about going to parties, dances, or any place where there will be people that I don't know well
41. **I am shy**

Scoring guidelines: a score of ≥ 25 may indicate the presence of an anxiety disorder. Scores higher than 30 are more specific. A score of 7 for items 1, 6, 9, 12, 15, 18, 19, 22, 24, 27, 30, 34, 38 may indicate panic disorder or significant somatic symptoms. A score of 9 for items 5, 7, 14, 21, 23, 28, 33, 35, 37 may indicate generalized anxiety disorder. A score of 5 for items 4, 8, 13, 16, 20, 25, 29, 31 may indicate separation anxiety disorder. A score of 8 for items 3, 10, 26, 32, 39, 40, 41 may indicate social anxiety disorder. A score of 3 for items 2, 11, 17, 36 may indicate significant school avoidance. A score of 3 or more on the five-item scale (in bold print) indicates a serious problem with anxiety.

SELECTING EFFECTIVE INTERVENTIONS

The following review summarizes the outcome research on anxiety disorders in children and adolescents. It is understood that practitioners who intend to learn and apply evidence-based approaches for internalizing disorders in general will consult specific authoritative sources (e.g., treatment manuals, practice texts) and adapt methods as the client's individual assessment profile, developmental stage, and circumstances necessitate. This section does not address every anxiety disorder, because of the amount of symptom overlap and co-occurrence among them (e.g., separation anxiety disorder, social anxiety disorder). Some distinctions among the disorders and related problems have more to do with context rather than substantial differences in symptom profile (e.g., bug phobias vs. school refusal), and key intervention approaches are often quite similar but require individual tailoring to a child and family as needed. In addition, treatment outcomes for other anxiety disorders, including agoraphobia, panic disorder, OCD, and PTSD, are covered briefly here, because those approaches have been described more thoroughly in previous chapters for adults and can be readily adapted to work with children and adolescents.

Major reviews of the literature overwhelmingly support cognitive-behavioral therapy (CBT) interventions as the most effective methods for ameliorating anxiety disorders in children and adolescents. CBT for children addresses problems related to anxiety through some combination of cognitive restructuring (i.e., reexamining and challenging anxiety-related thoughts realistically), relaxation and other coping methods, problem-solving strategies, guided exposure (imaginal or in vivo), and contingency management (e.g., collaborating with the family to use positive reinforcement) (Brown et al., 2008; Compton, Burns, Egger, & Robertson, 2002; Kazdin, 1994b; Kendall, 1993; King, Hamilton, & Ollendick, 1988; Ollendick & King, 1994b, 1998; Reynolds, 1992). Shaping children's behavior directly by guiding them into the anxiety-provoking situation until the fear extinguishes, and reinforcing those efforts, appears to be a well-established approach to achieve anxiety reduction, even without the use of preliminary anxiety-reduction techniques (e.g., relaxation training) (Ollendick & King, 1998). Nevertheless, in actual practice, covert (imaginal) and direct methods are likely to be combined. It has also become increasingly evident that incorporating psycho-education and cognitive-behavioral methods into a family therapy format may be preferred in some circumstances, although more research in this direction is needed (Northey, Wells, Silverman, & Bailey, 2003). Studies on the efficacy of treatment for childhood PTSD continue to increase (Compton et al., 2002; Dowd & McGuire, 2011).

More recent data continue to provide strong support for CBT with children and adolescents. Results of CBT for anxiety disorders in children and adolescents are quite strong and enduring; the results last, and gains are maintained (Brown et al., 2008). Ten-year follow-ups of adolescents into young adulthood (more than one-third minorities, including Hispanic Americans and African Americans) treated originally for phobias and other anxiety disorders (see Silverman, Kurtines, Ginsburg, Weems, Rabian et al., 1999) found that reductions in anxiety disorders maintained, and other co-occurring problems benefited as well (e.g., depression, substance abuse). These results were comparable to other longitudinal findings, and improvements were greater than those associated with prospective studies of adolescents (Saavedra, Silverman, Morgan-Lopez, & Kurtines, 2010).

Separation Anxiety, Social Anxiety, Generalized Anxiety, School Refusal, and Other Phobias

Last, Hansen, and Franco (1998) randomly assigned 56 children with school phobia to 12 weeks (1-hour session each) of either cognitive-behavioral intervention (i.e., combined graduated exposure and coping skills exercises, including self-talk carried out by parent and child) or an educational support group that combined information about school refusal, self-monitoring with diaries, and supportive listening. Unlike the CBT condition, no specific directives were provided regarding how to confront fear in the educational support group. Outcome measures included attendance records and standardized scales for measuring fear and depression, among other outcomes. There were no differences between the two groups in demographics or dropout rates. At post-treatment and follow-up, there were no significant differences in attendance or severity of symptoms between the two groups. However, the small sample size may have masked substantive clinical differences: post-treatment attendance was higher for the CBT group (65% vs. 48%), more students in the CBT group maintained improvement from pre-treatment to follow-up (65% vs. 40%), and fewer students in the CBT group showed no improvement (14% vs. 40%). Although the findings are suggestive, further controlled trials for school-refusal treatments are needed.

Barrett, Dadds, and Rapee (1996) conducted a similar test of CBT for children with a range of anxiety disorders (i.e., overanxious, separation and social anxiety disorder). The 79 children ranged from age 7 to age 14 and were recruited from community centers, schools, and medical and mental health practitioners, or referred from parents in response to advertisements. The children were randomly assigned to three groups: individual CBT, CBT plus family involvement (in which each of 12 sessions of 70 minutes were split between CBT and family sessions), and a wait-list control group (provided with the intervention after the waiting period). CBT was based on Kendall's (1994) work (described in detail later here), which combines a number of cognitive and behavioral coping-skills techniques. The CBT and family intervention included the same CBT method, and parents were taught to actively reinforce "courageous" behaviors and extinguish (i.e., ignore) excessive complaining or anxious behaviors in their children. Parents were also taught how to deal with upset, to gain awareness of their own anxiety-coping abilities, and to model better coping responses for their children through improved problem solving and communications. A battery of well-validated standardized measures was used, several of them identical to those employed in Kendall (1994). Results clearly demonstrated successful outcomes for both active treatment conditions, and results were maintained at 6 and 12 months. Of those who received CBT (with and without family involvement), 69.8% no longer met the diagnostic criteria for the disorders, and only 26% of wait-list clients no longer met the criteria. At 1-year follow-up, results revealed that 95.6% of participants who received individual and family intervention no longer met diagnostic criteria for their disorder, and both self-report and clinician ratings showed significantly more improvement than did reports for the group that received only CBT. However, the addition of family therapy appeared to benefit only younger children significantly (aged 7–10) than older children (aged 11–14). It appears that in treating anxiety disorders, the addition of the family educational component may be particularly important for younger children. A 6-year follow-up study with 52 of the original participants demonstrated that the vast majority of the children (85.7%) maintained gains overall, but the results of both CBT and CBT with family were ultimately comparable (Barrett, Duffy, Dadds, & Rapee, 2001). Thus, the data suggest that the inclusion of family members may be helpful in the short run.

In a study with 60 children who met similar diagnostic criteria for a range of anxiety disorders, Barrett (1998) compared group-format CBT with a group family format (with parents and children). The sample comprised 32 boys and 28 girls. About 25% of the sample was from non-English-speaking homes. Barrett (1998) employed the same intervention protocol (adapted to group format) and the same measures as used in Barrett et al. (1996). Children were randomly assigned to the three groups (group CBT, group family therapy, and wait list—who were treated later). The interventions were conducted over 12 weekly 2-hour sessions. As expected, the two active treatment groups saw significant improvement, with a marginally superior outcome for the family group. At 12-month follow-up, 85% of children who received the group family intervention no longer met their particular diagnosis for anxiety disorder. Overall, this and previously reviewed studies suggest that CBT is an effective intervention for children's anxiety disorders, that it can be equally effective when administered in group format (Silverman & Berman, 2001), and that the addition of parent education as part of the intervention may marginally improve outcomes. More research is needed to replicate these findings.

To examine whether CBT methods could be successfully implemented in a group format, Silverman, Kurtines, Ginsburg, Weems, Lumpkin et al. (1999) compared a group format with a wait-list control group. Fifty-six children (34 boys and 22 girls) with a mean age of 10, about half of whom were Hispanic, were randomly assigned to the treatment and control conditions (in a two-to-one ratio of treatment group to control). Children in the control condition were provided treatment within 8–10 weeks. The children had a variety of anxiety disorder diagnoses, including overanxious disorder (DSM-III-R), social anxiety disorder, and generalized anxiety. A combination of broad and narrow measures were used. In the group CBT format, parents and children met in separate groups for 40 minutes, and then children met with their parents together for 15 minutes. The therapeutic content in the two separate groups was similar. The CBT group used contingency management approaches to help parents reinforce their child's exposure to anxiety-provoking situations, and they practiced the use of coping responses. Results indicated that 64% of participants in the treatment group no longer met the diagnostic criteria, whereas only 13% in the control group did not. On the basis of CBCL scores, 82% of children improved to within the cutoff range for internalizing disorders, whereas only 9% of the control group did so. Symptom reductions were maintained at 12 months. The authors concluded that CBT can be effectively implemented in group format with the inclusion of parents.

In a controlled trial to compare the efficacy of contingency management (CM) to self-control (SC) therapy and an educational support (ES) condition, Silverman, Kurtines, Ginsburg, Weems, Rabian et al. (1999) recruited 104 children (aged 6–16; 54 boys) and their parents. About 33% of the sample was Hispanic American. Participants met DSM criteria for phobic disorder, most of which were simple phobias (e.g., nighttime fears, small animals, school, thunder and lightning, airplanes, loud noises), and most had another anxiety disorder. The investigators used a battery of well-validated scales. Treatment manuals were employed to guide all three interventions, which lasted for 10 sessions (40 minutes with child, 25 minutes with parents, and 15 minutes together). The CM condition emphasized teaching parents to use reinforcement principles to facilitate graduated exposure experiences for their child using a fear hierarchy. Self-management skills were based on Kendall's (1994) work, and the educational component included supportive listening and didactic material on phobias. Of original participants, 81% completed the study. All three conditions performed comparably well at completion and at 3-, 6-, and 12-month follow-ups. Findings were comparable across multiple measures that reflected various points of view (e.g., child, parent, practitioner). The authors speculated that participants in the ES condition took what they learned from the lectures and attempted self-directed exposure on their own. Future research is needed to replicate the findings and identify effective treatment components.

Panic Disorder and Agoraphobia

Research on treating panic and agoraphobia in children and adolescents is quite limited. However, the few studies that exist indicate that young people benefit substantially from cognitive-behavioral treatments that are very similar to those used with adults (with modifications made in engagement style and age-appropriate language). Key skills appear to be an emphasis on psychoeducation about what panic symptoms are, what causes them, and why they persist; cognitive restructuring via addressing distorted beliefs about the causes or effects of panicky feelings; breathing retraining to avoid hyperventilation; and exposure as needed to address avoidance of specific situations (Hoffman & Mattis, 2000). It appears that both brief intensive interventions (six extended sessions over 8 days) or 11 weekly sessions over 3 months appear to be effective at reducing panic; however, weekly visits also appear to be effective in reducing comorbid depression. Both interventions result in sustained improvements at 6-month follow-up. In general, this approach seems to help with other comorbid anxiety disorders as well, perhaps not a surprising finding, given the degree of shared symptoms (Chase, Whitton, & Pincus, 2012; Gallo, Chan, Buzzella, Whitton, & Pincus, 2012).

Obsessive-Compulsive Disorder

Cognitive-behavioral interventions and medication (e.g., serotonin reuptake inhibitors) alone or in combination have been demonstrated as treatments of choice for OCD (Manassis, 2000; March & Leonard, 1996; Piacentini & Bergman, 2000). Whether these work better in combination is a question that begs further research. March (1995) published a thorough review of the literature and identified 32 articles describing psychosocial interventions for OCD, 25 of which were qualitative case reports and 7 of which were single-subject designs. He concluded that exposure with response prevention (EXRP) is the most effective method to date and that inclusion of the family may help facilitate the treatment process and improve outcomes. Psychodynamic therapies have been demonstrated to be ineffective with OCD, and the empirical literature provides no support for unfounded claims regarding symptom substitution, dangers associated with interrupting compulsive rituals, uniformity of learned symptoms, and incompatibility between therapy and pharmacotherapy (March & Leonard, 1996). Although responses to EXRP are robust, many clients continue to improve after treatment (e.g., Fischer, Himle, & Hanna, 1998). However, over longer periods (e.g., 9–14 years after treatment), symptoms can return for many clients (e.g., Bolton, Luckie, & Steinberg, 1995).

More recent reviews of the literature, including meta-analyses, continue to show a confluence of findings that support exposure with response prevention and antidepressant medication as the treatment of choice for children with OCD, although some view EXRP as conferring greater benefit overall (Abramowitz, Whiteside, & Deacon, 2005; Geller, 2006; Turner, 2006; Watson & Rees, 2008). In an additional review, Barrett et al. (2008) found that EXRP resulted in remission rates ranging from 40% to 85%, and concluded that EXRP is the psychosocial treatment of choice for children and adolescents with OCD and can be delivered in a group family format as deemed necessary. More research is needed, however, to better understand the psychological mechanisms driving OCD, such as thought-action fusing (i.e., thinking about something bad makes one responsible for what happens) (Barrett et al., 2008; Turner, 2006). For example, a British sample ($N = 20$) revealed comparable large effect sizes in a controlled trial of EXRP (Bolton & Perrin, 2008). A later study with a larger sample ($N = 96$) of children showed that a brief (five-session) manualized intervention based on principles of OCD regarding cognitive distortions characterized by an exaggerated sense of responsibility was comparably effective as 12 sessions, and gains were maintained for at least 14 weeks beyond termination (Bolton et al., 2011). Notwithstanding criticism that the results of efficacy studies are not likely to transfer well to everyday practice, Farrell, Schlup, and Boschen (2010) demonstrated that EXRP delivered by busy generalist practitioners showed robust results in community practice (including parental involvement) in reducing symptoms and everyday functioning in 33 children and adolescents with OCD, as well as large effect sizes for core symptoms of OCD. Long-term maintenance of gains has also been reported for EXRP and other cognitive techniques. One study showed follow-ups to be overwhelmingly maintained even up to 7 years from individual and group-delivered CBT (i.e., psychoeducation, anxiety management, cognitive therapy, intensive EXRP) with family involvement (Barrett, Healy-Farrell, & March, 2004; O'Leary, Barrett, & Fjermestad, 2009).

The techniques for treating OCD in children are quite similar to those for treating adults (Franklin & Foa, 2008; Shafran, 1998). Children are gradually exposed to the feared situation that elicits anxiety (e.g., touching a kitchen garbage can), and then they are prevented from engaging in the compulsive ritual (e.g., repeated hand washing). The length of time for exposure to the feared situation accompanied by response prevention is extended gradually, and (as with adults) children monitor their anxiety level with a self-anchored scale (the Subjective Units of Distress Scale). A hierarchy of fears (e.g., from doorknob to garbage can to toilet bowl) is developed with the child, and family members are included to facilitate the treatment at home and learn how to avoid reinforcing the child's ritualistic behavior. Material reinforcements can be incorporated into the treatment as a reward for substantial compliance with response prevention. A multimodal approach incorporates EXRP, other cognitive coping and relaxation techniques, family psychoeducation, and medication (Abramowitz et al., 2005; Bolton et al., 1995; Shafran, 1998; Watson & Rees, 2008). The child's significant others who have the opportunity to observe and reinforce the child on a regular basis (e.g., parents, teachers) should also be included. Exposure with response prevention is an effective intervention for many children and adolescents but might require some booster sessions for clients who have more severe symptoms.

Post-Traumatic Stress Disorder

In their meta-analysis, Kowalik, Weller, Venter, and Drachman (2011) reported significant findings of CBT interventions with children in the reduction of both internalizing and externalizing behaviors and symptoms of PTSD. Comparison groups included nondirective supportive techniques, child-centered approaches, and wait-list controls. In their meta-analysis, Corcoran and Pillai (2000) found that parent-involved treatment of sexual abuse-related PTSD confers relatively small but significant advantages for parent-involved versus child-focused treatments. They also noted the relatively small number of sessions across studies (8–20 sessions) and suggested that the parent-child dyads might benefit from more treatment and/or booster sessions. In their review, Makely and Falcone (2010) also concluded that CBT is the most recommended treatment for childhood PTSD at this time. They also noted that although play, art, and other expressive therapies can be helpful ways to engage children in the assessment and treatment process, there is little evidence of long-term relief from PTSD symptoms from these interpretation-based approaches.

To offset some of the smaller-sample studies regarding treatment of PTSD related to child sex abuse, Cohen, Deblinger, Mannarino, and Steer (2004) conducted a randomized controlled trial at multiple sites comparing trauma-focused cognitive-behavioral treatment with child-focused treatment (a relatively nondirective approach to encourage child and parent to resolve post-trauma concerns such as lack of trust). The sample consisted of children between the ages of 8 and 14, 90% of whom had suffered other trauma in addition to sexual abuse and almost all of whom met PTSD diagnostic criteria (i.e., more severe cases). About 203 children (and 189 parents) receiving the trauma-focused treatment showed significantly greater reductions in PTSD symptoms, depression, shame, and other behavioral and emotional problems. Parents also showed greater reduction in abuse-related distress and depression, and improvements in parenting skills related to supporting the child. Twice as many children in the child-centered approach continued to meet criterion for PTSD compared with those in the CBT group. Follow-up evaluations at 6 and 12 months revealed solid maintenance for most gains (Deblinger, Mannarino, Cohen, & Steer, 2006).

Najavits, Gallop, and Weiss (2006) used an exploratory randomized controlled trial of the Seeking Safety treatment (Najavits, 2002), an approach using cognitive-behavioral skills to treat trauma, versus a self-selected treatment-as-usual group. Seeking Safety is designed along five basic principles: (1) safety as the priority; (2) integrated treatment of PTSD and substance use disorders; (3) a focus on ideals; (4) four content areas of cognitive, behavioral, interpersonal, and case management; and (5) attention to therapist processes. The study was conducted with a small sample of adolescent females (18 in treatment; 15 controls, 25 sessions over 3 months) who were diagnosed with both PTSD and substance use disorders. Results showed that those receiving the Seeking Safety treatment manifested substantially greater improvements (effect sizes in the moderate to high range) in both trauma-related symptoms and substance use. In addition, they showed additional improvements in nontargeted problems, including anorexia.

The procedure for graduated imaginal exposure for treatment of PTSD is quite similar to the process used for adults (Resick, Monson, & Rizvi, 2008; Smith et al., 1998) (see chapter 9). A script of the traumatic event is developed from the child's account (a tape can be helpful for homework exposure sessions). The child is also taught how to use a 0–10 SUDS scale to indicate level of anxiety, in order to manage it during the covert exposure sessions. Practitioners should take care not to overwhelm the child with anxiety during exposure in sessions. The script should be developed with sufficient sensory detail to allow for a realistic mental reenactment of the event. The child's level of arousal is stepped up carefully based on level of tolerance, but the goal is to gradually elicit a high level of anxiety. The child is taught relaxation and breathing exercises to hold the image (ideally) for more extended periods, in order to maintain imaginal exposure until the subjective level of anxiety (i.e., SUDS) decreases significantly. Homework is assigned to continue the imaginal exposure at home, with the assistance of family members if possible. In vivo exposure to circumstances that remind the child of the traumatic event may also become part of the treatment if behavioral avoidance of certain circumstances has become a significant problem (e.g., school where abduction occurred). Smith et al. (1998) point out that although uncontrolled studies of CBT for children's PTSD are generally positive, there are few data from controlled studies to date. Nevertheless, given the effectiveness of CBT for other anxiety disorders, it is considered the treatment of choice for PTSD at this time (Dowd & McGuire, 2011; Smith et al., 1998).

Can Trauma-Related Treatment Be Made Culturally Congruent?

Rolfsnes and Idsoe (2011) conducted a meta-analysis of 19 studies (all used comparison groups) across nine countries and concluded that school-based interventions with children and adolescents exposed to trauma can be effective. Of the studies, 16 were variations of cognitive-behavioral interventions. These findings raise the question of whether major modifications are needed to effectively adapt CBT-based interventions to other cultures. In reference to implementing Cognitive Behavioral Interventions for Trauma in Schools (CBITS), Ngo et al. (2008) pointed out that evidence for the effectiveness of culturally adapted intervention is quite mixed. Uncontrolled case studies of cognitive behavioral treatment for trauma in Native American children on a rural reservation in Montana showed promising results (Morsette et al., 2008). Although the authors made efforts aimed at cultural adaptation (e.g., involvement of elders), design limitations of the study precluded testing whether these modifications to CBITS made a difference in outcomes. Using a within-group longitudinal design (four measurement points), Goodkind, LaNoue, and Milford (2010) administered a culturally modified cognitive-behavioral approach (i.e., education, relaxation training, cognitive therapy) with 24 selected Native American adolescents who had been exposed to violence. Cultural modifications were characterized as surface changes (e.g., materials, channels of delivery, settings) to make the intervention more culturally congruent with participants' expectations. Results revealed improvements in PTSD symptoms, depression, and coping; however, improvements began to reverse at 3 months. The authors suggested that the cultural adaptation to the CBT treatment may not have had a positive impact. Nevertheless, the design precludes any robust conclusions about the efficacy of the treatment itself or the utility of the cultural adaptations. The superior efficacy and effectiveness of culturally adapted interventions versus out-of-the-box approaches appears, at this time, to be a hypothesis in need of further testing.

Exemplar Study: Controlled Trial for Children with Anxiety Disorders

Kendall (1994) conducted the first randomized clinical trial of a cognitive-behavioral intervention with children suffering from anxiety disorders. The methodology and the intervention have provided a foundation for many subsequent controlled trials. Forty-seven children referred from multiple community sources were included in the study. Twenty-seven children (aged 9–13) received treatment for 16–20 visits, and after 8 weeks, the 20 children in the control group were assigned to therapists for the same intervention. Of the initial treatment group, 52% were boys, 78% were white, and 22% were African American. All clients were diagnosed with one or more anxiety disorders, including overanxious disorder, separation anxiety disorder, and avoidant disorder. More than half were given an additional diagnosis of simple phobia, and about one-third experienced co-occurring depression. There were no differences between the treatment and control groups on major characteristics noted earlier. Seven doctoral candidates provided the cognitive-behavioral intervention and were trained in the procedure with an 85-page manual that detailed "(a) recognizing anxious feelings and somatic reactions to anxiety, (b) clarifying cognitions in anxiety-provoking situations (i.e., unrealistic or negative attributions and expectations), (c) developing a plan to help cope with the situation (i.e., modeling anxious self-talk into coping self-talk as well as determining what coping actions might be effective), and (d) evaluating performance and administering self-reinforcement as appropriate" (Kendall, 1994, p. 103). (The intervention procedures are detailed in the next section.)

Kendall's (1994) findings revealed significant improvements in almost all major indicators for the treatment group. Sixty-four percent of the treatment group versus 5% of the wait-list control group no longer met the criteria for anxiety disorders, and gains were maintained at 1-year follow-up. A long-term (2–5 years) follow-up study of 82% of eligible study participants revealed stable maintenance of gains over that period. Participants reported specific cognitive-behavioral skills as well as the relationship with the therapist as important aspects of the treatment experience (Kendall & Southam-Gerow, 1996). In a second randomized control trial of cognitive-behavioral methods, Kendall et al. (1997) compared 60 children (treatment group) with

34 wait-list controls. The children (aged 9–13) had a variety of anxiety disorders, including overanxious, avoidant, and separation anxiety disorders. After the intervention, more than half no longer met their pretreatment diagnosis, whereas only 6% of controls no longer met their diagnostic criteria. Gains were maintained at 1-year follow-up.

Description of CBT for Treating Anxiety for Children and Younger Adolescents

In general, the program (Kendall, 1992; Kendall, Korlander, Chansky, & Brady, 1992) combines traditional cognitive behavioral skills and adapts them for children and younger adolescents with anxiety disorders. Some of these techniques can be readily adjusted for older adolescents as well, or adult protocol can be employed. The core skills include relaxation combined with imagery designed for the child's individual needs, problem-solving skills for difficulties that appear to cause anxiety, role-playing, modeling, in vivo exposure, and contingency reinforcement (i.e., using positive reinforcement to gradually shape successful coping with anxiety). Therapists were encouraged to be flexible in the application of these skills to accommodate the needs of the individual child, and upon review, the investigators deemed treatment fidelity to be adequate. A battery of well-validated measures was employed. In addition, other behavioral observations were made using a seven-item, five-point scale to measure the quality of the child's perception of the therapeutic relationship.

Kendall and associates (Kendall, 1992; Kendall et al., 1992) have outlined the 16-week program schedule. Weeks 1–8 focus on four skill areas: an awareness of the physical sensations associated with anxiety; recognizing and evaluating self-talk when the child is anxious; learning problem-solving skills, including the use of constructive self-talk and coping skills; and engaging in self-evaluation and reward for overall performance. Skills are taught so that the children can demonstrate them through a series of "show that I can" (STIC) tasks:

- Session 1: Practitioners help put the child at ease, gauge child's understanding of problem and readiness to engage in treatment, develop a constructive rapport to allow for collaboration on the problem without pressure.

- Sessions 2–3: Practitioners help the child to identify and learn about his or her own emotional reactions, which may include some didactic methods such as looking at pictures of others and identifying what those people might be feeling and engaging in role-play to show how someone might act when sad, anxious, angry, and so forth. Practitioners must accommodate the child's ability to tolerate and understand what is being demonstrated in order to progress at the child's pace.

- Session 4: Once the child has learned to identify anxiety more accurately, that skill is used as a starting point for the child to learn how to use tension as a cue to engage in relaxation skills, including relaxing specific muscle groups and breathing exercises.

- Session 5: Practitioners help the child identify and articulate the self-talk he or she uses when anxious (i.e., the content of cognitive processes), challenge those cognitions, and replace them with coping self-talk that helps the child feel less anxious. One way to help the child articulate these "dysfunctional" thoughts and construct coping response alternatives is the use of cartoon characters and "thought balloons" that he or she can fill in with coping self-statements.

- Session 6: The child begins to engage in problem-solving strategies. The approach used in this program is to help the child identify situations, feelings, and thoughts regarding anxiety-provoking situations, and then explore a series of coping and problem-solving responses (actions) to a series of increasingly anxiety-provoking situations.

- Session 7: The goal is to help the child learn to self-evaluate fairly his or her performance (anxious children tend to have high standards and judge themselves harshly), and then give him- or herself a "pat on the back" for making a good effort and achieving partial successes.

- Session 8: The client reviews progress to date and solidifies what he or she has learned by summarizing the main points of the program using the acronym FEAR: feeling frightened (i.e., recognizing anxiety symptoms), expecting bad things to happen (i.e., recognizing anxious self-talk), identifying positive actions and attitudes (i.e., problem-solving and coping skills), and results and rewards (i.e., self-evaluation, "pat on the back" for a constructive response to a fearful situation). The steps learned in the first eight sessions are summarized on a wallet-size card, and the practitioner shares the coping plan with parents.

- Sessions 9–16: The child learns to build on his or her self-assessment and coping skills by implementing them with real anxiety-provoking problems covertly and in vivo in a graduated manner. The child is taught the use of SUDS and, after practicing covertly, confronts the fearful situation in vivo. The use of the SUDS scale is to help the child gauge his or her own fear and adjust the pace of exposure so that it is challenging but not overwhelming. As the child improves and achieves a tolerable level of anxiety at each stage by using cognitive-behavioral coping skills to deal with fear, the child can reward him- or herself as planned. Situations imaginally and in vivo must be realistic and specific to the child's fear, and the child must experience significant degrees of anxiety to learn to successfully cope with fears. Progress may be two steps forward, one step back, but practitioners should communicate optimism about the final outcome and always reward progress. Termination should be a time of evaluation, reward for successes, looking ahead to further challenges, and (if needed) occasional booster sessions. As the family situation warrants, the parent(s) can continue to reinforce the child's progress.

TREATMENT PLANNING AND EVALUATION

CASE STUDY: NOAH

Noah, a 9-year-old African American boy, was brought to the local mental health center because his aunt found him in his room sobbing. He was attempting to make a noose out of a bedsheet, and, he later admitted, that he was planning to hang himself in his closet. After disclosing his intentions to his aunt, she queried him about why he would want to do that. At about 4:30 p.m., Noah's mother, Nadine, came home from her shift as a nurse's aid in the local hospital, and everyone sat down together. The aunt's son, Jared (age 11), also came home from school, and got busy doing his homework at the kitchen table.

Three months earlier, Noah's cousin Damon (a 19-year-old son of another aunt) was killed as an innocent bystander in a drive-by shooting as a result of a feud between two rival gangs. Noah had been very close to him. He hung around Damon a lot and looked up to him. Noah's father had been out of the picture since Noah was about 3 years old. Noah had only vague recollections of his father, sharpened over the years only through seeing pictures of him and overhearing stories about him from his neighbors and his mom. Noah's mother and her sister got together and agreed to share the child-rearing and living expenses by moving in

together, at least for a while. A while turned into a few years. Noah and Jared got along well, and between two adults working different shifts, Noah's mother and aunt were able to cover child care, make ends meet, and develop a tight family unit.

Noah had always been somewhat of an anxious, quiet child. He did not have a behavior problem, but he caused his mother some concern because of his occasional odd behavior. He was shy and did not like to keep company with other kids. He spoke about one friend from school he had for three consecutive years. He played with his cousin Jared but shied away from other social events and school activities, and never mentioned that he had been invited to other kids' birthday parties. He spoke about vague fears now and again, usually based on something related to a TV show or something he read in a book (he was a good reader and had a complex and rich imagination). He complained of stomachaches off and on. His mother could never link his complaints to food, and it seemed to usually have something to do with going to an unfamiliar place or going to the doctor or dentist for routine care. Noah was extremely methodical and orderly with his personal belongings. His mother always felt it was a bit extreme, but she was one of the few parents who never complained about their children being messy, she said, not "minding" or not picking up after themselves. There were times she had to check on him when he was alone in his room (which he shared with Jared, who was often on the floor of the living room watching TV or playing video games). When she would knock and enter Noah's room, she would find him deeply engrossed in his play, talking aloud, providing the voice for the characters in his imaginary world of superhero and villains-playmates. When his mother called him for dinner, it would often be hard to extract him from his play. Once his mother, exasperated after having called him to dinner three times, stormed into his room and insisted that he come to the table immediately. When she went to prompt him by taking his hand, he started to scream that he could not leave until his work was done. "What work?" His toys had to be placed perfectly before he could let himself leave the room. Although Noah was a good student, his mother also noticed that he would get frustrated and bogged down in minutiae (e.g., getting a column of numbers perfectly aligned, his penmanship had to be perfect), and sometimes he would cry in frustration if he could not get it just so after spending useless hours trying. Another time she

found him sobbing on his knees next to his bed; he said, "I can't get my prayers right. I can't get them to be perfect for Jesus." His mother and aunt, who both regularly attended services with their boys, were concerned that maybe they had overdone it, although they did not have prayer services at home, and Jared, bored by church, never indicated that he cared about prayers one way or the other.

But trying to kill himself was another matter altogether. Although it had been 3 months since his cousin Damon had been buried, Noah seemed to become very upset about it all over again. Jared, a sharp listener, overheard his mom and aunt talking and offered an explanation: "They were talking about Damon on TV, and Noah was with me." As they talked to Noah they also found out that Damon had promised to take Noah to a baseball game when the season opened in the spring. When his mom spoke with Noah's teacher, she said that Noah had told her several times that he was going to a game with his cousin Damon. Noah, who had never been to a baseball game, was looking forward to it all winter. It was now baseball season, the kids in school were talking about their favorite players, but Noah would not be going with his best friend.

MFS Assessment: Defining Problems and Goals

After several visits with Noah's mother and aunt, and a few hours with Noah, the social worker, June, began to put together the pieces as best she could. It came out that Noah's father had been rather violent in the home when Noah was young. He had been abusive to Noah's mother, and although Noah said he did not recall any of these events, his mother strongly suspected that it might account for some of his fears. As a little boy, he would come out of his room late at night, apparently sleepwalking, after the couple had argued loudly (often with furniture being pushed or thrown, and considerable screaming and yelling, sometimes hitting). He also tended to have nightmares during that time, and he was often very afraid of being left with anyone (e.g., babysitter, family member) during the time he was aged 2.5 to 3. He would cry and scream if his mother left the house, and at times, he seemed inconsolable. After his father moved out, Noah settled down gradually, although some of this fears continued. Noah's mother reported problems with alcohol on both sides of the family, as well as (what appeared to be) depression on her mother's side. Noah's mother said she blamed herself because Noah did not have a father, and she was grateful when he was about 7 years old that Damon took him under his wing. After Noah's father left, she said she was a "nervous wreck" and that things were "unstable around here with babysitters and never knowing if I was going to be able to pay the rent." Things got better when she teamed up with her sister.

With more recent analysis, it appeared that Noah's depression, feelings of hopelessness, and thoughts of suicide may have resulted from a delayed reaction to the loss of Damon. He appeared to be somewhat emotionless and somewhat numb during the wake and funeral following Damon's death. But his thoughts and feelings about the loss seemed to be leaking out. In addition to his long-standing shyness, general fears, somatic complaints, and stress response and grief, the social worker, June, was also concerned about Noah's extreme worry about orderliness and his distress about not being about to "make it perfect" with his tidying up, his homework completion, and his nighttime prayers. Put together, Noah appeared to have a predisposition toward anxiety disorders and depressive symptoms, all of which were exacerbated by the recent trauma associated with the loss of Damon.

Although there appeared to be a direct link between the increase in depression and suicidal thoughts and Damon's death, the other problems appeared to be both temperamental and the result of exposure to intense fighting and intermittent violence in the home when Noah was younger. In addition, his mother noticed an increase in Noah's anxiety when he was expected to participate socially in school or make a presentation (show-and-tell), or after his mother worked double shifts (at which time both sisters hired another cousin as house-sitter for the evening). Changes in routine, unplanned events, and conflicts with another child in school, among other stressors, seemed to cause Noah to be more anxious, as suggested by an increase in compulsive orderliness, somatic complaints (e.g., attempts to feign illness to stay home from school), and general restlessness.

The results of these discussions with June, Noah, and his mom seemed to indicate that helping Noah deal with his intense sadness and thoughts about killing himself were the top priority. Second on the list seemed to be his general fears about school, and socializing with other children (e.g., after-school event or a birthday party). Third was his mother's concern about Noah's need to be "perfect." All agreed on three main goals for the intervention: help Noah resolve his grief over Damon as best he could, improve his socialization skills (reduce his social anxiety to a manageable level), and help him "lighten up" on his obsessive tendencies to be "perfect."

Selecting and Designing Interventions: Defining Strategies and Objectives

A series of step-by-step objectives were considered for each goal (table 12.1). To help Noah resolve some of his grief over Damon, the social worker planned a series of exercises that she and Noah started together to help him talk about Damon, his time with him, his good memories, and his fears and unspoken sorrow regarding how Damon died and how much he missed him. This process included putting together a scrapbook of their time together with drawings and a few photographs that Noah's mother had saved, as well as talking about the things that they had planned to do together. Mom gradually participated in reminiscing with Noah at home. Objectives for reducing his shyness included gradually introducing him to some of the after-school programs available. Noah would be encouraged to stay at the program with an adult for a "couple of minutes" to look around, and that amount of time was then gradually increased by a few minutes until he became more comfortable and found some acquaintances with whom he shared common interests. Another series of objectives focused on gradually reducing Noah's need for "perfection" by gradually modifying his extreme standards for homework, cleanup, and prayer by setting more reasonable standards.

Interventions to address and accomplish these goals included a cognitive approach to grief work, graduated exposure to reduce his shyness, and a combination of contingency management and exposure with response prevention to reduce his compulsive behavior. To facilitate these interventions, June worked closely with Noah to teach him anxiety management skills, including affect education (identification of feelings), tracking feelings over time and linking them to behaviors-in-situation, identifying some more troubling thoughts (e.g., "Nobody will like me," "If I don't tidy up just right, bad things will happen to Mom and me, and it will be my fault"); the practitioner worked carefully with Noah using drawings and action figures to tease out a hierarchy of fears and help set a course for "conquering" his fears one by one. Noah needed to learn to meditate, breathe, relax, and imagine himself more in control (just like one of his martial arts heroes), a key skill for him to have "superhero courage" to take on other challenges. After he was taught the SUDS scale (to measure courage), Noah was taught imaginal exposure to prepare to deal with social anxiety, see himself (covert rehearsal) saying "hi" to other kids, and to practice saying something positive to another child to initiate interaction (e.g., "that's a cool shirt"). The practitioner role-played some encounters with him and things to say if kids were mean or didn't want to play with him.

June, Mom, and Noah worked closely together on a careful hierarchy of steps for approaching other kids and reducing his compulsive "perfect" behavior. Noah's aunt was included so when his mom was not around she could reinforce his "time limits" for cleaning up, writing out his homework, and saying his prayers. They all understood what the rewards were on a daily basis (e.g., praise, a little more TV time) if Noah stuck to the time limits and left things "just a little bit messy." A consultation was planned between the pastor at the local church, Noah's mom, and Noah to talk about "prayer" (not to put Noah on the spot, but just to get an authoritative view of why praying doesn't have to be perfect). The pastor and his wife (who was also a social worker) understood immediately what was needed and made the encounter into a fun picnic on the church grounds with their own grandchildren. The meeting helped dispel some of Noah's more oppressive ideas about what he thought God wanted of him: "God wants you to have fun, Noah!" was a help-ful injunction from the pastor. The social worker June also had a phone con-versation with Noah's teacher (with whom June collaborated regularly). The teacher, very familiar with classroom contingency management, immediately got on board with the reinforcement schedule to allow Noah only limited time to "tidy up" his work and focused on praising the content of his work and discouraging him from being "too fussy." The after-school program mon-itor also agreed to record (by estimating) the number of minutes Noah played with other kids. This case management and networking paid off immediately, as there was little confusion among various players in Noah's life about what was expected of him. Over the following 2–3 months, Noah's mother and teacher reported considerable improvement. A sense of heavi-ness appeared to begin to lift. He learned to live with "good enough" tidying up, spent more time playing with other kids, and seemed less preoccupied with his grief.

Selecting Scales and Creating Indexes to Monitor and Evaluate Client Progress

The practitioner chose the CDRS-R (short form) because it seemed to address the right balance of anxious (social withdrawal) and depressive (anhedonia, depressed mood, self-esteem) symptoms. It also has a conversational format that seemed to lend itself to assessment with Noah, who was fairly articulate once he felt comfortable with an adult. Specific indexes included (at different points during the intervention depending on the achievement of different objectives) his intensity of sadness (0, "none," and 10, "extremely sad") regarding grief over Damon's death, any indications of suicidal thoughts (0,

TABLE 12.1   The Client Service Plan: Noah and His Family

Problems	Goals	Objectives (samples)	Interventions	Assessment and evaluation tools
Depression, grief, stress-related symptoms resulting from the death of his friend	Provide a normative degree of resolution for grief; resolve acute symptoms related to death, cognitive appraisal of the death, and further sense of danger	Carefully review child's understanding of circumstances of cousin's death and exaggerated fears of his own danger; review time with Damon and develop a scrapbook together	Cognitive therapy focused on resolving fears related to death and facilitating grief Coping skills to enhance relaxation through imagery and muscle relaxation; modeling and role-play of conversation and play; graduated exposure; contingency management with rewards for more playtime in after-school program	In addition to CDRS-R to cover most target symptoms, the following indexes were employed: • Index of suicidal ideation and index of hopelessness • Number of minutes playing with others in after-school program • Number of times he initiated conversation or play • Internal SUDS (level of "courage" to make friends) • Number of minutes spent organizing (at home and school) • Level of subjective anxiety (SUDS 0–10) experienced if things are not "perfect"
Shyness, social anxiety with kids at school	Increase comfort level and improve socialization skills to play after school for at least 1 hour	Graduated objectives: measured from a few minutes up to 60 minutes in after-school program; instructors record number of minutes		
Moderate OCD symptoms; perfectionism, excessive organizing to get things "just right"; feelings of responsibility for external events	Reduce expectations to be perfect; tolerate "messiness" with reduced anxiety and compulsive behaviors	Graduated objectives: to reduce level of perfectionism with regard to tidying up room, homework, prayer by reducing amount of organizing to 1–2 minutes daily at the end of each respective task	In addition to coping skills, EXRP exercised early on until he can "leave it alone"; daily rewards for reducing organizing time	

"none," and 10, "all the time"), level of hopelessness (0, "none," and 10, "extremely hopeless"), number of minutes he spent playing with another child in the after-school program, and amount of time he spent trying to make his room or his homework "perfect."

ASSESSMENT OF DEPRESSION IN CHILDREN AND ADOLESCENTS

Background Data

Symptoms of depression and depressive disorders cut across an array of conditions children suffer, and the indicators of depression are similar to those experienced by adults: sadness, dysphoric mood, pessimism, irritability, social withdrawal, loneliness, negative self-image, harsh self-criticism, sleep disturbances, and concerns about death, among others. There are differences between childhood and adult depressive symptoms as well. Symptoms such as somatic complaints, irritability, and social withdrawal may be more common in children, whereas psychomotor retardation, delusions, and hypersomnia are more likely to occur in adults. Depression may be associated with poor school performance and interpersonal problems. Other signs may be pessimism, irritability, and social difficulties (Fonseca & Perrin, 2001; Petti, 1989). Major depressive disorder appears to occur twice as frequently in adolescent females than in adolescent males (Compas, 1997), but dysthymia appears to occur equally in children of both sexes. Adolescents with major depression are more likely to abuse substances, and those who do are more likely to exhibit conduct disorder and other psychosocial distress (Buckstein, 1995; Buckstein, Brent, & Kaminer, 1989; King et al., 1996). More than one-third of nonreferred children are estimated to have experienced significantly depressed moods, and between 10% and 20% of children in the community may meet diagnostic criteria for depression.

Theories on the Causes of Depression in Children and Adolescents

As with theories of anxiety, theories of depression are developmentally multidimensional. Early psychoanalytic theories tended to overemphasize the role of early childhood trauma and frustration related to maternal neglect (e.g., introjected rage). Later formulations stressed interrupted attachment, separation, and loss (e.g., Bowlby, 1980). Cognitive theories, including Beck's (1976) cognitive triad (negative view of self, the environment, and the future) and learned helplessness (Seligman, 1975), focused primarily on the development of depression-causing attributions regarding one's ability to cope effectively with environmental challenges. Biological predispositions for disordered neurotransmitter dysfunction or hormonal changes during adolescence have been hypothesized to interact with environmental stressors over time (Garmezy, 1991). Although early loss may contribute to initial vulnerabilities to depression, temperament and other social and environmental stressors are probably at work in the etiology of childhood and adolescent depression (Goodyer, 1995; Harrington, 1995).

Cognitive theories of depression emphasize depression-causing cognitive structures and processes rather than developmental processes. However, whether a child becomes a depressed adolescent or adult depends on whether he or she develops a negative attribution style (Harrington, 1995; Harrington, Wood, & Verduyn, 1998). Developmental changes from early childhood into adolescence reveal a gradually increasing awareness of psychological states, including an awareness of depression and other emotions. It appears that children have difficulty reflecting critically on their own cognitive schema and "dysfunctional thinking" by comparing what they believe to be theoretically valid with verifiable evidence. Developmentally, they may not be ready or even amenable to critical cognitive self-appraisal until their early teens (Harrington, Wood, & Verduyn, 1998). Whether a negative attribution style is biologically predetermined or whether such cognitive structures are the result of a depression-prone temperament interacting with a harsh or critical environment is not known. Evidence suggests that environmental stressors and maltreatment are likely to increase the risk for depression in children and adolescents and are likely to have long-term effects that carry over into adulthood. However, the effects may also be mediated by a host of other social risk and protective factors. As with anxiety problems, this causal relationship between abuse and depression must be seen within its psychosocial context over time (Compas, Grant, & Ey, 1994; Downey, Feldman, Khuri, & Friedman, 1994). Although cognitive theories provide a critical focal point for understanding how depression-causing processes mediate life events and depressive symptoms, their role is probably better understood when familial and community and/or environmental factors (acute and chronic stressors) are considered as well (Harrington, 1995).

Although there are similarities and differences with regard to theories of anxiety and depression (Axelson & Birmaher, 2001; Compas, 1997; Harrington, Wood, & Verduyn, 1998), they appear to share a common multivariate framework for explaining risks and resiliencies related to depression by linking genetic predisposition, quality of early childhood family experiences, emergence of resilient or negative cognitive structures, and development of skills for coping with environmental stressors. Longitudinal research provides the strongest argument for linking these biopsychosocial influences in a transactional-developmental framework. For example, Duggal, Carlson, Sroufe, and Egeland (2001) conducted a longitudinal study of 168 socioeconomically at-risk children who grew into adolescence. The researchers examined the associations among early family context, maternal depression, and development of depression in the child. They used videotaped observational data to measure maternal interactional behaviors during childhood and adolescence. Early maternal stress and child abuse were shown to be significant correlates of childhood depression, accounting for 19% of variance. Maternal depression predicted adolescent depression in females but not males. However, early abuse and both early and later maternal stress were not significantly predictive of depression in adolescence. Results showed only modest continuity in depression from childhood through adolescence, suggesting that the causes of depression for children and adolescents may involve different factors and pathways.

Noting the consistent findings that females are diagnosed with higher rates of depression than males, Silberg et al. (1999) conducted a longitudinal study of twin males and females (at pre- and post-puberty) and demonstrated that negative life events contributed to depression in boys and had an even stronger effect on girls. For boys, any increase in depression appeared to be related to relatively recent negative life events (i.e., previous year), whereas for girls depression increased despite the lack of any particular negative life event. Genetic influences appeared to account for about 30% of variance for girls, which suggests that genetic factors play a predominant role in female depression. A 1-year longitudinal survey of a mixed-race sample of 240 children and their mothers (Garber, Little, Hilsman, & Weaver, 1998) showed that maternal depression alone did not predict suicidal symptoms in the child, but the child's negative perceptions of family environment did, and those perceptions mediated the causal effects of the mother's depression. Last, adolescent onset of major depressive episode appears to have predictive value into early adulthood. Risk factors appear to be higher for females, and for those with previous depressive episodes, depression in other family members, and co-occurring mental health symptoms (Lewinsohn, Rohde, Seeley, Klein, & Gotlib, 2000).

Sorting out the relative effects of biological predisposition to depression and environmental effects continues to be a challenge for longitudinal research. Nevertheless, a model is emerging, and it includes the following factors: (1) biological vulnerabilities rooted in the limbic system, endocrine (hormonal) system, and biological rhythms that affect sleep patterns; (2) lack of early maternal care, maternal depression, abuse and neglect, disruptive family relationships marked by lower levels of support and cohesion, conflict, hostility, rejection and criticism, parental conflict, and parental depression; (3) problems in cognitive schema, errors in reasoning, and attribution errors similar to those discussed with regard to adult depression (see chapter 6); (4) development of poor coping strategies and interpersonal deficits; (5) moderate to severe negative life events, including both traumatic events and common, everyday stressors (Cicchetti, Rogosch, & Toth, 1994; Compas, 1997; Duggal et al., 2001; Goodyer, 1995; Petti, 1989; Stark, Vaughn, Doxey, & Luss, 1999). One-factor theories for depression (e.g., bad genes, bad mothering, a traumatic event) have not shown good explanatory power for the development of a depressive disorder.

MFS Assessment of Depression and Depressive Disorders: Special Considerations

MFS assessment of depression follows a similar deductive process to assessment of anxiety disorder but is perhaps a bit more challenging. Unlike anxiety disorders, for which key symptoms are more readily observable, thoughts and feelings of depression may be more covert, and behavioral symptoms of withdrawal may not be perceived as a problem in an otherwise "good" child. In addition, it may be difficult for children to conceptualize specific aspects of depression, gauge their own level of depression, or articulate the nature of their unhappiness. Drawing pictures, playing with toys, and other methods can be useful for engaging children in assessment and helping them express their feelings and daily concerns, although interpretations should be confirmed by more objective means.

Multiple observations of the child conducted across different situations with data obtained from multiple informants can provide an accurate portrait of a child's struggles with depression. As in the case of anxiety disorders, the MFS assessment should cover the three major modes of expression: the child's cognitive appraisal of events in his or her life (e.g., expressions of hopelessness, pessimism, catastrophic expectations), physiological symptoms (e.g., somatic complaints, sleep disturbance), and behaviors often associated with depression (e.g., social withdrawal, suicidal threats, aggression). Descriptively, the adult diagnosis of depression applies fairly well to children, and depressive symptoms are similar for both children and adolescents. Suicide, however, is more likely to occur in adolescents than in younger children (Harrington, 1995; Reynolds, 1994).

Assessment of Suicide Risk in Children and Adolescents

More than 4,000 adolescents commit suicide every year (Centers for Disease Control and Prevention, CDC, 2014b). Given the rates of co-occurring depressive disorders and other childhood disorders, suicide should be routinely and carefully assessed in both children and adolescents. Guidelines for screening and assessment of potentially suicidal youth are readily available (American Academy of Child and Adolescent Psychiatry, AACAP, 2001a; Greenhill & Waslick, 1997). Key risk factors for child and adolescent suicide include pre-existing psychopathology (e.g., depression, bipolar disorder, aggressiveness, other mood disorders, substance abuse, personality disorder), stressful events (e.g., losses, academic crises, interpersonal upsets), problems with the law, family difficulties, and previous suicide attempts. Other predictive factors include history of running away, family history of suicide, history of child physical and/or sexual abuse, and being gay or lesbian. There is a particular need to be aware of the disproportionate risk of suicide in gay and lesbian youth, as well as a need for better-organized social supports to prevent it (Proctor & Groze, 1994). Boys commit suicide four times more often than girls do. With regard to cultural and racial differences, Native American and Alaskan Native adolescents commit more suicides than other racial groups, and Hispanic American rates of youth suicide exceed those for both African American and non-Hispanic white youth (CDC, 2014b).

Assessment of suicide in young people is quite similar to that of adults (see chapter 6). In addition to considering the foregoing risk factors, practitioners must consider suicide risk on a severity continuum of suicidal ideation, suicidal threats, and suicide attempts. Particular attention should be paid to history of previous attempts as well as the degree of potential lethality of the means contemplated, frequency and intensity of the ideation, and whether the client has a plan in place and has contemplated specific means of suicide. Intervention requires a continuum of options as well, with the general rationale beginning with acute emergency intervention, possible hospitalization followed by partial hospitalization (as needed), and follow-up outpatient intervention. As we will examine here, children and adolescents with depression respond quickly to CBT, and family psychoeducational methods may be a helpful adjunct to continued treatment. Referral and intervention decision points are all guided by considerations of the severity of the depression, co-occurring psychopathology (e.g., substance abuse), and available social supports (e.g., immediate family or others who can provide careful supervision).

Instruments for Assessing Depressive Disorders in Children and Adolescents

The Children's Depression Inventory (CDI) is one of the most widely used self-report measures for children (Kovacs, 1985). The CDI (derived from the Beck Depression Inventory, BDI; Beck, Ward, Mendelson, Mock, & Erbaugh, 1961) (Carlson & Cantwell, 1980; Kovacs, 1985) includes 27 items covering a broad range of depressive symptoms and related problems. Each item comprises three statements describing symptoms at three levels of intensity. In a three-part study, four domains related to depression were identified through factor analysis with a group of 216 children, balanced by gender and race: affective behavior, image ideation, interpersonal relations, and guilt-irritability (Helsel & Matson, 1984). Results showed no differences by gender and race, although age directly predicted greater depression. However, a later analysis of the scale employed a large community sample (more suitable for factor analysis than just clinic samples) and demonstrated a somewhat different factor structure from that of previous investigations (Craighead, Smucker, Craighead, & Ilardi, 1998). Results of the analysis suggested a five-factor scale that measured constructs related to depression (i.e., dysphoria and self-deprecation) as well as externalizing symptoms including school and social problems. Overall, the CDI is considered a useful and reliable instrument, and in its later revision, it has been shown to be robustly reliable and valid (Bae, 2012). It continues to be widely used, has been translated into various languages, and has been used to examine depressive symptoms in minority youth (Myers & Winters, 2002).

The Depression Self-Rating Scale (DSRS) (Birleson, 1981; Birleson, Hudson, Buchanan, & Wolff, 1987) is a self-report measure of moderate to severe depression in children and adolescents. It was initially developed with several samples of children, including those diagnosed as clinically depressed, residential patients, and a school-based population. The initial pool of 37 items was reduced through statistical analysis to 18. Children rate whether they have experienced the symptoms within a 1-week period on a three-point scale (0–2) of "never," "sometimes," or "most of the time." The initial study demonstrated good discriminant validity between depressed and nondepressed children (aged 7–13), good test-retest reliability (.80), and good split-half reliability (.86). The advantages of the DSRS are its brevity and utility as a treatment evaluation tool. Additional studies have demonstrated good utility and good sensitivity in that the DSRS correctly identifies children who have been diagnosed as depressed (Birleson et al., 1987). The DSRS has also been shown to have good cross-cultural validity (Kohrt et al., 2011). The factor structure of the DSRS was replicated and showed very good internal consistency with adolescents when compared with previous research (Ivarsson & Gillberg, 1997). A cutoff score of 15 is recommended as a screen for clinical depression.

The Children's Depression Rating Scale (CDRS) (Poznanski, Cook, & Carroll, 1979) was derived from the Hamilton Depression Rating Scale (see chapter 6). It was developed on the assumption that children's self-reports may not be as valid as the observations of experienced clinicians who use multiple sources of data. Because the assessment is conducted in an interview format, the practitioner can accommodate the child's cognitive level and language style. The initial study of the CDRS (Poznanski et al., 1979) was conducted with 30 hospitalized depressed children and demonstrated a high correlation between the scale and clinical diagnosis. The original version of the CDRS had 15 items, with a possible total score of 61 points. The items measured the following constructs: depressed mood, weeping, self-esteem, excessive guilt, morbid preoccupations, suicidal ideation, schoolwork, social withdrawal, irritability, anhedonia, speech tempo, appetite, sleep, hypoactivity, physical complaints, and fatigue. A revised version of the scale (Poznanski et al., 1984) includes 17 items, correlates significantly with global ratings of depression, and reveals good interrater and test-retest reliability. A five-item version that reflects DSM criteria measures dysphoric mood, anhedonia, social withdrawal, low self-esteem, and fatigue (Overholser, Brinkman, Lehnert, & Ricciardi, 1995). The CDRS (short form) was demonstrated to have high internal consistency ratings in two samples (.80 and .88), high interrater reliability (.93), and high correlations between short and long forms of the CDRS for both boys (.89) and girls (.92), and it correlated significantly with other valid depression scales. The revised CDRS (short form) is presented here as instrument 12.2.

INSTRUMENT 12.2   The Children's Depression Rating Scale–Revised Short Form

For a general time frame, try to assess the child's symptoms as they occurred over the previous 2 weeks. If the child has been recently hospitalized and this has disrupted their life (e.g., not sleeping well because of the new surroundings), then try to evaluate their symptoms as they appeared during the 2 weeks prior to their hospitalization. Also, if a problem has occurred for a long time (e.g., chronic school problems), *only score symptoms that appear to be related to emotional distress,* not some other problem (e.g., learning disability, drug abuse).

Item No. 1: Anhedonia (Capacity to Have Fun)

What do you like to do for fun? After school? On weekends? Do you have any hobbies? When was the last time you did the hobby? (Discuss the activities and note interest, involvement, enthusiasm.) How often do you have fun? (Note frequency of activities that are available.) When was the last time you really enjoyed yourself? Tell me about it. How often do you get bored? What do you do when you get bored? What do you like to watch on TV? Tell me about your favorite TV show. In the last month, has it been hard to get interested in most things? Have you still enjoyed the things you usually enjoy? Last week, did you find anything interesting? Enjoyable? Funny?

Scoring:
1. Interest and activities are appropriate for age, personality and social environment. Shows no appreciable change with present illness. Any feelings of boredom are transient.
2. Doubtful.
3. Describes some activities available several times a week but not on a daily basis. Shows interest but not enthusiasm.
4. Mild to moderate.
5. Is easily bored. Complains of "nothing to do." Participates in structured activities with a "going through the motions" attitude. May express interest primarily in activities that are (realistically) unavailable on a daily or weekly basis.
6. Moderate to severe.
7. Has no initiative to become involved in any activities. Primarily passive. Watches others play or watches TV, but shows little interest. Requires coaxing to get involved in activity. Shows no enthusiasm or real interest in activities.

So, it sounds like you have been feeling . . .

Item No. 2: Social Withdrawal

Do you have many friends? Are they at school or home? What things do you do with your friends? How often do you see them? Do you really have a close friend? What is the name of your best friend? How long have you known this person? How often have you seen this person in the past month (never, rarely, sometimes, frequently, always)? In the past month, how often have you shared *your* problems with him/her (never, rarely, sometimes, frequently, always)? In the past month, how often have they shared *their* problems with you (never, rarely, sometimes, frequently, always)? Do your friends ever call for you when you don't feel like doing anything? How often do you just want to be left alone and be by yourself? What do you do when a friend calls you, but you don't feel like doing anything?

Scoring:
1. Enjoys friendships with peers at school and home.
2. Doubtful.
3. May not actively seek out friendships but waits for others to initiate a relationship or may occasionally reject opportunities to play without a describable alternative.
4. Mild to moderate.
5. Frequently avoids or refuses opportunities for desirable interaction with others and/or sets up situations where rejection is inevitable.
6. Moderate to severe.
7. Does not currently relate to other children. States s/he has "no friends" or actively rejects new or former friends.

So, it sounds like you have been feeling . . .

Item No. 3: Excessive Fatigue

During the last month, what has your energy been like? How tired have you been feeling lately? Do you get tired more easily now than you used to? Have you been tired all the time? How often do you feel this way? Do you have little energy to do things or feel tired a lot? Do you feel tired even when you have had enough sleep? How often do you take naps during the day? How do you feel after a nap?

Scoring:
1. No unusual complaints of "feeling tired" during the day.
2. Doubtful.
3. Occasional complaints of fatigue that seen somewhat excessive and not related to boredom.
4. Mild to moderate complaint.
5. Daily complaints of feeling tired.
6. Moderate to severe.
7. Complains of feeling tired most of the day. May voluntarily take long naps without feeling refreshed. Fatigue interferes with play activities.

So, it sounds like you have been feeling . . .

Item No. 4: Self-Esteem

During the last month, how have you felt about yourself as a person? What are some things about yourself that you like? What kinds of things are you good at? What are some things about yourself that you do not like? Would you like to change anything about yourself? How do you feel about the way you look? How smart do you think you are compared to other kids your age? Have you been feeling down on yourself lately? Do you ever feel worthless as a person?

Scoring:

1. Describes self in primarily positive terms.
2. Doubtful.
3. Describes self with one important area where the child feels deficient.
4. Mild to moderate.
5. Describes self in preponderance of negative terms or gives bland answers to questions.
6. Moderate to severe.
7. Refers to self in derogatory terms. Reports that other children refer to him/her frequently by using derogatory nicknames and child puts self down.

So, it sounds like you have been feeling . . .

Item No. 5: Depressed Feelings

How has your mood been lately? How often have you felt sad? In the past month, how much of the time have you felt sad? How long have you felt this way? What seems to make you feel like that? When you feel unhappy, how long does it last? One hour? A few hours? A day? What kinds of things make you feel unhappy? How often do you feel like this? Every week? Every two weeks? When you've been feeling depressed, how bad has it been? Do other people know when you are sad?

Scoring:

1. Occasional feelings of unhappiness which quickly disappear.
2. Doubtful.
3. Describes sustained periods of unhappiness which appear excessive for the events described.
4. Mild to moderate.
5. Feels unhappy most of the time without major precipitating cause.
6. Moderate to severe.
7. Feels unhappy all of the time, accompanied by psychic pain (e.g., "I can't stand it")

So, it sounds like you have been feeling . . .

SELECTING EFFECTIVE INTERVENTIONS FOR CHILDREN AND ADOLESCENTS

CBT for children has shown solid benefits for moderately depressed children and adolescents, but results for seriously depressed children and adolescents are less impressive (Brown et al., 2008; Carr, 2009; Curry, 2001; Compton et al., 2002; Harrington, 1995; Stark et al., 1999). Although cognitive-behavioral therapies have garnered empirical support for successful outcomes with anxiety disorders, treatments for depressive disorders in young children lag behind (Tandon, Cardeli, & Luby, 2009). Using the methodological guidelines set forth by the Task Force on Promotion and Dissemination of Psychological

Procedures (1995), Kaslow and Thompson (1998) summarized the findings on psychosocial interventions for childhood and adolescent depression:

> Results from this review reveal that several psychosocial interventions programs, the majority of which are based on the cognitive-behavioral model, are effective in reducing depressive symptoms and alleviating depressive disorders in non-clinical samples of adolescents. Positive treatment effects are noted regardless of treatment modality (group, individual or family therapy) or nature or extent of parental involvement. Treatment effects generally are maintained at follow-up. However, because most of the studies were conducted in schools with non-referred youth with depressive symptoms and used relatively inexperienced clinicians, the generalizability of the findings across populations, settings, and clinician-experience level remains unclear. Further, because few between-group design studies have compared different interventions, it is premature to conclude that any specific intervention approach is most efficacious in reducing depression in youth. (p. 153)

Reviewers also stress the need to address co-occurring problems, such as anxiety disorders, and to consider using family formats more often (Birmaher, Ryan, Williamson, Brent, & Kaufman, 1996). Given the possibility that more than half of children suffering from anxiety or depression experience co-occurring symptoms of these disorders, practitioners must be eclectic in combining cognitive-behavioral methods (Kendall et al., 1992). Eclecticism may also extend to the inclusion of family therapy methods in the treatment of depression in young persons (Harrington, Whittaker, & Shoebridge, 1998). In a 10-year review, Birmaher et al. (1996) shared that cognitive-behavioral and behaviorally oriented family systems approaches were efficacious for childhood depression. Harrington (1995) notes that family therapy could be useful in a number of applications: practitioners can act as consultant to an otherwise healthy and intact family and provide advice and guidance regarding how to help their child cope with depression; family members can participate as adjunct therapists by helping the child-client follow through on therapeutic "homework" or otherwise facilitate treatment in other cooperative ways; other problems in the family affecting the child's well-being such as mental illness, substance abuse, domestic violence, marital problems, or other family dysfunction can be addressed. As Kovacs and Bastiaens (1995) point out, "Treatment of the parents' own disorders should be seriously considered in tandem with the psychotherapy of the youngster. It is difficult to see how one could expect a positive and *lasting* treatment response from a child whose parent is disturbed and is thereby probably unable to meet the youngster's needs" (p. 298). Last, although family factors have been associated with contributing to depression and its relapse, more research on the use of family therapy for depression in young persons is needed (Curry, 2001).

Interpersonal psychotherapy (IPT) may be another viable option for interventions with depressed youth. Harrington (1995) notes that IPT may be useful given its present and future focus, its emphasis on improving social relationships, and the fact that it deals with interpersonal disputes and role transitions—all areas that are developmentally pertinent to children and adolescents. Over the past 15 years, controlled research on IPT with depressed adolescents has increased, and evidence suggests that it is moderately effective and can be delivered over 8–12 sessions in community- and school-based settings (Klomek & Mufson, 2006). IPT also appears to be effective, at least in the short term, with comorbid anxiety and depressive disorders (Young et al., 2012). More research is needed to boost long-term outcomes (see chapter 6 for a description of IPT).

A series of key studies since the mid-1980s has shown modest support for the efficacy of CBT for depression and a growing interest in integrating CBT with family therapy. Reynolds and Coats (1986) randomly assigned thirty moderately depressed adolescents to three conditions: CBT condition with self-control skills (i.e., self-monitoring, self-evaluation, and self-reinforcement), relaxation training, or a wait-list control group. Both treatments demonstrated significant reductions in depression compared to the control group at 5-week follow-up. Stark, Reynolds, and Kaslow (1987) compared two behaviorally oriented treatments for children aged 9–12 with a wait-list control group. The first behavioral treatment group consisted of self-control (i.e., self-monitoring and evaluation, and coping skills practiced through homework assignments). The second group emphasized problem-solving skills (i.e., feelings education, social skills, and planned activities reinforced through homework assignments). Treatments were provided in small groups over 12 hourly sessions for 5 weeks. Both treatment groups resulted in positive outcomes (decreased depression), with results maintained at 5-week follow-ups. The control group showed little change. In a similar study, Kahn, Kehle, Jenson, and Clark (1990) showed that CBT and relaxation training had better outcomes than self-modeling over time. Fine, Forth, Gilbert, and Haley (1991) compared a social skills training group with a therapeutic support group. Both groups were conducted over 12 weekly meetings and showed comparable improvements at 9-month follow-up. Wood, Harrington, and Moore (1996) compared an individual CBT model (i.e., cognitive restructuring, social problem-solving, and coping skills for depression) with relaxation training with inpatient depressed children. In the short run, the CBT group showed better results, with improvements in symptoms and self-image. However, by 6-month follow-up, some of the CBT group had relapsed, and the relaxation group continued to improve.

Some investigators have evaluated CBT approaches in a psychoeducational format. For example, Lewinsohn, Clarke, Hops, and Andrews (1990) evaluated a school-based program for 59 depressed adolescents (aged 14–18) in a cognitive-behavioral psychoeducational group (i.e., coping with depression) conducted over 7 weeks of 14 evening sessions lasting 2 hours. In one group, parents participated by receiving separate instruction in skills for coping with depression and family problems. Parents of the second group of adolescents did not participate. Wait-list controls received the intervention at a later date. Both treatment groups showed comparable and significant clinical gains, and outcomes showed continued improvements at 2-year follow-up. In a more recent study, preliminary evidence of effectiveness was demonstrated for a 5-week program that combined family psychoeducation and teaching depressed children CBT skills (Asarnow, Scott, & Mintz, 2002).

Exemplar Study: CBT and Family Therapy for Depression

As with treatment of anxiety disorders in children and adolescents, recent controlled trials of CBT for depression have focused more on the potential differential effectiveness of family therapy alone or in combination with CBT. One randomized controlled trial (Brent et al., 1997) compared CBT, systemic behavioral family therapy (SBFT), and nondirective supportive therapy. The sample included 107 clinically depressed adolescents treated over 12–16 weeks. Participants were between the ages of 13 and 18, met DSM criteria for major depressive disorder, and scored 13 or higher on the Beck Depression Inventory. Other serious comorbid psychiatric disorders were ruled out. Of the eligible 122 adolescents, 107 agreed to be randomly assigned to treatment conditions, and 78 completed the study. All participants were provided with free treatment. Therapists had 6 months of intensive training in the intervention method they provided, master's degrees, and a median of 10 years practice experience. CBT was characterized by collaborative empiricism, teaching clients about the CBT model, monitoring and challenging dysfunctional thinking, and enhancing problem-solving and social skills. Systematic behavioral family therapy (SBFT) included functional family therapy (see chapter 13) combined with communication and problem-solving methods with an emphasis on homework practice. Nondirective supportive treatment (NST) emphasized relationship building, empathic responses, and expression of feelings. Therapists in this condition refrained from providing directive advice of any kind. Close supervision and fidelity checks (i.e., use of videos to rate adherence to the respective models) demonstrated good adherence to each treatment approach. Well-validated instruments were employed at multiple points in treatment. These included standardized measures based on the DSM, the BDI, a global assessment of functioning for children, and other indicators. Results demonstrated markedly superior remission for the CBT condition (60%) (i.e., absence of symptoms meeting the criteria for major depressive disorder) compared with the SBFT condition (38%) and the NST group (39%). There were no differences among the three groups on measures of suicidality or overall functional impairment. Parents' opinion of the credibility of CBT increased relative to that of SBFT.

The researchers noted a few limitations to the study. Because suicide attempters were referred out for emergency treatment, generalizations to suicidal adolescents are limited. In addition, given the need for experimental rigor in client selection, generalizations to young persons with co-occurring disorders is limited as well. The intense amount of supervision and quality-control checks in this study are also difficult to transfer to typical clinical service environments. In comparing the results of CBT to SBFT and NST, they noted that "having a good therapeutic relationship . . . may be necessary, but is not sufficient to result in optimal clinical improvement of adolescent depression. . . . [R]esults also indicate that insistence on the treatment of the family as a unit . . . will cause a certain proportion of families to refuse treatment" (Brent et al., 1997, p. 883). They also noted that the rapid remission of depressive symptoms is critical in youthful depression since it too often precipitates suicide attempts. The greater credibility shown by parents for the CBT approach is important since client satisfaction is linked to treatment adherence. They recommend that future studies compare psychotherapeutic drugs with and without CBT, and test these methods in typical practice settings.

Follow-up studies with this same sample, however, suggested that after 2 years, results from CBT and SBFT were comparable. Most of the young persons recovered with no discernible advantage from either of these two methods (Birmaher et al., 2000). Over the long haul, it may be that a good number of depressed adolescents may need more treatment, including, in some cases, antidepressant medication and continued family therapy, because of a number of predisposing factors, including severity of depression at intake, co-occurring disorders such as anxiety, maternal depression, and family difficulties (Brent, Kolko, Birmaher, Baugher, & Bridge, 1999; Brent et al., 1998; Renaud et al., 1998). Nevertheless, the superior short-term results of CBT should not be undervalued, given the importance of suicide risk early on in treatment. Future research should examine the differential contributions of CBT and family interventions for adolescents with and without the use of medications.

Finally, Kolko, Brent, Baugher, Bridge, and Birmaher (2000) conducted further analysis with these 107 depressed adolescents and found little evidence to link the specific therapeutic technique to the theoretically commensurate change processes (e.g., cognitive techniques should effect dysfunctional thinking, family techniques should change family functioning) and echo a point made throughout this text: the evidence supporting specific cause-effect linkages between intervention methods and their commensurate theoretical change processes is far from compelling. What is known, however, is that some psychosocial interventions are generally more effective than others, at least in the short run.

Descriptions of Comprehensive CBT Programs for Treatment of Depression in Children and Adolescents

CBT for children is based on the same theoretical and practice principles as CBT for adults, but it is oriented to the child's age and circumstances (Harrington, 1995; Harrington et al., 1998; Kovacs & Bastiaens, 1995). In addition to challenging and changing maladaptive cognitions directly, CBT for depression in children and adolescents usually involves other components as well: goal directedness; self-monitoring and evaluating; teaching specific skills such as social skills, self-reinforcement, and relaxation training; and practicing those skills through role-play, rehearsal, and homework exercises to solidify and generalize the effective use of those skills. Self-monitoring may be the most important skill for a young person to learn as part of cognitive-behavioral therapy. The emphasis is placed on first teaching children to accurately identify what they are feeling and then train themselves to focus on more positive thoughts and actions to break the cycle of negative thinking and reduce their depression. Identifying dysfunctional thoughts, such as consistently devaluing oneself, can be directly addressed through standard cognitive restructuring methods (e.g., Beck, 1976) (see chapter 6). First, the child identifies the dysfunctional automatic thought and then challenges it by answering the question: "Where is the evidence to support this belief?" Second, the child examines alternative explanations for upsetting thoughts or events. Third, the child is helped to challenge his or her negative expectations of the future. These assignments should be followed by "experiments" that are creatively developed between the practitioner and the child to test out and ultimately disconfirm the dysfunctional beliefs. Behavioral self-regulation skills (see Kanfer, 1970; Rehm, 1977) can help children reinforce themselves positively to successfully carry out certain behaviors or activities that are purposeful and help them feel better about themselves. Helping children learn to structure their activities can also help move them away from the depressive rumination often associated with inactivity.

Building on these core cognitive-behavioral techniques, Stark, Rouse, and Kurowski (1994) outlined a comprehensive program for working with the depressed child and (as needed) their family. On the basis of well-established self-control and cognitive-behavioral intervention methods, the goal of treatment is to identify those core themes (i.e., cognitive schemata) related to their dysfunctional thought processes. Key techniques include cognitive restructuring, cognitive modeling, self-instructional training, positive activity scheduling (e.g., fun and goal-oriented activities such as chores), relaxation training (i.e., muscle relaxation accompanied by imagery as needed), coping with behavioral problems including social skills deficits (e.g., lack of assertiveness), problem solving, behavioral assignments, self-reinforcement, and behavioral disconfirmation tasks to challenge core negative schemata and dysfunctional thinking. Family interventions are employed as needed.

In the early phase of treatment the practitioner takes much of the initiative in gauging the child's readiness to change, helping the child identify negative moods and the dysfunctional thoughts associated with depressive thinking, and helping the child challenge those thoughts, seek alternative plausible explanations, and replace the dysfunctional thoughts with more positive ways of looking at a situation. As the intervention progresses, the child is encouraged to take more of the initiative to identify dysfunctional thought processes, thus challenging and moving the child toward identifying the core depressive themes presumably associated with core negative schemata. As these are identified and challenged, the most powerful part of the intervention is emphasized: behavioral assignments to challenge and disconfirm beliefs. It is important that the practitioner work closely with parents and teachers, particularly to support the goals of the intervention. If it becomes apparent that there are problems in the family that are having a negative impact on the child, then those problems must be addressed directly. If, for example, the parent(s) are having trouble with parenting skills, they can improve by demonstrating more supportive parenting and effective, nonpunitive disciplinary practices. If a couple is having problems, a couple's intervention should be implemented, focusing on enhancing problem solving and communications. In brief, an effective approach to depression in children combines effective CBT methods with behaviorally oriented family therapy.

Harrington et al. (1998) have also formulated a multimodal approach (Depression Treatment Program) that includes a flexible application of cognitive-behavioral intervention methods tailored to the unique needs of the adolescent. Their program is designed for unipolar depressed adolescents between the ages of 11 and 18. Between 10 and 14 sessions are applied over 10 or 12 weeks (with four additional booster sessions). The adolescent is understood to have problems in three major domains: negative thinking (i.e., negative attributional style, low self-esteem), problems in social relationships (e.g., social inhibitions, withdrawal, conflict), and behavioral symptoms of depression (e.g., poor sleep, lower activity). Following a broad multidimensional assessment that includes the existence of co-occurring problems, a functional analysis is undertaken to help the adolescent learn to assess troubling thoughts, feelings, and behaviors and link them to depressive mood. The adolescent is then encouraged to become more active, engage in more positive behavior activities, and reward her- or himself for efforts in this area. Social problem solving is a priority, and the practitioner helps the adolescent apply standard problem-solving techniques to social difficulties (i.e., by brainstorming, coming up with possible solutions, putting them into action and evaluating them). As with the previous model, these methods ideally should be tailored to the needs of each young person.

Summary of Key Intervention Elements for Internalizing Disorders of Childhood and Adolescence

Although every child's individual plan is unique, effective psychosocial treatment for anxiety and depression should include some combination of the following:

- Educate children about their own emotional processes (i.e., helping them identify, differentiate, and understand their feelings)

- Teach self-monitoring of feelings and link their feelings (including physiological and/or somatic sensations) to their anxious and depressive thoughts (i.e., anxious or depressive self-talk) or situational factors

- Help children identify, examine, and challenge distorted cognitions associated with their anxieties and/or depression; help them learn to make connections between situations, fears, depressive thoughts, and their behaviors

- If children suffer from low activity due to depression (perhaps combined with anxiety and fearful avoidance behavior), develop a step-by-step plan to increase their activity level

- Build hierarchies of children's fears, worries, and perceived sources of anxiety

- Teach relaxation skills (which have been shown to be helpful for both anxiety and depression), which are a key coping skill to be employed with covert and in vivo exposure and practice

- Use covert (imaginal) rehearsal skills to play out (in the imagination) how they can approach an anxiety-producing situation

- Help them develop an approach hierarchy; that is, break down their plan to confront a fear into small steps with a plan to confront each step one at a time

- Teach children SUDS so they can gauge their own level of anxiety as they approach fearful thoughts or situations covertly or in vivo

- Model the new behaviors they agree to try out

- Engage in role-playing activities that help children rehearse new behaviors and prepare to address problems in vivo

- Guide children in gradually confronting the feared situation in vivo (if feasible), and work gradually up the fear hierarchy when they have successfully conquered each step; successful efforts are likely to enhance their sense of mastery (self-efficacy) in the problematic situation and increase confidence that they can do it again successfully

- Gradually increase the level of challenge (based on the fear hierarchy developed earlier), and children should practice their new coping skills (relaxation, breathing, self-talk) on their own or with significant others (as the situation dictates) in homework assignments

- Help children enhance their problem-solving skills in troubling or challenging situations related to their anxiety or depression (i.e., brainstorming, considering possible solutions, testing out the strategy, evaluating it)

- Work with the family, teachers, coaches, and/or other collaterals to reinforce children's efforts to confront their fears and reduce feelings of helplessness or inadequacy

- Use family sessions when possible to identify interactional patterns and other family problems that may be contributing to the child's distress or potential progress or be inadvertently sabotaging progress

- Teach all collaterals to use contingency management (i.e., tangible rewards, giving or withdrawing) to reinforce children's gains; make sure all adults involved in the treatment plan are on the same page (i.e., understand the contingencies for rewards or sanctions); depending on children's progress and age, encourage them to gradually take over the control of some contingencies by developing their own self-evaluation and self-regulation skills

- Help collaterals avoid behaviors that may reinforce children's anxiety and depression

- Use case management skills to coordinate the intervention with key collaterals (e.g., teachers, coaches) to ensure continuity in delivering the intervention plan

Medications for Internalizing Disorders in Children and Adolescents

With the exception of using SSRIs to treat OCD (e.g., Castellanos, 1998), there is little research to support the use of antidepressants (tricyclic antidepressants [TCAs] and SSRIs) or antianxiety drugs for treating internalizing disorders in children and adolescents (Birmaher et al., 1996; Compton et al., 2002; Pine & Grun, 1998). Nevertheless, these drugs, particularly antidepressants, are commonly prescribed for young persons. The prescribing of TCAs or SSRIs in children carries similar side effects as in adults: dry mouth, constipation, drowsiness, hypertension, and mania, among others. Overdoses resulting in possible coma or death are of particular concern with antidepressants. At best, antidepressants and anxiolytics may be useful as adjunctive treatments when combined with cognitive-behavioral interventions (Axelson & Birmaher, 2001; Stock, Werry, & McClellan, 2001). Although benzodiazapines and TCAs have been shown to be of little use in treating childhood anxiety disorders, results from trials of SSRIs have been more positive for social anxiety disorder and generalized anxiety disorder (Brown et al., 2008).

TREATMENT PLANNING AND EVALUATION

CASE STUDY: AKUTI

Akuti, a 15-year-old girl of Indian descent, was found vomiting in her bedroom after having taken a handful of antidepressant medication pills prescribed to her by the family physician. Her mother, Karuna, had entered the apartment, attached to the motel that she and her husband, Joseph, managed together, just in time to hear her daughter getting sick.

She called 911, and Akuti was taken to the local emergency room. After a gastric lavage, she was kept overnight for observation and released in the morning. The nurse on duty had conducted a brief screening for suicidal intent, and she gave Karuna and Joseph a referral to the local mental health center so that Akuti could be treated for depression. The nurse did not see any imminent risk of suicide but advised them to monitor Akuti closely until she was more thoroughly assessed by a mental health clinician. She was kept out of school for a few days and helped around the motel office doing routine chores under the close eye of her disapproving but worried father. The nurse also suggested that the family consider going together to family therapy to address the young girl's extreme concern over "disappointing my parents," as Akuti had told the nurse.

MFS Assessment: Defining Problems and Goals

Akuti's father, Joseph, emigrated to the United States from southwestern Kerala, India, 20 years earlier. He met his wife, Karuna, while he managed a motel and she worked in a nearby fabric store. They later married with the consent of Karuna's parents, who had come to the United States years before. Karuna's mother was Muslim and her father Hindu. Her grandparents lived and died in Rajasthan, and they raised Akuti's own parents on terrifying stories of postindependence Hindu-Muslim violence. Joseph had been raised Catholic but as a boy was equally comfortable giving *puja* at the local Hindu temple with his grandfather in a small village in Kerala. His parents had remained in Kerala. As a boy, he went to a primary school run by Catholic nuns. He placed a high value on being able to read and write well (as most people in highly literate Kerala did) and demanded nothing but excellence and straight As from Akuti, who attended a local Catholic high school. Karuna was a bit more circumspect on the matter of grades and a young girl's need for a social life, but Joseph, having worked his way out of rural poverty in Kerala, was adamant that his daughter would achieve nothing less than excellence. He was determined that she would become a top professional, perhaps a doctor.

Harris, an outpatient family therapist with an MSW, met Akuti and her parents at the mental health center for their first visit. Joseph immediately expressed dismay that Harris was not a psychiatrist and did not even have a PhD. Harris explained that most family therapy was provided at the clinic by trained master-level social workers who had 2 years of internship, that he had many years of experience, and that he would work closely with the psychiatrist on staff to diagnose and assess Akuti for depression and suicide risk. Joseph seemed mollified. Harris asked if it would be OK to get some background information about Akuti and her parents. They agreed. Joseph took the lead and told Harris about his upbringing, where he was from, and why he wanted his daughter to succeed in this country. Harris told Joseph that he had spent time in Kerala after college on a Fulbright grant and had visited the tea plantations; Joseph quickly recounted he had worked there as a boy. Harris went on to say how he had also visited the lush Keralan backwaters and spent time in Fort Kochi. Joseph brightened up immediately and told Harris about his experience working in the hotels in Fort Kochi and how many conversations with Western businessmen got him thinking about emigrating and working in the US hospitality industry. Joseph seemed to warm up to the situation, but then started to apologize for his daughter for "causing all this upset."

Harris then asked Karuna about her background. She was raised by working-class parents in the United States who owned a fabric and tailor business. After they retired, Karuna worked for the people who bought their business. She had several Indian friends in their neighborhood and seemed more at ease with Akuti's situation. Her story reflected a greater degree of acculturation to American cultural norms than did Joseph's. Harris turned to Akuti to ask her why she thought she was here. Immediately, Akuti began to cry and explain, " I don't want to disappoint my parents. I can't get straight As; it's too hard for me. I have no friends. All I do is study, but I can't get all As no matter what I do."

Harris asked Karuna when she thought the problem began: "About a year ago, when she entered high school. It's a Catholic high school run by nuns and they start right off talking about college and college-prep courses, entrance exams, and so forth. They put a lot of pressure on the kids." Joseph interrupted: "And so they should. That's why we sent her there: to study hard. That's the only way you can get anywhere. Do you want her working in the motel business or cutting fabric for rich people all her life?"

Harris interrupted: "It seems clear to me that you both care very deeply for your daughter and want her to have a bright future. I understand that. If I ever have children, I would want the same. May I ask Akuti something?" Her father nodded his assent. "Akuti, what is it that is troubling you the most, and what do you want your parents to understand about your current sadness?" Akuti responded: "I know they want me to be the best student in the class, but I need to have friends! They won't even let me bring a friend over to our place!" Again, she began to sob.

At that point Harris suggested that, to conduct a thorough assessment, it would be helpful if he could meet with Akuti alone for a while, and then with just her parents, so everyone could have a chance to speak freely. They all agreed. When they were alone, Harris asked Akuti how she was feeling about all this. She wiped her eyes and echoed her mother's observation that it all seemed to start last year in high school. "I've met new people, I've tried to make new friends, but my parents—mostly my father—won't let me go out after school and hang out with some of the girls I know. There are also some boys, too, that hang out with us sometimes. I like one of them but would never say that at home. My father would kill me." Harris asked her if she meant that he would physically hurt her. "I don't think so, he never has, but he can be scary when he is angry," she replied. Harris asked her what her mother did: "She tries to talk to Daddy and calm him down, but he does not like to take orders from Mom."

Harris proceeded with a more formal MFS assessment by first examining signs and symptoms of depression and some of the anxiety symptoms she seemed to have over the previous year, as well as the events leading up to her recent overdose. From what Akuti told him, it appeared that her mother had become alarmed a few months earlier upon seeing that her daughter had become withdrawn, and joyless, and she heard her crying in her room a lot. The family physician had given her a prescription for antidepressants, and Joseph insisted that she stay on them until she got better and her grades improved. Akuti's condition did not improve significantly; her grades actually began to decline; and her father became increasingly agitated and angry about the situation, further pressuring Akuti and isolating her further from any social contacts. Karuna had become increasingly alarmed and started arguing with Joseph, which further convinced him that he needed to take a firm stand.

Harris's suicide assessment indicated that, although Akuti was still depressed, she seemed relieved to have someone outside the family to talk to and indicated that she did not really want to hurt herself, although she was still pessimistic about any positive change in her life. As the assessment continued, it became clear that Akuti was also very anxious, particularly about not getting top grades, but also about "fitting in" with friends. She did have one good friend, however, also of Indian descent. Her friend's parents gave her more liberty than did Akuti's, but she could relate to her situation somewhat. Akuti reported that she had never consumed an alcoholic beverage, although there was whiskey in the home, "Dad's favorite," and she had never used other drugs. There were no other indications of serious mood disturbances other than her depression, which seemed congruent with respect to her worries about school performance and her social isolation. She seemed desperate and did not know where to go or what to do. "I'm just trapped," she said. Harris assured her that he would do what he could to help her parents understand what she needs and hope they can come to some kind of agreement. But as part of the deal, Akuti had to be honest with him about how she felt and whether she had any more thoughts of harming herself. She agreed and they shook hands. "You have my phone number on the card I gave you. Use it if you think you need to. Now, I need to spend some time with your parents."

The interview with Karuna and Joseph focused on their relationship and background together, their work, and their experience as parents raising Akuti. Joseph saw his role as husband and father as somewhat patriarchal, and he was the "boss" with respect to running the motel. He worried a lot about the future of the business, since the parent company of the chain he worked for was going to be absorbed by an international hospitality corporation; he worried that they might "bring in their own people" and push him out of work. As Akuti had indicated, he also liked his whiskey. "Yes, I developed a taste for it while working in Kochi hotels. You know, India consumes more whiskey than any other country in the world! Even the United States!" he boasted. Joseph denied his drinking was a problem, although he admitted to getting drunk once or twice a week. Upon further assessment, between the stress of the business and drinking too much, Joseph admitted that it did affect his mood somewhat. "Sometimes I can get a bit irritable. I admit it. I can be impatient, I suppose." Joseph agreed to monitor his drinking and see if he might cut back somewhat. Harris assured him that many people drink too much sometimes. "That doesn't mean you have to give it up, necessarily, but let's keep an eye on it and talk some more about it later." Joseph agreed to take this measured approach.

Karuna echoed that Joseph was "the boss" at work and at home but that it was not a problem for her. "That's the way it is with my Indian friends too, but we know how to get around that sometimes," she laughed. Even Joseph chuckled a bit: "Yes, it's true. I can be a bully sometimes. That's the way I was brought up. My father was king. That was it. No one challenged him. We knew what hard times were like. I have always wanted better for Karuna, and she knows we both want a whole lot better for Akuti." Harris asked them: "How about your daughter? How does she see the two of you together?" Karuna answered: "She knows she is well loved, but I think Joseph is too tough on her. She is a teenager now, and she needs friends. There is too much pressure on her." Joseph sighed, his impatience showing. "So, enough talk, what are we going to do about this problem of ours?"

Selecting and Designing Interventions: Defining Strategies and Objectives

Initially, Harris decided to work individually with Akuti for further assessment and to provide her with some sense of autonomy in addressing some of her fears and pessimism. In addition to a more in-depth qualitative MFS assessment (see table 12.2), Harris had Akuti complete the Beck Depression Inventory to get a baseline for her level of depression. He was particularly concerned with her initial level of hopelessness, although even in the second meeting she seemed more at ease. Harris initially focused on providing some psychoeducation regarding depression; signs of suicidal intent; and how the disparity among her social needs, academic goals, and parents' expectations could have a profound negative effect on her self-appraisal and mood. Cognitive therapy was used to address Akuti's own distorted beliefs about her own social anxieties, beliefs that were somewhat exaggerated because of her limited exposure to peers. Harris assured her that he would work with her parents to find the right balance. She seemed to like having someone else in her corner.

Harris worked separately for a few visits with Akuti's parents as well to help them better understand, in general, the social needs of young teenage girls. Through nonverbal communication (so as to not overtly contradict her husband), Karuna seemed to implicitly understand Harris's point. Harris deftly appealed to Joseph's reluctance to loosen up on his daughter's very limited social time by providing his opinion: colleges and (perhaps later) medical schools are no longer just interested in good grades; they want to admit students who are socially well adjusted and can get along with others as well. This formulation seemed to get Joseph's attention and soften his position somewhat. "We can talk about that," he said.

A few sessions of couples therapy provided a forum for a more egalitarian style of communication between Joseph and Karuna. Harris was still careful not to suggest that Joseph did not have final veto power but helped them negotiate, in principle at least, some "time off" for friends and socializing. Joseph was adamant that Akuti first bring up her grades. Harris took a calculated risk and suggested that, perhaps, with some socialization time, Akuti might feel better, her spirits could lift, and her grades would improve. Harris made his case again: "Everybody needs some motivation. Perhaps if she knows that a couple of times per week she can be with a friend or two, she might work in a more focused way. Being depressed can really sap your energy and concentration. She is really unhappy now, and thinks, 'Why should I study so hard? What's the point?'" Karuna subtly nodded in agreement. Joseph looked over at her, looked down at his lap, then up at Harris. "You might have a point. You are very persuasive, Harris. OK. Let's give that a try. But if you're wrong, and her grades don't come back up, we'll have to rein her in again."

The next few sessions were conducted as a family. Everyone agreed to the plan and to do their part in using the monitoring tools they had developed with Harris. Over the weeks, Akuti visibly brightened up after spending more time with friends. Her anxiety diminished, and she was more at ease about her schoolwork, which began to improve. Joseph began to loosen his stance somewhat with Akuti, focused more on his business concerns, and was more willing leave the social issues to Karuna and Akuti.

CHAPTER SUMMARY

Many young persons suffer substantial psychosocial disruption when symptoms of anxiety and depression are serious and chronic. These problems often co-occur. A number of valid and practical scales are available to enhance assessment and evaluation protocol with children suffering internalizing disorders, and interventions for these conditions are reasonably well developed and effective. Interventions for more severe depression, however, lag behind. The key effective elements in treating these two disorders

TABLE 12.2   The Client Service Plan: Akuti and Her Family

Problems	Goals	Objectives (samples)	Interventions	Assessment and evaluation tools
Akuti: depression, crying, withdrawn, thoughts of hopelessness, potential suicide risk, anxiety regarding school performance, social anxiety and fitting in with peers	Reduce symptoms of depression; reduce and/or eliminate suicidal ideation	Work with Akuti on a weekly calendar and/or contract to map homework and social time with at least one peer for parental approval	Psychoeducation on depression, suicidal thoughts; cognitive therapy (address dysfunctional thoughts about parental expectations, distinguish her needs from their fears, address distortions about social fears and expectations)	BDI (Akuti); self-monitor stressors, mood disturbances, any suicidal thoughts Develop self-anchored anxiety scale (0–10) around school performance and social anxiety
Karuna and Joseph: parenting differences regarding Akuti's social activities with peers	Agree with parents on achievable academic goals; increase time for peer socialization with parents' approval; improve overall communication (calmer, less directive) between parents and between parents and Akuti	Have Akuti discuss her schoolwork with both parents present for 3–5 minutes per day; plan twice-weekly visits with her girlfriend; once during the week and half day on Saturday	Exposure: gradually increase social contacts with friends and peers Psychoeducation on depression and adolescent academic and social developmental needs	Use self-anchored agreement scale (0–10) on mutual collaboration on Akuti's academic and social goals Have Joseph monitor and record (0–10) level of work-related stress and use a 7-day diary to monitor alcohol consumption and mood
Joseph: work-related stressors; possible moderate alcohol abuse	Agreement on academic and socialization goals for Akuti Encourage Joseph to research parent company; connect with other motel chain managers for support Help Joseph monitor alcohol and make "adjustments" for health reasons; consider alternatives for stress reduction	Contact one other motel manager in chain per week to compare notes about company's future directions; monitor moods and alcohol consumption (in ounces) on weekly calendar grid	Emotion-focused couples therapy to help parents communicate more effectively about Akuti's needs and goals Brief intervention around alcohol abuse and co-occurring stress, anxiety, and mood disturbance; refer Joseph for a physical with his family doctor	

overlap considerably, and practitioners should develop eclectic treatment plans that address the unique needs of individual clients. Families and other participants in the child's life should be included in the treatment whenever feasible to provide consistency and follow-through. Practitioners who employ MFS assessment and evidence-based interventions for internalizing disorders can feel confident that many of their young clients will achieve meaningful and lasting relief from anxiety and depression.

CHAPTER 13

CONDUCT DISORDER AND ADHD IN
CHILDREN AND ADOLESCENTS

The externalizing disorders of conduct disorder (CD) and attention-deficit hyperactivity disorder (ADHD) are among the most common diagnoses applied to children and adolescents. As with internalizing disorders, the symptoms and problems associated with externalizing disorders often co-occur, and the skills of applying effective interventions with these disorders overlap considerably. Thus, it makes heuristic sense to address them both in this chapter. However, because there are also some distinguishing features of CD and ADHD with respect to assessment and intervention, they are addressed separately here, in a way that reflects the current literature. Assessment for externalizing disorders emphasizes a detailed functional assessment that employs data from multiple points of view. In addition to addressing behavioral problems across multiple settings (e.g., school, home, community), a comprehensive assessment of a child with ADHD also requires testing for learning disabilities and academic deficits. Intervention with both CD and ADHD emphasizes the use of some combination of cognitive-behavioral skills, behavioral family therapy, and contingency management. In contrast to internalizing disorders, medications for young persons with ADHD have been shown to be effective, although data suggest that behavioral interventions might be needed for the longer-term maintenance of gains.

ASSESSMENT OF CONDUCT DISORDER

Background Data

The DSM-5 (American Psychiatric Association, APA, 2013) mentions four main categories of behaviors indicative of conduct disorder: aggressive conduct that causes or threatens physical harm to other people or animals, behaviors that cause property damage (e.g., arson), deceitfulness and/or theft, and serious rule violations (e.g., stays out all night, truancy from school). These behaviors often result in difficulties in social, academic, and occupational functioning. Young persons who manifest these behaviors might also show a characteristic callousness, a lack of empathy regarding others' feelings, and a considerable lack of remorse concerning the effects of their own behaviors. These latter characteristics in children predict adult psychopathy (see chapter 10). Low frustration tolerance, temper outbursts, and risk taking are common features of CD, and they may be associated with lower academic achievement, precocious sexual activity, early use of drugs and alcohol, and higher suicide risk. Oppositional defiant disorder (ODD) (described in more detail later) is a likely precursor to CD, and it is characterized by chronic disobedient, uncooperative, and disruptive behavior. Burke, Waldman, and Lahey (2010) demonstrated with longitudinal data that ODD is predictive of CD.

Juvenile delinquency must be distinguished from conduct disorder. *Juvenile delinquency* is a general term that refers to the delinquent acts engaged in by young people. Juvenile delinquency is fairly common, and usually does not lead to arrest. However, a subgroup of children and adolescents who engage in criminal activities such as assault, robbery, animal cruelty, and rape, among other offenses, are more likely to fit the criteria for conduct disorder rather than juvenile delinquency. Conduct disorder and juvenile delinquency are mostly associated with males, although female juvenile delinquency and conduct disorder should be considered equally serious. After committing a few offenses, it is likely that juveniles are on their way to an enduring problem as an adult. Most offenses are committed by recidivists who started young and gradually came to engage in more severe antisocial acts. Long-term outcomes for chronic offenders are generally considered bleak (Moore & Arthur, 1989).

Prevalence rates for CD are estimated at between 2% and 9%, and between 6% and 10% for ODD, with boys outnumbering girls by a ratio of at least four to one. CD appears to account for about half of all referrals to mental health clinics for childhood problems. Older boys are more likely to be diagnosed with CD than with ODD, and CD shows good stability over time from childhood, through adolescence, and into adulthood as antisocial personality disorder (APA, 2013; Baum, 1989; McMahon & Estes, 1997). The co-occurrence rates of ODD and CD are between 84% and 96%, and half or more of children with CD are likely to meet criteria for ADHD as well. Children with CD also appear to manifest academic deficiencies, problems with interpersonal relationships, and cognitive and problem-solving deficiencies (e.g., overinterpreting hostility in others). Animal cruelty is a particularly telling sign of CD (Miller, 2001). Children with CD, including some with ADHD, are also at an increased risk of becoming antisocial adolescents and adults with co-occurring mental health and substance abuse problems (Baily, 1998; Disney, Elkins, McGue, & Iacono, 1999; Kazdin, 1997; Molina, Smith, & Pelham, 1999; Riggs, Baker, Mikulich, Young, & Crowley, 1995; Weinberg, Rohdert, Colliver, & Glantz, 1998; White, Xie, Thompson et al., 2001).

CD also appears to be a predictor of entry into gangs. Evidence for this association is supported by several studies, including a 6-year longitudinal survey (Lahey, Gordon, Loeber, Stouthamer-Loeber, & Farrington, 1999) that demonstrated that almost 25% of African American boys, from a sample of 347 children in first, fourth, and seventh grades, had entered a gang by age 19. Factors related to gang initiation included increased levels of CD symptoms before gang entry, having delinquent friends in early adolescence, lower family income, and lack of parental supervision. Juvenile offenders, in general, were also at a higher risk than others in their age group for contracting HIV because of both drug abuse and risky sexual behavior (Malow, McMahon, Cremer, Lewis, & Alferi, 1997).

Cultural factors may buffer or worsen the long-term outcomes for behaviorally disordered children and adolescents. For example, Coatsworth et al. (2002) conducted a 3-year longitudinal study with 150 low-income adolescent girls (aged 12–14) and their families from different Hispanic ethnic subgroups. They found family support to be a key factor in mitigating the occurrence of behavioral problems. However, peer conflicts and conflicts between family members and peer group predicted more externalizing problems. More research is needed that examines cultural risk and protective factors associated with CD and other behavioral disorders in youth.

Growing Evidence for Comorbidity in Conduct Disorder

Chen, Thrane, Whitbeck, Johnson, and Hoyt (2007) conducted a cross-sectional study using interviews with delinquent youth living on the street and found that those with earlier onset of conduct disorder were more likely to be delinquent in various ways (e.g., stealing, drugs), more likely to engage in sexual behaviors for money, and more likely to be sexually victimized and exposed to violent acts. A Finnish study demonstrated that among both boys and girls (aged 12–17) hospitalized with a psychiatric disorder, those diagnosed with conduct disorders and co-occurring alcohol use disorders were several times more likely (four times for girls and nine times for boys) to engage in both self-harming behaviors and suicide attempts than were those patients with CD alone (Ilomaki, Rasanen, Villo, Hakko, & Study 70 Workgroup, 2007). On the basis of longitudinal data from the Avon Longitudinal Study of Parents and Children (ALSPAC), Barker, Oliver, and Maughan (2010) showed that four problem areas that manifested early in a child's development (i.e., hyperactivity, emotional difficulties, peer relational problems, and antisocial behaviors) were more strongly predictive of later conduct disorders than when these problems came about later in childhood. One 40-year longitudinal Danish study showed that children with either conduct disorder or attention-deficit hyperactivity disorder were about six times as likely to be diagnosed with alcoholism at age 40. The combination of CD and ADHD was even more strongly predictive of later alcohol dependence (Knop et al., 2009). One literature review underscored the comorbidity of conduct disorder and substance use disorders, noting the growing evidence for common genetic, neurophysiological, familial, and environmental risk factors (Connor & Lochman, 2010).

Theories

Although it has been long established that children with CD are at an increased risk of becoming antisocial adults (Robins, 1966), most children with ODD or CD do *not* become antisocial adults. Risk factors associated with CD include genetic predisposition, history of family psychopathology (e.g., psychopathy, substance abuse, criminality, mood disorder, schizophrenia, ADHD), disruptive parenting, conflicted family relationships, childhood abuse and/or neglect, early difficulties with behavioral self-control, problems with social competence that result in peer rejection, academic difficulties, poverty, and exposure to community violence (APA, 2000; Cadoret & Cain, 1980; Connor & Lochman, 2010; Grilo, Sanislow, Fehon, Martino, & McGlashan, 1999; Horne, Glaser, & Calhoun, 1999; Kazdin, 1997; McMahon & Frick, 2005). Signs of CD in younger children generally lead to more negative outcomes in the long term than does delinquency that begins in early adolescence (Herbert, 1998). "Late starters" tend to decrease such behaviors as they grow into adulthood (McMahon & Estes, 1997).

Conduct-disordered young persons appear to experience major cognitive distortions and difficulties in social problem solving. They also lean toward more action-oriented and physically aggressive solutions to problems rather than talking things out (Herbert, 1998; Kendall, 1993). Fraser (1996) summarized the main points in emerging cognitive theories of aggression and antisocial behavior in children. These psychosocial processes take into consideration the child's innate arousal level (i.e., temperament) and the child's own social learning experience (e.g., observing violent parents or other models, witnessing substance abuse and associated negative consequences). These experiences can affect the development of skills to cognitively appraise another's behavior (e.g., inaccurate appraisal of social cues, such as seeing or exaggerating hostile intent when not present or not significant) and lead to failure to consider long-term consequences of aggressive action. In addition, children may fail to learn the interpersonal coping skills necessary to engage in problem solving as a preferred method of resolving interpersonal conflict. Children who live in a violent home, for example, may have learned that using force is an appropriate way to achieve their short-term gains. Environmental factors that influence the development of aggressive behavioral style and conduct disorder also include exposure to community violence, poverty, and drug abuse.

Key Elements of Multidimensional-Functional-Systems Assessment of ODD and CD

Conduct disorder is described in the DSM-5 (APA, 2013) as a repetitive and persistent pattern of behavior in which an adolescent violates the basic rights of others or major age-appropriate societal norms or rules, as indicated by the presence of three (or more) of the following criteria in the previous 12 months (with at least one of these criteria present in the previous 6 months):

- Shows aggression toward people and animals, and often bullies, threatens, or intimidates others
- Often initiates physical fights
- Has used a weapon that can cause serious physical harm to others (e.g., bat, brick, gun)
- Has been physically cruel to people
- Has been physically cruel to animals
- Has stolen while confronting a victim (e.g., mugging, extortion, armed robbery)
- Has forced someone into sexual activity
- Has destroyed property (e.g., deliberately set fire with the intent to cause serious damage, deliberately destroyed others' property)
- Has engaged in deceitfulness or theft (e.g., broken into someone else's house or car)
- Often lies to obtain goods or favors or to avoid obligations (i.e., "cons" others)
- Has stolen items of nontrivial value without confronting a victim (e.g., shoplifting without breaking and entering, forgery).

A young person who meets these criteria may also have engaged in serious violations of rules, often stays out at night despite parental prohibitions, has run away from home overnight at least twice (or once without returning for a lengthy period), and is often truant from school. For a diagnosis of CD, these disturbances in behavior must have caused clinically significant impairments in social, academic, or occupational functioning. Some of these behaviors are likely to have begun before age 13. Other diagnostic specifiers (e.g., limited prosocial emotions, lack of remorse or guilt) suggest a burgeoning tendency toward psychopathy. It is very likely that an older adolescent who has demonstrated several of these behaviors with some consistency will meet the criteria for antisocial personality disorder at age 18.

Oppositional defiant disorder (ODD) is a recurrent pattern of negativistic, defiant, disobedient, and hostile behavior toward authority figures that persists for at least 6 months; it is characterized by the frequent occurrence of at least four of the following behaviors: losing one's temper; arguing with adults; refusing to comply with authorities; deliberately annoying others; blaming others (not taking responsibility); being easily annoyed by others; and demonstrating anger, resentfulness, or vindictiveness (APA, 2013). The young person's behavior is particularly marked by being stubborn and unwilling to compromise, ignoring the directives of adult authorities, and failing to take responsibility for his or her actions. To meet diagnostic criteria, the behaviors must result in problems related to social, academic, or occupational functioning. Adolescents who manifest these behaviors are also likely to suffer from low self-esteem, may have a history of hyper-motor activity, may have poor tolerance for frustration, are more likely to abuse alcohol and other drugs, and are more likely to meet criteria for diagnosis of conduct disorder. As is CD, ODD is often accompanied by a history of having at least one parent with similar behavioral disorders, often with a substance abuse problem as well; disruptive parenting; and a history of harsh, abusive, or neglectful parenting.

Individualized multidimensional-functional-systems (MFS) assessment is necessary because of the heterogeneity of symptoms among children with behavioral disorders (Ashford, Sales, & Reid, 2001; Kazdin, 1997; McMahon & Frick, 2005). Multidimensional measures targeting the child's unique problems are also more useful than single indexes for measuring treatment outcomes. As with internalizing disorders, externalizing disorders in children have come to be better understood not as dichotomous conditions (i.e., diagnoses) but as multidimensional problems in which multiple developmental (e.g., abuse and neglect) and environmental causes (e.g., crime, neighborhood violence) influence the child's thoughts (e.g., negative, hostile cognitions), feelings (e.g., depression, anger), and behaviors (e.g., defiance, aggression). The children's psychosocial functioning is affected on every level to varying degrees of severity, and these problems are understood to interact in complex ways in family, school, and community environments (McMahon & Estes, 1997).

A functional analysis delineates the patterns and sequencing of the antecedents and consequences associated with conduct-disordered behaviors (Herbert, 1998). This functional analysis is conducted in the context of the child's expected achievement levels for cognitive, behavioral, physical, and social development (Rutter, 1997). Noting whether the child is an early or late starter with respect to behavioral symptoms may be critical for predicting a diagnosis, as are the severity and type of conduct problems (e.g., school-yard fighting vs. stealing or harming animals) (McMahon & Estes, 1997). Functional analysis helps target goals and objectives for an individually tailored treatment plan. Therapeutic goals are likely to include changing cognitive distortions and attributional processes regarding a generally hostile or aggressive approach to family and peers, as well as improving social and general problem-solving skills to reduce conflict and increase prosocial behaviors.

A thorough examination of family functioning is also essential, as some of the antecedents (proximate causes) and consequences of conduct problems are likely to manifest at home. Parenting skills (e.g., nurturance, disciplining methods) should receive careful scrutiny, as should the child's response to parents' behaviors. In addition, the couple relationship (if relevant) should be examined (see chapter 11), as well as the presence of substance abuse, domestic violence, and other conflicts (e.g., custody battles). Parenting skills, in particular, deserve careful scrutiny. Foster and Robin (1997) summarize key areas of concern regarding parent-adolescent conflict: repeated, predominantly verbal disputes; disagreements that fail to resolve problems; unpleasant, angry interactions; and pervasive negative feelings (e.g., anger, hopelessness, mistrust) about family relationships. Families prone to experiencing adolescent-parent conflict tend to have poor communications and problem-solving skills, cognitive distortions about family relations, and poor cooperation between parents and other dysfunctional coalitions among family members (e.g., triangulation, severe disengagement). During the family assessment, the practitioner should make an effort to forge a strong working alliance so that the challenging work of changing the behaviors of both parents and children can be undertaken successfully. In addition to parental competence and overall family functioning, the assessment should take into account the larger social system: the child's functioning in school and in the community, as well as any involvement with the criminal justice system (Baily, 1998).

The practitioner should make every effort to employ multiple data sources (e.g., parents, siblings, teachers, coaches, physicians, law enforcement) and multiple methods (e.g., interviewing alone and with the family, direct observation in different settings, self-monitoring, adjunct use of behavioral rating scales and other relevant instruments) (Franz & Gross, 1998). The child may also be an important informant, but the validity and usefulness of the data depend on several factors, including age, cognitive capacities, and capacity for truth telling. McMahon and Estes (1997) suggest that if a child is younger than 10 years old, self-report may not be factually reliable, but the practitioner can learn much through brief periods of play or informal exchanges about the child's cognitive and emotional state. With older children, practitioners can learn more from their point of view on home, school, friends, clubs, and so on, as well as from how they feel about their relationships with others and how they feel about themselves.

Instruments

The Revised Behavior Problem Checklist (RBPC) (Quay, 1983) is one of the most thoroughly researched and widely used scales for measuring problem behaviors in children and adolescents. Its 89 items cover a range of behavioral dimensions: conduct disorder, personality disorder, inadequacy and immaturity, psychotic behavior, and socialized or delinquent personality. Test-retest reliability has generally been shown to be adequate, and like the Child Behavior Check List (CBCL), the RBPC discriminates between treatment and nontreatment groups. It can be filled out by parents, teachers, or other adult caregivers. Norms are available for teacher ratings from kindergarten through grade 12, and mother ratings for children aged 5–16. However, one study of the RBPC demonstrated low interrater reliability among various informants (i.e., mental health professionals, special education teachers, classroom teachers) for all subscales (i.e., conduct disorder, socialized aggression, attention problems, anxiety, psychotic behavior, motor tension) (Cutchen & Simpson, 1993). Lack of congruence among different informants, however, is not uncommon in the use of rating scales, including the CBCL and the Shortform Assessment for Children (SAC) (noted in chapter 12).

The Eyberg Child Behavior Inventory (ECBI) (Eyberg & Robinson, 1983; Eyberg & Ross, 1978) was developed to assess conduct disorders in children from age 2 to 12. Thirty-six items are rated on a seven-point scale to measure both frequency of occurrence (intensity score) and a dichotomous score (yes or no) to indicate whether respondents consider the behavior a problem (i.e., problem score). The problem score ranges from 0 to 36, and the severity score ranges from 36 to 252. Normative data are available. There are (slightly different) parent and teacher versions used to rate children's disruptive behaviors, and the scale takes less than 10 minutes to complete. Several studies have shown good psychometric properties, including excellent internal consistency, good to excellent test-retest and interrater reliability, good discriminant validity by distinguishing referred from nonreferred children, and good factorial stability by race and gender (Burns & Patterson, 1990; Burns, Patterson, Nussbaum, & Parker, 1991). A more recent analysis of the ECBI's factor structure (Burns & Patterson, 2000) revealed three subscales that reliably measured symptoms of ODD, CD, and ADHD. The ECBI is a reliable, valid, and useful measure of these behaviors and a useful scale for measuring treatment progress and outcomes, but differential diagnoses for the disorders should be made with formal diagnostic criteria. The proprietary ECBI may not be suitable for older adolescents with CD, as item content is oriented toward younger children (Collett, Ohan, & Myers, 2003).

The New York Teacher Rating Scale (NYTRS) (Miller, Klein et al., 1995) is a very promising addition to the collection of scales available for measuring behavior disorders in youth. It is specifically designed to measure ODD and CD. The original scale consisted of 90 items gleaned from several existing scales (e.g., RBPC, Conners rating scales) and was administered by teachers to more than 1,300 children in grades 1–10 and a small sample of children diagnosed with CD. Exploratory factor analysis reduced the scale to 36 items measuring four main factors: defiance, physical aggression, delinquent aggression, and peer relations. Another factor comprised four additional conduct items, and a two-item factor measured global impairment. To add to the scale's utility, two composite scores are computed (see instrument 13.1): the Antisocial Behavior Scale (ABS) and the Disruptive Behavior Scale (DBS). Means and standard deviations published in Miller, Klein et al. (1995) serve as normative data, and because there were no differences by class year, scores

INSTRUMENT 13.1   New York Teacher Rating Scale (NYTRS)

Please rate the child on the items below, using the average child in a regular classroom as your basis for comparison. Rate the child's behavior over the <u>previous four weeks</u>. Please answer all questions. For each item, indicate the degree of the problem. Not at all = 0; Just a little = 1; Pretty much = 2; Very much = 3.

	Not at all	Just a little	Pretty much	Very much
1. Defiant	0	1	2	3
2. Angry	0	1	2	3
3. Argues, quarrels with teachers	0	1	2	3
4. Acts "smart" (impudent or sassy)	0	1	2	3
5. Spiteful, vindictive	0	1	2	3
6. Loses temper	0	1	2	3
7. Disobedient, difficult to control	0	1	2	3
8. Tries to dominate others; bullies, threatens	0	1	2	3
9. Easily annoyed by others	0	1	2	3
10. Blames others; denies own mistakes	0	1	2	3
11. Deliberately annoys others	0	1	2	3
12. Lies	0	1	2	3
13. Breaks school rules	0	1	2	3
14. Destroys or defaces property	0	1	2	3
15. Acts violently to other children or adults (hits, pushes, etc.)	0	1	2	3
16. Starts physical fights	0	1	2	3
17. Gets involved in physical fights with peers	0	1	2	3
18. Physically cruel	0	1	2	3
19. Assaults others	0	1	2	3
20. Carries a knife or other weapon	0	1	2	3
21. Has used a knife or other weapon, in a fight	0	1	2	3
22. Has mugged someone	0	1	2	3
23. Sexual misbehavior (not masturbation)	0	1	2	3
24. Steals on the sly	0	1	2	3
25. Shakes down others for money or other belongings	0	1	2	3
26. Late to school or class	0	1	2	3
27. Truants	0	1	2	3
28. Others like to play with him/her	0	1	2	3
29. Peers seek his/her company	0	1	2	3
30. Is liked by peers	0	1	2	3
31. Helpful to others	0	1	2	3
32. Has at least one good friend	0	1	2	3
33. Is considerate with friends/companions	0	1	2	3
34. Shows remorse when does something wrong	0	1	2	3
35. How much of a conduct problem is the child at this time?	0	1	2	3

36. How much of an academic problem does
    the child have at this time?   0   1   2   3

Scoring instructions

Defiance scale = (items 1+2+3+4+5+6+7+8+9+10+11+12+13+14)/14
Physical aggression scale = (items 15+16+17+18+19)/5
Delinquent aggression scale = (items 20+21+22+23)/4
Peer relations scale = (items 28+29+30+31+32+33+34)/7 (Note: higher score indicates better functioning.)

Composite scales

Antisocial behavior scale = (items 15+16+17+18+19+20+21+22+23+24+25+26+27)/13
Disruptive behavior scale = (items 1+2+3+4+5+6+7+8+9+10+11+12+13+14+15+16+17+18+19+20+21+22+23+24+25+26+27)/27

Mean scores for conduct-disordered sample from L. S. Miller et al., 1995: Defiance, 1.75; physical aggression scale, 1.17; delinquent aggression, .11; peer relations, 1.0; for composite scales: ABS, .67; DBS, 1.53.

---

do not have to be adjusted. Internal consistency ratings for all subscales were shown to be good to excellent, with moderate to good test-retest reliability. As with other scales cited, interrater agreements tend to be moderate at best. The NYTRS has demonstrated good convergent validity with the RBPC, and it accurately identifies young persons with CD. It has also shown good sensitivity to behavioral interventions and would serve well as an evaluation tool. A parent version of the scale is also available (Collett et al., 2003; Miller & Kamboukos, 2000; Miller-Brotman, 2003).

SELECTING EFFECTIVE INTERVENTIONS

Several somewhat-overlapping interventions, often used in combination, have been shown to be effective with young people with CD. These include cognitive-behavioral therapy (CBT) (implemented individually and in family therapy), behaviorally oriented parenting skills, contingency management approaches, behavioral family therapy, and multisystemic approaches. Substance abuse in behaviorally disordered young people is a common co-occurring problem, and it is understood that these approaches are also suited for effectively addressing substance abuse. However, substance abuse in young people often presents as the primary problem (often not comorbid with conduct disorder). Therefore, interventions designed primarily for substance abuse by young people are addressed in chapter 16.

Cognitive-behavioral therapy, behavioral family therapy, and multisystemic approaches have accumulated a growing body of evidence as first-line treatments for ODD and CD, as well as comorbid conditions such as ADHD (Brown et al., 2008; Corcoran, 2008; Henggeler, Schoenwald, Borduin,

Rowland, & Cunningham, 2009; Sexton, 2011). Brestan and Eyberg (1998) reviewed the intervention literature for 82 studies involving 5,272 children and adolescents with conduct problems using Chambless and Hollon's (1998) methodological criteria to rate studies as "established" effective treatments or "probably efficacious." More than 50% of the studies reviewed included at least one comparison group, random assignment to groups, reliable measures, at least 12 or more participants in each group, and reports of the number of dropouts. Fewer than half of the studies reported using a treatment manual; conducted 6-month follow-ups; or reported descriptive statistics for participants' gender, race/ethnicity, and other factors. Those interventions deemed "established" had to meet the following criteria: positive results had to be demonstrated in at least two controlled studies in which treatment manuals were employed, and the replication study had to be conducted by researchers other than those who conducted the original controlled trial. "Probably efficacious" interventions were those that were demonstrated to be effective by at least two controlled studies, but the same (original) research team could have conducted the replication. Brestan and Eyberg (1998) concluded that only behaviorally oriented parent training programs could be considered "established" treatments. "Probably efficacious" interventions included an array of cognitive-behavioral skill-oriented approaches (e.g., anger control, problem-solving therapy) and multisystemic interventions. They suggested that future research include more girls with conduct disorders and increase research with racial/ethnic minority families and their children.

Farmer, Compton, Burns, and Robertson (2002) came to very similar conclusions in a 15-year review of interventions for children aged 6–12: their data show consistent positive outcomes for cognitive-behavioral and family-oriented treatments. They added that combining child-focused and family approaches may have discernible advantages. With regard to a larger community psychosocial focus, multisystemic approaches clearly garnered the preponderance of evidence for effectiveness with emotionally and behaviorally disordered adolescents, although more research is needed with younger children and adolescents. Gacono, Nieberding, Owen, Rubel, and Bodholdt (2001) echoed these conclusions in a 10-year review of the literature: behaviorally oriented individual and family approaches (particularly multisystemic therapy, or MST) appeared to be most effective for conduct-disordered youth. Serin and Preston (2001) recommended that the interventions be modified, tested, and implemented with adult offenders.

On the basis of a comprehensive review of 9 meta-analyses and 23 literature reviews spanning 50 years, Palmer (1996) concluded that confrontation (e.g., scared straight), traditional social casework, counseling, and psychodynamically oriented therapies showed very little evidence of effectiveness (i.e., reduction in recidivism). Programs that showed mixed results included diversionary programs (e.g., combination of case management, job program, and counseling), physical challenge programs (e.g., Outward Bound), restitution, vocational and educational training, and enhanced probation and parole monitoring. Overall, these "mixed" results showed only modest reductions in recidivism overall. Programs judged to be successful were predominantly behaviorally oriented approaches that included family interventions, contingency management, and other life-skills approaches. Multidimensional and ecologically valid strategies such as MST (Henggeler et al., 1998) provide a comprehensive framework for guiding effective eclectic interventions, and these approaches have also been applied to prevention programs for high-risk youth (Blechman & Vryan, 2000; Liddle & Hogue, 2000). However, despite the advances made in treatments for juvenile offenders, one area still has not been adequately addressed in outcome research: juvenile sex offenders. About 20% of sex offenses are committed by juveniles, and offenders are often diagnosed with co-occurring CD and ADHD (Bourke & Donohue, 1996). Nevertheless, evaluation research on the effectiveness of treatment programs for juvenile sex offenders has been largely descriptive in nature, and thus provides a poor basis for making treatment recommendations (Becker & Johnson, 2001).

Individual and Family Applications of Cognitive-Behavioral Therapies

Cognitive-behavioral therapy goals emphasize helping youths improve their abilities to signal their arousal state, accurately label their feelings, use self-inhibitory messages, slow down their responses, and better recognize hostile or nonhostile social cues. These approaches can be employed individually, but they have been incorporated more frequently into family approaches. The social worker plays an active role in modeling proper self-assessment and social responses and improving the young person's ability to empathize with others (Kendall, 1993; Webster-Stratton & Herbert, 1994). Cognitive-behavioral programs that emphasize problem solving, parent behavioral management training, and the effective use of contingency management skills (e.g., learning to provide nurturance, using rewards and sanctions more effectively) have been successful in helping aggressive and antisocial children (e.g., Corcoran, 2008; Fraser, Day, Galinsky, Hodges, & Smokowski, 2004; Kazdin, Bass, Siegel, & Thomas, 1989; Webster-Stratton & Herbert, 1994; Webster-Stratton, Hollinsworth, & Kolpacoff, 1989; Webster-Stratton, Kolpacoff, & Hollinsworth, 1988). Reviews of psychosocial interventions have outlined a well-established range of cognitive-behavioral methods for alleviating psychological and situational distress with children, adolescents, and their families (Alexander, Holtzworth-Munroe, & Jameson, 1994; Alexander & Parsons, 1982; Corcoran, 2008; Kazdin, 1994b; Kendall, 1993; Mann & Borduin, 1991; Ollendick & King, 1994a; Webster-Stratton & Herbert, 1994). Some research has demonstrated that successful interventions with children with conduct problems also improve the mental health of mothers (Hutchings, Appelton, Smith, Lane, & Nash, 2002).

Cognitive-behavioral coping skills have been successfully implemented in the context of behavioral family therapy (Alexander & Parsons, 1982; Alexander, Waldron, Newberry, & Liddle, 1988; Baily, 1998; Foster, 1994; Kazdin, 1994b, 1997; McMahon & Forehand, 1984; Northey, Wells, Silverman, & Bailey, 2003; Webster-Stratton & Herbert, 1994). These methods include helping parents to identify, relabel, and monitor child or adolescent problems, and to negotiate behavioral contracts with the child or adolescent. Psychoeducation is provided to help parents learn normative expectations for their child's behavior and to develop more effective parenting skills. Therapeutic methods employed to this end include role-playing and modeling effective nurturing and disciplining behavior, as well as effective parent-child communication, problem solving, and generalization of skills across different situations. A randomized study in Britain of parent training for at-risk children, based on the Webster-Stratton model (Webster-Stratton & Herbert, 1994), has shown significant benefits in terms of reducing child disruptive behavior and reducing stress and depression in young parents, with solid maintenance of gains in the experimental treatment group over 18 months (Bywater et al., 2009; Hutchings et al., 2007).

Behavioral and Structural Family Therapy

Literature reviews have consistently demonstrated that structural or behaviorally oriented family therapies are the most effective for improving children's conduct problems and generalizing those benefits to the family system (Alexander et al., 1994; Alexander & Parsons, 1982; Geismar & Wood, 1986; Gurman, Kniskern, & Pinsof, 1986; Hazelrigg, Cooper, & Borduin, 1987; Kazdin, 1997; Lebow & Gurman, 1995). Estrada and Pinsoff (1995) found uniformly robust results in support of parent management training for improving long-term gains in children's behavior, parents' skills, and parents' positive perceptions of their children. However, clients who experienced greater social and economic disruption in their lives were not helped as much by these interventions, a problem that may underscore the limitations of even the most effective psychosocial interventions (Chamberlain & Rosicky, 1995; Kazdin, 1997).

Multisystemic and Other Comprehensive Approaches

Combining CBT with long-term family and systemic supports in the community (e.g., schools and juvenile justice systems) has been strongly endorsed over the years (Bramblett, Wodarski, & Thyer, 1991; Christophersen & Finney, 1999; Harnish, Tolan, & Guerra, 1996; Horne et al., 1999). Multisystemic therapy, perhaps the most effective and best-defined comprehensive approach for conduct-disordered youth, combines individual CBT methods, behavioral family therapy, and community supports with contingency management strategies. MST has been shown to be effective in improving family functioning, as well as reducing psychiatric symptoms and recidivism in chronic juvenile offenders (Borduin, Henggeler, Blaske, & Stein, 1990; Borduin et al., 1995; Bourke & Donohue, 1996; Henggeler, Melton, & Smith, 1992; Henggeler, Melton, Smith, Schoenwald, & Hanley, 1993; Henggeler et al., 1986; Henggeler & Sheidow, 2003; Henggeler et al., 1998). MST has also shown positive gains for youth with co-occurring behavioral and substance use disorders (Henggeler et al., 2009).

Testing a similar comprehensive approach with low-income, at-risk youth using a quasi-experimental design, Mann and Reynolds (2006) demonstrated modest but significant gains 15 years after prevention efforts to reduce delinquency. The authors stated that family, social support, and school factors showed independent predictive value for lowering delinquency. The program included comprehensive services, including half-day and full-day preschool programming; parental participation at school; community outreach services; and physical, medical, and nutritional services over 6 years up to age 9.

Exemplar Outcome Study: MST with Juvenile Offenders

In their review of the literature, Borduin et al. (1995) pointed out that controlled studies of serious juvenile offenders have been relatively neglected. Although behavioral skills approaches have been shown to be promising, long-term results have not been impressive. Long-term maintenance of gains is likely to require more extensive intervention with social systems that go beyond the individual offender and his or her immediate family. Such strategies, such as MST, include the school, community, criminal justice, and other systems that can have an impact on the lives of these young persons. Their study was designed to have advantages over previous studies of MST by including a larger sample size, longer follow-up measures, improved measurement tools, and comparable treatment groups receiving about equal amounts of intervention. In the current study, the authors randomly assigned 176 clients (from an original consecutive referral group of 200) to either MST or an eclectic individual therapy (a loosely defined psychodynamic, client-centered, and supportive approach). The juvenile offender participants had at least one parent included in the study (mostly mothers), were 70% white and 30% black, had been arrested about four times on average for serious crimes, and were mostly of low socioeconomic status. All participants were voluntary but remained under the jurisdiction of the court during treatment. Of participants, 140 completed treatment (with no significant differences between the two groups on completion rates), and the MST group had an average of about 24 visits, whereas the individual eclectic intervention lasted almost 29 visits, a statistically significant advantage. MST was provided by graduate-level practitioners who were trained and supervised in the approach by the first author, and the individual eclectic control group received services from practicing clinicians in local mental health agencies. In the MST condition, all clients received interventions that involved more than one social system, whereas 90% of those who received individual treatment received only the individual therapy. Most assessments were conducted in the home for both treatment conditions, and both pre and post measures included an array of well-validated psychosocial measures, including the Symptom Check List (SCL-90), the RBPC, the Family Adaptability and Cohesion Evaluation Scales (FACES-II), and an array of observational measures, including videotapes of family interactions and checklists completed by the juvenile's teachers. State police records provided 4-year follow-up data on arrests.

Results demonstrated that, compared to the control group, MST significantly and substantively reduced key family correlates of antisocial behavior in the participants, improved psychosocial adjustment in family members, improved family relations, improved parents' psychological well-being, improved youth behavior, and resulted in substantially reduced rearrests after treatment. The success of MST did not vary by participant demographics (e.g., age, gender, race, income). The authors attributed the success of the model to its comprehensive nature and ecological validity. Those who received individual therapy were arrested more than twice as often and for more serious crimes than were those who received MST.

Reducing aggressive behavior is also a primary target of concern among those who work in residential settings such as group homes or psychiatric hospital programs. Behavioral approaches using contingency management have also been shown to be helpful in those circumstances as well. Wong (1999), for example, conducted an uncontrolled evaluation of a behavioral program in an inpatient multiservice treatment program with adolescents who had histories of severe emotional disturbance and violent behavior, three of whom had been adjudicated on homicide charges. These youths (10 females, 19 males) were on average age 15; were generally of below-average intelligence; and had a mixed assortment of diagnoses, including conduct disorder, ADHD, major depression, and bipolar disorder, among others. They also had numerous prior interventions. The behavioral intervention included structured teaching of prosocial interpersonal behaviors (i.e., engaging the youth; identifying the problem behavior; providing a rationale; demonstrating proper behavior to the youth—who would then practice the behavior; and providing corrective feedback and rewards as needed); a reinforcement system by which clients could earn points to obtain small privileges (e.g., snacks, music, magazines); a privilege system for improved performance and responsibility (e.g., gaining off-site passes for better behavior and school performance); the use of minimally to moderately restrictive interventions for aggressive behavior (e.g., from verbal prompts to restraints for out-of-control aggression); implementation of an increasingly enriched daily schedule (e.g., movies, sporting events); and weekly community meetings. The findings demonstrated gradual and significant reductions in the most severe problem behaviors. Because of the uncontrolled nature of the design, though, the relative effectiveness of the behavioral program cannot be judged, nor can specific effective elements of the program be identified. Nevertheless, the study serves as a good model for implementing behavioral skills interventions in a residential setting with some of the most severely disturbed aggressive youth.

Key Elements of Effective Practices with Conduct-Disordered Youth

Many practitioner-researchers have contributed to evidence-based practices with conduct-disordered children and their families. These approaches, for the most part, share common theoretical and practice elements, and they have been incorporated and integrated into multiple-level intervention strategies that are likely to include methods for addressing the child's individual behavior, the parent's skills, family functioning and well-being, and the broader system within which the child or adolescent's behavior has become a source of distress (e.g., school, community).

Kendall (1993), Kazdin (1994b), and others (e.g., Kazdin & Weisz, 1998) contributed much of the research on individual CBT approaches for children with CD, and Hanf (1970), Forehand and McMahon (1981), Webster-Stratton and Herbert (1994), and Patterson (1982) provided much of the foundation for parent management training and similar parenting-skills approaches that incorporate CBT skills. These methods are based on social cognitive and operant behavioral principles that stress the functional linkage between antecedent events, the child's behaviors, and subsequent reinforcement to increase prosocial behaviors and reduce negative or noncompliant behaviors. Parents learn about basic nurturing and effective limit setting through psychoeducation, modeling, and rehearsal with the practitioner (who provides verbal and/or videotaped feedback). The parent then practices these skills at home, monitors the results, and evaluates his or her performance in subsequent sessions. Webster-Stratton and colleagues (e.g., Webster-Stratton & Hancock, 1998) expanded these programs to incorporate additional communication and problem-solving techniques, marital therapy, stress management, and closer coordination with school personnel to maximize child and family well-being. In similar fashion, Henggeler et al. (1998) widened the scope of behavioral family systems approaches to include community reinforcement and contingency management with key collaterals in the schools and the criminal justice system. Because an adolescent's problems are often related to a host of factors, including family problems, association with antisocial peers, school difficulties, substance abuse, criminal acts, and a lack of community support factors, it is the basic premise of MST that these problems be addressed through a multiple-level intervention that is implemented in the youth's natural environment.

Practitioners should become familiar with available clinical texts and treatment manuals for these evidence-based interventions. However, the approaches share common elements and are frequently combined. Although Kazdin (1997) rightfully cautions against simply combining treatments with the expectation that they will yield superior effects, practitioners should learn these methods "by the book," but they should also be prepared to flexibly tailor intervention plan to the needs and circumstances of each child or adolescent and family. More research on matching eclectic models to problem type, severity, and other client characteristics is needed.

The following lists present the core elements of evidence-based practice with conduct-disordered youth:

CBT Skills

- Help the child more accurately read and interpret the behavior and feelings of others in social situations.
- Use Socratic questioning, clarification, gentle confrontation, and the testing out of dysfunctional cognitions.
- Teach self-instructional training, including self-talk to identify and track problem circumstances, and covertly reinforce behavioral self-control.
- Employ cognitive restructuring to help correct the child's distorted expectations and misappraisal of social situations, and replace those with prosocial cognitions.
- Through psychoeducation, modeling, role-play, and homework, help the child stop and think about his or her own immediate emotional reactions to social or other situational provocations in a more deliberate manner.
- Emphasize how to make self-statements about the problem, consider alternative responses, and engage in problem solving that will lead to solutions.
- Teach the child to self-monitor reactions and skills in social situations.
- Model cognitive processes by making prosocial verbal self-statements aloud in the presence of the child, help the child rehearse these skills by prompting with cues to practice the self-statements, and use modeling and role-play to rehearse the prosocial behaviors while delivering feedback and praise for successful use of skills.
- Help the child express feelings more effectively.
- Teach the child to control anger and related responses by early identification of anger-provoking cues and through use of constructive responses to avert aggressive encounters; reinforce the use of standard problem-solving skills in response to provocation.

- Teach the child covert desensitization so that the child can relax and visualize him- or herself identifying, processing, and responding to a potential problem situation in a prosocial manner.
- Model and role-play effective and assertive interpersonal skills.
- Guide in vivo desensitization procedures and assign homework for practicing the new skills in increasingly challenging social circumstances.
- Show the child how to reward him- or herself (self-reinforcement) for positive social responses and reductions in negative behaviors.
- Teach parents how to reinforce these skills at home.

Effective Parenting Skills

- Demonstrate nurturance (e.g., emotional and physical caring, playing) and positive disciplining skills (i.e., giving directives calmly through simple communications).
- Balance positive reinforcement for prosocial or constructive behaviors with proportionate sanctions or punishment as needed (e.g., losing points as part of contingency management contract, temporary loss of privileges).
- Use the following techniques to teach parents more effective child management:
  - Explain the rationale for the approach (e.g., using positive means to increase prosocial behaviors, reduce negative behaviors, and improve child-parent relationship).
  - Demonstrate the skills via role-playing.
  - Have parent(s) practice the skill as the therapist role-plays the child.
  - Explain the desired behavior to the child until the child demonstrates an understanding of it.
  - Have the child participate in role-plays to demonstrate the behavior.
  - Direct the parent to demonstrate the approach with the child (with coaching from practitioner) while the practitioner observes.
  - Allow the parent to practice without direct coaching.
  - Assign homework for the parent to practice skills at home, then review performance in the following session.
- Teach parents how to pinpoint problem behaviors and monitor them at home (e.g., recording compliance versus noncompliance).
- Teach parents how to shape the child's behavior by stringing together rewards and sanctions to increase the child's constructive and otherwise prosocial behaviors (parents likely need to be reminded that, at all times, their behavior must represent a model to their troubled child or adolescent).

- Teach parents how to monitor (or supervise) their children at all times, even when parents are away from home, such as knowing where their children are, what they are doing, whom they are with, and when they will return (children must be held accountable for these "mini-contracts").

- Demonstrate to parents how they can be flexible, particularly with older children, and practice problem-solving and negotiating strategies; help them understand that being an effective parent does not always mean "winning" every battle decisively.

- Assign specific homework tasks as the child's progress dictates.

- Direct parent management techniques toward improving the child's school behavior and performance if needed; arrange for regular communication between parent and teacher.

- Help parents design goals for their children that are achievable and specific. Adults (e.g., parents, teachers) involved in the treatment should be trained to apply praise and tangible rewards for prosocial behaviors.

Behavioral and Structural Family Therapy Skills

- Identify problem behaviors between family members, negotiate solutions, and improve positive interactions (particularly by reducing coercive interactions).

- Clarify roles in the family, alliances, and conflicted relationships.

- Demonstrate communication and problem-solving skills among all family members, and continually monitor and evaluate improvements.

- Provide couple interventions to improve communication and problem-solving (also on issues other than parenting differences).

- Facilitate the style, direction, and intensity of communications so they become increasingly constructive (e.g., one person speaks at a time, no interrupting, no global accusations, no name-calling).

- Negotiate straightforward contingency contracts to facilitate the couple relationship or parent management.

Broader Systems or Community-Based Contingency Management

- Engage in assertive case management as needed with social systems (e.g., schools, law enforcement, criminal justice) and arrange for other instrumental and social supports.

- Actively include teachers and other school personnel in the treatment plan to generalize and maintain prosocial behavioral improvements.

- Get all parties on the "same page" with regard to the contingency management plan: have a list of the problems and consistent responses (contingencies) for positive and negative behaviors; various participants in the intervention must stick to the contingency management plan (i.e., rewards and sanctions) so responses can be swift, fair, and consistent.

• Communicate often with collaterals to monitor intervention outcomes and make suitable adjustments in the treatment plan; coordinate the activities of teachers, physicians, law enforcement (e.g., juvenile probation), and the family; and keep all respective parties focused on the intervention goals for the child or adolescent (note that all parties should use the same performance ratings, such as child's behavioral goals, to consistently judge cross-situational progress; also, rewards and sanctions based on the child's behavior must be coordinated to prevent the youth from becoming confused or allowing him or her to play one person off another).

• Make arrangements for long-term follow-up, booster sessions, and other services to the extent that service policies and legal contingencies allow.

ASSESSMENT OF ATTENTION-DEFICIT HYPERACTIVITY DISORDER

Background Data

Attention-deficit hyperactivity disorder (ADHD), formerly categorized in the DSM-IV-TR (APA, 2000) under "attention-deficit and disruptive behavior disorders," is now classified in the DSM-5 as a neurodevelopmental disorder (APA, 2013). Nevertheless, the diagnostic category, well researched over the years, is relatively unchanged. ADHD is characterized by a constellation of cognitive and behavioral problems that cause dysfunction in social and academic roles. ADHD is marked by multiple symptoms of inattention, impulsive hyperactivity, or a combination of both. ADHD is highly comorbid with CD and ODD, which is why it is presented in this chapter. The child or adolescent with ADHD (it can also be diagnosed in adults) demonstrates several problems, such as lack of attention to tasks or sustaining attention for any length of time, lack of responsiveness to direct requests, trouble following through on chores or schoolwork, difficulty organizing tasks, avoidance of activities that require sustained mental effort, being disorganized and losing things necessary for completing tasks, being easily distracted by extraneous stimuli, and forgetfulness in daily activities. Hyperactivity and impulsivity problems are indicated by the child's excessive fidgeting with hands or feet, trouble staying seated, difficulty engaging quietly in leisure activities, and difficulty waiting his or turn, among others.

Situational factors also have a significant impact on the frequency and severity of symptoms associated with ADHD (Barkley, 1987). Other factors that may affect the child's performance include time of day, fatigue, amount of restraint required, level of extraneous stimulation in the environment, reinforcement schedule associated with the task, and presence or absence of adult supervision. Children with ADHD appear most challenged when persistence is required of them to perform the task or when they must exercise personal behavioral restraint. In addition to academic achievement, other problems associated with ADHD include intellectual difficulties, language development, anxiety, depression, problems with peers, and several physical problems (Barkley, 1997a).

Age also brings a different emphasis to ADHD symptoms. Children with ADHD are inclined to respond to the first thought that enters their mind, they do not sufficiently consider the effects of their behavior, and many find it difficult to delay gratification. The severity and frequency of these behaviors can vary over time in the same child. In addition to the impact on learning, speech, and language development, ADHD is also associated with problems related to sleep, emotional, interpersonal, and other behavioral problems (van der Krol, Oosterbaan, Weller, & Koning, 1998). Robin (1998a) notes that ADHD in adolescents may shed light on more serious problems related to conduct-disordered behaviors, including academic failure, serious behavioral problems in the family and community (e.g., poor communications, frequent outbursts and arguments, physical violence, noncompliance with parent expectations), and emotional disturbances (e.g., depression, sadness, low self-esteem possibly associated with constant frustration, repeated failures, not living up to others' expectations). Impulsivity in adolescents may also be associated with risk-taking behaviors that may make adolescents more prone to accidents and injuries. Robin (1998a) also notes other developmental and medical problems associated with ADHD, including other developmental delays and mild neurological deficits.

Estimates of ADHD in the population vary from 3% to 10% of children (APA, 2013; Pelham, Wheeler, & Chronis, 1998) and up to 5% or 6% of adults (APA, 2013; Spencer, Biederman, Wilens, & Faraone, 2002). One problem with current diagnostic criteria is the lack of available norms across different age groups, a condition that creates confusion in estimating prevalence and determining diagnosis. Estimates of the ratio of ADHD diagnosis of males and females range widely, from two to one to nine to one (APA, 2013; White, 1999). ADHD co-occurs with conduct disorders (van der Krol et al., 1998), bipolar disorder, substance abuse, and other learning disabilities (Spencer et al., 2002). ADHD symptoms also overlap with symptoms that characterize post-traumatic stress disorder (PTSD), which suggests the need for a comprehensive assessment to rule out traumatic events that may exacerbate problems that are characteristic of ADHD (Weinstein, Staffelbach, & Biaggio, 2000).

A childhood diagnosis of ADHD has a negative prognosis for future behavior problems (Pelham et al., 1998). Fischer, Barkley, Smallish, and Fletcher (2002) interviewed a group of young adults who had been diagnosed with ADHD as children. More than 90% of the original sample was located and interviewed (147 previously diagnosed with ADHD, 73 controls who had not). Although the follow-up data were based exclusively on self-reports, evidence strongly suggested that those who had been diagnosed with ADHD as children were much more likely to be diagnosed later with conduct disorder, a condition that also appeared to mediate a greater tendency to develop personality disorders (e.g., antisocial personality disorder, borderline personality disorder) as adults. The ADHD group appeared to be five times more likely to develop antisocial personality disorder than the control group.

There is a lack of research on the relationship among ADHD, race/ethnicity, and socioeconomic factors (Gingerich, Turnock, Litfin, & Rosen, 1998). Research is hampered by a lack of culturally sensitive norms, which has contributed to inaccurate estimations of rates of the disorder. However, some evidence suggests that ADHD is more likely to be diagnosed among African American youth, perhaps as a result of socioeconomic and other environmental stressors that may affect the cause and course of the disorder as well as access to effective treatment.

Theories on the Causes of ADHD

ADHD appears to be partly heredity, although an unstructured or chaotic environment can exacerbate symptoms (van der Krol et al., 1998). Genetics may explain about 75% of predisposition for the disorder, a rate higher than that of other disorders. Brain-imaging studies have demonstrated that areas of the brain that influence attention span are smaller and less active in persons with ADHD than in those without the disorder (Spencer et al., 2002). Other potential contributors to ADHD include parental psychopathology, low birth weight (possibly related to the mother's drinking or smoking during pregnancy), and in utero brain injuries. Although few research studies have focused on the links between personality traits and ADHD, some research suggests that children with ADHD are less aroused and more likely to seek external stimulation, even to the point of engaging in risky behaviors, than are children without ADHD (White, 1999). Persons with ADHD also appear to have lower inhibitory control and are more likely to suffer from anxiety disorders. Other research has suggested links between ADHD and creativity, but data show lower levels of conscientiousness, with a greater tendency toward behavioral disorders, including substance abuse. The link between temperament and ADHD (i.e., higher activity level, more distractibility and impulsivity) is well established. Longitudinal research on familial influences (including parental psychopathology) suggests that persons diagnosed with both ADHD and CD may be a distinct subtype from those with ADHD alone, although sorting out the relative influences of genetics and environmental influences is a challenge (Faraone, Biederman, Jetton, & Tsuang, 1997). Positive long-term outcomes, however, appear to be linked to higher levels of family cohesion, warmth, and support; higher socioeconomic status; and growing up in intact families with fewer children. The relationship among these biopsychosocial factors actually explains substantial amount of the variance when accounting for ADHD (White, 1999).

There have been advances in process theories of ADHD. Although previous theoretical work has addressed problems in behavioral inhibition and information processing in persons with ADHD, Barkley (1997a, 1997b) has offered a more unified and comprehensive approach to provide a sound theoretical foundation for further research. Poor behavioral inhibition related to neuropsychological dysfunction in the prefontal lobes of the brain is specified as the central deficiency in ADHD. In Barkley's model, behavioral inhibition (which is needed to regulate performance) is the central construct related to four other executive functions: working memory, self-regulation of affect, motivation and arousal, and internalization of speech and reconstitution (e.g., analysis and synthesis of behavior). The model assumes (1) that the capacity for behavioral inhibition develops before the other executive functions; (2) that the four executive functions developed at different times, have different trajectories, and are interactive; (3) that if the capacity for inhibition improves, then executive functions can improve (i.e., they are secondary to the primary role of inhibition); (4) that dysfunction in behavioral inhibition is primarily genetic in origin, but the social environment can affect its expression; and (5) that dysfunction in the four executive functions interacts reciprocally with deficits in the primary dysfunction in inhibition. The four executive functions regulate the relationship between cognitive information processing and behavioral performance (including sense of time and influence of the future over immediate consequences). The end result is a greater capacity for the individual to predict and control one's environment (and one's own behavior in it), and to optimize performance and outcomes. The optimal interaction of the executive functions permits more effective adaptive functioning in general. For the person with ADHD, there is serious disruption in these regulatory processes, as evidenced by core clinical symptoms described earlier.

Barkley (1997a, 1997b) has noted that the current descriptive clinical view does not consider an array of other cognitive deficits associated with the disorder. The purpose of the four main executive functions is to obtain better prediction and control over the individual's own behavior, more influence over the individual's environment, and ultimately better influence and prediction of future consequences. The difficulty in maintaining persistent attention appears to represent impairment in task-directed behavior, which is related to poor behavioral inhibition. This process results in the individual's difficulties in self-regulation. Distractibility in the child with ADHD appears to be related to difficulties in screening out interference: internal and external events that disrupt executive functions necessary for regulating self-control and persistence. The difficulty in completing tasks appears to be related to a lack of reinforcement and a tendency to go from one uncompleted task to the next. Thus, inattention is considered a secondary symptom of ADHD, the result of poor behavioral inhibition and difficulty in screening out interference. Future research on this model could be improved by the use of larger samples; an examination of gender differences, family history, and developmental factors; more consistency in defining ADHD; and more emphasis on the effects that these factors have on the performance deficits associated with ADHD.

Key Elements of MFS Assessment of ADHD

Diagnostic criteria (APA, 2013) for ADHD provide a choice of either multiple symptoms of inattention or multiple symptoms of hyperactivity or impulsivity. In either case, the child must exhibit six or more of the symptoms for at least 6 months. For inattention, these may include failure to pay close attention to schoolwork or making careless mistakes, difficulty sustaining attention in tasks or play, not listening when spoken to directly, showing poor follow-through or failing to finish chores or schoolwork, difficulty in organizing tasks, avoiding activities that involve sustained mental effort, often losing things necessary for completing tasks, being easily distracted by extraneous stimuli, and often being forgetful in daily activities. For hyperactivity-impulsivity, these may include the child often fidgeting with hands or feet, having trouble staying seated when expected, running around or climbing excessively when such behavior is not expected, having difficulty engaging quietly in leisure activities, often being "on the go" or driven as if by a motor, talking excessively, blurting out answers before questions are completed, having difficulty waiting his or her turn, and interrupting or intruding on others. Other necessary criteria include the existence of some symptoms prior to age 12; presence of the impairment in more than one setting; the symptoms must cause dysfunction in social, academic, or occupational roles; and the behaviors cannot be caused by other disorders (e.g., pervasive developmental disorder, anxiety disorder, PTSD). However, there are problems in applying DSM criteria across the board with children and adolescents (Robin, 1998a). Symptoms may manifest in different proportions in children versus older adolescents, and the criteria may result in accurate diagnosis of fewer girls with mild to moderate ADHD.

Because of the variability in the presentation of behaviors related to ADHD, MFS assessment is strongly recommended (AACAP, 1997a; Barkley, 1997a; Barkley & Edwards, 1998; Braswell & Bloomquist, 1991; Robin, 1998a, 1998b; Root & Resnick, 2003). Practitioners should include a careful diagnosis and assessment of academic performance and learning disabilities (with specialized testing and consultation). The assessment should also include the use of broad and narrow behavioral scales, input from multiple informants (e.g., parents, teachers), child interview, direct observation of the child, and a thorough medical examination to rule out any related physical problems (Barkley, 1997a). However, caution is in order with regard to the validity of much of the child's self-report. The child's behavior with the practitioner may not be a reliable indicator of their behavior in other circumstances, and diagnosis should never be made solely on the basis of the child interview. As part of the MFS assessment, the practitioner should pay careful attention to identifying co-occurring problems and disorders (e.g., effects of abuse, neglect or other trauma, substance abuse, anxiety disorders).

A careful functional assessment will help demonstrate any situational differences in the frequency and intensity of the child's or adolescent's behavioral problems over time. Identifying factors that precipitate an increase in problem behaviors and the situational factors that reinforce them can provide clues for effective intervention planning (Pfiffner & Barkley, 1998; Robin, 1998a, 1998b). A child who is well organized and demonstrates sustained attention and good comportment in school but is nervous, cannot follow through on homework assignments, or is behaviorally disruptive at home is less likely to have ADHD and more likely to be experiencing family problems—possibly psychological or physical abuse. Conversely, a child's behavior in school may suggest ADHD, but parents may see little evidence of distractibility or disruptive behavior in the home. Obtaining information from multiple informants across situations can highlight any inconsistencies and avoid premature diagnosis and unnecessary or incorrect treatment.

The MFS assessment should also include a thorough analysis of family functioning. Parents may tend to blame themselves for the child's difficulties, develop unrealistic expectations of the child, or have difficulty dealing with their anger and frustration with the child. Other parental difficulties that are likely to affect the child's behavior include unwittingly reinforcing the child's dysfunctional behavior or failing to reward the child for productive behavior. These patterns may be related to broader problems of parenting skill, including lack of effective disciplining techniques. Parental deficiencies in problem solving and communication may also interfere negatively with the intervention.

As with CD, developmental considerations should also inform the assessment of ADHD (Barkley, 1997a, 1997b; Robin, 1998a). Restlessness and inattention tend to occur in young children. By latency and early adolescence, however, other behavioral problems may begin to emerge, including difficulties with peers and conduct problems at home and in the community (e.g., excessive argumentativeness, aggressiveness). Older adolescents are at an increased risk of becoming involved in delinquent behavior and dropping out of school. If an adolescent continues to manifest signs of ADHD and co-occurring behavior disorders (e.g., CD), family conflicts are likely to increase. Young adults who express signs and symptoms related to ADHD may be at greater risk of other mental health difficulties (e.g., anxiety, depression), substance abuse, interpersonal problems, and occupational frustrations. These problems are likely to negatively affect youthful developmental processes, such as identity development, relationship building, and accomplishment of academic and occupational tasks.

Barkley and Edwards (1998) emphasize the importance of interviewing the parents and suggest that they can provide the most ecologically valid account of their child's behavior. The main purposes of the parent interview are to establish a good working rapport with the parents and child; provide parents with an opportunity to vent frustration regarding their attempts to cope with their child's difficulties; obtain information about the family, particularly the parents' and the child's behavior over time, as well as the child's health and academic history; assess the parents' psychological well-being, including the presence of other disorders, quality of the couple relationship, and the child's social functioning; and observe family interactions.

Because most children with ADHD have trouble with academic performance and classroom behavior, a detailed assessment of school performance is required. The assessment should target specific areas of concern regarding the student's behavior and academic performance; include a formal diagnostic evaluation, testing for ADHD and any related learning disabilities; initiate the development of an individual education plan (IEP); and arrange for special accommodations for the student to optimize learning and facilitate resolution of behavioral difficulties at school. The intervention plan should be specific regarding the goals for enhanced academic achievement. Regular reports on progress toward goals should pass from the school to the parents. The details of the student's plan may include procedures for taking notes in class, homework completion, test preparation, improved study habits, better time management, and environmental changes at home (e.g., time and place to study, better organization in study or homework space). Case management should facilitate regular communication among all parties to ensure consistency, thoroughness, and follow-through with the overall plan.

Because many children with ADHD are likely to experience specific learning difficulties and other academic deficiencies, specialized educational testing methods may be required to complete the assessment. Robin (1998a) points out that, in a practical sense, learning disabilities in the context of ADHD assessment refer to a significant discrepancy between scores on an IQ test (i.e., intellectual ability) and scores on academic achievement tests. The estimates of co-occurring learning disabilities and ADHD vary widely because of differences in definitions. Nevertheless, valid intelligence and achievements tests are available and routinely used by educational testing specialists. Social workers are likely to work with a school psychologist to coordinate the assessment and integrate data into a comprehensive report. The Wechsler Intelligence Scale for Children (WISC) may be used with standardized achievement tests that measure performance in verbal and written expression, mathematical reasoning, spelling, and other core academic performance domains. The Continuous Performance Test (CPT) should be used in conjunction with other assessment data. It may also be used to monitor medication response. According to Root and Resnick (2003), the CPT provides important information, including the child's ability to sustain attention and inhibit impulsivity, flexibility in thinking and reasoning, ability to shift attention, and ability to perform tasks continuously. The CPT "is designed to be extremely boring. It requires the child to perform a repetitive activity (waiting for specific letter or geometric shape to appear on a computer screen) in a sequence of presentations that lasts for 10 to 20 minutes. The CPT measures a specific aspect of sustained attention (the ability to attend and respond to a stimulus in a boring, repetitive activity)" (Swanson, 1992, p. 76; for a review, see O'Laughlin & Murphy, 2000). A poor performance on the CPT may suggest, but does not confirm, an ADHD diagnosis. Additional testing may be required to rule out other learning disabilities.

On the basis of data gleaned from diagnosis, educational and intelligence testing, classroom observation, and CPTs, children may be eligible for specialized services that would provide them with remedial assistance and other accommodations, such as modifications to their schedules, alternative homework assignments and methods of classroom testing, special tutoring, and other adjustments. These accommodations can improve both their learning experience and their academic performance.

Instruments for the Assessment of ADHD

Given the heterogeneity of symptoms and co-occurring problems associated with ADHD, the use of both broad (e.g., CBCL, SAC) and narrow scales is recommended. The CBCL subscale for measuring ADHD symptoms (Chen, Faraone, Biederman, & Tsuang, 1994) and the Child Attention Profile (Barkley, 1995), which includes items from the CBCL (teacher-report version) and items from the revised Conners (1997) rating scales, are considered among the most valid measures. Both parent and teacher versions of the Conners scale are available in short and long forms. Internal consistency measures are good to excellent for the Conners subscales, and the scale distinguishes children with and without the disorder. A large normative database has been developed for the Conners subscales for different age ranges, and it appears to be sensitive to change in symptom levels (Collett et al., 2003).

The Swanson, Nolan, and Pelham IV questionnaire (SNAP-IV) is based on DSM-IV criteria for ADHD diagnosis, is similar to other ADHD scales, and has been widely used in ADHD treatment research (Collett et al., 2003; Swanson, 1992). The short version of the scale focuses on ADHD and ODD symptoms. Longer versions of the scale cover a broader range of symptoms and behaviors. Although few psychometric studies have been conducted on the SNAP-IV, it has been used extensively in clinical research including the multisite Multi-Modal Treatment Study (MTA) (reviewed later here), it has been shown to have good to excellent internal consistency, and it is sensitive to client changes in treatment (for a review, see Collett et al., 2003).

The SNAP-IV, however, tends to overestimate the number of children in the general population with ADHD (Swanson et al., 2002). To correct this problem, a revised scale was developed that rates each item on a seven-point scale (from –3 to 0 to 3), from "far below average" to "far above average." The revised SNAP-IV—the Strengths and Weakness of ADHD Symptoms and Normal Behavior Scale (SWAN) (Swanson et al., 2002)—demonstrates improved distributional and structural characteristics, and it is considered a reliable, valid, brief, and easy-to-use instrument that complements assessment and evaluation with children suspected of having ADHD. The SWAN (extended version) and related materials are readily available for no charge online (www.adhd.net). The brief SWAN Rating Scale is presented here as instrument 13.2.

INSTRUMENT 13.2   Strengths and Weakness of ADHD Symptoms and
Normal Behavior Scale (SWAN)

Children differ in their abilities to focus attention, control activity, and inhibit impulses. For each item listed below, how does this child compare to other children of the same age? Please select the best rating based on your observations over the past month. Compared to other children, how does this child do the following:

	Far below	Below	Slightly below	Average	Slightly above	Above	Far above
1. Give close attention to detail and avoid careless mistakes							
2. Sustain attention on tasks or play activities							
3. Listen when spoken to directly							
4. Follow through on instructions and finish schoolwork/chores							
5. Organize tasks and activities							
6. Engage in tasks that require sustained mental effort							
7. Keep track of things necessary for activities							
8. Ignore extraneous stimuli							
9. Remember daily activities							
10. Sit still (control movement of hands/ feet or control squirming)							
11. Stay seated (when required by class rules/ social conventions)							
12. Modulate motor activity (inhibit inappropriate running/climbing)							
13. Play quietly (keep noise level reasonable)							

14. Settle down and rest
    (control constant activity)   ___ ___ ___ ___ ___ ___ ___

15. Modulate verbal activity
    (control excess talking)   ___ ___ ___ ___ ___ ___ ___

16. Reflect on questions
    (control blurting out answers)   ___ ___ ___ ___ ___ ___ ___

17. Await turn (stand in line and take turns)   ___ ___ ___ ___ ___ ___ ___

18. Enter into conversations and games
    (control interrupting/intruding)   ___ ___ ___ ___ ___ ___ ___

The seven-point response is scored +3 to –3 accordingly: far below average = +3, below average = +2, slightly below average = +1, average = 0, slightly above average = –1, above average = –2, far above average = –3. Subscale scores on the SWAN are calculated by summing the scores on the items in the specific subset (ADHD-Inattention and ADHD-Hyperactivity/Impulsivity), and by dividing by the number of items in each subscale to express the summary score as the average rating for all items in the subscale. Use the scorecard below to calculate each subscale. The average scores have been designed to reflect population norms. Scores "above or far above" average may indicate a problem in that area. Diagnosis is not confirmed by these scores, which give a relative measure of performance in each area (i.e., Inattention and Hyperactivity/Impulsivity). Changes in scores that increase over time would indicate a greater problem; scores that decrease would indicate improvement.

	ADHD-Inattention	**ADHD-Hyperactivity/Impulsivity**
	1___	10___
	2___	11___
	3___	12___
	4___	13___
	5___	14___
	6___	15___
	7___	16___
	8___	17___
	9___	18___
Total score =	___	___
Average =	___	___

SELECTING EFFECTIVE INTERVENTIONS

There currently is a good deal of consensus in the outcome literature that ADHD is optimally treated with psychostimulant medication combined with individual, family, and classroom-based behavioral interventions. Specifically, effective psychosocial interventions include cognitive-behavioral skills, for the child to engender better self-regulatory skills (e.g., anxiety management, better organization, staying on task, controlling disruptive or aggressive behaviors), behavioral family therapy (e.g., psychoeducation, family communication and problem solving, parenting skills with contingency management), and classroom contingency management (Anastopoulos, 1998; Anastopoulos, Smith, & Wein, 1998; Barkley, 1995, 2002; Braswell & Bloomquist, 1991; Hinshaw, Klein, & Abikoff, 1998; Kazdin, 1994a; Kendall, 1993; Pelham et al.,

1998; Rapport, 1992; Root & Resnick, 2003). Although there is strong consensus on the use of behavioral family therapy and classroom-based contingency management, there is some mixed evidence on the necessity of the intervention including individual CBT coping skills (Kendall, 1993; Root & Resnick, 2003).

Farmer et al. (2002) identified more than 130 studies of treatment outcomes for ADHD in youths between the ages of 6 and 12. On the basis of 28 studies that met strict methodological criteria, they concluded that the most effective psychosocial interventions were cognitive-behavioral therapy (including social skills training), parent management training, and contingency management programs. Although effect sizes were fairly large, indicating clinically significant results, data demonstrating generalization and maintenance of gains were less impressive. The authors recommended more research on minority children (who are very underrepresented in the research overall), more replication of studies, more follow-up data beyond 6 months, and more ecological validity in the studies.

Fabiano et al. (2009) conducted the most extensive meta-analysis (175 studies) to date of behavioral interventions for ADHD (which included high rates of comorbid CD), using both between- and within-group designs of treatments that included some combination of parent training, classroom management, and child-focused intervention. Results showed moderate to large effect sizes (especially for contingency management approaches) that could be attributed to the behavioral aspect of treatment (separate from medication), and the authors found little variance by gender, age, and other characteristics (i.e., good generalizability). Authors noted that their results are more representative of the larger literature as a whole, suggesting that, while not discounting the benefits of stimulant medication, behavioral interventions should be considered a first-line treatment.

Although various components of a multimodal approach to treating ADHD have shown moderate or larger effect sizes (Brown et al., 2008), including parent training, child skills training, classroom-based intervention, and medication, it is not clear that all students require or would benefit from a multimodal approach. In some cases medication has been shown to be sufficient, although a combined approach is more beneficial in many cases (Corcoran, 2008).

Illustrative controlled studies demonstrated both the efficacy of combined behavioral programs and their limitations when applied with more challenging populations. Barkley, Edwards, Laneri, Fletcher, and Meevia (2001) compared 18 sessions of problem-solving and communication intervention, behavior management training (9 sessions), and a combined intervention group (18 sessions) with adolescents diagnosed with both ADHD and ODD. At the treatment midpoint (9 weeks) and end point (18 weeks) there appeared to be some modest improvement overall. Outcome measures were mixed depending on who provided the behavioral ratings (mother, father, or adolescent). In addition, there was considerable attrition by the end of treatment, particularly for the problem-solving communication group (38%). In a randomized study of preschoolers identified as having high levels of aggression, hyperactivity, and other behavioral problems (Barkley et al., 2000), 158 students were randomly assigned to four conditions: parent training, classroom behavioral management, combined parent training and classroom management, and no treatment. Ratings included the CBCL as well as several standardized and well-validated behavioral and academic performance measures. Results showed that classroom behavioral management resulted in observable behavioral improvements in parent and teacher ratings. The module of parent training revealed no significant effects; results appeared to be largely due to high rates of attrition. When parent-training conditions were combined, 25% of all parents assigned to the program had attended 1–4 sessions; 29%, 5–8 sessions; and 13%, 9–14 sessions. However, those who did not attend the parenting sessions did not differ significantly on several variables from those who did attend at least one session. Although the contingency management procedures were shown to be effective in reducing hyperactive, impulsive, inattentive, and aggressive behaviors, the lack of response to the parent training was discouraging. These problems underscore the challenges of implementing such programs in typical school settings, where parents have not voluntarily sought treatment but where it has been offered to them because their children were screened as "high risk." A 2-year follow-up study revealed no lasting positive effects for the classroom behavioral management program (Shelton et al., 2000). Clearly, there is a need to improve long-term follow-up in the homes and classrooms of children and adolescents with CD and ADHD. In addition to effective skill-based interventions, families with greater psychosocial and financial challenges in their lives will need greater instrumental and social supports, as well as better links among parents, school, juvenile law enforcement, health-care, and other community resources (Webster-Stratton, 1997).

Families and Schools Together (FAST) is an example of a program that combines therapeutic techniques and community support for early intervention programs in low-income settings (McDonald et al., 1997, p. 153). The FAST program has been widely implemented in at least 26 states. Components of FAST include identifying at-risk children, sending paraprofessionals (e.g., FAST graduates) to parents' homes to exhort them to join FAST, and engaging in multifamily gatherings for eight sessions at the child's school. The gatherings follow a structured agenda of family activities, parental mutual support, parent-child play therapy, singing, sharing a meal, and other expressive activities. Incentives to attend the program include a free meal and transportation if needed. A formal graduation ritual is provided to enhance the status of being a FAST graduate. As graduates, participants may continue as members of FASTWORKS, a program of a series of monthly meetings intended to enhance social and family supports and maintain the social network. Over time FASTWORKS evolves into a self-generating, self-governing social support network, which is intended to enhance links among family, schools, and community. Uncontrolled outcome evaluation and testimonials provide only suggestive evidence for the effectiveness of these programs in improving child behavior, family functioning, and social supports.

Involving teachers in a multimodal approach appears to be a potent factor in enhancing treatment outcomes for young people with ADHD. Sherman, Rasmussen, and Baydala (2008) conducted a 40-year review of the literature on "teacher factors" that potentially affect outcomes of ADHD. They found compelling evidence that teacher involvement in the overall intervention approach was very important for successful outcomes (given the amount of time children spend in the classroom), and they found that being knowledgeable about ADHD, having a good level of acceptance of various treatments, having a positive approach to behavior management (i.e., less punitive), using hand gestures to assist in communicating lessons, and using daily report cards on selected students, all contributed to effective outcomes. They urged cooperative approaches between clinicians and teachers in treatment of ADHD and more research on collaborative interventions.

Exemplar Outcome Study: The Multi-Modal Treatment Study of Children with ADHD

The Multi-Modal Treatment Study of Children (MTA) project was the largest study of its kind on any childhood disorder. Its main purpose was to compare the relative efficacy of medication, home and school-based behavioral programs, and a summer program with children diagnosed with ADHD (Arnold et al., 1997; Richters et al., 1995). In response to the existing literature, which showed somewhat variable responses to stimulant medications and psychosocial interventions either alone or in combination, depending on client characteristics, a 5-year multisite multimodal investigation was conducted to address the following unanswered questions regarding the treatment of ADHD:

> Under what circumstances (co-morbid conditions, age, gender, family background) do which treatment combinations (medication, behavior therapy, parent training, school-based intervention) have what impacts (improvement, stasis, deterioration) on what domains of child functioning (cognitive, academic, behavioral, physical, peer relations, family relations), for how long (short term versus long term), to what extent (effect sizes, normal versus pathological range), and why (processes underlying change)? (Richters et al., 1995, p. 996)

Understanding the role of socioeconomic status and co-occurring disorders were also important goals of the study.

The MTA study was a randomized controlled trial of the treatment of more than 500 children (aged 7–9) with ADHD. It was conducted at six sites in the United States and Canada. Four treatment groups were developed for the study: (1) a community care (CC) control group of treatment as usual in local community mental health agencies (about 67% of those referred received medication); (2) a medication-only group (MED) that received 1 month of medication; (3) a behavioral intervention group (BEH) that received a three-part behavioral intervention of parent-training classes, an 8-week all-day summer training program, and school-based interventions that included consultation with the teacher, daily report cards, and help from a classroom aide; (4) and a combined behavioral intervention program (same as group 3) and medication group (COMB) (Root & Resnick, 2003).

The multivariate design called for a comprehensive multidimensional assessment battery at baseline, 3 months and 9 months, at 14 and 24-month end points (Arnold et al., 1997), which allowed for examination of the following variables and their relationship to treatment: severity of the disorder, role of co-occurring disorders, gender, socioeconomic status, race/ethnicity, parental psychopathology, domains of functioning on outcome, acceptability of treatment, and compliance with the intervention. Interventions selected for the study were based on the following criteria: state of the art, as demonstrated by evidence supporting at least short-term efficacy; manualized and conducive to implementation in real practice settings; and "sufficiently intense, integrated, and flexible to credibly stand alone" (Arnold et al., 1997, p. 867). Great effort was made to design programs that had high ecological validity and could be applied flexibly to accommodate the vagaries of practice in real-world settings with clients.

The design of the behavioral program module (BEH) reflected findings from existing outcome literature (Wells et al., 2000) and consisted of behavioral parent training, an 8-week all-day summer session for children, and a school-based contingency management intervention. The parent-training classes were implemented as a combination of group and individual sessions over the course of 27 weeks and included the skills reviewed here previously as well as introduction and overview, setting up school-home report cards, principles of learning and reinforcement, playing with and learning to reward children in a timely manner, giving effective commands, time-out procedures, token economy, stress or anger management (for parents), helping the child deal with peer relations, and several weeks of review and generalization of skills.

The school intervention included consultation with teachers and the 8-week summer-training program. The therapist-consultants who provided the parent training also served as teacher consultants, and paraprofessionals trained to support the classroom-based program served as counselors in the summer program. Therapist consultants met with teachers about 26 times.

During that time, they set up the daily report card that parents learned to use in the parent-training program, and they provided the link between parent (at home) and teacher (classroom). The teachers also learned basic behavior management skills to implement in the classroom (similar to the skills parents learned for home-based intervention), such as implementing and enforcing classroom rules, giving attention to positive behaviors, ignoring annoying negative behaviors, giving clear commands and soft reprimands, giving individualized instructional materials as needed, altering class structure, using reinforcement procedures such as token economies, and using time-out procedures.

The paraprofessionals received extensive training in behavior management techniques to help in the classroom and to serve as counselors in the summer program. Only two children were assigned to each paraprofessional counselor. Specific target behaviors were itemized for each child on the basis of consultation with the therapist-consultant. The paraprofessional's goal for each child was to shape and fade the child's behavior (i.e., to reduce prompting a behavior) so that the teacher and parent could increasingly concentrate on tasks evaluated on the daily report card (while simultaneously decreasing attention from the paraprofessional). The summer treatment program comprised an intensive group-oriented combination of both academic and recreational activities that filled the day from 8 a.m. to 5 p.m. Token economy and behavioral management methods were employed in a highly supportive atmosphere to improve behavioral and interpersonal performance. Well-established social skills training methods (i.e., instruction, role-play, modeling) were emphasized to improve peer relations. The program included a buddy system in which each child was paired with another child and had access to a "buddy coach" to help with work on relationship difficulties. The children were also taught group problem-solving skills when difficulties arose, and they received "sensitive" sports coaching. The daily report card was used during the summer program as well. This multicomponent behavioral module placed heavy emphasis on developing good alliances with parents and teachers and on establishing a "right" balance between adhering to the treatment model and being sufficiently flexible, to adapt interventions to the needs of individual children and their parents.

Root and Resnick (2003) summarized the results of this ambitious study. The combination of behavioral treatment and medication performed significantly better than behavioral treatment alone or treatment as usual in the community. At first look, the medication-only group and the COMB group appeared to be about equally successful. However, when Conners, Epstein, and March (2001) combined teacher and parent measures, the combination of medication and behavioral intervention revealed the best outcomes overall. Combining behavioral programs and psychostimulant medication may be advantageous when dealing with co-occurring problems associated with ADHD (e.g., conduct problems, depression, family problems, interpersonal difficulties), which psychostimulant medication alone may not optimally address.

More recent follow-up data on the MTA is also revealing. Taking into consideration real-world variation in treatment adherence over time, a 36-month follow-up to the MTA study (Jensen et al., 2007) showed that most subjects continued to improve over time. However, in contrast to the initial findings that the combination of medication management and behavioral interventions was, on the whole, the most effective approach, differences among different treatment components (e.g., medication, behavioral approaches) disappeared over time, thus calling into question the oft-claimed superiority of medication treatment. The authors suggested that the differences could be due to self-selection, or variability in stopping or restarting medication over time.

Descriptions of Effective Interventions

Although CBT skills alone do not appear robust enough to improve the behavior problems and academic performance of children with ADHD, they may add to the overall effectiveness of a comprehensive approach that includes home and school-based behavioral (contingency management) programs combined with medication. Many of the CBT skills reviewed in chapter 12 (for anxiety) (e.g., Kendall, 1994) and in this chapter for addressing ODD and CD may be useful for children and adolescents with ADHD. Cognitive-behavioral coping skills include verbal self-talk, self-monitoring and self-evaluation, cognitive modeling, problem solving, and other self-regulatory strategies. Braswell and Bloomquist (1991) and Van der Krol et al. (1998) suggest the use of combinations of the following skills: anxiety reduction to reduce stress and improve concentration; basic problem solving (i.e., define problem, develop a plan, anticipate obstacles, implement and evaluate the plan) to approach daily problems in a more organized, focused, and systematic manner; and environmental management (at home and at school) to reduce distractions and facilitate self-control, attention, and problem-solving. Parents should learn to coach their children in self-regulation skills at home and help them create an environment conducive to quiet concentration.

Parent training in contingency management methods has been shown to be very successful in reducing children's behavior problems and improving their academic performance, primarily in younger children with ADHD. In the clinic setting, parents are taught (e.g., through reading, direct instruction, modeling, role-play, videotapes) the basic effective parenting techniques that were examined in greater detail earlier in this chapter. Practitioners should consult with parents and teachers to coordinate home-based behavioral parenting skills with a complementary contingency management plan in the classroom. A consistent evaluation-feedback system should be set up among social worker, parent, and teacher to reinforce classroom performance through the use of daily report cards. More intensive contingency management approaches may be carried out in a specialized treatment facility or by specialists in a classroom setting. The key elements of effective psychosocial interventions for ADHD are as follows (Anastopoulos, 1998; Anastopoulos et al., 1998; Barkley, 2002):

- Psychoeducation is provided to teach parents about the causes, developmental course, and prognosis for ADHD. Books and videos can also be recommended or provided.

- The causes of oppositional or defiant behavior are explained. Parents learn to understand the systemic and interactional nature of behavioral problems in the home. These factors include child and parent characteristics, situational factors such as consequences for defiant behavior, and the role of stressful family events. The practitioner helps parents understand how negative coercive interactions reinforce oppositional or defiant behavior.

- Parents are taught more effective ways to attend to a child's behavior, in order to reduce off-task or negative behaviors and increase on-task and positive behaviors. The technique consists of verbal narration and occasional positive statements to the child. Attention is applied strategically only when the child displays on-task, prosocial, and otherwise positive behaviors. Parents learn to ignore unwanted behaviors.

- Parents are taught to attend to child compliance and independent play by breaking down complex tasks; managing environmental distractions; and giving simple, direct commands while providing immediate reinforcement for prompt compliance. Positive reinforcement is provided frequently to shape the child's ability to engage in longer periods of nondisruptive activity.

- A token home economy (i.e., reward program) is established in which a menu of rewards is negotiated, and a parent gives tokens only when the child promptly obeys the parent's directive. If the child does not comply with the first command, he or she must forfeit the tokens. Parents can award additional tokens for a child's initiative or particularly positive attitude.

- Parents learn to implement time-out procedures for noncompliance. Two serious violations are defined as a result of discussions regarding the child's particular disruptive behaviors. Parents learn to issue a command, wait 5 seconds, issue a warning, and wait another 5 seconds. If the child has not complied, the child goes into time-out. During the time-out, the child must remain in time-out for roughly 2 minutes per year of his or her age (e.g., 20 minutes for a 10-year-old); be quiet during time-out; and agree to comply with the original command. More time-out may result if the child continues to be oppositional or disruptive.

- Time-out procedures and previous lessons are reviewed. Time-out can be extended to more behaviors if needed.

- Parents learn to manage noncompliant behaviors in public places. Parents are taught to review basic rules of conduct for the child before entering into a public place, to give the child an activity to keep him or her occupied, to reinforce good behavior, and to institute punishment should the child engage in disruptive behavior. The time-out or loss of privileges is instituted immediately upon returning home.

- Parents collaborate with the school to improve the child's school behavior. Rewards and punishments are instituted on the basis of daily reports from school. The report card addresses specific behaviors of concern, and rewards and/or punishments are dispensed by the same principles noted earlier. In the classroom, the teacher (or an assistant) implements contingency management as follows: learning tasks are broken down into smaller components; stimulation in the learning environment is increased (e.g., use of more colorful or otherwise more visually stimulating materials); on-task behavior is rewarded; off-task or disruptive behaviors are sanctioned through time-out or loss of privileges (e.g., free time during recess).

- Parents review what they have learned, entertain scenarios about future problems, and discuss how they might handle them. A 1-month follow-up or booster session may be planned to review any problems that arise after the program.

Pfiffner and Barkley (1998) recommend some refinements in implementing contingency management programs:

- Instructions must be given in a concise, clear, and somewhat exaggerated manner, followed by the child repeating the instructions to demonstrate that he or she heard and understood them.

- Consequences (positive and negative) must immediately follow the specific target behavior in order to be effective.

- Consequences must be more frequent and of greater magnitude than would otherwise be expected for "normal" children.

- Positives are preferred over negative reinforcers.

- Reinforcers should be changed every 2–3 weeks so they don't lose their influence on behavior. Parents can return to a specific reward after having set it aside for a while.

- Anticipating environmental changes or changes in other contingencies, and helping the child to review rules of own conduct, is important for the child to cope adequately with transitions.

- The child should be helped to anticipate and plan ahead.

- Use a strategy that combines positive consequences (e.g., praise, tangible rewards, token economies) and negative consequences (e.g., reprimands, response cost, time-out).

- For maximum effectiveness, consequences must be immediate, brief, consistent, salient, and—in the case of positive consequences—delivered frequently.

- On-task behaviors should be immediately rewarded with warmly delivered praise or other tangible reinforcement; negative behaviors should be responded to with withdrawal of attention (ignoring) (i.e., negative reinforcement).

- Token economies are effective; negative consequences (i.e., punishment) include reprimands or response cost (something is taken away, such as a privilege). Punishment must be immediate, unemotional, and consistent.

- Overall, positive reinforcement is much preferred to negative reinforcement and should be used more frequently that negative reinforcers or punishment.

- Time-outs can also be used in various ways: the child may be isolated or moved to the periphery of the "action," and thus unable to obtain rewards; work materials may be put away; a clock that earns rewards during productive activity may be stopped during off-task or otherwise disruptive behavior.

- These same principles are used in the home as well, and ideally are coordinated between teachers and parents via the (initially) daily and (later) weekly report card. A list of target behaviors are listed on the report card; those behaviors are rated on a scale (e.g., poor, fair, good, excellent) that can be scored with points and summed to a total score.

- Expectations of the child's behavior and/or academic performance (e.g., completed homework) must be made clear, and rewards and/or sanctions at home for improvements and agreed-on ratings must be made equally clear (e.g., pizza; movie; TV time; or a special trip for long-term major goal achievement, such as 4 weeks of 90% adequate ratings).

Robin (1998b) has noted that there is little research regarding the pragmatics of how to sequence interventions with an adolescent and family dealing with ADHD, but experience and judgment can serve as guides. Priority should be give to acute behavioral problems (e.g., conduct disorder, substance abuse problems), moving toward a family psychoeducation model, arranging for medication evaluation, and then directly improving the child's behaviors through family behavior therapy (including parent management training) and contingency management intervention in the classroom. Parents' efforts at home must be carefully coordinated with the classroom intervention (via the daily report card) to focus on the child's social behaviors and academic performance. The intervention tends to be intensive in the beginning (10–20 visits), and then it ideally shifts to a long-term follow-up model with intermittent checkups over a longer period. In addition to coordinating both home-based and classroom efforts, close coordination should also include the efforts of other participants in the intervention: the prescribing physician, various school personnel (i.e., teachers, guidance counselors, special education personnel, school administration), and a testing specialist, among others.

Robin (1998a, 1998b) also recommends some general implementation guidelines for behavioral interventions, particularly with older children and adolescents. Practitioners, parents, and teachers (i.e., adults) should strive to be somewhat flexible and willing to negotiate on some matters with the adolescent. Adults should also give immediate and frequent positive feedback and encouragement when it is earned, as well as negative feedback (e.g., mild rebukes) when it is warranted. Adults should be consistent and follow through with feedback and contingencies (e.g., "When you finish your homework, you can go visit your friend"), keep to a plan of action, avoid giving lectures and unnecessary arguments, avoid personalizing the conflict or tension, and be ready to forgive. Adults should focus on achieving successes and moving forward, and they should avoid becoming bogged down by grudges. Adults should take the long view of the child's progress and see the goals of day-to-day interventions as enhancing accountability, responsibility, and independence. Parents particularly should strive to gradually relinquish directives and punishments as adolescents "earn" their independence and learn by coping with the consequences of their own behavior. Adults should model accountability and follow-through. With children and adolescents, adults should clearly distinguish those matters that are negotiable and those that are not, and adults should be flexible when possible. Adults should always give a good reason for directives or requests of the child, and they should explain their rationale for sanctions, restrictions, or punishments. Adults also should model good communication skills and monitor the young person's behaviors (e.g., "Where you going? Whom are you going to be with? What are you planning to do? When will you be back?"), and they should be ready to confront serious discrepancies between the adolescent's words and deeds.

Social workers, whether working in community agencies, private practice, or schools, should be prepared to work in an interdisciplinary environment to help provide a thorough MFS assessment and collaborate with a range of other professionals to facilitate implementation of evidence-based practices for children, adolescents, and their families. This collaboration is critical if evidence-based psychosocial interventions for ODD, CD, and ADHD are to be implemented successfully and maintained over time (Tourse & Sullick, 1999). There is still much work to do to enhance interprofessional collaboration in social work in schools (Mooney, Kline, & Davoren, 1999) and elsewhere.

Medication for ADHD

The use of stimulants for children diagnosed with ADHD is, perhaps, the most established use of medication for children both clinically and empirically. These medications include dextroamphetamine, methylphenidate, and pemoline (Kaplan & Sadock, 1998). The clinical usefulness of stimulant medication with children with ADHD has been known since the 1930s (American Academy of Child and Adolescent Psychiatry, AACAP, 2001b), and near consensus has been reached regarding the efficacy of these drugs for reducing the primary symptoms of ADHD; they improve on-task behavior and academic performance, and reduce disruptive behaviors (AACAP, 1997a; Barkley, 1997a; Brown et al., 2008; Farmer et al., 2002; Hinshaw et al., 1998). For example:

> In the classroom, stimulants decrease interrupting, fidgetiness, and finger-tapping and increase on-task behavior. At home, stimulants improve parent-child interactions, on-task behaviors, and compliance. In social settings, stimulants improve peer nomination rankings of social standing and increase attention during sports activities. Stimulants decrease response variability and impulsive responding on laboratory cognitive task, increase the accuracy of performance, and improve short-term memory, reaction time, math computation, problem-solving in games and sustained attention. (AACAP, 2001b, p. 1353)

Greenhill (1998) cited more than 160 studies demonstrating the efficacy and effectiveness of amphetamine drugs for the treatment of ADHD. Data reveal that between 50% and 70% of children show marked improvement in cognitive functioning, on-task concentration, disruptive behavioral indicators, and—to some degree—social functioning. Despite the success of stimulant medications for ADHD, there are some serious limitations in the use of these drugs: many children do not approach "normal" levels of functioning, although most are rated improved; long-term benefits are often not evident; they do not appear to improve peer relations in the long run; the drugs are not likely to resolve family problems often present in the lives of children with ADHD; they do not help a sizable proportion of youth (10%–20%) even in the short run; up to almost 33% of children show adverse responses; and many parents find drug treatment unacceptable for various reasons and do not comply with medical recommendations (Pelham et al., 1998; Wells et al., 2000). Although debate continues as to whether medication alone is sufficient to reduce the main symptoms of ADHD, there is notable evidence that psychosocial interventions reduce the need for medication (AACAP, 1997a; Farmer et al., 2002).

Other factors to consider when prescribing medication for children with ADHD include age, duration and severity of the problem, history and success of prior treatment efforts, normal levels of anxiety in the child, parental motivation, absence of stimulant abuse in the home, and likelihood of compliance with the regimen (Barkley, 1997a). Because there is little evidence that clearly guides prediction of the correct dose of medication, physicians generally begin with a lower dose and increase it gradually until reaching an optimum balance between therapeutic effectiveness and side effects (AACAP, 1997a; Greenhill, 1998). Immediate-release stimulant medication has a brief duration (3–5 hours) of action, so multiple daily dosing is required. Practical concerns include administering the drugs at different times over the course of the child's school day. In addition, given the rapid rise in the prescribing of these drugs in the United States, some have drawn attention to the risk of overprescribing primarily to control behavior without a thorough diagnostic assessment (outlined earlier). Contraindications include evidence of previous sensitivity to stimulants, heart disease, glaucoma, drug abuse, hypertension and hyperthyroidism, motors tics, and family history of Tourette's or other tic disorders. Although the drugs are very safe, potential side effects include irritability, moodiness, headaches, abdominal pain, and loss of appetite. Side effects can often be avoided or reduced by gradual adjustments in the dose. Withdrawals may result in rebound effects, such as excitability, talkativeness, irritability, and insomnia (AACAP, 1997a, 2001b). Despite these concerns, stimulant medications have provided relief for many young persons with ADHD and their families. Nevertheless, many young people who could benefit from them do not receive proper care. A large 7-year multistage survey of more than 100,000 client records demonstrated that almost 50% of young people eligible for psychostimulant medication were not prescribed these drugs. In addition, at least 25% of individuals prescribed these medications did not receive follow-up care (Hoagwood, Kelleher, Feil, & Comer, 2000).

TREATMENT PLANNING AND EVALUATION

CASE EXAMPLE: ENRIQUE

Enrique, or "Ricky," was a 9-year-old boy of Native American and Hispanic descent. His parents were never married, but he had met his father informally once or twice when he was younger. His father, of mixed Native American ancestry, was somewhat of a drifter—he left the reservation in the Southwest years earlier and moved around often, following his work. Ricky's mother, Margarita, raised him by herself but received help from family members, particularly her mother. Although Margarita had a serious problem with alcohol and other drugs when she was younger (including while pregnant with Ricky), she had been clean and sober for the previous 6 years and was an active member of her Pentecostal church, which she credits with

giving her a new life. Nevertheless, raising Ricky without his father had been challenging. Although he had always been "un jalepeño pequeño," it wasn't until the previous year or so that Margarita realized she could not handle him by herself, and it was getting tougher to find people she could ask to watch him now and then. Complaints from the teachers at Ricky's school were increasing. Margarita's friends, who had always said Ricky was a handful when they babysat, also heard about his conduct in school and counseled Margarita to get help for him. She had been reluctant and unwilling to acknowledge his escalating behavior and problems with schoolwork because she felt guilty about his problems. In previous counseling, a therapist had told her that Ricky's problems were the result of "poor attachment," because Margarita had been "unavailable" to him because of her previous drug problems. Her friends were more pragmatic: Ricky was getting older, was having more problems adjusting to his new school, and was becoming more difficult to handle. In addition to having difficulty sitting still and focusing on his schoolwork in class and at home, Ricky had recently gotten into fights with other kids at school, usually during lunch or on the playground after school (he said, "They deserved it for calling me names"). In addition, he had become somewhat belligerent with his mother when she asked him to do chores at home or turn off the TV to finish his homework.

As for his schoolwork, Ricky had been tested by the school psychologist, who said he had trouble with math and reading, but also that if he were a bit more in control, he could improve on some of these things through tutoring. Margarita had managed over the past few years to get an associate's degree in administration from a community college, and she had landed a good job at a university as assistant to a dean and later assistant to the president. She was fortunate to have good benefits to cover services for Ricky, who attended a school that could provide them. During the conversation with the school psychologist, Margarita discussed her early drug problems and expressed guilt over that period in her life,

wondering whether she had not been a good mother to Ricky. The psychologist pointed out that she should be proud of how she thrived under duress without a partner and how difficult it must have been to turn her life around. When observing Ricky with Margarita in the office, the psychologist also noted that he could tell how close the two of them were. She must have done more than a few things right, he told her. Ricky's most recent physical showed him to be healthy, but that testing together with the psychologist's diagnosis revealed that Ricky had all the signs of ADHD and was developing a behavioral problem. The psychologist told Margarita that there was every reason to be optimistic that Ricky could get better if he started a program of medication, behavioral therapy at home and in the classroom, and tutoring for his academic challenges. If Ricky's mom stuck with it, the intervention might also prevent future problems as well. Because Ricky was becoming somewhat belligerent and getting into fights with other kids (sometimes he was a bully), the psychologist was concerned that he may become increasingly conduct disordered. Dan, the social worker on the team at school, would teach behavioral management skills to Margarita and coordinate treatment with the psychologist (who would supervise a tutor on staff), the consulting psychiatrist (who would provide medication), and the teacher (who would implement a contingency management plan in the classroom).

MFS Assessment: Defining Problems and Goals

Dan thought that Ricky certainly met many of the criteria for ADHD and ODD. The problems had persisted for some time and appeared to be getting worse. Ricky demonstrated a consistent pattern of being argumentative and conflictual with other children and stubborn and oppositional when dealing with his mother and other adult authority figures, particularly teachers. He appeared easily frustrated when things didn't go his way. Many of the problems overlapped with his learning and behavioral problems in school. He was often very fidgety and "always in motion," according to his teachers; had a hard time focusing on one task at a time and finishing his work; often blurted out responses to questions; and had trouble waiting his turn in general. He was disorganized in his work, often complaining that someone took his materials; and he did not respond readily to commands from teachers when they attempted to set limits on his behavior or help him focus on his work. He clearly had become disruptive to those around him and was taxing the patience of his mother and his teacher. The fact that Ricky had moved to a new neighborhood and school certainly may have disrupted his sense of security and consistency. Although he had been a "handful" in his previous school, complaints from teachers and the assessment of the current school psychologist seemed to be more serious than before. Margarita did not know whether this change was because the school personnel felt differently about her son (who was one of few children of color) in the school or whether there had been a real change in his behavior.

In addition to the recent uprooting and changes in Ricky's life, Dan and Margarita speculated whether this inability to focus on tasks and control his behavior was "in his blood" given the problems of Ricky's father or whether Margarita's substance abuse problems during pregnancy may have caused some subtle neurological problems. Because Ricky had no overt signs of Fetal Alcohol Syndrome, this was mere speculation, and the social worker did not overemphasize it. Although the history of impulse problems and substance abuse in Ricky's family history was of concern as a possible explanation for his troubles, the assessment turned to more current and functional aspects of his difficulties.

As Dan discussed Ricky's behavior over the course of a typical day with Margarita and Ricky's teacher, he noticed some patterns. Ricky's mom reported that he was more cooperative in the morning when getting ready for school, and she had less trouble convincing him to get dressed, eat breakfast, and the like. The teacher also noticed that he was quieter in the morning, and that during the day as lunch approached, he became more restless, showed less ability to focus on his work, and began to interact negatively and more frequently with his classmates. The afternoons appeared to be the most difficult: he would often sigh loudly, and writhe and fidget in his seat as though he were coming out of his skin. It seemed that he could not wait for the end of class. It was during this time that he was the most difficult to control and was most likely to be sent out of the classroom.

Ricky's mother noted that when he got home he often seemed angry and depressed and could not bring himself to start his homework, and he often procrastinated well past dinner. He would bargain with her to watch TV or play video games, "just for a little while then I'll start my homework." Margarita, who often took work home from her new job, was stressed herself and often did not have the energy or patience to maintain limits and structure with Ricky. She often "caved in," so she could finish her own work, make dinner, clean up, and get him ready for bed. Ricky's teacher complained that his work was often carelessly completed, incomplete, or simply not done. These problems and complaints appeared to be occurring with increasing frequency and severity. He seemed to be becoming more easily provoked in school. One playground monitor started to refer to him as the "playground bully." When Ricky came home from school, his mother was becoming increasingly alarmed at the degree of his anger and his general defiance when she asked him to pick up his room or start his homework. She was becoming increasingly concerned because Ricky was growing quickly and becoming much stronger, and she was very worried about being able to handle him in a few years as he entered adolescence. The school psychologist and social worker also confirmed that this was a good time to get the problems under control.

After meeting with mother and son and consulting with the school psychologist and teacher, Dan set up a meeting to discuss a service plan to address Ricky's difficulties. They all agreed that the first priority was reducing his belligerent behavior. The second priority was to help him improve his work and study skills, at home and in the classroom. All agreed that through weekly school reports and occasional meetings, coordinated by the social worker, they could help Ricky gain control over his behavior and improve his grades. Ricky said he just "wanted the other kids to like me better," and he felt that if they did, all his problems would go away. Improving Ricky's social skills was added to the list of improvements that would become a part of his service plan.

Selecting and Designing the Interventions: Defining Strategies and Objectives

The social worker Dan explained to Margarita that Ricky's difficulties in focusing his attention, staying on task, controlling his behavior, relating better to other kids, and improving his mood and overall sense of well-being were interrelated. In addition, the interventions that had been shown to be most effective for these problems were quite similar and could be easily integrated (table 13.1). Dan explained that, in addition to possible medication, behavior therapy and contingency management, when applied by Margarita and Ricky's teacher in a coordinated and consistent way, was very likely to help Ricky improve control over his behavior and his school performance. The social worker also suggested that Ricky's mom learn some stress management skills (e.g., meditation, breathing exercises) for her own benefit and to teach them to Ricky to help him settle down and concentrate before he started his homework. Dan spent an entire session providing psychoeducation to Ricky's mother on what ADHD was and what the entire behavioral program intervention would entail. Because Dan and the teacher had collaborated on classroom contingency management skills before, the teacher was prepared to carry out her part of the plan, and she would report to Dan and Margarita on a regular basis.

Dan reviewed the plan with Margarita, which would include psychoeducation for her about clinical behavior therapy, parent management training (clarity and consistency in communicating expectations), contingency management (consistent use of rewards and sanctions with short- and long-term rewards), coordination with Ricky's teacher (who would use similar behavioral and contingency management skills), and medication. Specifics of the plan included the following:

- Relaxation and playtime after school. Margarita would pick Ricky up around 4:30 from the after-school program (near the campus where she worked). She would then solely devote her attention to Ricky for about 20 minutes, asking him about his day, providing some nurturance (perhaps with a snack), and (if he wanted to) engaging in a game of some kind. This time would help her check on Ricky's mood and needs and prepare him for a more structured schedule in the evening. A reward would be planned for the end of the evening if Ricky accomplished all tasks satisfactorily. This time also was used to review reports from school (she retrieved a scorecard every day from the school secretary) and his progress toward long-term goals.

- Margarita would "meditate" with Ricky for a few minutes before he began his homework. During this time, he was taught some basic relaxation and meditation skills to "settle down and be cool" before starting his work. Five minutes per day were allotted to this activity before he began his homework and chores. She would also have Ricky talk aloud about his plans to organize and complete his homework (e.g., "First, I'll do my spelling homework, 'cause that's easy; then, I have to draw a map of Italy and show where the big cities are; then I'll do my math homework, that's the hardest part.").

- Parent management training was reviewed to help Margarita focus on structuring Ricky's late afternoon and evening time. The social worker reviewed with her how to issue simple commands with assertive follow-through. She would also learn to ignore some of the less important but annoying behaviors (e.g., whining, complaining, sighing) to reduce the negativity that had begun to define their time together at home. Mom and Ricky agreed to the following: "I will ask you once to do a specific chore; I will ask you to repeat it to me to make sure you understand, and I will wait 3 minutes to see if you begin the chore. Depending on what it is, we will also agree on how long it will take, and I will hold you to that."

- Implementing a contingency management plan to help Ricky better self-regulate through a home economy by which he could earn points for accomplishing schoolwork and doing chores at home. The rules were spelled out clearly and posted on the refrigerator. The teacher would apply a similar plan with the same scoring guidelines, and the overall score was combined so Margarita could issue larger rewards or sanctions on weekends. If Ricky did not comply with the rules spelled out on accomplishing chores and homework, he would lose a point for the day. If he had trouble completing some of the homework (e.g., a particular math problem), he had to show partial work on filling it out. On the advice of the school psychologist, Ricky was encouraged to do as much of the work as he could and then return to the more challenging problems later to avoid becoming overly frustrated.

- A special education intern would engage in extra tutoring as part of the after-school program.

- If Ricky should engage in negative attention getting, bother other students, get into fights, or not respond to his mother's or teacher's commands readily at home or school, he would lose points. For physical fighting, he would lose 5 points. Ricky's teacher agreed to use the same point system for his classroom tasks. He can achieve a maximum of 10 points per day in school and 10 points per day at home, if he accomplishes all his respective tasks. For a 5-day school week, that means a total of 100 points. The team and Ricky agreed that they would start by expecting Ricky to achieve 15 points per day for him to obtain daily rewards at home (e.g., TV or computer time; modest monetary rewards toward an object he desires), and 75 points for a larger weekend reward (e.g., having a friend stay over, renting a movie and ordering pizza). Margarita and the teacher discussed how these points would be applied or withdrawn, given their slightly different circumstances, to maintain some consistency.

- The social worker Dan also devised a stress management plan for Margarita, so she could feel less overwhelmed and more in control. As Ricky became more cooperative, she was able to relax more, get her own chores done, and occasionally get babysitters to have an evening out herself (the same reward system applied when the babysitter was in charge).

- Finally, Ricky would be sent for a medication consult to see if medication for ADHD symptoms would be of assistance to him.

Selecting Scales and Creating Indexes to Monitor and Evaluate Client Progress

To establish a useful baseline for Ricky, a trained teacher's aide used the NYTRS and the SWAN to measure behavior problems and ADHD symptoms. Dan showed Margarita how to use the SWAN at home so they could have one baseline measure for each situation. The school psychologist performed a few continuous performance tests and standard academic tests to assess Ricky's learning problems and recommend remedial exercises to the special education intern. These indexes would be used to gauge Ricky's academic progress. As for unique measures of behavior, completion of chores, and doing homework at home and school, Margarita and the teacher agreed to use the same indexes on the daily scorecard (rated –1, 0, 1) for chores completed in a timely manner, completed homework, completed in-class work, and points for maintaining good relations with others in class. Zeros were given for not completing tasks or work, and points could be taken away (–1) for actively negative or oppositional behavior at home or school: being "mouthy" and defiant, or losing up to 5 points for fighting or being belligerent. Margarita picked up the simple score card when she picked up Ricky after school. They would sit and discuss his experiences and scores everyday. The social worker compiled all the data from standardized scales and specific indexes to monitor and evaluate behavioral and academic progress over the course of the intervention.

CHAPTER SUMMARY

Conduct problems and ADHD are among the more common and distressing problems for children, adolescents, and their families, and they have a major impact on schools and the community. MFS assessment reveals many factors that are amenable to effective intervention through a combination of individual skill building, family behavior therapy, and contingency management employed consistently at home, in the classroom, and in the community. Medication is also likely to be of considerable help to children with symptoms or diagnosis of ADHD. Effective case management is essential to ensure consistent collaboration with the overall service plan. Social workers are in a position to take on important leadership roles in implementing evidence-based practices for these children and their families.

TABLE 13.1 The Client Service Plan: Ricky and Margarita

Problems	Goals	Objectives (samples)	Interventions	Assessment and evaluation tools
Belligerent, oppositional, defiant behavior with adults (e.g., mom, teacher); not responding to reasonable commands to attend to tasks	Minimize oppositional behavior; increase cooperativeness to level suitable to age	Initiate response to requests in 5 seconds; consistently engage in request until task is accomplished (75% of the time on weekly scorecard)	Psychoeducation with mom on parent management and contingency management skills Implementation of parent management skills at home, with contingency management; similar contingency management plan implemented at school by teacher Mom implements relaxation and meditation skills to prepare Ricky for homework and chores after school daily Psychiatric consultation provided for possible ADHD medication Psychological testing provided for assessment of learning deficits; psych intern will tutor for 30 minutes three times weekly Teacher will continue to observe; social skills training considered if problem behaviors do not abate Case management and coordination of total service plan to be conducted by social worker as team leader	NYTRS and SWAN to assess classroom behavior and ADHD symptoms at home and school Indexes for daily performance developed by mom and teacher (combined 20 points per day, weekly 100-point scale), with items including accomplished in-class schoolwork, lack of negative social behaviors, homework, and chores Standardized tests for intelligence and math and reading aptitude provided and analyzed by school psychologist
Frequent fidgeting, difficulty concentrating and attending to tasks; disorganized at school; often "on the go" in the classroom	Reduce fidgeting and restlessness; improve concentration and organizational skills to accomplish tasks	Consistently complete work 75% of the time on weekly scorecard (includes disruptive behaviors such as not leaving seat, bothering others)		
Poor school performance; possible learning deficits in math and reading	Improve math and reading skills; obtain passing grades in all classes	Attend tutoring sessions to identify specific learning problems and learn new study strategies		
Social problems with other children; bothering them, provoking negative interactions, fighting	Reduce or eliminate fighting; improve social ties with classmates	Obtain no negative scores on weekly scorecard for provoking negative interactions with other children; no specific prosocial objectives suggested, pending results of contingency management intervention, which may eliminate negative interactions and improve relations with classmates		

CHAPTER 14

CHILD ABUSE AND NEGLECT

This chapter examines the biopsychosocial factors associated with the abuse and neglect of children, describes some of the more immediate consequences of abuse and neglect, examines the clinical and forensic aspects of assessment, and reviews the literature on prevention and reactive intervention strategies (i.e., intervening after child abuse has been confirmed). Given that internalizing and externalizing disorders may be, in part, a consequence of abuse and neglect, interventions for these problems are also relevant here, but they are reviewed in chapters 12 and 13. Current interventions are probably best viewed on a continuum that spans prevention, early intervention, and intervention to stop abuse and neglect and help victims cope with psychosocial consequences, although the demarcations on this continuum of care are often blurred in the literature.

ASSESSMENT

Background Data

Childhood abuse and neglect are co-occurring and overlapping constructs. A review of the literature defining child abuse and neglect (e.g., Kaplan, Pelcovitz, & Labruna, 1999; Pecora, Whittaker, Maluccio, & Barth, 2000; Wolfe & St. Pierre, 1989) reveals the following: Physical abuse includes both minor physical harm (e.g., scratches, bruises) and major physical harm (e.g., broken bones; head injuries; being struck with a hand or object; having been kicked, shaken, thrown, burned, stabbed, or choked by a parent or parent substitute). Psychological and emotional abuse includes verbal abuse, harsh physical punishments (e.g., being tied up, emotionally neglected, exposed to domestic violence, deliberately impeding normal emotional and psychological development of a child with inconsistent limits or unreasonable expectations). Child physical neglect includes failure to provide basic care (e.g., food, clothing, shelter, hygiene, basic medical care if available). Definitions of sexual abuse vary considerably, but a general consensus includes a range of increasingly severe forms, from voyeurism or exhibitionism to deliberately exposing a child to pornographic material; sexualized touching or kissing;

masturbation to, with, by, or in front of a child; giving or receiving oral sex; vaginal or anal penetration with fingers or objects; and vaginal or anal intercourse with a child. These events may be brought about through enticement, various forms of persuasion, threats, or physical force. Child psychological, emotional, physical, and sexual abuse often occur in the context of various forms of family violence, and researchers are beginning to acknowledge that it may make more sense to look at these as interrelated rather than discrete phenomena (Slep & Heyman, 2001). However, there are some clinical and forensic advantages to examining these forms of abuse separately.

Estimates of child abuse and neglect have varied over previous decades depending on definitions of maltreatment, whether data measured referrals or confirmed cases, and other methodological considerations (Pareda, Guilera, Forns, & Gomez-Benito, 2009a). Earlier reviews estimated that there were approximately 1 million confirmed cases of child abuse and neglect annually in the United States (Kaplan et al., 1999; Pecora et al., 2000; Putnam, 2003; US Department of Health and Human Services, USDHHS, 1996a, 1996b; Wolfe & McEachran, 1997). More recent data reveal that state and local child protective services (CPS) in the United States received an estimated 3.7 million referrals of children being abused or neglected (USDHHS, 2012), including 681,000 children (9.1 per 1,000) who were victims of maltreatment. Of these, 79% were victims of neglect, 18% of physical abuse, and 9% of sexual abuse. An additional 10% were victims of other types of maltreatment, including threatened abuse, a parent's drug or alcohol abuse, or lack of supervision. About 80% of maltreatment was at the hands of parents (45.1% men and 53.6% women). An estimated 1,750 children died from maltreatment in 2011, four-fifths of them younger than age 4, with fatalities of boys exceeding those of girls by about 50%. Rates of death per 100,000 children were as follows: 3.9 for African Americans, 2.6 for American Indian or Alaska Natives, 1.9 for Hispanics, 1.6 for non-Hispanic whites, 1.2 for Pacific Islanders, and 0.4 for Asians. The USDHHS report suggests that physical and sexual abuse might have declined by half or more, but other data suggest that reports of child abuse and neglect are underestimated (Finkelhor, Ormrod, Turner, & Hamby, 2005; Finkelhor, Turner, Ormrod, & Hamby, 2009; Theodore et al., 2005). It is unlikely that the experiences are mutually exclusive, as the categories of maltreatment suggest. Different forms of abuse and neglect are likely to overlap in a substantial proportion of cases, and reoccurrence of abuse probably exceeds 50%. About 50% of these children will enter foster care at some point, and close to 75% of an estimated 1 million children will be served by the child welfare system.

With regard to child sexual abuse, Americans' consciousness has increased significantly over the past 20 years (Wolfe & Birt, 1997). However, because of high-profile cases in past years involving false accusations of abuse (e.g., satanic ritual abuse) combined with the popularization of bogus treatment methods (e.g., rebirthing therapy), public backlash has dampened community concern and engendered considerable skepticism regarding the real neglect and violence perpetrated by adults on millions of children in the United States. Earlier reports estimated that approximately 100,000–200,000 reports of sexual abuse of children are documented annually, and prevalence estimates (based on adult retrospective reports) range from 15% to 30% of children (i.e., before age 18), including 12%–35% of females and 4%–9% of males (Pecora et al., 2000; Putnam, 2003). On the basis of a random sample of 930 adult women in one city in the western United States, Russell (1983) estimated that 16% of women had experienced at least one episode of intrafamilial sexual abuse, and 31% had experienced extrafamilial sexual abuse before the age of 18. Stepfathers were about eight times more likely to abuse their daughters than biological fathers (17% vs. 2%), and stepfathers' abuse tended to be more severe (Russell, 1984). In the first national survey of sexual abuse, Finkelhor, Hotaling, Lewis, and Smith (1990) estimated that up to 27% of women and 16% of men experienced sexual abuse during childhood.

A meta-analysis of international studies of child sexual abuse reported that 7.9% of men and 19.7% of women had suffered some form of sexual abuse before age 18 (Pareda et al., 2009b). Rates of childhood sexual abuse, in general, are most likely underestimated because data more likely reflect only confirmed cases (Swenson & Hanson, 1998). Surveys in the United States of adolescents and adults on their retrospective accounts of abuse find much higher rates than other estimates. For example, in a survey of children aged 10–16, Finkelhor and Dziuba-Leatherman (1994) found that 3.2% of girls and .6% of boys were sexually abused every year, and about 15% of girls and about 6% of boys reported having been sexually abused in their lifetime. On the basis of a thorough review of 47 surveys of clinical and community samples, Fergusson and Mullen (1999) found the average rates of childhood sexual abuse to range from 8% to 62% for females and 3% to 29% for males. Regarding children having experienced intercourse, rates were 1%–28% for females and 1%–14% for males. Divergent estimates of abuse are attributed to a lack of reliable definitions of the problem, a lack of reliable measures, sampling differences, and other methodological problems. On the basis of the results of several studies reviewed by Wolfe and Birt (1997), family members accounted for fewer than half of incidents of sexual abuse of girls and less than a third of those involving boys. More than half of sexual abuse appears to be a onetime event, and girls are two to three times more likely than boys to be abused. Girls are also more likely than boys to be abused by a family member over time. About 33% of cases of sexual abuse are disclosed during childhood, and those who do not disclose are motivated to keep silent through fear of retribution against themselves or persons in their family. Others keep silent because of shame; guilt; or a lack of understanding that the act was wrong, a belief often engendered through indoctrination by the abuser.

Risk factors correlated with child abuse and neglect generally are well documented and include parental history of having been a victim of abuse, single-parent households, lack of parental knowledge and skill in child care, maternal depression, other psychopathology on the part of the adult care-taker (e.g., major mental illnesses, personality disorders), substance abuse, couple violence, lack of social support, low educational status, unemployment and poverty, homelessness, lack of access to basic health care, living in crime-ridden neighborhoods, parental stress and poor coping skills, and having parents with an above-average number of children (Appel & Holden, 1998; Begel, Dumas, & Hanson, 2010; Dore, 1999; Gaudin, 1993; Gelles, 1997; Smokowski & Wodarski, 1996; Wolfe & McEachran, 1997; Zlotnick, Robertson, & Wright, 1999). Accumulated risk of abuse is greater than risk associated with any one factor. In general, one can assume that the higher the number of risk factors in a family, the greater is the risk of abuse or neglect. However, correlated risk factors are not proof of child abuse or neglect. In addition, there are no consistently identified differences in rates of abuse or neglect by race when socioeconomic factors are statistically controlled for. Definitions of abuse and neglect are also subject to considerable variability by local statutes, community, and cultural norms. For example, views regarding the "acceptable" use of corporal punishment range considerably given cultural and religious norms (Gelles, 1997).

In addition to the general risk factors for child abuse and neglect, correlates of sexual abuse include being female, a median age of 10–11, being prepubertal, living in an otherwise dysfunctional family environment (e.g., marital conflict, lack of supervision of children), and experiencing other forms of emotional and physical abuse (Fergusson & Mullen, 1999). To reiterate, however, these correlated factors do not confirm abuse, and determinations of sexual abuse must be made through careful clinical and forensic evidence gathering. Nevertheless, a confluence of multiple risk factors for child abuse and neglect should prompt practitioners to carefully pursue more in-depth assessments.

Evidence strongly suggests that the consequences of child abuse and neglect do increase risk for child maladjustment and future psychopathology as adults (Maniglio, 2009; Putnam, 2003). Abused and/or neglected adolescents who end up in foster care have much higher rates of mental health and substance use problems, and specifically they are much more likely to attempt suicide (Pilowsky & Wu, 2006). Problems associated with abuse and neglect include depression, anxiety, symptoms of post-traumatic stress disorder (PTSD), conduct disorders, substance abuse and other high-risk behaviors, attention-deficit hyperactivity disorder (ADHD), social and interpersonal deficits (including difficulties developing trusting relationships with others), and other intellectual and academic deficits. As adults, persons who were sexually abused as children may be at greater risk of problems such as substance abuse, eating disorders, borderline personality disorder, PTSD, and depression. Gender differences reveal a greater likelihood of emotional disturbances (internalizing disorders) in girls and more behavior problems (externalizing disorders) in boys (Dore, 1999; Kaplan et al., 1999; Kazdin, 1994a; Widom, 1998; Wolfe & St. Pierre, 1989). These various problems may also be related to witnessing violence in the home. Probably more than half of children in violent homes have witnessed their father's assaults on their mother, have been exposed to an array of psychologically and physically abusive behaviors, and are more likely to be abused themselves. Data from a nationally representative survey revealed that more than 33% of children had been a witness to violence or another form of indirect victimization (Finkelhor et al., 2005). In addition to the emotional problems listed already, these children are also more likely to engage in aggressive or violent behaviors. The intensity of the child's response may be related to the intensity and frequency of violence, the quality of the child's relationship to their caregivers, the content of the disagreements, whether the parents can demonstrate satisfactory problem-solving and conflict resolution skills, and whether the child is directly involved with the conflict (for a review, see Anderson & Cramer-Benjamin, 1999). The effects of witnessing couple violence can have long-term impacts on children well into adulthood. Research on these and other traumatic events and their effects on children have demonstrated a direct relationship between the degree of victimization and the severity of the child's emotional and behavioral symptoms (Milgram, 1989).

Children who have been sexually abused are at increased risk of many of the same emotional and behavioral symptoms suffered by children who have been abused in general, as well as increased risk of sexualized behaviors (e.g., public masturbation, flirtatiousness), adolescent promiscuity, running away, engaging in prostitution, and PTSD (Friedrich, 1993; O'Donohue, Fanetti, & Elliott, 1998; Kendall-Tacket, Williams, & Finkelhor, 1993; Putnam, 2003; Swenson & Hanson, 1998; Wolfe & Birt, 1997; Wolfe, Gentile, & Wolfe, 1989; Wolfe & Wolfe, 1988). Child sexual abuse in girls might also predict more severe symptoms in adult victims of sexual assault, and both PTSD symptoms and alcohol use independently predicted further sexual assault in a sample of more than 500 women surveyed twice at a 1-year interval (Ullman, Najdowski, & Filipas, 2009).

Sometimes, there are no indications of psychosocial consequences of sexual abuse at the time of assessment, and most abused and neglected children do not develop formal PTSD (Widom, 1999). As for the long-term effects of child sexual abuse, it is clear that, on the basis of severity, type, chronicity, and social response to abuse, there is general evidence that persons who experienced child sexual abuse are at increased risk of developing emotional, behavioral, and interpersonal problems in the long run. However, the link between childhood sexual abuse and adult psychopathology is nonspecific, and there is no direct link between child sexual abuse and the development of any specific disorder (e.g., dissociative disorders). As of yet, there is no homogenous set of core symptoms that can be identified as so-called sexual abuse syndrome (Alter-Reid, Gibbs, Lachenmeyer, Sigal, & Massoth, 1986; Fergusson & Mullen, 1999; Hillberg, Hamilton-Giachritsis, & Dixon, 2011; Swenson & Hanson, 1998). It is also not empirically justifiable to conclude that sexually abused children are likely to suffer more psychosocial difficulties than children who suffered other forms of physical abuse (for a review, see Swenson & Hanson, 1998).

There are a host of moderating and mediating factors that account for the lack of a simple linear relationship between the experience of child abuse (including sexual abuse) and the development of psychopathology in children (and, later, adults) (Ammerman, Cassisi, Hersen, & Van Hasselt, 1986; Briere, 1992; Conte & Schuerman, 1987; Fergusson & Mullen, 1999; Kendall-Tacket et al., 1993; McGloin & Widom, 2001; Milgram, 1989; Swenson & Hanson, 1998; Widom, 1998; Wolfe & Birt, 1997; Wolfe & Wolfe, 1988). Those factors include the following:

- The existence of other chronic adversities that often exist in homes with multiple problems, including poverty, unemployment, and parental substance abuse
- The type, frequency, severity, and duration of abuse
- Whether the abuse included sexual abuse
- The relationship of abuser to victim (e.g., father, stepfather, neighbor, stranger)
- Severity level of threats used (e.g., bodily harm, death) at the time of abuse
- Innate resilience or vulnerability due to temperament and child's coping abilities
- Cognitive appraisal of the abuse, the abuser, and related factors
- Response of familial and social supports around the child (e.g., denial, attempts to prevent the abuse or efforts by nonoffending adults to provide emotional support afterward)

In general, multiple types of maltreatment, duration of abuse, and the associated severity of events predict greater long-term psychosocial effects in adulthood (Higgins & McCabe, 2001). Manifest symptoms and behavioral consequences are also relative to developmental level. For example, younger children may experience night terrors and somatic and externalizing problems, and adolescents are more likely to exhibit depression, suicidal behaviors, and substance abuse (Swenson & Hanson, 1998). Although child abuse in its various forms appears to have some proportional relationship to future psychopathology and violence, most abused children do not become abusive parents or violent members of society. The host of factors noted already here may increase or decrease the likelihood of predicting who succumbs to the impact of childhood victimization and who does not. However, interpreting these research findings is hampered by several methodological shortcomings (Anderson & Cramer-Benjamin, 1999; Fantuzzo & Mohr, 1999; Johnson et al., 2002; Milgram, 1989; Widom, 1989; Wolfe & McEachran, 1997).

Theories

Wolfe and St. Pierre (1989) identified three major categories of relevant theories of child abuse and neglect: the psychiatric model, which posits that child abuse and neglect is predominantly the result of parental mental health problems; the sociocultural model, in which parents succumb to some of the negative influences of social and economic deprivation; and the social-interactional model, whereby an abusive parent's psychological state mediates environmental stressors that may lead to abuse. However, the distinction among these theories has faded as research has become more multidimensional (Wolfe & McEachran, 1997). The factors that explain the causes of child abuse and neglect and the consequences of abuse in the short and long term include a range of biological, familial, social, environmental, and economic factors as they interact over time (Azar, Povilaitis, Lauretti, & Pouquette, 1998; Belsky, 1993). Theories that overemphasize one group of factors over another must be qualified. Despite the assertion, for example, that environmental factors are predominantly to blame for child abuse and neglect (e.g., Garbarino, 1977, 1997; Garbarino & Kostelny, 1992), there is no reason to believe that child abuse is predominantly the result of social, political, economic, and cultural conditions. This emphasis on the "ecosystem" is apparently intended to take responsibility for child abuse off the shoulders of an individual parent (and affiliated adults) and place it exclusively on society as a whole. However, evidence demonstrates that no specific psychosocial factors are necessary or sufficient to account for child maltreatment. The combination and interactions of factors are complex, and they include the psychological characteristics of the parent (or caregiver) (e.g., temperament, learning history, childhood experience, modeling of his or her own parents, beliefs about child-rearing practices, parental psychopathology), characteristics of the child (e.g., behavioral disorders or temperamental problems related to prenatal conditions, other health problems), parent-child interactions (e.g., an irritable parent with a history of abuse in his or her own childhood attempting to discipline a naturally rambunctious child), social-cultural factors that condone violence, social stressors related to poverty, overcrowding, crime and violence, and the impact of these factors on the parents and their ability to cope. Intergenerational effects of these personal, interpersonal, and contextual factors have also been recognized. Longitudinal data, for example, have demonstrated that the more risk factors present (e.g., poverty, young single mothers, poor maternal mental and physical health, lack of paternal involvement, difficult childhood temperament), the more likely (by several orders of magnitude) it is that maltreatment will occur (e.g., Brown, Cohen, Johnson, & Salzinger, 1998). Although there is little doubt that poverty and the effects of living in a crime-ridden neighborhood can make raising children more challenging, engaging in child abuse and neglect is far from being the domain of the poor.

Other theories have focused on the psychological processes that account for pathological outcomes in children who have been sexually abused. Psychodynamic theorists such as Hartman and Burgess (1990) have offered their theories of how children psychologically process the abuse event. On a foundation that considers pre-trauma factors, characteristics of the abuse event, quality of the disclosure experience, and post-disclosure outcomes, they explain: "The premise of informational processing gives some clues to the intensity of defensive adjustment made by children who are assaulted over a prolonged period of time. Their initial distress is subdued by a level of cognitive operations that allows the abuse activities to be stored partially in past memory. It is merely speculation as to what the child goes through to do this" (Hartman & Burgess, 1990, p. 116). They then use the psychodynamic concepts of "encapsulation of the event, dissociation, splitting, ego fragmentation, and drive disharmony[,] . . . which shows how the traumatic event is processed and provides the conceptual link between the event experience and patterns of post-abuse adjustment (Hartman & Burgess, 1990, p. 117). Encapsulation of the event involves the child keeping the event (which may still be in progress) to him- or herself. Because encapsulation requires considerable psychological energy, the effects disrupt the child's normal psychosocial development, including sense of self and other self-regulatory activities. They theorize that the child then relies on the defense mechanisms of dissociation, splitting, denial, and "ego fragmentation" to deal with psychological stress associated with the abuse. They further aver that several possible outcomes to the event may ensue, including an integrated pattern (i.e., child sees the abuse realistically and is able to discuss it with some objectivity) and an avoidant pattern (i.e., child denies the event and refuses to discuss it). Avoidance may lead to stress and later psychological and social problems. A third possible outcome is a symptomatic pattern whereby the child develops long-term difficulty coping with the event, feels guilty, engages in self-blame, and may experience behavioral problems (e.g., acting out sexually). Should identification with the abuser occur, the child eventually impersonates the aggressor and masters the anxiety by antisocially exploiting others. The problems with this formulation are, first, the stages of the theory, and possible outcomes are largely descriptive and simply reflect possibilities documented in the empirical literature. However, the explanations regarding how these processes occur make reference to theoretical constructs and processes that are largely untestable and simply inferred from case-study observation. Little evidence has been forthcoming to substantiate psychodynamic explanations for how some children develop problems and others do not. No prospective research has identified the unconscious processes as predictive of child or adult psychopathology in abused versus nonabused groups.

Finkelhor's traumagenic model (Finkelhor, 1988; Finkelhor & Browne, 1985) proposed that four psychosocial dynamics associated with sexual abuse distort cognitive and emotional processes in children: traumatic sexualization (causing distorted views of sexual feelings and behavior), betrayal (causing general distrust of various persons associated with the abuse or the community response to it), powerlessness (a sense of learned helplessness, depression, and fear), and stigmatization (guilt and shame leading to other problems, such as withdrawal from others and substance abuse). Although a thoughtful theoretical model—and perhaps a useful way to organize potential long-term effects of child sexual abuse—there is little empirical evidence to support the model or the fact that these concepts reliably predict the behavioral outcomes associated with them. Again, as noted earlier, many factors are likely to significantly affect the long-term consequences of child sexual abuse.

Some theoreticians have emphasized the model of post-traumatic stress disorder (PTSD) to account for the long-term effects of child sexual abuse (e.g., Kendall-Tacket et al., 1993). Certainly, severe abuse, including sexual abuse, is a traumatizing event, and children have been shown to manifest core symptoms of PTSD in response to abuse, including intrusive thoughts, numbing, hyperarousal, and avoidance. However, in their review, Kendall-Tacket et al. (1993) suggest that the PTSD model is not always a good fit for several reasons: sexual abuse produces no traumatic symptoms that are necessarily unique compared to other traumatic events; other non-PTSD problems (e.g., running away, promiscuity) may result from sexual abuse; and many victims of child sexual abuse do not develop PTSD symptoms. O'Donohue et al. (1998) consider that the PTSD theory of child sexual abuse is still evolving and provides a useful model for understanding the consequences of abuse.

Key Elements of Multidimensional-Functional-Systems Assessment

The initial identification of suspected child abuse or neglect may come from a number of sources, including hospital emergency room staff, a police officer, physician, school nurse, social worker, other professional, or private citizen in the community. Many professionals, including social workers, are "mandated reporters," meaning that they are legally required to report suspected incidents of child abuse or neglect to state child protective services and/or the police. Once a report is filed, a child protective services worker initiates a more formal intake and investigation. Should an initial screening produce evidence of child abuse or neglect, a more thorough assessment should follow (Pecora et al., 2000).

Two major purposes of the child abuse and neglect assessment include the *clinical assessment*, to prepare the child and other family members for psychosocial intervention if needed, and the *forensic investigation*, to assist in prosecuting the person who abused the child. These methods may be applied in parallel fashion or be conducted simultaneously by an interdisciplinary child abuse investigatory team. Regardless of which specific role or combination of roles the social worker takes on, competent assessment of child maltreatment requires both clinical and legal knowledge, use of evidence-based risk assessment data, and the implementation of valid instruments to augment the qualitative assessment (Milner, Murphy, Valle, & Tolliver, 1998).

Assessment of child abuse and neglect requires a multidimensional and functional perspective to capture all relevant data related to the child, the parents or other caregivers, the child-parent relationship, and the relationship of the family to the social environment. With the primary concern being the child's safety and well-being, the interacting causes and consequences of abuse or neglect need to be linked causally over time. Input is required from multiple sources, including the child and family members, teachers, child protective workers, social workers, psychologists, physicians, teachers, law enforcement personnel, and neighbors. Data must also be obtained and collated with multiple methods, including face-to-face interviews, medical exams, observation of the adults and their children individually and together in the home and the consulting office, behavioral performance tests of parenting skills, observations of the couple's communication and problem-solving skills, and the use of standardized scales. Gradually, a more detailed and fine-grained analysis focuses on the behavior of the parents and other important adults in the child's life, the child's behavior, and an analysis of parent-child interactions, in order to determine the nature of their relationship and the parents' capacities for providing nurturance and positive disciplining over time (Wolfe & McEachran, 1997).

An assessment of overall family functioning includes identifying evidence of domestic violence, evaluating basic conditions of the home environment (e.g., safety, adequacy of the structure, overall cleanliness), and socioeconomic conditions (e.g., adequacy of food, clothing, shelter). An evaluation of overall family structure, communication styles and patterns, problem-solving skills, and coping capacities with crises and everyday stressors can be very telling. The use of a global family functioning scale such as Family Adaptability and Cohesion Evaluation Scales (FACES) (Olsen, Russell, & Sprenkle, 1989) can provide useful insights. The family's quality of relationships with extended family and level of social supports, friends, and other relations in the community can indicate their level of social integration, whether they allow themselves to be observed, or whether they have become increasingly isolated.

Assessment of individual adults in the household should include psychosocial history, including evidence of their own experiences as victims of abuse and neglect; history of domestic violence and substance abuse in their respective families of origin; and other traumatic events, sudden losses, and the like. Practitioners should examine parents' own relationships with family and peers during their adolescence; the quality of their own relationships through adolescence and early adulthood; and their own engagement in abusive behaviors, violence, criminality, or drug abuse (or successful adaptation in healthful relationships, educational, and occupational achievements). Any history of family members' prior involvement in mental health, substance abuse, criminal justice, or previous child protective services systems should also be identified and explained. A review of the parents' adult relationships and/or marital history should carefully include evidence of couple conflict, domestic violence, substance abuse, parenting style, custody arrangements, infidelities, financial problems, and so forth (on assessment of couples, see chapter 11).

A thorough psychosocial assessment of the parents' behavior should include level of parenting skills (both nurturance and positive discipline procedures) and any evidence of outright abuse (e.g., psychological abuse or emotional negligence, physical and sexual abuse) of previous or current children in their care. A thorough examination of each parent's relationship with his or her children should include the degree of empathy and caring the adult shows for the child, hostility, and evidence of harsh verbal or physical disciplining practices. The practitioner should assess each adult's expectations of the children and the perception of what behavioral norms the adult applies to their children given their respective ages. Practitioners can observe parenting skills (in the consulting office or, preferably, in the home) by asking adults to engage in play activities, provide normative discipline for some infraction of house rules, or demonstrate how they make a request for a child to accomplish a household task. Despite the seemingly contrived nature of this request (and expecting that parents would strive to perform at their best), these demonstrations can be quite telling, particularly if the practitioner is adept at putting the adults somewhat at ease. Observation and demonstration of parent-child interactions can be accompanied by videotaped role-plays to assess parenting style or the manner in which parents communicate with each other about their children or how they communicate with their children directly. Parents often attribute immediate "triggers" for child abuse to the child's behavior (e.g., difficult or oppositional behavior, excessive crying, screaming).

When interviewing an adult suspected of child abuse, there is good reason to be concerned (as with many "mandated" or involuntary clients) about the validity of his or her self-report. In estimating the validity of the initial report of abuse, the practitioner should pay particular attention to the following data: a known history of abuse, any delay in obtaining assistance for the injured child, any incongruity between the client's assertions and known evidence of abuse, and any variation in the client's narrative about what events actually occurred with regard to the abuse allegations (Wolfe & McEachern, 1997).

The assessment should cover the individual child's psychological and social functioning commensurate with the child's age and developmental level. Evidence of internalizing and externalizing disorders should be examined (see chapters 12 and 13), and adjunct instruments should be used as needed. The Shortform Assessment for Children (Glisson, Hemmelgarn, & Post, 2002) can provide a relatively brief yet comprehensive overview of significant symptoms (see appendix B). Although children may suffer from anxiety, depression, and behavioral disorders for various reasons, the practitioner can begin to make tentative cause-effect inferences between the child's functioning and the parent's behavior by observing the quality of parent-child interactions, the parent's communication style and disciplining practices, whether the child appears to be receiving sufficient emotional nurturance, the child's perception of parents' expectations of him or her, and the emotional expression of the child and parents in each other's presence. Other important indicators of child well-being include school performance; relations with peers; and overall health and adequate physical care, including food, clothing, and basic medical care, as well as regular adult supervision and/or school attendance, adequate personal hygiene, and any evidence of physical or sexual abuse (Kaplan et al., 1999; Pecora et al., 2000; Wolfe & McEachern, 1997). Although psychological, behavioral, and situational problems among family members, including children, can have multiple causes and can co-occur for various reasons, practitioners must build a case for child abuse by carefully linking the parent's behavior to evidence of psychological and physical abuse and/or neglect of the child in a gradual, logical, and evidence-driven fashion. Again, collating the results of multiple sources of data gathered using multiple methods can go a long way toward determining whether a child's problems are associated with parental neglect or physical abuse.

Although many medical examinations do not reveal confirmatory evidence of child abuse, it is an essential part of the assessment process. Reichert (1992) emphasizes the need to examine the child carefully for unexplained burns, bruises, scars, as well as torn, stained, or bloody clothing. Lesions, warts, abrasions, lacerations, and the like in the genital or anal areas may be readily observed in a medical examination. Practitioners should note any difficulty walking or sitting, pain with diapering or when held, bowel dysfunction (e.g., constipation, encopresis), somatic complaints, and any behavioral changes. Other medical indicators include marks of physical trauma near the child's mouth or genitals, evidence of abnormalities resulting from an anal examination, or positive test results for sexually transmitted diseases. The chances of obtaining compelling forensic evidence increase with a timely medical examination. Should a practitioner suspect abuse, he or she should make a referral to child welfare authorities as soon as possible. Most often, indications of abuse can be observed externally by the attentive medical professional, and many signs can be readily observed by nonmedical practitioners (e.g., marks on a child's face, arms, and legs).

Depending on the type and the severity of the abuse, a range of intervention options is possible, depending on availability of services. These may include simple monitoring of the case and family counseling at a local family service center, specialized services for the child and/or other family members (e.g., mental health, substance abuse treatment), or more intensive home-based multidimensional treatment (e.g., intensive family preservation services). In cases with a more acute concern for the immediate safety of the child, other services may be available: temporary out-of-home placement; foster and kinship care; residential care for the child; family reunification at some later date; and termination of parents' rights and permanent removal of the child to foster care, kinship care, or adoption. This continuum of services is likely to vary considerably from case to case and from state to state, given the variability in the application of assessment protocol and standards, regional benchmarks for what constitutes levels of abuse and neglect, and the availability of services all along the continuum of care (Pecora et al., 2000).

Despite promising developments in empirically validated approaches to child abuse assessment in general, "the application of scientifically informed techniques for the assessment of emotional, physical, and sexual abuse of children are not uniformly applied across jurisdictions in United States, and highly questionable assessment techniques continue to be employed" (Mart, 2010a, p. 266).

Special Considerations: Sexual Abuse Assessment

Should sexual abuse be suspected during the initial child abuse screening and assessment process, a specific sexual abuse assessment and investigation should follow. It is best to approach the assessment of child sexual abuse as a special evaluation procedure nested within a comprehensive child abuse and neglect assessment (O'Donohue et al., 1998; Swenson & Hanson, 1998; Wolfe & Birt, 1997). However, blending the roles of clinical practitioner, advocate, and forensic evaluator is generally not advised, as the evaluator must consider several hypotheses and examine all relevant evidence as objectively as possible. There is also considerable overlap in the requisite knowledge and skill between a valid clinical and forensic assessment, despite the fact that the data gleaned from the clinical assessment and forensic investigation are applied to somewhat different purposes (i.e., preparation for intervention vs. determining whether a crime has been committed). As with a child abuse and neglect assessment in general, the state-of-the-art sexual abuse evaluation requires a comprehensive (i.e., multidimensional) and interdisciplinary team approach that employs multiple data sources, including clinical interviews; scales; direct observation; medical and other physical evidence; and the self-reported observations of multiple sources, including the child, parents, the child with each parent, and significant others who have knowledge about the child.

The clinical assessment focuses on identifying and gauging the impact of sexual abuse on the psychosocial well-being of the child, family functioning, and other indications of abuse or neglect in order to plan the intervention (Swenson & Hanson, 1998). A team approach is likely to increase cross-validation of observations and help avoid biases interjected by one practitioner's taking on of different roles with different interviewees. If an allegation of abuse is made, the accused should be interviewed by a practitioner with expertise in interviewing child sexual abusers (McGleughlin, Meyer & Baker, 1999). The forensic investigation may be conducted by a law enforcement professional, child protective worker, social worker, or other mental health professional or team of professionals. The forensic assessment focuses on determining the validity of the accusation. The investigators also strive to determine the frequency, severity, and duration of the abuse; whether use of force or other forms of coercion occurred, the relationship of the alleged abuser to the child, the time and place and other situational factors associated with the abuse, the current safety of the child, the ability of other caretakers to protect and support the child, and the potential for further abuse.

Anywhere from 20% to 50% of initial allegations are ultimately not confirmed, and (contrary to common opinion) only a small percentage of allegations are related to custody conflicts (and these are no more likely to be confirmed than allegations of sexual abuse in general). When allegations are confirmed, many cases are not prosecuted for several reasons, including poor cooperation from the alleged victim and family, variations in state jurisprudence, and ambivalence as to the recognition of child abuse as a crime or a mental health problem. The investigation and trial experience for children can be very stressful, but most children report after the fact that it was worth doing, and there appears to be little long-term harm from the judicial experience itself (Wolfe & Birt, 1997).

A detailed history should be taken to cover the child's normative development and identify problems, specifically any that appear to be directly related to sexual abuse (e.g., evidence of sexual trauma, exposure to pornography or adult sexual behavior, precocious sexual behavior), and details about the parent's mental health, substance abuse, level of partner intimacy, and sexual history (McGleughlin et al., 1999; Swenson & Hanson, 1998). The History of Victimization Form (Wolfe, Gentile, & Bourdeau, 1987) covers a list of specific sexual abuse indicators, including solicitation to abuse, exhibitionism and forced viewing of sexually explicit material, sexual kissing, touching and fondling, digital penetration, giving and/or receiving oral stimulation to genitals, and intercourse. The relationship of the perpetrator to the child is identified, as is duration and frequency of each type of abuse, as well as the degree and types of coercion employed (e.g., blackmail, rewards, threats). Although there has been much controversy regarding the validity of children's memories of alleged sexual abuse, children's memories of the events are generally considered to be accurate, although the degree of accuracy depends on several factors, including age, type, and style of interview, as well as other situational factors. Prompts to anchor memory (e.g., "Where were you?" "Who was there?" "What were you wearing?") can help children recall events more accurately. (Controversies regarding the problems with assessing the validity of memory and "recovered" memory are considered further later in this chapter.)

There appears to be some consensus regarding forensic and clinical evaluations of allegations of sexual abuse. The list that follows here presents the main points to be addressed when conducting expert assessment (e.g., American Academy of Child and Adolescent Psychiatry, AACAP, 1990; American Academy of Pediatrics, 1991; American Professional Society on the Abuse of Children, 1990; American Psychological Association, 1994; Kuehnle, 1996; McGleughlin et al., 1999; O'Donohue & Fanetti, 1996; Saywitz, Goodman, & Lyon, 2002). Recommendations for practitioners conducting a sexual abuse assessment include the following:

- Build good rapport with the child and other principals involved.
- Be clear about whether the interview is forensic or clinical in nature and the respective importance of the content of the interview in the context of the overall legal process.
- Communicate the limits of confidentiality.
- Obtain proper training to testify in court.
- Obtain multiple reports from significant others (e.g., parents, teachers, police, doctors, school nurses, coaches).
- Include interviews with the child alone (except with very young children) and not in the presence of the alleged perpetrator of the abuse.
- Orient the interview to the correct developmental (cognitive, verbal) level of the child.
- Proceed from general to more specific questions without leading or suggesting the answers.
- Use open interviewing techniques that avoid leading, suggestive, or even coercive methods.
- Be informed about normative sexual activity or play among children and adolescents.
- Consider the timing and circumstances of the allegations, the disclosure, and the function and impact on the family or any divorce process (e.g., opportunities for the child being led or used as leverage in custody battles).
- Consider whether the child's sexual knowledge is congruent with his or her developmental level, or whether other circumstances may have exposed the child to sexual material (e.g., videotapes, magazines, witnessing adults having sex or children being abused).
- Judge whether the child's disclosure is congruent with the child's own language or other vocalizations mimicked from an adult.

- Examine whether the child's report is consistent within and between interviews.
- Determine the quality of the child's emotional response to the report.
- Videotape the investigative interview to avoid the stress of repeated interviewing.
- Recognize the ability and limitations of child's testimony in court and the potential for negative effects of testifying on the child.
- Make an effort to determine the child's ability to tell the truth and accurately recall events.
- Elicit facts about the abuse: what happened, how, when, where, and under which circumstances. Have the child report other relevant details (e.g., clothes, smells, body parts or unique physical details such as tattoos); query the child for circumstantial facts (e.g., "What was on television?" "Was it night or day?" "Who was home?").
- Ask the child to describe other details about the abuser's behaviors such as bribes or threats of reprisal.
- Determine the basic plausibility of the alleged abuse event by comparing the report to other known facts (e.g., the abuser was out of town that week).
- Be alert for denials of abuse and signs of coercion or pressure to claim or deny abuse originating from others.
- Be cautious and informed about the limitations of using drawings, play, anatomically correct dolls, and other forms of psychological testing that require interpretation of ambiguous stimuli (e.g., drawings, projective testing).
- Recognize the limitations and fallibility of memory, the role of suggestibility in changing memories, and the fact that memories are subject to distortion, and assess the child's overall competency and credibility.
- Understand that many problems children have are not unique indicators of sexual abuse (i.e., there is no sexual abuse syndrome); their distress or symptoms may indicate the occurrence of other problems.
- Use valid scales as adjuncts to the multidimensional interview.
- Obtain a thorough medical examination of the child.

Despite these well-documented guidelines, the empirical evidence supporting the validity of child sexual abuse assessments is lacking (McGleughlin et al., 1999). As noted earlier, there is no consistent symptom profile or syndrome for sexually abused children. Many symptoms are found in many non-sexually-abused children as well. Conversely, the absence of symptoms does not suggest that a child was not abused, as many sexually abused children manifest no symptoms. In addition, empirical examinations of interviewing skills with child sexual abuse demonstrate a high degree of inaccuracy in determining whether sexual abuse has occurred, partly because of the indeterminacy of child self-report. The testimony of sexual abuse experts cannot be taken at face value or dismissed out of hand. Standardized assessment protocols are not available for any specific age group, and instruments cannot be confirmatory any more than the self-report of individuals. Although careful interviewing of a child's narrative account may increase the validity of recall, suggestibility in children remains a serious concern. Research findings from confirmed cases of abuse can be misleading because they are based on non-representative groups of abused children. Overall, although a well-trained sexual abuse evaluator using evidence-based protocol can identify many cases of childhood sexual abuse accurately, there is still considerable room for false positives (i.e., false accusations of abuse) and false negatives (i.e., not confirming abuse when, in fact, it happened). Although the validity of assessment for mental health problems in general falls well short of 100% accuracy (e.g., diagnosing depression or anxiety disorders), the clinical and dispositional implications of these problems are not nearly as profound as they are in making decisions that may permanently alter the lives of children and their parents (O'Donohue et al., 1998). Social workers who perform clinical or forensic assessments of child sexual abuse and interventions are well advised to obtain specialized training from recognized professionals who engage in evidence-based assessment and intervention practices.

Controversial Issues and Methods in Child Sexual Abuse Assessment

There has been much controversy over the years regarding how to conduct interviews with children who have been sexually abused, which methods lead to false-positive and false-negative conclusions about abuse, the reliability of memory, and the use of drawings or dolls to evoke accurate recollections and details of sexual abuse. Key matters of concern are addressed in this section.

The Reliability and Validity of Memory and Recovered Memories. The reliability and validity of children's memories and the phenomena of repressed and recovered memories have been controversial topics in clinical practice for some time. In general, children's memories, particularly memories that have been consistently maintained over time, are considered fairly resistant to distortion. However, the likelihood of memory distortion is related to the following factors: the child is of preschool age; the child has been intimidated by authoritative persons; the child has experienced delay between the event and the time of recall, has been influenced by the suggestions of others; and the child has been affected by retroactive interference (e.g., memories of a previous abusive situation affects recall), autosuggestion (e.g., previously held beliefs about sexual abuse), and/or confabulation of information to fill memory gaps, among other reasons (Goodman, Bottoms, Shaver, & Qin, 1995; Wolfe & Birt, 1997). The general controversy in eliciting children's memories of abuse seems to lie somewhere on a continuum, ranging from nonleading open-ended questions to prompts, to leading questions. At the extreme, children can be pressured to answer questions a certain way, as in cross-examination of an adult witness in a criminal trial. There is compelling evidence that, in fact, memory can be unreliable and that children's reports of abuse (or absence of it) can be influenced or distorted through pressure or coercion. Even highly detailed investigatory interviews are fraught with reliability and validity problems because children's reports and memories can be manipulated. Most experts understand that validating an allegation of sexual abuse in a clinical or a forensic assessment is very challenging (e.g., AACAP, 1997a; Loftus, 1993, 1994; O'Donohue & Fanetti, 1996). They also recognize that although many memories of abuse are accurate, people do often forget or distort memories, and the recollection of memories once forgotten is certainly a *possibility*. Noting that many people who have been sexually abused always remember the event, Geraerts, Raymaekers, and Merckelbach (2008) reviewed the literature on recovered memories and concluded that slowly emerging recovered memories during therapy are likely to be due to suggestion and are more likely to be inaccurate and susceptible to false memories than are memories that arise spontaneously outside of therapy. In those cases, some people may have forgotten that they once remembered the abuse (Geraerts et al., 2009).

The problem with assessing repressed memory lies not in its possibility but in determining whether recovered memories can be accurately determined through clinical assessment techniques (e.g., any technique ranging from ordinary interviewing to memory regression work). These questions are important and must be determined by scientific inquiry, not uncontrolled case studies or conference testimonials. Because even the most skilled investigators employing "objective" evidence (e.g., medical evidence, eyewitnesses) have trouble making highly confident allegations of abuse, those who make their allegations based on highly questionable assumptions, unsubstantiated theories, and untested interviewing and diagnostic techniques are more likely to make false allegations (i.e., false positives) and are more likely to inaccurately dismiss the possibility that abuse actually has occurred (i.e., false negatives). Basing one's assessment on false assumptions (e.g., satanic ritualistic abuse is common); confusing correlation with causation (e.g., depression and low self-esteem are obvious indicators of sexual abuse); and/or using assessment techniques that lack scientific merit (e.g., body work, memory regression, dream analysis, projective testing and interpretation of children's drawings) make allegations of sexual abuse (in general) and recovered memories (specifically) much more risky. A good rule of thumb in making allegations of sexual abuse is to use evidence-based assessment guidelines that have been promoted by leading professional groups, to use a range of conventional assessment tools and protocols based on data gathered from multiple points of view, and—above all—to be conservative in making criminal allegations of child abuse. For a more thorough discussion of this critical topic, see Loftus (1993, 1994).

Despite much of the distortion promulgated in the field, scientific consensus regarding the repressed memory phenomenon has emerged (Eisen & Goodman, 1998; Knapp & VandeCreek, 2000). In brief:

- Child abuse in all its forms is harmful in the short and often in the long-run.
- Satanic ritual abuse of children is rare.
- Continuous memories of abuse are likely to be accurate.
- Some memories can be lost and recovered.
- Memories from infancy are highly unreliable.
- False memories can be created.
- Traumatized children are no more suggestible than nontraumatized children.
- Memory recovery techniques are not reliable.
- Child and adult emotional and behavioral disorders can be successfully treated without having first established whether sexual abuse actually occurred.
- The complex processes involved in the interaction of traumatic events and memory are not sufficiently understood to justify much confidence in "recovered memory" work.

Projective Techniques.   Projective testing is, at best, a questionable approach to assessment in the mental health field. However, its use in child abuse assessments (particularly sexual abuse) is highly controversial. These techniques include drawing methods (e.g., house-tree-person, draw-a-man), freehand drawing, interpretation of children's play, and Rorschach testing, among others. The fundamental problem with such tests (given their psychoanalytic origins) is that they require practitioners to make cause-effect interpretations from highly ambiguous data that can usually be interpreted in any number of ways. Although a denotative drawing by a young child (e.g., two people having sex) is reason for concern, interpretations of ambiguous material are more likely to be influenced by the expectations of the interpreter than what is necessarily on the mind of the child or relevant to their actual experience.

Reviews of methodologically sound research (e.g., Veltman & Browne, 2002) have concluded that, although the use of projective tests may be useful for stimulating discussion and evoking emotional expression, there is no evidence that the interpretation of children's impressionistic drawings, paintings, dreams, or play is a reliable or valid method for establishing allegations of sexual abuse or for diagnostic purposes, nor do these have any predictive value for psychosocial interventions. In general, evidence continues to emerge that investigative techniques that require children to draw or construct human figures fail to distinguish children who have been abused from those who have not (e.g., Williams, Wiener, & MacMillan, 2005). However, nuanced modifications of these approaches have been offered. Noting, for example, that free-recall memory is considerably more accurate than prompted recall, and that younger children are more prone to suggestibility than older children, Aldridge et al. (2004) used gender-neutral human-figure drawings with 90 children (72 girls) ranging from age 4 to 13 years to determine whether such drawings elicited more information from children and whether the child's age made a difference. They found that drawings elicited substantially more relevant details, especially in younger children, after the initial phase of the investigation (relying on unprompted free recall) had exhausted the child's memory. However, these details required more prompting with the human-figure drawing, an approach that is associated with less accurate recall and results from greater suggestibility in younger children. The authors recommended that, "to minimize contamination, therefore, it is preferable that human figure drawings be introduced as late as possible in investigative interviews, as they were here" (Aldridge et al., 2004, p. 309).

Anatomically Correct Dolls.   The use of anatomically correct dolls in well-trained hands has come to be considered useful as part of a comprehensive evidence-based assessment (Everson & Boat, 1994; Swenson & Hanson, 1998). According to Wolfe and Birt (1997), "Recent research evidence has quelled many of the concerns about anatomically correct dolls. Dolls do not elicit unfounded reports of sexual behavior or elicit excessive sexual behavior in free-play conditions with non-abused children; they are also useful in discriminating abused from non-abused children in terms of both sexual abuse disclosures and sexual play with the dolls" (p. 595). In general, the proper use of dolls elicits more valid disclosures of sexual abuse than do open-ended questions. When using the dolls to interview children, interviews should occur as soon as possible after the alleged event, multiple interviewers should be discouraged, practitioners should avoid leading questions, open-ended questioning of children is preferred, developmentally sensitive questions should be used with younger children (younger than age 6), and interviews should be videotaped (Lamb, 1994).

Wolfe and Birt (1997) concluded from their review of the empirical literature that anatomically correct dolls should be used to identify body parts (e.g., penis, vagina, buttocks), clarify previous statements, and help nonverbal or low-verbal children express themselves and describe an event after there has been indication of abuse activity. They affirm, though: "However, [al]though unusual behavior with dolls may be worthy of note in an evaluation report, such behavior without a direct report of sexual abuse should not be considered conclusive evidence of abuse" (Wolfe & Birt, 1997, p. 597).

The use of dolls to comfort a child, help break the ice in an interview, facilitate conversation, stimulate emotional expression, and help stimulate memory when narrating experiences is generally accepted as useful and reasonably valid as long as the interviewer does not lead the child. When used for these purposes, suggestiveness and interviewer error are relatively low (Everson & Boat, 1994; Swenson & Hanson, 1998).

As with projective and other interpretive methods, it may be best to characterize the proper use of anatomically correct dolls as facilitative, but not confirmatory, of abuse. Noting the lack of evidence in support of using anatomically correct dolls for forensic interviews with children who have allegedly been sexually abused, Hlavka, Olinger, and Lashley (2010) conducted a naturalistic study of 500 videotaped forensic interviews and found that interviewers perceived that the dolls helped clarify information, yielded better consistency from children, helped children distance themselves when describing abuse, and generally improved communication with children. This evidence, however, does not support or detract from claims that the use of anatomically correct dolls has highly predictive validity in corroborating abuse, but it does suggest that the dolls can facilitate the child's description of the alleged event.

Cultural Aspects in Assessment of Child Abuse and Neglect

Although some genuine efforts have been made to examine racial and ethnic differences regarding child abuse and neglect (e.g., Meston, Heiman, Trapnell, & Carlin, 1999; Moisan, Sanders-Phillips, & Moisan, 1997), research is marked by several methodological shortcomings, including lack of representativeness in samples, problems in defining ethnic subgroups and abuse and neglect, and lack of adequate statistical controls. Thus, practitioners should exercise caution in drawing conclusions about ethnic differences given the stigmatizing nature of child abuse allegations.

Despite the lack of consistent evidence in linking cultural factors to child abuse and neglect, there are important general recommendations that apply to social work practice with diverse populations. It is important to consider the cultural milieu of the community before engaging in child abuse and neglect interventions. The lack of compatibility between practitioners' beliefs, attitudes, and behaviors and those of their clients on matters of child-rearing practices, family norms, and rituals can impede efforts to help. Practitioners should strive to understand the cultural processes of the communities they intend to assist (O'Donnell, Wilson, & Tharp, 2002).

For example, noting the lack of research on family preservation services with Native Americans, Coleman, Unrau, and Manyfingers (2001) have provided some thoughtful suggestions. Assessment and successful engagement of Native American families requires some basic understanding of the tribe one is involved with; the importance of family (particularly with regard to intergenerational relationships that include ancestors); the communal view of extended family and their responsibility for raising the children; and the role of spirituality and importance of symbol, ceremony, and rituals (which can be readily incorporated into family interventions). Broader social and historical matters need to be understood and recognized as well. These include a keen sensitivity to the history of oppression and dislocation experienced by many tribes, continuing poverty and protracted periods of unemployment among many Native Americans, and the devastation wrought by addiction to alcohol and other drugs. An awareness of tribal history, sense of frustration, distrust, humiliation, and disempowerment is vital before practitioners can expect any level of acceptance. Specific knowledge and skills apply even on the micro level of engagement: basic familiarity with communication norms (e.g., significance of eye contact, acceptability of asking personal questions, readiness to endure long periods of silence during conversations).

As indicated in chapter 2, given the variability among all groups of people, no standard "diversity" methods apply to all relevant cases. Yet practitioners can open doors through showing patience, appreciating history and culture, and learning a bit of language *before* attempting to engage. When they do engage, they should be willing to ask questions and listen to answers before presuming to help.

Current Status of Risk Assessment of Child Abuse and Neglect

Currently, the state of the art for making risk assessments of child abuse and neglect in the field is embryonic. Most evidence suggests that even experienced practitioners do not accurately predict the likelihood of abuse given current practices in child welfare. In one prospective study of 446 at-risk families positively identified for child abuse and followed for 5 years (DePanfilis & Zuravin, 1999), results demonstrated that family stress, partner abuse, social support deficits, and child vulnerability factors were significantly predictive of later abuse. Further analysis of decisions to close these cases showed that workers were not using evidence-based criteria to support their decisions about the likelihood of reabuse. In addition, workers tended to concern themselves less with child neglect than with child abuse, despite the potentially greater consequences associated with neglect (DePanfilis & Zuravin, 2001).

In a three-wave survey of 432 children alleged to have been abused or neglected, Camasso and Jagannathan (2000) tested the reliability and predictive validity of a structured assessment tool (the Washington State Risk Assessment Matrix; Marks & McDonald, 1989) for predicting reoccurrence of abuse. They found poor reliability ratings and little reason to believe that subsequent abuse could be predicted with any confidence. However, they suggested that risk assessment scales be improved by shortening them to focus on items that have been shown to be predictive of abuse (e.g., chronicity of abuse, substance abuse problems) and by applying more rigorous psychometric standards to the selection of instruments (i.e., ensuring reliability and validity). A convergent validity study of 261 cases in the US Northwest (English & Graham, 2000) showed insignificant and otherwise weak correlations between child protective workers' judgments and research interviewers' ratings on an extensive battery of valid instruments for measuring multiple domains of child and parent well-being and functioning. Finally, a recent examination of child protective services decision-making patterns highlighted further concerns about workers' accurate identification of child abuse and neglect. Rossi, Schuerman, and Budd (1999) compared the decisions of 27 child welfare experts with those of 103 child protective services workers, and they based their coded decisions on 70 actual case summaries. Findings revealed little relationship between level of professional experience and pattern of decision making. The authors underscored the obvious risks inherent in making false-positive and false-negative decisions, and they noted the need for evidence-based standards to be developed for child protective service assessment, evaluation, and decision making.

Despite all that has been written regarding the importance of improving child protective services assessment, there is a lack of research on the matter. Recently, the first substantive descriptive survey of child protective evaluations in Illinois was conducted (Budd, Felix, Poindexter, Naik-Polan, & Sloss, 2002; Budd, Poindexter, Felix, & Naik-Polan, 2001). A random sample of about 200 African American, Hispanic, and Caucasian children was selected from child protective case rolls, and evaluations were conducted largely by doctoral-level psychologists. On the basis of case data using rigorous coding methods, Budd and colleagues (Budd et al., 2001; Budd et al., 2002) demonstrated the following: (1) multidimensional assessments including a range of methods and data collected over multiple sessions were not the norm; (2) there was a disproportionate focus on the child's attributes or developmental functioning but little ecological validity (i.e., getting collateral reports and/or observing the child in a range of other settings such as school or with peers); (3) despite their lack of validity, projective assessment methods were used in almost 90% of cases; (4) many reports did not make any assessment of the credibility of collected data; and (5) the purpose of the evaluation (i.e., clinical, forensic) was often not clear.

Regarding problems in child sexual abuse assessments specifically, mistakes in child sexual abuse interviews (Mart, 2010b) include the following: failure to develop rapport; lack of understanding of developmental capacities of the child; failure to use hypothesis testing; use of leading questions or suggestively reinforcing certain responses from the child; failure to develop contextual details surrounding the abuse; and failure to use structured interview protocols (see Lamb, Orbach, Hershkowitz, Epslin, & Horowitz, 2007). However, improvements are possible. A review of the literature has suggested that use of the child sex abuse interview protocol developed by the National Institute of Child Health and Human Development (NICHD), which emphasizes free-recall prompts and techniques to avoid "leading" or suggestive questions, improves the reliability and accuracy of such interviews, including with younger children (Lamb et al., 2007). To improve the ability of child protective workers to make informed decisions and reduce risk of harm to children, more aggressive efforts must be made to incorporate the training and use of evidence-based assessment tools into child welfare services.

Instruments to Screen For and Measure the Effects of Child Abuse and Neglect

Several standardized measures may enhance the assessment of risk for child abuse and neglect (Camasso & Jagannathan, 2000; Lyons, Doueck, & Wodarski, 1996; McDonald & Marks, 1991), but they must be used as part of a comprehensive multidimensional-functional-systems (MFS) assessment. In addition, broad and narrow scales are useful for measuring baseline severity of children's problems (whether related to abuse or not) and for monitoring and evaluating changes in the child's problems. PTSD scales, in particular, have become widely used for children who have suffered traumatic stressors such as child abuse. Other adjunctive tools should also be considered for assessing mental health, substance abuse, and other problems in children and adult family members, along with tools that measure family functioning (Combs-Orme & Thomas, 1997). Many relevant scales have been noted or more fully described in other chapters.

The Child Abuse Potential Inventory (CAPI) (Milner, 1994; Milner, Gold, & Wimberly, 1986; Milner et al., 1998; Walker & Davies, 2010) is a widely used screening device for child abuse that is self-administered by the parent. It has 160 items and contains a 77-item physical abuse scale (but is not intended to detect sexual abuse) and six other subscales: distress, rigidity, unhappiness, problems with child and self, problems with family, and problems with others. It also contains scales to detect lying or other inconsistencies. Overall reliabilities (internal consistency, split half, test-retest) for subscales have been good to excellent, and the CAPI accurately classifies physical abusers and nonabusers better than 80% of the time with various abusive populations. The scale also correlates with perception of behavior problems in the child, negative parent-child interactions (e.g., harsh and/or authoritarian discipline), low social supports, family conflict, and a lack of family cohesion. The CAPI also correlates with abuse-related life stress and with physiological and psychosocial indicators of abuse. Although more research is needed to determine its predictive validity for abuse, the CAPI scale does appear to be sensitive to change in clients when administered over time. Thus, the CAPI seems to be a useful adjunct to an MFS assessment for screening, monitoring, and evaluation.

Although not all abused and neglected children meet criteria for PTSD, even subclinical signs and symptoms (e.g., avoidance, arousal, numbing, dissociation) may be an indication that a child is under significant duress because of psychological or physical abuse and neglect. The Children's Impact of Traumatic Events Scale-Revised (CITES-R) (Nader, 1997; Wolfe & Gentile, 1991) is a structured interview instrument designed to measure children's cognitions regarding the effects of abuse. It is intended to be used with children aged 8–16, and it comprises 78 items (11 subscales). With older children it may be administered as a paper-and-pencil self-report scale. It takes between 20 and 40 minutes to administer. Many of the items were borrowed from other related scales, and several subscales were derived from factor analysis. The scale measures a number of important constructs, including PTSD symptoms, perceptions of social support following abuse, abuse attributions (e.g., guilty feelings), and eroticism. Scale items are scored (0–2) from "not true," "somewhat true," to "very true." Internal consistency reliabilities generally are in the acceptable range, although inadequate alpha coefficients have been noted for a few of the subscales (e.g., "dangerous world") (Crouch, Smith, Ezzell, & Saunders, 1999). Other data have shown moderate support for both the internal consistency and the concurrent validity of the CITES-R subscales with sexually abused children (Chaffin & Shultz, 2001).

The Trauma Symptom Checklist for Children (TSCC) (Briere, 1996; Nader, 1997) is a 54-item scale intended to measure the effects of trauma and child abuse in children aged 8–16. Subscales include measures of anger, anxiety, depression, dissociation, PTSD symptoms, and sexual concerns. Items are rated on a four-point frequency scale (0–3), from "never" to "sometimes," "lots of times," and "almost all the time." Subscales are in the acceptable range for internal consistency reliability, have shown good concurrent validity with other validated scales, and have demonstrated good discriminant validity with sexually abused (vs. nonabused) females. Population norms are available. With a group of 119 hospitalized adolescents, the TSCC subscales were shown to be reliable, and they correlated well with other independent measures of psychiatric distress; also, the PTSD subscale accurately distinguished sexually abused adolescents from those who were not sexually abused (Sadowski & Friedrich, 2000).

The Post-Traumatic Stress Disorder Reaction Index (PTSD-RI) is one of the most widely used and validated instruments for measuring PTSD symptoms in children and adolescents. Developed in the mid-1980s (Frederick, 1985), the initial administration of the PTSD-RI was in response to a fatal sniper attack on a children's school playground (Nader, Pynoos, Fairbanks, & Frederick, 1990; Pynoos et al., 1987). The PTSD-RI has been translated into several languages and has been used in many countries to assess trauma symptoms in children who have been subjected to natural disasters, sniper attacks, political violence and terrorism, exposure to atrocities; who have witnessed sexual assaults of their mother and/or suicide of an adolescent peer;

who have faced life-threatening medical illnesses; and who have suffered severe burn injuries, among other traumatic events, including the terrorist attack on the World Trade Center in New York City in 2001 (Steinberg, Brymer, Decker, & Pynoos, 2004).

Evolving with changes in DSM criteria for PTSD, the current PTSD-RI (Revision 1) is designed as a paper-and-pencil instrument to be used for screening young persons for PTSD symptoms, and it is also useful for monitoring and evaluating the effects of intervention. The items are thoughtfully designed to be easy to read with little or no prompting from the interviewer. It is divided into three parts. Part 1 contains dichotomous (yes or no) items that screen for lifetime traumatic events. Part 2 (13 items) provides an assessment of DSM-IV criteria: A1 (i.e., intense fear response to a traumatic event; items 15–21) and A2 (i.e., symptoms of reexperiencing; items 22–26), and item 27 (for dissociation). These 13 items relate directly to the traumatic event referenced in part 1 that the respondent marked as having bothered him or her "the most." (The list of traumatic events includes items related to child physical and sexual abuse.) Part 3 addresses symptoms of PTSD that correspond to DSM-IV criteria B, C, and D (i.e., intrusive thoughts, avoidance, and arousal). These 20 questions are specially designated to correspond with specific PTSD criteria. These items are scored on a continuous frequency scale (0–4) corresponding to "none," "little," "some," "much," and "most," and indicating the relative frequency with which the symptoms occurred during the previous month. A frequency scale guide is included to help children anchor their frequency estimates (instrument 14.1). A scoring sheet is also included (appendix G) to tabulate the subscale scores and total score corresponding to DSM-IV criteria.

The children's version is intended for use with those aged 7–12 years (see instrument 14.1). A parent version closely mirrors the children's version. There is also an adolescent version (minor alterations in language) for those older than age 12. (The adolescent and parent version are available from Dr. Pynoos.) Practitioners can administer the scale in a face-to-face format and detach the frequency scale guide so the child can easily follow along. The "past month" criteria can be modified as needed to suit the relevant time frame in reference to the traumatic event (e.g., "since the traumatic event," "in the past week since X occurred"). Under most circumstances the scale can be administered and scored in less than an hour. The scale should be administered by someone who has some training and familiarity with PTSD and diagnostic DSM-IV criteria, and who is at least a graduate student intern under the supervision of a licensed master's-level clinician.

The scoring guidelines for parts 1 and 2 are straightforward. In part 3, only those 17 items corresponding to the DSM-IV criteria are scored. Three of the items have alternate forms, and the one that the child scores higher is counted in the final scoring. The scoring guide helps the practitioner calculate the total PTSD severity score and scores for each DSM-IV criteria (B, C, and D). A cut score of 38 or more has been shown to have optimal sensitivity and specificity for detecting PTSD (Steinberg et al., 2004). The PTSD-RI has been shown to have very good to excellent internal consistency (e.g., Layne et al., 2001), good to excellent test-retest reliability (Pynoos et al., 1987), and good convergent criteria with DSM diagnosis (e.g., Pynoos et al., 1993). The PTSD-RI is an excellent screen and treatment evaluation tool. The different formatted versions of the PTSD-RI, associated training materials, and scoring aids are available from the authors (rpynoos@mednet.ucla.edu).

INSTRUMENT 14.1   Post-Traumatic Stress Disorder Reaction Index (PTSD-RI)

Below is a list of VERY SCARY, DANGEROUS OR VIOLENT things that sometimes happen to people. These are times where someone was HURT VERY BADLY OR KILLED, or could have been. Some people have had these experiences, some people have not had these experiences. Please be honest in answering if the violent thing happened to you, or if it did not happen to you.

FOR EACH QUESTION: Check "Yes" if this scary thing HAPPENED TO YOU.
Check "No" if it DID NOT HAPPEN TO YOU.

1. Being in a big earthquake that badly damaged the building you were in. Yes [   ] No [   ]

2. Being in another kind of disaster, like a fire, tornado, flood or hurricane. Yes [   ] No [   ]

3. Being in a bad accident, like a very serious car accident. Yes [   ] No [   ]

4. Being in a place where a war was going on around you. Yes [   ] No [   ]

5. Being hit, punched, or kicked very hard at home. (DO NOT INCLUDE ordinary fights between brothers & sisters.) Yes [   ] No [   ]

6. Seeing a family member being hit, punched or kicked very hard at home. (DO NOT INCLUDE ordinary fights between brothers & sisters.) Yes [   ] No [   ]

7. Being beaten up, shot at or threatened to be hurt badly in your town. Yes [   ] No [   ]

8. Seeing someone in your town being beaten up, shot at or killed. Yes [   ] No [   ]

9. Seeing a dead body in your town (do not include funerals). Yes [   ] No [   ]

10. Having an adult or someone much older touch your private sexual body parts when you did not want them to. Yes [   ] No [   ]

11. Hearing about the violent death or serious injury of a loved one. Yes [   ] No [   ]

12. Having painful and scary medical treatment in a hospital when you were very sick or badly injured. Yes [   ] No [   ]

13. OTHER than the situations described above, has
    ANYTHING ELSE ever happened to you that was
    REALLY SCARY, DANGEROUS OR VIOLENT?   Yes [ ] No [ ]

14. a. If you answered "YES" to only ONE thing in the above list of questions 1
       to 13, place the number of that thing (1 to 13) in this blank. _____

    b. If you answered "YES" to MORE THAN ONE THING, place the number of
       the thing that BOTHERS YOU THE MOST NOW in this blank. _____

    c. About how long ago did this bad thing (your answer to a or b) happen
       to you? _____

    d. Please write what happened: _____
       _____
       _____

**FOR THE NEXT QUESTIONS, please Check "Yes" or "No" to answer HOW
YOU FELT during or right after the bad thing happened that you just
wrote about in Question 14.**

15. Were you scared that you would die?   Yes [ ] No [ ]

16. Were you scared that you would be hurt badly?   Yes [ ] No [ ]

17. Were you hurt badly?   Yes [ ] No [ ]

18. Were you scared that someone else would die?   Yes [ ] No [ ]

19. Were you scared that someone else would be hurt badly? Yes [ ] No [ ]

20. Was someone else hurt badly?   Yes [ ] No [ ]

21. Did someone die?   Yes [ ] No [ ]

22. Did you feel very scared, like this was one of your
    most scary experiences ever?   Yes [ ] No [ ]

23. Did you feel that you could not stop what was
    happening or that you needed someone to help?   Yes [ ] No [ ]

24. Did you feel that what you saw was disgusting or gross? Yes [ ] No [ ]

25. Did you run around or act like you were very upset?   Yes [ ] No [ ]

26. Did you feel very confused?   Yes [ ] No [ ]

27. Did you feel like what was happening did not seem real
    in some way, like it was going on in a movie instead of
    real life?   Yes [ ] No [ ]

Here is a list of problems people sometimes have after very bad things happen.
Please THINK about the bad thing that happened to you that you wrote about
in Question 14 on page 2. Then, READ each problem on the list carefully. CIR-
CLE ONE of the numbers (0, 1, 2, 3 or 4) that tells how often the problem has
happened to you in the past month. Use the Rating Sheet on page 5 to help you
decide how often the problem has happened in the past month. PLEASE BE
SURE TO ANSWER ALL QUESTIONS.

HOW MUCH OF THE TIME DURING THE PAST MONTH

		None	Little	Some	Much	Most
1D4	I watch out for danger or things that I am afraid of.	0	1	2	3	4
2B4	When something reminds me of what happened, I get very upset, afraid or sad.	0	1	2	3	4
3B1	I have upsetting thoughts, pictures, or sounds of what happened come into my mind when I do not want them to.	0	1	2	3	4
4D2	I feel grouchy, angry or mad.	0	1	2	3	4
5B2	I have dreams about what happened or other bad dreams.	0	1	2	3	4
6B3	I feel like I am back at the time when the bad thing happened, living through it again.	0	1	2	3	4
7C4	I feel like staying by myself and not being with my friends.	0	1	2	3	4
8C5	I feel alone inside and not close to other people.	0	1	2	3	4
9C1	I try not to talk about, think about, or have feelings about what happened.	0	1	2	3	4
10C6	I have trouble feeling happiness or love.	0	1	2	3	4
11C6	I have trouble feeling sadness or anger.	0	1	2	3	4
12D5	I feel jumpy or startle easily, like when I hear a loud noise or when something surprises me.	0	1	2	3	4
13D1	I have trouble going to sleep or I wake up often during the night.	0	1	2	3	4
14AF	I think that some part of what happened is my fault.	0	1	2	3	4
15C3	I have trouble remembering important parts of what happened.	0	1	2	3	4
16D3	I have trouble concentrating or paying attention.	0	1	2	3	4
17C2	I try to stay away from people, places, or things that make me remember what happened.	0	1	2	3	4
18B5	When something reminds me of what happened, I have strong feelings in my body, like my heart beats fast, my head aches, or my stomach aches.	0	1	2	3	4

19C7 I think that I will not live a long life.

None Little Some Much Most
0   1   2   3   4

20AF I am afraid that the bad thing will happen again.

None Little Some Much Most
0   1   2   3   4

Frequency Rating Sheet

How often or how much of the time during the past month, that is since _____, does the problem happen?

None 0							Little 1							Some 2							Much 3							Most 4						
S	M	T	W	T	F	S	S	M	T	W	T	F	S	S	M	T	W	T	F	S	S	M	T	W	T	F	S	S	M	T	W	T	F	S
								X							X				X			X		X		X		X	X	X	X	X	X	X
															X						X		X		X			X	X	X	X			
												X					X				X		X		X			X	X			X	X	
																	X	X			X	X	X				X	X	X	X	X	X	X	X

Never	2 times a month	1–2 times a week	2–3 times a week	Almost every day

SELECTING EFFECTIVE INTERVENTIONS

This section provides a critical overview of interventions that span the continuum from prevention to early intervention to reactive interventions. The methods used along that continuum include individual treatment of the child affected by abuse and neglect, interventions with parents to improve their child-care skills, home-based interventions that address parenting and environmental conditions (e.g., safety) in the home, and ecosystemic programs that employ multiple modalities in the home and the community (e.g., interface with schools, criminal justice system). If parental rights are terminated, children may be referred to foster or kinship care or be made eligible for adoption, services that go beyond the scope of the current chapter.

Interventions targeting child abuse and neglect must be understood in the context of child welfare policy. Pecora et al. (2000) summarize important principles and notable legislation. The main principles of child welfare include the following:

- Ensuring child safety and promoting the psychosocial and economic well-being of child and family
- Empowering the family in directing their future well-being
- Paying due attention to the unique cultural context and needs of families
- Providing access to services
- Making the child welfare system accountable
- Facilitating efficient coordination of system resources

The goals of the child welfare system strive to balance child psychosocial and physical well-being with permanency planning for the family, a difficult and often contentious balance to maintain. Modern child welfare policy began to emerge in the 1960s in response to a growing national awareness of abused and neglected children, captured in the phrase "battered child syndrome" (Kempe, Silverman, Steele, Droegemueller, & Silver, 1962). This growing awareness inspired legislation to cope with the prevention of child abuse. Important child welfare legislation includes the following:

- The Child Abuse Prevention and Treatment Act (1974), which mandated reporting of child abuse and neglect, and provides funds for prevention and treatment demonstration projects
- Title XIX of the Social Security Act, which enhanced health-care services for low-income individuals and bolstered early childhood health-care services
- Adoption Assistance and Child Welfare Act of 1980, which was enacted to promote permanency planning for children
- Family Support Act of 1988, which gave further financial assistance for low-income families
- Adoption and Safe Families Act (1997), which was enacted to promote children's safety by reducing child abuse and neglect

In addition to a burgeoning body of research on the causes, prevention, and treatment of child abuse and neglect, all 50 states now have mandatory reporting laws for child abuse (Mattaini, McGowan, & Williams, 1996).

Preventing Child Abuse and Neglect

Wekerle and Wolfe (1993) examined more than 30 controlled studies evaluating prevention efforts for (primarily) young mothers to improve parenting skills as well as, secondarily, child developmental and behavioral competencies. The prevention efforts are premised on the notion that although there may be no obvious signs of neglect or abuse by (typically) poor, young single mothers, prevention may guard against problems that might arise later and interfere with a child's healthy psychosocial development. The studies reviewed were separated into three main categories: those that focused on parent competencies (i.e., intensive group intervention or home visits to provide support and parenting skills); parent-child support programs for new parents (i.e., home visits to provide information and support); and parent-child support for teen parents (i.e., group intervention or home visits to help improve attitudes and parenting skills). Although methodological limitations compromised the data, it appears that behavioral skills approaches that continue for up to 3 years hold more promise than general supportive, educational methods. However, results seem to show greater improvement in mothers' attitudes and skills than in improvements in children's well-being and development.

A meta-analytic review (MacLeod & Nelson, 2000) tested related hypotheses for 56 proactive and reactive programs designed to prevent or reduce child maltreatment. Proactive programs are designed to begin when the mother is pregnant, immediately after the birth of the child, or during early infancy. These interventions include home visiting and multicomponent social support and mutual aid. Community-based proactive programs include family support, child care and preschool education, and community development. Reactive programs are usually employed in early childhood in response to indicated child abuse or neglect. These programs include intensive family preservation (e.g., Homebuilders), multicomponent interventions (e.g., Project 12-Ways), social supports, and specific parent-training programs. The methodological criteria employed in the search included studies of children up to age 12 years; prevention programs only (excluding sexual abuse prevention programs); the use of prospective controlled designs; the use of studies only published in journals, books, and dissertations; outcome measures including indicators of out-of-home placement, child maltreatment, parental attitudes, observations of parents' behaviors, and measures of the home environment.

The authors of the review had expected the following findings to emerge from the analysis: programs using an ecological framework would be more successful than more targeted programs; empowerment and strengths-based interventions would be more effective than expert-driven, deficit-based interventions of longer duration and higher intensity; and interventions that employed both social and instrumental (concrete) supports would be more effective than those that employed a more targeted "professional helping approach." Findings of the meta-analysis revealed a total mean effect size for these programs of .41, which means that outcomes for clients in the experimental groups exceeded outcomes for 66% of those in the control groups, and longer interventions generally resulted in better outcomes overall. Effect sizes for proactive interventions tended to be higher at follow-up than when measures were taken post-intervention. However, the converse was true for reactive interventions. Interventions based on an ecological framework were not more successful than micro-level interventions. Although empowerment and strengths-based approaches had greater effect sizes than deficit-based approaches, many of the programs (e.g., family preservation services) generally used placement status as an outcome measure (thus conflating intervention and outcomes) but used measures of family, parent, or child well-being to gauge results. Last, social supports appeared to improve outcomes for proactive programs but had less impact in reactive programs, possibly because the social supports added an element of surveillance in cases where abuse had yet to occur. Overall, this meta-analytic review sheds a positive light on efforts to prevent and intervene with child abuse and neglect, but conclusions must be tempered with caution because of poorly defined program components and outcome measures.

A major review of outcome studies that focused exclusively on primary prevention programs for child neglect and physical abuse (nonsexual) revealed 11 studies that met rigorous methodological criteria (MacMillan, MacMillan, Offord, Griffith, & MacMillan, 1994a). Findings showed strong support for home visitation programs primarily targeted at the prenatal and early postnatal needs of poor, unmarried young mothers. In a second study focused on sexual abuse, MacMillan, MacMillan, Offord, Griffith, and MacMillan (1994b) showed that educationally oriented prevention programs can increase knowledge and safety skills regarding sexual abuse, but there is little evidence that such programs actually reduce rates of childhood sexual abuse. More recently, a meta-analysis of more than 40 evaluation studies revealed that early intervention programs for child abuse and neglect showed moderately positive results in improved parental skills and improved child functioning. However, this meta-analysis mixed nonrandomized and randomized studies (Geeraert, van den Noortgate, Grietens, & Onghena, 2004).

School-Based Prevention Strategies.   Although not explicitly developed for the purpose of reducing child abuse and neglect, programs that foster better school and community service integration may reduce some of the environmental risk factors that can lead to the neglect and abuse of children, including inadequate adult supervision of children; poor-quality day care; and parental stress symptoms due to overwork, poverty, and single-parent status, among other causes. The School program of the 21st Century (Zigler, 1989) was developed as a comprehensive year-round program of child care, early parent education, and family support for children and their parents from prenatal care to age 12. The program is based on several principles: creation of a stable and reliable child-care system, equal access for all children to quality child care, and adequate addressing of children's developmental (cognitive, emotional, social, and physical) needs. Finn-Stevenson, Desimone, and Chung (1998) reported that there were more than 500 such schools operating in at least 16 states and serving more than 250,000 families. The programs run year-round and are implemented after school lets out for the day and during school vacations and summers. The program includes outreach services in the community to provide in-home parent education and referral for other needed services. The results of a recent evaluation of two such schools covering the second to fourth years of the program (Finn-Stevenson et al., 1998) demonstrated several positive outcomes: reduced child-care costs for parents, reduced lost work hours, decreased parental stress, and an improved parent-child relationship. These outcomes imply promising influences on children's academic and psychosocial development and well-being.

Although child self-protection (awareness) programs in schools have shown that children learn the concepts associated with sexual abuse, little evidence suggests that these programs actually reduce child sexual abuse. Overall, prevention studies continue to suffer from serious methodological weaknesses (Finkelhor, 2009; Kenny, Capri, Thakkar-Kolar, Ryan, & Runyon, 2008; Topping & Barron, 2009).

Home-Visiting Programs.   Paraprofessional home-visiting programs can reduce rates of child abuse (Roberts, Kramer, & Suissa, 1996). In their review, Howard and Brooks-Gunn (2009) examined home-visiting programs to prevent child abuse and neglect. Although the results were mixed, they found them promising overall. Social workers often play a key role in home-visiting programs, sometimes teaming up with nurses or other health professionals. A narrative review in the United Kingdom and the United States of early intervention support services for vulnerable families with young children (Armstrong & Hill, 2001) found that while "voluntary" attendees (mostly young mothers and children) found the experience satisfying, "referred" clients found them to be stigmatizing, often viewing them as a "dumping ground." Nevertheless, these programs show some improvements in psychosocial adjustment for mothers and children. Longer-term programs (2 years or more) that provided education, occupational counseling, health education, and social support were found to be generally helpful. Although there are similarities in home-visiting programs, home health visitors give priority to the health of the young child but also provide emotional support and general advice on child rearing. Some of these programs have been targeted at mothers suffering from postpartum depression and/or other psychiatric problems, as well as low-birth-weight babies or those showing indications of failure to thrive. Overall, evidence from several quasi-experimental studies strongly suggests that children who are targeted by these programs make significant improvements in health and psychosocial adjustment in the long run. Many mothers in need have also accepted as positive the development of networking strategies, the enhancement of social supports, and the inclusion of paraprofessionals. In addition, the findings of uncontrolled studies suggest an increase in feelings of support and self-confidence, and fewer incidents of child abuse and neglect.

In one Australian study (Fraser, Armstrong, Morris, & Dadds, 2000), researchers conducted a controlled trial comparing in-home services with access to standard clinic health services in a group of young at-risk mothers. One hundred eighty-one mothers met the following criteria for being "high risk": single-parenthood status, victims of domestic violence, screening positive for child abuse and/or neglect, and experiencing financial stress and unstable housing. The cases were randomly assigned to an experimental early intervention home-visiting program intended to improve family and parent adjustment and to reduce incidents of child abuse and neglect. The program was specifically designed to promote a good working alliance with mothers, to improve mother-infant attachment, to enhance parenting skills, to promote healthful behaviors in the child, to reduce parental stress, to promote the use of social supports, and to reduce child abuse and neglect. The experimental program included intensive in-home services provided by a nurse, social worker, and paraprofessional assistants. A designated pediatrician coordinated services and provided care in a clinic setting and during in-home crisis situations. The experimental group received 20 or more home visits on average, and mothers with acute needs (e.g., low-birth-weight babies) received more home visits. Families receiving information about the availability of health and social services for the mother and child served as the control group.

Although the study demonstrated positive results in child, parent, and home adjustment measures after 6 months, there were no substantive differences in outcomes between the experimental and control interventions at 12 months. In the comparison group, only about 20% of the women consistently availed themselves of clinic services. No specific demographic factors predicted superior adjustment overall. In this case, it appears that access to standard child health-care services is as effective as intensive in-home care. Both interventions, when analyzed separately, also demonstrated a comparable reduction in child abuse potential.

Leventhal (1996) suggests a strategy for home visiting to prevent child abuse and neglect:

- Visits should begin early and occur frequently.
- Practitioners should emphasize the development of a sound working relationship.
- The home situation, including the child's needs (e.g., safety, health, nutrition), should be closely monitored.
- Practitioners should provide concrete services and supports for the family (e.g., transportation, housing, budgeting).
- Practitioners should model techniques to teach effective parenting skills.
- Attempts should be made to include males in the overall strategy.
- Interventions should be tailored to fit the needs of the particular family.

Given the reduction in available funds for such services, Leventhal (1996) suggests that the real question is "not whether we . . . can prevent these types of maltreatment from occurring (because the answer is yes), but whether we, as a society, can afford the resources to provide the necessary preventive services to families" (p. 647).

Child-Focused Interventions

Relatively little emphasis in the literature has been on directly treating abused and neglected children to improve their coping skills. Two prominent efforts are reviewed here. Fantuzzo et al. (1988) demonstrated that positive and prosocial peer-mediated play can result in more responsiveness in maltreated and withdrawn children. Thirty-nine children (about half non-Hispanic whites and half African Americans) who had been brought to the attention of child welfare professionals were randomly assigned to three groups. In group 1, "normal" peer children were taught to initiate prosocial behaviors toward the withdrawn child. In group 2, adult teacher aides prompted social interaction between the maltreated child and the peer. Group 3 served as a control condition. All treatment conditions included eight brief play sessions spread out over 3–4 weeks. Several observational measures were taken to rate four types of social interaction: behavioral initiations and responses and oral initiations and responses. By viewing videotaped samples, raters who were blind to the purposes and hypotheses of the study took measurements. Six-month follow-up data from classroom settings were available for about half of the sample. Results showed statistically significant improvements for children in the peer initiation treatment condition in both verbal and behavior initiations, and significant improvements in oral verbal initiations in the classroom setting. There were no significant effects in the adult-initiated or the controlled condition. Overall, the results support the use of peer social initiation strategies to help withdrawn children who have experienced neglect.

Culp, Heide, and Richardson (1987) conducted a controlled experiment in which 35 maltreated children were enrolled into a multiservice day-treatment program. The children were matched on age, gender, race, and problem category (i.e., abuse, neglect) with 35 maltreated children who did not receive services. Of the 70 children, 43% were female, 63% were African American and 37% white (non-Hispanic), and the mean age was 36 months. The program emphasized a strong teacher-child relationship and activities that focused on building self-esteem, enhancing caring peer relationships, coping with feelings, and engaging in multiple learning activities typical of preschool programs. The program was conducted for 6 hours per day, 5 days per week. Other services included individual child treatment, parent group counseling and educational services, individual therapy if needed, and a 24-hour telephone crisis service. Using cognitive, behavioral, interpersonal, and language development indicators, results demonstrated that the treatment group improved significantly more than the control group did. Percentile improvement scores were on average about 10–15 points higher for the treatment group post-treatment. A related study with a similar population and program (Culp, Richardson, & Heide, 1987) demonstrated that improvements were not related to race, but that girls benefited more than boys for reasons that were not explained. Although many of the skill-based programs to enhance children's coping skills were reviewed in chapters 12 and 13, the programs here are highlighted because they were tested specifically with children who were known to have been abused or neglected. Given the substantial rates of abuse and neglect in children who receive mental health services (regardless of the presenting problem), it is reasonable to suggest that interventions designed for internalizing and externalizing disorders in children would be beneficial for abused and neglected children as well. Nevertheless, there currently exists a lack of practice research that incorporates these skill-based approaches specifically for abused and neglected children.

Behavioral Family Therapy

A more extensive literature tests interventions designed to improve behavioral parenting skills for parents who have been identified as being abusive or neglectful (Barth, 2009; Gershater-Molko, Lutzker, & Sherman, 2002; Kazdin, 1994b; Wolfe & Wekerle, 1993). Some of these intervention methods have also been incorporated into broad-based ecobehavioral or other multimodal programs. These interventions share similar characteristics as those parent-child training programs reviewed in chapter 13 for use with conduct-disordered children and adolescents (e.g., Alexander & Parsons, 1982; Alexander, Holtzworth-Munroe, & Jameson, 1994; Gurman, Kniskern, & Pinsof, 1986; Hazelrigg, Cooper, & Borduin, 1987; Kazdin, 1997; Lebow & Gurman, 1995; McMahon & Forehand, 1984; Webster-Stratton & Herbert, 1994). Behavioral techniques such as psychoeducation, modeling, role-playing, practice, feedback, and reinforcement are intended to reduce the risk of abuse by helping parents to be more nurturing and to use more positive disciplining methods with children. Later developments to behavioral parent training included anger management, stress management, coping skills, anger control, and cognitive interventions to address the erroneous and unrealistic expectations some parents had of their children's behavior. Practitioners employing cognitive behavioral interventions can help parents avoid taking the child's provocative behavior as a personal affront and rather develop a more empathic understanding of the child's own emotional, physical, interpersonal, and/or situational needs (Corcoran, 2000). Controlled studies have shown that increasing parental self-control and other skills results in significantly improved emotional rapport between child and parent and a decrease in the child's negative and aggressive behaviors.

Wolfe and Sandler (1981) conducted a single-subject design with three parents referred through child protective services to evaluate the use of behavioral parent management techniques. In addition, contingency management (i.e., rewarding parents for consistent use of their newly learned parenting techniques) was employed as part of the intervention. The three case analyses revealed excellent results, which were maintained up to 12 months post-treatment. Watson-Perczel, Lutzker, Greene, and McGimpsey (1988) demonstrated with three single-subject evaluations of neglectful families that standard behavioral interventions (i.e., teaching, support, reinforcement, and contingency management) could be used to successfully help severely neglectful families (e.g., evidence of excrement, dead animals, swarms of cockroaches, decaying food) improve the safety, cleanliness, and health of the child's environment.

Schinke et al. (1986) conducted a matched-pairs experimental design in which the treatment group received a 2-hour stress management skills program for 10 weeks geared toward enhancing parents' self-control and improving interpersonal communication, positive disciplining skills, and skills for enhancing social supports. Although the authors reported significant improvements at post-test and at 6-month follow-ups, there were few details regarding measures employed. Nevertheless, the study offered one of the few skill-based brief interventions that could be readily employed in typical agency settings, and the results did include some follow-up data.

Several controlled trials provided substantial evidence for the potential of behavioral interventions to reduce abuse and neglect. Brunk, Henggeler, and Whelan (1987) compared group parent training with a multisystemic therapy (MST) for abusive and neglectful parents in an 8-week randomized controlled trial with an equal mix of white and African American parents. Results based on both standardized scales and videotaped observational measures showed significant improvements in both groups. However, there were also some differences: positive outcomes for MST included observational ratings showing significantly greater reductions in child abuse and neglect. Group parent training also resulted in enhanced social support for these parents and reduced isolation. Parent-training groups showed greater reduction in social isolation and improvement in their social well-being, whereas the multisystems group showed more improvements in parent-child relations. There were no follow-up measures taken, and the overlap in the results for both groups suggests considerable similarity between the two approaches, particularly in addressing parent-child management practices.

Whiteman, Fanshel, and Grundy (1987) investigated the effectiveness of a three-part cognitive-behavioral intervention with abusive parents who had trouble controlling their anger, often an antecedent to abuse. The investigators devised a skill-based intervention that exclusively targeted parents' thoughts, feelings, and behaviors related to anger control. Three specific cognitive-behavioral skills were investigated: cognitive restructuring (CR) (to change the parent's negative attributions regarding the child's behavior), stress management (SR) (to reduce arousal associated with anger), and problem-solving skills (PS) (to find more constructive ways to deal with the stresses of child rearing). Fifty-five subjects were randomly assigned (about evenly) to five groups: CR; SR; PS; a combined group of CR, SR, and PS; and a group that received agency treatment as usual. Participants were, on average, 33 years of age; poor; about 25% white, 25% Hispanic, and 50% African American; and 91% female. Realistic scenarios that would typically provoke an angry reaction on the part of the parent were portrayed and role-played. A scale that measured various dimensions of anger was developed as part of the study to evaluate the effects of the intervention. In addition, items adapted from previously published reliable scales were employed to measure affection, discipline, empathy, and irritating behaviors. Results suggested that the composite treatment package was the most effective intervention overall, although the relaxation training component probably did not account for much of the positive impact of the intervention. The authors concluded that because the current study included only six sessions of treatment, CBT packages provided for longer durations would likely yield even greater outcomes.

Wolfe, Edwards, Manion, and Koverola (1988) conducted a randomized trial comparing a child-care educational program (agency treatment as usual) with an education and parent training program based on McMahon and Forehand's (1981) model. Thirty young, poor, single mothers with young children (aged 9–60 months) completed the program, which lasted on average for 9 sessions. Trained graduate-level therapists with no prior parenting experience of their own provided the parent training interventions. Bachelor-level paraprofessionals conducted the educational component. Self-report measures included standardized instruments for quality of parenting and level of depression and observational measures of mother-child interaction, and standardized measures of child behavior were taken at pre-test, post-test, and follow-up. The parent-training intervention took place in a clinic setting. Education groups included 8–10 mothers and were conducted at the agency. Parent training included in vivo practice and an opportunity for parents to observe their own performance with their child on videotape, accompanied by constructive feedback. They were also provided with anxiety management and coping skills to improve interactions with their child. At 3-month follow-up, results indicated that those parents who received the behavioral parent training improved significantly more than did those who received just the educational component. However, for both groups, observational measures in the home were modestly positive but not significantly different. Reports at 12 months by child welfare workers on indicators of child care or abuse showed improvements for both groups as well. Overall, results strongly suggest that the addition of behavioral parent training to standard agency intervention improves outcomes for mothers of at-risk children. It is important to point out, however, that these mothers in need were carefully screened to rule out domestic violence, unsuitable housing, serious psychopathology, and substance abuse problems. In short, generalizing to situations of more severe trouble may not be warranted.

In a randomized controlled design, Meezan and O'Keefe (1998) compared the use of an eclectic combination of behaviorally oriented, psycho-educational, multifamily group therapy (MFGT) with traditional family services for 81 abusive and neglectful white, Hispanic, and African American families. Both groups also received case management to ensure adequate instrumental supports. Using a range of psychometrically sound scales to measure social supports, problem-solving skills, and attitudes toward child rearing, as well as knowledge of child development, family structure, and child abuse risk, both groups showed improvement, but the MFGT group showed more areas of improvement in potential of child abuse occurring and attitudes toward child rearing. Although it was difficult to discern whether the differences were due to differences in programmatic content or to the overall amount of service (i.e., the MFGT conditions received between three and five times as much face-to-face and phone contact during the study), and because there were no follow-up measures taken, it is hard to determine the durability of the changes. Nevertheless, one could argue the MFGT condition engendered better engagement in treatment than traditional services.

Interventions Designed Specifically for Children Who Have Been Sexually Abused

A small research literature on interventions with children who have been sexually abused has begun to emerge. It is also understood that, although a child's problems may be the direct result of sexual abuse, other contextual factors may contribute to their distress as well (e.g., poverty, dislocation, substance abuse, family conflict). Nevertheless, Swenson and Hanson (1998) make some basic recommendations regarding the unique practical aspects of treating a child who has been sexually abused. In the intervention, the practitioners should do the following:

- Assume that the child's safety has been secured, a thorough forensic and clinical assessment completed, and any crises stabilized

- Develop an empathic and sensitive relationship with the child to help him or her express feelings regarding the abuse

- Provide psychoeducation and cognitive interventions to help the child resolve erroneous beliefs about the abuse (e.g., "He told me it was my fault")

- Use anxiety and stress management techniques to help the child cope with residual anxiety and depression (e.g., night fears, feelings of guilt, worthlessness)

- Implement structural and behavioral family interventions to cope with other co-occurring problems through communication and problem-solving techniques, substance abuse treatment for those adolescents or adults who have remained in the home

- Provide a broader, multisystemic approach that includes clinical case management and other considerations, such as evidence of other abuse, neglect, and problems the child may have in school and the community.

Critics of sexual abuse intervention have accurately noted the lack of evidence to support psychodynamic approaches to treating children who have been sexually abused (Conte, 1984). However, according to literature reviews that include randomized controlled trials, interventions that have been shown to be effective with other internalizing and externalizing childhood disorders are also effective in reducing problems that are presumed to result from sexual abuse (Fergusson & Mullen, 1999; Finkelhor & Berliner, 1995; Nader, 2001; O'Donohue et al., 1998; Saywitz, Mannarino, Berliner, & Cohen, 2000). Multiple-baseline single-subject designs have revealed similar results (e.g., Farrell, Hains, & Davies, 1998). Finkelhor and Berliner (1995) noted several limitations in the sexual abuse treatment literature. In addition to the paucity of randomized trials, they noted the heterogeneity of problems experienced by children who have been abused sexually, the asymptomatic response of some who have not yet or will not develop symptoms, and the multiple-problem context in which sexual abuse often occurs.

In the case of a parent who is an abuser, the nonoffending parent may require intervention for any number of problems: reassessing his or her role in the family as parent, coping with the loss of his or her partner, and improving the relationship between the child victim and the nonoffending parent. Treatments for the offending parent are typically court mandated. As for some offending parents who remain or return to the home, some anecdotal literature on family therapy has described interventions whereby offenders recount their actions in manipulating the victim, apologize and take full responsibility for their behavior, redefine their role, and articulate different guidelines for their relationship with the victim and other family members. Given the high rates of co-occurring psychopathy in adult sex offenders, one must weigh carefully the likelihood of rehabilitation versus the risk of reoffending. Little research has been conducted on these types of family interventions after an offense has occurred (Swenson & Hanson, 1998).

Exemplar Study: A Controlled Trial of CBT and Family Therapy for Children Who Have Been Sexually Abused

The following controlled study illustrates an effective intervention for children who have been sexually abused. Thirty-six sexually abused children (aged 5–17), some of whom demonstrated PTSD symptoms, participated in a clinical study in which a cognitive-behavioral intervention (CBT) with family (i.e., parent or caregiver) involvement was compared to CBT without family involvement and a wait-list control group (King et al., 2000). Children received 20 sessions of CBT (50 minutes each), which focused largely on anxiety management, including hierarchical imaginal exposure and anxiety coping skills to address stressful memories and images related to abuse. Assertiveness and psychoeducation components were also included to help children learn personal safety skills and improve their sense of confidence. The family treatment condition emphasized problem-solving and communication skills for family members, and caregivers were taught contingency management skills to improve parenting. Parent and teacher training sessions were also coordinated by the practitioner. All treatments were geared toward children's developmental stage. Fidelity checks revealed high agreement between manual instructions and actual implementation. A range of standardized and validated indexes were employed to measure baseline assessment and outcome. These instruments measured the degree of PTSD symptoms, self-rated fear and anxiety, depression, and the child's perceived ability to cope with abuse-related symptoms. Results demonstrated very good improvement for both treatment groups compared to the control group. Although both the individual CBT and the CBT and family conditions showed comparable results in reduced PTSD symptoms, fear and anxiety, and global functioning at post-test and follow-up (12 weeks), practitioners found the family format more satisfying overall. In short, as with previous studies, CBT (with or without direct family involvement) was shown to be substantively effective in reducing symptoms associated with sexual abuse of children.

On the basis of results from relevant literature, Barth (2009) concluded that behaviorally oriented parental training and/or family interventions are the most effective approaches to reducing child abuse and neglect, but more resources must be brought to bear to improve research methods and to implement approaches in the field. For example, one randomized trial of a behavioral parent-training program (including parenting skills training and attention to financial and social supports) with parents on methadone maintenance showed a reduced potential for child abuse, improved attitudes toward more flexible parenting, and reduced child behavior problems (Dawe & Harnett, 2007).

Ecosystemic Approaches: Home-Based, Family Preservation, Family Reunification, and Other Multiservice Systems Models

Comprehensive multiservice ecobehavioral methods are typically some combination of home-based child and/or parent-focused interventions; enhanced social and instrumental supports; and other case management activities, which may include interactions with schools, medical professionals, and law enforcement personnel. The basic rationale of ecological approaches is the need to address the family's problems in their ecology in an integrated way on several interacting levels (i.e., individual, familial, community). In recent years, these methods have been provided in the context of the family preservation and reunification movement, where temporary placement of the child is sometimes part of the intervention.

The Homebuilders model (Kinney, Haapala, & Booth, 1991; Kinney, Madsen, Fleming, & Haapala, 1977) is perhaps one the most recognized family preservation interventions. This model, started in 1974 in Tacoma, Washington, is an intensive, in-home, brief, multiservice effort aimed to stabilize the family of the abused and/or neglected child by improving parenting skills, addressing mental health and substance abuse needs of individual family members, and providing case management to interface with larger social systems. As described in the initial program evaluation (Kinney et al.,

1977), a driving rationale for the development of this family preservation model was to prevent the removal of family members and avoid institutionalization of the child, given the associated emotional and financial costs. The Homebuilders concept was informed by research that showed that home-based interventions with families in crisis could prevent placement and institutionalization of the child. In that uncontrolled evaluation, 80 families were recruited who met the following criteria: they were in crisis, there appeared to be a high likelihood that some member would be removed, one member had expressed a strong desire to keep the family together, and staff would not be placed in a highly dangerous situation. After initial emotional and/or physical crises ebbed, workers focused on developing behaviorally defined problem definitions. In general, these problems included (in descending order of frequency) running away, truancy, school disruption, child abuse, other physical violence in the home, high suicide potential, and substance abuse, among others. The intervention comprised behavioral problem solving and skills training (e.g., communications training), advocacy and case management to improve community resources, and follow-up services for booster sessions if needed. More than 90% of participants were followed up on in a year. Virtually all cases avoided placement, the main goal of Homebuilders. However, many methodological weaknesses (e.g., lack of a control group; poorly defined interventions; lack of standardized outcome measures to evaluate the psychosocial functioning of children, adults, and overall family functioning) preclude definitive conclusions about the effectiveness of this program.

Walton (1997) conducted an experimental comparison only at post-test between child protective services (CPS) (i.e., treatment as usual) and CPS combined with 11 hours of family preservation services (FPS) in 132 randomly assigned cases. While the CPS investigators focused on allegations of abuse and neglect, the collaborating FPS workers emphasized strengths-based approaches to help the family take responsibility for strengthening itself, provided support, encouraged problem solving and decision making, accompanied parents to court, and established a network of services to increase child safety. Results showed that the experimental group cases were open for fewer days. The author concluded that home placement "hastened the closing of the case and the returning of total responsibility to the caregiver" (Walton, 1997, p. 456). On the basis of interviews 6 months after case determination, experimental services were deemed to have improved parents' (or caregivers') attitudes toward the agency. Participants said they were more satisfied with services, used more services and were more likely to use services, found counseling and other services more helpful, and appreciated the FPS services more than standard CPS services.

In a replication of this study with a similar randomized posttest-only experimental design (Walton, 2001) follow-up interviews were conducted with caretakers, caseworkers, administrators, and supervisors, and additional data gleaned from agency databases (e.g., abuse, neglect status, services used, custody history, caseworker demographics). Instruments included the Index of Parental Attitudes (Hudson, 1982b) and another interview questionnaire with no known psychometric qualities. As in the original study, the FPS intervention comprised engagement, problem-solving, and case management interventions provided in tandem with CPS services for an average of 14 hours. Attrition reduced the initial 97 experimental cases to 65, and the control cases from 111 to 60 families. Results demonstrated that, although there was no significant difference between the two groups in the number of children remaining in their homes, children in the FPS group were more likely to return to their home and stay longer. There was no difference between the two groups in the number of cases of substantiated abuse or services employed. The parents in the FPS group had significantly more problems regarding the parent-child relationship, yet they expressed more satisfaction with FPS workers, were more likely to view the services as helpful, and rated the FPS caseworkers higher. Other service-related data were reported as well, but no tests of significance were provided. There was no difference between the groups on additional referrals during the 6 months following the intervention. Although attempts to improve FPS services should be encouraged, there appears to have been relatively little methodological improvement in the research, thus frustrating any real attempts to determine the actual superiority of FPS versus standard child protective services. Others have cataloged the serious methodological flaws of family preservation programs (e.g., lack of control groups, poor measures) and have questioned the apparently exaggerated conclusions regarding successful outcomes (e.g., Lindsey, Martin, & Doh, 2002).

Pecora et al. (2000) outline the principles and assumptions of family reunification: (1) the primacy of the biological family as the preferred context for child rearing; (2) the family of origin is the best place to raise a child when the family is given adequate assistance; (3) separation from the biological family can have long-term negative consequences; (4) extended family members should be considered part of the family unit; (5) reunification is seen on a continuum from partial to full reconnection with the child's family; (6) children should be reunited in a timely manner, and early and consistent contact with their families of origin should be brought about as soon as is feasible; (7) if it becomes clear that the risks of reunification to the child's well-being far outweigh the potential benefits, termination of parental rights remains an option, although some connection may still be maintained. Evaluating whether a child should be reunified with his or her biological family requires a thorough assessment of the following considerations:

- The parents' and child's mutual expectations and willingness to be reunified with one another

- A thorough reevaluation of the parents' skills and competencies, as well as expectations; adequacy of the home; and the parents' ability to care for the child's psychological, emotional, and physical needs

- Resolution of the problems that brought about placement initially
- A gradual reintroduction of the child into the home with progressively longer visitations
- Dealing with temporary setbacks to progress
- Continued liaising with social service professionals, legal monitoring, and involvement with foster parents and other social supports

Overall, outcomes of family reunification programs are indeterminate at this time (Pecora et al., 2000). However, in one combined quantitative and qualitative study on the effectiveness of family reunification, Terling (1999) examined data collected on more than 1,500 cases over 4 years. An in-depth case-record analysis of 59 randomly selected cases was also conducted to provide a finer-grained view. Of reunified cases, 37% were shown to reenter the CPS system within 3.5 years. No differences in reentry rates were shown between whites and African Americans. A disturbing finding revealed that CPS worker assessments were not predictive of whether a child was likely to be further abused or neglected. In addition, when serious risks were documented in the case record, they were sometimes ignored. A close-up examination of 59 cases revealed that several factors were associated with reentry into the system: (1) previous and repeated involvement with CPS; (2) substance abuse in the parent or partner and a lack of sufficient time to succeed in recovery; (3) an inability to grasp basic parenting competencies; and (4) inadequate social support. The study also pointed up one particularly illuminating fact: removal of the perpetrator of child abuse from the home virtually eliminated the risk of that child being abused again.

Project 12-Ways (Lutzker, Bigelow, Doctor, Gershater, & Greene, 1998; Lutzker & Rice, 1984) is an ecobehavioral approach whereby assessment and intervention are conducted in the client's living environment (i.e., home, school, and other relevant community settings). The intervention may include several services, such as parent-child training, stress management, homemaker skills and budgeting, marital counseling, and infant health care. Some evidence suggests that families do benefit from participation in Project 12-Ways. Lutzker and Rice (1987) compared outcomes (further abuse and neglect) between Project 12-Ways and child protective services (i.e., treatment as usual) with 97 randomly selected families. Results showed some slight advantage for Project 12-Ways clients, but other methodological problems preclude definitive answers.

Lutzker, Bigelow, Doctor, Gershater et al. (1998) reported two replications of Project 12-Ways: Project SafeCare and Project Ecosystems. Project SafeCare included 3 of the 12 components of Project 12-Ways: home safety (e.g., identifying and correcting hazards), infant-child health care (e.g., recognizing and seeking prompt treatment), and bonding and stimulation (e.g., increasing positive parent-child interactions) (Lutzker, Bigelow, Doctor, & Kessler, 1998). Five weeks of service were provided for each component consecutively for a total of 15 weeks. In the evaluation, two groups of predominantly Hispanic families were served: a nonabusive at-risk group and a group with confirmed abuse and neglect referred by child welfare staff. Four single-subject case studies were conducted to test the efficacy of the program. Results indicated modest improvement in safety, health care, and parent-child behavior. Because of the methodological limitations, results must be viewed with caution. Project Ecosystems was implemented with developmentally disabled children in an urban setting and was also shown through single-subject designs to be reasonably effective (Lutzker, Bigelow, Doctor, Gershater et al., 1998). Both studies provided modest support for integrating behavioral interventions in a more ecologically valid systems approach (Gershater-Molko et al., 2002; Lutzker, Van Hasselt, Bigelow, Greene, & Kessler, 1998).

Overall, ecosystemic approaches to child welfare show mixed results. Those approaches that incorporate behavioral skill-based interventions have shown considerable promise. However, given the lack of clearly defined interventions, as well as the lack of standardized measures and randomized trials, firm conclusions cannot be drawn regarding the effectiveness of these models (AuClaire & Schwartz, 1986; Friedman, 1991; McDonald & Associates, 1990; Wells & Biegel, 1992).

Related Needs of Clients Receiving Child Welfare Services

Substance Abuse Services.   Substance abuse is a prevalent and challenging problem in families who encounter the child welfare system. Substance abuse is one of the main barriers to successful long-term outcomes in child welfare endeavors (Azzi-Lessing & Olsen, 1996; Semidei, Radel, & Nolan, 2001). Substance abuse and associated criminal problems among parents of abused and neglected children co-occur with a wide range of other difficulties, including mental illness, health problems (e.g., HIV), and domestic violence, among others. The consequences of children's exposure to the effects of substance abuse and addiction include increased risk of depression, anxiety problems, low self-esteem, learning difficulties, behavioral disorders, interpersonal problems, and substance abuse (Dore, Kauffman, Nelson-Zlupko, & Granfort, 1996). CPS services can be improved through training workers in valid assessment and monitoring substance abuse in their clients, improving integration with substance abuse services, and developing better collaboration with law enforcement and the criminal justice system (Semidei et al., 2001).

To date, little research on coordinating substance abuse services and child welfare has been conducted, although anecdotal evidence suggests that it is feasible (e.g., Gruber, Fleetwood, & Herring, 2001; McAlpine, Marshall, & Doran, 2001). In one study, substance-abusing women with children who were involved with child protective services were surveyed during or soon after receiving substance abuse services. Although there was both a low response rate to the survey and concerns about self-reporting bias, there was some suggestive evidence that matching services to the needs of the clients could result in better outcomes (Smith & Marsh, 2002). Some of the evidence-based approaches to treating couples or adolescents with a substance abuse problem could be readily incorporated into an ecobehavioral approach to dealing with child abuse and neglect. These methods include motivational enhancement therapy, coping skills approaches, behavioral couples and family interventions, and community reinforcement and contingency management approaches (see chapters 7 and 16).

Residential Programs.   Reviewers have noted that 24-hour residential treatment services serve a purpose in the child welfare system by providing a haven of last resort for many children, and giving them distance from the abusive, neglectful parents and the intense emotional conflict. This time-out gives them a chance to obtain emotional and psychological support, and it provides an opportunity to affiliate in a peer environment. Ideally, such stays are time limited, and parents are concurrently involved in treatment. Despite the rapid increase in small residential facilities for placement of abused and neglected children, relatively little research of adequate methodological quality has been conducted on such services. Therapeutic programs in the residential treatment facilities do not appear to result in sustainable benefits when children are released back to the community (Pecora et al., 2000; Smokowski & Wodarski, 1996).

Foster Care, Kinship Care, and Adoption.   Programs such as foster care, long-term group homes, and other residential treatment programs may be an option should attempts to prevent abuse, reduce it via intervention, preserve the family, or reunite the family fail. Termination of parental rights and adoption of the child by permanent foster parents is a possible outcome. Smokowski and Wodarski (1996) found that placements of long duration are associated with a combination of more severe child behavior problems, parental skill deficits, poverty, and lack of social supports. Although there are considerable methodological weaknesses in the data regarding psychosocial correlates of children in foster care, Horan et al. (1993) demonstrated in a review of the literature (from 1974 to 1989) that children who entered foster care have very high rates of serious mental health disorders and are in need of much more care than is currently available.

About 500,000 children are in foster care at any given time. They are taken from their families of origin for reasons ranging from inadequate parenting skills to serious physical or sexual abuse. The number of children in foster care continues to grow, and children of color, particularly African Americans, are disproportionately represented and are likely to remain in foster care longer than their white counterparts. Foster care is intended to be a temporary placement, and it refers not only to "family foster care" but also to temporary placement of a child in a group home or other residential settings. During this time, the initial problems that prompted the child's removal from the home can be ameliorated through psychosocial intervention, social services, and possibly adjudication, should criminal acts such as sexual abuse have occurred.

Problems that have plagued the foster-care system include excessive lengths of stay, drifting from one foster home to another, disproportionate representation of children of color, and long-term disruption in relationships with members of families of origin. Policies and procedures vary considerably from location to location. To improve consistency in foster care, more coordination is recommended among child protective services, the legal system, and other community service agencies:

> The major functions of family foster care include emergency protection, crisis intervention, assessment and case planning, reunification, preparation for adoption, and preparation for independent living. To implement such functions, these diverse forms of foster care are required, including emergency foster care, kinship foster care, placement with unrelated foster families, treatment foster care, foster care for medically fragile children, shared family foster care, and small family group home care. (Pecora et al., 2000, pp. 303–304)

There has been increasing discussion regarding the professionalizing of foster parenting. Such a strategy would involve improved recruitment, training, and evaluation of prospective foster parents; increased compensation considering level of expertise; greater specialization for foster care of children who have special medical or psychological needs; and greater liaising between professional foster parents, agencies, and perhaps biological parents (Pecora et al., 2000). In general, it has become widely accepted that, despite the problems and shortcomings of the US foster-care system, foster parents provide a critical service for children in need. However, there is little solid systematic evaluation research into foster care.

Kinship care (foster placement with relatives) has gained increasing interest as a viable alternative to child placement. The challenges of kinship services are similar to those of nonrelative foster care: initial assessment of caretakers, adequacy of the kinship relative's home situation, and the need for greater professionalization of kinship caretakers. In addition, evaluation has revealed similar mixed outcomes (Pecora et al., 2000). Ultimately, should reunification efforts fail, adoption may be the ideal permanent placement alternative, although not all child welfare professionals share that view. Kinship care appears to account for a good portion of the increase in foster care placements over the past 20 years, and several factors (e.g., child's age, gender, family income, geographical location) have been shown to be related to the likelihood of kinship placement (Grogan-Kaylor, 2000).

Although there are more prospective adoptive parents than there are available children, many children are not adopted because of the general preference for healthy, white babies in contrast to older children from racial minorities or those with special needs (Mather & Lager, 2000). Although there are prospective adoptive white parents who desire to adopt a child from another race or cultural background, such arrangements have met with considerable resistance. Many in minority communities feel that it is not in the best interests of the child to be raised in a cultural environment that is not their own. For example, the Indian Child Welfare Act (1978) was passed, in part, to stop the adoption of Native American children by non–Native American parents (Mather & Lager, 2000). Similar controversies have arisen in recent years regarding gay and lesbian couples adopting children. Many in the heterosexual community who are opposed to same-sex relationships on ostensibly religious or psychological grounds object to such arrangements. Nevertheless, there appears to be little evidence (perhaps because of a lack of research) that having been raised by otherwise nurturing adoptive parents of a different background is in any way detrimental to a child's psychosocial development. Those who wish to influence child welfare policy must weigh the risks and benefits of raising a child in a "different" family against significantly reducing the chances of a child ever having a home and a family to call his or her own.

Methodological Limitations of Child Abuse and Neglect Research and Recommendations for Improvements

Although ecobehavioral approaches that include behavioral skills training have shown promise, most research on community-based family programs designed to reduce child abuse and neglect suffers from serious methodological limitations (Bath & Haapala, 1993; Blythe, Salley, & Jayaratne, 1994; Corcoran, 2000; Courtney, 2000; Dore, 1993; Gaudin, 1993; Gershater-Molko et al., 2002; Howing, Kohn, Gaudin, Kurtz, & Wodarski, 1992; Kelly & Blythe, 2000; Lindsey et al., 2002; Oates & Bross, 1995; Smokowski & Wodarski, 1996; Wolfe & Wekerle, 1993). These limitations include poorly defined problems, lack of controlled randomized designs, poorly defined intervention methods, a lack of fidelity measures to gauge how consistently the interventions are applied, a striking lack of standardized assessment and outcome measures (including no measures of child well-being!), and lack of long-term follow-up, among others. Major design limitations are addressed briefly here in turn. First, measuring assessment and outcome requires the use of standardized scales to gauge the changing functioning level of children, adults, and family functioning as a whole. Many brief, reliable, and valid scales are readily available. These can be readily incorporated into the broader qualitative and/or narrative assessment. Although dispositional data are important (e.g., whether or not a child is placed), such indicators often reflect the expressed policy of the program (e.g., family preservation) but tell us little about the psychosocial welfare of children and the adults in their lives (e.g., domestic violence, drug abuse). In addition, risk assessment instruments, though not foolproof, would greatly reduce the arbitrariness that seems to plague decision making in child welfare. Second, interventions need to be clearly defined. Terms such as *strengthening* and *empowering* are vague. Evaluators need to know which actual professional skills are employed in order to test whether they produced the desired results. In addition, there is a substantial literature on effective behavioral child interventions, parent management training, and behavioral family therapy (see chapters 12 and 13) that is not in evidence in descriptions of community-based child welfare interventions or evaluation reports. Last, although controlled randomized trials would sharpen the focus on efficacy by comparing different approaches with similar populations, even uncontrolled studies would be greatly improved by employing good measures, clearly defined interventions, and adequate statistical modeling to account for client characteristics and allow for linkage of specific program components to outcomes.

Description of Effective Interventions for Child Abuse and Neglect

Unlike most of the other chapters in this book in which there are clear models of "best practices," the literature in the child welfare field is rather fragmented and inconclusive. What follows is an overview of potentially effective intervention "ingredients" for addressing child abuse and neglect. These elements could be applied in various combinations given the severity and complexity of a case, and after determining whether the case requires prevention (e.g., for at-risk single moms), early intervention (i.e., first signs of abuse), or reactive care for documented serious cases.

Essential components should include (as necessary):

- Conducting comprehensive forensic and clinical assessment for the child and the family, which incorporates the inputs of multiple sources and employs multiple methods, both qualitative and quantitative
- Teaching behavioral parenting skills (see chapter 13 for details)
- Teaching and monitoring adequate standards for maintaining the orderliness, safety, and cleanliness of a home, as well as maintaining basic hygiene (laundry, showering, grooming) of the child
- Teaching awareness of and responsibility for monitoring the child's safety when in the presence of other family members and in the community (e.g., how to watch after your kids)
- Teaching stress management skills to parents to better cope with anger and frustration, especially when dealing directly with children

- Teaching problem-solving and communications skills as part of behavioral couples therapy and structural and behavioral family therapy to improve marital relations and overall family functioning

- Providing case management services (including advocacy, schools, health-care professionals, other social services) to help parents enhance social and instrumental supports, facilitating the reciprocal exchange of information with other service providers on the welfare of the child and family to promote generalization of improvements, and facilitating contingency management programs to ensure adherence to drug treatment protocol and/or compliance with other court-ordered mandates (e.g., refraining from all forms of domestic violence) as required to maintain (i.e., preserve) or regain (e.g., reunify) custody of a child in placement

- Use integrated or contracted mental health and substance abuse services for parent(s) and adolescents as needed

- Facilitate placements such as brief hospital or residential stays, temporary foster care, and kinship care

How these services are applied will depend on state child welfare policies and funding, as well as the structure and organization of private, public, and contracted services. A key point is the need for greater interservice collaboration among child welfare agencies and the mental health, substance abuse, law enforcement, and criminal justice systems.

TREATMENT PLANNING AND EVALUATION

CASE EXAMPLE: MIKEY AND HIS MOM, JANET

Janet, a 28-year-old waitress at a rural highway diner, was driving home at about midnight after her shift when she was pulled over by a local police officer. She was arrested for driving under the influence of alcohol. The officer suspected that Janet was also using other substances, and he shined a flashlight on the passenger-side floor and noticed a spent wrapper of rolling papers and small squares of tinfoil. After further investigation, Janet admitted that she had a "very small" amount of cocaine in her possession, but that it belonged to her boyfriend. She was arrested and brought to the local police depart-

ment for processing. The officer allowed her to contact her sister to come pick her up. Upon arriving at home, her sister, Kara, discovered that Janet's 5-year-old son, Mikey, was home alone. She also noticed drug paraphernalia and beer bottles strewn about, the house dirty and in disarray, and Mikey sleeping on the couch with his wrist tied with a piece of rope to the couch leg. Very upset, she argued with Janet and insisted that Mikey come home with her to stay at her house. Janet tearfully relented. The next day, Kara contacted the child welfare department, and an investigation was immediately conducted.

The child welfare social worker, Rachel, saw the same disarray in the house the next day. Kara kept Mikey out of school for the day and met the social worker at Janet's home to discuss the situation. Janet apparently had left Mikey, as she often had, with her live-in boyfriend, Bret, who she thought was taking care of him. On further investigation, it seemed that Bret had a serious problem with alcohol and other drugs. The social worker took a close look at Mikey, rolled up his sleeves, and noticed welts and bruises up and down his arms. She found the same types of marks on his legs. When she asked Mikey if Bret hit him, he held back tears: "He's mean. He hits me all the time." Janet objected, saying, "He does not. He only hits him when he's being bad, when he doesn't do what we say." The child welfare worker informed her that a full investigation would have to be conducted. In the meantime, she recommended that Mikey stay with Janet's sister, Kara, temporarily until the investigation was completed.

Further assessment of the situation revealed that the boyfriend, Bret, had been living with Janet for about 18 months. Before that time, there had been no indications of abuse. After he moved in with Janet, their occasional drug use began to escalate, and things got out of hand. Janet worked evenings, and in the beginning Bret was pretty good about staying at home and watching after Mikey. As their drug use increased, though, both became more negligent with everyday duties, including housecleaning, taking care of Mikey, and making regular meals. The school nurse and Mikey's teacher had sent home notes of concern about Mikey's appearance and behavior. He was becoming increasingly withdrawn from the other children, and at times he became oppositional about the cleanup duties for which each child was responsible. Rachel's concern grew, and she sent Mikey for a medical evaluation to rule out any serious injuries, nutritional deficiencies, or other health problems. Although she had yet to detect any indicators that Mikey had been sexually abused, she spoke with the physician to include those considerations in her examination. Discussion with Janet revealed that, while Bret did have "sexually explicit materials around and did look at porn movies," none of them had anything to do with children (i.e., child pornography), and she didn't think he exposed Mikey to it. As Janet put it, "He may be a jerk, but he's not a pervert." Nevertheless, the social worker kept the possibility of sexual abuse in mind as she planned a more in-depth assessment. Since the social worker became involved, and Janet had gone to court for driving under the influence and drug possession, Bret had left town and had not been seen for more than a week. The police indicated that a warrant had been issued for his arrest on suspicion of child abuse and drug possession. The social worker accompanied Janet to court, and the judge put her on probation for a year, with the stipulation that she cooperate with child welfare services and obtain treatment for her drug abuse. Because the arrest for driving under the influence was her first such offense, she was fined and ordered to attend substance abuse classes as well. Rachel was told that reports on Janet's progress would be expected periodically over the course of the following 90 days to determine whether Janet would regain custody of Mikey. Her sister agreed to take in her nephew for that time, and Janet could visit him if accompanied by the social worker.

MFS Assessment: Defining Problems and Goals

The social worker, Rachel, was employed in a small rural agency that delivered most of the relevant services to clients in the community. Over the following few weeks, Rachel spent some time further assessing the situation by conducting interviews and making observations in Janet's home. She was also able to interview Mikey in private in Kara's home, to observe his behavior in Janet's presence, and to assess Janet's parenting skills. In addition, Rachel, who was well known in the community and had good collegial relations with other professionals, readily communicated with Mikey's teacher and physician, the court, and law enforcement to continue assessment and evaluation of the case. In addition to her substance abuse problems, Janet had a range of other troubles: her conflicted and sometimes violent relationship with Bret, her own family history of emotional neglect, having witnessed domestic violence between her parents, poor parenting skills, and financial problems. She was also considerably depressed. She did, however, appear to genuinely love Mikey, she was remorseful about her neglect of him, and she felt very guilty about the abuse her son had received at the hands of Bret. She also felt somewhat complicit in that she had gone along with Bret's "old-school discipline," as he called it. She regretted ever having let him punch Mikey on the arms and legs (Bret was careful not to hit Mikey in the face, so as to not leave any obvious bruises or wounds). Janet also seemed to have few social supports. She had drifted away from her sister over the years—her sister, "the perfect one," she said, with a comfortable home, three children, and a stable marriage.

The social worker employed a combination of assessment strategies: observation of Mikey at home alone and with his mom, "play assessment" (drawing and playing with action figures and other toys), and discussions with Janet and with Mikey's teacher. Rachel determined that Mikey was somewhat depressed, anxious, and withdrawn; had some difficulties getting along with his kindergarten peers; and demonstrated occasional outbursts in school, especially when asked to carry out a required task. He also wet his bed at night, which had been a source of provocation for Bret. Sometimes he went to school smelling of urine ("to teach him a lesson," said Bret). Because of his occasional dirty appearance and difficulty relating to the other kids, they shunned him and made fun of him. Mikey was lonely much of the time and didn't know where he fit in with the other kids. The medical test came back negative, and further examination of additional traumas, including sexual abuse, seemed to turn up no substantive data. Child trauma checklists were used as a guide to consider other forms of abuse. Also, Mikey said that he did see Janet and "stupid Bret" arguing vehemently sometimes, and "Bret hit mommy too. I wish I could beat Bret up."

Janet began receiving substance abuse treatment at the local mental health center and attending her classes (which were held there as well). She had not shown signs of withdrawal, and her heavier drug use had been a relatively recent development. She did not think she was going to have a hard time "giving it up," she said. "I'll do anything to get Mikey back." But she did confess to missing Bret. She knew, however, that if he came back there would be trouble. The social worker strongly encouraged Janet to continue with her treatment for substance abuse and obey the court mandate "to the letter" if she wanted to get Mikey back. Rachel was clear about her role as both therapist and court liaison, stressing to Janet that if she wanted to get Mikey back, she would have to work hard not to relapse, eliminate any use of corporal punishment, and take better care of his emotional and physical needs. Janet said she understood what was expected, and she thanked Rachel for "being straight" with her.

A functional analysis of Janet's situation revealed that, even without the influence of Bret present, her parenting skills could use considerable improvement. Part of the difficulty seemed to stem from the poor modeling Janet received from her own parents: "I can't blame them completely, since, I admit, Little Miss Perfect [i.e., her sister Kara] is a pretty good mom. I just become so frustrated at times. I never feel like I have enough time to do anything with him, and I lose my temper and start yelling. Then he cries and I feel bad about losing my cool." On one supervised visit, Kara dropped Mikey off with Janet and the social worker, and Janet was instructed to play a game that Mikey liked. She then helped Mikey clean his room. After that, they made lunch together. As Janet engaged in these activities with Mikey, Rachel made herself relatively unobtrusive (catching up on progress notes at the kitchen table), but she could observe the impatience in Janet's face during her playtime with Mikey, trying to orchestrate his every move rather than hanging back and just "being there" with him, as Rachel put it. Later, when Janet went to coach Mikey in cleaning up his room, she demonstrated a similar lack of patience. Although things remained relatively calm, upon interviewing Janet, Rachel knew that if she were not present as social worker, these types of situations could turn into yelling matches. If Bret were around, then the hitting might start. A concise functional analysis revealed serious difficulty in Janet's ability to provide a calm, nurturing, and fun environment for Mikey even for a brief period. She showed abrupt impatience when it came time for tasks or setting limits. These situations had become a daily event and would quickly escalate into a reciprocal negative exchange (with yelling and hitting becoming somewhat serious). Janet's reactions would upset Mikey and reinforce Janet's sense of incompetence as a parent. After a couple of weeks and several hours of assessment, the social worker discussed their time together so far, and with Janet's input, they summarized the problems and goals: Janet loved her son but had problems of her own, including substance abuse, depression, low self-confidence, a short temper, and a proneness to involve herself in psychologically and (sometimes) physically abusive relationships. Her parenting skills needed considerable improvement, and she was under much financial stress, which contributed to her "feeling stuck." Janet felt that she first had to clean herself up (i.e., get off drugs and alcohol), and to earn her son back, she would have to demonstrate that she could provide better nurturance and positive discipline for him. In the long run, she also agreed that she probably also needed to upgrade her criteria for selecting romantic partners.

Selecting and Designing the Intervention: Defining Strategies and Objectives

The overall service plan (table 14.1) included a multifaceted approach in the tradition of an ecobehavioral framework, but with specific attention paid to integrating evidence-based interventions in that framework. Components of the plan included (1) developing a solid relationship with Rachel, who was clear about her combined role of clinician, advocate, and court liaison; (2) learning behavioral parenting skills; (3) contingency management contracting with the courts; (4) case management with court, school, medical, and substance abuse services; (5) and improved social supports.

The parenting skills intervention (described in detail in chapter 13) included psychoeducation to provide Janet with developmental information regarding normative expectations for Mikey and to instruct her in better child nurturance and limit setting. Rachel also provided Janet with brief cognitive therapy to help Janet understand and cope better with negative feelings associated with her own abuse as a child. Janet and Rachel spent considerable time engaging Mikey in play and task-oriented activities to teach Janet how to put Mikey at ease, make him feel loved, and "invest in good feelings between them" so that getting him to obey the rules (e.g., cleanup, keeping his bedtime) would go more smoothly and be less of a source of anger and conflict. Specific objectives were designed to successfully spend 10, 20, and eventually 30 minutes of playtime a day with Mikey and deliver calm, clear directives for accomplishing his daily tasks (e.g., picking up toys, brushing his teeth, getting ready for bed). They developed a chart together to track his progress every day. If he did well, he received a 5-minute bedtime story and a "special present" at the end of the week if he did a "very good" job (i.e., met expectations for 4 of 5 days). Although the ground work for improving parenting skills was done during visits with Mikey at her sister's home, Janet did not fully practice and carry out all the components of the plan successfully until Mikey returned to her own home. During this time she reconciled somewhat with Kara, and was able to implement some of the bedtime rituals at Kara's house.

Rachel also taught Janet some basic stress management (e.g., brief mediation, imagery) to use when she said she felt like she was going to "lose it." She practiced three times a day and used imagery of being with Mikey when he returned home, remaining calm during playtime, helping Mikey cooperate with her around the house, and getting him ready for bed. Later, after Mikey returned home, she was able to keep a chart of stressful situations when caring for Mikey, what her actions were, what the outcomes were (of both her behavior and Mikey's), and how she evaluated her performance afterward. Her goal was to keep her verbal outbursts to a minimum and to reduce any pushing, pulling, or hitting behaviors to none. After Mikey returned and Janet had more opportunity to actually practice her new skills, Janet worked on the finer points: giving praise when Mikey did well (stressing the power and superiority of positive reinforcement over punishment), ignoring little annoying things, and taking time out for activities she enjoyed (all this with sobriety in mind). Janet also stressed the importance of maintaining a reasonably neat home and paying attention to Mikey's hygiene, clean clothing, and appearance. Rachel helped her design a simple time management chart to complete basic household chores in a timely manner. Communication between Janet and the teacher would be designed to get feedback about Mikey's behavior in school and in the after-school program.

Janet examined the potential for additional income supports and discovered that Mikey was eligible for health-care coverage at no cost with a state-sponsored health clinic. Nevertheless, Janet would continue to struggle financially unless she increased her income. They discussed making some adjustments and budgeting decisions. Now that Mikey was in school full-time (including the after-school program), Janet decided to work full-time and give up working evenings. She also found a more affordable apartment and decided to move ("I am not telling Bret where I'm going," she said). Consultation with Mikey's teacher revealed that there were two bachelor's-level volunteers (teachers in training) in the after-school program who were willing to work with Mikey on alternate days to help him with his social and behavioral problems (i.e., shyness, oppositional behavior). The social worker discussed a plan with them to help Mikey initiate cooperative play with one or two other children with whom he wanted to make friends and record (monitor and evaluate) their efforts. They would also record how Mikey obeyed the rules of the after-school program.

After the 90-day period expired, Janet and the social worker returned to court to give a generally positive report to the judge regarding some of the adjustments she had made. There appeared to be no further instances of substance abuse, she was no longer consorting with drug users in her personal life, and she felt she was ready to take her son home. Although Janet felt some softening of the anger she had felt toward her sister, she needed to make some new friends. New prospects included some of the other single mothers she was meeting at the after-school program and women whom she met in the single mother's support group she occasionally attended at the mental health center. The court mandated that her case remain open for the remainder of the year, and Rachel was required to file quarterly reports. Custody of her son would remain contingent on her continued progress.

Selecting Scales and Creating Indexes to Monitor and Evaluate Client Progress

The PTSD-RI was employed to screen for traumatic events and symptoms and the SAC to measure internalizing and externalizing symptoms at the start of the intervention and at 3-month intervals. In addition, several unique monitoring indexes and charts were employed to gauge Mikey's progress at home and in the after-school program, to help Janet improve her time management skills, and to engage in self-monitoring to complete household chores in a timely fashion.

TABLE 14.1   The Client Service Plan: Mikey and Janet

Problems	Goals	Objectives (samples)	Interventions	Assessment and evaluation tools
Mikey has bruises up and down his arms	Eliminate all forms of neglect and abuse; custody would be restored when situation resolved	Paraprofessionals model and coach Mikey to interact with another child with whom he wants to be friends	Child welfare places child with Janet's sister for 90 days; court-ordered interventions for Janet	For Mikey: PTSD-RI to screen for traumatic events and related symptoms; SAC to assess for internalizing and externalizing symptoms and problems
Mikey shows signs of depression and anxiety at home and in school; is oppositional (angry) at times in school	Alleviate depression and excess anxiety, improve Mikey's ability to socialize with other kids	Rachel instructs Kara how to use the bell-and-pad method to prevent bed-wetting; Kara paid for it and implements it with Mikey; praises him for dry days and provides encouragement for mishaps	Coach paraprofessionals to help Mikey improve social skills through gradual exposure	Behavioral observation to test social skills at school
Mikey wets his bed once or twice per week	Eliminate his bed-wetting		Use prompts and rewards to reduce oppositional behavior directed toward teacher	Design and implement a monitoring chart for his successes in responding to mother's directives; paraprofessionals also chart social skills and positive responses to classroom directives
Janet abuses alcohol, marijuana, and sometimes cocaine	Abstain from marijuana and cocaine (a stipulation for regaining custody); strongly encouraged Janet to abstain or at least minimize alcohol use	During visits with social worker present: Play board game for 10 minutes (even if "bored"), and gradually increase	Use bell-and-pad method; work with Janet's sister to use the device and reward Mikey for successful "dry" mornings	

Problems	Goals	Objectives (samples)	Interventions	Assessment and evaluation tools
She also shows signs of depression	Further assess depression and treat pharmacologically if needed	to 30 minutes; plan a directive to give to Mikey (e.g., clean plate after lunch) during visits and follow up with praise or a calm reminder; begin using chart to record his successes	Janet attends mandatory mental health and substance abuse treatment at community mental health center	Janet monitors her own completion of domestic duties, including physical care of Mikey's hygiene and appearance
Janet has a history of being abused in her family and in other relationships, and Bret occasionally pushed and hit her	Help her better understand effects of abuse history, current repetition, and seek alternative type of relationship		Cognitive therapy to address depression and examine abuse experiences and beliefs, expectations these experiences created for current relationships	
She shows serious deficits in her parenting skills, both nurturing and positive disciplining	Improve her parenting skills and eliminate need to use coercive methods		Janet attends educational women's support group	
Janet has financial problems commensurate with being of the "working poor"	In the long term reduce expenditures and improve working situation (i.e., work full-time)		Behavioral parenting skills program at home by social worker during visits and continues after custody restored; stress management skills	
			Free budgeting counseling (clinic's board member's firm provided pro bono classes once a month for low-income parents); seeks a full-time job	
			Case management functions include referrals, networking, advocacy, and coordinating services through contacts with court, schools, health care, and mental health center; court liaison was to ensure compliance with contingency management plan and periodically report results of treatment to court	

CHAPTER SUMMARY

The physical and sexual abuse of children, along with the neglect of their physical, psychological, and emotional needs, remains a prevalent problem. Multiple factors contribute to the likelihood of child abuse and neglect. Qualitative and quantitative methods are available that can improve both risk assessment and clinical assessment of abuse and neglect in child protective services and in clinical practice with children and adolescents who have been abused and neglected. Broad-based ecobehavioral interventions have been shown to be promising, but they are more likely to be effective over time if they include behavioral parenting skills; integrated substance abuse, mental health, and foster-care services; and consistent follow-up with contingency management programs linked to the criminal justice system. However, even with improvements in child welfare assessment, intervention, and evaluation methods, improving child welfare policy will require much greater national commitment to protect children and adolescents from abuse and neglect.

CHAPTER 15

EATING DISORDERS

Eating disorders, generally categorized as anorexia, bulimia, and binge-eating disorder, include a continuum of disorders marked by cognitive, behavioral, and physiological symptoms, including preoccupation with body image, problems with appetite, and dietary regulation. A range of other problems, including depression, substance abuse, personality disorders, and interpersonal difficulties, often co-occur with eating disorders. Eating disorders can be episodic or chronic, they range from moderate to severe, and they can be life threatening. A significant proportion of persons with primary anorexia are likely to die from the disorder even with aggressive medical care. However, many people struggling with bulimia nervosa and binge-eating disorder (but less so for those with anorexia) can improve significantly from evidence-based treatments, regain the ability to regulate dietary practices, and improve overall self-image and interpersonal adjustment. There are a range of well-developed assessment protocol and evidence-based practices, including cognitive-behavioral interventions and interpersonal psychotherapy. In recent years, it has been recognized that early intervention methods with adolescents and young adults can effectively interrupt the onset of an eating disorder.

ASSESSMENT

Background Data

There is ample literature available that describes the characteristics of eating disorders (American Psychiatric Association, APA, 2000; Fairburn, Cooper, Doll, Norman, & O'Connor, 2000; Fairburn & Wilson, 1993; Foreyt & Mikhail, 1997; Shekter-Wolfson, Woodside, & Lackstrom, 1997; Wilson, 2011). Three main categories of eating disorders have emerged in the empirical literature: anorexia nervosa, bulimia nervosa, and binge-eating disorder.

Anorexia Nervosa.   Persons diagnosed with anorexia nervosa (AN) have a morbid preoccupation with staying extremely thin; refuse to gain weight (remain below the 85th percentile for their weight class); and demonstrate serious cognitive disturbance in how they see their own body shape and size, with a particular fear of becoming "fat." If the onset of anorexia precedes puberty, the individual may not achieve menarche. If the onset follows puberty, the client may develop amenorrhea. Often, these clients do not see their preoccupation with being ultra-thin as a problem. The DSM-5 provides two subtypes of AN: "restricting," which is characterized by an almost exclusive emphasis on dieting, fasting, or excessive exercise, and "binge eating and/or purging," whereby the individual binge eats and then purges through self-induced vomiting or use of laxatives, diuretics, or enemas. Most persons with anorexia who binge eat also purge, although there are some who purge without bingeing. Persons with anorexia are often clinically depressed, and many show signs of obsessive-compulsive disorder. They often suffer from poor self-esteem, appear to be emotionally restricted, and are often preoccupied with needing to control their environment. Also, they can be somewhat inflexible in their thinking and adhere to perfectionist standards. Anorexia can result in a long list of medical problems, many of which can be detected in laboratory work-ups (e.g., electrolyte abnormalities). In addition, clinical problems can include constipation, emaciation, dry skin, hypotension, cardiovascular problems (e.g., arrhythmias), and osteoporosis. The onset of anorexia usually begins between the ages of 14 and 18 years. For some individuals, it requires hospitalization. Even with aggressive medical intervention, the mortality rate for persons with anorexia is greater than 10%. One prospective study of 39 adolescents with anorexia showed a 69% remission rate over 10 years (including all seven males in the sample), although many continued to have other psychiatric difficulties, including depression, anxiety, and substance abuse disorders (Herpertz-Dahlmann et al., 2001). Although anorexia appears to be a clinical syndrome in predominantly industrialized countries where society prizes thinness as a sign of beauty, persons from other cultures who assimilate and acculturate to these ideals may also become anorectic.

Bulimia Nervosa.   Bulimia nervosa (BN) is characterized by binge eating and compensatory methods to avoid weight gain (e.g., self-induced vomiting, laxatives, enemas). A "binge" is an ingestion of a greater-than-normal amount of food within a discrete period (e.g., 2 hours), often with an emphasis on high-carbohydrate, high-calorie foods (e.g., a dozen donuts, a layer cake). Usually persons with binge eating disorder are ashamed of their behavior, and bingeing often takes place in secret. Often, emotional upset, dysphoric mood, or an episode of interpersonal conflict precedes the binge-eating episode, and it is typically accompanied by a feeling of loss of personal control. Between 80% and 90% of binge eaters employ vomiting as a way to avoid weight gain. They are also preoccupied with body shape and weight. Their appearance plays a disproportionate role in their self-evaluation.

There are subtypes of bulimia: purging, in which the person regularly engages in vomiting or other compensatory behaviors (e.g., laxatives); and nonpurging, whereby the person engages in attempts to compensate for bingeing through excessive exercise or fasting but does not regularly engage in vomiting or use laxatives or other methods to eliminate what has been consumed. Those with bulimia tend to be within their normal weight range (more or less), and they may experience other co-occurring problems, such as depression, poor self-image, social anxiety disorder, and other anxiety problems. Persons with bulimia appear to be disproportionately more likely to have a substance abuse problem, and they often use stimulants for appetite suppression. Medical examination and laboratory findings are likely to detect other problems as well, such as electrolyte abnormalities, loss of tooth enamel (from gastric fluids eroding enamel as a consequence of vomiting), and menstrual irregularities. Bulimia tends to begin in late adolescence or early adulthood, and it may have a variable course over time. In general, if symptoms remit for a year, long-term outcomes are quite positive. Although some practitioners see similarities in excessive drinking and eating disorders as addictive processes, there are significant differences in etiology, psycho-physiological, and behavioral mechanisms (Wilson, 1993a), not least of which is the absence of any classic dependence syndrome (i.e., tolerance and withdrawal).

Binge-Eating Disorder.   Binge-eating disorder (BED) is similar to bulimia. However, in binge-eating disorder the client does not engage in compensatory behaviors (e.g., vomiting, use of laxatives) on a regular basis. Binge-eating disorder is more likely to be associated with persons who struggle with overweight or obesity. Many clinical samples for this disorder have been drawn from weight-control clinics. As in bulimia, in BED, binge-eating episodes are often precipitated by depression, upset, interpersonal conflict, or feelings of tension—all of which are relieved by bingeing. Often a weight problem is associated with poor self-image, low self-esteem, depression, anxiety, and dissatisfaction with work or relationships. There is also a disproportionate risk for personality disorder or substance abuse diagnoses. The problem appears to begin in late adolescence or early adulthood. Long-term prognosis for BED appears to be better than that for bulimia. In the first prospective study to compare long-term (5-year) outcomes of the two disorders, about 50% of those with bulimia retained an eating-disorder diagnosis, whereas only about 20% of the BED group did so (Fairburn et al., 2000). Binge eating is an important health risk behavior to focus on with young persons, as it is the core component of both bulimia nervosa and binge-eating disorder, and it may be related to a subtype of anorexia nervosa.

Epidemiological Data for Eating Disorders

Population estimates for eating disorders have been somewhat inconsistent over the past 20 years. Earlier community studies estimated the prevalence of

AN at about 1%, BN at 1%–3%, and BED at 2%–5% (Johnson, Tsoh, & Varnado, 1996); also, the vast majority (at least 90%) of persons suffering from eating disorders in general are female. Attia and Walsh (2007) reported AN rates between .5 and 1%, with females outnumbering males by 5–10 times. They also note that research suggests that AN might not be as culture bound as previously thought.

More recent data, based on the National Health and Nutrition Examination Survey (NHANES) study (Merikangas et al., 2010), estimated 12-month prevalence rates of eating disorders in young people (aged 8–15) to be about .1%, lower than previous estimates. However, the replication of the National Comorbidity Survey (NCS) (which included more than 10,000 adolescents) (Swanson, Crow, LeGrange, Swendsen, & Merikangas, 2011) found rates of eating disorders to be .3% for AN, .6% for BN, and 1.6% for BED. Diverging from previous data, those results showed that lifetime rates of AN were comparable by gender, although women reported about three times the rate of both BN and BED. Between 50% and 75% of respondents met criteria for some other psychiatric disorder as well.

However, surveys have also shown that those who manifest subclinical symptoms (i.e., do not meet diagnostic criteria) report extreme dietary restrictions and binge eating and purging behaviors in a range of 15% to 40% (Johnson et al., 1996), and unhealthy dietary practices have been estimated as present in as many as 80% of young persons (Fairburn & Beglin, 1990). Early symptoms of eating disorders appear to have significant predictive value. In a longitudinal study of 800 children and their mothers in the community, data on risk factors and symptoms associated with eating disorders were collected over four periods between the mid-1970s and the early 1990s. Symptoms in early adolescence strongly predict the development of bulimia nervosa in later adolescence and adulthood. Bulimia in late adolescence is even more predictive of adult bulimia. Early childhood conflicts around eating and mealtime appeared to have prognostic value for the development of later eating disorders (Kotler, Cohen, Davies, Pine, & Walsh, 2001). One prospective study showed young women in college to have comparable rates of eating-disordered attitudes and other symptoms as they did in their senior year of high school, but they may have increased dissatisfaction with body shape and size (Vohs, Heatherton, & Herrin, 2001).

Behaviors associated with eating disorders are related to various other psychosocial problems, including depression, anxiety disorders, substance abuse, obsessive-compulsive disorder, personality disorders, PTSD, and interpersonal problems. In addition, the behavioral consequences of eating disorders have a disruptive impact on work and school functioning (Kashubeck-West & Mintz, 2001; O'Brien & Vincent, 2003; Pratt, Phillips, Greydanus, & Patel, 2003). Although depression and anxiety appear prominent in both bingeing and non-bingeing eating disorders, substance abuse and borderline personality disorder seem to be more prominent in binge-eating disorders.

However, although correlations have been established between eating disorders and these other conditions, causal explanations remain a subject of speculation.

There is considerable mortality associated with eating disorders, particularly anorexia. Arcelus, Mitchell, Wales, and Nielsen (2011) conducted a meta-analysis covering the period 1966–2010 with 35 studies reporting mortality rates, in order to determine best estimates of mortality from eating disorders. They found mortality in persons with AN to be about .5%; in persons with BN, about .2%; and .3% for eating disorders not otherwise specified. Factors predicting death in patients with AN included co-occurring affective disorder, alcohol abuse, self-harm, and suicidal behavior. Franko and Keel (2006) came to very similar conclusions in their review.

Theories on the Causes of Eating Disorders

Evidence suggests that eating disorders result from several interacting biopsychosocial risk factors (Foreyt & Mikhail, 1997; Striegel-Moore, 1993; Striegel-Moore & Cachelin, 2001). Developmental trajectories of these disorders can be highly variable for individuals, and the factors may combine cumulatively to provide a dose-response relationship with eating disorders. Identified risk factors include genetics and other biological predispositions, gender, race, early maturation for women, high body-mass index, body size and shape, excessive dieting, family problems, and childhood sexual abuse (for BN), among others (Ferriero, Seoane, & Senra, 2011; Nichols & Viner, 2009; Pratt et al., 2003; Stice, 2002).

Family and twin studies demonstrate that eating disorders run in families in which a first-degree relative had an eating disorder (potentially supporting both social learning and genetic theories). Other biological evidence suggests that eating disorders are correlated with hormonal changes during puberty, depression (via genetic transmission), and metabolic dysfunction in an individual. Case-controlled studies (i.e., matching persons with and without an eating disorder on several variables such as age and gender) also suggest that personal risk factors (e.g., low self-esteem) are somewhat predictive. In terms of development, binge-eating behaviors emerge during late adolescence, perhaps motivated by dissatisfaction with one's body image and shape. Some feminist theorists have asserted that such factors are linked to the negative stress women bear regarding gender-role expectations, idealized images of feminine beauty, and social acceptance. Extreme dieting, binge eating, and purging may be ways for women to try to ensure acceptability and affirm their own identity. These difficulties may emerge in adolescence as a result of the cascading and interacting effects of biological changes, social stressors, struggles with self-esteem and identity development, conflicts with parents, and perfectionist demands to cope with academic performance and the drive toward independence.

Psychodynamic theorists have hypothesized that eating disorders are an expression of unresolved unconscious childhood conflicts, and as such, they are a defense against oral impregnation by the father, overidentifying with a negative maternal introject, or unresolved dependency needs, among other explanations. There currently is no scientific evidence that supports these opinions. Other, sociocultural, psychodynamic formulations have examined the links between differential developmental role expectations of adolescent females versus males to account for the onset of eating disorders as one compensatory effort to achieve an idealized norm of female beauty as a defense against rejection (Slater, Guthrie, & Boyd, 2001). However, this formulation is not a uniquely psychodynamic explanation. A more parsimonious explanation would likely involve social learning and culture-bound views of female beauty.

Cognitive theories have gained prominence in the theoretical and empirical literature regarding the cause and maintenance of eating disorders (e.g., Fairburn, 1997; Wilson, 2010, 2011). Cognitive distortions regarding body shape and weight, chronic negative self-evaluation, and poor self-esteem seem to dominate the thought processes of the person with eating disorders. These distortions are directly related to false beliefs about the value of highly restrictive diets, the "goodness" or "badness" of certain foods, and the assumed benefits of purging after eating as a form of weight control. Negative schema and dysfunctional thinking may extend to other aspects of life, including beliefs about interpersonal relations. The false beliefs among those with eating disorders regarding dieting can be considered a generalized manifestation of two dysfunctional forms of cognitive processing: dichotomous thinking and perfectionism. When clients with an eating disorder view their eating patterns in such rigid terms, the rules become fragile and easily broken, thus reinforcing the cycle of dietary restrictiveness and bingeing and purging. These lapses in keeping to the rules are often precipitated by periods of emotional stress, which are often associated with a conflict situation (e.g., fight with boyfriend). Positive and negative reinforcing behaviors meant to accommodate these beliefs (e.g., binge eating to cope with stress or feelings of inadequacy, purging to cope with fears of weight gain) help maintain the dysfunctional cognitions.

Racial and cultural factors in research on eating disorders have gained more attention in recent years given that eating disorders are more prevalent among white women (Pratt et al., 2003), although race is overused for classification; cultural and ethnic groupings are categories that may have more salience. Cultural beliefs may be related to negative cognitive schema about body image, and research on cultural influences may have implications for the disorder's etiology. Observing that eating disorders are among the most common problems for college women, Arriaza and Mann (2001) compared samples of white, Hispanic American, and Asian American young university women and found that although all groups have concerns about their body shape and overall appearance, young white women engage in more dietary restrictive behaviors commensurate with eating disorders. In the first community comparison between a recruited sample of African American and white women (mean age 31) with binge-eating disorder, Pike, Dohm, Striegel-Moore, Wilfley, and Fairburn (2001) used matched samples of African American and white women with and without an eating disorder to demonstrate that white women were more likely to demonstrate greater binge-eating frequency; dietary restrictiveness; and concerns about weight, body shape and eating. The authors surmised that because of less concern in these areas, African American women are at a lesser risk of developing bulimia nervosa. African American women, however, were more likely to be overweight and less likely to seek treatment for obesity, thus putting them at greater risk for other health problems. In the first college-based study to examine diagnostic rates of eating disorders in a representative sample of African American young women, Mulholland and Mintz (2001) found rates of anorexia (1%), bulimia (1%), and indications of eating disorders (i.e., symptoms—23%) to be comparable to estimates in the literature on college-aged white women. Mixed findings on race in the research may be partly explained by the use of different diagnostic criteria or the inclusion of subclinical symptoms (Kashubeck-West & Mintz, 2001).

Multidimensional-Functional-Systems Assessment

The diagnostic criteria for eating disorders in the DSM-5 (APA, 2013) are essentially unchanged from those of the DSM-IV, except for the following: for AN, the requirement of amenorrhea has been eliminated and criteria for judging low body weight have been modified; for both BN and BED, the frequency criteria for bingeing and purging (as required) have been lowered to once per week for 3 months rather than twice per week.

The diagnostic criteria for anorexia nervosa include a refusal to maintain normal body weight, intense fear of gaining weight, a gross disturbance in the way an individual perceives his or her body, and failure to recognize when one is very underweight. Diagnosis of bulimia nervosa (BN) is marked by recurrent episodes of binge eating a larger-than-normal amount of food in a 2-hour period, accompanied by a feelings of losing control over the behavior. Compensatory behaviors—that is, purging (e.g., vomiting, laxatives), excessive fasting, and/or excessive exercise—are used to prevent weight gain. Both bingeing and purging are used at least once a week for 3 months or more, and the client's self-evaluation is unduly influenced by his or her perception of body shape and weight. Binge-eating disorder is similar to BN, but the person does not engage in compensatory behaviors on any regular basis. In addition to the criteria for eating large amounts of food within a discrete period and a sense of lack of control over eating during the episode, the diagnosis includes three or more of the following: eating much more rapidly than normal, eating until uncomfortably full, eating large amounts when not physically feeling hungry, eating alone because of embarrassment over one's eating behavior, and feeling disgusted at oneself or guilty and/or depressed. A person meeting this diagnosis engages in binge eating at least once weekly for 3 months.

Anderson and Murray (2010) underscore the importance of conceptualizing the assessment of eating disorders as a multimodal process composed of a theoretical understanding of eating disorders, a functional assessment (the hows and whys of an individual's eating disordered thoughts, feelings, behaviors, and situational factors), as well as diagnosis and the use of specific instruments. In the context of conducting an MFS assessment, the eating disorder should also be seen in a broader context of overall functioning across psychological, social, and physical health domains, as well as being understood within a systems perspective whereby interpersonal relations both significantly affect and are affected by the behaviors of the person with an eating disorder.

Assessment should at a minimum capture the following data: weight history (i.e., highest, lowest, ideal), thoughts, opinions about the "ideal" body type, patterns of food restriction or bingeing (e.g., types of food, triggers, patterns), weight-control methods (e.g., vomiting, medications, exercise, laxatives), overall eating patterns (e.g., caloric intake, weighing practices), menstrual history, co-occurring problems (e.g., drug abuse, depression, self-harming behaviors, suicidal ideation, other impulsive or risk-taking behaviors), serious interpersonal conflicts, previous treatments (e.g., success, failure), trauma (e.g., sexual or physical abuse in childhood or adulthood), and a physical exam (Fairburn & Wilson, 1993; Foreyt & Mikhail, 1997; Schmidt, 1998). People with eating disorders might be secretive and embarrassed about discussing their problem, reluctant to cooperate with the assessment or preliminary recommendations, and/or oppositional and rebellious about treatment in general.

Self-monitoring is an indispensable and reasonably accurate tool, and it should be employed to enhance assessment, provide ongoing treatment monitoring of progress, and evaluate treatment outcomes. However, to obtain reliable and valid self-report, the client should be actively encouraged to learn and use self-monitoring techniques, not passively expected to do so spontaneously (Wilson, 1993a). Self-monitoring is usually conducted with a chart that can be tailored to the client's needs and expectations. As part of a comprehensive and ongoing assessment, self-monitoring of binge-eating episodes can help create an accurate data trail that describes days of the week, time of day, situation (e.g., where, with whom), state of mind and emotional distress (e.g., response to a negative event), substance use, type and amount of food consumed, response to the episode (e.g., purging, refraining from purging), and so forth. Monitoring begins as part of the initial assessment and continues for the duration of treatment. Self-monitoring may add to the client's sense of participation and control as a collaborative participant in their treatment. Benefits to the intervention for binge eating often occur quickly in treatment, and some of the benefits appear to be associated with the client's self-monitoring activities by which they can begin to track and make cause-effect connections between antecedent situational, cognitive or emotional events, and bingeing behavior. When applied skillfully in the context of a sound working alliance, self-monitoring can be an invaluable adjunct to the assessment, monitoring, and evaluation of treatment with clients who are struggling with binge-eating behaviors (Wilson & Vitousek, 1999).

Foreyt and Mikhail (1997) offer a version of a commonly used daily chart to help clients participate in the assessment and self-monitoring process (see table 15.1).

Self-monitoring provides a framework for the functional analysis of the pattern of binge eating and purging. The functional analysis informs the intervention plan by defining a chain reaction of interacting cognitive, behavioral, physiological, and situational factors. Accordingly, the client's anxieties about body shape and weight may trigger dieting behavior, then bingeing, and then purging to compensate for overeating (Fairburn & Wilson, 1993; Schmidt, 1998). Treatment directly targets both cognitive and behavioral aspects of the disorder. First, in collaboration with the client, practitioners must make a detailed analysis over the course of a week or two of antecedent events that appear to precipitate the binge-purge episode. These may include troubling thoughts, feelings, behaviors, and/or situations that cause distress or emotional upset that precipitate the binge. A client may simply feel stressed in general, have had a fight with a friend, have been rejected by a boyfriend, have been turned down for a job, have failed an exam, or any number of upsetting occurrences. Second, a detailed analysis should be con-

TABLE 15.1   Daily chart for self-monitoring eating patterns

Time of day	Place	With whom	Associated activities	Foods/liquors: include amounts	Feelings before, during and after eating	Purge yes/no: If yes, vomiting, laxatives, diuretics, etc.	Feelings before, during and after purge

ducted on the thoughts associated with the decision to binge and purge, type of food, and amount of food. Third, any consequences that ensue after the binge-purge episode should be recorded and reviewed. These might include feelings after bingeing and purging, substance abuse, suicidal thoughts, use of laxatives, or other reactions to the episode.

Instruments

Most experts in the field consider the Eating Disorder Examination (EDE) (Cooper & Fairburn, 1987; Grilo, Masheb, & Wilson, 2001; Smith, Marcus, & Eldredge, 1994; Wilson, 1993b) to be the gold standard for assessment of binge eating and other eating disorders. The EDE is a semistructured clinical research interview schedule that examines signs and symptoms of eating disorders retrospectively over 28 days, but it also includes time frames commensurate with DSM categories to provide diagnostic data for clinical and research purposes. For binge-eating disorder, the criteria had also been adapted to the DSM-IV's 6-month criteria as well (Grilo et al., 2001). The EDE divides overeating into several categories, including objective bulimic episodes (i.e., ingestion of large quantities of food with subjective loss of control), subjective bulimic episodes (i.e., eating quantities of food that are generally not considered extreme, but the client reports feelings of losing control), and objective overeating episodes (i.e., overeating without a subjective sense of losing control). Four subscales constitute the EDE: dietary restraint, eating concern, weight concern, and shape concern. Items are rated from 0 to 6, with higher scores indicating greater severity or frequency.

The EDE-Q (Fairburn & Beglin, 1994) is the self-report version of the EDE. Both scales have excellent psychometric properties (i.e., good internal consistency of subscales, as well as good interrater reliability and discriminant validity for diagnosing those with eating disorders). In a study using both community and patient samples, the self-report EDE-Q compared well with the EDE structured-interview format (Grilo et al., 2001). Agreement was very good on the more unambiguous behaviors of self-induced vomiting and laxative use, and there was "close agreement" on dietary restraint. However, there was more disagreement (though not clinically substantive) on "concerns about weight," and even more disagreement on concerns about shape. Overall, the EDE-Q provides a sound basis for conducting an initial screening commensurate with a provisional diagnosis.

In addition to the EDE, Kashubeck-West, Mintz, and Saunders (2001) reviewed several scales with solid psychometric properties, including the Eating Disorder Inventory (Cumella, 2006; Garner, Olmstead, & Policy, 1983) and the Bulimia Test-Revised (BULIT-R; Thelen, Farmer, Wonderlich, & Smith, 1991; Welch, Thompson, & Hall, 1993), perhaps among the better-known scales. The Yale-Brown-Cornell Eating Disorder Scale (YBCEDS) (Mazure,

Halmi, Sunday, Romano, & Einhorn, 1994) was designed to identify and measure a client's unique eating-disorder symptoms with eight core items. The scale also contains six items that measure motivation for change. The scale has shown good reliability and concurrent validity with other eating-disorder scales (Mazure et al., 1994), and it effectively distinguishes normal controls from restrained eating dieters and those who have recovered from eating disorders (Sunday & Halmi, 2000).

A recent addition to the collection of eating-disorder scales is the Eating Disorders Diagnostic Scale (EDDS). Scores on the EDDS can be used to diagnose anorexia, bulimia, and binge-eating disorders, and the scale provides a composite score that is useful for measuring overall symptoms and detecting changes in symptoms over time. The computerized scoring tool is available from Eric Stice via email (estice@ori.org). However, if the scale is primarily used to measure overall symptom level and monitor changes during intervention, the composite total score should be used. This global symptoms measure is calculated by simply summing all items (except height, weight, and birth control; 1 = yes, 0 = no).

The EDDS was initially developed in two consecutive studies (Stice, Telch, & Rizvi, 2000). In study 1, items derived from the EDE, the DSM, and the structured-interview version of the DSM were compiled and examined by 26 experts on eating disorders, then piloted with a combined group of college and high school students and clients in an eating-disorders clinic. Study 2 examined reliability and validity with a combined community and clinic sample of 367 females. Internal consistency reliability for the composite scale was .91 for the full sample. Overall accuracy rates for test-retest reliabilities exceeded 90%, and test-retest reliability for the composite score was very good (.87). Criterion validity was supported, with data showing the EDDS diagnoses to be congruent with diagnoses based on interviews more than 90% of the time. Correlations among the EDDS composite scores and subscales of the EDE and the YBCEDS were moderate and significant.

Four studies reported simultaneously (Stice, Fisher, & Martinez, 2004) further supported the reliability and validity of the EDDS (see instrument 15.1), including its predictive validity and sensitivity to change. Study 1 essentially replicated Stice et al. (2000), with more than 700 adolescent females who were somewhat younger than those in the original study. Study 2 demonstrated that the EDDS was sensitive to change with undergraduate women enrolled in a course on preventing eating disorders. Study 3 demonstrated that the EDDS was sensitive to clinical change, resulting from an intervention with 181 adolescent females with concerns about body image. Last, study 4 demonstrated that the EDDS predicted increased risk for the onset of binge eating and compensatory behaviors and the onset of depression. In summary, the EDDS shows excellent reliability as well as construct and criterion validity; is sensitive to clinical change; and has a high degree of utility in that it can be completed within the parameters of a typical interview with persons suffering from a range of eating-disorder symptoms.

INSTRUMENT 15.1   Eating Disorder Diagnostic Scale (EDDS)

Please carefully complete all questions.

Over the past 3 months . . .	Not at all		Slightly		Moderately		Extremely

1. Have you felt fat?   0   1   2   3   4   5   6

2. Have you had a definite fear that you might gain weight or become fat?   0   1   2   3   4   5   6

3. Has your weight influenced how you think about (judge) yourself as a person?   0   1   2   3   4   5   6

4. Has your shape influenced how you think about (judge) yourself as a person?   0   1   2   3   4   5   6

5. During the past 6 months have there been times when you felt you have eaten what other people would regard as an unusually large amount of food (e.g., a quart of ice cream) given the circumstances?   Yes   No

6. During the times when you ate an unusually large amount of food, did you experience a loss of control (feel you couldn't stop eating or control what or how much you were eating)?   Yes   No

7. How many DAYS per week on average over the past 6 MONTHS have you eaten an unusually large amount of food and experienced a loss of control?   0 1 2 3 4 5 6 7

8. How many TIMES per week on average over the past 3 MONTHS have you eaten an unusually large amount of food and experienced a loss of control?   0 1 2 3 4 5 6 7 8 9 10 11 12 13 14

During these episodes of overeating and loss of control did you . . .

9. Eat much more rapidly than normal?   Yes   No

10. Eat until you felt uncomfortably full?   Yes   No

11. Eat large amounts of food when you didn't feel physically hungry?   Yes   No

12. Eat alone because you were embarrassed by how much you were eating?   Yes   No

13. Feel disgusted with yourself, depressed, or very guilty after overeating?   Yes   No

14. Feel very upset about your uncontrollable overeating or resulting weight gain?   Yes   No

15. How many times per week on average over the past 3 months have you made yourself vomit to prevent weight gain or counteract the effect of eating?   0 1 2 3 4 5 6 7 8 9 10 11 12 13 14

16. How many times per week on average over
    the past 3 months have you used laxatives
    or diuretics to prevent weight gain or
    counteract the effects of eating?   0 1 2 3 4 5 6 7 8 9 10 11 12 13 14

17. How many times per week on average over
    the past 3 months have you fasted (skipped
    at least 2 meals in a row) to prevent weight
    gain or counteract the effects of eating?   0 1 2 3 4 5 6 7 8 9 10 11 12 13 14

18. How many times per week on average over
    the past 3 months have you engaged in
    excessive exercise specifically to counteract
    the effects of overeating episodes?   0 1 2 3 4 5 6 7 8 9 10 11 12 13 14

19. How much do you weigh? If uncertain, please give your best estimate. ____lbs.

20. How tall are you?   ___ feet ___ inches

21. Over the past 3 months, how many menstrual periods
    have you missed?   1 2 3 4 na

22. Have you been taking birth control pills during the
    past 3 months?   Yes   No

SELECTING EFFECTIVE INTERVENTIONS

Although no particular treatment approach has been found to be especially effective with AN (Vitousek, 2002; Wilson & Fairburn, 1998; Wilson, Grilo, & Vitousek, 2007), cognitive-behavioral therapy (CBT) and interpersonal psychotherapy (IPT) have emerged as comparably effective treatments for BN and BED (Hay & Claudino, 2010; Schmidt, 1998; Stein et al., 2001; Wilson, 2010, 2011; Wilson & Fairburn, 1993, 1998). Although most research on the treatment of eating disorders has occurred with adults, methods are readily adaptable to adolescents (Bowers, Evans, & van Cleve, 1996). However, many people still do not benefit sufficiently from the best-supported approaches (Wilson et al., 2007). Also, more research is needed on the efficacy of treatments for eating disorders among racial minorities (Stein et al., 2001).

Anorexia Nervosa.   Given the paucity of methodologically sound studies conducted on AN (Wilson et al., 2007), only a few are reported here. Eisler, Simic, Russell, and Dare (2007) conducted a 5-year follow-up of a randomized controlled trial (RCT) at Maudsley Hospital in England that compared conjoint family therapy (i.e., adolescents included) and separate family therapy (i.e., adolescents seen separately) with patients who had been diagnosed with AN. Follow-up measures revealed no recurrence of AN symptoms and no overall differences between the two groups. The authors cautioned that patients with highly critical parents (i.e., expressed emotion) might be better served by separate treatment early on. However, Gowers et al. (2007) found poor results in an RCT comparing inpatient, specialized out-patient (i.e., CBT), and treatment as usual in 167 adolescents with AN. Only about 33% of participants were improved at 2-year follow-up, and there were no substantive outcome differences among the three groups. Although theo-ries espoused by the family therapy movement (e.g., dysfunctional commu-nication patterns) on the causes of anorexia nervosa and other eating disor-ders have not been substantiated, including the family in treatment can be practical, especially with adolescent clients (Dare & Eisler, 2002). RCTs have provided modest support for the use of family therapy with anorexia but not for bulimia nervosa (e.g., Dare & Eisler, 2002; Eisler et al., 1997; McIntosh, Bulik, McKenzie, Luty, & Jordan, 2000). However, in their review, Attia and Walsh (2007) concluded that, although structured medical programs that focus on weight gain might be helpful, psychosocial treatments continue to show little promise for this serious disorder.

Bulimia Nervosa.   CBT and IPT are currently considered first-line approaches for treating BN (Wilson & Fairburn, 1993, 1998, 2010; Wilson et al., 2007). Steinhausen and Weber (2009), however, caution against being overly optimistic, because many patients do not fully recover. Nevertheless, CBT appears to be effective for more than 75% of clients, and more than 50% report successfully abstaining from bingeing and purging.

A series of controlled studies directly comparing IPT with CBT demon-strated comparable outcomes (e.g., Fairburn et al., 1991; Fairburn et al., 1995; Fairburn, Jones et al., 1993; Wilson et al., 2007). Relevant investigations have assessed the relative efficacy of three interventions: behavior therapy (BT) that focused exclusively on dietary changes, CBT, and IPT. Although initial out-comes showed CBT to be the superior treatment, follow-ups demonstrated comparable results for IPT as well. Although clients who received BT origi-nally did well, long-term results over several years deteriorated.

CBT for bulimia has also been successfully adapted to group formats (Kettlewell, Mizes, & Wasylyshyn, 1992; Shekter-Wolfson et al., 1997). One RCT comparing a combination of CBT and Motivational Interviewing fol-lowed by individual versus group CBT showed no long-term differences (2.5 years) for a sample of 225 people diagnosed (mostly) with bulimia nervosa. This study suggests that CBT is effective (i.e., it reduced bingeing and laxa-tive abuse) without a motivational enhancement component and regardless of whether it is delivered in individual or group format (Katzman et al., 2010).

Other approaches show some promise as well. Although research on family therapies for BN is limited, one RCT of 80 adolescents with BN showed family-based treatment to be more effective than supportive treatment at post-test and at 6-month follow-up on all measures of success (e.g., reduced bingeing, vomiting, and concerns about weight) (Le Grange, Crosby, Rathouz, & Leventhal, 2007). Another randomized controlled trial compared the Maudsley model of family therapy for BN (a problem-oriented approach gradually yielding control back to the patient) with a self-guided CBT approach, finding that both were substantially effective, with negligible differences overall (Schmidt et al., 2007).

In the first RCT of its type, at 3-month follow-up, Internet-based CBT (eight 45-minute sessions online with email support) was shown to be clearly superior to wait-listed control groups for students with BN and an unspecified eating disorder ($N = 76$) (Sanchez-Ortiz et al., 2011). Gains were well maintained post-treatment. Given the appeal, flexibility, and privacy of the Internet, this approach may be able to reach and assist many young people with eating disorders.

Binge-Eating Disorder.   Results of more recent narrative and meta-analytic reviews underscore the first-line status of CBT and IPT for treating BED (Vocks et al., 2010; Wilson, 2011; Wilson et al., 2007). As a recent example, Grilo, Masheb, Wilson, Gueorguieva, and White (2011) used a randomized trial to compare CBT and behavioral weight loss (BWL) with both BED and obesity in 125 patients. CBT was more effective for BED, and BWL was more effective with obesity through 12-month follow-up, although weight losses ultimately became almost negligible. The combination approach (CBT and BWL), however, did not prove superior in reducing BED behaviors.

As with other behavioral disorders, readiness to change can be correlated with better engagement and improved outcomes in treating eating disorders (e.g., Geller, Drab-Hudson, Whisenhunt, & Srikameswaran, 2004). Noting the importance of motivation, Cassin, von Ranson, Heng, Brar, and Wojtowitz (2008) compared a one-session motivational interview (MI) approach and accompanying self-guiding handbook to a handbook-only group of 108 women diagnosed with BED, and they followed both groups at intervals for up to 16 weeks. Those in the MI-and-handbook group improved about 2.5 times as much as the handbook-only group. The combination of a motivational approach to boost self-efficacy and a skills-based approach to changing eating behaviors also resulted in improvements in other areas of life (and more so in the MI group) including depression and self-esteem. The Internet program Student Bodies (described later in this chapter) has recently garnered further support via an RCT in which 105 adolescents, on average, showed (for the first time) substantial reductions in BED behaviors with moderate weight loss and maintenance of gains (Jones et al., 2008). Another study of 259 patients with BED showed that those receiving CBT had better short-term gains than those in a self-help group, but the differences were no longer significant at 12-month follow-up, and many clients continued to experience co-occurring symptoms (e.g., depression) (Peterson, Mitchell, Crow, Crosby, & Wonderlich, 2009). Results suggest that long-term follow-ups remain a challenge for practitioners, and support groups might have an important role to play in the delivery of cost-effective treatments.

Potential Change Processes in CBT and IPT.   Cognitive behavioral interventions for eating disorders focus on "identifying and changing specific beliefs, attributions, expectations, values, and cognitive distortions that contribute to the eating disorder. Cognitive and behavioral techniques are employed to teach adolescents to be more aware of their thoughts, feelings, and behaviors. . . . [T]hey learn to identify and label their emotions, as well as recurrent patterns of thinking" (Bowers et al., 1996, p. 236). Examining and challenging distorted dysfunctional cognitions related to eating disorders is a key component of CBT. Behavioral changes in eating habits are planned out carefully and in specific graded steps to help clients achieve optimal success.

Originally developed for treating depression (Klerman, Weissman, Rounsaville, & Chevron, 1984; Weissman, Markowitz, & Klerman, 2000), IPT focuses on interpersonal conflicts (i.e., usually a role dispute or role transition) and associated emotional distress that may precipitate binge eating. According to Weissman et al. (2000), "Subjects benefit from exploring their interpersonal options, practicing them in therapeutic role playing, and then trying them out with significant others. As the interpersonal problem area is addressed, bulimic symptoms resolve" (p. 318). In contrast to CBT practitioners, IPT practitioners do not emphasize bingeing, restricting, or purging behaviors as part of treatment.

Johnson et al. (1996) have suggested that change processes for IPT and CBT may overlap, in that both might be used to focus on interpersonal distress as a trigger (i.e., antecedent) for binge eating. Examinations of the change processes of CBT for eating disorders (see Wilson & Fairburn, 1993) reveal no definitive answers. However, possible explanations for how CBT works include the following: cognitive changes about body shape and weight; reduced dietary restraints, which subsequently reduces a tendency to binge; increased self-efficacy, which results in an improved ability to cope with normal eating and precipitating stressors; and alteration of reinforcement contingencies. It is possible that several processes work in concert, that different processes work for different clients, and that other change processes are at work, such as creating a sense of a "fresh start" in dealing with the problem, reducing depression, increasing interpersonal activities through greater social support, improving self-confidence and mood, and reducing interpersonal conflict, thus reducing social "triggers" to binge (Fairburn, 1993). However, definitive evidence for specific change processes in both CBT and IPT remain undetermined (Shekter-Wolfson et al., 1997; Smith et al., 1994; Wilson & Fairburn, 1993, 1998; Wilson et al., 2007). As mechanisms of change become clearer for CBT and IPT, the potential for patient-treatment matching grows as well (Wilson, 2011).

Fairburn, Cooper, and Shafran (2003) have proposed an extension of cognitive-behavioral theory that emphasized "transdiagnostic" core mechanisms of disordered eating in general. The concepts include clinical perfectionism, core low self-esteem, mood intolerance, and interpersonal difficulties. They argue that, cross-sectionally, eating disorders share common maintenance factors, and longitudinally, people with eating disorders (i.e., anorexia, bulimia, and atypical eating disorders) can drift from one diagnosis to another (e.g., people with bulimia nervosa might previously have met criteria for anorexia). They suggest that the four mechanisms can be targeted in treatment for any eating disorder, and as such, they are attempting to integrate core theoretical change processes of CBT and IPT into one approach that can be applied to any eating disorder. To test this theory, a two-site randomized controlled trial was conducted with 154 eligible participants who primarily had bulimia nervosa or atypical eating disorders. Fairburn et al. (2009) compared 20 weekly sessions of an enhanced CBT with the same enhanced CBT approach augmented to target those core mechanisms specifically, and they found generally good but equivalent gains for the two treatment conditions (in comparison to wait-list controls who did not improve). The authors suggested that the "broader" CBT (which specifically targeted the core mechanisms) showed some slight indications that it might have been more effective with those clients who showed greater psychopathology. At best, the findings must be deemed tentative, and the authors offer little support to suggest that this form of enhanced CBT effectively targets these specific mechanisms of change. In addition, the theory suggests that people with anorexia nervosa share the same core pathology, but people with anorexia were not included in the study, thus precluding a full test of the theory. Nevertheless, this transdiagnostic approach is theoretically in line with other research into change-process treatment (e.g., for anxiety disorders) that suggests the potential of designing interventions that target core common mechanisms of change.

Medication for Treating Eating Disorders.   In their review of the role of medication for eating disorders, Levine and Levine (2010) concluded that, although no medications have been shown to be definitively effective for AN, SSRIs might be helpful for some with BN. One meta-analysis and literature review showed moderate but short-term positive effects, and little evidence for long-term efficacy for the use of medications (e.g., antidepressants, anti-epilepsy and anti-obesity drugs) with BED (Reas & Grilo, 2008). Other reviews of the controlled studies (Wilson et al., 2007; Wilson & Fairburn, 1993, 1998) on the use of antidepressant medication have concluded the following:

- Antidepressant drugs are generally more effective than placebo.
- The relationship between dose of antidepressants and the response in BN treatment is unclear.
- SSRIs and tricyclic antidepressants (TCAs) appear to show comparable results.
- Clients who fail to respond favorably to one antidepressant may have better results with another.

- More research is needed in the following areas: long-term outcomes, effects on symptoms other than bingeing and purging, predictors of response to antidepressants, and the mechanisms by which these drugs are effective with BN.

- CBT appears to be more acceptable to clients than medication.

- CBT has lower dropout rates than medication treatment.

- CBT appears to be superior to a drug-treatment regimen that uses one type of antidepressant.

- Combined treatment of CBT and antidepressant is more effective than medication alone, but the combination of CBT and medication appears to provide few advantages over CBT alone.

- Combining CBT and medication may be superior when an important treatment goal is to reduce symptoms of anxiety and depression.

- Long-term maintenance of gains appears to be better with CBT than with medication.

- Although some medications alleviate symptoms related to treatment of eating disorders, including AN and BN, they are not considered first-line interventions.

Description of CBT for Bulimia Nervosa and Binge-Eating Disorder. Interventions for bulimia nervosa and binge eating can be reviewed in greater detail in various excellent texts (e.g., Fairburn, 1997; Fairburn, Marcus, & Wilson, 1993). CBT lasts for about 20 visits, and follow-up visits can be planned as needed. The main goals are to modify eating habits, eliminate purging, change the client's self-evaluation of body shape and weight, and maintain healthful dietary practices. Although core skills are represented here, practitioners need to rely on informed judgments to make adjustments given the client's diagnosis (bulimia vs. binge eating), the client's unique circumstances, and other co-occurring problems. Modifications to the core aspects of treatment, however, should not be done without good reason. The structure of the approach and the application of its core elements are essential for CBT to be effective (Wilson et al., 2007). The stages of treatment are cumulative in the sense that new skills are added as each stage is accomplished. Given the demands of the treatment and the inherent skepticism of clients about the efficacy of the intervention, a sound working relationship, a spirit of collaboration, and mutual trust and respect are essential for the intervention to work. Instilling a sense of commitment is critical so clients understand that there is hard work ahead and that they must take responsibility for working between visits to make substantive progress. Frequency of the visits may be modified should a more severely disturbed client need more intensive treatment (e.g., twice weekly at first). Normally, weekly visits are sufficient.

Current effective CBT approaches are based on Fairburn's (1981) formulation and were expanded by G. T. Wilson and others through the 1980s and 1990s. The main elements, briefly summarized, are as follows (Wilson & Fairburn, 1993, 1998):

- Develop a good therapeutic relationship.
- Teach clients self-monitoring skills for thoughts, feelings, behaviors, and situations associated with eating habits as well as actual eating patterns.
- Educate clients about the CBT model of BN and the need to reduce dysfunctional cognitions about the self, dietary restraint, and the need to change actual eating behaviors
- Develop an established routine of weekly weigh-ins
- Educate clients about regulating body weight and the potentially negative consequences of dieting and purging
- Develop and follow through on a plan of regular healthful eating habits
- Teach self-control (self-regulation) skills
- Teach problem-solving skills
- Modify rigid rules concerning "forbidden" foods
- Challenge and change cognitive distortions (cognitive restructuring) regarding eating habits, body shape, and weight
- Teach and carry out graduated exposure methods to increase acceptance of body weight and shape
- Instruct clients in relapse prevention skills (i.e., identifying triggers and having planned responses to at-risk situations)

The following lists provide more detailed analysis of how to implement CBT for bulimia and binge-eating disorder:

Stage 1
Stage 1 presents the CBT Model and modifies dietary practices (visits 1–8, approximately):

- Conduct a thorough assessment (see previous points on MFS assessment).
- Educate clients about the problems associated with binge eating and dietary restraint, how these practices are linked to mood and self-image problems, and why both practices need to be changed to overcome the problem. The interactions of extreme dietary restrictions, bingeing (and purging), mood disturbance, and low self-esteem are a vicious cycle that might persist until extreme dietary practices are brought under control. Help clients understand how CBT works (i.e., a combination of changing dysfunctional beliefs and attitudes about eating, body shape, and weight, and reinforcing those changes through improved and less restrictive dietary practices).

- Teach clients self-monitoring skills to track eating behaviors and associated thoughts, moods, behaviors, circumstances, and episodes of bingeing and purging (discussed earlier). This classic functional analysis helps practitioners and clients get a clear picture of the sequential, patterned links among binge eating (and purging), mood, self-image concerns, emotional distress, interpersonal problems, other stressors that may trigger binges, and the role of substance abuse problems, among other things. Develop a daily monitoring sheet with clients, which may help enhance compliance. Weekly detailed discussions of the monitoring sheets are also important.

- Conduct weekly weigh-ins. Clients should be encouraged to weigh themselves weekly (not be weighed by the practitioner); practitioners, though, can weigh the client during the first and last sessions of the intervention.

- Clients and practitioner should work together to develop a new dietary plan that is healthier and less restrictive (e.g., three regular meals with in-between snacks) and eliminate all purging behaviors (e.g., throwing away laxatives). Practitioners must continue to educate clients about the importance of normal eating and the avoidance of extreme dieting practices that tend to perpetuate the problem. Vomiting should be adamantly discouraged, and this practice usually disappears without much struggle when normal eating patterns return. Nevertheless, some of the coping skills employed (e.g., pleasurable distractions) can be used to avoid urges to binge and urges to vomit.

- Instruct clients in the use of coping skills. Distractions such as pleasant activities or seeking social supports can be planned as a way to reduce risks regarding bingeing and purging; clients can learn to anticipate at-risk situations (e.g., in late afternoon, after classes or work) and plan healthful alternative activities.

- Significant others and social supports should be included in the intervention. At this point, significant others (e.g., friends, relatives) can be interviewed to be included in clients' experiences to help clients be less secretive about the problem, provide social support, and provide an opportunity to see whether the client understands the treatment procedures by having them explain the intervention to their friends and family.

Stage 2
Stage 2 continues dietary modification and intensive use of cognitive interventions to modify dysfunctional beliefs regarding dietary practices and self-evaluation (about eight additional visits):

- Continue to address more "normal" (i.e., healthful) eating and the problem of avoiding "forbidden" foods by gradually reintroducing them into clients' diet. Increase the average amount of food consumed to avoid "fasting" and low energy. Clients should be less scrupulous about every calorie eaten and should eat in a wider array of circumstances. Overall, stage 2 concentrates on returning clients to normal healthful eating habits and modifying overly restrictive dietary rules.

- Continue practicing coping skills. Review basic problem-solving processes to help clients cope with at-risk episodes for relapse (e.g., identifying thoughts, feelings, behaviors, and circumstances that put them at risk, and finding alternative healthy coping responses).

- Teach and emphasize standard cognitive therapy techniques (e.g., Beck, 1976) to identify and disconfirm irrational thoughts through rational argument (e.g., challenge the thought "people think I am ugly and dislike me because I am not thin" by asking, "Where is the evidence to support this belief? What evidence discounts this belief?").

- Enact behavior changes through practicing and graduated exposure to disconfirm dysfunctional beliefs. Although cognitive challenges can be posed to confront dysfunctional beliefs about dieting and self-image, behavioral changes (i.e., graduated exposure using behavioral "experiments") are necessary to convincingly disconfirm beliefs. Not gaining weight on a normal diet while engaging in normal exercise (e.g., jogging a reasonable distance two or three times per week) and being less inhibited in one's dress or appearance in public (vs. hiding all of one's physical "imperfections") will help solidify gains in self-image and maintain normal dieting, as well as the reduction and/or elimination of bingeing and purging.

Stage 3

Stage 3 focuses on maintenance of gains and relapse prevention (three visits at 2-week intervals)

- Develop a relapse prevention plan. In stage 3, clients are assisted in standard relapse prevention. Clients should be taught to expect relapse but to avoid overreacting to it (e.g., thinking, "I'm a failure"). Encourage clients to quickly resume their normal eating regimen where they left off. A written plan may be useful for preparing for at-risk situations; also, brainstorm possible coping responses, including reaching out to helpful social supports to avoid potential pitfalls. For binge eaters for whom obesity is a key concern, these approaches are applicable, but modifications are in order (see Fairburn, Marcus, & Wilson, 1993).

Because those with binge-eating disorder present a different problem profile from those who have bulimia nervosa (i.e., less cognitive distortion about body shape and absence of purging), they have somewhat different intervention goals. The initial emphasis for obese clients is to stop binge eating, not to lose weight, and to develop realistic goals for weight loss. Nutritional counseling based on current scientific data is important, and it is critical to reinforce the avoidance of extreme diets of any kind. Healthful, regularly scheduled meals and regular exercise are strongly recommended. Clients should be helped to avoid "addiction" metaphors regarding food and instead focus on regular healthful eating habits with a wide variety of foods. Concern about body image and self-appraisal of attractiveness should be addressed realistically with attention paid to exercise, feeling better about oneself, avoiding unrealistic comparisons to thin and idealized images of female beauty, and emphasizing other aspects of one's self-worth in addition to physical attractiveness. Broad and long-term improvements in healthful living should be established during the last visits of treatment.

A Brief Description of IPT.   Several sources have described the IPT format (Fairburn, 1993; Weissman et al., 2000; see also chapter 6). The therapist is active in the early sessions, conducts a thorough assessment, and provides psychoeducation about eating disorders and the rationale for the intervention. During the first four sessions or so, the therapist takes a history of eating patterns, weight changes, bingeing, purging, and interpersonal functioning, and notes any apparent connections between interpersonal distress and the eating-disordered behaviors. An analysis of significant life events and any problems with depression or self-esteem are explored. The emphasis in treatment then shifts to an examination of efforts to constructively address the identified interpersonal conflicts on the assumption that relationship distress serves as a precipitant to binge-eating episodes (sessions 5–16). The onus of responsibility is on the client to address these problems between sessions, yet little attention is explicitly paid to the eating behaviors themselves. In the final two or three visits, client and therapist review progress, prepare to cope with possible relapses, and terminate. Research is needed to further examine the role of interpersonal distress as a precipitant to binge-purge cycles and the potential for increasing the efficacy of CBT by emphasizing the resolution of interpersonal conflict and distress as part of treatment (i.e., combining key elements of CBT and IPT). "Integrated" approaches to eating disorders have not been tested (Wilson et al., 2007), but they might enhance treatment outcomes. Future research might examine combining elements of IPT and CBT.

Prevention and Early Intervention with Disordered Eating.   With adolescents and young adults, there are good reasons to consider prevention and early intervention methods for eating disorders. There is a high rate of subclinical symptoms in young women particularly, and some may be in the early stages of developing a serious eating disorder. In addition, there are other co-occurring problems (e.g., substance abuse, depression, social anxiety) that are amenable to screening and early intervention. Some of these clients may be helped significantly by early identification and intervention, whereas others may be referred for treatment.

Levine and Piran (2001) reviewed 22 outcome studies of programs for the prevention of disordered eating. All studies were at least quasi-experimental in design, used repeated measures, and included at least a 1-month follow-up measure. The prevention programs included some combination of education, skill building, and environmental changes. Overall, results were generally modest but demonstrated that prevention programs could increase knowledge and improve attitudes and behaviors related to disordered eating. The authors called for more research and prevention programs that include efforts to improve organizational and community attitudes regarding healthful eating and general physical well-being.

In an earlier review of 20 investigations of programs designed to prevent eating disorders, Austin (2000) concluded that few firm recommendations could be made because of programmatic weaknesses and methodological flaws in the research. Feminist models, for example, used didactic and broad-based educational efforts to focus on environmental, cultural, and political factors that potentially increase a woman's risk for developing eating disorders. Other studies focused on making changes in the social environment, but again, methodological flaws muddled the findings. The author recommended further research to consider implementing prevention programs that might have a direct effect on the social environment, such as addressing social norms, changing curriculum content to target health-related issues, and providing healthier eating choices in schools and universities.

More recent reviews result in more optimism with regard to preventing disordered eating. Fingeret, Warren, Cepeda-Benito, and Gleaves (2006) reviewed more than 50 studies on the prevention of disordered eating. They found greater effects for increased knowledge than for attitudes and eating behaviors. However, there was some evidence that those at greater risk for eating disorders benefited more than those at lower risk. Using rigorous methodological criteria, Stice, Shaw, and Marti (2007) reviewed 66 studies on eating disorder prevention and found that 51% of eating disorder prevention programs reduced risk factors associated with eating disorders, and 29% reduced current or future eating pathology. However, overall effect sizes were generally small. Nevertheless, programs targeting selected groups (vs. universal programs) tended to show larger effect sizes for programs that were women-only; interactive and run by trained practitioners; and aimed at those older than age 15 and those at greater risk for eating disorder, depression, obesity, thin body idealization, dieting, and eating pathology. The authors rightly caution that these factors are more prudently interpreted as correlates of treatment effects.

Exemplar Outcome Research: A Series of Controlled Trials of the Student Bodies Program

Winzelberg et al. (1998) conducted an initial controlled trial of the psycho-education and behavior change program Student Bodies, an Internet-based prevention program designed to improve body image among university women. Initial results with 57 undergraduates demonstrated improvements in body image and other problem behaviors associated with binge eating. After making improvements in both the program and the study methodology, Winzelberg et al. (2000) conducted a second controlled trial of the same program with 48 undergraduates. The program lasted 8 weeks, and students were reassessed at 3-month follow-up. The program was educational in nature and included information on cultural determinants of beauty and CBT self-help methods for improving body satisfaction. The program consisted of interactive software that featured text, audio, and video components. Participants also used online self-monitoring devices and behavior change exercises, and they posted their reactions to the lessons each week. Online discussion groups enhanced social supports during the project. As for results, there were no significant differences in concerns about body shape as measured by standardized scales, but statistical differences did emerge at 3-month follow-up, although they were clinically modest in magnitude. Nevertheless, the Internet-based program demonstrated promising results and the feasibility of engaging young persons in an interactive program. In a related study, Celio et al. (2000) demonstrated that the Internet-based program described earlier was substantially more effective than a classroom-based didactic program that did not include the CBT skills component of the Internet-based program.

In a subsequent trial to test Student Bodies (Zabinski et al., 2001), the investigators narrowed their student selection criteria to those deemed to be at risk for an eating disorder. The 62 participants were randomly assigned to Student Bodies or to a no-treatment control group (offered the same program after the study). Measures were taken at baseline, post-test (8 weeks), and 10-week follow-up. Measures included the EDE-Q and a social support scale to test whether the program would negatively affect exposure to "live" social supports. Of participants, 56 (27 experimental, 29 control) completed the program, including follow-up assessments. The program components are described in Winzelberg et al. (2000).

Both groups improved significantly on self-assessment of body image and eating-disorder pathology. There were no significant differences between the two groups. However, reports from the treatment group indicated that they benefited from the intervention and felt a good deal of social support from the Internet-based bulletin board. The treatment group also showed slightly better improvements in body satisfaction, although the difference was not statistically significant. How does one account for successful outcomes in both the treatment and non-treatment groups? Zabinski et al. (2001) suggested that small sample size and variability in reported problems may have reduced the statistical power needed to demonstrate significant results. In addition, participants were screened for greater severity of symptoms than the general college population, and some symptoms may have regressed to the mean over time in both groups. Despite the modest results, this study of at-risk, young, college-age women supports the utility and potential efficacy of an Internet-based skill-oriented program to reduce cognitive and behavioral symptoms of eating disorders.

TREATMENT PLANNING AND EVALUATION
CASE STUDY: TINA

Tina was a 19-year-old white woman from a large working-class family (she was the youngest of seven children). Tina's family physician referred her to the social worker Peggy after Tina's mother caught her vomiting in the bathroom. After a brief discussion, Tina's mom discovered that Tina had been binge eating and purging for almost 2 years. Alarmed, her mother sent her to the family physician, who felt she needed counseling or psychotherapy. Despite this problem, Tina presented herself as cheerful and positive, and she reported that she did not see her bingeing and purging as a big problem; she knew "lots of girls" who were doing it. Tina attended community college (she wanted to become an executive in the fashion industry) and worked part-time in a dress store. She was involved in a romantic relationship with a young man whom she cared a lot about, and she very much wanted to please him. She had also been drinking alcohol and using cocaine on the weekends. She said her cocaine use was not a problem and that she didn't see what the big deal

was. Tina was saving up her money for plastic surgery to improve her appearance, although her friends wondered aloud what was concerning her. Tina had recently returned home after living away for a few years. She said she had money problems and just needed some time to get back on her feet. As she and her siblings had gradually left home, Tina's mother had gone to work full-time as a cashier in the local grocery store, after having been a full-time homemaker. Tina's dad had always worked hard, sometimes two jobs when all the children were at home, and he had not been around much. On the weekends he was often with his pals at the local tavern. Tina's parents generally got along, if for no other reason than to cooperate in raising their children, but they sometimes argued on the weekends. Two of Tina's brothers had substance abuse problems, and a sister had been diagnosed with schizophrenia. Two other sisters had finished college, and the rest of her siblings seemed to be working steadily and starting families of their own.

MFS Assessment: Defining Problems and Goals

Tina's bingeing and purging had been relatively continuous for 2 years. She reported that she started bingeing and purging after a sleepover with a girlfriend when she was 16 or 17 years old. She was impressed by her girlfriend's conviction that the only way to get a guy was to stay "as thin as possible." In addition to bingeing on "junk foods" and purging, she also began to take laxatives. About the same time, she met Steve, who became her steady boyfriend. Steve used drugs and introduced Tina to cocaine, which she referred to as the "ultimate diet drug." She also smoked pot and drank too much on the weekend, although this was intermittent. Steve sold cocaine to support his own drug habit. During the week, Tina would not drink or smoke pot while she was working and going to classes, but occasionally she would use cocaine to keep herself going. During her visit with the doctor, she discussed her drug use and a constant burning in her esophagus. The doctor explained that if she did not stop bingeing and purging, she would develop problems that would require serious medical attention. Tina had also not had a regular menstrual cycle for several months, a problem that caused her much concern. The physician gave her some medication for her esophageal irritation and some supplements (she was anemic), and referred her to a social worker who specialized in treatment of eating disorders.

As Tina discussed her problem history with the social worker Peggy, she began to cry. Peggy, taking a more detailed history, realized that Tina had apparently been unhappy with her relationship for a while and was worried about her bingeing and purging and her cocaine use, but she was afraid that she would not be able to stop. She appeared to be depressed and had not been sleeping well. The social worker told her she would have to stop using the cocaine first before her symptoms could be sorted out and before she could develop a more healthful dietary plan. In summarizing her situation, it appeared that Tina had several interacting, co-occurring problems that she needed to deal with: she had a long-standing lack of self-confidence, low self-esteem, and a distorted body image. Her bingeing and purging was starting to take a toll on her physically and was wreaking havoc on her sense of well-being. She was somewhat depressed; she was in a relationship with someone who was exploiting her; and her substance abuse was exacerbating her psychological, emotional, and interpersonal problems. She did have some good friends who were willing to give her support, even though they were increasingly puzzled by what they considered self-destructive behavior. She was ambitious and disciplined enough to hold down a steady job and take classes, and she was doing reasonably well. She was not suicidal and had never engaged in self-mutilating behaviors. She wanted to change what she was doing but wasn't sure where to begin.

Peggy suggested that they discuss in more detail what Tina wanted to accomplish from the intervention. The social worker laid out what she saw as the major problems (outlined earlier), and they discussed how Peggy thought that Tina's eating disorder, drug problem, unhappy relationship, and self-image were related. Tina agreed with the connections, and she got the clear impression that she first had to stop using drugs, which, she said, were "messing" her up. She had not yet developed a clear dependence syndrome—her use was fairly intermittent—but her drug use was affecting her mood, which in turn was preventing her from dealing constructively with other difficulties. The social worker and Tina decided together that a good course of action would be for Tina to take some time out at home for a period of supervised abstinence from drug use to clear her head, and then undertake a more detailed assessment of her bingeing and purging habit. Once Tina felt she was in more control of the recreational drug use and eating habits, she could take on larger concerns about her lack of self-confidence and the quality of relationships she wanted to have in her life. In the meantime, Tina agreed that it might be a good idea to reduce her contact with Steve by explaining that she needed some time to herself.

In coordination with the physician, who would continue to monitor Tina's physical symptoms, the social worker Peggy, with Tina's approval, had Tina's parents come to the next session. Because Tina was living at home and was not prepared yet to live independently, they agreed that involving her parents in her treatment, at least initially, might be helpful. With the support of her social worker, physician, and parents, Tina felt more confident that she could make some initial changes in her life. The first step was to have her stay at home for a week to "detoxify." Because she was between semesters, she did not have to miss classes. She told her employer that she had some "personal problems" to work out, and she requested a week off from work. Her mom took time off from her job at the supermarket. Tina scheduled two brief visits with her social worker during this first week and a follow-up visit with her physician. In the evening her dad spent some time with her. They went out to see a movie together, something she had never done alone with him. Her dad discussed his off-and-on drinking problems and stunned her with a confession that years earlier, when he was working in boiler maintenance in a hospital, he had become dependent on "uppers" to keep him going between two full-time jobs. She was open with him for the first time about her relationship with Steve, and her dad suggested that she think about choosing a better boyfriend. Her mom and dad got along well that week and seemed to be exclusively concerned about her well-being. As the week wore on Tina became somewhat bored, but she noticed that she was sleeping better and her spirits lifting. Her physician had also prescribed an antidepressant, but she did not expect to feel the effects for another week or so. She spent much of the time helping her mother around the house.

After her "detox week," Tina worked with Peggy to develop a more detailed assessment of her binge-purge cycle and come up with a more healthful dietary schedule. An analysis of her "typical" week showed that she had developed a fairly predictable pattern of getting herself "stressed out" at work and in school, and then trying the balance these demands by "making Steve happy." This last challenge was apparently a very difficult one: Steve was never satisfied with her looks, their sex life, or anything Tina did. He was particularly uninterested in her schooling, often describing it as a "waste of time," and he made fun of her job. Sometimes they drank or used cocaine together. If she was feeling down after a long day or had an argument with him on the phone, she was more likely to go home and binge on junk food and purge afterward. She always felt worse after purging, but she felt she didn't have any other choice. She feared she otherwise would "get disgustingly fat" and be even less acceptable to Steve. Often, between dealing with him, her mood swings, and daily stressors, Tina felt that she was out of control and just surviving from one day to the next. Although each week was a little different, the pattern was a variation on the same themes: keep going, get stressed out, feel badly about myself, binge and purge, use alcohol or cocaine to cope, and so on. She was bingeing and purging about three to four times per week. At some point she knew that the routine had to end, and she felt she was ready to do something about it.

Selecting and Designing the Intervention: Defining Strategies and Objectives

After identifying the problems and general intervention goals, the social worker Peggy discussed intervention options with Tina and suggested they choose initial objectives (see table 15.2). Tina already felt very much involved, and having survived the first week at home using the self-monitoring chart, she felt that she was collaborating well with Peggy. She also felt that she had a basic understanding of how her problems were related, which gave her a sense of control over some of the changes she was about to implement. Although the social worker had touched on it initially, she provided Tina with a more detailed explanation of how her mood, self-image, the drug use, and her binge-purge cycle were not only related; her bingeing and purging actually "kept the pattern going." They reviewed the details of the types of food Tina binged with, how much and how often, and then discussed in detail what a healthful, "normal" diet would look like. Tina was strongly encouraged to discontinue all bingeing and purging immediately and begin her "normal" diet. Given her distorted expectations about gaining weight and becoming "fat," her social worker discussed with her how her distorted view of herself might be related to how she feels about herself in general and to her feelings of not being acceptable or "good enough" for others.

Tina continued to self-monitor in the following few weeks and track her mood, negative cognitions about herself and her physical appearance, and urges to binge and purge. Although she made progress, she did slip up a few times, once after Steve confronted her while she was leaving class. She did not resume using cocaine, but she came home upset because Steve was very angry with her and made her feel like "a traitor." After discussing her momentary relapse with Peggy, however, she felt less guilty about it. Her social worker congratulated her for getting back on the plan with her new eating regimen and not resuming cocaine use with Steve. She weighed herself weekly and did not see any substantive change in her weight. This alleviated any fears that she would put on a lot of weight if she didn't purge. She began to exercise with a friend of hers, running once or twice during the week and alone on the weekend. She began to feel better about her body, beginning to see herself as "fit" rather than feeling the need to be "thin." In general, she spent more time with friends she had drifted away from since she started dating Steve, and she was feeling better about herself. Steve had called her several times, and with the exception of confronting her after school, Tina had not seen him. She was bargaining for more time when he angrily told her not to come around anymore. Although upset, Tina refrained from bingeing and purging, and she stayed on her regimen despite doubts about her decision not to see Steve.

As she continued to follow her dietary regimen, more or less, Tina's fears of relapse began to abate, and she became less concerned about gaining weight. More of her focus during visits turned to her feelings about herself and the types of relationships she had in the previous few years. She had felt for a long time that something was missing, that she was not satisfied, and that she spent too much time worrying about whether or not the other person was happy even when she was not. Peggy went with this new direction and felt that as long as Tina's self-monitoring and dietary regimen continued, and as long as she abstained from cocaine, it might be helpful for her to examine her self-image and relationship with Steve. This emphasis on interpersonal relationships revealed a distorted or disproportionate belief that it was basically up to Tina to make a relationship work, with little expectation of return on her part. As they examined these long-standing beliefs, Peggy challenged them and encouraged Tina to begin actively putting them to the test in everyday circumstances.

As the weeks passed, Tina seemed to grow in confidence that relapse would not be a major problem. The more she stayed with her current eating regimen and exercise, the better she felt about herself. She kept very busy as a way of coping, but she felt that doing so was all right for the time being. She was not ready to take on a new relationship, and she felt good about herself for not "caving in" when Steve called again. She surprised herself when she told him on the phone that she really didn't want to spend much more time with a "pot head." Although she felt a little guilty afterward, the feeling didn't last long. After 16 visits or so, Tina and Peggy agreed that it was, perhaps, time to back off from regular visits to once per month for a while. Tina was planning to stay at home for the rest of the school year, then think about her next move. She wanted to keep in touch with the social worker in the meantime (just as a safety net) until she felt she was ready to go it alone.

Selecting Scales and Creating Indexes to Monitor and Evaluate Client Progress

In addition to using the EDDS to monitor specific symptoms (using individual items) as well as the overall composite score to track progress, the social worker decided to also use the Hamilton Depression Rating Scale (HAM-D; see chapter 6) to keep an eye on Tina's level of depression. In addition, the development and use of her daily self-monitoring chart was integral to Tina's role in the intervention. The chart helped keep her on track, and as a self-monitoring tool, it helped her hone self-regulatory skills by not overreacting to upset, stopping to consider what she was thinking and feeling, gauging the degree of risk for bingeing and purging, considering healthier alternatives to bingeing and purging, and thinking about the negative consequences she would experience if she did give in to the urge (as well as the feeling of satisfaction and progress she would feel if she successfully bypassed the urge). Other indexes could have been used to monitor co-occurring substance use.

CHAPTER SUMMARY

Depending on type and severity, anorexia, bulimia nervosa, and binge-eating disorder can be among the most challenging disorders to treat. In addition, they often co-occur with other serious problems, including depression, anxiety disorders, and substance abuse. Assessment protocol requires an emphasis on detailed functional analysis of thoughts, feelings, and behaviors related to bingeing and purging. There are also several valid eating-disorder scales that can enhance assessment and provide a measure for monitoring progress. Cognitive-behavioral therapy and interpersonal psychotherapy for bulimia nervosa and binge-eating disorder are comparably effective, but anorexia nervosa remains a difficult, and often intractable, disorder.

TABLE 15.2   The Client Service Plan: Tina

Problems	Goals	Objectives (samples)	Interventions	Assessment and evaluation tools
Intermittent drug abuse: alcohol, marijuana, cocaine	Eliminate drug use; refrain from all illicit drug use; social drinking to be reconsidered at later date	Refrain from drug use immediately with supervision of family, physician, and social worker; begin self-monitoring urges to use and identifying feeling states	Combined use of CBT and IPT elements to address interpersonal distortions and their effect on self-image and mood	EDDS to assess and monitor individual and global bulimia symptoms; HAM-D to monitor depression
Bingeing and purging 3–4 times per week	Eliminate all bingeing and purging and associated laxative use	Self-monitoring of thoughts, feelings, situations associated with urge to binge or purge	Psychoeducation to help her better understand how problems are linked, how eating normally and exercising will help her stop urges to binge or purge	Self-monitoring chart to include self-anchored indexes to measure stress, emotional antecedents to binge or purge, and actual episodes of either; chart also used to monitor any use of alcohol or drugs
Poor self-esteem, distorted body image (thinks she's fat)	Improve self-esteem; develop healthier, more realistic body image through healthful diet and exercise	Eat normal amounts and types of food daily; have weekly weigh-in at home; begin exercising 2–3 times per week	Brief behavioral family therapy to incorporate parents' social support to help Tina detox for further assessment of mental status and mood	
Unassertive in relationships; allows herself to be exploited; feels she is not "good enough"	Develop better understanding of interpersonal distortions and reasons for being unassertive; improve quality of interpersonal relationships	Identify in daily charts thoughts, feelings about her relationship and how it is related to urges to binge or purge or get high; select daily opportunity to assert herself and discuss with social worker	Help develop detailed eating and exercise regimen; report weekly weigh-ins; develop self-monitoring chart with social worker and use daily	
			Interpersonal psychotherapy to examine distorted beliefs and expectations, understand how behavior in relationships affects her mood; role-play and practice assertiveness in community to be less compliant with others	
			Case management with physician on health status, testing, and medication	

CHAPTER 16

SUBSTANCE ABUSE AND CO-OCCURRING PROBLEMS IN ADOLESCENTS AND YOUNG ADULTS

Late adolescence and young adulthood are particularly potent times for psychosocial development. Changes during this time include greater emotional and sexual involvement with others, increases in academic or occupational responsibilities, the taking on of responsibility for one's own physical and economic survival, and eventually emancipation from one's parents. The outcome trajectory for this dynamic period that bridges adolescence and adulthood can move one toward psychosocial growth, stagnation, or decline. This time also typically ushers in the use of alcohol and other drugs, which can be accompanied by psychiatric and behavioral problems. The purpose of this chapter is to summarize what is currently known about epidemiology, co-occurring problems, risk factors, and theories about substance abuse, and to show practitioners how to conduct assessments (in addition to what was covered in chapter 7) and engage adolescents in early intervention and treatment for substance use problems.

ASSESSMENT

Background Data

Results from the Monitoring the Future Survey conducted over a span of 20 years with high school students show that about 44% of young people of high school age reported having used alcohol and/or other drugs. (Ilgen et al., 2011). Most of those surveyed used marijuana and cocaine, and they had comorbid mental health problems. Decades of survey data from community, high school, and college samples have shown that young people account for almost half (45%) of all adult drinking in the United States (Greenfield & Rogers, 1999), and young people in college consume as much alcohol as, if not more than, their noncollege cohorts (Gfoerer, Greenblatt, & Wright, 1997; O'Malley & Johnston, 2002). From 67% to 75% of college students drink alcohol (Griffin & Botvin, 2010), and about 40% are considered binge drinkers (i.e., consume five or more drinks in one sitting within the previous 2 weeks). Although rates of alcohol and drug use vary somewhat over the years, over decades they have remained relatively steady (Griffin & Botvin, 2010; Jager, Schulenberg, O'Malley, & Bachman, 2013; Nelson, Xuan, Lee, Weitzman, & Wechsler, 2009; O'Malley & Johnston, 2002).

There are an array of co-occurring psychiatric disorders as well as psychosocial and behavioral problems related to excessive substance use in high school and college student samples (e.g., Johnston, O'Malley, Bachman, & Schulenberg, 2013; O'Hare, 1990; Wechsler, Davenport, Dowdall, Moeykens, & Costillow, 1994; Wechsler et al., 2002). These problems include depression, suicide, anxiety disorders, interpersonal problems (e.g., fights, unplanned and unprotected sex), community disturbances such as criminal behavior (e.g., driving under the influence, vandalism), and other acute consequences (e.g., death by excessive alcohol consumption during fraternity hazing, alcohol-related accidents including falls and drowning). As are adult women, young women are also known to be at greater risk for the consequences of excessive drinking, including more co-occurring depression and anxiety, higher blood-alcohol levels than males, and greater vulnerability to victimization through sexual assault, among other problems (Amaro, 1995; Greenfield, Pettinati, O'Malley, Randall, & Randall, 2010; O'Hare, 1997b, 2001b; Wechsler, Dowdall, Davenport, & Rimm, 1995).

Despite evidence for widespread heavy drinking among young persons, most do not develop long-term addictions (Chen & Kandel, 1995; Fillmore, 1974, 1988), and it is difficult to predict which individuals will develop long-term problems. However, young persons do tend to underestimate the short-term acute risks involved with substance abuse (O'Hare & Tran, 1997; Perkins, 2002; Wechsler & McFadden, 1979; Wechsler et al., 1994). Awareness of youthful problem-drinking patterns and associated risk factors, such as disinhibited drinking, stress-related drinking, and high expectations of positive reinforcement from drinking, may also have prognostic value for future alcohol dependence (Bennett, McCrady, Johnson, & Pandina, 1999; Schuckit, 1998).

Drinking in one's senior year of high school is significantly predictive of college drinking (Yu & Shacket, 2001). Perhaps because of their relative inexperience and recent emancipation from parental oversight, college freshmen are of particular concern, as they appear to have more problems related to drinking than older college students do. Rates of binge drinking increased successively from 14% to 24% and then 32% in students in grades 8, 10, and 12, respectively, but they jumped to 39% when high school students entered college (US Department of Health and Human Services, 1999). It is not until young people move beyond this important transition from high school to college that the association between heavy drinking and problems begins to decline, through senior year and beyond (O'Neill, Parra, & Sher, 2001). These changes include reduced overall consumption, greater discretion regarding risky drinking situations (e.g., driving under the influence), and the development of other skills that may attenuate negative consequences of excessive use. Thus, freshman year may be a critical opportunity to reduce future harm associated with excessive drinking.

The National Survey on Drug Use and Health (Substance Abuse and Mental Health Services Administration, SAMHSA, 2013) reports lifetime prevalence rates for use of alcohol and other drugs (for those aged 12–17 in 2012) as follows: alcohol, 32.4%; any illicit drug, 24.2%; marijuana, 17%; psychiatric medication, 10%; inhalants, 6.5%; cocaine, 1.10%; and hallucinogens, 3.3%. There are lower percentages (less than 3.0% each) for ecstasy, tranquilizers, sedatives, and stimulants. Data from the Monitoring the Future Survey (Johnston et al., 2013) suggest some decrease in alcohol use in young people during the period 2008–2013 (i.e., a decline from 15.9% to 10.2% among grade 8 students, from 28.8% to 25.7% among grade 10 students, and from 43.1% to 39.2% among grade 12 students) as well as some decrease in binge drinking. From 2012 to 2013, decreases were observed in binge use of alcohol (defined as five or more consecutive drinks in the previous 2 weeks) among tenth graders, with a 5-year trend showing a significant decrease in all three grades. The survey also reported a long-term drop in nonmedical use of prescription medications, and a decrease in use of inhalants. However, the 5-year trend also revealed increased marijuana use from 5.8% to 7.0% among eighth graders, from 13.8% to 18.0% among tenth graders, and from 19.4% to 22.7% among twelfth graders, along with a concomitant decrease in perceived harm associated with smoking marijuana. The percentage of twelfth graders reporting past-year nonmedical use of amphetamines rose from 6.8% in 2008 to 8.7% in 2013, and current use among twelfth graders also increased from 2.9% in 2008 to 4.1% in 2013. Among twelfth graders, marijuana and hashish are by far the most popular drug (36.4%), followed by synthetic marijuana (7.9%), the stimulant Adderall (7.4%), the narcotic Vicodin (5.3%), cough medicine (5.0%), sedatives (4.8%), tranquilizers (4.6%), hallucinogens (4.5%), and ecstasy (4.0%)—with other drugs (e.g., cocaine, inhalants, oxycodone) trending at less than 3%.

Taking the long view, these data should be interpreted with caution. Preferred drug types cycle through various phases, and variations suggest substitution (e.g., cocaine, methamphetamine, ecstasy). Over the past few decades, taken as a whole, the use and abuse of alcohol and other drugs has not changed dramatically. In addition, given considerable differences in the pharmacological properties of these various substances, risks of overdose and death vary considerably as well. The increases in fatalities from narcotics (i.e., prescription pain medications) in the general population is alarming (as noted in chapter 7), whereas there is no evidence of mortality resulting from an overdose of marijuana. Resources aimed at reducing substance use and abuse might be better spent targeting severe consequences, health problems, and loss of life, rather than trying to reduce usage rates overall of what are very different substances.

Racial Differences in Substance Use.   The National Survey on Drug Use and Health (SAMHSA, 2013) has estimated rates of illicit drug use among persons aged 12 and older, by race, as follows: Asian Americans (3.7%), Native Hawaiians or Other Pacific Islanders (7.8%), Hispanics (8.3%), whites (9.2%), blacks (11.3%), American Indians or Alaska Natives (12.7%), and biracial or multiracial (14.8%). Among young people specifically, African American students use drugs significantly less than whites and binge drink less (12%) than Hispanic students (28%) and whites (36%), and whites use other drugs at higher rates than other minority groups, including marijuana, inhalants, LSD, heroin, barbiturates, amphetamines, and tranquilizers. However, in senior year, Hispanics have the highest usage rates for more "dangerous" drugs, including cocaine and crack. Again, these data should be interpreted with caution, as preferences for one class of drug or another come in and out of fashion. In a cross-sectional sample of more than 300 adjudicated adolescents in the western United States (white, African American, and Hispanic), Caldwell, Silver, and Strada (2010) found greater instances of substance use among whites.

Co-occurring Problems and Comorbid Disorders.   Substance abuse problems in young people are accompanied by a host of co-occurring problems, including a variety of mental health disorders and high-risk behaviors (The Methods for the Epidemiology of Child and Adolescent Mental Disorders [MECA] Study [Kandel et al., 1997; Kandel et al., 1999]). These include conduct disorder, depression, and anxiety disorders. The likelihood that youth engage in multiple co-occurring health-risk behaviors (e.g., failing to use seat belts, carrying weapons, smoking or using smokeless tobacco, abusing substances, engaging in risky sex) appears to increase with age. A nationally representative sample of adolescents (aged 12–21) demonstrated that although most young persons do not engage in multiple risky behaviors, about 33% of those aged 14–17 engaged in more than one type of high-risk behavior, as did about 50% of college-aged youth. Males in all ages engaged in more risky behaviors than females. Young people not attending school in the age ranges of 14–17 and 18–21 engaged in more health-risk behaviors than did those attending school (Brener & Collins, 1998). Longitudinal analyses (e.g., Tubman, Windle, & Windle, 1996) suggest that externalizing problems in children and adolescents are linked to increases in risky sexual behaviors and substance abuse.

On the basis of the National Epidemiologic Survey on Alcohol and Related Conditions study (i.e., a nationally representative sample), Blanco et al. (2008) found that, except for bipolar disorder (more common in noncollege cohorts), college students and their noncollege cohorts have comparable levels of psychiatric disorders and comparable rates of alcohol use disorders (even when controlling for sociodemographics). However, non-college students are more likely to have a drug-related disorder and receive treatment for that disorder. In a large study (pooled data from 77 treatment studies) of adults and adolescents in treatment, Chan, Dennis, and Funk (2010) found that, of adolescents presenting a substance use problem, 72%–82% also had a mental health problem. About 50% reported an internalizing disorder and up to 67% reported an externalizing disorder. Roberts, Roberts, and Xing (2007) reported on an epidemiological study conducted in the (racially/ethnically diverse) Houston metropolitan area and found high rates of psychiatric comorbidity among youth, particularly among those diagnosed with dependence, women, and older adolescents. There were no significant differences in comorbidity among racial/ethnic groups. Externalizing disorders and anxiety disorders were more likely to occur among those with substance abuse and dependence diagnoses, and mood disorders were more common among those with alcohol dependence. Adolescents with substance use problems, especially those with comorbid mental health problems, are particularly at risk for high-risk sexual behaviors, including contracting HIV from needle use and unprotected sex (Chan, Passetti, Garner, Lloyd, & Dennis, 2011). In a national sample of youth, Ford, Elhai, Connor, and Frueh (2010) found that young people who had been victimized by violence multiple times were at much greater risk for post-traumatic stress disorder (PTSD), depression, and substance use.

Youths with disabilities (e.g., emotional, learning, and mobility) are significantly more likely than youth without disabilities to engage in risky behaviors, including sexual activity and substance abuse. Those with emotional disabilities were six times as likely to attempt suicide in the previous 12 months and those with learning or mobility disabilities were three times as likely to attempt suicide (Blum, Kelly, & Ireland, 2001). Health-risk behaviors are also likely to be associated with higher rates of depression and anxiety, which further complicates the clinical picture (Murphy, Durako et al., 2001). Increased emotional distress appears to be related to maladaptive coping, which may include drug and alcohol abuse (Arthur, 1998; O'Hare & Sherrer, 2000). Despite most stressors being in the range of mild to moderate, some students suffer psychological problems severe enough to result in withdrawal from school (Weiner & Wiener, 1997). Although many young people have co-occurring substance abuse and mental health problems, only 10%–12% ever receive services (Cheng & Lo, 2010; Ilgen et al., 2011).

Risky Sex as a Co-occurring Problem with Substance Abuse.   Young people account for a significant proportion of new HIV/AIDS cases (Leigh, 1999) with those aged 20–24 contracting HIV infection at the highest rate (Centers for Disease Control and Prevention, CDC, 2014b). Despite the plethora of messages about safe sex, young people do not use condoms consistently (CDC, 2006), and knowledge of AIDS/HIV risk does not necessarily reduce risky behaviors (Koch, Palmer, Vicary, & Wood, 1999; Lewis, Malow, & Ireland, 1997; Staton et al., 1999). Excessive drinking among young people increases the likelihood of high-risk sexual behavior, thereby increasing the possibility of both contracting sexually transmitted diseases (STDs) and sexual assault (Abbey, McAuslan, & Ross, 1998; Carroll & Carroll, 1995; Cooper & Orcutt, 1997; Leigh & Schafer, 1993; O'Hare, 2005; O'Leary, Goodhart, Sweet Jemmott, & Boccher-Lattimore, 1992; Snipes & Benotsch, 2013; Tubman, Des Rosiers, Schwartz, & O'Hare, 2012). Although a disproportionate amount of the research on substance abuse and risky sex has been done with college students, similar findings with noncollege cohorts have emerged. In a 10-year longitudinal study of a racially/ethnically diverse (about half African American) and environmentally high-risk group (about half residing in high-crime neighborhoods), Guo et al. (2002) demonstrated that binge drinking at an early age predicted a higher number of sex partners later in adolescents, and marijuana use predicted increased likelihood of risky sexual practices (i.e., avoiding condom use).

Although cause-effect inferences should be made cautiously, more serious levels of behavioral risk factors seem to co-occur with a greater number of risky behaviors overall. For example, in addition to increased risk of STDs (including HIV), the total number of sex partners a young person has correlates with other risky behaviors, including substance abuse, carrying weapons, and violence in black and white males and females (Valois, Oeltmann, Waller, & Hussey, 1999). It also has become more evident that bisexual and gay and lesbian male and female adolescents share many of the same risks as their heterosexual counterparts, including those related to risky sex and substance abuse. However, bisexual and gay and lesbian adolescents appear more likely to have been sexually abused and more likely to have engaged in sexual activity at a younger age (Saewyc, Bearinger, Heinz, Blum, & Resnick, 1998). In the same study, data on bisexual and gay males demonstrated three to four times the rate of attempted suicide as heterosexual counterparts, estimated from general population data. Although there is variance among age, gender, race, and sexual orientation, young people present one of the more challenging but potentially fruitful opportunities for secondary intervention. However, much of the data on gay, lesbian, and bisexual youth were based on nonrepresentative samples. More recent research with larger and more representative samples suggests that findings that point toward greater risk might be premature, and the relationship between sexual orientation and substance use might be complicated by factors such as gender and other sociodemographic factors. That being said, lesbian girls appear to be at greater risk for abusing alcohol than heterosexual boys (Ziyadeh et al., 2007).

Theories

Theories relating to substance use in adults apply equally to adolescents, but the literature on adolescents draws attention to factors related to onset at that time of life when substance abuse generally begins. There have been several somewhat-overlapping theories offered to explain substance abuse in young persons (Buckstein, 1995; Jessor & Jessor, 1977; Schulenberg & Maggs, 2002; Zucker & Fitzgerald, 1991). These include genetic and social learning influences, the development of alcohol expectancies (i.e., beliefs about the positive or negative effects of alcohol or other drug abuse), parental modeling, inadequate relationships with parents, early onset of substance abuse problems, academic problems, conduct disorder and other problems with aggression, interpersonal conflict or other deviance, risky sexual behaviors, peer relations and poor social bonds, other co-occurring psychopathology (e.g., depression, other mental illnesses, eating disorders), and living in stressful environments (e.g., poverty, high crime). Of course, cultural factors are also correlated with substance abuse, as rates of substance use vary considerably by racial and cultural background. It is understood that the interactions of these potential risk factors are complex and not well understood. In general, they are cumulative in the sense that more risk factors increase the chances of developing a serious substance abuse problem or addiction.

Developmental theories relevant to the behavior of adolescents and young adults have been applied to alcohol abuse (Schulenberg & Maggs, 2002; Schulenberg, Maggs, Steinman, & Zucker, 2001). Developmental transitions are conceptualized as originating in the interaction of both distal and proximate influences on biological (i.e., physical) maturation, beliefs, expectancies and cultural context, family and other interpersonal experiences, personal values and goals. These activities interact and are reciprocally influenced by the environment around the individual. Physiological changes (alcohol tolerance), peer relations, increased sexual activity and a new broadening of social relations, new academic and occupational challenges among other transitional and/or developmental events present a whole range of opportunities for growth and adaptation or avoidance and psychosocial dysfunction. These developmental transitions include fundamental changes in pubertal and cognitive development, affiliative transitions (e.g., family, friends, romantic relationships), achievement transitions (e.g., school, work), and identity transitions (e.g., changes in self-definition, increased self-regulation). Schulenberg et al. (2001) identify overloaded coping abilities, an incongruity between developmental needs and circumstances, and the potentially growth-promoting aspects of risk-taking behavior as factors that may promote risky behaviors. A developmental perspective could inform prevention strategies by illuminating opportunities for prevention experts to interrupt and redirect certain risk behaviors or alter interpersonal and contextual factors that could have an impact on existing risk factors. Prevention strategies may be more effective if they target young people's important life transitions (e.g., going to college), use interventions that are salient to young people's specific problems (e.g., risky sex while drinking), and consider both students' freedoms and the need for students to be accountable for their behavior.

It is often stated that health-risk behaviors are directly related to peer-group affiliation (i.e., peer pressure). At least one study has demonstrated that young people's health-risk behaviors may be more influenced by peers than by parents (Beal, Ausiello, & Perrin, 2001). In cross-sectional and prospective research with inner-city African American youth, it was shown that parents' monitoring of their children's behavior was directly correlated with their child's risky behaviors, including sex, drug use, drug trafficking, truancy, and violence (Xiaoming, Stanton, & Feigelman, 2000a, 2000b). A recent longitudinal study showed that parent-child influences are reciprocal: adolescents' deviant behavior can have a negative impact on parenting capacities as well (Trucco, Colder, Wieczorek, Lengua, & Hawk, 2014). Those young persons considered "deviant" (e.g., nonconformists, "stoners," "burnouts") show the highest rates of risky behaviors, and once affiliated with troubled peer groups, they find it hard to extricate themselves (La Greca, Prinstein, & Fetter, 2001). As longitudinal multivariate research designs are brought to bear, the relationships among personal risk factors, parents, neighborhood characteristics, and peer relations with juvenile delinquency and substance abuse are proving reciprocally causal and complex (Trucco et al., 2014). As with other areas in the modern behavioral sciences, conclusions about why young people drink or use drugs should be understood as emerging within a multivariate context over time.

Social cognitive models have also had a large presence in the literature on youth drinking for some time, and they have been shown to be useful for linking motivations for drinking, alcohol expectancies of drinking effects, stress, and social and contextual variables as reciprocal determinants of problem drinking (e.g., Abrams & Niaura, 1987; Brown, Christiansen, & Goldman, 1987; Cooper, Russell, & George, 1988; Maisto, Carey, & Bradizza, 1999; Moos, 2007; O'Hare, 1998a). This model has demonstrated that interactions among physiological predisposition, beliefs, drinking behaviors, and preferred drinking contexts operate in complex ways. Cognitive, behavioral, and contextual factors are theoretically amenable to early intervention strategies. Four major developments in recent years have contributed to a social cognitive model of youthful drinking: (1) research on the structural and situational aspects of drinking (e.g., when, where, with whom), (2) alcohol expectancy research, (3) motives relating to substance use (e.g., partying vs. coping with emotional distress), and (4) research on high-risk drinking contexts. The first area has demonstrated that college drinking is primarily a social affair done in same- and mixed-gender peer groups in an atmosphere of general conviviality (Harford & Grant, 1987; O'Hare, 1990; Wechsler & McFadden, 1979). Older teens (twelfth graders) were shown to be more likely than younger adolescents to drink with peers in large groups and in someone else's home (Mayer, Forster, Murray, & Wagenaar, 1998). In one gender-comparison study of adult children of alcoholics in college, men appeared to be more inclined than women to drink in larger and same-sex groups, and convivial drinking appeared to be associated with better social adjustment (Senchak, Leonard, & Greene, 1998). The second area of research emphasizes important cognitive mediators of drinking, known as alcohol expectancies, which are beliefs in relatively specific types of reinforcement from drinking. Expectancy constructs as measured by the Alcohol Expectancy Questionnaire (AEQ) are correlated with drinking patterns, attitudes, and associated problems and drinking motives (Brown, 1985; Brown et al., 1987; Brown, Goldman, Inn, & Anderson, 1980; Cooper, 1994; Wall, Hinson, & McKee, 1998). The third theoretical area emphasizes high-risk drinking situations, including those associated with relapse during treatment and recovery (Marlatt & Gordon, 1985; Isenhart, 1993). Surveys of young persons not in treatment have consistently found that, although most young persons associate excessive drinking with convivial and celebratory experiences (Carey, 1993; O'Hare, 1997b), they also often abuse alcohol to cope with negative emotions such as anxiety, depression, and stress, which are associated with interpersonal problems (Cooper et al., 1988; Evans & Dunn, 1995; O'Hare, 1998a; O'Hare & Sherrer, 2005).

How problem drinking is defined also depends on the perspectives of the young person who drinks and others. Although most young persons drink as part of socializing (e.g., partying), negative consequences in the community (e.g., vandalism, excessive noise, car accidents, public urination) are likely to be defined as such by local police, campus neighbors, and school administrators. Young persons who drink as part of dating and sexual encounters may find that alcohol facilitates such encounters in a positive way or results in negative consequences (e.g., unprotected sex, date rape) (Abbey & Harnish, 1995; Cooper, 2002; Norris, 1994; O'Hare, 1998a). Young people who drink as a way of coping with negative emotions (e.g., depression, anxiety) are more likely to suffer from social and emotional problems related to drinking, and they may be at greater risk for more serious drinking problems in the long run (O'Hare & Sherrer, 2005; Schuckit, 1998). A social-cognitive perspective informs secondary prevention efforts. Practitioners can help young drinkers improve situational awareness of risks, make better estimates about the potential for harm to themselves or others, and enhance their coping skills in reducing consumption and/or altering the context of use to reduce negative consequences.

Theories have also been applied to risky sexual behaviors. Brown and Lourie (2001) provided a brief overview of the theories and methods that have shown promise for understanding and reducing HIV health-risk behaviors: the theory of reasoned action, the health belief model, and social cognitive theory (e.g., self-efficacy theory and transtheoretical model of change). Although there are some differences in these theories, they overlap considerably in their emphasis on the interaction of cognitive factors, consequential behaviors, and situational variability. They also share common implications for early intervention: providing new information, challenging existing dysfunctional cognitions, and enhancing self-efficacy and coping skills in at-risk situations.

Risky Sexual Behaviors and Substance Use.   Other risks are associated with substance abuse and sexual encounters. Estimates from several studies suggest than more than half of college women report having been sexually assaulted. About 5% report that the assault ended in a completed rape. About half of assaults appear to be alcohol related (often when both were drinking), and almost all assaults were committed by a man familiar to the woman (i.e., acquaintance rape) (Abbey, 2002). In a 1-year longitudinal study, frequent drinking and frequent binge drinking predicted additional sexual assault in freshman college women, but having been assaulted did not change drinking patterns (Mouilso, Fischer, & Calhoun, 2012). The theoretical explanations regarding alcohol use and sexual assault are not straightforward and involve complex interactions among cognitive, situational, cultural, and gender-based factors, among others (Abbey, 2002; Cooper, 2002; Leigh, 1999). Theoretical explanations for the link between risky sex and heavy drinking include general sensation seeking, impaired judgment, alcohol expectancies, and contextual factors related to sexual behaviors and drinking (Dermen & Cooper, 1994a, 1994b; Leigh, 1999; Norris, 1994; O'Hare, 1998a, 2005; Schafer & Leigh, 1996; Steele & Josephs, 1990).

Leigh (1990) demonstrated in a household survey that items related to the expectancy of sexual enhancement and disinhibition were associated with the likelihood of drinking during a specific sexual situation and the amount of alcohol consumed during the most recent sexual encounter. Dermen and Cooper (1994a) conducted a survey with a more representative sample of more than 900 adolescents (aged 13–19) to develop a scale that, in addition to sexual enhancement (Brown et al., 1980), included items relevant to disinhibition and specific risky sexual behaviors (e.g., unprotected sex). After validating the scale with confirmatory factor analysis, Dermen and Cooper (1994b) found that sex-specific expectancies were better than global alcohol expectancies in predicting specific sexual situations, but they were as useful or somewhat less useful than general global expectancies in predicting drinking at parties and on dates. Although men and women who drink in convivial and intimate circumstances share increased expectancies of enhanced sexual relations, men are more likely to engage in risky sexual *behaviors* (Cooper & Orcutt, 1997; Dermen, Cooper, & Agocha, 1998; Leigh & Aramburu, 1996; O'Hare, 1998a, 1999), and these situations carry greater risks of harm for young women (Abbey et al., 1998).

On the basis of a considerable amount of survey research (Abbey, 2002; Abbey et al., 1998; Cooper, 1992; Leigh, 1999; Mouilso et al., 2012; Norris, 1994; O'Hare, 1998a, 2001b; O'Leary, 1992), several interrelated factors appear to increase the likelihood of rape occurring. These factors, both general and related specifically to alcohol use, include the following:

- Social learning and personality disturbances on the part of the male (e.g., social learning processes that present sexual aggressiveness in a positive light, conduct- or impulse-disordered behaviors related to psychopathy, antisocial personality)

- Alcohol expectancies regarding sexual assertiveness or a belief in enhanced sexual experience through alcohol use

- Cultural and peer influences that encourage sexual aggressiveness and lack of consideration for a woman's prerogative to say no
- The belief that if a woman is drinking she is sexually more available
- The physiologically disinhibiting (and judgment-impairing) attributes of alcohol
- The use of alcohol intoxication as an excuse for aggressive sexual behavior (in the male) or as an excuse to hold a woman responsible for an assault (if she was drinking)

A multivariate model is emerging that outlines a useful assessment framework for early intervention, and it includes at a minimum the following factors: person variables (e.g., gender, age, cultural background), alcohol expectancies (social learning experiences regarding drinking and sexual behavior), physiological gender differences, history of impulsivity and sensation seeking related to drinking, patterns of excessive alcohol consumption, and situational factors that include heavy drinking and sexual encounters. Although drinking and risky sex may be correlated, their relationship is complex, and drawing explicit links between alcohol use and specific risky sexual behaviors has been difficult to demonstrate empirically (Abbey, 2002; Cooper, 2002).

Multidimensional-Functional-Systems Assessment of Substance Abuse and Risky Sex in Young Persons

Recognizing the somewhat arbitrary distinction between *abuse* and *dependence* (e.g., tolerance does not equate dependence), the authors of the DSM-5 have amended the diagnostic criteria by listing signs and symptoms of what are now categorized as "substance use disorders" (American Psychiatric Association, APA, 2013) without the previous distinction. In addition, youthful substance abuse is often transitory or context specific, and it does not often meet the former criteria of abuse and, less often, dependence (Chen & Kandel, 1995; Fillmore, 1974, 1988; Martin & Winters, 1998). Although long-term outcomes are always a concern, the focus of assessment and treatment with young people tends to be on more acute negative consequences of substance use and abuse, consequences that can be very serious and even fatal. Thus, assessment of substance abuse with adolescents and young adults should emphasize not just which substances are used and how often, but also how substance use might be related to other co-occurring psychiatric and psychosocial disorders.

A motivational interviewing style (Miller & Rollnick, 1991, 2013; see chapter 7) might be particularly well suited to work with young persons. A strategy that shows respect for their personal experiences, eschews an authoritative stance, and encourages them to make their own judgments regarding the pros and cons of substance use and other risky behaviors is likely to elicit a more positive response than is direct confrontation. Showing concern and interest in other problems in their life (e.g., relationships, school frustrations) that may or may not be directly related to substance use will also be met with more constructive engagement. If the young person lives at home, family interviews can be used conjointly, exclusively (for younger adolescents), or not at all, depending on the family situation.

Assessment of substance abuse in young persons demands the same multidimensional-functional-systems (MFS) assessment approach as with adults (see chapter 7), with the understanding that there is likely to be a generally shorter substance abuse history and the points of concern are likely to focus on situational risks for negative consequences associated with that time of life (e.g., peer relations, conflict with parents) rather than a clear dependence syndrome (although that is a possibility that should always be ruled out). An examination of signs of serious tolerance or withdrawal (dependence) should be conducted, along with a medical examination that includes tests for drug use and STDs (Buckstein, 1995). Type of substances used and careful estimates of quantity and frequency of consumption are very important, but they must be tied specifically to risks for acute health crises (e.g., alcohol poisoning) and other negative consequences, including psychological problems (e.g., depression, anxiety), interpersonal difficulties (e.g., fighting, risky sex, fights, accidents, family problems), academic and occupational deficits, general health concerns, and problems in the community (e.g., fights, vandalism, driving under the influence, other crimes). Because young people have problems that may be only coincidentally associated with substance use, detailed MFS assessment is needed to more closely tie their use to acute or chronic psychosocial problems.

Key questions guiding the MFS assessment are the same as for adults: Which substances? How much? How often? What are the psychological, emotional, interpersonal, and occupational or academic consequences? The interviewer should be prepared to probe areas that are most salient to young people's substance abuse and to the individual's own experiences. The use of alcohol and other drugs is not a random event, and a detailed analysis of the drugs used, with whom, where, when, and under which circumstances will go a long way toward functionally tying substance use to key antecedents such as a response to emotional distress, interpersonal problems, celebrations, circumstances that may incur special risks (e.g., drinking, smoking pot while driving), on the job, during school hours, or as a prelude to sexual encounters. A 2-week chart of daily use patterns with a special focus on problematic (excessive) use in risky circumstances will prove very helpful to early intervention planning. Because young persons tend to underestimate the inherent risk in substance abuse, it may also be helpful to have them compare their average consumption to established norms of their peers, who may not consume as much as the student assumes (Read, Wood, Davidoff, McLacken, & Campbell, 2002). In addition, perceived drinking norms also appear to vary by peer group identification (e.g., "jocks," "brains," "loners," "deviants") (Sessa, 2007). Helping young people "connect the dots" with regard to their psychological and emotional concerns, their expectancies of alcohol's effects, how much they think others with whom they identify are drinking, and the specific circumstances in which they abuse substances needs to be explored carefully.

Instruments

There are many alcohol screening, assessment, and diagnostic tools developed for work with adults (see chapter 7). Although some have shown some utility for older adolescents (e.g., the AUDIT; Fleming, Barry, & MacDonald, 1991; O'Hare & Sherrer, 1999), many are not sensitive to the acute or contextually specific substance use problems of young people. There are, however, several instruments designed for adolescents (Leccese & Waldron, 1994; Martin & Winters, 1998; White, Labouvie, & Papadaratsakis, 2005). Screens and assessment tools for adolescents tend to emphasize negative consequences of substance use associated with situational factors rather than long-term indications of substance dependence. However, there are limitations to relying on these "proxy" indicators of substance abuse (i.e., co-occurring problems such as depression or interpersonal distress). Many young persons, whether they drink or not, experience these problems. Thus, relying too heavily on co-occurring indicators may lead to a high level of false positives. Even firsthand accounts by significant others and "toxicology screens" can be misleading. Third parties may not be able to tell what substances were used, how much, or how often, and lab tests usually are not accurate indicators of quantity or frequency. Ultimately, there may be no adequate substitute for a thorough MFS assessment conducted in a comfortable environment where a young person can be open about use without fearing unreasonable reprisals.

Self-report instruments have been commonly used in survey research to detect and estimate the degree of negative consequences attributed to drinking (Wechsler et al., 1994; Wechsler et al., 2002). Although this approach may have some research utility, evidence of factorial validity and scale reliabilities are often not reported, and these data do not offer any validated taxonomy for categorizing different dimensions of problem drinking. Another instrument that addresses a range of psychosocial consequences associated with drinking, the Rutgers Alcohol Problem Inventory (RAPI) (White & Labouvie, 1989; White et al., 2005), has been shown to distinguish adolescent drinkers from problem drinkers and to correlate with various measures of abuse. It was also shown to be cross-culturally valid with First Nation (Mi'kmaq) adolescents in Nova Scotia (Noel et al., 2010). Other more comprehensive assessment instruments for substance abuse are available but often require a lengthy structured interview, which is not practical when routine brief assessment tools are needed. Given the high prevalence of abusive drinking among young persons, brief, valid, and reliable self-report screening devices are needed so that practitioners can quickly evaluate and refer problem-drinking young persons for further substance abuse assessment and intervention.

The College Alcohol Problem Scale–Revised (CAPS-r) was developed and replicated with college students, mostly freshmen who were adjudicated for breaking university drinking rules. Their age, status as freshmen, and the fact that they were "caught" suggests that this sample represents a group of young persons at particular risk for problem drinking (Maddock, Laforge, Rossi, & O'Hare, 2001; O'Hare, 1997a, 1998b). The original pool of 20 items was drawn from an array of instruments used in prominent college-drinking studies (e.g., Engs, 1977; O'Hare, 1990a; Wechsler & McFadden, 1979). Exploratory factor analysis (EFA) was used with two separate samples to replicate the analysis of the same 20 items. Ten items were extracted from the original CAPS version of the scale. Cronbach's alphas in both samples were comparable (social-emotional, .88, .89; community, .79, .76), and the CAPS demonstrated good concurrent validity with the quantity-frequency index, a version of the Michigan Alcoholism Screening Test, and the peak drinking index from the Alcohol Use Disorders Identification Test (O'Hare, 1997a, 1998b).

Using the same 20 items as in the original CAPS, Maddock et al. (2001) employed confirmatory factor analysis with a broader sample of university undergraduates to refine the original CAPS. The study resulted in an eight-item version, the CAPS–Revised (CAPS-r), which defines two subscales similar to the original one: personal problems (feeling sad, blue, and/or depressed; nervousness and/or irritability; feeling bad about oneself; and problems with appetite or sleeping) and social problems (engaged in unplanned sexual activity; drove under the influence; did not use protection when engaging in sex; and engaged in illegal activity associated with drug use). Internal consistency reliabilities were comparable to those of the original scale (i.e., personal problems = .79, social problems = .75). The current eight-item version requests that respondents estimate the frequency with which they have experienced specific alcohol-related problems over the previous year. Although there are no established norms, Maddock et al. (2001) surveyed more than 700 undergraduates in a university in the US Northeast, finding the following mean scores: personal problems (males 3.75, females 3.28), social problems (males 3.47, females 4.93), and total (males 7.17, females 8.22). The CAPS-r can be used in an interview or as a self-report, paper-and-pencil screen to identify personal and social problems related to drinking in young people. Scores from individual items, or subscales (personal, 1–4; social, 5–8) and the global score (the sum of all eight items), can be used to establish baseline measures for assessment and to monitor and evaluate client response to early intervention efforts (e.g., by changing instructions from "previous year" to "3 months" or the start of treatment, as needed). The CAPS-r also has been shown to be reliable and valid with non-adjudicated college students (Talbot, Umstattd, Usdan, Martin, & Geiger, 2009). The CAPS-r takes about 2–3 minutes to administer and requires only basic interviewing skills and knowledge of substance abuse problems.

INSTRUMENT 16.1   College Alcohol Problems Scale–Revised (CAPS-r)

Use the scale below to rate HOW OFTEN you have had any of the following problems over the past year <u>as a result of drinking alcoholic beverages</u>.

____1. Feeling sad, blue, or depressed

    1 Never   2 Yes, but not in the past year   3 1–2 times

    4 3–5 times   5 6–9 times   6 10 or more times

____2. Nervousness, irritability

    1 Never   2 Yes, but not in the past year   3 1–2 times

    4 3–5 times   5 6–9 times   6 10 or more times

____3. Caused you to feel bad about yourself

    1 Never   2 Yes, but not in the past year   3 1–2 times

    4 3–5 times   5 6–9 times   6 10 or more times

____4. Problems with appetite or sleeping

    1 Never   2 Yes, but not in the past year   3 1–2 times

    4 3–5 times   5 6–9 times   6 10 or more times

____5. Engaged in unplanned sexual activity

    1 Never   2 Yes, but not in the past year   3 1–2 times

    4 3–5 times   5 6–9 times   6 10 or more times

____6. Drove under the influence

    1 Never   2 Yes, but not in the past year   3 1–2 times

    4 3–5 times   5 6–9 times   6 10 or more times

____7. Did not use protection when engaging in sex

    1 Never   2 Yes, but not in the past year   3 1–2 times

    4 3–5 times   5 6–9 times   6 10 or more times

____8. Illegal activities associated with drug use

    1 Never   2 Yes, but not in the past year   3 1–2 times

    4 3–5 times   5 6–9 times   6 10 or more times

The Drinking Context Scale (DCS) (O'Hare, 1997b, 2001a; O'Hare & Sherrer, 2005) was developed with college students (mostly freshmen men and women) cited their first time for breaking university drinking rules. Drinking context is defined here as a composite of social, emotional, and situational factors in which the respondent estimates the likelihood of drinking excessively. The DCS employs a continuous measurement scale, anchors respondents' view of alcohol use in their own drinking experience rather than their belief in drinking effects, and emphasizes the likelihood of drinking excessively (as defined subjectively by the respondent). Initial exploratory factor analysis (EFA) resulted in three distinct subscales (convivial drinking, intimate drinking, and negative coping—or drinking to cope with negative emotions). The original scale accounted for 61.5% of variance, and subscales demonstrated excellent internal reliabilities (.93, .89, and .90). The three subscales were moderately correlated. Multiple analyses of variance demonstrated concurrent validity with the quantity-frequency index and a modified version of the Michigan Alcoholism Screening Test (O'Hare, 1997b). Later, a more rigorous assessment of the DCS's validity (O'Hare, 2001a) was conducted with a similar population by employing confirmatory factor analysis (CFA) with a much larger sample ($N = 505$) of participants in the same program. Results supported the validity and reliability of a nine-item version of the scale. Internal consistency reliabilities were calculated for the three factor subscales of the DCS; they are as follows: convivial drinking (.82), intimate drinking (.81), and negative coping (.85). The reliabilities are very good, considering the brevity of each subscale (longer scales tend to artificially inflate internal consistency coefficients). Moreover, Gonzalez, Bradizza, and Collins (2009) demonstrated that drinking to cope mediated suicidal ideation and alcohol consumption in underage college drinkers.

The DCS-9 (O'Hare, 2001a) is a brief instrument that can be used as a screening device to identify at-risk drinking in young persons, to augment assessment, and/or to monitor and evaluate early intervention efforts. Identifying risky drinking contexts can provide an assessment and outcome framework for treatment planning and evaluating coping-skills interventions

---

INSTRUMENT 16.2   Drinking Context Scale (DCS)

Based on your <u>personal experience</u>, how would you RATE THE CHANCES that you might find yourself <u>drinking excessively</u> in the <u>following circumstances</u>? (Use the following scale to rate your responses.)

Extremely High	High	Moderate	Low	Extremely Low
5	4	3	2	1

Convivial drinking

When I'm at a party or similar other get-together	5	4	3	2	1
When I'm at a concert or other public event	5	4	3	2	1
When I'm celebrating something important to me	5	4	3	2	1

Intimate drinking

When I'm with my lover	5	4	3	2	1
When I'm on a date	5	4	3	2	1
Before having sex	5	4	3	2	1

Negative coping

When I've had a fight with someone close to me	5	4	3	2	1
When I'm feeling sad, depressed or discouraged	5	4	3	2	1
When I'm angry with myself or someone else	5	4	3	2	1

(described later here). The individual items can be used as prompts in a qualitative interview to further explore excessive drinking in specific circumstances (e.g., when partying, before sex, when angry or depressed). The three subscales are easily summed, and a global measure of risky drinking can be obtained by summing all nine items. No special training is required beyond basic interviewing skills and a basic knowledge of alcohol problems in young persons. Although no norms have been established, mean scores for 505 college students (O'Hare, 2001a) adjudicated for underage drinking are convivial drinking (9.23), intimate drinking (5.42), and negative coping (4.30). Dividing each subscale total by 3 provides a relative mean that reflects the likelihood of drinking excessively in that context (e.g., 4 = high likelihood of drinking excessively). Dividing the total score (all nine items) by 9 also provides a relative mean reflecting the likelihood of drinking excessively.

SELECTING EFFECTIVE INTERVENTIONS

There are various approaches to preventing and mitigating the negative consequences of substance abuse in young people. These strategies include primary prevention, early (secondary) intervention, and tertiary intervention for those with more serious substance abuse problems. Much of the research on prevention and early intervention has been conducted on high school and college samples, but treatment research with other community-based samples has increased. These are presented here with the understanding that educational and community samples overlap to some degree.

Primary Prevention.   In general, there is little compelling evidence that broad-brush primary prevention strategies targeted at reducing college drinking and associated problems have yielded substantively positive results (Clapp, Segars, & Voas, 2002; Hanson & Engs, 1995; Moskowitz, 1989; Walters, Bennett, & Noto, 2000; Wechsler et al., 2002; Werch, Pappas, & Castellon-Vogel, 1996). Such programs usually provide information about health and behavioral risks associated with using alcohol and other drugs. It may be more cost-effective to identify those young persons who manifest problems with substance abuse, then offer personalized feedback and skill-based early intervention programs. Many substance use problems co-occur with other presenting problems (e.g., behavioral, academic, health, or mental health problems), which offers college personnel ample opportunities to identify students in trouble with alcohol and other drugs. The link between substance abuse and risky sex also suggests that practitioners who work with young persons incorporate good self-monitoring and coping skills to anticipate situations in which sexual activity is likely and work toward reducing negative consequences. In this section, the evidence for effective early intervention methods for adolescents and young adults who abuse alcohol and other drugs will be reviewed, and selected interventions will be described.

Evidence-based prevention programs that emphasize learning new coping skills are generally grounded in social-cognitive theory and often employ some combination of psychoeducation and cognitive-behavioral coping skills approaches. Botvin and associates (e.g., Botvin, Baker, Dusenbury, Tortu, & Botvin, 1990; Botvin, Griffin, Diaz, & Ifill-Williams, 2001; Griffin & Botvin, 2010) developed the Life Skills Training Program (LSTP), which has been shown in randomized trials to be effective at changing maladaptive cognitions linked to substance abuse. In their review of the literature, Griffin and Botvin (2010) summarized primary prevention programs that have shown evidence of effectiveness from controlled trials. First among them is Life Skills Training, a primary-prevention school-based program (junior high and high school) that aims to improve overall social skills, especially those for resisting use of tobacco, alcohol, and other drugs. Evidence from several controlled trials with white students and minority students, including follow-up data, show substantive evidence for reduced substance use. Griffin and Botvin (2010) also noted Project Toward No Drug Abuse, a 12-lesson program similar to LST but with more emphasis on harder drugs and reducing related violence.

In describing the rationale for LSTP, Botvin et al. (1990) emphasized the use of coping skills to help youths stop or avoid initiating drug use through a combination of psychoeducation, changing expectancies, and practicing drug-refusal skills. A 3-year randomized controlled study was undertaken to test the efficacy of LSTP. The goals of the program were to reduce cigarette smoking and use of alcohol and marijuana. Participants were educated about actual prevalence rates (i.e., providing "norms" to debunk the notion "everybody's doing it"), examined the social acceptability and negative consequences of use, and practiced substance-refusal skills to improve self-efficacy in social situations. Fifty-six schools participated in the study, and pre- and posttest data were successfully collected from more than 4,000 (mostly) white seventh graders. Students were randomly assigned to three conditions: LSTP (provided by a live trainer), a videotaped version of the training, and a no-treatment control group. LSTP is designed to be implemented in 12 modules over 15 class periods. Teaching techniques include lecture, demonstration, role-play and performance feedback, reinforcement, and homework assignments. Student participants are provided with booster sessions in the eighth and ninth grades to reinforce material learned in the seventh-grade training program. Teachers are trained in LSTP in a day-long workshop that includes use of a program manual. Fidelity checks were regularly made of randomly selected classroom presentations of the program. Outcome measures included standard quantity and frequency measures for substance use and standardized scales to assess changes in knowledge, assertiveness, and expectancies. Significantly less cigarette and marijuana smoking were found in both treatment conditions than in the control group, although overall mean differences were not substantive. In addition, no differences in alcohol consumption level were found between groups. Knowledge and attitudes toward substance use and the use of substance refusal skills appeared to show a significant mediating effect for the active treatments versus the control group. Although results from the initial study appear to be modest, long-term follow-up data demonstrated some positive effects lasting until the end of high school (Botvin, Baker, Dusenbury, Botvin, & Diaz, 1995). For those students who received reasonably complete versions of the intervention, there were 44% and 66% fewer drug and polydrug users, respectively, in the treatment group.

Exemplar Outcome Study: Generalizing Botvin et al.'s Work to Young Persons of Color

Building on earlier work with the Life Skills Program, Botvin et al. (2001) implemented a similar program in a randomized control trial (treatment vs. standard New York City prevention curriculum) with predominantly African American and Hispanic urban minority youth. The experimental program was similar to that described in Botvin et al. (1990); it was provided in 15 sessions to seventh graders, with 10 booster sessions in eighth grade. Standard indexes of alcohol consumption (including binge drinking), and drinking-related variables (e.g., knowledge, perceived benefits, normative expectations of peer use) were employed as outcome measures. Of participants, 80% completed pre- and posttest data at one year, although only 58% provided complete data in the second year of the program. As with the previous study, those who dropped out were also more likely to be heavier alcohol users, although attrition did not differ between the two treatment conditions. The intervention resulted in a 57% decrease in binge drinking at 1-year and 2-year follow-ups, as well as improved alcohol-related knowledge, attitudes, and peer drinking expectations. Thus, the study provides substantive evidence that skill-based, large-scale prevention programs based on reducing harm and designed initially for white students can be implemented effectively with urban students of color.

Overall, although these studies show the potential effectiveness of such programs, consistent implementation and attrition remain a considerable challenge. In some cases, those students with the greatest need for help may be those who are least likely to participate actively in such programs. For example, Moncher and Schinke (1994) implemented a similar cognitive-behavioral prevention approach to reduce smoking and smokeless tobacco use in Native American sixth and seventh graders but showed few significant results. Weisz and Black (2001) conducted a small quasi-experimental study that demonstrated that a violence prevention program could improve knowledge and attitudes regarding sexual assault and dating violence among African American youths in the inner city. Although results were promising, there remains a need for more controlled investigations of prevention and early intervention research with youth of color who have multiple problems.

Komro et al. (2007) carried out a large, multisite randomized controlled trial of prevention efforts (vs. prevention as usual) over 4 years (grades 6–9) in largely low-income African American and Hispanic neighborhoods in Chicago. The program included psychoeducation, a family focus, and community projects with more than 4,000 students. The design included excellent follow-up over time and a high level of parent and teacher participation. Underscoring the challenges of prevention technologies, the researchers found no significant reduction in substance use or related risk factors. However, they did note some promising evidence for the home-based intervention program (e.g., home-based activity workbooks, family-fun events).

Parental involvement in prevention strategies might be a key factor for improving prevention program outcomes. Koning et al. (2009) compared brief parent-involved psychoeducational prevention programs (e.g., rule setting) aimed to reduce risk of heavy drinking in 3,490 student participants in a randomized study in the Netherlands and found the parent-involved group (targeted at parents and children together) to be superior to either parents or children alone as well as the control group. Online prevention programs for college students are increasing, and these can involve parents as well. One randomized controlled trial included 279 dyads of parents (85% mothers, 94% white) and newly admitted freshmen. The parent-targeted prevention program focused on parents discussing prevention and alcohol reduction strategies with their son or daughter (Donovan, Wood, Frayjo, Black, & Surette, 2012). Results were promising: parents who used the online program discussed such matters more with their child, who also reported using more prevention strategies.

Early Intervention.   Evidence-based early intervention programs include some combination of motivational interviewing; psychoeducation about psychological, social, and health risks associated with substance use, examination of alcohol expectancies (i.e., beliefs in positive and negative effects of alcohol), comparison of the client's substance use with statistical peer norms, and cognitive-behavioral coping skills approaches (e.g., coping with at-risk situations, negative moods)—all targeted at the overall goal of reducing harm associated with substance use. A perspective of harm reduction is based on the assumption that many young persons with substance use problems will benefit from modifying their use and developing better health-promoting coping skills (Marlatt, 1996; Marlatt & Witkiewitz, 2002; Miller & Rollnick, 2013; Miller, Turner, & Marlatt, 2001). Rather than mandating abstinence (which can reduce a young person's likelihood of engaging in treatment at all), early intervention aimed to reduce harm addresses the relative risks associated with substance use and abuse, and targets problem and risk reduction along a continuum (including elective abstinence). A practitioner focused on reducing harm is less confrontational and emphasizes motivational engagement. The intervention follows a staged trajectory whereby the practitioner meets clients at their level of readiness to change and collaboratively negotiates intervention goals through a guided process of weighing the pros and cons of altering substance use patterns and related problem behaviors (Miller & Rollnick, 2013; Sobell, Cunningham, & Sobell, 1996). In college samples, this overall strategy has been formalized as the Brief Alcohol Screening and Intervention for College Students (BASICS) (Dimeff, Baer, Kivlahan, & Marlatt, 1999), which has yielded significant positive outcomes (Carey, Scott-Sheldon, Carey, & DeMartini, 2007).

Exemplar Study: Early Intervention for Substance-Abusing College Students.   Because high school heavy drinking tends to continue into early adulthood, college freshmen may be the most likely to benefit from early intervention methods (Marlatt & Witkiewitz, 2002). In one of the earlier cognitive-behavioral intervention studies for college students with mild to moderate drinking problems, Kivlahan, Marlatt, Fromme, Coppel, and Williams (1990) randomly assigned 43 moderate problem drinkers (mean of age 23) to three conditions: a moderation-oriented cognitive-behavioral therapy (CBT) skills course, an alcohol information class, and an assessment-only group. The CBT skills course (8 weeks) covered models of addiction, consequences of alcohol abuse, estimation of blood-alcohol levels, moderate-drinking skills, training in relaxation and nutrition as well as encouragement to engage in aerobic exercise, how to monitor and cope with risky drinking situations more assertively, challenges to erroneous alcohol expectancies (e.g., alcohol makes me sexier), and skills for relapse prevention in order to adhere better to self-imposed limits and rules concerning moderate drinking. The alcohol information class (also 8 weeks) consisted of a traditional medical-educational model that included films and lectures about the effects of alcohol and other drugs, family and legal aspects, and other related topics. Several drinking measures including self-monitoring charts were employed with all three groups. Data were collected at baseline, and at 4-, 8-, and 12-month follow-ups. Results showed no significant differences between groups, but there was an encouraging trend toward less drinking in the CBT skills group.

A later replication of this skills approach (Baer et al., 1992) compared a 6-week (90-minute) classroom training to individualized feedback based on motivational interviewing. Both treatment groups demonstrated comparable and substantive findings: an approximately 40% drop in alcohol consumption was maintained over 2 years.

Marlatt et al. (1998) tested the effectiveness of a very brief motivational interview (see Heather, 1995; Miller & Rollnick, 2013) with individualized feedback for college freshmen who had filled out questionnaires regarding drinking and associated problems after they had been admitted to university during their senior year of high school. Three hundred forty-eight students were randomly assigned to either brief intervention or an assessment-only control group. Those assigned to brief treatment (provided in the winter of their freshman year) were also given self-monitoring cards and asked to track their drinking on a daily basis 2 weeks before the intervention. The motivational intervention was used to review students' individual data, encourage students to compare their drinking with reported norms for peer drinking, examine personal risk factors for problem drinking (e.g., family history of substance abuse), have students draw conclusions about their personal drinking habits and potential problems, and have students consider modifying their drinking to reduce negative consequences. In keeping with motivational enhancement principles, arguing with the student and direct confrontation were avoided.

In the second year of the study, students were mailed personalized feedback (comparing their data with college norms) based on data collected at baseline and 6-month and 12-month follow-ups. Those participants categorized as "high" and "extreme" risk were contacted for further motivational interviewing, and many accepted. Overall, outcomes revealed that those high-risk students demonstrated significantly greater reductions in problem drinking than did students in the control group at 2-year follow-up. Nevertheless, clinical significance of the changes was modest, and the high-risk students were still reporting more drinking and drinking-related consequences than the average college student. At 2-year follow-up, high-risk students who had received the motivational-interview module were doing better than high-risk controls (Roberts, Neal, Kivlahan, Baer, & Marlatt, 2000), and the benefits continued to accrue throughout the years of college (Baer et al., 2001). Overall, students considered the intervention "user-friendly" and relevant to their everyday concerns. The program appeared to be useful as an initial prevention effort that, if unsuccessful, could be followed up with more intensive treatment as needed.

Murphy, Duchnick et al. (2001) and Borsari and Carey (2000) found similar results for brief intervention (i.e., motivational interview coupled with providing normative feedback) in randomized controlled trials. Overall, it appears that early intervention methods using motivational engagement, CBT skills, and harm reduction are the most promising approaches available to date for reducing substance use and related problems in adolescents and young adults (Larimer & Cronce, 2002), and benefits appear to extend to some community samples as well (Wachtel & Staniford, 2010). Turisi et al. (2009) compared an online administered BASICS program alone, BASICS and parent handbook, parent handbook alone, and assessment-only control group with 1,275 new college students (former high school athletes). They found some advantages in using the combined program for reducing high-risk drinking and/or problems associated with drinking (relative to other treatment groups). Schaus, Sole, McCoy, Mullett, and O'Brien (2009) tested a brief intervention approach (i.e., motivational interviewing, norms clarification, strategies to reduce risk) with more than 300 college students (50% female) who tested positive in a college health center for high-risk drinking after randomization to treatment and control groups. Over a 1-year follow-up, the brief intervention showed significantly less alcohol consumption, high-risk drinking, and problem-related behaviors. Attrition rates at follow-up were considerable but comparable between treatment and control groups. Dermen and Thomas (2011) used a very brief information-based motivational intervention (two sessions) to reduce alcohol consumption and/or HIV-risk behavior (and a combined intervention that addressed both) in 154 white (86%) college students and found that alcohol counseling alone did not reduce risky sexual behaviors, but targeted high-risk sex counseling did show some positive results in reducing unprotected sex at 15-month follow-up. Recently, in a large randomized trial with high-risk drinkers, BASICS showed solid decreases for college women and even better effects for men who were mandated for treatment, although attrition was considerable in both the treatment and comparison groups (DiFulvio, Linowsky, Mazziotti, & Puleo, 2012). The BASICS program was also shown to be robustly effective for Hispanic students as well, with minor modifications made for cultural congruency while maintaining high fidelity to the BASICS model (Tomaka, Palacios, Morales-Monks, & Davis, 2012). In both studies, higher-risk drinkers appeared to benefit more than lower-risk drinkers.

Descriptions of Effective Early Interventions

Early intervention programs for youths engaged in risky behaviors share many common elements. These approaches are typically brief (one or a few sessions), given in a classroom or counseling setting, and include a combination of the following: education on alcohol and its effects (physical and psychological factors), cognitive modification (i.e., changing erroneous expectancies and perceived norms regarding others' drinking, drug use habits), and training in coping skills (e.g., self-monitoring skills, setting and keeping targets for number of drinks, estimating blood-alcohol level, drink refusal, practicing safe sex). These programs emphasize psychoeducation and skills training to help young people survive this period of their lives by avoiding and negotiating high-risk situations to reduce negative consequences (harm to self or others) or to achieve and maintain abstinence. The list that follows here presents the key components of the well-regarded Alcohol Skills Training Program (ASTP), developed at the University of Washington (see Dimeff et al., 1999; Miller, Kilmer, Kim, Weingardt, & Marlatt, 2001). These components evolved into the BASICS program, and they exemplify the state of the art of early intervention programming for youth (relevant research was examined here earlier; e.g., Baer et al., 1992; Carey et al., 2007; Kivlahan et al., 1990; Marlatt et al., 1998):

- Component 1: Be flexible and approachable, and establish good rapport with students. Clearly communicate the philosophy of BASICS with an emphasis on making informed choices versus prohibition, and show respect for the choice of drinking goals that individuals make: moderation or abstinence. Confidentiality among members is stressed.

- Component 2: Help students assess their own use by identifying and gauging discrepancies between current drinking patterns (including reviewing the definition of a standard drink) and self-designed drinking goals; help them compare their own drinking to actual drinking norms in the college community. Students who appear to have more serious problems and may be developing a dependence on alcohol or other drugs should be referred for primary substance abuse intervention.

- Component 3: Provide information-based lecture and/or discussion regarding basic pharmacology and physiological processes associated with drinking alcohol: absorption, metabolism, blood-alcohol levels (BALs), tolerance, withdrawal, dependence, cross-tolerance (also see chapter 7 and other relevant texts on these topics).

- Component 4: Define and discuss BAL in more detail, along with psychophysiological effects of different BALs and factors that influence BAL (e.g., rate and amount of drinking, gender, weight).

- Component 5: Emphasize the psychological and behavioral effects associated with blood alcohol level and the "biphasic" response to alcohol (pleasing effects at lower levels, risks at higher levels). Students should also generate and examine their own positive and negative beliefs and expectancies regarding drinking. They are encouraged to judge their likely point of diminishing returns and to heed injunctions to avoid behaviors that are more likely to result in negative consequences at higher levels of consumption. Examine the role of tolerance as an indicator of a potentially serious problem, and examine the effects of alcohol when combined with other drugs.

- Component 6: Teach students to monitor their own drinking behavior. Now that participants are more knowledgeable about drinking and its effects, this knowledge needs to be put into action. Although the exercises do not require or encourage students to drink, participants are taught to monitor their own consumption rate (i.e., quantity, frequency) and effects. Self-monitoring also emphasizes an analysis of the context of drinking: where they were, with whom, in what situation, in what frame of mind, and so forth.

- Component 7: Participants review their self-monitoring charts relative to their initial self-assessments and standard BAL chart. Assist them in reassessing how much they drank (including reviewing their heaviest drinking episode), help them evaluate how well they performed relative to their initial self-assessment, and relate results to what they now know about alcohol metabolism and their own BAL estimates.

- Component 8: Help students review and debunk erroneous beliefs they may hold about the positive effects of drinking (i.e., alcohol expectancies). Help them gauge how much those effects (e.g., having a good time socially, enhancing sexual encounters, relieving stress) are the result of alcohol versus their own behavior.

- Component 9: Reinforce the notion of moderation and not exceeding a BAL above .05 or .06. The emphasis at this point is to focus on skills to enhance moderate drinking and to reduce risks associated with heavier drinking, including setting predetermined drinking limits, tracking the number of drink equivalents, spacing drinks over time, alternating drinks with nonalcoholic drinks, avoiding drinking games, using drink-refusal skills, and engaging in alternative nondrinking activities. Other skills include avoiding excessive drinking in situations where sexual activity is more likely and planning for alternative transportation if needed.

- Component 10: Summarize key points about the program, keep the floor open to follow-up questions, evaluate the program, and help students plan for the future should they consider changes in drinking habits down the road or require referrals for further help.

Targeting Risky Sexual Behaviors as Part of Early Intervention.   As with substance abuse, preventative health research has repeatedly demonstrated that information provision alone is not associated with reducing risky sexual behaviors (Basen-Engquist, 1992; O'Leary, 1992; Raj, 1996). Growing evidence, however, has suggested that applying social-cognitive principles and skills with at-risk young persons can enhance self-efficacy and coping skills regarding drinking and safer sex (Darkes & Goldman, 1993; O'Grady, Wilson, & Harman, 2009; Sikkema, Winett, & Lombard, 1995). Programs that enhance a young person's skills in recognizing antecedent factors (e.g., thoughts, feelings, behaviors, situations) and using skills to reduce substance abuse and avoid unplanned and/or unprotected sex have been shown to be moderately effective. Helpful strategies include debunking erroneous expectations that excessive drinking will improve sexual encounters, helping students learn to anticipate the potential risks of unplanned sexual encounters while drinking, setting specific drinking goals to encourage moderation or avoid ingesting large amounts of alcohol in short periods of time, rehearsing assertive behaviors that can reduce excessive alcohol use or avoid unplanned sexual encounters, and encouraging self-monitoring and evaluation as part of a prevention or early intervention strategy.

Treatments Focused Primarily on Community Samples in Settings outside Education.   Meta-analysis and narrative reviews of the literature on adolescent substance abuse treatments have revealed that, on the whole, behaviorally oriented family therapies and cognitive-behavioral skills approaches are most effective (Liddle & Dakof, 1995; Vaughn & Howard,

2004; Waldron, 1997). Deas and Clark (2009) reviewed randomized treatment studies for adolescents with substance use problems from 1990 to 2005. Of the 14 studies that met their rigorous criteria (e.g., randomization, comparison treatments, focus on adolescents), treatments that demonstrated evidence of effectiveness included behavioral family and multisystemic interventions, cognitive-behavioral interventions, and motivational interviewing. All interventions were based primarily on social-cognitive theory and behaviorally oriented interventions implemented with individuals, families, and/or the wider social system. They also reported that pharmacotherapy appears to have little role in substance abuse treatment with adolescents, except in the case of comorbid psychiatric disorders.

Individual Approaches.   Methodologically sound controlled studies on individual treatments for adolescent substance abusers outside of educational settings are few. In one controlled trial Monti et al. (1999) compared motivational interviewing with standard care (i.e., brief admonitions against drinking and driving) offered in a busy, urban hospital emergency room. Ninety-four participants aged 18–19 were randomly assigned to each condition. Measures were taken on alcohol use patterns, related problems, drinking and driving, and episodes of drinking and driving, among other related indicators. Retrospective baseline was taken over the previous 12 months, with further measures taken at baseline and 3- and 6-month (follow-up) intervals. Results showed that 6 months after their initial interview, the motivational interview group showed a significant reduction in drinking and driving and other social problems, and only half as many alcohol-related injuries as the control group. Department of Motor Vehicle records showed significantly fewer moving violations for the motivational group than the standard care group. Monti, Barnett, O'Leary, and Colby (2001), having reviewed the motivational enhancement literature with adolescents, concluded that motivational interviewing has shown benefits in harm reduction for alcohol and marijuana use for both older and younger adolescents, particularly with more resistant youths.

Another randomized controlled trial with a sample of 40 previously hospitalized adolescents (67% female, middle to upper-middle class) who had attempted suicide in the prior 3 months compared CBT with enhanced treatment by providers in the community using standardized measures taken up to 18 months post-enrollment. CBT showed superior results overall, particularly in fewer heavy-drinking days, fewer problems with marijuana abuse, fewer suicide attempts, and better overall functioning (Esposito-Smythers, Spirito, Kahler, Hunt, & Monti, 2011). Therapist and computer-assisted brief interventions have also shown promise via a randomized controlled trial for reducing both alcohol use and violence in a large-sample study conducted in an urban hospital emergency room (Walton et al., 2010).

Family-Based Approaches.   Behavior family therapy has been successfully employed with families of drug-addicted persons, including adolescents (Stanton & Shadish, 1997; Stanton, Todd, & Associates 1982), and has been the subject of much outcome research (Weinberg, Rohdert, Colliver, & Glantz, 1998). One meta-analysis of family interventions for a drug-abusing member focused on randomized controlled studies (Stanton & Shadish, 1997). A total of 15 studies covering about 3,500 clients and significant others met suitable criteria. Results of the analysis showed that marital and family interventions produced outcomes superior to individual, peer group, or family psychoeducation. They also appeared cost-effective when combined with methadone maintenance for heroin users. The strategies appeared to work equally well for adolescent and adult abusers, and demonstrated relatively higher levels of client retention.

The results of structural and behavioral family therapies with substance-abusing youth and their families have not been uniformly positive, however. Szapocznik, Kurtines, Foote, Perez-Vidal, and Hervis (1983) compared conjoint family therapy with family therapy conducted with individuals. Participants were Hispanic families and individuals, and treatment included follow-ups of 6–12 months on some families. There was considerable attrition in the study, and results showed some advantage for the individual intervention. In a later replication study, Szapocznik, Kurtines, Foote, Perez-Vidal, and Hervis (1986) demonstrated similar results with another sample of Hispanic families. Santisteban et al. (1996) later demonstrated that more emphasis on early engagement efforts could substantially improve treatment retention. In an uncontrolled trial of brief strategic family therapy (BSFT) with 122 mostly Hispanic young people (aged 12–14) and their families, Santisteban et al. (1997) demonstrated that an ethnically sensitive intervention delivered in 12–16 sessions of 90 minutes over 4–6 months was moderately effective at reducing conduct disordered behavior, improving family functioning, and reducing substance abuse. Practitioners made special efforts to address the cultural expectations of these primarily Hispanic families by being task oriented and showing an understanding of intergenerational tensions, family hierarchy, and acculturation stressors. Although more research is needed on culturally congruent interventions with conduct-disordered youth, evidence generally shows that outcomes of mainstream services for both minority and white young persons may be comparable with regard to changes in delinquency, school performance, self-esteem, behavior, interpersonal problems, anxiety, depression, and family functioning, among other outcomes (Wilson, Lipsey, & Soydan, 2003).

Waldron, Brody, and Slesnick (2001) called for combining individual CBT methods and behavioral family therapy for substance-abusing adolescents. The objectives of this approach include the need to reduce or eliminate substance use and other problem behaviors, and to improve family relationships.

They suggest three phases to the relatively brief (14 session) intervention: sessions 1–5 include engagement, motivational enhancement, and a thorough systems and individual functional assessment targeting key problems for a skill-building intervention. The whole family is seen during the first few visits, with two visits reserved for the adolescent alone. Behavior-change interventions are the focus of sessions 6–10, with the hour divided (15 and 45 minutes) for the individual and family, respectively. These sessions include a combination of behavioral family interventions similar to those noted earlier (see, e.g., Alexander, Holtzworth-Munroe, & Jameson, 1994) and individual approaches to coping skills, discussed in chapter 7 (see, e.g., Kadden, 1994; Monti et al., 2001). In the third phase (sessions 11–14) the intervention focuses on generalization of gains and relapse prevention.

In a multisite randomized study of brief family therapy with a large sample of racially diverse substance abusing adolescents, Robbins et al. (2011) compared BSFT (joining, restructuring, directing communications, problem solving) with treatment as usual in the community. They found that BSFT resulted in better engagement, retention, and family functioning and fewer drug-using days during the final 12-month observation period (although drug-using days were not substantially different overall). The authors noted that baseline levels of substance use were low (i.e., "floor effect," with little room for reduction in drug use) because many participants had been institutionalized before the study (for severe drug abuse). These data might have affected the ambiguous results on drug use.

Systems-Oriented Approaches.   Interventions with young substance use offenders often involve the criminal justice system, and racial minorities are disproportionately involved in that system. African American and Hispanic youth are more likely to be involved in the criminal justice system (e.g., arrest, probation, parole) than white substance-using youth when controlling for sociodemographic, substance use, and mental health factors (Godette, Malatu, Leonard, Randolf, & Williams, 2011). Ruiz, Stevens, Fuhriman et al. (2009) conducted an uncontrolled evaluation of a program combining drug-court supervision with cognitive-behavioral family treatment and reported that, by gender and race, adolescent clients showed some reduction in drug use but no reduction in sexual risk taking behaviors. The sample was relatively small ($N = 65$), and all data were self-reported. In another controlled trial comparing family court, drug court, and drug courts in combination with multisystemic treatment (MST) and contingency management (CM), Henggeler et al. (2006) showed the combination of drug court, MST, and CM to be most effective. Noting the lack of treatment research among homeless youth, Slesnick, Prestopnik, Meyers, and Glassman (2007) conducted a randomized comparison of the Community Reinforcement Approach (on social and concrete supports, including job referral, housing, and the like; see chapter 7) and community services (e.g., drop-in center, food, clothing, case management) with 180 youth living on the street in New Mexico (about 67% male). Although clients in both programs improved, those who engaged in the Community Reinforcement Approach showed twice as many reductions in substance use and depression and increased social stability by a factor of 4. However, they noted the lack of follow-up measurement to determine longer-term outcomes.

Overall, approaches that combine behavioral, family, and systems to sub-stance-abusing youth appear promising. However, data on the effectiveness of substance abuse interventions with young people outside of educational settings should be interpreted cautiously. Calabria, Shakeshaft, and Havard (2011) conducted an extensive review and found a host of methodological limitations, including lack of blind assessment, a heavy reliance on self-report, lack of consistent follow-ups, and high dropout rates.

The Relevance of Racial/Ethnic Factors in Treatment Outcomes. Noting that previous research on ethnic client-therapist matching has been methodologically weak, with mixed results overall, Flicker, Waldron, Turner, Brody, and Hops (2008) conducted a randomized controlled trial of func-tional family therapy with 86 adolescents and at least one parent (and a few siblings) to test whether racial/ethnic client-therapist matching would lead to better outcomes. Results revealed that both Hispanic and white clients reduced drug use, but there was no overall differences in drug use at follow-up between ethnically matched versus unmatched clients. However, within the Hispanic group, matched clients did somewhat better at follow-up than unmatched clients, a finding that did not occur with white clients. The authors speculated that acculturation to the "other" culture (i.e., white to Hispanic) might have accounted for the differential outcomes. As limitations, they noted the lack of a cultural competence measure and the likelihood that the study had too small a sample to support the design.

TREATMENT PLANNING AND EVALUATION

CASE EXAMPLE: ISABEL

Isabel, a 19-year-old college fresh-man, arrived in the health services offices to have a rash looked at. After a brief discussion and a few tests, the doctor told her she had contracted syphilis. Upset and tearful, the doc-tor assured her that, at this stage of the disease, she would be easily cured with proper treatment. She also told Isabel that she should insist that her sexual partners use a con-dom. A nurse took a little more his-tory and asked her about her sexual activity in more depth. The discus-sion led to screening for the use of alcohol and other drugs. Isabel reported that she liked to party with her friends, and on occasion, she engaged in unplanned sexual behavior. She said she had been sexually active since she was 14, and she thought she had learned to be careful. The nurse asked if she had been intoxicated at the time of these encounters, and Isabel reported that she probably wouldn't have slept with many of her partners unless she had been. The nurse suggested that Isabel make an appointment at the college counseling center to address the fact that she appeared to be placing herself at risk.

During her first visit with the social worker, Susan, Isabel discussed her conversation with the nurse and admitted that she perhaps had taken a few too many chances over the years. She felt fortunate that she had not contracted HIV. Susan queried her about the amount of alcohol she consumed before engaging in these "spontaneous sexual adventures," and Isabel told her that she usually got high (i.e., smoked marijuana) and had six or seven drinks. She said she never drove a car during these times but made sure she had a place to sleep. Often "it was some guy's place, so hanging out after the party was a good idea and usually led to other stuff." Susan asked how long Isabel had felt that she was drinking too much. She responded: "Since I was in high school, about 15 or 16."

MFS Assessment: Defining Problems and Goals

Susan said she wanted to get more background to understand better how this pattern of sexual activity and substance abuse had evolved. Isabel told Susan that she came from Guatemala illegally with her mother when she was 6 years old to visit her aunt in Texas. She never knew her biological father. When she arrived there, her mother told her that they would stay in the United States. After staying with her aunt for a little while, her mother met Jim and moved to the northeastern United States. Jim was a bit older than her mother and a long-haul truck driver, so he was gone for a week or so at a time. Isabel had the impression that her mother liked him, and he seemed nice to both of them. Isabel eventually went to school, although by the time she started, she was a little older than the other children. Later, she found out that her mother had paid a lawyer to straighten out the paperwork for them to stay in the United States. Her mother worked as a cleaning woman for companies that tended private homes, and she worked for catering companies and did other domestic service work. The relationship with Jim seemed to work out over time. He wasn't around much, and Isabel recalls many times feeling like a "regular family." She even remembers eventually calling him "Dad." Isabel learned to speak English very well when she was young, since she had started school fairly early and was an excellent student. She met other students from Guatemala in her classes and other Hispanic students, so she kept up her Spanish as well.

When she was about 12 years old, Jim began to treat her a bit differently and to show interest in her sexually. Isabel was very uncomfortable with Jim when he pressed up against her. She remembers Jim saying, "It's all right— we're not really having sex. I just need you to sit on my lap for a few minutes." He was never rough, he treated her "a little special" afterward, and she didn't want to upset her mother. Having heard about "stuff like this" in school, she knew it was wrong, but she was afraid of the problems that would result if she told her mother or any of the teachers her "secret."

Jim's conduct continued intermittently, usually when Isabel's mom was working late. After a few years, Isabel started dating other boys, and Jim didn't object much. She felt him pull away from her, but they said nothing about it. Isabel didn't discuss the situation with anyone, and she found herself more and more engaged with friends her own age. She was quite popular in high school and had many friends and acquaintances. She continued to do very well in school, applied for college, was accepted to several schools, and decided to go to one out of state.

When Susan asked her how she felt about moving away, Isabel responded that she felt a little sad, but she knew it was a good idea. She called her mother often and said her mother seemed to be happy with her situation. Although she had generally enjoyed herself in high school, she reported feeling "down in the dumps" at times now in college. Spending time with friends seemed to help, but she spent an increasing amount of time "getting high" with friends and drinking. She also found that she was very popular with male students, and she developed an active sex life. She liked to please them, was told she was "good at it," and felt she had an "edge" over the other girls. Despite her partying, she kept up her grades, and school remained important to her. She felt it would be a way to avoid having to work menial jobs like her mother. She was appreciative of her mother's struggles, felt lucky about going to college, and took little for granted.

Susan asked her how often she felt depressed, and Isabel said it seemed to come with heavier partying. She would feel lethargic for a day or so after, and she sometimes regretted her sexual encounters. But the feelings usually dissipated, more or less. She sometimes wondered if the pattern was a problem, but given the amount of partying she witnessed around the dorm, she didn't feel all that different from the others. The social worker then asked her why she came for counseling, if things weren't so bad. She responded, "Syphilis scared me, and there's still the HIV thing. I'm afraid I'll get drunk, do something stupid, and get AIDS. I also have found that the work is harder in college, and I am afraid that I might fall behind. It's just that it is hard to say no when you are used to partying with people. I guess I could slow it down a bit, but I'm just not sure how. I also don't know what to do about the sex thing. Sometimes I want to, sometimes I don't, but I often feel like it's expected of me. I've also never really had a steady boyfriend. That concerns me. Like, what's wrong with me? Why am I different? Sometimes it makes me feel lonely just having sex with these guys and forgetting about it," she said, laughing. The social worker responded that there appeared to be pros and cons to the whole situation. Partying and being with friends was fun, and sex could be enjoyable too, but there appeared to be drawbacks to her current repertoire. Susan reassured her that no one was putting any pressure on her to change. Susan said that Isabel seemed to know that some "adjustments" were in order, and perhaps they could discuss how she wanted to go about making them. Isabel expressed relief that she wasn't going to be "therapized to death" about her "issues" and agreed that the next step was up to her.

In the next session, Susan led a more detailed discussion about Isabel's moodiness, substance abuse, and casual sex. She asked Isabel to describe her "typical week" from one day to the next and to talk about her usual daily routine. According to Isabel, Mondays were a bit slow, but she commented, "Who likes Mondays anyway?" The social worker asked her to elaborate. "I usually get some school work done on Sundays, but not as much as I need to. I'm usually a little hung over, and I still feel the effects on Monday. I think it bothers my sleep." The social worker reflected: "So you start off with a deficit on Monday morning." Isabel continued, saying that Tuesdays and Wednesdays were productive. Without partying, she could get most of her work done: "I am actually feeling pretty good going into Thursday night. Then the partying starts." Isabel then described the next few days: dragging herself through her classes and "partying big-time" on Friday night: "That's when I usually get really messed up, hook up with someone, and wake up with some guy on Saturday morning. Saturdays are usually a lost day, and sometimes Saturday night I just go back to my dorm and hang out alone. Saturday night is more of a date night for some of the girls, but that hasn't been my thing."

Susan and Isabel tried to connect the dots. From Thursday evening through Sunday, it appeared that Isabel was feeling regretful about compromising her ability to get things done, feeling somewhat depressed about excessive drinking (six to eight mixed drinks, she estimated), and marijuana use, and feeling depressed and somewhat regretful and lonely in response to casual sex. The social worker quipped: "So, from Thursdays to Sunday it's sex, drugs, and rock and roll." Isabel responded: "I don't like that, or the way I am. I think I need to make some changes." They decided that next visit they would talk about what it was, specifically, that she would like to change.

In the following visit, they agreed that her moodiness, negative view of herself, mediocre academic performance, and risky sexual activities appeared to be related. The rest of the discussion focused on which problem to address first, and how to approach each problem in a stepwise manner. It seemed that the excessive drinking and pot smoking were the immediate catalyst. Perhaps Isabel could try cutting down a bit, changing her drinking patterns, slowing down her consumption, and being more careful about what (and how much absolute alcohol) she was actually consuming.

Susan decided to first summarize what they knew about the problem before they discussed a list of treatment priorities. Isabel appeared to be drinking more than she realized. When they discussed quantity, it became apparent that she was usually consuming mixed drinks that either she or someone else poured. Because she preferred vodka drinks, she knew the beverage was 80 proof (40% alcohol), but she didn't know how much she was actually drinking. She was under the impression they were "strong" drinks because she could really taste the vodka. So Isabel was probably consuming considerable more than she thought, maybe ten to twelve actual drink equivalents rather than six or seven. In reviewing the consequences of consumption, she felt that her drinking was contributing to her mild to moderate depression and increasing the chances of engaging in casual sex (which she only did when drunk), which in turn was adding to her negative opinions about herself and "getting in the way" of having a different kind of relationship with men; she also felt that substance abuse was compromising the quality of her work, because she lacked concentration and energy needed for her studies. This subpar academic performance was adding to her self-doubt and negative view of herself.

When the social worker and Isabel discussed the context of drinking, it appeared that it was partly to simply join in and have fun, but it was also done to set up casual sex with an undetermined partner. Often, she paid little heed to whether her partner was using protection. Although Isabel did not think she was deliberately using alcohol to cope with negative feelings, she considered the possibility that she had developed this pattern by drinking to cover up negative feelings about herself that she did not quite understand. They both agreed that she needed to assess the amount she drank more carefully, and that cutting down would likely have a positive impact on her mood, work, choice of sex partners, and how she felt about herself.

Selecting and Designing the Intervention: Defining Strategies and Objectives

Isabel agreed to engage in a period of self-monitoring for a week to examine the exact amount of alcohol she was consuming as well as her thoughts and feelings in the specific party circumstances she found herself in, and to carefully consider the consequences. The social worker suggested that she might consider cutting down or eliminating her marijuana use, and bringing condoms. They both designed a self-monitoring chart to record the day, amount of alcohol consumed (she agreed to pour her own drinks), situation, what she was thinking, how she was feeling, and any notable events. She also agreed to record any reflections the day after having had casual sex. This period would last 2 weeks, and she agreed to keep her visit the following week to provide a progress report and trouble-shoot any problems with self-monitoring (see table 16.1).

After the 2 weeks of self-assessment, they discussed the results. The first week, Isabel measured her own drinks and realized that she had been consuming much more than she thought. When she measured her own, she was less intoxicated, and although she was attracted to one of the young men at the fraternity party, she felt less inclined to "jump into bed" and that she was better able to exercise discretion. She did not know if this was due to actually drinking less or whether she was just paying more attention to the amount she was drinking and thinking about her choices. She also noticed in the second week that she drank a lot more, even though she was measuring her own drinks. She figured, "What the heck, I was good last week, and now I'm going to live it up." She did but reported a negative experience with a young man who became somewhat aggressive. She was very aggressive back and pushed him off, but she was shaken from the experience. She also recorded the next day, "I felt like crap about myself and didn't get a thing done all day. That kind of sums up my situation, don't you think?" Susan responded, "Sounds to me like you've been sorting these things out for yourself."

Isabel seemed more than ready to make some adjustments, so they agreed to get more specific about intervention objectives. They decided the first objective would be to cut alcohol consumption in half. Given her body weight, she could consume about four drinks over 6 hours in a night. This change would help keep her blood-alcohol level to a minimum and probably reduce her chances of making impulsive decisions. Susan suggested that she continue to pour and measure her own drinks (she poured out one shot of vodka back at home to see what it looked like at the bottom of a plastic cup) and drink more slowly during parties, occasionally topping off her drink with just a mixer. Isabel also decided to replace every other drink with seltzer and a twist. In the following 2 weeks she reported successfully cutting her consumption by about half and was feeling pretty good about getting more of her work done.

Her second objective was to avoid sleeping with anyone until she had gone on a date with him at least one time. By the fourth visit, she reported, "I haven't gone home with anyone. But I'm not sure how I feel about it." She had not yet agreed to date anyone, although she had been asked out. She decided to wait on making any decisions. This objective led to a more in-depth discussion about how she felt about men in general, and it became apparent that for much of her life she felt a mix of resentment but also a desire to please them and be liked in return. When Susan asked her to reflect on important relationships with men that she had in her life, she could only think of Jim, her "quasi stepfather," who she still felt some affection for; however, she also felt he had betrayed her: "he used me to get himself off." She decided that she might like to try a different type of arrangement with a male friend but was not ready to try "dating" yet. That objective would remain on hold for a while.

Her third objective was to improve the quality of her schoolwork. She decided that, because she was drinking less, she could get up earlier on weekend mornings and put in some more time in the library. She decided that she would spend 5 hours working on her schoolwork every Saturday morning and 5 hours on Sunday, in addition to the work she put in Monday through Wednesday. She felt that this would double her productivity.

Her fourth objective was to start feeling better physically, to have more energy, and to feel better about her appearance. The social worker told her that if she stuck with it, the effects of exercise were sure to reduce stress and symptoms of depression and to improve her sleep and concentration. She decided to join a women's exercise class on campus that combined aerobics and weight training. She saw herself as a physical person, but only intermittently had engaged in regular vigorous exercise. It would also give her the opportunity to meet some other new women friends.

CBT skills training conducted in a model of motivational enhancement and harm reduction seemed to be a promising approach given Isabel's particular constellation of problems. Motivational engagement, psychoeducation, self-monitoring, drinking moderation, cognitive therapy for depression, self-regulatory skills, and exercise for stress reduction seemed to be a promising package for Isabel's needs. Susan's application of motivational interviewing helped Isabel quickly engage in the process of weighing the pros and cons of her behaviors for herself rather than feeling lectured or judged about her behaviors. She was already thinking about changing when she came in, and the social worker helped her move forward in a more purposeful and focused way. Susan also helped her experience a relationship with a female as collaborator, in a give-and-take helping relationship, something she had not had very often. She knew that she often kept her distance from other women and preferred the company of men. But because her relationships with men were ephemeral, she often felt deeply alone. Self-monitoring helped her make tentative links among her current difficulties, and it even helped her obtain some insight into possible origins of problems she had been experiencing for a long time. Cognitive methods helped her challenge her expectancies about drinking and how she erroneously thought it was facilitating her encounters with men. An examination of the contextual aspects of her drinking also helped her understand the purpose it was serving: not just to have fun but also as a way to block out difficult feelings and fears about encountering men in a more meaningful kind of relationship. Planned drink refusal and moderation helped her reduce alcohol consumption overall, a change that had immediate positive effects on her behavior, mood, energy level, concentration, and academic performance. Regular vigorous exercise also helped her regulate stress and feel better about herself, and it provided an opportunity to make more women friends who followed a more balanced and healthful lifestyle. As Isabel made progress over the following few weeks, she was also able to begin to talk about her loneliness, her anger and resentment toward Jim, and her fears about encountering both men and women on a more honest and intimate level.

Selecting Scales and Creating Indexes to Monitor and Evaluate Client Progress

A uniquely designed self-monitoring chart served as an excellent assessment and evaluation tool, providing Isabel with the opportunity to focus on and accurately record actual number of drinks (once she measured how much absolute alcohol she was really consuming); daily mood (excellent, good, fair, poor); and situational factors related to her thoughts, feelings, and behaviors. She was able to examine these changes over time, and using the chart gave her a personal and critical role in evaluating her own progress. The initial use of the AUDIT revealed that her score was above the cutoff of 8 (see chapter 7) and well within the "problem drinking" range. The CAPS-r helped her identify that she was experiencing both personal (depression, feeling bad about herself) and social (risky sex activities) problems, partly as a result of drinking, and the DCS helped her identify circumstances in which she was drinking excessively. When used repeatedly, every 2 weeks or so, the self-monitoring chart and scales provided a helpful evaluative framework for judging her treatment progress.

TABLE 16.1   The client service plan for Isabel

Problems	Goals	Objectives (sample)	Interventions	Assessment and evaluation tools
Excessive alcohol consumption (10–12 drinks an evening once a week, less another day of week, sometimes accompanied by marijuana use	Reduce alcohol consumption to moderate level; reduce and/or eliminate marijuana use	Develop self-monitoring chart with social worker; record thoughts, feelings, behaviors, situational factors, and number of drinks; target objective is to reduce number of measured drinks (1.5 oz of alcohol per drink) to four drinks a night	Overall plan: motivational interviewing, CBT, moderation and self-regulation skills with harm reduction

Self-monitoring and moderation skills: estimating blood alcohol, moderation training (e.g., eat before, skip drinks, drink slowly); challenging alcohol expectancies about effects, examining drinking contexts and consequences

Cognitive therapy to focus on quality of relationships, fears and | AUDIT as screening tool to provide feedback on level of drinking problem

Self-monitoring indexes and charts to measure number of drinks, mood, behaviors, consequences, narrative reflections

CAPS-r for assessment and monitoring to estimate self-anchored personal and social problems related to drinking

DCS for assessment and monitoring to examine context-specific excessive drinking |
| Unplanned and (sometimes) unprotected sex | Avoid spontaneous sexual activity; always insist on protection | Have at least one date before sleeping with person; get to know him first | | |
| Lack of intimacy with others; no close female friends; little history of male intimate relationships | Develop better friendships and "dating" relationship before having sex | Plan at least one activity with a woman friend; plan a date with a male acquaintance | | |

Problems	Goals	Objectives (sample)	Interventions	Assessment and evaluation tools
Moderate symptoms of depression: poor concentration, sleep disturbance, dysphoric mood; negative feelings about herself	Alleviate symptoms of depression to a minimum: improve mood, sleep, concentration	Record and monitor mood as part of self-monitoring chart	inhibitions about intimacy, and experimenting with getting to know men before having sex; examine female relationships, sense of distance from other women	
Concerns about academic performance	Increase study time by 100%; grades will improve as a result	Structure five hours on Saturday and Sunday mornings to study at library	Consider further examination of feelings about having been molested by Jim, once drinking and risky sex are under control	
			Join exercise class on campus; exercise vigorously twice a week	
			Discuss self-regulation skills: problem solving and time management to encourage consistency and plan rewards after each study session	

CHAPTER SUMMARY

The excitement and adventure of adolescence and young adulthood also usher in risks that, though not unique to young people, increase considerably because of their inexperience and other psychosocial vulnerabilities associated with youth. Assessment for adolescents and young adults who abuse substances and engage in risky sexual behaviors should emphasize a contextually defined MFS analysis. Scales are available to help qualitatively probe details of a young person's risky behaviors and to provide quantitative data to gauge problem severity and to track changes over time. A combination of motivational interviewing; psychoeducation about drinking, drugs, and their effects; self-monitoring; and practicing moderation has been shown to be the most promising early intervention to date. Behavioral family and multisystemic approaches appear to hold the most potential for more serious substance use disorders. More outcome research and program evaluation, however, must be conducted with non-college community samples and with young persons of color, many of whom are at greater risk because of socioeconomic factors.

AFTERWORD
THE FUTURE OF EVIDENCE-BASED
PRACTICE FOR SOCIAL WORKERS

Expectations about the future of evidence-based practices in social work noted in the first edition of this book have continued to evolve over the 10 years since that book's publication, albeit more slowly than some would like to see. Although there has been considerable growth in controlled studies of psychosocial interventions for a variety of problems and, increasingly, with more diverse populations, the adoption of evidence-based practices by social workers continues to lag. In addition, much of the social work literature that addresses matters related to the training, education, and implementation of evidence-based practices tends to lack empirical rigor. With regard to some articles and books on the subject, some appear to have co-opted the term *evidence-based* as a marketing tool rather than to denote that the content within is based on sound research. As evidence-based practices continue to evolve, more rigorously tested approaches will come to supplant those based on weak evidence. Future advances will also continue to flow from interdisciplinary and multidisciplinary efforts. The complex needs of millions of people in the United States and elsewhere with mental health disorders require a broad, empirically sound, and interdisciplinary perspective.

Debates in social work also continue to question the role of research, speculate about broader philosophical or policy issues, and quibble over definitions or parameters of evidence-based practices. Nevertheless, using the collective findings of controlled empirical evidence to guide treatment selection will remain the keystone of evidence-based practice. Program evaluation should also play a greater role in optimizing service delivery. It is also understood that clinical judgment, ethical professional conduct, and client participation in treatment planning will remain essential ingredients in competent clinical practice. However, belaboring these aspects of care is unnecessary since they are relevant to good practice generally. What will continue to distinguish evidence-based interventions from others is the continued core focus of this second edition: the reliance on methodologically sound evidence to guide treatment planning.

Readers can also expect evidence-based practices to generalize well across countries and cultures with commonsense modifications made to increase cultural acceptability. Despite assertions from some that the use of standard research methods to test interventions is not a suitable approach for non-Western cultures, the adoption of evidence-based practices is growing and will continue to grow around the world. In some respects, emerging nations might have an advantage in adopting state-of-the-art practices more readily, as they are less bogged down by non-evidence-based authoritative traditions. They can hit the ground running by implementing best practices from the start and training a new cadre of practitioners in evidence-based approaches.

In summary, the emergence and evolution of evidence-based practices appears to be on solid footing, but full implementation still has a long way to go. However, progress will continue to be largely contingent on how vigorously social work education adapts to the evidence-based landscape. Incorporating technological advances into routine care to facilitate client contact and enhance treatment effectiveness will also be exciting to watch along with other scientific advances in understanding and treating mental health disorders. I fully expect that evidence-based practices will continue to grow and thrive as naysayers and non-evidence-based approaches simultaneously fade out of sight.

APPENDIXES

CLIENT ID# _____

RATE YOUR CLIENT'S WELL-BEING **OVER THE LAST 30 DAYS** USING THE
SCALE BELOW. SCORE EACH OF THE FOLLOWING AREAS. <u>USE EVERYTHING
YOU KNOW ABOUT THIS CLIENT BASED ON ALL SOURCES OF DATA.</u> (If you
provide treatment as part of a team, give a score based on team consensus.)

POOR	**IMPAIRED**	**MARGINAL**	**GOOD**	**EXCELLENT**
0	1	2	3	4

1. MENTAL STATUS: COGNITIVE FUNCTIONING: Consider the client's level of
hallucinations, delusions, disorientation, bizarre behavior or speech, memory problems, serious confusion or other symptoms of serious cognitive impairment. How would you rate their overall mental status?   **RATING** ___

_____

_____

_____

2. MENTAL STATUS: EMOTIONAL STATE: Consider the client's level of
depression, anxiety, obsessional thinking and overall emotional state. . . .
How would you rate their overall emotional condition?   **RATING** ___

_____

_____

_____

3. IMPULSE CONTROL: Think about your client's overall behavior. Consider
things such as their ability to express themselves effectively, ability to work at
things patiently, tendencies to verbally or physically lash out at others, run
away, harm themselves or proneness to impulsive, criminal, or drug-abusing
behavior. How would you rate their overall impulse control?   **RATING** ___

_____

_____

_____

4. COPING SKILLS: Think about your client's ability to cope with problems
and everyday stresses. How would you rate their ability to assess problem
situations, deal with "triggers", use stress reduction strategies, consider possible solutions to problems, perhaps reach out to others for help in order
to deal effectively with their difficulties?   **RATING** ___

_____

_____

_____

5. IMMEDIATE SOCIAL NETWORK (close friends, spouse, family): Consider
the quality of your client's relationships with those available friends, family,
spouse (as applicable). How would you rate the quality of the interaction
overall between your client and them with respect to closeness, intimacy,

general interpersonal satisfaction, effective communications, conflict, level of hostility, aggression, abuse?   **RATING** ___

---

6. *EXTENDED SOCIAL RELATIONSHIPS/NETWORK* (local community): Think about your client's relationships with persons outside their immediate family and social group. Consider their relationship to others in the community, their involvement in social groups, organizations, and general feeling of integration into the wider community in which they live. How would you rate their overall relationship with the community right now?   **RATING** ___

---

7. *RECREATIONAL ACTIVITIES:* Consider what the client does for fun (alone or social), hobbies, relaxation (reading, TV, video games, playing cards, etc.) and physical exercise (walking, jogging, biking, etc.). How would you rate the client's overall involvement in recreational activities?   **RATING** ___

---

8. *LIVING ENVIRONMENT:* Think about your client's current or (if client is institutionalized) most recent living environment. Consider such things as adequacy of food, clothing, shelter, and safety. How would you rate their overall living environment?   **RATING** ___

---

9. *USE OF ALCOHOL AND OTHER DRUGS:* Consider the clients use of alcohol, illicit substances (cocaine, heroin, marijuana, pcp, hallucinogens, etc.) and illicit use of prescription medication. Consider the following: how often do they use them, in what quantity, and what are the psychological, physical and social consequences associated with their use? How would you rate the client's overall functioning with regard to the use of alcohol and other drugs?   **RATING** ___

---

10. *HEALTH:* Consider the client's overall health. Aside from normal, transient illnesses, think about health habits, chronic primary health disorders, their opinion of their own health, ability to engage in their usual activities relatively free from discomfort, overall energy level, hospitalizations and treatments for illness other than psychiatric ones. How would you rate their health overall?   **RATING** ___

11. *INDEPENDENT LIVING/SELF CARE:* Consider how your client manages their household, takes care of personal hygiene, eats, sleeps and otherwise cares for themselves. How would you rate their performance in this area?   **RATING** ___

_____

_____

_____

12. *WORK (OR ROLE) SATISFACTION:* If the client works outside the home, is a homemaker or student, think for a moment about their work (or role) productivity. Considering the type of work or role in which they are engaged, how would you rate their overall work (role) productivity right now?   **RATING** ___

_____

_____

_____

PSYCHOLOGICAL WELL-BEING sub-scale score: Sum items 1-4 = _____

SOCIAL WELL-BEING sub-scale score: Sum items 5-8 = _____

TOTAL PSWS: Sum items 1-12 = _____

For relative severity scores on sub-scales:

PSYCHOLOGICAL WELL-BEING relative severity score: Sum items 1-4 and divide by 4 = _____

SOCIAL WELL-BEING relative severity score: Sum items 5-8 and divide by 4 = _____

Appendix B Shortform Assessment for Children

Date: _____/_____/_____ **Child's Name:** _____

Child's ID #: _____ **DOB:** ____/____/____ **Gender: M F**

Use the behaviors listed below to describe this child as you know him or her.

Mark ⓪ if the behavior never occurs, ① if the behavior sometimes occurs, and ② if the behavior occurs often.

⓪ = Never ① = Sometimes ② Often

Behavior		Behavior	
1. Has no respect for others	⓪ ① ②	25. Lacks self-confidence	⓪ ① ②
2. Doesn't follow rules	⓪ ① ②	26. Worries about health too much	⓪ ① ②
3. Is sad, unhappy, or feels down	⓪ ① ②	27. Attacks or hits others	⓪ ① ②
4. Is easily worried	⓪ ① ②	28. Hesitates to speak up in groups	⓪ ① ②
5. Is mean or cruel	⓪ ① ②	29. Yells or screams too much	⓪ ① ②
6. Steals from others	⓪ ① ②	30. Is quiet and doesn't share thoughts	⓪ ① ②
7. Fights a lot	⓪ ① ②	31. Is unsure of self or easily embarrassed	⓪ ① ②
8. Loses temper or throws tantrums	⓪ ① ②	32. Is aggressive	⓪ ① ②
9. Disobeys	⓪ ① ②	33. Has stomachaches without medical reason	⓪ ① ②
10. Curses or swears	⓪ ① ②	34. Stares into space or at nothing	⓪ ① ②
11. Is afraid he/she might do something bad	⓪ ① ②	35. Demands too much attention from others	⓪ ① ②
12. Is uncomfortable with attention from others	⓪ ① ②	36. Is irritable or stubborn	⓪ ① ②
13. Says he/she is not loved by anyone	⓪ ① ②	37. Has sudden mood swings	⓪ ① ②
14. Thinks he/she is worthless or second-rate	⓪ ① ②	38. Doesn't feel guilty about bad behavior	⓪ ① ②
15. Talks more than he/she should	⓪ ① ②	39. Is arrogant or over-bearing	⓪ ① ②
16. Hangs out with troublemakers	⓪ ① ②	40. Teases or provokes other children	⓪ ① ②
17. Has headaches without medical reason	⓪ ① ②	41. Destroys other people's things	⓪ ① ②
18. Cheats or lies	⓪ ① ②	42. Threatens or frightens others	⓪ ① ②
19. Is overly anxious or afraid	⓪ ① ②	43. Argues too much	⓪ ① ②
20. Blames him/herself too much	⓪ ① ②	44. Moves slowly or lacks energy	⓪ ① ②
21. Feels tired a lot	⓪ ① ②	45. Says he/she feels lonely	⓪ ① ②
22. Has pains without medical reason	⓪ ① ②	46. Is overly loud	⓪ ① ②
23. Keeps to him/herself a lot	⓪ ① ②	47. Is withdrawn and keeps apart from people	⓪ ① ②
24. Feels sick without medical reason	⓪ ① ②	48. Cries or appears tearful too much	⓪ ① ②

Comments:

Developed by: University of Tennessee
Children's Mental Health Services Research Center
with support from the National Institute of Mental Health

Your Name: _____

Your relationship to the child is (mark only one):
① mother ② father ③ teacher ④ relative
⑤ foster parent ⑥ agency caregiver
⑦ other (describe): _____

654

Before completing this scale, specify the number of client contacts this summary represents: _____

Using the scale below, score each item to estimate how often you actually use the following social work practice skill with this particular client. Under each item, describe more specifically the actual skill employed with this client.

| **Very often** | **Often** | **Moderately** | **Seldom** | **Never/almost never** |
| 4 | 3 | 2 | 1 | 0 |

Supportive/facilitative skills

1. Provided emotional support for my client   ___

_____

_____

2. Endeavored to increase their self-confidence   ___

_____

_____

3. Helped my client to feel good about her/himself   ___

_____

_____

4. Tried to increase their confidence that in the fact that I could really help them   ___

_____

_____

Insight facilitation skills

5. Helped them uncover troubling feelings   ___

_____

_____

6. Helped them learn from past experiences   ___

_____

_____

7. Explored how past relationships affect current problems   ___

_____

_____

8. Helped them learn from past attempts to solve problems   __

_____

_____

_____

Therapeutic coping skills

9. Taught them specific skills to deal with a certain problems   __

_____

_____

_____

10. Taught them how to manage their own problem behaviors   __

_____

_____

_____

11. Showed them how to reward themselves for progress with a problem   __

_____

_____

_____

12. Taught them how to monitor their own behaviors   __

_____

_____

_____

13. Collaborated with them on plans to cope with relapses of a problem   __

_____

_____

_____

Case management skills

14. Assessed their level of material resources   __

_____

_____

_____

15. Advocated on their behalf   __

_____

_____

_____

16. Made referrals to other services   __

_____

_____

_____

17. Gave them information about other services   ___

_____
_____
_____

18. Coordinated services for them with other agencies   ___

_____
_____
_____

Appendix D Substance Abuse Treatment Self-Efficacy Scale (SATSES)

Please indicate to what degree you feel confident in employing the following knowledge and skills relevant to alcohol and other drug abuse interventions. Use the scale below and place your number answer in the space provided to the right of each question.

There will also be a short vignette at the end of the questionnaire.

1 = **Very low** confidence to no confidence in my knowledge/skills
2 = **Low** confidence in my knowledge/skills
3 = **Moderate** confidence in my knowledge/skills
4 = **High** confidence in my knowledge/skills
5 = **Very High** confidence in my knowledge/skills

Assessment/Treatment Planning

How confident are you in . . .

1. Gathering data systematically from the client and other available collateral sources, using screening instruments and other methods that are sensitive to age, culture and gender. At a minimum, data should include: current and historic substance use; health, mental health, and substance-related treatment history; mental status; and current social environmental, and/or economic constraints on the client's ability to follow through successfully with an action plan?   _____

2. Determining the client's readiness for treatment/change and the needs of others involved in the current situation?   _____

3. Reviewing the treatment options relevant to the client's needs, characteristics, and goals?   _____

4. Constructing with the client and others, as appropriate, an initial action plan based on needs, preferences, and available resources.   _____

5. Selecting and using comprehensive assessment instruments that are sensitive to age, gender, and culture?   _____

6. Analyzing and interpreting the data to determine treatment recommendations?   _____

7. Obtaining and interpreting all relevant assessment information?   _____

8. Explaining assessment findings to the client and others potentially involved in treatment?   _____

9. Screening for AOD toxicity, withdrawal symptoms, aggression or danger to others, and potential for self-inflicted harm or suicide?   _____

10. Identifying appropriate strategies for each outcome?   _____

1 = **Very low**   2 = **Low**   3 = **Moderate**   4 = **High**   5 = **Very high**

How confident are you in . . .

Case Management

11. Establishing and maintaining professional relations with civic groups, agencies, other professionals, governmental entities, and the community-at-large in order to ensure appropriate referrals, identify service gaps, expand community resources, and help address unmet needs? _____

12. Continuously assessing and evaluating referral resources to determine their appropriateness? _____

13. Arranging referrals to other professionals, agencies' community programs, or other appropriate resources to meet client needs? _____

14. Exchanging relevant information with the agency/professional to whom the referral is being made, in a manner consistent with confidentiality regulations and generally accepted professionals standards of care? _____

15. Evaluating the outcome of the referral? _____

16. Initiating collaboration with referral sources? _____

Counseling—Individual

17. Establishing a helping relationship with the client characterized by warmth, respect, genuineness, concreteness and empathy? _____

18. Facilitating the client's engagement in the treatment/recovery process? _____

19. Encouraging and reinforcing all client actions that are determined to be beneficial in progressing toward treatment goals? _____

20. Working appropriately with the client to recognize and discourage all behaviors inconsistent with progress toward treatment goals? _____

21. Recognizing how, when, and why to use the client's significant others to enhance or support the treatment plan? _____

22. Facilitating the development of basic and life skills associated with recovery? _____

23. Adapting counseling strategies to the individual characteristics of the client, including (but not limited to): disability, gender, sexual orientation, developmental level, acculturation, ethnicity, age and health status? _____

1 = Very low   2 = Low   3 = Moderate   4 = High   5 = Very high

How confident are you in . . .

Counseling—Group

24. Performing the actions necessary to start a group, including determining group type, purpose, size, and leadership; recruiting and selecting members; establishing group goals and clarifying behavioral ground rules for participating; identifying outcomes; and determining criteria and methods for termination or graduation from the group? _____

25. Facilitating the entry of new members and the transition of exiting members? _____

26. Facilitating group growth within the established ground rules, and precipitate movement toward group and individual goals by using methods consistent with group type? _____

27. Describing and summarizing client behavior within the group for the purpose of documenting the client's progress and identifying needs/issues that may require modification of the treatment plan? _____

Ethics

28. Utilizing a range of supervisory options to process personal feelings and concerns about clients? _____

29. Conducting culturally appropriate self-evaluations of professional performance, applying ethical, legal, and professional standards to enhance self-awareness and performance? _____

30. Obtaining appropriate continuing professional education? _____

31. Assessing and participating in regular supervision and consultation sessions? _____

32. Developing and utilizing strategies to maintain physical and mental health? _____

Appendix E Addiction Severity Index

INSTRUCTIONS

1. Leave No Blanks – Where appropriate code items:

   X = question not answered
   N = question not applicable

   Use only one character per item.

2. Item numbers circled are to be asked at follow-up. Items with an asterisk are cumulative and should be rephrased at follow-up (see Manual).

3. Space is provided after sections for additional comments.

SEVERITY RATINGS

The severity ratings are interviewer estimates of the patient's need for additional treatment in each area. The scales range from 0 (no treatment necessary) to 9 (treatment needed to intervene in life-threatening situation). Each rating is based upon the patient's history of problem symptoms, present condition and subjective assessment of his treatment needs in a given area. For a detailed description of severity ratings' derivation procedures and conventions, see manual. **Note: These severity ratings are optional.**

SUMMARY OF PATIENT'S RATING SCALE

0 – Not at all
1 – Slightly
2 – Moderately
3 – Considerably
4 – Extremely

G1. I.D. NUMBER ☐☐☐☐

G2. LAST 4 DIGITS OF SSN ☐☐☐☐

G3. PROGRAM NUMBER ☐☐☐

G4. DATE OF
ADMISSION ☐☐☐☐☐
Mth. Day Year

G5. DATE OF
INTERVIEW ☐☐☐☐☐
Mth. Day Year

G6. TIME BEGUN ☐☐ : ☐☐

G7. TIME ENDED ☐☐ : ☐☐

G8. CLASS: ☐
1–Intake
2–Follow-up

G9. CONTACT CODE: ☐
1–In Person
2–Phone

G10. GENDER: ☐
1–Male
2–Female

G11. INTERVIEWER CODE ☐☐
NUMBER

G12. SPECIAL: ☐
1–Patient terminated
2–Patient refused
3–Patient unable to respond

GENERAL INFORMATION

NAME _____
CURRENT ADDRESS _____

G13. GEOGRAPHIC CODE ☐☐☐
G14. How long have you lived
at this address? ☐☐ ☐☐
Yrs. Mos.
G15. Is this residence owned
by you or your family? ☐
0–No 1–Yes
G16. DATE OF BIRTH ☐☐☐☐☐
Mth. Day Year
G17. RACE ☐
1–White (Not of Hispanic Origin)
2–Black (Not of Hispanic Origin)
3–American Indian
4–Alaskan Native
5–Asian of Pacific Islander
6–Hispanic–Mexican
7–Hispanic–Puerto Rican
8–Hispanic–Cuban
9–Other Hispanic
G18. RELIGIOUS PREFERENCE ☐
1–Protestant   4–Islamic
2–Catholic   5–Other
3–Jewish   6–None
(G19) Have you been in a ☐
controlled environment
in the past 30 days?
1–No
2–Jail
3–Alcohol or Drug Treatment
4–Medical Treatment
5–Psychiatric Treatment
6–Other _____
(G20) How many days? ☐☐

ADDITIONAL TEST RESULTS

G21. Shipley C.Q. ☐☐☐

G22. Shipley I.Q. ☐☐☐

G23. Beck Total Score ☐☐

G24. SCL-90 Total ☐☐☐

G25. MAST ☐☐

G26. _____ ☐☐☐

G27. _____ ☐☐☐

G28. _____ ☐☐☐

SEVERITY PROFILE

Problems	Medical	Employ/Support	Alcohol	Drug	Legal	Family/Social	Psychiatric
9							
8							
7							
6							
5							
4							
3							
2							
1							
0							

☐☐☐☐

MEDICAL STATUS

*(M1.) How many times in ☐☐ your life have you been hospitalized for medical problems? *(Include o.d.'s, d.t.'s, exclude detox.)*

M2. How long ago was ☐☐ ☐☐ your last hospitaliza- Yrs. Mos. tion for a physical problem?
0–No
1–Yes _____
Specify

M3. Do you have any chronic ☐ medical problems which continue to interfere with your life?

(M4.) Are you taking any pre- ☐ scribed medication on a regular basis for a physical problem? 0–No 1–Yes

(M5.) Do you receive a pension ☐ for a physical disability? *(Exclude psychiatric disability.)*
0–No
1–Yes _____
Specify

(M6.) How many days have you ☐☐ experienced medical prob- lems in the past 30 days?

For questions M7 & M8 please ask patient to use the Patient's Rating Scale

(M7.) How troubled or bothered ☐ have you been by these medical problems in the past 30 days?

(M8.) How important to you ☐ now is treatment for these medical problems?

Interviewer Severity Rating

M9. How would you rate the ☐ patient's need for medical treatment?

Confidence Ratings

Is the above information significantly distorted by:

(M10) Patient's misrepresen- ☐ tation?
0–No 1–Yes

(M11) Patient's inability to ☐ understand?
0–No 1–Yes

COMMENTS

EMPLOYMENT/SUPPORT STATUS

*(E1.) Education completed ☐☐ ☐☐ *(GED = 12 years)* Yrs. Mos.

*(E2.) Training or technical ☐☐ education completed Mos.

E3. Do you have a profession, ☐ trade or skill?
0–No
1–Yes _____
Specify

(E4.) Do you have a valid ☐ driver's license?
0–No 1–Yes

(E5.) Do you have an auto- ☐ mobile available for use? *(Answer No if no valid driver's license.)*
0–No 1–Yes

E6. How long was your ☐☐ ☐☐ longest full-time job? Yrs. Mos.

*(E7.) Usual (or last) occupation. ☐

_____
(Specify in detail)

(E8.) Does someone contribute ☐ to your support in any way?
0–No 1–Yes

(E9.) (ONLY IF ITEM E8 IS YES) ☐ Does this constitute the majority of your support?
0–No 1–Yes

E10. Usual employment ☐ pattern, past 3 years.
1–full time (40 hrs/wk)
2–part time (reg. hrs)
3–part time (irreg., daywork)
4–student
5–service
6–retired/disability
7–unemployed
8–in controlled environment

(E11.) How many days were ☐☐ you paid for working in the past 30? (include "under the table" work.)

How much money did you receive from the following sources in the past 30 days?

(E12.) Employment ☐☐☐☐ (net income)

(E13.) Unemployment ☐☐☐☐ compensation

(E14.) DPA ☐☐☐☐

(E15.) Pension, benefits or ☐☐☐☐ social security

(E16.) Mate, family or ☐☐☐☐ friends (money for personal expenses).

(E17.) Illegal ☐☐☐☐

(E18.) How many people depend ☐ on you for the majority of their food, shelter, etc.?

(E19.) How many days have you ☐ experienced employment problems in the past 30?

For questions E20 & E21 please ask patient to use the Patient's Rating Scale

(E20.) How troubled or ☐ bothered have you been by these employment prob- lems in the past 30 days?

(E21.) How important to you ☐ now is counseling for these employment problems?

Interviewer Severity Rating

E22. How would you rate the ☐ patient's need for employ- ment counseling?

Confidence Ratings

Is the above information significantly distorted by:

(E23.) Patient's misrepresen- ☐ tation?
0–No 1–Yes

(E24.) Patient's inability to ☐ understand?
0–No 1–Yes

COMMENTS

□□□□

DRUG/ALCOHOL USE

	Past 30 Days	Lifetime Use Yrs.	Rt of adm.
D1. Alcohol–any use at all	□□	□□	□
D2. Alcohol–To Intoxication	□□	□□	□
D3. Heroin	□□	□□	□
D4. Methadone	□□	□□	□
D5. Other opiates/ analgesics	□□	□□	□
D6. Barbiturates	□□	□□	□
D7. Other sed/ hyp/tranq.	□□	□□	□
D8. Cocaine	□□	□□	□
D9. Amphetamines	□□	□□	□
D10. Cannabis	□□	□□	□
D11. Hallucinogens	□□	□□	□
D12. Inhalants	□□	□□	□
D13. More than one substance per day (Incl. alcohol).	□□	□□	

Note: See manual for representative examples for each drug class

*Route of Administration:
1 = Oral, 2 = Nasal, 3 = Smoking,
4 = Non IV inj., 5 = IV inj.

D14. Which substance is the □□ major problem? *Please code as above or 00–No problem*; 15–Alcohol & Drug (Dual addiction); 16-Polydrug; *when not clear, ask patient.*

D15. How long was your last □□ period of voluntary abstinence from this major substance? *(00–never abstinent)*

D16. How many months ago □□ did this abstinence end? *(00–still abstinent)*

How many times have you:

*D17. Had alcohol d.t.'s □□

*D18. Overdosed on drugs □□

How many times in your life have you been treated for:

*D19. Alcohol Abuse: □□

*D20. Drug Abuse: □□

How many of these were detox only?

*D21. Alcohol □□

*D22. Drug □□

How much would you say you spent during the past 30 days on:

D23. Alcohol □□□□

D24. Drugs □□□□

D25. How many days have □□ you been treated in an outpatient setting for alcohol or drugs in the past 30 days? *(Include NA, AA).*

How many days in the past 30 have you experienced:

D26. Alcohol Problems □□

D27. Drug Problems □□

For questions D28–D31 please ask patient to use the Patient's Rating Scale

How troubled or bothered have you been in the past 30 days by these:

D28. Alcohol Problems □

D29. Drug Problems □

How important to you now is treatment for these:

D30. Alcohol Problems □

D31. Drug Problems □

Interviewer Severity Rating

How would you rate the patient's need for treatment for:

D32. Alcohol Abuse □

D33. Drug Abuse □

Confidence Ratings

Is the above information significantly distorted by:

D34. Patient's misrepresen- □ tation?
0–No 1–Yes

D35. Patient's inability to □ understand?
0–No 1–Yes

COMMENTS

_____
_____
_____
_____
_____
_____
_____
_____
_____
_____
_____
_____
_____

⊓⊓⊓   **LEGAL STATUS**

L1. Was this admission prompted
or suggested by the criminal
justice system (judge, proba-
tion/parole officer, etc.)
0–No 1–Yes   ☐

(L2.) Are you on probation or
parole?
0–No 1–Yes   ☐

How many times in your life have
you been arrested and <u>charged</u> with
the following:

*(L3.) Shoplifting/vandalism   ⊓⊓

*(L4.) Parole/probation   ⊓⊓
violations

*(L5.) Drug charges   ⊓⊓

*(L6.) Forgery   ⊓⊓

*(L7.) Weapons offense   ⊓⊓

*(L8.) Burglary, larceny, B&E   ⊓⊓

*(L9.) Robbery   ⊓⊓

*(L10.) Assault   ⊓⊓

*(L11.) Arson   ⊓⊓

*(L12.) Rape   ⊓⊓

*(L13.) Homicide, manslaughter   ⊓⊓

*(L14.) Prostitution   ⊓⊓

*(L15.) Contempt of court   ⊓⊓

*(L16.) Other   ⊓⊓

*(L17.) How many of these   ⊓⊓
charges resulted in
convictions?

How many time in your life have you
been charged with the following:

*(L18.) Disorderly conduct,   ⊓⊓
vagrancy, public
intoxication

*(L19.) Driving while intoxicated ⊓⊓

*(L20.) Major driving violations   ⊓⊓
(reckless driving, speeding,
no license, etc.)

*(L21.) How many months were   ⊓⊓
you incarcerated in   Mos.
your life?

L22. How long was your last   ⊓⊓
incarceration?   Mos.

L23. What was it for?   ⊓⊓
(*Use codes 3–16, 18–20.
If multiple charges,
code most severe*).

(L24.) Are you presently awaiting   ☐
charges, trial or sentence?
0–No 1–Yes

(L25.) What for? (*If multiple   ⊓⊓
charges, use most severe*).

(L26.) How many days in the   ⊓⊓
past 30 were you detained
or incarcerated?

(L27.) How many days in the   ⊓⊓
past 30 have you engaged
in illegal activities for profit?

*For questions L28 & L29 please
ask patient to use the
Patient's Rating Scale*

(L28.) How serious do you feel   ☐
your present legal problems
are? (*Exclude civil problems*)

(L29.) How important to you   ☐
now is counseling or referral
for these legal problems?

Interviewer Severity Rating

L30. How would you rate the   ☐
patient's need for legal
services or counseling?

Confidence Ratings

Is the information significantly
distorted by:

(L31.) Patient's misrepresentation? ☐
0–No 1–Yes

(L32.) Patient's inability to under- ☐
stand?
0–No 1–Yes

COMMENTS

▭▭▭▭

FAMILY/SOCIAL RELATIONSHIPS

(F1.) Marital Status   ☐
   1–Married   4–Separated
   2–Remarried   5–Divorced
   3–Widowed   6–Never Married

F2. How long have you   ▭▭ ▭▭
   been in this marital   Yrs. Mos.
   status? (*If never
   married, since age 18.*)

(F3.) Are you satisfied with   ☐
   this situation?
   0–No
   1–Indifferent
   2–Yes

*(F4.) Usual living arrangements   ☐
   (past 3 yr.)
   1–With sexual partner and
      children
   2–With sexual partner alone
   3–With children alone
   4–With parents
   5–With family
   6–With friends
   7–Alone
   8–Controlled environment
   9–No stable arrangements

F5. How long have you   ▭▭ ▭▭
   lived in these arrange-   Yrs. Mos.
   ments? (*If with parents
   or family, since age 18.*)

(F6.) Are you satisfied with   ☐
   these living arrangements?
   0–No
   1–Indifferent
   2–Yes

Do you live with anyone who:
   0–No 1–Yes

F7. Has a current alcohol   ☐
   problem?

F8. Uses non-prescribed drugs?   ☐

(F9.) With whom do you spend   ☐
   most of your free time:
   1–Family
   2–Friends
   3–Alone

(F10.) Are you satisfied with   ☐
   spending your free time
   this way?
   0–No
   1–Indifferent
   2–Yes

(F11.) How many close friends   ☐
   do you have?

Direction for F12–F26: Place "0" in
relative category where the answer
is clearly <u>no for all relatives in the
category</u>; "1" where the answer is
clearly <u>yes for **any** relative within
the category</u>; "X" where the answer
is <u>uncertain or "I don't know"</u> and
"N" where there <u>never was a relative
from that category.</u>

Would you say you have had close,
long lasting, personal relationships
with any of the following people in
your life:

F12. Mother   ☐
F13. Father   ☐
F14. Brothers/Sisters   ☐
F15. Sexual Partner/Spouse   ☐
F16. Children   ☐
F17. Friends   ☐

Have you had significant periods in
which you have experienced serious
problems getting along with:
0–No 1–Yes

	Past 30 Days	In Your Life
(F18.) Mother	☐	☐
(F19.) Father	☐	☐
(F20.) Brothers/Sisters	☐	☐
(F21.) Sexual partner/ spouse	☐	☐
(F22.) Children	☐	☐
(F23.) Other significant family _____	☐	☐
(F24.) Close friends	☐	☐
(F25.) Neighbors	☐	☐
(F26.) Co-Workers	☐	☐

Did any of these people (F18–F26)
abuse you? 0 = No 1 = Yes

	Past 30 Days	In Your Life
F27. Emotionally (make you feel bad through harsh words)?	☐	☐
F28. Physically (caused you physical harm)?	☐	☐
F29. Sexually (force sexual advances or sexual acts)?	☐	☐

How many days in the past 30 have
you had serious conflicts:

(F30.) With your family?   ▭▭

(F31.) With other people?   ▭▭
   (excluding family)

*For questions F32–F35 please
ask patient to use the
Patient's Rating Scale*

How troubled or bothered have you
been in the past 30 days by these:

(F32.) Family problems   ☐

(F33.) Social problems   ☐

How important to you now is treatment or counseling for these:

(F34.) Family problems   ☐

(F35.) Social problems   ☐

Interviewer Severity Rating

F36. How would you rate the   ☐
   patient's need for family
   and/or social counseling?

Confidence Ratings

Is the above information
significantly distorted by:

(F37.) Patient's misrepresentation?   ☐
   0–No 1–Yes

(F38.) Patient's inability to under- ☐
   stand?
   0–No 1–Yes

COMMENTS

_____
_____
_____
_____
_____
_____
_____
_____
_____
_____
_____
_____
_____
_____
_____
_____
_____

□□□□

How many times have you been
treated for any psychological or
emotional problems?

*(P1.)In a hospital   □□

*(P2.)As an Opt. or Priv. patient   □□

(P3.)Do you receive a pension   □
    for a psychiatric disability?
    0–No 1–Yes

Have you had a significant period
(that was not a direct result of drug/
alcohol use), in which you have:
0–No 1–Yes

	Past 30 Days	In Your Life
(P4.)Experienced serious depression	□	□
(P5.)Experienced serious anxiety or tension	□	□
(P6.)Experienced hallucinations	□	□
(P7.)Experienced trouble understanding, concentrating or remembering	□	□
(P8.)Experienced trouble controlling violent behavior	□	□
(P9.)Experienced serious thoughts of suicide	□	□
(P10.)Attempted suicide	□	□
(P11.)Been prescribed medication for any psychological emotional problem	□	□

PSYCHIATRIC STATUS

(P12.)How many days in the   □□
    past 30 have you
    experienced these
    psychological or
    emotional problems?

*For questions P13 & P14 please
ask patient to use the
Patient's Rating Scale*

(P13.)How much have you been   □
    troubled or bothered by
    these psychological or
    emotional problems in the
    past 30 days?

(P14.)How important to you   □
    now is treatment for these
    psychological problems?

*THE FOLLOWING ITEMS ARE TO BE
COMPLETED BY THE INTERVIEWER*

At the time of the interview, is patient:
    0–No 1–Yes

(P15.)Obviously depressed/   □
    withdrawn

(P16.)Obviously hostile   □

(P17.)Obviously anxious/nervous   □

(P18.)Having trouble with   □
    reality testing, thought
    disorders, paranoid thinking

(P19.)Having trouble compre-   □
    hending, concentrating,
    remembering

(P20.)Having suicidal thoughts   □

Interviewer Severity Rating

P21. How would you rate the   □
    patient's need for psychiatric/
    psychological treatment?

Confidence Ratings

Is the above information
significantly distorted by:

(P22.)Patient's misrepresentation? □
    0–No 1–Yes

(P23.)Patient's inability to under- □
    stand?
    0–No 1–Yes

COMMENTS

Appendix F Score Form, Borderline Personality Disorder Severity Index, Version IV

Interviewer: Date:

Client: Assessment no.:

Medication use:

4.4.A Regular use of alcohol:
4.5.A Regular use of soft drugs:
4.6.A Regular use of hard drugs:

1. Abandonment   **Notes**:

1.1	0 1 2 3 4 5 6 7 8 9 10	....
1.2	0 1 2 3 4 5 6 7 8 9 10	....
1.3	0 1 2 3 4 5 6 7 8 9 10	....
1.4	0 1 2 3 4 5 6 7 8 9 10	....
1.5	0 1 2 3 4 5 6 7 8 9 10	....
1.6	0 1 2 3 4 5 6 7 8 9 10	....
1.7	0 1 2 3 4 5 6 7 8 9 10	....

Mean: _____

2. Interpersonal relationships

2.1	0 1 2 3 4 5 6 7 8 9 10	....
2.2	0 1 2 3 4 5 6 7 8 9 10	....
2.3	0 1 2 3 4 5 6 7 8 9 10	....
2.4	0 1 2 3 4 5 6 7 8 9 10	....
2.5	0 1 2 3 4 5 6 7 8 9 10	....
2.6	0 1 2 3 4 5 6 7 8 9 10	....
2.7	0 1 2 3 4 5 6 7 8 9 10	....
2.8	0 1 2 3 4 5 6 7 8 9 10	....

Mean: _____

3. Identity

3.1	0 1 2 3 4	....
3.2	0 1 2 3 4	....
3.3	0 1 2 3 4	....
3.4	0 1 2 3 4	....
3.5	0 1 2 3 4	....
3.6	0 1 2 3 4	....
3.7	0 1 2 3 4	....
3.8	0 1 2 3 4	....

Mean × 2.5 = _____

4. Impulsivity

4.1	0 1 2 3 4 5 6 7 8 9 10	....
4.2	0 1 2 3 4 5 6 7 8 9 10	....
4.3	0 1 2 3 4 5 6 7 8 9 10	....
4.4	0 1 2 3 4 5 6 7 8 9 10	....

4.5	0 1 2 3 4 5 6 7 8 9 10	....
4.6	0 1 2 3 4 5 6 7 8 9 10	....
4.7	0 1 2 3 4 5 6 7 8 9 10	....
4.8	0 1 2 3 4 5 6 7 8 9 10	....
4.9	0 1 2 3 4 5 6 7 8 9 10	....
4.10	0 1 2 3 4 5 6 7 8 9 10	....
4.11	0 1 2 3 4 5 6 7 8 9 10	....

Mean: _____

5. Parasuicidal behaviour

5.1	0 1 2 3 4 5 6 7 8 9 10	....
5.2	0 1 2 3 4 5 6 7 8 9 10	....
5.3	0 1 2 3 4 5 6 7 8 9 10	....
5.4	0 1 2 3 4 5 6 7 8 9 10	....
5.5	0 1 2 3 4 5 6 7 8 9 10	....
5.6	0 1 2 3 4 5 6 7 8 9 10	....
5.7	0 1 2 3 4 5 6 7 8 9 10	....
5.8	0 1 2 3 4 5 6 7 8 9 10	....
5.9	0 1 2 3 4 5 6 7 8 9 10	....
5.10	0 1 2 3 4 5 6 7 8 9 10	....
5.11	0 1 2 3 4 5 6 7 8 9 10	....
5.12	0 1 2 3 4 5 6 7 8 9 10	....
5.13	0 1 2 3 4 5 6 7 8 9 10	....

Mean: _____

6. Affective instability

6.1	0 1 2 3 4 5 6 7 8 9 10	....
6.2	0 1 2 3 4 5 6 7 8 9 10	....
6.3	0 1 2 3 4 5 6 7 8 9 10	....
6.4	0 1 2 3 4 5 6 7 8 9 10	....
6.5	0 1 2 3 4 5 6 7 8 9 10	....

Mean: _____

7. Emptiness

7.1	0 1 2 3 4 5 6 7 8 9 10	....
7.2	0 1 2 3 4 5 6 7 8 9 10	....
7.3	0 1 2 3 4 5 6 7 8 9 10	....
7.4	0 1 2 3 4 5 6 7 8 9 10	....

Mean: _____

8. Outbursts of anger

8.1	0 1 2 3 4 5 6 7 8 9 10	....
8.2	0 1 2 3 4 5 6 7 8 9 10	....
8.3	0 1 2 3 4 5 6 7 8 9 10	....
8.4	0 1 2 3 4 5 6 7 8 9 10	....
8.5	0 1 2 3 4 5 6 7 8 9 10	....
8.6	0 1 2 3 4 5 6 7 8 9 10	....

Mean: _____

9. Dissociation and Paranoid ideation

9.1	0 1 2 3 4 5 6 7 8 9 10	....
9.2	0 1 2 3 4 5 6 7 8 9 10	....
9.3	0 1 2 3 4 5 6 7 8 9 10	....
9.4	0 1 2 3 4 5 6 7 8 9 10	....
9.5	0 1 2 3 4 5 6 7 8 9 10	....
9.6	0 1 2 3 4 5 6 7 8 9 10	....
9.7	0 1 2 3 4 5 6 7 8 9 10	....
9.8	0 1 2 3 4 5 6 7 8 9 10	....

Mean: _____

Total sum of means: _____

Appendix G   Scoring Worksheet for UCLA PTSD Index for DSM-IV, Revision 1: Child Version©

Subject ID# _____   **Age** _____   **Sex (circle): M   F**
# of days since traumatic event _____

CRITERION A-TRAUMATIC EVENT	PTSD SEVERITY: OVERALL SCORE
Exposure to Traumatic Event Questions 1–13: at least 1 "Yes" answer **YES NO** Type of Traumatic Event rated as most distressing (Question 14: write trauma type in the blank) _____ **Criterion A1 met** Questions 15–21: at least 1 "Yes" answer **YES NO** **Criterion A2 met** Questions 22–26: at least 1 "Yes" answer **YES NO** **Criterion A met** **YES NO** **Peritraumatic Dissociation** **YES NO** Question 27: answer "Yes"	Question #/Score Question #/Score 1.____ 12.____ 2.____ 13.____ 3.____ [Omit 14]. 4.____ 15.____ 5.____ 16.____ 6.____ 17.____ 7.____ 18.____ 8.____ 19.____ 9.____ [Omit 20]. *10. or 11.____ *(Sum the items from the above 2 columns, write sum below)* **(Sum total PTSD SEVERITY** **of scores) = _____ SCORE** *Place the highest Score from either Question 10 or 11 in the blank above: Score Question 10.___/ Score Question 11.___

CRITERION B (REEXPERIENCING) SX.	CRITERION C (AVOIDANCE) SX.

<u>Question #/DSM-IV Symptom</u> <u>Score</u>
3. (B1) Intrusive recollections   _____
5. (B2) Trauma/bad dreams   _____
6. (B3) Flashbacks   _____   # of Criterion B
2. (B4) Cues: Psychological   Questions with
   reactivity   _____   Score ≥ Symp-
18. (B5) Cues: Physiological   tom Cutoff:
   reactivity   ____ ____
 	
CRITERION B SEVERITY
SCORE (Sum of above scores): = _____
 	
DSM-IV CRITERION B MET:
(Diagnosis requires at least 1 "B" Symptom):   **YES   NO**
	<u>Question #/DSM-IV Symptom</u> <u>Score</u>
	9. (C1) Avoiding thoughts/feelings _____
	17. (C2) Avoiding activities/people _____
	15. (C3) Forgetting _____ # of Criterion C
	7. (C4) Diminished interest etc. _____ Questions with
	8. (C5) Detachment/estrangement _____ Scores ≥ Symp-
	*10. or 11. (C6) Affect restricted _____ tom Cutoff:
	
	19. (C7) Foreshort. future _____
	
	[*Place the highest Score from either Question 10 or 11 in the blank above.]
	
	CRITERION C SEVERITY
	SCORE (Sum of above scores): = _____
	
	DSM-IV CRITERION C MET:
	(Diagnosis requires at least 3 "C" Symptoms): **YES NO**

CRITERION D (INCREASED AROUSAL) SX.	DSM-IV PTSD DIAGNOSTIC INFO.

<u>Question #/DSM-IV Symptom</u> <u>Score</u>
13. (D1) Sleep problems   _____
4. (D2) Irritability/anger   _____
16. (D3) Concentration problems ____   # of Criterion D
1. (D4) Hypervigilance   _____   Questions with
12. (D5) Exaggerated startle   _____   Score ≥ Symp-
   tom Cutoff:
   ____
 	
CRITERION D SEVERITY
SCORE (Sum of above scores): = _____
 	
DSM-IV CRITERION D MET:
(Diagnosis requires at least 2 "D" Symptoms):   **YES   NO**
	
	DSM-IV FULL PTSD DIAGNOSIS LIKELY
	(Criteria A, B, C, D all met) **YES NO**
	
	PARTIAL PTSD LIKELY
	[Criterion A met and:
	Criteria (B + C) or (B + D) or (C + D)] **YES NO**

Addiction Severity Index (ASI)
The ASI and training materials are available free of charge at www.tresearch.org.
Reprinted with permission of Thomas McLellan.

Agoraphobia Scale
Contact: Lars-Goran Ost at ost@psychology.su.se.
Reprinted with permission from Ost, 1990.

Alcohol Use Disorders Identification Test (AUDIT)
Reprinted from USDHHS, 2003, pp. 311–314

Borderline Personality Disorder Severity Index (BPDSI)
Contact: Josephine Giesen-Bloo, Department of Medical, Clinical, and Experimental Psychology, University Maastricht, PO Box 616, NL-6200 MD Maastricht, The Netherlands; e-mail: j.giesen@dep.unimaas.nl.
Reprinted with permission of Josephine Giesen-Bloo.

Brief Psychiatric Rating Scale–Anchored (BPRS-A)
Contact: David Lachar, Department of Psychiatry and Behavioral Sciences, University of Texas, Houston Health Science Center, P.O. Box 20708, Houston, TX 77225; e-mail: david.lachar@uth.tmc.edu.
Reprinted with permission from Lachar et al., 2001.

Children's Depression Rating Scale–Revised Short Form (CDRS-r)
To obtain a copy, contact James Overholser, Department of Psychology, Case Western Reserve University, Cleveland, OH 44106-7123; e-mail: overholser@po.cwru.edu.
Reprinted with permission from Overholser, Brinkman, Lehnert, & Ricciardi, 1995.

College Alcohol Problems Scale–Revised (CAPS-r)
Copies of CAPS-r are available free of charge from oharet@bc.edu.
Reprinted from USDHHS, 2003, pp. 340–342

Drinking Context Scale (DCS-9)
Copies of DCS-9 are available free of charge from oharet@bc.edu.
Reprinted from USDHHS, 2003, pp. 359–362.

Drug Abuse Screening Test–10 (DAST-10)
To obtain a copy, contact Harvey Skinner, Department of Public Health Sciences, Faculty of Medicine, University of Toronto, 12 Queen's Park Crescent West, Toronto, Ontario M5S 1A8; e-mail: harvey.skinner@utoronto.ca.
Reprinted with permission of Skinner, 1982, and the Centre for Addiction and Mental Health, Toronto, Canada.

Eating Disorder Diagnostic Scale (EDDS)
A computerized scoring tool is available from Eric Stice at estice@ori.org.
Copyright 2000 by Eric Stice and Christy F. Telch. Reprinted with permission.

Geriatric Depression Scale (GDS)
The GDS is in the public domain.
Reprinted from Yesavage et al., 1983.

Hamilton Depression Rating Scale (HAM-D)
The HAM-D is in the public domain.
Reprinted from Hamilton, 1960.

Marital Disaffection Scale
Contact: Dr. Karen Kayser, University of Louisville.
Copyright 1990 by the National Council on Family Relations.
Reprinted with permission.

New York Teacher Rating Scale (NYTRS)
Contact: Laurie Miller-Brotman, New York University Child Study Center,
577 First Ave., New York, NY 10016; email: millel02@med.nyu.edu.
Reprinted with permission of Laurie Miller-Brotman.

Obsessive-Compulsive Inventory–Revised (OCI)
To obtain copies, contact Edna Foa, Center for the Treatment and Study of Anxiety,
University of Pennsylvania, 3535 Market St., Suite 600N, Philadelphia, PA 19104;
e-mail: foa@mail.med.upenn.edu.
Reprinted with permission of Edna B. Foa.

Post-Traumatic Stress Disorder Reaction Index (PTSD-RI)
The different formatted versions of the PTSD-RI, associated training materials,
and scoring aids are available from the authors at rpynoos@mednet.ucla.edu.
Contact: Robert Pynoos, UCLA Trauma Psychiatry Service, 300 UCLA Medical
Plaza, suite 2232, Los Angeles, CA 90095-6968, (310) 206-8973.
Copyright 1998 Pynoos, Rodriguez, Steinberg, Stuber, & Frederick.
Reprinted with permission of Robert Pynoos.

Practice Skills Inventory (PSI)
The PSI is available free of charge from oharet@bc.edu.
Copyright Tom O'Hare, 1997.

Psychosocial Well-Being Scale (PSWS)
The PSWS is available free of charge from oharet@bc.edu.
Copyright Tom O'Hare, 2002.

PTSD Symptom Scale Interview (PSS-I)
A manual is available from Nora Feeney and Edna Foa.
Contact: Edna B. Foa, Center for the Treatment and Study of Anxiety,
University of Pennsylvania, 3535 Market St., Suite 600N, Philadelphia, PA 19104;
e-mail; foa@mail.med.upenn.edu.
Reprinted with permission of Edna Foa.

Screen for Child Anxiety-Related Emotional Disorders (SCARED)
Contact: Boris Birmaher, Western Psychiatric Institute and Clinic,
Department of Child Psychiatry, 3811 O'Hara St., Pittsburgh, PA 15213;
e-mail: birmaherb@msx.upmc.edu.
Reprinted with permission of Boris Birmaher.

Shortform Assessment for Children (SAC)
The SAC scale and scoring software are available from Children's Mental
Health Services Research Center, Henson Hall, University of Tennessee,
Knoxville, TN 37996-3332.
Reprinted with permission of University of Tennessee Children's Mental
Health Services Research Center.

Strengths and Weakness of ADHD Symptoms and Normal Behavior Scale (SWAN)
The SWAN extended version and related materials are available without charge
from www.ADHD.net.
Copyright James M. Swanson, University of California, Irvine.
Reprinted with permission.

Substance Abuse Treatment Self-Efficacy Scale (SATSES)
The SATSES is available free of charge from Katie Kranz, kkranz@providence.edu,
or from Tom O'Hare at oharet@bc.edu.
Copyright Katherine M. Kranz. Reprinted with permission.

REFERENCES

Abbey, A. (2002). Alcohol-related sexual assault: A common problem among college students. *Journal of Studies on Alcohol, 63*, 118–128.

Abbey, A., & Harnish, R. (1995). Perception of sexual intent: The role of gender, alcohol consumption, and rape supportive attitudes. *Sex Roles, 32*, 297–313.

Abbey, A., McAuslan, P., & Ross, L. T. (1998). Sexual assault perpetration by college men: The role of alcohol misperception of sexual intent, and sexual beliefs and experiences. *Journal of Social and Clinical Psychology, 17*, 167–195.

Abbott, P. J., Weller, S. B., Delaney, H. D., & Moore, B. A. (1998). Community reinforcement approach in the treatment of opiate addicts. *American Journal of Drug and Alcohol Abuse, 24*, 17–30.

Abel, E. M. (2000). Psychosocial treatments for battered women: A review of empirical research. *Research on Social Work Practice, 10*, 55–77.

Ablon, J. S., & Jones, E. E. (2002). Validity of controlled clinical trials of psychotherapy: Findings from the NIMH Treatment of Depression Collaborative Research Program. *American Journal of Psychiatry, 159*, 775–783.

Abracen, J., Looman, J., & Langton, C. M. (2008). Treatment of sexual offenders with psychopathic traits: Recent research developments and clinical implications. *Trauma, Violence, and Abuse, 9*, 144–166.

Abramowitz, J. S., Brigidi, B. D., & Roche, K. R. (2001). Cognitive-behavioral therapy for obsessive compulsive disorder. *Research on Social Work Practice, 11*, 357–372.

Abramowitz, J. S., Whiteside, S. P., & Deacon, B. J. (2005). The effectiveness of treatment for pediatric obsessive-compulsive disorder: A meta-analysis. *Behavior Therapy, 36*, 55–63.

Abrams, D. B., & Niaura, R. S. (1987). Social learning theory. In H. T. Blane & K. E. Leonard (Eds.), *Psychological theories of drinking and alcoholism* (pp. 131–178). New York, NY: Guilford Press.

Abrams, D. J., Rojas, D. C., & Arciniegas, D. B. (2008). Is schizoaffective disorder a distinct categorical diagnosis? A critical review of the literature. *Neuropsychiatric Disease and Treatment, 4*, 1089–1109.

Abramson, L. Y., Seligman, M. E., & Teasdale, J. (1978). Learned helplessness in humans: Critique and reformulation. *Journal of Abnormal Psychology, 87*, 49–74.

Achenbach, T. M. (1991). *Manual for the Youth Self-Report and 1991 Profile*. Burlington, VT: University of Vermont Department of Psychiatry.

Achenbach, T. M. (1995). Empirically based assessment and taxonomy: Applications to clinical research. *Psychological Assessment, 7*, 261–274.

Acierno, R., Donohue, B., & Kogan, E. (1994). Psychological interventions for drug abuse: A critique and summation of controlled studies. *Clinical Psychology Review*, *14*, 417–442.

Adams, K. B., Matto, H. C., & LeCroy, C. W. (2009). Limitations of evidence based practice for social work education: Unpacking the complexity. *Journal of Social Work Education*, *45*, 165–186.

Adamson, S. J., Heather, N., Morton, V., Raistrick, D., & Slegg, G. P. (on behalf of the UKATT Research Team). (2010). Initial preference for drinking goal in the treatment of alcohol problems: II. Treatment outcomes. *Alcohol and Alcoholism*, *45*, 136–142.

Adamson, S. J., Sellman, J. D., & Frampton, C. (2009). Patient predictors of alcohol treatment outcome: A systematic review. *Journal of Substance Abuse Treatment*, *36*, 75–86.

Adoption and Safe Families Act (ASFA), Pub. L. No. 105-89.

Adoption Assistance and Child Welfare Act of 1980, Pub. L. No. 96-272.

Afifi, T. O., MacMillan, H., Cox, B. J., Asmundson, G. J. G., Stein, M. B., & Sareen, J. (2009). Mental health correlates of intimate partner violence in marital relationships in a nationally representative sample of males and females. *Journal of Interpersonal Violence*, *24*, 1398–1417.

Ainsworth, M. D., Blehar, M. C., Waters, E., & Wall, E. (1978). *Patterns of attachment: A psychological study of the strange situation*. Hillsdale, NJ: Erlbaum.

Aisenberg, E. (2008). Evidence-based practice in mental health care to ethnic minority communities: Has its practice fallen short of its evidence? *Social Work*, *53*, 297–306.

Albert, M., Becker, T., McCrone, P., & Thornicroft, G. (1998). Social networks and mental health service utilization: A literature review. *International Journal of Social Psychiatry*, *44*, 248–266.

Alcohol and Drug Abuse Institute. (2011). *The ADAI library*. Seattle, WA: University of Washington.

Alcoholics Anonymous. (1981). *Twelve steps and twelve traditions*. New York, NY: Alcoholics Anonymous World Services.

Aldridge, J., Lamb, M. E., Sternberg, K. J., Orbach, Y., Esplin, P. W., & Bowler, L. (2004). Using a human figure drawing to elicit information from alleged victims of child sexual abuse. *Journal of Consulting and Clinical Psychology*, *72*, 304–316.

Alessi, S. M., Rash, C., & Petry, N. M. (2011). Contingency management has also been shown to be efficacious with cocaine patients who engaged in pretreatment marijuana use. *Drug and Alcohol Dependence*, *118*, 62–67.

Alexander, J. F., Holtzworth-Munroe, A., & Jameson, P. B. (1994). The process and outcome of marital and family therapy: Research, review and evaluation. In A. E. Bergin & S. L. Garfield (Eds.), *The handbook of psychotherapy and behavior change* (4th ed., pp. 595–630). New York, NY: Wiley.

Alexander, J. F., & Parsons, B. V. (1982). *Functional family therapy: Principles and procedures*. Carmel, CA: Brooks/Cole.

Alexander, J. F., Waldron, H. B., Newberry, A. M., & Liddle, N. (1988). *Family approaches to treating delinquents*. Newbury Park, CA: Sage.

Alford, B. A., & Correia, C. J. (1994). Cognitive therapy of schizophrenia: Theory and empirical status. *Behavior Therapy*, *25*, 17–33.

Allen, J. P., & Mattson, M. E. (1993). Psychometric instruments to assist in alcoholism treatment planning. *Journal of Substance Abuse Treatment*, *10*, 289–296.

Alter-Reid, K., Gibbs, M. S., Lachenmeyer, J. R., Sigal, J., & Massoth, N. A. (1986). Sexual abuse of children: A review of the empirical findings. *Clinical Psychology Review*, *6*, 249–266.

Amaro, H. (1995). Love, sex and power. *American Psychologist*, *50*, 437–447.

Amaya-Jackson, L., & March, J. S. (1995). Posttraumatic stress disorder. In J. S. March (Ed.), *Anxiety disorders in children and adolescents* (pp. 276–317). New York, NY: Guilford Press.

Ambrogne, J. A. (2002). Reduced-risk drinking as a treatment goal: What clinicians need to know. *Journal of Substance Abuse Treatment*, *22*, 45–53.

American Academy of Child and Adolescent Psychiatry. (1990). *Guidelines for clinical evaluation of child sexual abuse*. Washington, DC: Author.

American Academy of Child and Adolescent Psychiatry. (1997a). Practice parameters for the forensic evaluation of children and adolescents who may have been physically or sexually abused. *American Academy of Child and Adolescent Psychiatry*, *36*, 423–442.

American Academy of Child and Adolescent Psychiatry. (1997b). Summary of the practice parameters for the assessment and treatment of children, adolescents, and adults with ADHD. *Journal of the American Academy of Child and Adolescent Psychiatry*, *36*, 1311–1317.

American Academy of Child and Adolescent Psychiatry. (2001a). Practice parameter for the assessment and treatment of children and adolescents with suicidal behavior. *Journal of the Academy of Child and Adolescent Psychiatry*, *40*, 24S–51S.

American Academy of Child and Adolescent Psychiatry. (2001b). Summary of the practice parameter for the use of stimulant medications in the treatment of children, adolescents, and adults. *Journal of the American Academy of Child and Adolescent Psychiatry*, *40*, 1352–1355.

American Academy of Pediatrics. (1991). Guidelines for the evaluation of the sexual abuse of children. *Pediatrics*, *87*, 254–260.

American Professional Society on the Abuse of Children. (1990). *Guidelines for psychosocial evaluation of suspected sexual abuse in young children*. Chicago, IL: Author.

American Psychiatric Association. (2000). *Diagnostic and statistical manual of mental disorders* (4th ed., text rev.). Washington, DC: Author.

American Psychiatric Association. (2013). *Diagnostic and statistical manual of mental disorders* (5th ed.). Washington, DC: Author.

American Psychological Association. (1994). Guidelines for child custody evaluations in divorce proceedings. *American Psychologist*, *49*, 677–680.

Ammerman, R. T., Cassisi, J. E., Hersen, M., & Van Hasselt, V. B. (1986). Consequences of physical abuse and neglect in children. *Clinical Psychology Review*, *6*, 291–310.

Amodeo, M., & Kay, J. L. (1997). Viewing alcohol and other drug use cross culturally: A cultural framework for clinical practice. *Families in Society*, *78*, 240–254.

Amodeo, M., Lundgren, L., Cohen, A., Rose, D., Chassler, D., Beltrame, C., & D'Ippolito, M. (2011). Barriers to implementing evidence-based practices in addiction treatment programs: Comparing staff reports on motivational interviewing, adolescent community reinforcement approach, assertive community treatment, and cognitive-behavior therapy. *Evaluation and Program Planning*, *34*, 382–389.

Anastopoulos, A. D. (1998). A training program for parents of children with attention-deficit/hyperactivity disorder. In J. M. Briesmeister & C. E. Schaefer (Eds.), *Handbook of parent training: Parents as co-therapists for children's behavior problems* (pp. 27–60). New York, NY: Wiley.

Anastopoulos, A. D., Smith, J. M., & Wien, E. E. (1998). Counseling and training parents. In R. A. Barkley (Ed.), *Attention-deficit hyperactivity disorder: A handbook for diagnosis and treatment* (pp. 373–393). New York, NY: Guilford Press.

Anderson, D. A., & Murray, A. D. (2010). Psychological assessment of eating disorders. In W. S. Agras (Ed.), *The Oxford handbook of eating disorders* (pp. 249–258). New York, NY: Oxford University Press.

Anderson, J., Moeschberger, M., Chen, M. S., Junn, P., Wewers, M. E., & Guthrie, R. (1993). An acculturation scale for Southeast Asians. *Social Psychiatry and Psychiatric Epidemiology*, *28*, 134–141.

Anderson, S. A. (2001). Clinical evaluation of violence in couples: The role of assessment instruments. *Journal of Family Psychotherapy*, *12*, 1–18.

Anderson, S. A., & Cramer-Benjamin, D. B. (1999). The impact of couple violence on parenting and children: An overview and clinical implications. *American Journal of Family Therapy*, *27*, 1–19.

Angermeyer, M. C., Kuhn, L., & Goldstein, J. M. (1990). Gender and the course of schizophrenia: Differences in treated outcomes. *Schizophrenia Bulletin*, *16*, 293–307.

Annis, H. M., & Davis, C. S. (1991). Relapse prevention. *Alcohol Health and Research World*, *15, 3*, 204–212.

Anthony, W. A., & Blanch, A. (1989). Research on community support services: What have we learned? *Psychosocial Rehabilitation Journal*, *12*, 55–81.

Annis, H. M. (1982). *Inventory of Drinking Situations*. Toronto, ON: Addiction Research Foundation.

Annis, H. M., & Davis, C. S. (1991). Relapse prevention. *Alcohol Health and Research World*, *15, 3*, 204–212.

Anton, R. F., O'Malley, S. S., Ciraulo, D. A., Cisler, R. A., Couper, D., Donovan, D. M., . . . Zweben, A. (2006). Combined pharmacotherapies and behavioral interventions for alcohol dependence—The COMBINE study: A randomized controlled trial. *JAMA*, *295, 17*, 2003–2017.

Antony, M. M., & Swinson, R. P. (2000). *Phobic disorders and panic in adults: A guide to assessment and treatment*. Washington, DC: American Psychological Association.

Appel, A. E., & Holden, G. W. (1998). The co-occurrence of spouse and physical child abuse: A review and appraisal. *Journal of Family Psychology*, *12*, 578–599.

Appelbaum, P. S. (1993). Legal liability and managed care. *American Psychologist*, *48*, 251–257.

Appelbaum, P. S. (1996). Law and psychiatry—*Jaffee vs. Redmond*: Psychotherapist-patient privilege in the federal courts. *Psychiatric Services*, *47*, 1033–1052.

Appelbaum, P. S. (2001). Thinking carefully about out-patient civil commitment. *Psychiatric Services*, *52*, 347–350.

Arcelus, J., Mitchell, A., Wales, J., & Nielsen, S. (2011). Mortality rates in patients with anorexia nervosa and other eating disorders. *Archives of General Psychiatry, 68*, 724–731.

Arch, J. J., & Craske, M. G. (2009). First-line treatment: A critical appraisal of cognitive behavioral therapy developments and alternatives. *Psychiatric Clinics of North America, 32*, 525–547.

Armstrong, C., & Hill, M. (2001). Support services for vulnerable families with young children. *Child and Family Social Work, 6*, 351–358.

Arnold, L. E., Abikoff, H. B., Cantwell, D. P., Conners, C. K., Elliott, G., Greenhill, L. L., . . . Wells, K. C. (1997). National Institute of Mental Health collaborative multimodal treatment study of children with ADHD (MTA): Design challenges and choices. *Archives of General Psychiatry, 54*, 865–870.

Arntz, A., van den Hoorn, M., Cornelis, J., Verheul, R., van den Bosch, W., & de Bie, A. (2003). Reliability and validity of the Borderline Personality Disorder Severity Index. *Journal of Personality Disorders, 17*, 45–59.

Arriaza, C. A., & Mann, T. (2001). Ethnic differences in eating disorder symptoms among college students: The confounding role of body mass index. *Journal of American College Health, 49*, 309–315.

Arroyo, J. A., Westerberg, V. S., & Tonigan, J. S. (1998). Comparison of treatment utilization and outcome for Hispanics and non-Hispanic whites. *Journal of Studies on Alcohol, 59*, 286–291.

Arthur, N. (1998). The effects of stress, depression, and anxiety on postsecondary students' coping strategies. *Journal of College Student Development, 39*, 11–22.

Asarnow, J. R., Scott, C. V., & Mintz, J. (2002). A combined cognitive-behavioral family education intervention for depression in children: A treatment development study. *Cognitive Therapy and Research, 26*, 221–229.

Ashford, J. B., Sales, B. D., & Reid, W. H. (2001). Political, legal, and professional challenges to treating offenders with special needs. In J. B. Ashford, B. D. Sales, & W. H. Reid (Eds.), *Treating adult and juvenile offenders with special needs* (pp. 31–49). Washington, DC: American Psychological Association.

Ashley, O., Marsden, M., & Brady, T. (2003). Effectiveness of substance abuse treatment programming for women: A review. *American Journal of Drug and Alcohol Abuse, 29*, 19–53.

Ashton, H. (2005). The diagnosis and management of benzodiazepine dependence. *Current Opinion in Psychiatry, 18, 3*, 249–255.

Asnaani, A., Gutner, C. A., Hinton, D. E., & Hofmann, S. G. (2009). Panic disorder, panic attacks and panic attack symptoms across race-ethnic groups: Results of the collaborative psychiatric epidemiology studies. *CNS Neuroscience and Therapeutics, 15*, 249–254.

Asnaani, A., Richey, J. A., Dimaite, R., Hinton, D. E., & Hofmann, S. G. (2010). A cross-ethnic comparison of lifetime prevalence rates of anxiety disorders. *Journal of Nervous and Mental Disease, 198*, 551–555.

Attia, A., & Walsh, B. T. (2007). Anorexia. *American Journal of Psychiatry, 164*, 1805–1810.

AuClaire, P., & Schwartz, I. (1986). *An evaluation of the effectiveness of intensive home-based services as an alternative to placement for adolescents and their families.* Minneapolis, MN: Hubert H. Humphrey Institute of Public Affairs, University of Minnesota.

Austin, S. B. (2000). Prevention research in eating disorders: Theory and new directions. *Psychological Medicine, 30*, 1249–1262.

Avison, W. R., & Gotlib, I. H. (1994). Introduction and overview. In W. R. Avison & I. H. Gotlib (Eds.), *Stress and mental health: Contemporary issues and prospects for the future* (pp. 3–12). New York, NY: Plenum Press.

Axelson, D. A., & Birmaher, B. (2001). Relation between anxiety and depressive disorders in childhood and adolescence. *Depression and Anxiety, 14*, 67–78.

Azar, S. T., Povilaitis, T. Y., Lauretti, A. F., & Pouquette, C. L. (1998). The current status of etiological theories in intrafamilial child maltreatment. In J. R. Lutzker (Ed.), *Handbook of child abuse research and treatment* (pp. 3–30). New York, NY: Plenum Press.

Azrin, N. H. (1976). Improvements in the community reinforcement approach to alcoholism. *Behaviour Research and Therapy, 14*(5), 339–348.

Azrin, N. H., Sisson, R. W., Meyers, R., & Godley, M. (1982). Alcoholism treatment by disulfiram and community reinforcement therapy. *Journal of Behavior Therapy and Experimental Psychiatry, 13*, 105–112.

Azzi-Lessing, L., & Olsen, L. J. (1996). Substance abuse–affected families in the child welfare system: New challenges, alliances. *Social Work, 41*, 15–23.

Babor, T. F., & Grant, M. (1989). From clinical research to secondary prevention: International collaboration in the development of the Alcohol Use Disorders Identification Test (AUDIT). *Alcohol Health and Research World, 13*(4), 371–374.

Babor, T. F., Higgins-Biddle, J. C., Saunders, J. B., & Monteiro, M. G. (2001). *The Alcohol Use Disorders Identification Test: Guidelines for use in primary care* (2nd ed.). Geneva, Switzerland: World Health Organization.

Babor, T. F., Kranzler, H. R., & Lauerman, R. J. (1989). Early detection of harmful alcohol consumption: Comparison of clinical, laboratory, and self-report screening procedures. *Addictive Behaviors, 13*, 139–157.

Babor, T., Stephens, R., & Marlatt, G. A. (1987). Verbal report methods in clinical research on alcoholism: Response bias and its minimization. *Journal of Studies on Alcohol, 48*, 410–424.

Bae, Y. (2012). Test review: Children's Depression Inventory 2 (CDI 2). *Journal of Psychoeducational Assessment, 30*, 304.

Baer, J. S., Kivlahan, D. R., Blume, A. W., Arthur, W., McKnight, P., & Marlatt, G. A. (2001). Brief intervention for heavy-drinking college students: 4-year follow-up and natural history. *American Journal of Public Health, 91*, 1310–1316.

Baer, J. S., Marlatt, G. A., Kivlahan, D. R., Fromme, K., Larimer, M. E., & Williams, E. (1992). An experimental test of three methods of alcohol risk reduction with young adults. *Journal of Consulting and Clinical Psychology, 60*, 974–979.

Bailley, S. E., Lachar, D., Rhoades, H. M., Diefenbach, G. J., Espadas, A., & Varner, R. V. (2004). Quantifying symptomatic change during acute psychiatric hospitalization using new subscales for the anchored Brief Psychiatric Rating Scale. *Psychological Services, 1*, 68–82.

Baily, V. (1998). Conduct disorders in young children. In P. Graham (Ed.), *Cognitive-behaviour therapy for children and families* (pp. 95–109). New York, NY: Cambridge University Press.

Baker, A., Bucci, S., Lewin, T. J., Kay-Lambkin, F., Constable, P. M., & Carr, V. J. (2006). Cognitive behavioural therapy for substance use disorders in people with psychotic disorders: Randomized controlled trial. *British Journal of Psychiatry, 188*, 439–448.

Baker, H. S., & Baker, M. N. (1987). Heinz Kohut's self-psychology: An overview. *American Journal of Psychiatry, 144*, 1–9.

Bandura, A. (1977). *Social Learning Theory*. Englewood Cliffs, NJ: Prentice Hall.

Bandura, A. (1986). *Social foundations of thought and action: A social cognitive theory*. Englewood Cliffs, NJ: Prentice-Hall.

Bandura, A. (1999). A sociocognitive analysis of substance abuse: An agentic perspective. *Psychological Science*, *10*, 214–217.

Barak, A., Hen, L., Boniel-Nissim, M., & Shapira, N. (2008). A comprehensive review and a meta-analysis of the effectiveness of Internet based psychotherapeutic interventions. *Journal of Technology in the Human Services*, *26*, 109–160.

Barber, J. G. (1995). Working with resistant drug abusers. *Social Work*, *40*, 17–23.

Barber, J. G., & Gilbertson, R. (1996). An experimental study of brief unilateral intervention for partners of heavy drinkers. *Research on Social Work Practice*, *6*, 325–336.

Barber, J. G., & Gilbertson, R. (1997). Unilateral interventions for women living with heavy drinkers. *Social Work*, *42*, 69–78.

Barker, E. D., Oliver, B. R., & Maughan, B. (2010). Co-occurring problems of early onset, persistent, childhood limited, and adolescent onset conduct problem youth. *Journal of Child Psychology and Psychiatry*, *51*, 1217–1226.

Barkley, R. A. (1987). *Defiant children: A clinician's manual for parent training*. New York, NY: Guilford Press.

Barkley, R. A. (1995). *Taking charge of ADHD: The complete authoritative guide for parents*. New York, NY: Guilford Press.

Barkley, R. A. (1997a). Attention-deficit/hyperactivity disorder. In E. J. Mash & L. G. Terdal (Eds.), *Assessment of childhood disorders* (pp. 71–129). New York, NY: Guilford Press.

Barkley, R. A. (1997b). Behavioral inhibition, sustained attention, and executive functions constructing a unifying theory of ADHD. *Psychological Bulletin*, *121*, 65–94.

Barkley, R. A. (2002). Psychosocial treatments for attention deficit/hyperactivity disorder in children. *Journal of Clinical Psychiatry*, *63*, 36–43.

Barkley, R. A., & Edwards, G. (1998). Diagnostic interview, behavior rating scales, and the medical examination. In R. A. Barkley (Ed.), *Attention-deficit hyperactivity disorder: A handbook for diagnosis and treatment* (pp. 263–293). New York, NY: Guilford Press.

Barkley, R. A., Edwards, G., Laneri, M., Fletcher, K., & Meevia, L. (2001). The efficacy of problem-solving communication training alone, behavior management training alone, and their combination for parent-adolescent conflict in teenagers with ADHD and ODD. *Journal of Consulting and Clinical Psychology*, *69*, 926–941.

Barkley, R. A., Shelton, T. L., Crosswait, C., Moorehouse, M., Fletcher, K., Barrett, S., . . . Metevia, L. (2000). Multimethod psychoeducational intervention for preschool children with disruptive behavior: Preliminary results at post-treatment. *Journal of Child Psychology and Psychiatry*, *41*, 319–332.

Barletta, J., Beamish, P., Patrick, M., Andersen, K., & Pappas, N. (1996). Obsessive-compulsive disorder: Emerging standard of care. *Psychotherapy in Private Practice*, *15*, 19–31.

Barlow, D. H. (1988). *Anxiety and its disorders: The nature and treatment of anxiety and panic*. New York, NY: Guilford Press.

Barlow, D. H. (1997). Cognitive-behavioral therapy for panic disorder: Current status. *Journal of Clinical Psychiatry*, *58*(suppl. 2), 32–35.

Barlow, D. H., Allen, L. B., & Choate, M. L. (2004). Toward a unified treatment for emotional disorders. *Behavior Therapy, 35*, 205–230.

Barnes, M. F. (1995). Sex therapy in the couples context: Therapy issues of victims of sexual trauma. *American Journal of Family Therapy, 23*, 351–360.

Barrett, P. M. (1998). Evaluation of cognitive-behavioral group treatments for childhood anxiety disorders. *Journal of Clinical Child Psychology, 27*, 459–468.

Barrett, P. M., Dadds, M. R., & Rapee, R. M. (1996). Family treatment of childhood anxiety: A controlled trial. *Journal of Consulting and Clinical Psychology, 64*, 333–342.

Barrett, P. M., Duffy, A. L., Dadds, M. R., & Rapee, R. M. (2001). Cognitive-behavioral treatment of anxiety disorders in children: Long-term (6-year) follow-up. *Journal of Consulting and Clinical Psychology, 69*, 135–141.

Barrett, P. M., Farrell, L., Pina, A. A., Peris, T. S., & Piacenti, J. (2008). Evidence-based psychosocial treatments for child and adolescent obsessive-compulsive disorder. *Journal of Clinical Child and Adolescent Psychology, 37*, 131–155.

Barrett, P., Healy-Farrell, L., & March, J. S. (2004). Cognitive-behavior family treatment of childhood obsessive compulsive disorder: A controlled trial. *Journal of the American Academy of Child and Adolescent Psychiatry, 43*, 46–62.

Barrios, B. A., & Hartmann, D. P. (1997) Fears and anxieties. In E. J. Mash & L. G. Terdal (Eds.), *Assessment of childhood disorders* (3rd ed., pp. 230–327). New York, NY: Guilford Press.

Barth, R. P. (2009). Preventing child abuse and neglect with parent training: Evidence and opportunities. *Future of Children, 19*, 95–118.

Bartolini, M., Coccia, M., Luzzi, S., Leandro, P., & Ceravolo, M. G. (2004). Motivational symptoms of depression mask preclinical Alzheimer's disease in elderly subjects. *Dementia and Geriatric Cognitive Disorders, 19*, 31–36.

Basen-Engquist, K. (1992). Psychosocial predictors of "safer sex" behavior in young adults. *AIDS Education and Prevention, 4*, 120–134.

Basic Behavioral Science Task Force. (1996). Basic behavioral science research for mental health: Sociocultural and environmental processes. *American Psychologist, 51*, 722–731.

Bastien, D. L. (2010). Pharmacological treatment of combat-induced PTSD: A literature review. *British Journal of Nursing, 19*, 318–321.

Bateman, A., & Fonagy, P. (1999). Effectiveness of partial hospitalization in the treatment of borderline personality disorder: A randomized controlled trial. *American Journal of Psychiatry, 156*, 1563–1569.

Bateman, A., & Fonagy, P. (2001). Treatment of borderline personality disorder with psychoanalytically informed partial hospitalization: An 18-month follow-up. *American Journal of Psychiatry, 158*, 36–42.

Bateman, A., & Fonagy, P. (2008). 8-year follow-up of patients treated for borderline personality disorder: Mentalization-based treatment versus treatment as usual. *American Journal of Psychiatry, 165*, 631–638.

Bateman, A., & Fonagy, P. (2009). Randomized controlled trial of outpatient mentalization-based treatment versus structured clinical management for borderline personality disorder. *American Journal of Psychiatry, 166*, 1355–1364.

Bath, H. I., & Haapala, D. A. (1993). Intensive family preservation services with abused and neglected children: An examination of group differences. *Child Abuse and Neglect, 17*, 213–225.

Baucom, D. H., & Epstein, N. (1990). *Cognitive-behavioral marital therapy*. New York, NY: Brunner/Mazel.

Baucom, D. H., Epstein, N., & Rankin, L. A. (1995). Cognitive aspects of cognitive behavioral marital therapy. In N. S. Jacobson & A. S. Gurman (Eds.), *Clinical handbook of couple therapy* (pp. 65–90). New York, NY: Guilford Press.

Baucom, D. H., Mueser, K. T., Shoham, V., Daiuto, A. D., & Stickle, T. R. (1998). Empirically supported couple and family interventions for marital distress and adult mental health problems. *Journal of Consulting and Clinical Psychology*, *66*, 53–88.

Baucom, K. J. W., Sevier, M., Eldridge, K. A., Doss, B. D., & Christensen, A. (2011). Observed communications in couples two years after integrative and traditional behavioral couple therapy: Outcome and link with five-year follow-up. *Journal of Consulting and Clinical Psychology*, *79*, 565–576.

Baum, C. G. (1989). Conduct disorders. In T. H. Ollendick & M. Hersen (Eds.), *Handbook of childhood psychopathology* (2nd ed., pp. 171–196). New York, NY: Plenum Press.

Baynes, D., Mulholland, C., Cooper, S. J., Montgomery, R. C., MacFlynn, G., Lynch, G., . . . King, D. J. (2000). Depressive symptoms in stable chronic schizophrenia: Prevalence and relationship to psychopathology and treatment. *Schizophrenia Research*, *45*, 47–56. doi: 10.1016/S0920-9964(99)00205-4.

Beach, S. R., & O'Leary, K. D. (1992). Treating depression in the context of marital discord: Outcome and predictors of response for marital therapy vs. cognitive therapy. *Behavior Therapy*, *23*, 507–528.

Beal, A. C., Ausiello, J., & Perrin, J. M. (2001). Social influences on health-risk behaviors among minority school students. *Journal of Adolescent Health*, *28*, 474–480.

Beauvais, F. (1998). American Indians and alcohol. *Alcohol Health and Research World*, *22*, 253–259.

Bebout, R., Drake, R., Xie, H., McHugo, G., & Harris, M. (1997). Housing status among formerly homeless dually diagnosed adults. *Psychiatric Services*, *48*(7), 936–941.

Beck, A. T. (1976). *Cognitive therapy and the emotional disorders*. New York, NY: New American Library.

Beck, A. T. (1996). Beyond belief: A theory of modes, personality and psychopathology. In P. M. Salkovskis (Ed.), *Frontiers of cognitive therapy* (pp. 1–25). New York, NY: Guilford Press.

Beck, A. T., Brown, G., Steer, R. A., & Weissman,, A. N. (1991). Factor analysis of the Dysfunctional Attitude Scale in a clinical population. *Psychological Assessment*, *3*, 478–483.

Beck, A. T., & Emery, G. (with Greenberg, R. L.). (1985). *Anxiety and phobias: A cognitive perspective*. New York, NY: Basic Books.

Beck, A. T., Rush, A. J., Shaw, B. F., & Emery, G. (1979). *Cognitive therapy of depression*. New York, NY: Guilford Press.

Beck, A. T., Steer, R. A., & Garbin, M. G. (1988). Psychometric properties of the Beck Depression Inventory: Twenty-five years of evaluation. *Clinical Psychology Review*, *8*, 77–100.

Beck, A. T., Ward, C. H., Mendelson, M., Mock, J., & Erbaugh, J. (1961). An inventory for measuring depression. *Archives of General Psychiatry*, *4*, 561–571.

Becker, J. V., & Johnson, B. R. (2001). Treating juvenile sex offenders. In J. B. Ashford, B. D. Sales, & W. H. Reid (Eds.), *Treating adult and juvenile offenders with special needs* (pp. 273–289). Washington, DC: American Psychological Association.

Beckerman, N. L., Letteney, S., & Lorber, K. (2000). Key emotional issues for couples of mixed HIV status. *Social Work in Health Care, 31*, 25–41.

Beckett, J. O., & Dungee-Anderson, D. (2000). Older persons of color: Asian-Pacific Islander Americans, African Americans, Hispanic Americans and American Indians. In R. L. Schneider, N. P. Kropf, & A. J. Kisor (Eds.), *Gerontological social work* (pp. 257–301). Belmont, CA: Wadsworth.

Beckman, L. J. (1994). Treatment needs of women with alcohol problems. *Alcohol Health and Research World, 18*, 206–211.

Bedell, J. R., Hunter, R. H., & Corrigan, P. W. (1997). Current approaches to assessment and treatment of persons with serious mental illness. *Professional Psychology: Research and Practice, 28*, 217–228.

Bedell, J. R., & Lennox, S. S. (1997). *Handbook for communication and problem-solving skills training: A cognitive-behavioral approach*. New York, NY: Wiley.

Bedregal, L. E., Sobell, L. C., Sobell, M. B., & Simco, M. (2006). Psychometric characteristics of a Spanish version of the DAST-10 and the RAGS. *Addictive Behaviors, 31*, 309–319.

Beekman, A., de Beurs, E., van Balkom, A., Deeg, D., van Dyck, R., & van Tilburg, W. (2000). Anxiety and depression in later life: Co-occurrence and communality of risk factors. *American Journal of Psychiatry, 157*, 89–95.

Begel, A. M., Dumas, J. E., & Hanson, R. F. (2010). Predicting child abuse potential: An empirical investigation of two theoretical frameworks. *Journal of Child and Adolescent Psychology, 39*, 208–219.

Beidas, R. S., & Kendall, P. C. (2010). Training therapists in evidence-based practice: A critical review of studies from a systems-contextual perspective. *Clinical Psychology: Science and Practice, 17*, 1–30.

Beidel, D. C., & Morris, T. L. (1995). Social phobia. In J. S. March (Ed.), *Anxiety disorders in children and adolescents* (pp. 181–211). New York, NY: Guilford Press.

Bellack, A. S., & DiClemente, C. C. (1999). Treating substance abuse among patients with schizophrenia. *Psychiatric Services, 50*, 75–80.

Bellack, A. S., Mueser, K. T., Gingerich, S., & Agresta, J. (1997). *Social skills training for schizophrenia: A step-by-step guide*. New York, NY: Guilford Press.

Bellamy, J. L., Bledsoe, S. E., Mullen, E. J., Fang, L., & Manuel, J. I. (2008). Agency-university partnership for evidence-based practice in social work. *Journal of Social Work Education, 44*, 55–75.

Bellamy, J. L., Mullen, E. J., Satterfield, J. M., Newhouse, R. P., Ferguson, M., Brownson, R. C., & Spring, B. (2013). Implementing evidence-based practice education in social work: A transdisciplinary approach. *Research on Social Work Practice, 23*, 426–436.

Belsky, J. (1993). Etiology of child maltreatment: A developmental-ecological analysis. *Psychological Bulletin, 114*, 413–434.

Benbenishty, R. (1996). Integrating research and practice: Time for a new agenda. *Research on Social Work Practice, 6*, 77–82.

Bennett, L. A., Janca, A., Grant, B. F., & Sartorius, N. (1993). Boundaries between normal and pathological drinking. *Alcohol Health and Research World, 17(3)*, 190–195.

Bennett, L. W. (1995). Substance abuse and the domestic assault of women. *Social Work, 40*, 760–771.

Bennett, M. E., McCrady, B. S., Johnson, V., & Pandina, R. J. (1999). Problem drinking from young adulthood to adulthood: Patterns, predictors and outcomes. *Journal of Studies on Alcohol, 60*, 605–614.

Benson, H. (1975). *The relaxation response*. New York, NY: Avon.

Bentley, K. J. (1998). Psychopharmacological treatment of schizophrenia: What social workers need to know. *Research on Social Work Practice, 8*, 384–405.

Bergmark, A. (2008). On treatment mechanisms: What can we learn from the COMBINE study? *Addiction, 103*, 703–705.

Berry, J. W. (1986). The acculturation process and refugee behavior. In C. L. Williams & J. Westermeyer (Eds.), *Refugee mental health in resettlement countries* (pp. 25–36). New York, NY: Hemisphere.

Betchen, S. (2007). Premature ejaculation: An integrative intersystems approach for couples. *Journal of Family Psychotherapy, 20*, 241–260.

Beutler, L. E., Clarkin, J. F., & Bongar, B. (2000). *Guidelines for the systematic treatment of the depressed patient*. New York, NY: Oxford University Press.

Bezirganian, S., Cohen, P., & Brook, J. S. (1993). The impact of mother-child interaction on the development of borderline personality disorder. *American Journal of Psychiatry, 150*, 1836–1842.

Bibb, J. L., & Chambless, D. L. (1986). Alcohol use and abuse among diagnosed agoraphobics. *Behavior Research and Therapy, 24*, 49–58.

Biederman, J., Rosenbaum, J. F., Chaloff, J., & Kagan, J. (1995). Behavioral inhibition as a risk factor. In J. S. March (Ed.), *Anxiety disorders in children and adolescents* (pp. 61–81). New York, NY: Guilford Press.

Birditt, K. S., Brown, E., Orbuch, T. L., & McIlvance, J. M. (2010). Marital conflict behaviors and implications for divorce over 16 years. *Journal of Marriage and Family, 72*, 1188–1204.

Birleson, P. (1981). The validity of depressive disorder in childhood and the development of a self-rating scale: A research report. *Journal of Child Psychology and Psychiatry, 22*, 73–88.

Birleson, P., Hudson, I., Buchanan, D. G., & Wolff, S. (1987). Clinical evaluation of a self-rating scale for depressive disorder in childhood (Depression Self-Rating Scale). *Journal of Child Psychology and Psychiatry, 28*, 43–60.

Birmaher, B., Brent, D. A., Chiappetta, L., Bridge, J., Monga, S., & Baugher, M. (1999). Psychometric properties of the Screen for Child Anxiety Related Emotional Disorders (SCARED): A replication study. *Journal of the American Academy of Child and Adolescent Psychiatry, 38*, 1230–1236.

Birmaher, B., Brent, D. A., Kolko, D. J., Baugher, M., Bridge, J., Holder, D., . . . Ulloa, R. E. (2000). Clinical outcome after short-term psychotherapy for adolescents with major depressive disorder. *Archives of General Psychiatry, 57*, 29–36.

Birmaher, B., Khetarpal, S., Brent, D., Cully, M., Balach, L., Kaufman, J., & Beer, S. M. (1997). The Screen for Child Anxiety Related Emotional Disorders (SCARED): Scale construction and psychometric characteristics. *Journal of the American Academy of Child and Adolescent Psychiatry, 36*, 545–553.

Birmaher, B., Ryan, N. D., Williamson, D. E., Brent, D. A., & Kaufman, J. (1996). Childhood and adolescent depression: A review of the past 10 years: Part II. *Journal of the American Academy of Child and Adolescent Psychiatry, 35,* 1575–1583.

Bisson, J. I., & Shepherd, J. P. (1995). Psychological reactions of victims of violent crime. *British Journal of Psychiatry, 167,* 718–720.

Black, B. (1995). Separation anxiety disorder and panic disorder. In J. S. March (Ed.), *Anxiety disorders in children and adolescents* (pp. 212–234). New York, NY: Guilford Press.

Black, D. W., Monahan, P., Baumgard, C. H., & Bell, S. E. (1997). Predictors of long-term outcome in 45 men with antisocial personality disorder. *Annals of Clinical Psychiatry, 9,* 211–217.

Blake, D. D., & Sonnenberg, R. T. (1998). Outcome research on behavioral and cognitive-behavioral treatments for trauma survivors. In V. M. Follette, J. I. Ruzek, & F. R. Abueg (Eds.), *Cognitive-behavioral therapies for trauma* (pp. 15–47). New York, NY: Guilford Press.

Blake, D. D., Weathers, F. W., Nagy, L. M., Kaloupek, D. G., Gusman, F. D., Charney, D. S., & Keane, T. M. (1995). The development of a clinician-administered PTSD scale. *Journal of Traumatic Stress, 8,* 75–90.

Blake, D. D., Weathers, F. W., Nagy, L. M., Kaloupek, D. G., Klauminzer, G., Charney, D. S., & Keanse, T. M. (1990). A clinician rating scale for assessing current and lifetime PTSD: The CAPS-1. *Behavior Therapist, 13,* 187–188.

Blanchard, E. B. (1994). Behavioral medicine and health psychology. In A. E. Bergin & S. L. Garfield (Eds.), *The handbook of psychotherapy and behavior change* (4th ed., pp. 701–733). New York, NY: Wiley.

Blanco, C., Okuda, M., Wright, C., Hasin, D. S., Grant, B. F., Liu, S., & Olfson, M. (2008). Mental health of college students and their non-college-attending peers. *Archives of General Psychiatry, 65,* 1429–1437.

Blankers, M., Koeter, M. W. J., & Schippers, G. M. (2011). Internet therapy versus Internet self-help versus no treatment for problematic alcohol use: A randomized controlled trial. *Journal of Consulting and Clinical Psychology, 79,* 330–341.

Blankertz, L. E., & Cnaan, R. A. (1994, December). Assessing the impact of two residential programs for dually diagnosed homeless individuals. *Social Service Review,* 536–560.

Blazer, D. G., & Wu, L. (2011). The epidemiology of alcohol use disorders and subthreshold dependence in a middle-aged and elderly community sample. *American Journal of Geriatric Psychiatry, 19,* 685.

Blechman, E. A., & Brownell, K. D. (1998). *Behavioral medicine and women: A comprehensive handbook.* New York, NY: Guilford Press.

Blechman, E. A., & Vryan, K. D. (2000). Prosocial family therapy: A manualized preventive intervention for juvenile offenders. *Aggression and Violent Behavior, 5,* 343–378.

Blonigen, D. M., Timko, C., Finney, J. W., Moos, B. S., & Moos, R. H. (2011). Alcoholics Anonymous attendance, decreases in impulsivity and drinking and psychosocial outcomes over 16 years: Moderated mediation from a developmental perspective. *Addiction, 106,* 1267–1277.

Bloom, M., Fischer, J., & Orme, J. G. (2009). *Evaluating practice: Guidelines for the accountable professional* (6th ed.). New York, NY: Pearson.

Blosnich, J. R., & Bossarte, R. M. (2009). Comparisons of intimate partner violence among partners in same-sex and opposite-sex relationships in the United States. *American Journal of Public Health, 99*, 2182–2184.

Blum, R. W., Kelly, A., & Ireland, M. (2001). Health-risk behaviors and protective factors among adolescents with mobility impairments and learning and emotional disabilities. *Journal of Adolescent Health, 28*, 481–490.

Blumenthal, S. J. (1994). Women and depression. *Journal of Women's Health, 3*, 467–479.

Blythe, B. J., Salley, M. P., & Jayaratne, S. (1994). A review of intensive family preservation services research. *Social Work Research, 18*, 213–224.

Bodholdt, R. H., Richards, H. R., & Gacono, C. B. (2000). Assessing psychopathy in adults: The Psychopathy Checklist–Revised and screening version. In C. B. Gacono (Ed.), *The clinical and forensic assessment of psychopathy: A practitioner's guide* (pp. 55–86). Mahwah, NJ: Erlbaum.

Bogerts, B. (1993). Recent advances in the neuropathology of schizophrenia. *Schizophrenia Bulletin, 19*, 431–445.

Bograd, M., & Mederos, F. (1999). Battering and couples therapy: Universal screening and selection of treatment and modality. *Journal of Marital and Family Therapy, 25*, 291–312.

Bohn, M. J., Babor, T. F., & Kranzler, H. R. (1995). Alcohol Use Disorders Identification Test (AUDIT): Validation of a screening instrument for use in medical settings. *Journal of Studies on Alcohol, 56*, 423–432.

Bohus, M., Haaf, B., Simms, T., Limberger, M. F., Schmahl, C., Unckel, C., . . . Linehan, M. M. (2004). Effectiveness of inpatient dialectical behavior therapy for borderline personality disorder: A controlled trial. *Behaviour Research and Therapy, 42*, 487–499.

Bolton, D., Luckie, M., & Steinberg, D. (1995). Long-term course of obsessive-compulsive disorder treated in adolescence. *Journal of the American Academy of Child and Adolescent Psychiatry, 34*, 1441–1450.

Bolton, D., & Perrin, S. (2008). Evaluation of exposure with response prevention for obsessive-compulsive disorder in childhood and adolescence. *Journal of Behavior Therapy, 39*, 11–22.

Bolton, D., Williams, T., Perrin, S., Atkinson, L., Gallop, C., Waite, P., & Salkovskis, P. (2011). Randomized controlled trial of full and brief cognitive-behavior therapy and wait-list for pediatric obsessive-compulsive disorder. *Journal of Child Psychology and Psychiatry, 52*, 1269–1278.

Bolton, J. M., & Robinson, J. (2010). Population-attributable fractions of axis I and axis II mental disorders for suicide attempts: Findings from a representative sample of the adult, noninstitutionalized US population. *American Journal of Public Health, 100*, 2473–2480. doi: 10.2105/AJPH.2010.192252.

Bond, G. R. (2004). Supported employment: Evidence for an evidence-based practice. *Psychiatric Rehabilitation Journal, 27*, 345–359.

Bond, G. R., Becker, D. R., Drake, R. E., Rapp, C. A., Meisler, N., Lehman, A. F., . . . Blyler, C. R. (2001). Implementing supported employment as an evidence-based practice. *Psychiatric Services, 52*, 313–322.

Bond, G. R., Drake, R. E., & Becker, D. R. (2008). An update on randomized controlled trials of evidence-based supported employment. *Psychiatric Rehabilitation Journal, 31*, 280–290.

Bond, G. R., Drake, R. E., & Becker, D. R. (2010). Beyond evidence-based practice: Nine ideal features of a mental health intervention. *Research on Social Work Practice, 20,* 493–501.

Bond, G. R., Drake, R. E., Mueser, K. T., & Becker, D. R. (1997). An update on supported employment for people with severe mental illness. *Psychiatric Services, 48,* 335–346.

Bongar, B., Maris, R. W., Berman, A. L., & Litman, R. E. (1992). Outpatient standards of care and the suicidal patient. *Suicide and Life-Threatening Behavior, 22,* 453–477.

Borduin, C. M., Henggeler, S. W., Blaske, D. M., & Stein, R. (1990). Multisystemic treatment of adolescent sexual offenders. *International Journal of Offender Therapy and Comparative Criminology, 35,* 105–114.

Borduin, C. M., Mann, B. J., Cone, L. T., Henggeler, S. W., Fucci, B. R., Blaske, D. M., & Williams, R. A. (1995). Multisystemic treatment of serious juvenile offenders: Long-term prevention of criminality and violence. *Journal of Consulting and Clinical Psychology, 63,* 569–578.

Borntrager, C. F., Chorpita, B. F., Higa-McMillan, C., & Weisz, J. R. (2009). Provider attitudes toward evidence-based practices: Are the concerns with the evidence or with the manuals? *Psychiatric Services, 60,* 677–681.

Borsari, B., & Carey, K. B. (2000). Effects of brief motivational intervention with college student drinkers. *Journal of Consulting and Clinical Psychology, 68,* 728–733.

Botvin, G. J., Baker, E., Dusenbury, L. D., Botvin, E. M., & Diaz, T. (1995). Long-term follow-up results of a randomized drug abuse prevention trial in a white middle-class population. *JAMA, 273,* 1106–1112.

Botvin, G. J., Baker, E., Dusenbury, L., Tortu, S., & Botvin, E. M. (1990). Preventing adolescent drug abuse through a multimodal cognitive-behavioral approach: Results of a 3-year study. *Journal of Consulting and Clinical Psychology, 58,* 437–446.

Botvin, G. J., Griffin, K. W., Diaz, T., & Ifill-Williams, M. (2001). Preventing binge drinking during early adolescence: One- and two-year follow-up of a school-based prevention intervention. *Psychology of Addictive Behaviors, 15,* 360–365.

Bouchery, E. E., Harwood, H. J., Sacks, J. J., Simon, C. J., & Brewer, R. D. (2011). Economic costs of excessive alcohol consumption in the U.S., 2006. *American Journal of Preventative Medicine, 41,* 516–524.

Bourke, M. L., & Donohue, B. (1996). Assessment and treatment of juvenile sex offenders: An empirical review. *Journal of Child Sexual Abuse, 5,* 47–70.

Bouton, M. E. (2000). A learning theory perspective on lapse, relapse and the maintenance of behavior change. *Health Psychology, 19,* 57–63.

Bowers, W. A., Evans, K., & van Cleve, L. (1996). Treatment of adolescent eating disorders. In M. A. Reinecke, F. M. Dattilio, & A. Freeman (Eds.), *Cognitive therapy with children and adolescents: A case book for clinical practice* (pp. 227–250). New York, NY: Guilford Press.

Bowlby, J. (1969). *Attachment and loss: Vol. 1. Attachment.* New York, NY: Basic Books.

Bowlby, J. (1980). *Attachment and loss: Vol. 3. Loss, sadness and depression.* New York, NY: Basic Books.

Bowman, M. L. (1999). Individual difference in posttraumatic distress: Problems with the DSM-IV model. *Canadian Journal of Psychiatry, 44*, 21–33.

Bradburn, N. M. (1969). *The structure of psychological well-being.* Chicago: Aldine.

Bradford, K. (2010). Screening for couples for intimate partner violence. *Journal of Family Psychotherapy, 21*, 76–82.

Bradshaw, W. (1996). Structured group work in individuals with schizophrenia: A coping skills approach. *Research on Social Work Practice, 6*, 139–153.

Brady, J. E., & Li, G. (2013). Prevalence of alcohol and other drugs in fatally injured drivers. *Addiction, 108*, 104–114.

Brady, K. T., & Sinha, R. (2005). Co-occurring mental and substance use disorders: The neurobiological effects of chronic stress. *American Journal of Psychiatry, 162*, 1483–1493. doi: 10.1176/appi.ajp.162.8.1483.

Bramblett, R., Wodarski, J. S., & Thyer, B. A. (1991). Social work practice with antisocial children: A review of current issues. *Journal of Applied Social Sciences, 15*, 169–182.

Brandt, J. R., Kennedy, W. A., Patrick, C. J., & Curtin, J. J. (1997). Assessment of psychopathy in a population of incarcerated adolescent offenders. *Psychological Assessment, 9*, 429–435.

Brannen, S. J., & Rubin, A. (1996). Comparing the effectiveness of gender-specific and couples groups in a court-mandated spouse abuse treatment program. *Research on Social Work Practice, 6*, 405–424.

Braswell, L., & Bloomquist, M. L. (1991). *Cognitive-behavioral therapy with ADHD children: Child, family, and school interventions.* New York, NY: Guilford Press.

Bray, J. W., Cowell, A. J., & Hinde, J. M. (2011). A systematic review and meta-analysis of health care utilization outcomes in alcohol screening and brief intervention trials. *Medical Care, 49*, 287–294.

Brems, C., & Johnson, M. E. (1997). Clinical implications of the co-occurrence of substance use and other psychiatric disorders. *Professional Psychology: Research and Practice, 28*, 437–447.

Brener, N. D., & Collins, J. L. (1998). Co-occurrence of health-risk behaviors among adolescents in the United States. *Journal of Adolescent Health, 22*, 209–213.

Brennan, P. L., & Moos, R. H. (1996). Late-life drinking behavior. *Alcohol Health and Research World, 20*, 197–204.

Brent, D. A. (2011). Preventing youth suicide: Time to ask how. *Journal of the American Academy of Child and Adolescent Psychiatry, 50*, 738–740.

Brent, D. A., Holder, D., Kolko, D., Birmaher, B., Baugher, M., Roth, C., . . . Johnson, B. A. (1997). A clinical psychotherapy trial for adolescent depression comparing cognitive, family and supportive therapy. *Archives of General Psychiatry, 54*, 877–885.

Brent, D. A., Kolko, D. J., Birmaher, B., Baugher, M., & Bridge, J. (1999). A clinical trial for adolescent depression: Predictors of additional treatment in the acute and follow-up phases of the trial. *Journal of the Academy of Child and Adolescent Psychiatry, 38*, 263–270.

Brent, D. A., Kolko, D. J., Birmaher, B., Baugher, M., Bridge, J., Roth, C., & Holder, D. (1998). Predictors of treatment efficacy in a clinical trial of three psychosocial treatments for adolescent depression. *Journal of the American Academy of Child and Adolescent Psychiatry, 37*, 906–914.

Breslau, N., Davis, G., Andreski, P., Federman, B., & Anthony, J. C. (1998). Epidemiological findings on post traumatic stress disorder and co-morbid disorders in the general population. In B. P. Dohrenwend (Ed.), *Adversity, stress and psychopathology* (pp. 319–330). New York, NY: Oxford University Press.

Breslau, N., Davis, G., Andreski, P., & Peterson, E. (1991). Traumatic events and posttraumatic stress disorder in an urban population of young adults. *Archives of General Psychiatry, 48*, 216–222.

Brestan, E. V., & Eyberg, S. (1998). Effective psychosocial treatments of conduct-disordered children and adolescents: 29 years, 82 studies, and 5,272 kids. *Journal of Clinical Child Psychology, 27*, 180–189.

Brewin, C. R., & Holmes, E. A. (2003). Psychological theories of posttraumatic stress disorder. *Clinical Psychology Review, 23*(3), 339–376.

Bride, B. E. (2001). Single-gender treatment of substance abuse: Effect on treatment retention and completion. *Social Work Research, 25*, 223–232.

Bridle, C., Spanjers, K., Patel, S., Atherton, N. M., & Lamb, S. E. (2012). Effect of exercise on depression severity in older people: Systematic review and meta-analysis of randomized controlled trials. *British Journal of Psychiatry, 201*, 180–185.

Briere, J. (1992). *Child abuse trauma: Theory and treatment of lasting effects.* Newbury Park, CA: Sage.

Briere, J. (1996). *Trauma Symptom Checklist for Children (TSCC).* Odessa, FL: Psychological Assessment Resources.

Brown, G. W. (1998). Loss and depressive disorders. In B. P. Dohrenwend (Ed.), *Adversity, stress and psychopathology* (pp. 358–370). New York, NY: Oxford University Press.

Brown, J., Cohen, P., Johnson, J. G., & Salzinger, S. (1998). A longitudinal analysis of risk factors for child maltreatment: Findings of a 17-year prospective study of officially recorded and self-reported child abuse and neglect. *Child Abuse and Neglect, 22*, 1065–1078.

Brown, L. K., & Lourie, K. J. (2001). Motivational interviewing and the prevention of HIV among adolescents. In P. M. Monti, S. M. Colby, & T. A. O'Leary (Eds.), *Adolescents, alcohol and substance abuse: Reaching teens through brief interventions* (pp. 244–274). New York, NY: Guilford Press.

Brown, R. (2010). Associations with substance abuse treatment completion among drug court participants. *Substance Use and Misuse, 45*, 1874–1891.

Brown, R. T., Antonuccio, D. O., DuPaul, G. J., Fristad, M. A., King, C. A., Leslie, L. K., ... Vitiello, B. (2008). *Childhood mental health disorders: Evidence base and contextual factors for psychological, psychopharmacological, and combined interventions.* Washington, DC: American Psychological Association.

Brown, S. A. (1985). Expectancies vs. background in the prediction of college drinking patterns. *Journal of Consulting and Clinical Psychology, 53*, 123–130.

Brown, S. A., Christiansen, B. A., & Goldman, M. S. (1987). The Alcohol Expectancy Questionnaire: An instrument for the assessment of adolescent and adult alcohol expectancies. *Journal of Studies on Alcohol, 48*, 483–491.

Brown, S., Goldman, M., Inn, A., & Anderson, L. (1980). Expectancies of reinforcement from alcohol: Their domain and relation to drinking patterns. *Journal of Consulting and Clinical Psychology, 48*, 419–426.

Brown, T. G., Werk, A., Caplan, T., & Seraganian, P. (1999). Violent substance abusers in domestic violence treatment. *Violence and Victims, 14*, 179–190.

Brownell, K. D., Marlatt, G. A., Lichtenstein, E., & Wilson, G. T. (1986). Understanding and preventing relapse. *American Psychologist, 41*, 765–782.

Brunk, M., Henggeler, S. W., & Whelan, J. P. (1987). Comparison of multisystemic therapy and parent training in the brief treatment of child abuse and neglect. *Journal of Consulting and Clinical Psychology, 55*, 171–178.

Buchanan, R. W. (1995). Clozapine efficacy and safety. *Schizophrenia Bulletin, 21*, 579–591.

Buchanan, R. W., Kreyenbuhl, J., Kelly, D. L., Noel, J. M., Boggs, D. L., Fischer, B. A., . . . Keller, W. (2010). The 2009 Schizophrenia PORT psychopharmacological treatment recommendations and summary statements. *Schizophrenia Bulletin, 36*, 71–93.

Buckstein, O. G. (1995). *Adolescent substance abuse: Assessment, prevention and treatment*. New York, NY: Wiley.

Buckstein, O. G., Brent, D. A., & Kaminer, Y. (1989). Comorbidity of substance abuse and other psychiatric disorders in adolescents. *American Journal of Psychiatry, 146*, 1131–1141.

Budd, K. S., Felix, E. D., Poindexter, L. M., Naik-Polan, A. T., & Sloss, C. F. (2002). Clinical assessment of children in child protection cases: An empirical analysis. *Professional Psychology: Research and Practice, 33*, 3–12.

Budd, K. S., Poindexter, L. M., Felix, E. D., & Naik-Polan, A. T. (2001). Clinical assessment of parents in child protection cases: An empirical analysis. *Law and Human Behavior, 25*, 93–108.

Buila, S. (2009). Evidence-based research on the effectiveness of psychosocial interventions for bipolar disorder. *Social Work in Mental Health, 7*, 572–586.

Burke, J. D., Waldman, I., & Lahey, B. B. (2010). Predictive validity of childhood oppositional defiant disorder and conduct disorder: Implications for DSM-V. *Journal of Abnormal Psychology, 119*, 739–751.

Burlew, K., Larios, S., Suarez-Morales, L., Holmes, B., Venner, K., & Chavez, R. (2011). Increasing ethnic minority participation in substance abuse clinical trials: Lessons learned in the National Institute on Drug Abuse's clinical trial network. *Cultural Diversity and Ethnic Minority Psychology, 17*, 345–356.

Burnett-Zeigler, I., Ilgen, M., Valenstein, M., Divin, K., Gorman, L., Blow, A., . . . Chermack, S. (2011). Prevalence and correlates of alcohol misuse among returning Afghanistan and Iraq veterans. *Addictive Behaviors, 36*, 801–806.

Burnette, D. (1998). Grandparents rearing grandchildren: A school-based small group intervention. *Research on Social Work Practice, 8*, 10–27.

Burnette, M. F., & Drake, R. E. (1997). Gender differences in patients with schizophrenia and substance abuse. *Comprehensive Psychiatry, 38*,109–116.

Burns, B., & Santos, A. B. (1995). Assertive community treatment: An update of randomized trials. *Psychiatric Services, 46*, 669–675.

Burns, G. L., & Patterson, D. R. (1990). Conduct problem behaviors in a stratified random sample of children and adolescents: New standardization data on the Eyberg Child Behavior Inventory. *Psychological Assessment: A Journal of Consulting and Clinical Psychology, 2*, 391–397.

Burns, G. L., & Patterson, D. R. (2000). Factor structure of the Eyberg Child Behavior Inventory: A parent rating scale of oppositional defiant behavior toward adults, inattentive behavior, and conduct problem behavior. *Journal of Clinical Child Psychology, 29*, 569–577.

Burns, G. L., Patterson, D. R., Nussbaum, B. R., & Parker, C. M. (1991). Disruptive behaviors in an outpatient pediatric population: Additional standardization data on the Eyberg Child Behavior Inventory. *Psychological Assessment: A Journal of Consulting and Clinical Psychology, 3,* 202–207.

Burns, T., Catty, J., Becker, T., Drake, R. E., Fioritti, A., Knapp, M., . . . Wiersma, D. (for EQOLISE group) (2007). The effectiveness of supported employment for people with severe mental illness: A randomized controlled trial. *Lancet, 370,* 1146–1152.

Busby, D. M., Christensen, C., Crane, D. R., & Larson, J. H. (1995). A revision of the dyadic adjustment scale for use with distressed and nondistressed couples: Construct hierarchy and multidimensional scales. *Journal of Marital and Family Therapy, 21,* 289–308.

Butler, A. C., Chapman, J. E., Forman, E. M., & Beck, A. T. (2006). The empirical status of cognitive behavioral therapy: A review of the meta-analyses. *Clinical Psychology Review, 26,* 17–31.

Butterfield, M. I., & Becker, M. E. (2002). Posttraumatic stress disorder in women: Assessment and treatment in primary care. *Women's Mental Health, 29,* 151–170.

Byers, A. L., Yaffe, K., Covinsky, K. E., Friedman, M. B., & Bruce, M. L. (2010). High occurrence of mood and anxiety disorders among older adults. *Archives of General Psychiatry, 67,* 489–496.

Bystritsky, A., Munford, P. R., Rosen, R. M., Martin, K. M., Vapnik, T., Gorbis, E. E., & Wolson, R. C. (1996). A preliminary study of partial hospital management of severe obsessive-compulsive disorder. *Psychiatric Services, 47,* 170–174.

Bywater, T., Hutchings, J., Daley, D., Whitaker, C., Yeo, S. T., Jones, K., . . . Edwards, R. T. (2009). Long-term effectiveness of a parenting intervention for children at risk of developing conduct disorder. *British Journal of Psychiatry, 195,* 318–324.

Cadoret, R., & Cain, C. (1980). Sex differences in predictors of antisocial behavior in adoptees. *Archives of General Psychiatry, 37,* 1171–1175.

Caetano, R. (1993). Ethnic minority groups and Alcoholics Anonymous: A review. In B. S. McCrady & W. R. Miller (Eds.), *Research on Alcoholics Anonymous: Opportunities and alternatives* (pp. 209–232). New Brunswick, NJ: Rutgers Center of Alcohol Studies.

Caetano, R., & Clark, C. L. (1998). Trends in alcohol consumption patterns among whites, blacks and Hispanics: 1984 and 1995. *Journal of Studies on Alcohol, 59,* 659–668.

Caetano, R., Clark, C. L., & Tam, T. (1998). Alcohol consumption among racial/ethnic minorities. *Alcohol Health and Research World, 22,* 233–241.

Caetano, R., Vaeth, P. A. C., & Ramisetty-Mikler, S. (2008). Intimate partner violence victim and perpetrator characteristics among couples in the United States. *Journal of Family Violence, 23,* 507–518.

Cahill, S., Carrigan, M., & Frueh, B. (1999). Does EMDR work? And if so, why? A critical review of the controlled outcome and dismantling research. *Journal of Anxiety Disorders, 13,* 5–33.

Calabria, B., Shakeshaft, A. P., & Havard, A. (2011). A systematic and methodological review of interventions for young people experiencing alcohol-related harm. *Addiction, 106,* 1406–1418.

Caldwell, R. M., Silver, N. C., & Strada, M. (2010). Substance abuse, familial factors, and mental health: Exploring racial and ethnic group differences among African-American, Caucasian, and Hispanic juvenile offenders. *American Journal of Family Therapy*, *38*, 310–321.

Callaway, J. T. (1998). Psychopharmacological treatment of dementia. *Research on Social Work Practice, 8*, 452–474.

Calzada, E. J., Basil, S., & Fernandez, Y. (2012). What Latina mothers think of evidence-based parenting practices: A qualitative study of treatment acceptability. *Cognitive and Behavioral Practice, 20*, 362–374.

Camasso, M. J., & Jagannathan, R. (2000). Modeling the reliability and predictive validity of risk assessment in child protective services. *Children and Youth Services Review, 22*, 873–896.

Campbell, D., & Stanley, J. (1963). *Experimental and quasi-experimental designs for research*. Chicago, IL: Rand McNally.

Canuso, C. M., Bossie, C. A., Zhu, Y., Youseff, E., & Dunner, D. L. (2008). Psychotic symptoms in patients with bipolar mania. *Journal of Affective Disorders, 111*, 164–169.

Caouette, J. D., & Guyer, A. E. (2014). Gaining insight into adolescent vulnerability for social anxiety from developmental cognitive neuroscience. *Developmental Social and Affective Neuroscience, 8*, 65–76.

Carey, K. B. (1993). Situational determinants of heavy drinking among college students. *Journal of Counseling Psychology, 40*, 217–220.

Carey, K. B. (1996a). Substance use reduction in the context of outpatient psychiatric treatment: A collaborative, motivational, harm reduction approach. *Community Mental Health Journal, 32*, 291–306.

Carey, K. B. (1996b). Treatment of co-occurring substance abuse and major mental illness. *New Directions for Mental Health Services, 70*, 19–31.

Carey, K. B., Cocco, K. M., & Simons, J. S. (1996). Concurrent validity of clinicians' ratings of substance abuse among psychiatric outpatients. *Psychiatric Services, 47*, 842–847.

Carey K. B., Scott-Sheldon, L. A. J., Carey, M., & DeMartini, K. S. (2007). Individual-level interventions to reduce college student drinking: A meta-analytic review. *Addictive Behaviors, 32*, 2469–2494.

Carey, K. B., & Teitelbaum, L. M. (1996). Goals and methods of alcohol assessment. *Professional Psychology: Research and Practice, 27*, 460–466.

Carey, M. P., Carey, K. B., & Kalichman, S. C. (1997). Risk for human immunodeficiency virus (HIV) infection among persons with severe mental illnesses. *Clinical Psychology Review, 17*, 271–291.

Carlson, B. E., & Russer-Hogan, R. (1991). Trauma experiences, stress, dissociation and depression in Cambodian refugees. *American Journal of Psychiatry, 148(11)*, 1548–1551.

Carlson, G. A., & Cantwell, D. P. (1980). A survey of depressive symptoms, syndrome and disorder in a child psychiatric population. *Journal of Child Psychology and Psychiatry, 21*, 19–25.

Carr, A. (2009). *What works with children, adolescents, and adults? A review of research on the effectiveness of psychotherapy*. New York, NY: Routledge.

Carroll, J. L., & Carroll, L. M. (1995). Alcohol use and risky sex among college students. *Psychological Reports, 76,* 723–726.

Carroll, L. (1865). *Alice's adventures in wonderland.* London, UK: Macmillan.

Carten, A. J. (1996). Mothers in recovery: Rebuilding families in the aftermath of addiction. *Social Work, 41,* 215–223.

Carter, G. L., Willcox, C. H., Lewin, T. J., Conrad, A. M., & Bendit, N. (2010). Hunter DBT project: Randomized controlled trial of dialectical behavior therapy in women with borderline personality disorder, *Australian and New Zealand Journal of Psychiatry, 44,* 162–173.

Carter, J. D., Joyce, P. R., Mulder, R. T., Sullivan, P. F., & Luty, S. E. (1999). Gender differences in the frequency of personality disorders in depressed outpatients. *Journal of Personality Disorders, 13,* 67–74.

Carter, R. T. (1995). *The influence of race and racial identity in psychotherapy: Toward a racially inclusive model.* New York, NY: Wiley.

Cassin, S. E., von Ranson, K. M., Heng, K., Brar, J., & Wojtowitz, A. E. (2008). Adapted motivational interviewing for women with binge eating disorder: A randomized controlled trial. *Psychology of Addictive Behaviors, 22,* 417–425.

Castellanos, F. X. (1998). Tic disorders and obsessive-compulsive disorder. In B. T. Walsh (Ed.), *Child psychopharmacology* (pp. 1–28). Washington, DC: American Psychiatric Press.

Castle, D., White, C., Chamberlain, J., Berk, M., Berk, L., Lauder, S., . . . Gilbert, M. (2010). Group-based psychosocial intervention for bipolar disorder: Randomized controlled trial. *British Journal of Psychiatry, 196,* 383–388.

Cattell, R. B. (1965). *The scientific analysis of personality.* Chicago, IL: Aldine.

Celio, A. A., Winzelberg, A. J., Eppstein-Herald, D., Wilfley, D., Springer, E. A., Dev, P., & Taylor, C. B. (2000). Reducing risk factors for eating disorders: Comparison of an Internet-based and classroom-delivered psychoeducational program. *Journal of Consulting and Clinical Psychology, 68,* 650–657.

Centers for Disease Control and Prevention. (2006). Youth risk behavior surveillance: United States—2005. *Morbidity and Mortality Weekly Report, 55,* 1–108.

Centers for Disease Control and Prevention. (2013a). *Alcohol-related disease impact (ARDI).* Atlanta, GA: Author.

Centers for Disease Control and Prevention. (2013b). *Policy impact: Prescription painkiller overdoses.* Retrieved from http://www.cdc.gov/homeandrecreational safety/rxbrief/.

Centers for Disease Control and Prevention. (2014a). *HIV surveillance report: Diagnoses of HIV infection and AIDS in the United States and dependent areas, 2011* (Vol. 23). Atlanta, GA: Author.

Centers for Disease Control and Prevention. (2014b). *Suicide prevention.* Retrieved from http://www.cdc.gov/violenceprevention/pub/youth_suicide.html.

Chaffin, M., & Shultz, S. K. (2001). Psychometric evaluation of the Children's Impact of Traumatic Events Scale–Revised. *Child Abuse and Neglect, 25,* 401–411.

Chamberlain, P., & Rosicky, J. G. (1995). The effectiveness of family therapy in the treatment of adolescents with conduct disorders and delinquency. *Journal of Marital and Family Therapy, 21,* 441–459.

Chambless, D. L., & Gillis, M. M. (1996). Cognitive therapy of anxiety disorders. In K. S. Dobson & K. D. Craig (Eds.), *Advances in cognitive-behavioral therapy* (pp. 116–144). Thousand Oaks, CA: Sage.

Chambless, D. L., & Hollon, S. D. (1998). Defining empirically supported therapies. *Journal of Consulting and Clinical Psychology*, *66*, 7–18.

Chambless, D. L., & Ollendick, T. H. (2001). Empirically supported psychological interventions: Controversies and evidence. *Annual Review of Psychology*, *52*, 685–716.

Chan, Y., Dennis, M. L., & Funk, R. R. (2010). Prevalence and comorbidity of major externalizing and internalizing problems among adolescents and adults presenting to substance abuse treatment. *Journal of Substance Abuse Treatment*, *34*, 14–24.

Chan, Y., Passetti, L. L., Garner, B. R., Lloyd, J. J., & Dennis, M. L. (2011). HIV risk behaviors: Risky sexual activities and needle use among adolescents in substance abuse treatment. *AIDS and Behavior*, *15*, 114–124.

Chase, R. M., Whitton, S. W., & Pincus, D. B. (2012). Treatment of adolescent panic disorder: A nonrandomized comparison of intensive versus weekly CBT. *Child and Family Behavior Therapy*, *34*, 305–323.

Chatterjee, S., Pillai, A., Jain, S., Cohen, A., & Patel, V. (2009). Outcomes of people with psychotic disorders in a community-based rehabilitation programme in rural India. *British Journal of Psychiatry*, *195*, 433–439.

Chemtob, C. M., Tolin, D. F., van der Kolk, B. A., & Pitman, R. K. (2000). Eye movement desensitization and reprocessing. In E. B. Foa, T. M. Keane, & M. J. Friedman (Eds.), *Effective treatments for PTSD: Practice guidelines from the international society for traumatic stress studies* (pp. 139–154). New York, NY: Guilford Press.

Chen, K., & Kandel, D. (1995). The natural history of drug use from adolescents to the mid-thirties in a general population sample. *American Journal of Public Health*, *85*, 41–47.

Chen, L., Eaton, W., Gallo, J., Nestadt, G., & Crum, R. (2000). Empirical examination of current depression categories in a population-based study: Symptoms, course and risk factors. *American Journal of Psychiatry*, *157*, 573–580.

Chen, W. J., Faraone, S. V., Biederman, J., & Tsuang, M. T. (1994). Diagnostic accuracy of the Child Behavior Checklist Scales for attention-deficit hyperactivity disorder: A receiver operating characteristics analysis. *Journal of Consulting and Clinical Psychology*, *62*, 1017–1025.

Chen, X., Thrane, L., Whitbeck, L. B., Johnson, K. D., & Hoyt, D. R. (2007). Onset of conduct disorder, use of delinquent subsistence strategies, and street victimization, among homeless and runaway adolescents in the Midwest. *Journal of Interpersonal Violence*, *22*, 1156–1183.

Cheng, T. C., & Lo, C. C. (2010). Mental health service and drug treatment utilization: Adolescents with substance use/mental disorders and dual diagnosis. *Journal of Child and Adolescent Substance Abuse*, *19*, 447–460.

Cheung, Y. W. (1990). Ethnicity and alcohol/drug use revisited: A framework for future research. *International Journal of the Addictions*, *25*, 581–605.

Chien, W. T., & Wong, K. (2007). A family psycho-education group program for Chinese people with schizophrenia in Hong Kong. *Psychiatric Services*, *58*, 1003–1006.

Child Abuse Prevention and Treatment Act (CAPTA), Pub. L. No. 93-247, 42.

Christensen, A., Jacobson, N. S., & Babcock, J. C. (1995). Integrative behavioral couple therapy. In N. S. Jacobson & A. S. Gurman (Eds.), *Clinical handbook of couple therapy* (pp. 31–64). New York, NY: Guilford Press.

Christensen, H., Griffiths, K. M., Mackinnon, A. J., & Brittliffe, K. (2006). Online randomized controlled trial of brief and full cognitive behavior therapy for depression. *Psychological Medicine, 36,* 1737–1746.

Christophersen, E. R., & Finney, J. W. (1999). Oppositional defiant disorder. In R. T. Ammerman, M. Hersen, & C. G. Last (Eds.), *Handbook of prescriptive treatments for children and adolescents* (2nd ed., pp. 102–113). Boston, MA: Allyn & Bacon.

Chou, K. L. (2009). Panic disorder in older adults: Evidence from the National Epidemiologic Survey on Alcohol and Related Conditions. *International Journal of Geriatric Psychiatry, 25,* 822–832.

Chow, W., Law, S., Andermann, L., Yang, J., Leszcz, M., Wong, J., & Sadavoy, J. (2010). Multi-family psycho-education group for assertive community treatment clients and families of culturally diverse background: A pilot study. *Community Mental Health Journal, 46,* 363–371.

Cicchetti, D., Rogosch, A., & Toth, S. L. (1994). A developmental psychopathology perspective on depression in children and adolescents. In W. M. Reynolds & H. F. Johnston (Eds.), *Handbook of depression in children and adolescents* (pp. 123–141). New York, NY: Plenum Press.

Clapp, J. D., Segars, L., & Voas, R. (2002). A conceptual model of the alcohol environment of college students. *Journal of Human Behavior in the Social Environment, 5,* 73–90.

Clark, D. A., & Beck, A. T. (with Alford, B. A.). (1999). *Scientific foundations of cognitive theory and therapy of depression.* New York, NY: Wiley.

Clark, D. A., & Beck, A. T. (2010). Cognitive theory and therapy of anxiety and depression: Convergence with neurobiological findings. *Trends in Cognitive Sciences, 14,* 418–424.

Clark, R. E., Ricketts, S. K., & McHugo, G. J. (1999). Legal system involvement and costs for persons in the treatment for severe mental illness and substance abuse disorders. *Psychiatric Services, 50,* 641–647.

Clarkin, J. F., Levy, K. N., Lenzenweger, M. F., & Kernberg, O. F. (2007). Evaluating three treatments for borderline personality disorder: A multiwave study. *American Journal of Psychiatry, 164,* 922–928.

Clavarino, A., Hayatbakhsh, M. R., Williams, G. M., Bor, W., O'Callaghan, M., & Najman, J. M. (2011). Depression following marital problems: Different impacts on mothers and their children? A 21-year prospective study. *Social Psychiatry and Psychiatric Epidemiology, 46,* 833–841.

Cleckley, H. (1941). *The mask of sanity.* St. Louis, MO: Mosby.

Clum, G. A., Broyles, S., Borden, J., & Watkins, P. L. (1990). Validity and reliability of the Panic Attack Symptoms and Cognitions Questionnaires. *Journal of Psychopathology and Behavioral Assessment, 12,* 233–245.

Coatsworth, J. D., Pantin, H., McBride, C., Briones, E., Kurtines, W., & Szapocznik, J. (2002). Ecodevelopmental correlates of behavior problems in young Hispanic females. *Applied Developmental Science, 6,* 126–143.

Cocco, K. M., & Carey, K. B. (1998). Psychometric properties of the Drug Abuse Screening Test in psychiatric outpatients. *Psychological Assessment, 10,* 408–414.

Coccozelli, C., & Hudson, C. G. (1989, December). Recent advances in alcoholism diagnosis and treatment assessment research: Implications for practice, *Social Service Review,* 533–552.

Coffey, S. F., Dansky, B. S., Falsetti, S. A., Saladin, M. E., & Brady, K. T. (1998). Screening for PTSD in a substance abuse sample: Psychometric properties of a modified version of the PTSD Symptom Scale self-report. *Journal of Traumatic Stress, 11*, 393–399.

Cohen, J. A., Deblinger, E., Mannarino, A. P., & Steer, R. A. (2004). A multi-site randomized controlled trial for children with sex abuse-related PTSD symptoms. *Journal of the Academy of Child and Adolescent Psychiatry, 43*, 393–402.

Coid, J., & Ullrich, S. (2010). Antisocial personality disorder is on a continuum with psychopathy. *Comprehensive Psychiatry, 51*, 426–433.

Cole, P. M., Llera, S. J., & Pemberton, C. K. (2009). Emotional instability, poor emotional awareness, and the development of borderline personality disorder. *Development and Psychopathology, 21*, 1293–1310.

Coleman, H., Unrau, Y. A., & Manyfingers, B. (2001). Revamping family preservation services for native families. *Journal of Ethnic and Cultural Diversity in Social Work, 10*, 49–68.

Collett, B. R., Ohan, J. L., & Myers, K. M. (2003). Ten-year review of scales: VI. Scales assessing externalizing behaviors. *Journal of the American Academy of Child and Adolescent Psychiatry, 42*, 1143–1170.

Colonnesi, C., Draijer, E. M., Stams, G. J. J. M., Van der Bruggen, C. O., Bögels, S. M., & Noom, M. J. (2011). The relation between insecure attachment and child anxiety: A meta-analytic review. *Journal of Clinical Child and Adolescent Psychology, 40*, 630–645.

Combs-Orme, T., & Thomas, K. H. (1997). Assessment of troubled families. *Social Work Research, 21*, 261–269.

Compas, B. E. (1997). Depression in children and adolescents. In E. J. Mash & L. G. Terdal (Eds.), *Assessment of childhood disorders* (3rd ed., pp. 197–229). New York, NY: Guilford Press.

Compas, B. E., Grant, K. E., & Ey, S. (1994). Psychosocial stress and child and adolescent development. In W. M. Reynolds & H. F. Johnston (Eds.), *Handbook of depression in children and adolescents* (pp. 509–523). New York, NY: Plenum Press.

Compton, S. N., Burns, B. J., Egger, H. L., & Robertson, E. (2002). Review of the evidence base for treatment of childhood psychopathology: Internalizing disorders. *Journal of Consulting and Clinical Psychology, 70*, 1240–1266.

Compton, W. M., Cottler, L. B., Abdallah, A. B., Phelps, D. L., Sptiznagel, E. L., & Horton, J. C. (2000). Substance dependence and other psychiatric disorders among drug dependent subjects: Race and gender correlates. *American Journal on Addictions, 9*, 113–125.

Compton, W. M., Thomas, Y. F., Stinson, F. S., & Grant, B. F. (2007). Prevalence, correlates, disability, and comorbidity of DSM-IV drug abuse and dependence in the United States: Results from the National Epidemiologic Survey on Alcohol and Related Conditions. *Archives of General Psychiatry, 64*(5), 566–576.

Conners, C. K. (1997). *Conners' Rating Scales–Revised technical manual.* North Tonawanda, NY: Multi-Health Systems.

Conners, C. K., Epstein, J., & March, J. (2001). Multimodal treatment of ADHD (MTA): An alternative outcome analysis. *Journal of the American Academy of Child and Adolescent Psychiatry, 40*, 159–167.

Connor, B. D., & Lochman, J. E. (2010). Comorbid conduct disorder and substance use disorders. *Clinical Psychology: Science and Practice, 17*, 337–349.

Conte, H. R., Plutchik, R., Karasu, T. B., & Jerrett, I. (1980). A self-report border-line scale: Discriminative validity and preliminary norms. *Journal of Nervous and Mental Disease*, *168*, 428–435.

Conte, J. (1984, May–June). Progress in treating the sexual abuse of children. *Social Work*, 258–263.

Conte, J., & Schuerman, J. (1987). The effects of sexual abuse on children: A multi-dimensional view. *Journal of Interpersonal Violence*, *2*, 380–390.

Cooke, D. J., & Michie, C. (1997). An item response theory analysis of the Hare Psychopathy Checklist–Revised. *Psychological Assessment*, *9*, 3–14.

Cooper, M. L. (1994). Motivations for alcohol use among adolescents: Develop-ment and validation of a four factor model. *Psychological Assessment*, *6*(2), 117–128. doi: 10.1037/1040-3590.6.2.117.

Cooper, M. L. (2002). Alcohol use and risky sexual behavior among college stu-dents and youth: Evaluating the evidence. *Journal of Studies on Alcohol*, *63*, 101–117.

Cooper, M. L., & Orcutt, H. K. (1997). Drinking and sexual experience on first dates among adolescents. *Journal of Abnormal Psychology*, *106*, 191–202.

Cooper, M. L., Russell, M., & George, W. H. (1988). Coping, expectancies and alcohol abuse: A test of social learning theory formulations. *Journal of Abnor-mal Psychology*, *97*, 218–230.

Cooper, Z., & Fairburn, C. (1987). The eating disorder examination: A semi-structured interview for the assessment of the specific psychopathology of eat-ing disorders. *International Journal of Eating Disorders*, *6*, 1–8.

Corcoran, J. (2000). Family interventions with child physical abuse and neglect: A critical review. *Children and Youth Services Review*, *22*, 563–591.

Corcoran, J. (2008). *Mental health treatments for children and adolescents*. New York, NY: Oxford University Press.

Corcoran, J., & Pillai, V. (2000). A meta-analysis of parent-involved treatment for child sexual abuse. *Research on Social Work Practice*, *18*, 453–464.

Corcoran, K. J., & Gingerich, W. J. (1994). Practice evaluation in the context of managed care. *Research on Social Work Practice*, *4*, 326–337.

Corcoran, K., Gingerich, W. J., & Briggs, H. E. (2001). Practice evaluation: Setting goals and monitoring change. In H. E. Briggs & K. Corcoran (Eds.), *Social work practice: Treating common client problems* (pp. 66–84). Chicago, IL: Lyceum Books.

Corcoran, K., & Vandiver, V. (1996). *Maneuvering the maze of managed care: Skills for mental health practitioners*. New York, NY: Free Press.

Corin, E., Thara, R., & Padmavati, R. (2005). Shadows of culture in psychosis in South India: A methodological exploration and illustration. *International Re-view of Psychiatry*, *17*, 75–81.

Corrigan, E. (1985). Gender differences in alcohol and other drug use. *Addictive Behaviors*, *10*, 313–317.

Corrigan, P. (1997). Behavior therapy empowers persons with severe mental ill-ness. *Behavior Modification*, *21*, 45–61.

Corwin, M. (1996, January). Early intervention strategies with borderline clients. *Families in Society: The Journal of Contemporary Human Services*, 40–49.

Costanzo, P., Miller-Johnson, S., & Wencel, H. (1995). Social development. In J. S. March (Ed.), *Anxiety disorders in children and adolescents* (pp. 82–108). New York, NY: Guilford Press.

Costello, E. J., & Angold, A. (1988). Scales to assess child and adolescent depression: Checklists, screens, and nets. *Journal of the American Academy of Child and Adolescent Psychiatry*, 27, 726–737.

Cournos, F., & McKinnon, K. (1997). HIV seroprevalence among people with severe mental illness in the United States: A critical review. *Clinical Psychology Review*, 17, 259–269.

Courtney, M. E. (2000). Research needed to improve the prospects for children in out-of-home placement. *Children and Youth Services Review*, 22, 743–761.

Craig, T. K. J., Johnson, S., McCrone, P., Afuwape, S., Hughes, E., Gournay, K., . . . Thornicroft, G. (2008). Integrated care for co-occurring disorders: Psychiatric symptoms, social functioning, and service costs at 18 months. *Psychiatric Services*, 59, 276–282.

Craighead, L. W., Craighead, W. E., Kazdin, A. P., & Mahoney, M. J. (Eds.) (1994). *Cognitive and behavioral interventions: An empirical approach to mental health problems*. Boston, MA: Allyn & Bacon.

Craighead, W. E., Smucker, M. R., Craighead, L. W., & Ilardi, S. S. (1998). Factor analysis of the Children's Depression Inventory in a community sample. *Psychological Assessment*, 10, 156–165.

Crane, D. R., Middleton, K. C., & Bean, R. A. (2000). Establishing criterion scores for the Kansas Marital Satisfaction Scale and the Revised Dyadic Adjustment Scale. *American Journal of Family Therapy*, 28, 53–60.

Craske, M. G. (1996a). Cognitive-behavioral approaches to panic and agoraphobia. In K. S. Dobson & K. D. Craig (Eds.), *Advances in cognitive-behavioral therapy* (pp. 145–173). Thousand Oaks, CA: Sage.

Craske, M. G. (1996b). An integrated treatment approach to panic disorder. *Bulletin of the Menninger Clinic*, 60, A87–A104.

Craske, M. G. (1997). Fear and anxiety in children and adolescents. *Bulletin of the Menninger Clinic*, 61, A4–A36.

Craske, M. G. (1999). *Anxiety disorders: Psychological approaches to theory and treatment*. Boulder, CO: Westview Press.

Craske, M. G., & Barlow, D. H. (2008). Panic disorder and agoraphobia. In D. H. Barlow (Ed.), *Clinical handbook of psychological disorders* (4th ed., pp. 1–64). New York, NY: Guilford Press.

Craske, M. G., & Zoeller, L. A. (1995). Anxiety disorders: The role of marital therapy. In N. S. Jacobson & A. S. Gurman (Eds.), *Clinical handbook of couple therapy* (pp. 394–410). New York, NY: Guilford Press.

Crawford, T. N., Cohen, P. R., Chen, H., Anglin, D. M., & Ehrensaft, M. (2009). Early maternal separation and the trajectory of borderline personality disorder symptoms. *Development and Psychopathology*, 21, 1013–1030.

Crits-Christoph, P. (1998). Psychosocial treatment for personality disorders. In P. E. Nathan & J. M. Gorman (Eds.), *A guide to treatments that work* (pp. 544–553). New York, NY: Oxford University Press.

Crouch, J. L., Smith, D. W., Ezzell, C. E., & Saunders, B. E. (1999). Measuring reactions to sexual trauma among children: Comparing the Children's Impact of Traumatic Events Scale and the Trauma Symptom Checklist for Children. *Child Maltreatment*, 4, 255–263.

Crowell, S. E., Beauchaine, T. P., & Linehan, M. M. (2009). A biosocial developmental model of borderline personality: Elaborating and extending Linehan's theory. *Psychological Bulletin*, 135, 495–510.

Cuijpers, P., Reynolds, C. F., Donker, T., Li, J., Andersson, G., & Beekman, A. (2012). Personalized treatment of adults depression: Medication, psychotherapy, or both? A systematic review. *Depression and Anxiety, 29*, 855–864.

Culp, R. E., Heide, J., & Richardson, M. T. (1987). Maltreated children's developmental scores: Treatment versus nontreatment. *Child Abuse and Neglect, 11*, 29–34.

Culp, R. E., Richardson, M. T., & Heide, J. S. (1987). Differential developmental progress of maltreated children in day treatment. *Social Work, 32*, 497–499.

Cumella, E. J. (2006). Review of the Eating Disorder Inventory–3. *Journal of Personality Assessment, 87*, 116–117.

Cummings, S. M. (2003). The efficacy of an integrated group treatment program for depressed assisted living residents. *Research on Social Work Practice, 13*, 608–621.

Cunningham, J. A., Sobell, L. C., Sobell, M. B., & Kapur, G. (1995). Resolution from alcohol problems with and without treatment: Reasons for change. *Journal of Substance Abuse, 7*, 365–372.

Cunningham, M. D., & Reidy, T. J. (1998). Antisocial personality disorder and psychopathy: Diagnostic dilemmas in classifying patterns of antisocial behavior in sentencing evaluations. *Behavioral Sciences and the Law, 16*, 333–351.

Cunningham, M. D., & Reidy, T. J. (1999). Don't confuse me with the facts: Common errors in violence risk assessment at capital sentencing. *Criminal Justice and Behavior, 26*, 20–43.

Curry, J. F. (2001). Specific psychotherapies for childhood and adolescent depression. *Biological Psychiatry, 49*, 1091–1100.

Cusack, K. J., Morrissey, J. P., Cuddeback, G. S., Prins, A., & Williams, D. M. (2010). Criminal justice involvement, behavioral health service use, and costs of forensic assertive community treatment: A randomized trial. *Community Mental Health Journal, 46*, 356–363.

Cutchen, M. A., & Simpson, R. G. (1993). Interrater reliability among teachers and mental health professionals when using the revised Behavior Problem Checklist. *Journal of Psychoeducational Assessment, 11*, 4–11.

Daeppen, J. B., Bertholet, N., Gaume, J., Fortini, C., Faouzi, M., & Gmel, G. (2011). Efficacy of brief motivational intervention in reducing binge drinking in young men: A randomized controlled trial. *Drug and Alcohol Dependence, 113*, 69–75.

Daghestani, A. N., Dinwiddie, S. H., & Hardy, D. W. (2001). Antisocial personality disorders in and out of correctional and forensic settings. *Psychiatric Annals, 31*, 441–446.

Dahl, A. A. (1995). Commentary on borderline personality disorder. In J. Livesley (Ed.), *The DSM-IV personality disorders* (pp. 158–164). New York, NY: Guilford Press.

Daiuto, A. D., Baucom, D. H., Epstein, N., & Dutton, S. S. (1998). The application of behavioral couples therapy to the assessment and treatment of agoraphobia: Implications of empirical research. *Clinical Psychology Review, 18*, 663–687.

Daley, D. (1987). Relapse prevention with substance abusers. *Social Work, 32*, 159–163.

Dalgleish, T. (2004). Cognitive approaches to posttraumatic stress disorder: The evolution of multirepresentational theorizing. *Psychological Bulletin, 130*(2), 228–260.

Dang, J. N. (2008). *Statistical analysis of alcohol-related driving trends, 1982–2005*. Washington, DC: US Department of Transportation, National Highway Traffic and Safety Administration.

Dare, C., & Eisler, I. (2002). Family therapy and eating disorders. In C. G. Fairburn & K. D. Brownell (Eds.), *Eating disorders and obesity: A comprehensive handbook* (2nd ed., pp. 314–319). New York, NY: Guilford Press.

Darkes, J., & Goldman, M. S. (1993). Expectancy challenge and drinking reduction: Experimental evidence for a mediational process. *Journal of Consulting and Clinical Psychology, 61*, 344–353.

Dauber, S., Neighbors, C., Dasaro, C., Riordan, A., & Morgenstern, J. (2012). Impact of intensive case management on child welfare system involvement for substance-dependent parenting women on public assistance. *Child and Youth Services Review, 34*, 1359–1366.

Davidson, K., Norrie, J., Tyrer, P., Gumley, A., Tata, P., Murray, H., & Palmer, S. (2006). The effectiveness of cognitive behavior therapy for borderline personality disorder: Results from the Borderline Personality Disorder Study of Cognitive Therapy (BOSCOT) trial. *Journal of Personality Disorders, 20*, 450–465.

Davidson, P. R., & Parker, K. C. (2001). Eye movement desensitization and reprocessing (EMDR): A meta-analysis. *Journal of Consulting and Clinical Psychology, 69*, 305–316.

Dawe, S., & Harnett, P. (2007). Reducing potential for child abuse in methadone-maintained parents: Results from a randomized controlled trial. *Journal of Substance Abuse Treatment, 32*, 381–390.

Dawes, R. M. (1989). *House of cards: Psychology and psychotherapy built on myth*. New York, NY: Free Press.

Day, A., Chung, D., O'Leary, P., & Carson, E. (2009). Programs for men who perpetrate domestic violence: An examination of the issues underlying the effectiveness of intervention programs. *Journal of Family Violence, 24*, 203–212.

Deas, D., & Clark, A. (2009). Current state of treatment for alcohol and other drug use disorders in adolescents. *Alcohol Research and Health, 32*, 76–82.

Deblinger, E., Mannarino, A. P., Cohen, J. A., & Steer, R. A. (2006). A follow-up study of a multisite, randomized, controlled trial for children with sexual abuse-related PTSD symptoms. *Journal of the Academy of Child and Adolescent Psychiatry, 45*, 1474–1484.

De Bonis, M., De Boeck, P., Lida-Pulik, H., Hourtane, M., & Feline, A. (1998). Self-concept and mood: A comparative study between depressed patients with and without borderline personality disorder. *Journal of Affective Disorders, 48*, 191–197.

Deckel, A. W., Hesselbrock, V., & Bauer, L. (1996). Antisocial personality disorder, childhood delinquency, and frontal brain functioning: EEG and neuropsychological findings. *Journal of Clinical Psychology, 52*, 639–650.

Del Boca, F. K., & Darkes, J. (2003). The validity of self-reports of alcohol consumption: State of the science and challenges for research. *Addiction, 98*(2, suppl.), 1–12.

Denis, C. M., Cacciola, J. S., & Alterman, A. I. (2013). Addiction Severity Index (ASI) summary scores: Comparison of the recent status scores of the ASI-6 and the composite scores of the ASI-5. *Journal of Substance Abuse Treatment, 45,* 444–450.

Denis, C., Fatse, M., Beltran, V., Bonnet, C., Picard, S., Combourieu, I., . . . Auriacombe, M. (2012). Validity of the self-reported drug use section of the Addiction Severity Index and associated factors used under naturalistic conditions. *Substance Use and Misuse, 47,* 353–363.

DePanfilis, D., & Zuravin, S. J. (1999). Predicting child maltreatment recurrences during treatment. *Child Abuse and Neglect, 8,* 729–743.

DePanfilis, D., & Zuravin, S. J. (2001). Assessing risk to determine the need for services. *Children and Youth Services Review, 23,* 3–20.

Dermen, K. H., & Cooper, M. L. (1994a). Sex-related alcohol expectancies among adolescents: I. Scale development. *Psychology of Addictive Behaviors, 8,* 152–160.

Dermen, K. H., & Cooper, M. L. (1994b). Sex-related alcohol expectancies among adolescents: II. Prediction of drinking in social and sexual situations. *Psychology of Addictive Behaviors, 8,* 161–168.

Dermen, K. H., Cooper, M. L., & Agocha, V. B. (1998). Sex-related expectancies as moderators of the relationship between alcohol use and risky sex in adolescents. *Journal of Studies on Alcohol, 59,* 71–77.

Dermen, K. H., & Thomas, S. N. (2011). Randomized controlled trial of brief interventions to reduce college students' drinking and risky sex. *Psychology of Addictive Behaviors, 25,* 583–594.

Derogatis, L. R., & Melisaratos, N. (1983). The Brief Symptom Inventory: An introductory report. *Psychological Medicine, 13,* 595–605.

Desai, R., Harpaz-Rotem, H., Najavits, L., & Rosenheck, R. (2008). Impact of the seeking safety program on clinical outcomes among homeless female veterans with psychiatric disorders. *Psychiatric Services, 59,* 996–1003.

Dessaulles, A., Johnson, S. M., & Denton, W. H. (2003). Emotion-focused therapy for couples in the treatment of depression: A pilot study. *American Journal of Family Therapy, 31,* 345–353.

DeVellis, R. F. (2000). *Scale development: Theory and applications.* Thousand Oaks, CA: Sage.

Devilly, G., & Spence, S. (1999). The relative efficacy and treatment distress of EMDR and a cognitive behavioral trauma treatment protocol in the amelioration of post-traumatic stress disorder. *Journal of Anxiety Disorders, 13,* 131–157.

Dick, L. P., & Gallagher-Thompson, D. (1996). Late-life depression. In M. Hersen & V. B. Van Hasselt (Eds.), *Psychological treatment of older adults: An introductory text* (pp. 181–208). New York, NY: Plenum Press.

Dickerson, F. B. (1997). Assessing clinical outcomes: The community functioning of persons with serious mental illness. *Psychiatric Services, 48,* 897–902.

DiClemente, C. C., Bellino, L. E., & Neavins, T. M. (1999). Motivation for change and alcoholism treatment. *Alcohol Research and Health, 23,* 86–92.

DiClemente, C. C., Carbonari, J. P., Montgomery, R. P. G., & Hughes, S. O. (1994). The Alcohol Abstinence Self-Efficacy Scale. *Journal of Studies on Alcohol, 55,* 141–148.

DiClemente, C. C., & Hughes, S. O. (1990). Stages of change profiles in outpatient alcoholism treatment. *Journal of Substance Abuse, 2*, 217–235.

Diefenbach, G. J., Abramowitz, J. S., Norberg, M. M., & Tolin, D. F. (2007). Changes in quality of life following cognitive-behavioral therapy for obsessive-compulsive disorder. *Behaviour Research and Therapy, 45*, 3060–3068.

DiFulvio, G. T., Linowski, S. A., Mazziotti, J. S., & Puleo, E. (2012). Effectiveness of the Brief Alcohol Screening and Intervention for College Students (BASICS) program with a mandated population. *Journal of American College Health, 60*, 269–280.

Dimeff, L. A., Baer, J. S., Kivlahan, D. R., & Marlatt, G. A. (1999). *Brief Alcohol Screening and Intervention for College Students: A harm reduction approach.* New York, NY: Guilford Press.

Dimidjian, S. Martell, C. R., Addis, M. E., & Herman-Dunn, R. (2008). Behavioral activation for depression. In D. H. Barlow (Ed.), *Clinical handbook of psychological disorders* (4th ed., pp. 328–364). New York, NY: Guilford Press.

Dinh, T. Q., Yamada, A. M., & Yee, B. W. K. (2009). A culturally relevant conceptualization of depression: An empirical examination of the factorial structure of the Vietnamese Depression Scale. *International Journal of Social Psychiatry, 55*, 496–505.

Disney, E. R., Elkins, I. J., McGue, M., & Iacono, W. G. (1999). Effects of ADH, conduct disorder, and gender on substance use and abuse in adolescence. *American Journal of Psychiatry, 156*, 1515–1521.

Dixon, L., Adams, C., & Lucksted, A. (2000). Update on family psychoeducation for schizophrenia. *Schizophrenia Bulletin, 26*, 5–20.

Dixon, L. B., Dickerson, F., Bellack, A. S., Bennett, M., Dickinson, D., Goldberg, R. W., . . . Kreyenbuhl, J. (2010). The 2009 Schizophrenia PORT psychosocial treatment recommendations and summary statement. *Schizophrenia Bulletin, 36*, 48–70.

Dixon, L. B., & Lehman, A. F. (1995). Family interventions for schizophrenia. *Schizophrenia Bulletin, 21*, 631–643.

Dixon, L. B., Lehman, A. F., & Levine, J. (1995). Conventional antipsychotic medications for schizophrenia. *Schizophrenia Bulletin, 21*, 567–577.

Dixon, L. B., McFarlane, W. R., Lefley, H., Lucksted, A., Cohen, M., Falloon, I., . . . Sondheimer, D. (2001). Evidence-based practices for services to families of people with psychiatric disabilities. *Psychiatric Services, 52*, 903–910.

Dobson, K. S. (Ed.) (2009). *Handbook of cognitive behavioral therapies* (3rd ed.). New York, NY: Guilford Press.

Dobson, K. S. (1989). A meta-analysis of the efficacy of cognitive therapy for depression. *Journal of Consulting and Clinical Psychology, 57*, 414–419.

Dobson, K. S., & Craig, K. D. (Eds.) (1996). *Advances in cognitive-behavioral therapy.* Thousand Oaks, CA: Sage.

Dobson, K. S., & Jackman-Cram, S. (1996). Common change processes in cognitive-behavioral processes for depression. In K. S. Dobson & K. D. Craig (Eds.), *Advances in cognitive-behavioral therapy* (pp. 63–82). Thousand Oaks, CA: Sage.

Doering, S., Horz, S., Rentrop, M., Fischer-Kern, M., Schuster, P., Benecke, C., . . . Buchheim, P. (2010). Transference-focused psychotherapy v. treatment by community psychotherapists for borderline personality disorder: Randomized controlled trial. *British Journal of Psychiatry, 196*, 389–395.

Dohrenwend, B. P. (1998). Overview of evidence for the importance of adverse environmental conditions in causing psychiatric disorders. In B. P. Dohrenwend (Ed.), *Adversity, stress and psychopathology* (pp. 523–538). New York, NY: Oxford University Press.

Dohrenwend, B. P., & Dohrenwend, B. S. (1974). Social and cultural influences on psychopathology. *Annual Review of Psychology, 25*, 417–452.

Dohrenwend, B. P., Levav, I., Shrout, P. E., Schwartz, S., Naveh, G., Link, B. G., . . . Stueve, A. (1998). Ethnicity, socioeconomic status, and psychiatric disorders: A test of the social causation-social selection issue. In B. P. Dohrenwend (Ed.), *Adversity, stress and psychopathology* (pp. 285–318). New York, NY: Oxford University Press.

Donabedian, A. (1980). *Explorations in quality assessment and monitoring: Vol. 1. The definition of quality and approaches to its assessment.* Ann Arbor, MI: Health Administration Press.

Donovan, D. (1999). Assessment strategies and measures in addictive behaviors. In B. S. McCrady & E. S. Epstein (Eds.), *Addictions: A comprehensive guidebook* (pp. 187–215). New York, NY: Oxford University Press.

Donovan, E., Wood, M., Frayjo, K., Black, R. A., & Surette, D. A. (2012). A randomized controlled trial to test the efficacy of an on-line, parent-based intervention for reducing the risks associated with college-student alcohol use. *Addictive Behaviors, 37*, 25–35.

Dore, M. M. (1993, November). Family preservation and poor families: When "homebuilding" is not enough. *Families in Society: The Journal of Contemporary Human Services*, 545–556.

Dore, M. M. (1999). Emotionally and behaviorally disturbed children in the child welfare system: Points of preventive intervention. *Children and Youth Services Review, 21*, 7–29.

Dore, M. M., Kauffman, E., Nelson-Zlupko, L., & Granfort, E. (1996, December). Psychosocial functioning and treatment needs of latency-age children from drug-involved families. *Families in Society: The Journal of Contemporary Human Services*, 595–603.

Dorfman, R. A., Lubben, J. E., Mayer-Oakes, A., Atchison, K., Schweitzer, S. O., DeJong, F. J., & Matthias, R. E. (1995). Screening for depression among a well elderly population. *Social Work, 40*, 295–304.

Dowd, H., & McGuire, B. E. (2011). Psychological treatment of PTSD in children: An evidence-based review. *Irish Journal of Psychology, 32*, 25–39.

Downar, J., & Kupar, S. (2008). Biological theories. In K. T. Mueser & D. V. Jeste (Eds.), *Clinical handbook of schizophrenia* (pp. 25–34). New York, NY: Guilford Press.

Downey, G., Feldman, S., Khuri, J., & Friedman, S. (1994). Maltreatment and childhood depression. In W. M. Reynolds & H. F. Johnston (Eds.), *Handbook of depression in children and adolescents* (pp. 481–508). New York, NY: Plenum Press.

Dozois, D. J., Dobson, K. S., & Ahnberg, J. L. (1998). A psychometric evaluation of the Beck Depression Inventory–II. *Psychological Assessment, 10*, 83–89.

Draine, J. (1997). A critical review of randomized field trials of case management for individuals with serious and persistent mental illness. *Research on Social Work Practice, 7*, 32–51.

Drake, R. E. (1998). Brief history, current status, and future place of assertive community treatment. *American Journal of Orthopsychiatry*, *68*, 172–175.

Drake, R. E., Alterman, A. I., & Rosenberg, S. R. (1993). Detection of substance use disorders in severely mentally ill patients. *Community Mental Health Journal*, *29*, 175–192.

Drake, R. E., Green, A. I., Mueser, K. T., & Goldman, H. H. (2003). The history of community mental health treatment and rehabilitation for persons with severe mental illness. *Community Mental Health Journal*, *39*(5), 427–440.

Drake, R. E., McHugo, G. J., Clark, R. E., Teague, G. B., Xie, H., Miles, K., & Ackerson, T. H. (1998). Assertive community treatment for patients with co-occurring severe mental illness and substance use disorder: A clinical trial. *American Journal of Orthopsychiatry*, *68*, 201–215.

Drake, R. E., Mercer-McFadden, C., Mueser, K. T., Hugo, G. J., & Bond, G. R. (1998). Review of integrated mental health and substance abuse treatment for patients with dual disorders. *Schizophrenia Bulletin*, *24*, 589–608.

Drake, R. E., & Mueser, K. T. (1996). Alcohol-use disorder and severe mental illness. *Alcohol Health and Research World*, *2*, 87–93.

Drake, R., & Mueser, K. T. (2002). Co-occurring alcohol use disorder and schizophrenia. *Alcohol and Health*, *26*, 99–102.

Drake, R. E., & Mueser, K. T. (2000). Psychosocial approaches to dual diagnosis. *Schizophrenia Bulletin*, *26*, 105–118.

Drake, R. E., Mueser, K. M., Clark, R. E., & Wallach, M. A. (1996). The course, treatment, and outcome of substance disorder in persons with severe mental illness. *American Journal of Orthopsychiatry*, *66*, 42–51.

Drake, R. E., Osher, F. C., & Wallach, M. A. (1989). Alcohol use and abuse in schizophrenia: A prospective community study. *Journal of Nervous and Mental Disease*, *177*, 408–414.

Drake, R. E., Rosenberg, S. D., & Mueser, K. T. (1996). Assessing substance use disorder in persons with severe mental illness. *New Directions for Mental Health Services*, *70*, 3–17.

Drake, R. E., & Wallach, M. A. (2000). Dual diagnosis: 15 years of progress. *Psychiatric Services*, *51*(9), 1126–1129.

Drake, R. E., Yovetich, N. A., Bebout, R. R., Harris, M., & McHugo, G. J. (1997). Integrated treatment for dually diagnosed homeless adults. *Journal of Nervous and Mental Disease*, *180*, 298–305.

Duan, C., & Hill, C. E. (1996). The current state of empathy research. *Journal of Counseling Psychology*, *43*, 261–274.

Duggal, S., Carlson, E. A., Sroufe, L. A., & Egeland, B. (2001). Depressive symptomatology in childhood and adolescence. *Development and Psychopathology*, *13*, 143–164.

Dumaine, M. L. (2003). Meta-analysis of interventions with co-occurring disorders of severe mental illness and substance abuse: Implications for social work practice. *Research on Social Work Practice*, *13*(2), 142–165.

Dutta, R., Boydell, J., Kennedy, N., Van Os, J., Fearon, P., & Murray, R. M. (2007). Suicide and other causes of mortality in bipolar disorder: A longitudinal study. *Psychological Medicine*, *37*(6), 839–847.

Dutton, D. G., Bodnarchuk, M., Kropp, R., Hart, S. D., & Ogloff, J. P. (1997). Client personality disorders affecting wife assault post-treatment recidivism. *Violence and Victims*, *12*, 37–50.

Dutton, D. G., Starzomski, A., & Ryan, L. (1996). Antecedents of abusive personality and abusive behavior in wife assaulters. *Journal of Family Violence, 11*, 113–132.

Dzieglielewski, S. F., & Leon, A. M. (1998). Pharmacological treatment of major depression. *Research on Social Work Practice, 8*, 475–490.

Dziegielewski, S. F., Resnick, C., Nelson-Gardell, D., & Harrison, D. F. (1998). Treatment of sexual dysfunctions: What social workers need to know. *Research on Social Work Practice, 8*, 685–697.

D'Zurilla, T. J., & Goldfried, M. R. (1971). Problem solving and behavior modification. *Journal of Abnormal Psychology, 78*, 107–126.

Eack, S. M., Hogarty, G. E., Greenwald, D. P., Hogarty, S. S., & Keshavan, M. S. (2011). Effects of cognitive enhancement therapy on employment outcomes in early schizophrenia: Results from a 2-year randomized trial. *Research on Social Work Practice, 21*, 32–42.

Edelstein, B., Staats, N., Kalish, K. D., & Northrop, L. E. (1996). Assessment of older adults. In M. Hersen & V. B. Van Hasselt (Eds.), *Psychological treatment of older adults: An introductory text* (pp. 35–68). New York, NY: Plenum Press.

Edenfield, T. M., & Saeed, S. A. (2012). An update on mindfulness meditation as a self-help treatment for anxiety and depression. *Psychology Research and Behavior Management, 12*, 131–141.

Edmond, T., Rubin, A., & Wambach, K. G. (1999). The effectiveness of EMDR with adult female survivors of childhood sexual abuse. *Social Work Research, 23*, 103–116.

Ehlers, A., & Clark, D. M. (2000). A cognitive model of posttraumatic stress disorder. *Behavior Research and Therapy, 38*, 319–345.

Eisen, M. L., & Goodman, G. S. (1998). Trauma, memory, and suggestibility in children. *Development and Psychopathology, 10*, 717–738.

Eisen, S. V., Dill, D. L., & Grob, M. C. (1994). Reliability and validity of a brief patient-report instrument for psychiatric outcome evaluation. *Hospital and Community Psychiatry, 45*, 242–247.

Eisen, S. V., Normand, S., Belanger, A., Spiro, A., & Esch, D. (2004). The Revised Behavior and Symptom Identification Scale (BASIS-R): Reliability and validity. *Medical Care, 42*, 1230–1241.

Eisler, I., Dare, C., Russell, G. F., Szmukler, G., le Grange, D., & Dodge, E. (1997). Family and individual therapy in anorexia nervosa. *Archives of General Psychiatry, 54*, 1025–1030.

Eisler, I., Simic, M., Russell, G. F., & Dare, C. (2007). A randomized controlled treatment trial of two forms of family therapy in adolescent anorexia nervosa: A five-year follow-up. *Journal of Child Psychology and Psychiatry, 48*, 552–560.

El-Bassel, N., Ivanoff, A., Schilling, R. F., Gilbert, L., Borne, D., & Chen, D. (1995). Preventing HIV/AIDS in drug-abusing incarcerated women through skills building and social support enhancement. *Social Work Research, 19*, 131–141.

Elbogen, E. B., & Tomkins, A. J. (2000). From the psychiatric hospital to the community: Integrating conditional release and contingency management. *Behavioral Sciences and the Law, 18*, 427–444.

Elkin, I. (1994). The NIMH treatment of depression collaborative research program: Where we began and where we are. In A. E. Bergin & S. L. Garfield (Eds.), *The handbook of psychotherapy and behavior change* (4th ed., pp. 114–142). New York, NY: Wiley.

Elkin, I., Parloff, M. B., Hadley, S. W., & Autry, J. H. (1985). NIMH treatment of depression collaborative research program: Background and research plan. *Archives of General Psychiatry, 42*, 305–316.

Elkin, I., Shea, M. T., Watkins, J. T., Imber, S. D., Sotsky, S. M., Collins, J. F., . . . Parloff, M. B. (1989). National Institute of Mental Health Treatment of Depression Collaborative Program: General effectiveness of treatments. *Archives of General Psychiatry, 46*, 971–982.

Elliot, R. (2010). Psychotherapy change process research: Realizing the promise. *Psychotherapy Research, 20*, 123–135.

Ellis, A. (1962). *Reason and emotion in psychotherapy*. Secaucus, NJ: Citadel.

Ellison, C., Burdette, A. M., & Wilcox, W. B. (2010). The couple that prays together: Race and ethnicity, religion, and relationship quality among working-age adults. *Journal of Marriage and Family, 72*, 963–975.

Emmelkamp, P. M. G. (1994). *Behavior therapy with adults*. In A. E. Bergin & S. L. Garfield (Eds.), *The handbook of psychotherapy and behavior change* (4th ed., pp. 379–427). New York, NY: Wiley.

Emmelkamp, P. M. G., & Vedel, E. (2010). Commentary—Psychological treatments for antisocial personality disorder: Where is the evidence that group treatment and therapeutic community should be recommended? *Personality and Mental Health, 4*, 30–33.

Emrick, C. (1974). A review of psychologically oriented treatment of alcoholism: I. The use and interrelationships of outcome criteria and drinking behavior following treatment. *Quarterly Journal of Studies on Alcohol, 35*, 523–549.

Emrick, C. (1982). Evaluation of alcoholism psychotherapy methods. In E. M. Pattison & E. Kauffman (Eds.), *The encyclopedic handbook of alcoholism* (chap. 95). New York, NY: Gardner Press.

Emrick, C. (1993). Alcoholics Anonymous: What is currently known? In B. S. McCrady & W. R. Miller (Eds.), *Research on Alcoholics Anonymous: Opportunities and alternatives* (pp. 41–78). New Brunswick, NJ: Rutgers Center of Alcohol Studies.

English, D. J., & Graham, J. C. (2000). An examination of relationships between children's protective services social worker assessment of risk and independent LONGSCAN measures of risk constructs. *Children and Youth Services Review, 22*, 897–933.

Engs, R. C. (1977). Drinking patterns and drinking problems of college students. *Journal of Studies on Alcohol, 38*, 2144–2156.

Epstein, N. H., Baucom, D. H., & Daiuto, A. (1997). Cognitive-behavioural couples therapy. In W. K. Halford & H. J. Markham (Eds.), *Clinical handbook of marriage and couples intervention* (pp. 415–449). New York, NY: Wiley.

Erikson, E. H. (1950). *Childhood and society*. New York, NY: Norton.

Erlenmeyer-Kimling, L. (1996). A look at the evolution of developmental models of schizophrenia. In S. Matthysse, D. L. Levy, J. Kagan, & F. M. Benes (Eds.), *Psychopathology: The evolving science of mental disorder* (pp. 229–252). New York, NY: Cambridge University Press.

Eronen, M., Angermeyer, M. C., & Schulze, B. (1998). The psychiatric epidemiology of violent behavior. *Social Psychiatry and Psychiatric Epidemiology, 33*, S13–S23.

Esposito-Smythers, C., Spirito, A., Kahler, C. W., Hunt, J., & Monti, P. (2011). Treatment of co-occurring substance abuse and suicidality among adolescents: A randomized trial. *Journal of Consulting and Clinical Psychology, 79*, 728–739.

Essock, S. M., Frisman, L. K., & Kontos, N. J. (1998). Cost-effectiveness of assertive community treatment teams. *American Journal of Orthopsychiatry, 68*, 179–190.

Estrada, A. U., & Pinsoff, W. M. (1995). The effectiveness of family therapies for selected behavioral disorder of childhood. *Journal of Marital and Family Therapy, 21*, 403–440.

Evans, D. M., & Dunn, N. J. (1995). Alcohol expectancies, coping responses and self-efficacy judgments: A replication and extension of Cooper et al.'s 1988 study in a college sample. *Journal of Studies on Alcohol, 56*, 186–193.

Everson, M. D., & Boat, B. W. (1994). Putting the anatomical doll controversy in perspective: An examination of the major uses and criticisms of the dolls in child sexual abuse evaluations. *Child Abuse and Neglect, 18*, 113–129.

Eyberg, S. M., & Robinson, E. A. (1983). Conduct problem behavior: Standardization of a behavioral rating scale with adolescents. *Journal of Clinical Child Psychology, 12*, 347–357.

Eyberg, S. M., & Ross, A. W. (1978). Assessment of child behavior problems: The validation of a new inventory. *Journal of Clinical Child Psychology, 7*, 113–116.

Eysenck, H. J. (1952). The effects of psychotherapy: An evaluation. *Journal of Consulting Psychology, 16*, 319–324.

Eysenck, H. J. (1960). *The structure of human personality*. London, UK: Routledge and Kegan Paul.

Fabiano, G. A., Pelham, W. E., Coles, E. K., Gnagy, E. M., Chronis-Toscano, A., & O'Connor, B. C. (2009). A meta-analysis of behavioral treatments for attention-deficit/hyperactivity disorder. *Clinical Psychology Review, 29*, 129–140.

Fairburn, C. G. (1981). A cognitive-behavioural approach to the treatment of bulimia. *Psychological Medicine, 11*, 707–711.

Fairburn, C. G. (1993). Interpersonal psychotherapy for bulimia nervosa. In G. L. Klerman & M. M. Weissman (Eds.), *New applications of interpersonal psychotherapy* (pp. 353–378). Washington, DC: American Psychiatric Association.

Fairburn, C. G. (1997). Eating disorders. In D. M. Clark & C. G. Fairburn (Eds.), *Science and practice of cognitive behaviour therapy* (pp. 209–241). New York, NY: Oxford University Press.

Fairburn, C. G., & Beglin, S. J. (1990). Studies of the epidemiology of bulimia nervosa. *American Journal of Psychiatry, 147*, 401–408.

Fairburn, C. G., & Beglin, S. J. (1994). Assessment of eating disorders: Interview or self-report questionnaire? *International Journal of Eating Disorders, 16*, 363–370.

Fairburn, C. G., Cooper, Z., Doll, H. A., Norman, P., & O'Connor, M. (2000). The natural course of bulimia nervosa and binge eating disorder in young women. *Archives of General Psychiatry, 57*, 659–665.

Fairburn, C. G., Cooper, Z., Doll, H. A., O'Connor, M. E., Bohn, K., Hawker, D. M., . . . Palmer, R. L. (2009). Transdiagnostic cognitive-behavioral therapy for eating disorders: A two-site trial with 60-week follow-up. *American Journal of Psychiatry, 166*, 311–319.

Fairburn, C. G., Cooper, Z., & Shafran, R. (2003). Cognitive behaviour therapy for eating disorders: A "transdiagnostic" theory and treatment. *Behavior, Research and Therapy, 41*, 509–528.

Fairburn, C. G., Jones, R., Peveler, R. C., Carr, S. J., Solomon, R. A., O'Connor, M. E., . . . Hope, R. A. (1991). Three psychological treatments for bulimia nervosa. *Archives of General Psychiatry*, *48*, 463–469.

Fairburn, C. G., Jones, R., Peveler, R. C., Hope, R. A., & O'Connor, M. (1993). Psychotherapy and bulimia nervosa: Longer-term effects of interpersonal psychotherapy, behavior therapy, and cognitive behavior therapy. *Archives of General Psychiatry*, *50*, 419–428.

Fairburn, C. G., Marcus, M. D., & Wilson, G. T. (1993). Cognitive-behavior therapy for binge eating and bulimia nervosa: A comprehensive treatment manual. In C. G. Fairburn & G. T. Wilson (Eds.), *Binge eating: Nature, assessment and treatment* (pp. 361–404). New York, NY: Guilford Press.

Fairburn, C. G., Norman, P. A., Welch, S. L., O'Connor, M. E., Doll, H. A., & Peveler, R. C. (1995). A prospective study of outcome in bulimia nervosa and the long-term effects of three psychological treatments. *Archives of General Psychiatry*, *52*, 304–312.

Fairburn, C. G., & Wilson, G. T. (Eds.) (1993). *Binge eating: Nature, assessment and treatment*. New York, NY: Guilford Press.

Falloon, R. H., & Coverdale, J. H. (1994). Cognitive-behavioural family interventions for major mental disorders. *Behaviour Change*, *11*, 213–222.

Falloon, R. H., Roncone, R., Malm, U., & Coverdale, J. H. (1998). Effective and efficient treatment strategies to enhance recovery from schizophrenia: How much longer will people have to wait before we provide them? *Psychiatric Rehabilitation Skills*, *2*, 107–127.

Fals-Stewart, W., & Clinton-Sherrod, M. (2009). Treating intimate partner violence among substance abusing dyads: The effect of couples therapy. *Professional Psychology: Research and Practice*, *40*(3), 257–263.

Fals-Stewart, W., Lam, W., & Kelly, M. L. (2009). Learning sobriety together: Behavioral couples therapy for alcoholism and drug abuse. *Journal of Family Therapy*, *31*, 115–125.

Fals-Stewart, W., O'Farrell, T., & Birchler, G. (1997). Behavioral couples therapy for male substance-abusing patients: A cost outcomes analysis. *Journal of Consulting and Clinical Psychology*, *65*, 789–802.

Family Support Act of 1988, Pub. L. No. 100-485.

Fantuzzo, J. W., Jurecic, L., Stovall, A., Hightower, A. D., Goins, C., & Schachtel, D. (1988). Effects of adult and peer social initiations on the social behavior of withdrawn, maltreated preschool children. *Journal of Consulting and Clinical Psychology*, *56*, 34–39.

Fantuzzo, J. W., & Mohr, W. K. (1999). Prevalence and effects of child exposure to domestic violence. *Future of Children*, *9*, 21–32.

Faraone, S. V., Biederman, J., Jetton, J. G., & Tsuang, M. T. (1997). Attention deficit disorder and conduct disorder: Longitudinal evidence for a familial subtype. *Psychological Medicine*, *27*, 291–300.

Farmer, E. M. Z., Compton, S. N., Burns, B. J., & Robertson, E. (2002). Review of the evidence base for treatment of childhood psychopathology externalizing disorders. *Journal of Consulting and Clinical Psychology*, *70*, 1267–1302.

Faroud, T., Edenberg, H. J., & Crabbe, J. (2010). Genetic research: Who is at risk for alcoholism? *Alcohol Research and Health*, *33*, 64–75.

Farrell, L., Schlup, B., & Boschen, M. J. (2010). Cognitive-behavioral treatment of childhood obsessive-compulsive disorder in community-based clinical practice: Clinical significance and benchmarking against efficacy. *Behaviour Research and Therapy*, *48*, 409–417.

Farrell, S. P., Hains, A. A., & Davies, W. H. (1998). Cognitive behavioral interventions for sexually abused children exhibiting PTSD symptomatology. *Behavior Therapy*, *29*, 241–255.

Farrington, D. P. (2000). Psychosocial predictors of adult antisocial personality and adult convictions. *Behavioral Sciences and the Law*, *18*, 605–622.

Fava, G. A., Rafanelli, C., Grandi, S., Canestrari, R., & Morphy, M. A. (1998). Six-year outcome for cognitive behavioral treatment of residual symptoms in major depression. *American Journal of Psychiatry*, *155*, 1443–1445.

Fava, M., Rankin, M. A., Wright, E. C., Alpert, J. E., Nierenberg, A. A., Pava, J., & Rosenbaum, J. F. (2000). Anxiety disorders in major depression. *Comprehensive Psychiatry*, *41*, 97–102.

Fazel, S., Bains, P., & Doll, H. (2006). Substance abuse and dependence in prisoners: A systematic review. *Addiction*, *101*, 181–191.

Feit, M. D., & Cuevas-Feit, N. M. (1996). An overview of social work practice with the elderly. In M. J. Holosko & M. D. Feit (Eds.), *Social work practice with the elderly* (2nd ed., pp. 3–20). Toronto, ON: Canadian Scholar's Press.

Ferguson, C. J. (2010). Genetic contributions to antisocial personality and behavior: A meta-analytic review from an evolutionary perspective. *Journal of Social Psychology*, *150*, 160–180.

Fergusson, D. M., & Mullen, P. E. (1999). *Childhood sexual abuse: An evidence-based perspective* (Developmental Clinical Psychology and Psychiatry Series No. 40). Thousand Oaks, CA: Sage.

Ferriero, F., Seoane, G., & Senra, C. (2011). A prospective study of risk factors for the development of depression and disordered eating in adolescents. *Journal of Clinical Child and Adolescent Psychology*, *40*, 500–505.

Field, C. A., & Caetano, R. (2005). Intimate partner violence in the U.S. general population. *Journal of Interpersonal Violence*, *20*, 463–469.

Fillmore, K. M. (1974). Drinking and problem drinking in early adulthood and middle age: An exploratory 20-year follow-up study. *Quarterly Journal of Studies on Alcohol*, *35*, 819–840.

Fillmore, K. M. (1988). *Alcohol use across the life course*. Toronto, ON: Addiction Research Foundation.

Fine, S., Forth, A., Gilbert, M., & Haley, G. (1991). Group therapy for adolescent depressive disorder: A comparison of social skills and therapeutic support. *Journal of the American Academy of Child and Adolescent Psychiatry*, *30*, 79–85.

Fingeret, M. C., Warren, C. S., Cepeda-Benito, A., & Gleaves, D. H. (2006). Eating disorder prevention research: A meta-analysis. *Eating Disorders*, *14*, 191–213.

Finkelhor, D. (1988). The trauma of child sexual abuse: Two models. *Journal of Interpersonal Violence*, *2*, 348–366.

Finkelhor, D. (2009). The prevention of childhood sexual abuse. *Future of Children*, *19*, 169–194.

Finkelhor, D., & Berliner, L. (1995). Research on the treatment of sexually abused children: A review and recommendations. *Journal of the American Academy of Child and Adolescent Psychiatry*, *34*, 1408–1423.

Finkelhor, D., & Browne, A. (1985). The traumatic impact of sexual abuse: A conceptualization. *American Journal of Orthopsychiatry, 55,* 530–541.

Finkelhor, D., & Dziuba-Leatherman, J. (1994). Children as victims of violence: A national survey. *Pediatrics, 94,* 413–420.

Finkelhor, D., Hotaling, G., Lewis, I. A., & Smith, C. (1990). Sexual abuse in a national survey of adult men and women: Prevalence, characteristics, and risk factors. *Child Abuse and Neglect, 14,* 19–28.

Finkelhor, D., Ormrod, R., Turner, H., & Hamby, S. L. (2005). The victimization of children and youth: A comprehensive national survey. *Child Maltreatment, 10,* 5–25.

Finkelhor D., Turner, H., Ormrod, R., & Hamby, S. L. (2009). Violence, abuse, and crime exposure in a national sample of children and youth. *Pediatrics, 124,* 1411–1423.

Finley, L. (1998). The cultural context: Families coping with severe mental illness. *Psychiatric Rehabilitation Journal, 21,* 230–240.

Finney, J. W., & Moos, R. H. (1991). The long-term course of treated alcoholism: I. Mortality, relapse and remission rates and comparisons with community controls. *Journal of Studies on Alcohol, 51,* 44–54.

Finney, J. W., Moos, R. H., & Timko, C. (1999). The course of treated and untreated substance use disorders: Remission and resolution, relapse and mortality. In B. S. McCrady & E. E. Epstein (Eds.), *Addictions: A comprehensive guidebook* (pp. 30–49). New York, NY: Oxford University Press.

Finn-Stevenson, M., Desimone, L., & Chung, A. (1998). Linking child care and support services with the school: Pilot evaluation of the school of the 21st century. *Children and Youth Services Review, 20,* 177–205.

Fischer, D. J., Himle, J. A., & Hanna, G. L. (1998). Group behavioral therapy for adolescents with obsessive-compulsive disorder: Preliminary outcomes. *Research on Social Work Practice, 8,* 629–636.

Fischer, J. (1973). Is casework effective? A review. *Social Work, 18,* 5–20.

Fischer, J. (1981). The social work revolution. *Social Work, 26,* 199–207.

Fischer, J. (1993). Empirically-based practice: The end of ideology? *Journal of Social Service Research, 18,* 19–64.

Fischer, M., Barkley, R. A., Smallish, L., & Fletcher, K. (2002). Young adult follow-up of hyperactive children: Self-reported psychiatric disorders, comorbidity, and the role of childhood conduct problems and teen CD. *Journal of Abnormal Child Psychology, 30,* 463–475.

Fishbein, D. H. (2000). Introduction. In D. H. Fishbein (Ed.), *The science, treatment, and prevention of antisocial behaviors: Application to the criminal justice system* (pp. 1-1 to 1-8). Kingston, NJ: Civic Research Institute.

Fisher, W. H., Packer, I. K., Grisso, T., McDermeit, M., & Brown, J. K. (2000). From case management to court clinic: Examining forensic system involvement of persons with severe mental illness. *Mental Health Services Research, 2,* 41–49.

Fitzpatrick, T. R. (1998). Bereavement events among elderly men: The effects of stress and health. *Journal of Applied Gerontology, 17,* 204–228.

Fleming, M. F., Barry, K. L., & MacDonald, R. (1991). The Alcohol Use Disorders Identification Test (AUDIT) in a college sample. *International Journal of the Addictions, 26,* 1173–1185.

Fletcher, B. W., Tims, F. M., & Brown, B. S. (1997). Drug Abuse Treatment Outcome Study (DATOS): Treatment evaluation research in the United States. *Psychology of Addictive Behaviors, 11,* 216–229.

Flicker, S. M., Waldron, H. B., Turner, C. W., Brody, J. L., & Hops, H. (2008). Ethnic matching and treatment outcome with Hispanic and Anglo substance-abusing adolescents in family therapy. *Journal of Family Psychology, 22*, 439–447.

Floyd, A. S., Monahan, S. C., Finney, J. W., & Morley, J. A. (1996). Alcoholism treatment outcome studies, 1980–1992: The nature of the research. *Addictive Behaviors, 21*, 413–428.

Floyd, F. J., Haynes, S. N., & Kelly, S. (1997). Marital assessment: A dynamic functional-analytic approach. In W. K. Halford & H. J. Markham (Eds.), *Clinical handbook of marriage and couples intervention* (pp. 349–377). New York, NY: Wiley.

Foa, E. B., Dancu, C. V., Hembree, E. A., Joycox, L. H., Meadows, E. A., & Street, G. P. (1999). A comparison of exposure therapy, stress inoculation training, and their combination for reducing posttraumatic stress disorder in female assault victims. *Journal of Consulting and Clinical Psychology, 67*, 194–200.

Foa, E. B., Huppert, J. D., & Cahill, S. P. (2006). Emotional processing theory: An update. In B. O. Rothbaum (Ed.), *Pathological anxiety: Emotional processing in etiology and treatment* (pp. 3–24). New York, NY: Guilford Press.

Foa, E. B., Huppert, J. D., Leiberg, S., Langner, R., Kichic, R., Hajcak, G., & Salkovskis, P. M. (2002). The Obsessive-Compulsive Inventory: Development and validation of a short version. *Psychological Assessment, 14*, 485–496.

Foa, E. B., & Kozak, M. J. (1986). Emotional processing of fear: Exposure to corrective information. *Psychological Bulletin, 99*, 20–35.

Foa, E. B., & Kozak, M. J. (1996). Obsessive compulsive disorder. In C. Lindemann (Ed.), *Handbook of the treatment of the anxiety disorders* (pp. 137–171). Northvale, NJ: Aronson.

Foa, E. B., Kozak, M. J., Salkovskis, P. M., Coles, M. E., & Amir, N. (1998). The validation of a new obsessive-compulsive disorder scale: The obsessive-compulsive inventory. *Psychological Assessment, 10*, 206–214.

Foa, E. B., & Meadows, E. A. (1997). Psychosocial treatments for posttraumatic stress disorder: A critical review. *Annual Review of Psychology, 48*, 449–480.

Foa, E. B., Riggs, D. S., Dancu, C. V., & Rothbaum, B. O. (1993). Reliability and validity of a brief instrument for assessing post-traumatic stress disorder. *Journal of Traumatic Stress, 6*, 459–473.

Foa, E. B., & Rothbaum, B. O. (1998). *Treating the trauma of rape: Cognitive-behavioral therapy for PTSD*. New York, NY: Guilford Press.

Foa, E. B., Rothbaum, B. O., Riggs, D. S., & Murdock, T. B. (1991). Treatment of post-traumatic stress disorder in rape victims: A comparison between cognitive-behavioral procedures and counseling. *Journal of Consulting and Clinical Psychology, 59*, 715–723.

Foa, E. B., & Tolin, D. F. (2000). Comparison of the PTSD Symptom Scale–Interview version and the Clinician Administered PTSD Scale. *Journal of Traumatic Stress, 13*, 181–191.

Fokias, D., & Tyler, P. (1995). Social support and agoraphobia: A review. *Clinical Psychology Review, 15*, 347–366.

Follette, V. M., Ruzek, J. I., & Abueg, F. R. (1998). A contextual analysis of trauma: Assessment and treatment. In V. M. Follette, J. I. Ruzek, & F. R. Abueg (Eds.), *Cognitive-behavioral therapies for trauma* (pp. 3–14). New York, NY: Guilford Press.

Folstein, M. F., Folstein, S., & McHugh, P. R. (1975). Mini-mental state: A practical method for grading the cognitive state of patients for the clinician. *Journal of Psychiatric Research, 12*, 189–198.

Fonagy, P., Steele, M., Steele, H., Leigh, T., Kennedy, R., Mattoon, G., . . . Gerber, A. (1996). The relation of attachment status, psychiatric classification, and response to psychotherapy. *Journal of Consulting and Clinical Psychology, 64*, 22–31.

Fonagy, P., Target, M., & Gergely, G. (2000). Attachment and borderline personality disorder: A theory and some evidence. *Psychiatric Clinics of North America, 23*, 103–122.

Fonseca, A. C., & Perrin, S. (2001). Clinical phenomenology, classification and assessment of anxiety disorders in children and adolescents. In W. K. Silverman & P. D. A. Treffers (Eds.), *Anxiety disorders in children and adolescents: Research, assessment and intervention* (pp. 126–158). New York, NY: Cambridge University Press.

Forbes, D., Lloyd, D., Nixon, R. D. V., Elliot, P., Varker, T., Perry, D., . . . Creamer, M. (2012). A multisite randomized controlled effectiveness trial of cognitive processing therapy for military-related posttraumatic stress disorder. *Journal of Anxiety Disorders, 26*, 442–452.

Forcehimes, A. A., Venner, K. L., Bogenschutz, M. P., Foley, K., Davis, M. P., Houck, J. M., . . . Begaye, P. (2011). American Indian methamphetamine and other drug use in the Southwestern United States. *Cultural Diversity and Ethnic Minority Psychology, 17*, 366–376.

Ford, J., Elhai, J. D., Connor, D. F., & Frueh, B. C. (2010). Poly-victimization and risk of posttraumatic, depressive, and substance use disorders and involvement in delinquency in a national sample of adolescence. *Journal of Adolescent Health, 46*, 545–552.

Forehand, R. L., & McMahon, R. J. (1981). *Helping the non-compliant child: A clinician's guide to parent training.* New York, NY: Guilford Press.

Foreyt, J. P., & Mikhail, C. (1997). Anorexia nervosa and bulimia nervosa. In E. J. Mash & L. G. Terdal (Eds.), *Assessment of childhood disorders* (3rd ed., pp. 683–716). New York, NY: Guilford Press.

Forth, A. E., Hart, S. D., & Hare, R. D. (1990). Assessment of psychopathy in male young offenders. *Psychological Assessment: A Journal of Consulting and Clinical Psychology, 2*, 342–344.

Foster, S. L. (1994). Assessing and treating parent-adolescent conflict. In M. Hersen, R. Eisler, & P. Miller (Eds.), *Progress in behavior modification* (pp. 53–72). New York, NY: Academic Press.

Foster, S. L., & Robin, A. L. (1997). Family conflict and communication in adolescence. In E. J. Mash & L. G. Terdal (Eds.), *Assessment of childhood disorders* (3rd ed., pp. 627–682). New York, NY: Guilford Press.

Fraenkel, P. (1997). Systems approaches to couple therapy. In W. K. Halford & H. J. Markham (Eds.), *Clinical handbook of marriage and couples intervention* (pp. 379–413). New York, NY: Wiley.

Frances, A. J., & Nardo, J. M. (2013). ICD-11 should not repeat the mistakes made by DSM-5. *British Journal of Psychiatry, 203*, 1–2.

Frances, R. J., & Miller, S. I. (Eds.) (1998). *Clinical textbook of addictive disorders.* New York, NY: Guilford Press.

Franklin, M. E., Abramowitz, J. S., Kozak, M. J., Levitt, J. T., & Foa, E. B. (2000). Effectiveness of exposure and ritual prevention for obsessive-compulsive disorder: Randomized compared with non-randomized samples. *Journal of Consulting and Clinical Psychology*, *68*, 594–602.

Franklin, M. E., & Foa, E. B. (2008). Obsessive-compulsive disorder. In D. H. Barlow (Ed.), *Clinical handbook of psychological disorders* (pp. 164–215). New York, NY: Guilford Press.

Franklin, M. E., & Foa, E. B. (2011). Treatment of obsessive compulsive disorder. *Annual Review of Clinical Psychology*, *7*, 229–243.

Franklin, C., & Jordan, C. (2011). *Clinical assessment for social workers: Quantitative and qualitative methods* (3rd ed.). Chicago, IL: Lyceum Books.

Franklin, C., Streeter, C., & Springer, D. (2001). Validity of the FACES IV family assessment measure. *Research on Social Work Practice*, *11*, 576–596.

Franko, D. L., & Keel, P. K. (2006). Suicidality in eating disorders: Occurrence, correlates and clinical implications. *Clinical Psychology Review*, *26*, 769–782.

Franz, D., & Gross, A. M. (1998). Assessment of child behavior problems: Externalizing disorders. In A. S. Bellack & M. Hersen (Eds.), *Behavioral assessment: A practical handbook* (4th ed., pp. 361–377). Boston, MA: Allyn & Bacon.

Fraser, J. A., Armstrong, K. L., Morris, J. P., & Dadds, M. R. (2000). Home visiting intervention for vulnerable families with newborns: Follow-up results of a randomized controlled trial. *Child Abuse and Neglect*, *11*, 1399–1429.

Fraser, M. (1996, January). Cognitive problem solving and aggressive behavior among children. *Families in Society: The Journal of Contemporary Human Services*, 19–31.

Fraser, M. W., Day, S. H., Galinsky, M. J., Hodges, V. G., & Smokowski, P. R. (2004). Conduct problems and peer rejection in childhood: A randomized trial of the Making Choices and Strong Families programs. *Research on Social Work Practice*, *14*, 313–324.

Frederick, C. J. (1985). Selected foci on the spectrum of posttraumatic stress disorders. In J. Laube & S. A. Murphy (Eds.), *Perspectives on disaster recovery* (pp. 110–130). East Norwalk, CT: Appleton-Century-Crofts.

Fredman, N., & Sherman, R. (1987). *Handbook of measurements for marriage and family therapy*. New York, NY: Brunner/Mazel.

Freedman, D. (2001). False prediction of future dangerousness: Error rates and psychopathy checklist—revised. *Journal of the American Academy of Psychiatry and the Law*, *29*, 89–95.

Freeman, E. M. (1991). Addictive behaviors: State of the art issues in social work treatment. In E. M. Freeman (Ed.), *The addiction process: Effective social work approaches* (pp. 1–9). New York, NY: Longman.

Freeston, M. H., Ladouceur, R., Gagnon, F., Thibodeau, N., Rheaume, J., Letarte, H., & Bujold, A. (1997). Cognitive-behavioral treatment of obsessive thoughts: A controlled study. *Journal of Consulting and Clinical Psychology*, *65*, 405–413.

Frese, F. J., Stanley, J., Kress, K., & Vogel-Scibilia, S. (2001). Integrating evidence-based practices and the recovery model. *Psychiatric Services*, *52*, 1462–1468.

Freud, A. (1946). *The ego and the mechanisms of defense*. New York, NY: International Universities Press.

Freud, S. (1923). *The ego and the id*. London, UK: Hogarth.

Freud, S. (1938). *The basic writings of Sigmund Freud*. New York, NY: Random House.

Freud, S. (1966). *Introductory lectures on psychoanalysis*. New York, NY: Norton. (Originally published 1920)

Friedman, L. H. (1991). Evaluating the impact of intensive family preservation services in New Jersey. In K. Wells & D. Biegel (Eds.), *Family preservation services: Research and evaluation* (pp. 47–71). Newbury Park, CA: Sage.

Friedman, M. (1997). Posttraumatic stress disorder. *Journal of Clinical Psychiatry, 58*(9, suppl.), 33–36.

Friedrich, W. N. (1993). Sexual victimization and sexual behavior in children: A review of recent literature. *Child Abuse and Neglect, 17,* 59–66.

Fritzler, B. K., Hecker, J. E., & Losee, M. C. (1997). Self-directed treatment with minimal therapist contact: Preliminary findings for obsessive-compulsive disorder. *Behaviour Research and Therapy, 35,* 627–631.

Frueh, B. C., Brady, K. L., & de Arellano, M. A. (1998). Racial differences in combat-related PTSD: Empirical findings and conceptual issues. *Clinical Psychology Review, 18,* 287–305.

Frueh, B. C., Grubaugh, A. L., Cusack, K. J., Kimble, M. O., Elhai, J. D., & Knapp, R. G. (2009). Exposure-based cognitive–behavioral treatment of PTSD in adults with schizophrenia or schizoaffective disorder: A pilot study. *Journal of Anxiety Disorders, 23,* 665–675.

Fuller, R. K., & Hiller-Sturmhofel, S. (1999). Alcoholism treatment in the United States: An overview. *Alcohol Research and Health, 23,* 69–77.

Fulwiler, C., & Ruthazer, R. (1999). Premorbid risk factors for violence in adult mental illness. *Comprehensive Psychiatry, 40,* 96–100.

Furby, L., Weinrott, M. R., & Blackshaw, L. (1989). Sex offender recidivism: A review. *Psychological Bulletin, 105,* 3–30.

Furman, W., & Flanagan, A. S. (1997). The influence of earlier relationships on marriage: An attachment perspective. In W. K. Halford & H. J. Markham (Eds.), *Clinical handbook of marriage and couples intervention* (pp. 179–202). New York, NY: Wiley.

Fusco, R. A. (2010). Intimate partner violence in interracial couples: A comparison to white and ethnic minority monoracial couples. *Journal of Interpersonal Violence, 25,* 1785–1800.

Gacono, C. B., Nieberding, R. J., Owen, A., Rubel, J., & Bodholdt, R. (2001). Treating conduct disorder, antisocial, and psychopathic personalities. In J. B. Ashford, B. D. Sales, & W. H. Reid (Eds.), *Treating adult and juvenile offenders with special needs* (pp. 99–129). Washington, DC: American Psychological Association.

Gainsbury, S., & Blaszczynski, A. (2008). A systematic review of Internet-based therapy for the treatment of addictions. *Clinical Psychology Review, 31,* 490–498.

Gallo, K. P., Chan, P. T., Buzzella, B. A., Whitton, S. W., & Pincus, D. B. (2012). The impact of an 8-day intensive treatment for adolescent panic disorder and agoraphobia on comorbid diagnoses. *Behavior Therapy, 43,* 153–159.

Galvan, F. H., & Caetano, R. (2003). Alcohol use and related problems among ethnic minorities in the United States. *Alcohol Research and Health, 27,* 87–94.

Gambrill, E. (1990). *Critical thinking in clinical practice*. San Francisco, CA: Jossey-Bass.

Gambrill, E. (1995). Less marketing and more scholarship. *Social Work Research*, *19*, 38–47.

Gambrill, E. (2001). Social work: An authority-based profession. *Research on Social Work Practice*, *11*, 166–175.

Gambrill, E. (2004). Contributions of critical thinking and evidence-based practice to the fulfillment of the ethical obligations of professionals. In H. E. Briggs & T. L. Rzepnicki (Eds.), *Using evidence in social work practice: Behavioral perspectives* (pp. 3–19). Chicago, IL: Lyceum Books.

Gambrill, E. (2006). Evidence-based practices and policy: Choices ahead. *Research on Social Work Practice*, *16*, 338–357.

Garbarino, J. (1977, November). The human ecology of child maltreatment: A conceptual model of research. *Journal of Marriage and the Family*, 721–735.

Garbarino, J. (1997). The role of economic deprivation in the social context of child maltreatment. In M. E. Helfer, R. S. Kempe, & R. D. Krugman (Eds.), *The battered child* (5th ed., pp. 49–60). Chicago, IL: University of Chicago Press.

Garbarino, J., & Kostelny, K. (1992). Child maltreatment as a community problem. *Child Abuse and Neglect*, *16*, 455–464.

Garber, J., Little, S., Hilsman, R., & Weaver, K. R. (1998). Family predictors of suicidal symptoms in young adolescents. *Journal of Adolescence*, *21*, 445–457.

Garfield, S. L. (1996). Some problems associated with "validated" forms of psychotherapy. *Clinical Psychology: Science and Practice*, *3*, 218–229.

Garmezy, N. (1991). Resilience in children's adaptation to negative life events and stressed environments. *Pediatric Annals*, *20*, 459–466.

Garner, D. M., Olmstead, M. P., & Policy, J. (1983). Development and validation of a multidimensional eating disorder inventory for anorexia nervosa and bulimia. *International Journal of Eating Disorders*, *2*, 15–34.

Gaudin, J. M. (1993). Effective intervention with neglectful families. *Criminal Justice and Behavior*, *20*, 66–89.

Gearon, J. S., Kaltman, S. I., Brown, C., & Bellack, A. S. (2003). Traumatic life events and PTSD among women with substance use disorders and schizophrenia. *Psychiatric Services*, *54*, 523–528. doi: 10.1176/appi.ps.54.4.523.

Geeraert, L., van den Noortgate, W., Grietens, H., & Onghena, P. (2004). Effects of family early prevention programs for families with young children at risk for physical child abuse and neglect: A meta-analysis. *Child Maltreatment*, *9*, 277–291.

Geismar, L., & Wood, K. (1986). *Family and delinquency: Resocializing the young offender*. New York, NY: Human Sciences Press.

Geller, D. A. (2006). Obsessive compulsive and spectrum disorders in children and adolescents. *Psychiatric Clinics of North America*, *29*, 353–370.

Geller, J. (1995). A biopsychosocial rationale for coerced community treatment in the management of schizophrenia. *Psychiatric Quarterly*, *66*, 219–235.

Geller, J., Drab-Hudson, D. L., Whisenhunt, B. L., & Srikameswaran, S. (2004). Readiness to change dietary restriction predicts outcomes in the eating disorders. *Eating Disorders: The Journal of Treatment & Prevention*, *12*, 209–224.

Gelles, R. J. (1997). *Intimate violence in families* (3rd ed.). Thousand Oaks, CA: Sage.

Gelles, R. J., & Cornell, C. P. (1990). *Intimate violence in families* (2nd ed.). Newbury Park, CA: Sage.

Gellis, Z. D., McGinty, J., Tierney, L., Jordan, C., Burton, J., & Misener, E. (2007). Randomized controlled trial of problem-solving therapy for minor depression in home care. *Research on Social Work Practice, 18,* 596–606.

Gendreau, P. (1996a). Offender rehabilitation: What we know and what needs to be done. *Criminal Justice and Behavior, 23,* 144–161.

Gendreau, P. (1996b). The principles of effective intervention with offenders. In A. T. Harland (Ed.), *Choosing correctional options that work: Defining demand and evaluating the supply* (pp. 117–130). Thousand Oaks, CA: Sage.

Geraerts, E., Lindsay, D. S., Merckelbach, H., Jelici, M., Raymaekers, L., Arnold, M. M., & Schooler, J. W. (2009). Cognitive mechanisms underlying recovered-memory experiences of child sexual abuse. *Psychological Science, 20,* 92–98.

Geraerts, E., Raymaekers, L., & Merckelbach, H. (2008). Recovered memories of child sexual abuse: Current findings and their legal implications. *Legal and Criminological Psychology, 3,* 165–176.

Gerbasi, J. B., Bonnie, R. J., & Binder, R. L. (2000). Resource document on mandatory outpatient treatment. *Journal of the American Academy of Psychiatry and the Law, 28,* 127–144.

Gershater-Molko, R. M., Lutzker, J. R., & Sherman, J. A. (2002). Intervention in child neglect: An applied behavioral perspective. *Aggression and Violent Behavior, 7,* 103–124.

Geschwind, N., Peeters, F., Drukker, M., van Os, J., & Wichers, M. (2011). Mindfulness training increases momentary positive emotions and reward experience in adults vulnerable to depression: A randomized controlled trial. *Journal of Consulting and Clinical Psychology, 79,* 618–628.

Gfoerer, J. C., Greenblatt, J. C., & Wright, D. A. (1997). Substance use in the US college-age population: Differences according to educational status and living arrangement. *American Journal of Public Health, 87,* 62–65.

Giesen-Bloo, J. H., Wachters, L. M., Shouten, E., & Arntz, A. (2010). The Borderline Personality Disorder Severity Index–IV: Psychometric evaluation and dimensional structure. *Personality and Individual Differences, 49,* 136–141.

Gingerich, K. J., Turnock, P., Litfin, J. K., & Rosen, L. E. (1998). Diversity and attention deficit hyperactivity disorder. *Journal of Clinical Psychology, 54,* 415–426.

Ginzburg, K., Ein-Dor, T., & Solomon, Z. (2010). Comorbidity of posttraumatic stress disorder, anxiety and depression: A 20–year longitudinal study of war veterans. *Journal of Affective Disorders, 123,* 249–257.

Glasgow, R. E. (2009). Critical measurement issues in translational research. *Research on Social Work Practice, 19,* 560–568.

Glasner-Edwards, S., & Rawson, R. (2010). Evidence-based practices in addiction treatment: Review and recommendations for public policy. *Health Policy, 97,* 93–104.

Gleason, W. J. (1997). Psychological and social dysfunctions in battering men: A review. *Aggression and Violent Behavior, 2,* 43–52.

Glisson, C., Hemmelgarn, A. L., & Post, J. A. (2002). The Shortform Assessment for Children: An assessment and outcome measure for child welfare and juvenile justice. *Research on Social Work Practice, 12,* 82–106.

Gloria, A. M., & Peregoy, J. J. (1996). Counseling Latino alcohol and other substance users/abusers. *Journal of Substance Abuse Treatment, 13,* 119–126.

Gmel, G., & Rehm, J. (2003). Harmful alcohol use. *Alcohol Research and Health, 27,* 52–62.

Godette, D. C., Malatu, M. S., Leonard, K. J., Randolf, S., & Williams, N. (2011). Racial/ethnic disparities and determinants of criminal justice involvement among youth in substance abuse treatment programs. *Journal of Correctional Healthcare*, *17*, 294–308.

Godley, S. H., Finch, M., Dougan, L., McDonnell, M., McDermeit, M., & Carey, A. (2000). Case management for dually diagnosed individuals involved in the criminal justice system. *Journal of Substance Abuse Treatment*, *18*, 137–148.

Gold, M. (1994). Neurobiology of addiction and recovery: The brain, the drive for the drug, and the 12-step fellowship. *Journal of Substance Abuse Treatment*, *11*, 93–97.

Gold, P. B., Meisler, N., Santos, A. B., Carnemolla, M. A., Williams, O. H., & Keleher, J. (2006). Randomized trial of supported employment integrated with assertive community treatment for rural adults with severe mental illness. *Schizophrenia Bulletin*, *32*, 378–395.

Goldberg, L. R. (1993). The structure of phenotypical personality traits. *American Psychologist*, *48*, 26–34.

Goldfried, M. R. (1980). Toward the delineation of therapeutic change principles. *American Psychologist*, *35*, 991–999.

Goldfried, M. R. (1995). *From cognitive-behavior therapy to psychotherapy integration*. New York, NY: Springer.

Goldfried, M. R. (2010). The future of psychotherapy integration: Closing the gap between research and practice. *Journal of Psychotherapy Integration*, *20*, 386–396.

Goldman, A., & Greenberg, L. (1992). Comparison of integrated systemic and emotionally focused approaches to couples therapy. *Journal of Consulting and Clinical Psychology*, *60*, 962–969.

Goldman, S. J., D'Angelo, E. J., & DeMaso, D. R. (1993). Psychopathology in the families of children and adolescents with borderline personality disorder. *American Journal of Psychiatry*, *150*, 1832–1835.

Goldstein, H. (1986). A cognitive-humanistic approach to the court-ordered vs. voluntary hard-to-reach client. *Social Casework*, *67*, 27–36.

Goldstein, J. M., & Tsuang, M. T. (1990). Gender and schizophrenia: An introduction and synthesis of findings. *Schizophrenia Bulletin*, *16*, 179–183.

Goldstein, R. B., Grant, B. F., Ruan, W. J., Smith, S. M., & Saha, T. D. (2006). Antisocial personality disorder with childhood- vs. adolescent-onset conduct disorder: Results from the National Epidemiologic Survey on Alcohol and Related Conditions. *Journal of Nervous and Mental Disease*, *194*, 667–675.

Gomberg, E. S. L. (1994). Risk factors for drinking over a woman's life span. *Alcohol Health and Research World*, *18*, 220–227.

Gonzalez, H. M., Tarraf, W., Whitfield, K. E., & Vega, W. A. (2010). The epidemiology of major depression and ethnicity in the United States. *Journal of Psychiatric Research*, *44*, 1043–1051.

Gonzalez, V. M., Bradizza, C. M., & Collins, R. L. (2009). Drinking to cope as a statistical mediator in the relationship between suicidal ideation and alcohol outcomes among underage college drinkers. *Psychology of Addictive Behaviors*, *23*, 443–451.

Goodheart, C. D., Kazdin, A. E., & Sternberg, R. J. (2006). *Evidence-based psychotherapy: Where practice and research meet*. Washington, DC: American Psychological Association.

Goodkind, J. R., LaNoue, M. D., & Milford, J. (2010). Adaptation and implementation of cognitive behavioral intervention for trauma in schools with American Indian youth. *Journal of Clinical Child and Adolescent Psychology, 39,* 858–872.

Goodman, G., Bottoms, B., Shaver, P. R., & Qin, J. (1995). *Factors affecting children's susceptibility versus resistance to false memory.* Paper presented at the biennial meeting of the Society for Research in Child Development, Indianapolis, IN.

Goodman, L. A., Salyers, M. P., Mueser, K. T., Rosenberg, S. D., Swartz, M., Essock, S. M., . . . Swanson, J. (2001). Recent victimization in women and men with severe mental illness: Prevalence and correlates. *Journal of Traumatic Stress, 14*(4), 615–632.

Goodman, S. H., Sewell, D. R., Cooley, E. L., & Leavitt, N. (1993). Assessing levels of adaptive functioning: The Role Functioning Scale. *Community Mental Health Journal, 29,* 119–131.

Goodman, W., Price, L., Rasmussen, S., Mazure, C., Fleischmann, R. L., Hill, C. L., . . . Charney, D. (1989). The Yale-Brown Obsessive Compulsive Scale. *Archives of General Psychiatry, 46,* 1006–1011.

Goodson, J., Helstrom, A., Halpern, J. M., Ferenschak, M. P., Gillihan, S. J., & Powers, M. B. (2011). Treatment of posttraumatic stress disorder in U.S. combat veterans: A meta-analytic review. *Psychological Reports, 109,* 573–599.

Goodwin, D. W. (1985). Genetic determinants of alcoholism. In J. H. Mendelson & N. K. Mello (Eds.), *The diagnosis and treatment of alcoholism* (pp. 65–87). New York, NY: McGraw-Hill.

Goodyer, I. M. (1995). Life events and difficulties: Their nature and effects. In I. M. Goodyer (Ed.), *The depressed child and adolescent: Developmental and clinical perspectives* (pp. 171–193). New York, NY: Cambridge University Press.

Gopaul-McNicol, S., & Brice-Baker, J. (1998). *Cross-cultural practice: Assessment, treatment and training.* New York, NY: Wiley.

Gorman-Smith, D., & Tolan, P. (1998). The role of exposure to community violence and developmental problems among inner-city youth. *Development and Psychopathology, 10,* 101–116.

Gortner, E. T., Gollan, J. K., Dobson, K. S., & Jacobson, N. S. (1998). Cognitive-behavioral treatment for depression: Relapse prevention. *Journal of Consulting and Clinical Psychology, 66,* 377–384.

Gossop, M., & Moos, R. (2008). Substance misuse among older adults: A neglected but treatable problem. *Addiction, 103,* 347–348.

Gottman, J. M. (1993a). The roles of conflict engagement, escalation, and avoidance in marital interaction: A longitudinal view of five types of couples. *Journal of Consulting and Clinical Psychology, 61,* 6–15.

Gottman, J. M. (1993b). A theory of marital dissolution and stability. *Journal of Family Psychology, 7,* 57–75.

Gottman, J. M. (1998). On the etiology of marital decay and its consequences: Comments from a clinical psychologist. In T. N. Bradbury (Ed.), *The developmental course of marital dysfunction* (pp. 423–426). New York, NY: Cambridge University Press.

Gottman, J. M., Levenson, R. W., Gross, J., Frederickson, B. L., McCoy, K., Rosenthal, L., . . . Yoshimoto, D. (2003). Correlates of gay and lesbian couples' relationship satisfaction and relationship dissolution. *Journal of Homosexuality, 45,* 23–43.

Gould, N. (2010). Integrating qualitative evidence in practice guideline development: Meeting the challenge of evidence-based practice for social work. *Qualitative Social Work*, *9*, 93–109.

Gowers, S. G., Clark, A., Roberts, C., Griffiths, A., Edwards, V., Claudine, B., . . . Barrett, B. (2007). Clinical effectiveness for treatments of anorexia nervosa in adolescents: Randomized controlled trial. *British Journal of Psychiatry*, *191*, 427–435.

Grados, M. (2010). The genetics of obsessive-compulsive disorder and Tourette syndrome: An epidemiological and pathway-based approach for gene discovery. *Journal of the American Academy of Child and Adolescent Psychiatry*, *49*, 810–819.

Graham, H. L., Maslin, J., Copello, A., Birchwood, M., Mueser, K., McGovern, D., & Georgiou, G. (2001). Drug and alcohol problems amongst individuals with severe mental health problems in an inner city area of the UK. *Social Psychiatry and Psychiatic Epidemiology*, *36*, 448–455.

Graham, N., Kimonis, E. R., Wasserman, A. L., & Kline, S. M. (2011). Associations among childhood abuse and psychopathy facets in male sexual offenders. *Personality Disorders: Theory, Research and Treatment*, 1–10.

Grant, B. F., & Dawson, D. A. (1999). Alcohol and drug use, abuse and dependence: Classification, prevalence and comorbidity. In B. S. McCrady & E. E. Epstein (Eds.), *Addictions: A comprehensive guidebook* (pp. 9–29). New York, NY: Oxford University Press.

Grant, B. F., Dawson, D. A., Stinson, F. S., Chou, S. P., Dufour, M. C., & Pickering, R. P. (2004). The 12-month prevalence and trends in DSM-IV alcohol abuse and dependence: United States, 1991–1992 and 2001–2002. *Drug and Alcohol Dependence*, *74*, 223–234.

Grant, B. F., Goldstein, R. B., Chou, S. P., Huang, B., Stinson, F. S., Dawson, D. A., . . . Compton, W. M. (2009). Sociodemographic and psychopathologic predictors of first incidence of DSM-IV substance use, mood and anxiety disorders: Results from the wave 2 National Epidemiologic Survey on Alcohol and Related Conditions. *Molecular Psychiatry*, *14*, 1051–1066.

Grant, B. F., & Harford, T. C. (1995). Comorbidity between DSM-IV alcohol use disorders and major depression: Results of a national survey. *Drug and Alcohol Dependence*, *39*, 197–206.

Grant, B. F., Harford, T. C., Dawson, D. A., Chou, P., Dufour, M., & Pickering, R. (1994). NIAAA's Epidemiologic Bulletin No. 35: Prevalence of DSM-IV alcohol abuse and dependence: United States, 1992. *Alcohol Health and Research World*, *18*, 243–248.

Grant, B. F., & Pickering, R. P. (1996). Comorbidity between DSM-IV alcohol and drug use disorders: Results from the National Longitudinal Alcohol Epidemiologic Survey. *Alcohol Health and Research World*, *20*, 67–72.

Grant, B. F., Stinson, F. S., Hasin, D. S., Dawson, D. A., Chou, S. P., Ruan, W. J., & Huang, B. (2005). Prevalence, correlates and comorbidity of bipolar I disorders and axis I and II disorders: Results from the National Epidemiologic Survey on Alcohol and Related Conditions. *Journal of Clinical Psychiatry*, *66*, 1205–1215.

Gray, M., Joy, E., Plath, D., & Webb, S. A. (2013). Implementing evidence-based practice: A review of the empirical research literature. *Research on Social Work Practice*, *23*, 157–166.

Green, B. A. (2009). Culture and mental health assessment. In S. Eshun & R. A. R. Gurung (Eds.), *Culture and mental health: Sociocultural influence, theory, and practice* (pp. 19–34). West Sussex, UK: Wiley-Blackwell.

Greenberg, L., Warwar, S., & Malcomb, W. (2010). Emotion-focused couples therapy and the facilitation of forgiveness. *Journal of Marital and Family Therapy*, *36*, 28–42.

Greenfield, S. F., Back, S. E., Lawson, K., & Brady, K. T. (2010). Substance abuse in women. *Psychiatric Clinics of North America*, *33*, 339–355.

Greenfield, S. F., Pettinati, H. M., O'Malley, S., Randall, P., & Randall, C. L. (2010). Gender differences in alcohol treatment: An analysis of outcome from the COMBINE study. *Alcoholism: Clinical and Experimental Research*, *34*(10), 1803–1812.

Greenfield, S. F., Rosa, C. R., Putnins, S. I., Green, C. A., Brooks, A. J., Calsyn, D. A., . . . Winhusen, T. (2011). Gender research in the National Institute on Drug Abuse National Treatment Clinical Trials Network: A summary of findings. *American Journal of Drug and Alcohol Abuse*, *37*, 301–312.

Greenfield, T. K., & Rogers, J. D. (1999). Who drinks most of the alcohol in the U.S.? The policy implications. *Journal of Studies on Alcohol*, *60*, 78–89.

Greenhill, L. L. (1998). Attention-deficit/hyperactivity disorder. In B. T. Walsh (Ed.), *Child psychopharmacology* (pp. 29–64). Washington, DC: American Psychiatric Press.

Greenhill, L. L., Pine, D., March, J., Birmaher, B., & Riddle, M. (1998). Assessment measures in anxiety disorders research. *Psychopharmacology Bulletin*, *34*, 155–164.

Greenhill, L. L., & Waslick, B. (1997). Management of suicidal behavior in children and adolescents. *Psychiatric Clinics of North America*, *20*, 641–666.

Gregory, R. J., Chlebowski, S., Kang, D., Remen, A. L., Soderberg, M. G., & Stepkovitch, J. (2008). A controlled trial of psychodynamic psychotherapy for co-occurring borderline personality disorder and alcohol use disorder. *Psychotherapy: Theory, Research, Practice, Training*, *45*, 28–41.

Grencavage, L. M., & Norcross, J. C. (1990). Where are the commonalities among the therapeutic common factors? *Professional Psychology: Research and Practice*, *21*, 372–378.

Griffin, K. W., & Botvin, G. J. (2010). Evidence-based interventions for preventing substance use disorders in adolescents. *Child and Adolescent Psychiatric Clinics of North America*, *19*, 505–526.

Griffin, R. (1991, February). Assessing the drug-involved client. *Families in Society: The Journal of Contemporary Human Services*, 87–94.

Grilo, C. M., Masheb, R. M., & Wilson, G. T. (2001). A comparison of different methods for assessing the features of eating disorders in patients with binge eating disorder. *Journal of Consulting and Clinical Psychology*, *69*, 317–322.

Grilo, C. M., Masheb, R. M., Wilson, G. T., Gueorguieva, R., & White, M. A. (2011). Cognitive-behavioral therapy, behavioral weight loss, and sequential treatment for obese patients with binge eating disorder: A randomized controlled trial. *Journal of Consulting and Clinical Psychology*, *79*, 675–685.

Grilo, C. M., Sanislow, C., Fehon, D. C., Martino, S., & McGlashan, T. H. (1999). Psychological and behavioral functioning in adolescent psychiatric inpatients who report histories of childhood abuse. *American Journal of Psychiatry*, *156*, 538–543.

Groenenberg, I., Sushma, S., Green, B. S., & Fleming, S. E. (2013). Family environment in inner-city African-American and Latino parents/caregivers: A comparison of the reliability of instruments. *Journal of Child and Family Studies*, *22*, 288–296.

Grogan-Kaylor, A. (2000). Who goes into kinship care? The relationship of child and family characteristics to placement into kinship foster care. *Social Work Research*, *24*, 132–141.

Grote, N. K., Swartz, A., Geibel, S. L., Zuckoff, A., Houck, P. R., & Frank, E. (2009). A randomized controlled trial of culturally relevant, brief interpersonal psychotherapy for perinatal depression. *Psychiatric Services*, *60*, 313–321.

Grubaugh, A. L., Zinzow, H. M., Paul, L., Egede, L. E., & Freuh, B. C. (2011). Trauma exposure and posttraumatic stress disorder n adults with severe mental illness: A critical review. *Clinical Psychology Review*, *31*, 883–899. doi: 10.1016/j.cpr.2011.04.003.

Gruber, K. J., Fleetwood, T. W., & Herring, M. W. (2001). In-home continuing care services for substance-affected families: The Bridges Program. *Social Work*, *46*, 267–277.

Grych, J. H., & Fincham, F. D. (1990). Marital conflict and children's adjustment: A cognitive contextual framework. *Psychological Bulletin*, *108*, 267–290.

Gryczynski, J., Mitchell, S. G., Peterson, T. R., Gonzales, A., Moseley, A., & Schwartz, R. P. (2011). The relationship between services delivered and substance use outcomes in New Mexico's Screening, Brief Intervention, Referral and Treatment (SBIRT) initiative. *Drug and Alcohol Dependence*, *118*, 152–157.

Guarnaccia, P. J. (1997). A cross cultural perspective on anxiety disorders. In S. Friedman (Ed.), *Cultural issues in the treatment of anxiety* (pp. 1–20). New York, NY: Guilford Press.

Guarnaccia, P. J., & Parra, P. (1996). Ethnicity, social status, and families' experiences of caring for a mentally ill family member. *Community Mental Health Journal*, *32*, 243–260.

Gumley, A., O'Grady, M., McNay, L., Reilly, J., Power, K., & Norrie, J. (2003). Early intervention for relapse in schizophrenia: Results of a 12-month randomized controlled trial of cognitive behavioural therapy. *Psychological Medicine*, *33*, 419–431.

Gunderson, J. G. (1984). *Borderline personality disorder*. Washington, DC: American Psychiatric Association.

Gunderson, J. G., Ronningstam, E., & Smith, L. E. (1995). Narcissistic personality disorder. In J. Livesley (Ed.), *The DSM-IV personality disorders* (pp. 201–212). New York, NY: Guilford Press.

Gunderson, J. G., Zanarini, M. C., & Kisiel, C. L. (1995). Borderline personality disorder. In J. Livesley (Ed.), *The DSM-IV personality disorders* (pp. 141–157). New York, NY: Guilford Press.

Guntrip, H. (1969). *Schizoid phenomena, object relations and the self*. New York, NY: International Universities Press.

Guo, J., Chung, I., Hill, K. G., Hawkins, J. D., Catalano, R. F., & Abbott, R. D. (2002). Developmental relationships between adolescent substance use and risky sexual behavior in young adulthood. *Journal of Adolescent Health*, *31*, 354–362.

Gupta, R. (2000). Treatment of depression in an elderly Asian Indian male: A cognitive behavioral approach. *Clinical Gerontologist*, *22*, 87–90.

Gurman, A. S., Kniskern, D. P., & Pinsof, W. M. (1986). Research on marital and family therapies. In S. L. Garfield & A. E. Bergin (Eds.), *Handbook of psychotherapy and behavior change* (3rd ed., pp. 565–626). New York, NY: Wiley.

Gutierrez, L. M. (1990). Working with women of color: An empowerment perspective. *Social Work, 35,* 149–153.

Haas, S. M., & Stafford, L. (1998). An initial examination of maintenance behaviors in gay and lesbian relationships. *Journal of Social and Personal Relationships, 15,* 846–855.

Hadas-Lidor, N., Weiss, P., & Redlich, D. (2011). "Keshet": Enhancing cognitive communication skills in families. *Psychiatric Services, 62,* 562.

Hahlweg, K., & Markman, H. J. (1988). Effectiveness of behavioral marital therapy: Empirical status of behavioral techniques in preventing and alleviating marital distress. *Journal of Consulting and Clinical Psychology, 56,* 440–447.

Halford, W. K. (1998). The ongoing evolution of behavioral couples therapy: Retrospect and prospect. *Clinical Psychology Review, 18,* 613–633.

Halford, W. K., & Bouma, R. (1997). Individual psychopathology and marital distress. In W. K. Halford & H. J. Markham (Eds.), *Clinical handbook of marriage and couples intervention* (pp. 291–322). New York, NY: Wiley.

Halford, W. K., Hahlweg, K., & Dunne, M. (1990). The cross-cultural consistency of marital communication associated with marital distress. *Journal of Marriage and the Family, 52,* 487–500.

Hall, G. C. (1995). Sexual offender recidivism revisited: A meta-analysis of recent treatment studies. *Journal of Consulting and Clinical Psychology, 63,* 802–809.

Hamberger, L. K., & Hastings, J. E. (1991). Personality correlates of men who batter and nonviolent men: Some continuities and discontinuities. *Journal of Family Violence, 6,* 131–147.

Hamilton, M. (1959). The assessment of anxiety states by rating. *British Journal of Medical Psychology, 32,* 50–55.

Hamilton, M. (1960). A rating scale for depression. *Journal of Neurology, Neurosurgery and Mental Science, 105,* 985–987.

Hanf, C. (1970). *Shaping mothers to shape their children's behavior.* Portland, OR: University of Oregon Medical School.

Hankin, B., Abramson, L., Moffitt, T. E., Silva, P., McGee, R., & Angell, K. (1998). Development of depression from preadolescence to young adulthood: Emerging gender differences in a 10-year longitudinal study. *Journal of Abnormal Psychology, 107,* 128–140.

Hanson, D. J., & Engs, R. C. (1995). Collegiate drinking: Administrator perceptions, campus policies and student behaviors. *National Association of Student Personnel Administrators, 32,* 106–115.

Hare, R. D. (1991). *The Hare Psychopathy Checklist–Revised manual.* Toronto, ON: Multi-Health Systems.

Hare, R. D. (1999). Psychopathy as a risk factor for violence. *Psychiatric Quarterly, 70,* 181–197.

Hare, R. D., Harpur, T. J., Hakstian, A. R., Forth, A. E., Hart, S. D., & Newman, J. (1990). The psychopathy checklist: Reliability and factor structure. *Psychological Assessment: A Journal of Consulting and Clinical Psychology, 2,* 338–341.

Hare, R. D., & Hart, S. D. (1995). Commentary on antisocial personality disorder: The DSM-IV field trial. In J. Livesley (Ed.), *The DSM-IV personality disorders* (pp. 127–134). New York, NY: Guilford Press.

Hare, R. D., McPherson, L. M., & Forth, A. E. (1988). Male psychopaths and their criminal careers. *Journal of Consulting and Clinical Psychology, 56*, 710–714.

Hare, R. D., & Neumann, C. S. (2009). Psychopathy: Assessment and forensic implications. *Canadian Journal of Psychiatry, 54*, 791–802.

Hare, R. D., & Neumann, C. S. (2010). The role of antisociality in the psychopathy construct: Comments on Skeem and Cooke (2010). *Psychological Assessment, 22*, 446–454.

Harford, T., & Grant, B. F. (1987). Psychosocial factors in adolescent drinking contexts. *Journal of Studies on Alcohol, 48*, 551–557.

Hargreaves, W. A., Shumway, M., Hu, T.-W., & Cuffel, B. (1998). *Cost-outcome methods for mental health*. San Diego, CA: Academic Press.

Harned, M. S., Chapman, A. L., Dexter-Mazza, E. T., Murray, A., Comtois, K. A., & Linehan, M. M. (2008). Treating co-occurring axis I disorders in recurrently suicidal women with borderline personality disorder: A 2-year randomized trial of dialectical behavior therapy versus community treatment by experts. *Journal of Consulting and Clinical Psychology, 76*, 1068–1075.

Harnish, L. D., Tolan, P. H., & Guerra, N. G. (1996). Treatment of oppositional defiant disorder. In M. A. Reineke, F. M. Dattilio, & A. Freeman (Eds.), *Cognitive therapy with children and adolescents: A casebook for clinical practice* (pp. 62–78). New York, NY: Guilford Press.

Harpur, T. J., Hakstian, A. R., & Hare, R. D. (1988). Factor structure of the Psychopathy Checklist. *Journal of Consulting and Clinical Psychology, 56*, 741–747.

Harrington, R. (1995). *Depressive disorder in childhood and adolescence*. New York, NY: Wiley.

Harrington, R., Whittaker, J., & Shoebridge, P. (1998). Psychological treatment of depression in children and adolescents: A review of treatment research. *British Journal of Psychiatry, 173*, 291–298.

Harrington, R., Wood, A., & Verduyn, C. (1998). Clinically depressed adolescents. In P. Graham (Ed.), *Cognitive-behaviour therapy for children and families* (pp. 156–193). New York, NY: Cambridge University Press.

Harris, M. (1996). Treating sexual abuse trauma with dually diagnosed women. *Community Mental Health Journal, 32*(4), 371–385.

Harris, E. C., & Barraclough, B. (1997). Suicide as an outcome for mental disorders. A meta-analysis. *British Journal of Psychiatry, 170*, 205–228. doi: 10.1192/bjp.170.3.205.

Hart, C. L., & Ksir, C. (2013). *Drugs, society and human behavior* (15th ed.). New York, NY: McGraw-Hill.

Hart, S. D., & Hare, R. D. (1989). Discriminant validity of the psychopathy checklist in a forensic psychiatric population. *Psychological Assessment: A Journal of Consulting and Clinical Psychology, 1*, 211–218.

Hart, S. D., Kropp, P. R., & Hare, R. D. (1988). Performance of male psychopaths following conditional release from prison. *Journal of Consulting and Clinical Psychology, 56*, 227–232.

Hartman, C. R., & Burgess, A. W. (1990). Sexual abuse of children: Causes and consequences. In D. Ciccetti & V. Carlson (Eds.), *Child maltreatment: Theory and research on the causes and consequences of child abuse and neglect* (pp. 95–128). New York, NY: Cambridge University Press.

Hartmann, D. P., Roper, B. L., & Bradford, D. C. (1979). Some relationships between behavioral and traditional assessment. *Journal of Behavioral Assessment*, *1*, 3–21.

Harvey, P. D. (2011). Assessment of everyday functioning in schizophrenia. *Innovations in Clinical Neuroscience*, *8*, 21–24.

Hasin, D. S. (1991). Diagnostic interviews for assessment: Background, reliability, validity. *Alcohol Health and Research World*, *15*(4), 293–301.

Hasin, D. S., Goodwin, R. D., Stinson, F. S., & Grant, B. F. (2005). Epidemiology of major depressive disorder: Results from the national epidemiologic survey on alcoholism and related conditions. *Archives of General Psychiatry*, *62*, 1097–1106.

Hasin, D. S., Stinson, F. S., Ogburn, E., & Grant, B. F. (2007). Prevalence, correlates, disability, and comorbidity of DSM-IV alcohol abuse and dependence in the United States: Results from the National Epidemiologic Survey on Alcohol and Related Conditions. *Archives of General Psychiatry*, *64*, 830–842.

Haskett, M. E., Miller, J. W., Whitworth, J. M., & Huffman, J. M. (1992, October). Intervention with cocaine-abusing mothers. *Families in Society: The Journal of Contemporary Human Services*, 451–461.

Hasking, P. A., & Oei, T. P. S. (2007). Alcohol expectancies, self-efficacy and coping in an alcohol-dependent sample. *Addictive Behaviors*, *32*, 99–113.

Hastings, J. E., & Hamberger, L. K. (1988). Personality characteristics of spouse abusers: A controlled comparison. *Violence and Victims*, *3*, 31–47.

Hawkins, K. A., & Sinha, R. (1998). Can line clinicians master the conceptual complexities of dialectical behavior therapy? An evaluation of a state department of mental health training program. *Journal of Psychiatric Research*, *32*, 379–384.

Hawton, K., Sutton, L., Haw, C., Sinclair, J., & Deeks, J. J. (2005). Schizophrenia and suicide: Systematic review of risk factors. *British Journal of Psychiatry*, *187*, 9–20.

Hawton, K., Sutton, L., Haw, C., Sinclair, J., & Harriss, L. (2005). Suicide and attempted suicide in bipolar disorder: A systematic review of risk factors. *Journal of Clinical Psychiatry*, *66*, 693–704. doi: 10.1192/bjp.187.1.9.

Hawton, K., Zahl, D., & Weatherall, R. (2003). Suicide following deliberate self-harm: Long-term follow-up of patients who presented to a general hospital. *British Journal of Psychiatry*, *182*, 537–542. doi: 10.1192/bjp.182.6.537.

Hay, P. J., & Claudino, A. M. (2010). Evidence-based treatment for the eating disorders. In W. S. Agras (Ed.), *The Oxford handbook of eating disorders* (pp. 452–479). New York, NY: Oxford University Press.

Hayashida, M. (1998). An overview of outpatient and inpatient detoxification. *Alcohol Health and Research World*, *22*, 44–46.

Hayes, R. L., Halford, W. K., & Varghese, F. T. (1995). Social skills training with chronic schizophrenic patients: Effects on negative symptoms and community functioning. *Behavior Therapy*, *26*, 433–449.

Haynes, S. N. (1998). The changing nature of behavioral assessment. In A. S. Bellack & M. Hersen (Eds.), *Behavioral assessment: A practical handbook* (pp. 1–21). Boston, MA: Allyn & Bacon.

Hazelrigg, M. D., Cooper, H. M., & Borduin, C. M. (1987). Evaluating the effectiveness of family therapies: An integrative review and analysis. *Psychological Bulletin*, *101*, 428–442.

Health Insurance Portability and Accountability Act of 1996, Pub. L. No. 104-191.

Heath, A. C. (1995). Genetic influences on alcoholism risk: A review of adoption and twin studies. *Alcohol Health and Research World, 19,* 166–171.

Heath, D. B. (1991). Uses and misuses of the concept of ethnicity in alcohol studies: An essay on deconstruction. *International Journal of the Addictions, 25* (5a–6a), 607–628.

Heather, N. (1995). Brief intervention strategies. In R. K. Hester & W. R. Miller (Eds.), *Handbook of alcoholism treatment approaches: Effective alternatives* (2nd ed., pp. 105–122). Boston, MA: Allyn & Bacon.

Heineman-Pieper, M. (1985). The future of social work research. *Social Work Research and Abstracts, 21,* 3–11.

Heinssen, R. K., Levendusky, P. G., & Hunter, R. H. (1995). Client as colleague: Therapeutic contracting with the seriously mentally ill. *American Psychologist, 50,* 522–532.

Helsel, W. J., & Matson, J. L. (1984). The assessment of depression in children: The internal structure of the Child Depression Inventory (CDI). *Behaviour Research and Therapy, 22,* 289–298.

Helzer, J. E., & Pryzbeck, T. R. (1988). The co-occurrence of alcoholism with other psychiatric disorders in the general population and its impact on treatment. *Journal of Studies on Alcohol, 49,* 219–224.

Hemmelgarn, A. L., Glisson, C., & Sharp, S. R. (2003). The validity of the Short-form Assessment for Children (SAC). *Research on Social Work Practice, 13,* 510–530.

Hemsley, D. R. (1996). Schizophrenia: A cognitive model and its implications for psychological intervention. *Behavior Modification, 20*(2), 139–169.

Hendrick, S. (1981). Self-disclosure and marital satisfaction. *Journal of Personality and Social Psychology, 40,* 1150–1159.

Hendrick, S. (1988). A generic measure of relationship satisfaction. *Journal of Marital and Family Therapy, 50,* 93–98.

Hendrick, S. S., Dicke, A., & Hendrick, C. (1998). The Relationship Assessment Scale. *Journal of Social and Personal Relationships, 15,* 137–142.

Henggeler, S. W., Halliday-Boykins, C. A., Cunningham, P. B., Randall, J., Shapiro, S. B., & Chapman, J. E. (2006). Juvenile drug court: Enhancing outcomes by integrating evidence-based treatments. *Journal of Consulting and Clinical Psychology, 74,* 42–54.

Henggeler, S. W., Melton, G. B., & Smith, L. A. (1992). Family preservation using multisystemic therapy: An effective alternative to incarcerating serious juvenile offenders. *Journal of Consulting and Clinical Psychology, 60,* 953–961.

Henggeler, S. W., Melton, G. B., Smith, L. A., Schoenwald, S. K., & Hanley, J. H. (1993). Family preservation using multisystemic treatment: Long-term follow-up to a clinical trial with serious juvenile offenders. *Journal of Child and Family Studies, 2,* 283–293.

Henggeler, S. W., Rodick, J. D., Borduin, C. M., Hanson, C. L., Watson, S. M., & Urey, J. R. (1986). Multisystemic treatment of juvenile offenders: Effects on adolescent behavior and family interactions. *Developmental Psychology, 22,* 132–141.

Henggeler, S. W., Schoenwald, S. K., Borduin, C. M., Rowland, M. D., & Cunningham, P. B. (1998). *Multisystemic treatment of antisocial behavior in children and adolescents.* New York, NY: Guilford Press.

Henggeler, S. W., Schoenwald, S. K., Borduin, C. M., Rowland, M. D., & Cunningham, P. B. (2009). *Multisystemic therapy for antisocial behavior in children and adolescents* (2nd ed.). New York, NY: Guilford Press.

Henggeler, S. W., & Sheidow, A. J. (2003). Conduct disorder and delinquency. *Journal of Marital and Family Therapy, 29*, 505–522.

Henry, W. P., Strupp, H. H., Schacht, T. E., & Gaston, L. (1994). Psychodynamic approaches. In A. E. Bergin & S. L. Garfield (Eds.), *The handbook of psychotherapy and behavior change* (4th ed., pp. 467–508). New York, NY: Wiley.

Hepworth, D. H., Rooney, R. H., Rooney, G. D., & Strom-Gottfried, K. (2012). *Direct social work practice: Theories and skills* (9th ed.). Belmont, CA: Brooks/Cole.

Herbert, M. (1998). Adolescent conduct disorders. In P. Graham (Ed.), *Cognitive-behaviour therapy for children and families* (pp. 194–216). New York, NY: Cambridge University Press.

Herman, J. (1992). *Trauma and recovery*. New York, NY: Basic Books.

Herman, S. E., Frank, K. A., Mowbray, C. T., Ribisl, K. M., Davidson, W. S., Bootsmiller, B., . . . Luke, D. A. (2000). Longitudinal effects of integrated treatment on alcohol use for persons with serious mental illness and substance abuse disorders. *Journal of Behavioral Health Services and Research, 27*, 286–302.

Herman, D. B., Susser, E. S., & Struening, E. L. (1998). Homelessness, stress and psychopathology. In B. P. Dohrenwend (Ed.), *Adversity and psychopathology* (pp. 132–141). New York, NY: Oxford University Press.

Herpertz-Dahlmann, B., Muller, B., Herpertz, S., Heussen, N., Hebebrand, J., & Remschmidt, H. (2001). Prospective 10-year follow-up in adolescent anorexia nervosa—course, outcome, psychiatric comorbidity, and psychosocial adaptation. *Journal of Child Psychology and Psychiatry, 42*, 603–612.

Hersen, M. (1985). Single-case experimental designs. In A. S. Bellack, M. Hersen, & A. E. Kazdin (Eds.), *International handbook of behavior modification and therapy* (pp. 85–124). New York, NY: Plenum Press.

Hesselbrock, M. N., Babor, T. F., Hesselbrock, V., Meyer, R. E., & Workman, K. (1983). "Never believe an alcoholic"? On the validity of self-report measures of alcohol dependence and related constructs. *International Journal of the Addictions, 18*, 593–609.

Hesselbrock, M. N., Hesselbrock, V. M., & Epstein, E. E. (1999). Theories of etiology of alcohol and other drug use disorders. In B. S. McCrady & E. E. Epstein (Eds.), *Addictions: A comprehensive guidebook* (pp. 50–74). New York, NY: Oxford University Press.

Hides, L., Samet, S., & Lubman, D. I. (2010). Cognitive behavior therapy (CBT) for the treatment of co-occurring depression and substance use: Current evidence and directions for future research. *Drug and Alcohol Review, 29*, 508–517.

Higgins, D. J., & McCabe, M. P. (2001). Multiple forms of child abuse and neglect: Adult retrospective reports. *Aggression and Violent Behavior, 6*, 547–578.

Higgins, S. T., Budney, A. J., Bickel, W. K., Foerg, F. E., Donham, R., & Badger, G. J. (1994). Incentives improve outcome in outpatient behavioral treatment of cocaine dependence. *Archives of General Psychiatry, 51*, 568–576.

Higgins, S. T., Budney, A. J., Bickel, W. K., Hughes, J. R., Foerg, F., & Badger, G. (1993). Achieving cocaine abstinence with a behavioral approach. *American Journal of Psychiatry, 150*(5), 763–769.

Higgins, S. T., & Petry, N. M. (1999). Contingency management. *Alcohol Research and Health*, *23*, 122–127.

Higgins, S. T., Sigmon, S. C., & Heil, S. H. (2008). Drug abuse and dependence. In D. H. Barlow (Ed.), *Clinical handbook of psychological disorders* (4th ed., pp. 547–577). New York, NY: Guilford Press.

Higgins, S., Sigmon, S., Wong, C., Heil, S., Badger, G., Donham, R., . . . Anthony, S. (2003). Community reinforcement for cocaine-dependent outpatients. *Archives of General Psychiatry*, *60*, 1043–1052.

Higgins, S., Wong, C., Badger, G., Ogden, D., & Dantona, R. (2000). Contingent reinforcement increases cocaine abstinence during outpatient treatment and 1 year follow-up. *Journal of Consulting and Clinical Psychology*, *68*, 64–72.

Hill, C. E., Nutt, E. A., & Jackson, S. (1994). Trends in psychotherapy process research: Samples, measures, researchers, and classic publications. *Journal of Counseling Psychology*, *4*, 364–377.

Hillberg, T., Hamilton-Giachritsis, C., & Dixon, L. (2011). Review of meta-analyses on the association between child sexual abuse and adult mental health difficulties: A systematic approach. *Trauma, Violence, and Abuse*, *12*, 38–49.

Hingson, R., & Winter, M. (2003). Epidemiology and consequences of drinking and driving. *Alcohol Research and Health*, *27*, 63–78.

Hinshaw, S. P., Klein, R. G., & Abikoff, H. (1998). Childhood attention deficit hyperactivity disorder: Nonpharmacological and combination treatments. In P. E. Nathan & J. M. Gorman (Eds.), *A guide to treatments that work* (pp. 26–41). New York, NY: Oxford University Press.

Hlavka, H. R., Olinger, S. D., & Lashley, J. L. (2010). The use of anatomical dolls as a demonstration aid in child sex abuse interviews: A study of forensic interviewers' perceptions. *Journal of Child Sexual Abuse*, *19*, 519–553.

Hoagwood, K., Kelleher, K. J., Feil, M., & Comer, D. M. (2000). Treatment services for children with ADHD: A national perspective. *Journal of the American Academy of Child and Adolescent Psychiatry*, *39*, 198–206.

Hobbs, J. D. J., Kushner, M. G., Lee, S. S., Reardon, S. M., & Maurer, E. W. (2011). Meta-analysis of supplemental treatment for depressive and anxiety disorders in patients being treated for alcohol dependence. *American Journal of Addictions*, *20*, 319–329.

Hochhausen, N. M., Lorenz, A. R., & Newman, J. P. (2002). Specifying the impulsivity of female inmates with borderline personality disorder. *Journal of Abnormal Psychology*, *111*, 495–505.

Hodge, M. A. R., Siciliano, D., Withey, P., Moss, B., Moore, G., Judd, G., . . . Harris, A. (2010). A randomized controlled trial of cognitive remediation in schizophrenia. *Schizophrenia Bulletin*, *36*, 419–427.

Hoffman, E. C., & Mattis, S. G. (2000). A developmental adaptation of panic control treatment for panic disorder in adolescence. *Cognitive and Behavioral Practice*, *7*, 253–261.

Hoffman, K. J., & Sasaki, J. E. (1997). Comorbidity of substance abuse and PTSD. In C. S. Fullerton & R. J. Ursano (Eds.), *Post-traumatic stress disorder: Acute and long-term responses to trauma and disaster* (pp. 159–174). Washington, DC: American Psychiatric Press.

Hogarty, G. E. (2002). *Personal therapy for schizophrenia and related disorders*. New York, NY: Guilford Press.

Hogarty, G. E., Kornblith, S. J., Greenwald, D., DiBarry, A. L., Cooley, S., Flesher, S., . . . Ulrich, R. (1995). Personal therapy: A disorder-relevant psychotherapy for schizophrenia. *Schizophrenia Bulletin, 21*, 379–393.

Hogue, A., & Dauber, S. (2013). Assessing fidelity to evidence-based practices in usual care: The example of family therapy for adolescent behavior problems. *Evaluation and Program Planning, 37*, 21–30.

Holahan, C. J., & Moos, R. H. (1994). Life stressors and mental health. In W. R. Avison & I. H. Gotlib (Eds.), *Stress and mental health: Contemporary issues and prospects for the future* (pp. 213–238). New York, NY: Plenum Press.

Holahan, C. J., Moos, R. H., Holahan, C. K., Cronkite, R. C., & Randall, P. K. (2004). Unipolar depression, life context vulnerabilities, and drinking to cope. *Journal of Consulting and Clinical Psychology, 72*(2), 269–275. doi: 10.1037/0022-006X.72.2.269.

Holden, G., Cuzzi, L., Rutter, S., Rosenberg, G., & Chernack, P. (1996). The hospital social work self-efficacy scale: Initial development. *Research on Social Work Practice, 6*, 353–365.

Holder, H., Longabaugh, R., Miller, W. R., & Rubonis, A. V. (1991). The cost effectiveness of treatment for alcoholism: A first approximation. *Journal of Studies on Alcohol, 52*, 517–540.

Hollon, S. D., & Beck, A. T. (1994). Cognitive and cognitive-behavioral therapies. In A. E. Bergin & S. L. Garfield (Eds.), *The handbook of psychotherapy and behavior change* (4th ed., pp. 428–466). New York, NY: Wiley.

Hollon, S. D., & Carter, M. (1994). Depression in adults. In L. Craighead, W. Craighead, A. Kazdin, & M. Mahoney (Eds.), *Cognitive and behavioral interventions: An empirical approach to mental health problems* (pp. 89–104). Needham Heights, MA: Allyn & Bacon.

Hollon, S. D., DeRubeis, R. J., Evans, M. D., Wiemer, M. J., Garvey, M. J., Grove, W. M., & Tuason, V. B. (1992). Cognitive therapy and pharmacotherapy for depression. *Archives of General Psychiatry, 49*, 774–781.

Hollon, S. D., & Kendall, P. C. (1980). Cognitive self-statements in depression: Development of an automatic thoughts questionnaire. *Cognitive Therapy and Research, 4*, 383–395.

Hollon, S. D., Shelton, R. C., & Davis, D. D. (1993). Cognitive therapy for depression: Conceptual issues and clinical efficacy. *Journal of Consulting and Clinical Psychology, 61*, 270–275.

Hollon, S. D., Shelton, R. C., & Loosen, P. T. (1991). Cognitive therapy and pharmacotherapy for depression. *Journal of Consulting and Clinical Psychology, 59*, 88–99.

Holtzworth-Munroe, A., Bates, L., Smutzler, N., & Sandin, E. (1997). A brief review of the research on husband violence: Part I. Maritally violent versus nonviolent men. *Aggression and Violent Behavior, 2*, 65–99.

Holtzworth-Munroe, A., Smutzler, N., & Bates, L. (1997). A brief review of the research on husband violence: Part III. Sociodemographic factors, relationship factors, and differing consequences of husband and wife violence. *Aggression and Violent Behavior, 2*, 285–307.

Holtzworth-Munroe, A., Smutzler, N., & Sandin, E. (1997). A brief review of the research on husband violence: Part II. The psychological effects of husband violence on battered women and their children. *Aggression and Violent Behavior, 2*, 179–213.

Holzel, L., Harter, M., Reese, C., & Kriston, L. (2011). Risk factors for chronic depression: A systematic review. *Journal of Affective Disorders, 129,* 1–13.

Hooper, S. R., & March, J. S. (1995). Neuropsychology. In J. S. March (Ed.), *Anxiety disorders in children and adolescents* (pp. 35–60). New York, NY: Guilford Press.

Hopko, D. R., Lachar, D., Bailley, S. E., & Varner, R. V. (2001). Assessing predictive factors for extended hospitalization at acute psychiatric admission. *Psychiatric Services, 52,* 1367–1373.

Hopps, J. G., Pinderhughes, E., & Shankar, R. (1995). *The power to care: Clinical practice effectiveness with overwhelmed clients.* New York, NY: Free Press.

Hor, K., & Taylor, M. (2010). Suicide and schizophrenia: A systematic review of rates and risk factors. *Journal of Psychopharmacology, 24*(11S4), 81–90. doi: 10.1177/1359786810385490.

Horan, S., Kang, G., Levine, M., Duax, C., Luntz, B., & Tasa, C. (1993). Empirical studies on foster care: Review and assessment. *Journal of Sociology and Social Welfare, 20,* 131–154.

Horne, A. M., Glaser, B. A., & Calhoun, G. B. (1999). Conduct disorders. In R. T. Ammerman, M. Hersen, & C. G. Last (Eds.), *Handbook of prescriptive treatments for children and adolescents* (2nd ed., pp. 84–101). Boston, MA: Allyn & Bacon.

Horowitz, M. J. (1997). *Stress response syndromes: PTSD, grief and adjustment disorders* (3rd ed.). Northvale, NJ: Aronson.

Horvath, A. O., & Greenberg, L. S. (1989). Development and validation of the working alliance inventory. *Journal of Counseling Psychology, 36,* 223–233.

Hotaling, G. T., & Sugarman, D. B. (1986). An analysis of risk markers in husband to wife violence: The current state of knowledge. *Violence and Victims, 1,* 101–124.

Hotopf, M., Sharp, D., & Lewis, G. (1998). What's in a name? A comparison of four psychiatric assessments. *Social Psychiatry and Psychiatric Epidemiology, 33,* 27–31.

Houston-Vega, M. K., Nuehring, E. M., & Daguio, E. R. (1997). *Prudent practice: A guide for managing malpractice risk.* Washington, DC: NASW Press.

Howard, K. S., & Brooks-Gunn, J. (2009). The role of home visiting programs in reducing child abuse and neglect. *Future of Children, 19,* 119–146.

Howard, M. O., McMillen, C. J., & Pollio, D. E. (2003). Teaching evidence-based practice: Toward a new paradigm for social work education. *Research on Social Work Practice, 13,* 234–259.

Howells, K., & Day, A. (2002). Grasping the nettle: Treating and rehabilitating the violent offender. *Australian Psychologist, 37,* 222–228.

Howing, P. T., Kohn, S., Gaudin, J. M., Kurtz, P. D., & Wodarski, J. S. (1992). Current research issues in child welfare. *Social Work Research, 28,* 5–12.

Howing, P. T., Wodarski, J. S., Gaudin, J. M., & Kurtz, P. D. (1989). Effective interventions to ameliorate the incidence of child maltreatment: The empirical base. *Social Work, 34,* 330–338.

Hser, Y., Maglione, M., Polinsky, M. L., & Anglin, M. D. (1998). Predicting drug treatment entry among treatment-seeking individuals. *Journal of Substance Abuse Treatment, 15,* 213–220.

Huang, B., Dawson, D. A., Stinson, F. S., Hasin, D. S., Ruan, W. J., Saha, T. D., . . . Grant, B. F. (2006). Prevalence, correlates, and comorbidity of nonmedical prescription drug use and drug use disorders in the United States: Results of the National Epidemiologic Survey on Alcohol and Related Conditions. *Journal of Clinical Psychiatry*, 67(7), 1062–1073.

Hubbard, R. L., Craddock, S. G., Flynn, P. M., Anderson, J., & Etheridge, R. M. (1997). Overview of 1-year follow-up outcomes in the Drug Abuse Treatment Outcome Study (DATOS). *Psychology of Addictive Behaviors, 11*, 261–278.

Hudson, C. G. (2009). Decision-making in evidence-based practice: Science and art. *Smith College Studies in Social Work, 79*, 155–174.

Hudson, W. (1982a). *The clinical measurement package*. Homewood, IL: Dorsey Press.

Hudson, W. (1982b). Scientific imperatives in social work research and practice. *Social Service Review, 56*, 246–258.

Hudson, W. W., & McMurty, S. L. (1997). Comprehensive assessment in social work practice: The Multi-Problem Screening Inventory. *Research on Social Work Practice, 7*, 79–98.

Humphreys, K. (1999). Professional interventions that facilitate 12-step self-help group involvement. *Alcohol Research and Health, 23*, 93–98.

Hurford, I. M., Marder, S. R., Keefe, R. S. E., Reise, S. P., & Bilder, R. M. (2011). A brief cognitive assessment tool for schizophrenia: Construction of a tool for clinicians. *Schizophrenia Bulletin, 37*, 538–545.

Hurley, D. (1991). Women, alcohol and incest: An analytical review. *Journal of Studies on Alcohol, 52*, 253–268.

Hurley, K., Huscroft-D'Angelo, J., Trout, A., Griffith, A., & Epstein, M. (2014). Assessing parenting skills and attitudes: A review of the psychometrics of parenting measures. *Journal of Child and Family Studies, 23*, 812–823.

Huss, M. T., & Langhinrichsen-Rohling, J. (2000). Identification of the psychopathic batterer: The clinical, legal and policy implications. *Aggression and Violent Behavior, 5*, 403–422.

Hutchings, J., Appelton, P., Smith, M., Lane, E., & Nash, S. (2002). Evaluation of two treatments for children with severe behaviour problems: Child behaviour and maternal mental health outcomes. *Behavioural and Cognitive Psychotherapy, 30*, 279–295.

Hutchings, J., Gardner, F., Bywater, T., Daley, D., Whitaker, C., Jones, K., . . . Edwards, R. T. (2007). Parenting intervention for Sure Start services for children at risk of developing conduct disorder: Pragmatic randomized controlled trial. *British Medical Journal, 334*, 678–682.

Huxley, N. A., Rendall, M., & Sederer, L. (2000). Psychosocial treatments in schizophrenia: A review of the past 20 years. *Journal of Nervous and Mental Disease, 188*, 187–201.

Hyler, S., Skodol, A., Kellman, H., Oldham, J., & Rosnick, L. (1990). Validity of the Personality Diagnostic Questionnaire–Revised: Comparison with two structured interviews. *American Journal of Psychiatry, 147*, 1043–1048.

Iervolino, A. C., Rijsdijk, F. V., Cherkas, L., Fullana, M. A., & Mataix-Cols, D. (2011). A multivariate twin study of obsessive-compulsive symptom dimensions. *Archives of General Psychiatry, 68*, 637–644.

Ilgen, M. A., Schulenberg, J., Kloska, D. D., Czyz, E., Johnston, L., & O'Malley, P. (2011). Prevalence and characteristics of substance abuse treatment utilization by U.S. adolescents: National data from 1987 to 2008. *Addictive Behaviors, 36*, 1349–1352.

Ilomaki, E., Rasanen, P., Villo, K., Hakko, H., & Study 70 Workgroup (2007). Suicidal behavior in adolescents with conduct disorder: The role of alcohol dependence. *Psychiatry Research, 150*, 305–311.

Inciardi, J. A., Martin, S. S., Butzin, C. A., Hooper, R. M., & Harrison, L. D. (1997). An effective model of prison-based treatment for drug-involved offenders. *Journal of Drug Issues, 27*, 261–278.

Indian Child Welfare Act of 1978, Pub. L. No. 95-608.

Ironson, G., Freund, B., Strauss, J., & Williams, J. (2002). Comparison of two treatments for traumatic stress: A community-based study of EMDR and Prolonged Exposure. *Journal of Clinical Psychology, 58*, 113–128.

Isenhart, C. E. (1993). Psychometric evaluation of a short form of the Inventory of Drinking Situations. *Journal of Studies on Alcohol, 54*, 345–349.

Ivarsson, T., & Gillberg, C. (1997). Depressive symptoms in Swedish adolescents: Normative data using the Birleson Depression Self-Rating Scale (DSRS). *Journal of Affective Disorders, 42*, 59–68.

Jacobsen, E. (1938). *Progressive muscle relaxation*. Chicago, IL: University of Chicago Press.

Jacobson, N. S. (1991). Behavioral vs. insight-oriented marital therapy: Labels can be misleading. *Journal of Consulting and Clinical Psychology, 59*, 142–145.

Jacobson, N. S., & Addis, M. E. (1993). Research on couples and couple therapy: What do we know? Where are we going? *Journal of Consulting and Clinical Psychology, 61*, 85–93.

Jacobson, N. S., Christensen, A., Prince, S. E., Cordova, J., & Eldridge, K. (2000). Integrative behavioral couple therapy: An acceptance-based promising new treatment for couple discord. *Journal of Consulting and Clinical Psychology, 68*, 351–355.

Jacobson, N. S., Dobson, K. S., Truax, P. A., Addis, M. E., Koerner, K., Gollan, J. K., . . . Prince, S. E. (1996). A component analysis of cognitive-behavioral treatment for depression. *Journal of Consulting and Clinical Psychology, 64*, 295–304.

Jacobson, N. S., Holtzworth-Munroe, A., & Schmaling, K. B. (1989). Marital therapy and spouse involvement in the treatment of depression, agoraphobia and alcoholism. *Journal of Consulting and Clinical Psychology, 57*, 5–10.

Jacobson, N. S., & Margolin, G. (1979). *Marital therapy: Strategies based on social learning and behaviour exchange principles*. New York, NY: Guilford Press.

Jager, A. D. (1999). Forensic psychiatry. *International Medical Journal, 6*, 249–253.

Jager, J., Schulenberg, J. E., O'Malley, P. M., & Bachman, J. G. (2013). Historical variation in drug use trajectories across the transition to adulthood: The trend toward lower intercepts and steeper, ascending slopes. *Development and Psychopathology, 25*, 527–543.

James, P. S. (1991). Effects of a communication training component added to an emotionally focused couples therapy. *Journal of Marital and Family Therapy, 17*, 263–275.

Jani, J. S., Ortiz, L., & Aranda, M. P. (2009). Latino outcome studies in social work: A review of the literature. *Research on Social Work Practice, 19*,3, 179–194.

Jansson, L., & Ost, L. (1982). Behavioral treatments for agoraphobia: An evaluative review. *Clinical Psychology Review*, *2*, 311–336.

Jensen, C. (1994). Psychosocial treatment of depression in women: Nine single-subject evaluations. *Research on Social Work Practice*, *4*, 267–282.

Jensen, P. S., Arnold, L. E., Swanson, J. M., Vitiello, B., Abikoff, H. B., Greenhill, L. L., . . . Hur, K. (2007). 3-year follow-up of the NIMH MTA study. *Journal of the Academy of Child and Adolescent Psychiatry*, *46*, 989–1002.

Jerrell, J. M., & Ridgely, M. S. (1995). Comparative effectiveness of three approaches to serving people with severe mental illness and substance abuse disorders. *Journal of Nervous and Mental Disease*, *183*, 566–576.

Jessor, R., & Jessor, S. L. (1977). *Problem behavior and psychosocial development: A longitudinal study of youth*. New York, NY: Academic Press.

Johnson, D. L. (1997). Overview of severe mental illness. *Clinical Psychology Review*, *17*, 247–257.

Johnson, J. L., Sher, K. J., & Rolf, J. E. (1991). Models of vulnerability to psychopathology in children of alcoholics. *Alcohol Health and Research World*, *15*, 33–42.

Johnson, P. L., & O'Leary, D. K. (1996). Behavioral components of marital satisfaction: An individualized assessment approach. *Journal of Consulting and Clinical Psychology*, *64*, 417–423.

Johnson, R. M., Kotch, J. B., Catellier, D. J., Dufort, V., Hunter, W., & Amaya-Jackson, L. (2002). Adverse behavioral and emotional outcomes from child abuse and witnessed violence. *Child Maltreatment*, *7*, 179–186.

Johnson, S. M. (2003). The revolution in couple therapy: A practitioner-scientist perspective. *Journal of Marital and Family Therapy*, *29*, 365–384.

Johnson, S. M. (2007). The contribution of emotionally-focused couples therapy. *Journal of Contemporary Psychotherapy*, *37*, 47–52.

Johnson, S. M., & Greenberg, L. S. (1985a). Differential effects of experiential and problem solving interventions in resolving marital conflict. *Journal of Consulting and Clinical Psychology*, *53*, 175–184.

Johnson, S. M., & Greenberg, L. S. (1985b). Emotionally focused couples therapy: An outcome study. *Journal of Marital and Family Therapy*, *11*, 313–317.

Johnson, S. M., & Greenberg, L. S. (1988). *Emotionally-focused therapy for couples*. New York, NY: Guilford Press.

Johnson, S. M., & Greenberg, L. S. (1995). The emotionally focused approach to problems in adult attachment. In N. S. Jacobson & A. S. Gurman (Eds.), *Clinical handbook of couple therapy* (pp. 121–141). New York, NY: Guilford Press.

Johnson, V. W. (1973). *I'll quit tomorrow*. New York, NY: Harper and Row.

Johnson, W. G., Tsoh, J. Y., & Varnado, P. J. (1996). Eating disorders: Efficacy of pharmacological and psychological interventions. *Clinical Psychology Review*, *16*, 457–478.

Johnston, C. W., & Alozie, N. O. (2001). The effect of age on criminal processing: Is there an advantage in being "older"? *Journal of Gerontological Social Work*, *34*, 65–82.

Johnston, L. D., O'Malley, P. M., & Bachman, J. G. (1996). *National survey results on drug use: Monitoring the future study (1975–1994): Vol. 2. College students and young adults*. Rockville, MD: National Institute for Alcohol Abuse and Alcoholism.

Johnston, L. D., O'Malley, P. M., Bachman, J. G., & Schulenberg, J. E. (2013). *Monitoring the Future national survey results on drug use, 1975–2012: Vol. 2. College students and adults ages 19–50*. Ann Arbor, MI: Institute for Social Research, University of Michigan.

Joint Commission on the Accreditation of Healthcare Organizations. (2004). *Comprehensive Accreditation Manual for Behavioral Healthcare, 2004–2005*. Oakbrook Terrace, IL: Author.

Jones, A. C., & Chao, C. M. (1997). Racial, ethnic and cultural issues in couples therapy. In W. K. Halford & H. J. Markham (Eds.), *Clinical handbook of marriage and couples intervention* (pp. 157–178). New York, NY: Wiley.

Jones, E. E., & Pulos, S. M. (1993). Comparing the process in psychodynamic and cognitive-behavioral therapies. *Journal of Consulting and Clinical Psychology, 61*, 306–316.

Jones, M., Luce, K. H., Osborne, M. I., Taylor, K., Cunning, D., Doyle, A. C., . . . Taylor, C. B. (2008). Randomized controlled trial of an Internet-facilitated intervention for reducing binge eating and overweight in adolescents. *Pediatrics, 121*, 453–462.

Jordan, C. E., & Walker, R. (1994). Guidelines for handling domestic violence cases in community mental health centers. *Psychiatric Services, 45*, 147–151.

Joseph, S., Williams, R., & Yule, W. (1997). *Understanding post-traumatic stress: A psychosocial perspective on PTSD and treatment*. New York, NY: Wiley.

Joutsenniemi, K., Moustgaard, H., Koskinen, S., Ripatti, S., & Maritikainen, P. (2011). Psychiatric comorbidity in couples: A longitudinal study of 202,959 married and cohabiting individuals. *Social Psychiatry and Psychiatric Epidemiology, 46*, 632–633.

Kadden, R. M. (1994). Cognitive-behavioral approaches to alcoholism treatment. *Alcohol Health and Research World, 18*, 279–286.

Kagan, J. (1989). Temperamental contributions to social behavior. *American Psychologist, 44*, 668–674.

Kagan, J. (1997). Conceptualizing psychopathology: The importance of developmental profiles. *Development and Psychopathology, 9*, 321–334.

Kahn, J. S., Kehle, T. J., Jenson, W. R., & Clark, E. (1990). Comparison of cognitive-behavioral, relaxation and self-modeling interventions for depression among middle school students. *School Psychology Review, 19*, 196–211.

Kandel, D. B., Johnson, J. G., Bird, H. R., Canino, G., Goodman, S. H., Lahey, B. B., . . . Schwab-Stone, M. (1997). Psychiatric disorders associated with substance use among children and adolescents: Findings from the Methods for the Epidemiology of Child and Adolescent Mental Disorders (MECA) Study. *Journal of Abnormal Child Psychology, 25*, 121–132.

Kandel, D., Johnson, J., Bird, H., Weissman, M., Goodman, S., Lahey, B., . . . Schwab-Stone, M. (1999). Psychiatric comorbidity among adolescents with substance use disorders: Findings from the MECA study. *Journal of the American Academy of Child and Adolescent Psychiatry, 35*, 743–751.

Kanfer, F. H. (1970). Self-monitoring: Methodological limitations and clinical applications. *Journal of Consulting and Clinical Psychology, 35*, 148–152.

Kantrowitz, J. L. (1995). Outcome research in psychoanalysis: Review and reconsiderations. In T. Shapiro & R. N. Emde (Eds.), *Research in psychoanalysis: Process, development, outcome* (pp. 313–328). Madison, CT: International Universities Press.

Kaplan, H. I., & Sadock, B. J. (1998). *Synopsis of psychiatry* (8th ed.). Baltimore, MD: Williams and Wilkins.

Kaplan, S. J., Pelcovitz, D., & Labruna, V. (1999). Child and adolescent abuse and neglect research: A review of the past 10 years: Part I. Physical and emotional abuse and neglect. *Journal of the American Academy of Child and Adolescent Psychiatry, 38*, 1214–1222.

Karls, J. M., & Wandrei, K. E. (Eds.) (1994). *The PIE classification system for social functioning problems*. Washington, DC: NASW Press.

Karney, B. R., & Bradbury, T. N. (1995). The longitudinal course of marital quality and stability: A review of theory, method and research. *Psychological Bulletin, 11*, 3–34.

Karno, M., Golding, J. M., Sorenson, S. B., & Burnam, M. A. (1988). The epidemiology of obsessive-compulsive disorder in five US communities. *Archives of General Psychiatry, 45*, 1094–1099.

Kashubeck-West, S., & Mintz, L. B. (2001). Eating disorders in women: Etiology, assessment, and treatment. *Counseling Psychologist, 29*, 627–634.

Kashubeck-West, S., Mintz, L. B., & Saunders, K. J. (2001). Assessment of eating disorders in women. *Counseling Psychologist, 29*, 662–694.

Kaslow, N. J., & Thompson, M. P. (1998). Applying the criteria for empirically supported treatment to studies of psychosocial interventions for child and adolescent depression. *Journal of Clinical Child Psychology, 27*, 146–155.

Kassel, J. D., Wardle, M. C., Heinz, A. J., & Greenstein, J. E. (2010). Cognitive theories of drug effects on emotion. In J. D. Kassel (Ed.), *Substance abuse and emotion* (pp. 61–82). Washington, DC: American Psychological Association. doi: 10.1037/12067-003.

Katzman, M. A., Bara-Carril, N., Rabe-Hesketh, S., Schmidt, U., Troop, N., & Treasure, J. (2010). A randomized controlled two-stage trial in the treatment of bulimia nervosa, comparing CBT vs. motivational enhancement in phase 1 followed by group vs. individual CBT in phase 2. *Psychosomatic Medicine, 72*, 656–663.

Kay, S. R., Fiszbein, A., & Opler, L. (1987). The positive and negative syndrome scale (PANSS) for schizophrenia. *Schizophrenia Bulletin, 13*, 261–276.

Kayser, K. (1996). The Marital Disaffection Scale: An inventory for assessing emotional estrangement in marriage. *American Journal of Family Therapy, 24*, 83–88.

Kayser, K. (1997). Couples therapy. In J. R. Brandell (Ed.), *Theory and practice in clinical social work* (pp. 254–287). New York, NY: Free Press.

Kazdin, A. E. (1978). Methodological and interpretive problems of single-case experimental designs. *Journal of Consulting and Clinical Psychology, 46*, 629–642.

Kazdin, A. E. (1994a). Methodology, design and evaluation in psychotherapy research. In A. E. Bergin & S. L. Garfield (Eds.), *The handbook of psychotherapy and behavior change* (4th ed., pp. 19–71). New York, NY: Wiley.

Kazdin, A. E. (1994b). Psychotherapy for children and adolescents. In A. E. Bergin & S. L. Garfield (Eds.), *The handbook of psychotherapy and behavior change* (4th ed., pp. 543–594). New York, NY: Wiley.

Kazdin, A. E. (1997). Practitioner review: Psychosocial treatments for conduct disorder in children. *Journal of Child Psychology and Psychiatry, 38*, 161–178.

Kazdin, A. E. (1998). *Research design in clinical psychology* (3rd ed.). Boston, MA: Allyn & Bacon.

Kazdin, A. E. (2002). *Research design in clinical psychology* (4th ed.). New York, NY: Pearson.

Kazdin, A. E., Bass, D., Siegel, T., & Thomas, C. (1989). Cognitive-behavioral therapy and relationship therapy in the treatment of children referred for antisocial behavior. *Journal of Consulting and Clinical Psychology, 57,* 522–535.

Kazdin, A. E., & Kendall, P. C. (1998). Current progress and future plans for developing effective treatments: Comments and perspectives. *Journal of Clinical Child Psychology, 27,* 217–226.

Kazdin, A. E., & Weisz, J. R. (1998). Identifying and developing empirically supported child and adolescent treatments. *Journal of Consulting and Clinical Psychology, 66,* 19–36.

Kazdin, A. E., & Wilson, G. T. (1980). *The evaluation of behavior therapy: Issues, evidence and research strategies.* Lincoln, NE: University of Nebraska Press.

Keane, T. M. (1998). Psychological effects of military combat. In B. P. Dohrenwend (Ed.), *Adversity, stress and psychopathology* (pp. 52–65). New York, NY: Oxford University Press.

Keane, T. M., Caddell, J., & Taylor, K. (1988). Mississippi Scale for Combat-Related Post-Traumatic Stress Disorder: Three studies in reliability and validity. *Journal of Consulting and Clinical Psychology, 56,* 85–90.

Kelly, J. L., & Petry, N. M. (2000). HIV risk behaviors in male substance abusers with and without antisocial personality disorder. *Journal of Substance Abuse Treatment, 19,* 59–66.

Kelly, S., & Blythe, B. J. (2000). Family preservation: A potential not yet realized. *Child Welfare, 79,* 29–42.

Kempe, C. H., Silverman, F. N., Steele, B. F., Droegemueller, W., & Silver, H. K. (1962). The battered child syndrome. *JAMA, 181,* 17–24.

Kendall, P. C. (1992). *Anxiety disorders in youth: Cognitive behavioral interventions.* Boston, MA: Allyn & Bacon.

Kendall, P. C. (1993). Cognitive-behavioral therapies with youth: Guiding theory, current status, and emerging developments. *Journal of Consulting and Clinical Psychology, 61,* 235–247.

Kendall, P. C. (1994). Treating anxiety disorders in children: Results of a randomized clinical trial. *Journal of Consulting and Clinical Psychology, 62,* 100–110.

Kendall, P. C., Flannery-Schroeder, E., Panichelli-Mindel, S. M., Southam-Gerow, M., Henin, A., & Warman, M. (1997). Therapy for youths with anxiety disorders: A second randomized clinical trial. *Journal of Consulting and Clinical Psychology, 65,* 366–380.

Kendall, P. C., Korlander, E., Chansky, T. E., & Brady, E. U. (1992). Comorbidity of anxiety and depression in youth: Treatment implications. *Journal of Consulting and Clinical Psychology, 60,* 869–880.

Kendall, P. C., & Southam-Gerow, M. A. (1996). Long-term follow-up of a cognitive-behavioral therapy for anxiety-disordered youth. *Journal of Consulting and Clinical Psychology, 64,* 724–730.

Kendall-Tackett, K. A., Williams, L. M., & Finkelhor, D. (1993). Impact of sexual abuse on children: A review and synthesis of recent empirical studies. *Psychological Bulletin, 113,* 164–180.

Kennedy, G. J., Metz, H., & Lowinger, R. (1996). Epidemiology and inferences regarding the etiology of late-life suicide. In G. J. Kennedy (Ed.), *Suicide and depression in late life* (pp. 3–22). New York, NY: Wiley.

Kenny, M. C., Capri, V., Thakkar-Kolar, R. R., Ryan, E. E., & Runyon, M. K. (2008). Child sexual abuse: From prevention to self-protection. *Child Abuse Review*, *17*, 36–54.

Kernberg, O. F. (1975). *Borderline conditions and pathological narcissism*. New York, NY: Aronson.

Kernberg, O. F. (1976). *Object relations theory and clinical psychoanalysis*. New York, NY: Aronson.

Kernberg, O. F. (1999). The psychotherapeutic treatment of borderline patients. In J. Derksen, C. Maffei, & H. Groen (Eds.), *Treatment of personality disorders* (pp. 167–182). New York, NY: Kluwer Academic/Plenum.

Kersten, K. (1990). The process of marital disaffection: Interventions at various stages. *Family Relations*, *39*, 257–265.

Kertzman, S. G., Treves, I. A., Treves, T. A., Vainder, M., & Korczyn, A. D. (2002). Hamilton Depression Scale in Dementia. *International Journal of Psychiatry in Clinical Practice*, *6*, 91–94.

Kessler, R. C., Birnbaum, H., Demler, O., Falloon, I. R. H., Gagnon, E., Guyer, M., . . . Wu, E. Q. (2005). The prevalence and correlates of nonaffective psychosis in the National Comorbidity Survey Replication (NCS-R). *Biological Psychiatry*, *58*(8), 668–676.

Kessler, R. C., Borges, G., & Walters, E. E. (1999). Prevalence of and risk factors for lifetime suicide attempts in the National Comorbidity Survey. *Archives of General Psychiatry*, *56*, 617–626. doi: 10.1001/archpsyc.56.7.617.

Kessler, R. C., Chiu, W. T., Jin, R., Ruscio, A. M., Shear, K., & Walters, E. E. (2006). The epidemiology of panic attacks, panic disorder, and agoraphobia in the National Comorbidity Survey Replication. *Archives of General Psychiatry*, *63*, 415–424.

Kessler, R. C., Crum, R. M, Warner, L. A., Nelson, C. B., Shulenberg, J., & Anthony, J. C. (1997). Lifetime co-occurrence of DSM-III-R alcohol abuse and dependence with other psychiatric disorders in the National Comorbidity Survey. *Archives of General Psychiatry*, *54*, 313–321.

Kessler, R. C., McGonagle, K., Zhao, S., Nelson, C., Hughes, M., Eshleman, S., . . . Kendler, K. (1994). Lifetime and 12-month prevalence of DSM-III-R psychiatric disorders in the United States. *Archives of General Psychiatry*, *51*, 8–19.

Kessler, R. C., Nelson, C. B., McGonagle, K., Edlund, M. J., Frank, R. G., & Leaf, P. (1996). The epidemiology of co-occurring addictive and mental disorders: Implications for prevention and service utilization. *American Journal of Orthopsychiatry*, *66*, 17–31.

Kessler, R. C., Rubinow, D. R., Holmes, C., Abelson, J. M., & Zhao, S. (1997). The epidemiology of DSM-III-R bipolar I disorder in a general population survey. *Psychological Medicine*, *27*, 1079–1089.

Kessler, R. C., Sonnega, A., Bromet, E., Hughes, M., & Nelson, C. B. (1995). Post-traumatic stress disorder in the National Comorbidity Survey. *Archives of General Psychiatry*, *52*, 1048–1060.

Kettlewell, P. W., Mizes, J. S., & Wasylyshyn, N. A. (1992). A cognitive-behavioral group treatment of bulimia. *Behavior Therapy*, *23*, 657–670.

Kety, S. S. (1996). Genetic and environmental factors in the etiology of schizophrenia. In S. Matthysse, D. L. Levy, J. Kagan, & F. M. Benes (Eds.), *Psychopathology: The evolving science of mental disorder* (pp. 477–487). New York, NY: Cambridge University Press.

Kilpatrick, D. G., & Resnick, H. S. (1993). Post traumatic stress disorder associated with exposure to criminal victimization in clinical and community populations. In *Post traumatic stress disorder: DSM-IV and beyond* (pp. 113–146). Washington, DC: American Psychiatric Press.

Kilpatrick, D. G., Resnick, H. S., Saunders, B. E., & Best, C. L. (1998). Rape, other violence against women, and post-traumatic stress disorder. In B. P. Dohrenwend (Ed.), *Adversity, stress and psychopathology* (pp. 161–176). New York, NY: Oxford University Press.

Kilpatrick, D. G., Saunders, B. E., Amick-McMullan, A., Best, C. L., Veronen, L. J., & Resnick, H. S. (1989). Victim and crime factors associated with the development of crime-related post-traumatic stress disorder. *Behavior Therapy, 20,* 199–214.

Kilpatrick, D. G., Saunders, B. E., Veronen, L. J., Best, C. L., & Von, J. M. (1987). Criminal victimization: Lifetime prevalence, reporting to police, and psychological impact. *Crime and Delinquency, 33,* 479–489.

King, C. A., Ghaziuddin, N., McGovern, L., Brand, E., Hill, E., & Naylor, M. (1996). Predictors of comorbid alcohol and substance abuse in depressed adolescents. *Journal of the Academy of Child and Adolescent Psychiatry, 35,* 743–751.

King, D. W., Leskin, G. A., King, L. A., & Weathers, F. W. (1998). Confirmatory factor analysis of the clinician-administered PTSD scale: Evidence for the dimensionality of posttraumatic stress disorder. *Psychological Assessment, 10,* 90–96.

King, N. J., Hamilton, D. I., & Ollendick, T. H. (1988). *Children's phobias: A behavioural perspective.* Chichester, UK: Wiley.

King, N. J., Tonge, B. J., Mullen, P., Myerson, N., Heyne, D., Rollings, S., . . . Ollendick, T. H. (2000). Treating sexually abused children with posttraumatic stress symptoms: A randomized controlled trial. *Journal of the American Academy of Child and Adolescent Psychiatry, 39,* 1347–1355.

Kingdon, D. G., & Turkington, D. (1991). The use of cognitive behavior therapy with a normalizing rationale in schizophrenia. *Journal of Nervous and Mental Disease, 179,* 207–211.

Kinney, J., Haapala, D. A., & Booth, C. (1991). *Keeping families together: The Homebuilders model.* New York, NY: Aldine de Gruyter.

Kinney, J., Madsen, B., Fleming, T., & Haapala, D. A. (1977). Homebuilders: Keeping families together. *Journal of Consulting and Clinical Psychology, 45,* 667–673.

Kinzie, J. D., Manson, S. M., Do, T. V., Nguyen, T. T. L., Bui, A., & Than, N. P. (1982). Development and validation of a Vietnamese-language depression rating scale. *American Journal of Psychiatry, 139,* 1276–1280.

Kirisci, L., Moss, H. B., & Tarter, R. E. (1996). Psychometric evaluation of the Situational Confidence Questionnaire in adolescents: Fitting a graded item response model. *Addictive Behaviors, 21,* 303–317.

Kirk, S. A. (1999). Good intentions are not enough: Practice guidelines for social work. *Research on Social Work Practice, 9,* 302–310.

Kitano, H. H. (1989). Alcohol and Asian-Americans. In T. D. Watts & R. Wright (Eds.), *Alcoholism in minority populations* (pp. 143–156). Springfield, IL: Thomas.

Kivlahan, D. R., Marlatt, G. A., Fromme, K., Coppel, D. B., & Williams, E. (1990). Secondary prevention with college drinkers: Evaluation of an alcohol skills training program. *Journal of Consulting and Clinical Psychology*, *58*, 805–810.

Klee, L., Schmidt, C., & Ames, G. (1991). Indicators of women's alcohol problems: What women themselves report. *International Journal of the Addictions*, *26*, 879–895.

Klein, W. C., & Bloom, M. (1995). Practice wisdom. *Social Work*, *40*, 799–807.

Klerman, G. L., & Weissman, M. M. (1993). *New applications of interpersonal psychotherapy*. Washington, DC: American Psychiatric Association.

Klerman, G. L., Weissman, M. M., Rounsaville, B. J., & Chevron, E. S. (1984). *Interpersonal psychotherapy of depression*. New York, NY: Basic Books.

Klinkenberg, W. D., & Calsyn, R. J. (1998). Gender differences in the receipt of aftercare and psychiatric hospitalization among adults with severe mental illness. *Comprehensive Psychiatry*, *39*(3), 137–142.

Klomek, A. B., & Mufson, L. (2006). Interpersonal psychotherapy for depressed adolescents. *Child and Adolescent Psychiatric Clinics of North America*, *15*, 959–975.

Klosko, J. S., & Sanderson, W. C. (1999). *Cognitive-behavioral treatment of depression*. Northvale, NJ: Aronson.

Klostermann, K., Kelley, M. L., Milletich, R. J., & Mignone, T. (2011). Alcoholism and partner aggression among gay and lesbian couples. *Aggression and Violent Behavior*, *16*, 115–119.

Klug, G., Hermann, G., Fuchs-Nieder, B., Panzer, M., Haider-Stipacek, A., Zapotoczky, H. G., & Priebe, S. (2010). Effectiveness of home treatment for elderly people with depression: Randomized controlled trial. *British Journal of Psychiatry*, 463–467.

Knapp, S., & VandeCreek, L. (2000). Recovered memories of childhood abuse: Is there an underlying professional consensus? *Professional Psychology: Research and Practice*, *31*, 365–371.

Knight, K., Hiller, M. L., & Simpson, D. D. (1999). Evaluating corrections-based treatment for the drug-abusing criminal offender. *Journal of Psychoactive Drugs*, *31*, 299–304.

Knop, J., Penick, E. C., Nickel, E. J., Mortensen, E. L., Sullivan, M. A., Murtaza, S., . . . Gabrielli, W. F. (2009). Childhood ADHD and conduct disorder as independent predictors of male alcohol dependence at age 40. *Journal of Studies on Alcohol and Other Drugs*, *70*, 169–177.

Kobak, K. A., Greist, J. H., Jefferson, J. W., Katzelnick, D. J., & Henk, H. J. (1998). Behavioral versus pharmacological treatments of obsessive compulsive disorder: A meta-analysis. *Psychopharmacology*, *136*, 205–216.

Koch, P. B., Palmer, R. F., Vicary, J. R., & Wood, J. M. (1999). Mixing sex and alcohol in college: Female-male HIV risk model. *Journal of Sex Education and Therapy*, *24*, 99–108.

Kohn, R., Dohrenwend, B. P., & Mirotznik, J. (1998). Epidemiological findings on selected psychiatric disorders in the general population. In B. P. Dohrenwend (Ed.), *Adversity, stress and psychopathology* (pp. 235–284). New York, NY: Oxford University Press.

Kohrt, B. A., Jordans, M. J., Tol, W., Luite, N. P., Maharjan, S. M., & Upadhaya, N. (2011). Validation of cross-cultural child mental health and psychosocial research instruments: Adapting the Depression Self-Rating Scale and Child PTSD Symptom Scale in Nepal. *BMC Psychiatry, 11*, 127–144.

Kolko, D. J., Brent, D. A., Baugher, M., Bridge, J., & Birmaher, B. (2000). Cognitive and family therapies for adolescent depression: Treatment specificity, mediation, and moderation. *Journal of Consulting and Clinical Psychology, 68*, 603–614.

Kolves, K., Ide, N., & de Leo, D. (2010). Suicidal ideation and behavior in the aftermath of marital separation: Gender differences. *Journal of Affective Disorders, 120*, 48–53.

Komro, K. A., Perry, C. L., Veblen-Mortenson, S., Farbakhsh, K., Toomey, T. L., Stigler, M. H., . . . Williams, C. L. (2007). Outcomes from a randomized controlled trial of a multi-component alcohol use prevention intervention for urban youth: Project Northland Chicago. *Addiction, 103*, 606–618.

Kondrat, D. C., & Teater, B. (2012). The looking-glass self: Looking at relationship as the mechanism of change in case management of persons with severe mental illness. *Families in Society, 93*, 271–278.

Koning, I. M., Vollenbergh, W. A. M., Smit, F., Verdurman, J. E. E., van den Eijnden, R. J. J. M., . . . Engels, R. C. M. E. (2009). Preventing heavy alcohol use in adolescents (PAS): Cluster randomized trial of a parent and student intervention offered separately and simultaneously. *Addiction, 104*, 1669–1678.

Koolaee, A. K., & Etemadi, A. (2010). The outcome of family interventions for the mothers of schizophrenia patients in Iran. *International Journal of Social Psychiatry, 56*, 634–646.

Kopelowicz, A. (1997). Social skill training: The moderating influence of culture in the treatment of Latinos with schizophrenia. *Journal of Psychopathology and Behavioral Assessment, 19*, 101–108.

Koss, M. (1993). Detecting the scope of rape: A review of prevalence research methods. *Journal of Interpersonal Violence, 8*, 198–222.

Koss-Chioino, J. (1999). Depression among Puerto Rican women: Culture, etiology and diagnosis. *Hispanic Journal of Behavioral Sciences, 21*, 330–350.

Kotler, L. A., Cohen, P., Davies, M., Pine, D. S., & Walsh, B. T. (2001). Longitudinal relationships between childhood, adolescent, and adult eating disorders. *Journal of the American Academy of Child and Adolescent Psychiatry, 40*, 1434–1440.

Kovacs, M. (1985). The Children's Depression Inventory (CDI). *Psychopharmacology Bulletin, 21*, 995–998.

Kovacs, M., & Bastiaens, L. J. (1995). The psychotherapeutic management of major depressive and dysthymic disorders in childhood and adolescence: Issues and prospects. In I. M. Goodyer (Ed.), *The depressed child and adolescent: Developmental and clinical perspectives* (pp. 281–310). New York, NY: Cambridge University Press.

Kovacs, M., Rush, A. J., Beck, A. T., & Hollon, S. D. (1981). Depressed outpatients treated with cognitive therapy or pharmacotherapy: A one-year follow-up. *Archives of General Psychiatry, 38*, 34–39.

Kowalik, J., Weller, J., Venter, J., & Drachman, D. (2011). Cognitive behavioral therapy for treatment of pediatric posttraumatic stress disorder: A review and meta-analysis. *Journal of Behavior Therapy and Experimental Psychiatry, 42*, 405–413.

Kranz, K. (2003). Development of the Alcohol and Other Drug Self-Efficacy Scale. *Research on Social Work Practice, 13,* 724–741.

Kranz., K., & O'Hare, T. (2006). The Substance Abuse Treatment Self-Efficacy Scale: A confirmatory factor analysis. *Journal of Social Service Research, 32,* 109–121.

Kreyenbuhl, J., Buchanan, R. W., Dickerson, F. B., & Dixon, L. B. (2010). The Schizophrenia Patient Outcomes Research Team (PORT): Updated treatment recommendations 2009. *Schizophrenia Bulletin, 36,* 94–103.

Kroger, C., Schweiger, U., Sipos, V., Arnold, R., Kahl, K. G., Schunert, T., . . . Reinecker, H. (2006). Effectiveness of dialectical behavior therapy for borderline personality disorder in an inpatient setting. *Behaviour Research and Therapy, 44,* 1211–1217.

Kudler, H. S., Blank, A. S., & Krupnick, J. L. (2000). Psychodynamic therapy. In E. B. Foa, T. M. Keane, & M. J. Friedman (Eds.), *Effective treatments for PTSD: Practice guidelines from the international society for traumatic stress studies* (pp. 176–198). New York, NY: Guilford Press.

Kuehnle, K. (1996). *Assessing allegations of child sexual abuse.* Sarasota, FL: Professional Resource Press.

Kulhara, P., Avasthi, A., Grover, S., Sharan, P., Sharma, P., Malhotra, S., & Gill, S. (2010). Needs of Indian schizophrenia patients: An exploratory study from India. *Social Psychiatry and Psychiatric Epidemiology, 45,* 809–818.

Kulka, R. A., Schlenger, W. E., Fairbank, J. A., Hough, R. L., Jordan, B. K., Marmar, C. R., & Weiss, D. S. (1988). *National Vietnam Veterans Readjustment Study (NVVRS): Description, current status, and initial PTSD prevalence estimates.* Research Triangle Park, NC: Research Triangle Institute.

Kulkarni, M., Porter, K. E., & Rauch, S. A. M. (2012). Anger, dissociation, and PTSD among male veterans entering into PTSD treatment. *Journal of Anxiety Disorders, 26,* 271–278.

Kuno, E., Rothbard, A. B., Averyt, J., & Culhane, D. (2000). Homelessness among persons with serious mental illness in an enhanced community-based mental health system. *Psychiatric Services, 51,* 1012–1016.

Kurdek, L. A. (1998). Relationship outcomes and their predictors: Longitudinal evidence from heterosexual married, gay cohabitating, and lesbian cohabitating couples. *Journal of Marriage and the Family, 60,* 553–568.

Kurtz, M., & Mueser, K. T. (2008). A meta-analysis of controlled research on social skills training for schizophrenia. *Journal of Consulting and Clinical Psychology, 76,* 491–504.

Kutchins, H., & Kirk, S. A. (1988). The business of diagnosis: DSM-III and clinical social work. *Social Work, 33,* 215–220.

Kutchins, H., & Kirk, S. A. (1997). *Making us crazy: The psychiatric bible and the creation of mental disorders.* New York, NY: Free Press.

Kutscher, E. C. (2008). Antipsychotics. In K. T. Mueser & D. V. Jeste (Eds.), *Clinical handbook of schizophrenia* (pp. 159–167). New York, NY: Guilford Press.

Lachar, D., Bailley, S. E., Rhoades, H. M., Espadas, A., Aponte, M., Cowan, K. A., . . . Wassef, A. (2001). New subscales for an anchored version of the Brief Psychiatric Rating Scale: Construction, reliability, and validity in acute psychiatric admissions. *Psychological Assessment, 13,* 384–395.

La Greca, A. M., Prinstein, M. J., & Fetter, M. D. (2001). Adolescent peer crown affiliation: Linkages with health-risk behaviors and close friendships. *Journal of Pediatric Psychology, 26,* 131–143.

Lahey, B. B., Gordon, R. A., Loeber, R., Stouthamer-Loeber, M., & Farrington, D. P. (1999). Boys who join gangs: A prospective study of predictors of first gang entry. *Journal of Abnormal Child Psychology, 27*, 261–276.

Lamb, H. R., & Weinberger, L. E. (1998). Persons with severe mental illness in jails and prisons: A review. *Psychiatric Services, 49*, 483–492.

Lamb, H. R., & Weinberger, L. E. (2008). Mental health courts as a way to provide treatment to violent persons with severe mental illness. *JAMA, 300*, 722–724.

Lamb, M. (1994). *The investigation of child sexual abuse: An interdisciplinary consensus statement*. Bethesda, MD: National Institute of Child Health and Human Development.

Lamb, M. E., Orbach, Y., Hershkowitz, Y., Epslin, P. W., & Horowitz, D. (2007). A structured forensic interview protocol improves the quality and informativeness of investigative interviews with children: A review of research using the NICHD investigative interview protocol. *Child Abuse and Neglect, 31*, 1201–1231.

Lambert, M. J., & Bergin, A. E. (1994). The effectiveness of psychotherapy. In A. E. Bergin & S. L. Garfield (Eds.), *The handbook of psychotherapy and behavior change* (4th ed., pp. 143–189). New York, NY: Wiley.

Lambert, M. J., & Ogles, B. M. (2004). The efficacy and effectiveness of psycho-therapy. In M. J. Lambert (Ed.), *Bergin and Garfield's handbook of psycho-therapy and behavior change* (pp. 139–193). New York, NY: Wiley.

Lambert, M. J., Shapiro, D. A., & Bergin, A. E. (1986). The effectiveness of psycho-therapy. In S. L. Garfield & A. E. Bergin (Eds.), *The handbook of psychotherapy and behavior change* (3rd ed., pp. 157–211). New York, NY: Wiley.

Lane, S. D., & Cherek, D. R. (2000). Biological and behavioral investigation of aggression and impulsivity. In D. H. Fishbein (Ed.), *The science, treatment, and prevention of antisocial behaviors: Application to the criminal justice system* (pp. 5-1 to 5-21). Kingston, NJ: Civic Research Institute.

Lapierre, S., Erlangsen, A., Waern, M., De Leo, D., Oyama, H., Scocco, P., . . . International Research Group for Suicide among the Elderly (2011). A systematic review of elderly suicide prevention programs. *Crisis: The Journal of Crisis Intervention and Suicide Prevention, 32*, 88–98.

Larimer, M. E., & Cronce, J. M. (2002). Identification, prevention and treatment: A review of individual-focused strategies to reduce problematic alcohol consumption by college students. *Journal of Studies on Alcohol, 63*, 148–163.

Larimer, M. E., Palmer, R. S., & Marlatt, G. A. (1999). Relapse prevention: An overview of Marlatt's cognitive-behavioral model. *Alcohol Research and Health, 23*, 151–159.

Last, C. G. (1989). Anxiety disorders. In T. H. Ollendick & M. Hersen (Eds.), *Handbook of childhood psychopathology* (2nd ed., pp. 219–227). New York, NY: Plenum Press.

Last, C. G., Hansen, C., & Franco, N. (1998). Cognitive-behavioral treatment of school phobia. *Journal of the American Academy of Child and Adolescent Psychiatry, 37*, 404–411.

Lawrence, E., & Bradbury, T. N. (2001). Physical aggression and marital dysfunction: A longitudinal analysis. *Journal of Family Psychology, 15*, 135–154.

Lawrence, E., Eldridge, K. A., & Christensen, A. (1998). The enhancement of traditional behavioral couples therapy: Consideration of individual factors and dyadic development. *Clinical Psychology Review, 18*, 745–764.

Lawrence, R., Bradshaw, T., & Mairs, H. (2006). Group cognitive behavioural therapy for schizophrenia: A systematic review of the literature. *Journal of Psychiatric and Mental Health Nursing, 13*, 673–681.

Layne, C. M., Saltzman, W. R., Savjak, N., Popovic, T., Music, M., Djapo, N., . . . Houston, R. (2001). Trauma/grief focused group psychotherapy: School-based postwar intervention with traumatized Bosnian adolescents. *Group dynamics: Theory, Research and Practice, 5*, 277–290.

Lazarus, R. S., & Folkman, S. (1984). *Stress, appraisal and coping*. New York, NY: Springer.

Le, N., Perry, D. F., & Stuart, E. A. (2011). Randomized controlled trial of a preventive intervention for perinatal depression in high-risk Latinas. *Journal of Consulting and Clinical Psychology, 79*, 135–141.

Lebow, J. (2000). What does the research tell us about couples and family therapies? *Psychotherapy in Practice, 56*, 1083–1094.

Lebow, J., & Gurman, A. S. (1995). Research assessing couple and family therapy. *Annual Review of Psychology, 46*, 27–57.

Leccese, M., & Waldron, H. B. (1994). Assessing adolescent substance use: A critique of current measurement instruments. *Journal of Substance Abuse Treatment, 11*, 553–563.

Leda, C., & Rosenheck, R. (1995). Race in the treatment of homeless mentally ill veterans. *Journal of Nervous and Mental Disease, 183*, 529–537.

Lee, C., Gavriel, H., Drummond, P., Richards, J., & Greenwald, R. (2002). Treatment of PTSD: Stress inoculation training with prolonged exposure compared to EMDR. *Journal of Clinical Psychology, 58*, 1071–1089.

Le Grange, D., Crosby, R. D., Rathouz, P. J., & Leventhal, B. L. (2007). A randomized controlled comparison of family-based treatment and supportive psychotherapy for adolescent bulimia nervosa. *Archives of General Psychiatry, 64*, 1049–1056.

Lehman, A. (1988). A quality of life interview for the chronically mentally ill. *Evaluation and Program Planning, 11*, 51–62.

Lehman, A. (1995). Vocational rehabilitation in schizophrenia. *Schizophrenia Bulletin, 21*, 645–656.

Lehman, A. F. (2010). Adopting evidence-based practices: Our hesitation waltz. *Schizophrenia Bulletin, 36*, 1–2.

Lehman, A. F., McNary, S. W., & O'Grady, K. E. (1997). Measuring subjective life satisfaction in persons with severe and persistent mental illness: A measurement quality and structural model analysis. *Psychological Assessment, 9*, 503–507.

Lehman, A. F., Steinwachs, D. M., & Co-investigators of the PORT Project (1998). At issue—Translating research into practice: The schizophrenia patient outcomes research team (PORT) recommendations. *Schizophrenia Bulletin, 24*, 1–10.

Lehman, C., Brown, T. A., & Barlow, D. H. (1998). Effects of cognitive-behavioral treatment for panic disorder with agoraphobia on concurrent alcohol abuse. *Behavior Therapy, 29*, 423–433.

Leichsenring, F. (1999). Development and first results of the Borderline Personality Inventory: A self-report instrument for assessing borderline personality organization. *Journal of Personality Assessment, 73*, 45–63.

Leichsenring, F. (2009). Psychodynamic psychotherapy: A review of efficacy and effectiveness studies. In R. A. Levy & J. S. Ablon (Eds.), *Handbook of evidence-based psychodynamic psychotherapy* (pp. 3–27). New York, NY: Humana Press.

Leichsenring, F., Leibing, E., Kruse, J., New, A. S., & Leweke, F. (2011). Borderline personality disorder. *Lancet, 377*, 74–84.

Leigh, B. C. (1990). The relationship of sex-related alcohol expectancies to alcohol consumption and sexual behavior. *British Journal of the Addictions, 85*, 919–928.

Leigh, B. C. (1999). The risks of drinking among young adults: Peril, chance, adventure: Concepts of risk, alcohol use and risky behavior in young adults. *Addiction, 94*, 371–383.

Leigh, B. C., & Aramburu, B. (1996). The role of alcohol and gender in choices and judgments about hypothetical sexual encounters. *Journal of Applied Social Psychology, 26*, 20–30.

Leigh, B. C., & Schafer, J. C. (1993). Heavy drinking occasions and the occurrence of sexual activity. *Psychology of Addictive Behaviors, 7*, 197–200.

Leventhal, J. M. (1996). Twenty years later: We do know how to prevent child abuse and neglect. *Child Abuse and Neglect, 20*, 647–653.

Levine, M. M. P., & Levine, R. L. (2010). Psychiatric medication: Management, myths and mistakes. In M. Maine, B. H. McGilley, & D. W. Bunnell (Eds.), *Treatment of eating disorders: Bridging the research-practice gap* (pp. 111–126). New York, NY: Elsevier.

Levine, M. P., & Piran, N. (2001). The prevention of eating disorders: Toward a participatory ecology of knowledge, action, and advocacy. In R. H. Striegel-Moore & L. Smolak (Eds.), *Eating disorders: Innovative directions in research and practice* (pp. 233–253). Washington, DC: American Psychological Association.

Levinger, G. (1976). A social psychological perspective on marital dissolution. *Journal of Social Issues, 32*, 21–47.

Levy, L. B., & O'Hara, M. W. (2010). Psychotherapeutic interventions for depressed, low-income women: A review of the literature. *Clinical Psychology Review, 30*, 934–950.

Lewis, J. E., Malow, R. M., & Ireland, S. J. (1997). HIV/AIDS risk in heterosexual college students: A review of a decade of literature. *Journal of American College Health, 45*, 147–158.

Lewis, R. E., Walton, E., & Fraser, M. W. (1995). Examining family reunification services: A process analysis of a successful experiment. *Research on Social Work Practice, 5*, 259–282.

Lewisohn, P. M. (1974). A behavioral approach to depression. In R. J. Freidman & M. M. Katz (Eds.), *The psychology of depression: Contemporary theory and research* (pp. 157–178). Washington, DC: Winston/Wiley.

Lewinsohn, P. M., Clarke, G. N., Hops, H., & Andrews, J. (1990). Cognitive-behavioral treatment for depressed adolescents. *Behavior Therapy, 21*, 385–401.

Lewinsohn, P. M., Rohde, P., Seeley, J. R., Klein, D. N., & Gotlib, I. (2000). Natural course of adolescent major depressive disorder in a community sample: Predictors of recurrence in young adults. *American Journal of Psychiatry, 157*, 1584–1591.

Lex, B. (1994). Alcohol and other drug abuse among women. *Alcohol Health and Research World, 18*, 212–219.

Liberman, R. P., & Kopelowicz, A. (2005). Recovery from schizophrenia: A concept in search of research. *Psychiatric Services, 56*, 735–742.

Liberman, R. P., Kopelowicz, A., & Young, A. S. (1994). Biobehavioral treatment and rehabilitation of schizophrenia. *Behavior Therapy, 25*, 89–107.

Liberto, J. G., Oslin, D. W., & Ruskin, P. E. (1992). Alcoholism in older persons: A review of the literature. *Hospital and Community Psychiatry*, *43*, 10, 975–984.

Liberto, J. G., Oslin, D. W., & Ruskin, P. E. (1996). Alcoholism in older populations. In L. L. Carstensen, B. A. Edelstein, & L. Dornbrand (Eds.), *The practical handbook of clinical gerontology* (pp. 324–348). Thousand Oaks, CA: Sage.

Liddle, H. A., & Dakof, G. A. (1995). Efficacy of family therapy for drug abuse: Promising but not definitive. *Journal of Marital and Family Therapy*, *21*, 511–543.

Liddle, H. A., & Hogue, A. (2000). A family-based, developmental-ecological preventive intervention for high-risk adolescents. *Journal of Marital and Family Therapy*, *26*, 265–279.

Liepman, M. R. (1993). Using family influence to motivate alcoholics to enter treatment: The Hohson Institute Intervention Approach. In T. J. O'Farrell (Ed.), *Treating alcohol problems: Marital and family interventions* (pp. 54–77). New York, NY: Guilford Press.

Lindahl, K. M., Clements, M., & Markman, H. (1998). Development of marriage: A 9-year perspective. In T. N. Bradbury (Ed.), *The developmental course of marital dysfunction* (pp. 205–236). New York, NY: Cambridge University Press.

Lindahl, K. M., Malik, N. M., & Bradbury, T. N. (1997). The developmental course of couples' relationships. In W. K. Halford & H. J. Markham (Eds.), *Clinical handbook of marriage and couples intervention* (pp. 203–224). New York, NY: Wiley.

Lindsey, D., Martin, S., & Doh, J. (2002). The failure of intensive casework services to reduce foster care placements: An examination of family preservation studies. *Child and Youth Services Review*, *24*, 743–775.

Linehan, M. M. (1993a). *Cognitive-behavioral treatment of borderline personality disorder*. New York, NY: Guilford Press.

Linehan, M. M. (1993b). *Skills training manual for treating borderline personality disorder.* New York, NY: Guilford Press.

Linehan, M. M., Armstrong, H. E., Suarez, A., Allmon, D., & Heard, H. L. (1991). Cognitive-behavioral treatment of chronically parasuicidal borderline patients. *Archives of General Psychiatry*, *48*, 1060–1064.

Linehan, M. M., Comtois, K. A., Murray, A. M., Brown, M. Z., Gallop, R. J., Heard, L., . . . Lindenboim, N. (2006). Two-year randomized controlled trial and follow-up of dialectical behavior therapy vs. therapy by experts for suicidal behaviors and borderline personality disorder. *Archives of General Psychiatry*, *63*, 757–766.

Linehan, M. M., & Dexter-Mazza, E. T. (2008). Dialectical behavior therapy for borderline personality disorder. In D. H. Barlow (Ed.), *Clinical handbook of psychological disorders: A step-by-step treatment manual* (4th ed., pp. 365–420). New York, NY: Guilford Press.

Linehan, M. M., Heard, H. L., & Armstrong, H. E. (1993). Naturalistic follow-up of a behavioral treatment for chronically parasuicidal borderline patients. *Archives of General Psychiatry*, *50*, 971–974.

Linehan, M. M., Kanter, J. W., & Comtois, K. A. (1999). Dialectical behavior therapy for borderline personality disorder. In D. S. Janowsky (Ed.), *Psychotherapy indications and outcomes* (pp. 93–118). Washington, DC: American Psychiatric Press.

Linehan, M. M., Tutek, D. A., Heard, H. L., & Armstrong, H. E. (1994). Interpersonal outcome of cognitive behavioral treatment for chronically suicidal borderline patients. *American Journal of Psychiatry*, *151*, 1771–1776.

Lipsey, M. W., & Wilson, D. B. (1993). The efficacy of psychological, educational, and behavioral treatment: Confirmation from meta-analysis. *American Psychologist*, *48*, 1181–1209.

Litten, R. Z., & Allen, J. P. (1999). Medications for alcohol, illicit drug, and tobacco dependence. An update of research findings. *Journal of Substance Abuse Treatment*, *16*, 105–112.

Locke, H., & Wallace, K. (1959). Short marital adjustment and prediction tests: Their reliability and validity. *Marriage and Family Living*, *2*, 251–255.

Loevinger, J. (1976). *Ego development: Conceptions and theories*. San Francisco, CA: Jossey-Bass.

Loftus, E. F. (1993). The reality of repressed memories. *American Psychologist*, *48*, 518–537.

Loftus, E. F. (1994). The repressed memory controversy. *American Psychologist*, *49*, 443–445.

Lohr, J., Lilienfeld, S., Tolin, D., & Herbert, J. (1999). Eye movement desensitization and reprocessing: An analysis of specific versus nonspecific treatment factors. *Journal of Anxiety Disorders*, *13*, 185–207.

Longabaugh, R., Donovan, D. M., Karno, M. P., McCrady, B. S., Morgenstern, J., & Tonigan, J. S. (2005). Active ingredients: How and why evidence-based alcohol behavioral treatment interventions work. *Alcoholism: Clinical and Experimental Research*, *29*, 235–247.

Longabaugh, R., & Morgenstern, J. (1999). Cognitive-behavioral coping-skills therapy for alcohol dependence: Current status and future directions. *Alcohol Research and Health*, *23*, 78–85.

Longo, M., Wickes, W., Smout, M., Harrison, Cahill, S., & White, J. M. (2009). Randomized controlled trial of dexamphetamine maintenance for the treatment of methamphetamine dependence. *Addiction*, *105*, 146–154.

LoPiccolo, J. (1994). Sexual dysfunction. In L. W. Craighead, W. E. Craighead, A. E. Kazdin, & M. J. Mahoney (Eds.), *Cognitive and behavioral interventions: An empirical approach to mental health problems* (pp. 183–196). Boston, MA: Allyn & Bacon.

Lordan, E. J., Kelley, J. M., Peters, C. P., & Siegfried, R. J. (1997). Treatment placement decisions: How substance abuse professionals assess and place clients. *Evaluation and Program Planning*, *20*, 137–149.

Losel, F., & Schmucker, M. (2005). The effectiveness of treatment for sexual offenders: A comprehensive meta-analysis. *Journal of Experimental Criminology*, *1*, 117–146.

Lowe, L. A. (1998). Using the Child Behavior Checklist in assessing conduct disorder: Issues of reliability and validity. *Research on Social Work Practice*, *8*, 286–301.

Lu, W., Fite, R., Kim, E., Hyer, L., Yanos, P. T., Mueser, K. T., & Rosenberg, S. D. (2009). Cognitive-behavioral treatment of PTSD in severe mental illness: Pilot study replication in an ethnically diverse population. *American Journal of Psychiatric Rehabilitation*, *12*, 73–91.

Lu, W., Mueser, K. T., Rosenberg, S. D., & Jankowski, M. K. (2008). Correlates of adverse childhood experiences among adults with severe mood disorders. *Psychiatric Services*, *59*, 1018–1026. doi: 10.1176/appi.ps.58.2.245.

Luborsky, L., Singer, B., & Luborsky, L. (1975). Comparative studies of psychotherapies: Is it true that "everyone has won and all must have prizes?" *Archives of General Psychiatry, 32*, 995–1008.

Lutzker, J. R., Bigelow, K. M., Doctor, R. M., Gershater, R. M., & Greene, B. F. (1998). An ecobehavioral model for the prevention and treatment of child abuse and neglect: History and applications. In J. R. Lutzker (Ed.), *Handbook of child abuse research and treatment* (pp. 239–266). New York, NY: Plenum Press.

Lutzker, J. R., Bigelow, K. M., Doctor, R. M., & Kessler, M. L. (1998). Safety, health care, and bonding within an ecobehavioral approach to treating and preventing child abuse and neglect. *Journal of Family Violence, 13*, 163–185.

Lutzker, J. R., & Rice, J. M. (1984). Project 12-Ways: Measuring outcome of a large in-home service for treatment and prevention of child abuse and neglect. *Child Abuse and Neglect, 8*, 519–524.

Lutzker, J. R., & Rice, J. M. (1987). Using recidivism data to evaluate Project 12-Ways: An ecobehavioral approach to the treatment and prevention of child abuse and neglect. *Journal of Family Violence, 2*, 283–289.

Lutzker, J. R., Van Hasselt, V. B., Bigelow, K. M., Greene, B. F., & Kessler, M. L. (1998). Child abuse and neglect: Behavioral research, treatment and theory. *Aggression and Violent Behavior, 3*, 181–196.

Lyons, J. S., Howard, K. I., O'Mahoney, M. T., & Lish, J. D. (1997). *The measurement and management of clinical outcomes in mental health*. New York, NY: Wiley.

Lyons, P., Doueck, H. J., & Wodarski, J. S. (1996). Risk assessment for child protective services: A review of the empirical literature on instrument performance. *Social Work Research, 20*, 143–155.

MacDonald, B. J. (1998). Issues in therapy with gay and lesbian couples. *Journal of Sex and Marital Therapy, 24*, 165–190.

MacDonald, G., Sheldon, B., & Gillespie, J. (1992). Contemporary studies of the effectiveness of social work. *British Journal of Social Work, 22*, 615–643.

Mackey, R. A., & O'Brien, B. A. (1998). Marital conflict management: Gender and ethnic differences. *Social Work, 43*, 128–140.

MacLeod, J., & Nelson, G. (2000). Programs for the promotion of family wellness and the prevention of child maltreatment: A meta-analytic review. *Child Abuse and Neglect, 24*, 1127–1149.

MacMillan, H. L., MacMillan, J. H., Offord, D. R., Griffith, L., & MacMillan, A. (1994a). Primary prevention of child physical abuse: A critical review, part I. *Journal of Child Psychology and Psychiatry, 35*, 835–856.

MacMillan, H. L., MacMillan, J. H., Offord, D. R., Griffith, L., & MacMillan, A. (1994b). Primary prevention of child sexual abuse: A critical review, part II. *Journal of Child Psychology and Psychiatry, 35*, 857–876.

Maddock, J. E., Laforge, R. G., Rossi, J. S., & O'Hare, T. (2001). The College Alcohol Problem Scale. *Addictive Behaviors, 26*, 385–398.

Magee, W. J., Eaton, W., Wittchen, H., McGonagle, K., & Kessler, R. (1996). Agoraphobia, simple phobia, and social phobia in the national comorbidity survey. *Archives of General Psychiatry, 53*, 159–168.

Magill, M., & Ray, L. A. (2009). Cognitive-behavioral treatment with adult alcohol and illicit drug users: A meta-analysis of randomized controlled trials. *Journal of Studies on Alcohol and Drugs, 70*, 516–527.

Mahler, M. M. (1968). *On human symbiosis and vicissitudes of individuation.* New York, NY: International Universities Press.

Mahoney, M. J. (1977). Reflections on the cognitive-learning trend in psychotherapy. *American Psychologist, 32*, 5–13.

Maisto, S., Carey, K., & Bradizza, C. (1999). Social learning theory. In K. E. Leonard & H. T. Blane (Eds.), *Psychological theories of drinking and alcoholism* (pp. 106–163). New York, NY: Guilford Press.

Maisto, S. A., Carey, M. P., Carey, K. B., Gordon, C. M., & Gleason, J. R. (2000). Use of the AUDIT and the DAST-10 to identify alcohol and drug use disorders among adults with severe and persistent mental illness. *Psychological Assessment, 12*, 186–192.

Makely, A. T., & Falcone, R. A. (2010). Post traumatic stress disorder in the pediatric trauma patient. *Seminars in Pediatric Surgery, 19*, 292–299.

Maletzky, B. M., & Steinhauser, C. (2002). A 25-year follow-up of cognitive/behavioral therapy with 7,275 sexual offenders. *Behavior Modification, 26*, 123–147.

Malow, R. M., McMahon, R., Cremer, D. J., Lewis, J. E., & Alferi, S. M. (1997). Psychosocial predictors of HIV risk among adolescent offenders who abuse drugs. *Psychiatric Services, 48*, 185–187.

Manassis, K. (2000). Childhood anxiety disorders: Lessons from the literature. *Canadian Journal of Psychiatry, 45*, 724–730.

Manassis, K. (2001). Child-parent relations: Attachment and anxiety disorders. In W. K. Silverman & P. D. A. Treffers (Eds.), *Anxiety disorders in children and adolescents: Research, assessment and intervention* (pp. 255–272). New York, NY: Cambridge University Press.

Maniglio, R. (2009). The impact of child sexual abuse on health: A systematic review of reviews. *Clinical Psychology Review, 29*, 647–657.

Mann, B. J., & Borduin, C. M. (1991). A critical review of psychotherapy outcome studies with adolescents: 1978–1988. *Adolescence, 26*, 505–541.

Mann, E. A., & Reynolds, A. J. (2006). Early intervention and juvenile delinquency prevention: Evidence from the Chicago longitudinal study. *Social Work Research, 30*, 153–167.

Manoleas, P. (Ed.) (1996). *The cross-cultural practice of clinical case management in mental health.* New York, NY: Haworth Press.

March, J. S. (1995). Cognitive-behavioral psychotherapy for children and adolescents with OCD: A review and recommendations for treatment. *Journal of the Academy of Child and Adolescent Psychiatry, 34*, 7–18.

March, J. S., & Leonard, H. L. (1996). Obsessive-compulsive disorder in children and adolescents: A review of the past 10 years. *Journal of the American Academy of Child and Adolescent Psychiatry, 35*, 1265–1273.

March, J. S., Leonard, H. L., & Swedo, S. E. (1995). Obsessive-compulsive disorder. In J. S. March (Ed.), *Anxiety disorders in children and adolescents* (pp. 251–275). New York, NY: Guilford Press.

Marcus, R. F., & Swett, B. (2002). Violence and intimacy in close relationships. *Journal of Interpersonal Violence, 17*, 570–586.

Marino, R., Stuart, G. W., & Minas, I. H. (2000). Acculturation of values and behavior: A study of Vietnamese immigrants. *Measurement and Evaluation in Counseling and Development, 33*, 21–41.

Markowitz, J. C. (1999). Developments in interpersonal psychotherapy. *Canadian Journal of Psychiatry, 44*, 556–561.

Marks, I. M. (1987). *Fears, phobias and rituals: Panic, anxiety and their disorders*. New York, NY: Oxford University Press.

Marks, J., & McDonald, T. (1989). *Risk assessment in child protective services. Predicting recurrence of child maltreatment*. Portland, ME: University of Southern Maine, National Child Welfare Resource Center Management and Administration.

Marlatt, G. A. (1996). Harm reduction: Come as you are. *Addictive Behaviors, 21*, 779–788.

Marlatt, G. A., Baer, J. S., Kivlahan, D. R., Dimeff, L. A., Larimer, M. E., Quigley, L. A., . . . Williams, E. (1998). Screening and brief intervention for high-risk college student drinkers: Results from a 2-year follow-up assessment. *Journal of Consulting and Clinical Psychology, 66*, 604–615.

Marlatt, G. A., & George, W. (1984). Relapse prevention: Introduction and overview of the model. *British Journal of the Mental Health Problems and Alcohol Abuse Addictions, 79*, 261–273.

Marlatt, G. A., & Gordon, J. R. (1985). *Relapse prevention: Maintenance strategies in the treatment of addictive behaviors*. New York, NY: Guilford Press.

Marlatt, G. A., & Witkiewitz, K. (2002). Harm reduction approaches to alcohol use: Health promotion, prevention, and treatment. *Addictive Behaviors, 27*, 867–886.

Marlowe, M. J., O'Neill-Byrne, K., Lowe-Ponsford, F., & Watson, J. P. (1996). The Borderline Syndrome Index: A validation study using the Personality Assessment Schedule. *British Journal of Psychiatry, 168*, 72–75.

Marsella, A. J., Friedman, M. J., & Spain, E. H. (1996). Ethnocultural aspects of PTSD: An overview of issues and research directions. In A. J. Marsella, M. J. Friedman, E. T. Gerrity, & R. M. Scurfield (Eds.), *Ethnocultural aspects of posttraumatic stress disorder* (pp. 105–130). Washington, DC: American Psychological Association.

Marshall, C., & Rossman, G. B. (1995). *Designing qualitative research* (2nd ed.). Thousand Oaks, CA: Sage.

Marshall, W. L. (1996). Assessment, treatment and theorizing about sex offenders: Developments during the past twenty years and future directions. *Criminal Justice and Behavior, 23*, 162–199.

Marshall, W. L., Ward, T., Mann, R. E., Moulden, H., Fernandez, Y. M., Serran, G., & Marshall, L. (2005). Working positively with sexual offenders: Maximizing the effectiveness of treatment. *Journal of Interpersonal Violence, 20*, 1096–1114.

Mart, E. G. (2010a). Common errors in assessment of allegations of child sexual abuse. *Journal of Psychiatry and the Law, 38*, 325–343.

Mart, E. G. (2010b). Special issue introduction: Assessment and testimony in child abuse cases. *Journal of Psychiatry and the Law, 38*, 265–269.

Martens, W. H. (2000). Antisocial and psychopathic personality disorders: Causes, course, and remission, a review article. *International Journal of Offender Therapy and Comparative Criminology, 44*, 406–430.

Martin, C. S., & Winters, K. C. (1998). Diagnosis and assessment of alcohol use disorders among adolescents. *Alcohol Health and Research World, 22,* 95–106.

Martin, S. S., Butzin, C. A., & Inciardi, J. A. (1995). Assessment of a multistage therapeutic community for drug involved offenders. *Journal of Psychoactive Drugs, 27,* 109–116.

Masters, W., & Johnson, V. (1970). *Human sexual inadequacy.* Boston, MA: Little, Brown.

Masterson, J. F. (1981). *The narcissistic and borderline personality disorders: An integrated developmental approach.* New York, NY: Brunner/Mazel.

Mather, J. H., & Lager, P. B. (2000). *Child welfare: A unifying model of practice.* Belmont, CA: Brooks/Cole.

Mattaini, M. A. (1996). The abuse and neglect of single-case designs. *Research on Social Work Practice, 6,* 83–91.

Mattaini, M. A., McGowan, B. G., & Williams, G. (1996). Child maltreatment. In M. A. Mattaini & B. A. Thyer (Eds.), *Finding solutions to social problems: Behavioral strategies for change* (pp. 223–266). Washington, DC: American Psychological Association.

Mattson, M. E., Allen, J., Longabaugh, R., Nickless, C., Connors, G. J., & Kadden, R. M. (1994). A chronological review of empirical studies matching alcoholic clients to treatment. *Journal of Studies on Alcohol, 55,* 16–29.

Maxfield, L., & Hyer, L. (2002). The relationship between efficacy and methodology in studies investigating EMDR treatment of PTSD. *Journal of Clinical Psychology, 58,* 23–41.

Mayer, R. R., Forster, J. L., Murray, D. M., & Wagenaar, A. C. (1998). Social settings and situations of underage drinking. *Journal of Studies on Alcohol, 59,* 207–215.

Mazure, C. M., Halmi, K. A., Sunday, S. R., Romano, S. J., & Einhorn, A. M. (1994). The Yale-Brown-Cornell Eating Disorder Scale: Development, use, reliability and validity. *Journal of Psychiatric Research, 28,* 425–445.

Mazzucchelli, T., Kane, R., & Rees, C. (2009). Behavioral activation treatments for depression in adults: A meta-analysis and review. *Clinical Psychology Science and Practice, 16,* 383–411.

McAlpine, C., Marshall, C. C., & Doran, N. H. (2001). Combining child welfare and substance abuse services: A blended model of intervention. *Child Welfare, 80,* 129–149.

McCarthy, B. W., Ginsberg, R. L., & Fucito, S. M. (2006). Resilient sexual desire in heterosexual couples. *Family Journal, 14,* 59–64.

McCarthy M. L. (2007). Prescription drug abuse up sharply in the USA. *Lancet, 369,* 1505–1506.

McClintock, S. M., Brandon, A. R., Husain, M. M., & Jarrett, R. (2011). A systematic review of the combined use of electroconvulsive therapy and psychotherapy for depression. *Journal of ECT, 27,* 236–243.

McCollum, E. E., & Stith, S. M. (2008). Couples treatment for interpersonal violence: A review of outcome research literature and current clinical practices. *Violence and Victims, 23,* 187–201.

McConnaughy, E. A., DiClemente, C. C., Prochaska, J. O., & Velicer, W. F. (1989). Stages of change in psychotherapy: A follow-up report. *Psychotherapy, 26*(4), 494–503.

McCracken, S. G., & Marsh, J. C. (2008, July). Practitioner expertise in evidence-based decision-making. *Research on Social Work Practice, 18*, 301–310.

McCrady, B. S. (2008). Alcohol use disorders. In D. H. Barlow (Ed.), *Clinical handbook of psychological disorders* (4th ed., pp. 496–546). New York, NY: Guilford Press.

McCrady, B. S., & Epstein, E. E. (Eds.) (1999). *Addictions: A comprehensive guidebook*. New York, NY: Oxford University Press.

McCrady, B. S., Epstein, E. E., Cook, S., Jensen, N., & Hildebrandt, T. (2009). A randomized trial of individual and couple behavioral alcohol treatment for women. *Journal of Consulting and Clinical Psychology, 77*(2), 243–256.

McCrady, B. S., Noel, N. E., Abrams, D. B., Stout, R. L., Nelson, H. F., & Hay, W. M. (1986). Comparative effectiveness of three types of spouse involvement in out-patient behavioral alcoholism treatment. *Journal of Studies on Alcohol, 47*, 459–467.

McDonald and Associates. (1990). *Evaluation of AB1562 in home care demonstration projects* (Vol. 1). Sacramento, CA: Author.

McDonald, L., Billingham, S., Conrad, T., Morgan, N., & Payton, E. (1997, March–April). Families and schools together (FAST): Integrating community development with clinical strategies. *Families in Society: The Journal of Contemporary Human Services*, 140–155.

McDonald, T., & Marks, J. (1991, March). A review of risk factors assessed in child protective services. *Social Service Review*, 112–132.

McDonough, M., & Kennedy, N. (2002). Pharmacological management of obsessive-compulsive disorder: A review for clinicians. *Harvard Review of Psychiatry, 10*, 127–137.

McFarlane, A. C., & Girolamo, G. D. (1996). The nature of traumatic stressors and the epidemiology of posttraumatic reactions. In B. A. Van der Kolk, A. C. McFarlane, & L. Weisaeth (Eds.), *Traumatic stress: The effects of overwhelming experience on mind, body and society* (pp. 129–154). New York, NY: Guilford Press.

McFarlane, A. C., & Yehuda, R. (1996). Resilience, vulnerability, and the course of post traumatic reactions. In B. A. Van der Kolk, A. C. McFarlane, & L. Weisaeth (Eds.), *Traumatic stress: The effects of overwhelming experience on mind, body and society* (pp. 155–181). New York, NY: Guilford Press.

McFarlane, W. R., Lukens, E., Link, B., Dushay, R., Deakins, S. A., Newmark, M., . . . Toran, J. (1995). Multiple-family groups and psychoeducation in the treatment of schizophrenia. *Archives of General Psychiatry, 52*, 679–687.

McGleughlin, J., Meyer, S., & Baker, J. (1999). Assessing sexual abuse allegations in divorce, custody, and visitation disputes. In R. M. Galatzer-Levy & L. Kraus (Eds.), *The scientific basis of child custody decisions* (pp. 357–388). New York, NY: Wiley.

McGloin, J. M., & Widom, C. S. (2001). Resilience among abused and neglected children grown up. *Development and Psychopathology, 13*, 1021–1038.

McGlynn, F. D., & Rose, M. P. (1998). Assessment of fear and anxiety. In A. S. Bellack & M. Hersen (Eds.), *Behavioral assessment: A practical handbook* (pp. 179–209). Boston, MA: Allyn & Bacon.

McGuire, A. B., Kukla, M., Green, A., Gilbride, D., Mueser, K. T., & Salyers, M. P. (2013, November). Illness management and recovery: A review of the literature. *Psychiatric Services*, 1–9.

McGuire, J., & Hatcher, R. (2001). Offense-focused problem solving: Preliminary evaluation of a cognitive skills program. *Criminal Justice and Behavior, 28*, 564–587.

McGurk, S. R., Mueser, K. T., DeRosa, T. J., & Wolfe, R. (2009). Work, recovery, and comorbidity in schizophrenia: A randomized controlled trial of cognitive remediation. *Schizophrenia Bulletin, 35*, 319–335.

McGurk, S. R., Twamley, E. W., Sitzer, D. I., McHugo, G. J., & Mueser, K. T. (2007). A meta-analysis of cognitive remediation in schizophrenia. *American Journal of Psychiatry, 164*, 1791–1802.

McHugh, R. K., Smits, J. A. J., & Otto, M. W. (2009). Empirically supported treatments for panic disorder. *Psychiatric Clinics of North America, 32*, 593–610.

McHugo, G. J., Drake, R. E., Burton, H. L., & Ackerson, T. H. (1995). A scale for assessing the stage of substance abuse treatment in persons with severe mental illness. *Journal of Nervous and Mental Disease, 183*, 762–767.

McHugo, G. J., Hargreaves, W., Drake, R. E., Clark, R. E., Xie, H., Bond, G. R., & Burns, B. (1998). Methodological issues in assertive community treatment studies. *American Journal of Orthopsychiatry, 68*, 246–260.

McIntosh, V. V., Bulik, C. M., McKenzie, J. M., Luty, S. E., & Jordan, J. (2000). Interpersonal psychotherapy for anorexia nervosa. *International Journal of Eating Disorders, 27*, 125–139.

McKellar, J. D., Harris, A. H., & Moos, R. H. (2006). Predictors of outcome for patients with substance-use disorders five years after treatment dropout. *Journal of Studies on Alcohol, 67*(5), 685–693.

McKinney, C. M., Caetano, R., Rodriguez, L. A., & Okoro, N. (2010). Does alcohol involvement increase the severity of intimate partner violence? *Alcoholism: Clinical and Experimental Research, 34*, 655–658.

McKinnon, M. C., Cusi, A. M., & MacQueen, G. M. (2013). Psychological factors that may confer risk for bipolar disorder. *Cognitive Neuropsychiatry, 18*, 1–2.

McLellan, A. T., Luborsky, L., O'Brien, C. P., & Woody, G. E. (1980). An improved diagnostic instrument of substance abuse patients: The Addiction Severity Index. *Journal of Nervous and Mental Disease, 168*, 26–33.

McLellan, A. T., Luborsky, L., Woody, G. E., & O'Brien, C. P. (1983). Predicting response to alcohol and drug abuse treatment: The role of psychiatric severity. *Archives of General Psychiatry, 40*, 620–625.

McMahon, R. J., & Estes, A. M. (1997). Conduct problems. In E. J. Mash & L. G. Terdal (Eds.), *Assessment of childhood disorders* (3rd ed., pp. 130–193). New York, NY: Guilford Press.

McMahon, R. J., & Forehand, R. (1984). Parent training for the non-compliant child: Treatment outcome, generalization, and adjunctive therapy procedures. In R. F. Dangel & R. A. Polster (Eds.), *Parent training: Foundations of research and practice* (pp. 298–328). New York, NY: Guilford Press.

McMahon, R. J., & Frick, P. J. (2005). Evidence-based assessment of conduct problems in children and adolescents. *Journal of Clinical Child and Adolescent Psychology, 34*(3), 477–505.

McMain, S. F., Links, P. S., Gnam, W. H., Guimond, T., Cardish, R. J., Korman, L., & Streiner, D. L. (2009). A randomized trial of dialectical behavior therapy versus general psychiatric management for borderline personality disorder. *American Journal of Psychiatry, 166*, 1365–1374.

Mechanic, D. (1996). Emerging issues in international mental health services research. *Psychiatric Services, 47*, 371–375.

Mechanic, D., Schlesinger, M., & McAlpine, D. D. (1995). Management of mental health and substance abuse services: State of the art and early results. *Milbank Quarterly, 73*, 19–55.

Meeks, T. W., Vahia, I. V., Lavretsky, H., Kulkarni, G., & Jeste, D. V. (2011). A tune in "A minor" can "be major": A review of epidemiology, illness course and public health implications of subthreshold depression in older adults. *Journal of Affective Disorders, 129*, 126–142.

Meezan, W., & O'Keefe, M. (1998). Evaluating the effectiveness of multifamily group therapy in child abuse and neglect. *Research on Social Work Practice, 8*, 330–353.

Meichenbaum, D. (1974). *Cognitive behavior modification.* Morristown, NJ: General Learning Press.

Meissner, W. W. (1978). The conceptualization of marriage and family dynamics from a psychoanalytic perspective. In T. J. Paolino & B. S. McCrady (Eds.), *Marriage and marital therapy* (pp. 25–28). New York, NY: Brunner/Mazel.

Mercer, C. C., Mueser, K. T., & Drake, R. E. (1998). Organizational guidelines for dual disorders programs. *Psychiatric Quarterly, 69*, 145–168.

Merikangas, K. R., He, J. P., Brody, D., Fisher, P. W., Bourden, K., & Koretz, D. S. (2010). Prevalence and treatment of mental disorders among U.S. children in the 2001–2004 NHANES. *Pediatrics, 125*, 75–81.

Merikangas, K. R., & Pato, M. (2009). Recent developments in the epidemiology of bipolar disorder in adults and children: Magnitude, correlates, and future directions. *Clinical Psychology Science and Practice, 16*, 121–133.

Messias, E. L., Chen, C., & Eaton, W. W. (2007). Epidemiology of schizophrenia: Review of findings and myths. *Psychiatric Clinics of North America, 30*, 323–338.

Meston, C. M., Heiman, J. R., Trapnell, P. D., & Carlin, A. S. (1999). Ethnicity, desirable responding, and self-reports of abuse: A comparison of European- and Asian-Ancestry undergraduates. *Journal of Consulting and Clinical Psychology, 67*, 139–144.

Meyers, R. J., & Smith, J. E. (1995). *Clinical guide to alcohol treatment: The community reinforcement approach.* New York, NY: Guilford Press.

Middleton, K., & Craig, C. D. (2012). A systematic literature review of PTSD among female veterans from 1990 to 2010. *Social Work and Mental Health, 10*, 233–252.

Miklowitz, D. J. (2008). Bipolar disorder. In D. H. Barlow (Ed.), *Clinical handbook of psychological disorders: A step-by-step treatment manual* (4th ed., pp. 421–462). New York, NY: Guilford Press.

Miklowitz, D. J., Simoneau, T. L., George, E. L., Richards, J. A., Kalbag, A., Sachs-Ericsson, N., & Suddath, R. (2000). Family-focused treatment of bipolar disorder: 1-year effects of a psycho-educational program in conjunction with pharmacotherapy. *Biological Psychiatry, 48*, 582–592.

Milgram, N. A. (1989). Children under stress. In T. H. Ollendick & M. Hersen (Eds.), *Handbook of childhood psychopathology* (2nd ed., pp. 399–415). New York, NY: Plenum Press.

Miller, B. C. (1995). Characteristics of effective day treatment programming for persons with borderline personality disorder. *Psychiatric Services, 46,* 605–608.

Miller, C. (2001). Childhood animal cruelty and interpersonal violence. *Clinical Psychology Review, 21,* 735–749.

Miller, E. T., Kilmer, J. R., Kim, E. L., Weingardt, K. R., & Marlatt, G. A. (2001). Alcohol skills training for college students. In P. M. Monti, S. M. Colby, & T. A. O'Leary (Eds.), *Adolescents, alcohol and substance abuse: Reaching teens through brief interventions* (pp. 183–215). New York, NY: Guilford Press.

Miller, E. T., Turner, A. P., & Marlatt, G. A. (2001). The harm reduction approach to the secondary prevention of alcohol problems in adolescents and young adults: Considerations across a developmental spectrum. In P. M. Monti, S. M. Colby, & T. A. O'Leary (Eds.), *Adolescents, alcohol and substance abuse: Reaching teens through brief interventions* (pp. 58–79). New York, NY: Guilford Press.

Miller, J. C. (2008). 12-step treatment for alcohol and substance abuse revisited: Best available evidence suggests a lack of effectiveness or harm. *International Journal of Mental Health and Addiction, 6,* 568–576.

Miller, L. S., & Kamboukos, D. (2000). Symptom-specific measures for disorders usually first diagnosed in infancy, childhood, or adolescence. In J. A. Rush Jr. (Ed.), *Handbook of psychiatric measures: Task force for the handbook of psychiatric measures* (pp. 325–356). Washington, DC: American Psychiatric Association.

Miller, L. S., Klein, R. G., Piacentini, J., Abikoff, H., Shah, M. R., Samoilov, A., & Guardino, M. (1995). The New York Teacher Rating Scale for disruptive and anti-social behavior. *Journal of the American Academy of Child and Adolescent Psychiatry, 34,* 359–370.

Miller, W., Meyers, R., & Tonigan, J. (1999). Engaging the unmotivated in treatment for alcohol problems: A comparison of three strategies for intervention through family members. *Journal of Consulting and Clinical Psychology, 67,* 688–697.

Miller, W. R. (1992). Effectiveness of treatment for substance abuse. *Journal of Substance Abuse Treatment, 9,* 93–102.

Miller, W. R., & Hester, R. K. (1986). Inpatient alcoholism treatment: Who benefits? *American Psychologist, 41,* 794–805.

Miller, W. R., & Kurtz, E. (1994). Models of alcoholism used in treatment: Contrasting AA and other perspectives with which it is often confused. *Journal of Studies on Alcohol, 55,* 159–166.

Miller, W. R., Meyers, R. J., & Hiller-Sturmhofel, S. (1999). The community-reinforcement approach. *Alcohol Research and Health, 23,* 116–120.

Miller, W. R., & Rollnick, S. (Eds.) (1991). Dealing with resistance. In W. R. Miller & S. Rollnick (Eds.), *Motivational Interviewing: Preparing people for change* (pp. 100–112). New York, NY: Guilford Press.

Miller, W. R., & Rollnick, S. (2013). *Motivational interviewing: Helping people change* (3rd ed.). New York, NY: Guilford Press.

Miller-Brotman, L. S. (2003). *New York Teacher Rating Scale.* Available from Laurie Miller Brotman, Institute for Children at Risk, New York University Child Study Center, NY.

Milligan, K., Niccols, A., Sword, W., Thabane, L., Henderson, J., & Smith, A. (2010). Maternal substance use and integrated treatment programs for women with substance abuse issues and their children: A meta-analysis. *Substance Abuse Treatment, Prevention and Policy, 5,* 21.

Millon, T., & Davis, R. (1995). Conceptions of personality disorders: Historical perspectives, the DSMS, and future directions. In J. Livesley (Ed.), *The DSM-IV personality disorders* (pp. 3–28). New York, NY: Guilford Press.

Milner, J. S. (1994). Assessing physical child abuse risk: The Child Abuse Potential Inventory. *Clinical Psychology Review, 14,* 547–583.

Milner, J. S., Gold, R. G., & Wimberley, R. C. (1986). Prediction and explanation of child abuse: Cross-validation of the child abuse potential inventory. *Journal of Consulting and Clinical Psychology, 54,* 865–866.

Milner, J. S., Murphy, W. D., Valle, L. A., & Tolliver, R. M. (1998). Assessment issues in child abuse evaluations. In J. R. Lutzker (Ed.), *Handbook of child abuse research and treatment* (pp. 75–115). New York, NY: Plenum Press.

Milrod, B., Leon, A. C., Busch, F., Rudden, M., Schwalberg, M., Clarkin, J., . . . Shear, M. K. (2007). A randomized controlled clinical trial of psychoanalytic psychotherapy for panic disorder. *American Journal of Psychiatry, 164,* 265–272.

Minkoff, K. (2000). *Dual diagnosis: An integrated model for the treatment of people with co-occurring psychiatric and substance disorders in managed care systems.* [Videotaped lecture]. Brookline Village, MA: Mental Illness Education Project.

Mitchell, C. G. (1999). Treating anxiety in a managed care setting: A controlled comparison of medication alone versus medication plus cognitive-behavioral group therapy. *Research on Social Work Practice, 9,* 188–200.

Mitchell, C. G. (2001). Patient satisfaction with manualized versus standard interventions in a managed care context. *Research on Social Work Practice, 11,* 473–484.

Mitte, K. (2005). A meta-analysis of the efficacy of psycho- and pharmacotherapy in panic disorder with and without agoraphobia. *Journal of Affective Disorders, 88,* 27–45.

Moffitt, T. E., Caspi, A., Dickson, N., Silva, P., & Stanton, W. (1996). Childhood-onset versus adolescent-onset antisocial conduct problems in males: Natural history from ages 3 to 18 years. *Development and Psychopathology, 8,* 399–424.

Moisan, P. A., Sanders-Phillips, K., & Moisan, P. M. (1997). Ethnic differences in circumstances of abuse and symptoms of depression and anger among sexually abused black and Latino boys. *Child Abuse and Neglect, 21,* 473–488.

Molina, B. S. G., Smith, B. H., & Pelham, W. E. (1999). Interactive effects of attention deficit hyperactivity disorder and conduct disorder in early adolescent substance abuse. *Psychology of Addictive Behaviors, 13,* 348–358.

Mollica, R. F., Poole, C., & Tor, S. (1998). Symptoms, functioning, and health problems in a massively traumatized population: The legacy of the Cambodian tragedy. In B. P. Dohrenwend (Ed.), *Adversity, stress and psychopathology* (pp. 34–51). New York, NY: Oxford University Press.

Mollica, R. F., Wyshak, G., de Marneffe, D., Khuon, F., & Lavelle, J. (1987). Indochinese versions of the Hopkins Symptom Checklist-25: A screening instrument for the psychiatric care of the refugees. *American Journal of Psychiatry*, *144*, *4*, 497–500.

Monahan, J. (1996). Violence prediction: The past twenty and the next twenty years. *Criminal Justice and Behavior*, *23*, 107–120.

Moncher, M., & Schinke, S. (1994). Group intervention to prevent tobacco use among Native American youth. *Research on Social Work Practice*, *4*, 160–171.

Monga, S., Birmaher, B., Chiappetta, L., Brent, D., Kaufman, J., Bridge, J., & Cully, M. (2000). Screen for Child Anxiety-Related Emotional Disorders (SCARED): Convergent and divergent validity. *Depression and Anxiety*, *12*, 85–91.

Monson, C. M., Taft, C. T., & Fredman, S. J. (2009). Military-related PTSD and intimate relationships: From description to theory-driven research and intervention development. *Clinical Psychology Review*, *29*, 707–714.

Montgomery, L., Burlew, A. K., Kosinski, A. S., & Forcehimes, A. A. (2011). Motivational enhancement therapy for African-American substance users: A randomized controlled trial. *Cultural Diversity and Ethnic Minority Psychology*, *17(4)*, 357–365.

Monti, P. M., Barnett, N. P., O'Leary, T. A., & Colby, S. M. (2001). Motivational enhancement for alcohol-involved adolescents. In P. M. Monti, S. M. Colby, & T. A. O'Leary (Eds.), *Adolescents, alcohol and substance abuse: Reaching teens through brief interventions* (pp. 145–182). New York, NY: Guilford Press.

Monti, P. M., Colby, S. M., Barnett, N. P., Spirito, A., Rohsenow, D. J., Myers, M., . . . Lewer, W. (1999). Brief intervention for harm reduction with alcohol-positive older adolescents in a hospital emergency department. *Journal of Consulting and Clinical Psychology*, *67*, 989–994.

Monti, P. M., & Rohsenow, D. J. (1999). Coping-skills training and cue-exposure therapy in the treatment of alcoholism. *Alcohol Research and Health*, *23*, 107–115.

Mooney, J. F., Kline, P. M., & Davoren, J. C. (1999). Collaborative interventions: Promoting psychosocial competence and academic achievement. In R. W. C. Tourse & J. F. Mooney (Eds.), *Collaborative practice: School and human service partnerships* (pp. 105–135). Westport, CT: Praeger.

Moore, D. R., & Arthur, J. L. (1989). Juvenile delinquency. In T. H. Ollendick & M. Hersen (Eds.), *Handbook of childhood psychopathology* (2nd ed., pp. 197–217). New York, NY: Plenum Press.

Moore, M. E., & Hiday, V. A. (2006). Mental health court outcomes: A comparison of re-arrest and re-arrest severity between mental health court and traditional court participants. *Law and Human Behavior*, *30*, 659–674.

Moorey, S. (1989). Drug abusers. In J. Scott, J. Williams, & A. T. Beck (Eds.), *Cognitive therapy in clinical practice: An illustrative casebook* (pp. 157–182). London, UK: Routledge.

Moos, R. H. (2007). Theory-based processes that promote the remission of substance use disorders. *Clinical Psychology Review*, *27*, 537–551.

Moos, R. H., & Moos, B. S. (1992). *Life Stressors and Social Resources Inventory–Adult Form manual*. Palo Alto, CA: Center for Health Care Evaluation, Department of Veterans Affairs and Stanford University Medical Centers.

Moos, R. H., & Moos, B. S. (1998). The staff workplace and the quality and outcome of substance abuse treatment. *Journal of Studies on Alcohol, 59*, 43–51.

Morgenstern, J., Labouvie, E., McCrady, B., Kahler, C., & Frey, R. (1997). Affiliation with Alcoholics Anonymous after treatment: A study of its therapeutic effects and mechanisms of action. *Journal of Consulting and Clinical Psychology, 65*, 768–777.

Morrison, A. P. (2008). Cognitive-behavior therapy. In K. T. Mueser & D. V. Jeste (Eds.), *Clinical handbook of schizophrenia* (pp. 227–238). New York, NY: Guilford Press.

Morrow-Howell, N., Becker-Kemppainen, S., & Lee, J. (1998). Evaluating an intervention for the elderly at increased risk of suicide. *Research on Social Work Practice, 8*, 28–46.

Morse, G. A., Calsyn, R. J., Klinkenberg, W. D., Helminiak, T. W., Wolff, N., Drake, R. E., . . . McCuddin, S. (2006). Treating homeless clients with severe mental illness and substance use disorders: Costs and outcomes. *Community Mental Health Journal, 42*, 373–404.

Morse, G. A., Calsyn, R. J., Klinkenberg, W. D., Trusty, M. L., Gerber, F., Smith, R., Temelhoff, B., & Ahmad, L. (1997). An experimental comparison of three types of case management for homeless mentally ill persons. *Psychiatric Services, 48*, 497–503.

Morsette, A., Swaney, G., Stolle, D., Schuldberg, D., van den Pol, & Young, M. (2008). Cognitive Behavior Intervention for Trauma in Schools (CBITS): School-based treatment on a rural American Indian reservation. *Journal of Behavior Therapy and Experimental Psychiatry, 40*, 169–178.

Moskowitz, J. M. (1989). The primary prevention of alcohol problems: A critical review of the research literature. *Journal of Studies on Alcohol, 50*, 54–88.

Mouilso, F. R., Fischer, S., & Calhoun, K. S. (2012). A prospective study of sexual assault and alcohol use among first-year college women. *Violence and Victims, 27*, 78–94.

Mowbray, C. T., Oyserman, D., Bybee, D., McFarlane, P., & Rueda-Riedle, A. (2001). Life circumstances of mothers with serious mental illness. *Psychiatric Rehabilitation Journal, 25*(2), 114–123.

Mowrer, O. A. (1960). *Learning theory and behavior*. New York, NY: Wiley.

Mueser, K. T., Bond, G. R., Drake, R. E., & Resnick, S. G. (1998). Models of community care for severe mental illness: A review of research on case management. *Schizophrenia Bulletin, 24*, 37–74.

Mueser, K. T., Corrigan, P. W., Hilton, D. W., Tanzman, B., Schaub, A., Gingerich, S., . . . Herz, M. (2002). Illness, management and recovery: A review of the research. *Psychiatric Services, 53*, 1272–1284.

Mueser, K. T., Deavers, F., Penn, D. L., & Cassisi, J. E. (2013). Psychosocial treatments for schizophrenia. *Annual Review of Clinical Psychology, 9*, 465–497.

Mueser, K. T., Drake, R. E., & Bond, G. R. (1997). Recent advances in psychiatric rehabilitation for patients with severe mental illness. *Harvard Review of Psychiatry, 5*, 123–137.

Mueser, K. T., & Gingerich, S. (2013a). Illness management and recovery. In V. L. Vandiver (Ed.), *Best practices in community mental health* (pp. 29–46). Chicago, IL: Lyceum Books.

Mueser, K. T., & Gingerich, S. (2013b). Treatment of co-occurring psychotic and substance use disorders. *Social Work in Public Health*, 28, 424–439.

Mueser, K. T., & Glynn, S. M. (1999). *Behavioral family therapy for psychiatric disorders* (2nd ed.). Oakland, CA: New Harbinger.

Mueser, K. T., Glynn, S. M., Cather, C., Xie, H., Zarate, R., Smith, L. F., . . . Feldman, J. (2013). A randomized controlled trial of family intervention for co-occurring substance use and severe psychiatric disorders. *Schizophrenia Bulletin*, 39, 658–672.

Mueser, K. T., Goodman, L. A., Trumbetta, S. L., Rosenberg, S. D., Osher, F. C., Vidaver, R., . . . Foy, D. W. (1998). Trauma and post-traumatic stress disorder in severe mental illness. *Journal of Consulting and Clinical Psychology*, 66, 493–499. doi: 10.1037/0022-006X.66.3.493.

Mueser, K. T., Noordsy, D. L., Drake, R. E., & Fox, L. (2003). *Integrated treatment for dual disorders: A guide to effective practice*. New York, NY: Guilford Press.

Mueser, K. T., Rosenberg, S. D., Drake, R. E., Miles, K. M., Wolford, G., Vidaver, R., & Carrieri, K. (1999). Conduct disorder, antisocial personality disorder and substance use disorders in schizophrenia and major affective disorders. *Journal of Studies on Alcohol*, 60, 278–284.

Mueser, K. T., Rosenberg, S. D., Goodman, L. A., & Trumbetta, S. L. (2002). Trauma, PTSD, and the course of severe mental illness: An interactive model. *Schizophrenia Research*, 53, 123–143. doi: 10.1016/S0920-9964(01)00173-6.

Mueser, K. T., Rosenberg, S. D., Xie, H., Jankowski, M. K., Bolton, E. E., Lu, W., . . . Wolfe, R. (2008). A randomized controlled trial of cognitive-behavioral treatment for posttraumatic stress disorder in severe mental illness. *Journal of Consulting and Clinical Psychiatry*, 76, 259–271.

Mullen, E. J. (1995). Pursuing knowledge through qualitative research. *Social Work Research*, 19, 29–32.

Mullen, E. J., & Shuluk, J. (2010). Outcomes of social work intervention in the context of evidence-based practice. *Journal of Social Work*, 11, 49–63.

Mulholland, A. M., & Mintz, L. B. (2001). Prevalence of eating disorders among African American women. *Journal of Counseling Psychology*, 48, 111–116.

Murphy, D. A., Durako, S. J., Moscicki, A., Vermund, S. H., Ma, Y., Schwarz, D. F., . . . Adolescent Medicine HIV/AIDS Research Network. (2001). No change in health risk behaviors over time among HIV infected adolescents in care: Role of psychological distress. *Journal of Adolescent Health*, 29, 57–63.

Murphy, J. G., Duchnick, J. J., Vuchinich, R. E., Davison, J. W., Karg, R. S., Olson, A. M., . . . Coffey, T. T. (2001). Relative efficacy of a brief motivational intervention for college student drinkers. *Psychology of Addictive Behaviors*, 15, 373–379.

Murthy, R. S., Kumar, K. V. K., Chisholm, D., Thomas, T., Sekar, K., & Chandrashekar, C. R. (2005). Community outreach for untreated schizophrenia in rural India: A follow-up study of symptoms, disability, family burden and costs. *Psychological Medicine*, 35, 341–351.

Myers, K., & Winters, N. C. (2002). Ten-year review of scales: II. Scales for internalizing disorders. *Journal of the American Academy of Child and Adolescent Psychiatry*, 41, 634–659.

Myric, H., & Anton, R. F. (1998). Treatment of alcohol withdrawal. *Alcohol Health and Research World*, 22, 38–46.

Nader, K. O. (1997). Assessing traumatic experiences in children. In J. P. Wilson & T. M. Keane (Eds.), *Assessing psychological trauma and PTSD* (pp. 291–348). New York, NY: Guilford Press.

Nader, K. (2001). Treatment methods for childhood trauma. In J. P. Wilson, M. J. Friedman, & J. D. Lindy (Eds.), *Treating psychological trauma and PTSD* (pp. 278–334). New York, NY: Guilford Press.

Nader, K., Pynoos, R. S., Fairbanks, L. A., & Frederick, C. (1990). Children's PTSD reactions one year after a sniper attack at their school. *American Journal of Psychiatry, 147*, 1526–1530.

Najavits L. M. (2002). *Seeking safety: A treatment manual for PTSD and substance abuse.* New York, NY: Guilford Press.

Najavits, L. M., Gallop, R. J., & Weiss, R. D. (2006). Seeking safety therapy for adolescent girls with PTSD and substance use disorder: A randomized controlled trial. *Journal of Behavioral Health Services and Research, 33*, 453–463.

Najavits, L. M., Weiss, R. D., & Liese, B. S. (1996). Group cognitive-behavioral therapy for women with PTSD and substance use disorder. *Journal of Substance Abuse Treatment, 13*, 13–22.

Naleppa, M. J., & Reid, W. J. (1998). Task-centered case management for the elderly: Developing a practice model. *Research on Social Work Practice, 8*, 63–85.

Nasr, T., & Kausar, R. (2009). Psycho-education and the family burden in schizophrenia: A randomized controlled trial. *Annals of General Psychiatry, 8*. Published online. doi: 10.1186/1744-859X-8-17.

Nathan, P. E., & Gorman, J. M. (Eds.) (1998). *A guide to treatments that work.* New York, NY: Oxford University Press.

Nathan, P. E., & Gorman, J. M. (Eds.) (2007). *A guide to treatments that work* (3rd ed.). New York, NY: Oxford University Press.

Nathan, P. E., & McCrady, B. S. (1987). Bases for the use of abstinence as a goal in the behavioral treatment of alcohol abusers. *Drugs and Society, 1*, 109–131.

National Center for Health Statistics. (2014). *Health, United States, 2013: With special feature on prescription drugs.* Hyattsville, MD: Author.

National Institute of Alcohol Abuse and Alcoholism. (2006). *Quick reference instrument guide.* Retrieved from http://pubs.niaaa.nih.gov/publications/Assessing Alcohol/quickref.htm.

National Institute of Mental Health. (2013). *Mental health medications.* Washington, DC: Author.

Naugle, A. E., & Follette, W. C. (1998). A functional analysis of trauma symptoms. In V. M. Follette, J. I. Ruzek, & F. R. Abueg (Eds.), *Cognitive-behavioral therapies for trauma* (pp. 48–76). New York, NY: Guilford Press.

Negy, C., & Snyder, D. K. (1997). Ethnicity and acculturation: Assessing Mexican American couples' relationships using the Marital Satisfaction Inventory–Revised. *Psychological Assessment, 9*, 414–421.

Nelson, T. D., & Steele, R. G. (2007). Predictors of practitioner self-reported use of evidence-based practices: Practitioner training, clinical setting, and attitudes toward research. *Administration and Policy in Mental Health and Mental Health Services Research, 34*, 319–330.

Nelson, T. F., Xuan, Z., Lee, H., Weitzman, E. R., & Wechsler, H. (2009). Persistence of heavy drinking and ensuing consequences at heavy drinking colleges. *Journal of Studies on Alcohol and Other Drugs, 70*, 726–734.

Nelson-Zlupko, L., Dore, M. M., Kauffman, E., & Kaltenbach, K. (1996). Women in recovery: Their perceptions of treatment effectiveness. *Journal of Substance Abuse Treatment, 13*, 51–59.

Newman, F. L., Howard, K. I., Windle, C. D., & Hohmann, A. A. (1994). Introduction to the special section on seeking new methods in mental health services research. *Journal of Consulting and Clinical Psychology, 62*, 667–669.

Ngo, V., Langley, A., Kataoka, S. H., Nadeem, E., Escudero, P., & Stein, B. D. (2008). Providing evidence-based practice to ethnically diverse youth: Examples from the Cognitive Behavior Intervention for Trauma in Schools (CBITS) program. *Journal of the Academy of Child and Adolescent Psychiatry, 47*, 858–862.

Ngo, D., Tran, T. V., Gibbons, J. L., & Oliver, J. M. (2001). Acculturation, premigration traumatic experiences and depression among Vietnamese Americans. *Journal of Human Behavior in the Social Environment, 3*, 225–242.

Nicassio, P. M. (1983). Psychosocial correlates of alienation: Study of a sample of Indochinese refugees. *Journal of Cross-Cultural Psychology, 14*(3), 337–351.

Nichols, D. E., & Viner, R. M. (2009). Childhood risk factors for lifetime anorexia nervosa by age 30 years in a national birth cohort. *American Academy of Child and Adolescent Psychiatry, 48*, 791–799.

Nieuwenhuizen, C., Schene, A. H., Boevink, W. A., & Wolf, J. R. L. M. (1997). Measuring the quality of life of clients with severe mental illness: A review of instruments. *Psychiatric Rehabilitation Journal, 20*, 33–41.

Niles, B. L., Klunk-Gillis, J., Ryngala, D. J., Silberbogen, A. K., Paysnick, A., & Wolf, E. J. (2012). Comparing mindfulness and psychoeducation treatments for combat-related PTSD using a telehealth approach. *Psychological Trauma: Theory, Research, Practice, and Policy, 4*, 538–547.

Nishith, P., Nixon, R. D. V., & Resick, P. A. (2005). Resolution of trauma-related guilt following treatment of PTSD in female rape victims: A result of cognitive processing therapy targeting comorbid depression? *Journal of Affective Disorders, 86*, 259–265.

Noel, M., O'Connor, R. M., Boudreau, B., Mushquash, C. J., Comeau, M. N., Stevens, D., & Stewart, S. H. (2010). The Rutgers Problem Alcohol Index (RAPI): A comparison of cut-points in First Nations Mi'kmaq and non-Aboriginal adolescents in rural Nova Scotia. *International Journal of Mental Health and Addiction, 8*, 336–350.

Noel, N. E., & McCrady, B. S. (1993). Alcohol focused spouse involvement with behavioral marital therapy. In T. J. O'Farrell (Ed.), *Treating alcohol problems: Marital and family interventions* (pp. 210–235). New York, NY: Guilford Press.

Nordstrom, G., & Berglund, M. A. (1987). A prospective study of successful long-term adjustment in alcohol dependence: Social drinking versus abstinence. *Journal of Studies on Alcohol, 48*, 95–103.

Norris, F. H. (1990). Screening for traumatic stress: A scale for use in the general population. *Journal of Applied Social Psychology, 20*, 1704–1718.

Norris, F. H. (1992). Epidemiology of trauma: Frequency and impact of different potentially traumatic events on different demographic groups. *Journal of Consulting and Clinical Psychology, 60*, 409–418.

Norris, F. H., & Riad, J. K. (1997). Standardized self-report measures of civilian trauma and post traumatic stress disorder. In J. P. Wilson & T. M. Keane (Eds.), *Assessing psychological trauma and PTSD* (pp. 7–42). New York, NY: Guilford Press.

Norris, J. (1994). Alcohol and female sexuality: A look at expectancies and risks. *Alcohol Health and Research World, 18*, 197–201.

Northey, W. F., Wells, K. C., Silverman, W. K., & Bailey, C. E. (2003). Childhood behavioral and emotional disorders. *Journal of Marital and Family Therapy, 29*, 523–545.

Nowinski, J. (1999). Self-help groups for addictions. In B. S. McCrady & E. E. Epstein (Eds.), *Addictions: A comprehensive guidebook* (pp. 328–346). New York, NY: Oxford University Press.

Nunes-Dinis, M., & Barth, R. P. (1993). Cocaine treatment and outcome. *Social Work, 38*, 611–617.

Nurius, P. S., & Gibson, J. W. (1990). Clinical observation, inference, reasoning and judgment in social work: An update. *Social Work Research and Abstracts, 26*, 18–25.

Nusslock, R., Abramson, L., Harmon-Jones, E., Alloy, L., & Coan, J. (2009). Psychosocial interventions for bipolar disorder: Perspective from the behavioral approach system (BAS) dysregulation theory. *Clinical Psychology Science and Practice*, 449–469.

Nygaard, R. L. (2000). The dawn of therapeutic justice. In D. H. Fishbein (Ed.), *The science, treatment, and prevention of antisocial behaviors: Application to the criminal justice system* (pp. 23-1 to 23-18). Kingston, NJ: Civic Research Institute.

Oates, R. K., & Bross, D. C. (1995). What have we learned about treating child physical abuse? A literature review of the last decade. *Child Abuse and Neglect, 19*, 463–473.

O'Brien, K., & Vincent, N. K. (2003). Psychiatric comorbidity in anorexia and bulimia nervosa: Nature, prevalence, and causal relationships. *Clinical Psychology Review, 23*, 57–74.

Odiah, C., & Wright, D. (2000). Forensic practice in the helping professions: Advocate and adversary roles as a threat to therapeutic alliances and fiduciary relations. *Journal of Offender Rehabilitation, 31*, 57–68.

O'Donnell, C. R., Wilson, K. K., & Tharp, R. G. (2002). The cross-cultural context: Lessons from community development projects. In G. B. Melton, R. A. Thompson, & M. A. Small (Eds.), *Toward a child-centered neighborhood-based child protection system: A report of the consortium on children, families and the law* (pp. 104–114). Westport, CT: Praeger.

O'Donohue, W., & Fanetti, M. (1996). Assessing the occurrence of child sexual abuse: An information processing, hypothesis testing approach. *Aggression and Violent Behavior, 1*, 269–281.

O'Donohue, W., Fanetti, M., & Elliott, A. (1998). Trauma in children. In V. M. Follette, J. I. Ruzek, & F. R. Abueg (Eds.), *Cognitive-behavioral therapies for trauma* (pp. 355–382). New York, NY: Guilford Press.

Oei, T. P. S., & Shuttlewood, G. J. (1996). Specific and nonspecific factors in psychotherapy: A case of cognitive therapy for depression. *Clinical Psychology Review, 16*, 83–103.

O'Farrell, T. J., Choquette, K. A., & Cutter, H. S. (1998). Couples relapse prevention sessions after behavioral marital therapy for male alcoholics: Outcomes during the three years after starting treatment. *Journal of Studies on Alcohol, 59*, 357–370.

O'Farrell, T. J., Choquette, K. A., Cutter, H. S. G., Brown, E. D., & McCourt, W. F. (1993). Behavioral marital therapy with and without additional couples relapse prevention sessions for alcoholics and their wives. *Journal of Studies on Alcohol, 54*, 652–666.

O'Farrell, T. J., & Fals-Stewart, W. (1999). Treatment models and methods: Family models. In B. S. McCrady & E. E. Epstein (Eds.), *Addictions: A comprehensive guidebook* (pp. 287–305). New York, NY: Oxford University Press.

O'Farrell, T., & Fals-Stewart, W. (2000). Behavioral couples therapy for alcoholism an drug abuse. *Journal of Substance Abuse Treatment, 18*, 51–54.

O'Farrell, T., & Fals-Stewart, W. (2003). Alcohol abuse. *Journal of Marital and Family Therapy, 29*, 121–146.

O'Farrell, T. J., & Schein, A. Z. (2011). Behavioral couples therapy for alcoholism and drug abuse. *Journal of Family Psychotherapy, 22*, 193–215.

Ogborne, A. C., Wild, T. C., Braun, K., & Newton-Taylor, B. (1998). Measuring treatment process beliefs among staff of specialized addiction treatment services. *Journal of Substance Abuse Treatment, 15*, 301–312.

Oggins, J., Leber, D., & Veroff, J. (1993). Race and gender differences in black and white newlyweds' perceptions of sexual and marital relations. *Journal of Sex Research, 30*, 152–160.

O'Grady, M. A., Wilson, K., & Harman, J. J. (2009). Preliminary findings from a brief, peer-led safer sex intervention for college students living in residence halls. *Journal of Primary Prevention, 30*, 716–731.

O'Hare, T. (1990). Drinking in college: Consumption patterns, problems, sex differences and legal drinking age. *Journal of Studies on Alcohol, 51*, 536–541.

O'Hare, T. (1991). Integrating research and practice: A framework for implementation. *Social Work, 36*(3), 220–223.

O'Hare, T. (1992). The substance-abusing chronically mentally ill: Prevalence, assessment, treatment and policy concerns. *Social Work, 37*, 185–187.

O'Hare, T. (1993). Alcohol consumption and presenting problems in an outpatient mental health clinic. *Addictive Behaviors, 18*, 57–65.

O'Hare, T. (1995). Differences in Asian and white drinking: Consumption level, drinking contexts and expectancies. *Addictive Behaviors, 20*, 261–266.

O'Hare, T. (1996a). Court-ordered vs. voluntary clients: Problem differences and readiness for change. *Social Work, 41*, 417–422.

O'Hare, T. (1996b). Readiness for change: Variation by intensity and domain of client distress. *Social Work Research, 20*, 13–17.

O'Hare, T. (1997a). Measuring excessive alcohol use in college drinking contexts: The Drinking Context Scale. *Addictive Behaviors, 22*, 469–477.

O'Hare, T. (1997b). Measuring problem drinking in first time offenders: Development and validation of the College Alcohol Problem Scale. *Journal of Substance Abuse Treatment, 14*, 383–387.

O'Hare, T. (1998a). Alcohol expectancies and excessive drinking contexts in young adults. *Social Work Research, 22*, 44–50.

O'Hare, T. (1998b). Replicating the College Alcohol Problem Scale with college first offenders. *Journal of Alcohol and Drug Education, 43*, 75–82.

O'Hare, T. (2001a). The Drinking Context Scale: A confirmatory analysis. *Journal of Substance Abuse Treatment, 20*, 129–136.

O'Hare, T. (2001b). Substance abuse and risky sex in young people: Validating the risky sex scale. *Journal of Primary Prevention, 22*, 89–101.

O'Hare, T. (2002). Evidence-based social work practice with mentally ill persons who abuse alcohol and other drugs. *Social Work in Mental Health, 1*, 43–62.

O'Hare, T. (2005). Risky sex and drinking contexts in freshman first offenders. *Addictive Behaviors, 30*, 585–588.

O'Hare, T. (2009). *Essential skills of social work practice: Assessment, intervention, and evaluation.* Chicago, IL: Lyceum Books.

O'Hare, T., Bennett, P., & Leduc, D. (1991). Reliability of self-reported alcohol use by community clients. *Hospital and Community Psychiatry, 42*, 406–408.

O'Hare, T., & Collins, P. (1997). Development and validation of a scale for measuring social work practice skills. *Research on Social Work Practice, 7*(2), 228–238.

O'Hare, T., Collins, P., & Walsh, T. (1998). Validating the Practice Skills Inventory with experienced clinical social workers. *Research on Social Work Practice, 552–563.*

O'Hare, T., & Geertsma, J. (2013). Using the Practice Skills Inventory in real time: Implications for evaluating evidence-based practices. *Best Practices in Mental Health, 9*, 52–66.

O'Hare, T., & Shen, C. (2012). Substance use motives and severe mental illness. *Journal of Dual Diagnosis, 8*, 1–9.

O'Hare, T., & Shen, C. (2013). Abstinence self-efficacy in people with severe mental illness. *Journal of Substance Abuse Treatment, 45*, 76–82.

O'Hare, T., Shen, C., & Sherrer, M. V. (2010). High-risk behaviors and drinking-to-cope as mediators of lifetime abuse and PTSD symptoms in clients with severe mental illness. *Journal of Traumatic Stress, 23*, 255–263.

O'Hare, T., Shen, C., & Sherrer, M. (2013a). Differences in trauma and posttraumatic stress symptoms in clients with schizophrenia spectrum and major mood disorders. *Psychiatry Research, 205*, 85–89.

O'Hare, T., Shen, C., & Sherrer, M. (2013b). Lifetime trauma and suicide attempts in people with severe mental illness. *Community Mental Health Journal.* Published online. doi: 10.1007/s10597-013-9658-7.

O'Hare, T., Shen, C., & Sherrer, M. (2013c). Lifetime trauma and suicide attempts in people with severe mental illness. *Community Mental Health Journal.* Published online.

O'Hare, T., & Sherrer, M. (1999). Validating the Alcohol Use Disorder Identification Test with college first offenders. *Journal of Substance Abuse Treatment, 17*, 113–119.

O'Hare, T., & Sherrer, M. (2000). Co-occurring stress and substance abuse in college first offenders. *Journal of Human Behavior in the Social Environment, 3*, 29–44.

O'Hare, T., & Sherrer, M. V. (2005). Assessment of youthful problem drinkers: Validating the Drinking Context Scale (DCS-9) with freshman first offenders. *Research on Social Work Practice, 15*, 110–117.

O'Hare, T., & Sherrer, M. V. (2009). Lifetime traumatic events and high-risk behaviors as predictors of PTSD symptoms in people with severe mental illnesses. *Social Work Research, 33*, 209–218.

O'Hare, T., & Sherrer, M. V. (2011). Subjective distress associated with sudden loss in clients with severe mental illness. *Community Mental Health Journal, 47*, 646–653. doi: 10.1007/s10597-011-9382-0.

O'Hare, T., Sherrer, M., Connery, H., Thornton, J., LaButti, A., & Emrick, K. (2003). Further validation of the Psycho-Social Well-Being Scale. *Community Mental Health Journal, 39*, 115–129.

O'Hare, T., Sherrer, M., Cutler, J., McCall, T., Dominique, K., & Garlick, K. (2002). Validating the Psychosocial Well Being Scale among mentally ill clients with substance abuse problems. *Social Work in Mental Health, 1*, 15–30.

O'Hare, T., Sherrer, M. V., LaButti, A., & Emrick, K. (2004). Validating the Alcohol Use Disorders Identification Test with persons who have serious mental illness. *Research on Social Work Practice, 14*, 36–42.

O'Hare, T., Sherrer, M. V., & Shen, C. (2006). Subjective distress from stressful events and high-risk behaviors as predictors of PTSD symptoms severity in clients with severe mental illness. *Journal of Traumatic Stress, 19*, 375–386. doi: 10.1002/jts.20131.

O'Hare, T., & Tran, T. V. (1997). Predicting problem drinking in college students: Gender differences and the CAGE questionnaire. *Addictive Behaviors, 22*, 13–21.

O'Hare, T., & Tran, T. V. (1998). Substance abuse among Southeast Asians in the U.S.: Implications for practice and research. *Social Work in Health Care, 26*, 69–80.

O'Hare, T., Tran, T. V., & Collins, P. (2002). Validating the Practice Skills Inventory: A confirmatory factor analysis. *Research on Social Work Practice, 12*, 653–668.

O'Keane, V. (2000). Evolving model of depression as an expression of multiple interacting risk factors. *British Journal of Psychiatry, 177*, 482–483.

O'Laughlin, E. M., & Murphy, M. J. (2000). Use of computerized continuous performance tasks for assessment of ADHD: A guide for practitioners. *Independent Practitioner, 20*, 282–287.

O'Leary, A. (1992). Self-efficacy and health: Behavioral and stress-physiological mediation. *Cognitive Therapy and Research, 16*, 229–245.

O'Leary, A., Goodhart, F., Sweet Jemmott, L., & Boccher-Lattimore, D. (1992). Predictors of safer sex on the college campus: A social cognitive theory analysis. *Journal of American College Health, 40*, 254–263.

O'Leary, E. M. M., Barrett, P., & Fjermestad, K. W. (2009). Cognitive behavior family treatment for childhood obsessive-compulsive disorder: A 7-year follow-up study. *Journal of Anxiety Disorders, 23*, 973–978.

O'Leary, K. D., Barling, J., Arias, I., Rosenbaum, A., Malone, J., & Tyree, A. (1989). Prevalence and stability of physical aggression between spouses: A longitudinal analysis. *Journal of Consulting and Clinical Psychology, 57*, 263–268.

O'Leary, K. D., & Beach, S. R. (1990). Marital therapy: A viable treatment for depression and marital discord. *American Journal of Psychiatry, 147*, 183–186.

O'Leary, K. D., Malone, J., & Tyree, A. (1994). Physical aggression in early marriage: Prerelationship and relationship effects. *Journal of Consulting and Clinical Psychology, 62*, 594–602.

Olff, M., Langeland, W., Draijer, N., & Gersons, B. P. R. (2007). Gender differences in posttraumatic stress disorder. *Psychological Bulletin, 133*(2), 183–204.

Ollendick, T. H. (1983). Reliability and validity of the Revised Fear Survey Schedule for Children (FSSC-R). *Behaviour Research and Therapy, 21*, 685–692.

Ollendick, T. H., & Hirshfeld-Becker, D. R. (2002). The developmental psychopathology of social anxiety disorder. *Biological Psychiatry, 1*, 44–58.

Ollendick, T. H., & King, N. J. (1994a). Diagnosis, assessment and treatment of internalizing problems in children: The role of longitudinal data. *Journal of Consulting and Clinical Psychology, 62*, 918–927.

Ollendick, T. H., & King, N. J. (1994b). Fears and their level of interference in adolescents. *Behaviour Research and Therapy, 32*, 635–638.

Ollendick, T. H., & King, N. J. (1998). Empirically supported treatments for children with phobic and anxiety disorders: Current status. *Journal of Child Psychology, 27*, 156–167.

Ollendick, T. H., Mattis, S. G., & King, N. J. (1993). Panic in children and adolescents: A review. *Journal of Child Psychology and Psychiatry, 35*, 113–134.

Olsen, D. H., Russell, C., & Sprenkle, D. (1989). *Faces III manual*. St. Paul, MN: Family Social Science, University of Minnesota.

O'Malley, P. M., & Johnston, L. D. (2002). Epidemiology of alcohol and other drug use among American college students. *Journal of Studies on Alcohol, 63*, 23–39.

O'Neill, S. E., Parra, G. R., & Sher, K. J. (2001). Clinical relevance of heavy drinking during the college years: Cross-sectional and prospective perspectives. *Psychology of Addictive Behaviors, 15*, 350–359.

Oosterlaan, J. (2001). Behavioural inhibition and the development of childhood anxiety disorders. In W. K. Silverman & P. D. A. Treffers (Eds.), *Anxiety disorders in children and adolescents: Research, assessment and intervention* (pp. 45–71). New York, NY: Cambridge University Press.

Orford, J. (1990). Alcohol and the family. In H. Annis, H. D. Cappell, F. B. Glaser, M. S. Goodstadt, & L. T. Kozlowski (Eds.), *Research advances in alcohol and drug problems* (Vol. 10, pp. 81–155). New York, NY: Plenum.

Orlinsky, D. E., Grawe, K., & Parks, B. K. (1994). Process and outcome in psychotherapy: *Noch einmal*. In A. E. Bergin & S. L. Garfield (Eds.), *The handbook of psychotherapy and behavior change* (4th ed., pp. 270–376). New York, NY: Wiley.

Orlinsky, D. E., & Howard, K. I. (1986). Process and outcome in psychotherapy. In S. L. Garfield & A. E. Bergin (Eds.), *The handbook of psychotherapy and behavior change* (pp. 311–384). New York, NY: Wiley.

Olsen, D. H., Russell, C., & Sprenkle, D. (1989). *Faces III manual*. St. Paul, MN: Family Social Science, University of Minnesota.

Osborn, D. P. J. (2001). The poor physical health of people with mental illness. *Western Journal of Medicine, 175*(5), 329–332.

Osher, F. C., & Kofoed, L. (1989). Treatment of patients with psychiatric and psychoactive substance abuse disorders. *Hospital and Community Psychiatry, 40*, 1025–1030.

Ossana, S. M. (2000). Relationship and couples counseling. In R. M. Perez, K. A. DeBord, & K. J. Bieschke (Eds.), *Handbook of counseling and psychotherapy with lesbian, gay, and bisexual clients* (pp. 275–302). Washington, DC: American Psychiatric Association.

Ost, L. (1990). The agoraphobia scale: An evaluation of its reliability and validity. *Behaviour Research and Therapy, 28*, 323–329.

Ost, L., & Treffers, P. D. A. (2001). Onset, course, and outcome for anxiety disorders in children. In W. K. Silverman & P. D. A. Treffers (Eds.), *Anxiety disorders in children and adolescents: Research, assessment and intervention* (pp. 293–312). New York, NY: Cambridge University Press.

Otto-Salaj, L. L., Heckman, T. G., Stevenson, L. Y., & Kelly, J. A. (1998). Patterns, predictors and gender differences in HIV risk among severely mentally ill men and women. *Community Mental Health Journal, 34(2)*, 175–190.

Oudman, E. (2012). Is electroconvulsive therapy (ECT) effective and safe for treatment of depression in dementia? A short review. *Journal of ECT, 28*, 34–38.

Overall, J. E., & Gorham, D. R. (1962). The Brief Psychiatric Rating Scale. *Psychological Reports, 10*, 799–812.

Overholser, J. C., Brinkman, D. C., Lehnert, K. L., & Ricciardi, A. M. (1995). Children's Depression Rating Scale–Revised: Development of a short form. *Journal of Clinical Child Psychology, 24*, 443–452.

Owens, G. P., Walter, K. H., Chard, K. M., & Davis, P. A. (2011). Changes in mindfulness skills and treatment response among veterans in residential PTSD treatment. *Psychological Trauma: Theory, Research, Practice and Policy, 4*, 221–228.

Pagano, M. E., White, W. L., Kelly, J. F., Stout, R. L., & Tonigan, S. J. (2013). The 10–year course of Alcoholics Anonymous participation and long-term outcomes: A follow-up study of outpatient subjects in Project MATCH. *Substance Abuse, 34*, 51–59.

Pagelow, M. D. (1992). Adult victims of domestic violence: Battered women. *Journal of Interpersonal Violence, 7*, 87–120.

Pagoto, S. L., Kozak, A. T., Spates, C. R., & Spring, B. (2006). Systematic desensitization for an older woman with a severe specific phobia. *Clinical Gerontologist, 30*, 89–98.

Pagura, J., Stein, M. B., Bolton, J. M., Cox, B. J., Grant, B., & Sareen, J. (2010). Comorbidity of borderline personality disorder and posttraumatic stress disorder in the U.S. population. *Journal of Psychiatric Research, 44*, 1190–1198.

Palmer, B. A., Pankratz, S., & Bostwick, J. M. (2005). The lifetime risk of suicide in schizophrenia. *Archives of General Psychiatry, 62*, 247–253. doi: 10.1001/archpsyc.62.3.247.

Palmer, T. (1996). Programmatic and nonprogrammatic aspects of successful intervention. In A. T. Harland (Ed.), *Choosing correctional options that work: Defining the demand and evaluating the supply* (pp. 131–182). Thousand Oaks, CA: Sage.

Pandina, R. J., & Johnson, V. (1990). Serious alcohol and drug problems among adolescents with a family history of alcoholism. *Journal of Studies on Alcohol, 51(3)*, 278–282.

Pareda, N., Guilera, G., Forns, M., & Gomez-Benito, J. (2009a). The international epidemiology of child sexual abuse: A continuation of Finkelhor (1994). *Child Abuse and Neglect, 33*, 331–342.

Pareda, N., Guilera, G., Forns, M., & Gomez-Benito, J. (2009b). The prevalence of child sexual abuse in community and student samples: A meta-analysis. *Clinical Psychology Review, 29*, 328–338.

Paris, J. (1995). Commentary on narcissistic personality disorder. In J. Livesley (Ed.), *The DSM-IV personality disorders* (pp. 213–217). New York, NY: Guilford Press.

Paris, J. (1997a). Antisocial and borderline personality disorders: Two separate diagnoses or two aspects of the same psychopathology? *Comprehensive Psychiatry*, *38*, 237–242.

Paris, J. (1997b). Childhood trauma as an etiological factor in the personality disorders. *Journal of Personality Disorders*, *11*, 34–49.

Paris, J. (2009). The treatment of borderline personality disorder: Implications of research on diagnosis, etiology and outcome. *Annual Review of Psychology*, *5*, 277–290.

Pasch, L. A., & Bradbury, T. N. (1998). Social support, conflict, and the development of marital dysfunction. *Journal of Consulting and Clinical Psychology*, *66*, 219–230.

Patrick, J., Links, P., Reekum, R. V., & Mitton, M. J. (1995). Using the PDQ-R scale as a brief screening measure in the differential diagnosis of personality disorder. *Journal of Personality Disorders*, *9*, 266–274.

Patterson, G. R. (1982). *Coercive family process*. Eugene, OR: Castalia Press.

Patterson, T. L., Bucardo, J., McKibbin, C. L., Mausbach, B. T., Moore, D., Barrio, C., . . . Jeste, D. V. (2005). Development and pilot testing of a new psychosocial intervention for older Latinos with chronic psychosis. *Schizophrenia Bulletin*, *31*, 922–930.

Pattison, E. M., Sobell, M. B., & Sobell, L. C. (1977). *Emerging concepts of alcohol dependence*. New York, NY: Springer.

Pecora, P. J., Whittaker, J. K., Maluccio, A. N., & Barth, R. P. (2000). *The child welfare challenge: Policy, practice, and research* (2nd ed.). New York, NY: Aldine de Gruyter.

Peele, S. (1989). *The diseasing of America: Addiction treatment out of control*. New York, NY: Lexington Books.

Pelham, W. E., Wheeler, T., & Chronis, A. (1998). Empirically supported psychosocial treatments for attention deficit hyperactivity disorder. *Journal of Clinical Child Psychology*, *27*, 190–205.

Penn, D. L., & Mueser, K. T. (1996). Research update on the psychosocial treatment of schizophrenia. *American Journal of Psychiatry*, *153*, 607–617.

Penn, D. L., Meyer, P. S., Evans, E., Wirth, R. J., Cai, K., & Burchinal, M. (2009). A randomized controlled trial of group cognitive-behavioral therapy vs. enhanced supportive therapy for auditory hallucinations. *Schizophrenia Research*, *109*, 52–59.

Perkins, W. (2002). Surveying the damage: A review of research on consequences of alcohol misuse in college populations. *Journal of Studies on Alcohol*, *63*, 91–100.

Persons, J. B., & Fresco, D. M. (1998). Assessment of depression. In A. S. Bellack & M. Hersen (Eds.), *Behavioral assessment: A practical handbook* (pp. 210–231). Boston, MA: Allyn & Bacon.

Peruzzi, N., & Bongar, B. (1999). Assessing risk for completed suicide in patients with major depression: Psychologists' views of critical factors. *Professional Psychology: Research and Practice*, *30*, 576–580.

Peterson, C. B., Mitchell, J. E., Crow, S. J., Crosby, R. D., & Wonderlich, S. A. (2009). The efficacy of self-help group treatment and therapist-led group treatment for binge eating disorder. *American Journal of Psychiatry*, *166*, 1347–1354.

Petrakis, I., Gonzalez, G., Rosenheck, R., & Krystal, J. (2002). Comorbidity of alcoholism and psychiatric disorders. (2002). *Alcohol Research and Health*, *26*, 81–89.

Petrides, G., Tobias, K. G., Kellner, C. H., & Rudorfer, M. V. (2011). Continuation and maintenance electroconvulsive therapy for mood disorders: Review of the literature. *Neuropsychobiology*, *64*, 129–140.

Petry, N., Martin, B., Cooney, J., & Kranzler, H. (2000). Give them prizes, and they will come: Contingency management treatment of alcohol dependence. *Journal of Consulting and Clinical Psychology*, *68*, 250–257.

Petti, T. A. (1989). Depression. In T. H. Ollendick & M. Hersen (Eds.), *Handbook of childhood psychopathology* (2nd ed., pp. 229–246). New York, NY: Plenum Press.

Pfiffner, L., & Barkley, R. A. (1998). Treatment of ADHD in school settings. In R. A. Barkley (Ed.), *Attention-deficit hyperactivity disorder: A handbook for diagnosis and treatment* (pp. 458–490). New York, NY: Guilford Press.

Piacentini, J., & Bergman, R. L. (2000). Obsessive-compulsive disorder in children. *Psychiatric Clinics of North America*, *23*, 519–533.

Pickens, R. W., & Svikis, D. S. (1991). Genetic contributions to alcoholism diagnosis. *Alcohol Health and Research World*, *15*(4), 272–277.

Pietrzak, R. H., Goldstein, R. B., Southwick, S. M., & Grant, B. F. (2011). Prevalence and axis I comorbidity of full and partial posttraumatic stress disorder in the United States: Results from wave 2 of the National Epidemiologic Survey on Alcohol and Related Conditions. *Journal of Anxiety Disorders*, *25*, 456–465.

Pike, K. M., Dohm, F. A., Striegel-Moore, R. H., Wilfley, D., & Fairburn, C. G. (2001). A comparison of black and white women with binge eating disorder. *American Journal of Psychiatry*, *158*, 1455–1460.

Pilecki, B., Arentoft, A., & McKay, D. (2011). An evidence-based causal model of panic disorder. *Journal of Anxiety Disorders*, *25*, 381–388.

Pilling, S., Bebbington, P., Kuipers, E., Garety, P., Geddes, J., Martindale, B., . . . Morgan, C. (2002). Psychological treatments in schizophrenia: II. Meta-analyses of randomized controlled trials of social skills training and cognitive remediation. *Psychological Medicine*, *32*, 783–791.

Pilling, S., Bebbington, P., Kuipers, E., Garety, P., Geddes, J., Orbach, G., & Morgan, C. (2002). Psychological treatments in schizophrenia: I. Meta-analysis of family intervention and cognitive behaviour therapy. *Psychological Medicine*, *32*, 763–782.

Pilowsky, P. J., & Wu, L. W. (2006). Psychiatric symptoms and substance use disorders in a nationally representative sample of American adolescents involved with foster care. *Journal of Adolescent Health*, *38*, 351–358.

Pinderhughes, E. (1989). *Understanding race, ethnicity and power: The key to efficacy in clinical practice*. New York, NY: Free Press.

Pine, D. S., & Grun, J. (1998). Anxiety disorders. In B. T. Walsh (Ed.), *Child psychopharmacology* (pp. 115–148). Washington, DC: American Psychiatric Press.

Polman, A., Bouman, T. K., van Hout, W. J. P. J., de Jong, P. J., & den Boer, J. A. (2010). Processes of change in cognitive-behavioral treatment of obsessive compulsive disorder: Current status and some future directions. *Clinical Psychology and Psychotherapy*, *17*, 1–12.

Pomeroy, E. C., Kiam, R., & Abel, E. M. (1999). The effectiveness of a psychoeducational group for HIV-infected/affected incarcerated women. *Research on Social Work Practice, 9*, 171–187.

Pompili, M., Tondo, L., Grispini, A., De Pisa, E., Lester, D., Angeletti, G., . . . Tatarelli, R. (2006). Suicide attempts in bipolar disorder patients. *Clinical Neuropsychiatry: Journal of Treatment Evaluation, 3*(5), 327–331.

Pottick, K. J., Hansell, S., & Barber, C. C. (1998). An inpatient measure of adolescent and child psychosocial services and treatment. *Social Work Research, 22*, 217–231.

Powers, M. B., Halpern, J. M., Ferenschak, M. P., Gillihan, S. J., & Foa, E. B. (2010). A meta-analytic review of prolonged exposure for posttraumatic stress disorder. *Clinical Psychology Review, 30*, 635–641.

Powers, M. B., Vedel, E., & Emmelkamp, P. M. G. (2008). Behavioral couples therapy (BCT) for alcohol and drug use disorders: A meta-analysis. *Clinical Psychology Review, 28*, 952–962.

Poznanski, E. O., Cook, S. C., & Carroll, B. J. (1979). A depression rating scale for children. *Pediatrics, 64*, 442–450.

Poznanski, E. O., Grossman, J. A., Buchsbaum, Y., Banegas, M., Freeman, L., & Gibbons, R. (1984). Preliminary studies of the reliability and validity of the Children's Depression Rating Scale. *Journal of the American Academy of Child Psychiatry, 23*, 191–197.

Prasadarao, P. S. D. V. (2009). International perspectives on culture and mental health. In S. Eshun & R. A. R. Gurung (Eds.), *Culture and mental health: Sociocultural influence, theory, and practice* (pp. 149–178). West Sussex, UK: Wiley-Blackwell.

Pratt, H. D., Phillips, E. L., Greydanus, D. E., & Patel, D. R. (2003). Eating disorders in the adolescent population: Future directions. *Journal of Adolescent Research, 18*, 297–317.

Prendergast, M. L., Anglin, M. D., & Wellisch, J. (1995). Treatment for drug-abusing offenders under community supervision. *Federal Probation, 59*, 66–75.

Prins, P. J. M. (2001). Affective and cognitive processes and the development and maintenance of anxiety and its disorders. In W. K. Silverman & P. D. A. Treffers (Eds.), *Anxiety disorders in children and adolescents: Research, assessment and intervention* (pp. 23–44). New York, NY: Cambridge University Press.

Prochaska, J. O., & DiClemente, C. C. (1986). Toward a comprehensive model of change. In W. R. Miller & N. Heather (Eds.), *Treating addictive behaviors* (pp. 3–27). New York, NY: Plenum.

Prochaska, J. O., DiClemente, C. C., & Norcross, J. C. (1992). In search of how people change: Applications to addictive behaviors. *American Psychologist, 47*, 1102–1114.

Proctor, C. D., & Groze, V. K. (1994). Risk factors for suicide among gay, lesbian, and bisexual youth. *Social Work, 39*, 504–513.

Project Match Research Group. (1997). Matching alcoholism treatments to client heterogeneity: Project Match post treatment drinking outcomes. *Journal of Studies on Alcohol, 58*, 7–29.

Project Worth. (1997). Current approaches to drug treatment for women offenders. *Journal of Substance Abuse Treatment, 15*, 151–163.

Putnam, F. W. (2003). Ten-year research update review: Child sexual abuse. *Journal of the American Academy of Child and Adolescent Psychiatry, 42*, 269–278.

Pynoos, R. S., Frederick, C., Nader, K., Arroyo, W., Eth, S., Nunez, W., . . . Fairbanks, L. (1987). Life threat and posttraumatic stress in school-age children. *Archives of General Psychiatry, 44*, 1057–1063.

Pynoos, R., Goenjian, A., Tashjian, M., Karakashian, M., Manjikian, R., Manoukian, G., . . . Fairbanks, L. A. (1993). Posttraumatic stress reactions in children after the 1988 Armenian earthquake. *British Journal of Psychiatry, 163*, 239–244.

Quay, H. C. (1983). A dimensional approach to behavior disorder: The Revised Behavior Problem Checklist. *School Psychology Review, 12*, 244–249.

Quigley, L. A., & Marlatt, G. A. (1996). Drinking among young adults: Prevalence, patterns and consequences. *Alcohol Health and Research World, 20*, 185–196.

Quinsey, V. L., Harris, G. T., Rice, M. E., & Lalumiere, M. L. (1993). Assessing treatment efficacy in outcome studies of sex offenders. *Journal of Interpersonal Violence, 8*, 512–523.

RachBeisel, J., Scott, J., & Dixon, L. (1999). Co-occurring severe mental illness and substance use disorders: A review of recent research. *Psychiatric Services, 50*, 1427–1434.

Rachman, S. (1980). Emotional processing. *Behaviour Research and Therapy, 18*, 51–60.

Raj, A. (1996). Identification of social cognitive variables as predictors of safer sex behavior and intent in heterosexual college students. *Journal of Sex and Marital Therapy, 22*, 247–259.

Ran, M., Xiang, M., Chan, C., Leff, J., Simpson, P., Huang, M., . . . Li, S. (2003). Effectiveness of psychoeducational intervention for rural Chinese families experiencing schizophrenia. *Social Psychiatry and Psychiatric Epidemiology, 38*, 69–75.

Randolph, F. L., Ridgway, P., & Carling, P. J. (1991). Residential programs for persons with severe mental illness: A nationwide survey of state-affiliated agencies. *Hospital and Community Psychiatry, 42*, 1111–1115.

Rapoport, J. L., Swedo, S. E., & Leonard, H. L. (1992). Childhood obsessive-compulsive disorder. *Journal of Clinical Psychiatry, 53*, 11–16.

Rapport, M. D. (Ed.) (1992). Treatment of children with attention-deficit hyperactivity disorder (ADHD). *Behavior Modification, 16* (Special Series).

Rauch, S., Grunfeld, T., Yadin, E., Cahill, S., Hembree, E., & Foa, E. (2009). Changes in reported physical health symptoms and social function with prolonged exposure therapy for chronic posttraumatic stress disorder. *Depression and Anxiety, 26*, 732–738.

Ray, O., & Ksir, C. (1999). *Drugs, society and human behavior* (8th ed.). New York, NY: McGraw-Hill.

Raytek, H. S., McCrady, B. S., Epstein, E. E., & Hirsch, L. S. (1999). Therapeutic alliance and the retention of couples in conjoint alcoholism treatment. *Addictive Behaviors, 24*, 317–330.

Read, J. P., Wood, M. D., Davidoff, O. J., McLacken, J., & Campbell, J. F. (2002). Making the transition from high school to college: The role of alcohol-related social influence factors in students' drinking. *Substance Abuse, 23*, 53–65.

Reamer, F. (1992). The impaired social worker. *Social Work, 37*, 165–170.

Reamer, F. (1995). Malpractice claims against social workers: First facts. *Social Work*, *40*, 595–601.

Reamer, F. G. (2000). The social work ethics audit: A risk-management strategy. *Social Work*, *45*, 355–365.

Reamer, F. G. (2012). *Boundary issues and dual relationships in the human services*. New York, NY: Columbia University Press.

Reas, D. L., & Grilo, C. M. (2008). Review and meta-analysis of pharmacotherapy for binge eating disorder. *Obesity*, *16*, 2024–2038.

Rector, N., Seeman, M., & Segal, Z. (2003). Cognitive therapy for schizophrenia: A preliminary randomized controlled trial. *Schizophrenia Research*, *63*, 1–11.

Reger, M. A., & Gahm, G. A. (2009). A meta-analysis of the effects of Internet- and computer-based cognitive-behavioral treatments for anxiety. *Journal of Clinical Psychology*, *65*, 53–75.

Regier, D. A., Farmer, M. E., Rae, D. S., Locke, B. Z., Keith, S. J., Judd, L. L., & Goodwin, F. K. (1990). Comorbidity of mental disorders with alcohol and other drug abuse. *JAMA*, *264*, 2511–2518.

Rehm, J., Gmel, G., Sempos, C., & Trevisan, M. (2003). Alcohol-related morbidity and mortality. *Alcohol Research and Health*, *27*, 39–51.

Rehm, L. P. (1977). A self-control model of depression. *Behavior Therapy*, *8*, 787–804.

Reichert, S. K. (1992). Medical evaluation of the sexually abused child. In M. E. Helfer, R. S. Kempe, & R. D. Krugman (Eds.), *The battered child* (5th ed., pp. 313–328). Chicago, IL: University of Chicago Press.

Reid, W. J. (1997a). Evaluating the dodo's verdict: Do all interventions have equivalent outcomes? *Social Work Research*, *21*, 5–18.

Reid, W. J. (1997b, June). The future of clinical social work. *Social Service Review*, 200–213.

Reid, W. J. (2001). The scientific and empirical foundations of clinical practice. In H. E. Briggs & K. Corcoran (Eds.), *Social work practice: Treating common client problems* (pp. 36–53). Chicago, IL: Lyceum Books.

Reid, W. J., & Hanrahan, P. (1982). Recent evaluations of social work: Grounds for optimism. *Social Work*, *27*, 328–340.

Renaud, J., Brent, D. A., Baugher, M., Birmaher, B., Kolko, D. J., & Bridge, J. (1998). Rapid response to psychosocial treatment for adolescent depression: A two-year follow-up. *Journal of the American Academy of Child and Adolescent Psychiatry*, *37*, 1184–1190.

Resick, P. A., Monson, C. M., & Rizvi, S. L. (2008). Posttraumatic stress disorder. In D. H. Barlow (Ed.), *Clinical handbook of psychological disorders* (4th ed., pp. 65–122). New York, NY: Guilford Press.

Resick, P. A., Nishith, P., Weaver, T. L., Astin, M. C., & Feuer, C. A. (2002). A comparison of cognitive processing therapy, prolonged exposure and a waiting condition for the treatment of posttraumatic stress disorder in female rape victims. *Journal of Consulting and Clinical Psychology*, *70*, 867–879.

Resnick, H. S., Kilpatrick, D. G., Dansky, B. S., Saunders, B. E., & Best, C. L. (1993). Prevalence of civilian trauma and post traumatic stress disorder in a representative national sample of women. *Journal of Consulting and Clinical Psychology*, *61*, 984–991.

Resnick, S. G., Bond, G. R., & Mueser, K. T. (2003). Trauma and posttraumatic stress disorder in people with schizophrenia. *Journal of Abnormal Psychology*, *112*, 415–423. doi: 10.1037/0021-843X.112.3.415.

Reynolds, C. F., Frank, E., Perel, J. M., Imber, S. D., Cornes, C., Miller, M. D., . . . Kupfer, D. J. (1999). Nortriptyline and interpersonal psychotherapy as maintenance therapies for recurrent major depression: A randomized controlled trial in patients older than 59 years. *JAMA*, *281*, 39–45.

Reynolds, W. M. (1994). Assessment of depression in children and adolescents by self-report questionnaires. In W. M. Reynolds & H. F. Johnston (Eds.), *Handbook of depression in children and adolescents* (pp. 209–234). New York, NY: Plenum Press.

Reynolds, W. M., & Coats, K. I. (1986). A comparison of cognitive-behavioral therapy and relaxation training for the treatment of depression in adolescents. *Journal of Consulting and Clinical Psychology*, *54*, 653–660.

Rice, L. N., & Greenberg, L. S. (1984). The new research paradigm. In *Patterns of change: Intensive analysis of psychotherapy process* (pp. 7–25). New York, NY: Guilford Press.

Rice, M. (1997). Violent offender research and implications for the criminal justice system. *American Psychologist*, *52*, 414–423.

Rice, M., & Harris, G. (1995). Violent recidivism: Assessing predictive validity. *Journal of Consulting and Clinical Psychology*, *63*, 737–748.

Richey, C. A. (1994). Social support training. In D. K. Granvold (Ed.), *Cognitive and behavioral treatment: Methods and applications* (pp. 299–338). Pacific Grove, CA: Brooks/Cole.

Richters, J. E., Arnold, L. E., Jensen, P. S., Abikoff, H., Conners, C. K., Greenhill, L. I., . . . Swanson, J. M. (1995). NIMH collaborative multisite multimodal treatment study of children with ADHD: I. Background and rationale. *Journal of the American Academy of Child and Adolescent Psychiatry*, *34*, 987–1000.

Ries, R. K., Galanter, M., & Tonigan, J. S. (2008). Twelve-step facilitation. In M. Galanter & H. D. Kleber (Eds.), *The American Psychiatric Publishing textbook of substance abuse treatment* (4th ed., pp. 373–386). Arlington, VA: American Psychiatric Publishing.

Rife, J. C., & Belcher, J. R. (1994). Assisting unemployed older workers to become reemployed: An experimental evaluation. *Research on Social Work Practice*, *4*, 3–13.

Riggs, P. D., Baker, S., Mikulich, S. K., Young, S. E., & Crowley, T. J. (1995). Depression in substance-dependent delinquents. *Journal of the American Academy of Child and Adolescent Psychiatry*, *34*, 764–771.

Riggs, D. S., & Foa, E. B. (1993). Obsessive compulsive disorder. In D. H. Barlow (Ed.), *Clinical handbook of psychological disorders: A step-by-step manual*. New York, NY: Guilford Press.

Robbins, M. S., Feaster, D. J., Horigan, V. E., Bachrach, K., Berlew, K. A., Carrion, I., . . . Werstlein, R. (2011). Brief strategic family therapy versus treatment as usual: Results of a randomized multisite trial for substance using adolescents. *Journal of Consulting and Clinical Psychology*, *79*, 713–727.

Roberts, A. R., & Brownell, P. (1999). A century of forensic social work: Bridging the past to the present. *Social Work*, *44*, 359–369.

Roberts, I., Kramer, M. S., & Suissa, S. (1996). Does home visiting prevent childhood injury? A systematic review of randomised controlled trials. *British Medical Journal, 312,* 29–33.

Roberts, L. J., Neal, D. J., Kivlahan, D. R., Baer, J. S., & Marlatt, G. A. (2000). Individual drinking changes following a brief intervention among college students: Clinical significance in an indicated preventive context. *Journal of Consulting and Clinical Psychology, 68,* 500–505.

Roberts, L. J., Shaner, A., & Eckman, T. A. (1999). *Overcoming addictions: Skills training for people with schizophrenia.* New York, NY: Norton.

Roberts, R. E., Roberts, C. R., & Xing, Y. (2007). Comorbidity of substance use disorders and other psychiatric disorders among adolescents: Evidence from an epidemiologic survey. *Drug and Alcohol Dependence, 88S,* S4–S13.

Robin, A. L. (1998a). *ADHD in adolescents: Diagnosis and treatment.* New York, NY: Guilford Press.

Robin, A. L. (1998b). Training families with ADHD adolescents. In R. A. Barkley (Ed.), *Attention-deficit hyperactivity disorder: A handbook for diagnosis and treatment* (pp. 413–457). New York, NY: Guilford Press.

Robins, L. N. (1966). *Deviant children grown up.* Baltimore, MD: Williams and Wilkins.

Robins, C. J., & Hayes, A. M. (1993). An appraisal of cognitive therapy. *Journal of Consulting and Clinical Psychology, 61,* 205–214.

Rock, M. (2001). Emerging issues with mentally ill offenders: Causes and social consequences. *Administration and Policy in Mental Health, 28,* 165–180.

Rodgers, B., Korten, A., Jorm, A., Jacomb, P., Christensen, H., & Henderson, A. (2000). Non-linear relationships in associations of depression and anxiety with alcohol use. *Psychological Medicine, 30,* 421–432.

Rogers, C. (1951). *Client-centered therapy.* Boston, MA: Houghton-Mifflin.

Rogers, S., & Silver, S. (2002). Is EMDR an exposure therapy? A review of trauma protocols. *Journal of Clinical Psychology, 58,* 43–59.

Rogers, S., Silver, S., Goss, J., Obenchain, J., Willis, A., & Whitney, R. (1999). A single session, group study of exposure and eye movement desensitization and reprocessing in treating posttraumatic stress disorder among Vietnam War veterans: Preliminary data. *Journal of Anxiety Disorders, 13,* 119–130.

Rolfsnes, E. S., & Idsoe, T. (2011). School-based intervention programs for PTSD symptoms: A review and meta-analysis. *Journal of Traumatic Stress, 24,* 155–165.

Ronan, K. R., & Deane, F. P. (1998). Anxiety disorders. In P. Graham (Ed.), *Cognitive-behaviour therapy for children and families* (pp. 74–94). New York, NY: Cambridge University Press.

Rooney, R. H. (1992). *Strategies for working with involuntary clients.* New York, NY: Columbia University Press.

Rooney, R. H., & Bibus, A. A. (2001). Clinical practice with involuntary clients in community settings. In H. E. Briggs & K. Corcoran (Eds.), *Social work practice: Treating common client problems* (pp. 391–406). Chicago, IL: Lyceum Books.

Root, R. W., & Resnick, R. J. (2003). An update on the diagnosis and treatment of attention-deficit/hyperactivity disorder in children. *Professional Psychology: Research and Practice, 34,* 34–41.

Rosa-Alcazar, A. I., Sanchez-Meca, J., Gomez-Conesa, A., & Marin-Martinez, F. (2008). Psychological treatment of obsessive-compulsive disorder: A meta-analysis. *Clinical Psychology Review, 28,* 1310–1325.

Rosen, A. (2003). Evidence-based social work practice: Challenges and promise. *Social Work Research, 27,* 197–208.

Rosen, R. C., & Leiblum, S. R. (1995). Treatment of sexual disorders in the 1990s: An integrated approach. *Journal of Consulting and Clinical Psychology, 63,* 877–890.

Rosenberg, H., & Davis, L. (1994). Acceptance of moderate drinking by alcohol treatment services in the United States. *Journal of Studies on Alcohol, 55,* 167–172.

Rosenberg, S. D., Drake, R. E., Wolford, G. L., Mueser, K. T., Oxman, T. E., Vidaver, R. M., . . . Luckoor, R. (1998). Dartmouth Assessment of Lifestyle Instrument (DALI): A substance use disorder screen for people with severe mental illness. *American Journal of Psychiatry, 155,* 232–238.

Rosenberg, S. D., Lu, W., Mueser, K. T., Jankowski, M. K., & Cournos, F. (2007). Correlates of adverse childhood events in adults with schizophrenia spectrum disorder. *Psychiatric Services, 58,* 245–253. doi: 10.1176/appi.ps.58.2.245.

Rosenheck, R., & Fontana, A. (1996). Ethnocultural variations in service use among veterans suffering from PTSD. In A. J. Marsella, M. J. Friedman, E. T. Gerrity, & R. M. Scurfield (Eds.), *Ethnocultural aspects of post-traumatic stress disorder* (pp. 483–504). Washington, DC: American Psychological Association.

Rossi, P. H., & Freeman, H. E. (1993). *Evaluation: A systematic approach.* Thousand Oaks, CA: Sage.

Rossi, P. H., Schuerman, J., & Budd, S. (1999). Understanding decisions about child maltreatment. *Evaluation Review, 23,* 579–598.

Rothbaum, B. O., Foa, E. B., Riggs, D. S., Murdock, T., & Walsh, W. (1992). A prospective examination of post-traumatic stress disorder in rape victims. *Journal of Traumatic Stress, 5,* 455–475.

Rothbaum, B. O., Meadows, E. A., Resick, P., & Foy, D. W. (2000). Cognitive-behavioral therapy. In E. B. Foa, T. M. Keane, & M. J. Friedman (Eds.), *Effective treatments for PTSD: Practice guidelines from the international society for traumatic stress studies* (pp. 60–83). New York, NY: Guilford Press.

Rounsaville, B. J., Dolinsky, Z. S., Babor, T. F., & Meyer, R. E. (1987). Psychopathology as a predictor of treatment outcome in alcoholics. *Archives of General Psychiatry, 44,* 505–513.

Roy-Byrne, P., Dafadakis, C., Ries, R., Decker, K., Jones, R., Bolte, M. A., . . . Mark, H. (1995). A psychiatrist-rated battery of measures for assessing the clinical status of psychiatric inpatients. *Psychiatric Services, 46,* 347–352.

Royse, D., & Thyer, B. A. (1996). *Program evaluation: An introduction.* Chicago, IL: Nelson-Hall.

Royse, D., Thyer, B. A., & Padgett, D. K. (2009). *Program evaluation: An introduction* (5th ed.). Belmont, CA: Wadsworth.

Roysircar, G. (2009). Evidence-based practice and its implications for culturally sensitive treatment. *Multicultural Counseling and Development, 37,* 66–82.

Rubin, A. (1985). Practice effectiveness: More grounds for optimism. *Social Work, 30,* 469–476.

Rubin, A. (1991). The effectiveness of outreach counseling and support groups for battered women: A preliminary evaluation. *Research on Social Work Practice*, *1*, 332–357.

Rubin, A. (1992). Is case management effective for people with serious mental illness? A research review. *Health and Social Work*, *17*, 138–150.

Ruef, A. M., Litz, B. T., & Schlenger, W. E. (2000). Hispanic ethnicity and risk for combat-related posttraumatic stress disorder. *Cultural Diversity and Ethnic Minority Psychology*, *6*, 235–251.

Ruiz, B., Stevens, S., Fuhriman, J., Bogart, J., & Korchmaros, J. D. (2009). A juvenile drug court model in southern Arizona: Substance abuse, delinquency, and sexual risk outcomes by gender and race/ethnicity. *Journal of Offender Rehabilitation*, *48*(5), 416–438.

Ruscio, A. M., Stein, D. J., Chiu, W. T., & Kessler, R. C. (2010). The epidemiology of obsessive-compulsive disorder in the National Comorbidity Survey Replication. *Molecular Psychiatry*, *15*, 53–63.

Russell, D. E. H. (1983). The incidence and prevalence of intrafamilial and extrafamilial sexual abuse of female children. *Child Abuse and Neglect*, *7*, 133–146.

Russell, D. E. H. (1984). The prevalence and seriousness of incestuous abuse: Stepfathers vs. biological fathers. *Child Abuse and Neglect*, *8*, 15–22.

Rutter, M. (1997). Nature-nurture integration: The example of anti-social behavior. *American Psychologist*, *52*, 390–398.

Rutter, M., & Rutter, M. (1993). *Developing minds: Challenge and continuity across the life span*. New York, NY: Basic Books.

Ruwaard, J., Schrieken, B., Schrijver, M., Broeksteeg, J., Dekker, J., Vermeulen, H., & Lange, A. (2009). Standardized web-based cognitive behavioural therapy of mild to moderate depression: A randomized controlled trial with a long-term follow-up. *Cognitive Behaviour Therapy*, *38*, 206–221.

Ryan, C. S., Sherman, P. S., & Judd, C. M. (1994). Accounting for case manager effects in the evaluation of mental health services. *Journal of Consulting and Clinical Psychology*, *62*, 965–974.

Ryan, T. (1998). Perceived risks associated with mental illness: Beyond homicide and suicide. *Social Science Medicine*, *46*,2, 287–297.

Ryle, A. (1997). The structure and development of borderline personality disorder: A proposed model. *British Journal of Psychiatry*, *170*, 82–89.

Ryle, A., & Golynkina, K. (2000). Effectiveness of time-limited cognitive analytic therapy of borderline personality disorder: Factors associated with outcome. *British Journal of Medical Psychology*, *73*, 197–210.

Saavedra, L. M., Silverman, W. K., Morgan-Lopez, A. A., & Kurtines, W. M. (2010). Cognitive-behavioral treatment for childhood anxiety disorders: Long-term effects on anxiety and secondary disorders in young adulthood. *Journal of Child Psychology and Psychiatry*, *51*, 924–934.

Sabo, A. (1997). Etiological significance of associations between childhood trauma and borderline personality disorder: Conceptual and clinical implications. *Journal of Personality Disorders*, *11*, 50–70.

Sackett, D. L., Straus, S. E., Richardson, W. S., Rosenberg, W., & Haynes, R. B. (2000). *Evidence-based medicine: How to practice and teach EBM*. New York, NY: Churchill Livingstone.

Sadowski, C. M., & Friedrich, W. N. (2000). Psychometric properties of the trauma symptom checklist for children (TSCC) with psychiatrically hospitalized adolescents. *Child Maltreatment, 5*, 364–372.

Saewyc, E. M., Bearinger, L. H., Heinz, P. A., Blum, R. W., & Resnick, M. D. (1998). Gender differences in health and risk behaviors among bisexual and homosexual adolescents. *Journal of Adolescent Health, 23*, 181–188.

Safford, F. (1997). Differential assessment of dementia and depression in elderly people. In F. Safford & G. Krell (Eds.), *Gerontology for health professionals: A practice guide* (2nd ed., pp. 56–73). Washington, DC: NASW Press.

Safran, J. D. (1998). (Ed.), *The widening scope of cognitive therapy: The therapeutic relationship, emotion, and the process of change.* Northvale, NJ: Aronson.

Safren, A. A., O'Cleirigh, C., Tan, J. Y., Raminani, S. R., Reilly, L. C., Otto, M. W., & Mayer, K. H. (2009). A randomized controlled trial of cognitive behavior therapy for adherence and depression (CBT-AD) in HIV-infected individuals. *Health Psychology, 28*, 1–10.

Safren, S. A., Gonzalez, R. E., Horner, K. J., Leung, A. W., Heimberg, R. G., & Juster, H. R. (2000). Anxiety in ethnic minority youth: Methodological and conceptual issues and review of the literature. *Behavior Modification, 24*, 147–183.

Saha, S., Chant, D., & McGrath, J. (2007). A systematic review of mortality in schizophrenia: Is the differential mortality gap worsening over time? *Archives of General Psychiatry, 64*(10), 1123–1131. doi: 10.1001/archpsyc.64.10.1123.

Salekin, R. T., Worley, C., & Grimes, R. D. (2010). Treatment of psychopathy: A review and brief introduction to the mental model approach for psychopathy. *Behavioral Sciences and the Law, 28*, 235–266.

Salkovskis, P. M. (1985). Obsessional-compulsive problems: A cognitive-behavioural analysis. *Behaviour Research and Therapy, 23*, 571–583.

Salkovskis, P. M. (1989). Cognitive-behavioural factors and the persistence of intrusive thoughts in obsessional problems. *Behaviour Research and Therapy, 27*, 677–682.

Sallee, F. R., & March, J. S. (2001). Neuropsychiatry of paediatric anxiety disorders. In W. K. Silverman & P. D. A. Treffers (Eds.), *Anxiety disorders in children and adolescents: Research, assessment and intervention* (pp. 90–125). New York, NY: Cambridge University Press.

Sallee, R., & Greenawald, J. (1995). Neurobiology. In J. S. March (Ed.), *Anxiety disorders in children and adolescents* (pp. 3–34). New York, NY: Guilford Press.

Salmon, P. (2001). Effects of physical exercise on anxiety, depression, and sensitivity to stress: A unifying theory. *Clinical Psychology Review, 21*, 33–61.

Salyers, M. P., McGuire, A. B., Rollins, A. L., Bond, G. R., Mueser, K. T., & Macy, V. R. (2010). Integrating assertive community treatment and illness management and recovery for consumers with severe mental illness. *Community Mental Health Journal, 46*, 319–329.

Salzer, M. S., Nixon, C. T., Schut, L. J. A., Karver, M. S., & Bickman, L. (1997). Validating quality indicators: Quality as relationship between structure, process and outcome. *Evaluation Review, 21*, 292–309.

Sanchez-Craig, M. (1980). Random assignment to abstinence or controlled drinking in a cognitive-behavioral program: Short-term effects on drinking behavior. *Addictive Behaviors, 5*, 35–39.

Sanchez-Craig, M., & Lei, H. (1986). Disadvantages of imposing the goal of abstinence on problem drinkers: An empirical study. *British Journal of Addiction*, *81*, 505–512.

Sanchez-Ortiz, V. C., Munro, C., Stahl, D., House, J., Startup, H., Treasure, J., . . . Schmidt, U. (2011). A randomized controlled-trial of Internet-based cognitive-behavioral therapy for bulimia nervosa or related disorders in a student population. *Psychological Medicine*, *41*, 407–417.

Sanchez-Meca, J., Rosa-Alcazar, A. I., Marin-Martinez, F., & Gomez-Conesa, A. (2010). Psychological treatment of panic disorder with or without agoraphobia: A meta-analysis. *Clinical Psychology Review*, *30*, 37–50.

Sanders, M. R., Markie-Dadds, C., & Nicholson, J. M. (1997). Concurrent interventions for marital and children's problems. In W. K. Halford & H. J. Markham (Eds.), *Clinical handbook of marriage and couples intervention* (pp. 509–535). New York, NY: Wiley.

Sanders, M. R., Nicholson, J. M., & Floyd, F. J. (1997). Couples' relationships and children. In W. K. Halford & H. J. Markham (Eds.), *Clinical handbook of marriage and couples intervention* (pp. 225–253). New York, NY: Wiley.

Sanjuan, P., & Langenbucher, J. (1999). Age-limited populations: Youth, adolescents and older adults. In B. McCrady & E. Epstein (Eds.), *Addictions: A comprehensive guidebook* (pp. 477–498). New York, NY: Oxford University Press.

Santisteban, D. A., Coatsworth, D., Perez-Vidal, A., Mitrani, V., Jean-Gilles, M., & Szapocznik, J. (1997). Brief structural/strategic family therapy with African-American and Hispanic high-risk youth. *Journal of Community Psychology*, *25*, 453–471.

Santisteban, D. A., Szapocznik, J., Perez-Vidal, A., Kurtines, W. M., Murray, E. J., & LaPeriere, A. (1996). Efficacy of interventions for engaging youth/families into treatment and some factors that may contribute to differential effectiveness. *Journal of Family Psychology*, *10*, 35–44.

Sarason, I. G., Pierce, G. R., & Sarason, B. R. (1994). General and specific perceptions of social support. In W. R. Avison & I. H. Gotlib (Eds.), *Stress and mental health: Contemporary issues and prospects for the future* (pp. 151–177). New York, NY: Springer.

Sarwer, D. B., & Durlak, J. A. (1997). A field trial of the effectiveness of behavioral treatment for sexual dysfunctions. *Journal of Sex and Marital Therapy*, *23*, 87–97.

Saunders, J. B., Aasland, O. G., Amundsen, A., & Grant, M. (1993). Alcohol consumption and related problems among primary health care patients: WHO collaborative project on early detection of persons with harmful alcohol consumption—I. *Addiction*, *88*, 349–362.

Saunders, J. B., Aasland, O. G., Babor, T. F., de la Fuente, J. R., & Grant, M. (1993). Development of the Alcohol Use Disorders Identification Test (AUDIT): WHO collaborative project on early detection of persons with harmful alcohol consumption—II. *Addiction*, *88*, 791–804.

Sauter, J., & Franklin, C. (1998). Assessing post-traumatic stress disorder in children: Diagnostic and measurement strategies. *Research on Social Work Practice*, *8*, 251–270.

Saxon, A. J., Wells, E. A., Fleming, C., Jackson, T. R., & Calsyn, D. A. (1996). Pre-treatment characteristics, program philosophy and level of ancillary services as predictors of methadone maintenance treatment outcome. *Addiction*, *91*, 1197–1209.

Sayers, S. L., & Sarwer, D. B. (1998). Assessment of marital dysfunction. In A. S. Bellack & M. Hersen (Eds.), *Behavioral assessment: A practical handbook* (pp. 293–314). Boston, MA: Allyn & Bacon.

Saywitz, K. J., Goodman, G. S., & Lyon, T. D. (2002). Interviewing children in and out of court: Current research and practice implications. In J. E. B. Meyers, L. Berliner, J. Briere, C. T. Hendrix, C. Jenny, & T. A. Reid (Eds.), *The APSAC handbook on child maltreatment* (2nd ed., pp. 349–377). Thousand Oaks, CA: Sage.

Saywitz, K. J., Mannarino, A. P., Berliner, L., & Cohen, J. A. (2000). Treatment for sexually abused children and adolescents. *American Psychologist*, *55*, 1040–1049.

Schafer, J., & Leigh, B. C. (1996). A comparison of the factor structures of adolescent and adult alcohol effect expectancies. *Addictive Behaviors*, *21*, 403–408.

Scharff, J. S. (1995). Psychoanalytic marital therapy. In N. S. Jacobson & A. S. Gurman (Eds.), *Clinical handbook of couple therapy* (pp. 164–196). New York, NY: Guilford Press.

Schaus, J. F., Sole, M. L., McCoy, T. P., Mullett, N., & O'Brien, M. C. (2009). Alcohol screening and brief intervention in a college student health center: A randomized controlled trial. *Journal of Studies of Alcohol and Other Drugs*, *16*, 131–141.

Scherer, M. W., & Nakamura, C. Y. (1968). A fear survey schedule for children (FSS-C): A factor analytic comparison with manifest anxiety (CMAS). *Behaviour Research and Therapy*, *6*, 173–182.

Schilling, R. F., El-Bassell, N., Hadden, B., & Gilbert, L. (1995). Skills-training groups to reduce HIV transmission and drug use among methadone patients. *Social Work*, *40*, 91–101.

Schinke, S. P., Schilling, R. F., Kirkham, M. A., Gilchrist, L. D., Barth, R. P., & Blythe, B. J. (1986). Stress management skills for parents. *Journal of Child and Adolescent Psychotherapy*, *3*, 293–298.

Schliebner, C. T. (1994). Gender-sensitive therapy: An alternative for women in substance abuse treatment. *Journal of Substance Abuse Treatment*, *11*, 511–515.

Schmidt, N. B., & Keough, M. E. (2009). Treatment of panic. *Annual Review of Clinical Psychology*, *6*, 241–256.

Schmidt, U. (1998). Eating disorders and obesity. In P. Graham (Ed.), *Cognitive-behaviour therapy for children and families* (pp. 262–281). New York, NY: Cambridge University Press.

Schmidt, U., Lee, S., Beecham, J., Perkins, S., Treasure, J., Yi, I., Winn, S., Robinson, P., . . . Eisler, I. (2007). A randomized controlled trial of family therapy and cognitive behavior therapy guided self-care for adolescents with bulimia nervosa and related disorders. *American Journal of Psychiatry*, *164*, 591–598.

Schniering, C. A., Hudson, J. L., & Rapee, R. (2000). Issues in the diagnosis and assessment of anxiety disorders in children and adolescents. *Clinical Psychology Review*, *20*, 453–478.

Schnurr, P., Friedman, M., Engel, C., Foa, E., Shea, M., Chow, B., . . . Bernardy, N. (2007). Cognitive behavior therapy for posttraumatic stress disorder in women: A randomized controlled trial. *JAMA*, *297*, 820–830.

Schonbrun, Y. C., & Whisman, M. A. (2010). Marital distress and mental health care service utilization. *Journal of Consulting and Clinical Psychology*, *78*, 732–736.

Schottenbauer, M. A., Glass, C. A., & Arnkoff, D. B. (2007). Decision-making and psychotherapy integration: Theoretical considerations, preliminary data, and implications for future research. *Journal of Psychotherapy Integration*, *17*, 225–250.

Schottenfeld, R., Moore, B., & Pantalon, M. V. (2011). Contingency management with community reinforcement approach or twelve-step facilitation drug counseling for cocaine dependent pregnant women or women with young children. *Drug and Alcohol Dependence*, *118*, 48–55.

Schroder, A., Heider, J., Zaby, A., & Gollner, R. (2013). Cognitive behavioral therapy versus progressive muscle relaxation training for multiple somatoform symptoms: Results of a randomized controlled trial. *Cognitive Therapy and Research*, *37*, 296–306.

Schuckit, M. (1998). Biological, psychological and environmental predictors of the alcoholism risk: A longitudinal study. *Journal of Studies on Alcohol*, *59*, 485–494.

Schulenberg, J. E., & Maggs, J. L. (2002). A developmental perspective on alcohol use and heavy drinking during adolescence and the transition to young adulthood. *Journal of Studies on Alcohol*, *63*, 54–70.

Schulenberg, J., Maggs, J. L., Steinman, K. J., & Zucker, R. A. (2001). Development matters: Taking the long view on substance abuse etiology and intervention during adolescence. In P. M. Monti, S. M. Colby, & T. A. O'Leary (Eds.), *Adolescents, alcohol and substance abuse: Reaching teens through brief interventions* (pp. 19–57). New York, NY: Guilford Press.

Schumm, J. A., O'Farrell, T. J., Murphy, C. M., & Fals-Stewart, W. (2009). Partner violence before and after couples-based alcoholism treatment for female alcoholic patients. *Journal of Consulting and Clinical Psychology*, *77*, 1136–1146.

Schwartz, A., & Schwartz, R. M. (1993). *Depression: Theories and treatment*. New York, NY: Columbia University Press.

Schwartz, J. (1998). Neuroanatomical aspects of cognitive-behavioural therapy response in obsessive-compulsive disorder: An evolving perspective on brain and behaviour. *British Journal of Psychiatry*, *173*(35, suppl.), 38–44.

Scogin, F., & McElreath, L. (1994). Efficacy of psychosocial treatments for geriatric depression: A quantitative review. *Journal of Consulting and Clinical Psychology*, *62*, 69–74.

Scott, J., Garland, A., & Moorhead, S. (2001). A pilot study of cognitive therapy in bipolar disorders. *Psychological Medicine*, *31*, 459–467.

Scott, J., Paykel, E., Morriss, R., Bentall, R., Kinderman, P., Johnson, T., . . . Hayhurst, H. (2006). Cognitive-behavioral therapy for severe and recurrent bipolar disorder. *British Journal of Psychiatry*, *188*, 313–320.

Scott, J. E., & Dixon, L. B. (1995). Assertive community treatment and case management for schizophrenia. *Schizophrenia Bulletin*, *21*, 657–668.

Seghal, B., Young, A., Gillem, A. R., Saules, K., Grey, M. J., & Nabors, N. A. (2011). Practicing what we know: Multicultural counseling competence among clinical psychology trainees and experienced multicultural psychologists. *Cultural Diversity and Ethnic Minority Psychology*, *17*, 1–10.

Seligman, L. (1998). *Selecting effective treatments: A comprehensive, systematic guide to treating mental disorders*. San Francisco, CA: Jossey-Bass.

Seligman, M. E. (1975). *Helplessness: On depression, development and death.* San Francisco, CA: Freeman.

Seltzer, M. (1971). The Michigan Alcoholism Screening Test: The quest for a new diagnostic instrument. *American Journal of Psychiatry, 127,* 1653–1658.

Semidei, J., Radel, L. F., & Nolan, C. (2001). Substance abuse and child welfare: Clear linkages and promising responses. *Child Welfare, 80,* 109–128.

Senchak, M., Leonard, K. E., & Greene, B. W. (1998). Alcohol use among college students as a function of their typical social drinking context. *Psychology of Addictive Behaviors, 12,* 62–70.

Serin, R. C., & Brown, S. L. (2000). The clinical use of the Hare Psychopathy Checklist–Revised in contemporary risk assessment. In C. B. Gacono (Ed.), *The clinical and forensic assessment of psychopathy: A practitioner's guide* (pp. 251–268). Mahwah, NJ: Erlbaum.

Serin, R. C., & Preston, D. L. (2001). Managing and treating violent offenders. In J. B. Ashford, B. D. Sales, & W. H. Reid (Eds.), *Treating adult and juvenile offenders with special needs* (pp. 249–271). Washington, DC: American Psychological Association.

Sessa, F. M. (2007). Peer crowds in a commuter college sample: The relation between self-reported alcohol use and perceived peer crowd norms. *Journal of Psychology, 141,* 293–305.

Sexton, T. L. (2011). *Functional family therapy in clinical practice: An evidence-based treatment approach for working with troubled adolescents.* New York, NY: Routledge.

Shadish, W. R., Montgomery, L. M., Wilson, P., Wilson, M. R., Bright, I., & Okwumabua, T. (1993). Effects of family and marital psychotherapies: A meta analysis. *Journal of Consulting and Clinical Psychology, 61,* 992–1002.

Shadish, W. R., & Sweeney, R. B. (1991). Mediators and moderators in meta-analysis: There's a reason we don't let dodo birds tell us which psychotherapies should have prizes. *Journal of Consulting and Clinical Psychology, 59,* 883–893.

Shafran, R. (1998). Childhood obsessive-compulsive disorder. In P. Graham (Ed.), *Cognitive-behaviour therapy for children and families* (pp. 45–73). New York, NY: Cambridge University Press.

Shalev, A. Y. (1996). Stress versus traumatic stress: From acute homeostatic reactions to chronic psychopathology. In B. A. Van der Kolk, A. C. McFarlane, & L. Weisaeth (Eds.), *Traumatic stress: The effects of overwhelming experience on mind, body and society* (pp. 77–101). New York, NY: Guilford Press.

Shalev, A. Y. (2009). Posttraumatic stress disorder and stress-related disorders. *Psychiatric Clinics of North America, 32,* 687–704.

Shalev, A. Y., Bonne, O., & Eth, S. (1996). Treatment of posttraumatic stress disorder: A review. *Psychosomatic Medicine, 58,* 165–182.

Shapiro, F. (1996). Eye movement desensitization and reprocessing (EMDR): Evaluation of controlled PTSD research. *Journal of Behavioral and Experimental Psychiatry, 27,* 209–218.

Shapiro, F. (2002). EMDR 12 years after its introduction: Past and future research. *Journal of Clinical Psychology, 58,* 1–22.

Shea, M. T., Elkin, I., Imber, S. D., Sotsky, S. M., Watkins, J. T., Pilkonis, P. A., . . . Parloff, M. B. (1992). Course of depressive symptoms over follow-up: Findings from the National Institute of Mental Health Treatment of Depression Collaborative Program. *Archives of General Psychiatry*, *49*, 782–787.

Shedler, J. (2010). The efficacy of psychodynamic psychotherapy. *American Psychologist*, *65*, 98–109.

Sheehan, T., & Owen, P. (1999). The disease model. In B. S. McCrady & E. E. Epstein (Eds.), *Addictions: A comprehensive guidebook* (pp. 268–286). New York, NY: Oxford University Press.

Shekter-Wolfson, L. F., Woodside, D. B., & Lackstrom, J. (1997). Social work treatment of anorexia and bulimia: Guidelines for practice. *Research on Social Work Practice*, *7*, 5–31.

Shelton, T. L., Barkley, R. A., Crosswait, C., Moorehouse, M., Fletcher, K., Barrett, S., . . . Metevia, L. (2000). Multimethod psychoeducational intervention for preschool children with disruptive behavior: Two-year post-treatment follow-up. *Journal of Abnormal Child Psychology*, *28*, 253–266.

Shenton, M. E. (1996). Temporal lobe structural abnormalities in schizophrenia: A selective review and presentation of new magnetic resonance findings. In S. Matthysse, D. L. Levy, J. Kagan, & F. M. Benes (Eds.), *Psychopathology: The evolving science of mental disorder* (pp. 51–99). New York, NY: Cambridge University Press.

Sher, K. (1987). Stress dampening response. In H. Blane & K. Leonard (Eds.), *Psychological theories of drinking and alcoholism* (pp. 227–271). New York, NY: Guilford Press.

Sher, K. (1997). Psychological characteristics of children of alcoholics. *Alcohol Health and Research World*, *21*, 247–254.

Sherman, J., Rasmussen, C., & Baydala, L. (2008). The impact of teacher factors on achievement and behavioral outcomes of children with attention-deficit/hyperactivity disorder (ADHD): A review of the literature. *Educational Research*, *50*, 347–360.

Sherrer, M. V. (2011). The role of cognitive appraisal in adaptation to traumatic stress in adults with serious mental illness: A critical review. *Trauma, Violence and Abuse*, *12*, 151–167.

Sherrer, M. V., & O'Hare, T. (2008). Clinical case management. In K. Mueser & D. Jeste (Eds.), *Clinical handbook of schizophrenia* (pp. 309–318). New York, NY: Guilford Press.

Shoevers, R. A., Beekman, A., Deeg, D., Geerlings, M., Jonker, C., & Van Tilburg, W. (2000). Risk factors for depression in later life: Results of a prospective community based study (AMSTEL). *Journal of Affective Disorders*, *59*, 127–137.

Shulman, L. (1992). *The skills of helping: Individuals, families and groups*. Itasca, IL: Peacock.

Siegel, D. (1984). Defining empirically based practice. *Social Work*, *29*, 325–331.

Sigvardsson, S., Cloninger, R., Bohman, M., & von Knorring, A. (1982). Predisposition to petty criminality in Swedish adoptees. *Archives of General Psychiatry*, *39*, 1248–1253.

Sikkema, K. J., Winett, R. A., & Lombard, D. N. (1995). Development and evaluation of an HIV-risk reduction program for female college students. *AIDS Education and Prevention*, 7, 145–159.

Silberg, J., Pickles, A., Rutter, M., Hewitt, J., Simonoff, E., Maes, H., . . . Eaves, L. (1999). The influence of genetic factors and life stress on depression among adolescent girls. *Archives of General Psychiatry*, 56, 225–232.

Silverman, W. K., & Berman, S. L. (2001). Psychosocial interventions for anxiety disorders in children: Status and future directions. In W. K. Silverman & P. D. A. Treffers (Eds.), *Anxiety disorders in children and adolescents: Research, assessment and intervention* (pp. 313–334). New York, NY: Cambridge University Press.

Silverman, W. K., Kurtines, W. M., Ginsburg, G. S., Weems, C. F., Lumpkin, P. W., & Carmichael, D. H. (1999). Treating anxiety disorders in children with group cognitive-behavioral therapy: A randomized controlled trial. *Journal of Consulting and Clinical Psychology*, 67, 995–1003.

Silverman, W. K., Kurtines, W. M., Ginsburg, G. S., Weems, C. F., Rabian, B., & Serafini, L. T. (1999). Contingency management, self-control, and education support in the treatment of childhood phobic disorders. *Journal of Consulting and Clinical Psychology*, 67, 675–687.

Silverman, W. K., & Serafini, L. T. (1998). Assessment of child behavior problems: Internalizing disorders. In A. S. Bellack & M. Hersen (Eds.), *Behavioral assessment: A practical handbook* (4th ed., pp. 342–360). Boston, MA: Allyn & Bacon.

Silverstein, S. M., & Bellack, A. S. (2008). A scientific agenda for the concept of recovery as it applies to schizophrenia. *Clinical Psychology Review*, 28, 1108–1124.

Simon, G. E., Hunkeler, E., Fireman, B., Lee, J. Y., & Savarino, J. (2007). Risk of suicide attempt and suicide death in patients treated for bipolar disorder. *Bipolar Disorders*, 9(5), 526–530. doi: 10.1111/j.1399-5618.2007.00408.x.

Simon, L. M. (1997). Do criminals specialize in crime types? *Applied and Preventive Psychology*, 6, 35–53.

Simon, L. M. (1998). Does criminal offender treatment work? *Applied and Preventive Psychology*, 7, 137–159.

Simons, A. D., Gordon, J. S., Monroe, S. M., & Thase, M. E. (1995). Toward an integration of psychologic, social, and biologic factors in depression: Effects on outcome and course of cognitive therapy. *Journal of Consulting and Clinical Psychology*, 63, 369–377.

Simpson, D. D., Joe, G. W., Rowan-Szal, G. A., & Greener, J. M. (1997). *Journal of Substance Abuse Treatment*, 14, 565–572.

Simpson, E. B., Pistorello, J., Begin, A., Costello, E., Levinson, J., Mulberry, S., . . . Stevens, M. (1998). Use of dialectical behavior therapy in a partial hospital program for women with borderline personality disorder. *Psychiatric Services*, 49, 669–673.

Sinadinovic, K., Berman, A. H., Hasson, D., & Wennberg, P. (2010). Internet-based assessment and self-monitoring of problematic alcohol and drug use. *Addictive Behaviors*, 35, 464–470.

Singh, J. P., Serper, M., Reinharth, J., & Faxel, S. (2011). Structured assessment of violence risk in schizophrenia and other psychiatric disorders: A systematic review of the validity, reliability, and item content of 10 available instruments. *Schizophrenia Bulletin*, 37, 899–912.

Sisson, R., & Azrin, N. (1986). Family-member involvement to initiate and promote treatment of problem drinkers. *Journal of Behaviour Therapy and Experimental Psychiatry, 17*, 15–21.

Skeem, J. L., & Cooke, D. J. (2010). One measure does not a construct make: Directions toward reinvigorating psychopathy research—Reply to Hare and Neumann (2010). *Psychological Assessment, 22*, 455–459.

Skinner, H. A. (1982). The Drug Abuse Screening Test. *Addictive Behaviors, 7*, 363–371.

Skodol, A. E., Bender, D. S., Morey, L. C., & Oldham, J. M. (2013). The ironic fate of the personality disorders in DSM-5. *Personality Disorders: Theory, Research, and Treatment, 4*, 342–349.

Skriner, L. C., & Chu, B. C. (2014). Cross-ethnic measurement invariance of the SCARED and CES-D in a youth sample. *Psychological Assessment, 26*, 332–337.

Slater, J. M., Guthrie, B. J., & Boyd, C. J. (2001). A feminist theoretical approach to understanding health of adolescent females. *Journal of Adolescent Health, 28*, 443–449.

Slep, A. M. S., & Heyman, R. E. (2001). Where do we go from here? Moving toward an integrated approach to family violence. *Aggression and Violent Behavior, 6*, 353–356.

Slesnick, N., Prestopnik, J. L., Meyers, R. J., & Glassman, M. (2007). Treatment outcome for street-living, homeless youth. *Addictive Behaviors, 32*, 1237–1251.

Sloan, R. B., Staples, F. R., Cristol, A. H., Yorkston, N. J., & Whipple, K. (1975). *Psychotherapy vs. behavior therapy*. Cambridge, MA: Harvard University Press.

Smith, B. D., & Marsh, J. C. (2002). Client-service matching in substance abuse treatment for women with children. *Journal of Substance Abuse Treatment, 22*, 161–168.

Smith, D. E., Marcus, M. D., & Eldredge, K. L. (1994). Binge eating syndromes: A review of assessment and treatment with an emphasis on clinical application. *Behavior Therapy, 25*, 635–658.

Smith, G. R., Fischer, E. P., Nordquist, C. R., Mosley, C. L., & Ledbetter, N. S. (1997). Implementing outcomes management systems in mental health settings. *Psychiatric Services, 48*, 364–368.

Smith, M. L., Glass, G. V., & Miller, T. I. (1980). *The benefits of psychotherapy*. Baltimore, MD: Johns Hopkins University Press.

Smith, P., Perrin, S., & Yule, W. (1998). Post-traumatic stress disorder. In P. Graham (Ed.), *Cognitive-behaviour therapy for children and families* (pp. 127–142). New York, NY: Cambridge University Press.

Smith, S. L., Sherrill, K. A., & Colenda, C. C. (1995). Assessing and treating anxiety in elderly persons. *Psychiatric Services, 46*, 36–42.

Smith, T. E., Bellack, A. S., & Liberman, R. P. (1996). Social skills training for schizophrenia: Review and future directions. *Clinical Psychology Review, 16*, 599–617.

Smokowski, P. R., & Wodarski, J. S. (1996). The effectiveness of child welfare services for poor, neglected children: A review of the empirical evidence. *Research on Social Work Practice, 6*, 504–523.

Snipes, D. J., & Benotsch, E. G. (2013). High-risk cocktails and high-risk sex: Examining the relation between alcohol mixed with energy drink consumption, sexual behavior, and drug use in college students. *Addictive Behaviors, 38*, 1418–1423.

Snyder, D. K., & Wills, R. M. (1989). Behavioral versus insight-oriented marital therapy: Effects on individual and interspousal functioning. *Journal of Consulting and Clinical Psychology, 57*, 39–46.

Snyder, D. K., Wills, R. M., & Grady-Fletcher, A. (1991). Long-term effectiveness of behavioral vs. insight-oriented marital therapy. *Journal of Consulting and Clinical Psychology, 59*, 146–149.

Sobell, L. C., Cunningham, J. A., & Sobell, M. B. (1996). Recovery from alcohol problems with and without treatment: Prevalence in two population surveys. *American Journal of Public Health, 86*, 966–972.

Sobell, L. C., Toneatto, T., & Sobell, M. B. (1994). Behavioral assessment and treatment planning for alcohol, tobacco, and other drug problems: Current status with an emphasis on clinical applications. *Behavioral Therapy, 25*, 533–580.

Soler, J., Pascual, J. C., Tiana, T., Cebria, A., Barrachina, J., Campins, M. J., . . . Perez, V. (2009). Dialectical behavior therapy skills training compared to standard group therapy in borderline personality disorder: A 3-month randomized controlled clinical trial. *Behaviour Research and Therapy, 47*, 353–358.

Solomon, P. (1992). The efficacy of case management services for the severely mentally disabled clients. *Community Mental Health Journal, 28*, 163–180.

Solomon, S. D., & Davidson, J. R. T. (1997). Trauma: Prevalence, impairment, service use and cost. *Journal of Clinical Psychiatry, 58*(suppl. 9), 5–11.

Song, J. Y., Yu, H. Y., Kim, S. H., Hwang, S. S., Cho, H., Kim, Y. S., . . . Ahn, Y. M. (2012). Assessment of risk factors related to suicide attempts in patients with bipolar disorder. *Journal of Nervous and Mental Disease, 200*, 978–984.

Sowers-Hoag, K. M. (1997). Case management with the elderly. In F. Safford & G. Krell (Eds.), *Gerontology for health professionals: A practice guide* (2nd ed., pp. 74–92). Washington, DC: NASW Press.

Spangler, D., Simons, A., Monroe, S., & Thase, M. (1996). Gender differences in cognitive diathesis-stress domain match: Implications for differential pathways to depression. *Journal of Abnormal Psychology, 105*, 653–657.

Spangler, D., Simons, A., Monroe, S., & Thase, M. (1997). Response to cognitive-behavioral therapy in depression: Effects of pretreatment cognitive dysfunction and life stress. *Journal of Consulting and Clinical Psychology, 65*, 568–575.

Spanier, G. B. (1976). Measuring dyadic adjustment: New scales for assessing the quality of marriage and similar dyads. *Journal of Marriage and Family Therapy, 38*, 15–28.

Spence, S. H. (1997). Structure of anxiety symptoms among children: A confirmatory factor-analytic study. *Journal of Abnormal Psychology, 106*, 280–297.

Spencer, T. J., Biederman, J., Wilens, T. E., & Faraone, S. V. (2002). Overview and neurobiology of attention-deficit/hyperactivity disorder. *Journal of Clinical Psychiatry, 63*, 3–9.

Springer, S. A., Azar, M. M., & Altice, F. L. (2011). HIV, alcohol dependence, and the criminal justice system: A review and call for evidence-based treatment for released prisoners. *American Journal of Drug and Alcohol Abuse, 37*, 12–21.

Sprock, J., & Yoder, C. (1997). Women and depression: An update on the report of the APA task force. *Sex Roles, 36*, 269–303.

Srebnik, D., Hendryx, M., Stevenson, J., Caverly, S., Dyck, D. G., & Cauce, A. M. (1997). Development of outcome indicators for monitoring the quality of public mental health care. *Psychiatric Services, 48*, 903–909.

Sroufe, L. A. (1997). Psychopathology as an outcome of development. *Development and Psychopathology, 9*, 251–268.

Stake, R. E. (1995). *The art of case study research*. Thousand Oaks, CA: Sage.

Staley, D., & El-Guebaly, N. (1990). Psychometric properties of the Drug Abuse Screening Test in a psychiatric patient population. *Addictive Behaviors, 15*, 257–264.

Stanley, M. A., Beck, J. G., Novy, D. M., Averill, P. M., Swann, A. C., Diefenbach, G. J., & Hopko, D. R. (2003). Cognitive-behavioral treatment of late-life generalized anxiety disorder. *Journal of Consulting and Clinical Psychology, 71*, 309–319.

Stanley, M. A., & Turner, S. M. (1995). Current status of pharmacological and behavioral treatment of obsessive-compulsive disorder. *Behavior Therapy, 26*, 163–186.

Stanton, M. D., & Shadish, W. R. (1997). Outcome, attrition, and family-couples treatment for drug abuse: A meta-analysis and review of the controlled, comparative studies. *Psychological Bulletin, 122*, 170–191.

Stanton, M. D., Todd, T. C., & Associates (1982). *The family therapy of drug abuse and addiction*. New York, NY: Guilford Press.

Stark, K. D., Reynolds, W. M., & Kaslow, N. (1987). A comparison of the relative efficacy of self-control therapy and a behavioral problem-solving therapy for depression in children. *Journal of Abnormal Child Psychology, 15*, 91–113.

Stark, K. D., Rouse, L. W., & Kurowski, C. (1994). Psychological treatment approaches for depression in children. In W. M. Reynolds & H. F. Johnston (Eds.), *Handbook of depression in children and adolescents* (pp. 275–307). New York, NY: Plenum Press.

Stark, K. D., Vaughn, C., Doxey, M., & Luss, L. (1999). Depressive disorders. In R. T. Ammerman, M. Hersen, & C. G. Last (Eds.), *Handbook of prescriptive treatments for children and adolescents* (2nd ed., pp. 114–140). Boston, MA: Allyn & Bacon.

Staton, M., Leukefeld, C., Logan, T. K., Zimmerman, R., Lynam, D., Milich, R., . . . Clayton, R. (1999). Risky sex behavior and substance use among young adults. *Health and Social Work, 24*, 147–153.

Steele, C. M., & Josephs, R. A. (1990). Alcohol myopia: Its prized and dangerous effects. *American Psychologist, 45*, 921–933.

Steffens, D. C. (2013). Exercise for late life depression? It depends. *Lancet, 382*, 4–5.

Stein, D. J., Denys, D., Gloster, A. T., Hollander, E., Leckman, J. F., Rauch, S. L., & Phillips, K. A. (2009). Obsessive-compulsive disorder: Diagnostic and treatment issues. *Psychiatric Clinics of North America, 32*, 665–685.

Stein, L. I., & Test, M. A. (1980). Alternatives to mental hospital treatment: I. Conceptual model, treatment program, and clinical evaluation. *Archives of General Psychiatry, 37*, 392–397.

Stein, R. I., Saelens, B. E., Dounchis, J. Z., Lewczyk, C. M., Swenson, A. K., & Wilfley, D. E. (2001). Treatment of eating disorders in women. *Counseling Psychologist, 29*, 695–732.

Steinberg, A. M., Brymer, M. J., Decker, K. B., & Pynoos, R. S. (2004). The University of California at Los Angeles Post-Traumatic Stress Disorder Reaction Index. *Current Psychiatry Reports, 6*, 96–100.

Steinglass, P., Bennett, L. A., Wolin, S. J., & Reiss, D. (1987). *The alcoholic family*. New York, NY: Basic Books.

Steinhausen, H., & Weber, S. (2009). Outcomes of bulimia nervosa: Findings from one-quarter century of research. *American Journal of Psychiatry, 166,* 1331–1341.

Steketee, G. S. (1993). *Treatment of obsessive compulsive disorder.* New York, NY: Guilford Press.

Steketee, G. (1997). Disability and family burden in obsessive-compulsive disorder. *Canadian Journal of Psychiatry, 42,* 919–928.

Steketee, G., Chambless, D. L., & Tran, G. Q. (2001). Effects of axis I and II comorbidity on behavior therapy outcome for obsessive-compulsive disorder with agoraphobia. *Comprehensive Psychiatry, 42,* 76–86.

Steketee, G., Siev, J., Fama, J. M., Keshaviah, A., Chosak, A., & Wilhelm, S. (2011). Predictors of treatment outcome in modular cognitive therapy for obsessive-compulsive disorder. *Depression and Anxiety, 28,* 333–341.

Steketee, G., & Shapiro, L. J. (1995). Predicting behavioral treatment outcome for agoraphobia and obsessive compulsive disorder. *Clinical Psychology Review, 15,* 317–346.

Stern, A. (1938). Psychoanalytic investigation and therapy in the borderline group of neuroses. *Psychoanalytic Quarterly, 7,* 467–489.

Stern, M. I., Herron, W. G., Primavera, L. H., & Kakuma, T. (1997). Interpersonal perceptions of depressed and borderline patients. *Journal of Clinical Psychology, 53,* 41–49.

Stevens, J. R. (1992). Abnormal reinnervation as a basis for schizophrenia: A hypothesis. *Archives of General Psychiatry, 49,* 238–243.

Stewart, S. H. (1996). Alcohol abuse in individuals exposed to trauma: A critical review. *Psychological Bulletin, 120,* 83–112.

Stice, E. (2002). Risk and maintenance factors for eating pathology: A meta-analytic review. *Psychological Bulletin, 128,* 825–848.

Stice, E., Fisher, M., & Martinez, E. (2004). Eating Disorder Diagnostic Scale: Additional evidence of reliability and validity. *Psychological Assessment, 16,* 60–71.

Stice, E., Shaw, H., & Marti, C. N. (2007). A meta-analytic review of eating disorder prevention programs: Encouraging findings. *Annual Review of Clinical Psychology, 3,* 207–231.

Stice, E., Telch, C. F., & Rizvi, S. L. (2000). Development and validation of the Eating Disorder Diagnostic Scale: A brief self-report measure of anorexia, bulimia, and binge eating disorder. *Psychological Assessment, 12,* 123–131.

Stiles, P. G., & McGarrahan, J. F. (1998). The Geriatric Depression Scale: A comprehensive review. *Journal of Clinical Geropsychology, 4,* 89–110.

Stith, S. M., & McCollum, E. E. (2011). Conjoint treatment of couples who have experienced intimate partner violence. *Aggression and Violent Behavior, 16,* 312–318.

Stith, S. M., Rosen, K. H., & McCollum, E. E. (2003). Effectiveness of couples treatment for spouse abuse. *Journal of Marital and Family Therapy, 29,* 407–426.

Stock, S. L., Werry, J. S., & McClellan, J. M. (2001). Pharmacological treatment of paediatric anxiety. In W. K. Silverman & P. D. A. Treffers (Eds.), *Anxiety disorders in children and adolescents: Research, assessment and intervention* (pp. 335–367). New York, NY: Cambridge University Press.

Stoffelmayer, B. E., Mavis, B. E., & Kasim, R. M. (1994). The longitudinal stability of the Addiction Severity Index. *Journal of Substance Abuse Treatment, 11,* 373–378.

Strachan, M., Gros, D. F., Ruggiero, K. J., Lejuez, C. W., & Acierno, R. (2012). An integrated approach to delivering exposure-based treatment for symptoms of PTSD and depression in OIF/OEF veterans: Preliminary findings. *Behavior Therapy, 43,* 560–569.

Strachan, M., Gros, D. F., Yuen, E., Ruggiero, K. J., Foa, E. B., & Acierno, R. (2012). Home-based telehealth to deliver evidence-based psychotherapy in veterans with PTSD. *Contemporary Clinical Trials, 33,*402–409.

Strean, H. S. (1986). Psychoanalytic theory. In F. J. Turner (Ed.), *Social work treatment: Interlocking theoretical approaches* (3rd ed., pp. 19–45). New York, NY: Free Press.

Streeter, C. L., & Franklin, C. (1992). Defining and measuring social support: Guidelines for social work practitioners. *Research on Social Work Practice, 2,* 81–99.

Striegel-Moore, R. H. (1993). Etiology of binge eating: A developmental perspective. In C. G. Fairburn & G. T. Wilson (Eds.), *Binge eating: Nature, assessment and treatment* (pp. 144–172). New York, NY: Guilford Press.

Striegel-Moore, R. H., & Cachelin, F. M. (2001). Etiology of eating disorders in women. *Counseling Psychologist,* 635–661.

Strohl, A. (2009). Physical activity, exercise, depression and anxiety disorders. *Journal of Neural Transmission, 116,* 777–784.

Stuart, R. B. (1969). Operant-interpersonal treatment of marital discord. *Journal of Consulting and Clinical Psychology, 33,* 675–682.

Stuart, R. B. (1980). *Helping couples change.* New York, NY: Guilford Press.

Stueve, A., Dohrenwend, B. P., & Skodol, A. E. (1998). Relationships between stressful life events and episodes of major depression and nonaffective psychotic disorders: Selected results from a New York risk factor study. In B. P. Dohrenwend (Ed.), *Adversity, stress and psychopathology* (pp. 341–357). New York, NY: Oxford University Press.

Stutzman, S. V., Bean, R. A., Miller, R. B., Day, R. D., Feinauer, L. L., Porter, C. L., & Moore, A. (2011). Marital conflict and adolescent outcomes: A cross-ethnic group comparison of Latino and European-American youth. *Children and Youth Services Review, 33,* 663–668.

Suarez-Morales, L., Martino, S., Bedregal, L., McCabe, B. E., Cuzmar, I. Y., Paris, M., . . . Szapocznik, J. (2010). Do therapist cultural characteristics influence the outcome of substance abuse treatment for Spanish-speaking adults? *Cultural Diversity and Ethnic Minority Psychology, 16,* 199–205.

Substance Abuse and Mental Health Services Administration. (2013). *Results from the 2012 National Survey on Drug Use and Health: Summary of national findings* (NSDUH Series H-46, HHS Publication No. SMA 13–4795). Rockville, MD: Author.

Sue, S., & Zane, N. (1987). The role of culture and cultural techniques in psychotherapy: A critique and reformation. *American Psychologist, 42, 1,* 37–45.

Sue, S., & Zane, N. (2006). How well do both evidence-based practices and treatment as usual services satisfactorily address the various dimensions of diversity? In J. C. Norocross, L. E. Beutler, & R. F. Levant (Eds.), *Evidence-based practices in mental health: Debate and dialogue on the fundamental questions* (pp. 329–374). Washington, DC: American Psychological Association.

Sue, S., Zane, N., & Young, K. (1994). Research on psychotherapy with culturally diverse populations. In A. E. Bergin & S. L. Garfield (Eds.), *Handbook of psychotherapy and behavior change* (pp. 783–820). New York, NY: Wiley.

Sullivan, P. F., Neale, M. C., & Kendler, K. S. (2000). Genetic epidemiology of major depression: Review and meta-analysis. *American Journal of Psychiatry, 157,* 1552–1562.

Sullivan, W. P., Hartmann, D. J., Dillon, D., & Wolk, J. L. (1994, February). Implementing case management in alcohol and drug treatment. *Families in Society: The Journal of Contemporary Human Services,* 67–73.

Sunday, S. R., & Halmi, K. A. (2000). Comparison of the Yale-Brown-Cornell eating disorders scale in recovered eating disorder patients, restrained dieters, and non-dieting controls. *International Journal of Eating Disorders, 28,* 455–459.

Sundel, M., & Sundel, S. S. (1998). Pharmacological treatment of panic disorder. *Research on Social Work Practice, 8,* 426–451.

Swanson, J. M. (1992). *School-based assessments and interventions for ADD students.* Irvine, CA: KC Publishing.

Swanson, J. M., Schuck, S., Mann, M., Carlson, C., Hartman, K., Sergeant, J., . . . McCleary, R. (2002). *Categorical and dimensional definitions and evaluation of symptoms of ADHD: The SNAP and the SWAN ratings scales.* Retrieved from http://www.adhd.net.

Swanson, S. A., Crow, S. J., LeGrange, D., Swendsen, J., & Merikangas, J. R. (2011). Prevalence and correlates of eating disorders in adolescents: Results from the National Comorbidity Survey Replication adolescent supplement. *Archives of General Psychiatry, 68,* 714–723.

Swartz, M. S., Burns, B. J., Hiday, V. A., George, L. K., Swanson, J., & Wagner, H. R. (1995). New directions in research on involuntary outpatient commitment. *Psychiatric Services, 46,* 381–385.

Swartz, M. S., Swanson, J. W., Hiday, V. A., Borum, R., Wagner, H. R., & Burns, B. J. (1998). Violence and severe mental illness: The effects of substance abuse and nonadherence to medication. *American Journal of Psychiatry, 155,* 226–231.

Swenson, C. C., & Hanson, R. F. (1998). Sexual abuse of children: Assessment, research and treatment. In J. R. Lutzker (Ed.), *Handbook of child abuse research and treatment* (pp. 475–499). New York, NY: Plenum Press.

Swenson, C. R., Sanderson, C., Dulit, R. A., & Linehan, M. M. (2001). The application of dialectical behavior therapy for patients with borderline personality disorder on inpatient units. *Psychiatric Quarterly, 72,* 307–324.

Szapocznik, J., Kurtines, W. M., Foote, F. H., Perez-Vidal, A., & Hervis, O. (1983). Conjoint versus one-person family therapy: Some evidence for the effectiveness of conducting family therapy through one person. *Journal of Consulting and Clinical Psychology, 51,* 889–899.

Szapocznik, J., Kurtines, W. M., Foote, F. H., Perez-Vidal, A., & Hervis, O. (1986). Conjoint versus one-person family therapy: Further evidence for the effectiveness of conducting family therapy through one person with drug-abusing adolescents. *Journal of Consulting and Clinical Psychology, 54,* 395–397.

Talbot, L. L., Umstattd, M. R., Usdan, S. L., Martin, R. J., & Geiger, B. F. (2009). Validation of the College Alcohol Problem Scale—revised (CAPS-r) for use with non-adjudicated first-year students. *Addictive Behaviors, 34,* 471–473.

Tandon, M., Cardeli, E., & Luby, J. (2009). Internalizing disorders in early childhood: A review of depressive and anxiety disorders. *Child and Adolescent Psychiatric Clinics of North America, 18,* 593–610.

Tandon, R., Keshavan, M. S., & Nasrallah, H. A. (2008a). Schizophrenia—"Just the facts": What we know in 2008. Part I: Overview. *Schizophrenia Research*, *100*, 4–19.

Tandon, R., Keshavan, M. S., & Nasrallah, H. A. (2008b). Schizophrenia—"Just the facts": What we know in 2008: Part II. Epidemiology and etiology. *Schizophrenia Research*, *102*, 1–18.

Tarrier, N., & Barrowclough, C. (1995). Family interventions in schizophrenia and their long-term outcomes. *International Journal of Mental Health*, *24*, 39–53.

Tarrier, N., Sommerfield, C., Pilgrim, H., & Faragher, B. (2000). Factors associated with outcome of cognitive-behavioural treatment of chronic post-traumatic stress disorder. *Behaviour Research and Therapy*, *38*, 191–202.

Tarter, R., Vanyokov, M., Giancola, P., Dawes, M., Blackson, T., Miezzich, A., & Clark, D. (1999). Etiology of early age onset substance use disorder: A maturational perspective. *Development and Psychopathology*, *11*, 657–683.

Task Force on Promotion and Dissemination of Psychological Procedures. (1995). Training in and dissemination of empirically-validated psychological treatments: Report and recommendations. *Clinical Psychologist*, *48*, 3–23.

Taylor, E. H. (1987). The biological basis of schizophrenia. *Social Work*, *32*, 155–121.

Taylor, S. (1995). Assessment of obsessions and compulsions: Reliability, validity and sensitivity to treatment effects. *Clinical Psychology Review*, *15*, 261–296.

Taylor, S., & Clark, D. A. (2009). Transdiagnostic cognitive-behavioral treatments for mood and anxiety disorders: Introduction to the special issue. *Journal of Cognitive Psychotherapy: An International Quarterly*, *23*, 3–5.

Taylor, S., Thordarson, D., Maxfield, L., Fedoroff, I. C., Lovell, K., & Ogrodniczuk, J. (2003). Comparative efficacy, speed, and adverse effects of three PTSD treatments: Exposure therapy, EMDR, and relaxation training. *Journal of Consulting and Clinical Psychology*, *71*, 330–338.

Teague, G. B., Bond, G. R., & Drake, R. E. (1998). Program fidelity in assertive community treatment: Development and use of a measure. *American Journal of Orthopsychiatry*, *68*, 216–232.

Teasdale, J. D. (1995). Clinically relevant theory: Integrating clinical insight with cognitive science. In P. M. Salkovskis (Ed.), *Frontiers of cognitive therapy* (pp. 26–47). New York, NY: Guilford Press.

Tehrani, J. A., Brennan, P. A., Hodgins, S., & Mednick, S. A. (1998). Mental illness and criminal violence. *Social Psychiatry and Psychiatric Epidemiology*, *33*, S81–S85.

Tenhula, W. N., Bennett, M. E., & Kinaman, J. E. S. (2009). Behavioral treatment of substance abuse in schizophrenia. *Journal of Clinical Psychology: In Session*, *65*, 831–841.

Tengstrom, A., Grann, M., Langstrom, N., & Kullgren, G. (2000). Psychopathy (PCL-R) as a predictor of violent recidivism among criminal offenders with schizophrenia. *Law and Human Behavior*, *24*, 45–58.

Teri, L. (1996). Depression in Alzheimer's disease. In M. Hersen & V. B. Van Hasselt (Eds.), *Psychological treatment of older adults: An introductory text* (pp. 209–222). New York, NY: Plenum Press.

Terling, T. (1999). The efficacy of family reunification practice: Reentry rates and correlates of reentry for abused and neglected children reunited with their families. *Child Abuse and Neglect, 23*, 1359–1370.

Test, M. A., Burke, S., & Wallach, L. S. (1990). Gender differences of young adults with schizophrenic disorders in community care. *Schizophrenia Bulletin, 16*, 331–344.

Thase, M. E., Friedman, E. S., Fasiczka, A. L., Berman, S. R., Frank, E., Nofzinger, E. A., & Reynolds, C. F. (2000). Treatment of men with major depression: A comparison of sequential cohorts treated with either cognitive-behavioral therapy or newer generation anti-depressants. *Journal of Clinical Psychiatry, 61*, 466–472.

Thelen, M. H., Farmer, J., Wonderlich, S., & Smith, M. (1991). A revision of the Bulimia-Test: The BULIT-R. *Psychological Assessment: A Journal of Consulting and Clinical Psychology, 3*, 119–124.

Theodore, A. D., Chang, J. J., Runyan, D. K., Hunter, W. M., Bangdewala, S. I., & Agans, R. (2005). Epidemiologic features of the physical and sexual maltreatment of children in the Carolinas. *Pediatrics, 115*, e331–e337.

Thibaut, J. W., & Kelly, H. H. (1959). *The social psychology of groups.* New York, NY: Wiley.

Thomas, C., & Corcoran, J. (2001). Empirically-based marital and family interventions for alcohol abuse: A review. *Research on Social Work Practice, 11*, 549–575.

Thomas, E. J., & Ager, R. D. (1993). Unilateral family therapy with spouses of uncooperative alcohol abusers. In T. J. O'Farrell (Ed.), *Treating alcohol problems: Marital and family interventions* (pp. 3–33). New York, NY: Guilford Press.

Thomas, E. J., & Santa, C. A. (1982). Unilateral family therapy for alcohol abuse: A working conception. *American Journal of Family Therapy, 10, 3*, 49–58.

Thompson, L. W. (1996). Cognitive-behavioral therapy and treatment for late-life depression. *Journal of Clinical Psychiatry, 57*, 29–37.

Thorpe, G. L., & Olson, S. L. (1997). *Behavior therapy* (2nd ed.) Boston, MA: Allyn & Bacon.

Thyer, B. A. (1995). Effective psychosocial treatments for children: A selected review. *Early Child Development and Care, 106*, 137–147.

Thyer, B. A. (2001). Evidence-based approaches to community practice. In H. E. Briggs & K. Corcoran (Eds.), *Social work practice: Treating common client problems* (pp. 54–65). Chicago, IL: Lyceum Books.

Thyer, B. A. (2004). Science and evidence-based social work practice. In H. E. Briggs & T. L. Rzepnicki (Eds.), *Using evidence in social work practice: Behavioral perspectives* (pp. 74–89). Chicago, IL: Lyceum Books.

Thyer, B. A., & Myers, L. A. (2010). The quest for evidence-based practice: A view from the United States. *Journal of Social Work, 11*, 8–25.

Title XIX of the Social Security Act, Pub. L. No. §§ 1396-1396, 1965.

Tolin, D. F., & Foa, E. B. (2006). Sex differences in trauma and posttraumatic stress disorder: A quantitative review of 25 years of research. *Psychological Bulletin, 132*(6), 37–85.

Tomaka, J., Palacios, R., Morales-Monks, S., & Davis, S. E. (2012). An evaluation of the BASICS alcohol risk reduction model among predominantly Hispanic college students. *Substance Use and Misuse, 47*, 1260–1270.

Topping, K. J., & Barron, I. G. (2009). School-based child sexual abuse prevention programs: A review of effectiveness. *Review of Educational Research*, *79*, 431–463.

Tourse, R. W. C., & Sullick, J. (1999). The collaborative alliance: Supporting vulnerable children in school. In R. W. C. Tourse & J. F. Mooney (Eds.), *Collaborative practice: School and human service partnerships* (pp. 59–78). Westport, CT: Praeger.

Tran, T. V. (1993). Psychological traumas and depression in a sample of Vietnamese people in the United States. *Health and Social Work*, *18*, *3*, 184–194.

Tran, T. V. (1997). Exploring the equivalence of factor structure in a measure of depression between black and white women: Measurement issues in comparative research. *Research on Social Work Practice*, *7*, 500–517.

Tran, T. V. (2009). *Developing cross-cultural measurement*. New York, NY: Oxford University Press.

Treadwell, K. R. H., Flannery-Schroeder, E. C., & Kendall, P. C. (1995). Ethnicity and gender in relation to adaptive functioning, diagnostic status, and treatment outcome in children from an anxiety clinic. *Journal of Anxiety Disorders*, *9*, 373–384.

Trimble, J. E. (1990). Ethnic specification, validation prospects, and the future of drug use research. *International Journal of the Addictions*, *25*(2A), 149–170.

Truax, C. B., & Carkhuff, R. R. (1967). *Toward effective counseling and psychotherapy*. Chicago, IL: Aldine.

Trucco, E. M., Colder, C. R., Wieczorek, W. F., Lengua, L. J., & Hawk, L. W. (2014). Early adolescent alcohol use in context: How neighborhoods, parents, and peers impact youth. *Development and Psychopathology*, *26*, 425–436.

Trull, T. J., Sher, K. J., Minks-Brown, C., Durbin, J., & Burr, R. (2000). Borderline personality disorder and substance use disorders: A review and integration. *Clinical Psychology Review*, *20*, 235–253.

Tryer, P. (1995). Are personality disorders well classified in DSM-IV? In J. Livesley (Ed.), *The DSM-IV personality disorders* (pp. 29–42). New York, NY: Guilford Press.

Tsui, M. (2000). The harm reduction approach revisited. *International Social Work*, *43*, 243–251.

Tubman, J., Des Rosiers, S. E., Schwartz, S. J., & O'Hare, T. (2012). The use of the risky sex scale among adolescents receiving treatment services for substance use problems: Factor structure and predictive validity. *Journal of Substance Abuse Treatment*, *43*, 359–365.

Tubman, J. G., Windle, M., & Windle, R. C. (1996). Cumulative sexual intercourse patterns among middle adolescents: Problem behavior precursors and concurrent health risk behaviors. *Journal of Adolescent Health*, *18*, 182–191.

Tuliatos, J., Perlmutter, B., & Holden, G. (Eds.) (2001). *Handbook of family measurement techniques* (Vol. 2). Thousand Oaks, CA: Sage.

Turisi, B., Larimer, M. E., Mallett, K. A., Kilmer, J. R., Ray, A. E., Mastroleo, N. R., . . . Montoya, H. (2009). A randomized clinical trial evaluating a combined alcohol intervention for high risk college students. *Journal of Studies on Alcohol and Other Drugs*, *70*, 555–567.

Turkat, I. (1992). Behavioral intervention with personality disorders. In S. M. Turner, K. S. Calhoun, & H. E. Adams (Eds.), *Handbook of clinical behavior therapy* (2nd ed., pp. 117–134). New York, NY: Wiley.

Turner, A. P., & Jacupcak, M. (2010). Behavioral activation for treatment of PTSD and depression in an Iraqi combat veteran with multiple physical injuries. *Behavioural and Cognitive Psychotherapy*, *38*, 355–361.

Turner, C. M. (2006). Cognitive-behavioural theory and therapy for obsessive-compulsive disorder in children and adolescents: Current status and future directions. *Clinical Psychology Review*, *26*, 912–938.

Turner, W. M., & Tsuang, M. T. (1990). Impact of substance abuse on the course and outcome of schizophrenia. *Schizophrenia Bulletin*, *16*, 87–95.

Tutty, L. M. (1996). Post-shelter services: The efficacy of follow-up programs for abused women. *Research on Social Work Practice*, *6*, 425–441.

Tversky, A., & Kahneman, D. (1974). Judgment under uncertainty: Heuristics and biases. *Science*, *183*, 1124–1131.

The Twelve Steps of Alcoholics Anonymous. (1981). Service Material from the General Service Office. Alcoholics Anonymous World Services, Inc.

Tyson, E. H., & Glisson, C. (2005). A cross-ethnic validity study of the Shortform Assessment for Children (SAC). *Research on Social Work Practice*, *15*, 97–109.

Tyson, K. B. (1992). A new approach to relevant scientific research for practitioners: The heuristic paradigm. *Social Work*, *37*, 541–556.

Uba, L. (1994). *Asian Americans: Personality, patterns, identity and mental health*. New York, NY: Guilford Press.

Uehara, E. S. (1994). Race, gender, and housing inequality: An exploration of the correlates of low-quality housing among clients diagnosed with severe and persistent mental illness. *Journal of Health and Social Behavior*, *35*, 309–321.

Uehara, K., Morelli, P., & Abe-Kim, J. (2001). Somatic complaint and social suffering among survivors of the Cambodian killing fields. *Journal of Human Behavior in the Social Environment*, *3*, 243–262.

Ullman, S. E., Najdowski, C. J., & Filipas, H. H. (2009). Child sexual abuse, post-traumatic stress disorder, and substance use: Predictors of sexual revictimization in adult sexual assault survivors. *Journal of Child Sexual Abuse*, *18*, 367–385.

Umbricht, D., & Kane, J. M. (1995). Risperidone: Efficacy and safety. *Schizophrenia Bulletin*, *21*, 593–606.

US Department of Health and Human Services. (1996a). *Child maltreatment 1994: Reports from the states to the National Center on Child Abuse and Neglect*. Washington, DC: US Government Printing Office.

US Department of Health and Human Services. (1996b). *Third national incidence study of child abuse and neglect: Final report (NIS-3)*. Washington, DC: US Government Printing Office.

US Department of Health and Human Services. (1997). *Ninth special report to Congress on alcohol and health*. Washington, DC: US Government Printing Office.

US Department of Health and Human Services. (1998). *National Household Survey on Drug Abuse: Population estimates, 1997*. Washington, DC: US Government Printing Office.

US Department of Health and Human Services. (1999). *National survey results on drug use from the Monitoring the Future Study (1975–1998)*. Washington, DC: US Government Printing Office.

US Department of Health and Human Services. (2000). *10th special report to Congress on alcohol and health*. Washington, DC: US Government Printing Office.

US Department of Health and Human Services. (2012). *Child Maltreatment 2011*. Available from http://www.acf.hhs.gov/programs/cb/research-data-technology/statistics-research/child-maltreatment.

US Department of Justice. (2000). *Extent, nature, and consequences of intimate partner violence: Findings from the National Violence against Women Survey*. Washington, DC: Author.

US Department of Justice. (2001). *National Institute of Justice Research in brief— Documenting domestic violence: How health care providers can help victims*. Washington, DC: Author.

Utsey, S. O., & Ponterotto, J. G. (1996). Development and validation of the Index of Race Relations (IRRS). *Journal of Counseling Psychology, 43*, 490–501.

Vaillant, G. (1983). *The natural history of alcoholism*. Cambridge, MA: Harvard University Press.

Vaillant, G., & Hiller-Sturmhöfel, S. (1996). The natural history of alcoholism. *Alcohol Health and Research World, 20*, 152–161.

Valois, R. F., Oeltmann, J. E., Waller, J., & Hussey, J. R. (1999). Relationship between number of sexual intercourse partners and selected health risk behaviors among public high school adolescents. *Journal of Adolescent Health, 25*, 328–335.

Van Balkom, A. J., De Haan, E., Van Oppen, P., Spinhoven, P., Hoogduin, A. L., & Van Dyck, R. (1998). Cognitive and behavioral therapies alone versus in combination with fluvoxamine in the treatment of obsessive compulsive disorder. *Journal of Nervous and Mental Disease, 186*, 492–499.

Van den Bree, M. B. M., Svikis, D. S., & Pickens, R. W. (2000). Antisocial personality and drug use disorders—are they genetically related? In D. H. Fishbein (Ed.), *The science, treatment, and prevention of antisocial behaviors: Application to the criminal justice system* (pp. 1–19). Kingston, NJ: Civic Research Institute.

Van der Kolk, B. A., Weisaeth, L., & Van der Hart, O. (1996). History of trauma in psychiatry. In B. A. Van der Kolk, A. C. McFarlane, & L. Weisaeth (Eds.), *Traumatic stress: The effects of overwhelming experience on mind, body and society* (pp. 47–73). New York, NY: Guilford Press.

Van der Krol, R. J., Oosterbaan, H., Weller, S. D., & Koning, A. E. (1998). Attention deficit hyperactivity disorder. In P. Graham (Ed.), *Cognitive-behaviour therapy for children and families* (pp. 32–44). New York, NY: Cambridge University Press.

Van Etten, M., & Taylor, S. (1998). Comparative efficacy of treatments for posttraumatic stress disorder: A meta-analysis. *Clinical Psychology and Psychotherapy, 5*, 126–144.

Van Hook, M. (1999). Women's help-seeking patterns for depression. *Social Work in Health Care, 29*, 15–34.

Van't Veer-Tazelaar, P. J., van Marwijk, H. W. J., van Oppen, P., van Hout, H. P. J., van der Horst, H. E., Cuijpers, P., . . . Beekman, A. T. F. (2009). Stepped-care prevention of anxiety and depression in late life. *Archives of General Psychiatry, 66*, 297–304.

Vasquez, M. J. T. (1994). Latinas. In L. Comas-Diaz & B. Greene (Eds.), *Women of color: Integrating ethnic and gender identities in psychotherapy* (pp. 114–138). New York, NY: Guilford Press.

Vaughn, M. G., & Howard, M. O. (2004). Adolescent substance abuse treatment: A synthesis of controlled evaluations. *Research on Social Work Practice, 14,* 325–335.

Vaughn, M. J., & Matyastik Baier, M. E. (1999). Reliability and validity of the Relationship Assessment Scale. *American Journal of Family Therapy, 27,* 137–147.

Veltman, M. V. M., & Browne, K. D. (2002). The assessment of drawings from children who have been maltreated: A systematic review. *Child Abuse Review, 11,* 19–37.

Verheul, R., van den Bosch, L. M. C., Koeter, M. W. J., de Ridder, M. A. J., Stijnen, T., & van den Brink, W. (2003). Dialectical behavior therapy for women with borderline personality disorder: 12-month randomized clinical trial in the Netherlands. *British Journal of Psychiatry, 182,* 135–140.

Verhulst, F. C. (2001). Community and epidemiological aspects of anxiety disorders in children. In W. K. Silverman & P. D. A. Treffers (Eds.), *Anxiety disorders in children and adolescents: Research, assessment and intervention* (pp. 273–292). New York, NY: Cambridge University Press.

Vickerman, K. A., & Margolin, G. (2009). Rape treatment outcome research: Empirical findings and state of the literature. *Clinical Psychology Review, 29,* 431–448.

Vidrine, J. I., Reitzel, L. R., Figueroa, P. Y., Velasquez, M. M., Mazas, C. A., Cinciripini, P. M., & Wetter, D. W. (2013). Motivation and Problem Solving (MAPS): Motivationally-based skills training for treating substance use. *Cognitive and Behavioral Practice, 20,* 501–516.

Vien, A., & Beech, A. R. (2006). Psychopathy: Theory, measurement, and treatment. *Trauma, Violence and Abuse, 7,* 155–174.

Vink, D., Aartsen, M. J., & Schoevers, R. A. (2008). Risk factors for anxiety and depression in the elderly: A review. *Journal of Affective Disorders, 106,* 29–44.

Vitelli, R. (1997). Comparison of early and late start models of delinquency in adult offenders. *International Journal of Offender Therapy and Comparative Criminology, 4,* 351–357.

Vito, G. F., & Tewksbury, R. A. (1998). The impact of treatment: The Jefferson county (Kentucky) drug court program. *Federal Probation, 62,* 46–51.

Vitousek, K. B. (2002). Cognitive-behavioral therapy for anorexia nervosa. In C. G. Fairburn & K. D. Brownell (Eds.), *Eating disorders and obesity: A comprehensive handbook* (2nd ed., pp. 308–313). New York, NY: Guilford Press.

Vocks, S., Tuschen-Caffier, B., Pietrowsky, R., Rustenbach, S. J., Kersting, A., & Herpertz, S. (2010). Meta-analysis of the effectiveness of psychological and pharmacological treatments for binge eating disorder. *International Journal of Eating Disorders, 43,* 205–217.

Vohs, K. D., Heatherton, T. F., & Herrin, M. (2001). Disordered eating and the transition to college: A prospective study. *International Journal of Eating Disorders, 29,* 280–288.

Vreven, D. L., Gudanowski, D. M., King, L. A., & King, D. W. (1995). The civilian version of the Mississippi PTSD Scale: A psychometric evaluation. *Journal of Traumatic Stress, 8,* 91–109.

Wachtel, P. L. (1977). *Psychoanalysis and behavior therapy: Toward an integration.* New York, NY: Basic.

Wachtel, P. L. (1987). *Action and insight*. New York, NY: Guilford Press.

Wachtel, T., & Staniford, M. (2010). The effectiveness of brief interventions in the clinical setting in reducing alcohol misuse and binge drinking in adolescents: A critical review of the literature. *Journal of Clinical Nursing, 19*, 605–620.

Wakefield, J. C. (1997). When is development disordered? Developmental psychopathology and the harmful dysfunction analysis of mental disorder. *Development and Psychopathology, 9*, 269–290.

Wakefield, J. C., & Kirk, S. A. (1995). Unscientific thinking about scientific practice: Evaluating the scientist-practitioner model. *Social Work Research, 20*, 83–95.

Walborn, F. S. (1996). *Process variables*. Pacific Grove, CA: Brooks/Cole.

Waldron, H. B. (1997). Adolescent substance abuse and family therapy outcome: A review of randomized trials. In T. H. Ollendick & R. J. Prinz (Eds.), *Advances in clinical child psychology* (Vol. 19, pp. 199–234). New York, NY: Plenum Press.

Waldron, H. B., Brody, J. L., & Slesnick, N. (2001). Integrative behavioral and family therapy for adolescent substance abuse. In P. M. Monti, S. M. Colby, & T. A. O'Leary (Eds.), *Adolescents, alcohol and substance abuse: Reaching teens through brief interventions* (pp. 216–243). New York, NY: Guilford Press.

Walitzer, K. S., Dermen, K. H., & Barrick, C. (2008). Facilitating involvement in Alcoholics Anonymous during out-patient treatment: A randomized clinical trial. *Addiction, 104*, 391–401.

Walker, C. A., & Davies, J. (2010). A critical review of the psychometric evidence base of the Child Abuse Potential Inventory. *Journal of Family Violence, 25*, 215–227.

Wall, A., Hinson, R. E., & McKee, S. A. (1998). Alcohol outcome expectancies, attitudes towards drinking, and the theory of planned behavior. *Journal of Studies on Alcohol, 59*, 409–419.

Walsh, T. C. (1997). Alcoholic offenders: A gender comparison. *Alcoholism Treatment Quarterly, 15*, 29–41.

Walters, S. T., Bennett, M. E., & Noto, J. V. (2000). Drinking on campus: What do we know about reducing alcohol use among college students? *Journal of Substance Abuse Treatment, 19*, 223–228.

Walton, E. (1997). Enhancing investigative decisions in child welfare: An exploratory use of intensive family preservation services. *Child Welfare, 76*, 447–461.

Walton, E. (2001). Combining abuse and neglect investigations with intensive family preservation services: An innovative approach to protecting children. *Research on Social Work Practice, 11*, 627–644.

Walton, M. A., Chermack, S. T., Shope, J. T., Bingham, C. R., Zimmerman, M. A., Blow, F. C., & Cunningham, R. M. (2010). Effects of brief intervention for reducing violence and alcohol misuse among adolescents: A randomized controlled trial. *JAMA, 304*, 527–535.

Ware, J. E., Kosinski, M., & Keller, S. D. (1996). A 12–item short form health survey: Construction of scales and preliminary tests of reliability and validity. *Medical Care, 34*, 220–233.

Watson, H. J., & Rees, C. S. (2008). Meta-analysis of randomized, controlled treatment trials for pediatric obsessive-compulsive disorder. *Journal of Child Psychology and Psychiatry, 49*, 489–498.

Watson, J. C., Gordon, L. B., Stermac, L., Kalogerokos, R., & Steckley, P. (2003). Comparing the effectiveness of process-experiential with cognitive-behavioral psychotherapy in the treatment of depression. *Journal of Consulting and Clinical Psychology*, *71*, 773–781.

Watson-Perczel, M., Lutzker, J. R., Greene, B. F., & McGimpsey, B. J. (1988). Assessment and modification of home cleanliness among families adjudicated for child neglect. *Behavior Modification*, *12*, 57–81.

Weaver, T. L., & Clum, G. A. (1993). Early family environments and traumatic experiences associated with borderline personality disorder. *Journal of Consulting and Clinical Psychology*, *61*, 1068–1075.

Webb, J. A., McKelvey, R. S., & Strobel, R. (1997). Replication and extension of a risk profile for Amerasian youth. *Journal of Traumatic Stress*, *10*, 645–654.

Webster-Stratton, C. (1997, March–April). From parent training to community building. *Families in Society: The Journal of Contemporary Human Services*, 156–171.

Webster-Stratton, C., & Hancock, L. (1998). Training for parents of young children with conduct problems: Content, methods and therapeutic processes. In J. M. Briesmeister & C. E. Schaefer (Eds.), *Handbook of parent training: Parents as co-therapists for children's behavior problems* (2nd ed., pp. 98–152). New York, NY: Wiley.

Webster-Stratton, C., & Herbert, M. (1994). *Troubled families, problem children— Working with parents: A collaborative process*. New York, NY: Wiley.

Webster-Stratton, C., Hollinsworth, T., & Kolpacoff, M. (1989). The long-term effectiveness and clinical significance of three cost-effective training programs for families with conduct-problem children. *Journal of Consulting and Clinical Psychology*, *57*, 550–553.

Webster-Stratton, C., Kolpacoff, M., & Hollinsworth, T. (1988). Self-administered videotape therapy for families with conduct-problem children: Comparison with two cost-effective treatments and a control group. *Journal of Consulting and Clinical Psychology*, *56*, 558–566.

Wechsler, H., Davenport, A., Dowdall, G., Moeykens, B., & Costillow, S. (1994). Health and behavioral consequences of binge drinking in college. *JAMA*, *272*, 1672–1677.

Wechsler, H., Dowdall, G., Davenport, A., & Rimm, E. (1995). A gender-specific measure of binge drinking among college students. *American Journal of Public Health*, *85*, 982–985.

Wechsler, H., Lee, J. E., Kuo, M., Seibring, M., Nelson, T. F., & Lee, H. (2002). Trends in college binge drinking during a period of increased prevention efforts: Findings from 4 Harvard School of Public Health College Alcohol Study surveys: 1993–2001. *Journal of American College Health*, *50*, 203–217.

Wechsler, H., & McFadden, M. (1979). Drinking among college students in New England: Extent, social correlates, and consequences of alcohol use. *Journal of Studies on Alcohol*, *40*, 969–996.

Weinberg, N., Rohdert, E., Colliver, J., & Glantz, M. (1998). Adolescent substance abuse: A review of the last 10 years. *Journal of the American Academy of Child and Adolescent Psychiatry*, *37*, 252–261.

Weiner, E., & Wiener, J. (1997). University students with psychiatric illness: Factors involved in the decision to withdraw from their studies. *Psychiatric Rehabilitation Journal*, *20*, 88–91.

Weinstein, D., Staffelbach, D., & Biaggio, M. (2000). Attention-deficit hyperactivity disorder and posttraumatic stress disorder: Differential diagnosis in childhood sexual abuse. *Clinical Psychology Review, 20*, 359–378.

Weisner, C., Matzger, H., & Kaskutas, L. (2003). How important is treatment? One-year outcomes of treated and untreated alcohol-dependent individuals. *Addiction, 98*, 901–911.

Weisner, C., & Schmidt, L. (1993). Alcohol and drug problems among diverse health and social service populations. *American Journal of Public Health, 83*, 824–829.

Weiss, B., Catron, T., Harris, V., & Phung, T. (1999). The effectiveness of traditional child psychotherapy. *Journal of Consulting and Clinical Psychology, 67*, 82–94.

Weiss, R. L., & Heyman, R. E. (1997). A clinical-research overview of couples interactions. In W. K. Halford & H. J. Markham (Eds.), *Clinical handbook of marriage and couples intervention* (pp. 13–42). New York, NY: Wiley.

Weissman, M. M., Markowitz, J. C., & Klerman, G. L. (2000). *Comprehensive guide to interpersonal psychotherapy*. New York, NY: Basic Books.

Weisz, A. N., & Black, B. M. (2001). Evaluating a sexual assault and dating violence prevention program for urban youths. *Social Work Research, 25*, 89–102.

Weisz, J. R., Donenberg, G. R., Han, S. S., & Weiss, B. (1995). Bridging the gap between lab and clinic in child and adolescent psychotherapy. *Journal of Consulting and Clinical Psychology, 63*, 688–701.

Weisz, J. R., & Hawley, K. M. (1998). Finding, evaluating, refining, and applying empirically supported treatments for children and adolescents. *Journal of Child Clinical Psychology, 27*, 206–216.

Weisz, J. R., Weiss, B., Alicke, M. D., & Klotz, M. L. (1987). Effectiveness of psychotherapy with children and adolescents: A meta-analysis for clinicians. *Journal of Consulting and Clinical Psychology, 55*, 542–549.

Wekerle, C., & Wolfe, D. A. (1993). Prevention of child physical abuse and neglect: Promising new directions. *Clinical Psychology Review, 13*, 501–540.

Welch, G., Thompson, L., & Hall, A. (1993). The BULIT-R: Its reliability and clinical validity as a screening tool of DSM-III-R bulimia nervosa in a female tertiary education population. *International Journal of Eating Disorders, 14*, 95–105.

Wells, K., & Biegel, D. E. (1992). Intensive family preservation services research: Current status and future agenda. *Social Work Research and Abstracts, 28*, 21–27.

Wells, K. B., Astrachan, B. M., Tischler, G. L., & Unutzer, J. (1995). Issues and approaches in evaluating managed mental health care. *Milbank Quarterly, 73*, 57–75.

Wells, K. C., Pelham, W. E., Kotkin, R. A., Hoza, B., Abikoff, H. B., Abramowitz, A., & associates (2000). Psychosocial treatment strategies in the MTA study: Rationale, methods, and critical issues in design and implementation. *Journal of Abnormal Child Psychology, 28*, 483–505.

Werch, C. E., Pappas, D. M., & Castellon-Vogel, E. A. (1996). Drug use prevention efforts at colleges and universities in the United States. *Substance Use and Misuse, 31*, 65–80.

Westen, D., Novotny, C. M., & Thompson-Brenner, H. (2004). The empirical status of empirically supported psychotherapies: Assumption, findings, and reporting in controlled clinical trials. *Psychological Bulletin, 130*, 631–663.

Westenberg, P. M., Siebelink, B. M., & Treffers, P. D. A. (2001). Psychosocial developmental theory in relation to anxiety and its disorders. In W. K. Silverman & P. D. A. Treffers (Eds.), *Anxiety disorders in children and adolescents: Research, assessment and intervention* (pp. 72–89). New York, NY: Cambridge University Press.

Wexler, D. B. (1991). Inducing therapeutic compliance through the criminal law. In D. B. Wexler & B. J. Winick (Eds.), *Essays in therapeutic jurisprudence* (pp. 187–218). Durham, NC: Carolina Academic Press.

Wexler, H. K. (1995). The success of therapeutic communities for substance abusers in American prisons. *Journal of Psychoactive Drugs, 27,* 57–66.

Whaley, A. L. (1998). Cross-cultural perspective on paranoia: A focus on the black American experience. *Psychiatric Quarterly, 69,* 325–343.

Whaley, A. L., & Davis, K. E. (2007). Cultural competence and evidence-based practice in mental health services. *American Psychologist, 62,* 563–574.

Wheaton, B. (1994). Sampling the stress universe. In W. R. Avison & I. H. Gotlib (Eds.), *Stress and mental health: Contemporary issues and prospects for the future* (pp. 77–114). New York, NY: Plenum Press.

White, H. R., & Labouvie, E. W. (1989). Towards the assessment of adolescent problem drinking. *Journal of Studies on Alcohol, 50,* 30–37.

White, H. R., Labouvie, E. W., & Papadaratsakis, V. (2005). Changes in substance use during the transition to adulthood: A comparison of college students and their noncollege age peers. *Journal of Drug Issues, 35,* 281–305.

White, H. R., Xie, M., Thompson, W., Loeber, R., & Stouthamer-Loeber, M. (2001). Psychopathology as a predictor of adolescent drug use trajectories. *Psychology of Addictive Behaviors, 15,* 210–218.

White, J. D. (1999). Personality, temperament and ADHD: A review of the literature. *Personality and Individual Differences, 27,* 589–598.

Whiteman, M., Fanshel, D., & Grundy, J. F. (1987). Cognitive-behavioral interventions aimed at anger of parents at risk of child abuse. *Social Work, 32,* 469–474.

Widiger, T. A., & Corbitt, E. M. (1995). Antisocial personality disorder. In J. Livesley (Ed.), *The DSM-IV personality disorders* (pp. 103–126). New York, NY: Guilford Press.

Widom, C. S. (1998). Childhood victimization: Early adversity and subsequent psychopathology. In B. P. Dohrenwend (Eds.), *Adversity and psychopathology* (pp. 81–95). New York, NY: Oxford University Press.

Widom, C. S. (1999). Posttraumatic stress disorder in abused and neglected children grown up. *American Journal of Psychiatry, 156,* 1223–1229.

Widom, C. S., Czaja, S. J., & Paris, J. (2009). A prospective investigation of borderline personality disorder in abused and neglected children followed up into adulthood. *Journal of Personality Disorders, 23,* 433–446.

Widom, C. S., & Toch, H. (2000). The contribution of psychology to criminal justice education. In D. H. Fishbein (Ed.), *The science, treatment, and prevention of antisocial behaviors: Application to the criminal justice system* (pp. 3–1 to 3–19). Kingston, NJ: Civic Research Institute.

Wild, D., Furtado, T., & Angalakuditi, M. (2012). The translation and cultural adaptation of the Child Behavior Checklist for use in Israel (Hebrew), Korea, the US (Spanish), India (Malayalam and Kannada), and Spain. *Psychology Research and Behavior Management, 5,* 51–56.

Wilk, D. (1994). Women and alcoholism: How a male-as-norm bias affects research, assessment and treatment. *Health and Social Work, 19*, 29–35.

Williams, K. E., Chambless, D. L., & Steketee, G. (1998). Behavioral treatment of obsessive-compulsive disorder in African Americans: Clinical issues. *Journal of Behavior Therapy and Experimental Psychiatry, 29*, 163–170.

Williams, S. D., Wiener, J., & MacMillan, H. (2005). Build-a-person technique: Examination of the validity of human-figure features as evidence of child sexual abuse. *Child Abuse and Neglect, 29*, 701–713.

Wills, T., Sandy, J., & Yaeger, A. (2000). Temperament and adolescent substance use: An epigenetic approach to risk and protection. *Journal of Personality, 68*, 1127–1151.

Wilsnack, S. C., Wilsnack, R. W., & Hiller-Sturmhöfel, S. (1994). How women drink: Epidemiology of women's drinking and problem drinking. *Alcohol Health and Research World, 18*, 173–184.

Wilson, G. T. (1993a). Assessment of binge eating. In C. G. Fairburn & G. T. Wilson (Eds.), *Binge eating: Nature, assessment and treatment* (pp. 227–249). New York, NY: Guilford Press.

Wilson, G. T. (1993b). Binge eating and addictive disorders. In C. G. Fairburn & G. T. Wilson (Eds.), *Binge eating: Nature, assessment and treatment* (pp. 97–122). New York, NY: Guilford Press.

Wilson, G. T. (1995). Behavior therapy. In R. J. Corsini & D. Wedding (Eds.), *Current psychotherapies* (5th ed., pp. 197–228). Itasca, IL: Peacock.

Wilson, G. T. (1996). Empirically-validated treatments: Realities and resistance. *Clinical Psychology: Science and Practice, 3*, 241–244.

Wilson, G. T. (2010). Cognitive behavior therapy for eating disorders. In W. S. Agras (Ed.), *The Oxford handbook of eating disorders* (pp. 331–347). New York, NY: Oxford University Press.

Wilson, G. T. (2011). Treatment of binge eating disorder. *Psychiatric Clinics of North America, 34*, 773–783.

Wilson, G. T., & Fairburn, C. G. (1993). Cognitive treatments for eating disorders. *Journal of Consulting and Clinical Psychology, 61*, 261–269.

Wilson, G. T., & Fairburn, C. G. (1998). Treatments of eating disorders. In P. E. Nathan & J. M. Gorman (Eds.), *A guide to treatments that work* (pp. 501–530). New York, NY: Oxford University Press.

Wilson, G. T., Grilo, C. M., & Vitousek, K. M. (2007). Psychological treatment of eating disorders. *American Psychologist, 62*, 199–216.

Wilson, G. T., & Vitousek, K. M. (1999). Self-monitoring in the assessment of eating disorders. *Psychological Assessment, 11*, 480–489.

Wilson, S. J., Lipsey, M. W., & Soydan, H. (2003). Are mainstream programs for juvenile delinquency less effective with minority youth than majority youth? A meta-analysis of outcomes research. *Research on Social Work Practice, 13*, 3–26.

Windle, M. (1996). Effect of parental drinking on adolescents. *Alcohol Health and Research World, 20*, 181–184.

Winzelberg, A. J., Eldredge, K. L., Eppstein, D., Wilfley, D., Dasmahapatra, R., Dev, P., & Taylor, C. B. (2000). Effectiveness of an Internet-based program for reducing risk factors for eating disorders. *Journal of Consulting and Clinical Psychology, 68*, 346–350.

Winzelberg, A. J., Taylor, C. B., Sharpe, T., Eldredge, K. L., Dev, P., & Constantinou, P. S. (1998). Evaluation of a computer-mediated eating disorder intervention program. *International Journal of Eating Disorders, 24,* 339–349.

Witkin, S. L. (1998). The right to effective treatment and the effective treatment of rights: Rhetorical empiricism and the politics of research. *Points and Viewpoints in Social Work, 43,* 75–80.

Wolfe, D. A., Edwards, B., Manion, I., & Koverola, C. (1988). Early intervention for parents at risk of child abuse and neglect: A preliminary investigation. *Journal of Consulting and Clinical Psychology, 56,* 40–47.

Wolfe, D. A., & McEachran, A. (1997). Child physical abuse and neglect. In E. J. Mash & L. G. Terdal (Eds.), *Assessment of childhood disorders* (3rd ed., pp. 523–568). New York, NY: Guilford Press.

Wolfe, D. A., & Sandler, J. (1981). Training abusive parents in effective child management. *Behavior Modification, 5,* 320–335.

Wolfe, D. A., & St. Pierre, J. (1989). Child abuse and neglect. In T. H. Ollendick & M. Hersen (Eds.), *Handbook of childhood psychopathology* (2nd ed., pp. 377–398). New York, NY: Plenum Press.

Wolfe, D. A., & Wekerle, C. (1993). Treatment strategies for child physical abuse and neglect: A critical progress report. *Clinical Psychology Review, 13,* 473–500.

Wolfe, R., Morrow, J., & Fredrickson, B. L. (1996). Mood disorders in older adults. In L. L. Carstensen, B. A. Edelstein, & L. Dornbrand (Eds.), *The practical handbook of clinical gerontology* (pp. 274–303). Thousand Oaks, CA: Sage.

Wolfe, V. V., & Birt, J. (1997). Child sexual abuse. In E. J. Mash & L. G. Terdal (Eds.), *Assessment of childhood disorders* (3rd ed., pp. 569–623). New York, NY: Guilford Press.

Wolfe, V. V., & Gentile, C. (1991). *Children's Impact of Traumatic Events Scale–Revised (CITES-R).* London, ON: Department of Psychology, London Health Sciences.

Wolfe, V. V., Gentile, C., & Bourdeau, P. (1987). *History of Victimization form* [Unpublished assessment instrument]. London, ON: London Health Sciences Centre.

Wolfe, V. V., Gentile, C., & Wolfe, D. A. (1989). The impact of sexual abuse in children: A PTSD formulation. *Behavior Therapy, 20,* 215–228.

Wolfe, V. V., & Wolfe, D. A. (1988). The sexually abused child. In E. J. Mash & L. G. Terdal (Eds.), *Behavioral assessment of childhood disorders* (2nd ed., pp. 670–714). New York, NY: Guilford Press.

Wolford, G. L., Rosenberg, S. D., Drake, R. E., Mueser, K. T., Oxman, T. E., Hoffman, D., . . . Carrieri, K. L. (1999). Evaluation of methods for detecting substance use disorder in persons with severe mental illness. *Psychology of Addictive Behaviors, 13,* 313–326.

Wolpe, J. (1958). *Psychotherapy by reciprocal inhibition.* Stanford, CA: Stanford University Press.

Wolpe, J. (1973). *The practice of behavior therapy.* Elmsford, NY: Pergamon.

Wong, C. W. (2013). Collaborative empiricism in culturally sensitive cognitive behavior therapy. *Cognitive and Behavioral Practice, 20,* 390–398.

Wong, K. K., Chiu, R., Tang, B., Mak, D., Liu, J., & Chiu, S. N. (2008). A randomized controlled trial of a supported employment program for persons with long-term mental illness in Hong Kong. *Psychiatric Services, 59,* 84–90.

Wong, S. E. (1999). Treatment of antisocial behavior in adolescent inpatients: Behavioral changes and client satisfactionn. *Research on Social Work Practice, 9*, 25–44.

Wong, Y. J., Kim, S. H., & Tran, K. K. (2010). Asian Americans' adherence to Asian values, attributions about depression, and coping strategies. *Cultural Diversity and Ethnic Minority Psychology, 16*, 1–8.

Wood, A., Harrington, R., & Moore, A. (1996). Controlled trial of a brief cognitive-behavioural intervention in adolescent patients with depressive disorders. *Journal of Child Psychology and Psychiatry and Allied Disciplines, 37*, 737–746.

Wood, K. (1978). Casework effectiveness: A new look at the research evidence. *Social Work, 23*, 437–457.

World Health Organization. (2010). *mhGAP intervention guide for mental, neurological and substance use disorders in non-specialized health settings: Mental Health Gap Action Programme (mhGAP)*. Geneva, Switzerland: Author.

World Health Organization. (2012). *World Suicide Prevention Day 2012*. Retrieved from http://www.who.int/mediacentre/events/annual/world_suicide_prevention_day/en/.

Wright, K. N. (1993). Alcohol use by prisoners. *Alcohol Health and Research World, 17*, 157–161.

Xiang, Y., Weng, Y., Li, W., Gao, L., Chen, G., Xie, L., . . . Ungvari, G. (2007). Efficacy of the community re-entry module for patients with schizophrenia in Beijing, China: Outcome at 2-year follow-up. *British Journal of Psychiatry, 190*, 49–56.

Xiaoming, L., Stanton, B., & Feigelman, S. (2000a). Impact of perceived parental monitoring on adolescent risk behavior over 4 years. *Journal of Adolescent Health, 27*, 49–56.

Xiaoming, L., Stanton, B., & Feigelman, S. (2000b). Perceived parental monitoring and health risk behaviors among urban low-income African-American children and adolescents. *Journal of Adolescent Health, 27*, 43–48.

Yates, B. T. (1996). *Analyzing costs, procedures, processes, and outcomes in human services* (Applied Social Science Research Methods Series No. 42). Thousand Oaks, CA: Sage.

Yesavage, J. A., Brink, T. L., Rose, T. L., Lum, O., Huang, V., Adey, M., & Leirer, V. O. (1983). Development and validation of a geriatric depression screening scale: A preliminary report. *Journal of Psychiatric Research, 17*, 37–49.

Young, J. E., Rygh, J. L., Weinberger, A. D., & Beck, A. T. (2008). Cognitive therapy for depression. In D. H. Barlow (Ed.), *Clinical handbook of psychological disorders: A step-by-step manual* (4th ed., pp. 250–305). New York, NY: Guilford Press.

Young, J. F., Makeover, H. B., Cohen, J. R., Mufson, L., Gallop, R. J., & Benas, J. S. (2012). Interpersonal psychotherapy-adolescent skills training: Anxiety outcomes and impact of comorbidity. *Journal of Clinical Child & Adolescent Psychology, 41*, 640–653.

Young, R. C., Biggs, J. T., Ziegler, V. E., & Meyer, D. A. (1978). A rating scale for mania: Reliability, validity and sensitivity. *British Journal of Psychiatry, 133*, 429–435.

Yu, J., & Shacket, R. W. (2001). Alcohol use in high school: Predicting students' use and alcohol problems in four-year colleges. *American Journal on Drug and Alcohol Abuse, 27*, 775–793.

Yudko, E., Lozhkina, O., & Fouts, A. (2007). A comprehensive review of the psychometric properties of the Drug Abuse Screening Test. *Journal of Substance Abuse Treatment, 32,* 189–198.

Yule, W., Perrin, S., & Smith, P. (2001). Traumatic events and post-traumatic stress disorder. In W. K. Silverman & P. D. A. Treffers (Eds.), *Anxiety disorders in children and adolescents: Research, assessment and intervention* (pp. 212–234). New York, NY: Cambridge University Press.

Zabinski, M. F., Pung, M. A., Wilfley, D. E., Eppstein, D. L., Winzelberg, A. J., Celio, A., & Taylor, C. B. (2001). Reducing risk factors for eating disorders: Targeting at-risk women with a computerized psychoeducational program. *International Journal of Eating Disorders, 29,* 401–408.

Zanarini, M. C. (2009). Psychotherapy of borderline personality disorder. *Acta Psychiatrica Scandinavica, 120,* 373–378.

Zanarini, M. C., Frankenburg, F. R., Reich, B., Marino, M. F., Haynes, M. C., & Gunderson, J. G. (1999). Violence in the lives of adult borderline patients. *Journal of Nervous and Mental Disease, 187,* 65–71.

Zigler, E. F. (1989). Addressing the nation's child care crisis: The school of the twenty-first century. *American Journal of Orthopsychiatry, 59,* 484–491.

Zimmermann, G., Favrod, J., Trieu, V. H., & Pomini, V. (2005). The effect of cognitive behavioral treatment on the positive symptoms of schizophrenia spectrum disorders: A meta-analysis. *Schizophrenia Research, 77,* 1–9.

Zimmerman, M. (2012). Is there adequate empirical justification for radically revising the personality disorders section for DSM-5? *Personality Disorders: Theory, Research and Treatment, 3,* 444–457.

Zinbarg, R. E., Barlow, D. H., Brown, T. A., & Hertz, R. M. (1992). Cognitive-behavioral approaches to the nature and treatment of anxiety disorders. *Annual Review of Psychology, 43,* 235–267.

Ziyadeh, N. J., Prokop, L. A., Fisher, L. B., Rosario, M., Field, A. E., Camargo, C. A., & Austin, S. B. (2007). Sexual orientation, gender, and alcohol use in a cohort study of U.S. adolescent girls and boys. *Drug and Alcohol Dependence, 87,* 119–130.

Zlotnick, C., Robertson, M. J., & Wright, M. (1999). The impact of childhood foster care and other out-of-home placement on homeless women and their children. *Child Abuse and Neglect, 23,* 1057–1068.

Zucker, R. A., & Fitzgerald, H. E. (1991). Early developmental factors and risk for alcohol problems. *Alcohol Health and Research World, 15,* 18–24.

Zucker, R. A., & Gomberg, E. S. L. (1986). Etiology of alcoholism reconsidered: The case for a biopsychosocial process. *American Psychologist, 41*(7), 783–793.

INDEX

About the Author

Thomas O'Hare is associate professor at Boston College. He has an MSW and a Ph.D. from Rutgers University. He has worked as a clinical social worker and served as director of quality assurance for the South Shore Mental Health Center in Charlestown, Rhode Island. He has written and contributed to numerous articles, many of which focus on co-occurring mental health and substance abuse problems in young adults and persons with serious mental illnesses. Professor O'Hare is a longtime advocate of evidence-based social work practices. He was awarded a Fulbright-Nehru grant to teach and conduct research at Ragajiri School of Social Work, Kerala, India, in 2013.